Dictionary of Literary Biography

Documentary Series

Walter McDonald, John M. Del Vecchio, edited by Ronald Baughman (1991)

10 *The Bloomsbury Group*, edited by Edward L. Bishop (1992)

11 *American Proletarian Culture: The Twenties and The Thirties*, edited by Jon Christian Suggs (1993)

12 *Southern Women Writers: Flannery O'Connor, Katherine Anne Porter, Eudora Welty*, edited by Mary Ann Wimsatt and Karen L. Rood (1994)

13 *The House of Scribner, 1846-1904*, edited by John Delaney (1996)

14 *Four Women Writers for Children, 1868-1918*, edited by Caroline C. Hunt (1996)

15 *American Expatriate Writers: Paris in the Twenties*, edited by Matthew J. Bruccoli and Robert W. Trogdon (1997)

16 *The House of Scribner, 1905-1930*, edited by John Delaney (1997)

17 *The House of Scribner, 1931-1984*, edited by John Delaney (1998)

18 *British Poets of The Great War: Sassoon, Graves, Owen*, edited by Patrick Quinn (1999)

19 *James Dickey*, edited by Judith S. Baughman (1999)

See also DLB 210

Yearbooks

1980 edited by Karen L. Rood, Jean W. Ross, and Richard Ziegfeld (1981)

1981 edited by Karen L. Rood, Jean W. Ross, and Richard Ziegfeld (1982)

1982 edited by Richard Ziegfeld; associate editors: Jean W. Ross and Lynne C. Zeigler (1983)

1983 edited by Mary Bruccoli and Jean W. Ross, associate editor Richard Ziegfeld (1984)

1984 edited by Jean W. Ross (1985)

1985 edited by Jean W. Ross (1986)

1986 edited by J. M. Brook (1987)

1987 edited by J. M. Brook (1988)

1988 edited by J. M. Brook (1989)

1989 edited by J. M. Brook (1990)

1990 edited by James W. Hipp (1991)

1991 edited by James W. Hipp (1992)

1992 edited by James W. Hipp (1993)

1993 edited by James W. Hipp, contributing editor George Garrett (1994)

1994 edited by James W. Hipp, contributing editor George Garrett (1995)

1995 edited by James W. Hipp, contributing editor George Garrett (1996)

1996 edited by Samuel W. Bruce and L. Kay Webster, contributing editor George Garrett (1997)

1997 edited by Matthew J. Bruccoli and George Garrett, with the assistance of L. Kay Webster (1998)

1998 edited by Matthew J. Bruccoli, contributing editor George Garrett, with the assistance of D. W. Thomas (1999)

Concise Series

Concise Dictionary of American Literary Biography, 7 volumes (1988-1999): *The New Consciousness, 1941-1968; Colonization to the American Renaissance, 1640-1865; Realism, Naturalism, and Local Color, 1865-1917; The Twenties, 1917-1929; The Age of Maturity, 1929-1941; Broadening Views, 1968-1988; Supplement: Modern Writers, 1900–1998.*

Concise Dictionary of British Literary Biography, 8 volumes (1991-1992): *Writers of the Middle Ages and Renaissance Before 1660; Writers of the Restoration and Eighteenth Century, 1660-1789; Writers of the Romantic Period, 1789-1832; Victorian Writers, 1832-1890; Late-Victorian and Edwardian Writers, 1890-1914; Modern Writers, 1914-1945; Writers After World War II, 1945-1960; Contemporary Writers, 1960 to Present.*

Concise Dictionary of World Literary Biography, 20 volumes projected (1999-): *Ancient Greek and Roman Writers; German Writers.*

Dictionary of Literary Biography® • Volume Two Hundred Fourteen

Twentieth-Century Danish Writers

Dictionary of Literary Biography® • Volume Two Hundred Fourteen

Twentieth-Century Danish Writers

Edited by
Marianne Stecher-Hansen
University of Washington

A Bruccoli Clark Layman Book
The Gale Group
Detroit • San Francisco • London • Boston • Woodbridge, Conn.

To Andreas,
To Inger Tranberg and Knud P. Stecher,
and to my students

Contents

Plan of the Series

. . . Almost the most prodigious asset of a country, and perhaps its most precious possession, is its native literary product—when that product is fine and noble and enduring.

Mark Twain*

The advisory board, the editors, and the publisher of the *Dictionary of Literary Biography* are joined in endorsing Mark Twain's declaration. The literature of a nation provides an inexhaustible resource of permanent worth. We intend to make literature and its creators better understood and more accessible to students and the reading public, while satisfying the standards of teachers and scholars.

To meet these requirements, *literary biography* has been construed in terms of the author's achievement. The most important thing about a writer is his writing. Accordingly, the entries in *DLB* are career biographies, tracing the development of the author's canon and the evolution of his reputation.

The purpose of *DLB* is not only to provide reliable information in a convenient format but also to place the figures in the larger perspective of literary history and to offer appraisals of their accomplishments by qualified scholars.

The publication plan for *DLB* resulted from two years of preparation. The project was proposed to Bruccoli Clark by Frederick G. Ruffner, president of the Gale Research Company, in November 1975. After specimen entries were prepared and typeset, an advisory board was formed to refine the entry format and develop the series rationale. In meetings held during 1976, the publisher, series editors, and advisory board approved the scheme for a comprehensive biographical dictionary of persons who contributed to North American literature. Editorial work on the first volume began in January 1977, and it was published in 1978. In order to make *DLB* more than a reference tool and to compile volumes that individually have claim to status as literary history, it was decided to organize volumes by

From an unpublished section of Mark Twain's autobiography, copyright by the Mark Twain Company

topic, period, or genre. Each of these freestanding volumes provides a biographical-bibliographical guide and overview for a particular area of literature. We are convinced that this organization—as opposed to a single alphabet method—constitutes a valuable innovation in the presentation of reference material. The volume plan necessarily requires many decisions for the placement and treatment of authors who might properly be included in two or three volumes. In some instances a major figure will be included in separate volumes, but with different entries emphasizing the aspect of his career appropriate to each volume. Ernest Hemingway, for example, is represented in *American Writers in Paris, 1920–1939* by an entry focusing on his expatriate apprenticeship; he is also in *American Novelists, 1910–1945* with an entry surveying his entire career, as well as in *American Short-Story Writers, 1910–1945, Second Series* with an entry concentrating on his short stories. Each volume includes a cumulative index of the subject authors and articles. Comprehensive indexes to the entire series are planned.

Since 1981 the series has been further augmented by the *DLB Yearbooks,* which update published entries and add new entries to keep the *DLB* current with contemporary activity. There have also been *DLB Documentary Series* volumes which provide biographical and critical source materials for figures whose work is judged to have particular interest for students. One of these companion volumes is devoted entirely to Tennessee Williams.

We define literature as the *intellectual commerce of a nation:* not merely as belles lettres but as that ample and complex process by which ideas are generated, shaped, and transmitted. *DLB* entries are not limited to "creative writers" but extend to other figures who in their time and in their way influenced the mind of a people. Thus the series encompasses historians, journalists, publishers, book collectors, and screenwriters. By this means readers of *DLB* may be aided to perceive literature not as cult scripture in the keeping of intellectual high priests but firmly positioned at the center of a nation's life.

DLB includes the major writers appropriate to each volume and those standing in the ranks behind

xiii

them. Scholarly and critical counsel has been sought in deciding which minor figures to include and how full their entries should be. Wherever possible, useful references are made to figures who do not warrant separate entries.

Each *DLB* volume has an expert volume editor responsible for planning the volume, selecting the figures for inclusion, and assigning the entries. Volume editors are also responsible for preparing, where appropriate, appendices surveying the major periodicals and literary and intellectual movements for their volumes, as well as lists of further readings. Work on the series as a whole is coordinated at the Bruccoli Clark Layman editorial center in Columbia, South Carolina, where the editorial staff is responsible for accuracy and utility of the published volumes.

One feature that distinguishes *DLB* is the illustration policy—its concern with the iconography of literature. Just as an author is influenced by his surroundings, so is the reader's understanding of the author enhanced by a knowledge of his environment. Therefore *DLB* volumes include not only drawings, paintings, and photographs of authors, often depicting them at various stages in their careers, but also illustrations of their families and places where they lived. Title pages are regularly reproduced in facsimile along with dust jackets for modern authors. The dust jackets are a special feature of *DLB* because they often document better than anything else the way in which an author's work was perceived in its own time. Specimens of the writers' manuscripts and letters are included when feasible.

Samuel Johnson rightly decreed that "The chief glory of every people arises from its authors." The purpose of the *Dictionary of Literary Biography* is to compile literary history in the surest way available to us—by accurate and comprehensive treatment of the lives and work of those who contributed to it.

The *DLB* Advisory Board

Introduction

The two decades following the turn of the century have been described by Danish critic Bo Hakon Jørgensen as a "skyggezone" (a gray area) in Danish literature. Some literary historians have argued that the true division between nineteenth- and twentieth-century Danish literature is marked most decisively by World War I. The confusion regarding periodization arises from the fact that the currents of and the counterreactions to *Det moderne Gennumbrud* (the Modern Breakthrough) of 1871, the literary movement promulgated by the critic and scholar Georg Brandes that introduced naturalism and realism to Denmark, were still strong at the turn of the century. Furthermore, the older generation of nineteenth-century writers, both the realists of the 1880s such as Henrik Pontoppidan and Herman Bang and the symbolist poets of the 1890s such as Sophus Claussen and Johannes Jørgensen, continued to publish important works well into the first decades of the twentieth century. Nevertheless, the year 1900 is a useful demarcation, for it marks the arrival in Europe of a distinctively modern worldview—incorporating artistic, intellectual, cultural, and scientific influences—that came to shape Danish literature for an entire century. While a single trend, movement, or zeitgeist does not define the first two decades of the century, many competing and concurrent trends came into play: naturalism and realism, symbolism and Romanticism, social orientation and psychological introspection. The new weltanschauung, or comprehensive worldview, that began to emerge in Denmark at the turn of the century is a reflection of a society in transition. The forces of industrialization and urbanization began to transform Danish society from a rural agrarian culture to a modern industrialized welfare state, a process that took half the century to complete. The new perspective was also inseparably tied to developments in the sciences: Max Planck published the quantum theory in 1900; Albert Einstein, the theory of relativity in 1905; and Niels Bohr, the theory of the atom in 1913. These new scientific conceptions of the relationship between time and space, matter and energy, macrocosms and microcosms shattered the ordered nineteenth-century conception of the physical world and shifted the perspective on man's relationship to his surroundings. Just as Einstein's theory of relativity questioned the concept of a harmonious physical universe, so did Sigmund Freud's theories raise doubts about the conception of man as a rational being. Freud's pioneering work, *Interpretation of Dreams* (1900), introduced the notion of the subconscious and the idea that human action was often guided by irrational impulses. Another reaction to the destruction of the concept of an ordered physical universe was the development of Expressionism in the pictorial arts. An artistic movement whose members sought to portray emotion rather than depict objective reality, Expressionism replaced aesthetic harmony with exaggeration, distortion, and dissonance, reflecting a shattered worldview. Although not all of these radical developments in the arts, science, and culture were immediately reflected in the literature of the day, the seeds were sown that would shape the direction of Danish literature in the following decades.

The various trends and impulses of the pre–World War I decades—in hindsight they are considered aspects of early modernism—are illustrated most brilliantly in the work of Johannes V. Jensen. His work is a reaction against the socially oriented naturalism of the Modern Breakthrough, an embracing of a new scientific conception of humankind (specifically biological determinism) as well as a harbinger of a new aesthetic awareness. In Jensen's magnificent historical novel, *Kongens Fald* (1901; translated as *The Fall of the King,* 1933), the reader finds a merging of naturalism with symbolism, of Romanticism with nihilism, and of psychological introspection with a national and regional consciousness. His cultivation of a "concrete" reality, technology, the machine, speed, and the moment—and, not least, his idealization of America—is illustrative of the cultural optimism that was characteristic of the early years following the turn of the century. With his *Digte* (Poems, 1906) and the many collections of short prose texts he called *myter* (myths), he laid the foundations of modernism in Danish poetry and prose and became one of the most innovative spirits in Danish literature and cultural life.

If there is one predominant tendency that is characteristic of Danish literature between 1900 and 1920, it is the democratization of the literary institution. Whereas throughout the nineteenth century most successful writers were sons of the educated bourgeoisie, the clergy, or the upper class, in the early 1900s working-class and women writers joined the ranks of the literary establishment. Writers from the rural provinces and from the working classes of Denmark are best represented in this volume by Jeppe Aakjær, Marie Bregendahl, Thit Jensen, and Martin Andersen Nexø. In particular, the rise of a vigorous regional literature, or *hjemstavnsdigtning,* was nurtured in Denmark by the emancipation of Danish smallholders and the *folkehøjskoler* (folk high-schools), voluntary residential schools for adults with a curriculum influenced by National Romanticism and folk culture, founded in 1844 at Rødding by N. F. S. Grundtvig, the theologian, poet, and popular educator.

Aakjær's *Vredens Børn* (Children of Wrath, 1904), depicting the harsh working conditions of servants and farm laborers, represents this new combination of social criticism and regionalism. Nexø, Denmark's first influential socialist writer, portrays the plight of the working class in novels that remain the most important in this genre. Although Nexø does not typify regional literature, he was, like Aakjær, a product of the Grundtvigian *folkehøjskole* milieu. Nexø's *Pelle Erobreren* (4 volumes, 1906–1910; translated as *Pelle the Conqueror,* 4 volumes, 1913–1916), one of the most widely translated works in Danish literature, attempts to counter the bourgeois individualism of the nineteenth-century bildungsroman and expresses Nexø's solidarity with the proletariat.

A new generation of woman writers also made a striking entrance into the literary scene at the turn of the century. Bregendahl, Agnes Henningsen, Thit Jensen, and Karin Michaëlis, all advocates of woman's liberation from conventional roles, wrote about women's lives, psychology, and identity from an early feminist perspective. Michaëlis's novel *Den farlige Alder* (1910; translated as *The Dangerous Age,* 1911), describing the mental agony of a divorced, menopausal woman, acquired international fame and was translated into twenty languages. Bregendahl represents a bridge between regional literature and a new female perspective in *En Dødsnat* (1912; translated as *A Night of Death,* 1931), which depicts the death of a farm woman in childbirth as seen through the eyes of her many children. Bregendahl, Henningsen, Jensen, and Michaëlis all achieved long and prolific literary careers that extended well into the mid-twentieth century.

The outbreak of World War I was as great a shock to the Danes as it was to the rest of the western world. Denmark recognized that the era of peace at her southern border, which had begun at the end of the Franco-Prussian War of 1871, had now come to an end. The outbreak of World War I shattered the optimism and idealism of the early years of the century. The technological and scientific advances that had promised a brighter future for humankind now aided armed conflict and mass destruction. Regardless of Denmark's neutral status, the war caused a shattering of ideals and a realignment of thinking, which found expression in Danish literature of the 1920s and 1930s. At the same time, the chaos of the postbellum era encouraged cultural and political debates and artistic experimentation. The seeds of change that had been sown before the war came to fruition during the decades that followed it.

Danish literature between the two world wars was shaped by several different literary currents, distinguishing the "disillusioned" decade of the 1920s from the politicized 1930s. It is no accident that the first part of Tom Kristensen's classic novel *Hærværk* (1930; translated as *Havoc,* 1968), which offers a portrait of the 1920s as a period of ambiguity, is titled "Mellem Meninger" (Among Opinions). The 1920s is often regarded as a decade without a clear literary program or movement, a decade characterized by skepticism, uncertainty, and nihilism and by the feeling that the old ideals and ideologies (both political and aesthetic) no longer apply to modern life. Particular to this decade is the introduction of modern aesthetics, especially inspired by Expressionism in the pictorial arts, for which the Danish periodical *Klingen* (1917–1921) served as an important vehicle. The 1920s became a period for lyrical experimentation and innovation in Danish poetry. Kristensen, with his lyrical expressionism, was a central figure of the decade; his debut collection, *Fribytterdrømme* (Dreams of a Freebooter, 1920), offers examples of Expressionistic technique, including inspiration from Cubism and Dadaism. His early novels depict the chaos of urban life in a manner that is characteristic of the European modernist novel. His famous novel *Hærværk,* in which the protagonist must experience chaos and devastation in order to achieve a standpoint, is a monument to the "lost generation" of the 1920s. Jacob Paludan, another key figure in the 1920s, offers a more conservative reaction to the decade. His novels may be read as a protest against the superficiality and materialism of modern civilization and mass culture, the results of industrialization and capitalism. His major work, *Jørgen Stein* (2 volumes, 1932, 1933; translated, 1966), depicts the disillusioned generation as "årgangen som snublede i starten" (the generation that stumbled at the start). A third representation of the decade occurs in Knud Sønderby's debut *Midt i en Jazztid* (In the Middle of a Jazz Age, 1931), which depicts the leisure-class youth of the 1920s, liberated from the morals and ideals of the prewar generation; the novel came to be considered a Danish parallel to F. Scott Fitzgerald's depiction of the Jazz Age.

By the late 1920s the politicization of Danish literature that came to characterize the era of the Great

Depression had begun. Marxist philosophy as well as the theories of Freud (whose major works were translated into Danish in 1920) became predominant intellectual influences in the cultural debates and literature of this decade. By the end of the decade the intellectual Left began to articulate a new literary program in journals such as the socialist *Clarté*. Marxism won over a younger generation of writers who advocated a politically engaged literature. An early manifestation of a new socialist, Marxist-inspired literature was Hans Kirk's *Fiskerne* (The Fishermen, 1928), which delineates the development of a community of fishermen. A collective novel, where the focus is not on a single hero but rather on a group of people, *Fiskerne* represents a radical break with the conventional bildungsroman that centers on the development of an individual protagonist. The compositional form of *Fiskerne*—regarded by early critics as a literary articulation of socialist ideology—became extremely popular in the 1930s and inspired a series of collective novels; H. C. Branner, Martin A. Hansen, William Heinesen, and Hans Scherfig all published collective novels. However, not all of these collective novels were directly inspired by Marxism, and many tended to describe the breakdown of the solidarity of a community rather than a socialist utopia.

The idea that the arts—not least, literature—should work to transform or reform society was certainly not new to Danish literature, but it was radicalized by the Depression and by the threat of Fascism. In 1933 Adolf Hitler was elected chancellor in Germany, the same year Denmark's Social Democratic prime minister Thorvald Stauning won the support of the Venstre (Liberal) Party and passed important social reforms which improved the lot of workers and the unemployed. *Socialrealisme* (social realism) became the dominant literary trend of the decade; and the novel, the preferred genre. Among the most significant movements in Denmark of the late 1920s and 1930s is *Kulturradikalisme* (Cultural Radicalism). Based on the architectural concept of functionalism, Cultural Radicalism espouses the belief that rationality and functionality should shape social development; its goal is a democratic state in which every individual—man, woman, and child—is given the freedom to develop naturally to his or her fullest potential. The movement's journal, *Kristisk Revy* (1926–28), edited by the architect and cultural critic Poul Henningsen, and later *Kulturkampen,* the organ of a core group of anti-Nazist intellectuals such as Piet Hein, had considerable influence on writers of the period.

Many of the literary concerns of the 1930s may be understood within the broad context of Cultural Radicalism, the movement of the intellectual Left. A new understanding of the importance of childhood experiences and education—inspired directly by the theories of Freud—were part of the cultural debates and literary concerns of the decade. The child and childhood became important concerns for writers of the period. Branner's collective novel *Legetøj* (Toys, 1936), for example, makes use of Freudian theory to demonstrate how childhood experiences may inhibit the healthy development of the individual, leading to power-seeking, even Nazism, in adulthood. Childhood as an important motif is also evident in Tove Ditlevsen's *Barndommens Gade* (Street of Childhood, 1943), as the title suggests. The criticism of prevailing pedagogic views and of education is directly reflected in Scherfig's *Det forsømte Foraar* (1940; translated as *Stolen Spring,* 1986), a scathing satire on the authoritarian Danish school system of the World War I era. In the 1930s children's education was considered one of the battlefields of the antifascist cultural struggle. Sexuality and women's liberation were also important topics of debate during the interwar period and related to the agenda of Cultural Radicalism. Danish women were granted the right to vote in 1915, and an equal rights law went into effect in 1921 at a time when many women were entering the work force. Under the Social Democratic government, child-rearing was regarded for the first time as society's concern. An active public lecturer, Thit Jensen was one of the driving forces in a movement that called for birth control and sex education to better the lot of women.

Drama, with its potential to engage the public directly in moral and political questions, became a favored genre of the decade. In the 1930s the Danish theater experienced a dramatic revival, particularly through the works of Kaj Munk and Kjeld Abell, whose works reflected the political currents of the decade Munk's *Ordet* (1932; translated as *The Word,* 1953), a contemporary religious drama in the naturalistic tradition, has become a classic in Danish theater and a motion picture classic in Carl Dreyer's adaptation. Although Munk's dramas of the early 1930s idealized strong dictatorial leaders—initially he admired Hitler and Benito Mussolini—in the latter part of the decade, he rejected anti-Semitism and, after the German occupation of Denmark began in April of 1940, he became one of the most outspoken and fearless Danish opponents of Nazism. Abell was a greater innovator in the Danish theater; his dramas broke with the naturalistic tradition and experimented with new dramatic technique. In *Anna Sophie Hedvig* (1939, translated 1944), a play in which he alludes to the Spanish Civil War, he takes up the question of the ethical responsibility of the individual faced with fascist tyranny.

As in any national literature, there are masterpieces in Danish literature that fall outside the dominant literary or cultural currents of a given period. Such is the case of the writings of the Faroese author Jørgen-Frantz Jacobsen, whose only novel, *Barbara* (1939; translated as *Barbara,* 1939), set on the Faroe Islands in the late eighteenth century, tells the story of a destructively passionate woman. The Faroese Islands, situated roughly equidistant to Norway, Scotland, and Iceland have been under Danish rule since the Viking Age. Although the Faroese people gained limited self-government in 1948, they still have extensive historic and literary ties with Denmark. The two most widely read Faroese authors, William Heinesen and Jacobsen, chose to publish in Danish rather than their native Faroese; Jacobsen's *Barbara* became a best-seller in Denmark and one of the most widely translated works of the decade.

The work of Karen Blixen, whose *Seven Gothic Tales* (1934) and *Out of Africa* (1937) won international recognition, is another of the anomalies of Danish literature during the Depression. Blixen, who published in England and America under the pen name Isak Dinesen, defended the old-fashioned art of storytelling and clashed with the contemporary preference for socially engaged literature. Rather than relying on the works of Marx and Freud, she drew on those of Friederich Nietzsche and Søren Kierkegaard, as well as the *Arabian Nights,* presenting herself as a modern-day Scheherazade. Only after World War II, when her exotic tales were understood as modern existentialist parables, did she come to be recognized as one of the most influential Danish artists of the twentieth century.

The occupation of Denmark by Nazi Germany in 1940 is the most significant turning point in the history and culture of modern Denmark. National Socialism—the ideology of *Blot und Boden* (Blood and Soil)—never gained a significant foothold in Danish soil; therefore, the arrival of occupying German forces on 9 April 1940 served to galvanize intellectuals and writers, whether they were Marxists, anti-Fascist radicals, Christians, or nonreligious humanists. For the first years of the war, the Danish government engaged in a *samarbejdspolitik* (policy of collaboration) with Hitler, who intended to display Denmark as a "model protectorate" under the Third Reich. However, many Danes were resistant to this political compromise. As an underground resistance to the occupying forces grew, the iron fist of the Nazi regime tightened. By August 1943 acts of sabotage and resistance against the Nazi Wehrmacht had increased to such an extent that the Danish puppet government resigned. The resistance movement became more effectively organized, even boasting the rescue of some seven-thousand Danish Jews, who were smuggled into neutral Sweden in October 1943, and the resistence remained active throughout the remainder of the occupation. Danish literature was put under German censorship during the war, a circumstance which led to the flourishing of an illegal press as well as a tendency to

hide anti-Fascist allegories in works that passed through German censorship. Martin A. Hansen's *Jonatans Rejse* (Jonatan's Journey) and Branner's *Drømmen om en Kvinde* (The Dream of a Woman), novels published in 1941 under censorship, contain such anti-German sentiments and dramatize the tension between good and evil, life and death. *Der brænder en Ild* (A Fire Is Burning), published illegally in 1944, an anthology of essays and poems by such distinguished writers as Abell, Branner, Hansen, Ditlevsen, and Piet Hein, became a landmark for intellectual and spiritual resistance during the occupation.

World War II is a watershed in Danish literature. The occupation—besides galvanizing national feeling through a collective experience of hardship—forced the abstract questions of ethics and spirituality into the tangible realm of everyday life. Immediately following the liberation, publications dealing with firsthand experiences of the war were popular, such as letters, diaries, or documentary accounts of resistance fighters or concentration camp prisoners. In the 1950s, experiences of the occupation were articulated artistically in novels such as Branner's *Ingen kender natten* (1955; translated as *No One Knows the Night,* 1958) and Tage Skou-Hansen's *De nøgne træer* (1957; translated as *The Naked Trees,* 1959). In postwar Danish writing, the war continued to serve as a frequent literary motif well into the 1960s. In 1962 Scherfig published *Frydenholm,* a bitter and satirical indictment of the treatment of Danish Communists during the occupation. Scherfig, along with Kirk and Nexø, had spent part of the war imprisoned in Hørserød, an internment camp in Denmark.

Although Denmark survived the occupation with its culture, historical cities, and population largely intact—without the physical devastation and bombardment experienced by other European nations—World War II created a deep sense of pessimism and, among writers, a generation of skeptics. The liberation on 5 May 1945 brought relief but also the onset of the Cold War in a world now divided between Eastern and Western blocs and threatened by nuclear weapons. In postwar Danish literature the outer drama of the war and the occupation was now transformed into an inner conflict within the individual. The war had demonstrated the inadequacies of political ideologies to solve problems inherent to human nature. It had meant a loss of meaning and values. It seems natural that after the war writers were drawn to existentialism, which offered a way for the individual to create meaning in existence through his own actions and choices.

Heretica (Heresy, 1948–1953), a journal closely identified with the literary modernism represented by writers such as Stéphane Mallarmé, Rainer Maria Rilke, and T. S. Eliot, became the forum for a new literary movement that rejected the ideological dogmatism of the 1930s. The "heretics" were both poets and prose writers such as Thorkild Bjørnvig, Martin A. Hansen, Frank Jæger, Ole Sarvig, Skou-Hansen, Ole Wivel, and, of course, Blixen, who was regarded as a kind of artistic mentor. These writers saw themselves in a revolt against established intellectual beliefs: the scientific worldview of naturalism in general, and the materialism of Marxism, in particular. They sought to divorce the human dilemma from the "external" circumstances of society and politics in order to articulate a deeper religious or metaphysical understanding of life. The dominant genre of the *Heretica* movement was poetry, with Bjørnvig, one of the first editors of the journal, holding a central position as a visionary poet in the symbolist tradition. His significance is comparable to Sophus Claussen's role in the 1890s. Bjørnvig's poetry is neither strictly metaphysical nor religious but deals with the fundamental conditions of human existence–love, transformation, and death–as articulated in his well-known collection, *Anubis* (1955), the title alluding to an Egyptian god of death. The philosophy of the heretical protest is best described as a humanist existentialism, drawing its inspiration from Kierkegaard and Jean-Paul Sartre. The major prose work of the *Heretica* group, and one of the most debated books of the postwar period, is Hansen's *Løgneren* (1950; translated as *The Liar,* 1954). It is the quintessential existentialist novel depicting a pivotal moment in a man's life in which he recognizes his life as a deception and ultimately chooses the ethical resolution.

While the *Heretica* generation maintained the dominant influence during the immediate postwar period, the Cultural Radicals founded *Dialog* (1950–1961), a journal intended to counter *Heretica*. It profiled the views of the intellectual left wing and among its most important contributors were Kirk and Scherfig, both of whom remained steadfast in their socialist convictions following the war.

After the war, spelling reforms–initiated by the Socialist minister of education, Hartvig Frisch–were enacted in 1948. Nouns, which formerly had been written with initial capitals, as in German, were now lower cased. The spelling of the Danish special vowel *aa* was changed to *å*. Some older or conservative authors, such as Blixen, objected to these changes and continued to use the pre–1948 orthography in their works. In 1984 the Danish government allowed local governments, in cities such as Aarhus and Aalborg, to return to their original spellings of place names. Because of these changes, many apparent inconsistencies continue to appear in works of Danish literature.

By 1960 the process of industrialization and urbanization that had begun in Denmark at the turn of the century was completed. The country was now a modern industrialized welfare state. In Danish literature, the criticism and rejection of modern urban life and an increasingly alienating existence serve as a frequent theme after the late 1950s. The war had left Europe in a deep cultural crisis. During the 1950s this crisis came to be regarded as permanent and led to a feeling of absolute alienation. The literary trends that emerged in the 1960s reflect a blending of this modernist sensibility with the existentialist perspective of the older *Heretica* generation.

The literary trends and the cultural climate of the 1960s may be framed within the context of *Ny-radikalisme* (New Radicalism), a political movement of the 1960s with ties to the Cultural Radicalism of the 1930s. New Radicalism grew out of the heightened social and political awareness that typified the 1960s in the West. In Denmark, the movement protested against the self-satisfied norms of the welfare society, bourgeois materialism, and membership in the North Atlantic Treaty Organization, among other matters. Similar to the Cultural Radicals of the 1930s, the New Radicals of the 1930s embraced the sexual revolution and educational reform. These radical sympathies and modernist poetics merged to form the dominant literary trend of the 1960s that some Danish literary historians have called *Ny-radikale modernisme* (New Radical Modernism). During the late 1950s and early 1960s, the periodical *Vindrosen,* edited by two of the period's central figures, Klaus Rifbjerg and Villy Sørensen, became the dominant literary and cultural organ of this second generation of postwar modernism. Torben Brostrøm, who later shared the editorship of *Vindrosen* with Niels Barfoed, was a leading critic of the period, chronicling its artistic vision.

Poetry is central to the modernist tradition in Danish postwar literature. In the hands of such poets as Bjørnvig, Per Højholt, Klaus Rifbjerg and Benny Andersen, poetry in the 1960s became less metaphysical and more involved in the external world. Rifbjerg's collection *Konfrontation* (Confrontation, 1960), central to postwar Danish modernist poetry, lends its title to a generation of "*Konfrontation* poets." The poetic text is regarded as the manifestation of the confrontation of the mind of the poet with the details of the concrete world. Unlike the reflective *Heretica* poet, the *Konfrontation* poet registers impressions of modern life, confronting material and concrete things as a way of coming to terms with the modern world. Andersen, who debuted in 1960 with his ironic depictions of the alienated modern individual and his humorous observations on the details of ordinary life, also belongs to this generation of modernist poets.

A contrary poetic trend emerged in the mid 1960s, representing another aspect of the modernistic tradition. *Systemdigtning* (Systemic poetry) or metapoetry, concentrating on the poetic language itself, functions under the assumption that language cannot adequately depict the external world but is ultimately self-reflexive. Language and linguistic associations are the central focus of the metapoetic text, which eliminates the individuality of the poet. No other Danish poet has pursued Systemic poetry with more consistency and greater innovation than Højholt. His *Min hånd 66* (My Hand 66), a radically experimental work published in 1966, explores linguistic associations with a playfulness and humor that have become Højholt's artistic signature. Another of the foremost Systemic poets of the postwar decades is Inger Christensen, whose highly successful work *Det* (It, 1969) combines metapoetry with social criticism and a utopian vision. Henrik Nordbrandt, difficult to categorize within a single poetic movement, has drawn inspiration from *Systemdigtning* as well as other traditions in Danish modernist poetry.

The isolated condition of the modern individual is also one of the predominant concerns of Danish prose narratives of the 1950s and 1960s. As in poetry, the postwar sensibility called for new forms of expression in prose. As early as 1953 Sørensen's first published work, *Sære historier* (translated as *Tiger in the Kitchen and Other Strange Stories,* 1957), introduced a new genre of fantastic stories that influenced an entire generation of "sære fortællere" (strange storytellers), a term coined by Thomas Bredsdorff in his 1968 work of that title, which presented this new generation of writers. The fantastic narrative breaks with realism in order to follow its own strange logic in a symbolic world often reminiscent of the tales of Hans Christian Andersen and ancient myth. However, the fantastic stories of the postwar period are distinctively modernist in the manner of Franz Kafka—one of Sørensen's sources of inspiration—in that they are based on a worldview that is fundamentally shattered. This distinction is vividly illustrated in Sørensen's tale "En glashistorie" (A Tale of Glass, 1964), a darkly pessimistic inversion of Andersen's Romantic tale "Sneedronningen" (The Snow Queen, 1845). The fantastic tales of this period demonstrate a heightened psychological sense, the plot often driven by the repressed desires or irrational urges of the subconscious. Peter Seeberg is another master of this genre. In *Eftersøgningen og andre noveller* (The Search and Other Stories, 1962), a work that shows the influence of Albert Camus and Samuel Beckett, Seeberg depicts humans as faced with an absence of meaning in seemingly absurd quests for existential guideposts.

Another literary trend in Denmark during the late 1950s and 1960s is a return to a naturalistic or psycho-logical realism; it is particularly well demonstrated in two very successful novels, both published in 1958, dealing with the themes of puberty and sexual awakening. Rifbjerg's *Den kroniske uskyld* (The Chronic Innocence) and Leif Panduro's *Rend mig i traditionerne* (translated as *Kick Me in the Traditions,* 1961) both deal with coming-of-age in a confusing and at times hypocritical adult world. In their focus on the significance of sexual development, these novels demonstrate the continued influence of Freudian concepts in modern Danish prose.

The youth and student rebellions of 1968 mark a turning point in Danish society and a further radicalization of literary trends. The worldwide political and social upheavals of the late 1960s—including international protests against the Vietnam War, the Civil Rights and Free Speech movements in the United States, and the Cultural Revolution in China—strengthened the Left in Scandinavia and inspired a debate about engaged literature. Danish critics refer to the period from 1968 to the mid 1970s as "Virkeligheden der voksede" (The Reality that Grew), referring to the increasing politicization of literature. The individual is no longer regarded as an isolated entity but as a member of a social unit. Literary realism, with strong ties to the social realism of the 1930s, reemerged. Politicized works produced during this decade reassessed the writer's role in society and included much authentic factual information about contemporary economic, political, and social conditions. *Arbejderlitteratur* (worker's literature), workplace reports, memoirs, interview- and debate-books, and documentary accounts from the developing world became popular in Scandinavia at this time. In retrospect, most of the politicized documentaries of the period have mainly historical interest as part of a particular episode in Danish literature. Historical documentary fiction, on the other hand, which became a popular new genre during this period in Denmark, continues to hold readers. Thorkild Hansen's best-selling documentary works take up historical questions regarding Denmark's ventures in exploration and colonialism. In particular, his trilogy of books on the Danish slave trade, written between 1967 and 1970, reflects the growing awareness during the decade of the role of western imperialism in the developing world. Ebbe Kløvedal Reich, a central figure in the 1970s, links the student rebellion of 1968 with several grassroots movements and antiauthoritarian, left-wing platforms. His fanciful historical narratives depicting Denmark's history and mythology are contributions to the heated public debate about national culture and identity that surrounded Denmark's decision to join the European Common Market in 1972. In the decades which have followed, Reich has continued to cultivate Danish national identity in historical works in which the Roman Empire represents by analogy the expanding European Union.

Ny-realisme (New Realism) became a predominant trend in prose works during the 1970s, offering more precise depictions of social reality than in the psychologically oriented realism of the preceding decade. While not explicitly political, these new realistic works are set in accurately depicted social milieu and tend to depict the private conflicts of the middle class. The work of Christian Kampmann, for example, demonstrates this development from psychological individualism, for example in his short stories *Blandt venner* (Among Friends, 1962), to socially critical novels of the 1970s that depict the private crises of the Danish bourgeoisie. The early works of Henrik Stangerup also demonstrate the tendencies of New Realism. *Manden der ville være skyldig* (1973; translated as *The Man Who Wanted To Be Guilty,* 1982), for example, deals with a man who is not allowed to be guilty because the guardians of the Welfare State deprive him of responsibility for his own life.

Not least of the significant developments of the late 1960s and 1970s was the flourishing of women's literature. As a result of the efforts of the Women's Movement and of the heightened social consciousness of the decade, women gained significant ground in Denmark in the 1970s. The right to free abortions was achieved in 1973, and new laws regarding equal pay went into effect in 1976. In the course of the 1970s the number of female members of parliament increased from 10 to 25 percent. In the literary establishment, women writers—at least in a numerical sense—finally gained the equality which had been denied them for so long. There are many women writers of great talent in Denmark today; in the twenty-first century, it will hopefully become meaningless to distinguish categorically between men and women writers. While it is impossible in this volume to cover all of the women who have contributed to Danish literature in the last decades of the twentieth century, some of the most representative and influential figures have been included.

Elsa Gress, one of the few female members of the most elite Danish authors' society, Det Danske Akademi (The Danish Academy), held a central position in Danish letters and criticism for four decades. Prolific in many genres, she joined the fierce polemic regarding the role of women with her essay *Det uopdagede køn* (The Undiscovered Sex) in 1964; although she formally rejected the Women's Movement, her controversial opinions often placed her at the center of the debate. On the opposite side of the spectrum, Suzanne Brøgger has continued to contribute her original perspective to the discussion of women's roles, identity, and sexuality since the 1970s. In her first book, *Fri os fra kærligheden*

(1973; translated as *Deliver Us from Love,* 1976), she attacks modern morality, monogamous love, and the nuclear family, and in *Crème Fraîche* (Sour Cream, 1978) she describes her erotic adventures. Brøgger seems to have taken to heart Blixen's 1953 oration in which she advised postwar women to lay down their weapons and repossess their femininity. Dorrit Willumsen, who debuted in the mid 1960s, became one of the most significant Danish prose writers of the late twentieth century. Firmly rooted in modernist tradition, Willumsen's early novels often depict women alienated as sex objects in a depersonalized male-oriented consumer society. Kirsten Thorup also holds a central position in modern Danish literature; in particular, her generational novels such as *Himmel og helvede* (Heaven and Hell, 1982) have established her reputation as an astute chronicler of Danish life and society during the postwar decades.

By the 1980s Denmark was well on its way to transforming itself from a modern industrial state to a technological information society. Whereas the 1960s and 1970s may be remembered for political activism and idealism, the 1980s and 1990s may—with historical hindsight—be identified with individualism, political apathy, and nostalgia. Because of economic recessions in the 1970s and growing unemployment, the tax burden of the welfare state began to fall heavily on those who worked, since students, the unemployed, children, and the elderly, who comprised over half the population, paid no taxes. For the first time since the Social Democratic Party took power during the Depression era, a Conservative majority won power in the Danish parliament in 1982. Poul Schlüter's election as prime minister marked a turn to the Right in Danish politics, a movement toward privatization and a tightening of the public sector. Almost simultaneously with the dissipation of the Cold War—marked most dramatically by the dissolution of the Soviet Union and the reunification of Germany—Denmark reluctantly joined the European Union in 1993. Within the context of these dramatic social and political realignments, it is interesting to note the resurgence of many traditional literary genres and modes during the last two decades of the century, although it is too early to predict which literary trends will eventually come to characterize these decades.

In the 1980s a new generation of lyrical poets emerged who experimented with postmodern aesthetics and impulses from painting, punk and New Wave music, and sculpture. The passionate tone, subjectivity, and sensuality of this poetry bears likeness to the older Danish poetic traditions, particularly to the Symbolists and the *Heretica* poets. Pia Tafdrup, whose 1985 anthology, *Transformationer: Poesi 1980–85* (Transformations: Poetry 1980–1985), introduced the new generation, emerged in the 1990s as a leading figure in Scandinavian poetry. Her work is also representative of *Kropsmod-ernisme* (Modernism of the Body), a new tendency in postmodern poetry that employs the sensations of the physical body as a basis for exploring the conditions of existence.

Biographical and historical fiction experienced a revival during this period. The biographical novel, a fictive narrative based on an historical personage, became particularly popular among women writers who revisited the destinies of notable artists, writers, or nobility of past centuries. Willumsen has made important contributions to this genre with two successful novels: *Marie: En roman om Madame Tussauds liv* (1983; translated as *Marie: A Novel About the Life of Madame Tussaud,* 1986), about the woman who founded the wax museum in London, and *Bang: En roman om Herman Bang* (Bang: A Novel about Herman Bang, 1996), an award-winning novel about the life of the Danish writer Herman Bang. Henrik Stangerup's trilogy of novels, *Vejen til Lagoa Santa* (1981; translated as *The Road to Lagoa Santa,* 1984), *Det er svært at dø i Dieppe* (1985; translated as *The Seducer: It is Hard To Die in Dieppe,* 1990) and *Brøder Jacob* (1991; translated as *Brother Jacob,* 1993), depicting three remarkable Danish historical figures according to Kierkegaard's notion of the aesthetic, ethical, and religious existence, is among the most distinguished work in this genre. The biographical genre, with its focus on authentic persons of the historical past, might be viewed as a revolt against the alienating tendencies of modernist prose, which addresses the potential of language itself but fails to offer the reader heroes and heroines.

A Romantic yearning for good stories with engaging plots and remarkable protagonists is also evident in the emergence of the predominant literary movement of the late twentieth century, magic realism. Although magic realism is a critical term that was first applied to Latin American literature, the term is well suited to describe a Danish homegrown variety of fantastic narratives. Related to the *sære historier* (strange stories) of the 1960s, these magical narratives suspend the strictures of realism in order to merge elements of myth, fairy tale, ghost story, or murder mystery into the plot. Hanne Marie Svendsen made her mark as a magic realist with her award-winning novel *Guldkuglen* (1985; translated as *The Gold Ball,* 1989). The tendencies of magic realism are also evident in Ib Michael's cycle of novels *Vanillepigen* (The Vanilla Girl, 1991), *Den tolvte rytter* (The Twelfth Knight, 1993) and *Brev til månen* (Letter to the Moon, 1995), which won critical acclaim in Denmark. In postmodern Danish literature, a highly creative merging of genres is evident in the fantastical narratives of the late century. Peter Høeg's *Frøken Smillas fornemmelse for sne* (1992; translated as *Smilla's Sense of*

Snow, 1993), which became an international best-seller, masterfully blends the genres of science fiction, the crime thriller, and the fantastic narrative. Characteristic of the work of Høeg and Michael is the metafictional aspect of the narrative, a self-conscious commentary on and clever interplay between various genres. One of William Heinesen's literary masterpieces should be mentioned: *Laterna Magica: Nye Erindringsnoveller* (Magic Lantern: New Fictive Recollections, 1985; translated as *Laterna Magica,* 1987), a collection of fantastic stories and timeless tales set on the Faroe Islands, represents a native Scandinavian form of magic realism and places a period at the end of a long and fruitful literary career that spanned nearly the entire twentieth century. The combination of linguistic artistry and intellectual sophistication, of ancient myth and folk ballad, of sincere pathos and wry wit, and of social commentary and a universalist perspective make *Laterna Magica* one of the crowning achievements of modern Danish literature.

In broad strokes, these are some of the principal lines of Danish literature of the twentieth century. An effort has been made to include the most representative and influential figures of the century in this volume. Some consideration has also been given to authors whose writing is available in English translation. In Denmark, the literature of the twentieth century is detailed in no fewer than five volumes in the third edition of *Danske digtere i det 20. århundrede* (Danish Writers of the 20th Century, 1982), edited by Torben Brostrøm and Mette Winge.

–Marianne Stecher-Hansen

Acknowledgments

This book was produced by Bruccoli Clark Layman, Inc. Karen L. Rood is senior editor for the *Dictionary of Literary Biography* series. Jan Peter F. van Rosevelt was the in-house editor. He was assisted by Charles Brower, Samuel W. Bruce, and Sara Parker.

Production manager is Philip B. Dematteis.

Administrative support was provided by Ann M. Cheschi, Tenesha S. Lee, and Joann Whittaker.

Accounting was done by Angi Pleasant.

Copyediting supervisor is Phyllis A. Avant. Senior copyeditor is Thom Harman. The copyediting staff includes Ronald D. Aiken II, Brenda Carol Blanton, Worthy B. Evans, Melissa D. Hinton, William Tobias Mathes, Jennifer S. Reid, and Michelle L. Whitney.

Editorial assistant is Margo Dowling.

Editorial trainee is Carol A. Fairman.

Indexing specialist is Alex Snead.

Layout and graphics supervisor is Janet E. Hill. Graphics staff includes Zoe R. Cook.

Office manager is Kathy Lawler Merlette.

Photography editors are Charles Mims, Scott Nemzek, Alison Smith, and Paul Talbot. Digital photographic copy work was performed by Joseph M. Bruccoli.

SGML supervisor is Cory McNair. The SGML staff includes Tim Bedford, Linda Drake, Frank Graham, and Alex Snead.

Systems manager is Marie L. Parker.

Kimberly Kelly performed data entry.

Typesetting supervisor is Kathleen M. Flanagan. The typesetting staff includes Karla Corley Brown, Mark J. McEwan, and Patricia Flanagan Salisbury. Freelance typesetter is Delores Plastow.

Walter W. Ross and Steven Gross did library research. They were assisted by the following librarians at the Thomas Cooper Library of the University of South Carolina: Linda Holderfield and the interlibrary-loan staff; reference-department head Virginia Weathers; reference librarians Marilee Birchfield, Stefanie Buck, Stefanie DuBose, Rebecca Feind, Karen Joseph, Donna Lehman, Charlene Loope, Anthony McKissick, Jean Rhyne, and Kwamine Simpson; circulation-department head Caroline Taylor; and acquisitions-searching supervisor David Haggard.

The editior of this volume wishes to thank The Danish Literature Information Centre for providing a translation subsidy; Tiina Nunnally and Steven Murray of Fjord Press of Seattle for assistance with illustrative materials, translations, and for valuable advice in general; the publishing firms of Gyldendal, Borgen, and Vindrose, for providing illustrative materials and their help in contacting the subjects of these entries; Anna Broemel for assistance with compiling illustrations for the volume; Mark Mussari for helpful editorial assistance; and Linda Norkool and my colleagues at the Department of Scandinavian Studies at the University of Washington for assisting my work in many ways. I also wish to extend my heartfelt thanks to the in-house volume editor, Jan Peter F. van Rosevelt, for his dedicaton and editorial talents, which greatly enhanced this volume. Finally, I am grateful to my fellow scholars in the field of Danish literature–in North America and Europe–for their substantial contributions to this volume.

Dictionary of Literary Biography® • Volume Two Hundred Fourteen

Twentieth-Century Danish Writers

Dictionary of Literary Biography

Jeppe Aakjær
(10 September 1866 – 22 April 1930)

Timothy R. Tangherlini
University of California, Los Angeles

BOOKS: *Missionen og dens Høvding* (Copenhagen: J. Erslev, 1897);

Bondens Søn: Skildringer fra Fjends Herred (Copenhagen: V. Oscar Søtofte, 1899);

Derude fra Kjærene: Digte (Copenhagen: V. Oscar Søtofte, 1899);

Vadmelsfolk: Hedefortællinger (Copenhagen: V. Oscar Søtofte, 1900);

Fjandboer: Fortællinger fra Heden (Copenhagen: Gyldendal, 1901);

Ruskantate: Studenter samfundet, 26 September 1903 (Copenhagen: O. C. Olsen, 1903);

Steen Steensen Blichers Livs-Tragedie i Breve og Aktstykker, 3 volumes in 36 parts (Copenhagen & Christiana: Gyldendal, 1903–1904);

Vredens Børn: Et Tyendes Saga (Copenhagen: Gyldendal, 1904);

Fra Jul til Sanct Hans: Historier (Copenhagen: Gyldendal, 1905);

Fri Felt: En Digtsamling (Copenhagen: Gyldendal, 1905);

Rugens Sange og Andre Digte (Copenhagen: Gyldendal, 1906);

Livet paa Hegnsgaard: Bondekomedie i fire Akter (Copenhagen: Gyldendal, 1907);

Paa Aftægt: En Fortælling (Copenhagen: Gyldendal, 1907);

Hvor Bønder bor: Tolv Smaahistorier (Copenhagen: Gyldendal, 1908);

Muld og Malm: En Digtsamling (Copenhagen & Christiania: Gyldendal, 1909);

Ulvens Søn: Skuespil i fire Akter (Copenhagen: Gyldendal, 1909);

Den Sommer og den Eng: Digte (Copenhagen: Gyldendal, 1910);

Af Gammel Jehannes hans Bivelskistaarri: En bette Bog om stur' Folk (Copenhagen: Gyldendal, 1911);

Jeppe Aakjær (courtesy of Gyldendal Publishers)

Frederik Tapbjergs Plovgilde: Udvalgte Fortaellinger (Copenhagen & Christiania: Gyldendal, 1911);

Naar Bønder elsker: Skuespil i fem Akter (Copenhagen & Christiania: Gyldendal, 1911);

Hytter i Alle Lande: Et Foredrag (Copenhagen: Skandinavisk Boghandel, 1912);

3

Jævnt Humør: Smaahistorier (Copenhagen: Gyldendal, 1913);

Esper Tækki: En Sallingbo-Empe (Copenhagen: Gyldendal, 1913);

Sommer-Taler (Copenhagen: Gyldendal, 1913);

Arbejdets Glæde: En Fortælling om Bønder (Copenhagen: Gyldendal, 1914);

Fir' Fjandbo-Saang: Ett for Lett og ett for Laang (Holstebro: Printed by Niels P. Thomsen, 1915);

Hedevandringer (Copenhagen & Christiania: Gyldendal, 1915);

Jens Langkniv: Af Fjends Herreds Krønike Bog (Copenhagen: Gyldendal, 1915);

Hvor der er gjærende Kræfter: Landarbejderroman (Copenhagen & Christiana: Gyldendal, 1916);

Livog Sang: Digte i Udvalg (Copenhagen: Gyldendal, 1916);

Vejr og Vind og Folkesind: Digte (Copenhagen: Gyldendal, 1916);

En Skarns Præst og Andre Syndere: Kulturbilleder fra Hjemstavnen (Copenhagen: Pios Vignet-Bøger, 1917);

Himmelbjærgpræsten: Et Skuespil (Copenhagen & Christiania: Gyldendal, 1917);

Fremtidens Bondehjem (Copenhagen: Gyldendal, 1918);

Ravperler, Julen 1918 (Holstebro: Printed by Niels P. Thomsen, 1918);

Af min Hjemstavns Saga: Lidt Bondehistorie (Copenhagen & Christiana: Gyldendal, 1919);

Glimmersand: Smaavers, Julen 1919 (Holstebro: Printed by Niels P. Thomsen, 1919);

Mit Regnebræt: En Selvbibliografi (Copenhagen: Det Akademiske Antikvariat, 1919);

En Daad (Copenhagen: Gyldendal, 1920);

Rejserids af Viborg Amt, Julen 1920 (Holstebro: Printed by Niels P. Thomsen, 1920);

Hjærtegræs og Ærenpris: Digtsamling (Copenhagen: Gyldendal, 1921);

Den ny Klokke: En Historie fra Heden, Julen 1921 (Holstebro: Printed by Niels P. Thomsen, 1921);

Pigen fra Limfjorden: Roman (Copenhagen: Danske Forfatteres Forlag, 1921);

Min første Jul: En Skizze, Julen 1922 (Holstebro: Printed by Niels P. Thomsen, 1922);

Bonden og hans Jord: Et Digt, Julen 1923 (Holstebro: Printed by Niels P. Thomsen, 1923);

Po fir glowende Pæl: Fra jen si bitte Tid: En Sagnsamling (Copenhagen: Gyldendal, 1923);

Hejmdals Vandringer: Et Højsommerdigt (Copenhagen: Gyldendal, 1924);

I Oplysningens Tjeneste: Et Ungdomsminde Julen 1924 (Holstebro: Printed by Niels P. Thomsen, 1924);

Kongenshus: En Luftspejling, Julen 1925 (Holstebro: Printed by Niels P. Thomsen, 1925);

Rejsegildet: Skuespil i 5 Akter (Copenhagen: Gyldendal, 1925);

St. St. Blicher: Hans Personlighed og hans Muse Julen 1926 (Holstebro: Printed by Niels P. Thomsen, 1926);

Min hædersdag paa Kjøbenhavns Raadhus 10 September 1926 (Holstebro: Printed by Niels P. Thomsen, 1927);

Under Aftenstjernen: Digte (Copenhagen: Gyldendal, 1927);

En bristet Drøm: Blicher og Himmelbjærgfesterne (Copenhagen: Gyldendal, 1927);

Fra min Bitte-Tid: En Kulturhistorisk Selvbiografi (Copenhagen: Gyldendal, 1928);

Svenske Jacob og hans Vise, Julen 1928 (Holstebro: Printed by Niels P. Thomsen, 1928);

Drengeaar og Knøsekaar: Kilderne springer og Bækken gaar (Copenhagen: Gyldendal, 1929);

Før det dages: Minder fra Halvfemserne (Copenhagen: Gyldendal, 1929);

Langs Karupaaens Bred: Studier fra Hjemstavnen (Copenhagen: Gyldendal, 1929);

Markedet og Markedsviser (Holstebro: Printed by Niels P. Thomsen, 1929);

Fra Agermuld og Hedesand: Studier fra Hjemstavnen (Copenhagen: Gyldendal, 1930);

Konge, Adel og andre Sallingboer: Studier fra Hjemstavnen (Copenhagen: Gyldendal, 1930);

En Samling Breve og Papirer udgivet som Manuskript, edited by George Saxild (Copenhagen: Gyldendal, 1931);

Gammel Brug og Gammel Brøde: Studier fra Hjemstavnen (Copenhagen: Gyldendal, 1931);

Spildkorn: Dedicationer og Smaavers, collected and edited by Solveig Aakjær (Copenhagen: Printed by Niels P. Thomsen, 1931);

Digte og Noveller: Spredte Fund i Jenles Bibliothek i Maj 1932 (Copenhagen: Gyldendal, 1932);

Fra Sallingland til Øresund: Studier fra Hjemstavnen, edited by August F. Schmidt (Copenhagen: Gyldendal, 1932);

Muld og Mænd: Studier fra Hjemstavnen (Copenhagen: Gyldendal, 1932);

Efterladte Erindringer: Fra Tiden Omkring Aarhundred-Skiftet og Fremefter, edited by Saxild (Copenhagen: Gyldendal, 1934);

Bjergmands-snak (Lemuig: Privattryk, 1949).

Editions and Collections: *Skrifter,* 10 volumes (Copenhagen, 1912–1913);

Samlede Værker, 8 volumes in 7 (Copenhagen & Christiania: Gyldendal, 1918–1919);

Samlede Digte: Mindeudgave, edited by Svend Aakjær, 3 volumes (Copenhagen: Gyldendal, 1931);

Over den Blanke Aa: Udvalgte Prosaværker, 2 volumes, edited by Svend Aakjær (Copenhagen: Gyldendal, 1938)–comprises *Vadmeisfolk; Bondens aon; Af Gammel Johannes hans Bivelskistaarr; Arbejdets Glæde;*

Jyske folkeminder, edited by Bengt Holbek, Danmarks folkeminder, no. 76 (Copenhagen: Munksgaard, 1966);

De stille folk: Sociale Artikler og Fortællinger, edited by Solvejg Bjerre and Hans Jørn Christensen (Copenhagen: Gyldendal, 1980);

Digte af Jeppe Aakjær, edited by Asger Schnack (Copenhagen: Hans Reitzel, 1988).

Editions in English: *Four Poems,* translated by J. A. Peehl (N.p.: W. Wakeslee, 1917)–comprises "Clear View," "Jutland," "Jutland's Heath," and "The Land of Heather";

"A Song of the Rye," translated by Robert S. Hillyer, *American-Scandinavian Review,* 12 (1924): 669.

Songs of the Heath, translated by J. Glyn Davies (Llanfairfeachan, Wales: H. Glyn Davies, 1962);

"Off for the Day," translated by W. Glyn Jones in *Contemporary Danish Prose,* edited by Elias Bredsdorff (Copenhagen: Gyldendal, 1958; Westport, Conn.: Greenwood Press, 1974), pp. 29–40.

OTHER: *Fræ wor Hjemmen: Vers og Prose i Jydsk Mundart,* edited by Aakjær (Aarhus: Det Jydske Forlag, 1902);

Jydsk Stævne: Et Aarsskrift, edited by Aakjær (Aarhus, 1902);

Danmark: Illustretet Almanak udgivet af den danske Presse, edited by Aakjær and Gustave Hetsch (Copenhagen, 1919–1924);

Steen Steensen Blichers Samlede Skrifter, 33 volumes, edited by Aakjær and others (Copenhagen: Gyldendal, 1920–1934).

The three short lines that Jeppe Aakjær wrote during his early student years as the motto for the new flag of Catilina, the Social Democratic student association, "Fra Folket vi kommer, til Folket vi gaar, dets Lykke skal være vor Lov" (From the folk we come, to the folk we go, its good fortune shall be our law), summarize the ideas that shaped his long authorship. Aakjær was one of a group of authors from Jutland who emerged on the literary scene during the first decades of the twentieth century. They were loosely grouped by critics as the "Jutland movement" or as "folkelige realister" (folk realists) since their realistic mode of writing had a strong connection to the rural folklife of the Jutlandic peasantry. This new *hjemstavnslitteratur* (regional literature) became a significant literary movement in Denmark even though the authors, as Aakjær himself points out in his memoirs, hardly formed a cohesive group. Instead, they were bound together by their love of the rural regions of Jutland. Other than Aakjær, authors

Front cover for Aakjær's 1924 poem about a wandering Jutlander

who are considered to be part of this group include Johannes V. Jensen–perhaps the most successful of the authors in the loosely affiliated movement–and his sister, Thit Jensen; Marie Bregendahl, to whom Aakjær was married for seven years; Knud Hjortø; Johan Skjoldborg; Martin Andersen Nexø, best known for his four-volume socialist novel, *Pelle Erobreren* (Pelle the Conqueror, 1906–1910); Thøger Larsen; and Jakob Knudsen.

Later in life, Aakjær was somewhat puzzled by the lack of a leader for the "Jutland movement." In his memoirs, he complains,

> Alle de andre Litteraturretninger havde fra første Færd haft en Fører. Romantikken havde Johan Ludvig Heiberg og adskillige andre. Realismen fra '70erne havde altid Georg Brandes, den utrætteligste Lansedrager, for den ny Tid. Halvfemsernes Maaneskindsmænd havde C. E. Jensen . . . Men den jydske Retning fik ikke sin egen Kritiker. Den Mand kom aldrig frem og har ikke vist sig endnu, der forstod den inderste Nerve i den jydske Retnings Litteratur.

> (All of the other literary movements had, from the very beginning, a guide. Romanticism had Johan Ludvig Heiberg and assorted others. Realism from the 1870s always had Georg Brandes, the most tireless point man for the new age. The 1890s moonlight men had C. E. Jensen . . . The Jutlandic school never had its own

critic. That man never came forward, and still hasn't to this day, who understood the innermost nerve in the Jutlandic school's literature.)

Despite this lack of a critical guide, authors from this movement were extraordinarily influential in twentieth-century Danish literature.

Jeppe Aakjær is perhaps best remembered today in Denmark as the author of the lyrics of popular folk songs. After N. F. S. Grundtvig and B. S. Ingemann, Aakjær's songs constitute the largest group in the 1989 edition of the *Folkehøjskolens Sangbog* (Folk High School Songbook). Often, poems he had composed were set to music while, at other times, he wrote lyrics intended specifically for songs. These words were set both to familiar folk melodies and new compositions alike. His myriad contributions to Danish popular music include funerary verses in honor of Sophus Schandorf, the well-known author, and Viggo Hørup, the journalist and radical politician; "The Revolutionary Student," which was used as the fight song of the University of Copenhagen student association for many years; and other songs such as "Se dig ud en Sommer dag" (Look Outside on a Summer Day, 1905), "Storken" (The Stork, 1912), "Historiens Sang" (History's Song, 1917), and "Goddaw ijen" (Good Day Again, 1919). His songs were so popular that the well-known critic Thomas Bredsdorff said to Aakjær in their last conversation, "Hvor maa det være velsignet at vide, at man er den danske Sanger, der har skrevet omtrent al den Sang, som et helt Slægtled synger!" (It must be a blessing to know that one is the Danish bard who has written just about every song that an entire generation is singing!).

Although today Aakjær's songs completely overshadow the rest of his literary production, he is the author of seven novels, five plays, dozens of short stories, many historical essays printed in collections and the popular press, as well as several collections of poetry and a multivolume literary biography of the great nineteenth-century Danish poet Steen Steensen-Blicher. In fact, it is paradoxical that an author who made no secret of his inability to play a single instrument or read musical notation is now best remembered for songs.

Aakjær was born Jeppe Jensen on 10 September 1866 in the small village of Aakjær in Jutland; in 1906 he changed his name to that of his birth village, a fairly common practice in Denmark. One of eight children, his father, Jens Peder Jensen, was a farm owner who came from a long line of farmers. Aakjær himself experienced early on the difficult toil of rural life that was to become a major focus of his literary endeavors. At a young age he was sent off to tend cattle as a herdsboy and, as he grew older, took up the more demanding work of a farmhand. In his memoirs he remembers these early days with a mixture of nostalgia and bitterness. His mother, Cathrine Marie, was a hardworking farmwife whom he remembers singing ballads and other folk songs to her many children. His father, who was a staunch supporter of the *Venstre* (Liberal) party, inspired both Aakjær's interest in politics and strong democratic leanings from an early age.

Aakjær's grandfather also lived at the farm under a quasi-retirement arrangement known as *aftægt,* in which a parent cedes to their child the rights to the farm in return for room and board. These arrangements, which were quite common in late-nineteenth-century Denmark, often became strained. In some cases the elderly parent was used as unpaid labor and received little in the way of lodgings and care. In other cases the parent became a millstone around the grown child's neck, contributing little to the economy of the farm and demanding a great deal. Aakjær's own experiences with the cruel aspects of the pensioner's system came in the form of his grandfather's tyranny, drinking, and swearing, which cast a pall over his childhood home. These experiences with the *aftægt* system—and his condemnation of it—appeared in many of his writings, particularly the novels *Paa Aftægt: En Fortælling* (In Retirement: A Story, 1907), *Vredens Børn: Et Tyendes Saga* (Children of Wrath: A Servant's Saga, 1904) and *Bondens Søn: Skildringer fra Fjends Herred* (The Peasant's Son: Pictures from the Fjend District, 1899).

Even though schooling had been made mandatory for Danish children at the beginning of the nineteenth century, in practice many children in rural areas received little education since their help was needed on their parents' farms. Throughout his youth, Aakjær's schooling was not particularly rigorous. This circumstance changed, however, when a young teacher named Niels Jakobsen came to the school at Fly where Aakjær was a student. In 1882 Jakobsen arranged for Aakjær to attend Staby *folkehøjskole* (Folk High School)—the *folkehøjskoler* are residential schools for adults with a curriculum influenced by folk culture. In 1884 Jakobsen managed to convince Aakjær's parents to allow him to travel to Copenhagen to study at *Blaagaards Seminarium* (Blaagaard's Teacher's College). In the intervening two years, Aakjær studied with Jakobsen, with the ultimate goal being a teaching degree. Aakjær, however, left the teacher's college without finishing his teaching credential, quitting after his preliminary examinations.

Aakjær's first literary activities were in late adolescence when, in 1883, at the age of seventeen, he began contributing material for Evald Tang Kristensen's journal, *Skattegraveren* (The Treasure Hunter), after seeing an advertisement in *Højskolebladet* (The *folke* High School Magazine). Kristensen's journal was dedicated

Aakjær in his study at Jenle

to publishing collected folklore–ballads, fairy tales, legends, jokes, riddles, and descriptions of folklife–from an informal network of collectors throughout Jutland. Young Aakjær was intrigued by the stories he heard on the farms where he worked, and he began in earnest to collect these tales. Over the course of several years, Aakjær contributed more than three hundred folk narratives, riddles, and songs, and the vast majority of these found their way into Kristensen's journal or other published works. For example, at least seventy-seven legends that Aakjær sent to Kristensen were included in his *Jydske Folkeminder VIII: Sagn og Overtro fra Jylland* (Jutlandic Folklore VIII: Legends and Superstition from Jutland, 1886). In addition, Aakjær provided Kristensen with a list of potential informants in the Fly area, and Kristensen sought many of these people out on a highly successful fieldwork trip. In return for Aakjær's extraordinary help and enthusiasm, Kristensen sent Aakjær copies of the issues in which his recordings appeared, as well as some of his other books–primarily folklore collected from people in Jutland.

Even after Aakjær stopped collecting folklore when he moved to Copenhagen in 1884 to prepare for his preliminary examinations for higher education, the two corresponded, albeit with less and less frequency. Kristensen was mildly critical of Aakjær's collections and felt that Aakjær was unsuccessful in his attempts to duplicate the contours of the Jutlandic dialect, although he praised him for trying. Aakjær later became known as a master of reproducing the Jutlandic dialects in his written works. Indeed, this wish to capture the nuances of folk speech became one of Aakjær's overwhelming concerns. Later in life, the two men became great admirers of each others' work, and it was clear that Kristensen felt that Aakjær was one of very few literary men who truly understood the nature of the rural folk. At Kristensen's eightieth birthday party Aakjær sang his translation of the traditional Scots song in the version popularized by Robert Burns as "Auld Lang Syne," and this, more than all of the speeches made in Kristensen's honor, was the most moving moment of the day, according to those in attendance.

Many of the legends Aakjær collected made their way into his later novels and short stories, the clearest example of this transition being *Po fir glowend Pæl: Fra jen si bitte Tid: En Sagnsamling* (On Four Glowing Posts: From My Childhood: A Myth Collection, 1923). Set on a foggy summer night in Davbjærg Daas, the work is both a retelling of twenty-six of the many legends that he had collected as a young man and a masterful description of the people who told the stories. In it, Aakjær captures the immediacy of folk performance, coupled to the sounds of the Jutlandic dialect. In Aakjær's earlier work *Bondens Søn* one also finds legend narratives woven into the story. His attention to aspects of folklife also emerge in this novel, providing a rich description of the daily life of his farm-working characters. In his novel *Jens Langkniv: Af Fjends Herreds Krønike bog* (Jens Longknife: From the Chronicle of the Fjend District, 1915) Aakjær further combines his appreciation of folk legend and belief with his historical training, including a fascinating exploration of the role of witchcraft in sixteenth-century Denmark. His preoccupation with themes from Danish legend emerges in his poetry as well, the best example of this being "Bjergmands-Snak" (Mound-dweller's Talk, 1949), written on the occasion of a festival and read by the popular Danish actor Valdemar Mæs. The long poem, somewhat reminiscent of Hans Christian Andersen's tale *Elverhøj* (The Hill of the Elves, 1845), is presented as the words of a mound-dweller, a sometimes threatening supernatural being in Danish folklore, and weaves together many of the popular stories of these creatures.

Aakjær, like many young men and women at the turn of the century, was lured to Copenhagen by the cultural and educational opportunities the city offered. His move to Copenhagen in 1884 marked not only the end of his fledgling career as a folklorist but also the beginning of his literary career. In Copenhagen he was inspired by the social and intellectual movements of the time. He became intellectually engaged by the ideas of Brandes and Hørup and politically awakened by his first political hero, the Jutlandic politician Jens Busk. However, after completing his preliminary examinations in 1886, Aakjær returned from the capital to Jutland, splitting his time between his parents' farm, Per Odgaard's farm, and Esper Andersen's dairy, where he often spent time writing during his visits to his home province. He also embarked on a lecture tour of Jutland, speaking primarily at *folkehøjskoler,* lecturing about the new ideas that were emerging in the intellectual circles of Copenhagen. His lectures had a strong political slant to them and were often directed at waking the spirit of resistance among the cotters and day laborers. This spirit of resistance, coupled to his passionate critique of religion, was considered by the local authorities

to be seditious, and one of these lectures in Viborg landed him in jail for nearly three weeks. In later years Aakjær often emerged as the spokesperson for various social movements, particularly the *husmandsbevægelse* (cotters' movement) and the *tyendebevægelse* (servants' movement).

During the winter of 1887–1888, Aakjær studied at Askov *Folkehøjskole,* one of the many folk high schools that dotted the Danish countryside. His stay at the school, however, seemed to have been of little importance to him. From 1888 to 1890, he worked as a teacher at Elbæk *friskole* (free school) in eastern Jutland but decided not to pursue a career as a schoolteacher. In 1899, in a speech titled "Ungdom og Politik" (Youth and Politics), Aakjær expressed his growing concern with social injustice, a position that emerges again and again in his writings. He ended the speech with words that guided him for the rest of his life: "Jeg vil ikke gjøre Uret, og jeg vil ikke finde mig i Uret." (I will not commit injustices, and I will not tolerate injustice.) Besides the ideas of Brandes, other strong influences on Aakjær included Charles Darwin, whose works he read in J. P. Jacobsen's translations, and the social philosophies of Henry George and Karl Marx, especially Marx's *Das Kapital* (1867, 1885, 1894), which had a significant influence on Aakjær's developing sense of worldwide injustice. In his memoirs he recounts how Marx's work inspired him to fight for the democratization of the human spirit and the socialist transformation of society. Many of Aakjær's works, such as *Vredens Børn* and *Arbejdets Glæde: En Fortælling om Bønder* (The Joy of Work: A Story about Peasants, 1914), reflect his deep concern with the agrarian proletariat and his strong desire to improve their condition. This social political engagement is perhaps one of the most characteristic aspects of Aakjær's authorship.

In 1890 Aakjær was drafted; first placed in the infantry in Skive, he was later sent to a barracks in Copenhagen. After six weeks, however, he was discharged because of a problem with his vision. He returned to teaching at Elbæk *friskole* for the remainder of 1890 and part of 1891, then tried his hand working as a teacher at Morten Pontoppidan's *folkehøjskoler* in 1891 and 1892 but found it difficult to earn enough money to support himself and decided once again that he was not interested in being a teacher. In 1892, with the help of friends, he returned to Copenhagen to continue his studies, intending to earn a degree in history. He married Marie Bregendahl in 1893; she was an author herself and another future member of the Jutlandic school. After seven years and one son, Svend Aakjær, the marriage ended. Even many years later, Aakjær still seemed bitter about the relationship, making only slight reference to it in his final volume of

Godaw igjen
Jeppe

End'le jenle eller som Franskmændene siger Enfin seuls
Jeppe Aakjær vender hjem fra Festerne

Caricature of Aakjær by Alfred Schmidt for the magazine Blæksprutten; *he is returning to Jenle from Copenhagen, where he was honored for his
writing in a celebration on 10 September 1926; the original caption reads "Finally Jenle, or as the French say,
'Alone at Last.' Jeppe Aakjær returns from the parties."*

memoirs. During these student years he became deeply involved in the politics of the student association, and at one point he was elected to its executive committee, a position he held for several years. In 1895 he passed his *studentereksamen,* and in 1896 he received his *candidatus* degree. For the next two years, he studied history at the University of Copenhagen, but economic difficulties forced him to abandon his studies and become a professional writer.

In order to support himself during his studies, Aakjær began working for various newspapers in Copenhagen. His first job was as a copyeditor at the Left Reform Party newspaper, *Politiken,* which was run by one of Denmark's leading cultural figures, Edvard Brandes, brother of Georg Brandes. While there, Aakjær first drew attention to himself with his early cultural historical work, *Missionen og dens Høvding* (The Mis-

sion and Its Chieftain, 1897). The title alludes in a derogatory fashion to the Inner Mission, an evangelical Lutheran movement founded by Vilhelm Beck, but the critique in the book extends far beyond a simple attack on this fundamentalist movement. Rather, Aakjær sets his sights on the oppressive nature of Christianity in general. The work is markedly polemical and reveals Aakjær's deep distaste for what he calls an "anachronistic" conservative Lutheranism. Instead, he emphasizes concepts of fairness and proposes that Christianity, with its emphasis on confession, often deters this human will to justice. Aakjær found the Inner Mission particularly dangerous since most of its supporters lived in the rural areas he loved. In his later works, especially his novels, Aakjær frequently included criticism of the stultifying nature of Christianity, especially that of the Lutheran Church.

Edvard Brandes was impressed with Aakjær's work and promoted him to the position of contributor at *Politiken*. Aakjær later switched to the newspaper *København*, but his journalistic career did not develop significantly until 1899, when he became a parliamentary correspondent for the social democratic newspaper, *Provinspresse*, a position he kept until 1903. Aakjær later complained about the poor treatment he received from the various newspapers and felt that they had robbed him of time that could have been better spent writing. Brandes, however, continued to be supportive of Aakjær and wrote several positive reviews of his work—a positive review from Brandes was a significant boost for the career of a young author in Denmark.

Aakjær continued his attack on the Inner Mission in his first major literary work, his 1899 novel, *Bondens Søn*. The novel, which is strongly autobiographical, recounts the story of Jens, a young man who grows up in poverty in rural Jutland. He leaves home and heads to Copenhagen but still feels the oppressive hand of the conservative Christianity that was beaten into him by his grandfather. After some time in the city, the protagonist returns home on a visit, accompanied by a girl-friend from Copenhagen. Rather than giving him a warm welcome, the townspeople reveal their deep provincialism and react negatively to the personal freedoms of the city as personified by Jens. He is not, however, beaten by the conservatism of his hometown. Although he eventually takes over his father's farm and marries his hometown sweetheart, he remains apart from the traditional peasant culture. The book is informed by Aakjær's strong distrust of Christianity and his experiences as a student in Copenhagen. While some critics have dismissed the work as naive, it reveals Aakjær's first concerted attempt to address issues of both political and cultural importance and an effort to portray rural Jutlandic life in a critical and nuanced fashion.

Aakjær had originally hoped that the important publishing firm of Gyldendal would accept the work, but his initial queries were quickly rebuffed, even though Peter Nansen, an editor at Gyldendal, had earlier encouraged him to submit his work. Aakjær instead found a bookstore owner, V. Oscar Søtofte, who was willing to take a chance on him and publish this first novel. Søtofte soon thereafter published a collection of Aakjær's verse, *Derude fra Kjærene* (Out There from the Watering Holes, 1899). The relationship was never quite what Aakjær had expected or hoped for, and he felt that Søtofte was unwilling to market his work properly, complaining about the "tasteless" cover Søtofte had chosen for *Bondens Søn*. A disagreement arose between the two over the publication of Aakjær's collection of short stories describing rural Jutlandic life.

While Aakjær wanted the stories published as a single book, Søtofte felt that the ensuing volume would be far too large and persuaded Aakjær to break the work up into two shorter volumes, only the first of which, *Vadmelsfolk: Hedefortællinger* (Homespunfolk: Heath Stories, 1900), was published by Søtofte. *Vadmelsfolk* was published shortly before Christmas in 1900, but Aakjær did not benefit from the increased sales of the holiday season, since few shoppers were aware of the book. Aakjær was sorely disappointed by the marketing and sales of his works, and his relationship with Søtofte fell apart.

Aakjær, however, had attracted attention to his literary abilities with these first few volumes and the long-sought-after publishing relationship with Gyldendal finally materialized. *Fjandboer: Fortællingen fra Heden* (Fjand Dwellers: Stories from Heden, 1901), which comprised the remaining stories, was the first work Aakjær published with Gyldendal. His main contact and editor at Gyldendal was Nansen, the man who had refused *Bondens Søn*. Although Aakjær felt that Gyldendal, over the years, occasionally let him down or was overly demanding, their association provided him with a steady income, and Aakjær published virtually all of his books with the firm, the one notable exception being *Pigen fra Limfjorden: Roman* (The Girl from Limfjord: Novel, 1921), which he published with Danske Forfatteres Forlag, a smaller house. At the beginning of his publishing relationship with Gyldendal, Aakjær arranged with Nansen that he would receive a 150-kroner advance at the beginning of each month, a sum that brought him just above the subsistence level. With this financial arrangement, Aakjær was finally able to abandon most of his journalistic commitments and concentrate on his literary writing. However, the arrangement also meant that Aakjær had to produce a significant amount of material for the press, and he soon found himself in debt to Gyldendal. By 1910 he owed the press 8,000 kroner—even though he received nearly 10,000 kroner for the popular edition of his collected works, an edition that sold close to seventy thousand copies, he immediately had to return most of the money to the press. Aakjær, however, had managed to retain the rights to all of his works, which was not common practice at that time.

At the turn of the century, Aakjær launched himself into a work that was to take control of his life for several years, namely his monumental literary biography, *Steen Steensen Blichers Livs-Tragedie i Breve og Aktstykker* (Steen Steensen Blicher's Life Tragedy in Letters and Documents, 1903–1904). Aakjær spent hours in archives study throughout the country, following leads, writing letters, collating information, and looking into the smallest nooks and crannies in Blicher's past. For example, in his memoirs Aakjær recounts the excitement of digging through the archives at a women's prison and discovering that Blicher's character Lange Margrethe was based on a real person. The result of Aakjær's obsessive historical research is an extraordinarily thorough accounting of Blicher's life and literary endeavors. The biography was sold by subscription, a common practice at the time, and eventually totaled thirty-six small volumes. Despite Aakjær's enthusiasm and Gyldendal's support for the project, subscriptions were disappointing, with only six hundred copies subscribed, instead of the expected two to three thousand. Critical reception, however, was quite positive, and eventually the work came to be considered a significant contribution to Danish literary history.

In 1905 and 1906 Aakjær published several collections of poetry, namely *Fri Felt: En Digtsamling* (Open Field: A Poem Collection, 1905) and *Rugens Sange og Andre Digte* (Songs of the Rye and Other Poems, 1906). The latter is considered by many to be among his finest works and includes Aakjær's best-known poem, "Jens Langkniv" (Jens Longknife). He wrote the majority of the poems in this collection while staying at the house of his good friends Johanne and Sigurd Rambusch. Unlike his socially and politically aware short stories and novels, Aakjær's poems tend to dwell on the beauty of rural life. His poems are imbued with a lyricism that captures the spirit of peasant life at the same time that it revels in the natural beauty of rural Denmark. Nowhere is this more clearly seen than in the first thirteen poems of the verse cycle *Rugens Sange*. Aakjær mentions that he always drew inspiration for his poems on long walks under the open sky, occasionally stopping to jot down the verses or stomping out the rhythm with his feet. Later, he would rework the lines, but the original inspiration always came while he was out in the very landscape that he wrote about. Aakjær, in his rural poetry, owes a great debt to the works of the Scottish poet Robert Burns, a poet whom Aakjær felt had managed to capture the nuances of rural dialects, the beauty of the natural landscape, the emotional life of the farmers, and the contours of day-to-day existence in his verse. Indeed, Aakjær was so taken by Burns's poetry that in 1898 he translated a great deal of his verse into Danish. Later, Aakjær visited Scotland to wander in the same places that Burns had. Aakjær attempted to capture some of the humor of Burns's *Tam O' Shanter* (1789) in his own humorous piece, *Esper Tække: En Sallingbo-Empe* (Esper Tække: A Salling Imp, 1913).

In 1906 Aakjær was awarded a fellowship, the *Anckerske Legat,* and set off on a long journey through Europe with his friend Lauritz Larsen. After a jaunt through continental Europe, he returned with Larsen to Denmark and then set out on his own for Scotland. The three months he spent there were truly inspira-

Cover for the final, posthumously published volume of Aakjær's memoirs, edited by Georg Saxild

tional, and through this trip he solidified his artistic connection to Burns. During his stay in Scotland, however, he suffered a relapse of an intestinal problem that plagued him for most of his life and prevented him from seeing as much of Scotland as he had wished. While Aakjær never wrote any works directly related to his travels, he mentions in his memoirs the extraordinary influence his trips abroad had on his poetic perspective. After his fellowship year was over, Aakjær only managed to travel abroad one more time before his death. In 1913 he traveled to Germany, Holland, Belgium, and England accompanied by his son. While on the first trip he had been bored by museums, on this trip he spent nearly two weeks wandering through the collections of the British Museum. A painful blister on his foot, however, curtailed the trip, and they returned to Denmark without revisiting his by then beloved Scotland.

In 1905, the year before he set out on his European travels, Aakjær had purchased fifty-five acres near Salling which, in 1907, became his farm, Jenle. In the same year he married the artist, Nanna Krog, whom he had met several years earlier in Copenhagen. Their marriage was long and happy. Together, they had two children, a son, Esben, and a daughter, Solvejg. In 1908 Aakjær was voted a state-supported stipend of 800 kroner a year, and this stipend, combined with the income from Gyldendal, assured him of economic security for the rest of his life. In 1910 Aakjær made Jenle the site for annual folk festivals, known as the Jenlefest, attended by several thousand people each year. Among the attendees at these festivals were local farmers, prominent politicians, and noted figures in Danish intellectual, artistic, and literary life. Despite his growing literary prominence, Aakjær remained true to his political and social ideals, and this was reflected in the political spirit of these festivals. In 1916, as a fiftieth-birthday present, Aakjær received six acres of heather-covered hills that abutted the original property. Due to Aakjær's failing health, the last of these festivals took place in 1929.

In 1907 Aakjær wrote the first of his dramatic pieces, *Livet paa Hegnsgaard: Bondekomedie i fire Akter* (Life at Hegns Farm: Rural Comedy in Four Acts), in which he attempted to capture the spirit of rural life not on the pages of a book, but rather in the living representation of the theater. Aakjær had actually written the majority of this first play many years earlier, in 1901, but when it was rejected by the Folketeater (People's Theater) in Copenhagen, he put it aside. Not until 1907 did he consider writing for the stage again. With encouragement from a friend, he finished the fourth act of *Livet paa Hegnsgaard,* and by 1908 the piece was a commercial success. Although Aakjær was a bit disappointed in the inability of most actors to capture the nuances of the Jutlandic dialect, he continued to write for the stage, following with the play *Ulvens Søn: Skuespil i fire Akter* (The Wolf's Son: Play in Four Acts, 1909), which engaged many of the social themes he had addressed in his earlier novel, *Vredens Børn.* The following year, Aakjær wrote *Naar Bønder elsker: Skuespil i fem Akter* (When Peasants Love: Play in Five Acts, 1911) a play that he considered to be his best even though critical and popular receptions were not nearly as enthusiastic as they had been for his first play. Aakjær wrote two more plays during his career, *Himmelbjærgpræsten: Et Skuespil* (The Minister of Himmelbjærg: A Play, 1917) and *Rejsegildet: Skuespil i 5 Akter* (The Going-Away Party: Play in 5 Acts, 1925), but neither of these were ever performed.

In 1911 Aakjær also published one of his more controversial pieces, *Af Gammel Jehannes hans Bivelski-staarri: En bette Bog om stur' Folk* (From Old Jehanne's Bible Stories: A Little Book about Big Folk, 1911). Aakjær bases the narrator on one of the many excellent storytellers he knew from his home province. In the book the narrator tells several biblical stories, but he relates them in Jutlandic dialect and changes the stories to fit his social and cultural environment. While some critics accused Aakjær of blasphemy, he felt that his stories captured the folk reception of the widely known Bible stories, making them more accessible to ordinary people. Aakjær continued with his social criticism and critique of institutional religions in several later novels and short-story collections, most notable among these being *Hvor der er gjærende Kræfter: Landarbejderroman* (Where There Are Fermenting Powers: Farmworker Novel, 1916) and *Af min Hjemstavns Saga: Lidt Bondehistorie* (From My Provincial Saga: Little Farmer Story, 1919). He also published several more poetry collections, including *Vejr og Vind og Folkesind: Digte* (Rain and Wind and Folkspirit: Poems, 1916), *Hjærtegræs og Ærenpris: Digtsamling* (Quaking Grass and Speedwell: Poem Collection, 1921) and *Under Aftenstjernen: Digte* (Under the Evening Star: Poems, 1927), all of which continued in the vein of his earlier verse.

Toward the end of his life, Aakjær turned his attention to writing his memoirs and rekindled his interest in local history. His memoirs, which detail both life in rural Denmark and the struggles of an author, eventually filled four volumes: *Fra min Bitte-Tid: En Kulturhistorisk Selvbiografi* (From My Childhood: A Cultural Historical Autobiography, 1928), *Drengeaar og Knøseaar: Kilderne Springer og Bækken gaar* (Boyhood Years and Laddish Years: The Wells Spring and the Stream Flows, 1929), *Før det dages: Minder fra Halvfemserne* (Before Dawn: Memories from the Nineties, 1929), and *Efterladte Erindringer: Fra Tiden Omkring Aarhundred-Skiftet og Fremefter* (Posthumous Memories: From Times around the Turn of the Century and Afterwards, 1934). Most of these were written from his sickbed. Although he recovered in 1928 from a dangerous bout with gangrene, he died two years later of a heart attack while working in the garden of his farm. His cultural and historical explorations of his home provinces eventually comprised the six-volume *Studier fra Hjemstavnen* (Studies from the Province, 1929–1932).

Aakjær's contributions to Danish literature, literary and cultural history, folklore, and popular culture were substantial. His political commitment to the disenfranchised members of the rural economy was a constant feature throughout his long career. Perhaps the lack of critical attention to his work in subsequent years can be attributed to his engagement in his prose with problems of the day. His poetry, which focused more on the beauty of rural life, has accordingly had greater staying power. Even today, his poems, which were often set to music, play an important part in the cultural life of most Danes.

Letters:

Solvejg Aakjær Bjerre, ed., *Breve fra Jeppe Aakjær 1883–1899* (Copenhagen: Gyldendal, 1944);

Aakjær Bjerre, ed., *En brevveksling mellem Jeppe Aakjær og Henrik Cavling* (Herning: Poul Kristensen, 1988);

Kamma Aakjær, ed., *Drøm og drama: Breve mellem Jeppe Aakjær og hans søskende* (Videbæk: Farfars Forlag, 1990).

Bibliography:

Jeppe Aakjær, *Mit Regnebræt: En Selvbibliografi* (Copenhagen: Gyldendal, 1919).

Biographies:

K. K. Nicolaisen, *Jeppe Aakjær: En lille Biografi og Karakteristik* (Copenhagen: Gyldendal, 1913);

Reinhard Fuchs, *Der dänische Bauerndichter Jeppe Aakjær* (Gütersloh, 1940).

References:

J. Christian Bay, *Jeppe Aakjær's Minde* (Chicago: Danish-American Association, 1930);

Solvejg Bjerre, *Livet på Jenle: 1905–1926: Nanna og Jeppe Åkjærs hjem* (Copenhagen: Hans Reitzel, 1985);

Bjerre, *Man lever jo dog kun når man arbejder* (Holstebro, 1966);

Bjarne Nielsen Brovst, *Jeppe Aakjær på Askov Højskole 1887–1888* (Herning: Poul Kristensen, 1988);

Brovst, *Jeppe Aakjær og en kusine: En dokumentarisk skildring* (Copenhagen: Hernov, 1985);

Brovst, *Jeppe Aakjærs 17 dage i Viborg arrest 1887* (Herning: Poul Kristensen, 1987);

Hans Jørn Christensen, ed., *Vredens Børn: En montage*, Pædagogisk arbejdsmapper, no. 33 (Kongerslev: GMT, 1979);

"Det folkelige gennembrud," in *Dansk Litteratur Historie*, volume 7, edited by Gunhild Agger and others (Copenhagen: Gyldendal, 1990), pp. 33–74;

Johannes Nørgaard Frandsen, "En skælven i et ydmygt sind: Jeppe Aakær, *Rugens Sange*," in *Læsninger i Dansk Litteratur*, volume 3, edited by Inger-Lise Hjordt-Vetlesen and Finn Frederik Krarup (Odense: Odense University Press, 1997), pp. 76–94;

Inger Lise Hjordt-Vetlesen, *Flugtens fængsel: Længsler og bindinger i Jeppe Aakjærs romaner* (Odense: Odense University Press, 1981);

Peder Jensen, *Jeppe Aakjærs første artikel* (Odder, 1966);

Evald Tang Kristensen, *Minder og Oplevelser,* 4 volumes (Viborg: Forfatterens Forlag, 1923–1927);

Hans Jørn Nielsen, *Til folket vi går: Omkring nogle Aakjær-sange* (Aalborg: Institut for Sprog, Kommunikation og Kulturhistorie, 1982);

Felix Nørgaard, *Jeppe Aakjær: En Introduktion til hans Forfatterskab* (Copenhagen: Gyldendal, 1941);

August F. Schmidt, *Fra Sallingland til Øresund* (Brabrand: Eget Forlag, 1932);

Schmidt, *Jenle og Jenlefesterne* (Brabrand: Eget Forlag, 1935);

Schmidt, *Jeppe Aakjær: Nogle Oplysninger om hans Forfatterskab* (Brabrand: Eget Forlag, 1933);

Hakon Stangerup and F. J. Billeskov Jansen, "Jeppe Aakjær," in *Dansk Litteratur Historie*, volume 3, edited by P. H. Traustedt (Copenhagen: Politikens Forlag, 1966), pp. 498–505;

Waldemar Westergaard, "Jeppe Aakjær," *American-Scandinavian Review,* 12, no. 11 (1924): 665–669.

Papers:

Many of Jeppe Aakjær's papers are in Det Kongelige Bibliotek (The Royal Library), Copenhagen. His folklore collections, which he had sent to Evald Tang Kristensen, are filed under his original name, Jeppe Jensen, in the Dansk folkemindesamling (Danish Folklore Archive) in Det Kongelige Bibliotek.

Kjeld Abell

(25 August 1901 – 5 March 1961)

John Lingard
University College of Cape Breton

BOOKS: *Melodien der blev væk: Larsens Komedie i 21 Bille-der* (Copenhagen: Monde, 1935); translated by Frances Sinclair and Ronald Adam as *The Melody that Got Lost* (London: Allen & Unwin, 1939);

Eva aftjener sin Barnepligt: Komedie i ll billeder (Copen-hagen: Nyt Nordisk Forlag, 1936);

Paraplyernes Oprør (Copenhagen: W. Hansen, 1937);

Anna Sophie Hedvig: Skuespil i 3 Akter (Copenhagen: Nyt Nordisk Forlag, 1938); translated as *Anna Sophie Hedvig* in *Scandinavian Plays of the Twentieth-Century,* Second Series, edited by Alrik Gustafson (Prince-ton: Princeton University Press, American-Scan-dinavian Foundation of New York, 1944), pp. 223–229;

Judith: Skuespil i 6 Billeder (Copenhagen: Nyt Nordisk Forlag, 1940);

Silkeborg: Skuespil af Kjeld Abell (Copenhagen: Thaning & Appel, 1946);

Dage Paa en sky: Skuespil i 3 Akter (Copenhagen: Thaning & Appel, 1947); translated by A. I. Roughton as *Days on a Cloud,* in *The Genius of the Scandinavian Theater,* edited by Evert Sprinchorn (New York: New American Library, 1964), pp. 466–535;

Teaterstrejf i Påskevejr (Copenhagen: Thaning & Appel, 1948);

Miss Plinckby's kabale: Lystspil i 3 akter (Copenhagen: Thaning & Appel, 1949);

Vetsera blomstrer ikke for enhver: Skuespil i 3 akter (Copen-hagen: Thaning & Appel, 1950);

Fodnoter i støvet: Glimt fra en rejse (Copenhagen: Thaning & Appel, 1951);

Den blå pekingeser (Copenhagen: Thaning & Appel, 1954);

Andersen; eller, Hans livs eventyr (Copenhagen: Thaning & Appel, 1955);

Fire skuespil af Kjeld Abell (Copenhagen: Thaning & Appel, 1955)—comprises *Melodien der blev væk; Eva aftjener sin Barnepligt, Judith;* and *Dronning går igen,* translated by J. F. S. Pearce as *The Queen on Tour,* in *Contemporary Danish Plays: An Anthology,* edited by

Kjeld Abell (courtesy of Gyldendal Publishers)

Elias Bredsdorff (London: Thames & Hudson / Copenhagen: Gyldendal, 1955), pp. 105–171;

De tre fra Minikoi (Copenhagen: Thaning & Appel, 1957); translated by Roughton as *Three from Mini-koi* (London: Secker & Warburg, 1960);

Kameliadamen: Skuespil i 3 akter inspiret af Alexandre Dumas' roman af samme navn (Copenhagen: Thaning & Appel, 1959);

Skriget (Copenhagen: Gyldendal, 1961).

Editions and Collections: *Anna Sophie Hedvig: Skuespil i 3 akter,* edited by Niels Heltberg (Copenhagen: Nyt Nordisk Forlag, 1951);

Synskhedens gave: Prosa og vers af Kjeld Abell, edited by Bredsdorff (Copenhagen: Gyldendal, 1962);

Den blå pekingeser, edited, with an introduction, by Nils Kjærulf (Copenhagen: Gyldendal, 1965).

PLAY PRODUCTIONS: *Enken i spejlet: Ballet,* Copenhagen, The Royal Theater, 20 November 1934;

Melodien der blev væk, Copenhagen, Riddersalen, 6 September 1935; adapted as *The Melody that Got Lost,* London, Embassy Theatre, 26 December 1936;

Eva aftjener sin barnepligt, Copenhagen, The Royal Theater, 8 December 1936;

Anna Sophie Hedvig, Copenhagen, The Royal Theater, 1 January 1939;

Judith, Copenhagen, The Royal Theater, 10 February 1940;

Dronning gaar igen, Copenhagen, The Royal Theater, 5 March 1943;

Silkeborg, Copenhagen, Det Ny Teater, 1 March 1946;

Dage paa en Sky, Copenhagen, The Royal Theater, 11 December 1947;

Miss Plinckby's kabale, Copenhagen, The Royal Theater, 13 February 1949;

Vetsera blomstrer ikke for enhver, Copenhagen, Frederiksberg Theater, 12 November 1950;

Den blå pekingeser, Copenhagen, The Royal Theater, 16 December 1954;

Skriget, Copenhagen, The Royal Theater, 2 November 1961.

MOTION PICTURES: *Millionærdrengen,* screenplay by Abell, Palladium Productions, 1936;

Tak fordi du kom, Nick, screenplay by Abell, Palladium Film, 1941;

Regnen holdt op, screenplay by Abell, Palladium Film, 1942;

Ta' Briller paa, screenplay by Abell, Palladium Film, 1942.

Kjeld Abell was the great source of renewal in twentieth-century Danish drama. As playwright, essayist, and set designer, he worked tirelessly to create a modern theater free from the constraints of realism and alive to the issues of its day. While only two of Abell's plays, *Melodien der blev væk: Larsens Komedie i 21 Billeder* (The Lost Melody: Larsen's Comedy in Twenty-one Scenes, 1935; translated as *The Melody that Got Lost,* 1936), and *Anna Sophie Hedvig Skuespil i 3 Akter* (Anna Sophie Hedvig: Play in Three Acts, 1938; translated 1944) won international recognition, H. C. Branner could justly claim: "Det var Kjeld Abell som gjorde dansk teater levende og nutidigt" (It was Kjeld Abell who made Danish theater living and contemporary) by politicizing its subject matter and revolutionizing its form.

Abell was born in Ribe, Jutland, Denmark, on 25 August 1901 to Peter Abell, a high-school teacher, and his wife, Susanne Jørgensen. In 1910 the family moved to Odense, and then in 1912 to Copenhagen. After Abell graduated from the Metropolitan School in 1919, he studied at the Academy of Art where he was able to develop his considerable talents as a graphic artist, painter, and designer. In 1920 Gustav Reinhardt's production of August Strindberg's *Spöksonaten* (*The Ghost Sonata,* 1907) was Abell's introduction to symbolist theater, and its impact on the young theater artist is vividly recalled in *Teaterstrejf i påskevejr* (Theater Sketches in Easter Weather, 1948): "Pludselig blev tanker klippet over. Jeg holdt op at tænke. I de korte øjeblikke katastrofen skete, var der kun tid at føle. Jeg følte med øjne, ører, hele personen" (Suddenly thought was disconnected. I stopped thinking. In the brief moments during which the catastrophe took place, there was only time to feel. I felt with my eyes, my ears, my whole being). Abell went on to study political science at the University of Copenhagen. To pay his way, he found work in the police fingerprint department, which almost certainly influenced his literal and metaphoric use of *gerningstedet* (the scene of the crime) in several of his plays. After receiving his degree, he left with his wife, Grete, for Paris where their son, Jacob, was born, and where Abell began his theatrical career as a designer. His encounter with French symbolist theater and cinema would have lasting importance to him, as would the new ballet created by the revolutionary choreographers Sergei Diaghileff and Georges Balanchine.

In 1930 Abell followed Balanchine to Copenhagen to design sets for a season of ballet at the Royal Theater, which soon became his second home. There too, his own ballet, *Enken i spejlet: Ballet* (The Widow in the Mirror: Ballet) was successfully presented in 1934. Here, in what Abell called "Det ordløse teater hvor man lærer rummet at kende" (The wordless theater where you learn to interpret space), he introduced his audience to many of the ideas and images that were to characterize his plays: the individual trapped by her past; a mirror- or picture-frame as an image of entrapment and loneliness; music and dance as metaphors for desire and freedom: "Enken sprænger spejlrammet og lever" (The widow bursts the mirror-frame and lives).

While many of his contemporaries believed that cinema would replace theater, Abell insisted that "Filmen gav theatret en mulighed for at leve videre. Det var filmen der viste theatret at det igen burde blive

Drawing by Abell published on the back cover of his first play, Melodien der blev væk: Larsens
Komedie i 21 Billeder *(1935)*

rigtigt teater" (Film gave theater an opportunity to survive. It was film which showed theater that it must again become real theater). Unlike motion pictures, theater should not, indeed could not, be realistic; instead, "teatret bør altid være den frie tankes fantastiske fristed" (theater must always be the free imagination's fantastic sanctuary). Just as Abell's characters are often seen breaking away from some kind of frame, so the dramatist must escape the constraints of a "kølig og graa" (cool and grey) realism framed by the proscenium arch, to restore living contact with the audience. In his important essay "Realisme–?" (Realism–?, 1935), Abell claims that if this escape can be achieved, "der skal sejres paa begge sider af rampen" (there will be victory on both sides of the footlights).

On 6 September 1935 Abell's first play, *Melodien der blev væk: Larsens Komedie i 21 Billeder,* opened at Riddersalen. In *Melodien der blev væk,* Abell tells the story of Larsen, an average middle-class clerk, who is haunted by fragments of a life-enhancing melody. Using the techniques of epic and expressionist theater, Abell shows the audience Larsen at the office, at home with his wife Edith and her rather ghastly parents, or trying to enjoy a bourgeois picnic in the woods. Eventually, Larsen and Edith discover the full melody that leads them "langt ud i det fri" (far out into nature), leaving behind Larsen's in-laws who are now blindfolded and deaf to the music of life.

More satirical review than drama, *Melodien der blev væk* nonetheless includes many of the ideas, techniques, and strengths and weaknesses of Abell's later plays. The goal of the action is freedom–here freedom from middle-class conformity, materialism, and a nine-to-five office routine. Abell is good at displaying the defects of this world. In two office scenes, for example, three typists, each called Froken Møller and wearing a photographic mask, sing a "skrivemaskinesang" (typewriter song) and perform a "Danse du Bureau"(office dance), looking like "hjerneløse mekaniske dukker" (brainless mechanical dolls). In a scene titled "Søndag" (Sunday), banality darkens into pathos when Edith defends her right to use linen napkins: "Jeg vil bruge mine ting mens de er pæne og ny" (I want to use my things while they are fine and new). The author is not, however, so successful at demonstrating ways of escape. One of his most perceptive and loyal critics, Frederik Schyberg, argued that the happy ending was "scenisk svag" (theatrically weak), and that "Dens logik holdt ikke stik" (Its logic did not hold true).

With all its flaws, *Melodien* had an extraordinary impact on its first audiences. "De af os, der var unge," Carl Johan Elmqvist writes, "da Kjeld Abell i 1935 fik sit store gennembrud med *Melodien der blev væk* . . . blev ikke de samme mennesker, som vi ville være blevet uden *Melodien*. Forestillingen havde jo i en sjælden grad publikumstække, men den havde først og fremmest ungdomstække, fordi den virkede lige saa ung som vi selv og lokkede toner frem i os, som vi knapt vidste, at vi rummede" (Those of us who were young in 1935 when Kjeld Abell had his great breakthrough with *Melodien der blev væk* . . . became different people from what we would have been without *Melodien*. The production had of course unusual audience appeal, but it appealed first and foremost to the young, because it seemed just as young as we were ourselves and struck chords in us we hardly knew we had). The play ran for 594 performances in Copenhagen and was produced in Norway, Sweden, and England. Several satirical pieces in review format were to follow *Melodien der blev væk*, the most substantial being *Eva aftjener sin Barnepligt: Komedie i 11 Billeder* (Eve Serves her Childhood: Comedy in Eleven Scenes) in 1936, a popular if self-indulgent piece in which the biblical Eve walks out of a Renaissance painting to remake her own life.

Anna Sophie Hedvig, Abell's next major work, premiered on 1 January 1939. It is, in his own words, a "*tilsyneladende* gammeldags" (*apparently* old-fashioned) three-act problem play whose realism was "født af tiden" (born of the times). Ever since German rearmament in 1935, Abell had been trying to warn Denmark of the threat from the south. In his play, he suggests that tyranny can only be overcome through violence.

Anna Sophie Hedvig, a middle-aged high-school teacher, has murdered a vicious, child-hating, female colleague who was about to become principal. Apart from two flashbacks to the scene of the crime, the play takes place in the living room of Anna's cousin who is married to a wealthy entrepreneur. During a cocktail-hour conversation about the Spanish Civil War, Hoff, the guest of honor, remarks that "et oplyst, kultiveret, moderne menneske kan ikke slaa ihjel" (an enlightened, cultivated, modern person cannot kill). This compels Anna to confess and defend her action:

det var som om jeg pludselig fra min lille verden så ind i den store–den fra viserne–den vi hører om og taler om–men som er så langt borte–den verden, hvor det ikke er mord at slå ihjel–hvor en enestes mening skal være alles–det var hende, der ville angribe min verden–måtte jeg ikke forsvare den–inden hun angreb–?– –må vi ikke forsvare vores små verdener–?–er det ikke dem, der tilsammen er den store

(it was as if I suddenly looked out of my little world into the big world–the one in the newspapers–the one we hear about and talk about–but which is so far away–that world where it isn't murder to kill–where one person's opinion must be shared by all–it was she who wanted to attack my world–wasn't I meant to defend it–before she attacked–?– – –aren't we meant to defend our small worlds–?–isn't it those that make up the big one).

After her story has been told, the stunned company divides sharply over what action they should take. Anna's cousin and nephew boldly step out of line to take her side, but Hoff and his frightened host agree to hand her over to the police. With its intriguing plot, politically urgent message, and well-individualized characters, *Anna Sophie Hedvig* was Abell's second theatrical triumph, his first at the Royal Theater, and has become a classic of modern Danish drama.

Even after the outbreak of war, there were Scandinavians who clung to the belief that the kind of political tyranny they read about in the newspapers was still "far away." Such complacency may have prompted Abell to choose for his first wartime play the apocryphal legend of Judith and Nebuchadnezzer's general Holofernes, who places her city under siege. The analogies between Denmark and Bethulia, between Hitler and Holofernes, are striking, but Abell's *Judith: Skuespil i 6 Billeder* (Judith: Play in Six Scenes, 1940) does not exploit them with sufficient resonance or clarity. This failure is largely because Abell sidetracks the central political conflict with a frame narrative involving a modern couple, which is only tenuously linked to the Bible story, and, more seriously, alters the famous climax: this Judith does not assassinate Holofernes; he is killed instead by a procuress who has posed as Judith's maid. The resulting sense of audience disappointment probably contributed to the box-office failure of the play. It is hard not to agree with Schyberg's review: "Hvem er Judith, naar hun ikke er den Judith, der slog Holofernes ihjel? Hun er ingen" (Who is Judith, when she is not the Judith who killed Holofernes? She is no one).

During the first years of the occupation, Abell produced three screenplays for feature films, as well as working as a director at Tivoli. His next play, *Dronning går igen* (The Queen Walks Again, 1943; translated as *The Queen on Tour*, 1955) was produced in 1943. It is on

Abell in 1936 standing in front of one of his set designs (Nordfoto)

the surface a realistic murder mystery, set in a country inn. A man's body has been found on a nearby road, and the chief suspect is Mirena Pritz, an actress who happens to carry a revolver and has just arrived at the inn still wearing her Gertrude costume from a touring production of William Shakespeare's *Hamlet* (1603). For two acts, the detective genre is skillfully sustained. In the third, Mirena delivers a thinly veiled appeal to the latter-day Hamlets in her audience:

> jeg saa en verden der ikke lod sig bortforklare, en verden behersket af Macbeth's og Claudius' brutale efterkommere, en verden lukket inde i et ubarmhjertigt Kronborg med fortiden vandrende som genfærd pa bastionerne og fremtiden hvilende i den veges haand—og op af det Kronborg rejste sig min fæstning, ikke til forsvar—nej, angreb!—jeg ville komme og jeg kom som den trojanske hest—dækket af de store, de berømte, de knæsatte navne red jeg ind i selve det elendigste provinshul med dolken parat i hvert ord.

> (I saw a world that could not be explained away, a world controlled by the brutal successors of Macbeth and Claudius, a world shut inside a cruel Elsinore with its past wandering like ghosts on the ramparts and its

future resting in the weak man's hand—and up from that Elsinore my own fortress rose, not for defense—no, for attack!—I planned to come and I did come like the Trojan horse—under cover of the assumed names of the great and the famous, I rode into the most wretched provincial hole with a dagger hidden in every word).

Reviewers in what Johan Faltin Bjørnsen calls "en slik Ulvetid" (that time of the wolves) could not respond openly to this challenge. It was safer to address aesthetic matters: Bodil Ipsen's strong performance of Mirena and the seemingly bathetic revelation that there has been no murder after all. This, however, must have been Abell's point: the real murders were taking place outside the theater. In retrospect, *Dronning går igen* seems one of Abell's more durable plays. Its clever interweaving of the detective plot with a system of Shakespearean allusion and coded resistance message makes it worthy of revival and reappraisal.

On 29 August 1943, the Germans declared a state of emergency in Denmark and took hundreds of Danish citizens, Abell among them, hostage, placing them in an internment camp at Horserød. Shortly after their release, the great Danish playwright Kaj Munk was murdered by the Gestapo on 4 January 1944. The next evening, Abell courageously interrupted a performance at the Royal Theater to speak from the stage in Munk's memory. The audience's reaction was recorded in a letter written by Bent Suenson to Abell the following day: "Jeg var i teatret i gaar og vil gerne sige dig, hvor smukt de ord, du sagde virkede, paa mig og dem, der var med mig. Intet, tror jeg, kunne have gjort et stærkere indtryk end disse tilstræbt stilfærdige og smukke ord" (I was in the theater yesterday and would like to tell you what a beautiful effect the words you said had on me and those who were with me. Nothing, I believe, could have made a stronger impression than those well-chosen, quiet, and beautiful words). Abell left the theater fifteen minutes before the arrival of the Gestapo and was active in the resistance for the remainder of the war. A photograph taken in the summer of 1944 shows him effectively disguised with bleached hair, moustache, and steel-rimmed glasses.

Out of these experiences came a new play, *Silkeborg* (1946), about the Martensen-Smiths, a family that is tragically divided by the occupation. The play opens and closes in 1900 near Himmelbjerget where a student has a waking dream about the family through three generations. Inside this frame, the plot centers on events surrounding a British weapons drop in which Jørgen, the son, takes part. The pickup miscarries, and the Gestapo track Jørgen and his friend Ulriksen back to the Martensen-Smiths' home, where Ulriksen is killed. Jørgen's mother, Git, once had an affair with a

Abell at work in Copenhagen in July 1944, while in hiding from the Gestapo

Germanized Dane called Carl Otto who is now serving with the occupation forces, though he is anti-Nazi. He chooses this night to visit Git, and later appears, in uniform, to help Jørgen evade the Gestapo. Misunderstanding the situation and traumatized by his mother's apparent treason, Jørgen shoots Carl Otto and runs out into the night.

Silkeborg is one of Abell's strongest plays. There is a new, caustic quality to the dialogue and a powerful film-noir atmosphere of violence and fear. Frederick J. Marker rightly praises the skill with which the "private" scene between Git and Carl Otto is charged with "wider ideological and ethical concerns."

Dage Paa en sky: Skuespil i 3 Akter (Days on a Cloud: Play in Three Acts, 1947; translated 1964) is the first of three postwar plays that form a kind of trilogy against suicide. A scientist, driven by guilt and despair over the atomic bomb, has jumped from a plane to end his life. The action turns a few seconds of free fall into a flashback on his life, and a mythical exploration of love and hate. The cloud of the title is inhabited by Aphrodite and her attendant goddesses who are at war with Zeus and inspire the scientist with a wish to live. As he pulls the ripcord on his parachute and floats to earth, Aphrodite seems set fair to defeat Olympic tyranny.

The surrealist setting is one of Abell's finest, with "gennemsigtige tempelruiner og væltede søjler" (transparent temple ruins and overturned columns), together with "faldefærdige balustre, tilsyneladende kun holdt sammen af visne efeuranker" (crumbling balustrades, apparently only held together by withered ivy vines). This new balance of imagination and self-discipline is not as evident in the dialogue, which often betrays Abell's love of passionate, but dramatically inappropriate rhetoric. The reviewers praised Holger Gabrielson's sensitive production, but the dramatist was attacked for what some took to be communism, despite the play's appeal to individual love and freedom.

After *Miss Plinckby's kabale: Lystspil i 3 akter* (Miss Plinckby's Game of Patience: Comedy in Three Acts, 1949), a well-crafted and underrated excursion into drawing-room comedy, the trilogy continued with *Vetsera blomstrer ikke for enhver* (Vetsera Does not Bloom for Everyone, 1950). Set in an isolated *landsted* (country villa), *Vetsera blomstrer ikke for enhver* marks a return to Abell's symbolic realism. The cool grey neoclassical facade of the house is replaced in act 2 by an eerie garden room redolent of "et forfald der er standset" (an arrested decay). The villa thus reflects the aristocratic pose of its recently deceased owner, which masked emotional sterility and despair. Obsessed with the legendary suicide pact of Maria Vetsera and Prince Rudolph of Austria, the owner, David, had tried to persuade a working-class girl named Vetsera to join him in a similar pact. After she rejected this sinister offer, he lacked the courage for direct suicide and drank himself to death instead. His sister-in-law Alice had once loved him but was repelled by his drift into self-destruction. The action moves toward her personal exorcism of David's ghost, aided by the more "common" but more courageous Vetsera.

Vetsera blomstrer ikke for enhver was Abell's one real box office and critical failure. All that reviewers found to praise were Bodil Ipsen's performance of Alice and Helge Refn's expert realization of the house. Svend Kragh-Jacobsen pointed to many borrowings from the plays of Henrik Ibsen, August Strindberg, Eugene O'Neill, Jean Giraudoux, and Jean Anouilh; and Hans Brix criticized the prolixity of the dialogue. While it is probable that Abell's borrowings form a corrective pastiche of dramatists who had valorized self-destruction, *Vetsera blomstrer ikke for enhver* is, unfortunately, not strong enough to take on Ibsen, O'Neill, or Anouilh at their own game.

The last play in this trilogy, *Den blå pekingeser* (The Blue Pekingese, 1954), opened at the Royal Theater, with Mogens Wieth and Bodil Kjer in the leading roles of André and Tordis Eck. Like many of Abell's heroines, Tordis feels herself trapped in a series of mirrors and portraits. She calls herself "en indrammet datter" (a daughter in a frame), and even her friend and former lover, André, whose name is a pun on *andre* (other people), describes her as "en person i et billede som vi betragede udefra" (someone in a picture whom we looked at from the outside). When the play begins, Tordis has retreated to a weird viking-gothic mansion on a Baltic island, where she tries to kill herself, but spoils "den fuldendte forbrydelse" (the perfect crime) by sending a coded suicide note to André. The island is cut off from Sjælland by a fierce storm, but he manages to get a message sent to Tordis's doctor who saves her life.

This skeletal plot would not have made a full-length play if Abell had not, in Branner's words, "ophævede naturalismens love for tid og sted og lod os se det sceniske nu i dets sammenhæng med fortid og fremtid" (canceled the naturalistic rules of time and place and let us see the scenic present in its connection with the past and future). As André waits for news of Tordis, the action moves between real time and place in a café near the Royal Theater and a symbolist vision of the island "befolket af genfærd, genfærd af døde, genfærd af ufødte" (peopled by ghosts, ghosts of the dead, ghosts of the unborn).

Den blå pekingeser had a great success with its first public and may well be Abell's masterpiece. The long second-act speeches are undoubtedly too rhetorical to be truly dramatic. They are built from Abell's favorite kind of sentences, which Schyberg calls serpentine, where "billederne snubler over hinanden og tilsidst hverken er til at hitte ud af eller ind i" (the images stumble over each other and are in the end impossible to make head or tail of). On the other hand, the interweaving of André's narrative in the café with dramatized scenes on the island is brilliant, especially in act 1. Just as striking are the play's dreamlike landscape—imaginatively realized in the first production by Erik Nordgreen's design—and a fascinatingly original soundscape that includes storm effects, a piano concerto by Wolfgang Amadeus Mozart, a waltz by Niels Viggo Bentzon, and the bells of an invisible Pekingese. Here, more successfully than in any other play, Abell succeeded in turning the stage into "the free imagination's fantastic sanctuary."

Abell died suddenly on 5 March 1961. His last play, *Skriget* (The Scream), was produced in November of that year. The main characters are birds who inhabit or invade the bell tower of a country church: two owls, Tuwit and her mate Tuhuh; an Australian vulture named Arthur; and a domesticated crow that once betrayed the owls into captivity. The story of Tuwit's revenge on Crow is juxtaposed with a human drama, at first narrated by the birds, involving an organist who seems to have lost his wife's affection and his ability to play. This plot climaxes with a terrifying cry that marks the turning point of the whole play. The organist's wife has heard the cry in a radio broadcast of the service and rushes to the church to be reunited with her husband. Meanwhile Arthur has gathered together a large flock of birds that peck Crow to death outside the tower.

Like the last or near-last plays of Shakespeare, Ibsen, and Strindberg, *Skriget* suspends received conventions to bring a privately imagined judgment day to the stage. Abell's chosen target is mankind's inability to perceive and respect a deep connectedness between all living things: "Altid sir de noget de ikke mener," remarks Tuwit about her human captors, "—men lytter man sig ned under det de ikke mener, lytter sig helt ned, er sproget det samme som i den vingede verden, dernede kan ikke lyves, for dernede er ingen ord" (they always say something they don't mean—but if you listen down underneath what they don't mean, listen right down, the language is the same as in the winged world, there can be no lies down there, because down there there are no words).

Though Abell undercuts his theme in the second part by introducing human characters, *Skriget* is often genuinely funny and wise. While Harald Engberg greeted the play with puzzled respect, H. C. Branner suggested that as soon as the curtain rises, "må man åbne seg" (you must open yourself) to Abell's world, "hvor der ikke gjaelder nogen anden logik end den digteriske" (where no other logic prevails than that of the poetic).

Nils Kjærulf believed that Abell's reputation as Munk's successor began to wane during the 1950s, when a negative reaction to his late symbolic manner set in. By 1965, however, Kjærulf could report that "*radioteatret* har gjort en stor indsats for at rehabilitere Kjeld Abell ved en række fortjenstfulde opførelser af både ældre og nyere værker. Og har man lyttet til dem, vil man have fornemmet, hvor *levende* og *nærværende* en dramatiker han stadig er" (*radio theater* has gone a long way toward rehabilitating Kjeld Abell with a series of excellent productions of both older and newer works. And if you have listened to them, you will have felt how *living* and *contemporary* a dramatist he still is). Although Abell has never caught on in the English-speaking world in the way that Ibsen and Strindberg have, his plays and theater essays form a fascinating contribution to twentieth-century drama.

Letters:
Elias Bredsdorff, ed., *Kjeld Abell: Et brevportraet* (Copenhagen: Spektrum, 1993).

References:
Johan Faltin Bjørnsen, *Kjeld Abell: Hans idéer og verker* (Oslo: Solum, 1978);

H. C. Branner, "Paradokset Kjeld Abell," in *En bog om Kjeld Abell,* edited by Sven Møller Kristensen (Copenhagen: Gyldendal, 1961), pp. 162–165;

Elias Bredsdorff, introduction to A. I. Roughton's translation of *Days on a Cloud,* in *The Genius of the Scandinavian Theater,* edited by Evert Sprinchorn (New York: New American Library, 1964), pp. 466–476;

Bredsdorff, *Kjeld Abells billedkunst* (Copenhagen: Gyldendal, 1979);

Allen E. Hye, "Fantasy + Involvement = Thought: Kjeld Abell's Conception of Theater," *Scandinavian Studies,* 63 (Winter 1991): 30–49;

Frederick J. Marker, *Kjeld Abell* (Boston: Twayne, 1976);

Marker and Lise-Lone Marker, "Three New Voices," and "Playwriting in Transition," in their *A History of Scandinavian Theatre* (Cambridge: Cambridge University Press, 1996), pp. 262–268, 310–317;

Frederick Schyberg, *Kjeld Abell* (Copenhagen: Thaning & Appel, 1947);

Schyberg, *Teatret i krig* (Copenhagen: Gyldendal, 1949);

Schyberg, *Ti aars teater* (Copenhagen: Gyldendal, 1939).

Benny Andersen
(7 November 1929 –   )

Leonie Marx
University of Kansas

BOOKS: *Den musikalske ål: Digte* (Copenhagen: Borgen, 1960);

Kamera med køkkenadgang: Digte (Copenhagen: Borgen, 1962);

Den indre bowlerhat: Digte (Copenhagen: Borgen, 1964);

Puderne: Noveller (Copenhagen: Borgen, 1965); translated by Andersen and others as *The Pillows* (Copenhagen: Borgen / Willimantic, Conn.: Curbstone, 1983);

Portrætgalleri: Digte (Copenhagen: Borgen, 1966);

Os, illustrated by Lise Roos (Copenhagen: Borgen, 1966);

Snøvsen og Eigil og katten i sækken, illustrated by Signe Plesner Andersen (Copenhagen: Borgen, 1967);

Tykke-Olsen m.fl.: Fortællinger og monologer (Copenhagen: Borgen, 1968);

Det sidste øh og andre digte (Copenhagen: Borgen, 1969);

Den hæse drage (Copenhagen: Borgen, 1969);

Snøvsen på sommerferie, illustrated by Signe Plesner Andersen (Copenhagen: Borgen, 1969);

Lejemorderen og andre spil (Copenhagen: Borgen, 1970)– comprises *Lejemorderen, Glassplinten, Faders kop;*

Her i reservatet: Digte (Copenhagen: Borgen, 1971);

Man sku' være noget ved musikken, by Andersen and Henning Carlsen (Copenhagen: Borgen, 1972);

Snøvsen og Snøvsine, illustrated by Signe Plesner Andersen (Copenhagen: Borgen, 1972);

Svantes viser: En sanghistorie (Copenhagen: Borgen, 1972);

Barnet der blev ældre og ældre: Kronikker og erindringer (Copenhagen: Borgen, 1973);

Undskyld hr., hvor ligger naturen? Børnelytterroman, illustrated by Kim Plesner Andersen (Copenhagen: Borgen, 1973);

Personlige papirer: Digte (Copenhagen: Borgen, 1974);

En lykkelig skilsmisse, by Andersen and Carlsen (Copenhagen: Borgen, 1975);

Nomader med noder: Digte m.m. (Copenhagen: Borgen, 1976);

Under begge øjne: Digte (Copenhagen: Borgen, 1978);

Orfeus i undergrunden (Copenhagen: Borgen, 1979);

Benny Andersen (courtesy Vindrose Publishers)

Himmelspræt eller kunsten at komme til verden: Digte (Copenhagen: Borgen, 1979);

Kolde fødder (Copenhagen: Rhodos, 1980);

På broen: Roman i ni episoder (Copenhagen: Borgen, 1981);

Oven visse vande (Copenhagen: Borgen, 1981);

Over skulderen: Blå historier (Copenhagen: Borgen, 1983);

Ebberød bank: Folkekomedie i fem afdelinger, by Andersen and Steen Albrechtsen (Graasten: Drama, 1984);

Snøvsen hopper hjemmefra, illustrated by Signe Plesner Andersen (Copenhagen: Borgen, 1984);

Hymner og ukrudt, by Andersen and Povl Dissing (Copenhagen: Borgen, 1985);

Tiden og storken: Digte (Copenhagen: Borgen, 1985);

Hyddelihat: Børnekomedie med sange, by Andersen, Dissing, and Eva Madsen (Copenhagen: Borgen, 1986);

Over adskillige grænser, by Andersen and Dissing (Copenhagen: Borgen, 1988);

Lille pige med stor effekt (Copenhagen: Borgen, 1989);

Chagall & skorpiondans: Digte, prosadigte, prosa m.m. (Copenhagen: Borgen, 1991);

Denne kommen og gåen: Digte, prosadigte, prosa (Copenhagen: Borgen, 1993);

Snøvsen ta'r springet, by Andersen and Jørgen Vestergaard (Copenhagen: Borgen, 1994);

Verdensborger i Danmark og andre digte om danskere (Copenhagen: Borgen, 1995); translated by Cynthia La Touche Andersen as *Cosmopolitan in Denmark and Other Poems about the Danes* (Copenhagen: Borgen, 1995);

Verden uden for syltetøjsglasset: Digte, illustrated by Maria Bramsen (Copenhagen: Borgen, 1996);

Skynd dig langsomt (Copenhagen: Borgen, 1998).

Collections and Editions: *Man burde burde: Digte 1960–69,* edited by Niels Barfoed (Copenhagen: Borgen, 1971);

Andre sider: Et udvalg af tilsidesatte digte gennem årene, edited by Thorkild Borup Jensen (Copenhagen: Borgen, 1987);

Det er spilleme ikke kedeligt: Et udvalg af Benny Andersens yndlingshumor, edited by Andersen (Frederiksberg: Fisker, 1991);

Snøvsen, photography by John Johansen and Jørgen Vestergaard Andersen (Copenhagen: Borgen, 1992)–comprises *Snøvsen og Eigil og katten i sækken, Snøvsen på sommerferie, Snøvsen og Snøvsine, Snøvsen hopper hjemmefra;*

Forår i Central Park, illustrated by Maria Bramsen (Copenhagen: Gyldendal, 1995);

Alle historierne om Snøvsen, illustrated by Signe Plesner Andersen (Copenhagen: Borgen, 1997)–comprises *Snøvsen og Eigil og katten i sækken, Snøvsen på sommerferie, Snøvsen og Snøvsine, Snøvsen hopper hjemmefrategninger;*

Samlede digte: Digte 1960–1996 (Copenhagen: Borgen, 1998).

Editions in English: *Selected Poems,* translated by Alexander Taylor (Princeton: Princeton University Press, 1975);

Selected Stories, translated by Jack Brondum and others (Willimantic, Conn.: Curbstone, 1983)–comprises "The Pants," "Hiccups," "Layer Cake" from *Puderne;* "Fats-Olsen," "A Happy Fellow" from *Fats Olsen m.fl.;* "The Speaking Strike" from *På broen.*

PLAY PRODUCTION: *Regn med sol,* by Andersen, Klaus Rifbjerg, and Leif Panduro, Rønne, Rønne Teater, 20 June 1975.

MOTION PICTURES: *Familien med de 100 børn,* music by Andersen, Zepia Film, 1972;

Man sku være noget ved musikken, screenplay by Andersen and Henning Carlsen, Henning Carlsen Film/ Nordisk Film, 1972;

Da Svante forsvandt, screenplay by Andersen and Carlsen, Dagnat Productions, 1975;

Danmark er lukket, screenplay adapted from Andersen's play *Orfeus i undergrunden* by Andersen and Dan Tschernia, Focus Film/Det Danske Filminstitut, 1980;

Snøvsen ta't springet, screenplay by Andersen and Jørgen Vestergaard, Nordisk Film, 1994.

TELEVISION: "Glassplinten," script by Andersen, Danmarks Radio, 9 November 1969;

Faders kop, script by Andersen, Danmarks Radio, 10 October, 1970;

Huset på Christianshavn, series, written by Andersen and others, Nordisk Film/Danmarks Radio, 1970;

"Tykke-Olsen," script by Andersen, Danmarks Radio, 20 May 1970.

RECORDINGS: *Svantes viser,* Andersen and Povl Dissing, Copenhagen, Abra Cadabra/Metronome, 1973;

Da Svante forsvandt, by Andersen, Copenhagen, Exlibris, 1975;

Oven visse vande, by Andersen and Dissing, Copenhagen, Exlibris, 1981;

Hymner og ukrudt, by Andersen and Dissing, Copenhagen, Rosen, 1984;

Noder i flere farver, Copenhagen, Rosen, 1986;

Over adskillige grænser, by Andersen and Dissing, Copenhagen, Rosen, 1988;

I al slags vejr, by Andersen and Dissing, Copenhagen, Pladecompagniet A/S, 1990;

Skynd dig langsomt, by Andersen, Dissing, and Jens Jefsen, Viborg, Kavan, 1998.

OTHER: *Nikke Nikke Nambo og andre danske børnerim og remser,* edited, with an afterword, by Andersen, illustrated by Harry Vedøe (Copenhagen: Borgen, 1963);

Bram Stoker, *Dracula,* translated by Andersen (Copenhagen: Borgen, 1963);

Lille Peter Dille og andre udenlandske børnerim og remser, translated and edited by Andersen, illustrated by Harry Vedøe (Copenhagen: Borgen, 1964);

Peter Weiss, *Afsked med forældrene,* translated by Andersen (Copenhagen: Bing, 1964);

Weiss, *Forfølgelsen af og mordet på Jean Paul Marats,* translated by Andersen (Copenhagen: Bing, 1965);

Weiss, *Forundersøgelsen,* translated by Andersen (Copenhagen: Bing, 1966);

Ord om Vietnam: En internationel antologi, edited by Andersen and others (Stockholm: Bonniers / Oslo: Gyldendal, 1967);

Weiss, *Samtalen mellem de tre gående,* translated by Andersen (Copenhagen: Bing, 1967);

August Strindberg, *Et drømmespil,* translated by Andersen (Copenhagen: Borgen, 1967);

Sylvia Plath, *Sengebogen,* translated by Andersen (Copenhagen: Forum, 1978);

Anthony Paul, *Tigeren der mistede sine striber,* translated by Andersen (Copenhagen: Forum, 1980);

Lars Forssell, *Ole med harmonikaen,* translated by Andersen (Copenhagen: Carlsen, 1985);

Jamaica Kincaid, *Annie John,* translated by Andersen and Cynthia La Touche Andersen (Copenhagen: Gyldendal, 1986).

Benny Andersen is widely recognized as a modern author who has won a large international circle of readers because he expresses his social and philosophical concerns with a kind of humor that highlights the compelling nature of his themes. The fact that his works have been translated into several languages, including English, German, Italian, Czech, Swedish, and Norwegian, illustrates the broad reception of his poetry and prose among linguistically and culturally diverse audiences.

Born 7 November 1929 to Svend Aage and Gudrun Andersen in the Copenhagen suburb of Søborg and baptized Benny Allan Andersen, he grew up during economically and politically difficult times. As a teenager he experienced the events of World War II during the German occupation of Denmark from 1940 to 1945. The tensions created by this foreign occupation and the Danish resistance to it, particularly in the Copenhagen General Strike of 1944 with its street barricades, and, subsequently, the liberation of Denmark by Allied forces in May 1945 made a deep impression on Andersen, as revealed in his later works.

As the eldest of four children in a close-knit working-class family, he had to leave school in 1944 and take various jobs to contribute to the family income. During the previous year his family had purchased a piano by installments, and Andersen had begun taking music lessons from his father's cousin. While working as a messenger for a cheese shop and later for a company manufacturing radiator gauges, he attended evening school, enabling him to receive his high school diploma in 1948. At about this time, after Andersen had begun an office career in an advertising firm, he developed a keen interest in lyric poetry, then the dominant literary genre in Denmark. He received encouragement in writing his own poems from Signe Plesner, a graphic artist whom he had met in evening school and who became his wife in 1950. Andersen decided against continuing in an office career; instead he followed his musical interests by working as a bar pianist, at first in Danish provincial towns and subsequently traveling through Scandinavia as a member of a musical trio. In 1957 the trio played aboard a Norwegian ocean liner bound for New York, where Andersen visited Minton's Playhouse in Harlem. During these years of travel with his family—a daughter, Lisbet Anja, was born in 1950 and a son, Kim, in 1957—Andersen used his spare time to write poetry. Beginning in 1952, his poems appeared in major Danish literary journals, initially in *Heretica.* The Copenhagen publisher Jarl Borgen discovered Andersen's poetry in the pages of *Hvedekorn* (Grains of Wheat) and in 1960 published Andersen's first volume of poetry, *Den musikalske ål: Digte* (The Musical Eel: Poems). Andersen settled with his family in Copenhagen and worked as a bar pianist in the Frederiksberg section of town. From the time his second volume of poetry, *Kamera med køkkenadgang: Digte* (Camera with Kitchen Privileges: Poems), appeared in 1962, he devoted himself primarily to literary pursuits.

Considering Andersen's debut as a poet in the influential literary-cultural journals of the early postwar period, it is not surprising to see his initial proximity to the modernist phase associated with *Heretica* (1948–1953). More importantly, however, it is significant to observe how he turned away from it. Characteristic of the poets associated with *Heretica,* such as Ole Sarvig and Thorkild Bjørnvig, was their intensive use of symbolism. This aesthetic position had resulted in poetry that increasingly came under attack as introverted and obscure. It was no longer acceptable as a valid aesthetic basis for the poets of the second phase of Danish modernism, who broke with the tradition of late symbolism. They resorted instead to experimentation with antithetical elements as they searched for at least partial clarity in a chaotic world, as Finn Stein Larsen pointed out in *Modernismen i dansk litteratur* (Modernism in Danish Literature, 1969). Although his reading of symbolist poets such as Rainer Maria Rilke, Charles-Pierre Baudelaire, and Arthur Rimbaud left traces in Andersen's early work, he developed his own style during the 1950s, moving away from introverted symbolism to the disquieting lyrical images of poets such as Edith Södergran, thus adding his voice to the second phase of Danish modernism.

Den musikalske ål, Andersen's 1960 collection, includes poetry from nearly a decade of writing and lays the thematic foundation for his subsequent works and his stance as an author. "Landstation" (Rural Station), originally published in *Heretica* in 1952 and translated by Alexander Taylor in *Selected Poems* (1975), reveals that even in his early poetry Andersen accepted antithetical aspects of life without attempting to formulate a symbolic synthesis. By drawing attention to one of the most basic contrasts of the modern experience, the meeting of civilization with nature's unadulterated elementary forces, he accentuates a situation that holds fundamental importance for his work. He places the city dweller in "Landstation" into the open landscape of Jutland, where he stands face to face with a powerful force—the cyclical renewal of life after winter:

Et stjernetegn af vildgæs
styrter over himlen.
Er det mit navn der slynges hæst herned
spottende og fordrejet?

Tøvende, som for at granske,
hvor meget du endnu tør se
kommer en ko uden tøjr
imod dig gennem pløret.
Føder fåmælt en kalv i sneen.

Du vender svimmel om,
går vild i dette fremmede land.
Glemmer sti og ærinde.
Mærker blot hvor Jyllands tunge jord
fatter om dine blanke sko.

(A constellation of wild geese
streaks across the heavens.
Is it my name that in their harsh,
mocking and distorted way they fling down?

Hesitating, as if to investigate
how much you still dare see,
a cow loose from her tether comes
toward you through the mud.
Silently gives birth to a calf in the snow.

You turn back, dizzy,
lose your way in this strange land.
Forget path and errand.
Notice only how the thick earth of Jutland
clutches your shiny shoes.)

The elemental forces of nature and the animals who live in tune with them are perceived as far superior to the representative of civilization, who suddenly does not feel stable in his "shiny shoes," his civilized existence. Without roots in these forces, the impact this encounter has on the speaker equals a moment of imbalance, a sudden spell of dizziness, when his existential loneliness

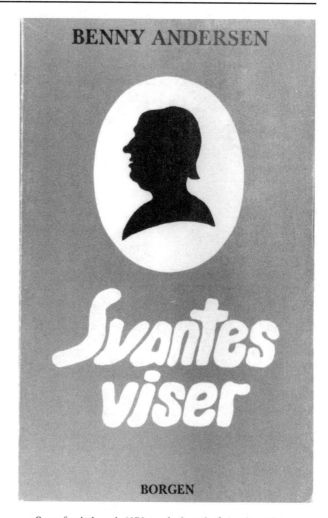

Cover for Andersen's 1972 novel, about the fictional poet Svante

enters his consciousness with overwhelming force. In contrast to nature, he lacks that strong sense of one direction and stands apart with his freedom of choice. For him, there are no religious ties to heaven, whose "hvide døre" (white doors) signal both the overcast sky and thereby the closed doors of heaven. The experience is similar to Søren Kierkegaard's encounter with Jutland's heath as he noted it in his journal of 1840 or to that of Andersen's speaker in "Atlanten på fastende hjerte" (The Atlantic on an Empty Stomach, 1962) from *Kamera med køkkenadgang*. Jutland's nature triggers a disquieting sensation in the visitor who is accustomed to the more confined spaces of the city or the gentle landscape of Zealand. The open landscape without fixed points of orientation, like the open ocean, evokes an unbalancing glimpse of existence at large, causing the viewer to feel dizzy or sick, to experience physical and existential nausea. In this situation of uncertainty, which is voiced in many variations in Andersen's poetry, the commitment to work toward balance in life without a religious safety

Andersen at the piano with guitarist Povl Dissing and bassist Jens Jefsen (courtesy of Arte Booking)

net is emphasized in *Den musikalske ål* by "Lige før vinter" (Just before Winter). For the speaker of the poem, heaven is not an option; instead he must come to exist "hinsides tanken om frelse" (beyond the thought of salvation). On this basis, the task of searching for at least partial clarity or some balance in life is projected as a challenge that can easily catch the individual off guard.

Another prominent feature of Andersen's writing is his ability to transfer this challenge from the philosophical plane to that of concrete everyday experiences. In ordinary life, basic dispositions, like the negation of reality in favor of an ideal, are exposed and linked with the failure to work for meaningful balance within oneself and in interactions with others. Thus, philosophical insights are often related to the practical everyday sphere with a deceiving simplicity. They come to light in many poems through encounters that blend the serious with the comic, with humor, satire, and irony. In *Den musikalske ål*, for instance, small portraits from nature build on Hans Christian Andersen's metaphor of the duck pond for society. For example, the musical eel of the title poem, symbolic of the aesthete, leaves the pond in anger over the dissonant water landing of the duck and thereby

escapes from reality, a position that is clearly rejected in the poems in this volume.

While most of the poems in *Den musikalske ål* reveal what might be called an uncanny dimension of life that is often placed at a distance through humor, the four long prose poems at the end of the volume signal an intensely felt, all-pervasive threat to existence. This heightened sense of danger was paralleled by the Cold War atmosphere, the worldwide growth of industrialization, and expanding consumerism. The younger generation of writers, particularly those who were associated, as was Andersen, with the journal *Vindrosen* (The Compass), were concerned with the seemingly decreasing quality of life. For Andersen the creative process becomes a means to increase the quality of daily life in view of an environment that appears to be critically out of balance. His ethical and literary commitment centers on the thematic complex of existential and social balance in life with the challenge to choose genuine individual development and to reach out to others. This commitment forms the common ground for his works.

In his subsequent volumes of poetry, Andersen varies a small number of major themes, expanding them and demonstrating their complexity by means of his psychological insight and his detailed perception of his surroundings. He expands his technique of reversing commonly held views of what constitutes a significant or insignificant event by creating a different perspective on the linguistic level. In *Den musikalske ål* the unusual focus of a subjective impression in "Sommerdag" (Summerday) leads to the temporary reversal of natural laws: "Solen er standset / foran en syngende lærke" (The sun has stopped / in front of a singing lark). This linguistic technique is increasingly applied to the material in *Kamera med køkkenadgang*, in which he achieves a perspective that contrasts with widespread norms by changing the word order of common idioms, as in the line: "børn af uønskede forældre" (children of unwanted parents) in "I baren" (In the Bar); by thus defamiliarizing a fixed idiom such as "unwanted children," he alters an established focus on society. While Andersen continues the satirical mode in *Den indre bowlerhat: Digte* (The Bowler Hat Within: Poems, 1964), he focuses more on the complexity of life as it daily confronts the individual. The necessity to activate individual potential and to recognize misguided norms is emphasized here with a particular focus on inhibitions that must be overcome, as in the poem "Godhed" (Goodness). Here Andersen applies comic exaggeration to the speaker's method of trying to be good to others, because the speaker's efforts take place in the solitude of his room, where he conscientiously practices opening his arms, timing with his watch the speed he achieves. The ironic punchline of the poem reveals that satisfaction with a good practice session has become a substitute for the higher value of actually reaching out to other people. This satisfaction leaves the speaker in a state of grotesque self-isolation.

Such tragicomic depiction is characteristic of Andersen's works: in *Portrætgalleri* (Portrait Gallery, 1966) with emphasis on the challenge to choose self-development in order to avoid stagnation, and, with a closer look at the poet in society, in *Det sidste øh og andre digte* (The Last Um and Other Poems, 1969). Here "Tumling" (Toddler) illustrates the labor it takes to meet this constant challenge to keep moving. Cumbersome human efforts at gaining balance in life are conveyed through a contrasting arrangement of active and passive verbs. The poem was written during a period of the late 1960s when, as a result of the concrete poetry movement, poets experimented with typographical arrangement of a poem on the page to underscore its theme. Thus "Tumling," a poem of thirty-eight lines, includes fifteen lines of varying length centered on a vertical axis in order to simulate the staggering movement of a small child who is still learning to walk and has to conquer each fraction of an inch. It underscores the individual's imperfect attempts to achieve balance in life, but also the constant effort of the small steps it requires in order not to simply settle down, but to gain "ny svimmelhed" (new dizziness). With *Her i reservatet: Digte* (Here on the Reserve: Poems, 1971) Andersen adds a polemical dimension that is presented in a dialectical pattern. The three different viewpoints are the outside observer's, the inside perspective of the inhabitants of the reserve, and the historiographer's perspective one hundred years later. From the historiographer's vantage point, the Denmark of 1971 resembles a bygone golden age, when people could influence their lives by making choices. Such nostalgia begs the question as to what sense of social responsibility guides contemporary twentieth-century decisions. It is noteworthy that, possibly in the spirit of this question, Andersen's poetry in *Personlige papirer: Digte* (Personal Papers: Poems, 1974) expresses his code of ethics more directly through a stated hope of bridging the experience of emptiness with warmth and meaningful contact. This openness developed at a time of personal changes for Andersen, when he and his wife Signe separated and divorced. His openness increased further in the 1980s under the encouragement of Cynthia La Touche Andersen, whom he married in 1981.

Often the very titles of Andersen's works invite his readers to participate in a different way of seeing. They create awareness by formulating uncommon combinations or by playing on well-known fixed phrases and titles, suggesting another perspective, usually by slightly altering the expression and thus enticing the reader to discover or rediscover another, less familiar angle of a particular theme. In the 1978 collection, *Under begge øjne:* *Digte* (Under Both Eyes: Poems), this invitation extends from the title to the composition of the poems and to their layout as "dobbel-digte" (double-poems) in one section. Here the reader is instructed that the poems on the same subject, but each with different thematic emphasis, need to be read simultaneously—under both eyes, so to speak. The complexity of a theme becomes more visible if one absorbs its contrasting sides. In the pair "Gammel mand i lys" (Old Man in the Light) as opposed to "Gammel mand i skygge" (Old Man in the Shadow), for example, it is as if one recalled the negative of a picture while looking at the developed print.

Throughout Andersen's works one can find a preoccupation with the theme of balance in life. This theme is given high visibility in many poems, particularly those dealing with time, which, in its fleeting quality, parallels open space in its resistance to human efforts to measure and control it. Examples of this preoccupation are "Tiden" (Time), from *Her i reservatet,* the poem "Klokken" (The Clock), and the title poem, "Tiden og storken," from *Tiden og storken: Digte* (Time and the Stork: Poems, 1985). As the title of *Tiden og storken* suggests, time plays a central role in this volume; in many poems it is a subtext to times that are not changing for the better, while in others the theme is the acceptance of the paradoxical quality of time, as in "Afsked og ny aftale" (Farewell and New Understanding).

Characteristic of Andersen's works since the late 1970s is a more direct depiction of the necessity to make a choice in the spirit of Kierkegaard. That is, by choosing continually to develop an authentic and socially responsible self, the individual may achieve genuine interaction with others. Of particular importance in this regard is the publication of his ninety-page volume *Himmelspræt eller kunsten at komme til verden: Digte* (Blanket-Toss or the Art of Coming into the World: Poems, 1979). In the sixty-page title poem Andersen presents love and trust between two people, in the smallest social unit, as a model to be developed in a larger context in order to cope with existential nausea and despair over a deeply troubled environment. This model of human interdependence extends from the personal to the national and to the global level. It must counterbalance and counteract one-dimensional attitudes such as those that cause others to be viewed as enemies because they are different and therefore are seen as threats to a narrow view of security. This theme permeates Andersen's work of the 1980s and 1990s.

The serious tenor underlying Andersen's poems plays a much larger role in his short stories in which many characters are obsessed with ensuring some stability and safety wherever individual need and design might find it. This obsession signals a precarious balance that can be observed in many of their lives. Frequently Andersen's characters seek refuge in more or less tangi-

Cover for Andersen's 1996 collection of poems, most of which deal with growing up during World War II

reversion to the oral phase of infancy and emphasizes how starved he is for contact with others, a need that is also exemplified by his wish to be caught by a living hand when he reaches into someone's pocket. It is a desperate way of reaching out for help while gradually settling deeper into isolation. He only senses that somewhere between early childhood and adulthood a critical change had taken place in him that had led to his current situation. This is precisely what has happened to many of the characters depicted in Andersen's short stories: during adolescence, a mistake crept into their lives, causing them to rely on shortcuts such as accepting secondhand opinions and values instead of taking the longer route of working out their own values. As a result, they usually fail to develop their full potential in making meaningful contact with their surroundings. Andersen highlights how such failure comes to haunt people because they cannot find happiness or personal fulfilment after having accepted the easy solutions of society to obtain social balance. They have merely assumed a role in their public lives, while they are secretly tormented by a sense that something essential is lacking in their existence. Outwardly, they function like well-greased cogs in society's machinery, but psychologically, they are approaching a breaking point.

Andersen cannot be accused of failing to indicate an alternative to this subjugation of the individual to society. Even in Andersen's early stories "Bruddet" (The Break) and "Hustelefonen" (The Extension Phone), use- and efficiency-oriented norms in the workplace determine the model for the adolescent, who tries hard to become an accepted and respected member of a society that is largely indifferent toward individuality. In stories such as "Bruddet" Andersen emphasizes dramatically how vital it is for the young person not merely to wait for directives and not to depend on secondhand feelings but to begin to see, listen, and feel for himself in order to find his course in life.

The story collections *Tykke-Olsen m.fl.: Fortællinger og monologer* (Fats-Olsen et al: Short Stories and Monologues, 1968) and *Over skulderen: Blå historier* (Over the Shoulder: Blue Stories, 1983) also present a broad spectrum of distraught individuals who are struggling with social pressures and the choices with which they are confronted. Depicted as well are individuals who have made the wrong choice, such as the protagonist in the story "Særpræget" (Cachet). Consequently, they either feel helpless and lost or the characters actually contribute to the inhumane sides of their social environment, so that it becomes a small-scale replica of a world engaged in cold war as in "Varmedrunken" (The Hot Water Bottle). In this story a young husband harasses an older woman, a refugee whom he and his wife have taken in, but who he thinks is imposing on them after she has fallen ill. This

ble substitutes for that missing security and certainty about the course of their lives. Usually they resort to objects or unusual behavior as safety valves and engage in absurd enterprises to find temporary comfort; for the most part, they are depicted as sadly unable to make a better choice. The comic elements in their characters derive from a problematic lack of balanced proportions regarding individual or group behavior, and this lack is matched by various techniques of exaggeration.

Typical examples are "Bukserne" (The Pants) and "Passagen" (The Passage) from the 1965 collection *Puderne: Noveller* (The Pillows: Short Stories). In the first story the protagonist's preference since childhood for wearing secondhand clothes is linked with his failure to develop an identity of his own. His failure is portrayed as life-threatening because it leads him to the brink of suicide, a symbolic depiction of the vital necessity that a genuine personal identity represents for both individuals and the society to which they belong. In the second story a more extreme case is depicted: Lars Hansen, the protagonist, resorts to picking people's pockets for objects that he can substitute for human company and a new life, such as the lady's glove that he fills with red sago pudding so he can suck on the fingers. His behavior is a

theme is expanded to a larger scale in the title story, "Tykke-Olsen," where attention is called to the closed-mindedness of an entire provincial town.

Most often, these glimpses of someone's everyday life are shown through the eyes of a first-person speaker or narrator. This narrative stance allows a particularly close observation of a given angle of individual struggle in society, including self-observation, providing the reader with an inside view of an individual's existential experiences in modern Denmark.

Svantes viser: En sanghistorie (Svante's Songs: A Story in Song, 1972) could be taken as a case in point, but here there is a focus on the position of the author in society. Andersen splits his authorial persona into two different personalities in the tale of Svante. Presenting the story as a documentary allows Andersen to depict himself in it as Svante's friend and critic; this documentary device allows him to represent two seemingly contrasting points of view, that of the poet and that of an editor who provides meaningful criticism. In reality, these two are complementary points of view in which Andersen engages. Svante seems to indulge in the luxury of private problems, like unhappy love and nostalgia for harmonious country life in an idealized Sweden. With his joy in the simple things of life and his horror over a consumer society that makes him sick, he isolates himself from society. Appearing in the early 1970s, a time when critics demanded the author's active involvement in solving social problems, Svante appears to be a complete anachronism. While he does have to step out of his escapist attitude and move from distant aesthete to ethically involved person, his poems are important in their concern with small problems affecting the quality of daily life. They should be read alongside the works of other authors who concentrate on social and political issues, such as drug addiction, slums, and the Common Market. By publishing Svante's songs–both within the tale and in actual life–Andersen claims a place for this kind of poetry and song. It is a position of protest against a narrowly defined view of socially engaged literature. And it is a position confirmed by the enormous success of Svante's songs in Denmark, some of which are among Andersen's songs that were selected for inclusion in the seventeenth edition of *Folkehøjskolens sangbog* (Songbook of the Folk High Schools, 1989). Andersen frequently performs these songs at the piano in a duo or trio with the singer and guitarist Povl Dissing in the role of Svante.

Andersen contributed to the debate over the Common Market with a play, *Orfeus i undergrunden* (Orpheus in the Underground, 1979). Although his stature as an author rests primarily on his poetry and on his prose, this play about a modern Danish Orpheus stands out from his plays in *Lejemorderen og andre spil* (The Hired Assassin and Other Plays, 1970) and the play *Kolde fødder*

(Cold Feet, 1980). In *Orfeus i undergrunden,* which was later adapted as a motion picture, *Danmark er lukket* (Denmark Is Closed, 1980), Andersen takes an outspoken stance against Denmark's membership in the European Common Market, projecting a future in which the Danish state no longer exists, thereby complementing and taking a step further the concerns he had formulated earlier in *Her i reservatet.*

The difficulty of balancing the child's world with that of the adult during adolescence, a theme familiar from the short stories, comes to light in its many facets in *På broen: Roman i ni episoder* (On the Bridge: Novel in Nine Episodes, 1981) particularly given the historical setting of that novel–Denmark's occupation by German forces from 1940 to 1945. If the adolescent grows up into a maladjusted adult, dominated by fear and self-interest, and goes on suppressing his knowledge of other, more-humane possiblities of interacting, then he is bound to be haunted by this neglect. If his problems in life are only covered up by resorting to substitutes for the real solution, it leads to the kind of self-betrayal with consequences for others that Henrik Ibsen termed "livsløgen," the "lie of life." Andersen provides many examples of this theme in his works. The novel exemplifies how crucial it is to develop a genuine personality like that of the protagonist of *På broen,* young Erling, who has a personality open to the possibilities and ambiguities of life. Andersen makes this necessity clear by contrasting the two friends, Erling and Allan. Allan, the stronger one, who has a one-dimensional view of life, bears Andersen's middle name and is also depicted as sharing Andersen's social milieu and upbringing, which suggests that Andersen includes himself in the struggles he depicts.

Sensing the right course of action and making the right choice on the spur of the moment are qualities especially associated with the world of children, in which utilitarian norms do not yet dominate. In this regard, the volumes about the fantastic little creature "Snøvs" have, in the tradition of Hans Christian Andersen, a great deal to say both to the children who listen to these stories and to the adults who read these stories to them. The Snøvs stories are a prime example of the project Benny Andersen is engaged in: taking himself at his word and language at its word. His play with the literal meaning of expressions achieves multiple, humorous perspectives. The figure of Snøvs, for instance, exemplifies the creative world of children in which there are almost unlimited possibilities, as in the humorous creation of a lonely creature, Snøvs, derived from the idiomatic expression "at gå fra snøvsen" (to go crazy). Together with the children Eigil and Pernille, Snøvs shows adult behavior and perspectives that should not be followed, in order to bring about a more humane social environment. The children's behavior also illustrates that they can spontane-

*Andersen reading from his works at the University of Minnesota, 6
October 1997 (photograph by Leonie Marx)*

stantly must choose to come into the world and choose to be with others in the time span they have between birth and death.

Verden uden for syltetøjsglasset: Digte (The World Outside the Jelly Jar: Poems, 1996) represents a return to the events Andersen witnessed during the 1940s. In it, Andersen provides glimpses of an adolescence that, despite insecurities and historical battles, seemed to be paradoxically sheltered, a transitional, pupated phase in life that held great hopes for future development.

A careful reading of Andersen's works as a whole will elucidate that even the humorous poems, which highlight situations that are both sad and amusing, are based on the same ethical foundation as are his serious works. Like the author and philosopher Villy Sørensen, Andersen is concerned with the confrontation between individual and society, the experience of angst and nothingness, and the many self-betraying strategies available to people who do not wish to develop as individuals. What Søren Baggesen in *Modernismen i dansk litteratur* noted about Sørensen's prose also holds for Andersen's poetic language. Both have learned from Hans Christian Andersen's use of language that it can be a means to "forvandle den trivielle hverdagslige ydre verden i et indre poetisk univers, hvor tingene får mening uden at miste deres tingslighed" (turn the trivial external world of the everyday into an inner poetic universe, where objects acquire a meaning without losing their nature as objects). In Benny Andersen's works, objects can mirror a person's attitudes, fears, or evasions.

As one of the authors in Danish modernism's second phase, Andersen is engaged in an existentialist project. His roots lie in Kierkegaard's philosophy, yet he does not provide a replica of a Kierkegaardian system. Rather, he provides his readers with an ethical view that can serve as the beginning of a more authentic way of life. With his tragicomic method, Andersen entices the reader to accept a philosophy of life transmitted through comic, ironic, or satirical techniques—even if this means that he also has to take the risk of being read one-dimensionally: that is, for entertainment only. That his message has not fallen on deaf ears is evident in the broad critical acclaim and numerous recognitions he has received, among them his acceptance in 1972 into the prestigious Det Danske Akademi (The Danish Academy).

Andersen frequently goes on tour in Denmark and abroad reading from his poetry and playing his songs on the piano. In 1981 he appeared at the Roskilde Music Festival, playing with Jens Jefsen, and in 1985 he returned to the festival with Povl Dissing and his band. In 1983 and 1985 he toured the United States, and in 1997 he completed another tour of Canada and the United States, during which he appeared on Garrison

ously reach out to others. Through both his themes and his experimentation with language, Andersen's books for children are intimately connected with his work for adult readers.

Two of his three poetry collections from the 1990s, *Chagall & skorpiondans: Digte, prosadigte, prosa m.m.* (Chagall and the Dance of Scorpions: Poems, Prose Poems, Prose, and So On, 1991) and *Denne kommen og gåen: Digte, prosadigte, prosa* (This Coming and Going: Poems, Prose Poems, Prose, 1993), include longer prose poems as well as short prose pieces, many of which sustain a highly reflective mood and an awareness of death. But the mode of personal reflections in the latter volume blends a tongue-in-cheek affirmation of both life and death with an appreciation of life's complexity. In this book Andersen cleverly exposes society's absurdities, particularly the misguided hostility toward people who have immigrated to Denmark. One can hardly find a better reminder that such hostile attitudes are at once grave and ridiculous mistakes than in the poem "Mit liv som indvandrer" (My Life as an Immigrant). Birth and death are here depicted as an immigration process that includes everyone. One might say immigration never ceases since humans con-

Keillor's popular radio program, *A Prairie Home Companion,* and concluded by attending a conference on his works at the University of Minnesota.

Amiable and with a gentle approach to others, Andersen is a well-liked guest. Intent on practicing tolerance, he does not, however, hesitate to voice his deep indignation over the oppression and ill treatment of other people, be it in foreign war zones or at home in Denmark. Often he has taken issue with a misdirected nationalism and an animosity toward immigrants in Denmark who differ in their skin color and cultural habits. He employs a technique of unobtrusively exposing the comic elements inherent in such hostility toward others; for instance, in "Skabsvenskere" (Closet Swedes) he focuses on the fact that Danish national identity is not clear-cut but rather a highly complex matter in view of the many periods of immigration to Denmark throughout the centuries.

Andersen's social awareness, so characteristic of his work from the beginning of his literary career, received a new impetus through his marriage to Cynthia La Touche in 1981. Since then his works reflect an expanded consciousness regarding the many different possible perspectives on an issue, a development to which Cynthia La Touche Andersen's experiences and personality contributed greatly. Originally from Barbados, she settled in Denmark in 1961. She has the complex perspective of an immigrant who grew up in the West Indies in a culture with a strong British imprint, and, as a nurse and midwife in the city of Copenhagen, she has experienced Danish society at many different levels. It is not surprising that a common interest in the West Indies led to their collaboration in translating into Danish the novel *Annie John* (1985) by Jamaica Kincaid. Another form of collaboration was Cynthia La Touche Andersen's translation into English of her husband's collection *Verdensborger i Danmark og andre digte om danskere* (1995; translated as *Cosmopolitan in Denmark and Other Poems about the Danes,* 1995). Benny Andersen's sustained popularity in Denmark can be attributed to the fact that his works function like a mirror of society, a mirror that presents his contemporaries with a complex view of individual and social flaws, one magnified by a comic strategy that includes self-irony.

Interview:

Jette Kromann, "Benny Andersen," in her *Digtere på bånd,* volume 1 (Copenhagen: Borgen, 1966), pp. 7–46.

Bibliography:

Arne Kyhnau and Karen Larsen, *Benny Andersen: En bibliografi* (Copenhagen: Danmarks Biblioteksskole, 1982).

References:

Uffe Andreasen, "Benny Andersen," in *Danske digtere i det 20. århundrede,* 5 volumes, edited by Torben Broström and Mette Winge (Copenhagen: Gad, 1982), IV: 239–252, 400–401;

Søren Baggesen, "Prosa," in *Modernismen i dansk litteratur,* edited by Jørn Vosmar (Copenhagen: Fremad, 1969), pp. 119–191;

Niels Barfoed, "Benny Andersen: *Den musikalske ål,*" *Vindrosen,* 7 (1960): 586;

Johs. Nørregaard Frandsen, "Længslernes ridder. Benny Andersen: *Svantes viser,*" in *Læsninger i dansk litteratur,* volume 4, edited by Anne-Marie Mai and Knud Bjarne Gjesing (Odense: Odense Universitetsforlag, 1997), pp. 326–345, 373–374;

Thorkild Borup Jensen, *Benny Andersen: et forfatterskabsportræt* (Copenhagen: Borgen, 1987);

Finn Stein Larsen, "Lyrik," in *Modernismen i dansk litteratur,* edited by Vosmar (Copenhagen: Fremad, 1969), pp. 13–117;

Leonie Marx, *Benny Andersen: A Critical Study* (Westport, Conn.: Greenwood Press, 1983);

Marx, *Sproget taget på ordet: En studie i Benny Andersens forfatterskab* (Copenhagen: Borgen, 1986);

Keld Zeruneith, "Ironiens frygtløse distance," in *Analyser af moderne dansk lyrik,* 2 volumes (Copenhagen: Borgen, 1976), II: 82–97.

Thorkild Bjørnvig

(2 February 1918 –   )

Per Dahl
University of Århus

Translated by Hanne Ejsing Jørgensen

BOOKS: *Stjærnen bag Gavlen* (Copenhagen: Gyldendal, 1947);

Martin A. Hansens Digtning, with a bibliography by Ole Wivel (Copenhagen: Wivels Forlag, 1949);

Evigt Foraar: Digte (Copenhagen: Gyldendal, 1954);

Anubis: Digte (Copenhagen: Gyldendal, 1955);

Rainer Maria Rilke og tysk Tradition (Copenhagen: Gyldendal, 1959);

Figur og ild: Digte (Copenhagen: Gyldendal, 1959);

Begyndelsen: Essays (Copenhagen: Gyldendal, 1960);

Kains Alter: Martin A. Hansens Digtning og Tænkning (Copenhagen: Gyldendal, 1964);

Forsvar for Kains Alter: En kritisk Efterskrift (Copenhagen: Gyldendal, 1965);

Vibrationer: Digte (Copenhagen: Gyldendal, 1966);

Ravnen (Copenhagen: Gyldendal, 1968; revised edition, Copenhagen: Brøndum, 1990);

Udvalgte digte (Copenhagen: Gyldendal, 1970);

Oprør mod neonguden: Et essay om beat (Copenhagen: Gyldendal, 1970);

Virkeligheden er til: Litterære essays (Copenhagen: Gyldendal, 1973);

Pagten: Mit venskab med Karen Blixen (Copenhagen: Gyldendal, 1974; revised and enlarged edition, 1985); translated by Ingvar Schousboe and William Jay Smith as *The Pact: My Friendship with Isak Dinesen* (Baton Rouge: Louisiana State University Press, 1983; London: Souvenir, 1984);

Delfinen: Miljødigte 1970–75 (Copenhagen: Gyldendal, 1975);

Det religiøse menneskes ansigter (Copenhagen: Brøndum, 1975);

Stoffets krystalhav: Digte, photographs by Meta May Holboe (Copenhagen: Schønberg, 1975);

Morgenmørke: Digte (Copenhagen: Gyldendal, 1977; enlarged and illustrated edition, Copenhagen: Brøndum, 1979);

Også for naturens skyld: Økologiske essays (Copenhagen: Gyldendal, 1978);

courtesy of Birgit Bjørnvig

Barnet og dyret i industrisamfundet: Et essay (Copenhagen: Gyldendal, 1979);

Abeguder: Miljødigte 1975–80 (Copenhagen: Gyldendal, 1981);

Den dobbelte lykke: Digte (Copenhagen: Brøndum, 1982);

Kentaur (Århus: Centrum, 1983);

Solens have og skolegården: Erindringer 1918–33 (Copenhagen: Gyldendal, 1983);

Hjørnestuen og månehavet: Erindringer 1934–38 (Copenhagen: Gyldendal, 1984);

Gammelt og nyt under solen (Copenhagen: Brøndum, 1986);

Jordens hjerte: Erindringer 1938–46 (Copenhagen: Gyldendal, 1986);

Gennem regnbuen (Copenhagen: Gyldendal, 1987);

Ønsket: Erindringer 1946–48 (Copenhagen: Gyldendal, 1987);

Den følende planet: Syv essays 1959–86 (Copenhagen: Gyldendal, 1988);

Epimetheus: Miljødigte 1980–90 (Copenhagen: Gyldendal, 1990);

Digtere (Copenhagen: Gyldendal, 1991);

Siv vand og måne (Copenhagen: Gyldendal, 1993);

Samlede digte, 1947–93 (Copenhagen: Gyldendal, 1998).

Edition in English: *The World Tree,* selected and translated by Paula Hostrup-Jensen, edited by Sven H. Rossel (Seattle: Mermaid Press, 1993).

OTHER: Franz Werfel, *Kunstens Kald,* selected and translated, with an introduction, by Bjørnvig (Copenhagen: Wivels Forlag, 1948);

Rainer Maria Rilke, *Udvalgte Digte,* volume 1, selected and translated, with an introduction, by Bjørnvig (Copenhagen: Wivels Forlag, 1949; revised edition, Copenhagen: Gyldendal, 1963);

Rilke, *Duino elegier. Udvalgte digte,* volume 2, selected and translated, with an introduction, by Bjørnvig (Copenhagen: Gyldendal, 1957; revised, 1982);

Rilke, *Sene Digte. Udvalgte digte,* volume 3, selected and translated, with an introduction, by Bjørnvig (Copenhagen: Gyldendal, 1958);

Martin A. Hansen, *Lykkelige Kristoffer,* edited, with an afterword, by Bjørnvig (Copenhagen: Gyldendal, 1963);

Gottfried Benn, *Glasblæseren og andre Essays,* selected, with an introduction, by Bjørnvig, translated by Jørgen Elbek (Copenhagen: Gyldendal, 1965);

Hansen, *Martsnat,* edited, with an afterword, by Bjørnvig (Copenhagen: Gyldendal, 1965);

Dansk lyrik, 2 volumes, selected, with an afterword, by Bjørnvig (Copenhagen: Gyldendal, 1965; revised, with an introduction, by Bjørnvig, 1968);

Hansen, *Ved Korsvejen: Litterære Essays,* edited by Bjørnvig and Ole Wivel (Copenhagen: Gyldendal, 1965);

Hansen, *Verdensromanen: Historiske Essays,* edited by Bjørnvig and Wivel (Copenhagen: Gyldendal, 1966);

Friedrich Hölderlin, *Brød og vin og andre digte,* selected and translated, with an introduction, by Bjørnvig (Copenhagen: Brøndum, 1970; revised edition, Copenhagen: Gyldendal, 1992);

Frank Jæger, *Miraklernes bog: Kasserede Digte,* edited, with an introduction, by Bjørnvig (Copenhagen: Gyldendal, 1977);

Rilke, *Udsat på hjertets bjerge: Digte,* translated and selected, with an introduction, by Bjørnvig (Copenhagen: Gyldendal, 1995)—comprises revision of *Udvalgte digte,* volumes 1, 2, and 3;

Tigersalmeß. Digte om vilde dyr, poems by Robinson Jeffers, Loren Eiseley, Margaret Atwood, and Ted Hughes, selected and translated, with an introduction, by Bjørnvig (Copenhagen: Gyldendal, 1995).

Thorkild Bjørnvig's works comprise poetry, translations, literary criticism, essays, and memoirs; between 1949 and 1993 he produced more than thirty-five books. His collections of poems with their complex themes of eroticism, nature, and the role of humans in the cosmos make him a central figure in modern Danish literature. Furthermore, his involvement with the ecology movement and his close friendships with Karen Blixen (Isak Dinesen) and Martin A. Hansen have attracted great attention, in Denmark and elsewhere, while his highly esteemed translations of Friedrich Hölderlin and Rainer Maria Rilke have made these two central European poets accessible to Scandinavian readers.

Thorkild Strange Bjørnvig was born in Aarhus (after 1948, spelled Århus) on 2 February 1918; his father, Theodor Frese Bjørnvig, was a factory inspector and was married to Adda Thomine Hummel Jensen. Thorkild spent the first thirty years of his life in Aarhus, partly in town and partly in a summer house near Aarhus Bay. The first years in school were difficult for this delicate boy, who in a naive way took everything literally. In 1934 he entered high school at Aarhus *Katedralskole* (cathedral school) but failed after two years, repeated a grade, and eventually graduated with mediocre marks in 1938. Although not excelling academically, Bjørnvig developed friendships in Heimdall, the high-school student union, and was encouraged to begin writing poetry. In January 1940 his first published poem appeared in the local newspaper.

After leaving school Bjørnvig studied Comparative Literature at the University of Aarhus together with his friend, Bjørn Poulsen. Under the guidance of Jens Kruuse, Ernst Frandsen, and Heinrich Fauteck, and later Erik Lunding and Paul Krüger, his talent slowly began to unfold and the student group *Musiske Studenter* (Artistic Students), which he joined in 1941, provided a productive environment. Here he made friends with the future author Tage Skou-Hansen, among others, and the group performed plays by writers such as Maxwell Anderson, William Butler Yeats, Christopher Isherwood, and W. H. Auden.

Eventually Bjørnvig focused on studying German literature, especially the works of Johann Wolfgang von Goethe, Hölderlin and Rilke. In 1944 the University of Copenhagen organized an essay competition for which Bjørnvig wrote an essay on Rilke and German tradition, which won a gold medal in 1946. This essay was not published until 1959, following publication of the last volume of Bjørnvig's three-volume translation of Rilke's works.

ANUBIS

DIGTE AF

THORKILD
BJØRNVIG

GYLDENDAL
1956

Title page for the second edition of Bjørnvig's third collection of poetry, which was inspired by a statue of Anubis, the jackal-headed Egyptian god of death

In the fall of 1946 Bjørnvig married the twenty-four-year-old librarian Grete Damgaard Petersen. He met Martin A. Hansen, a writer who was to become a special friend and colleague to Bjørnvig, and in February 1947 he received an M.A. in Comparative Literature. In 1949 Bjørnvig published his first introduction to Hansen's writings, *Martin A. Hansens Digtning* (The Literary Writings of Martin A. Hansen, 1949).

But Bjørnvig wanted to write poetry, not criticism. In 1940 he had submitted a collection of poems to the Danish publishing house of Gyldendal and another collection in 1943, but both were turned down. Hansen now assisted him in his third attempt, and in the fall of 1947 the first of Bjørnvig's collections, *Stjærnen bag Gav-len* (The Star behind the Gable) was published. The reception was overwhelming, and Bjørnvig was immediately regarded as an important Danish poet. Readers

were particularly drawn by his strophic and rhymed forms, which depict erotic experiences reflected in nature, as in the poem "September," translated by Paula Hostrup-Jensen:

Fra Vandet stiger
Goplens rene
Klokkebevægelse
gennem mit Indre.
Nældens Takvinge
lukker sig sort
paa Bjælken, for roligt
at overvintre.

(The bell-like movement
Of jellyfish rises
Up through my body
From the watery deep.
The tortoiseshell butterfly
Folds up black
On the rafter, preparing
For winter sleep.)

Shortly after his graduation Bjørnvig served in the Danish civil emergency service. Part of the time was spent as a driver at the refugee aid center, Mission Danoise, in Rastatt on the border between France and Germany; during his stay here he met Rilke's publisher, Anton Kippenberg, in Marburg. In the beginning of 1948 Bjørnvig moved to Sletten in Vedbæk, north of Copenhagen, and here he entered into a close literary collaboration with Bjørn Poulsen, the beginning of the so-called *Vedbæk-parnas* (Parnassus of Vedbæk), as the *Heretica* group, which was to have a major influence on postwar Danish literature, was known. Bjørnvig's translations of the works of Rilke began in a collaboration with writer and publisher Ole Wivel, who in 1945 had started Wivels Forlag (Wivel Publishers), substantially supported by Knud W. Jensen (who later funded Gyldendal and created the impressive Louisiana Museum of Modern Art on the north Zealand coast). This new group of writers launched a literary journal, *Heretica* (1948–1953), for which Bjørnvig and Poulsen served as editors the first two years.

In their manifesto soliciting contributors, this group of writers advocated an aesthetic view of life, which differed from both rationalism and orthodox religion. This view of life, according to the *Heretica* manifesto, "bæres af en søgen efter nye vækstpunkter i åndslivet, som nu efter afslutningen af den anden verdenskrig er ved at stivne i forældede politiske og videnskabelige problemstillinger" (is borne by a search for new spheres of development in spiritual and intellectual life, which–since after World War II–has been calcified in antiquated political and scientific concerns). As a confirmation of the *Heretica* manifesto, Bjørnvig published the essay "Begyndelsen–en Improvisation" (The Initiation–an Improvisation) in the first issue of the journal. The essay is a utopian sketch of man's aesthetic education and of those people who "uden Ængstelse atter og atter tør bearbejde og muligvis omstøde Bund og Grænse i deres første Erfaringer" (without fear, over and over again dare work with and perhaps even destroy the limits of their primeval experiences). This idea of "an aesthetic human" implies an individual and existential awareness reaching beyond the dogmatism of the Cold War era. *Heretica* attracted attention far beyond the narrow literary circles in Denmark and fascinated the most important of the modern writers of the decade, creating a debate about the so-called cultural crisis.

Toward the end of 1947 Bjørnvig was introduced to Karen Blixen; an intense personal and artistic relationship developed between the two of them. It was a master-pupil relationship that both of them considered a kind of "pact." Fragments of their "Covenant Letters" appear in the book that Bjørnvig wrote about this relationship more than twenty years later: *Pagten: Mit venskab med Karen Blixen* (1974; translated as *The Pact: My Friendship with Isak Dinesen,* 1983), and in their correspondence, which was finally published in 1996 as part of Blixen's collected letters, *Karen Blixen i Danmark: Breve 1931–62* (Karen Blixen in Denmark: Letters 1931–1962). Bjørnvig wrote in *Pagten* about his meeting with Blixen that he was "berust af en mægtigere forventning til livet end jeg nogensinde havde kendt. Det var som at møde et menneske af en art, jeg kun havde hørt om i myten og historien" (intoxicated with a tremendous expectation of life, greater than I had ever known before. It was like meeting a person of the kind I had heard about in myth and history).

After suffering a concussion in Paris during the spring of 1950, Bjørnvig stayed as a convalescent with Blixen at her Rungstedlund estate during the following fall and again–after having studied for a few months in Bonn, Germany–during the fall of 1951. Then he slowly extricated himself from the relationship; "the pact" was broken in the summer of 1952 although Bjørnvig maintained sporadic contact with Blixen until her death in 1962. In his 1991 book *Digtere* (Poets), Bjørnvig commented on the relationship: "Karen Blixen havde opfattet min kone Grete som en hindring for min udfoldelse, Martin [A. Hansen] som en forudsætning. Den ene ville skille os, den anden holde os sammen" (Karen Blixen saw my wife Grete as a hindrance for my development, and Martin [A. Hansen] as a condition for it. One of them would divide us, while the other would keep us together).

In the early 1950s Bjørnvig was slowly working on the poems that were to be part of his third collection,

Anubis: Digte (Anubis: Poems, 1955). These poems were inspired by a statue of Anubis, the jackal-headed Egyptian god of death, that Bjørnvig saw at the Ny Carlsberg Glyptotek (New Carlsberg Sculpture Gallery) in Copenhagen. In several poems in *Anubis* Bjørnvig deals with problems of death and suicide; the great poem "Barndommens Hus" (House of Childhood)–written at Rungstedlund–and the title poem "Anubis" conclude with a vision of the cosmos, expressed in "Anubis" as "at tænke Himmelrummet med min Krop" (imagining the vault of heaven with my body). The ecstacy of creation, the opposite of death, is epitomized in a compressed sonnet about Vincent van Gogh, "Cypresser under natlig Himmel" (Cypresses beneath a Night Sky).

In the 1950s Bjørnvig published little; however, in a productive interplay between poetry and research, and between lyrical inspiration and academic reflection, Bjørnvig worked on his doctoral thesis about European modernism he had begun and put aside earlier, and on the collection *Figur og ild: Digte* (Figure and Fire: Poems, 1959). Following several poems dealing with modern alienation (for example, a series of sonnets about Friedrich Nietzsche) and with eroticism as the intermediate link, in the last part of *Figur og ild* Bjørnvig unfolds his central themes of nature and the cosmos. Bjørnvig's approach here ranges from analysis and description to experience and expression, while the settings of the poems shift from the city into the countryside. The scenery depicted is that of Kandestederne in northern Jutland, where in the mid 1950s Bjørnvig worked for long periods each spring and fall. In the poem "Halcyonic," which deals with the calm sea in a late fall afternoon, the subject takes on a new vision:

O Klarhed mellem Efteraar og Vinter
sent ved Havet.
Vilde Farver efter Stormen
fylder Øjenene til de er genfødt
og alene tror paa disse Farver: Grønt og Purpur,
intet andet.
Og Stjærnerne, de første føles
som Glædesstød, som Mørkets Gave
og Mildhed længe efter
i søvnløse Lemmer.

(O late-day brightness beside the sea
Between autumn and winter.
After the storm the eyes are filled
With violent colors till they are reborn,
Believing in these colors alone:
Green and purple,
Nothing else.
And the stars: the first ones feel
Like stabs of joy, like a gift of darkness
And, afterwards, as gentleness
In sleep-loosened limbs.)

In many of the best poems in *Figur og ild,* such as "Kandestederne," "Klitspejlet" (The Dune Mirror), "Dag og Nat" (Day and Night), and "Ahorntræet" (The Maple Tree), an inspired balance between the first-person narrator and the surrounding world is articulated in an almost ecstatic form. *Figur og ild* incorporates modernistic forms and language; Bjørnvig is no longer tied to tradition, and his poems are now expressive rather than reflexive.

Figur og ild, perhaps the best of his poetry collections, won Bjørnvig the Søren Gyldendal Award in 1960. On 28 November 1960 he joined fifteen other prominent writers in founding Det Danske Akademi (The Danish Academy), and he has since become the member with the most seniority.

As early as the mid 1950s Bjørnvig had recorded global perspectives on the postwar pollution of the environment; in his collection *Begyndelsen: Essays* (The Initiation: Essays, 1960) a negative view of nature is articulated, along with a defense of the proposition that human beings, both physically and mentally, live by seeing nature as something strange and different. This proposition led to a great deal of debate, and at first some accused Bjørnvig of suffering from a Romantic fear of industrialization. But his view of nature also led to a collaborative working relationship with the prominent theologian K. E. Løgstrup, a relationship shaped by their mutual respect for nature and one in which the two freely exchanged ideas.

Begyndelsen comprises critical reflections on modern civilization. The longest essay in the collection is a strikingly original analysis of the phenomenon of "aesthetic idiosyncrasy," which originates in the psychological phenomenon that something in another person—irrespective of who this person is or what he or she has done—causes unspeakable disgust. The loathing fills the observer's universe so that he is involuntarily fascinated by the object of his disgust and seeks it out, with the loathing eventually becoming a motive for abuse or even murder. Bjørnvig illustrates the "aesthetic idiosyncrasy" through various striking examples, drawn from works as diverse as Edgar Allan Poe's short story "The Tell-Tale Heart" (1843) and the writings of D. H. Lawrence and Graham Greene.

Bjørnvig wrote an important article about modernism, "Moderniteten som holdning" (Modernity as an Attitude), that was published in *Louisiana Revy* (January 1962) and later collected in *Virkeligheden er til: Litterære essays* (Reality Exists: Literary Essays, 1973). In "Moderniteten som holdning" Bjørnvig defines modernism as "et sakralt provisorium, udtryk for indsigter og erfaringer, som ellers er blevet hjemløse og nægtet realitet i verden, som den er i dag" (a sacred provisional arrangement, expressing insights and experiences other-

wise turned homeless and denied reality in the world of today).

With a pre-ecological view of nature and with the understanding of modernism as a "sacred provisional arrangement," Bjørnvig began working on an analysis of Hansen's work in 1961, completing the first draft of his critical study in April 1963. Bjørnvig's general thesis is that an "uforsonlig konflikt mellem kunst og kristendom" (relentless conflict between art and Christianity) caused Hansen to stop writing fiction. Bjørnvig documented his argument through a series of textual analyses inspired by New Criticism. This critical study, *Kains Alter: Martin A. Hansens Digtning og Tænkning* (Cain's Altar: Martin A. Hansen's Writings and Thoughts, 1964), was submitted as a six-hundred-page doctoral dissertation; in December 1964 Bjørnvig defended his dissertation at the University of Århus. The dissertation sparked a widespread and intense literary and theological debate in Denmark, to which Bjørnvig himself contributed in *Forsvar for Kains Alter: En kritisk Efterskrift* (In Defense of Cain's Altar: A Critical Afterword, 1965).

In 1966 one of Bjørnvig's less notable collections of poems, *Vibrationer: Digte* (Vibrations: Poems), was published. In several of the poems Bjørnvig seems to be repressing a genuine openness. In "Solopgang" (Sunrise) the narrator is an unintegrated spectator and observer of himself, removed from life-giving nature:

Og Sol paa Sol paa Sol staar op
i det graa, vækker Uro, en vag
Bevægelse opad in Vævene, Nerverne,
en bedragerisk Springflod i Blodet,
refleksagti Haab—
men Hjærtet svinger sig ikke mer med,
det bliver hernede,
bliver paa Stedet.

(And sun after sun after sun rises
in greyness, creating unrest, a vague
movement upwards through nerves and tissue,
a treacherous spring tide in your blood,
a conditioned hope—
but the heart is not joining in,
it is stuck,
it stays put.)

Two years later *Ravnen* (The Raven, 1968), a major poem cycle, was published. Bjørnvig had worked on these poems since his high-school days; the collection is a nearly perfect piece of art—and also nearly inaccessible to the reader because of the many condensed mythological and literary allusions. When he republished the collection twelve years later, Bjørnvig confessed in a postscript that he had "strøget enkelte strofer, som jeg givetvis forstod, da

Bjørnvig with Karen Blixen (Isak Dinesen), ca. 1950 (photograph by Knud Jensen)

jeg skrev dem, men knap forstår i dag og da slet ikke nødvendigheden af dem" (deleted some of the verses, which I most likely had understood when I wrote them, but hardly understand today, nor can I see why they should be there). *Ravnen* is perhaps Bjørnvig's most important work, one in which he most consciously realizes himself. The first drafts date from 1937 and some of the sections were composed in the early 1940s, but the majority of the poems were written during two long stays in Rome in 1963 and 1964, when Bjørnvig experienced a mental crisis.

Bjørnvig had begun writing *Ravnen* on the east-facing Århus Bay. The last songs were written on the island of Samsø, where he had rented a small house (also facing east) during the winter and spring of 1966–1967. It was with a sense of homecoming that he finished the poems, commenting on them in 1973 in the periodical *Dansk Ud yn*:

Endelig var jeg ankommet til min østkyst, vandrede der morgen efter morgen i planettimen før solens opgang, ja boede, mens jeg sad og skrev sidste afsnit, mere mellem stjærnebilleder og morgenrøden end mellem vægge, eksatisk henrykket af et og et eneste– ligesom i sommeren '41–: Jordens og himlens, stjærnekonstellationernes og planeterne generøse urørlige og ufattelige skønhed, hele livet værd at få lov at se og være i.

(Finally I had arrived on my eastern coast, and I wandered there dawn after dawn in the planetary hour before sunrise, nay, I lived, while writing the last section, more among the constellations and the first blush of dawn than within walls, in ecstactic joy over one single thing–like the summer of '41–: The generous, untouchable and incomprehensible beauty of the earth, the sky, the stars and the planets, worth my entire life just to watch and to be in.)

Ravnen was intended to answer the question: "Who am I?" Even the first poem deals with the problem of personal identity:

Et sted må den findes, skabelsesplanen
en brændende stjernenat under mit liv,
et væsen, som fatter mig ufbrudt og tydeligt,
hele min værens rene motiv

(Somewhere it must exist, the blueprint of creation
A shining, starry night under my life,
A creature who clearly understands me all the time,
The pure motive for all my being.)

Bjørnvig had once read this section to Karen Blixen and wrote about it in *Pagten:*

Den egentlige dybere og hårdere dialog mellem Karen Blixen og mig . . . gik om identitetsproblematikken, om spørgsmålet: Hvem er jeg?–Karen Blixen mente, at man erfarede svaret ved sin placering i historien forstaaet som fortælling . . . jeg ved vor relation til kosmos.

(The fundamental dialogue between Karen Blixen and me . . . concerned the problem of identity, the question: Who am I? Karen Blixen thought the answer was found in one's place in history understood as a tale . . . I, in our relation to the cosmos.)

According to Bjørnvig's perspective, the mind and the senses are created in the image of the universe and correspond to it.

With *Ravnen* Bjørnvig had written and lived through his inspiration from nature and the cosmos, and this was marked by the publishing of *Udvalgte digte* (Selected Poems, 1970). In this collection he evaluates a phase in his lyrical writings. The poems are not presented chronologically, but arranged thematically, culminating with the last section, "Cosmos."

After *Figur og ild* Bjørnvig had published a poetics of modernism; in the same way, *Ravnen* was followed by two lectures on religious experiences at the University of Copenhagen in 1971, later published as *Det religiøse menneskes ansigter* (The Faces of the Religious Human Being, 1975). The lectures provoked criticism from his friend Løgstrup, who maintained that although Bjørnvig had had experiences of a religious nature, these experiences remained anonymous and temporary, and they never became confessional doctrines. In 1973 several of Bjørnvig's literary essays and analyses, many on Danish and European modernism, were collected in a major work with the characteristic title *Virkeligheden er til* (Reality Exists).

The ecstatic dimension he experienced in nature made Bjørnvig—much to the surprise of many of his academic readers—respond positively toward the youth rebellion and rock music; he interpreted this movement as a renewed phrasing of the inspiration and utopian impulses of "initiation" in his *Oprør mod neonguden: Et essay om beat* (Rebellion against the Neon God: An Essay on Beat, 1970). It was, however, less surprising that in the same year he published *Brød og vin og andre digte* (Bread and Wine and Other Poems), a powerful translation of Friedrich Hölderlin's highly inaccessible poems, commemorating the bicentennial of Hölderlin's birth.

In 1969 his marriage with Grete Bjørnvig had ended in divorce, and in 1970 Thorkild Bjørnvig married the thirty-four-year-old Birgit Nielsen, a teacher who later became a politician in the European Union. Since 1973 the couple has lived at the most northern point of the island of Samsø, near where Bjørnvig had finished writing *Ravnen*. The author Thorkild Hansen was their neighbor for several years.

Under the influence of his second wife, Bjørnvig's view of nature gradually became more consciously ecological, and this shift resulted in a series of striking and frequently topical poems on ecology, many written for publication in newspapers or for meetings of environmental activists. In the three collections of ecological poems, *Delfinen: Miljødigte 1970–75* (The Dolphin: Environmental Poems 1970–1975, 1975), *Abeguder: Miljødigte 1975–80* (Monkey Gods: Environmental Poems 1975–1980, 1981), and *Epimetheus: Miljødigte: 1980–90* (Epimetheus: Environmental Poems 1980–1990, 1990), Bjørnvig abandons his earlier meditative self-reflexive style and appeals directly to the reader. The strict forms were also abandoned in favor of free verse, almost prose, with a tone that is frequently one of angry protest. The poems are all filled with informative and factual statements, with copious and instructive notes, frequently based on study tours to the United States, Scotland, Iceland, and the Hebrides. Bjørnvig did not appeal to the readers in vain; the poems gained him new readers, gave rise to debates, and intensified the concern in Denmark for ecological matters. The collections were sold and republished in editions of unusual size for poetry.

The poems on ecology are paralleled in *Også for naturens skyld: Økologiske essays* (For Nature's Sake, as Well: Ecological Essays, 1978). In the introduction Bjørnvig writes: "Jeg har efter evne forsøgt at påvirke mine medmenneskers fantasi og forestillingskraft gennem anskuelighed og eksempler. Mit ubevidste og bevidste mål har været: at tænke anskueligt" (To the best of my ability I have tried to influence my fellowmen's imagination through lucid examples. My unconscious and conscious aim has been: clear perception). The following year an honorary doctorate was conferred on Bjørnvig by the University of Lund in Sweden, and he published a small collection of essays, *Barnet og dyret i industrisamfundet: Et Essay* (The Child and the Animal in Industrial Society: An Essay, 1979).

Despite all the poems on ecology, Bjørnvig did not lose track of his own personal identity as a poet. In the collection *Morgenmørke: Digte* (Morning Darkness: Poems, 1977) he returns to experiences and structures from *Ravnen*, although these poems are more subdued and less mythological. The poems are also more confessional insofar as they include scenes from a marriage that ends in divorce and the description of the start of a new relationship. In between are pure nature poems, such as "Hebridebugt" (Hebridean Bay):

Klippernes halvcirkel sandbreddens halvmåne om de atlantiske dønninger,
her bliver begrænsning og rum i eet til en åbning;
bag mig er klodens trængsel og tomheden over den,

foran mig hvirvlende dyb af ædelstensklarhed:
. . . .
gennem sådanne åbninger drager jordkloden ånde.

(Half-circle of rock, half-moon of sand embracing the
    Atlantic rollers,
limitation and space uniting into an opening;
behind me the congested globe with the void above,
in front of me the gemlike clarity of the swirling deep:
. . . .
through openings like these the globe draws breath.)

The poems are no longer rhymed, though many of them are related to another strict form, the hexameter—so a discreet tension is created between rhythm and meter.

In 1981 Bjørnvig was hospitalized for a minor operation, and there he wrote a poem about his relationship to the writings of Goethe, "Første nat på hospitalet" (First Night at the Hospital), which also deals with the theme of death. He realizes—eventually—that he is now too old to die young and is reconciled to the idea of being torn between the future and the past "i en sidste svævende grunden over / menneskelig mulighed, vækst, forandring og troskab / natlige afgrunde, hvisken og kærlighedssamhør, / østlig vækkende uro, opfyldelsens ro i vest." (in a final unresolved pondering over / human potential, growth, change and fidelity, / nocturnal depths, whispers and loving togetherness, / easterly awakening unrest, the calm of fulfillment in the west). The poem is included in the collection *Gennem regnbuen* (Through the Rainbow, 1987).

The 1974 publication of *Pagten* demonstrated Bjørnvig's nearly photographic memory and his ability to relive his friendship with Blixen in detail. From 1983 to 1987 Bjørnvig followed up on his memoir with four more volumes of memoirs, comprising almost a thousand pages, recalling the years from 1918 to 1948, when *Pagten* begins. He also wrote a series of profiles of Danish authors, many of whom he had known personally, collected in *Digtere,* including figures such as Tove Ditlevsen, Frank Jæger, and Knud Sønderby.

In connection with his seventy-fifth birthday in 1993, a collection of his poems, selected and translated by Paula Hostrup-Jensen, was published in English as *The World Tree,* and Bjørnvig also published his collection of poems, *Siv vand og måne* (Water, Rushes, and the Moon), a work that revealed his continuing ability to record and express his impressions. The collection opens with four poems dedicated to Hölderlin, depicting Hölderlin's life from a young, ecstatic poet, through his love for "Diotima" until his breakdown, followed by thirty-

five years of insanity. Then follow twenty poems titled "Rejsen" (The Journey) and finally four subdued, intensely lyrical poems. In 1995 his Rilke translations were published in a selected and revised edition, *Rainer Maria Rilke: Udsat på hjertets bjerge: Digte,* and the following year the prestigious European Aristeion Prize was bestowed upon Bjørnvig.

In "Blade af en uført dagbog" ("Pages from an Unkept Diary") Bjørnvig maintains,

Alt genoplever jeg, fysisk svagere, aftagende–psykisk stadig tydeligere, i forklarelse. Om eftermiddagen og tidligt på aftenen stadig trættere. Indtil den sidste fortætning før søvnen. Så nær stjernehimlen som aldrig før, først med åbne, så med lukkede øjne. Og endelig borte, i legemlighedens sødme, i svæven ud over dens omrids.

(I relive everything, physically weaker and declining–yet mentally more and more lucid–transfigured. In the afternoon and early evening increasingly weary. Until the final concentration before sleep. Never before so near the starry sky, first with my eyes open, then closed. And gone–in the sweetness of corporeality, drifting beyond its contours.)

These lines echo the conclusion of *Ravnen,* published twenty-five years earlier—itself based on an idea from 1938. There is a coherence and cohesiveness in Thorkild Bjørnvig's whole body of work.

Letters:
Karen Blixen i Danmark: Breve 1931–62, volumes 1–2, edited by Frans Lasson and Tom Engelbrecht (Copenhagen: Gyldendal, 1996).

Interviews:
Claus Clausen, "Thorkild Bjørnvig," Claus Clausen, *Digtere i Forhør 1966* (Copenhagen: Gyldendal, 1966), pp. 33–59;

Tom på Thuro: En samtale mellem Tom Kristensen og Thorkild Bjørnvig (Odense: Andelsbogtykkeriet i Odense, 1971);

Lisbeth Wissing, "Nye erkendelser," in her *Mod nye erkendelser* (Copenhagen: Information, 1992), pp. 28–29;

Erik A. Nielsen and Marianne Barlyng, "Nattergaledigteren: En samtale med Thorkild Bjørnvig," in *I kentaurens tegn,* edited by Marianne Barlyng (Copenhagen: Gyldendal, 1993), pp. 263–297.

References:
Marianne Barlyng, ed., *I kentaurens tegn: En bog om Thorkild Bjørnvigs universer* (Copenhagen: Gyldendal, 1993);

Torben Brostrøm, "Thorkild Bjørnvig," in *Danske digtere i det 20. århundrede,* third edition, volume 3, edited by Torben Brostrøm and Mette Winge (Copenhagen: Gad, 1981), pp. 326–346;

Per Dahl, *Thorkild Bjørnvigs tænkning* (Copenhagen: Gyldendal, 1976);

Anders Ellegaard, "Det sakrale provisorium. Thorkild Bjørnvig: Figur og Ild," in *Læsninger i dansk litteratur,* volume 4, edited by Anne-Marie Mai and Knud Bjarne Gjesing (Odense: Odense Universitetsforlag, 1997), pp. 160–177;

Björn Julén, "Thorkild Bjørnvig," in *Danske digtere i det 20. århundrede,* second edition, volume 3, edited by Frederik Nielsen and Ole Restrup (Copenhagen: Gad, 1965), pp. 273–289;

Johnny Kondrup, *Erindringens udveje: Studier i moderne dansk selvbiografi* (Copenhagen: Amadeus, 1994), pp. 246–325;

Ole Wivel, *Romance for valdhorn* (Copenhagen: Gyldendal, 1972);

Wivel, *Tranedans* (Copenhagen: Gyldendal, 1975).

Papers:

A small collection of Thorkild Bjørnvig's correspondence is held by Det Kongelige Bibliotek (The Royal Library), Copenhagen.

Karen Blixen
(Isak Dinesen)
(17 April 1885 – 7 September 1962)

Linda G. Donelson

and

Marianne Stecher-Hansen
University of Washington

BOOKS: *Seven Gothic Tales,* as Isak Dinesen (New York: Harrison Smith & Robert Haas; London: Putnam, 1934); translated by Blixen as *Syv fantastiske Fortællinger* (Copenhagen: C. A. Reitzel, 1935);

Out of Africa, as Dinesen (London: Putnam, 1937; New York: Random House, 1938); translated by Blixen as *Den afrikanske Farm,* as Blixen (Copenhagen: Gyldendal, 1937);

Winter's Tales, as Dinesen (New York: Random House; London: Putnam, 1942); translated by Blixen as *Vinter-Eventyr,* as Blixen (Copenhagen: Gyldendal, 1942);

Gengældelsens Veje, as Pierre Andrézel, as translated by Clara Svendsen (Copenhagen: Gyldendal, 1944); translated by Blixen as *The Angelic Avengers,* as Dinesen (London: Putnam, 1946; New York: Random House, 1947);

Last Tales, as Dinesen (New York: Random House; London: Putnam, 1957); translated by Blixen as *Sidste Fortællinger,* as Blixen (Copenhagen: Gyldendal, 1957);

Anecdotes of Destiny, as Dinesen (New York: Random House; London: Joseph, 1958); translated by Blixen as *Skæbne-Anekdoter* (Copenhagen: Gyldendal, 1958);

Sandhedens Hævn: En Marionet-komedie (Copenhagen: Glydendal, 1960); translated by Donald Hannah as "The Revenge of Truth," in his *"Isak Dinesen" and Karen Blixen: The Mask and the Reality* (New York: Random House, 1971), pp. 179–204;

Skygger på Græsset (Copenhagen: Gyldendal, 1960); translated by Blixen as *Shadows on the Grass,* as Dinesen (New York: Random House; London; Joseph, 1961);

On Mottoes of My Life (Copenhagen: Ministry of Foreign Affairs, 1962);

Karen Blixen (photograph by Rie Nissen; courtesy of Gyldendal Publishers)

Osceola, edited by Clara Svendsen, Gyldendals Julebog 1962 (Copenhagen: Gyldendal, 1962);

Ehrengard, as Dinesen (New York: Random House; London: Joseph, 1963); translated by Svendsen (Copenhagen: Gyldendal, 1963);

Essays (Copenhagen: Gyldendal, 1965); enlarged as *Mit livs mottoer og andre essays* (Copenhagen: Gyldendal, 1978); translated by P. M. Mitchell and W. D. Paden as *Daguerreotypes and Other Essays,* as Dinesen (Chicago: University of Chicago Press, 1979); enlarged again as *Samlede essays* (Copenhagen: Gyldendal, 1985);

Efterladte Fortællinger, edited, with an afterword, by Frans Lasson (Copenhagen: Gyldendal, 1975); enlarged and translated by P. M. Mitchell and W. D. Paden as *Carnival: Entertainments and Posthumous Tales,* as Dinesen (Chicago: University of Chicago Press, 1977; London: Heinemann, 1978); enlarged again as *Kongesønnerne og andre efterladte fortællinger,* edited by Frans Lasson (Copenhagen: Gyldendal, 1985);

Moderne ægteskab og andre betragtninger, foreword by Lasson (Copenhagen: Gyldendal, 1981); translated by Anne Born as *On Modern Marriage: And Other Observations,* as Dinesen (New York: St. Martin's Press, 1986).

Editions and Collections: *Babettes gæstebud,* translated by Jørgen Claudi (Copenhagen: Fremdad, 1957);

Fra det gamle Danmark: Udvalgte fortællinger, 2 volumes (Copenhagen: Gyldendal, 1963);

Out of Africa, introduction by Alan Moorehead (New York: Time, 1963);

Mindeudgave, 7 volumes (Copenhagen: Gyldendal, 1964)—comprises *Fantastiske Fortællinger,* 2 volumes; *Den afrikanske Farm; Vintereventyr,* 2 volumes; *Skæbneanekdater; Gengældelsens veje;*

Et Udvalg, edited by Merete Klenow With (Copenhagen: Gyldendal/Dansklærerforeningen, 1964);

Den afrikanske farm, edited, with an afterword, by Aage Henriksen (Copenhagen: Gyldendal, 1970);

"Det drømmende Barn" og andre fortællinger, edited by Else Cederborg (Copenhagen: Gyldendal/Dansklærerforeningen, 1979);

Sorg-Agre og Vejene omkring Pisa, afterword by Susanne Fabricius (Copenhagen: Gyldendal/Dansklærerforeningen, 1987).

OTHER: Truman Capote, *Holly,* with an introductory essay by Blixen (Copenhagen: Gyldendal, 1960);

Olive Schriener, *The Story of an African Farm,* with an introductory essay by Dinesen (New York: Limited Editions Club, 1961);

Basil Davidson, *Det genfundne Afrika,* with an introductory essay by Blixen (Copenhagen: Gyldendal, 1962);

Hans Christian Andersen, *Thumbelina and Other Fairy Tales,* with an introductory essay by Dinesen (London & New York: Macmillan, 1962).

Karen Blixen is the most widely recognized figure in twentieth-century Danish letters, eliciting greater critical and popular attention than any other Danish writer of this century. The scholarly studies dealing with her life and works number well over four hundred publications. Interest in her fiction has remained unabated since *Seven Gothic Tales* (1934), her debut published under the pseudonym Isak Dinesen. Wearing a bearskin coat, stylish attire, and a flamboyant hat, Blixen won international renown in the 1940s and 1950s with her collections of tales. While only one hundred thousand copies of *Out of Africa* (1937) were printed in her lifetime, more than a million and a half copies have been sold during the last two decades of the century. Sydney Pollack's 1985 motion-picture adaptation of this book won an Academy Award and has been seen by more than fifty million viewers around the world. From an early age Dinesen worked to establish her own personal myth and her place in world literature. As a result, the relationship between her life and works has been the subject of considerable attention, including many memoirs and biographies. Relatives and friends, scholars and critics have all sought to offer the "true" picture of Karen Blixen's life and persona. Four volumes of selected letters, which document her entire adult life, have been published posthumously. Studies published in the 1980s and 1990s reveal that the relationship between this author's life and works continues to be the subject of intense critical inquiry and revisionism.

Blixen's works are the literary expressions of her views on art, nature, and identity. She drew much of her philosophy from the nineteenth-century Romantic school of writers, who believed that man in his most godlike form has a strong connection to nature and that the primitive and the aristocrat share an innate creativity or intuitiveness. She was also inspired by Søren Kierkegaard, who was skeptical of established religion and thus saw man as isolated in his relation to God. She also admired Friedrich Nietzsche as a poet; her aesthetics—not least her use of parody—bear a remarkable likeness to his ideals. Raised as a Unitarian, Dinesen rejected the dualism of the Protestant tradition, but she was well versed in the Bible, and many witty reinterpretations of events of the Old and New Testaments occur in her tales.

The author was born Karen Christentze Dinesen 17 April 1885 on a rural estate north of Copenhagen. The wooded property called *Rungstedlund* faces east toward the Øresund, the channel dividing Denmark and Sweden. Its timber and stucco manor house was once an inn–the celebrated eighteenth-century Danish poet Johannes Ewald lived there for a time. Dinesen grew up inspired by literature. Her grandfather Adolph Wilhelm Dinesen had been a friend of the writer Hans Christian Andersen. Her father, Wilhelm Dinesen, wrote *Jagtbreve* (1888; translated as *Boganis' Letters from the Hunt*, 1987) and *Paris under Communen* (Paris under the Commune, 1871), works acclaimed by the greatest critic of his day, Georg Brandes. Many of Dinesen's family, including her sister Ellen, her aunt Mary Bess Westenholz, and her brother, Thomas, were writers. From youth she had been steeped in Nordic mythology. As a child she loved ghost stories and magic, and she devoured stories of the supernatural, especially those exalting the mystical powers of women.

Dinesen's father was not titled, but his first cousins, the Krag-Juel-Vind-Frijs's, were related to the Danish royal family. Her mother, Ingeborg Westenholz Dinesen, was the daughter of a wealthy shipowner. Later Dinesen made much of the contrast between her hedonistic and aristocratic paternal relatives and her practical and prosperous maternal ones. Her father committed suicide in 1895, when Karen Dinesen was ten years old. According to the family legend, he took his life because he had contracted syphilis. It was widely known that the disease could lead to a slow death from madness. Karen, his second daughter, nicknamed "Tanne," had been his favorite child, and his death left a lasting impression on her psyche.

The death of Dinesen's father left an extended family of women to support each other materially and spiritually. Her grandmother and her aunts, who lived at a neighboring estate, helped with the moral supervision and education of the children. Dinesen showed a special aptitude for painting and, after the age of eighteen, took classes at the Academy of Art in Copenhagen. Several of her paintings survive, including beautiful portraits of Africans. Although painting never became more than a pastime for her, her writing was profoundly influenced by the artist's perspective, relying on colors and images to express sensations and emotions.

Dinesen was also interested from an early age in writing. As a child she often kept her sisters awake at night with the stories she invented. She also wrote marionette comedies that were performed by the entire family. In 1907, when she was twenty-two years old, two of her stories were published under the pseudonym "Osceola" in Danish literary journals, "Pløjeren" (The Ploughman) in *Gads Danske Magasin* and "Eneboerne" (The Hermits) in *Tilskueren*. In 1909 "Familien de Cats"

Blixen in 1913, a year before she went to Africa and married Bror von Blixen-Finecke (photograph by Juncker-Jensen)

(The de Cats Family) was also published in *Tilskueren*. Later collected in *Osceola* (1962), these early tales display elements that appear over and over in the author's stories: a concern for identity, a sympathy with nature, and a reverence for the story as art. In "Pløjeren" Dinesen describes a heroine about her own age who copes with the enthusiasm of her lover by setting him to the practical enterprise of plowing his land. "Eneboerne" reveals Dinesen's fascination with the unity of nature, as symbolized by the sea, and her penchant for eroticism. The young woman's lover is a ghost who consummates their love by drowning her. Years later, "Sandhedens Hævn" (The Revenge of Truth, 1926), a tale illustrating the importance of ideals, was published, and republished in book form in 1960.

As a young woman, Dinesen lived in romantic frustration. While still taking art classes in Copenhagen, she developed a friendship with Daisy Frijs, the daughter of her father's titled cousin, and Frijs's young aristocratic friends. She began a flirtation with Hans von Blixen-Finecke, her second cousin, the son of Baron Blixen of Sweden. Hans was an officer in the

Swedish military and a champion horseman. When Hans Blixen abandoned her for a fiancée eight years younger, Dinesen decided to marry Hans's twin brother, Bror. Bror is said to have been competitive, the kind of man who would enjoy winning his brother's sweetheart. This rash determination to reach the object of her desire through a substitute would later be represented allegorically in many of Dinesen's stories dealing with the theme of vicarious achievement.

With the encouragement of relatives, Dinesen and Bror Blixen embarked on a grand plan to start a pioneer coffee farm in East Africa. Little is known about their courtship, except that Bror later gave Dinesen credit for the idea of going to Africa. They were married on 14 January 1914 in Mombasa, on the coast of British East Africa. She wore a safari helmet and a shantung suit. Many have questioned why Dinesen married Bror—she herself emphasized the importance of gaining the title "Baroness," but she also insisted that she was in love with Bror. Late in life she told her secretary, Clara Svendsen, that if she could relive one moment it would be to go on safari again with Bror.

The lasting record of the author's saga in Africa lies not in her writings meant for publication but in her vast correspondence with her family during the period 1914–1931, large portions of which have been published as *Breve fra Afrika 1914–31* (1978; translated as *Letters from Africa 1914–1931,* 1981). For the years immediately following her marriage her only writing that survives are these letters, written two or more per week, addressed to her mother, her sisters, her uncle Aage, her brother, Thomas, and her aunt Bess.

The Blixens set up housekeeping on seven hundred acres of woodland, twelve miles southwest of Nairobi. The farm lay at an elevation of 6,200 feet, near the Ngong Hills, a range of low mountains forming a barrier against the Rift Valley. With the help of 1,200 Africans, the land was cleared and prepared for coffee seedlings. The Blixens could expect no crop from the coffee trees for three to five years. In their living arrangements they relied on household servants: a cook, Esa; a houseman, Juma; and a personal servant, Farah, as well as several young Africans who performed odd jobs. In *Out of Africa* Blixen refers to this as a "feudal" system of labor, but she and Bror were merely following the pattern they had known in their childhood on the large estates in Scandinavia.

Only a year after her marriage, sometime in the early months of 1915, Blixen learned she had syphilis. Later she told her family that her husband had given her the illness, but she never said how he had acquired the infection. Her letters suggest that she made a suicide attempt in February of that year. Several weeks later she turned up in Paris, looking for a specialist in venereal diseases. She eventually made her way through war-torn Europe back to Denmark, where a venerealogist, Carl Rasch, found her to be suffering from syphilis and poisoning from the treatment (mercury tablets) given to her in Nairobi. Through a series of injections of intravenous arsenic—a new treatment for the illness—Blixen grew better. Reexaminations by Rasch in 1919 and 1925 revealed no further evidence of syphilis; however, despite the doctor's assurances, Blixen continued to believe she would never recover from the illness. Syphilis appears time and again in Blixen's writings and features prominently in the popular myth that gathered around her after she rose to literary prominence. She could not escape the irony that she had been victimized by the same illness that had led to her father's death. She spent much of her later life developing a philosophy to cope with the implications of the diagnosis. In 1926 she wrote to her brother, Thomas: "Hvis det ikke lød saa væmmeligt, kunde jeg f. Ex. sige at det for mig, saadan som Verden nu engang er, var værd at have haft Syphilis for at være blevet 'Baroness'" (If it did not sound so beastly I might say that, the world being as it is, it was worth having syphilis in order to become a "Baroness").

After spending most of 1915 and 1916 in Denmark, Blixen reconciled with her husband. They returned to their African farm with a new bankroll provided by her relatives. Under the aegis of a new family company, the Karen Coffee Corporation, they bought two additional farms. Karen Blixen's letters over the next two years seesawed between optimism and exasperation. A series of droughts precluded any profits from the large capital input. Bror was gone frequently, chasing other investments. Toward the end of 1918 she found consolation in a new friendship, with Denys Finch Hatton, an Englishman recently returned from the war. Son of Henry Stormont Finch Hatton, thirteenth Earl of Winchelsea, and educated at Eton and Oxford, he was the quintessential English aristocrat: lanky, well read, witty, teasing, and a shrewd judge of people. She wrote to Thomas about Finch Hatton in 1918: "Jeg har nemlig haft den Lykke paa mine gamle Dage at møde mit Ideal levendegjort i ham" (I have been so fortunate in my old age to meet my ideal realized in him).

Shortly after the war ended, Karen separated permanently from Bror (they divorced in 1925). The immediate cause was not Finch Hatton, but Bror's continuing infidelities. After Bror left, she protected herself from loneliness by writing stories. In *Out of Africa,* she explains that she was forced into a program of writing: "I was young, and by instinct of self-preservation, I had to collect my energy on something. . . . I began in the evenings to write stories, fairy-tales and romances, that would take my mind a long way off, to other countries and times." Several notebooks filled with outlines and jottings survive from her years in Africa; many of these stories were later revised and published in her first collection, *Seven Gothic Tales.*

Blixen had been left with complete responsibility for two 4,500-acre coffee farms. In 1920 the Karen Coffee Corporation made her managing director of the corporation. Not one year out of seventeen yielded a profit. She took out more loans, sold off some of her land, and convinced her family that the exotic investment would eventually pay off. In 1924 Finch Hatton began staying in her house while he was in Nairobi–a few months out of every year. She miscarried his child in 1922 and another in 1926. He was not interested in marriage. It was not until the death of his best friend, Berkeley Cole, in 1925 that Finch Hatton spent more time with Blixen. In 1928 he entertained his friend, Edward, Prince of Wales (later King Edward V until he abdicated and became Duke of Windsor) at her house–an event described in *Out of Africa.* He also bought an airplane and flew Blixen over her farm, which she describes as her "most transporting pleasure" in Africa. By 1929 a cascade of events had begun that would bring an end to Blixen's farming life. A loan promised by Finch Hatton never materialized. The collapse of the stock market sent coffee and land prices spiraling downward. Locusts descended on the land, and drought exhausted Blixen's last hopes for recovery. Finally, she had to sell out to a developer in Nairobi. A few weeks later, on 14 May 1931, Finch Hatton died in the crash of his light airplane.

Shortly before she left Kenya for good, Blixen sent some finished stories to a publisher. In a letter to Thomas, she explained that she had begun writing a book during these difficult months and that she had been writing in English as she thought it would be more "profitable" (although she feared that she would have difficulties with the language). During and after her return to Denmark in 1931 she wrote and refined more stories. In several of them she hints that she died spiritually when she left Africa. It was, as she suggests in "The Deluge at Norderney" (1934; translated as "Syndfloden over Norderney," 1935), as if in leaving Africa she had gone away from the "one real place and hour" of her life. During a difficult readjustment to living at home under her mother's kind and critical eye, she continued to send her stories to publishers. She offered the tales under the pen name Isak Dinesen–the name "Isak" in Hebrew means "the one who laughs."

In 1932 Blixen used Thomas Dinesen's acquaintance with the American writer, Dorothy Canfield Fisher, to contact an American publisher. After two years of negotiations and revisions, her first volume of

Cover for the 1935 Danish edition of Blixen's first book, the short-story collection originally published in English as Seven Gothic Tales *(1934)*

stories was published by the publishing firm of Robert Haas and Harrison Smith (which later became Random House) in New York. The foreword to the English edition was written by Canfield Fisher, who played along with the author's pseudonym and her desire for anonymity: "The author is a Continental European, writing in English although that is not native to his pen." Chosen as the Book-of-the-Month, *Seven Gothic Tales,* published in April 1934, established Blixen's reputation as "Isak Dinesen" and laid the financial foundation for her future writing. In October 1934 the prestigious editor Constant Huntington at Putnam's oversaw a British edition of the tales.

As Dinesen was dissatisfied with the attempts of Danish translators, she hit upon a method of translating the works herself, a method which she practiced throughout the remainder of her career: with the English "original" in front of her, she freely improvised a Danish version while dictating to a stenographer. In this manner, two original versions of each of her major works were created. In the winter of 1935 she noted:

"jeg kan dansk,–ikke alene ligesaa godt som engelsk, men jeg vil næsten tillade mig at sige: saa godt som nogen dansk Skribent" (I know Danish–not only as well as English, but I will venture to say, as well as any Danish writer). Danish publishers, however, were more reluctant to print this collection of exotic tales and feared that the Danish public might find her book "aristokratisk and forfinet" (aristocratic and refined), as critic Otto Rung remarked. Through her brother-in-law, Knud Dahl, the director of C. A. Reitzel's publishing house, the Danish edition *Syv fantastiske Fortællinger* was published on 25 September 1935. As her publishers and critics (and the author) had feared, the book was not well received in Denmark.

Dinesen called the tales "gothic" because of their tragic and supernatural elements. They were designed not to frighten, but rather to make a profound statement. Their gothic nature arises from the author's sense of whimsy; even in her most tragic story, Dinesen wanted the reader to discover a joke. Setting the tales in the mid-nineteeth century, she hoped, would render the stories mythical. To reinforce this vision, she wrote each tale as a collection of intricately woven inset stories resembling, in structure, *The Thousand and One Nights*.

The American edition of the collection begins with "The Deluge at Norderney," the tale of a flood of near biblical proportions on the Atlantic coast of Holstein in 1835. Four aristocratic vacationers, marooned in a hayloft by the rising waters, spend a night telling stories that reveal their true identities. Each lets his or her "mask" fall while they await the Day of Judgment. Because it so elegantly articulates–through the free-flowing conversations of the characters–Dinesen's artistic and philosophical vision, "The Deluge at Norderney" is considered one of her most significant tales. The characters are doomed by the rising waters, but they do not lose their sense of humor. Taken together, the inset tales record the journey from innocence to philosophical maturity. The young woman Calypso is the first of many characters who realizes her true nature by gazing into a mirror. In studying an erotic painting, she comes to understand the power and pleasure of being a woman. Miss Nat-og-Dag (Miss Night-and-Day) articulates the author's credo that "truth is for tailors and shoemakers . . . . I, on the contrary, have always held that the Lord has a penchant for masquerades." Miss Malin's self-created role as "the grand courtesan of her time" illustrates the power of the imagination: in reality a virgin, she holds "a firm faith in a past of colossal licentiousness." The Cardinal tells the inset tale, "The Wine of the Tetrarch," which explains how the robber Barabbas met his fate, going free so that Christ might be crucified. In the dramatic denouement of "The Deluge at Norderney," the Cardinal removes a bandage

from his face to reveal that he is really the actor Kasparson in disguise. He has played many varying roles in his life: "I have lived long enough, by now," he says, "to have learned, when the devil grins at me, to grin back." Central to *Seven Gothic Tales* is the concept of the mask, which is illustrated most obviously in the conversations between Miss Malin and Kasparson. According to Kasparson (whose motto is "disguise yourselves"), the new "bourgeois king" of France, Louis Philippe, is contemptuous because he lacks charlatanry: "he is genuinely reliable all through."

"The Old Chevalier" ("Den gamle vandrende Ridder") takes place "in the early days of the 'emancipation of woman.'" In this story about a failed love affair, a man becomes involved with a prostitute, Nathalie, who has never before offered herself for money; she appears as an innocent, trading favors for shelter. In the most charming and sensuous scene in the tale, the young Baron von Brackel undresses the girl, allowing for a witty digression on the significance of a woman's clothing as a symbol of identity, the idea that in that age "a woman was . . . a work of art, the product of centuries of civilization." He falls in love, but Nathalie seems oblivious to his passion. She leaves after their encounter, having fulfilled her role. The tale ends enigmatically, leaving the reader uncertain about whether the girl was indeed a prostitute or an innocent. The narrator learns from the experience that the importance lies in the role playing: "We two had played. A rare jest had been offered me and I had accepted it; now it was up to me to keep the spirit of our game until the end." The story also offers the author's sometimes curious views on the role of independent women: "most women, when they feel free to experiment with life, will go straight to the witches' Sabbath. I myself respect them for it, and do not think that I could ever really love a woman who had not, at some time or other, been up on a broomstick."

One tale especially lends a gothic element to *Seven Gothic Tales*. "The Monkey" ("Aben") is the story of a virgin prioress who exchanges her soul with that of an ape. The tale parodies the Gothic genre with its characters, settings, and themes. Boris von Schreckenstein is the decadent and melancholy hero of the tale. A homosexual scandal has brought him to the cloister to ask his aunt (the prioress) to arrange a marriage for him. The heroine of the tale, Athena Hopballehus–Boris's intended wife–is a giantess, likened to the ancient goddess of war and daughter of Zeus. Her mighty figure makes her role as the pursued female comical. "The Monkey" verges on the burlesque when Dinesen parodies the supper of seduction: "Boris was looking at Athena. . . . He liberated the maiden of her strong and fresh flesh together with her clothes, and imagined that he

Denys Finch Hatton, the British adventurer who was Blixen's lover in Kenya

might be very happy with her, that he might even fall in love with her, could he have her in her beautiful bones alone." Fortified by an aphrodisiac, Boris pursues innocent Athena to the bedroom. After rolling on the floor together, restrained by the girl's strength, Boris succeeds only in grating his teeth against Athena's. The next morning a pale, innocent Athena responds to the admonitions of the prioress, "What?" she asked, "Shall I have a child from that?"

Beyond the lighthearted parody of Gothic conventions, "The Monkey" delivers a more profound statement on Dinesen's artistic vision. In the final scene of metamorphosis, the "double nature" of the prioress is revealed, a shocking union between civilized refinement and primitive instinct, between the European and the African. In a concluding quotation from Virgil, the "true" prioress admonishes Athena and Boris: "discite justitiam, et non temnere divos" (obey the law, and do not offend the gods). Obey both Apollo and Dionysus, implies the author; accept the irrational, unconscious, and instinctual forces in human life, and "let the monkey in."

"The Roads Round Pisa" ("Vejene omkring Pisa") demonstrates many themes that appear repeatedly in Dinesen's tales. It is the story of a mistake. Its inset tales give clues to a chain of events that the reader at first finds incomprehensible. Only when all the pieces of the puzzle have been revealed do the characters in the story realize the full extent of their misunderstanding. The tale is woven throughout with erotic images. Prince Potenziani, impotent and fearing that his young wife will demand an annulment, secretly employs his friend, Count Nino, to take his place in the marital bed. Ironically, on the same night, the wife sneaks away and substitutes a friend in her place. Ignorant about the switch, the prince blames the count for not carrying out his promise to impregnate his wife. A duel ensues, interrupted only when Prince Potenziani realizes how badly he has misunderstood the course of events. He declares, "Always we fail because we are too small. . . . Too small I have been, too small for the ways of God." He dies, his gun firing skyward—in a gesture of spiritual fulfillment.

In "The Dreamers" ("Drømmerne") Dinesen again uses the concept of identity to offer a way to cope with tragedy. A famous opera singer, Pellegrina Leoni, loses her voice in a fire. Afterwards she pursues a life of constantly changing roles: whore, artist-revolutionary, and finally, saint. The tale is narrated by the three men who fall in love with the variously disguised Pellegrina. Pellegrina is accompanied by a mysterious shadow figure, Marcus Cocoza, and in the end she tells her companion: "I will not be one person again, Marcus, I will be always many persons from now. Never again will I have my heart and my whole life bound up with one woman, to suffer so much." The author later said that the diva's loss of voice symbolized her loss of her farm and her life in Africa; in this story she evaluates how to go on living. The storyteller Mira Jama in the tale says, "Dreaming is the well-mannered people's way of committing suicide."

"The Supper at Elsinore" ("Et Familieselskab i Helsingør") presents a commentary on the aesthetic versus the ethical life. Two sisters hold a conversation with the ghost of their dead brother, Morten, who disappeared from home years earlier. In the intervening time he has had many adventures as a pirate and gunrunner on the high seas. The tale contrasts the attitudes of the sister, Fanny, who resents not having lived such a full life, and the other sister, Eliza, who rejoices vicariously in Morten's adventures. The story seems to criticize Fanny's failure to live according to her instincts, but it also suggests that a story can provide for readers what they cannot experience themselves.

In "The Poet" ("Digteren") Dinesen satirizes those who believe they have power over destiny. The poet in the tale is a councilor in a bourgeois Danish town, who has a grandiose belief in his own talent for creating a story. His complicated interference in the love affair of a young couple causes the lovers to murder him. The killing, which comes about inadvertently, dooms the lovers. At the denouement, the woman cries, "You poet!," sarcastically referring to the councilor's inept matchmaking. Only the councilor, as he dies, realizes that fate has wrought a story greater than he could have invented. "The Poet" demonstrates Dinesen's overarching philosophy that any life is a story, "the men and women of this earth . . . are only the plaster of God, and we, the artists, are his tools, and when the statue is finished in marble or bronze, he breaks us all up."

Seven Gothic Tales won immediate criticial acclaim in the Anglo-American world. Dinesen's British publisher, Constant Huntington, wrote to the author: "To my mind Seven Gothic Tales is the most important work in literature that has appeared in the English language this century . . . if it made a success in America, it should make ten times greater success in England where its details and allusions are near and more familiar." Indeed, Dinesen's elegant and highly original English prose, imaginative, exotic characters, and storytelling technique, captivated her Anglo-American readership. The Americans and the British immediately recognized and appreciated her parodic use of the Gothic genre and her allusions to the Romantic age.

However, Syv fantastiske Fortællinger was poorly received in Denmark, where the fantastic stories clashed with the preferred social realism of the Depression era. In the words of one young Danish critic, Frederick Schyberg, writing in the conservative daily newspaper Berlingske Tidende (25 September 1935), the author was guilty of "coquetry and shallowness, caprice and mystification, false effects and snobbery, name dropping, and pastiche." Dinesen is said to have kept a copy of this review, tattered and yellow, for the rest of her life, showing it to friends and admirers and asking for their response. That Dinesen used historical settings for her tales (most often the eighteenth and nineteenth centuries) to create a distance from her subjects and to allow for a certain artistic freedom has been noted repeatedly by critics. According to Donald Hannah, "the past is the dimension in which she felt her imagination could range most freely." However, early Danish critics readily perceived the author as an elitist opposed to the democratic ideals of modern Denmark. As a result, "the Baroness"–as she was known in her native land–was for decades regarded by many as a hopeless devotee of the ancien régime.

Almost from the moment she had made her permanent return to Denmark in 1931, Dinesen had conceived of a book "about the Masai." In 1935, directly following the publication of Syv fantastiske Fortællinger, she took up this project with intensity. She responded impatiently to prompting from her editor, Robert Haas, that she was creating an important work and could not be rushed. She retreated to a hotel at Skagen, at the northern tip of the Jutlandic peninsula, and wrote most of Out of Africa there during the winter months of 1936–1937. Putnam's in 1937 published Out of Africa to critical acclaim, and in 1938 the Random House edition appeared in the United States. Upon completing the English edition, Dinesen quickly dictated a Danish version of the book to her stenographer, Ulla Petersen, and the work was published and enthusiastically received in Denmark as Den afrikanske Farm (1937).

This new book was written differently from Seven Gothic Tales. The faceless narrator of the tales now displays an urbane, lyrical voice–the aristocratic, witty, and self-deprecating tone one might imagine characteristic of Dinesen's private conversation. Out of Africa is written like a dream, or reminiscence. In a dream "things happen without any interference" from the artist, who only records the kaleidoscope of events. She begins the narrative as if she were in an airplane, looking down upon her farm. "Looking back on a sojourn in the African high-lands, you are struck by your feeling of having lived for a time up in the air." Aerial imagery foreshadows the descriptions of her flights with Finch Hatton and paints an idyllic setting for this story of nostalgia.

Dinesen shapes this story of her African experience both as pastoral and as paradise lost. In the first of five parts, "Kamante and Lulu," the author depicts a pastoral idyll: the farm, the natives, and the animals. She describes the African boy Kamante as a wounded eccentric. She has learned from him, as from the Book of Job, to be stoic: "The Negro is on friendly terms with destiny, having been in her hands all his time"—in contrast to the white man, "of whom the majority strive to insure themselves against the unknown and the assaults of fate." A bushbuck (miniature antelope), Lulu, an aristocrat of the forest, represents the union of the farm with nature. Dinesen also describes the natives, from whom she learns how to live. They have "the sense of risks in life," she writes with admiration. Africa teaches you that "God and the Devil are one."

In the second section, "A Shooting Accident on the Farm," Dinesen introduces conflict, revealing the contrasting worldviews of the settler and the African. A small boy is severely injured by an inadvertent gunshot, which inaugurates a series of episodes of bad luck on the farm. This tragic event highlights the relationships between the various African tribes on and near Dinesen's farm: the Kikuyu, the Somali, and the Masai. She depicts the Masai, a warrior tribe of lion hunters, as the indigenous aristocrats: "Their style is not an assumed manner, nor an imitation of a foreign perfection. . . . It has grown from the inside, and is an expression of the race and its history." She also idealizes the values of pre-industrial societies in contrast to the shallowness of the modern age: "Perhaps the white men of the past, indeed of any past, would have been in better understanding and sympathy with the coloured races than we, of our Industrial Age, shall ever be."

In the third part, "Visitors to the Farm," Dinesen describes European, Asian, and African visitors, the last representing the Old Order of civilization. She includes literary characterizations of her English friends Berkeley Cole and Denys Finch Hatton. *Out of Africa* reaches its climax in the chapter "Wings," in which lion hunting with Finch Hatton is depicted as an erotic adventure: "Come now . . . and let us go and risk our lives unnecessarily," and flying with him brings the pattern of life into view: "This was the idea. And now I understand everything."

Cover for the 1937 Danish edition of Blixen's best-known book, published earlier that year in English as Out of Africa

In part four, "From an Immigrant's Notebook," the themes of the book are presented in a series of anecdotes and parables that encapsulate the wisdom Dinesen acquired in Africa. In "The Roads of Life" she illustrates, through a children's story, how perspective gives meaning to a man's troubles. His meandering and stumbling, when seen from an upstairs window, trace the beautiful figure of a stork. In "Of Pride" another fundamental concept underlying authorship is articulated when the Nietzschean concept of *amor fati* is tied to Dinesen's notion of aristocratic pride: "Pride is faith in the idea that God had, when he made us. A proud man is conscious of the idea, and aspires to realize it. . . . His success is the idea of God, successfully carried though, and he is in love with his destiny."

Part five, "Farewell to the Farm," is short and swift; the catastrophes that befell Dinesen, both natural and personal, are telescoped into the conclusion: falling coffee prices, grasshopper plagues, the sale of the farm, the sudden death of Finch Hatton, and the disintegration of the Old Order, represented by the burial of Chief Kinanjui. In *Isak Dinesen's Art: The Gayety of Vision*

(1964) Robert Woodrow Langbaum has described the aesthetic structure of *Out of Africa* as a "five-part classical tragedy"—four parts "idyll" and one part "Fall."

Central to *Out of Africa* is Dinesen's idealization of the aristocrat and the aristocratic spirit, but her definition of the aristocrat has little to do with socio-economic distinctions. She depicts not only Finch Hatton and Cole but also characters belonging to the proletariat—such as old Dane Knudsen and the actor Emmanuelson—as "aristocrats." For her the aristocrat stands as a symbol for what is highest in life, the man closest to God. It is someone who is free of the need for striving, someone who faces life freely, without petty concerns. Dinesen's aristocrat is the person with a sense of place in history, the person with style, and the person with an understanding of art. In *Out of Africa* she writes: "The true aristocracy and the true proletariat of the world . . . are both in understanding with tragedy. . . . They differ in this way from the bourgeoisie of all classes, who deny tragedy, who will not tolerate it, and to whom the word of tragedy means in itself unpleasantness." In Dinesen's writing "bourgeois" is anything that speaks of necessity or banality. It is the obsession for law and order, for rules, for morality. It is the cautious, the humorless, the narrow, or any attitude that limits the imagination. "People who have no pride," she writes, "are not aware of any idea of God in the making of them" and they accept "their happiness, and even their own selves, at the quotation of the day."

Out of Africa was received with resounding approval from readers. The lyrically narrated story proved a distraction from the burdens of the Great Depression. Robert Haas called the book one of the most important of his publishing career. The critics agreed, and the Book-of-the-Month Club edition alone sold fifty thousand copies. In Denmark, the naturalness of *Den afrikanske Farm* won the author a solid reputation. Over the decades, many of the critical assessments of *Out of Africa* have centered on the question of genre: is this book fact or fiction, memoir or novel, history or myth? While the work was originally read as an authentic memoir of the Danish author's life in Africa, critics have long since established it as a literary work of art. Clearly, *Out of Africa*, written five years after the author's return to Denmark, presents an idealized view of her life on the pioneer coffee farm, revealing almost no information about her conflicts with her husband, her struggles with her family in Denmark, her complicated relationships with close friends, and her difficult interactions with the Africans. The critic Langbaum has called *Out of Africa* an "authentic pastoral, perhaps the best prose pastoral of our time"; whereas Susan Hardy Aiken in *Isak Dinesen and the Engendering of Narrative* (1990) has argued that it is "situated between dis-

courses," defying categorization within a conventional genre. Indeed, *Out of Africa* is a finely crafted work that blends elements of autobiography, novel, memoir, travel book, and myth into a poetic prose narrative.

In *Out of Africa* Dinesen proclaimed her grief at leaving Kenya, but it is not clear how sincere her desire was to return. Just prior to the outbreak of World War II, she had planned to visit Farah. She had received the Tagea Brandt Fellowship, which would have covered her expenses. The hostilities in Europe prevented her going, and Farah died before the war ended. She never attempted to go to Kenya again.

During the German Occupation of Denmark, Dinesen managed to publish *Winter's Tales,* a collection of eleven stories designed to answer William Shakespeare's *The Winter's Tale* (circa 1611), resembling the great drama in its symbolism equating the sea with desire. The collection was published in 1942 in England and America, and in Denmark as *Vinter-Eventyr.* In fact, when Dinesen had completed the English manuscript, she personally took it to the British Embassy in Stockholm, where it was forwarded in a diplomatic mail pouch to London and subsequently to Robert Haas in New York. Dinesen claims that she was not aware of the publication of *Winter's Tales* until after the Liberation in 1945, when she received a flood of letters from American soldiers who had read the Armed Services paperback edition of her stories during the war.

Since its publication, critics in Denmark and America have regarded *Winter's Tales* as the most "Danish" of the author's books. In *Isak Dinesen: The Life of a Storyteller* (1982), Judith Thurman notes that *Winter's Tales* is "somber and introspective . . . filled with a poetic feeling . . . for the Danish landscape." Seven of the eleven stories are set in Scandinavia. "Sorrow-acre" ("Sorg-Agre"), the masterpiece of *Winter's Tales,* celebrates the Danish landscape, its rural life, and Nordic mythology. The second story in the English edition, it develops around two plots. The frame story is based on an authentic folktale from Southern Jutland that tells of a boy who has committed a crime and has been sentenced by the manorial lord. The lord is merciful and allows the boy's mother to atone for his crime: if she can reap an entire rye field from sunrise to sunset, her son will be redeemed. Although the task seems humanly impossible (it is ordinarily the work of three men), she harvests the entire field by sunset. Dinesen depicts Anne-Marie's effort not as torment, but as sweet fulfillment: "there was not . . . the slightest trace of fear or pain . . . amongst all the grave and concerned faces of the field hers was the only one perfectly calm, peaceful and mild." Having completed the day's work and ensured her son's freedom, she drops dead. Her feat is

1.

I had a farm in Africa, at the foot of the Ngong Hills. The Equator ran across these highlands a hundred miles to the North, but the farm lay at an altitude of over six thousand feet. In the day-time you felt that you had got high up, near to the sun, but the mornings and afternoons were limpid and restful, and the nights were cold.

The geographical position and the height of the land combined to create a landscape, which had not got its like in all the world. There was no fat on it and no luxuriance anywhere; it was Africa distilled up through six thousand feet, like the strong and refined essence of a continent. The colours here were dry and burnt, like the colours in pottery. The trees had got a light delicate foliage, and the structure of it was different to that of the trees in Europe, it did not grow in bows or cupolas, but in horizontal layers, and the formation gave to the tall solitary trees a likeness to the palms, or a heroic and romantic air, like fullrigged ships, and to the edge of a wood a strange appearance; as if the whole wood were faintly vibrating. Upon the grass of the great plains the crooked bare old thorn-trees were scattered, and the grass was spiced like thyme and bog-myrtle, in some places the scent was so strong, that it smarted in the nostrils. All the flowers, which you found on the plains or upon the creepers and liana in the Native forest were diminutive, like the flowers on the downs, - only just in the beginning of the long rains a number of big, massive, heavy-scented lilies sprang out on the plains. The views were immensely wide. Everything that you saw made for greatness and freedom, and unequalled nobility.

First page of the typescript for Out of Africa, *with annotations Blixen made while preparing the Danish version of the novel (courtesy of the Rungstedlund Foundation; used by permission of Random House)*

commemorated in the naming of the field, "Sorrow-acre."

The second, or covert, plot in "Sorrow-acre" deals with the young nobleman Adam, his uncle the manorial lord, and the lord's young wife. The only son of the lord, the heir to the manor, has died, and the old lord has married the young bride intended for his son. Her duty is to produce an heir in order to carry on the aristocratic lineage. Adam, just returned from England, encounters his uncle on the morning of the mowing of the rye field and engages him in conversations about the virtues of the ancient Norse gods versus the classical gods of antiquity and about the nature of comedy and tragedy. The lord argues that "The true art of the gods is the comic." Adam begs his uncle to halt the drama in the rye field, but the old lord responds that he has given the peasant woman, Anne-Marie, his word. In the course of the day, the young wife of the lord engages the company of her "nephew." The tale implies that Adam will beget a child with his young aunt, cuckolding the old lord. As the sun sets, the old lord oversees the peasant woman, who dies after reaping her last sheaf. Anne-Marie's death is depicted as a heroic meeting with destiny.

The suggestive power of "Sorrow-acre" has invited many critical readings. Most Dinesen scholars agree that the tale illustrates the concept of the "aristocratic spirit" and imply that Anne-Marie's superhuman feat demonstrates the Nietzschean concept of *amor fati* in its most extreme manifestation. In *The World of Isak Dinesen* (1961), Eric O. Johannesson finds in this tale "the most dramatic illustration of the aristocratic philosophy of life" and suggests that "the conversations between Adam and his uncle are evidently designed to illustrate the differences between two worlds . . . between the feudal and aristocratic eighteenth century and the sentimental and humanitarian nineteenth century." Langbaum notes that Dinesen "does not sentimentalize the old order, or gloss over the hardness of the reality she is out to justify" and calls the interaction between the lord and the peasant the "last dance of the dying order." In her 1981 essay "Dinesen's 'Sorrow-acre': Tracing the Woman's Line," Aiken has offered a feminist reevaluation of the tale, demonstrating how the author cleverly uses the noblewomen in the story to undermine the "myth of patrilinear succession."

The fulfillment of destiny in a courageous, heroic gesture is an idea central to *Winter's Tales*. In "The Heroine" ("Heloïse") a powerful and sensuous figure comes to symbolize the combined ideals of aristocracy and femininity. On the eve of the Franco-Prussian War of 1870–1871, a noble French woman saves a group of citizens fleeing from advancing Prussian armies (a plot alluding to the author's situation in Occupied Denmark). An insolent German officer, aroused by the lady's "great beauty," offers to free the refugees if she will come before him "dressed like the goddess Venus." Apparently unperturbed, she counters his bluff. The prisoners are released, among them a young man named Frederick, who has fallen in love with her. Years later, when Frederick attends a popular cabaret show in Paris, the climax is marked by "the appearance of the goddess Diana herself, with nothing on at all." Astonished, Frederick recognizes the "heroine," through whose inspiration the refugees had attained their "salvation."

In other tales in the collection, powerful women present fascinating and at times threatening figures. One such character is the old Lapp woman who appears in "The Sailor-boy's Tale" ("Skibsdrengens Fortælling"). This story borrows an allusion from "The Dreamers," describing a falcon caught in the rigging of a ship. Simon, a young sailor, climbs high on the mast and frees the falcon. The falcon turns on him, drawing blood from his hand. He falls, but in a dramatic reversal the falcon transforms herself into an old Lapp named Sunniva and saves the sailor. "The Sailor-boy's Tale," with its folktale motif, was intended by the author to be the first tale in the collection (as it is in the Danish edition); it announces the Nordic setting and the theme of nature.

In "The Pearls" ("En Historie om en Perle") Dinesen tells a tale of newlyweds; the prudent and cautious Jensine believes that she can teach her husband, the aristocratic Alexander, to give up his "fearlessness." Instead, Jensine eventually learns to overcome her fear of eroticism and death (both represented by the towering mountains of Norway). In the conclusion, she learns to appreciate the idea that immortality is achieved in the stories that are passed along with the pearl necklace she inherits.

"The Invincible Slave-owners" ("De standhaftige Slaveejere") is a clever tale concerning an aristocrat and her servant, Miss Rabe and Mizzi—they are actually sisters—who playfully exchange roles. Keeping the world at arm's length, they lightheartedly act out a drama of intrigue and danger. The point of the story is one of Dinesen's favorites: that of the relationship between master and servant as a "union of opposites." The two proud sisters, who alternate roles as master and servant, are inseparable.

A few of the stories in *Winter's Tales* deal with "lost" or orphaned children who end up in families in which they are unable to fulfill their destinies. These tales, such as "The Dreaming Child" ("Det drømmende Barn") and "Alkmene," seem related to the Greek myths about magical children begotten by a god upon mortals. In "The Dreaming Child" a small boy perishes

Blixen with some of her servants and their children at her farm in Kenya

when his stepparents fail to encourage his imaginative talent. Little Jens is born in the slums, the illegitimate son of a prostitute. He is adopted by a bourgeois couple, the thoroughly unimaginative Emilie and Jakob Vandmann. Like Jensine in "The Pearls," they represent the prudish, cautious, and conventional morality of the bourgeoisie, with its "scrupulous regard for the truth." The child eventually dies: "like a small brook which falls into the ocean, Jens gave himself up to, and was absorbed in, the boundless, final unity of dream." The child becomes an embodiment of the figure of the artist-dreamer in Dinesen's fiction, one whose imaginative talent must be nurtured. This theme is further emphasized in "Alkmene," a story about a free and innocent girl–likened to the Greek goddess–who is taught about

good and evil by her moralistic stepparents. Eventually she is no longer able to experience the sensual side of existence, and she relinquishes herself to a bourgeois work ethic that shuts out joy and love.

"The Fish" ("Fra det gamle Danmark") is one of the most important statements of Dinesen's spirituality. It is set in medieval Catholic Denmark during a period of strife between the monarchy and the nobility. King Erik Glipping finds his country in chaos, overrun by hostile noblemen. Pondering the riddle of man's existence on earth, he embarks on a spiritual quest and gradually reconciles himself to the inevitability of his own death. A brief epilogue to the English edition explains that King Erik was murdered in 1286 by a party of rebellious vassals. According to national legend, the killing was an act of revenge by the High Constable, who believed that the king had seduced his wife, Lady Ingeborg. In the tale, the king is journeying to the sea, engaged in a theological discussion in which he rejects the Christian dogma of humility, "the Lord did not . . . try His hand sufficiently on the conditions of man. . . . He might have tried himself at the circumstances of a great lord." At the seaside, a pagan thrall offers the king a fish (both a Christian and an ancient fertility symbol), in the entrails of which the ring of Lady Ingeborg is discovered. In wearing her ring, the king seals his fate, but not before he has understood his position in the universe in an epiphanic vision of the heavens and earth: "the sea and the sky joined without the faintest line of division, and became but the universe, unfathomable space."

The meeting of sensuous desires with the waters of the sea is a theme repeated in "Peter and Rosa" ("Peter og Rosa"). The story is set in mid-nineteenth-century Denmark and opens with a description of the freezing of the Sound between Denmark and Sweden, a scene paralleling the harsh winter of 1940–1941. Peter and Rosa reject the confining parsonage of their childhood: "fatal influences were . . . admonishing them to give up the vain and dangerous task of living." In an effort to embrace life and nature, they walk out onto the frozen sound. At the moment of self-realization, the ice cracks and they drown in the icy waters. The reader recalls Peter's earlier remark: "When you drown in the sea, it is all the seas of the world that take you. It seems to me that that is grand."

The essential motifs and themes of *Winter's Tales* are encapsulated in the "blue story," an inset tale in "The Young Man with the Carnation" ("Den unge Mand med Nelliken"). In this story within a story, Lady Helena spends a lifetime searching for a particular shade of blue. Having been forced to separate from the object of her desire, she spends the rest of her life longing for the "blue state" of happiness, which she had experienced at sea with a young sailor. Wherever she travels, she claims, on the opposite side of the earth another ship sails: "We two are like the reflection of one another, in the deep sea, and the ship of which I speak is always exactly beneath my own ship, on the opposite side of the globe." Lady Helena longs to unite with her male "reflection"; she can do so only by drowning: "In the end my ship will go down, to the center of the globe, and at the very same hour the other ship will sink as well . . . and there, in the midst of the world, we two shall meet." This "blue story" embodies longing, desire, and the sea, motifs that appear in the entire collection.

The frame story for *Winter's Tales*, "The Young Man with the Carnation," concerns Charlie Despard, a young disgruntled artist–who also appears in the final tale in the collection. Charlie's first book has been a success, but he is worried about the success of his second book. He is portrayed in the throes of wrestling with his responsibility as a writer and is in danger of lapsing into despair. In *Karen Blixens Eventyr: Med en Excurs om Pierre Andrézel* (Karen Blixen's Tales: With an Excursus on Pierre Andrézel, 1949)–the first scholarly study of Dinesen's works–Danish critic Hans Brix suggests that the author must have identified closely with the young artist's situation, as even his initials resemble her own (Karen Christentze Dinesen). The concluding story, "A Consolatory Tale" ("En opbyggelig Historie"), presents a more confident Charlie in a conversation with the adept storyteller Aeneas Snell. He has learned that he must accept his trials and successes as part of life's unity. Dinesen uses an inset tale, "The Tale of the False Caliph," about a prince and his doppelgänger, a beggar named Fath, to explain to the young Charlie that opposites must compliment one another: "'My master,'" said Fath, "'you and I, the rich and the poor of this world, are two locked caskets, of which each contains the key to the other.'" The locked caskets express the principle of interdependence that also ties together the stories in *Winter's Tales*. It is Dinesen's notion of an inherent balance in life that comes from the fearless acceptance of life's tragedies, a concept also articulated in "Sorrow-Acre" in the young Adam's realization that "life and death, happiness and woe, the past and the present, were interlaced within the pattern. . . . And out of the contrasting elements concord rose." *Winter's Tales* is considered one of Dinesen's masterpieces. It was critically acclaimed both in Denmark and in the Anglo-American world and was the author's favorite of her works. It constitutes the most poetic synthesis of Dinesen's artistic vision.

Dinesen had completed *Winter's Tales* while in poor health, and she continued to suffer debilitating symptoms. She had been intermittently ill ever since she went to Africa. At first she suffered from dysentery and anemia, but after the death of her mother in 1939 she was troubled by intermittent abdominal spasms, for which her doctors could find no cause. She was preoccupied with the fear that she had not recovered from syphilis, and in Africa she had dosed herself frequently with an elixir of arsenic for a wide variety of symptoms. The medicine seems to have undermined her health. Her physicians tried to relieve her pain in 1946 with an operation that severed some spinal nerves, but she continued to suffer abdominal spasms. Dinesen's doctors never found any evidence of tabes dorsalis–syphilitic deterioration of the spine.

By this time Dinesen had acquired a loyal secretary, Clara Svendsen (later Clara Selborn), who encouraged her writing and took dictation. During World War II Svendsen helped the author with a parodic Gothic novel, *Gengældelsens Veje* (1944), published first in Danish under the pseudonym Pierre Andrézel. The title page states that the work was "translated by Clara Svendsen"–Dinesen wished it to appear that the book was written by a mysterious Frenchman and translated into Danish. Published under German censorship in Denmark, she insisted that it was written only "to have a little fun" and always referred to the novel as her "illegitimate child." When the English edition, *The Angelic Avengers,* was published in 1946, American reviewers saw in the work an anti-Nazi allegory, noting that the story of the two innocent young girls imprisoned like "caged canaries" by the evil Mr. Pennhallow might represent Denmark's status as a "model protectorate" under Hitler's regime. The baroness insisted that she had had no such intentions. Neither was she happy when the book was chosen as a Book-of-the-Month Club selection. To her comic dismay, the melodramatic story sold well, including ninety thousand copies in the United States alone.

The idea that Dinesen's works might include anti-Nazi allegories may be linked to her firsthand impressions of Hitler's Germany. "Breve fra et Land i Krig" (Letters from a Land at War), an essay first published in the journal *Heretica* in 1948, includes her cleverly critical observations on the culture of Nazism, on the internal organization of a totalitarian state and its propaganda, architecture, and theater. After a month-long stay in Berlin as a foreign correspondent for the Danish daily *Politiken,* Dinesen returned to Denmark in early April 1940 and, on the eve of the Occupation, wrote this essay, which she claims lay forgotten in a desk drawer until after the war. Written at a time when the Danish press was under political censorship, "Breve fra et Land i Krig" offers an outsider's impressions of Hitler's Germany prior to the war. A closer view of the author's opinions on politics and art may be gained from her collected letters published in 1996, *Karen Blixen i Danmark: Breve 1931–62* (Karen Blixen in Denmark: Letters 1931–62), which are yet to be translated into English.

In the early 1950s Dinesen began a series of readings of her work on the radio, and her deep, smoky voice became well known in Scandinavia. Her first talk, broadcast on 1 and 7 January 1951 was called "Daguerrotypier" (Daguerreotypes); it was published the same year as a pamphlet and posthumously alongside her other important talks and lectures in *Essays* (1965; translated as *Daguerreotypes and Other Essays,* 1979). In "Daguerrotypier" Dinesen illustrates the ideals and values of the hierarchical nineteenth-century society of her youth. She describes the historical roles of woman–as saint, whore, and witch–with the intent to interpret these female representations for a younger generation. In 1953 she delivered the talk "En Baaltale med 14 Aars Forsinkelse" (Oration at a Bonfire, Fourteen Years Late, 1954) to a Danish teachers' seminary–she had been asked in 1939 to speak at an international women's conference, and her response came fourteen years later. In her oration, Dinesen urged women of her day to develop in their own way and not to imitate patterns established by men, arguing that the dissimilarity of traditional male and female roles forms a "union" of opposites: "Jeg tror, at den gensidige Inspiration Mand og Kvinde imellem har været den mægtigste Drivkraft i vor Slægts Historie" (I think that the mutual inspiration of man and woman has been the most powerful force in the history of the race). Already in *Moderne ægteskab og andre betragtninger* (1981; translated as *On Modern Marriage: And Other Observations,* 1986), written in 1923–1924, she had introduced the notion that the ideal relationship develops only where there is distance and dissimilarity between men and women. Her statement in the oration, "jeg er ikke Kvindesagskvinde" (I am not a feminist), was viewed for decades as a reactionary declaration; instead, feminist critics of the 1990s have pointed out that the statement should be read as Dinesen's commentary on the early feminist movement as represented by the Danish Women's Society, of which her spinster aunt Bess Westenholtz was a fervent member. In her oration Dinesen comments on the early feminist movement of the mid-nineteenth century, in which women "gjorde deres Indtog i Forklædning, i en mental og psykisk Mandsdragt" (made their entry in disguise, in a costume which intellectually or psychologically represented a male). She urges women of the postwar era to lay down the weapons of the early women's movement and advises them to repossess their femininity; a woman today, she says "frejdigt kan opslaa sin Ridderhjelm og vise Verden, at hun er Kvinde og ingen formummet Skælm" (can confidently open her visor and show the world that she is a woman and no disguised rogue).

In the 1940s and early 1950s Dinesen developed a purely spiritual flirtation with a group of young Danish literati, among them Ole Wivel, Thorkild Bjørnvig, and Aage Henriksen, who courted her advice and talent. She also lent them her support in starting the literary journal *Heretica* that debuted in 1948. Her relationship with the young Bjørnvig was later described as a demonic pact between master and pupil in Bjørnvig's memoir *Pagten: Mit Venskab med Karen Blixen*

Dust jacket for the Danish edition of Blixen's 1958 collection of stories, published earlier that year in English as Anecdotes of Destiny

(1974; translated as *The Pact: My Friendship with Isak Dinesen*, 1983).

Then nearly seventy years old, the author, still addressed as "the Baroness," was considered—in the words of Hans Brix—"Denmark's most important living writer." In 1954, when Ernest Hemingway accepted the Nobel Prize in literature, he deferred in his speech to three others whom he felt should have won it before him, one was "that beautiful writer, Isak Dinesen." Dinesen was considered a leading contender for the Nobel Prize but never won it. During the 1950s her health continued to fail. In 1956 she underwent an operation to remove a stomach ulcer, but in the process a third of her stomach was removed, and afterwards her health deteriorated dramatically from malnutrition.

With Clara Svendsen's help, however, Dinesen was able to publish another collection, *Last Tales* (translated as *Sidste Fortællinger*), in 1957. The opening tale, "The Cardinal's First Tale" ("Kardinalens første Historie") introduces the figure of Cardinal Salviati, whose personality combines the roles of poet and priest, embodying the Apollonian and Dionysian principles. The tale ends with an important discourse on the art of

the story, in which the artist-priest defends the story-teller's art against that of the novel: "The divine art is the story. In the beginning was the story." The poet-priest reappears in "The Cardinal's Third Tale" ("Kardinalens tredie Historie"), in which he tells the tale of the frigid Scotswoman Lady Flora Gordon, who "shrank from any touch, physical or mental." Moved by discussions with a Catholic priest, she gradually exchanges a rigid Protestant understanding of life for a more sensual Catholic vision and an appreciation of symbolism. By kissing the foot of the statue of St. Peter, she contracts syphilis vicariously. In the end, she ponders the symbolic significance of the syphilitic sore on her lip, whether it be a "rose" or a "seal."

"The Blank Page" ("Det ubeskrevne Blad") associates femininity with the art of storytelling. The narrator, an old woman, shares the secret of the craft: "Where the storyteller is loyal, eternally and unswervingly loyal to the story, there, in the end, silence will speak. Where the story has been betrayed, silence is but emptiness." To illustrate this point, she tells the tale of the blank page. In an old convent of the Carmelite Order, the sisters grow flax and manufacture a linen so fine that it is used for bridal sheets for the young princesses of Portugal. The blood-stained piece of linen, having been publicly displayed on the morning after the wedding, is given back to the convent to be framed and hung in a long gallery at the convent. There is one canvas in the midst of the long row that attracts more attention than all the others for it is "snow-white from corner to corner, a blank page." Several suggestive possibilities present themselves to the reader: does the blank page suggest that the princess circumvented sexual initiation by telling tales in the manner of Scheherazade and stayed her own death; does the pure white linen suggest that the princess was not a virgin at the time of consummation; or does it symbolize the mystery of the Immaculate Conception?

"The Blank Page" is the most succinct illustration of the craft of the story as practiced by Dinesen; it is powerfully suggestive, but the central enigma remains unresolved, allowing "silence to speak." In the 1980s and 1990s the tale became a favorite among feminist critics. In "'The Blank Page' and the Issues of Female Creativity" (1981), Susan Gubar suggests that the stained canvases may be regarded as "female art" and that the enigmatic white sheet relates a story of "female resistance" (escape from the bridal bed) and the author's rejection of the patriarchal order. This brand of feminist criticism, which views woman as victim, fails to appreciate the implied sense of feminine superiority in Dinesen's tales.

In "New Gothic Tales," the second section of *Last Tales,* Dinesen returns to material and themes from

Seven Gothic Tales. It includes "The Caryatids, an Unfinished Tale" ("Karyatiderne. En ufuldendt Historie"), a nightmarish tale about witchcraft and incest. In "Echoes" ("Ekko") the author addresses the problematic relationship between herself and the poet Bjørnvig. She later admitted to the Danish critic Aage Kabell that the story was a spiritual analysis of their falling out. Pellegrina Leoni, the character from "The Dreamers," is used to illustrate the interchange between mentor and disciple. The title evokes the music of ideas that played between the two artists.

"New Winter's Tales," the final section of *Last Tales,* presents three fine tales with Danish settings. "A Country Tale" ("En Herregaardshistorie") is an elaboration on the themes of "Sorrow-acre"; it deals with manorial culture and the relationship between lord and peasant. Dinesen makes the point here that individual responsibility is inherited with the appointed social role. The point is dramatized through the old motif of changelings: the wrong people have inherited the roles of lord and peasant and thus stand wrongfully accused of a crime.

Dinesen considered "Copenhagen Season" ("Ib og Adelaide") a "short novel." It offers an historical context for her father's youth and for the manners of the aristocratic society of Denmark in 1870. In this love story about Ib and Adelaide, Dinesen underlines again the theme of redemption through regained innocence: "It is only when one gets up to [the aristocrat's] lofty social level that one will again meet with keenness of the senses as with *savoir vivre*. For what is the end of all higher education? Regained naiveté."

"Converse at Night in Copenhagen" ("Samtale om Natten i København") returns to the theme of the opening story of *Last Tales*–it is the sort of tale that is antithetical to the contemporary novel, namely, *mythos*. Set in 1767, the story is a conversation between the mad King Christian VII of Denmark, the drunken poet Johannes Ewald, and a prostitute in whose room the three accidentally meet. The conversation articulates Dinesen's credo, the idea that the poet bears a responsibility to humankind and to God to give back "an earthy reflection of . . . heavenly existence."

In the early 1950s Dinesen heard that writing short stories for American magazines could be lucrative. She wrote a series of witty tales published in *Ladies Home Journal;* they appeared in the collection *Anecdotes of Destiny* (translated as *Skæbne-Anekdoter*) in 1958. Among these tales was "Babette's Feast" ("Babettes Gæstebud"), which was adapted in Gabriel Axel's 1987 Danish motion picture; it won the Academy Award for Best Foreign Film. The tale is set in a remote fishing village in northern Norway, where Dinesen effectively contrasts the ethical existence of two young pious sisters against the aesthetic life of their two suitors, a Swedish lieutenant and a French opera singer. Years later, the aging spinster sisters give refuge to a French woman, Babette, who, unbeknownst to them, was once a great culinary artist in Paris. She displays the transformative powers of an artist-priestess by preparing a gourmet French dinner for a gathering of dour Norwegian Protestants. The comedy turns on the conversation at the table, where the orgiastic meal is consumed "without any sign of either surprise or approval, as if they had been doing so every day for thirty years." A state of bliss and spiritual salvation, nevertheless, is attained by this partaking in the pleasures of the flesh.

Also in *Anecdotes of Destiny* is "The Diver" ("Dykkeren"), in which the concept of time becomes a central hardship to mankind after the fall from Paradise. Mira Jama, the storyteller introduced in "The Dreamers," has learned through his friendship with a fish, a maker of pearls, that fish can travel in any direction. In the water a journey cannot be traced, so the fish–symbolizing the spiritually liberated–suffer no consequences for their actions. Man is anchored to events, however, and from such events arise guilt, tragedy, unhappiness–and stories. Without time, authors would not be able to capture life's comedies and tragedies.

Another important story in *Anecdotes of Destiny* is "Tempests" ("Storme"). In this tale, Malli, a woman of heroic proportions both physically and mystically, is chosen to play the figure Ariel in Shakespeare's well-known drama. As Dinesen portrays her, she is neither human nor goddess but a creature in between, an artist. Like the author, she cannot find her place in life and is never destined for romantic love, but she is able to inspire others to join in the fantasies she creates.

"The Immortal Story" ("Den udødelige Historie") develops the theme introduced in "The Poet" and "Echoes" concerning the role of the meddler–a figure deluded about his omnipotence, who tries to usurp the role of the gods in a younger person's life by forcing his own dreams or plans onto another's destiny. As in the author's own experience with the young Bjørnvig, the effort backfires. The story inspired the 1968 Hollywood motion picture *The Immortal Story,* directed by Orson Welles.

In 1959, in the face of failing health, barely able to stay on her feet, and occasionally hospitalized and placed on intravenous fluids, the seventy-four-year-old author spent four months on tour in the United States. She was feted by New York high society, applauded in the American press, and courted by such luminaries as Nobel laureate Pearl S. Buck, the poet E. E. Cummings, and the actress Marilyn Monroe. Fashion photographers captured Dinesen's luminous eyes, her extreme thinness, her wry and wrinkled expression, and her long cigarettes. In January 1958 she was the guest of honor at The National Institute and the American Academy of Arts and Letters, where she delivered "On Mottoes of My Life" ("Mit Livs Mottoer"), later published as an essay in *Mit livs mottoer og andre essays* (1978; translated as *Daguerrotypes and Other Essays,* 1979). Demonstrating her stature as a master raconteur, Dinesen recited from memory her stories "The King's Letter" ("Barua a Soldani") and "The Wine of the Tetrarch" to audiences in New York, Boston, and Washington, D.C.

In 1960 Dinesen's *Skygger på Græsset* (translated as *Shadows on the Grass,* 1961), a brief sequel to *Out of Africa,* was published. It reveals what had happened in the interim to her African friends. The last work she sent to her publisher in 1962 was "Ehrengard," a tale answering Kierkegaard's notorious "Forførerens Dagbog" (The Diary of a Seducer, 1843). In Dinesen's tale, the chapters are titled as musical movements, and her premise, differing from Kierkegaard's, is that art and life are one. "The whole attitude of the artist towards the universe is that of a seducer," says Herr Cazotte, the painter in the story. He decides to seduce the beautiful and innocent Ehrengard—not literally, but figuratively, by capturing her naked image on canvas. Seduction in Dinesen's work means to bring to ultimate fulfillment or to elicit one's greatest potential. Artists must "draw forth, like the violinist with the bow upon the strings, the full abundance and virtue of the instrument within our hands." In a series of deceptions and comic twists, the girl in the tale becomes fulfilled in a greater and more symbolic way than the artist intended. The tale stresses Dinesen's viewpoint that life is story and that fate has a more grand conception of life than any artist could invent.

Dinesen has been criticized for being a "snob" by those who do not understand her vision of the aristocrat as the upholder of civilization—the collective memory of the wisdom bequeathed to humans through the centuries. She quoted Goethe: "Den, som ikke kan føre sit Regnskab over 3000 Aar, lever kun fra Haanden og i Munden" (He who cannot account for three thousand years is living from hand to mouth). The outward manifestation of this wisdom is manner and style. While style may be a mask, Dinesen believed it revealed the soul, or true nature, of the individual. The mask allows the wearer to live up to his or her own highest ideal. As the character Kasparson says in "The Deluge at Norderney," "Not by the face shall the man be known, but by the mask." The mask is the answer to the fundamental question in the existentialist canon, "Who am I?" As the Cardinal (Kasparson) points out to Miss Malin,

"The witty woman, Madame, chooses for her carnival costume one which ingeniously reveals something in her spirit or heart which the conventions of her everyday life conceal." Dinesen was photographed in the costume of Pierrot, a clown figure in the *commedia dell'arte.* The Italian drama, in which stock figures wearing masks improvise upon a theme, illustrates her philosophy of art.

Karen Blixen died of malnutrition on 7 September 1962 at Rungstedlund in Denmark, where she was born. For those who find Dinesen's stories challenging, the narrator of "The Dreamers" has a reply: "It is not a bad thing in a tale that you understand only half of it." Her inset stories never let the reader forget that a story is under way, and such is the manner in which the symbolism of events makes its greatest impression. Dinesen's unique brand of wit arises from the fact that the audience always knows she is conjuring.

Letters:
Breve fra Afrika 1914–31, 2 volumes, edited by Frans Lasson (Copenhagen: Gyldendal, 1978); translated by Anne Born as *Letters from Africa, 1914–1931,* as Dinesen (Chicago: University of Chicago Press, 1981);
Karen Blixen i Danmark. Breve 1931–62, 2 volumes, edited by Frans Lasson and Tom Engelbrecht (Copenhagen: Gyldendal, 1996).

Interviews:
Eugene Walter, "Isak Dinesen," *Paris Review* (Autumn 1956): 43–59;
Niels Birger Wamberg, "Karen Blixen (Interview, March 1960)," in his *Samtaler med danske digtere* (Copenhagen: Gyldendal, 1968), pp. 40–48.

Bibliographies:
Liselotte Henriksen, *Karen Blixen: En bibliografi/Isak Dinesen: A Bibliography* (Copenhagen: Gyldendal, 1977);
Aage Jørgensen, *Litteratur om Karen Blixen. En bibliografi* (Århus: Center for Undervisning og Kulturformidling, 1998).

Biographies:
Parmenia Migel, *Titania: The Biography of Isak Dinesen* (New York: Random House, 1967);
Judith Thurman, *Isak Dinesen: The Life of a Storyteller* (New York: St. Martin's Press, 1982);
Olga Anastasia Pelensky, *Isak Dinesen: The Life and Imagination of a Seducer* (Athens: Ohio University Press, 1991);

Linda G. Donelson, *Out of Isak Dinesen in Africa: Karen Blixen's Untold Story* (Iowa City: Coulsong, 1995).

References:

Susan Hardy Aiken, "Dinesen's 'Sorrow-Acre': Tracing the Woman's Line," *Contemporary Literature,* 25, no. 2 (1984): 156–186;

Aiken, *Isak Dinesen and the Engendering of Narrative* (Chicago: University of Chicago Press, 1990);

Thorkild Bjørnvig, *Pagten: Mit Venskab med Karen Blixen* (Copenhagen: Gyldendal, 1974); translated by Ingvar Schousboe and William Jay Smith as *The Pact: My Friendship with Isak Dinesen* (Baton Rouge: Louisiana State University Press, 1983);

Bror Blixen-Finecke, *The African Hunter* (London: Cassell, 1937);

Hans Brix, *Karen Blixens Eventyr: Med en Excurs om Pierre Andrézel* (Copenhagen: Gyldendal, 1949);

Else Brundbjerg, *Kvinden, kætteren, kunstneren Karen Blixen* (Copenhagen: Carit Andersens forlag, 1986);

Thomas Dinesen, *My Sister, Isak Dinesen,* translated by Joan Tate (London: Joseph, 1975);

Mogens Fog, "Karen Blixens Sygdomshistorie," in *Blixeniana 1978,* edited by Hans Andersen and Frans Lasson (Copenhagen: Karen Blixen Selskabet, 1978), pp. 139–146;

Susan Gubar, "'The Blank Page' and the Issues of Female Creativity," *Critical Inquiry,* 8, no. 2 (1981): 242–263;

Donald Hannah, *"Isak Dinesen" and Karen Blixen: The Mask and the Reality* (London: Putnam; New York: Random House, 1971);

Aage Henriksen, "Karen Blixen and Marionettes," translated by William Mishler, in *Isak Dinesen/Karen Blixen: The Work and the Life* (New York: St. Martin's Press, 1988), pp. 18–39;

Liselotte Henriksen, *Karen Blixen: En håndbog* (Copenhagen: Gyldendal, 1988);

Hans Holmberg, *Ingen skygge uden lys: Om livets veje og kunstens i nogle fortællinger af Karen Blixen* (Copenhagen: Reitzels, 1995);

Susan Horton, *Difficult Women, Artful Lives: Olive Schreiner and Isak Dinesen, In and Out of Africa* (Baltimore: Johns Hopkins University Press, 1995);

Eric O. Johannesson, *The World of Isak Dinesen* (Seattle: University of Washington Press, 1961);

Marianne Juhl and Bo Hakon Jørgensen, *Diana's Revenge: Two Lines in Isak Dinesen's Authorship,* translated by Anne Born (Odense: Odense University Press, 1985);

Aage Kabell, *Karen Blixen debuterer* (Munich: Wilhelm Fink Verlag, 1968);

Robert Woodrow Langbaum, *Isak Dinesen's Art: The Gayety of Vision* (New York: Random House, 1964);

Frans Lasson and Clara Svendsen, eds., *The Life and Destiny of Isak Dinesen* (London: Joseph, 1970);

Mark Mussari, "Farvens klang: Color Spaces in Strindberg, Branner, Dinesen and Bjørneboe," dissertation University of Washington, 1999;

Mogens Pahuus, *Karen Blixens livsfilosofi: En fortolkning af forfatterskabet* (Ålborg: Ålborg University Press, 1995);

Olga Anastasia Pelensky, ed., *Isak Dinesen: Critical Views* (Athens: Ohio University Press, 1993);

Tone Selboe, *Kunst og erfaring: En studie i Karen Blixens forfatterskap* (Odense: Odense University Press, 1996);

Clara Svendsen, *Notater om Karen Blixen* (Copenhagen: Gyldendal, 1974);

Sara Stambaugh, *The Witch and the Goddess in the Stories of Isak Dinesen: A Feminist Reading* (Ann Arbor: University of Michigan Research Press, 1988);

Marianne Stecher-Hansen, "Both Sacred and Secretly Gay: Isak Dinesen's 'The Blank Page,'" *Pacific Coast Philology,* 29, no. 1 (September 1994): 3–13;

Anders Westenholz, *The Power of Aries: Myth and Reality in Karen Blixen's Life,* translated by Lise Kure-Jensen (Baton Rouge: Louisiana State University Press, 1987);

Thomas R. Whissen, *Isak Dinesen's Aesthetics* (Port Washington, N.Y. & London: Kennikat Press, 1973);

Ole Wivel, *Karen Blixen: Et uafsluttet selvopgør* (Copenhagen: Lindhardt & Ringhof, 1987);

Gurli A. Woods, ed., *Isak Dinesen and Narrativity Reassessments for the 1990s* (Ottawa: Carleton University Press, 1994).

Papers:

Karen Blixen's letters and manuscripts are housed in the Karen Blixen Archives at Det Kongelige Bibliotek (The Royal Danish Library), Copenhagen. Her private library and selected manuscripts are displayed at the Karen Blixen Museum at Rungstedlund, Denmark.

H. C. Branner

(23 June 1903 – 24 April 1966)

Mark Mussari
University of Washington

BOOKS: *Legetøj: En Roman om en Forretning* (Copenhagen: Gyldendal, 1936);

Barnet leger ved Stranden (Copenhagen: Povl Branner, 1937);

Om lidt er vi borte (Copenhagen: Povl Branner, 1939)—includes "Et Barn og et Mus," translated by Evelyn Heepe as "A Child and a Mouse," in *Modern Danish Authors,* edited by Heepe and Niels Heltberg (Copenhagen: Scandinavian Publishing, 1946), pp. 83–98; "Sidst i august," translated by Heepe as "At the End of August," in her *Swans of the North, and Short Stories by Modern Danish Authors* (Copenhagen: Gad, 1953), pp. 35–50;

Drømmen om en Kvinde: Roman (Copenhagen: Povl Branner, 1941);

Historien om Børge (Copenhagen: Gyldendal, 1942); translated by Kristi Planck as *The Story of Börge,* Library of Scandinavian Literature, no. 23 (New York: Twayne, 1973);

To Minutters Stilhed (Copenhagen: Povl Branner, 1944)—includes "De tre Musketerer," translated by A. I. Roughton as "The Three Musketeers," in *Contemporary Danish Prose: An Anthology,* edited by Bredsdorff and F. J. Billeskov Jansen (Copenhagen: Gyldendal, 1958), pp. 270–281;

Digteren og Pigen (Copenhagen: Carit Andersen, 1945); translated by Villy Sørensen and Anne Born as *The Poet and the Girl* (Copenhagen: Wind-flower Press, 1980);

Angst (Copenhagen: Boghallen, 1947); translated by Sørensen and Born as *Anguish* (Copenhagen: Wind-flower Press, 1980);

Rytteren: Roman (Copenhagen: Branner & Korch, 1949); translated by Roughton as *The Riding Master: A Novel* (London: Secker & Warburg, 1951); republished as *The Mistress* (New York: New American Library, 1953);

Søskende: Skuespil i tre akter (Copenhagen: Branner & Korch, 1952); translated by Roughton as *The Judge,* in *Contemporary Danish Plays: An Anthology,* edited by Elias Bredsdorff (Copenhagen: Gylden-

H. C. Branner

dal / London: Thames & Hudson, 1955), pp. 495–557;

Bjergene: 2 noveller (Copenhagen: Gyldendal, 1953)—includes "Bjergene," translated by Sørensen and Born as *The Mountains* (Copenhagen: Wind-flower Press, 1982);

Ingen kender natten (Copenhagen: Gyldendal, 1955); translated by Roughton as *No Man Knows the Night* (London: Secker & Warburg, 1958);

Vandring langs floden: Prosastrykker (Copenhagen: Gyldendal, 1956);

Kunstens uafhængighed (Copenhagen: Gyldendal, 1957);

Thermopylæ: Skuespil i fire akter (Copenhagen: Gyldendal, 1958); translated by Pat Shaw as *Thermopylæ: A Play in Four Acts,* in *Modern Nordic Plays, Denmark,* introduction by Per Olsen (New York: Twayne, 1974), pp. 21–74;

Et spil om kærligheden og døden (Copenhagen: Gyldendal, 1960);

Ariel: Noveller (Copenhagen: Gyldendal, 1964);

Fem radiospil: Eftemæle, Natteregn, Hundrede kroner, Jeg elsker dig, Mørket mellem træerne (Copenhagen: Gyldendal, 1965);

H. C. Branner: Et udvalg, compiled by Sven Møller Kristensen and Karen Margrethe Branner, Gyldendals Julebog, 1966 (Copenhagen: Gyldendal, 1966)– comprises "To minutters stilhed," "Oluf Høegs skæbne," "Hans Majestæt," "Trommerne";

Tre skuespil: Rytteren, Søskende, Thermopylæ (Copenhagen: Gyldendal, 1968);

Drømmeren—og andre noveller, edited by Flemming Reislev (Frederiksberg: Fisker Schou, 1997).

Editions and Collections: *De blaa Undulater* (Copenhagen: Thejls Bogtryk, 1957);

Røde heste i sneen: Et H.C. Branner-udvalg, for realskolen og tilsvarende undervisningstrin, edited by L. Nordentoft and Jørn Vosmar (Copenhagen: Gyldendal, 1962);

Sidst i august: Et H.C. Branner-udvalg, for gymnasier og seminarier, edited by Nordentoft and Vosmar (Copenhagen: Gyldendal, 1962);

To minutters stilhed: H.C. Branner, edited, with an afterword, by Vosmar (Copenhagen: Gyldendal, 1964);

Digteren og pigen/Glimt af mig selv (Copenhagen: Carit Andersen, 1972);

Hannibals træsko—og andre noveller, edited by Jørn E. Albert (Copenhagen: Gyldendal, 1995).

Editions in English: *Two Minutes of Silence: Selected Short Stories,* translated by Vera Lindholm Vance (Madison: University of Wisconsin Press, 1966).

PLAY PRODUCTIONS: *Rytteren,* Stockholm, Lilla Dramaten, 5 April 1950; Copenhagen, Det nye Teater, February 1952;

Søskende, Stockholm, Kungliga Dramatiska Teatern, 13 December 1951; Copenhagen, Det Kongelige Teater, 5 January 1952; adapted as *The Judge,* New York, Theatre Marquee, 13 May 1958;

Thermopylæ, Copenhagen, Det Kongelige Teater, 1958.

MOTION PICTURES: *Jeg elsker dig,* screenplay by Branner, Nordisk Film, 1957;

Søskende, screenplay by Branner, Flamingo Film, 1966.

RADIO: *Efterspil,* script by Branner, Danmarks Radio, 13 September 1932;

En nytåskbkke, script by Branner, Danmarks Radio, 1 January 1959.

TELEVISION: *Et brev tilen søn,* script by Brenner, 1961;

Matador, script by Branner, 1965.

OTHER: Alice Tisdale Hobart, *Yang og Yin,* translated by Branner (Copenhagen, 1937);

Illés Kaczér, *Afrikas Aand dør ikke: En Nerges Roman,* translated by Branner (Copenhagen, 1938);

Hobart, *Kinas Lamper slukkes,* translated by Branner (Copenhagen, 1940);

Hobart, *Olie til Kinas Lamper,* translated by Branner (Copenhagen, 1941);

"Trommerne," in *Ny nordisk Novellekunst: Danmark, Finland, Island, Norge, Sverige* (Copenhagen: C. A. Reitzel, 1942);

Hele vejen rundt: Tolv amerikanske noveller, translated by Branner (Copenhagen: Povl Branner, 1943);

Franz Kafka, *Processen,* translated by Branner (Copenhagen: Gyldendal, 1945);

Hobart, *Floden,* translated by Branner (Copenhagen, 1945);

Johan Borgen, *Far og Mor og os,* translated by Branner (Copenhagen: Gyldendal, 1946);

Arthur Koestler, *Mørke midt paa Dagen,* translated by Branner (Copenhagen, 1946);

Koestler, *Tyv i Natten: Beretning om et Eksperiment,* translated by Branner (Copenhagen, 1947);

W. Somerset Maugham, *Livs Mosaik,* translated by Branner (Copenhagen: Virum, 1947);

En engelsk Bog tilegnet Kai Friis Møller, edited by Branner, Kjeld Abell, and Christian Elling (Copenhagen: Gyldendal, 1948);

Koestler, *Gladiatorerne,* translated by Branner (Copenhagen, 1948);

Kafka, *Slottet: På dansk,* translated by Branner (Copenhagen: Gyldendal, 1949);

"Humanismens krise," in *Humanismens krise,* Mennesket i tiden, no. 1 (Copenhagen: Hans Reitzel, 1950), pp. 8–30;

Gløder i mørke: Tretten noveller af unge danske forfattere, edited by Branner (Copenhagen: Gyldendal, 1953);

L. P. Hartley, *Gudernes sendebud: På dansk,* translated by Branner (Copenhagen: Gyldendal, 1954);

Thomas Mann, *Den bedragne,* translated by Branner (Copenhagen: Carit Andersen, 1954);

"Barndommens mose," in *Glimt af barndommen* (Copenhagen: Hans Reitzel, 1955), pp. 9–18;

Friedrich Dürrenmatt, *Den gamle dame besøger byen: Tragikomedie i tre akter,* translated by Branner (Copenhagen: Gyldendal, 1959);

Harold Pinter, *Vice værten,* translated by Branner (Copenhagen: Arena, 1961);

Truman Capote, *Nye stemmer, nye steder,* translated by Branner (Copenhagen: Gyldendal, 1963);

Arthur Miller, *Efter Syndefaldet,* translated by Branner (Copenhagen: Wangel, 1964).

SELECTED PERIODICAL PUBLICATIONS–
UNCOLLECTED: "Prometheus," *Politikens Magasin* (4 December 1932);

"Hvad er Sandhed?" *Politikens Magasin* (3 February 1935);

"Tre mænd vender hjem," *Politikens Magasin* (19 July 1936).

In 1955 H. C. Branner contributed an essay called "Barndommens mose" (Childhood's Bog) to *Glimt af barndommen* (Glimpse of Childhood), an anthology of childhood memories by prominent Danish authors. In this essay Branner recalls his fourth birthday, when he first became aware of a mysterious bog in the woods near his home. Synesthesia is at work as the adult Branner steps off the evening train and smells the swampish water: "Ved den lugt bliver jeg igen en lille dreng og lever et øjeblik i en verden fuld af brændende sol og kulsort mørke, en verden, hvor alt muligt, hvor liv og død og guder og uhyrer er ting til at tage og føle på" (At that smell I become a little boy again and live for a moment in a world full of burning sun and coal-black darkness, a world where everything is possible, where life and death and gods and monsters become tangible things). Throughout his career as one of the premiere voices in twentieth-century Danish literature, Branner returned to the imaginative possibilities of his childhood bog, where he found the wellspring of imagery and ideas that came to define his insightful, expressionist body of work.

Little biographical material is available about Branner, a private person who avoided publicity. One personal portrait is offered by the Danish critic Emil Frederiksen in his 1966 monograph on Branner's work: "Hans klare øjne havde et følsomt undersøgende og ret nøgternt blik og røbede en intelligens, der var anlagt både til åndfuld intuition og skarp analyse. Der var både noget hjerteligt imødekommende og venligt skeptisk i hans store smil" (His clear eyes had a sensitively examining and rather sober glance and revealed an intelligence that was suited for both brilliant intuition and sharp analysis. There was both something heartily forthcoming and kindly skeptical in his great smile). The man behind the smile is more difficult to identify.

Hans Christian Branner was born in Ordrup, a suburb of Copenhagen, on 23 June 1903, the son of the schoolmaster Christian Branner and Fanny Frederiksen. In the autobiographical essay "Glimt af mig selv" (Glimpse of Myself, 1944) he cited a childhood habit of lying in bed in the darkness and inventing stories "om Guder og Konger og Prinsesser" (about gods and kings and princesses) as the first sign of his literary proclivities. Listening to adults speaking in the living room below, Branner recalled that their strange words became "Besværgelser og Trylleformularer, ladet med mystisk Kraft" (incantations and magic charms, charged with mystic power). This early sense of otherworldliness and of language's puissance would eventually become hallmarks of Branner's literary output. In his book *Ideologi og æstetik i H. C. Branners sene forfatterskab* (Ideology and Aesthetics in H. C. Branner's Late Authorship, 1980), Erik Skyum-Nielsen described the pictorial nature of Branner's writing as "en vilje eller hang til at se billeder i alt og metaforisere oplevelsen" (a will or propensity to see pictures in everything and to make metaphors out of experience).

In 1921 Branner completed his *studentereksamen* (upper-secondary-school final examination) at Ordrup Gymnasium; infatuated with the stage, he then joined a traveling theater company for an unsuccessful and unhappy turn as an actor. From 1923 to 1932 he worked for the publishing firm of Jespersen & Pio in the warehouse division. During these years, Branner did not write, but his marriage in 1930 to Karen Margrethe Moldrup reawakened his early dreams of becoming an author. In 1932, with Karen's support, Branner quit his job and committed himself to writing. As he recalled later: "Jeg vidste ikke, om jeg kunde skrive. Men jeg vidste omsider, at der ikke var noget andet, jeg kunde" (I didn't know whether I could write. But I knew, at last, that there was nothing else I could do).

Branner published "Surdejen" (The Leaven, 1932) in the periodical *Politikens Magasin* on 4 September 1932. "Surdejen" marks his entry into the short-story genre, a genre that he helped revive in Denmark. Nearly sixty-five years later, in an article appearing in the Danish weekly *Weekendavisen* (24 April 1997), the critic Søren Schou called "Surdejen" a "mesterstykke" (masterpiece). He pointed to Branner's early use of one of his favorite themes, that of childhood trauma casting a long shadow over adulthood.

"Surdejen" concerns the childhood memory of Johan Sebastian Ankerstjerne, a prominent diplomat and reluctant author who has written a popular but misunderstood play. As a boy Ankerstjerne had attended a liberal school where teachers prided themselves in their openness and humanity. Branner warns, though: "Men løftede man bare en Smule paa Tradi-

tionens Rosenguirlander, stødte man straks paa Tyran-
niets Jernlænke" (But if the rosy festoons of tradition
were lifted slightly, one stumbled immediately upon
tyranny's iron chain). A school competition for the
best-written essay serves as the catalyst to uncovering
hidden repression in the institution: the protagonist
wins third prize with an essay that is a scathing attack
on the school, but when the headmaster reads it to the
school assembly, the essay has been censored with all of
the inflammatory passages removed. The young Ankerstjerne learns quickly that, despite boasting of their tolerance, the schoolmasters whitewash that which they
find offensive. The present misinterpretation of his play
merely echoes his childhood experience.

The short story "To Minutters Stilhed" (Two
Minutes of Silence), appearing in *Politikens Magasin* on 2
July 1933, deals with a couple, the evocatively named
Valdemar and Ragna Skjold-Lassen, who live beyond
their economic means in a suburban neighborhood.
Throughout the first three-quarters of the story, they
are depicted not as individuals but as members of their
neighborhood, a group obsessed with interior redeco-
rating and barbecues. As the story progresses, Branner
closes in on the emotional crisis faced by the husband at
the moment of his wife's death. Paralyzed with sorrow,
"en Gipsfigur" (a clay figure), Valdemar "var mere et
Billede paa Skræk og Forundring end paa plastisk Sorg,
han sad der som en tragisk Skuespiller, der pludselig
rives ud af Rollen i Teatret" (was more a picture of fear
and amazement than of elegant sorrow; he sat there like
a tragic actor who is suddenly torn out of his role in the
theater). In this one brief scene, Branner crafts a portrait of arrested emotion (the husband has forgotten
how to cry) in the middle of a story concerning the
vacuity and ultimate self-destruction brought on by
accumulating social position beyond one's means
(Ragna literally dies from the effort to keep up with the
neighbors). Despite his seeming epiphany of sorrow, by
the end of the tale Valdemar shows signs of his old
class-grubbing self as he ingratiates himself to a neighbor, a corporate magnate.

In "To Minutters Stilhed" there are elements that
appear in Branner's later works. For example, the characters' names, almost humorously historical, indicate
their representative function. Branner also composes
many long, run-on sentences, dependent on the
repeated use of *og* (and), a technique the Danish critic
Hans Hertel has called "ophobningsstil" (style of accumulation). This linguistic technique intimates the
stream-of-consciousness style that Branner employs in
his novels. Thematically, the story reveals inklings of
Branner's eventual move away from social realism with
its indictment of capitalistic greed toward existentialism.

*Cover for Branner's first short-story collection, which includes "De blaa
Undulater," his best-known story*

Branner honed his writing style in several short
stories published over the next few years in *Politikens
Magasin* and the Danish weekly *Berlingske Aftenavis*. He
merged a growing psychological insight with the predominant literary form of the early 1930s, *kollektivro-
manen* (the collective novel), a trend reflecting the
Marxist-driven social realism that defined both art and
literature at that time. Branner worked one of those
early short stories, "Isaksen" (1933), concerning the
plot to oust an alienated worker in a stationery company, into his first published novel, *Legetøj: En Roman om
en Forretning* (Toys: A Novel about a Business, 1936).
Branner wrote the book quickly, beginning it in October and completing the novel in November of 1936. In
a 1961 interview with Niels Birger Wamberg, he later
described this time as "det mest intense liv, jeg nogen
sinde har levet. Så man virkelig *så* og *følte* tingene; så
man virkelig var grebet af en slags inspiration, der fik
alt til at arbejde i samme takt, i samme rytme" (the most
intense life I have ever lived. I really *saw* and *felt* things—
I was seized by a kind of inspiration that got everything
to work at the same time, in the same rhythm). He also

cited the influence of Knut Hamsun, whose work he greatly admired, on the form of the novel and admitted he had "haft Hamsun med under armen hele vejen gennem bogen" (had Hamsun by my side throughout the book).

Reflecting the collectivist style perfected by Hans Kirk in *Fiskerne* (The Fishermen, 1928), in *Legetøj* Branner presents the machinations of management in the Kejser toy firm as a microcosm of modern class-driven society. The clash between power struggle and fear of unemployment speaks directly to historical developments in Europe at that time. The author's critical spotlight reveals Fascism and Nazism as acute consequences of humanity's misguided lust for power. The firm's executive manager, the appropriately named Herman Kejser (in Danish, *Kejser* means "emperor"), even lectures his underlings that "den enkelte er intet, forretningen er alt" (the individual is nothing, the business is everything). Branner paints a disturbing portrait of a Nazi in the everyday workplace, in his depiction of Kejser's unscrupulous right-hand man, Johan Feddersen, who terrorizes the firm and seizes control. It was not his last such portrait. In a 1961 interview Branner commented on the character of Feddersen:

Ham har vi alle mødt, ham kender vi alle. Det er ham, der kører på landevejen med 110 kilometers fart og er en fare for sine omgivelser. Han er den hårde, den dygtige, den smarte, den hensynsløse, den effektive—den mennesketype er jo ikke mindre fremtrædende i dag, end den var dengang.

(We have all met him, we all know him. He's the one driving on the highway at 110 kilometers, who is a danger for his surroundings. He's the hard one, clever, smart, ruthless, effective—that type of person who is no less prominent today than he was at that time.)

In *Legetøj* Branner counterpoints the male characters' drive to gain power with the innocent Klara Kvistgaard, whose strength is the true spine of the firm and who inspires one worker, Martin Lind, to experience a spiritual breakthrough. Lind's revelation arrives in the form of an interior dialogue made while he stares at himself in a mirror, in one of Branner's initial uses of the doppelgänger image, the split personality that he felt defined modern humanity. Critic Emil Frederiksen has observed that "i selve digterens personlighed er der foregået et lignende spil mellem angst og magt, underlegenhed og selvhævdelse, voksenhed og barnlighed; det er det spil hele *Legetøj* handler om" (in the author's personality itself a similar play between angst and power, inferiority and self-assertion, has taken place; all of *Legetøj* deals with this play).

Despite his emphasis in the novel on group dynamics, Branner also delves into the characters' home lives and personal backgrounds, thus departing somewhat from the purely materialist foundations of the collective novel. To Branner, the fear manifesting itself in the characters' interaction in the hierarchical workplace (that is, the sociopolitical arena) owes much to their repressed childhoods, one of the initial signs of a psychoanalytic perspective emerging in his work. His development along this line also parallels that of the Danish painters of the 1930s, who moved away from social realism in order to cultivate a psychologically oriented expressionism.

Branner soon began to view the lust for power that stands central to *Legetøj* as a product of human fear and loneliness. In his second novel, *Barnet leger ved Stranden* (The Child Plays on the Shore, 1937), the failed marriage of the narrator, Claus Bøje, and the death of his rebellious son compel him to retrace the emotional steps of his life in the form of a diary. The notions of arrested childhood development that Branner had toyed with in his first novel take center stage in *Barnet leger ved Stranden,* in many ways his most Freudian work. In the main character's self-analysis, somewhat akin to the Norwegian Aksel Sandemose's approach in *En Flyktning krysser sitt Spor* (1933; translated as *A Fugitive Crosses His Tracks,* 1936), Bøje reveals an infantile helplessness through his overly developed, orally fixated, sense of taste. An authoritarian father, another recurring motif in Branner, looms behind his emotional impotence.

In Bøje's wife, Birgitte, Branner creates a figure similar to Klara in *Legetøj*. Birgitte possesses a healthy sexual vitality which Bøje, trapped in a puritanical state of mind, cannot abide. In *Barnet leger ved Stranden* Branner offers his most explicit statement on the positive role of women:

Saadan gør Kvinder det der er nødvendigt. De gør det uden Glæde og uden Bevidsthed om at udrette noget stort, maaske endda helt i Blinde, men de gør det selv under Krige og Jordskælv. Og naar Mennesket hidtil har reddet sig ud af sin Ødelæggelse og ogsaa vil redde sig i Fremtiden, saa er det kun fordi der altid vil være Kvinder til at gøre det som er nødvendigt.

(Thus, women do what is necessary. They do it without joy and without consciousness of performing something great, possibly even in the dark, but they do it even in war and earthquakes. And if humanity until now has saved itself from its own destruction and will also save itself in the future, it is only because there will always be women to do that which is necessary.)

Branner is less Freudian in his second novel, and instead flirts with existentialism. One character extols the virtues of undergoing psychoanalysis while she loans books on Sigmund Freud to Bøje, only to be put in her place by Branner's voice of reason, the alcoholic Dr. Torsteinson. He warns her that the mystery of life is one of its essential elements and that there is no fulfillment in the search for complete freedom from all inhibitions. As Bøje helps Torsteinson travel through a blizzard to deliver a baby, Branner uses two of his favorite images, a childbirth and a snowstorm, to symbolize Bøje's final breakthrough in his attempt to win back Birgitte. In his 1959 monograph on Branner, Jørn Vosmar noted that *Barnet leger ved Stranden* is Branner's "svageste bog . . . Symbolikken er lidt for massiv" (weakest book . . . The symbolism is a little too massive). In his 1966 monograph, however, Frederiksen argued that thanks to the careful composition of the novel it is "rig på store og små tilfredstillelser" (rich in great and small pleasures).

In September 1939 Branner published a short-story collection, *Om lidt er vi borte* (In a Little While We Are Gone), which the Danish literary critic Hans Hertel has called "tiårets bedste novellesamling" (the decade's best short-story collection). An aural image from the title story—the encroaching sound of marching boots, is an image Branner had first used in a short story from 1933, "To Minutters Stilhed"—best represents the sense of social and emotional urgency that helps to define each of the collection's ten stories. Branner's unmatched insight into the workings of a child's mind manifests itself most notably in "Et Barn og et Mus" (translated as "A Child and a Mouse," 1946) and "De blaa Undulater" (translated as "The Blue Parakeets," 1966).

In "Et Barn og et Mus" Branner introduces the character of four-year-old Børge, whom he later employs as the main character in his novel *Historien om Børge* (1942; translated as *The Story of Börge*, 1973). Though maintaining the third-person narrative form, Branner switches to an interior perspective and captures the imaginative wanderings of a child's mind. Branner imbues these descriptions with observations in an adult narrative voice, and a dual perspective emerges seamlessly in the writing. As he comments in "Et Barn og et Mus," Børge's mind is "propfuld af den Slags Hemmeligheder som Minderne om Barndommen altid taber paa Marchen frem" (brimming with the kind of secrets that memories of childhood always lose sight of in the march forward). Much of Branner's writing attempts to reach into forgetfulness and retrieve those secrets. After the child announces his wondrous discovery of a little mouse in the attic, his parents set a trap to destroy the creature; when he finds the dead mouse,

H. C. BRANNER

TO MINUTTERS STILHED

KØBENHAVN
POVL BRANNERS FORLAG
M.CM.XLIV

Title page for Branner's 1944 collection of short stories, most of which are about childhood

Børge experiences deceit and death for the first time. The child's subsequent retreat to a fetal position under a hedge constitutes another recurring image in Branner's writing.

In "De blaa Undulater," which was adapted for Danish television by the director Astrid Henning-Jensen in 1965, Branner takes a turn toward symbolism, focusing on the relationship between two children, Katrine and Nils, and two parakeets, a gift to Katrine from her weak father. In "De blaa Undulater," a study of repressed and paralyzed emotion, Branner presents a haunting tale in which the spiteful Katrine ultimately gives the birds, the last object of affection in her loveless home, to her weaker friend and neighbor, Nils. In his *H. C. Branners tidlige forfatterskab* (H. C. Branner's Early Authorship, 1975), Leo Ottosen described the piece as "en moderne psykologisk novelle struktureret over en syndefaldsmyte" (a modern psychological short story structured around a lapsarian myth). One of Branner's finest stories, republished in 1957 in a special separate edition, "De blaa Undulater" offers profound insight into the machinations of a child's consciousness.

The title story, "Om lidt er vi borte" (translated as "In a Little While We Shall Be Gone," 1942), consists of a series of life pictures witnessed by a young married man who, anxious about the approaching war, has left home. Employing expressionistic and surreal imagery, Branner crafts a tale of emotional and temporal plasticity. His nameless protagonist is emblematic of Denmark's precarious position in World War II, as he wanders through a stormy, dreamlike Copenhagen, a setting perfectly suited to Branner's growing tendency to move the focus to the character's specific psychological response. In addition, a new shadow begins to cross his characters' paths: the inevitability of death in a mutable life. Returning home from his long night of the soul, the protagonist can only hold tightly to his wife in a world from which they soon may be gone.

In her essay "Det sociale menneske. Knuth Becker og H. C. Branner" (The Social Person: Knuth Becker and H. C. Branner, 1967), Anne-Katrine Gudme has commented that Branner's characters in his short stories "lever som i et glimt fra en blitzpære, de går over i éns erindring som mennesker der har levet et eneste livsøjeblik skarpt og endegyldigt igennem" (live as in the glimmer from a flashbulb; they pass into memory as people who have lived through a single moment in life sharply and definitively). This comparison also captures the expressionistic nature of his style.

In 1941 Branner returned to the novel form with *Drømmen om en Kvinde: Roman* (The Dream of a Woman: Novel), which was received with mixed reviews. Still, the novel, with its overriding theme of birth and death, moved Branner firmly into the existential literary tendency that surfaced in Denmark with such force during World War II. Branner also experimented with a new stream-of-consciousness approach in the structure of the novel. The surface narrative concerns two couples who meet to play bridge, but the narrative also enters their minds, a twilight area between dream and reality, and an interior landscape where past and present are played out simultaneously. It is late August 1939, and catastrophes are occurring throughout the world.

The hostess, Merete Rude, looks forward to the birth of her first child, though doctors have warned her that it will be a difficult delivery. Meanwhile, the lawyer Knud Mortimer has come to Copenhagen to be operated on for stomach cancer. Each is possessed by the inevitability of her and his respective condition. When Merete's husband Niels returns home late from work, he pauses outside his house and stares into a window at the bridge players. Bathed in a Hopperesque green light, they remind Niels of fish in an aquarium, an image that Branner employs many times in his writing.

Later that night, Mortimer suffers a painful attack, and his wife, Charlotte, takes him back to their hotel.

In the second half of the novel, Mortimer dies in his hotel room. At the end of his life, Mortimer finally realizes that the massive power of death cannot be fully comprehended. He also experiences an epiphany about the acquisition of material objects: "Man taler om det der har varig værdi, man taler om det faste og sikre og mener *ting*. Som om der fandtes noget mere flygtigt og usikkert end *ting!*" (We speak of what has lasting worth, we talk about the permanent and secure, and mean *things*. As if there existed anything more transitory and uncertain than *things!*). At the moment of his death, Mortimer has become reconciled to his life. Meanwhile, at the hospital, Merete gives birth to a seemingly stillborn son who is revived at the last minute by her doctor. Niels receives two bits of news: he is a father, and World War II has begun.

Jorn Vosmar has suggested that *Drømmen om en Kvinde* represents a stylistic breakthrough for Branner. According to Vosmar, "Den lange, blide rytme, de modulerede overgange og et indhold, der bølger mellem drøm og virkelighed, det bliver fra nu af kendetegnet på Branners følsomme prosa" (The long, gentle rhythm, the modulated transitions and a content that undulates between dream and reality—this becomes, from now on, characteristic of Branner's sensitive prose).

Branner's next novel, *Historien om Børge,* published in 1942, was originally presented as twelve radio readings during the German Occupation of Denmark (1940–1945). Returning to the imaginatively fertile setting of childhood development, Branner tells the story of four-year-old Børge's relationship to his mother and his dying father, a spectral figure whose fading presence, represented in the image of a toy ship, sets the course for the boy's later development. In some of his deftest writing, Branner maintains a dual focus, with Børge's perceptions and the narrative presence merging in a tour de force of psychological insight. After the boy is sent to live with an emotionless aunt and uncle, he passes from innocence to acceptance and understanding of his father's death.

Børge's development as an independent being is adroitly rendered in the arcing image of the novel: the ship. At the conclusion of the book, his mother takes the boy on board a vessel sailing up the Øresund. After Børge steals to the upper deck, the captain discovers him and, inviting the child in, allows him to steer: "Han styrede hele Skibet med alle Mennesker. Han mærkede det mellem sine Hænder: Skibet, Verden, alle Mennesker" (He steered the whole ship with all the people. He felt it between his hands: the ship, the world, all the people). As Emil Frederiksen pointed out, "Her har [Branner] formet sin klareste prosa, ikke sin mest karakteristiske, men den, der kommer klassisk dansk nærmest" (Here he [Branner] has formed his clearest prose, not his most characteristic, but that which comes closest to classic Danish).

In Danish prose, Branner is perhaps the author whose name is most associated with World War II. The war had a profound effect on his art and shifted his focus from psychology to existentialism. In a 1964 interview published in the Swedish journal *Santid och framtid* Branner commented:

> Kriget gav mig anledning att ställa frågan: Vad är egentligen psykologi? Psykologi är förhållandet mellan människor. Kriget bragte en de existentiella problemen in på livet. För att kunna gå vidare måste man ta sitt ansvar och sin skuld på sig.

> (The war gave me the opportunity to pose the question: What is psychology, really? Psychology is the relationship between people. The war brought the existential problem close to life. To endure, one must accept one's responsibility and guilt.)

Although Branner took no actual part in the resistance movement, several of his works directly address the Danish experience during the German Occupation. In 1942 he contributed "Trommerne" (The Drums), a nightmarish monologue, to a pan-Scandinavian collection, *Ny nordisk Novellekunst: Danmark, Finland, Island, Norge, Sverige* (New Nordic Short Story: Denmark, Finland, Iceland, Norway, Sweden). The narrator, a writer, must face the impotence of words and the chasm between art and the reality of war to overcome his angst, which has resulted in his wife's departure; the monologue is addressed to her. Through his wanderings through the threatening night, described in disturbingly German expressionistic terms, the narrator realizes that the drumming he hears is both outside and inside him. A stripe of blue-green sky, a slim vision of hope, ultimately compels him to reconnect with humanity. The surreal, Kafkaesque elements in the story owe much to Branner's familiarity with Franz Kafka's writing; he translated both *The Trial* (1945) and *The Castle* (1949) into Danish. Branner contributed an expanded, altered version of "Trommerne," a piece called "Angst" (Angst; translated as *Anguish,* 1980), to the Danish resistance movement's illegal publication *Der brænder en Ild* (There is a Fire Burning) in 1944. "Angst" was also published in a separate volume in 1947 and later republished with the novella "Bjergene" in *Bjergene: 2 noveller* (The Mountains: Two Stories, 1953).

Branner returned again to the short-story form in his next collection, *To Minutters Stilhed* (Two Minutes of Silence, 1944), in which many of the tales feature children. The ship image from *Historien om Børge* reappears

Front cover of Branner's 1949 novel, about a married woman who cannot recover emotionally from witnessing the death of her lover, a riding instructor who was thrown from his horse

in "Skibet" (translated as "The Ship," 1966), a story told in retrospect by a man plagued by discomfiting memories of his weak, ambitionless father. After he is taunted by a sibling into breaking a model ship, one of the few connections between him and his father, the boy fears, and simultaneously longs for, retribution. When that retribution does not arrive and the child is left disappointed, Branner compels the reader (along with the adult narrator) to ponder the weakness of relying on discipline and power for personal fulfillment. The story, first published in 1940, also depicts the attraction to Fascism and Nazism as rooted in an infantile need for rules and restrictions and a fear of self-dependence.

The anguish of puberty takes center stage in the humorous "De tre Musketerer" (translated as "The Three Musketeers," 1958), in which three twelve-year-old boys, teetering on the brink of sexual awakening, conspire to steal the photograph of a local beauty in an attempt to disarm the evil charms of this neighborhood Circe. In both "Røde Heste i Sneen" (Red Horses in the Snow) and "Den første Morgen" (The First Morning) the main characters, a fifteen-year-old boy and a newlywed man, discover that the transforming power of love, in the form of an innocent kiss and sex, respectively, is tied inextricably to an awareness of death, the two themes that often merge in Branner's most thoughtful works.

Branner crafted one of his most pensive tales in "Sidst i August" (translated as "At the End of August," 1953), a story that he expanded into "Bjergene" (translated as *The Mountains,* 1982), the longer title novella of the 1953 volume *Bjergene: 2 noveller.* In an attempt to recapture the romance that once defined their ten-year-old marriage, a couple vacationing in France just before the outbreak of World War II is determined to reach the Pyrennes. They briefly rekindle their earlier passion in a small café, but despite the husband's stubborn denial of the possibility of war, the impending conflict forces them to remain in Paris. In the end the weight of the world is too heavy for their romantic plans, and they turn back to Denmark. When the husband bemoans the fact that they never got to see the mountains, his wife replies, in an existential lament, "Er det ikke ligegyldigt . . . Er det ikke fuldkommen ligeyldigt nu, om du og jeg faar de Bjerge at se" (Does it really matter . . . isn't it completely irrelevant now, whether or not you and I get to see the mountains).

The title story, "To Minutters Stilhed," is an expressionistic reworking of the earlier tale of the same name (from 1933), about a man's inability to deal with his wife's death. Branner now focuses on the emotional paralysis stemming from the character's obsession with what others think. He composes even longer run-on sentences built on the repeated use of *og* (and) as a reflection of mental peregrination. One image melts into another, in the style of Virginia Woolf or James Joyce. The differences in the two versions of the story, written some ten years apart, also reflect Branner's development as an author. Whereas the original version began with a long section depicting the couple's vacuous suburban lifestyle, in which they interact on a purely collective level, the 1944 version focuses only on the husband's reaction to his wife's death. Now, it is his angst that serves as the main focus. Branner has pared the story down to one of his essential tenets: the small, telling moments of a person's life ultimately carry more significance than he or she can consciously discern.

Reviewing *To Minutters Stilhed,* the noted critic and author Tom Kristensen observed, "Der er ikke det Emne, Branner ikke formår at trænge sig ind i, og han kender Mænd og Kvinder og Børn lige godt, som om han havde alle tre Slags Sind i sig" (There is no subject Branner cannot penetrate, and he knows men and women and children equally well, as if he had all three kinds of temperaments within him).

Branner published what would become his most provocative work, *Rytteren: Roman* (The Horseman: Novel, 1949; translated as *The Riding Master: A Novel* 1951). He had originally composed it as both a short story and a play, which would later be reworked and staged, but its concerns carried the weight of a novel. In *Rytteren* Branner tells the story of Susanne, a thirty-two-year-old woman whose affair with Hubert, a riding instructor whom she saw thrown to his death by an untamed horse, has paralyzed her emotional development. Now living with Clemens, a middle-aged doctor who struggles to help her achieve emotional balance, Susanne exists in a limbolike state of attachment to the dead riding master. Clemens had known Hubert when they were boys, and the soft-spoken, guilt-ridden doctor and the deceased riding master seem as diametrically opposed as any two characters in literature. Like many of Branner's creations, they also function as representatives of distinctly different responses to life: in Susanne's case, the choice of life or death. Branner portrays her movement from despair to discovery in the five sections of the novel depicting five parts of the day: Morning, Noon, Afternoon, Evening, and Night.

Suicidal and spiteful, particularly toward Clemens and his nurse, the colorless and subservient Berta, Susanne has misplaced the focus in her life. In her attraction to the unrestricted sexuality symbolized by Hubert, Susanne reflects one of Branner's firmest convictions. The infatuation with complete freedom from all responsibility, which frequently leads to nihilism, stems from weakness reflecting both selfishness and arrested development. Still, this weakness masquerades as hedonism and strength. Branner quickly establishes Hubert (who has no major scenes; even in flashbacks he is markedly laconic) as a centaur figure from a prelapsarian, misty land of animal happiness, in which horses (that is, the sexual urges) run free.

Branner makes Susanne's choice even more difficult by depicting her alternative, Clemens, as a somewhat sexless, seemingly weak man, guilt-ridden by the knowledge that his mother died during his birth. His commitment to others, however, has arisen from this overly dutiful sense of responsibility that now defines his life: ". . . hvis jeg ikke var skyld i den og måtte bære ansvaret for den ville alting være meningsløst" (if I wasn't guilty in it and didn't have to bear the responsibility for it, everything would become meaningless). Thus, despite its unhealthy mental origins, Clemens's actual concern for the welfare of others makes him the strongest character in the book. Symbolically, he represents, to Branner, the only viable option for Susanne—modern humanity.

Social commentary steps into this psychological landscape in the form of two characters, also former friends of Hubert, who offer Susanne their own myopic responses to life: the nazi-like Herman, who has usurped Hubert's role as the riding master, and the pill-popping, free-spirited Michala, a parody of the salon communist common in Europe at this time. As weak as Susanne seems in the beginning of the novel, her own hidden strength slowly surfaces in her interactions with these two extreme characters. In his most scathing depiction of Nazism, Branner exposes the discipline-loving Herman, his hair described as a "helmet" and his rug worn from his jackbooted pacing, as nothing more than an overgrown infant in love with force. Herman, who unsuccessfully attempts to rape Susanne, defines power as "Frygt og kun frygt!" (Fear and only fear!); by the end of the scene, however, he is kneeling on the floor eating sugar cubes out of her hand.

Discipline is replaced with hedonism in Michala, who has covered her walls with colorful pictures done by children because she worships an infantile notion of irresponsible freedom: "Friheden for alt det forbandede der hedder godt og ondt, skyld og uskyld, ret og uret" (Freedom from every damn thing known as good and evil, guilt and innocence, right and wrong). Once Susanne exposes as a lie Michala's claim that Hubert had once tried to rape her, she too is reduced to kneeling in front of Susanne and crying, her head in Susanne's lap.

After Susanne returns to Clemens's apartment, she attempts to commit suicide by taking sleeping pills, but realizes, in her last moments of consciousness, that there will be no reuniting with Hubert, only a vast nothingness. Clemens saves her, however, thus resurrecting her from the emotionally paralytic state in which she has been arrested. She finally understands that her relationship with Hubert, who had been unfaithful and uncommitted, was itself a dead end and that one of them had to "die"; he died because, as she can now see, she was the strongest. Clemens, the pudgy clownlike figure in the striped suit, has signaled the way; the other characters remain trapped in the hell of their own self-absorption and fear. Branner takes a characteristic step away from psychoanalysis in *Rytteren;* it is not dwelling in the past that saves Susanne, rather, it is the epiphany about the responsibility Clemens represents that provides her with the strength to go on.

Reaction to Branner's novel was swift and initially laudatory. Tom Kristensen noted that had *Rytteren* been written in English, Branner would have awakened the next day to world fame. The internationally recognized author Karen Blixen (Isak Dinesen) took issue with some of Branner's contentions, however, and expressed her concerns in an essay written the following year and eventually published in *Bazar* in 1958. Given her love for the solipsistic, courageous individual, Blixen could not abide the figure of Clemens as a beacon of salvation, particularly since Susanne does not seem to take any active part in his transformative power. Blixen felt that Branner had mythologized Clemens's role to that of the supranormal helper in a folktale. She contended that the doctor has healed Susanne at the expense of her passionate side. Critics have often turned to Blixen's essay as the final word on *Rytteren.*

In "Samtale med en klovn" (Conversation with a Clown), published in *Politikens Kronik* (1 January 1950), Branner addressed the ongoing discussion about *Rytteren* by presenting a conversation between an author and a clown in which the author ridicules the notion that Clemens was intended as a Christ figure. In his hobo's hat and oversized galoshes, the clown represents the artistic attempt to convey inexpressible truths outside the realm of human logic: he dances at one point. Although an illusory representation of goodness in an exaggerated version of Clemens, the little clown insists that he is nevertheless an undeniable part of the author. In a 1964 interview with the Swedish journalists Frederic and Boel Fleisher, Branner attempted, once more, to clarify the confusion regarding the character of Clemens: "Clemens var bara ett utkast till en människa, ett experiment. Han har många svagheter. Och framför allt: han är ingen hjälte!" (Clemens was only the rough draft of a person, an experiment. He has many weaknesses. And above all: he is no hero!)

Later in 1950 Branner's essay "Humanismens krise" (The Crisis of Humanism) appeared in the volume of the same title, along with Martin A. Hansen's "Eneren og massen" (The One and the Masses). Branner had first presented his essay as a talk in Germany when he toured that war-torn country in 1946. "Humanismens krise" shares much in common with *Rytteren,* and both are characterized by a postwar ideology. In the essay Branner, addressing growing global tensions, uses the East and West as representatives of opposing forces, individual growth, and membership in a larger community that need to be united, declaring:

I en verdenssituation, hvor modsætningsforholdet mellem Øst og Vest har låst den politiske tænkning fast i tre-kanten frygt-had-aggression, findes der ikke andre udgangspunkter for åndelig forbindelse og kulturel udveksling mellem parterne end en diskussion om idealbegreber som kristendom og humanisme.

(In a world situation, where the opposing relationship between East and West has locked the political thinking into the triad of fear-hate-aggression, one can find no other starting point for spiritual connection and cul-

Branner signing copies of his novel Rytteren, *shortly after publication in December of 1949*

tural exchange between the parties than a discussion about ideal concepts such as Christianity and humanism.)

Branner holds up the true humanist as one who struggles to synthesize these opposites within his or her own personality. The religious concepts of goodness and moral rectitude are united with a strong social consciousness. For Branner, the emphasis falls on individual responsibility, manifested in a commitment to pacifism, atavistic of the figure of Christ.

Branner's work reached a new pinnacle of achievement in his innovative and haunting novel *Ingen kender natten* (1955; translated as *No Man Knows the Night*, 1958). *Ingen kender natten*, set in a time of heightened tension during World War II, is one of the finest Danish novels dealing with the German Occupation. Branner took the title from an old Danish psalm by B. S. Ingemann, "Ingen kender dagen før sol går ned" (No one knows the day before the sun goes down). Its alluringly nightmarish quality owes much to the surreal, shadowy, and curvilinear mental landscape developed in the first half of the novel. Written in a stream-of-consciousness style and moving between two seemingly opposed characters whose fates entwine nevertheless, the novel both

embraces and dissects all of Branner's previous concerns.

As the novel opens, Simon, a Communist resistance fighter, is fleeing the Gestapo, who relentlessly pursue him in the night. His former lover, the destitute Lydia, has betrayed him to the Germans. Meanwhile, Tomas, the drunken son-in-law of Gabriel, sits in a large suburban villa where he nurses his stupor and his inertia, both consequences of his meaningless life of writing advertising copy and his passionless marriage. Tomas bears the burden of a more sickly form of guilt than Clemens in *Rytteren*. As a young man Tomas had watched his mother die but had not called for help (her death was actually a suicide). She had been a possessive, sexually abusive parent, an overwhelming force, but at the moment of her death he realized that she was nothing more than a painted child. This description also applies to Tomas's wife, the infantile Daphne, Gabriel's daughter.

Gabriel, a wealthy manufacturer and one of Branner's infamous "døde voksner" (dead grown-ups), is a person whose existence has been defined by advertising; the acquisition of material things has taken over his life. He is reminiscent of Mortimer in *Drømmen om en Kvinde*. At one point in his longest speech, Gabriel provides a disturbingly accurate picture of a vacuous world driven by consumerism and commercialism. He is moving, inescapably, toward the heart attack he fears.

The paths of Tomas and Simon cross when Simon breaks into Gabriel's villa and becomes the catalyst to Tomas's final leap into action, and thus meaning, in his life (Gabriel keels over and dies precisely at the moment of Simon's break-in). During the course of the stream-of-consciousness narrative in the novel, a melange of psychological exposé and characterization, the two men actually begin and end each other's sentences, though their worlds initially seem unrelated. Employing the doppelgänger theme and thus playing on the sibling motif he has used throughout his work, Branner transforms the two seemingly disparate characters into "brothers." Simon tells himself to "Get up" when he stumbles from exhaustion just before entering the villa and passing out. These are also Tomas's first words to him when he discovers the resistance fighter in the house.

With his decision to help Simon and later a group of refugees hiding in a desolate building in Copenhagen, Tomas finally breaks the spell that has rendered him a nonparticipant in his own existence. As he warns himself in a final crucial moment, "Husk hvem du er, du har før dræbt mennesker ved at sidde stille og vente" (Remember who you are, you have already killed people by sitting still and waiting). Once he springs into action, Tomas moves inexorably toward the terrifying truth that losing one's life can provide, paradoxically, the meaning of existence. He becomes the avatar of Branner's own words in a New Year's radio talk in 1959: "For livet er ikke noget som *er,* men noget som *sker*" (For life is not something that *is,* but something that *happens*).

Tomas is reborn when he meets Lene, a fugitive and the strongest character in the book, a woman who has overcome an abusive stepfather, whom she now nurses, and who provides the sexual and emotional depth absent from Tomas's previously vacuous life of wealth and inactivity. Extending the biblical imagery of the characters' names, Branner reveals that Lene's full name is Martha Maria Magdalena. Unlike other repressed female characters in the novel, Lene is the embodiment of womanhood; her sexual nature is not stunted but regenerative. Through her and the example she sets, Tomas acquires the strength to sacrifice himself in his final attempt to save the other refugees. In his insightful critique of the novel in *Digtning og livssyn* (Writing and Outlook, 1960), Sven Møller Kristensen commented that the central theme of *Ingen kender natten* is "det uforløste og vildfarende menneskelige behov for hengivelse, behovet for kontakt, samhørighed, sammennes-kelighed" (the pent-up and searching human need for surrender, the need for contact, solidarity, together-ness).

In 1956 Branner gave a speech, "Kunstens uaf-hængighed" (The Independence of Art), at the Danish Student Union in Copenhagen; the talk was later pub-lished as an essay in *Politiken,* 25 November 1956, and then republished in book form in 1957. The talk had been prompted by the Soviet invasion of Hungary, which had resulted in an outcry from many prominent European intellectuals. Branner had seen hope in the opening of connections between the Soviet Union and the Western world, especially in the production and publication of works by Arthur Miller and Jean Paul Sartre. The brutal repression of the Hungarian people seemed to dash those hopes and inspired Branner's talk. Viewing the world as trapped between an impossi-ble war and an impossible peace, Branner was most appalled by the silence of many artists. "Kunsteren er hverken sjælesørger, pædagog eller profet, han kan ikke lære mennesker hvad de skal tænke og tro, eller hvor-dan de skal leve deres liv; hans opgave er at leve og udtrykke sin tid, være dens bevidsthed og samvit-tighed" (The artist is neither spiritual advisor, peda-gogue, nor prophet. He cannot teach people what they should think or believe, or how they should live their lives. His duty is to live and express his time, to be its consciousness and its conscience).

Branner takes a hard stand against purely materi-alist views of existence:

Hvis en marxist vil fortælle mig, at der ikke findes åndelig frihed, hvor der ikke findes frihed for nød og frygt og uvidenhed, saa må jeg give ham ret. Men når han deraf drager den slutning, at aåndfriheden må komme i anden række, at man må fjerne nøden og frygten og uvidneheden før man kan tillade mennesker at tænke og ytre sig frit, må jeg protestere. For der kan heller ikke findes frihed for nød og frygt og uvidenhed, hvor der ikke findes åndelig frihed.

(If a Marxist wants to tell me that no spiritual freedom can exist where there is no freedom from need and fear and ignorance, I must agree. But when, from this, he draws the conclusion that spiritual freedom must be secondary, that one must remove need and fear and ignorance before one can allow people to think and express themselves freely, I must protest. For there can surely be found no freedom from need and fear and ignorance where no spiritual freedom exists.)

Branner's 1956 essay constitutes an elegant cry against political repression.

On New Year's Day 1959 Branner gave a per-sonal, heartfelt talk, *En nytårs Klokke* (A New Year's Chime), about the advent of the new year on Danish radio (the speech appeared in *Politiken,* 4 January 1959). He recalled the first time war's shadow crossed his life, as a child in 1914:

krigen var kommet ind i mit liv og den har været der lige siden. Min barndom blev borte i den. Hele min ungdom var efterkrigstid, mellemkrigstid og førkrig-stid. Så blev også den borte i den sidste store krig og nu, i min sene manddom, er det den kolde krigs tid. Men skønt jeg har været i krig næsten hele mit liv, har jeg alligevel ikke haft mod til at se den i øjnene.

(the war had come into my life and it has been there ever since. My childhood became lost in it. All my youth was the time after the war, the time between the wars and the time before the war. That too was lost in the last great war, and now, in my late manhood, it is the time of the Cold War. Yet, although I have been in war nearly all my life, I have, nevertheless, never had the courage to look it straight in the eyes.)

Branner's last published prose, *Ariel: Noveller* (Ariel: Stories), a collection of four short stories, appeared in 1964. In the title piece a husband awakes in the bed of his mistress, but after a passionate scene of erotic pleasure, he slips out into the morning fog and eventually wends his way back home. His wife, though waiting for him, does not reproach him. Suffering from an undisclosed paralyzing illness, she tells her errant husband that she feels reborn with the breaking sun. As he carries her through their living room, he experiences a momentary awakening of the spirit, the brief lifting of the veil of time and space, and then he drops back into reality, stumbling under the burden of carrying his paralyzed wife. Finally, the husband buries himself in his wife's arms and cries like a baby, succumbing to pure sorrow. In its attempt to convey inexpressable emotions and sensations, "Ariel" functions as a modernist story. Skyum-Nielsen has observed that Branner, in his later production, writes like his contemporaries, who "fra den tidligere modernisme overtager opfattelsen af forfatteren som medium for en indre eller højere førsproglig virkelighed" (from earlier modernism take over the conception of the author as a medium for an inner or higher pre-linguistic reality).

In addition to his stellar reputation as a prose writer, Branner also established himself as a dramatist during the course of his career. Much of his reputation as a dramatist rests on his early radio plays, a genre to which his finely tuned ear for natural dialogue seemed especially suited. "Efterspil" (Epilogue), his first radio drama, was broadcast only nine days after the publication of his first short story in 1932; it has never been published. His second radio play, "Eftermæle" (Reputation), broadcast a year later, won Branner a second prize in Danish State Radio's national competition. He would produce five more radio plays–"Natteregn" (Night Rain, 1937); "Hundrede kroner" (A Hundred Crowns, 1949); "Jeg elsker dig" (I Love You, 1956), adapted as a 1957 motion picture for which Branner wrote the screenplay; "Et spil om kærligheden og døden" (A Play about Love and Death, 1960); and "Mørket mellem træerne" (The Darkness between the Trees, 1965)–and two television plays, "Et brev til en søn" (A Letter to a Son, 1961) and "Matador" (1965).

Branner also produced three stage plays during his career, and Søskende: Skuespil i tre akter (Siblings: Play in Three Acts, 1952; translated as The Judge, 1955), his first major work after Rytteren, remains his most effective and most widely read. Branner counterpoints the highly symbolic nature of the characters with a naturalistic setting, thus borrowing a technique from Swedish dramatist August Strindberg's chamber plays. In Søskende Branner presents the story of three grown siblings who have been called to their childhood home to see their father, an aging judge near death. The judge, alternately a sign for the superego, an inhuman discipline, and the God of the Old Testament, never appears on stage; instead, he bangs a staff on the floor above the action. A nurse, Sister Agnes, serving as a go-between, runs up and down the steps, reporting the old man's status and relating his dying words.

The three grown siblings represent distinct responses to the controlling patriarch. The oldest brother, Arthur, has lived a sexless life of conformity and rules, revealing an unresolved connection to the father. His concern over career advancement, though,

seems to take precedence over his fealty to the dying judge. Irene, the vivacious daughter, has never seen her father as anything but an old man who needed love and, thus, is not bound to his presence in her life. Still, her marriage to a wealthy but undemonstrative man who made money as a collaborator during the war has brought her to the brink of adultery. The judge's youngest son, Michael, a rebellious, ironic Christ figure, has chosen a hedonistic, nihilistic life on the sea, indicating that he remains just as bound to the father's tyranny as his duty-bound older brother. Suffering from insomnia and incapable of establishing any lasting relationships in his life, Michael represents the bad boy hiding behind the rebel's swagger. Obeisance to order defines Arthur's life; Michael nurses an infatuation for complete freedom; and Irene's marriage needs attending. For one brief moment the three main characters rhapsodize about abandoning their present lives and living together out in the country. Arthur even discloses a secret passion to escape his professional aspirations and become a gardener. In this scene Branner parodies the Danish affection for nature and the long literary tradition of characters who retire to sylvan settings in a futile attempt to escape ethical responsibilities.

In Søskende, Branner breathes a final sigh into the presence of reliable attributes in modern life. In the pale light of the closing scene, the characters are left on their own in a frighteningly dark existential state. Discussing Søskende in his 1961 article "Bergman, Branner, and Off-stage Dying," Richard Vowles observed that the play's "fusion of symbolism and naturalism permits the most accurate dramatic statement . . . of man's skirmish with the exasperating ambiguities of the superego."

Søskende premiered in Stockholm on 13 December 1951 with the great Alf Sjöberg directing; the play had its Danish premiere in Copenhagen on 5 January 1952. In February of 1952 Branner's dramatic adaptation of Rytteren was staged at Copenhagen's Det nye Teater (it had already premiered at Stockholm's Lilla Dramaten on 5 April 1950). In Thermopylæ: Skuespil i fire akter (1958; translated as Thermopylæ: A Play in Four Acts, 1974), his final stage production, Branner takes another characteristic step away from humanism. In Thermopylæ, with its strong social sensibility, Branner owes more to the plays of Henrik Ibsen than to those of Strindberg; he points to the weakness of an uncompromising humanism that reduces high ideals into freedom from responsibility. Set during World War II, the play presents the figure of an academic humanist whose voice has no effect in the struggle between his sons, one an avowed Communist and one a Nazi supporter. Stefan Fischer is a revered professor of cultural history and an enlightened liberal. As the play progresses, Stefan's lectures on democracy place him in a precarious position with both the Gestapo and the resistance movement. Both camps see him as too extreme. In his refusal to flee to Sweden, another sign of his uncompromising commitment to an idea, he brings destruction to his home. As in *Søskende*, the two sons cannot live up to their father's ideals, an unyielding humanism that seems, perhaps, too removed from the real world. In the end the father's attempt to remain distant from acute political realities contributes to one son's death at the hands of the other son.

Branner's writing brought him much success and garnered many accolades. He became a member of the board of the Danish Author's Union in 1940 and a recipient of the *Finansloven* (literally, "Financial Promise"), an annual state grant, in 1941. He served as editor of the periodical *Perspektiv* from 1953 to 1955. Throughout his career he received several honors, among them the Holberg Medal (1954), the Adam Oehlenschäger Award (1955), the Holger Drachmann Award (1955), the H. C. Andersen Medal (1960), and the Playwright's Prize (1961). He also served as a member of the Danish Academy and the Danish Author's League and as president of the Danish Playwrights Guild.

H. C. Branner once expressed his concern that schizophrenia would become the accepted mental state for modern humanity. Throughout his writing he struggled to provide solutions to the paralyzing mental division that seemed to define contemporary existence. In his later works, such as the short story "Ariel," he attempted to address modern life directly. As Skyum-Nielsen noted in his 1980 monograph, "Men når den centrale modernistiske 'splittelse'-erfaring er fælles fra generation til generation, er det private oplevelsesunivers, inden for hvilket den søges harmoniseret, det også" (Although the central modernist experience of alienation remains common from generation to generation, so does the universe of private experience, within which harmony is sought). That private experience moved increasingly into the spotlight in Branner's work.

In a 1961 interview Branner admitted that "Det er de færreste mennesker, der nogen sinde opnår den harmoni, den balance mellem sindets kræfter, som det vel betyder at blive voksen" (Only few people ever achieve the harmony, that balance between the mind's powers, that truly indicates maturity). His characters grew to be symbols for those powers, signposts for the crucial alternatives facing modern humanity. His contribution remains a singular one in the history of Danish letters.

Interviews:

Boel Fleisher and Frederic Fleisher, "Möte med H. C. Branner," *Samtid och framtid,* 21 (1964): 165–170;

Niels Birger Wamberg, "H. C. Branner," in his *Samtale med danske digtere* (Copenhagen: Gyldendal, 1968), pp. 110–121.

References:

Poul Bager, "H. C. Branner: Af Skrevet i Vand," in his *Læsninger af ud valgte texte* (Copenhagen: Centrum, 1991);

Karen Blixen, "H. C. Branner: *Rytteren,*" *Bazar,* 1 (1958): 51–63; *Bazar,* 2 (1958): 71–94;

Mogens Brøndsted, "Barnet hos H. C. Branner," *Edda,* 59 (1959): 111–160;

Jørgen Egebak, "H. C. Branner," in *Danske digtere i det 20. århundrede,* volume 2, edited by Torben Brostrøm and Mette Winge (Copenhagen: Gad, 1980), pp. 357–383;

Henning Fonsmark, *H. C. Branner. En introduktion* (Copenhagen: Gyldendal, 1951);

Emil Frederiksen, *H. C. Branner* (Copenhagen: Gyldendal, 1966);

Anne-Katrine Gudme, "Det sociale menneske. Knuth Becker og H. C. Branner," in *Tilbageblik på 30'erne: Litteratur, teater, kulturdebat 1930–39: En antologi,* volume 2, edited by Hans Hertel (Copenhagen: Stig Vendelkær, 1981), pp. 118–127;

Sven Møller Kristensen, "Ingen kender natten," in his *Digtning og livssyn: Fortolkninger af syv danske værker* (Copenhagen: Gyldendal, 1960), pp. 180–199;

T. L. Markey, *H. C. Branner* (New York: Twayne, 1973);

Mark Mussari, "H. C. Branner and the Colors of Consciousness," *Scandinavian Studies,* 71 (1999): 44–66;

Leo Ottosen, *H. C. Branners tidlige forfatterskab* (Copenhagen: Gyldendal, 1975);

René Rasmussen, "Det grædende barn: Børn hos H. C. Branner," *Litteraturens børn: Barndomsskildringer i dansk litteratur,* edited by Niels D. Lund and Winge (Copenhgaen: Høst, 1994), pp. 95–112;

Claus Secher, "Humanismens sande krise: En analyse af H. C. Branners *Rytteren,*" *Analyser af danske romaner,* volume 3, edited by Jørgen Holmgaard (Holstebro: Borgens, 1977), pp. 202–234;

Erik Skyum-Nielsen, *Ideologi og æstetik i H. C. Branners sene forfatterskab* (Copenhagen: Gyldendal, 1980);

Skyum-Nielsen, "To minutters skønhed, tredive års opbyggelighed," in *Læsninger i Dansk Litteratur,* volume 4, edited by Inger-Lise Hjordt-Vetlesen and Finn Frederik Krarup (Odense: Odense University Press, 1997), pp. 25–40;

Jørn Vosmar, *H. C. Branner* (Copenhagen: Gyldendal, 1959);

Richard Vowles, "Bergman, Branner, and Off-Stage Dying," *Scandinavian Studies,* 33 (1961): 1–9;

Niels Birger Wamberg, "Lidt om H. C. Branners poetiske rekvisitter," *Ord och bild,* 68 (1959): 436–445.

Marie Bregendahl

(6 November 1867 – 22 July 1940)

Helle Mathiasen
University of Arizona

BOOKS: *Hendrik i Bakken: Et Billede* (Copenhagen: Gyldendal, 1904);

En Dødsnat (Copenhagen & Christiania: Gyldendal, 1912); translated by Margery Blanchard as *A Night of Death* (New York: Knopf, 1931);

Billeder af Sødalsfolkenes liv, 7 volumes (Copenhagen & Christiania: Gyldendal, 1914–1923; republished as *Sødalsfolkene,* 2 volumes, 1935)—comprises *Alvilda* (1914), *Peter Guldgraver og hans eneste Ven* (1917), *Tre gamle Kvinder* (1918), *Blandt de Unge* (1919), *I Fest og Trængsler* (1921), *Mens Aarene gik* (1922), *Den gamle Provst* (1923);

I de lyse Nætter (Copenhagen: Aschehoug, 1920);

Mens Aarene gik– (Copenhagen: Gyldendal, 1922);

I Haabets Skær: Fire Fortællinger (Copenhagen: Gyldendal, 1924);

Med aabne Sind: To smaa Pigers Oplevelser og Indtryk (Copenhagen: Gyldendal, 1926)–includes "Skellet," translated by W. Glyn Jones as "The Boundary," in *Contemporary Danish Prose,* edited by Elias Bredsdorff (Copenhagen: Gyldendal, 1958), pp. 41–48;

Thora: En Novelle (Copenhagen: Gyldendal, 1926);

Den blinde Rytter (Copenhagen: Gyldendal, 1927); translated by Norma Farquhar as "Borghild" in *Scandinavian Women Writers,* edited by Ingrid Clareus (New York: Greenwood Press, 1989), pp. 53–71;

Naar Julen er nær: Noveller og Skitser (Copenhagen: Aschehoug, 1927);

Holger Hauge og hans Hustru: Roman fra en historisk Tid, 2 volumes (Copenhagen: Jespersen & Pio, 1934);

Møllen og andre Fortællinger (Odense: Flensted, 1936);

Mors Bog (Odense, 1936);

Smaa Kommentarer til Aakjærs Erindringer (Copenhagen: Nyt Nordisk, 1936);

Filtret Høst: Spredte Stemninger og Udbrud (Copenhagen: Gyldendal, 1937);

Birgitte Borg (Copenhagen: 1941).

courtesy of Kirsten Aakjær

Editions: *En dødsnat,* commentary by Lena Flarup, Brigitte Rugholm and Peter Rugholm (Herning: Forlaget Systime, 1984);

En dødsnat, edited by Esther Kielberg, afterword and notes by Mette Winge (Copenhagen: Borgen/ Danske Sprog og Litteraturselskab, 1992).

Marie Bregendahl holds a secure position as one of the leading Danish novelists in the generation that evolved around the Danish poet and novelist Johannes V. Jensen, the Swedish novelist Selma Lagerlöf, and the Norwegian author Sigrid Undset. Like these writers, Bregendahl used her birthplace in the countryside as the setting for her fiction, describing economic and cultural changes in the lives of farmers and peasants before and during industrialization. Bregendahl captured a peasant culture in transition from isolation to involvement in modern European politics. As did her British contemporary Thomas Hardy, she created an imaginary landscape, resembling her birthplace, peopled with a vast gallery of characters of all ages; with supreme skill she focused on individual men and women as they underwent the transformations of their era. Like other European writers of her generation, Bregendahl spent her childhood in the country and moved to the city as a young person, creating from her urban exile a fictional world presented in a style of tragic realism.

The eldest of eight children, Marie Sørensen was born 6 November 1867 in Fly, south of Skive, and raised on Bregendahl Farm in northern Jutland; her father, Peder Sørensen, and mother, Ane Kathrine Christensen, were farmers. Her parents married in 1866, when her mother was twenty-one and her father was thirty-seven. In 1894 the family changed its name to Bregendahl; *Gaarden Bregendahl* (Bregendahl Farm) had been in the family for centuries, and after Peder Bregendahl's death it passed to his eldest son. Marie attended the village school and was confirmed in the Danish Evangelical-Lutheran Church. Her first literary influence was her mother, a lover of the Norwegian writer Bjørnsterne Bjørnson's songs and stories. Early trauma changed Bregendahl's idyllic farm childhood to adult toil when her mother died in 1879 at age thirty-four during the birth of her ninth child, necessitating Marie Bregendahl's responsibility for her younger siblings. Bregendahl was almost twelve at the time.

Her intellectual awakening occurred during a stay at Vrigsted Folkehøjskole (folk high school) near Vejle in 1886–1887. The *folkehøjskoler* are voluntary residential schools for adults with a curriculum influenced by folk culture, founded in 1844 at Rødding as part of a movement to counteract the elitism that N. F. S. Grundtvig, the religious and social reformer, saw as perpetuating social injustice. In her writings Bregendahl repeatedly emphasizes the importance of the Grundtvigian *folkehøjskole* as a vehicle for the education of Danish farmers and peasants, including herself. Getting away from the strenuous work of farming, and being given the opportunity to write and read, was a turning point for the young girl.

While a folk-high-school student, Bregendahl met and fell in love with the poet Jeppe Aakjær, the son of a local smallholder. During their passionate courtship Bregendahl and Aakjær carried on a voluminous correspondence. Her letters show her growing awareness of new currents in Danish culture of the 1890s: Darwin-

ism, sexual politics, criticism of the Danish church, and the freethinking views of Georg Brandes, the radical critic and scholar. In addition, writing these letters helped Bregendahl grow as an author, as she expressed her feelings and thoughts to Aakjær.

Bregendahl and Aakjær moved to Copenhagen in 1892. They married 11 July 1893, and a son, Svend, was born on 20 January 1894. While her husband studied in preparation for his *studentereksamen* (secondary school diploma), Bregendahl became the family breadwinner, first working as a domestic servant, then managing a boardinghouse.

The seven-year marriage failed in 1900 and the couple separated. Thirty-six years later, in *Smaa Kommentarer til Aakjærs Erindringer* (Small Comments on Aakjær's Memoirs, 1936), Bregendahl wrote:

> Om Punktet, Aakjær og hans første Hustru skal jeg indskrænke mig til at sige, at enhver, der har kendt os begge, vel bare læst os, –vil være klar over, at vi var to bundforskellige Mennesker, og da de Vilkaar, hvorunder vi skulde realisere det vanskelige Problem, der hedder et Ægteskab, ikke lettede Forholdene for os, kan det vist siges, at være en naturlig Sag, at Forbindelsen brast.

> (On the issue of Aakjær and his first wife I will only say that anyone who has known us both or even just read our work–will realize that we were two radically different human beings and since the conditions under which we were to realize the difficult problem called a marriage did not make it easier for us, it is only natural that the relationship failed.)

On 22 January 1907, Jeppe Aakjær obtained a divorce, as he wished to remarry. Bregendahl spent the rest of her life in Copenhagen as a single mother and struggling author.

In 1897, before the divorce and in dire need of money to support her husband and son, Bregendahl had sent a story, "Fru Elviras Seng" (Mrs. Elvira's Bed) to the Copenhagen critic and political activist Edvard Brandes, brother of Georg Brandes, for publication in his daily newspaper, *Politiken*. Brandes did not publish the story but returned her manuscript with a polite note in which he made encouraging remarks about Bregendahl's talent. Next, she wrote a collection of short stories and a play that also remained unpublished. She published her first short fiction, "Ved Lars Skræders Sygeseng," (By the Sickbed of Lars the Tailor), in Aakjær's *Jydsk Stævne: Et Aarskrift* (Jutlandic Gathering: A Literary Annual, 1902), which includes works by Jutlandic authors. Bregendahl also wrote many articles for Danish newspapers and magazines and proofread for them at night to support herself and her son. Bregendahl was thirty-seven years old, however, before her

Bregendahl and her son, Svend Aakjær, in 1894 (courtesy of Kirsten Aakjær)

first novel, *Hendrik i Bakken: Et Billede* (Hendrik in the Hill: A Portrait, 1904) was published.

Hendrik i Bakken was praised by contemporary reviewers for its artistry. The title character, Hendrik, and his wife, Mariane, live on a large farm in the wind-blown region of northern Jutland. Hendrik is a nasty, solitary, taciturn, and slovenly individual. He loves his wife dearly but cannot show it. Mariane suffers from his stubborn silence. The pivotal event in their marriage is a dance party Mariane permits the workers to hold while her husband is away at the cattle market. The farmhands and the women servants carry on in high spirits, and the best dancer invites Mariane to join him, knowing she loves to dance, and she does—enjoying herself as if she were a young girl again. Hendrik's return ruins the party, however, and the dancing stops.

Sickened by Hendrik's hostility and further debilitated by the subsequent deaths of two of her young children, Mariane dies of grief. Hendrik refuses his wife a proper country funeral. The narrator's compassion for Mariane and even for Hendrik heightens the tragedy of this mismatched marriage, fated to occur and fated to fail. Bregendahl denied using her parents as models for Hendrik and Mariane, although similar pairs of loving but unhappy spouses appear in several of her other works.

After *Hendrik i Bakken,* Bregendahl stopped writing while she raised her son and managed her brother's household and dairy in Copenhagen. She later remarked, "Men saa holdt jeg op med at skrive—i hele 8 Aar. Hvorfor, Aah jo, Kampen for Tilværelsen! Penge ejede jeg ikke, og min Søn skulde opdrages ordentligt" (But then I stopped writing—for 8 long years. Why? Oh well, the struggle for existence! I had no money, and my son needed to be raised properly.)

After this eight-year lacuna, Bregendahl was able to recommence writing because of a small inheritance. Her literary breakthrough came with the publication of *En Dødsnat* (1912; translated as *A Night of Death,* 1931). Fifteen years later she recalled that she made 800 kroner from this book. Highly praised by Norwegian novelist and Nobel Prize winner Sigrid Undset and now considered a Danish classic, *En Dødsnat* is the powerful story of young Anne Gram's death during the birth of her eighth child. The action takes place during the 1870s, on a day near harvest time from late afternoon to early morning. The setting is a large farm in northern Denmark. The point of view is that of Gram's eldest daughter, Lise, twelve years old, the same age as Bregendahl was when she lost her mother in childbirth. Anne Gram's confinement and death are mirrored in the other characters' dialogue, but especially in Lise's feelings. Witnessing her mother's fear of death provokes Lise's first spiritual crisis. Her Bible lessons have taught her that acceptance of God's will is required for salvation, but with the other children Lise hears her mother's screams of protest from a distance:

Og ind imellem kom der nu bedende Raab til Gud og Frelseren om at give hende Hjælp og Styrke, thi hun kunne ikke blive ved at holde sin Pine ud.

"Aa, Gud i Himlen hjælpe mig!—Herre Jesus Christ, jeg holder det ikke ud!—Jeg holder ikke Pinen ud!—Hjælp mig!—Hjælp mig!" raabte hun i sin Nød og Vaande.

Og Klageraabene skar igennem den smukke Aftenstilhed, som nu imod Solnedgangstid hvilede over den store Have. Gang paa Gang kom disse jamrende Skrig farende derned til Børneklyngen og sønderrev al Havens, ja, al Høstaftenens Fred og Ro.

(And now from time to time they heard entreating cries to God and the Savior for help and strength, for she could no longer endure the pain.

"Oh, God in heaven help me!–Lord Jesus Christ, I cannot bear it!–I cannot bear the pain!–Help me!–Help me!" she cried out of her need and agony.

And her laments cut through the beautiful evening silence which now at sunset lay over the large garden. Time and again these groaning cries flew down to the children and tore apart all the peace of the garden, yes, all the peace and quiet of that harvest evening.)

Walking from her grandmother's cottage to her parents' bedroom in the main building of the farm, Lise moves closer and closer to the site of her mother's suffering until she sees her mother, who has just died. Lise understands the tragedy of her mother's suffering and death; she feels guilty for not always behaving lovingly toward her mother, and realizes that now she must assume responsibility for her mother's work of raising the children and managing the farm. In *En Dødsnat,* Bregendahl deftly delineates the nature and significance of peasant-women's work before industrialization, and the novel also stands out because of its realistic depiction of childbirth. For Bregendahl, creating a story out of her own childhood trauma may have been therapeutic.

In an interview she gave to a reporter from *Politiken* on 3 November 1937, shortly before her seventieth birthday, Bregendahl explained why she had to stay in Copenhagen to write: "Jeg har boet i København i 49 Aar, og da jeg begyndte at skrive, var det let, fordi jeg kun havde en graa Mur udenfor Vinduerne. Intet forstyrrede mig" (I have lived in Copenhagen for 49 years, and when I started to write, it was easy, because I only had a grey wall outside my windows. Nothing disturbed me). Life in Copenhagen with its deprivations and financial pressures—her father did not help to support his daughter or grandson—compelled Bregendahl to write. The city also furnished her with characters that she developed in her fiction. Bregendahl often said that she was not a regional writer; in fact, she considered this term a denigration of her achievement, remarking in an interview published in *Nationaltidende* on 5 November 1937: "Jeg skriver ikke om Bønder! Jeg skriver om mennesker" (I do not write about peasants! I write about people). She largely disclaimed having been influenced by any earlier writers, but critics and historians have pointed out resemblances between her settings and plots and those of Steen Steensen Blicher, the nineteenth-century Danish writer. Bregendahl herself acknowledged both Johannes V. Jensen and Henrik Pontoppidan as sources of inspiration.

Many of the characters from her earlier novels reappear in *Billeder af Sødalsfolkenes liv* (Pictures of the Life of the People of Sødal, 1914–1923), a novel in seven volumes and Bregendahl's longest work. The story takes place between 1864 and 1885. The Jutlandic setting resembles that of *Hendrik i Bakken* and *En Dødsnat,* as do the finely rendered details of landscape and weather, and of peasant life and speech. In her preface to the first volume of *Billider af Sødalsfolkenes liv,* Bregendahl confirms that some of her previous characters reappear here; indeed, she makes the separate plots coalesce by the use of these recurring characters. She writes that she prefers to call her narratives *billeder* (pictures); the separate events in this work are pictured or mirrored in the consciousness of observers, either as groups or individuals. This technique of shifting points of view, *kollektiv spejling* (collective mirroring), recalls Bregendahl's approach in *En Dødsnat* where she used various points of view to present Anne Gram's death in childbirth. In *Billeder af Sødalsfolkenes liv,* Bregendahl conclusively establishes her gift for the evocation of character and atmosphere, and she excels in developing memorable individuals. In the opening pages of the first book, *Alvilda* (1914), Bregendahl sets the mood of tragic realism. The title character, Alvilda, appears on the crest of a hill in Sødal, a lone figure striding against the wind. Her story is then told in flashback.

The tragic realism of *Billeder af Sødalsfolkenes liv* includes the miserable lives of women such as Alvilda who have chosen to love the wrong man. These peasant heroines have become trapped between loyalty to their families and their desire for freedom from family restrictions. In several of the stories the woman chooses a male stranger to help her escape from her familiar milieu; however, in nearly every case each woman's love is denigrated by her partner, resulting in the woman's insanity or death. This pattern of tragic alliance in Bregendahl's writing began in *Hendrik i Bakken,* continued in *En Dødsnat,* and finds fresh expression in *Billeder af Sødalsfolkenes liv.* Countering this theme are several stories depicting happy young peasants celebrating weddings, flirting, dancing, kissing, and making love during the light summer nights.

The final volume in *Billeder af Sødalsfolkenes liv* is *Den gamle Provst* (The Old Rural Dean, 1923). This book represents a departure for Bregendahl in two ways: here she discusses the increasing political power of nineteenth-century Danish peasants, and she focuses on a male protagonist. The author portrays Johan Frederik Richardt as an old man obsessed with himself; he believes his two daughters lie to him, and he thinks the people of Sødal reject him. His life seems wasted, and painful memories haunt the old dean as he remembers his failures and lies. Bregendahl exposes the hypocrisy

MARIE BREGENDAHL

SØDALSFOLKENE

GYLDENDAL

Cover for the first book of the two-volume 1935 edition of Bregendahl's epic novel of rural life, originally published in seven volumes as Billeder af Sødalsfolkenes liv *(1914–1923)*

of this pillar of the rural community–*Den gamle Provst* is a social commentary on the corrupt paternalism of a provincial culture.

The volume about the old rural dean concludes the series of pictures of the lives of the people of Sødal. At the time of publication Bregendahl explains that this story was always meant to conclude *Billeder fra Sødalsfolkenes liv,* saying that *Den gamle Provst* was intended to give a glimpse of the political upheavals in Denmark around 1885 with sketches of some of the prominent leaders and political figures, but concentrating on the old, paternalistic, rural dean, Johan Frederik Richardt. With this story Bregendahl expanded her pictures of Danish rural life to include serious consideration of national social and political issues.

In a different vein, for her next work Bregendahl chose to write about the psychology of young girls. *Med aabne Sind: To smaa Pigers Oplevelser og Indtryk* (With an Open Mind: Two Little Girls' Experiences and Impressions, 1926) is a collection of six stories featuring two contrasting characters, the young sisters Elsebet and Grethe. The author illustrates their maturation in a series of astutely observed tragedies mirrored in the girls' feelings. The style is that of *Billeder af Sødalsfolkenes liv:* a familiar and local nar-

rator tells stories in a measured tempo. The point of view regularly shifts to that of the young girls. The events described–a fire, a suicide by hanging, and the death of an impoverished woman–are horrible, both in themselves and in their effect on the young girls. The final story, "I de lange mørke Nætter," (In the Long Dark Nights) is set in Lofoten, Norway. Elsebet and Grethe have grown old. Elsebet remembers an event from their childhood, when Anders, a servant boy on their farm, was dismissed for petty theft. Anders has recently been sentenced to eight years in jail for robbery. Grethe minimizes the event, while Elsebet feels responsible. Jolted by the memory, Elsebet realizes, too late, that she was responsible for Anders's dismissal. This theme of guilt and remorse for past betrayal echoes the story about the old rural dean.

Bregendahl was conscious of her mission as social historian. In 1937 she remarked:

Mange siger, at *Sødalsfolkene* er mit Hovedværk. Jeg mener snarere, det er *Holger Hauge.* . . . jeg vilde give et Billede af dansk Bondeliv i Overgangen fra den gamle Tid til Mejerierne og Andelsvæsnet. Bogen skulde være et Monument for den Tid.

(Many say that *Sødalsfolkene* is my major work. I think it is rather *Holger Hauge.* . . . I wanted to present a picture of Danish peasant life during the transition from the old days to the dairies and cooperative movement. The book was intended as a monument to that time.)

The full title of the book, *Holger Hauge og hans Hustru: Roman fra en historisk Tid* (Holger Hauge and His Wife: Novel from an Historic Time, 1934), underscores Bregendahl's intent to write social history. The action of this novel occurs from 1877 to 1901, during a time of major changes in Danish agriculture. These new developments included the reclamation of the Jutland heath for cultivation, the rise of cooperative dairies, and the industrialization of Danish agriculture. *Holger Hauge og hans Hustru* is informed by Bregendahl's understanding of the cost of such reforms as she recreates the resistance of the old guard of Danish farmers to the "new man," Holger Hauge. Most movingly, she portrays the sacrifice of Holger Hauge's wife, Kirstine Vendelbo, who represents the old peasant values that must give way to the new market economy.

Holger Hauge og hans Hustru is an ambitious novel demonstrating Bregendahl's understanding of the human psyche, both female and male. In addition, the author also reflects on the intellectual currents of the 1890s articulated by the new ideas of Georg Brandes. From a feminist perspective *Holger Hauge og hans Hustru* is a tribute to the single mother. Where other female characters in Bregendahl's earlier fiction had succumbed to their husbands and lovers, Kirstine, a widowed mother of two and the future wife of Holger Hauge, supports her children by working as a dairymaid. When she chooses Holger, she enters into a partnership. In her quiet way, she becomes the agent of change in the peasant society of Sødal. The couple share a deep physical attraction, and both are intelligent and ambitious; however, the rapid changes in the community demand that Kirstine sacrifice her ambitions and happiness to ensure Holger's success.

Kirstine feels her life is confining but she nevertheless chooses to put all her energy into becoming the most respected peasant woman in her community. In her marriage to Holger, Kirstine suffers in silence because she understands that she can only achieve power through a man. After several years, Kirstine's anger projects itself as hatred of Holger sexuality, health, and masculinity. She becomes sick and dies prematurely. Holger is devastated by her death—only after he has lost her does he realize his wife's worth. In an epilogue to the novel, set at the beginning of World War I, twenty-five years after Kirstine's death, the reader learns that Holger has become rich, owning factories and driving an automobile. However, he sells his factories and other possessions to return to his farm. Meeting an old friend, Rørdam, at Kirstine's grave, he says: "Jeg synes ikke der har været noget ved det Stykke liv, jeg har levet, siden Kirstine døde" (I don't think life has had any meaning since Kirstine died). He has known other women since Kirstine, but feels only half alive without his wife: "En Mand er en Mand, en Kvinde en Kvinde, men et *Menneske,*—et Menneske, Rørdam, det er en Mand *og* en Kvinde." (A man is a man, a woman a woman, but a *human being*—a human being, Rørdam, that is a man *and* a woman.)

The brief autobiography, *Smaa Kommentarer til Aakjærs Erindringer,* appeared in 1936, two years after the publication of *Holger Hauge og hans Hustru.* This volume is Bregendahl's response to negative comments about her family made by her former husband in his memoirs. In a self-deprecating tone, Bregendahl counters Aakjær's disparaging remarks about her parents, her sister, and herself. She tells several anecdotes about helping Aakjær both financially and through her connections in Copenhagen.

Bregendahl's last novel, *Birgitte Borg* (1941), was published posthumously. The action begins in 1864 after the Danish army was defeated by the Germans at Dybbøl, and the setting is a large farm in an area similar to Sødal. The novel is permeated with love of home and work, detailing especially the toil of farm wives. Bregendahl describes the women's spinning, slaughtering of sheep, salting and preserving, smoking of meats, making of butter and cheese, cooking, washing, baking, and brewing. The young Birgitte Borg loses her mother in a tragic accident. This theme of loss, together with Bregendahl's chronicle of peasant life and toil before industrialization, recalls both *Hendrik i Bakken* and *En Dødsnat.*

On her seventieth birthday Bregendahl was still living in Copenhagen. She was working and full of vitality, noting in the *Nationaltidende* interview

Jeg blev Forfatter i en moden Alder, og jeg lagde straks en Plan, som jeg vilde følge, naar jeg skrev. Jeg har fulgt min Plan. Men jeg har det værste tilbage! Derfor bryder jeg mig Pokker om Halvfjerdsaarsalderen. Det afgørende er at faa skrevet det, som skal skrives. Det er det, det gælder om. Jeg har det værste tilbage. Det siger jeg, og det staar jeg ved. . . .

(I became a writer late in life, and I immediately made a plan to follow in my writing. I have followed my plan. But the worst is left to do! That is why I don't care a damn about being in my seventies. The important thing is to write that which must be written. That is what it is all about. The worst is left to do. That is what I say and that is what I mean. . . .)

Marie Bregendahl died of peritonitis 22 July 1940, a few months after the beginning of the German Occupation of Denmark during World War II. During her seventy-three years she succeeded in transforming herself from a farmer's daughter to a major Danish author. Work was a means of self-expression for Bregendahl. She was a single mother and working woman whose five novels and ten volumes of short stories, including *En Dødsnat, Billeder af Sødalsfolkenes liv,* and *Holger Hauge og Hans Hustru* have become classics in Denmark. Her writings display a schooled artistry in their portrayal of the human psyche, with Bregendahl's modern technique of mirroring the impact of events in her characters' feelings, and they commemorate a now-extinct peasant way of life. Both in her life and her works Bregendahl proved how painful and exhilarating it can be to live a full human life. In the *Nationaltidende* interview, three years before her death, she told a journalist, "Saa længe Danmark bestaar, tror jeg nok, det vil være af Betydning for mine Medmennesker, hvad jeg skriver!" (As long as Denmark exists, I dare to believe that what I write will be meaningful to my fellow human beings!) The continued popularity of her works and recent scholarly studies have confirmed Bregendahl's eminence as a literary artist.

Interviews:

"Hos Marie Bregendahl," *Sorø Amtstidendes Søndagslæsning* (16 February 1913);

"Marie Bregendahl," *Bogvennen* (1914): 384–385;

Inger Bræstrup, "Marie Bregendahls ny Bog," *Politiken* (20 November 1921);

"Efteraarslitteraturen. En Samtale med Marie Bregendahl," *Aalborg Venstreblad* (27 October 1923);

Aage, "Forfatterinden Marie Bregendahl," *Sorø Amtstidende* (4 November 1927);

Vidi, "Marie Bregendahl om sit Liv og sin Digtning," *Politiken* (3 November 1937);

"Jeg ved, at jeg har det værste tilbage," *Nationaltidende* (5 November 1937).

Biography:

Bjarne Nielsen Brovst, *Jeppe og Marie: En romanbiografi om Jeppe Aakjær og Marie Bregendahl* (Copenhagen: Centrum, 1988).

References:

P. M. Andersen, *Marie Bregendahl* (Copenhagen: Gyldendal, 1946);

Anette Bøtter-Jensen, "Barndomslandets generobring: Tab og vinding hos fire kvindelige bondeforfattere," M.A. thesis, Odense University, 1987;

Jørgen Falgaard, "Marie Bregendahl og det gamle bondemiljø. Nogle aspekter af hendes Sødalsdigtning," *Extracta,* 4 (1972): 86–91;

Emil Frederiksen, "Marie Bregendahl," *Danske digtere i det 20. aarhundrede,* volume 1, edited by Ole Restrup (Copenhagen: Gad, 1955), pp. 7–25;

Birgitte Hesselaa, "Marie Bregendahl," *Danske digtere i det 20. århundrede,* volume 1, edited by Torben Brostrøm and Mette Winge (Copenhagen: Gad, 1980), pp. 183–196;

Peder Hesselaa, *Marie Bregendahl* (Copenhagen: Haase, 1939);

Inger-Lise Hjordt-Vetlesen, "At blive digter," *Nordisk kvindelitteraturhistorie,* volume 3, edited by Elisabeth Møller Jensen and others (Copenhagen: Rosinante-Munksgaard, 1996), pp. 104–112;

Hjordt-Vetlesen, *Ord der løfter sig: Om latteren i Marie Bregendahls fortællinger* (Odense: Menneske og Natur, Humanistisk Forskningscenter, Odense University, 1993);

Frank Rojkjær Pedersen, "Marie Bregendahl: *Billeder af Sødalsfolkenes liv,*" *Skrifter fra Instituttet for Litteraturhistorie,* 2, no. 4 (1981): 56–67;

Carl Raaschou, "Bonde-og almuesindet hos Marie Bregendahl," *Skivebogen,* 58 (Skive: Skive Folkeblads Bogtrykkeri, 1967): 25–57;

Povl Schmidt and Jørgen Gleerup, eds., *Drift og socialitet: Analyse af fortællinger og malerier om hverdagslivet på landet i det 19. århundredes slutning samt kulturhistorisk bibliografi* (Odense: Odense University Press, 1983);

Schmidt, *Indføling og afstand: artikler og essays* (Copenhagen: Rosinante-Munksgaard, 1989);

Anne Mygind Sørensen, "At være kvinde i en brydningstid: Fiktion og virkelighed–Birgitte Borg og Marie Bregendahl," M.A. thesis, Odense University, 1987.

Papers:

The major collection of Marie Bregendahl's papers is at Det Kongelige Bibliotek (The Royal Library), Copenhagen.

Suzanne Brøgger

(18 November 1944 –   )

Tanya Thresher
University of Wisconsin–Madison

BOOKS: *Fri os fra kærligheden* (Copenhagen: Rhodos, 1973); translated by Thomas Teal as *Deliver us from Love* (New York: Delacorte, 1976; London: Quartet, 1977);

Kærlighedens veje & vildveje (Copenhagen: Rhodos, 1975)—includes "Ingenmandsland," translated by Christine Badcock as "No Man's Land" in *No Man's Land: An Anthology of Modern Danish Women's Literature,* edited by Annegret Heitmann (Norwich, U.K.: Norvik Press, 1987), pp. 109–127;

Creme Fraiche: En Føljeton (Copenhagen: Rhodos, 1978);

En gris som har været oppe at slås kan man ikke stege (Copenhagen: Rhodos, 1979); translated by Marina Allemano as *A Fighting Pig's Too Tough To Eat* (Norwich, U.K.: Norvik Press, 1997);

Brøg: 1965–1980 (Copenhagen: Rhodos, 1980);

Tone: Epos (Copenhagen: Rhodos, 1981);

Ja: Føljeton (Copenhagen: Rhodos, 1984);

Den pebrede susen: Flydende fragmenter og fixeringer (Copenhagen: Rhodos, 1986);

Edvard og Elvira: En ballade (Copenhagen: Rhodos, 1988);

Kvælstof: 1980–1990 (Copenhagen: Rhodos, 1990);

Min verden i en nøddeskal, illustrated by Fleur Brofos Asmussen (Copenhagen: Rhodos, 1991);

Efter orgien: En tragedi, translated by Ann-Mari Seeberg (Stockholm: Wahlström Widstrand, 1991); republished as *Efter orgiet: En tragedie* (Copenhagen: Rhodos, 1992);

Paradisets mave (Copenhagen: Høst & Søn, 1993);

Transperence: Føljeton (Copenhagen: Gyldendal, 1993);

Vølvens spådom (Brøndum: Aschehoug, 1994);

Løvespor: Essays, edited by Birthe Meldgård Mortensen (Copenhagen: Gyldendal, 1995);

Jadekatten: En Slægtssaga (Copenhagen: Gyldendal, 1997);

Et frit og muntert lig (Copenhagen: Brøndum, 1998).

PLAY PRODUCTIONS: *Efter orgien,* Stockholm, Kungliga Dramatiska Teatern, 23 October 1991; produced again, Copenhagen, Det Kongelige Teater, 15 March 1993; produced again as *After the Orgy,*

Suzanne Brøgger (photograph by Gregers Nielsen; from the dust jacket for Tone: Epos, *1981)*

Washington, D.C., Church Street Theater, 23 September 1992;

Dark, Frederiksberg, Betty Nansen Teatret, 11 October 1994.

In *Creme Fraiche: En Føljeton* (Crème Frâiche: A Feuilleton, 1978) Danish novelist and essayist Suzanne Brøgger tells of a Chinese potter who throws himself into the kiln to supply more oxygen to the glaze on a bowl. Just like the Chinese potter, Brøgger throws her whole being into her work in order to bring life and literature as close together as possible. The desire to live as she writes and write as she lives means that Brøgger writes from an intensely personal vantage point. She mixes autobiography, philosophical reflection, fiction, and documentation into a textual synthesis that is often difficult to categorize.

Brøgger's works are constantly developing, as her writing process matures and old selves and old language are cast off. Each text thus becomes an examination of the validity of previous texts, part of an internal dialogue that constantly questions and redefines itself. Happy to explore various literary genres, Brøgger has written five novels, five collections of essays and stories, two plays, one epic poem, a ballad, and two children's books, along with countless pieces of journalism. She mixes genres together and juxtaposes the lyrical with the prosaic, the elegant with the bawdy, and the trivial with the deeply philosophical. Her work is therefore difficult to categorize, but some critics have designated her mode of writing as creative nonfiction or fictional autobiography. As an ambiguous autobiographer writing predominantly in the first person, the narrator forces the reader to become a voyeur, and this voyeuristic aspect of her writing has caused some readers to find Brøgger's work unnerving. Consequently Brøgger has suffered harsh criticism throughout her career. Nevertheless, her work has been translated into fourteen languages and stands out as uniquely different from the works of her Danish contemporaries.

Even as a child she felt different from those around her. The eldest daughter of Ove Preis and Lilian Henius, Suzanne Preia was born in Copenhagen on 18 November 1944. She was educated at Bernadotteskolen until she was fourteen, when she moved with her mother and stepfather to Bangkok and Ceylon, taking her stepfather's name. Already conscious of her appearance, Brøgger worked as a teenage model in Bangkok and had short modeling stints in Copenhagen. She returned to Denmark in order to attend Th. Langs Boarding School in Silkeborg and to take her university entrance examination.

Although Brøgger had been writing since she was fifteen, it was not until she was thirty years old that she made her literary debut. Prior to this she had been combining her university studies with journalism, a career she held for the greater part of a decade. She traveled widely in the Soviet Union and in the Middle and Far East, working as a reporter. Believing in the importance of creating the writer before the writing, Brøgger emphasized not what she wrote, but rather from where she was writing. She decided that it was necessary to write from an exposed place where one was forced to compromise oneself.

Her first book, *Fri os fra kærligheden* (1973; translated as *Deliver us from Love,* 1976), targets the bourgeois family and marriage for their inability to allow individual freedom—in particular erotic freedom. A mixture of journalism and fiction, the book comprises fifteen reflective essays that question established attitudes toward sex, love, religion, and death. As the title of the book implies, Brøgger advocates a move away from the kind of love the West has valued—the kind of love connected with marriage, and hence, for Brøgger, with unlived life, isolation, and "cannibalism," by which Brøgger means "possessive repression." Brøgger defines love rather as an attraction between human beings, or a meeting between people full of possibilities for adventure and change.

Claiming that traditional value systems have become outdated, Brøgger concentrates on the female role in society. In an essay titled "Det naturlige er nu det kønneste" (Just Be Natural) she makes the point that there is no such thing as a natural woman. Stating that appearances are our real identities, she claims that the only true women—apart from some examples in psychiatric wards—are transvestites, as they play the feminine role to the hilt. On a more defiant note, Brøgger describes the rape of her narrator by police officers in Uzbekistan in the essay "Voldtægt" (Rape). The piece received much press attention, which concentrated on the violation and the apparent ease with which the narrator resigned herself to her fate rather than on the attitude of the male aggressors or the powerlessness of the victim.

Brøgger presents female experience as one side of a combined male/female spectrum in this work. Because she never fully explores a uniquely female experience, which was so fundamental to the women's movement at the time, Brøgger was highly criticized by feminists during the 1970s and 1980s. Despite the book's popularity in Denmark, where fifty thousand copies were sold by 1979, and in France, where there were three editions in print by that same year, the book never became popular in the United States, where feminists were reluctant to accept Brøgger as a serious social commentator. Radical feminists viewed her writing as detrimental to the cause; they accused Brøgger of bourgeois individualism and of being the victim of male fixations.

Nevertheless, in 1974 Brøgger was invited by the Dansk Kuindesamfond (Danish Women's Society) to give a *båltale* (bonfire speech) at their seventy-fifth anniversary at Copenhagen's city hall. The speech, "At ville eller ikke ville" (To Want or Not To Want), which was later published in *Kærlighedens veje & vildveje* (Love's Paths and Pitfalls, 1975), was controversial and highly criticized. In it Brøgger claimed that emancipation was a matter of will and that if women really wanted to, they could liberate themselves from repression. Rather than revolt against patriarchal society on its own terms, Brøgger challenged women to cast off their fear of change and admonished them to take their sexuality seriously.

In form and content *Kærlighedens veje & vildveje* is an extension of Brøgger's previous work. It also introduces characters and themes that appear in later works, such as the milliner Fru Nynne, who is a prototype for the protagonist in the epic poem *Tone: Epos* (1981). Where this collection of reflective essays differs somewhat from its predecessor is perhaps in such utopian texts as "Ingenmandsland" (translated as "No Man's Land," 1987). Like Virginia Woolf, Brøgger calls for a new place for women in this piece, but her place far exceeds the "room of one's own" that Woolf envisioned. Brøgger wants a new, creative land, an empty space that does not exclude people on the grounds of gender and that lies beyond a binary oppositional system. In spite of the utopian call, a discerning reader notices a certain discrepancy between this essay and the fictive and autobiographical essays in both collections. Nevertheless, the strength in these two collections lies in their challenge to scrutinize contemporary culture and to break free of the fear of change.

Creme Fraiche, the first part of a trilogy that also comprises *Ja: Føljeton* (Yes: Feuilliton, 1984) and *Transperence: Føljeton* (Transparency: Feuilliton, 1993), is a book about change. It relates the coming-of-age of its unnamed first-person narrator, who shares many biographical details with Brøgger, such as her parents' divorce, her schooling, her interviews with famous people when working as a reporter, and her travels in the Far East. Because of the obvious correspondence between the heroine and Brøgger, the work is difficult to categorize as either autobiography or fiction, and again it has led to much speculation about Brøgger's private life.

Rather than choose women's suffering as the subject of her text, as did so many women writers of the time, Brøgger relates the story of an ecstatic journey around the world by her sexually charged heroine. Although not as morally provoking as her previous texts, this picaresque tale once more pushes the female role to its limits. The irony of the feminine mask is again explored as the protagonist has to masquerade as a drag queen in order to be admitted into a New York gay club. As the heroine enters the world of Eros in exotic settings, she also gives fine descriptions of other characters and life at a Danish boarding school. With the tiger as a symbol for herself, the heroine celebrates her own strength, independence, and wildness. Using a technique that has become typical in her work, Brøgger also explores a second consciousness in the text–in this case, the adolescent

Cover for Brøgger's 1975 collection of essays, which includes the controversial 1974 address in which she asserted women could be liberated without challenging traditional institutions

heroine's lover and adviser in the ways of life, Max. Dialogue and letters supposedly written by Max allow him to speak in his own voice and disclose opinions about the heroine. The heroine's obvious vitality and joy of life has been read as a narcissistic trait, and the book ends with a warning that this fantastic journey of erotic self-discovery will have to end and that the heroine must find a place to land from her flights of fancy.

Brøgger's next book, *En gris som har været oppe at slås kan man ikke stege* (1979; translated as *A Fighting Pig's Too Tough to Eat,* 1997), is an exploration of that landing, a complement to the cosmopolitan *Creme Fraiche* depicting a more tranquil lifestyle. More condensed than its predecessor, it consists of brief aphoristic pictures of the narrator's life in the Danish village of Løve, West Zealand, where Brøgger has lived since 1970. The poetic narrative is interwoven

SUZANNE BRØGGER
EFTER ORGIET

R H O D O S

*Cover for the first Danish edition (1992) of Brøgger's first play,
originally published in Swedish the previous year*

with observations on the Cluny Tapestries of the Lady and the Unicorn and with Rainer Marie Rilke's comments on these images. Dedicated to the five senses and a nondescript sixth, "A mon seul désir" (To my only desire), the text explores concepts of otherness, change, and textuality. On one level the cosmopolitan narrator represents the Other in this disappearing rural community, standing in sharp contrast to her neighbors, Signe and Axel. On another level, however, it is possible to identify the narrator with the Lady from the tapestries, about whom the text repetitively asks, "Er hun den samme dame? Eller er hun en anden?" (Is she the same

lady? Or is she another?). Finally, the narrative self becomes one with the collective outcry against this vanishing culture.

Brøgger has labeled this text as an anthropological study in alterity, a meeting place of two different worlds that exist side by side. Death is a predominant theme, but it is not depicted negatively as long as it is not a living death. As a celebration of rural life, the text makes use of the soap-opera genre and includes much trivia about the everyday lives of the villagers—their successes at bingo and their relationships to one another. The text is also full of sensual imagery and cunning dialogue. It remains one of Brøgger's most popular works.

Brøg: 1965–1980 (Brew: 1965–1980, 1980) is a retrospective scrapbook that, with its eclectic collection of essays, interviews, and travel pieces from 1965 until 1980, indicates Brøgger's long-lasting links to freelance journalism. The title is both a play on the author's surname and an allusion to witchcraft, which Brøgger deems necessary to society. In the essay "Hvad skal vi med Hexe?" (Who Needs Witches?) Brøgger reveres witchcraft as a subversive way of pursuing pleasure. Brøgger's identification with and interest in witches allies her with Karen Blixen (Isak Dinesen), who has been a model for Brøgger and about whom there is a profound analysis in this collection. The central essay, "Karen Blixen og lidenskaben" (Karen Blixen and Passion), calls attention to Blixen's overlooked essay "Moderne ægteskab og andre betragtninger" (1981; translated as *On Modern Marriage and Other Observations,* 1986), written in the 1920s, which deals with many of the themes Brøgger has explored in her own work. Comparing this work to Blixen's letters and life, Brøgger analyses Blixen's relationship to free love and concludes that Blixen was able to modernize old values and create her own destiny.

Similar in theme to Blixen's essay, the final essay in the collection, "Forførelse og hengivelse" (Seduction and Submission), is a sharp critique of sexuality in Western society. Brøgger claims that Eros has had his wings clipped in our age and that sexuality has been reduced to the purely mechanical. Rather than contradicting her previous work, which celebrated free love, this piece is a lament over the fact that sexual emancipation, in which Brøgger so obviously sees magical powers, has been cut off from inner freedom. As society is now unable to be carried away by Eros, Brøgger anticipates an implosion of all its values.

Tone, for which Brøgger was awarded *De Gyldne Laurbær* (The Golden Laurels) prize in 1982, is a celebration of life as desire and creativity, and it is a rhythmical, poetical portrait of an ideal woman, the costumier Tone Bonnén. Graphically represented as free verse, this "kvindekvad til alle i trange tider" (woman's ballad for all those in need in difficult times) is an epic poem that paints a portrait of Tone and traces her life and death through brief anecdotes told by a third-person narrator, her family, and acquaintances. The poem constructs an historical frame around the story, which is enhanced by the many mythical allusions in the text, the archaic turns of phrase, and the internal rhyming so closely associated with skaldic verse. This quality is cleverly juxtaposed with the jovial jargon of the Copenhagen dialect, and together these stylistic turns give the piece a certain timeless quality.

Tone is a woman larger than life; rather like the tart she is named after, she "var den, der var mest af alt i" (was the one there was most of everything in). The piece chronicles her life from childhood, through an unhappy marriage and abandonment by her husband, to several affairs, sickness, and eventually death. After being freed from her marriage, Tone lives a bohemian life, breaking norms and enriching those around her. Refusing to let herself be tied down, Tone spreads her love to many people, fusing sexual love with love of humankind. Her bohemian life is balanced by a centered, well-organized self, which makes her a strong, creative individual. The final third of the book is devoted to an unsentimental description of Tone's long struggle with cancer and her death. On her deathbed she decides to remarry, and her yearning for love is finally satisfied as Eros enters her life. At the end of the poem, the balloon symbolizing her death rises into the sky to the words of a New York gospel choir, "Only love to give, only love to give." Tone's death becomes a movement into eternity and the precondition of the poem itself.

Ja also shows a movement from something into nothing. It begins with a statement rejecting the protagonist from *Creme Fraiche* and promising to trace a development "fra fix stjerne til–sort hul" (from a fixed star to–a black hole). *Ja* explores what happens when the erotic vagabond depicted in *Creme Fraiche* feels the need to belong to a community. It chronicles a metamorphosis from outer emancipation through an implosion to a cosmic space where ecstasy and stability, love and freedom are no longer opposites, and body and spirit become one. Indebted to Taoist belief, it celebrates reality as a never-ending cyclical fluctuation between opposites.

The greater part of this four-hundred-page novel explores the depths and pain of an unhappy relationship between the female protagonist, Mischka, and her obstetrician lover. The protagonist experi- ences claustrophobia in the relationship, and she is constantly marginalized by her lover, who is jealous of her independence as a professional writer. She consequently becomes ambivalent toward her own identity. In an attempt to satisfy her lover, she says yes to his every whim, but eventually she reaches point zero in the relationship–graphically shown in the text by a page full of zeros.

In keeping with the biblical motifs so prominent in the book, the protagonist symbolically buries herself, but arises after three days. Her new persona is christened in a ceremonial orgy at a mystical French castle, where the protagonist reaches beyond herself and becomes totally receptive to life. The union of her body and her spirit and her newfound openness to the cosmos is shown graphically as the text splits into a stream-of-consciousness account of the orgy and a list of "JA's" in the margin. After having learned that the snake, so often associated with sin in Western Christianity, is a symbol of development and enlightenment in Taoism, she returns to Palestine. The book ends as it began, in Jerusalem, where the main character symbolizes her multiplicity by giving herself a male name, Mischka, and where she gets a wing tattooed on her heel. The wing symbolizes not only freedom from stasis, but also further connects the protagonist to the mythical, seductive Lillith, Adam's first wife, who rejected convention. The text ends with an insert story by the Arabic Kung Fu Olympic champion, Aznan, the story of "Den tomme hand"(The Empty Hand), which emphasizes the practice and dedication required to empty yourself to the world and become receptive to everything.

Many readers considered this book too long, confusing, and fragmented because of its pastiche of texts and styles, typographical experimentation, and labyrinthine story line. The main story is framed, and there are inset stories, digressions, letters from a Greek Orthodox Priest, and frequent quotations from Søren Kierkegaard, Edith Södergran, and Jonathon Schell, to name but a few. The quotations primarily address the acknowledged ambiguity of science and are complemented by the repeated use of the Hebrew phrase "Halvay shayaamod" (May this one last), attributed to God after his twenty-sixth attempt at creating the world. These quotations give the book a universal quality intended to offset the personal one in the main story.

The narrator, who is writing her story in a little black book similar to the one the reader is holding, uses flashback effects and irony to distance herself from the narration. Her frequent comments to the reader, along with the other stylistic effects, challenge

Cover for the English edition of Brøgger's novel En gris som har været oppe at slås kan man ikke stege *(1979)*

Brøgger believes it is possible for her writing to bear witness to the creative energy she calls "den pebrede susen" (the peppery sough) and that it might do so by using life's ordinary turns of phrase and sacred humbleness.

Writing is also a central theme in her next essay collection, *Kvælstof: 1980–1990* (Nitrogen: 1980–1990, 1990), but here this intensifying life experience is connected with death, which, in turn, is regarded as a necessary prerequisite for life. In "Om at kysse hesten" (Kissing the Horse) Brøgger claims that as long as we have biography, which she defines loosely as the ability to reflect humanity's evolution and enlightenment through language, then we have the remains of the concept of civilization. In "Den indre posedame" (The Inner Bag Lady) creativity is likened to the alarm a body sounds when it is becoming infected—in other words, it is a matter of life and death. The inner bag lady, whose persona is to be revived in Brøgger's dramatic debut, *Efter orgiet: En tragedie* (After the Orgy: A Tragedy, 1992) is clearly a persona Brøgger incarnates as; "hun kan ikke indoptages og blive salonfähig, for hun inkarnerer det uacceptable, det urovækkende, det forarglige og det forvirrende. Kort sagt, det spejl, som måske er uundværligt, og hvorom vi siger: Det burde ikke være her" (she cannot be reintegrated and made respectable, for she is the incarnation of the unacceptable, the disturbing, the shocking, and the confusing; in short, the mirror that perhaps is indispensable and about which we say: It ought not be here).

With its introduction of the concept of the inner bag lady and its several essays devoted to death and virus, *Kvælstof* provided fertile ground for Brøgger's next project, the tragedy *Efter orgiet*. The play was commissioned by Dramaten, the royal theater in Stockholm, premiering there in 1991 under the direction of Bibi Anderson, and was first published in a Swedish translation that same year. It received mixed reviews but has since been performed in several theaters in Denmark and has been translated into English by Lone Thygesen Blecher and George Blecher. Although unpublished, this translation was used for a performance in Washington, D.C., at the Church Street Theater as part of Scena Theater's 1992 New European Play Festival, where it won the Scena Drama Award for best play.

The play is a requiem mass for the sexual revolution that shows society in the shadow of pestilence. Using the AIDS epidemic as a referent, the piece demonstrates how the desire to release sexuality and the subsequent misuse of that sexuality have created a death wish that has become part of each individ-

the reader to do as the protagonist: to empty his or her mind of all preconceived ideas of the novel as genre and to be receptive to this new, holistic approach.

The collection *Den pebrede susen* (1986) continues the discussion of the dissolution of the self—the turning away from binary oppositions to a spiritual level akin to the religious state in Kierkegaardian philosophy, a non-dualistic experience of the transcendence of the self. Perhaps reflective of Brøgger's situation, this movement is closely allied with writing. Listening attentively to the peppery sough around her, Brøgger again reflects on her rural life in "Jeg lever som jeg skriver" (I Live as I Write and I Write as I Live) and investigates her childhood and Jewish heritage in "Om at gå over floden. Inspirationskilder og forudsætninger" (Crossing the River: Premises and Sources of Inspiration). In spite of claiming "Ord er slet ikke nok, ord er nærmere til skade, fordi de lukker og bekræfter der hvor de skulle åbne og chokere" (Words are not at all effective, words are actually harmful because they close off or confine when they should open up and shock),

ual's body. Rather than dealing directly with AIDS, the play is a critique of civilization played out in different *bardos,* or death realms, as in the Tibetan Book of the Dead. The relationship between death and sex is represented by the four major characters: a family consisting of Rigor and Mortis and their daughter, Vulva, and son, Lem (Dick). The frank depiction in the play of sexual freedom borders on becoming a catalogue of sexual perversion and deviance, and yet the work also exposes society's underlying prejudices about the HIV virus. Suggesting many far-fetched possible causes for the virus (for example, a green ape), the piece also describes the modern conspiracy to cover up the truth and deny individuals the right to an identity. Brøgger criticizes the fashion and cosmetic industries in particular, as they encourage an artificially constructed identity, and she asks her audience to remember that "den som kender alt, men mangler sig selv, mangler alt" (the person who knows everything, but is missing oneself, is missing everything).

The play is organized as a series of long monologues in four acts, each of which ends with a meditation on one of the four elements. The mythical figure Hecate, who unifies past, present, and future, acts as the narrator. In keeping with the Greek leitmotif in the play, the monologues of the main characters are interrupted and commented upon by a chorus, which also sings popular children's songs. These songs, along with the meditations, require audience participation, which Brøgger sees as one of the defining aspects of theater. For her, the advantages of theater over any other genre lies in its communality and its cathartic possibilities.

Brøgger once more surprised the Danish public in 1991 when she married assistant professor and author Keld Zeruneith. The marriage was heralded in Danish newspapers with such chiding headlines as "Ægteskabsmodtstander overgiver sig: Suzanne Brøgger gift," (Opponent of Marriage Gives Up: Suzanne Brøgger Married). The birth of a daughter fathered by Zeruneith in the mid 1980s had already sparked curiosity as to whether Brøgger was indeed rejecting the strong ideals against family and marriage portrayed in her first two books. On a literary level, the arrival of her daughter signaled a move for Brøgger into yet another genre, that of children's books. *Min verden i en nøddeskal* (My World in a Nutshell, 1991) is a fairy-tale account of the life, history, and culture of different countries around the world, and *Paradisets mave* (The Belly of Paradise, 1993) is told from the point of view of a fetus.

The year 1993 also marked the publication of the concluding part of Brøgger's trilogy, which had begun with *Creme fraiche* and *Ja. Transperence* was nominated for the Nordic Council's Literature Prize and continues Brøgger's exploration of alienation and quest for freedom in a spiritual sense. In this work the unnamed protagonist searches for her own voice with the help of an exiled Tibetan lama and by taking music lessons. She is also forced to face the madness in herself in the form of a crazy woman who attempts to steal the narrator's identity and in a man calling himself Jesus who camps on her doorstep. After lengthy battles with these doppelgänger figures, the narrator finally achieves a state of transparency, where the self dissolves and the individual is able to reach out to another human being.

In 1994 Brøgger showed her ability to link Nordic mythology to the world at large while she also demonstrated her adaptability as an artist. She translated from Old Norse *Volupspá,* the prophecy of the Nordic Sybil, Volva, which depicts the creation of the world and the apocalypse. In "Post" (Post), the only new essay in the collection *Løvespor* (Lion Tracks, 1995), Brøgger interprets the poem as a contemporary tale of existential growth that vibrates around conflict and opposition. It shows how one must fight through fire in order to reach a state of illumination.

The power of fire and its regenerative properties is again examined in Brøgger's second, and as yet unpublished, dramatic piece, *Dark,* which premiered at the Betty Nansen Theater, Frederiksberg, on 11 October 1994 under the direction of Katrine Wiedemann. A modern rewriting of the story of the Virgin of Orléans, Joan of Arc, *Dark* examines martyrdom in society. Brøgger's protagonist, Janne, is a singer from the world of pop music whose androgyny takes the form of anorexia, but rather than being martyred at the stake, Janne is consumed by a fire from within. Since *Dark,* Brøgger has continued to explore the dramatic medium and has written texts for two musical performance pieces.

Brøgger's *Jadekatten: En Slægtssaga* (The Jade Cat: A Family Saga, 1997) is a novel about a family. In more than six hundred pages it follows the fortunes of a Danish Jewish family through snapshots of the various family members. They travel from Denmark to Chicago, through Latvia and into Sweden, changing as their milieu changes, watching Europe change with them. As historical events in Europe are ever present in the text, the microfamily narrative is consciously linked with a macro-European perspective, while neither is compromised at the expense of the other. Tracing the links between family life and the course of history, Brøgger has again returned to her well-practiced medley of fiction and autobiography.

As Brøgger is often the subject of her sharply provocative writing and as she practices a highly conscious enactment of her own public image, she has become a myth in the eyes of the Danish public. Rather like her literary forerunner Blixen, Brøgger has successfully crafted a persona of mystery and camouflage. She continuously changes her public image and has thus attracted public curiosity of the sort usually reserved for movie stars or royalty. Yet, unlike Marilyn Monroe, about whom Brøgger writes in *Kærlighedens veje og vildveje,* she escapes entrapment in the myth she creates by constantly reinventing it. The intense public interest in Brøgger has not been without its share of controversy and scandal, especially as her work is often sprinkled with intimate revelations and confessions rather in the style of her role models Henry Miller and Anaïs Nin. Yet, this public display of her most private life, which has resulted in her being labeled a bourgeois sex priestess, has not led to a lack of political commitment or existential insight. Throughout her work, Brøgger questions social, political, and historical change and searches for a deeper understanding of the human spirit.

Interviews:

Karen-Maria Bille and Helle-Vibeke Riisgård, "Begærets alvor," *Teater-et,* no. 63 (1993): 22–24;

Peter Øvig Knudsen, "Suzanne Brøgger. Audiens," in *Børn skal ikke lege under fuldmånen* (Brøndum: Ashcehoug, 1995), pp. 61–91.

References:

Marina Allemano, "Figures, True Stories and Literary Patchwork: The Brøggeresque Subject," *Scandinavica,* 32, no. 2 (1993): 203–225;

Susanne Dygaard, "Skriftens liv: Om positioner og positionsskift hos Suzanne Brøgger," *Den blå port,* no. 13 (1989): 38–48;

Scott de Francesco, "The Reception of Suzanne Brøgger in Denmark and the United States," in *Literary Communication and Reception,* edited by Zorau Konstantinovic, Manfred Naumann, and Hans Robert Jauss (Innsbruck: AMOE/Institut für Sprachwissenschaft der Universität Innsbruck, 1980), pp. 371–375;

Birthe Haarder, "Magten og begæret," *Kultur og klasse,* 17, no. 3 (1990): 29–47;

Jens Kistrup, "Det sku' være forbudt at lade sig byde," in *Blixen Brøgger og andre danske damer* (Viby: Centrum, 1985), pp. 61–70; translated by W. Glyn Jones as "You Shouldn't Be Allowed to Put Up With It," in *Out of Denmark* (Copenhagen: Det Danske Selskab, 1985), pp. 77–88;

Jette Lundbo Levy, "Kniven og såret," *Forum: Tidskrift for køn og kultur,* 15, no. 4 (1995): 14–19;

Christen Nisted and Ole Thornye, "Kærlighed, kaos–kosmos? Om Suzanne Brøggers roman JA og hendes 'føljeton,'" *Kritik,* 18, no. 7 (1985): 85–100;

Bjarne Sandstrøm, "Personlighedens råderum: En læsning af Suzanne Brøggers Tone som portrætdigt," *Kritik,* 15, no. 60 (1982): 24–39;

May Schack, "Besværgelsens heroiske kraft: Om forsvarsmekanismer og Suzanne Brøggers forfatterskab," *Kritik,* 14, no. 58 (1981): 7–28.

Inger Christensen
(16 January 1935 –   )

Thomas Satterlee
University of Miami

BOOKS: *Lys: Digte* (Copenhagen: Gyldendal, 1962)–
includes "Læner mit ømt natten" and "I bjergenes
Vilde ensomhed," translated by Alexander Taylor
as "Leaning Against the Night" and "In the Wild
Mountain Solitude," in *Contemporary Danish Poetry:
An Anthology,* edited by Line Jensen and others
(Copenhagen: Gyldendal / Boston: Twayne,
1977), pp. 260, 261; "Hvad er min døde sprokne
Krop," and "Sorg," translated by Nadia Chris-
tensen as "What is My Dead Cracked Body" and
"Sorrow," in *Contemporary Danish Poetry: An Anthol-
ogy,* edited by Jensen and others (Copenhagen:
Gyldendal / Boston: Twayne, 1977), pp. 261, 262;

Græs: Digte (Copenhagen: Gyldendal, 1963);

Evighedsmaskinen (Copenhagen: Gyldendal, 1964);

Azorno: Roman (Copenhagen: Gyldendal, 1967);

Det (Copenhagen: Gyldendal, 1969)–selections translated by Inger Christensen and Suzanne Nied as
"Inger Christensen: 'Stage: connectivities, vari-
abilities'; 'Epilogos,' from *It,*" in *No Man's Land: An
Anthology of Modern Danish Women's Literature,* edited
by Annegret Heitmann (Norwich, U.K.: Norvik
Press, 1987), pp. 69–107;

Intriganterne: Et teaterstykke (Copenhagen: Gyldendal,
1972);

Det malede værelse: En fortælling fra Mantua (Copenhagen:
Brøndum, 1976); translated by Denise Newman
as *The Painted Room* (London: Harvill, 2000);

Brev i april (Copenhagen: Brøndum, 1979);

alfabet (Copenhagen: Gyldendal, 1981) translated by Nied
as *alphabet* (London: Bloodaxe Books, 2000);

Del af labyrinten: Essays (Copenhagen: Gyldendal, 1982);

Den store ukendte rejse, illustrated by Vibe Vestergaard
(Copenhagen: Gad, 1982);

En vinteraften i Ufa og andre spil (Copenhagen: Gyldendal,
1987);

Septemberfortællingerne, by Christensen and others
(Copenhagen: Brøndum, 1988);

Mikkel og hele menageriet, illustrated by Lillian Brøgger
(Copenhagen: Høst, 1990);

Inger Christensen in 1969 (photograph by Gregers Nielsen)

Sommerfugledalen: Et requiem (Copenhagen: Brøndum,
1991); translated by Nied as *The Valley of Butterflies*
(Dublin: Dedalus, 1999);

Hemmelighedstilstanden (Copenhagen: Gyldendal, 1999).

Collections and Editions: *Alfabet: Digte,* afterword by
Claus Engstrom (Copenhagen: Gyldendal, 1988);

Digte af Inger Christensen, selected by Asger Schnack
(Copenhagen: Hans Reitzel, 1988);

Lys og græs (Copenhagen: Gyldendal, 1989);

Samlede digte (Copenhagen: Gyldendal, 1998).

RADIO: *En aften på Kgs. Nytorv: Et radiospil,* script by
Christensen, Danmarks Radio, 12 December
1975;

Stor og lille scener af Botho Strauss, translation by Chris-
tensen, adaptation by Anders Carlberg of Botho
Strauss's *Gross und Klein, Radioteatret,* Danmarks
Radio, 1981;

Penelopes væv: Et musikdrama for radio, translation by Christensen of a script by Nicole Macé, *Radioteatret,* Danmarks Radio, 1982;

Jeg elsker min elskede: Radiospil, translation by Christensen of Fay Weldon's *I Love My Love, Radioteatret,* Danmarks Radio, 1983.

TELEVISION: *Ægteskabet mellem lyst og nød: Et TV-spil,* script by Christensen, *TV-Teaterafdelingen,* Danmarks Radio, 10 December 1975;

Ørknens luftsyn et TV-spil, script by Christensen, *TV-Teaterafdelingen,* Danmarks Radio, 25 May 1975;

Kasimir og Karoline: Et folkestykke, translation by Christensen of Ödön von Horváth's *Kasimir und Karoline, TV-Teaterafdelingen,* Danmarks Radio, 1982;

Brændende tålmodighed: Et skuespil, translation by Christensen of Antonio Skármeta's *Ardiente paciencia, TV-Teaterafdelingen,* Danmarks Radio, 1983.

OTHER: *Ny tysk prosa,* selected and translated by Christensen and Poul Borum (Copenhagen: Stig Vendel-Kaers Forlag, 1965);

Tove Ditlevsen, *Noveller,* edited by Christensen (Copenhagen: Gyldendal, 1977);

Krig eller fred?: Temanummer om sikkerhedspolitik, edited by Christensen, Niels I. Meyer, and Ole Thyssen (Copenhagen: Gyldendal, 1981).

TRANSLATIONS: Max Frisch, *Bin eller rejsen til Peking* (Copenhagen: Gyldendal, 1967);

Euripides, *Medea* (Copenhagen: Gyldendal, 1973);

Jürgen Fuchs, *Daglige notater: Digte* (Copenhagen: Albatros, 1980);

Marilynne Robinson, *Hus og hjem* (Copenhagen: Gyldendal, 1982);

Wislawa Szymborska, *Lots hustru og andre kvinder: Digte,* translated by Christensen and Janina Katz (Copenhagen: Brøndum, 1982);

Rainer Werner Fassbinder, *Den brændende by Rainer Werner Fassbinder (efter Lope de Vega)* (Århus: Arkona, 1983);

Staffan Seeberg, *Hvor havet begynder: Roman* (Charlottenlund: Rosinante, 1983);

Virginia Woolf, *Tre guineas* (Charlottenlund: Rosinante, 1983);

Slavko Janevski, Blaze Koneski, and Mateja Matevski, *Den forstenede Orfeus tre makedonske digtere,* translated by Christensen and Jane Kabel (Copenhagen: Brøndum, 1985).

Since the 1960s Inger Christensen has been one of the most important and most popular poets in Denmark. Her contribution to Danish literature includes novels, short stories, essays, plays (for stage, radio, and television), and children's books; but she is best known for her poetry. Christensen has published six volumes of poetry, each successive volume gaining her greater recognition as a poet of remarkable originality. Her poetry appeals to a wide audience: politicians and political demonstrators alike have quoted from some of her well-known poems, and two of her collections have been set to music.

Inger Christensen was born on 16 January 1935, the daughter of Adolf Christensen, a tailor, and Erna Christensen, a factory worker. She was raised in a working-class neighborhood of Vejle, a provincial town in Jutland. The first in her family to attend a gymnasium, a secondary school that prepares students for the university, Christensen recalls being the only child from the working class in her entire school. Moving between school and home was, therefore, a strain for her, and she remembers being teased in school for her dialect and instructed to pronounce works "correctly." When she brought her educated speech home, however, she was promptly put in her place. Christensen's parents were neither artists nor inclined toward the arts, yet she credits them with instilling in her one of her most recognizable qualities as an artist: the desire to create a sense of order, a trait which becomes especially clear in her third volume of poetry.

In 1954 Christensen graduated from the gymnasium and began her training as an elementary-school teacher at Århus Seminarium (Teacher's College), where she received her teacher certification in 1958. Christensen had chosen a career in teaching because she thought it would give her free time for her writing, but during her years at the teacher's college she began to doubt whether she wanted to be a writer. These doubts led her to study medicine at the university, with the intention of becoming a doctor. Although she ultimately returned to her original career choice, the classes she took in chemistry, physics, math, and physiology made a strong impression on her and eventually found their way into her poetry.

While attending college, Christensen published her earliest poems in *Hvedekorn* (Grains of Wheat), a literary journal in which many Danish poets begin their careers. It was through letters she exchanged with the editor of this publication that Christensen learned of Poul Borum, another young poet who also lived in Århus. The relationship between the two writers quickly grew serious, and within half a year of their meeting, Poul proposed to her "på bagperronen af en linje 8 på Ringgaden" (on the back of a number 8 bus on Ring Street). They were married on 8 August 1959.

Literary ambitions filled their early years together, and both Christensen and Borum have published accounts describing their shared devotion to liter-

Christensen in 1981 (photograph by Gregers Nielsen)

ature. Both loved to read poetry aloud, and when a new book by a Danish poet came out they would buy the book, rush home, light candles, and then fight over who would be the first to read it to the other. Reading and writing were their chief passions. Books were stacked throughout their apartment, and, as Christensen recalls, they "sov neden under et landskab af bøger" (slept under a landscape of books). With Borum, Christensen encountered the work of several poets for the first time, including several Swedish poets as well as T. S. Eliot and Ezra Pound. Two of her favorite poets were Rainer Maria Rilke and Arthur Rimbaud. For the first years of their married life, Christensen and Borum lived in Knebel, where she taught at a *folkejskole* (public elementary school). Then in the mid 1960s the two taught together at the *Kunsthøjskole* (Art College) in Holbæk, where their students included Henrik Nordbrandt, who later distinguished himself as one of Denmark's leading poets. After teaching at the *Kunsthøjskole* for three semesters, Christensen devoted herself to full-time writing.

Christensen's first two volumes of poetry appeared a few years after she married. The majority of the poems in *Lys: Digte* (Light: Poems, 1962) and *Græs: Digte* (Grass: Poems, 1963) are short lyrical poems that make frequent use of nature imagery and symbolism.

For several of the poems in *Lys,* Christensen found inspiration from modern painters, such as Jackson Pollock, Paul Klee, and Marc Chagall. In a 1986 interview with Jan Kjærstad, a novelist and a reporter from the Norwegian journal *Vinduet,* Christensen said of *Lys* that it concerns "kjærlighet, også om de mørke sidene–av lyset" (love, also about the dark sides–of the light). The theme of love runs through poems in *Græs* also, but here Christensen's work begins to take on a more philosophical tone, evident especially in the long prose poem "Møde" (Meeting), in which the poet seems as concerned with the meaning of the words as the message that the words signify.

If "Mode" was a departure from her earlier works, it was also a signal of where Christensen's work would lead–toward more expansive writing and a greater emphasis on the connections between language, self, and reality. Shortly after *Græs,* Christensen published the novels *Evighedsmaskinene* (The Perpetual Motion Machine, 1964) and *Azorno* (1967). In these novels Christensen continues themes begun in her poetry, but she also challenges her earlier ideas. In *Evighedsmaskinen,* for example, the protagonist, Ulrik, questions whether he has read the world correctly when assuming that reality always has a front and a back, a literal and a symbolic meaning. Unlike Christensen's earliest poems, in which symbolic relationships go unchallenged, in this novel she explores alternative ways of understanding one's relationship to the world. As Ulrik discovers:

> Ligegyldigt nu at tale om en bagside; der er to sider, og de er fuldstændig ens. Og der ligger absolut ikke noget symbolsk i den opdageslse, at det ikk er et spejl; det ér nemlig et spejl. I hver lille fugl, hver fisk, hver blomst, hver del af en redes runding, i hvert stykke siv og knækket vinge, hver krog af en gren eller rod ser Ulrik et ansigt, som er hans, mængder af små bite ansigter og bagved dem det store ansigt, som stadigvæk er hans, tåget, forsvindende som søen, tilgroet med røddre, grene, siv o redre, igen oregroet. . . .

> (No matter now to speak of a backside; there are two sides, and they are completely the same. And there is absolutely nothing symbolic in the discovery that it's not a mirror; it is precisely a mirror. In every bird, every fish, every flower, every part of the weave of a nest, in every piece of reed and broken wing, every corner of a branch or root, Ulrik sees a face, which is his, many tiny little faces, and behind them the large face, which is still his, the fog disappearing like the lake, overgrown with roots, branches, reeds and nests, again overgrown. . . .)

Christensen's third book of poetry, *Det* (It, 1969), focuses on language as a complex creative act in which humans are simultaneously the creators and the created. In *Det* Christensen explores the limits of language, while at the same time attempting to transcend these limits. Along with its concern with linguistics, the book also addresses several philosophical issues of the 1960s, including French structuralism and the antipsychiatry movement in Britain.

Det is a 239-page poem consisting of three sections: "Prologos" (a long prose poem); "Logos" (a mixture of free-verse, traditional form, and shorter prose poems); and "Epilogos" (a long free-verse poem). This description, however, only begins to account for the book's rich complexity. The section entitled "Logos," for instance, is further divided into three subsections, and each of these subsections contains eight sub-subsections composed of eight poems apiece. To organize this middle section of *Det,* Christensen drew on the work of the Danish linguist Viggo Brøndal, who proposed that languages use specific prepositions to describe relationships. From his book *Præpositionernes theori* (A Theory of Prepositions, 1940), Christensen borrowed eight terms describing relation-types; these terms, Christensen believed, could also apply to the ways in which writing itself creates relationships as the writer continues to write and the work grows.

Det can be read from start to finish as one act of creation, beginning somewhere before words and consciousness are fully formed (Prologos), leading to the Creation itself, which is both the word and the world it creates (Logos), and ending at a stage after creation is complete and the word stands on its own (Epilogos). Besides indirectly addressing the subject of creation through its structure, *Det* also represents the poet's own creation myth in which words serve as the basic elements in building a new world. Some critics have compared the book with Genesis. The comparison may be apt, but through much of *Det* Christensen draws not on the standard language and symbols of religion but on that of the theater, which she uses to frame her more modern creation myth. And while Christensen orders her creation in place, she observes and comments on its artificiality: many of the props are plastic; the rain is fake; a machine generates the wind. In the latter part of the middle section of the book, Christensen includes a series of eight prose poems that, at first, resemble the Genesis story of creation. An undefined "they" create and find to be good such things as sand, snow, and water. These poems are soon replaced, however, by another series of prose poems in which "they" turn out to be doctors and patients in a psychiatric hospital.

Given its formal structure, critics have placed *Det* within the realm of Danish *systemdigtning* (systematic poetry), an offshoot of concrete poetry in which the poet invents a grammatical or mathematical system to serve as the organizing principle of the poem. In many ways *Det* fits this description. Not only has Christensen used Brøndal's grammatical categories in lending form to her poem, but she also has imposed other mathematical restrictions for herself. Like the "Logos" section, the long prose poem at the beginning of the book has been divided into subsections, each subsection containing a predetermined number of shorter prose poems whose line lengths also have been predetermined. Moreover, every line of the Prologos contains exactly sixty-six characters.

Yet, critics also have noticed that *Det* tends to transcend its genre. Many have noted that within her restrictive form Christensen seems remarkably free, open to surprising possibilities and unusual associations. One critic has suggested that the best way to read Christensen's type of *systemdigtning* is to think of it as a musical composition in which the composer follows a formal structure but constantly creates variations and original phrasings. Few critics are satisfied simply to label *Det* as "concrete poetry," searching instead for qualifications and superlatives, as P. M. Mitchell did in his *A History of Danish Literature* (1971) when he called *Det* the "triumphant apex" of concrete poetry.

Thirty-five years old when *Det* was published, Christensen saw her career soar with the publication of this work, her third book of poetry. Her first two poetry collections and her two novels had gone largely unnoticed, but Danish critics hailed *Det* as the book of the decade and Christensen as the most original writer of the 1960s. Her preeminent place among contemporary Danish writers at the time—a reputation based almost solely on the success of *Det*—is perhaps best seen on the cover of *A Decade of Danish Literature: 1960–1970,* which bears a page from *Det* as its cover illustration. When, in 1981, more than a decade after its initial publication, popular musician Pia Raug set portions of *Det* to music, appeal for Christensen's work continued to be strong, and the album sold more than thirty-five thousand copies.

In an interview conducted in 1995, Christensen was asked by Peter Øvig Knudsen to comment on *Det*. She admitted that, looking back on it, she felt ambivalent about the book. In her words, "Den indeholder så mange voldsomme og skræmmende elementer, at man på et senere, roligere stadie i sit liv tænker, 'hvad fan er det for en kvinde, som har skrevet den . . . ?' Men alligevel forstår jeg hende" (It contains so many violent and frightening elements that one, at a later, calmer stage in one's life thinks, "what the devil kind of woman wrote that. . . ?" But still I understand her). Nevertheless, *Det* remains one of Christensen's most popular books; and in spite of the author's reservations about it, *Det* might even be called her signature work since it includes Christensen's first sustained effort at writing the kind of poetry that, as it matured, gained continued praise from critics.

Perhaps the most defining characteristic of Christensen's poetry is her ability to place complicated technical restrictions on herself and to meet these restrictions in a way that seems so effortless that the reader forgets they exist. Her poems, in contrast to the strict systems they follow, seem light and often lighthearted. Words grow on the page, one after the other, in a kind of spontaneous and organic beauty that is unexpected from a poem encumbered with such severe mathematical and grammatical prerequisites. Christensen has remarked that writing for her involves a trancelike state, and that after she has written a poem she is often surprised by what appears on the page. This openness to the process of writing and to the surprises that the process offers further characterizes her work.

Brev i april (Letter in April, 1979), Christensen's fourth book of poems, appeared ten years after *Det,* and in the interim between these books two important events occurred in Chistensen's life. In 1973 she

and Poul had a son, Peter, who would play an important role in *Brev i april;* but in 1976, after seventeen years of marriage, Christensen and Borum divorced. They continued, however, to play an active role in each other's work until Borum's death in the summer of 1996. Borum, who founded the Forfatterskolen (Writer's School) in Copenhagen and who was noted as a critic as well as a writer, praised Christensen's poetry in his volume *Danish Literature: A Short Critical Survey* (1979).

Brev i april is, like *Det,* one long poem divided into sections, and it, too, follows a specific system. The poem consists of seven main sections, and each of the main sections has five parts. The parts are numbered, but their order changes from section to section. The careful reader, however, will notice that the five parts under each section are related to the five parts under other sections. Bound by common motifs, it is possible to read the first part of each of the seven sections as a continual poem; likewise with the other parts. Moreover, Christensen has arranged the poem so that the numbered part that ends one section begins the next section, thus providing a bridge between the sections. According to Christensen, her system is based on a work by the French composer Olivier Messiaen.

Christensen's most autobiographical work of poetry, *Brev i april* is based on the experiences of traveling in France with her young son. Although the extensive use of nature imagery has caused some readers to assume that Christensen wrote the book in the country, she in fact wrote *Brev i april* while she and Peter were in Paris. Her son's presence is central to the poem since his crayon drawings and his ability to turn reality into magic become the catalyst for the poet's own imagination, as well as a departure point for her meditations on language and the world. The poem is infused with the poet's fascination with the bonding that takes place between a mother and a son. Focusing on such tender moments, Christensen is at once a visionary who grasps the mystery all around her and a keen observer who notices such particulars as the way in which her son's breathing intermingles with the sounds she makes while writing the poem on the back of one of the boy's drawings. Here, as in all of her poems, Christensen pays special attention to the connections, the relationships, in her world.

Although the primary relationship in *Brev i april* is the one between mother and son, Christensen explores other relationships as well. As she did in *Det,* in *Brev i april* Christensen investigates the relationship between language and the world. But unlike the narrative voice of the earlier book, the voice in

Dust jacket for Christensen's 1998 collected poems

Brev i april seems much less sure of the ability of humans to construct the world out of words. As the speaker of this poem suggests, human beings may have gone wrong in the basic act of naming things: "Hvem ved / om granatæblet / ved med sig selv, / at det hedder / noget andet" (Who knows / whether the pomegranate / itself knows / that it is called / something else). Based on this possibility, the speaker wonders if she herself might have another name, then realizes that like the pomegranate she, too, is part of the world. Unlike the arrogance demonstrated in *Det*–where the poet speaks words and the world falls into order–the speaker in Christensen's fourth book of poetry finds herself in a more humble relationship with the world. At one point this voice even suggests that perhaps "tingene / ved med sig selv / at vi hedder / noget andet" (things / themselves know / that we are called / something else). This playful reversal throws a new light on the relationship between language and the world and shows how Christensen develops her theme over several books, almost as if she were continuing an argument with herself.

Christensen's fascination with language continues in her fifth poetry collection, *alfabet* (Alphabet, 1981). Whereas *Det* focused on words as the building blocks of language, and language as the raw material

for the world, *alfabet* reveals the structure behind words themselves, and instead of imposing her creative powers on the world, Christensen searches the world for the things that already exist in it. In her 1995 interview with Peter Øvig Knudsen, Christensen described the relationship between *Det* and *alfabet* in the following words: "For mig er *alfabet* kritik af verdensbilledet i *Det,* hvor et menneske udkaster en lille modelverden, som det tror at have et vist overblik over" (For me, *alfabet* is a critique of the worldview in *Det,* in which a person forms a little model world that she believes she has a certain overview of).

As do her previous two books of poetry, *alfabet* follows an established system, although it took Christensen years to find the right organizing principle for this book. The work began with the poet's love for certain words, which she had been collecting in notebooks. In preparation for *alfabet,* and without quite knowing what she was preparing herself for, Christensen read several dictionaries and encyclopedias, writing down those words that struck her as meaningful. After collecting these words and wanting to work them into a poem somehow, she searched for a way to arrange them. The solution came to her one day before Easter while she was sitting on a park bench with shopping bags on either side of her. Christensen could vaguely remember a mathematical system she had read of someplace. When a friend came over to talk to her, she described the system to him, and he told her that it was the number system of the medieval Italian mathematician Leonardo Fibonacci that she had in mind.

Along with the alphabet itself, Christensen used Fibonacci's number system to organize *alfabet.* The book is comprised of fourteen poems, beginning with the letter *A* and ending with *N.* Following Fibonacci's system, the A poem has one line and the B poem two lines. From then on, the number of lines in each poem is determined by the sum of the lines in the two poems that precede it. Thus the C poem, for instance, has three lines (the sum of A and B). Although Christensen found this system rather strict at first, she later discovered that it presented opportunities for her to include many of her favorite words. Her guiding principle in composing the book was that the words in the book must correspond to objects that actually exist in the world.

Christensen begins the book by simply pointing out the existence of apricot trees, then goes on to observe other plant and animal life. By the fourth poem, however, destructive forces begin to appear in the work: "dræberne findes; duerne, duerne; / dis, dioxin og dagene; dagene / findes; dagene døden; og digtene" (killers exist; doves, doves / haze, dioxin and days; days / exist; days death; and poems). Creative and destructive forces coexist throughout the work, but Christensen's original impulse in writing the book has remained the same: to show the multiplicity of things in the world, to let them stand on their own as themselves, and to suggest to the reader how fragile and precious the world is.

Critics were quick to praise *alfabet,* and Uffe Harder went as far as to call it "perhaps the most beautiful book Inger Christensen has written so far." Many readers speculated on why Christensen ends the book with the letter N. For her part, Christensen offered an explanation that begins with her characteristic sense of humor and ends in common sense: "Nej, det var fordi, der var deadline! . . . Desuden er der ikke så mange gode ord med o, p og q, så jeg frygtede at gå videre" (No, it was because there was a deadline! . . . Moreover, there aren't so many good words that begin with o, p and q, so I was afraid to go further).

If Christensen's explanation is to be taken seriously, *alfabet* represents the one time when she was not completely successful in managing one of her systems. If she in fact abandoned *alfabet* out of fear, it was with renewed confidence that she wrote her next poetry collection, whose system is perhaps the most restrictive of any she has chosen. *Sommerfugledalen: Et requiem* (The Valley of Butterflies: A Requiem, 1991) is a crown of sonnets, fifteen in all, and each one interwoven with the previous. Two quatrains and two tercets compose each sonnet, and Christensen follows an ABAB CDCD EFE GFG rhyming pattern through most of the poems. Moreover, the last line of the each sonnet reappears as the first line of the one following it; the fifteenth sonnet repeats, in order, the first lines of the preceding fourteen poems.

The year following the publication of *alfabet,* Christensen provided further explanation of her artistic intentions and assumptions in *Del af labyrinthen: Essays* (A Part of the Labyrinth: Essays, 1982), a book of essays titled after lines from *Brev i april:* "Jeg tænker, / altså er jeg del / af labyrinten" (I think, / I too am a part / of the labyrinth). In these essays Christensen develops and clarifies themes that appear in her poetry. In one essay she discusses Dante and notes that art leads the artist to a sense of unity, a notion that her own poetry supports. In other essays she questions the rights of humans to assume the role of creators rather than the role of created and to presume that their perceptions of the world are correct. As she had pointed out in *Brev i april,* the things of the world may not answer to the names that humans assign them.

As she had done with *alfabet,* Christensen wrote *Sommerfugledalen* in stages, without knowing where she might go next. Originally, she wrote the sonnet that appears as the fifteenth poem in the collection as a commemorative poem for the twenty-fifth anniversary of one of her publishers, Brøndum. It was later, while she discussed poetry with students in Hamburg, that Christensen thought to use the poem as a master sonnet in a crown of sonnets. Writing the book drew on her lifelong fascination with butterflies, and Christensen spent hours absorbed in technical books about butterflies, just as she had pored through dictionaries and encyclopedias to write *alfabet. Sommerfugledalen* includes a good deal of the factual knowledge she had gained in her research, and scientists have praised the work for its accuracy.

Naturally, the rich symbolic possibilities of a work such as *Sommerfugledalen* could hardly be lost on a poet who has pursued the relationship between language and the world since her earliest work. Throughout the book butterflies serve as a symbol both for death and for the writing process, which follow a parallel course with the butterflies beginning as early as the chrysalis stage. At one point in the poem, death merges with the butterfly and looks down on the speaker from the wing of a butterfly. Rather than finding this disturbing, Christensen sees the image in all its wonderful possibilities: "Men er det ikke en trøst, at det bare er en sommerfugl? . . .en forvandling" (But isn't it a comfort that it's only a butterfly?. . . a transformation).

With *Sommerfugledalen* Christensen came full circle as an artist. She incorporated the symbolism that characterized her early work in *Lys* and *Græs* with the mature voice that has pondered the limits of language and found its place in the world that it so eloquently evokes.

Christensen's work has won many prizes, including the prestigious Kritikerprisen (Critic's Prize) in 1969 and Gyldne Laurbær (Golden Laurels) in 1970, both for *Det.* She was made a member of Det Danske Akademi (The Danish Academy) in 1978. In 1994 she was awarded the Nordic Prize of the Swedish Academy and the Austrian State Prize for Literature. She has been a member of the Bielefelder Colloquium since 1994, and of the Académie Européenne de Poésie since its founding in 1996.

Christensen's work has been translated into German and French, and although a complete collection of her work has yet to appear in English translation, several individual poems have been included in journals and anthologies published in the United States and Great Britain. Notably, Susanna Nied's translation of selections from Christensen's fifth book, *alfabet,* won the American-Scandinavian Foundation Prize for 1982; a selection of Nied's translations appeared in the December 1982 issue of *Scandinavian Review.*

Asked in her interview with Knudsen to explain her intentions as an artist, Christensen made a statement with which her readers are likely to agree: "I dag kan jeg se, at det først og fremmest var en søgen efter det smukke i sproget" (Today I can see that it was first and foremost a search for the beauty in language).

Interviews:

Jan Kjærstad, "En kombinasjon av verden og meg selv. Intervju med Inger Christensen," *Vinduet,* 40 (1986): 2–9;

Peter Øvig Knudsen, "Tilfældets poet," in *Børn skal ikke lege under fuldmånen: Forfatterportrætter* (Copenhagen: Brøndum, 1995), pp. 225–255.

References:

Birgit Abild and Lisbeth Bonde, "Angst og system i *alfabet,*" in *Litteratur & Samfund,* 36 (September 1983): 8–27;

Marriane Bødker, "Ormenes tisken. Om Inger Christensens *alfabet,*" in *Digtning fra 80'erne til 90'erne,* edited by Anne-Marie Mai (Copenhagen: Borgen, 1993), pp. 118–132;

Poul Borum, *Danish Literature: A Short Critical Survey* (Copenhagen: Det Danske Selskab, 1979);

Borum, "Dengang i halvstredserne," in *Til Inger Christensen på tresårsdagen, den 16 januar 1995* (Copenhagen: Gyldendal, 1995), pp. 7–9;

Uffe Harder, "Inger Christensen and Other Women Poets," in *Out of Denmark: Isak Dinesen/Karen Blixen 1885–1985 and Danish Women Writers Today,* edited by Bodil Wamberg (Copenhagen: The Danish Cultural Institute, 1985), pp. 139–153;

Mads Fedder Henkiksen, "Blikket i Fokus: Projektioner på og fra Inger Christensens sonetkrans," in *Sprogskygger: Læsninger i Inger Christensens forfatterskab,* edited by Lis Wedell Pape (Århus: Århus University Press, 1995), pp. 86–209;

Iben Holk, ed., *Tegnverden: En bog om Inger Christensens forfatterskab* (Viby: Centrum, 1983);

Hans Lyngby Jepsen, *Ny dansk prosa: Fra Tove Ditlevsen til Anders Bodelsen og Inger Christensen* (Copenhagen: Vendelkær, 1972);

Svend Erik Larsen, "The Creative Language: Viggo Brøndal–100 Years," *Scandinavian Studies,* 60 (1988): 325–345;

P. M. Mitchell, *A History of Danish Literature,* revised edition (New York: Kraus-Thomson Organization, 1971), p. 313;

Susanna Nied, "Letting Things Be: Inger Christensen's *alphabet,*" *Scandinavian Review,* 70 (December 1982): 24–26;

Nied, "Light and Grass: Poems by Inger Christensen," M.A. thesis, San Diego State University, 1979;

Gudmund Roger-Henrichsen, *A Decade of Danish Literature: 1960–1970* (Copenhagen: Ministry of Foreign Affairs, 1972);

Sven H. Rossel, *A History of Danish Literature* (London & Lincoln: University of Nebraska Press, 1992);

Asger Schnack, *Tre kvindelige lyrikere: Et essay* (Copenhagen: Nansensgade Antikvariat, 1991);

Mette Soeborg, *Med sprogets proces: Diskurs og udsigelse i Inger Christensens forfatterskab* (Copenhagen: Institut for Litteraturvidenskab, 1983).

Tove Ditlevsen

(14 December 1917 – 7 March 1976)

Mette Winge

Translated by Tiina Nunnally

BOOKS: *Pigesind* (Copenhagen: Rasmus Naver, 1939);
Man gjorde et Barn Fortræd (Copenhagen: Athenæum, 1941);
Lille Verden: Digte (Copenhagen: Athenæum, 1942);
Barndommens Gade (Copenhagen: Athenæum, 1943);
Den fulde Frihed: Noveller (Copenhagen: Athenæum, 1944);
For Barnets Skyld (Copenhagen: Athenæum, 1946);
Blinkende Lygter: Digte (Copenhagen: Athenæum, 1947);
Dommeren: Noveller (Copenhagen: Athenæum, 1948)–includes "Appelsiner," translated by Ann and Peter Thornton as "Oranges," in *Contemporary Danish Prose,* edited by Elias Bredsdorff (Copenhagen: Gyldendal, 1958), pp. 352–357;
Paraplyen (Copenhagen: Hasselbalch, 1952);
Vi har kun hinanden: Radioroman (Copenhagen: Hasselbalch, 1954);
Kvindesind (Copenhagen: Hasselbalch, 1955);
Foraar (Copenhagen: Hasselbalch, 1956);
Annelise–tretten år (Copenhagen: Høst, 1959);
Flugten fra opvasken (Copenhagen: Hasselbalch, 1959);
To som elsker hinanden: Rad (Copenhagen: Hasselbalch, 1960);
Hvad nu, Annelise? (Copenhagen: Høst, 1960);
Den hemmelige rude: Digte (Copenhagen: Hasselbalch, 1961)–includes "Søndag," translated by Knud Mogensen and Kurt Hansen as "Sunday," in *Contemporary Danish Poetry: An Anthology,* edited by Line Jensen and others (Copenhagen: Gyldendal / Boston: Twayne, 1977), pp. 83–85;
Den onde lykke (Copenhagen: Hasselbalch, 1963);
Digte i udvalg (Copenhagen: Hasselbalch, 1964);
Barndom: Erindringer (Copenhagen: Hasselbalch, 1967);
Ungdom: Erindringer (Copenhagen: Hasselbalch, 1967);
Ansigterne (Copenhagen: Gyldendal, 1968); translated by Tiina Nunnally as *The Faces* (Seattle: Fjord Press, 1991);

Tove Ditlevsen (photograph by Nordfoto)

De voksne: Digte (Copenhagen: Gyldendal, 1969)–includes "Skilsmisse 1," "Skilsmisse 3," "Selvportræt 1," and "Selvportræt 4," translated by Ann Freeman as "Divorce 1," "Divorce 3," "Self-Portrait 1," and "Self-Portrait 4," in *Contemporary Danish Poetry,* edited by Jensen and others (Copenhagen: Gyldendal / Boston: Twayne, 1977), pp. 83–86, 90–94;

Med venlig hilsen Tove Ditlevsen: Spørgsmål og svar fra Familie Journalens brevkasse (Copenhagen: Gyldendal, 1969);

Gift: Erindringer (Copenhagen: Gyldendal, 1971);

Det runde værelse (Copenhagen: Gyldendal, 1973)—includes "Du som ingen" and "Det runde værelse," translated by Kurt Hansen as "You Who Someone" and "The Round Room" in *Contemporary Danish Poetry,* edited by Jensen and others (Copenhagen: Gyldendal / Boston: Twayne, 1977), pp. 87–89;

Min nekrolog og andre skumle tanker (Copenhagen: Gyldendal, 1973);

Paranteser (Copenhagen: Gyldendal, 1973);

Tove Ditlevsen om sig selv (Copenhagen: Gyldendal, 1975);

Vilhelms værelse (Copenhagen: Gyldendal, 1975);

En sibylles bekendelser (Copenhagen: Gyldendal, 1976);

Til en lille pige: Efterladte digte (Copenhagen: Gyldendal, 1978).

Editions and Collections: *Kærlighedsdigte* (Copenhagen: Hasselbalch, 1950);

Udvalgte digte (Copenhagen: Hasselbalch, 1954);

Frygt: Noveller i udvalg (Copenhagen: Hasselbalch, 1968);

Noveller, edited by Inger Christensen (Copenhagen: Gyldendal, 1977)—comprises *Den fulde Frihed; Dommeren; Paraplyen; Den onde lykke;*

Det tidlige forar: Barndom, ungdom (Copenhagen: Gyldendals Traneboger, 1984);

Samlede digte (Copenhagen: Gyldendal, 1996);

En æggesnaps—og andre noveller, edited by Jørn E. Albert (Copenhagen: Gyldendal, 1997).

Editions in English: *Complete Freedom and Other Stories: Selected Stories,* translated by Jack Brondum (Willimantic, Conn.: Curbstone Press, 1982)—comprises "Complete Freedom," "Angst (I)," "A Young Girl Becomes a Grandmother," "The Allotment Garden," "Break Time," "Two on a String," "Depression," "Oranges," "Angst (II)," "A Good Deal," "The Dagger";

Early Spring, translated by Tiina Nunnally (Seattle: Scal Press, 1985; London: The Women's Press, 1986)—comprises *Barndom; Ungdom.*

OTHER: Else Holmelund Minarik, *Bjørnefar kommer hjem,* translated by Ditlevsen, illustrated by Maurice Sendak (Copenhagen: Thorkild Beck, 1960);

Minarik, *Lille bjørns ven,* translated by Ditlevsen, illustrated by Sendak (Copenhagen: Thorkild Beck, 1961);

Min yndlingslæsning, edited by Ditlevsen (Copenhagen: Vendelkærs Forlag, 1964);

Tove Ditlevsen læser højt, edited by Ditlevsen, illustrated by Helle Skipper (Copenhagen: Hasselbalch, 1966).

Tove Ditlevsen's position as a writer was unusual for a Danish author. From the moment that her first book was published, shortly before the German occupation of Denmark in 1940, she attracted the attention of readers and the media—both the newspapers and the tabloids. The interest of reporters in Ditlevsen remained unabated, partly because she was always ready to answer their calls—if she did not call on them first—and partly because she never hid from the world that she had great personal problems. She talked about her problems openly, never concealing that she had been a drug addict, that she had attempted suicide, that she wanted to be married but at the same time could not bear it—in short, that her life was anything but perfect. She was willing to reveal much about herself, without resorting to histrionics, and her increasingly ravaged face showed what toll her life had taken on her.

Another reason for the ceaseless interest in Ditlevsen was the fact that she, unlike many authors, became directly involved in the lives of other people. She did so through her advice column, which she wrote primarily for women, usually on topics such as the sexual and marital problems of women. Her readers felt that she, as both a person and a writer, was much closer to them and their ordinary daily lives than were the majority of other authors.

Tove Irma Margit Ditlevsen was born 14 December 1917 to Ditlev and Alfrida Ditlevsen. She came from the working class, which she always perceived as having harmed her. She had no idea, for example, of how one was supposed to behave in "polite society." For a long time, for instance, she would order only mock turtle soup whenever she was invited out by a man, because that was the only dish that she knew how to eat properly.

Her home in Copenhagen was in most respects a traditional working-class home, although it was not entirely traditional because of her father's great interest in reading. Ditlev Ditlevsen was a foundry stoker and boiler attendant, and in contrast to many other Danish workers in the period during and after World War I, he was seldom unemployed. However, the family still had to live modestly in a small two-room apartment in the Vesterbro section of Copenhagen, a typical, rough, working-class neighborhood.

Tove Ditlevsen's father, a rather reserved man, wanted to be a journalist, but he never managed to become one. All his life he carried with him this unfulfilled dream and suffered from it, and yet he was unwilling to give his children the opportunity to realize their own dreams for a different kind of life. He did not permit his son, Edvin, to continue his studies, and his daughter, Tove, was not allowed to do so either. He felt that it was even more useless to waste any time on her education since girls were merely supposed to get married.

Ditlevsen's relationship with her father was not, however, as burdensome or difficult as the relationship she had with her mother. Alfrida Ditlevsen, née Mundus, was a brash Copenhagen woman whose greatest desire was to have fun, and when life did not give her what she yearned for, she became distraught and hostile toward her children, especially her daughter. Although Ditlevsen's father also failed her in every instance where his support would have been crucial (in particular when it began to dawn on her that she wanted to write and had the talent for it), her relationship with him was not as complicated nor as strained as was her relationship with her mother.

Ditlevsen's relationship with her mother was apparently the most difficult and insurmountable thing in her life. This difficulty was true not only during her childhood but also later on because the traumas that she suffered reached far into her adult life. Her interaction with her mother determined the shape of Ditlevsen's entire life and work. In one of her books of memoirs, *Tove Ditlevsen om sig selv* (Tove Ditlevsen About Herself, 1975), Ditlevsen describes this relationship as the "trembling and insecure" feelings that she had toward her mother during her childhood.

Alfrida Ditlevsen was an extremely complex person. She was temperamental and self-absorbed, and apparently she never made the slightest attempt to try to understand her daughter. She also cruelly rebuffed her daughter's attempts at physical contact, so that Ditlevsen became fearful and insecure.

These parents had an enormous impact on the author: the father who shut her out instead of supporting her and the mother who alternated between cold silence and, less frequently, a more agreeable mood—personality shifts that constantly confused her daughter. Her parents were the reason that Ditlevsen early in her life chose to withdraw into herself, into a figurative inner room or untouched sanctum—*Det runde værelse* (The Round Room, 1973), which is the title of her last poetry collection. There she felt free—free to dream, free to play with words and images, and free to create "slender sentences," as she expressed it. It was within this inner room, or universe, that her writing was conceived, and the inner sanctum was the place where Ditlevsen preferred to live, because inside she was as happy as a child who has been hurt can manage to be.

Ditlevsen's writings reveal that her childhood was both a specific time period and a state of mind, to which she returns again and again in all of her works: poems, short stories, novels, and various types of newspaper and magazine columns. Her childhood meant everything to her; it was the source from which she retrieved experiences, situations, and—first and foremost—moods. Her childhood, with all its pain and loneliness, pro-

vided Ditlevsen with a source that she could draw upon throughout her life, even though it always hurt to bring forth these dearly bought "treasures."

In the novel *Ansigterne* (1968; translated as *The Faces,* 1991), the reader encounters this childhood scene:

Det regnede fra en himmel, hun aldrig mere skulle se. Det var hendes barndoms himmel, som aftenstjernen prikkede hul i med et klart, spinkelt lys, der faldt ind over vindueskarmen i soveværelset, hvor hun sad med optrukne ben og fortabte sig i blide drømme. Bag hende var mørket og lugten af sved, søvn og støv. Bag hende var sengen med den tunge, klamme dyne, der var som låget på en kiste. Bag hende var hendes fars og mors uldne nattestemmer fra den kønnets verden, som hun ikke forstod. Bag hende stod den indespærrede nat og gærede som tilproppet syltetøj, der ikke kom luft til . . .

(It was raining from a sky that she would never see again. It was the sky of her childhood, and the evening star pricked a hole in it with a bright, delicate light that flooded the windowsill in her bedroom where she sat with legs drawn up and lost herself in gentle dreams. Behind her was the darkness and the fear and the smell of sweat, sleep, and dust. Behind her was the bed with its heavy, clammy quilt that was like the lid on a coffin. Behind her were her father's and mother's woolen nighttime voices from the world of sex, which she did not understand. Behind her was the imprisoned night, fermenting like a sealed jar of jam that no air could reach. . . .)

It is striking how often it rains in Ditlevsen's childhood universe. This thought occurred to a bright schoolchild, who once asked the author if it could really be true that it had always rained during her childhood. Ditlevsen replied affirmatively: "Jeg gav hende ret. Men forklarede, at regnvejret altid havde passet så godt til min sørgmodighed og tankefulde stemning, og at der findes 'Et sindets vejr, som er uafhængig af, hvordan vejret er i virkeligheden'" (I said that she was right, but explained that rain had always suited my melancholy and meditative mood, and that there exists "A weather of the soul that is not dependent on what the weather is like in reality"). The mood in Ditlevsen's descriptions of childhood is always melancholy, full of pain and fear, and childhood is even viewed as a narrow coffin, one from which it is impossible to escape. In another passage fear is directly linked to childhood: "Angsten er gammel den / lugter af barndom" (Fear is old / it smells of childhood).

Ditlevsen left school in 1932 with a middle-level certificate, having completed the ninth grade. She first took a job as a maid, as was then the custom for many young girls from working-class homes or farms. Later she worked in a warehouse, where she packaged tin

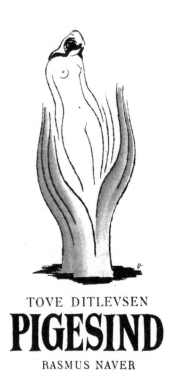

TOVE DITLEVSEN

PIGESIND

RASMUS NAVER

Cover for Ditlevsen's first book, a collection of poetry published in 1939

boxes, and then she became a typist. No matter where she was working, she would steal time to write. She wrote on little scraps of paper and took no real interest in the generally mindless work that was assigned to her. She continued to write because early on she had decided to become an author, later writing "Jeg havde jo min stædige drøm om at blive digter, og den slap jeg ikke et øjeblik af syne" (I had my stubborn dream about becoming a writer, and not for a moment did I let it slip from view).

The problem was that she had no idea how to go about achieving this dream. With her working-class background she knew—for this was one of the pieces of wisdom that her parents had instilled in her—that it was not enough to write, as she was already doing wherever and whenever she could. Something more was needed, and this "something more" was a husband. As a product of her time and environment, Ditlevsen was completely convinced that a woman could not make it without help. A woman had a fierce need for a man, but not just any man—she needed a man with influence. So when Ditlevsen met Viggo F. Møller, a man who had influence, and a certain literary influence at that, she accepted his proposal of marriage almost at once.

Møller was the editor of *Vild Hveds* (Wild Wheat), an important literary journal that helped establish the reputations of young poets, and it was in this journal that Ditlevsen's first poem, "Til mit døde barn" (Until My Dead Child), appeared in 1937. He was much older than Ditlevsen, but he was also a wealthy man whose apartment had a totally modern bathroom—at that time an unheard-of luxury. Møller helped Ditlevsen to publish her first poetry collection, *Pigesind* (A Girl's Soul), which appeared in 1939. On 9 April 1940 the German army invaded Denmark; twenty days later, Ditlevsen and Møller were married.

Pigesind, with its melancholy poems about life's brief joys, women's yearnings, and the longing for love, was well received. Critics, in particular, were enchanted by the overall wistful mood, by the gentle folk-ballad tone present in a number of the poems, and by Ditlevsen's lovely, classical style. *Pigesind* was a success, although the author later claimed that the reception was only mediocre because only about one hundred copies were sold of the five hundred copies printed; however, from then on Ditlevsen was a well-known figure, and not just in literary circles.

Ditlevsen's marriage to a man twenty years her senior was never consummated, as Møller was impotent. The two were ill-matched, and Ditlevsen quickly disappeared from her husband's life—to her satisfaction, but to Møller's great sorrow and undisguised bitterness. He felt used, and with good reason. The marriage—which ended in divorce in 1942—did, however, prove lucrative for Ditlevsen in many ways. With Møller's help she had been swept into the literary spotlight, and she quickly became one of the celebrated young writers of the day. Her bright and beautiful appearance also contributed greatly to her rapid rise to fame.

Møller had helped Ditlevsen to select the poems for her first collection, and he also gave her other literary advice. He was the one who suggested that she try to write a novel. Ditlevsen later said that before she started she did not really know what the novel was going to be about. "Jeg begyndte ligesom i et hjørne, og så kom ordene af sig selv uden nogen bevidst tankevirksomhed. Jeg følte det ikke som noget arbejde, det var bare vidunderligt" (I just started in one corner, and then the words appeared on their own, without any conscious thought. It did not feel like work to me; it was simply wonderful).

Her first novel was *Man gjorde et Barn Fortræd* (A Child Was Harmed, 1941). It is a realistically told story about a young girl named Kirsten who feels frightened and alienated because of a shadow she perceives to be hovering over her life. She feels that she is burdened with something unbearable, something that is gnawing at her. Because of this feeling, she has problems in her relationships with men. Gradually she realizes that the shadow is a man who sexually assaulted her when she was a child. She finds him and confronts him. This encounter gives her an insight into both her own feelings and her complicated relationship with her parents:

> Hun var klogere end de. Paa en eneste Dag var hun blevet det. Hun var ikke længere hæmmet, usikker og ængstelig. Hun havde rørt ved Livets inderste Hemmelighed, det havde gjort hende klog og stærk.

> (She was wiser than they were. This had happened in a single day. She was no longer inhibited, unsure of herself, or fearful. She had touched the innermost secret of life; it had made her wise and strong.)

Man gjorde et Barn Fortræd is a quiet novel, simply told, one that perhaps has certain stylistic imperfections, but in it Ditlevsen's narrative voice is confident, and her psychological insights and understanding are shrewd.

Over the years many readers believed that the author had been subjected to a similar sexual assault, but she always denied that the novel was literally autobiographical. As a child growing up in Vesterbro, Ditlevsen saw many examples of perverse sexuality directed at children; however, for Ditlevsen, to "do harm" does not apply exclusively to physical assaults. Throughout all of her works, she writes of a harm that is more psychological than physical. When the novel was published, there were many works on the market that were based on or inspired by Sigmund Freud's writings, and literary critics labeled Ditlevsen's novel "Freudian." But Ditlevsen always maintained that at the time she wrote the novel she had no knowledge of Freud or his theories.

While she was writing the novel, Ditlevsen continued to write poems, since poetry, she said, was her most natural form of expression. Many requests and invitations were sent to the young writer from newspapers and magazines asking for new poems. She was popular, and she understood how to supply the editors with what they wanted. She herself called these commissioned poems "my trick poems," and she included only a few of them in her published collections.

Ditlevsen was in the midst of a sort of lyrical outpouring, and so her next book was, logically enough, a poetry collection. It was called *Lille Verden: Digte* (Little World: Poems, 1942), and it became an even bigger hit with the public than had been *Man gjorde et Barn Fortræd*. It is in *Lille Verden* that her most quoted and most popular poems are found. This collection differs from her first poetry collection, *Pigesind*, in that the poems are far more erotic; they are the poems of a mature woman, and sexual desire coupled with moods of jealousy pervade several of the poems.

Lille Verden includes the most famous of Ditlevsen's poems, entitled "The Eternal Three," which opens with the often-quoted lines:

> Der er to mænd i verden,
> der bestandig krydser min vej.
> Den ene er ham jeg elsker,
> den anden elsker mig.

> (There are two men in the world,
> who cross my path constantly.
> One is the man that I love,
> the other one loves me.)

The reviews of *Lille Verden* were mixed, and the condescending tone in some of them would prove to be a widespread and common attitude in reviews of Ditlevsen's poetry, especially those by male critics. Several reviewers claimed that her poetry went far beyond the boundaries of what Niels Kaas Johansen in *Information* (28 November 1947) called the "excruciatingly banal." The critics' aversion to her poetry was primarily due to the fact that she was a traditionalist at a time when modernism was emerging in poetry. Over the course of the next ten to fifteen years modernism became the dominant trend in Danish poetry. For many years Ditlevsen refused to enter into any kind of experimentation with modernist techniques, remarking:

> Jeg følte aldrig trang til at bryde ud i sang om rustne vandrør, kloak-afløb og andre lidet poetiske fænomener, som gav mig indtryk af, at næsten alle landets digtere pludselig havde kastet sig over blikkenslagerfaget.

> (I never felt the urge to break into song about rusty pipes, sewer run-off, or other unpoetic phenomena, which gave me the impression that almost all of the poets in the country had suddenly taken up the plumbing trade.)

That a Swedish reviewer, in connection with *Lille Verden,* would call Ditlevsen "poetry's cocktail lounge pianoplayer" clearly indicates how harsh the criticism could be toward traditionalists in general and toward Ditlevsen in particular.

One of the poems in the collection is "Barndommens Gade," which can be regarded as a precursor to the most widely read of Ditlevsen's novels, the book of the same name, *Barndommens Gade* (My Childhood Street, 1943). "Barndommens Gade" refers to a specific street in Copenhagen–Istedgade–where many people, many passions, a great deal of misery, and much solace are to be found. It is a street sparkling with colors, even in the dark, and it is a street that does not let go of its children–because the street becomes part of them. The street exists as a

Ditlevsen and her first husband, literary editor Viggo F. Møller (courtesy of Gyldendal Publishers)

real place with buildings, traffic, and people, but it is also a psychological landscape:

> Jeg er din Barndoms Gade,
> jeg er dit Væsens Rod.
> Jeg er den bankende Rytme
> i alt hvad du længes mod.
>
> (I am your childhood street,
> I am the root of your soul.
> I am the thudding rhythm
> in all that you long for.)

It might be said that the poetic assertion in these lines applies not only to the poem and the subsequent novel of the same name, but that the "thudding rhythm" of this "childhood street" resonates through all of Ditlevsen's work.

The novel *Barndommens Gade,* which presents a broad, social-realistic portrait of working-class life in Copenhagen between the world wars, is the story of Ester's adolescence and daily life on a completely ordinary and shabby street in Copenhagen. Ester is shaped, for good and bad, by this street she detests. At the same time, however, she cannot tear herself away from it. As an adult she tries to do so, but it pulls her back: "Hun vender sig i trods fra Gaden og ved ikke at hun altid fører den med sig–i Øjnene, i Stemmen i sit farende

hjemløse Sind" (She turns defiantly away from the street, not knowing that she will always carry it with her–in her eyes, in her voice, in her wandering, homeless soul).

Later she acknowledges that she and the street belong together, and the novel ends with a description in which the street is perceived as a living being: "Gaden strækker sig, kælent gabende som en mæt og elsket Kvinde, med Dagningens matte Gloire om det dæmrende Haar, der flagrer i Blæsten som de brogede Blade paa Enghaveplads" (The street stretches, yawning endearingly like a satisfied and beloved woman, with the muted halo of the dawn encircling her luminous hair, which flutters in the breeze like the colorful leaves on Enghave Square).

The main character has many autobiographical traits, but Ditlevsen neglected to equip Ester, who is described as a budding artist, with the one essential prerequisite: talent. This attribute she gives instead to Ester's brother. Ditlevsen later explained that this was because even as an adult she was afraid of getting in trouble with her mother, who never bothered to hide her negative opinions about her daughter's "scribblings." In 1986 *Barndommens Gade* was made into a motion picture, written and directed by Astrid Henning-Jensen, with the well-known Danish actress Sofie Gråbøl playing the lead role.

One of Ditlevsen's trademarks as an author is her terse prose style; in her short stories she effectively depicts a person's entire life situation in only a few lines. Ditlevsen demonstrates this style in her first story collection, *Den fulde Frihed: Noveller* (1944; translated as *Complete Freedom and Other Stories* in 1982, although this anthology includes additional stories). In *Den fulde Frihed* is the story "Kolonihaven" (The Allotment Garden), which has become a classic text and is included in many literary anthologies for Danish schoolchildren.

The story is about an old man, a widower, who has been given an allotment garden by his children, who want to keep him busy. Their gift implies that they will not have to worry so much about their father and his state of mind anymore, let alone waste their precious time on him. The father–an old blue-collar worker–sees through them, however, and has a difficult time showing the gratitude expected of him. Ditlevsen later said that she had no scruples about using some of her father's traits for the old workman, but she would never dare to base a character on her mother. This claim was not entirely true, however, as the main character in *Ansigterne* bears some resemblance to Ditlevsen's mother.

Ditlevsen had gradually developed a great insight into the nature of love and women's emotions, but she had a gift for depicting men's feelings as well. *Den fulde Frihed* includes thirteen stories that are extremely different, and yet they all touch on the problem of how someone can both preserve her freedom and at the same time live in an emotionally binding relationship with another person. Ditlevsen maintains that if personal freedom cannot be preserved, a married couple could end up walking, talking, and eating in exactly the same way. Alternately, an individual might end up like the respectable bookkeeper in Ditlevsen's story "En uheldig Dag" (An Unlucky Day) who lives a life burdened with obligations both at work and at home and whose only breathing space is the walk home from the office. When his wife calls one day to say that she will pick him up at the office, he becomes panic-stricken–his only breathing space has been taken away from him.

The story "Foraar" (Spring) depicts a man's sudden epiphany when, as usual, he meets the woman he loves at the café where they often go, on a completely ordinary day when she looks as she always does and there is nothing obviously different. It is on that completely ordinary day, however, that he realizes that she is leaving him:

> Han saa ud i Luften og lod hende tale. Han sad og mistede hende Stykke for Stykke og havde ingen Mulighed mere for at naa hende. Han skulde aldrig mere røre hende, aldrig mere kysse hende. Han kunde ikke tage hendes Haand og sige: Naa, gamle Tøs, lad

det nu være godt–hun var mere uopnaaelig, end før han lærte hende at kende.

> (He stared into space and let her talk. He sat there, losing her bit by bit, and had no chance of ever reaching her again. He would never touch her again, never kiss her. He could not take her hand and say: Well, old girl, don't you worry about that–she was more unattainable now than before he got to know her.)

"En ung Pige bliver Bedstemoder" (A Young Girl Becomes a Grandmother) is about a woman who has allowed others to treat her like a child all her life; she has never really grown up. Then one day she suddenly realizes that she is about to become a grandmother, and she grows so confused that she is about to lose her grip on life. She is afraid of other people's expectations, and her only dream is to "blive kørt ind paa et Sidespor" (be driven off onto a side track) so that she can unobtrusively figure out who she really is.

The German occupation of Denmark during World War II and the living conditions that ensued are depicted in a few works by Ditlevsen. In the novel *For Barnets Skyld* (For the Child's Sake, 1946) the author depicts a divorce and its effects on a child–an older girl–and her mother. The mother tries to create a new life for herself and her daughter, but her attempt fails. Her interests conflict with those of her daughter, and the girl, abetted by her father, brings about a catastrophe in which the mother's new lover is shot during the last days of the Occupation. In this novel Ditlevsen has again incorporated much of the fear and uncertainty from her own childhood, and she presents a scathing portrait of the way in which parents pretend to make decisions for "the sake of the child" when they are simply doing what suits them best. Not much attention was paid to the novel; many felt that Ditlevsen had moved too far away from the territory with which she was most familiar: the children and adults from "her street."

Another work in which the war is reflected is the poem "De tyske soldater" (The German Soldiers), subtitled "Foraaret 1945" (Spring, 1945). In this poem Ditlevsen paints a sympathetic picture of the pitiful groups of weary and defeated German soldiers who, after the Allied liberation of Denmark, are on their way out of the country on foot. The poem was published in the Danish press in 1945 and was included in Ditlevsen's next poetry collection, *Blinkende Lygter: Digte* (Flickering Lights: Poems, 1947). The poem provoked an angry torrent from many readers, who thought it was both sentimental and offensive because it was unpatriotic.

Ditlevsen's *Blinkende Lygter* was the poetry collection that won Ditlevsen her greatest audience. When it was first published, more than ten thousand copies

Ditlevsen, ca. 1950 (courtesy of Gyldendal Publishers)

example, the poem "Børnene" (The Children) describes the youngsters, first as a sweet anticipation, then as an eye reflecting the moon, then as scampering feet.

Ditlevsen's next two books were short-story collections, the first called *Dommeren: Noveller* (The Judge: Stories, 1948). The second, which came out a few years later, was titled *Paraplyen* (The Umbrella, 1952). Because of her marital problems and the periods of psychological illness from which Ditlevsen suffered during this time, there was a longer lapse between publication of her books than previously.

Dommeren, the first of the two collections, includes her most popular and most quoted story: "En ægge-snaps" (An Eggnog). In the story, Ditlevsen describes how suspicions of a minor theft are about to destroy the trust and love, never openly expressed, between two people—a single mother and her daughter. But the trust is restored, and the mother says the words that can dissolve the child's fear: "Du kan jo røre dig en ægge-snaps" (Why don't you go ahead and make yourself an eggnog). In all its terseness, it is a remarkable, unsentimental story.

The same is true of the story "En flink dreng" (A Nice Boy) from the collection *Paraplyen*. Here the setting is neither on the street nor in a city apartment but in a gamekeeper's house in the country. It is about a child (in this case an adopted son) who realizes that he is not loved, or at least he is loved less than the "real" child. The story also describes the egotism and thoughtlessness of two adults, as seen from the child's point of view.

Typical of the stories in these collections is their ruthless tone. In general, Ditlevsen's characters are never particularly happy. In her stories they either have been or will be exposed to genuine love, so they are hungry for affection; but they never receive the love, tenderness, or understanding that might open them up. For this reason their lives are often sterile, and their surroundings seem petty and constricted.

Ditlevsen's pessimism increased at the same time as she became more and more critical of the institution of marriage, which she had long regarded as central to both her own life and the lives of all women. This development was connected with her own experiences and her exceedingly peculiar marriages, which were virtually put on display for the public eye. Her second tumultuous marriage, to Ebbe Munk on 9 December 1942, had produced a daughter, Helle, born in 1943, but the marriage lasted only a few years. On 26 November 1945 Ditlevsen married Dr. Carl Rydberg, and they had a son, Michael, a year later. However, this marriage proved to be the most disastrous of all—Ryberg freely prescribed drugs for his wife, thus plunging Ditlevsen into a harrowing nightmare of drug addic-

were printed—an enormous number for a Danish book and a staggering figure for a poetry collection. If the public was pleased, the critics were surly. One aggressive young critic said of *Blinkende Lygter* that "Tove Ditlevsen åbenbart ikke ønskede at deltage i sin generations stileksperimenter" (Tove Ditlevsen obviously did not want to participate in her generation's stylistic experiments). He also ridiculed her extensive use of four-line, rhymed stanzas and weak end rhymes. Furthermore, he claimed that her themes were unexciting.

This attitude was typical of male literary critics during the 1960s. It became fashionable to deride and ridicule Ditlevsen and her work. Her so-called unexciting themes were exciting for many people, however; with her wealth of human and, in particular, female experience, she spoke of fundamental conditions in life.

In this collection the best poems are again those with themes pertaining to women's lives: love relationships seen from the woman's point of view, the relationship to a child or children, the joy over a new dress, and the fear of losing a loved one—in particular, a child. For

tion, which she barely survived. The marriage ended in 1950.

Vi har kun hinanden (We Have Only Each Other, 1954) is the name of a work that Ditlevsen wrote at the request of Danmarks Radio; originally read in a series of radio broadcasts, it was later published as a novel. She did not care for this type of commissioned work, but she later explained that she was in great need of money. *Vi har kun hinanden* marks a transition in her work since it is the first of a series of novels in which she takes a critical look at marriage. In this novel Ditlevsen still expresses a certain optimism and a belief in the curative powers of sexual maturity, as well as faith that together, two people can actually establish a "refuge" in life. The male protagonist (one of the best male characters that Ditlevsen ever created) emphasizes that people should never say that they have "only" each other: "Du skal ikke sige 'kun'. Bare: Jeg har dig! ligesom når man leger tagfat. Du må altid sørge for at have noget andet også, uden for mig, noget der bare er dit" (You should not say "only." Simply: I've got you! Just like when you play tag. You should always make sure that you have something else too, separate from me, something that is yours alone).

During the following years Ditlevsen continued to shift from one genre to another. For a while her main interest was still poetry, but the hostility that critics had shown toward her particular style of poetry made her quite cautious. In 1955, however, the collection *Kvindesind* (The Soul of a Woman) was published; it represents a further development of her poetic themes. The title was well chosen, since it both indicates a connection with her debut collection, *Pigesind,* and signals that a development has occurred. The young girl has not only become the adult woman, but she is growing old. Even though the mirror reveals that time has passed and that the years have caught up with her body, Ditlevsen shows that inside the aging woman in the mirror resides a young girl. "Hvor er mine drømme? Og hvor er min tyveårs glæde" (Where are my dreams? And where is my twenty-year-old joy?) asks the narrative voice. In the same poem the painful recognition is formulated in this way: "Der bor en ung kvinde i mig, som ikke vil dø" (There lives inside me a young woman who will not die). Another theme is the sexual passion that the mature woman knows, in contrast to the innocence of the young woman. The costs are high, however, taking the form of those destructive impulses that are embodied in any type of passion. In 1956 Ditlevsen was awarded the prestigious *De Gylden Laurbær* (The Golden Laurels) by the Danish Book Dealers' Association for *Kvindesind.*

Although Ditlevsen firmly rejected the modernistic mode in her poetry, she was still affected by it, and in a series of poems in *Kvindesind* it is evident that she is using a different technique or style–a style that has connections to the modernism that she had previously repudiated so strongly. In contrast to her older poems with their set rhyme scheme and careful end rhymes, in *Kvindesind* there are poems with long lists of words and a new, unique staccato rhythm. The critics pointed out that in this collection there were several fine, solid poems but that the collection as a whole seemed more scattered than her previous books.

Flugten fra opvasken (Flight from the Dishes, 1959) is in many ways a central work, not only for Ditlevsen but also for Danish literature in general because it is an early and ruthless examination of the special situation and dilemmas of the family and particularly of women. "Family–I hate you" could be the subtitle for each of these twenty-one prose pieces. One of the essays is about the family living room, which in Ditlevsen's description becomes a claustrophobic space from which no one can escape:

> Ganske uanset hvor mange værelser der er i et hus eller i en lejlighed, vil familien altid klumpe sammen i en enkelt stue, når dens medlemmer ikke netop sover. Den plage, det er aldrig at kunne hengive sig til ensomhed og meditation, eksisterer således ikke kun i storbyens slumkvarterer, men er en egenskab, en lovbundethed i selve begrebet *familie*. Dag for dag, år for år, sidder man i samlingsstuen og indsuger det samme støv, den samme kedsomhed, den samme lugt af middagsmad, sved, indelukkethed, bøger, aviser, gammel tobak og våde fødder. Man stirrer på de samme vægge og kan hverken se dem eller tingene mere . . .

> (No matter how many rooms there are in a house or an apartment, the family always bunches up together in a single room when the members are not asleep. The torment of never being able to retreat into solitude or meditation exists not only in the slums of the big cities; it is a characteristic, a law, of the very concept of *family*. Day after day, year after year, you sit in the communal room and inhale the same dust, the same boredom; the same smell of dinner, sweat, stale air, books, newspapers, old tobacco, and wet feet. You stare at the same walls without being able to see them or anything else anymore. . . .)

Ditlevsen's desperation meant that she had made the leap out of the family room, although she had not joined the feminist revolt that was emerging during the 1960s and that would noisily erupt into the so-called red-stocking movement of the 1970s. It might be said that in terms of the situation and dilemmas of women, Ditlevsen spoke in two contradictory voices for the rest of her life. One protested loudly against isolation; the other murmured words of resignation and implied that, when it came right down to it, a woman's place was in

*Ditlevsen and her fourth husband, newspaper editor
Victor Andreasen*

working-class neighborhoods. In 1959 Ditlevsen was awarded the Børnebogspris (Children's Book Prize) of the Danish Ministry of Culture for *Annelise–tretten år.* Since the book was an enormous hit, Ditlevsen wrote the sequel, *Hvad nu, Annelise?,* published the following year. In this book the children move out to the northern part of Copenhagen, but it is clear that Ditlevsen does not have the same feeling for this setting that she felt toward the Vestrebro district.

Ditlevsen's marital problems not only continued but also grew worse during her stormy relationship with her fourth husband, Victor Andreasen, a newspaper editor and government official. They were married in 1951 and had a son, Peter, in 1954. Although the marriage lasted until 1973, it became an increasingly troubled relationship. A prelude of what was to come can be found in Ditlevsen's novel based on her 1959 radio drama, *To som elsker hinanden* (Two Who Love Each Other), published as a novel in 1960. The title comes from an often-quoted Danish love poem from the 1890s by Viggo Stuckenberg, and the rest of the stanza reads: "kan gøre hinanden mer' ondt / end alle de argeste fjender" (can cause each other more harm / than all the fiercest enemies). The novel is about three people: a man who is a rather weary and decrepit literary critic who starts a relationship with a young girl just as his wife, who is in her forties, discovers that she is pregnant. The wife is also tired–tired of him and tired of his lies and indifference; but although he does not have many sympathetic qualities, she still loves him, almost in spite of herself. In one passage their marriage is described as a prison with two prisoners and two guards. The third person in this dramatic triangle, the husband's lover, is a nice, ordinary girl who has fallen passionately in love with the older man and who patiently listens to him talk about his miserable marriage.

The marital crisis delineated in the story is concretely and effectively symbolized by the house they live in, where everything is in chaos and falling apart–the furnace does not work and everyone is freezing. At the end of the novel, when the married couple seem to be settling down again, the state of the house improves–even the furnace starts working again.

In the poetry collection *Den hemmelige rude: Digte* (The Secret Window: Poems, 1961) and the story collection *Den onde lykke* (Malicious Joy, 1963) there are rumblings of revolt against the conventional woman's role. The poetic "I" who speaks in the poems refuses any longer to be locked inside of the myths that shape the lives of men and women–in particular, the typical woman's role of the caregiver. In addition to these poems of rebellion, the collection includes six poems in which Ditlevsen plays with familiar motifs taken from

the home. This contradiction made her position ambivalent, and the women's movement had a hard time accepting Ditlevsen.

Annelise–tretten år (Annelise–Thirteen Years Old, 1959) and *Hvad nu, Annelise?* (What Now, Annelise?, 1960) are two children's books that Ditlevsen was commissioned to write. They were quite different from other works written for children and young people at that time, when most children's books were about middle-class life and set far away from the big-city neighborhoods that Ditlevsen had made the specialty of her writing.

In *Annelise–tretten år* Annelise and her little brother, Jens, temporarily move in with an aunt and uncle in the Vesterbro district because their mother is ill. The move is something of a shock for them, since neither their aunt nor uncle thinks it necessary to provide breakfast or milk for schoolchildren, and they think money is something that is best spent on beer and strong liquor. The story is about how the sensible Annelise manages to handle things for herself and her little brother, at the same time as she discovers the positive values–including friendship–that can be found in

fairy tales; for example, there are poems about a witch and others about Cinderella and Rapunzel.

Den onde lykke is comprised of eleven stories, all of which deal with fear, suppressed people, and homelessness. The man, the husband, is the chief enemy; the victims are his wife and children. The women of the stories are especially imperiled, and they find neither love nor tenderness. One example of this lack of caring is the attitude shown by the husband of the title story:

> Han lå og betragtede sin endnu sovende kone, alvorlig og intenst, som om hun repræsenterede en matematisk opgave, der skulle løses, før han kunne beskæftige sig med andre ting. Han følte altid en vis ømhed for hende, lige før han vækkede hende om morgenen. Den gik hurtigt over, og hun fik det sjældent at mærke.

> (He lay there observing his still sleeping wife, solemnly and intently, as if she represented a mathematical problem that had to be solved before he could move on to other things. He always felt a certain tenderness for her right before he woke her up in the morning. It passed quickly, and she seldom felt it.)

"Måden" (The Way), is about a woman who cannot handle "all" of her husband; she can only stand part of him at a time. The part she has the most difficulty handling is his nose. So when the "nose day" approaches, her persona falls apart: "Hendes lod blev ubærlig, og der måtte ske et eller andet. Det begyndte snigende. En morgen da hun kravlede rundt flæbende og besiddelsesløs, famlende efter sit centrifugalt splittede jeg . . ." (Her lot became unbearable, and something had to happen. It began insidiously. One morning when she was crawling around, sniveling, possessing nothing, fumbling for her centrifuged, scattered self . . .). This is Ditlevsen's first short story told in a nonrealistic manner. Along with the story "De små sko" (The Little Shoes), it anticipates the two novels about marriage: *Ansigterne,* which appeared five years later, and her last novel, *Vilhelms værelse* (Vilhelm's Room, 1975).

In the judgment of the critic Henning Fousmarch, writing for *Berlingske Aftenœuir* (4 October 1963), *Den onde lykke* was more like a catalogue of failed relationships than a well-composed collection of stories. This appraisal was not entirely fair, however, since *Den onde lykke* revealed an author who was in the process of whittling away her earlier traditional style of writing in favor of a style that corresponded to the exploded forms of consciousness that she now was trying to reveal.

Den onde lykke was, in a sense, a call to arms. But before the final confrontation with Andreasen, her fourth and last husband, Ditlevsen turned once more to her childhood, which she both clung to and wished to escape. This time her return to her childhood came not in the form of a novel or poem or story but in two memoirs called *Barndom: Erindringer* (Childhood: Memoirs, 1967) and *Ungdom: Erindringer* (Youth: Memoirs, 1967); both are translated in one volume as *Early Spring,* 1985.

If Ditlevsen's earlier "snapshots" of her rain-soaked childhood are compared with the two volumes of memoirs, there are no great differences in terms of content—in a sense, the story had already been told. Both *Barndom* and *Ungdom,* however, are written with much greater conciseness and with a more delicate linguistic polish than in her earlier fiction; the reader realizes that in these books the author has made great strides artistically.

The fact that her childhood was something that Ditlevsen could not, or rather would not, let go of is explicitly stated in her memoirs, as in *Barndom,* where she writes: "Hvor man end vender sig hen, støder man mod sin barndom og slår sig, for den er kantet og hård, og holder først op, når den har sønderevet én fuldstændig" (Wherever you turn, you run up against your childhood and hurt yourself because it's sharp-edged and hard, and stops only when it has torn you completely apart). There is a great deal of quiet and indirect social indignation in the first book of memoirs. One example is the passage where her brother finds the book in which she has been writing poems; at first he jokes about it, but then he suddenly falls onto the bed, sobbing. Life is too hard for him; his boss and the other men at his workplace are constantly after him—the apprentice at the bottom of the workplace hierarchy. He cannot bear it, and it is impossible for him to have any kind of privacy. Tove tells him: "'Jeg kan jo heller ikke have noget for mig selv, og det kan far og mor heller ikke. De er ikke engang alene, når de—når de—'" (I can't have anything for myself either, you know—and neither can Father or Mother. They're not even alone when they . . . when they . . .).

Ungdom covers the years from the time Tove left school at age sixteen until she had her first poem published. In this volume the rainy haze has lifted, and the reader has a distinct impression of a vulnerable but strong individual with a tenacious will to become a writer—a will that does not allow itself to be defeated by her surroundings or by the rather confused and chaotic life that she leads as an exploited maid, warehouse worker, and office girl.

Barndom and *Ungdom* did not exactly cause a sensation, partly because Ditlevsen had written about her childhood and adolescence many times before, in both fictional form (*Barndommens Gade*) and in various autobiographical essays, including *Flugten fra opvasken*. The restrained reception by readers and the media was soon replaced, however, by the uproar that greeted the publi-

Cover for Ditlevsen's 1968 poetry collection and the cover for the 1991 translation

cation of her third volume of memoirs four years later; this time the subject was her married life, with the ambiguous title *Gift: Erindringer* (1971)–*gift* is a word that in Danish means both "married" and "poison."

Before the third volume of memoirs was published, Ditlevsen demonstrated that even though she was in many ways miserable and had to fight hard to keep the demons at bay in her life, she was in the midst of a dramatic artistic development. That is what her readers–and the critics–would discover when the novel *Ansigterne* came out in 1968, followed by the poetry collection *De voksne: Digte* (The Grown-Ups: Poems) a year later.

Ansigterne is generally considered the finest of Ditlevsen's novels. It is a book about a woman's marriage and her nervous breakdown; it is a novel that examines the female artist's difficult situation. Several earlier works foreshadow this novel. In the story collection *Den onde lykke* several of the same props can be found in the story "De små sko," which has a mid-

dle-aged woman as its protagonist. She feels irrelevant and superfluous, and she stays at home because her husband says that it "wouldn't pay" for her to have a job. She and her husband both feel life slipping away from them. The wife develops a friendship with their young maid because she suspects her husband of being unfaithful, but this relationship turns tragic when she confuses a dream she has–of the maid throwing poison at her son–with reality. The story "The Way," in the same collection, also foreshadows the disintegration of a psyche, which is the central theme in *Ansigterne*.

The female protagonist in *Ansigterne*, Lise Mundus (named for Ditlevsen's mother, whose maiden name was Mundus) is an author, and her situation is all too familiar to women writers. She is in the midst of a creative crisis, partly because she is torn between the demands of her home and her husband and her own deep need to withdraw into an inner sanctum in order to create. To get out of her painful predicament, Lise

Mundus flees into madness. She does this not only because of her own unresolved situation, but also because she cannot cope with having to take a stand on the world's misery, as she is required to do. The person who demands her involvement and appeals to her global consciousness is the maid, Gitte. She represents the new youth, the youth that Ditlevsen's generation felt had taken power after 1968. Gitte asks all the questions that Lise Mundus would prefer to ignore–about issues such as the Vietnam War and the problems in the developing countries. Lise cannot, will not, answer these questions; in other ways she is also unable to cope with her life or her marriage, so she breaks down and becomes psychotic.

Ditlevsen effectively allows the reader to experience this psychosis from the "inside," since the narrative point of view is always connected to Lise. The reader participates in the hallucinations, hears the same voices behind the ventilation grating in the hospital rooms, and experiences human faces not as faces but as masks. The novel's conclusion is relatively positive. Gitte is fired, and the reader has the feeling that Lise and her husband might have a future together. *Ansigterne* proved to be a different type of novel, one that shocked readers, both because of its insight into the nature of insanity and because of the style in which it was written.

In the poetry collection *De voksne* Ditlevsen again made use of new tones as she renounced her traditional style by eliminating all rhymes and traditional verse construction. None of the poems in the collection is rhymed, and all of them have varying verse lengths. Ditlevsen touches on the themes of fear, death, divorce, and loneliness. In many poems there is also an unspoken feeling that hell is not represented by other people; rather, it is always part of yourself. And in this late collection her childhood reappears, once again associated with fear–the fear that is the main theme of her literary works:

> Angsten er gammel den
> lugter af barndom den
> har ingen genstand
> vækkes af blikke og ord og
> af pludselig støj
> lever i gentagne drømme hvor
> den som man elsker
> viser det dræbende had han
> skjuler om dagen.

> (Fear is old it
> smells of childhood it
> has no object
> awakened by glances and words and
> by sudden noise
> lives in repeated dreams where
> the one you love
> shows the deadly hatred he
> conceals by day.)

The collection prompted loud applause from the leading Danish poetry critics, who were all serious-minded men. It also drew the acclaim of the supporters of modernism and the opponents of all old-fashioned structured poetry: those critics who had been full of disdain for Ditlevsen's earlier efforts. In their eyes, Ditlevsen had finally seen the light of modernism.

All the media attention to which Ditlevsen had been subjected earlier in her career was overshadowed by what happened when her third volume of memoirs, *Gift,* appeared in 1971. Many people were scandalized because in this volume she not only recounted the story of her tumultuous marital life with her first three husbands, but she also ruthlessly exposed to ridicule all of the men with whom she had ever had a relationship. Tabloid and newspaper reporters immediately responded to the scent of scandal and eagerly reported stories of threatened lawsuits.

The brilliantly ambiguous Danish title, *Gift,* refers not only to the institution of marriage but also to the addiction that Ditlevsen was unable to escape for many years, thanks to the devastating amounts of prescription drugs supplied by her third husband, Rydberg. In addition to her withering depictions of her former husbands, Ditlevsen describes in scathing detail her lovers, including the well-known Danish poet Piet Hein. When a journalist asked Ditlevsen whether she should have been more discreet, she replied with the quick-wittedness that is said to be particularly characteristic of Copenhageners: If only people knew what she had *not* written about. The public uproar, however, prompted Ditlevsen to suffer another nervous breakdown.

Barndom, Ungdom, and *Gift* represent not only a milestone in Ditlevsen's own career; in many ways they rank among the finest memoirs written in Danish. It is not an exaggeration to say that in terms of sheer quality, they are on a par with *Min fynske Barndom* (My Funen Childhood, 1927), the memoir written by the famous composer Carl Nielsen, and with the novelist Martin Andersen Nexø's four-volume autobiography, published 1932–1939.

The fact that Ditlevsen's memoirs have such a strong impact is partly due to her highly developed technique of exclusion. Everything that does not serve to link her people, her milieu, and her memories into one great emotional arc has been scraped away. In these works she fully mastered and demonstrated the art of restriction and her talent for paring her narrative down to the essentials.

When her publisher, Gyldendal, launched a series of books about modern Danish authors, intended for use in the public schools, someone had the idea of asking Ditlevsen whether she would consider writing about herself. She agreed, and the short book titled *Tove Ditlevsen om sig selv,* which appeared in 1975, is a splendidly informative and much-quoted work, ranking almost on a par with her memoirs. In this book she remarks, for example, that the reader will search in vain for nature in her works because she never had any knack at writing about it. Once, she says, she ventured to write about a swallow that flew off with a worm in its yellow beak, but when this description prompted a storm of protests from ornithologists, she refrained from writing any more about birds or nature.

Tove Ditlevsen was in every sense a highly unusual person. Although she was ill for long periods of time, she never failed to write her advice column for *Familie Journalen* (The Family Journal), a popular magazine. Her advice was much in demand, and it was primarily women who sought her help. Almost all of them asked her about problems with relationships or marriages. Ditlevsen's answers were usually candid and clear, but she typically did not encourage women to leave their husbands, even though their marriages might be quite terrible. She had a fundamental belief that men and women thrived best in marriage and that women did not need to educate themselves in the same way as men did. In principle, women belonged within the four walls of home. With these views Ditlevsen distanced herself sharply from the women's movement, which gained prominence in Denmark after 1968.

Several of the advice columns that Ditlevsen wrote were collected in a book called *Med venlig hilsen Tove Ditlevsen: Spørgsmål og svar fra Familie Journalens brevkasse* (Sincerely, Tove Ditlevsen: Questions and Answers from *Familie Journalen*'s Advice Column, 1969). These essays demonstrate her courage to go right to the heart of whatever problem was presented to her; they also reveal her conservativism in terms of women's issues.

In addition to answering questions for the advice column, Ditlevsen also wrote other columns in the daily newspapers for many years. They were popular because her quick wit and lack of pretense remained intact even during her periods of depression. Many of these articles were collected in several volumes: *Min nekrolog og andre skumle tanker* (My Obituary and Other Gloomy Thoughts, 1973), *Paranteser* (Parentheses, 1973), and *En sibylles bekendelser* (Confessions of a Sibyl, 1976). In several of the essays, Ditlevsen makes humorous observations; in some she sputters with irritation; and in still others she expresses a gentle astonishment at the behavior of her fellow human beings.

In her last poetry collection, *Det runde værelse* (1973), Ditlevsen only partially continued with the exploded verse form with which she had experimented in *De voksne*. The book has a pervasively somber tone, and the narrative "I" of the poems seems worn out and alienated. Here too there is a solidarity with the weak, with those whom other people do not and will not understand.

Ditlevsen's last book was the novel *Vilhelms værelse* (1975), which can almost be read as a sequel to the memoir *Gift*. At the end of *Gift*, the narrator is saved from her addiction by her fourth husband. In the memoir he appears as a rescuing angel, but in the novel it becomes apparent that the angel also possesses diabolic traits. *Vilhelms værelse* is a grotesque and harsh story, but in brief passages it is also exceedingly funny. The novel is not by any means a solid work of art; it is often uneven, shaky, and confusing, but like many of Ditlevsen's less successful works, it shows glimpses of what a remarkable author she was.

One of Ditlevsen's biographers, Jens Andersen, has claimed that *Vilhelms værelse* is not really a novel; rather, it is more like "en vild og voldsom teksthybrid, der side om side med nøglehulskiggeriet og den grotesk-satirisk beskrivelse af et ægteskabs kremering handler om sin egen besværlige tilblivelse mellem alle mulige forskellige former for tekst" (a wild and violent hybrid text which, alongside the peeping in keyholes and the grotesque-satirical description of the last convulsions of a marriage, deals with its own difficult genesis among all possible forms of text).

The newspaper *Politiken,* for which Ditlevsen was writing, had decided to help publicize *Vilhelms værelse* by printing an excerpt from the book that featured the protagonist, Lise Mundus, selling her sensational memoir articles to a newspaper. For readers, it was difficult to distinguish between the various narrators, but they did agree on one thing: that this time Ditlevsen might well have gone completely mad, but she had done so in an incredibly entertaining way. The book became a great publishing success, even before the reviewers had a chance to pass judgment.

Vilhelms værelse is Ditlevsen's final statement about herself, her marriages, and her life. And it also includes some hints that with the publication of this book she herself was on her way out of life: "Hun gav sig omsider til at elske verden, men kun fordi den skulle udslettes sammen med hende" (At long last she allowed herself to love the world, but only because it was going to be obliterated along with her).

Tove Ditlevsen committed suicide 7 March 1976. It has been said of Ditlevsen that she is the great author of banality. This remark should be understood to mean that she is traditional, bordering on the banal, in terms of her choice of subject matter, since she writes almost exclusively about the relationship between parents and children, about the complicated and often banal interplay between men and women, about the man who betrays, about the children who grow up and disappear, about emptiness and empty hands. Ditlevsen is also traditional in her choice of narrative styles; it was only late in her career that she began to experiment with techniques, both in her poetry and her prose. The story that Ditlevsen tells throughout her work is basically the same. It is the story about the "harmed" child and the difficult life. The child, whether a girl or a boy, also collides with life as an adult—a life that is harsh and for the most part joyless. The joys that people do find are, in most cases, transformed and become bitter experiences. The child in Ditlevsen's works is always a version of the author herself because, in her case, life and writing were one.

Ditlevsen's gift resides first and foremost in the fact that she was able to make banality and traditionalism into a genuine, artistic trademark. She had great artistic and human integrity, and the person and the artist cannot be separated from each other. When Ditlevsen appeared in the media and revealed who she was and how harshly life had dealt with her, the world and her readers perceived her as genuine.

Her language was individual, simple, and at the same time sophisticated and surprising, even if many critics (especially male critics) misinterpreted her simplicity and regarded her style as superficial and flat. It was through Ditlevsen's simple language that banality was elevated to a great and universal literary art, and her books have never lost their hold on Danish readers.

Bibliography:

Ellen Margrethe Jensen, *Tove Ditlevsen: En bibliografi* (Copenhagen: Danmarks Biblioteksskole, 1976).

Biographies:

Harald Mogensen, ed., *Om Tove Ditlevsen: En bog skrevet af venner og andre der kendte hende* (Copenhagen: Forum, 1976);

Margit Mørk, *Kender du Tove Ditlevsen* (Copenhagen: Grafisk, 1986);

Erik Thygesen, *Tove Ditlevsen: 13 ansigter* (Copenhagen: Tiderne Skifter, 1986);

Jens Andersen, *Til døden os skiller: Et portræt af Tove Ditlevsen* (Copenhagen: Gyldendal, 1997);

Karen Syberg, *Tove Ditlevsen: Myte og liv* (Copenhagen: Tiderne Skifter, 1997).

Letters:

Ester Nagel, *Husmor og skribøse: En brevveksling med Tove Ditlevsen* (Charlottenlund: Rosinante, 1986);

Victor Andreasen, ed., *Kære Victor: Breve fra Tove Ditlevsen til Victor Andreasen 1972–1976* (Copenhagen: Gyldendal, 1993).

Interview:

Malin Lindgrenen: "Han, hun og ægteskabet," *Søndags-BT,* 13 January 1961.

References:

Lise Busk-Jensen, "Tove Ditlevsen," in *Nordisk kvindelitteraturhistorie,* 5 volumes, edited by Elisabeth Møller Jensen and others (Copenhagen: Rosinante, 1996), III: 482–493;

Stig Dalager and Anne-Marie Mai, "Tove Ditlevsen," in *Danske kvindelige forfattere,* 2 volumes, edited by Dalager and Mai (Copenhagen: Gyldendal, 1982), I: 112–122;

Susanne Knudsen, "Tove Ditlevsen," in *Imellem—skidt og skrift* (Copenhagen: Gyldendal, 1989), pp. 157–223;

Anne Birgitte Richard, *Kvindelitteratur og kvindesituation: Socialisering, offentlighed og æstetik: En undersøgelse af kvinders litterære produktionsvilkar med analyser af Tove Ditlevsen og Jette Drewsen* (Copenhagen: Gyldendal, 1976);

Lis Thorbjørnsen, ed., *Med venlig hilsen Tove Ditlevsen* (Copenhagen, Hasselbalch, 1969);

Mette Winge, "Tove Ditlevsen," in *Danske digtere i det 20. århundrede,* volume 3 (Copenhagen: Gad, 1981): pp. 241–256.

Elsa Gress

(17 January 1919 – 18 July 1988)

Lanae H. Isaacson

BOOKS: *Strejftog: Essays* (Copenhagen: K. E. Hermann, 1945);

Mellemspil (Copenhagen: Schultz, 1947);

Concertino (Fredensborg: Arena/Forfatternes Forlag, 1955);

Jorden er ingen stjerne (Fredensborg: Arena/Forfatternes Forlag, 1956);

Nye strejftog: Essays og epistler (Fredensborg: Arena/Forfatternes Forlag, 1957);

Elysisk aften—At være kætter: Essays (Fredensborg: Arena/Forfatternes Forlag, 1959);

Prometheus på flugt: Essays (Fredensborg: Arena/Forfatternes Forlag, 1961);

Er der nogen der hører efter? Essays (Fredensborg: Arena/Forfatternes Forlag, 1964);

Habiba og andre noveller (Copenhagen: Spectator, 1964);

Det uopdagede køn: Essays (Copenhagen: Spectator, 1964);

Mine mange hjem: Erindringsbog (Copenhagen: Spectator, 1965);

Det professionelle menneske: Essays og artikler 1941–1966, edited, with an introduction, by Hans Hertel (Copenhagen: Gyldendal, 1966);

Om Kløfter: Essays (Fredensborg: Arena/Forfatternes Forlag, 1967);

Boxiganga: Teater som livsform (Copenhagen: Spectator, 1968);

Lurens toner: Børnebog, by Gress and David Gress (Copenhagen: Spectator, 1968);

Fugle og frøer: Afsnit og epistler (Copenhagen: Arena/Forfatternes Forlag, 1969);

Den sårede Filoktet (Copenhagen: Forlaget Drama, 1970);

Fuglefri og fremmed: Erindringsbilleder (Copenhagen: Gyldendal, 1971);

Apropos virkeligheden: Essays (Copenhagen: Gyldendal, 1972);

Compañia: Erindringsbilleder (Copenhagen: Gyldendal, 1976);

Dramatikeren Soya: Tale ved overrækkelsen af Det danske Akademis store pris d. 28.11.1975 (Copenhagen: Borgen, 1976);

Salamander (Copenhagen: Gyldendal, 1977);

Elsa Gress in 1986 (photograph by Gregers Nielsen; courtesy of Gyldendal Publishers)

Engagement: Epistler og essays om kunst og liv og andet mere, illustrated by Clifford Wright (Copenhagen: Gyldendal, 1977);

Dæmoniske damer og andre figurer: Dramatiske tekster (Copenhagen: Gyldendal, 1979);

Fanden til Forskel: Essays, monologer og dialoger (Copenhagen: Gyldendal, 1979);

Vist koster det noget: Erindringsbog (Copenhagen: Berlingske, 1980);

Udsigter og indsigter, illustrated by Wright (Copenhagen: Mistral, 1981);

Viser og ballader, by Gress and Palle Gress (Toftlund: SiSu, 1982);

Blykuglen: Epistler og essays (Copenhagen: Gyldendal, 1984);

Henrik Stangerup, by Gress and others (Odense: Odense Universitetsforlag, 1986);

Simurghen (Copenhagen: Gyldendal, 1986); translated by Gress as *The Simurg* (London & New York: Quartet, 1989).

Edition in English: *Philoctetes Wounded and Other Plays,* translated by Gress (Glumson: DECENTER/Åso Gl. Skole, 1969).

PLAY PRODUCTIONS: *Den sårede filoktet,* Glumsø, DECENTER, 1969;

Ditto Daughter, Hollins College, Roanoke, Va., 30 April 1971; revised as *Ditto Dotter,* Frederiksberg, Riddersalen, 14 October 1976);

Liv, Copenhagen, Boldhusteater, 4 December 1974;

M.I.M.I.R.: Libretto til musik drama, script by Gress, music by Tom O'Horgen, Copenhagen, Det Kongelige Teater, 1974;

Donny Johnny: Play in 2 Parts, script by Gress, music by James Wilson, New York, St. Clement's Theater, 1975;

Kristi Himmelfartsfesten. Et vulkanstykke, Gladsaxe, Gladsaxe Teater, 1983.

MOTION PICTURES: *En by ved navn København,* screenplay by Gress and others, Danish Film Office/Minerva Film/Statens Filmcentral, 1960;

Boxiganga, screenplay by Gress, Copenhagen, 1967.

RADIO: *Hvis,* script by Gress, Danmarks Radio, 1947;

En negers Komediehus, script translated by Gress from a work by Adrienne Kennedy, Danmarks Radio, 1966.

TELEVISION: *Den sårede filoktet,* script by Gress, Danmarks Radio, 1974;

Erindring om fremtiden, script by Gress, Danmarks Radio, TV-teaterafdelingen, 1988;

Balladen om Carl Dreyer: TV-spil, script by Gress, Danmarks Radio, TV-teaterafdelingen, 1988.

TRANSLATIONS: Joan Grant, *Den røde Fjer* (Copenhagen, 1947);

Arnold J. Toynbee, *Historien i et nyt Lys* (Copenhagen, 1948);

Toynbee, *Kulteren for domstolen* (Copenhagen, 1949);

Arturo Barea, *Roden* (Copenhagen, 1950);

Louis Guilloux, *Drømmen om barndommen* (Copenhagen, 1950);

Willard Savoy, *En fremmed i landet* (Copenhagen, 1950);

Edna Ferber, *Giganten* (Copenhagen, 1953);

Ritchie Calder, *I kamp mod junglen* (Copenhagen, 1954);

Omar Khayyám, *Rubâijât* (Copenhagen: Spectator, 1960);

Jack Kerouac, *Vejene* (Fredensborg: Arena, 1960);

John Steinbeck, *Øst for Paradis,* translated by Gress and Mogens Knudsen (Copenhagen: Gyldendal, 1960);

Erskine Caldwell, *Jenny* (Copenhagen: Grafisk Forlag, 1961);

Aldous Huxley, *Essays* (Copenhagen: Aschehoug, 1961);

Huxley, *Ø: En Roman* (Copenhagen, 1962);

John Updike, *Hare Hop* (Copenhagen: Gyldendal, 1963);

Norbert Wiener, *Menneske og automat: Kybernettiken og samfundet* (Copenhagen: Gyldendal, 1963);

The Limfjord: Its Towns and Peoples, translated by Gress and Percy Wait (Copenhagen: Det Danske Selskab, 1964);

Ebbe Neergaard, *The Story of Danish Film* (Copenhagen: Det Danske Selskab, 1963);

Huxley, *Litteratur og videnskab* (Copenhagen: Rosenkilde & Bagger, 1964);

Under månens skive: Poetisk postil, translated and edited by Gress (Copenhagen: Spectator, 1964);

Philip Roth, *Farvel, Columbus* (Copenhagen: Gyldendal, 1965);

Updike, *I morgen og i morgen og så videre* (Copenhagen: Gyldendal, 1965);

Richard Wright, *Vidner* (Copenhagen: Gyldendal, 1966);

Marshall McLuhan, *Mennesket og medierne* (Copenhagen: Gyldendal, 1967);

Syv forfattere skriver til Århus Håndsætterklub i anledning af 50 års jubilæet 1969, translated by Gress and others (Viby J: Ravnsbjerg Tryk, 1969);

Paul Foster, *Tom Paine: Et spil i to dele* (Copenhagen, 1969);

F. Scott Fitzgerald, *Natten er blid,* translated by Gress and Helga Vang Lauridsen (Copenhagen: Gyldendal, 1972);

Lawrence Durrell, *Alexandria-kvartetten* (Copenhagen: Gyldendal, 1974);

Virginia Woolf, *Eget værelse,* translated by Gress and David Gress-Wright (Copenhagen: Samleren, 1978).

OTHER: Charles Dickens, *Oliver Twist,* translated by L. Moltke, foreword by Gress (Geneva: Edito Bøger, 1971);

Charlotte Brontë, *Jane Eyre,* translated by Aslaug Mikkelsen, foreword by Gress (Virum: Edito Bøger, 1971);

Dickens, *Pickwick Klubben,* translated by Moltke, foreword by Gress (Virum: Edito Bøger, 1971);

Lidija Dombrovska Larsen, *De vingede øjine: Digte, tegninger, gouacher,* foreword by Gress (Copenhagen: Ildfugl, 1973);

James Wilson, *Aria to Ariel; or, Grinning at the Devil,* libretto by Gress (Copenhagen: Henrik Nebelong, 1989).

Considered by many to be Denmark's literary grande dame, Elsa Gress established her reputation with three successive works: *Strejftog* (Incursions, 1945), a collection of essays on art and aesthetics; *Hvis* (If, 1947), a now lost radio play about suicide; and *Mellemspil* (Entr'Acte, 1947), a novel about a young girl's search for a new life in dreary post–World War II London. Following *Strejftog, Hvis* and *Mellemspil* demonstrated Gress's talents for tackling stylistic and formal challenges. *Mellemspil,* a work in which everything is, according to Henrik Stangerup, "beskrevet ud fra–inde fra–hovedpersonens følsomme sind, i pastelagtige farver, i rids, flygtige, næsten japansk" (described from–and within–the protagonist's sensitive mind, in pastel colors, in outlines, fleeting, nearly Japanese), won the 1947 Schultz Literature Prize for best novel. Throughout her life Gress, who Stangerup characterizes as a "kæmpende humanist på tværs af tre tiårs filosofiske, litterære og kulturpolitiske strømninger, nationale såvel som internationale" (a fighting humanist spanning three decades of philosophical, literary, and cultural-political trends, on the national and international plane), remained an insightful essayist, one of a few Danes who practiced the form with finesse; an enthusiastic dramatist; a novelist and short-story writer who utilized her knowledge of the Anglo-American world; and an autobiographer whose memoir of childhood, *Mine mange hjem: Erindringsbog* (My Many Homes: A Memoir, 1965), Stangerup describes as "et erindringsværk på linie med de smukkeste i dansk litteratur, fra Johanne Luise Heibergs og til Carl Nielsens og Asta Nielsens" (a memoir on a par with the loveliest in Danish literature, from Johanne Luise Heiberg's up to Carl Nielsen's and Asta Nielsen's).

The youngest of three siblings, Judith Elisa Gress was born 17 January 1919 in Frederiksberg, Copenhagen, to Edvard Tobias Gress, an upper-class gentleman of independent but dwindling means, and Elisa Hedevig Pallesen Gress, the daughter of a wealthy but eventually ruined merchant from Vendsyssel, Johan Andreas Brun Pallesen. Ostensibly the daughter of a patrician family living in fancy Ordrup, Gress attended Ordrup Gymnasium. *Mine mange hjem* depicts the balancing act Gress and her entire family, particularly her self-sacrificing mother, constantly performed. Well-educated but entirely unsuited to practical work, hopelessly neurotic, and with self-destructive tendencies to compulsive gambling, Edvard Gress managed to reduce his inheritance and his wife's to mere memory; his wife kept the family afloat by sacrificing family possessions and by keeping an array of lodgers in rented villas, even in tiny apartments. Gress paints a grim picture of a precarious, solitary childhood in a dysfunctional family of "fattige millionærer" (poor millionaires) whose inheritance and links to the past gradually dissolved into fleeting memories.

After receiving her secondary-school diploma in 1937, Gress traveled extensively for two years, living a vagabond life in Germany, France, and England. Gress experienced the ominous rise of Fascism and National Socialism firsthand. Increasingly, her focus turned to England; her orientation, which Stangerup characterizes as "angelsaksisk . . . i et land hvis litterære og filosofisk-teologiske tradition er overvejende tysk" (Anglo-Saxon . . . in a land whose literary and philosophical-theological tradition is overwhelmingly German), was unlike that of most Danes. Gress returned to the University of Copenhagen in 1939; she studied English literature and wrote an acclaimed thesis, "Omkring Klassicismens Gennembrud i Engelsk Litteratur" (Concerning the Classical Breakthrough in English Literature), for which she received the University Gold Medallion in 1942. Gress received her master of arts degree in comparative literature in 1944. Her years at the university were marred by the war, the suicide of her troubled older brother, Palle, and her family's continuing financial decline. Gress's own demanding teaching, translation, and writing schedule and her activities in the resistance movement in occupied Denmark added to her stress and led to a complete nervous collapse and hospitalization during the course of her studies.

Immediately after World War II, Gress returned to England to recuperate from the war and Palle's death, to write freelance articles, and eventually to work for the BBC (British Broadcasting Corporation). (Gress's work with the BBC later aroused suspicion during her stay in the United States, since many Americans at the time regarded the BBC as a base for international communism.) In *Fuglefri og fremmed: Erindringsbilleder* (Free as a Bird and Foreign: Scenes Remembered, 1971) Gress describes the London years as the impetus for her prizewinning 1947 novel, *Mellemspil;* in London, Gress mapped out a new identity, began a new life among people also recovering and beginning anew: *Mellemspil* marks Gress's own "sand[e] dokumentation af indre tilstande, og af de ydre tilstande der betinger dem og betinges af dem" (true documentation of inner states, and of the external conditions which determined them and were determined by them). *Mellemspil* and Gress's later novels, *Concertino* (1955) and *Jorden er ingen stjerne* (The Earth Is No Star, 1956), drew on the author's experiences in academic and literary circles in Europe and New York as a peripatetic intellectual making her way in the world according to her principles of engagement and eclecticism.

In 1951 Gress made her first trip to the United States in order to study at Columbia University on a Rockefeller grant; Gress participated in New York's artistic and intellectual life, with side excursions to other East Coast cities, the Rocky Mountains, and Pennsylvania. Gress later claimed that her doctoral seminars at Columbia could not compete with the actual experience of living in the United States. Like her protagonist, Judith, in *Jorden er ingen stjerne,* Gress became involved with a married intellectual, Richard Lewis, a professor at Columbia. Pregnant with her first son, David, she returned home to Denmark late in 1952 after arousing U.S. government suspicions regarding her war and postwar activities and consequently losing her visa. Gress met with warm acceptance and support in Denmark and also with a few unexpected difficulties, notably financial problems, as a single mother.

With the publication of Gress's first essays in *Strejftog,* the author found firm support from her editor, Karl-Erik Hermann, who went on to publish many of her books, including *Concertino* and *Jorden er ingen stjerne,* at his new firm, Arena. *Concertino* is not so much a novel as it is an essay on the cultural scene, the Cold War, the atomic bomb, political and artistic trends, and humanism—Gress's abiding principle—in a post–World War II environment. In the novel a group of intellectuals and academics have gathered somewhere in Europe. Gress often sets the stage for the encounter of New and Old Worlds in an indeterminate but generally festive and dynamic European locale, which functions as a catalyst for a meeting of minds.

In 1954 Gress visited Tunis as part of a women's delegation overseeing the French occupation of North Africa. Undertaking such a journey meant leaving fifteen-month-old David in the hands of the family's protectress, the indomitable Ane Cathrine Mørck, who figures prominently in *Mine mange hjem.* In Tunis, Gress was profoundly shocked,

Cover for Gress's 1947 novel, based on her experiences in London after World War II

as was her entire group, by the misery behind the facade of exotic beauty. The occupying French government remained largely indifferent; private philanthropy could do little to cope, given the enormity of the problem; and local Moslem strictures complicated international efforts to help. The poverty was exacerbated by the Tunisians' xenophobia and hatred of minorities, particularly of the local Jewish community. Before she left Tunis and returned to Denmark, Gress was made to sign an affidavit stating that she had not observed any objectionable conditions.

In many ways *Jorden er ingen stjerne* seems a thinly veiled account of the author on her own in the New World; like Gress, Judith is a Danish student who falls for a neurotic, financially hard-pressed academic, Bob Barker (modeled on Richard Lewis), a

Poster for Gress's first produced play, performed in English in Roanoke, Virginia, in 1967

man clinging to the skirts and fortune of his infantile wife, Grace; also like Gress, Judith loses her visa as a result of the State Department's growing suspicion of her and leaves New York pregnant and happy–or at least remarkably resigned–to be so. Gress captures a certain New York milieu and time, depicting the flawed motivations and values, the self-promotion schemes, shallow pseudo-intellectualism, and social and emotional complacency of an upper-class academic society out of sync with the life of the mind.

The novel is framed by Judith's remarks to her unborn child, a meld of the Old World and the New. The child's presence in this way throughout the novel lifts the circumstances of Judith's relationship with Barker from their quotidian simplicity and gives them an inevitable, even transcendental quality. The casual affair becomes something serious, almost as though the nascent life will control his parents and determine the course of events, as Judith recognizes: "Jo, du havde smedet endnu et par led i din dobbeltlænke, og fra nu af holdt du ikke op at klirre os om ørene med den–for ham af og til, for mig uafladeligt. Gå tilbage til 'friheden' kunne ingen af os nu" (Yes, you had cast a couple of links more in your double chain, and from now on you would not stop tickling our ears with it–his now and then, mine con-

stantly. None of us could go back to "freedom" now). In the wake of the failed affair a new, composite force emerges to control Judith, just as Gress's son, David, shaped the author's own destiny.

Other strengths of *Jorden er ingen stjerne* lie in Gress's description of scene and her use of detail and drama. Gress opens with the scene vaguely set in "et sted i Europa" (a place in Europe), a meeting of the Old and New Worlds on familiar turf. Other scenes– a Thanksgiving party in the country, a secretive rendezvous–set the stage for Barker and Judith's affair. Gress received accolades for her clear-eyed depiction of the symbiosis linking the United States and Denmark in an elaborate, often intricate pas de deux.

In 1956, after a brief stay in England, Gress married an American artist, Clifford Wright, whom she had met during her stay in New York; the couple had two children: Barbara in 1957 and Jonathan in 1958. Wright illustrated several of Gress's works, most notably her collections of essays and letters, *Engagement: Epistler og essays om kunst og liv og andet mere* (Engagement: Letters and Essays on Art, Life, and Other Matters, 1977) and *Udsigter og indsigter* (Views and Insights, 1981); the couple built a wide circle of artistic, literary, and theatrical friends. In the ensuing years Gress explored American culture, attacking antihumanism, emphasizing compassion, and depicting "de rigtige poeter og de oprigtige, bragende dygtige romanforfattere" (the true poets and the just, stunningly brilliant novelists). Gress's essays on American literature and culture, a kind of reformulation of *Concertino,* appeared in the collection *Nye strejftog* (New Incursions, 1957); subsequent collections of essays on politics, art, and aesthetics appeared at regular intervals: *Elysisk aften–At være kætter* (Elysian Evening–To Be a Heretic, 1959); *Prometheus på flugt* (Prometheus in Flight, 1961); *Er der nogen der hører efter? Essays* (Is Anyone Listening? Essays, 1964); and *Det uopdagede køn: Essays* (The Undiscovered Sex, Essays, 1964).

With *Det uopdagede køn,* a work whose title intentionally recalls Simone de Beauvoir's *Le deuxième sexe* (The Second Sex, 1949), Gress joined the fierce debate concerning the role of women. She stresses individualism and humanism, attributing the failures of many women as mothers to their immaturity and lack of understanding. In Gress's view, few women qualify for motherhood. Her emphases on individualism and humanism led her to reject de Beauvoir's ethical stance and her acceptance of prevailing societal values. Her belief in maturity, intelligence, and biological predisposition as necessary requirements for motherhood, on the other hand, put her at odds with more-radical feminists and their contempt for an inherently patriarchal society and its values.

In 1966 Hans Hertel published the best of Gress's essays in a compilation, *Det professionelle menneske: Essays og artikler 1941–1966* (The Professional Person: Essays and Articles, 1941–1966). Gress continued to write essays during the late 1960s and 1970s; collections from those years include *Om kløfter* (Concerning Chasms, 1967), *Fugle og frøer: Afsnit og epistler* (Birds and Frogs: Passages and Letters, 1969), and *Apropos virkeligheden* (Apropos Reality, 1972).

In addition to *Er der nogen der hører efter?* and *Det uopdagede køn,* Gress published a collection of innovative and engaging short stories, *Habiba og andre noveller* (Habiba and Other Stories), in 1964. The title story, "Habiba," draws on an incident Gress witnessed during her visit to Tunis: a young Arab prostitute stabbed a man to death for making her child cry. In "Habiba" the Arab girl stoically faces a French judge determined to get to the bottom of the story. Habiba accepts her long imprisonment in Melassine Prison willingly, even with relief, so long as she is allowed to keep her baby. Gress describes the simple story in such vivid detail that the reader empathizes with Habiba, sharing her pathetic sense of relief over her verdict.

One of the most intriguing short stories of the collection, "Ravnen flyver om aftenen" (The Raven Flies in the Evening), concerns a man on the verge of suicide who receives a chain letter guaranteeing him luck and happiness. In a fit of vindictiveness the man alters the letter so that it promises inevitable bad luck even if the chain is unbroken; the man–a writer by profession–sends copies to his wife, his rival, his publisher, and his best friend and then carries through on his plan to kill himself. After his death, misfortune spreads in concentric rings, farther and farther from its origin. "Ravnen flyver om aftenen" is bizarre, clever, and also funny, enlivened by a sense of melodrama.

In 1965, in recognition of her contributions to Danish national cultural and literary debate, Gress received the Jeanne and Henri Nathansen Literary Prize and the Kollegernes ærespris (Colleagues' Award of Honor). She received the Tage Brandt Travel Grant the following year.

Mine mange hjem re-creates Gress's Depression-era childhood with great accuracy, although the book also has a timeless quality. It is an account of a difficult time with difficult parents who still managed to give their children freedom and individuality, "en frihed måske, en uortodoks holdning afgjort" (a freedom perhaps, definitely an unorthodox stance). Central to Gress's childhood was her mother, who constantly shared enthusiasm and interests with her children, Palle and Elsa, engaging them in life and in whatever possibilities and challenges life held. This engagement held especially true when it came to reading "bøger og digte, hun selv havde tudet over som barn og ung" (books and poems she had wept over herself as a child and young girl).

In *Mine mange hjem* an especially dramatic event signals financial losses and social and economic downturn for the Gresses: the Pallesen family estate in Jutland burns completely to the ground, leaving a smoldering remnant of what was once a gilded age and a symbol of the start down a slippery slope to wandering, to unfilled needs, to many homes. The fact that the family remained together throughout these hardships was an enormous influence on Gress's own creativity and talent.

Edvard Gress only occasionally worked as a secretary, but he devoted much misplaced energy to futile efforts to win back the Gress fortune. A dangerously neurotic man who lived in constant fear of bacteria–so much so that he even washed money as well as his hands–Gress's father turned over the entire household to his long-suffering wife, who had the practical sense to sell the family's material possessions to keep a roof over their heads. With the death

ELSA GRESS

Compañia

FØRSTE BIND

Erindringsbilleder

Whatever we have been,
in some sort we still are ...
C. S. LEWIS

GYLDENDAL

Title page for the first volume of Gress's 1976 autobiography

of Gress's mother after years of overwork and untreated diabetes, the family unit dissolved, and Gress began her own peripatetic search for a home, eventually the artistic and literary one described in the two-volume *Compañia: Erindringsbilleder* (1976).

Mine mange hjem is filled with memorable characters, or rather, Gress makes them memorable with her skill for description and detail. Most notable is the family's faithful housekeeper-cum-nanny, Ane Cathrine Mørck, who more or less sacrifices her own life for the sake of the Gresses; at times living with the family, Mørck provided stability and security for them all, especially Gress, well into the author's adulthood. The Gress home, wherever it might be, was also haunted by the ghost of Gress's older sister, Lily, whose early death left a void never quite filled by her younger siblings. Lily was the family paragon; as such, she is constantly held up to Gress, who never quite measures up to "det unikum af intelli-

gens, godhed, blidhed og ynde" (that unity of intelligence, goodness, sweetness, and delight). Lily's death is a much harder loss for the family to accept: everything else—all the moves, the strange lodgers, the lost family heirlooms and homes—pales in comparison.

Increasingly, Gress began to direct her attention to theater and cinema, in large measure because of her association with director Tom O'Horgan, about whom she remarks in volume 2 of *Compañia*: "Tom laver ikke teater, han *er*" (Tom does not do theater, he *is* theater). O'Horgan was the inspiration for Roy Roscoe, the protagonist in Gress's novel *Salamander* (1977), a work dealing with the theater, dramatic artists, and the elusive, ephemeral spark of creativity. O'Horgan went on to direct a 1974 television adaptation of Gress's drama about the Danish painter Nicolai Abildgaard, *Den sårede Filoktet* (1970; translated as *Philoctetes Wounded,* 1969). An underground movie based on Gress's play *Boxiganga: Teater som livsform* appeared in 1967; the following year the play was published in an edition that included remarks by Gress on the theater in Danish and English. Gress has never quite caught on as a playwright and director. Still, her play about pregnancy, *Liv* (Life, 1974), was produced at the Boldhusteater; her fantasy on sexual roles and values, *Ditto daughter,* debuted at Hollins College, in Roanoke, Virginia, in 1967 and was subsequently performed at Cambridge University in a production directed by David Gress and at Riddersalen, in Frederiksberg under the playwright's own direction as *Ditto Dotter.* Other dramas from Gress's pen include *Donny Johnny: Play in 2 Parts* (1975), based on the long poem *Don Juan* (1819–1824), by George Gordon, Lord Byron, and a frightening view of the Apocalypse, *M.I.M.I.R: Libretto til musik drama* (M.I.M.I.R.: Libretto to a Musical Drama, 1974). In 1981 O'Horgan and Gress collaborated on a new production for Danish television, *Erindring om fremtiden* (Memory about the Future, 1988), in which past and present collide in a nightmarish setting. The text for this work originally appeared in Gress's 1979 collection of essays, *Fanden til Forskel: Essays, monologer og dialoger* (Hell of a Difference: Essays, Monologues and Dialogues).

During the late 1960s and early 1970s Gress, Wright, and their circle of artistic, theatrical, and literary colleagues formalized what Gress terms in volume 2 of *Compañia* "vores elastiske kollektiv . . . en hård kerne af husvenner" (our elastic collective . . . a hard kernel of friends of the house). Gress, Wright, and friends came up with the name DECENTER for the collective, a bit of a pun suggesting an alternative to hierarchy and centralization and also the idea that

> det gode, det levende, det spændende det kvalitative ikke er bundet til bestemte storbycentre, som i dag snarere kvæler end fremmer det kreative liv, men . . . alt det kan opstå hvor som helst givende og modtagende sjæle, idémennesker og kunstnere kommer sammen og arbejder sammen på uformel, ubunden vis.

> (good things, life, excitement, quality are not bound to specific metropolitan centers, which today strangle instead of encourage creative life, but . . . all that can occur wherever generous and receptive souls, people of ideas and artists, come together and work together in informal, unrestrictive fashion.)

Gress describes the activities and interests of DECENTER and her circle of literary and artistic friends in volume 2 of *Compañia,* which deals with Gress's postwar life in America, her studies at

Columbia, her many travels, and her subsequent marriage. As documented in *Mine mange hjerne, Fuglefri og fremmed,* and *Compañia,* adversity seems to have been a constant in Gress's life, although Gress bore such adversity with creativity, compassion, and a love of event and drama. Another book of memoirs, with the appropriate title *Vist koster det noget: Erindringsbog* (Of Course It Costs Something: A Memoir), appeared in 1980.

The late 1960s and early 1970s brought many honors to Gress: in 1969 she won the Poul Hennigsen Prize and the following year, the Årets Radise. She was also awarded the Kritikerprisen (Critics' Prize) for *Fuglefri og fremmed* in 1971; the Jeanne and Henri Nathensen Memorial Grant and the Selskabet for de skjønne og nyttige Videnskabers Pris (Prize from the Society for the Promotion of Art and Science) in 1973; the Søren Gyldendal Prize in 1974; and, in 1976, the Holberg Medal. Gress was also elected to the Danish Academy in 1975. During this period she continued to write the essays collected in *Engagement, Fanden til Forskel, Udsigter og indsigter,* and *Blykuglen: Epistler og essays* (Bullets of Lead: Letters and Essays, 1984).

In the essay "'Mit Amerika'–1976–en fødselsdagsskål" ("My America"–1976–a Birthday Toast) from *Engagement,* Gress readily confesses her ambivalence concerning America, the home of "det store flertal af mine venner samt mange af mine bedste fjender" (the great majority of my friends as well as many of my best enemies). For Gress, the United States is unlike any traditional nation, Denmark or England, for example, for "at være amerikaner indebærer altid et valg–om ikke ens eget valg, så en nær forfaders eller formoders valg" (to be an American always involves a choice–if not one's own choice, then the choice of a close paternal or maternal ancestor).

In her toast to America, Gress describes the United States as a reconfigured Europe filled with new possibilities and new directions; she also holds the United States up as a warning for "hvordan vore idéer tager sig ud som realiseret virkelighed" (how our ideas will develop in reality). Gress ends her essay with a tribute to the Declaration of Independence. She applauds the openness of American society, its endless possibilities, the fact that "der kan vokse roser på møddingerne i mit USA" (roses can grow in the compost piles of my USA).

Gress moves to firmer ground in "Hygge," an essay devoted to the quintessential quality of Danish culture, which appeared in *Udsigter og indsigter.* Based on a speech given to visiting Japanese dignitaries at the Tokai Center in Vedbæk, the essay defines *hygge* as the inherent Danish ability to create harmony, inner peace, and warmth for oneself and others. Many of the essays of *Udsigter og indsigter* reflect Gress's compassion and concern for others.

Gress's 1977 novel, *Salamander,* coincides with her involvement in drama and her acquaintance with O'Horgan. Roy Roscoe is a gifted and selfish artist who cruelly manipulates the members of his own experimental theater group. Lisa Branner, a young member of the company, risks her writing career and the love of her family to follow Roscoe; hers is one of the many torn lives Roscoe leaves in his wake. Gress focuses on the artist and his transcendental experience with creativity, "denne ynde og glæde og styrke over ham, der gjorde ham tidløs, uældet, og som Lisa aldrig ville blive træt af at se og føle. En ildånd, Salamander" (this delight and happiness and strength over him, making him timeless, ageless, something Lisa never tired of seeing and feeling. A spirit of fire, Salamander). *Salamander* also explores what happens when an experimental theatrical company loses its artistic fire. Ephemerally, the company functions as Roy's world, with a common code for all its members. The group inevitably loses its raison d'être, however, and Roy coldly moves on, as he has always done.

Gress's final novel, *Simurghen* (1986; translated as *The Simurg,* 1989), offers a procession of tableau of literary and artistic persona and scenes from Gress's peripatetic, intense, and dramatic life. In it Gress describes the intellectuals she met in New York and elsewhere. Gress died on 18 July 1988 in Copenhagen, not long after she had completed an English translation of *Simurghen* for publication.

Gress's *Mine mange hjem* serves as an antidote to the notion that all childhood memoirs depict an idyllic time of wonder, discovery, peace, and security.

Gress paints a memorable picture of a frightened, insecure childhood; yet, despite the family's instability, Gress's mother managed to bestow on her children a sense of "de mange hjems samlende kraft . . . tryllekredsen, hjemmet i hjemmene" (the collective power of the many homes . . . the magic circle, the home in the homes). Elsa Gress's touching memoir of her early years will surely endure when her novels, her many essays, her fiery polemic, and her earnest attempts at theater have faded from memory.

Biography:
Lis Thorbjørnsen, "En fritænker," in *Fem digterportrætter* (Copenhagen: Kristeligt Dagblad, 1970), pp. 62–89.

References:
Michael Bruun Andersen, ed., *Dansk litteraturhistorie: Velfærdsstat kulturkritik,* volume 8 (Copenhagen: Gyldendal, 1985), pp. 516–520;

Michael Cotta-Schonberg and Helga Vang Lauridsen, eds., *Nærværende: En bog om Elsa Gress* (Copenhagen: Gyldendal, 1990);

Stig Dalager and Anne-Marie Mai, *Danske kvindelige forfattere–fra Adda Ravnkilde til Kirsten Thorup: Udvikling og perspektiv,* volume 2 (Copenhagen: Gyldendal, 1982), pp. 55, 136, 140;

Ragnar Kvam, "Elsa Gress og Decentristene," *Samtiden,* 85 (1976): 417–424;

Sven H. Rossel, ed., *A History of Danish Literature* (Lincoln: University of Nebraska Press, 1992), pp. 441–442;

Henrik Stangerup, "Elsa Gress," in *Danske digtere i det 20. århundrede,* third edition, 5 volumes, edited by Torben Brostrøm and Mette Winge (Copenhagen: Gad, 1980), IV: 377–389.

Martin A. Hansen

(20 August 1909 – 27 June 1955)

Faith Ingwersen
University of Wisconsin at Madison

BOOKS: *Nu Opgiver Han* (Copenhagen: Gyldendal, 1935);

Kolonien (Copenhagen: Gyldendal, 1937);

Jonatans Rejse (Copenhagen: Gyldendal, 1941; revised editions, 1948, 1950);

Lykkelige Kristoffer (Copenhagen: Gyldendal, 1945); translated by John Jepson Egglishaw as *Lucky Kristoffer* (New York: American-Scandinavian Foundation/Twayne, 1974);

Tornebusken (Copenhagen: Gyldendal, 1946)—includes "Paaskeklokken," translated by H. Wayne Schow as "Easter Bells," in his *Against the Wind: Stories by Martin A. Hansen* (New York: Unger, 1979), pp. 207–273;

Agerhønen (Copenhagen: Gyldendal, 1947)—includes "Agerhønen," translated by Janet Beverley as "The Partridge," in *Adam* (London), 16, no. 188 (November 1948): 28–31; "Martsnat," translated by Lydia Cranfield as "March Night," in *Norseman,* 8 (January–February 1950): 54–60; "Bogen," translated by Cranfield as "The Book," in *Norseman,* 10 (May–June 1952): 192–197; "Offer," translated by Evelyn Heepe as "Sacrifice," in her *Swans of the North: Short Stories by Modern Danish Authors* (Copenhagen: Gad, 1953), pp. 51–75; "Høstgildet" translated by Heepe and Jean Koefoed as "Harvest Feast," in *New World Writing* (New York: New American Library of World Literature, 1955), pp. 110–125; "Soldaten og Pigen," translated by Richard B. Vowles as "The Soldier and the Girl," in *Accent: A Quarterly of New Literature,* 27, no. 1 (Winter 1957); "Fuglene," translated by K. R. Keigwin as "The Birds," in *Contemporary Danish Prose: An Anthology,* edited by Elias Bredsdorff (Copenhagen: Gyldendal, 1958), pp. 331–351; "Morgenstunden," translated by Martha Lepawsky as "The Morning Hour," in *Literary Review: Denmark Number,* 8, no. 1 (Autumn 1964): 31–39; "Uglen," translated by Schow as "The Owl," in *Against the Wind* (New York: Unger, 1979), pp. 21–30; "Fædrene," translated and

Martin A. Hansen (photograph by Gregers Nielson; courtesy of Gyldendal Publishers)

abridged by Faith Ingwersen as "Martin A. Hansen: From 'The Fathers,'" in *Translation: The Journal of Literary Translation,* 9 (Fall 1982): 35–45;

Tanker i en Skorsten (Copenhagen: Gyldendal, 1948);

Leviathan (Copenhagen: Wivels Forlag, 1950);

Løgneren (Copenhagen: Gyldendal, 1950); translated by Egglishaw as *The Liar* (Letchworth, Herts, U.K.: Dent, 1954);

Kirkebanken: Et udkast (Askov: Askov Boghandel, 1952);

Orm og Tyr (Copenhagen: Wivels Forlag, 1952);

Kringen: Billeder fra øvre Gudbrandsdal (Copenhagen: Gyldendal, 1953);

Paradisæblerne og andre historier (Copenhagen: Forlaget Fremad, 1953)—includes "Paradisæblerne," translated by Marion Marzolf as "The Paradise Apples," in *American-Scandinavian Review,* 52, no. 1 (March 1964): 72–78;

Dansk vejr (Copenhagen: Steen Hasselbalch, 1953);

Rejse paa Island (Copenhagen: Carit Andersens, 1954);

Konkylien, edited by Vera Hansen and Ole Wivel (Copenhagen: Gyldendal, 1955)—includes "Aasynet," translated by Niels Lyhne Jensen and James McFarlane as "The Countenance," in *Norseman,* 13, no. 5 (September-October 1955): 328–333; "Daniel," "Haavn," and "Den Retfærdige," translated by Schow as "The Just," in his *Against the Wind* (New York: Unger, 1979), pp. 146–159, 160–193, 79–103;

Gyldendals julebog 1955: Martin A. Hansen, edited by Wivel and Vera Hansen (Copenhagen: Gyldendal, 1955);

Midsommerkrans, edited by Vera Hansen and Wivel (Copenhagen: Gyldendal, 1956);

Af folkets Danmarkshistorie: Seks kapitler fortalt for ungdommen, edited by Vera Hansen and Wivel (Copenhagen: Gyldendal, 1957)—includes "Bygmesteren kommer for at rejse en kirke i landsbyen," translated by John Christianson as "The Master Stonecutter Builds a Danish Parish Church," in *American-Scandinavian Review,* 50, no. 4 (December 1962): 362–372;

Martin A. Hansen fortæller, edited by Hans Røpke and Wivel (Copenhagen: Gyldendal, 1958);

Efterslæt: Sidste noveller og skildringer, edited by Thorkild Bjørnvig and Wivel (Copenhagen: Gyldendal, 1959)—includes "Gartneren, Dyret og Barnet," translated by Hallberg Hallmundsson as "The Gardener, the Beast and the Child," in *An Anthology of Scandinavian Literature: From the Viking Period to the Twentieth Century,* edited by Hallmundsson (New York: Macmillan/Collier, 1965), pp. 87–95;

Ved korsvejen: Litterære essays, edited by Bjørnvig and Wivel (Copenhagen: Gyldendals Uglebøger, 1965);

Martsnat, edited by Bjørnvig (Copenhagen: Dansklærerforeningen-Gyldendal, 1965);

Verdensromanen: Historiske essays, edited by Bjørnvig and Wivel (Copenhagen: Gyldendals Uglebøger, 1966);

Martin A. Hansen og skolen, edited by Røpke and Wivel (Copenhagen: Gyldendal, 1968);

Isen bryder: Novelleforlægget til Løgneren, edited by Wivel (Haslev: Gyldendals Bogklub, 1969);

Martin A. Hansen: Hemmlighedens kunstner, compiled by Anders Thyrring Andersen and Jørgen Jørgensen (Copenhagen: Gyldendal, 1991).

Edition: *Mindeudgave,* 10 volumes (Copenhagen: Gyldendal, 1961)—comprises *Nu opgiver han; Kolonien; Jonatans rejse; Lykkelige Kristoffer; Tornebusken; Agerhønen; Tanker i en Skorsten; Løgneren; Noveller fra Konkylien og Efterslæt; Skildringer fra Midsommerkrans og Efterslæt.*

Editions in English: "Agerhønen," translated by Erik J. Friis as "The Partridge," in *American-Scandinavian Review,* 43 (December 1955): 383-386;

"Bogen," translated by Villy Sørensen and Anne Born as *The Book,* (Copenhagen: Wind-flower Press, 1978), pp. 7–19;

"Dansk Klima og dansk Folkekarakter," translated by anonymous as "Wind, Weather and Men's Minds," in *Danish Foreign Office Journal,* no. 12 (June 1954): 1–3;

"Soldaten og Pigen," translated by James E. Anderson as "The Soldier and the Girl," *American-Scandinavian Review,* 60, no. 1 (March 1972): 63–67;

"Brev til en Begynder," translated by P. M. Mitchell as "Letter to a Beginner," in *Literary Review,* 6 (Summer 1963): 431–440;

"Paradisæblerne," translated by Faith Ingwersen as "Paradise Apples" in *Anthology of Danish Literature: Bilingual Edition,* edited by F. J. Billeskov Jansen and Mitchell (Carbondale & Edwardsville: University of Illinois Press, 1971), 2: 528–547;

Against the Wind: Stories by Martin A. Hansen, translated by H. Wayne Schow (New York: Ungar, 1979).

RADIO: *Løgneren,* script by Hansen, Danmarks Radio, 1950.

POEM: "Menneske," *Heretica,* 1 (1948), pp. 356–364.

One cold midnight in April 1947, Martin A. Hansen was walking through the woods on his way from the Norwegian railway station of Roa to the house where he and his wife were staying. The walk felt to him like the silent wandering of the dead toward a final, unknown destination. On his way he saw three figures who seemed as though they were characters from two of his own novels—characters he had created to be wanderers through history. At the point where he met them, his waiting and watching wife had seen a light that she assumed to be a lantern he was carrying. He carried no light, however, nor had he been accompanied by others. Not until he lay on his deathbed in June 1955 was he able to analyze this vision through a story that came to be called "The Guests." In this story the narrator is visited by two ghosts, one who was inspired by the writer in wartime to transgress ordinary ethics and kill the other. The two spirits want the writer to shoulder his part of the guilt. To bear responsibility for what one writes became one of the major themes in Hansen's works.

Jens Alfred Martin Hansen was born on 20 August 1909 on Sealand, the largest of the Danish islands, although he came to identify a small, fertile peninsula in the parish of Strøby on the southeastern part of that island as a reflection of his country's past and the ideal for his world. He perceived his country and its ethical dilemmas as caught between the admonitions of the past and the ambiguity of the modern world. The ethical problems that arose at the end of World War II challenged his religious beliefs and his faith in God, himself, and the changing culture. These problems resonated in the troubled minds and hearts of Hansen's countrymen, and he seemed to them to speak not only for Danes but for all those who found themselves in the disturbing postwar world. The problems of alienation and the individual's struggle for meaning in an age in which the individual was ethically compromised were reflected in the style of European modernism. Hansen, who knew the works of Knut Hamsun, Marcel Proust, Franz Kafka, James Joyce, and André Gide, tried, by using highly symbolic and sometimes radically experimental forms, to acknowledge, analyze, and deal with the cultural and existential crises of the age. Along with other young writers, he came to see such an attempt as the application of an "ethical pessimism," through which curative values could be rediscovered. The urgency evident in the ambiguities of good and evil to be found in his works, as well as the excitement of his experimentations in style, the suggestiveness of his symbols, the democracy of his focus, and, ultimately, his seeming postulation of hope–all made him, for nearly forty years, one of the most influential, critically analyzed, and popular writers not only in Denmark but throughout Scandinavia.

Hansen's parents were of peasant stock and were native to the Stevns region. Though the post–World War I years were difficult economically, they managed in 1918 to acquire a little farm of their own. Stevns, with its old-fashioned villages, tended fields, dusty roads, and dark woods, came to represent to Hansen the cultural heritage of the peasantry. Hansen's biographer, Ole Wivel, detects in Hansen's writing an inner conflict derived from the characters of his parents, who represented an opposition of forces that could be traced to the antithetical geography of the areas from which they came within the region. Hansen's father, Hans Peter Hansen, came from the agricultural area near the sea, whereas his mother, Karen Christine Mariane Mathiasen, came from the forested hinterland. In

Hansen's literary world, tending fields denoted personal reliability and social responsibility–toward family, country, and culture–which in itself was an allegiance to the land. Such an ethical attitude was contrasted to the individualistic and aesthetic: the overly pensive, the superstitious, the impulsive, the sexual, the wild, the demonic, the visionary–in short, the poetically inspirational. Hansen voiced this view quite succinctly in an article in the *Berlingske Aftenavis* newspaper (18 November 1944) titled "Uafsluttet Efterskrift" (Unfinished Postscript):

> Der var Marker, Hegn, Skov, Strand, Aa, Eng, Kær. Og to Magter i alt. I Marken, som Mennesker dyrkede med deres bedste Vilje, havde det fredsæle, det gode Overtaget, den var Aand, Helle. I det "vilde" havde det farlige og djævelske Magt og drog derfor mest. I Aaen, i Kær og Krat boede et eller andet, man ikke saa, men følte sig advaret imod af sit Indre. . . . Intet at høre, intet at se, men det er der, Kulden, Ødelæggeren. Naturens onde Side, Maskinafsindet uden Maal og Med, den aandløse umaadelige Formerelse, der truer al Aand. Oplevelsen af dette Drama og Ens egen Rolle i det kunde siden nær være blevet glemt under Skønhed, under rig Lyrik, vor Litteraturs sidste og skønne Hedenskab.

> (There were fields, hedgerows, forest, beach, creek, meadow, fen. And [there were] two powers in all this. In the field, which human beings cultivated to the best of their ability, the peace-loving and the good had the upper hand; the field was spirit, sanctuary. In the "wild," the dangerous and devilish ruled, and the wild was therefore the more enticing. In creek, fen, and thicket lived something one did not see, but against which one felt an inner warning. . . . Nothing could be heard; nothing could be seen; but it was there: the coldness, the destroyer, the evil side of nature. Aimless, mechanical insanity; a soulless, illimitable propagation that threatens all spirit. The experiencing of that drama and one's own role in it could later nearly be forgotten beneath beauty, beneath a rich lyricism, our literature's last and lovely paganism.)

Hansen attended school until he was fourteen. As was the custom, he was then sent off to live and work on other farms. Leaving the region at seventeen, he enrolled at Haslev Seminarium (teachers' college). There, radicalized by the intellectual climate of the late 1920s, he felt estranged from his old culture, with its conservatism and its restrictive "Inner-Mission" Lutheran heritage. He became an admirer of what was viewed as a robust materialism in the Darwinistic writings of Johannes V. Jensen, as well as what was seen as a religious quest for self-knowledge in the writings of Søren Kierkegaard.

*Self-portrait by Hansen (Martin A. Hansen Collection,
Det Konginglike Bibliotek)*

In 1931, a year after Hansen's graduation from college, he was employed at Blaagaard Seminarium in Copenhagen. Although the district was poor and he had begun teaching in the midst of the Great Depression, Hansen continued his work at the school until 1945, when at last he could support himself by writing. His pedagogic techniques were to become the subject of later articles and were directly referred to, and indirectly applied in, his literary works.

Depending on medicine to alleviate the headaches he had suffered since his first year in Haslev and to combat the exhaustion he felt after too little sleep, Hansen wrote diligently at night, and in the same year that he married Vera Louise Marie Jensen and served five months in the Danish military, he also published his first novel, *Nu Opgiver Han* (Now He Gives Up, 1935). It was followed by a sequel, *Kolonien* (The Colony, 1937). Both books were written in the style of social realism common to the 1930s. They address issues surrounding the occupation of farming, which was undergoing the changes brought about by both the declining economy during the Great Depression and subsequent technical advances.

Nu Opgiver Han treats the general context of village, farms, and day laborers but concentrates on the

strife between two brothers: Kristen, a community leader who quickly adapts to the changing times and sells his farm, and Lars Jørn, who keeps to the old ways. Each of them has two children. Kristen has a daughter, who is a spoiled and citified young woman, and a son, who is the leader of a fascistic farm movement. Lars Jørn has two sons: the older briefly moves to South America, and the younger, Niels, wants to modernize the farm and turn it into a Marxist collective. Niels is capable, pragmatic, outspoken, and enormously energetic; he is a "man of the future." He is contrasted with another able and intelligent man, Thorvald, the farm foreman, who is too reflective and thus self-defeating. He is not a man Niels would want in his commune, and split between his ideals and his actions with regard to sexuality, Thorvald ultimately kills himself by not having the awareness to save himself from drowning. Thus, for the introspective young man, the psychological danger of the sexual, which always seems to be viewed in a dualistic light, finds voice in Hansen's first work.

The book ends with the arson of the farm and Niels's realization that his father will now have to give up. *Kolonien* treats Niels's struggle to make the communal experiment successful. Niels, too, becomes exhausted by his experiment. Most of his helpers have been inept, self-centered, or petty, and, faced by followers who do not live up to serving the ideal, Niels begins to subvert the notion of equality and to subordinate them to the goal of the commune's success in farming. After the destruction of their crops in a storm, Niels, who has become a much more introspective man, gives up.

Hansen had begun to feel that, although extreme political ideologies such as communism were antireligious—rejecting the maladies of cult, worship, and symbol—they were much like evangelical Protestant movements. Naturalism and its outgrowth, Social Realism, with their emphasis on a social and psychological description of the human being, were ready to castigate traditional religious worship, but they were also ready to accept vaguely religious moods and nature mysticism in its place. Hansen wanted the freedom to treat the wondrous in both old and new ways, to treat the individual and his fate during disastrous times. In 1937 Hansen made his first notes for the novel *Jonatans Rejse* (Jonatan's Journey, 1941; revised in 1948 and 1950).

In the spring of 1939 Hansen's first child, Hans-Ole, was born. In September, amidst recurrent rumors of war, Hansen was briefly recalled to military service. Denmark was occupied by Germany on 9 April 1940, but to Hansen's chagrin he was not called to defend his country. Unable to write for some time after the arrest of some of his friends, he finally took up again, for the third time, what was to be his most satiric work: the seemingly innocent fairy tale of Jonatan the smith, told with gallows humor. Hansen starts out with an optimistic, level-headed protagonist who seems to possess a sly innocence; as the lighthearted story progresses it becomes more of a picaresque novel with a hero who is somewhat deaf to its apocalyptic overtones. The language draws on folksy saws, literary maxims, and biblical proverbs—often furnishing the reader with contradictory wisdom. The charm of the language lies in its use of a surprise in emphasis, whether by understatement or exaggeration or incongruity. In *Jonatans Rejse* social realism—tempered perhaps by the influence of such writers as Hans Christian Andersen or Selma Lagerlöf—has become clothed in the garb of folklore, in what was perhaps Hansen's favorite of his works.

Jonatan, who suffers from minor sins—drinking, bragging, showing off, and an impulsiveness that exaggerates them—is both shrewd and naive. The devil has acted as his apprentice, but he has cuckolded Jonatan and introduced modern frivolities to the public, causing the moral decline of Jonatan's village and, with Jonatan's unwitting help, eventually of his country. Jonatan lures the devil into a bottle and makes his journey to present the bottle to the king, who should know how to avert the danger it represents. Since Jonatan is charming and means well, the reader is only too glad to accompany him on that journey through the old culture, into modern civilization, and back again.

Jonatan encounters a constantly changing cast of eccentrics. He involves himself in the troubles of others through curiosity and a desire to be helpful. Although he preaches, cajoles, and chides, he is slow to confront wrongdoing and often pursues the wrong actions. In fact, while on his journey, Jonatan frequently calls upon the devil to help him. The first person Jonatan helps is a doctor who is deep in debt; after having stolen money to pay more debts, he has hanged himself. Jonatan cuts him down and saves his life, then uses the bottle to produce the stolen money, and returns it. That act sets in motion Jonatan's ultimate fate. He is arrested for the theft and put in jail by the police chief, who feels akin to the alleged criminal but believes in punishment. His jailer, who is concerned with law, not justice, wishes to be a judge. Jonatan's bottle is stolen by the doctor and jailer, and, after he is temporarily released from jail, he follows them. On the way, he meets, among others, a young man called Askelad (Ash Lad, the masculine counterpart of Cinderella), who proclaims that he is a genius and will accomplish great scientific works; he therefore takes what he wants without fear of the consequences. He does fear that he may run out of time, however. The city is to be Askelad's great laboratory, and there he and Jonatan part for a time.

Jonatan becomes involved with an anarchist and her political opponents, a fanatical conservationist who waters weeds, a secret society (which includes a naïf, a misanthrope, a cynic, an idealist, an arms inventor, a musician, an ailing poet, a religious dignitary, a newspaper editor, and a wealthy industrialist). Although Jonatan tries to help the neighborhood poor and to give the bottle to the king, none of his acts has the desired outcome. Arrested and tried for the original crime, Jonatan finds that the devil is the best witness in his defense. Jonatan, refusing to expose the doctor, assumes his guilt and serves the sentence.

Jonatan has done a few good deeds, but he has also caused a case of raving madness and an unjust imprisonment, and facilitated two cases of adultery, a case of abandonment, several thefts, innumerable acts of dishonesty, and much civil strife. Although somewhat disjointed, the story of his journey is held together by certain themes: each character seems to typify a fixed idea, a strength that is also a weakness. Evil seems to be brought about by a lack of reflection, whereby virtue becomes vice. The poet in the secret society argues that to avoid decline and death one embraces an ideal, but in this ever changing world, ideals become distorted and doomed to falsehood. Evil serves as the exaggeration of desire; it brings judgment on that desire. The

Cover for the 1950 revised edition of Hansen's 1941 novel, about a blacksmith who puts the devil in a bottle

smith's idea is that evil is something apart from the person, who can control and use it for the good. The devil, however, assures Jonatan that evil works through the human being. In the course of the tale Jonatan the smith is transformed from a good-natured man to a sorcerer's apprentice and, finally, to a sorcerer. He takes on the attributes of both the devil and death. The moral decline brought about by the devil's activities in the village is paralleled by Jonatan's actions in the city. Although the poetic derives from nature, it, like the city—a living organism that is both wonderful and terrible, an aberration and possessing a blind will—is an expression of man's striving but also contains the seed of destruction. Evil becomes so paradoxical that it seems rather to be amoral, and one might see Jonatan's journey as a *felix culpa* (a "fortunate fall" from innocence into a state of sin that makes redemption possible).

If Hansen's subject is the eternal struggle against evil, he surely manages to depict the ambiguities involved. In other works he examines the same themes in altered forms—the corruption of modern society, the exercise of a seductive/sexual power over others, the ambiguous motives behind one's good deeds, and the similarity of good and evil. The metaphor of the journey would next appear in his writings as historic legend, played out in a past time of war.

In the years between 1941 and 1945, however, Hansen became more and more involved in supporting the Resistance movement. His daughter, Mette-Lise, was born in 1943, but by the fall of 1944 Hansen had left home and was living in hiding. He had written articles for the underground magazine *Folk og Frihed* (People and Freedom), in which he advocated action against the Nazis and their Danish collaborators. In "Dialog om Drab og Ansvar" (Dialogue on Killing and Duty, 1944–1945) he justified as a necessity the liquidation of Danish informers, who were betraying their fellow Danes to the occupation forces. He was convinced that, once the war was over, the nation would shoulder the responsibility for those actions and would thereby exonerate all those who had been forced by circumstance to suspend their culture's ethical laws. Hansen, having lost his father—symbolically representative of those laws—in March 1945, felt further distressed to find that, among the dead at war's end on 5 May 1945, there were those who had acted upon his words but were not officially exonerated. His own responsibility for their fate came to haunt him, and although he maintained the need of exercising a spiritual resistance, he came to distrust the artist who seduced others spiritually through the power of language.

The moral crisis Hansen endured was reflected in a proposed work, "Kains Alter" (Cain's Altar)—the draft of which he wrote in December 1945 and January 1946. It was to span the years from the 1800s to the modern age and portray a family through three generations. He intended to use his own family and memories. His fictional return to Stevns would be that of the author as ravager and exploiter—a spiritual criminal. Finally, however, Hansen came to view "guilt" as the negative expression of responsibility—the maintainance of the cultural values of one's forebears and the past; he saw it as binding one to humanity rather than separating one from it. He expressed his belief in tradition in several articles written in February and March 1946 and later included in the collection *Ved korsvejen* (At the Crossroad, 1965). With his newly won ethical perspective on his vocation, Hansen gave up the "Kains Alter" project.

Although the account of Jonatan was introduced and concluded by an "editor"—who claimed to have a mote in his eye that disturbed his vision and caused him to make a mistake in the book of life, provoking much suffering for those who believed him—*Lykkelige Kristoffer* (1945; translated as *Lucky Kristoffer,* 1974) purports to be an account by an elderly merchant named Martin writing in the late 1500s in the besieged city of Marberg. Its tumultuous events span the early 1520s to 1570, years of war between Sweden and Denmark that had begun with the partial dissolution of the Nordic union of 1397 and ended with the Reformation. Involved were four Danish kings and one Swedish, with added troops from the Hanseatic city of Lübeck and German mercenaries under a leader from Holstein.

Most of the tale that Martin chronicles takes place in the confusion of those years and on what was then Danish territory. Martin has taken up his pen after thirty years, when Sweden and Denmark have gone to war once more. In 1563 the Danish king decided to reclaim the Swedish throne, but by 1570 he found reconquering Sweden to be impossible.

In his youth Martin had been a novice in a cloister at Elsinore and received a minor degree as a cleric in Copenhagen. He has cut his career short, moved to the miserable Skrokhult estate in Halland, where he has become the tutor of the young Kristoffer. Meanwhile, he has collected and examined plants for their medical properties and taken notes on them for a treatise. The ironic and rather nihilistic Martin is also an observer of, and experimenter with, the lives of others, and he envies their spontaneity and exciting lives. Like the artist, he feels he can identify with the minds of others—all except those who represent a constant purity in their integrity. Also like the artist, he is not entirely honest in his retelling of events. He has filled Kristoffer's mind with romantic visions of heroes who fight and die for great causes, so the young knight, after seeing a vision of St. George, sets out for the south to fulfill his destiny by fighting for justice. With the two of them travels the real master of the estate, the old warrior Paal, who has trained the boy in swordfighting and who has an ongoing feud with him, and an old Catholic monk, who must travel south to answer Lutheran complaints against him. Along the way they are accosted by jittery soldiers; held prisoners at Vaabenhöj, the estate of untrustworthy nobility; and plundered by a local farmer and a band of rabble that has taken up robbery.

In the robbers' camp they meet the beautiful young Anna and the scientist Thygonius—the monk Mattias's philosophical antagonist. When Mattias celebrates the mass, he is tortured and hanged. The sheriff's men attack the robbers and take the travelers to Hälsingborg, where they are again imprisoned. Upon their escape and before crossing the sound to Sealand, Kristoffer and Paal duel and Paal is slain. Kristoffer then sets off alone, while Martin stays at the cloister in Elsinore, until he is sent on to Copenhagen to warn the Catholic spiritual leader Paulus Heliæ that his life is threatened. In Copenhagen, although Kristoffer is

lovesick over Anna, he eventually finds a cause for which he would lay down his life: as troops finally storm the besieged city, the knight dies defending the house of the prelate.

Martin's account of his companions in the war stops at this point, although the reader learns that Martin subsequently married Anna (who was unfaithful to him) and became both wealthy and influential. Sitting in another besieged city, he has chosen to stay to finish his account, although it will mean his death. It seems to give meaning to the past as well as to him: his chronicle is an analysis of and an antidote to the poison of the age.

The account may be seen on several levels: the transition of the Medieval Age, with its knights and saintly monks, into the Renaissance; the destruction of old values during an age of great upheaval; a recognition of the eternal ambiguity of mankind's circumstances; and a recognition of the importance of the artist's contribution to culture. Martin, the cleric-turned-cynic-turned-chronicler, has given up what seemed to be his calling several times. Perhaps he combines them all in his final days of writing: the religious, the medical, and the educational are present in his account of the past; the reader may find a needed understanding of the world and a salve for the soul in its pages. Nature—like the uncommitted early Martin—is a Janus head: it both destroys and heals. When Martin lost his notes on plants, his attempt to confront and overcome that ambiguity in nature was abandoned. Now he tries to write to exorcise that same ambiguity that has destroyed his culture. He pays homage to the past and his friends who were willing to sacrifice themselves for ideals. He, too, would leave something for others in the form of this chronicle—to which he gives the pure Kristoffer's name—and through it he seeks his own cultural redemption.

Both Jonatan's and Martin's journeys end after their protagonists have a supernatural experience. Though Jonatan flies with the devil and witnesses his desire for destruction, Martin sees the Virgin Mary and is nearly overcome by the fragrance of violets. Culture, like nature, bears within it the promise of spring and rebirth, but Martin seems at last overwhelmed by symbols of both.

Hansen's next work was *Tornebusken* (The Thornbush, 1946), which comprises three long stories set in modern times. They are thematically and cyclically related and employ parallel symbols. Hansen's experiments with fictional form in these three stories made the work one of the most important in modernist Danish prose. On the surface, the first story, "Paaskeklokken" (translated as "Easter Bells" in *Against the Wind: Stories by Martin A. Hansen*, 1979), is realistically told and takes place in the old farming community. This time the struggle is between personal values that represent religious/ethical viewpoints rather than ideological beliefs. Riding the bell's wave of sound, the reader is introduced to the minds of the characters—a farm family and their farmhands, teachers and their spouses, and the minister and the sexton—who seem to be awakened to a longing for purity or a wish to be truthful to themselves and honest in their dealings with others. While the Easter service takes place in the church—and after the consummation of a mutual seduction between Johan, the foreman of Linde Farm, and Ingrid, the daughter at the farm—a pagan ritual is enacted between Johan and an enraged bull. The manipulative Johan, who would simply use Ingrid and the family farm in his rise to power, needs to risk much in the gamble of life. He cleanses himself in a ritual battle, a bullfight, and his gamble becomes a drama of death—which makes catharsis and rebirth possible for others. Johan's belief in the power of death is both at odds with and similar to the spirit of church ritual. Only through understanding the suffering of others can one help them and oneself: one needs to be needed.

The cryptic "Midsommerfesten" (The Midsummer Festival) is Hansen's most structurally complex work. It takes place on several levels: there is the real, contemporary author (Hansen) who writes this story at the end of the war; there is another, fictional, author who, with the help of an imaginary woman reader, is writing a story during World War II; there is the story they write in which the characters reflect both the author and woman reader, but the action of which takes place before the war; and there is the reader who is reading the story after the war.

One hot day a young man named Georg meets two women, Klara and Alma, who are on their way to meet their dates at a town festival. He helps them fetch water at an ancient farm and then, sensing his dying grandfather's need for him to do something, goes his way. At the festival nearly all the men connected with the entertainment are named Georg, and the protagonist feels a particular kinship to one of them, an injured black boxer whom he urges to continue fighting beyond his endurance. He meets the women again, rejects the infatuated young Klara, and asks Alma, who is in her mid thirties and has left husband and children, to accompany him to Blood Hill, a site touched by either God or Satan, according to legend. The almost vampiric Georg tells her about his family: his dying grandfather who seems to expect something of him; his father who, though innocent, was imprisoned and finally brought to believe in his own guilt, and who thus became a criminal with regard to the law. Georg and Alma discuss two kinds of "sacred" crime: the destruc-

tion of oneself for others and the destruction of others for oneself; these are the crimes of Christ and Satan. In discussing the mystery of suffering, Georg discloses that he has been a writer who has manipulated others—such as the black boxer and Klara—and conducted experiments in causing them to suffer. He sees that Alma is no longer ready to commit the sacred crime of suicide and promises that in their life together he will make her suffer in every way he can. She, however, intends to return to her husband and thus to help Georg against himself.

Discovering that his grandfather's watch has stopped, signifying his death, Georg admits that he did not love Alma and cannot stand the fact that she realizes he can no longer hurt her. He longs for war, and Satan—who seeks his salvation in the endless suffering of others—can use a man like Georg. Alma, by maintaining that she will always believe in and thereby keep alive the goodness within Georg, represents the forgiveness of the persecuted toward the persecutor, and thus the miracle of salvation. Since, for Georg, Christ and Satan are as alike as twins and the division between good and evil is arbitrary, to choose or accept a fate imposes a meaning on the cosmic mystery: nature's erotically seductive, annihilating emptiness. To seek redemption is also the artist's attempt to impose meaning on the world's amorality; it may lead to the sacred crime of suffering on behalf of another and thus impose meaning on the world by the acceptance of a fate.

The author, who has been uncertain how to begin or continue his story, has had to answer to the portraits on the wall, to an imaginary critic, and to readers. He chooses a woman reader, Alma, because women, who have resisted pessimism and committed sacred crimes, understand writing. The author and Alma, in turn, assume the role of Jonah, who must preach what he does not want to preach—ordained destruction. In this age, the message is that Heaven and Hell do not exist, but Hell cannot die, for it exists in the thwarted ideal of justice and in a recognition of the world's evil. The nihilistic state of mind, where gods are dead or dying, re-creates this hell. If one's writing does not serve good over evil, one is responsible for the wrongs others have suffered. Yet, one of the many reasons the author gives for writing is to unmask hellish forms of bloodthirsty idealism. Perhaps having a fate is one of them, since it is the author who has created the sick god for whom he at last, Leviathan-like, casts "the woman" out to preach a sermon of possible hope to the damned—the readers of the finished tale.

It is wartime, and the conscience-stricken writer of the would-be story of Georg, who has learned that some of his friends have been arrested, sits alone at night feeling that something in particular is expected of him. He writes to analyze the manipulative role of the author, the dying cultural belief in goodness, and finding a possible redemption of humankind in a nihilistic universe. He opens himself to the criticism of an imagined reader, Alma, who—if transformed by what she reads—may take over the story and redeem the world by changing it, thus justifying the striving of the artistic impulse.

"Septembertaagen" (September Fog), the final story of the trilogy, is almost as cryptically experimental as is "Midsommerfesten." It is made up of two entwined narrative strands: the experiences of a young soldier on maneuvers before World War II and those of a child whose father had gone on maneuvers during World War I. The experiences are those of the same unnamed protagonist, who in both instances is enshrouded in fog. The child's father has joined the troops passing through the village, and the frightened boy, who calls out to him and can see his bootprints everywhere, cannot find him. Feeling angry and hurt, he lies to join a group of older boys, who tease him over a lack of bravery. To prove himself he eats the supposedly lethal flowers of the laburnum bush; only then does he realize that he has not lived up to his duty to his family, the duty to endure for the sake of the living. The "someone" who finally seems to be with him is death, and all ends in the fog of a dim and ghostly state. Being a helpless prey to the attraction of death is the demonic, which thrives in a fear of the good, true, and real, as well as the test of suffering. To long for death or war, however, is to become destructive to oneself and others. As an adult the man realizes that the laburnum bush symbolizes guilt—the emotional cost of defeat and retreat, a disappointed death wish, and a loss of faith through a loss of the "father."

Tornebusken is cyclical, turning from spring to midsummer to autumn, as well as from morning to noon, from noon to midnight, and from midnight to morning. The scene changes from the farming milieu, to the provincial town, to soldiers displaced from their traditional setting. Time is in part depicted as ritual occasions: the Eucharist, Marriage, and Extreme Unction. The narrator goes from being omniscient to interrupting the story and expressing his opinions in dramatic asides to carrying on a first-person narrative in an inner monologue. In the second story there are characters whose minds he cannot enter; in the third he merely guesses what is going on in the minds of the others and describes himself as a reporter of protocol. His role expands while diminishing in importance to the reality he describes. Characters in one story will often have counterparts in others. They are awakened to their participation in the cycle by the sound of a bell, the town festival band, or a haunting, taunting tune of war. All the protagonists have longed for war. The theme throughout is that evil

Hansen's son, Hans-Ole, and Hansen's father, Hanse Peter, in Stroby, summer 1940 (Martin A. Hansen Collection, Det Konginglike Bibliotek)

may seek suffering and death, but an acceptance of suffering for others may lead to their rebirth and the transformation of evil. Symbolized by the bull, the flowers, and the fog, death is not evil but a part of nature, which combines good and evil: suffering, death, and rebirth. The cyclical drama is eternal.

Hansen's first collection of short stories, *Agerhønen* (The Partridge), appeared in 1947. *Tornebusken* and *Agerhønen* had been planned as one volume and share many of the same themes. The latter work is divided into three sections, representing the stages on life's way, from the anticipation present in a rural childhood and youth to the adult's attempt to find meaning and finally to the nihilist's desire for death or a rebirth in a fellowship with others through suffering. The stories progress from the realistic to the nightmarish. The volume opens with "Agerhønen" (translated as "The Partridge," 1948), in which Providence provides a small miracle by sending a storm-driven partridge to a hungry family. Although a partridge also appears in two other stories, its final appearance is as a dead and rotting bird in the last story.

"Offer" (translated as "Sacrifice," 1953) takes the reader back to a period of plague and starvation. Upon consulting a witch, the desperate people have decided upon a sacrifice of innocents to put an end to the horror. They dig a grave for two young children and put food in it, but only the young woman Anna, the bailiff's wife, can summon the courage to explain to the children why their fate is important. The children are buried alive and Anna drowns herself. Though desperation has brought these people to abandon the law in their attempt to survive, they have left Anna, who was the instrument of their collective will, to take upon herself their common responsibility and to bear their blame.

The deaths in this chilling, brutal story contrast with that of the old man in "Fædrene" (translated as "The Fathers," 1982). The old man is a philologist who has made the study of the Septuagint his life's work, and he now walks through a rainy, foggy countryside, carrying his umbrella, his reading glasses, and his Bible. As so often in Hansen's works, such imagery reflects the mind, and the reader comes to realize that the old man is actually in a hospital dying. On this last journey he has returned to the landscape of his forebears. He meets three men who are looking for a thief who has stolen the family Bible; they prove to be his dead father, grandfather, and great-grandfather, each somehow younger than the last. The querulous, unsteady old man regains a childlike eagerness in their company and is allowed to stay with them. As he strains to be of help in the heavy work of lifting flour sacks, he becomes blind and invisible. This story of a mythical homecoming leaves the question of the nature of death open. The past carries with it certain expectations of the living, but if they can embrace these expectations, it is also comforting to the living. The past remains vibrant until the memory of it disappears. The old man's apparent rebirth ends in death.

"Manden fra Jorden" (The Man from the Earth) is told in the first person, but the narrator does not give his name, perhaps because such facts are only important to a life for which he feels indifference. He finds himself standing in a field, and as he walks on, he discards his belongings. He is apparently not cognizant of who he is, where he has come from, or where he is going. Upon finding a decaying partridge, he also leaves his shoes behind. When he comes to a forest, he finds a cow licking at the roots of an ash tree and revealing the form of a naked, hairy man. He must battle the man, but he is so detached that he soon loses and allows the man to shove him into the hole at the base of the ash tree and then throw dirt on him. The man heads back the way the narrator had come, where he had left his shoes and the partridge. While the narrator falls asleep, he hopes that the pretty ash may thrive. In Old Norse mythology the cow Audhumla licked Bure, the ancestor of the gods, into existence from ice blocks, whereas the first human beings were created from the ash tree. The protagonist, indifferent to life, accepts his fate of becoming one with nature. The newly risen man carries the future within him, and although he represents brute force and a negation of culture, he will undoubtedly acquire the accoutrements of culture as he travels back the way the protagonist has come. He, too, however, may one day find his acquired knowledge to be meaningless and in his spiritual exhaustion return to be reburied under the ash. Nature thus fulfills the death wish inherent in culture. Although extinction may be horrifying to the cultural mind, it may spell harmony to the nihilistic mind. The stories of *Agerhønen,* like those of the foregoing volume, are complex and ambiguous attempts to find an existential truth.

Although Hansen's collection of essays *Tanker i en Skorsten* (Thoughts in a Chimney, 1948) aroused critical interest, it was another work that achieved an enormous public acclaim. *Løgneren* (1950; translated as *The Liar,* 1954) was a novel commissioned to be read on Danmarks Radio; it also appeared as a newspaper serial.

This mysterious novel—Hansen's last—is based on an unfinished short story, "Isen Bryder" (The Ice Breaks), and takes place on an island called Sandø (Sand Island), which has been cut off from the outer world by ice for forty days. The time is shortly after World War II, and the main action covers three days: the late afternoon of Friday, 13 March, to the evening of Monday, 16 March. The novel is in the form of a diary, with an epilogue written a year later summing up the intervening events. The diarist, Johannes Vig (roughly translated as "John the Evader"), and who warns against slurring his names together into "Johannes Suig" ("John Fraud"), writes about his hopes and fears and his activities—which he both justifies and calls into doubt for an imaginary honest young friend, Natanael (with whom the reader is meant, in part, to identify). In clarifying or obscuring the truth, Vig draws upon the Bible, the Icelandic sagas, Nordic myth, folktales, and Danish literature (including the works of Kierkegaard). Vig is not only the postman, vicar, schoolteacher, Good Samaritan, and protector of the island, but also its guest, drunk, hunter (of the snipe, or sexual desire, and the seal, or death), and its evil spirit; he sees the island as a Leviathan imprisoning him like a Jonah. His final goal is to be its naturalist and historian, capturing its nature and past culture for its inhabitants.

In the epilogue Vig admits that he has filled twenty notebooks with his writings about the island and added five more to that number in the past year. He also adds that he had not written his diary entries concurrently with the events described but had done so long after the action. Across these notebooks he has written the words "The Liar." The reader is left to interpret the whole account.

The fog of "Septembertaagen" reappears in *Løgneren,* but the season has changed to that of late winter. Vig, like Georg in "Midsommerfesten," finds himself caught between two women, a younger and an older, married woman, in this case named Annemari and Rigmor, respectively. He refuses to declare his affection to Annemari until the ice breaks, but by then she is ready to depart, and it is too late. He makes a pact with Rigmor never again to act upon his affection for her, either. Vig is caught between his past actions and his present decisions and between his lack of faith in God and his wish to believe. In fact, he calls himself an unbeliever who believes what he does not believe and a man who cannot change. Vig also declares to Natanael that art is what he cares about and that he slyly eases others on until they surprise the meaning in his equations. Hansen's nihilistic modern protagonists crave and demand meaning in life, even if it costs suffering or death; and in *Løgneren,* as in *Tornebusken,* the protagonist's dilemma is elucidated through scenes of the church service and a pagan place of sacrifice–and, in Vig's case, spiritual self-sacrifice. The church service that takes place on Sunday, 15 March, with the reading of Luke 24–26, is about the unclean spirit that, once driven out of a man, returns with seven others to inhabit him, and Vig feels as if he is that spirit–or one of those old Nordic spirits dispossessed by Christianity. For Vig, as a teacher and an author, meaning in life is something he can pass on to his readers. For him to do so, however, he must give up his own desires and martyr himself–setting an example of the good, the right, and the binding of nature by culture–by means of his harpoon-like pen. His continuing work on Sandø may be truth, but he calls his notebooks about his life a lie.

From 1950 to 1952 Hansen and the poet and critic Ole Wivel coedited the new journal *Heretica.* It lasted six years and was a dominant force on the literary scene. Its youthful contributors, in attempting to face and analyze the postwar existential crisis while distrusting most political solutions, brought European modernism to the journal. Hansen contributed substantially to modernism through his use of symbolic and experimental forms. Although these authors were seeking to find new values for their deeply troubled culture, they were felt by the political left to be indifferent to social ills.

Hansen's many essays testify to his need to express himself directly to his readers. They deal with literature, history (*Tanker i en Skorsten*), mythology, and philosophy (*Leviathan,* 1950). In some of his

Cover for the 1957 paperback edition of Hansen's last novel (1950), which was commissioned as a serial by Danmarks Radio and read on the air in 1950

travel books, Hansen seems mainly concerned with recording the age-old battle between nature and culture, even though he vividly describes his impressions of landscapes. If a common denominator can be found for these diverse works, it is Hansen's insistence on a sense of ethics. He knew that nihilism is a seductive force, and as a counterforce he proposed what he had called "ethical pessimism." To advocate optimism would be naive at a time when evil was a major presence, but to advocate a pessimism that called for ethics and refused to yield to nihilism and evil in spite of their power was a stance that Hansen felt could contribute to postwar culture.

Two years after the fictional Johannes Vig had dedicated himself to writing a history of Sand Island, Hansen wrote his own cultural history: *Orm og Tyr* (Serpent and Bull, 1952). In 1950 Hansen had taken his family to live in the vicarage of the village of Allerslev, which lies in the midst of the ancient Lejre region on Sealand. Lejre is filled with burial mounds that testify to its importance during Nordic antiquity; in fact, it may have once been the seat of Danish kings. In *Orm og Tyr* Hansen turns to the impact Christianity had on the Nordic mind, by changing a culture that was in decline and in which nature was filled with the demonic and the restless dead to one in which the dead could rest in peace. Both life and death became harmoniously meaningful. Around 1250 Christianity underwent a change that was reflected in the transformation of architecture and art from the Romanesque to the Gothic. Dualism, a spiritual split between thought and emotion, replaced Christianity's former basic element of joy, and Hansen felt that the peasant's harmony gave way to the monk's alienation from this world. This estrangement again allowed the fate of the dead to be at odds with life, and that re-encroachment of demonic nature resulted in nihilistic reflections. A legend seemed to point the way to overcome this state: a serpent from the forest surrounds the church, and the parishioners raise a young bull, a tame animal, to destroy it. The peasant upholders of culture destroy the spiritual threat through the bull, which dies afterward. The concepts of death and rebirth are to be understood both metaphysically and psychologically. The legend is an exorcism, and Hansen's use of it is an invocation of that past as a source of tradition that can help the present and the future. He describes the tale as rising birdlike from the evening of a vigorous but waning age and shining in light that has already faded below. So, too, the innumerable Danish medieval churches still had an existential function in the traditions of the modern age. Hansen believed that one could transcend personal and familial memory and discover the essence of past traditions: memory becomes the supranatural remembrance of past ages.

Hansen viewed Odin, the Nordic All Father and the god of poetry, as having become dispossessed, a demon spirit haunting the night. Hansen turned from fiction and put his powers into the service of culture. Although in 1953 he published a collection of earlier short stories, *Paradisæblerne og andre historier* (The Apples of Paradise and Other Stories), no more were to appear until after his death. The eight volumes of essays and stories, new and old, published in the following thirteen years were edited by his wife, Vera, and his friends Ole Wivel, Thorkild Bjørnvig, and Hans Røpke.

Two stories may convey the tenor of Hansen's final fiction: the title story of his last collection, "Paradisæblerne" (translated as "The Paradise Apples," 1964), and the nightmarish tale "Gartneren, Dyret og Barnet" (translated as "The Gardener, the Beast and the Child," 1965), from the posthumously

published *Efterslæt* (Winnowings, 1959). In "Paradisæblerne," a young boy who visits his grandmother meets an old gamekeeper and a school chum whose fates seem to presage his own coming isolation and purposelessness. Angry, defiant, and fearful, he dares fate, first by going on thin ice and then by fumbling for apples he has thrown in the fog. He twice escapes drowning, and sensing that Providence has saved him, he feels ashamed as he once more takes the right path home. His grandmother's belief in both him and Providence seems to prevent his own nihilism and rebelliousness from destroying him.

In "Gartneren, Dyret og Barnet," a gardener works at twilight tying up roses. Indifferent to his work and to his little boy, he wishes to step away from the idyllic scene and to have the freedom of boyhood for himself. Hiding in the darkness, where all seems clammy, decaying, and palely voluptuous, the gardener watches his frightened son rush off calling him. While wishing to forget and drowse, the man sees a large animal bounding off in the same direction as his son, and he runs after it. He comes to a garden center that looks bombed out and has become a weed-filled dump with large predators prowling about. He sees himself in their eyes and wants to live by their law. By taking one more step away, he could slip into forgetfulness and liberation, and he knows that if he attacks the beasts, he may be slain, but he would achieve peace. Although the beasts' prey proves not to be his son, he knows that the boy will now find his father to be more horrific than the beasts, for, in him, the son will see the painful wonder of death. By his irresponsibility and his nihilism, as well as his own bestial nature, he has psychologically wounded another person, an act that is a sacred crime. Although he at last calls out to the boy, it is too late to prevent or undo the effect of his rejection of his role as a cultural being for the demonic freedom of the wild and destructive. The gardener has set his mark upon the boy—that of a "sickness unto death"—and must live with the resulting guilt.

Hansen nevertheless seemed to hope it was not too late for modern man, split between supporting civilizing culture and avoiding all responsibility. From 1952 to 1954 Hansen dedicated himself to travel descriptions of Denmark, Norway, and Iceland—though he found troubling the formidable nature of Iceland, which could conquer all human endeavor. It was not until he lay dying from uremic poisoning that, in the midst of his suffering and bouts of unconsciousness, he again feverishly tried to write down the tales that swirled in his mind. He died on 27 June 1955.

One might say that, true to his ambiguous nature as an artist, Martin A. Hansen left a cultural heritage: that of someone who dared to offer the possibility of achieving, through dutiful sacrifice, spiritual hope. Although in his story "The Guests" he interprets his own characters' accompanying him at night through the Norwegian forest as bespeaking past guilt, the characters—by appearing to take on a life of their own and lighting his way—seem to testify with intrinsic humor, charm, and irony to his incomparable ability as an artist. For thirty to forty years critics favoring social realism found Hansen to be reactionary, but with their decline, both the man and his existential ambiguities have begun to be rediscovered.

Bibliography:

Henrik Denman, "Det bibliografiske arbejde," *Martin A. Hansen i nutids lys,* edited by Denman and Henrik Kettel (Roskilde: The Authors, 1990), pp. 30–34.

Biographies:

Ole Wivel, *Martin A. Hansen,* 2 volumes (Copenhagen: Gyldendal, 1967, 1969);

Jan Nissen, *Den unge Martin A. Hansen: Dokumenter og kommentarer—en forfatterbiografisk studie* (Copenhagen: Gyldendal, 1974);

Bjarne Nielsen Brovst, *Martin A. Hansen: Bondesøn og digter* (N. p.: Centrum and B. N. Brovst, 1991);

Nielsen Brovst, *Martin A. Hansens ungdom, i digte, breve og dagbøger, fra 1929–1945* (Herning: Poul Kristensens Forlag, 1992).

References:

Thorkild Bjørnvig, *Martin A. Hansen* (Copenhagen: Wivels Forlag, 1948);

Bjørnvig, *Kains Alter: Martin A. Hansens digtning og tænkning* (Copenhagen: Gyldendal, 1965);

Erik M. Christensen, *Ex auditorio: Kunst og ideer hos Martin A. Hansen* (Fredensborg: Forfatternes Forlag Arena, 1965);

Aage Henriksen, *Gotisk tid: Fire litterære afhandlinger* (Haslev: Gyldendal, 1971);

Faith Ingwersen, "The Truthful Liars: A Comparative Analysis of Knut Hamsun's *Mysterier* and Martin A. Hansen's *Løgneren,*" dissertation, University of Chicago, 1974;

H. Wayne Schow, "Kierkegaardian Perspectives in Martin A. Hansen's *The Liar,*" *Critique* (Atlanta), 15, no. 3 (1974): 53–65;

Faith and Niels Ingwersen, *Martin A. Hansen* (New York: Twayne for G. K. Hall, 1976);

Niels Ingwersen, introduction to Hansen's *Lucky Kristoffer,* translated by John Jepson Egglishaw (New York: American-Scandinavian Foundation / Twayne, 1974), pp. 5–22;

Finn Stein Larsen, "Leviathans Kontur: Om den episke mønsterdannelse i Martin A. Hansens *Løgneren,*" in *Omkring Løgneren,* Værkserien 5, edited by Ole Wivel (Copenhagen: Hans Reitzels Forlag, 1971), pp. 128–151;

Göran Printz-Påhlson, "The Liar: The Paradox of Fictional Communication in Martin A. Hansen," *Scandinavian Studies,* 36 (November 1964): 263–280;

Henrik Ljungberg, *Den falske dagbog* (Copenhagen: Gyldendal, 1994, 1995).

Thorkild Hansen
(9 January 1927 – 4 February 1989)

Marianne Stecher-Hansen
University of Washington

BOOKS: *Minder svøbt i Vejr: En Studie i Jacob Paludans Digtning* (Copenhagen: Hasselbalch, 1947);

Resten er Stilhed: Variationer over et Tema af Shakespeare (Copenhagen: Gyldendal, 1953);

Pausesignaler (Copenhagen: Gyldendal, 1959);

Syv seglsten (Copenhagen: Gyldendal, 1960);

En kvinde ved en flod (Copenhagen: Gyldendal, 1961);

Det lykkelige Arabien: En dansk ekspedition 1761–67 (Copenhagen: Gyldendal, 1962); translated by James and Kathleen McFarlane as *Arabia Felix: The Danish Expedition of 1761–1767* (New York: Harper & Row, 1964; London: Collins, 1964);

Jens Munk (Copenhagen: Gyldendal, 1965; republished, 2 volumes, 1969); translated and abridged by James McFarlane and John Lynch as *North West to Hudson Bay: The Life and Times of Jens Munk* (London: Collins, 1970); republished as *The Way to Hudson Bay: The Life and Times of Jens Munk* (New York: Harcourt, Brace & World, 1970);

Jens Munks minde-ekspedition, by Hansen and Peter Seeberg (Copenhagen: Gyldendal, 1965);

Slavernes kyst, illustrated by Birte Lund (Copenhagen: Gyldendal, 1967);

Slavernes skibe, illustrated by Lund (Copenhagen: Gyldendal, 1968);

Rejsedagbøger (Copenhagen: Gyldendal, 1969)—comprises revised editions of *Pausesignaler, Syv seglsten, En kvinde ved en flod;*

Slavernes øer, illustrated by Lund (Copenhagen: Gyldendal, 1970);

Vinterhavn: Nye rejsedag bøger (Copenhagen: Gyldendal, 1972);

De søde piger: Dagbog 1943–47 (Copenhagen: Gyldendal, 1974);

Sidste sommer i Angmagssalik, illustrated by Sven Havsteen-Mikkelsen (Copenhagen: Gyldendal, 1978);

Processen mod Hamsun, 3 volumes (Copenhagen: Gyldendal, 1978);

Samtale med Dronning Margrethe (Copenhagen: Forum, 1979);

Thorkild Hansen, 1978 (photograph by Kurt Petersen, Nordfoto)

Kurs mod solnedgangen: Nye rejsedagbøger (Copenhagen: Gyldendal, 1982);

Søforhør: Nærbillede af Thorkild Hansen (Copenhagen: Lindhardt & Ringhof, 1982);

Enemærker: Samlede digte og aforismer, 2 volumes, afterword by Lars Peter Rømhild (Copenhagen: Brøndum, 1989);

Et atelier i Paris: Dagbog 1947–52, 2 volumes (Copenhagen: Gyldendal, 1990);

Thorkild Hansens billeder: Tekster og Fotografier (Copenhagen: Gyldendal, 1990);

Artikler fra Paris 1947–52, edited by Gitte Jæger and Rømhild (Copenhagen: Gyldendal, 1992);

Øer: Dagbøger fra Færøerne 1966 og fra Kykladerne 1972, edited by Jæger and Rømhild (Copenhagen: Gyldendal, 1993);

Mellem Brøndkjær og Nørholm: Dagbog fra Hamsun-årene 1975–78, edited by Jæger and Rømhild (Copenhagen: Gyldendal, 1996);

Havblik midt på dagen: Artikler 1952–62, edited by Jæger and Rømhild (Copenhagen: Gyldendal, 1998).

Thorkild Hansen was an early proponent and master of documentary fiction; his major works published in the 1960s became best-sellers in his native Denmark and were extremely popular throughout Scandinavia. Focusing on obscure figures and forgotten episodes in Denmark's past, he wrote engaging historical accounts of the Danish expedition to Arabia in 1761–1767 and of a seventeenth-century Danish voyage to discover a Northwest Passage from Europe to Asia. His magnum opus is a trilogy of works on the Danish slave trade. Like the earlier author Johannes V. Jensen, Hansen is one of the great travelers in modern Danish letters; his works reach back into history and out into the far corners of the globe. His technique—involving extensive research into authentic documents and expeditions to the historical loci—was highly innovative in his day. Hansen deliberately walked a tightrope between fact and fiction, demonstrating his great skill as a novelist as well as his impressive talent as an historian. More daring and provocative than other documentary writers of the period, he undertook ambitious and controversial topics while challenging the disciplinary boundaries between history and fiction with all the hazards involved.

Perhaps more than any other writer in postwar Danish letters, Hansen's private life has attracted considerable attention, particularly since his death in 1989. Private documents (such as personal letters and journals) fascinated him and inspired his projects, enabling him to reconstruct and interpret the destinies of historical figures. However, when the discrepancies between his own published journals and the facts of his early life were brought to light, Danish critics called his "documentary method" into question. Some critics have suggested that, by publishing his own (thoroughly edited) journals, Hansen intended to make himself the most memorable protagonist in his works.

Thorkild Hansen was born in Copenhagen on 9 January 1927. He grew up in Virum, an upper-middle-class suburb north of Copenhagen. His father, Jørgen Hansen, was an architect, his mother, Thyra Andersen, a homemaker. Thorkild was the eldest of three children with a sister, Vibeke, and brother, Povl. He attended Holte Gymnasium (secondary school) during the German occupation of Denmark and graduated in the spring of 1945 with an emphasis in mathematics.

Between 1945 and 1947, demonstrating considerable talent at a young age, Hansen studied literature under Paul V. Rubow, F. J. Billeskov Jansen, and Ejnar Thomsen at the University of Copenhagen; already in 1946 he wrote a critical study of the Danish author Jacob Paludan, *Minder svøbt i Vejr: En Studie i Jacob Paludans Digtning* (Weather-shrouded Memories: A Study in Jacob Paludan's Fiction, 1947). Hansen's modest debut did not go unnoticed. On 4 August 1947, at the age of twenty, he embarked on a sophisticated intellectual apprenticeship: he went to Paris, taking with him a scholarship (to support studies at the Sorbonne) as well as an agreement with the popular Danish daily *Ekstra Bladet.* Ole Calving, the paper's editor in chief, had—the very same day—offered Hansen a job as a foreign correspondent. The sojourn in Paris was to have lasted six months; instead, Hansen remained in Paris for five years. There he immersed himself in contemporary French literature and existentialist philosophy, meeting such luminaries as Albert Camus, André Gide, Jean-Paul Sartre, and André Malraux. He wrote about French literature, theater, cinema, and cultural life, sending hundreds of articles to *Ekstra Bladet,* where Calving paid him well for his contributions. A selection of Hansen's many articles from Paris was published posthumously as *Artikler fra Paris 1947–52* (Articles from Paris 1947–52, 1992). While in Paris, Hansen also wrote about classical French literature, completing a collection of critical-philosophical essays dealing with figures from Michel de Montaigne to Marcel Proust, *Resten er Stilhed: Variationer over et Tema af Shakespeare* (The Rest is Silence: Variations on a Shakespearean Theme), published by Gyldendal in 1953 after Hansen's return to Copenhagen.

Yet another work was the result of Hansen's literary apprenticeship in Paris: his journals, *Et atelier i Paris: Dagbog 1947–52* (A Studio in Paris: Diary 1947–52), which were published posthumously in two volumes in 1990. These Parisian journals followed as volumes two and three in a series that Hansen began publishing in 1974 with *De søde piger: Dagbog 1943–1947* (The Sweet Girls: Diary, 1943–47), which chronicles Hansen's life as a student in Denmark during the German occupation and up to the point of his departure for Paris. *Et atelier i Paris* continues the story, describing how, upon arriving in Paris, Hansen developed a close friendship with a French industrialist, Baron Jean Seillière (in fact, it was Seillière who provided Hansen with the atelier, or studio, in which he lived for five years). Hansen was

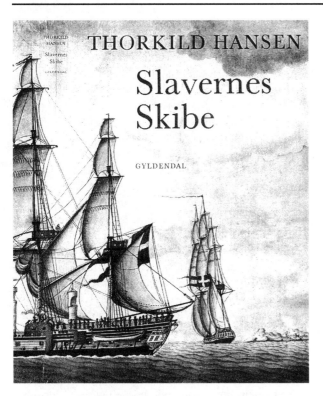

THORKILD HANSEN

Slavernes
Skibe

GYLDENDAL

*Dust jacket for the second book in Hansen's trilogy about Danish
involvement in the slave trade*

introduced to the upper circles of French society and accompanied his Maecenas on trips to southern Europe and to North Africa. In 1951 Hansen met and (rather suddenly it seems) married a twenty-three-year-old Danish woman, Birte Lund, who had been working in Paris as an au pair. In 1952 the couple returned to Copenhagen and settled into a middle-class existence. Hansen made a living as a critic and journalist for the newspaper *Information* for the next ten years, supporting his family, which eventually included two daughters, Marie and Vera. A selection of Hansen's important journalistic articles from this period was published posthumously as *Havblik midt på dagen: Artikler 1952–62* (Calm Seas at Midday: Articles 1952–62, 1998). In 1955 the family was able to move from a small apartment in the city to a comfortable house (called "Pilar") by Lake Furesø, north of Copenhagen.

In the late 1950s and early 1960s the themes and concerns of Hansen's authorship began to emerge; he published three journals based on his travels, thoroughly reworked and artistically condensed in the manner that was to become his trademark. *Pausesignaler* (Interval Signals, 1959) consists of impressionistic sketches from postwar Europe recorded in lyrical prose; Hansen drew the material from his travels in Germany, France, Italy, Greece, and Spain in the early 1950s. But, rather than being a travelogue in a conventional sense,

Pausesignaler is Hansen's description of an internal journey and an articulation of his aesthetic sensibilities. In the next two books, *Syv seglsten* (Seven Seals of Stone, 1960) and *En kvinde ved en flod* (A Woman by a River, 1961), Hansen turned to the documentary format and the expedition theme that were to become his artistic forte. Both books were based on firsthand experience in expeditions to far corners of the world. In 1960 Hansen participated in an archaeological expedition, headed by the Danish professor P. V. Glob, to Failaka Island off the coast of Kuwait; *Syv seglsten* is based on Hansen's experience during this expedition. The following year Hansen joined a Scandinavian expedition to Nubia, which was funded by UNESCO and was part of an international effort to rescue Egyptian temples threatened by the building of the Aswan High Dam; this experience is documented in *En kvinde ved en flod*. In his account of the damming of the Nile, Hansen portrays Western civilization at odds with nature and indigenous cultures. Most strikingly, these two travel books demonstrate how Hansen turns away from abstract concerns to an encounter with "concrete" reality. *Pausesignaler, Syv seglsten,* and *En kvinde ved en flod* were revised and published as a collected edition, *Rejsedagbøger* (Travel Journals, 1969).

Det lykkelige Arabien: En dansk ekspedition 1761–67 (1962; translated as *Arabia Felix: The Danish Expedition of 1761–1767,* 1964) is a reconstruction of the Danish expedition to Arabia in 1761–1767 and marks Hansen's literary breakthrough. This work won Hansen recognition as a leading writer of the period and introduced a new genre of documentary-historical fiction to Danish letters. With the successful publication of *Det lykkelige Arabien,* Hansen was able to give up his position at *Information* and to live for the rest of his life from his earnings as an independent writer.

The events of the eighteenth-century expedition to Yemen provided Hansen with fascinating material. In January 1761 a six-man expedition had set sail from Copenhagen to explore the cultural, philological, and scientific wonders and curiosities of the Near East. A philologist, Frederick Christian von Haven, was charged with the expedition's most important mission, the visit to the Sinai Peninsula in order to study the sacred Arabic manuscripts at St. Catherina's Monastery at Mount Sinai; a scientist, Peter Forsskål, was assigned to collect and classify exotic specimens of plants and animals from the entire region; and a mathematician and cartographer, Carsten Niebuhr, was appointed leader of the expedition with the task of charting the geography of the region. The expedition team also included an artist, a doctor, and a servant. All but one of the expedition members perished within months of arriving in Arabia in 1763. Niebuhr, the sole survivor, was able to salvage some of the expedition's valuable findings before making a miraculous solo journey home to Denmark. In Copenhagen the scholarly and scientific findings drew little attention, and the Arabian Expedition, which had been financed in hopes of winning Denmark cultural prestige in Enlightenment Europe, soon sunk into oblivion.

When Hansen began his investigation of this scientific expedition, he discovered an abundance of source materials, much of which had been neglected for nearly two hundred years. Among them were letters, diaries, and scholarly works from the expedition that filled three enormous boxes stored in the Rigsarkivet (National Archives of Denmark) as well as many scientific specimens and documents housed in Det kongelige zoologiske Museum (the Royal Danish Zoological Museum). Judging from the bibliography to *Det lykkelige Arabien,* Hansen made extensive use of the available materials.

In Hansen's hands the participants in the Arabian Expedition are shaped into literary characters and the events and internal conflicts are molded into a plot. Hansen emphasizes the expedition's difficult start and its internal problems, already evident before the departure from the harbor of Copenhagen. He describes the many hardships of the expedition and the weaknesses within the group. He portrays the philologist von Haven as a vain and incompetent academician who bungles the expedition's important mission to Mount Sinai. In striking contrast to von Haven, Hansen depicts the natural scientist Forsskål and the astronomer and cartographer Niebuhr as the two scholarly geniuses of the expedition. He casts von Haven (who at one point attempts to poison the other members of the expedition) in the role of the antagonist and blames the officialdom in Copenhagen for ineptitude and indifference. Death is depicted as overshadowing the entire expedition, eventually claiming the lives of five of its members. Hansen singles out Niebuhr as the sole individual who understands the fundamental conditions of human existence and depicts his humble resignation to his destiny as an alternative to the ultimately futile quest for happiness in distant lands.

In *Det lykkelige Arabien,* Niebuhr comes to illustrate Camus's concept of *l'homme absurde* (the absurd man)— the person whose life and work is without meaning. In Hansen's description of Niebuhr, living and dying in a state of anonymity and oblivion becomes crucial to accepting destiny. Hansen comments, "Den, der vil se, må selv være usynlig. Den, der vil huske, må leve ubemærket og glemt" (He who wants to see, must be invisible. He who wants to remember must live unnoticed and forgotten). When Niebuhr at last returns to Copenhagen and gains a small measure of recognition for his

achievements, he rejects a prestigious position and a title of nobility and instead chooses to return to his native Dietmarsk. There he lives quietly for thirty-five years as a parish clerk until he dies peacefully at the age of eighty-two. Hansen suggests that the Arabian desert has taught Niebuhr about the fundamental realities of existence:

> Vejen opad er uden interesse. Sandheden kan ikke svæve. Den ligger paa jorden for vore fødder, æsler og mennesker tramper hen over den og sviner den til, men det spiller ingen rolle, den bliver liggende paa jorden, den er paa en maade jorden selv, spændt ud under os som et sikkerhedsnet, dybere end den kan vi aldrig falde. Derfor er der ikke grund til frygt. Der findes ingen nederlag.

> (The road upwards is without interest. Truth cannot float in the air. It lies on the ground beneath our feet; donkeys and people trample on it and soil it, but that doesn't matter. Truth stays on the ground, in a way it is the earth herself, stretched out under us like a safety net; we can never fall any deeper. Therefore there is no reason for fear. Defeat does not exist.)

The portrait of Niebuhr in *Det lykkelige Arabien* is influenced by the existentialist outlook of postwar Europe, an outlook central to Hansen's authorship. Hansen suggests that Niebuhr's humble industriousness is his triumph over defeat; his struggle, albeit ultimately futile, is heroic. The Nietzschean concept of *amor fati* (love of destiny) in Hansen's authorship takes on an absurdist dimension, inspired in particular by Camus's *Le Mythe de Sisyphe* (The Myth of Sisyphus, 1942; translated, 1955). In his 1947 essay dealing with Camus, "Pest" (Plague), Hansen writes, "Sisyfos, det er arbejderen, kontoristen, vor tids menneske, hvis værk er uden mening. Men når Sisyfos går ned fra bjerget, er han alligevel lykkelig" (Sisyphus, he is the worker, the office clerk, a person of our times, whose work is without meaning. But when Sisyphus walks down the mountain, he is nevertheless happy). Like Camus's Sisyphus, Niebuhr is ultimately depicted in *Det lykkelige Arabien* as a contented man; there is no defeat in his return to the hinterland of Dietmarsk. Niebuhr's destiny illustrates the victory of the individual over worldly ambition, the idea—in the author's own words—that "the road upwards is without interest."

Hansen's first historical work received positive reviews. On the occasion of the book's publication, 16 October 1962, renowned critic and author Tom Kristensen, writing in the Danish daily *Politiken,* lauded Hansen as "en fin stilist med episk kraft og kritisk sans og historisk forståelse" (a fine stylist with epic power, critical sense and historical understanding) and predicted optimistically the likelihood of Hansen's book

Hansen and his second wife, Gitte Jæger, walking near their home on the island of Samsø, summer 1978 (photograph by Erik Friis)

becoming The Book of the Month, if translated into English. Other critics praised Hansen's ability to shape dry historical documents into an exciting and readable narrative while at the same time allowing the facts to speak for themselves. Since its initial publication in 1962, *Det lykkelige Arabien* has been republished in several editions and translated into the other Scandinavian languages, as well as English, French, and Italian.

Hansen's next documentary novel, a work about the Northwest Expedition of 1619–1620 led by Captain Jens Munk, forms a counterpart to his book about the Arabian Expedition. At the center of *Jens Munk* (1965; translated and abridged as *North West to Hudson Bay: The Life and Times of Jens Munk,* 1970) is a venture in the history of Danish exploration and imperialism, an account of an event often overlooked in conventional national historiography. *Jens Munk* won Hansen further recognition as an influential documentary writer in Scandinavia. At the same time, the conspicuously fictive aspects of this historical reconstruction stirred up a debate among Danish

critics regarding the boundary between historiography and historical fiction.

Hansen claimed that he first heard Munk's name in 1963 in a radio program, which included a reading from the captain's diary written at Hudson Bay in 1620, and that he began writing *Jens Munk* eight days later. In 1964, with the support of the National Museum of Canada, Hansen organized a research expedition with writer and archaeologist Peter Seeberg to study the conditions at the site of Munk's winter camp at the mouth of the Churchill River. According to Hansen, the initial problem facing the project was a matter of "alt for sparsomme kilder, der nødvendiggjorde en alt for rigelig 'meddigtning,' om du vil, så rigelig, at bogen ville miste sit dokumentariske præg og blive en roman" (a great scarcity of sources, necessitating, so to speak, an excess amount of "improvisation"–so excessive that the book would lose its documentary character and turn into a novel). The challenge Hansen encountered in writing *Jens Munk* was the necessity of distancing himself from the narrator's role in order to objectify the presentation of the facts and to maintain the appearance of authenticity.

Hansen was attracted to the history of the seventeenth-century Danish seafarer and Arctic explorer Munk by the epistemological challenge that the scanty historical material presented and by the character himself, whose story he viewed as a fascinating allegory. Munk, the illegitimate son of a Danish nobleman, served as an explorer, captain, and soldier under Denmark's notorious King Christian IV. A Renaissance monarch, Christian IV pursued an ambitious policy of foreign commerce and expansion, which included attempts to gain Swedish territory. In an effort to promote lucrative trade with the Far East, he entrusted Captain Munk with the task of discovering a navigable waterway through the North American Continent. According to the historical record, Munk's two vessels were stranded by the winter ice on the west coast of Hudson Bay. Fifty-seven crewmen perished, and only Munk and two others survived. Scuttling the mother ship, *Enhiørningen* (The Unicorn), the three men managed to sail an open boat across the Atlantic to Bergen. Following his return to Denmark, Munk was denounced by Christian IV and died ignominiously.

The expedition to Hudson Bay in 1964 made it possible to study the factual conditions at the site of Munk's winter camp. At the mouth of the present-day Churchill River (formerly *Rivière Danoise* or *Rivière Monk*) Hansen and his team were able to locate the exact site of Munk's encampment, to unearth artifacts, and to verify details in the historical record. The scholarly results of the expedition were published by Hansen and Seeberg as *Jens Munks minde-ekspedition* (The Jens Munk Memorial Expedition) in 1965. Hansen's journal from the expedition was later reworked and published as *Vinterhavn: Nye rejsedagbøger* (Winter Harbor: New Travel Diaries, 1972).

The documentary works of the 1960s and 1970s differ from conventional historiography in that they often depict the author as a researcher engaged in an epistemological quest. The narrator in such works often assumes the role of an omniscient storyteller who evaluates documents, comments on the significance of events, and structures the facts into a meaningful plot. Hansen tended to reject the term "historical novel" and maintained that his works were reliable documentary accounts of history. In *Jens Munk* he makes use of a fictive narrator, *kronikeren* (the chronicler), who enables him to comment on the particular difficulties involved in apprehending a past reality.

The plot of *Jens Munk* delineates a downward curve of defeat and death in oblivion, a kind of deterministic fatalism. The protagonist both embraces his destiny and rises in fruitless rebellion against it. As a paradigm of the human condition, the story illustrates Hansen's tragic view of existence. The author reluctantly confirms such "literary" interpretations of *Jens Munk:*

> Der gik faktisk to år efter, at bogen var trykt og udgivet, før det gik op for mig, at denne historie om en mand, der atter og atter måtte begynde forfra selvfølgelig var en ny version af den myte om Sisyfos, jeg kendte til bevidstløshed fra Camus.

> (Actually two years passed after the book was printed and published, before it dawned on me that this story about a man who had to start over and over again was, of course, a new version of the Sisyphus myth which I knew from Camus like the back of my hand.)

Given Hansen's tendency to emphasize the accuracy and factuality of his historical works, it is not surprising that he should attempt to deflate literary interpretations of them. *Jens Munk* does express immediate concerns of the author connected with his views of history: the idea that history, in the words of the narrator in the conclusion of *Jens Munk,* is not "et produkt af resultater og sejre, men en sum af begyndelser, dette vedvarende bølgeslag af slægter, der skyller op og trækker sig tilbage" (a product of results and victories; it is the sum of beginnings, that continuous surging of the waves of generations who swell up and then recede). Munk's story of failure and defeat thus provides an antidote to the traditional glorification of the national past and its heroes.

In Hansen's *Jens Munk* the protagonist's personal downfall is seen as an extended metaphor for Denmark's decline. Munk's defeat, King Christian IV's downfall, and the Kalmar War (1611–1613)–the last Danish military victory–are presented as parallel events. Turning points in Munk's life are often described by "the chronicler" against the background of momentous changes in Denmark's destiny. In this regard, it is tempting to compare *Jens Munk* to Johannes V. Jensen's novel *Kongens Fald* (1900–1901; translated as *The Fall of the King,* 1933), a similarity immediately noted by the critics upon the publication of *Jens Munk.* In both works Denmark's destiny of defeat and decline is closely tied to the fates of the protagonists. In both works the protagonists are presented as dreamers, or *fantaster,* a pervasive motif in Danish literature.

In *Jens Munk* Hansen invents the figure of the chronicler, who both provides the facts and attempts to imbue them with meaning. Hansen's fascinating account of this explorer from Danish history is a fine demonstration of his method, a masterpiece in the documentary genre, but also a striking example of metahistory. *Jens Munk* became Hansen's second best-seller,

Kap. 4.   PAGINA   *104.*

                    ← *cvor* →

nogle ivrige stemmer oppe paa dækket. Erichsen beordrede lavmælt geværskytterne i

▮▮▮stilling. Saa fik matroserne besked paa ▮▮▮▮▮▮▮▮ at ro nærmere.

          Det var mandag aften, den 6. august 1753. Der blæste en svag sydvestlig vind.

Den lille regntid i Guinea var endnu ikke begyndt, himlen var skyfri og dækket med

stjerner. Maanen var i tiltagende, 1 døgn efter første kvarter, og 6 timer bagefter

solen. Lidt over middag var den staaet op i øst, og da solen gik ned, hang den ▮▮▮

paa midten af sin bane, kun 22° syd for zenith. Det havde været let for kaptajn Erich=

sen og hans folk at orientere sig efter mørkets frembrud, nu kl. 11 saa de halvmaanen

(paa det samme sted,   *nogle*

staa ildrød bag skibet, hvor de ▮▮▮▮timer forinden havde set solen. Der var da gaaet

halvandet døgn,

▮▮▮▮▮ siden kaptajn Erichsen havde opgivet sit skib. Nu fik han det tilbage igen.

Det hele gik saa hurtigt, at han knap huskede, hvad der skete, og de følgende begi=

venheder optager kun en lille plads i vidneforklaringerne. Han huskede, at geværskyt=

terne ▮▮▮▮affyrede en enkelt salve efter nogle negre, der skyndsomt forlod skibet i

deres kanoer. Han huskede, hvorledes han kort efter entrede "Patientia" i skæret fra

matrosernes fakler. Og han huskede, at der aldrig før i hans liv havde mødt ham et

værre syn.

          Da slaven Qvabena 38 timer forinden til sin forbløffelse ▮▮▮▮▮▮▮▮▮ *saa,*

▮▮▮▮ at de hvide havde opgivet kampen, greb han en ▮▮▮økse i kaptajnens geværkiste

                                                           snart
og huggede sig gennem skottet ind til negerlasten. Det tykke skillerum var brudt ned,

Coffi sprang igennem hullet og begyndte at frigøre mændene fra deres lænker, Qvabena

løb op paa det folketomme dæk, overhuggede ▮▮▮▮▮▮▮▮ surringerne paa storlugen, aab=

nede den og kaldte de stærkeste til sig. Nogle ▮▮▮▮fik fat i kaptajnens flintebøs=

ser, resten gav sig til at bakse med de svære jernkanoner. Snart rullede de første

skud hen over vandet i retning af den flygtende redningsbaad, Qvabena selv fyrede løs

gennem vinduerne i agterkahytten. Men afstanden var for stor, kampen var afsluttet, *og*

                                        dækket
nu begyndte der et andet skuespil om bord. Nede paa slave▮▮▮ havde negrene hjulpet

til med at befri deres kammerater, efterhaanden som de selv kom af med lænkerne, og

da Qvabena indstillede skydningen væltede de nøgne mennesker, mænd, kvinder og børn

mellem hinanden, op gennem luger, trapper og lejdere, op paa dækket. Man hørte den

Page from the corrected print-out for Hansen's Slavernes skibe *(Collection of Gitte Jæger)*

and was translated into English, French, Polish, and Hungarian.

In *Slavernes kyst* (The Slave Coast, 1967), *Slavernes skibe* (The Slave Ships, 1968), and *Slavernes øer* (The Slave Islands, 1970) Hansen takes up the question of the Danish role in the African slave trade and in slavery on Danish-owned West Indian sugar plantations in the seventeenth, eighteenth, and early nineteenth centuries. Of Hansen's works dealing with Denmark's history of exploration and colonialism, the slave trilogy is his most ambitious and most thoroughly researched project. In order to gain a firsthand impression of former slave forts, the sea voyage, and the sugar plantations, Hansen made fact-finding expeditions to West Africa in 1965 and to the Virgin Islands (formerly the Danish West Indies) in 1967; he was accompanied by his wife, Birte Lund, who illustrated the trilogy with sketches from the historical localities.

In the slave trilogy Hansen challenges the cherished notion that Denmark was the first European nation to abolish its slave trade. On 16 March 1792 Denmark had in fact decreed a prohibition on the importation of slaves into its West Indian colonies. However, Hansen reminds his Scandinavian readers that, under pressure from slave owners in the West Indies, the Danish government suspended the implementation of this decree and that the official ban on the Danish slave trade only went into effect in 1807, prompted by the example of the British government, which outlawed the slave trade within the British Empire in that year. The abolition of slavery in the Danish colonies did not occur until decades later with the Emancipation Act of 1848.

Hansen's choice of subject matter and perspective can be seen as a direct response to the political climate of the 1960s. In a decade when the United States was a favorite target for its treatment of African Americans and its imperialist role in Southeast Asia, Hansen shifted the focus to his native land and, in doing so, touched a sensitive nerve in the national consciousness. The slave trilogy was awarded the Nordisk Råds Litteraturpris (the Nordic Council's Literary Award) in 1971; the wording of the commission's rationale for awarding the prize seems colored by the political concerns of the decade: "med historisk sakkundskap och konstnärlig kraft ett exempel på de rika ländernas utsugning av de fattiga länderna levandegöres" (an example of the wealthy countries' exploitation of the impoverished countries is illustrated with historical expertise and powerful artistry). Prior to the publication of Hansen's trilogy, Denmark's role in ending the slave trade had been held up as cause for national pride. Hansen's trilogy may be read as a response to the cursory treatment that Denmark's involvement in the slave trade had received in history textbooks.

Hansen's slave trilogy is ambitious in scope; more than one thousand pages in length, it spans nearly 250 years of Danish colonial history. *Slavernes kyst,* the first volume of the trilogy, gives a history of Danish Guinea. Hansen points out that the Danish state maintained five forts–Christiansborg, Augustaborg, Fredensborg, Kongensteen, and Prindsensteen–on the so-called Slave Coast (the coast between the Gold Coast and Benin) primarily for the purpose of securing slave labor for its West Indian colonies. He traces the history of Danish involvement on the Guinea Coast from the establishment of the West Indian-Guinean Company in 1672 to the sale of the Danish forts and territorial claims to England in 1850 for £10,000. *Slavernes kyst* is structured around the documentary accounts of seven Danish colonialists: an officer, two pastors, a slave trader, a doctor, a bookkeeper, and a governor; each describes from his perspective the conditions under which Africans were sold into slavery, auctioned off at Danish forts, purchased by slave captains, branded, held in captivity, and packed into the holds of slave ships. Hansen pays particular attention to the personal motivations, sympathies, and antipathies of the Danes who were involved in this trade. He also chronicles the staggering loss of Danish lives on the Slave Coast, the long line of pastors, civil servants, governors, and doctors who died of malaria, cholera, yellow fever, and unknown causes, often within months of arriving in Africa.

Slavernes skibe, the second volume of the trilogy, describes the infernal conditions aboard the Danish slave ships that transported the African prisoners from the Danish forts of Guinea to the Danish forts in the West Indies. Of the thousands of slaves transported on Danish ships, Hansen estimates that one-fifth perished under way, a mortality rate that indicates the conditions on board. The author describes how the Africans were packed into the hold lying naked on raw wooden shelves only seventy centimeters in height. The slave ships sailed slowly on the nearly windless Middle Passage, with the Atlantic crossing often taking two months. The individual accounts of a boatswain, a helmsman, a slave captain, and a ship's doctor provide insights into daily events aboard the ships. *Slavernes skibe* contains a wealth of information on maritime history, the conditions of life on board, the perils of the Middle Passage, slave uprisings and mutinies, and the auctions upon arrival at the Danish fort in Christiansted.

Slavernes øer, the final volume of the slave trilogy, is a tour de force that chronicles the entire history of the Danish West Indies, the islands of St. Croix, St. Jan, and St. Thomas, from the arrival of the first Danish colonists in 1671 to the sale of the islands to the United

Dust jacket for the collection of Hansen's articles on literature, published in 1998

States in 1917. *Slavernes øer* casts new light on significant historical events on the islands: the St. Jan uprising of 1733 led by an African chieftain, the influence of the Pietist Herrnhutian missionaries, the trial of the insurgent slaves of the uprising of 1759 in Christiansted, and the Emancipation Act of 1848. The role of the governor of the Danish West Indies, Peter von Scholten, in bringing about the Emancipation Act of 1848 is central to the work. Hansen also describes the inhuman working conditions on the sugar plantations and in the sugar mills, depicting the profitable production of sugar as the economic mainstay that perpetuated the barbarous practice of African slave labor.

Hansen's vivid descriptions of the harsh conditions of the slaves in the sugar mills caused literary critics of the early 1970s to nod their heads and speak approvingly of the underlying Marxist perspective in Hansen's trilogy. However, the author himself pointed out that Marxist economic theory is simply a useful tool—among other tools—in describing the slave trade: "de marxistiske økonomiske teorier . . . indgår i rækken af de hjælpemidler, der står til rådighed, hvor det drejer sig om et så økonomisk struktureret stof som dette, men de er ikke de eneste" (Marxist economic theories . . . are included in the number of tools available when one is dealing with an economically structured material such as this, but they are not the only tools). Hansen's refusal to subscribe to the predominantly Marxist ideol-

ogy of the decade is evident in his use of literary allusions; the title page of each volume features a quote by such highly unfashionable figures as Johan Wolfgang von Goethe regarding the freedom and the dignity of the individual, representing a challenge to the prevailing political climate in Denmark.

In his portrait of Africa and the Africans, Hansen evokes Isak Dinesen's *Out of Africa* (1937; translated, by Karen Blixen, as *Den afrikanske Farm,* 1937), the best-known work in Danish letters devoted to Africa prior to the slave trilogy. While Dinesen's novel is an idealization of European imperialism and a sentimental portrait of the African spirit, Hansen's trilogy is a denunciation of colonialism and a condemnation of the European exploitation of the Africans. Dinesen's nostalgic opening line, "I had a farm in Africa at the foot of the Ngong Hills," is utilized to great effect as a leitmotiv in Hansen's trilogy. The factuality and acerbity of Hansen's work serves as an antidote to the sentimentality and nostalgia of Dinesen's portrait of the European experience in Africa.

The figure of Peter von Scholten, the governor general of the Danish West Indies, is central to *Slavernes øer;* in fact, Hansen's depiction of von Scholten may have renewed interest in this historical figure, who subsequently became the subject of a full-length Danish feature motion picture, *Peter von Scholten,* produced by Nina Crone in 1987, with a screenplay written by Sven

Holm that seems to have drawn on Hansen's trilogy. According to legend, von Scholten promised his mulatto mistress, Anna Heergaard, that he would emancipate the African slaves in the Danish West Indies. Hansen builds on this legend, depicting the governor's promise to his mistress as the motivation behind his role in the emancipation. Hansen has pointed out that von Scholten is in a sense "the protagonist" and "end result" of the trilogy. In the concluding volume Hansen demonstrates how the governor was punished by the Danish state for proclaiming the abolition of slavery.

The slave trilogy is arguably Hansen's finest and most influential work. The extensive research, the scholarly method, and the detached narrative stance that characterize the trilogy demonstrate Hansen's true stature as an historical writer whose work has proved seminal. On 20 October 1970 in the Danish paper *Berlingske tidende,* historian Kristian Hvidt praised the author's ability to combine the imaginative and factual aspects of historical writing in *Slavernes øer:* "Kombinationen af den suveræne skribent og den fantasifulde, men dog kritiske historiker er sjælden" (The combination of the superior writer and the imaginative, but nevertheless critical historian, is rare). Other critics of the day observed that *Slavernes øer* not only was eminently well written but it also contained many valuable new insights into the history of the Danish colonies. In fact, Hansen's trilogy contributed to a shift of perspective in later accounts of Danish imperialist ventures and provided a corrective to traditional historiography. With regard to the famous Ordinance of 1792 that prohibited the importation of slaves into Danish possessions, it is notable that historians since 1970 are careful to point out that the notion of Denmark's humanitarian leadership is questionable. Hansen's prizewinning trilogy reached a larger reading public and scholarly community in Scandinavia than had any earlier work dealing with Denmark's slave trade and tropical colonies. Not only did Hansen succeed in touching a sensitive nerve in the Danish national consciousness, but he also injected new vigor into the scholarly debate regarding Denmark's role in the history of slavery. The slave trilogy has been translated into Swedish, Norwegian, Icelandic, and French; the work remains untranslated into English, though it would be of great interest to the English-speaking world.

The reception of the slave trilogy and the award by the Nordic Council in 1971 marked the peak of Hansen's career as a writer. He had attained the status of a public figure who frequently articulated his views on politics and literature. Between 1972 and 1982 he participated in many missions with the Red Cross, traveling to South and North Vietnam, Bangladesh, Western Sahara, Zambia, Rhodesia, Malaysia, Uganda, Algeria, and Poland. Hansen also found time to travel for pleasure and to gain new impressions for his work, in 1966 to the Faroe Islands, in 1972 to Greece, in 1973 to East Greenland, in 1974 to Egypt, and in 1975 to Italy. Throughout his adult life, Hansen kept diaries, recording what he saw and experienced, people he met, and books he read; his many travels were recorded in particular. During his lifetime he published several travel journals such as *Sidste sommer i Angmagssalik* (Last Summer in Angmagssalik, 1978), an account of his impressions of eastern Greenland. A second collection of travel journals was published as *Kurs mod solnedgangen: Nye rejsedagbøger* (Course toward the Setting Sun: New Travel Journals, 1982), which includes revised editions of the earlier *Vinterhavn* and *Sidste sommer i Angmagssalik,* as well as a third part that covers Hansen's missions with the Red Cross between 1971 and 1982. In his reflections on human life and history, Hansen is always an astute observer who registers his impressions soberly, often with a twist of irony.

While his career was at its high point, Hansen's marriage to Birte Lund suffered. After nearly twenty years of marriage the couple separated in 1970, and Hansen moved with thirty-three-year-old Gitte Jæger to "Brøndkjær," a new home that he had built on the Danish island of Samsø. For the next decade Hansen and Jæger (wed in 1978) made their home on Samsø; the couple lived as neighbors to the important author Thorkild Bjørnvig, raised sheep, and made frequent visits to their Copenhagen apartment. While living at Brøndkjær, Hansen launched the research for his next major work; it was to deal with the case against the Nobel laureate and Nazi sympathizer Knut Hamsun. In 1975 Hansen and Jæger traveled to Norway to conduct research for this book; the difficult three-year process of researching and writing the Hamsun book is chronicled in the posthumously published diary, *Mellem Brøndkjær og Nørholm: Dagbog fra Hamsun-årene 1975–78* (Between Brøndkjær and Nørholm: Diary from the Hamsun years 1975–78, 1996).

Hansen's critics had received the slave trilogy as a work written in the spirit of the leftist politics of the 1960s. However, the reception of his next work, the three-volume *Processen mod Hamsun* (The Case against Hamsun, 1978), eight years later brought about an abrupt decline in Hansen's reputation as a documentarist; it proved to be his last significant work. In certain respects, Hansen's aims and intentions in his Hamsun project were similar to those he had in his successful slave trilogy. He sought to touch a sensitive nerve in national consciousness, this time that of the Norwegians, specifically with regard to the war-crimes trials and the treatment of Nazi collaborators following

Hansen in Africa on a 1979 mission with the Danish Red Cross (Collection of Gitte Jæger)

World War II. Evident again is Hansen's effort to target the "establishment" (this time the government and judicial bureaucracy of postwar Norway) and his effort to undermine the accepted notion of Scandinavian egalitarian humanism. For the readers of *Processen mod Hamsun,* however, Hansen's subject matter represented a different ideological focus. In defending Hamsun it seemed to many Scandinavian readers and critics that Hansen defended Nazism and Nazi collaborators. Whereas the slave trilogy had placed Hansen to the left of the political spectrum, the work on Hamsun shifted him, in the eyes of many critics and readers, to the extreme right (in other words, the "wrong" side).

Hamsun, unlike most of his countrymen, supported Imperial Germany and the Central Powers during World War I, and Nazi Germany after 1933 and during the occupation of Norway by German troops in World War II. Membership in Vidkun Quisling's Nasjonal Samling (National Union) Party after 8 April 1940 was made a criminal offense by the Norwegian government-in-exile in London, and party members began to be arrested soon after the liberation of Norway by the Allies in May 1945. The eighty-six-year-old Knut Hamsun and his wife, Marie, were among those first arrested.

Obviously, Thorkild Hansen intended to deflate the widespread and comfortable myth that Hamsun's fascist convictions were the expressions of an old man suffering from dementia. This myth was widely held in

Scandinavia and abroad and was traceable to the psychiatric examination requested by the Norwegian government in 1946, which concluded that Hamsun was a man of "varigt svækkede åndsevner" (permanently impaired mental faculties). Hansen certainly recognized the human tendency to whitewash national heroes and was determined to uncover the true and the "sane" Hamsun behind the popular myth, perpetuated in literary histories and textbooks.

Hansen was well aware that a book on Knut Hamsun's trial would be political dynamite, but he was gripped by the story of Hamsun. In his eyes it embodied all the conflicts of our age: "modsætningen mellem den enkelte og de mange, mellem kunst og politik, og selvfølgelig især mellem mand og kvinde" (the opposition between the individual and the masses, between art and politics, and of course, especially between man and woman). Perhaps Hansen's attraction to the case of Hamsun also had deeper and more personal roots in his own experiences during World War II. In *De søde piger: Dagbog 1943–47* he describes his own sentiments as a student during the German occupation of Denmark. On 3 April 1945 he notes that he has just completed a study of Hamsun's *Markens grøde* (1917; translated as *Growth of the Soil,* 1921) and comments, "Nu siger de, Hamsun er nazist. Det lyder utroligt, men hvorfor ikke? . . . Det gode ved digterne er det, der bliver tilbage, når meningerne er trukket fra" (Now they are saying that Hamsun is a Nazi. It sounds incredible, but why not? . . .

The good thing about poets is that which remains, when the opinions are withdrawn). Already evident here is Hansen's view on the separate roles of art and politics, the idea that a writer remains a great artistic genius, regardless of any "unfashionable" political opinions. Politics are transitory, art is immortal. This perspective on art is consistent with Hansen's stance throughout the 1960s and early 1970s, a period during which he was often under fire for his "outdated" existentialist views.

Knut Hamsun, as portrayed by Thorkild Hansen, emerges as a supremely tragic figure. Indeed, many of the facts speak for themselves: Hamsun was nearly deaf and isolated during the war, naively stubborn in his political views, ignorant of the realities of the war, and too proud and honorable to blame others for his errors. The ninety-year-old author's memoirs *Paa gjengrodde stier* (1949; translated as *On Overgrown Paths,* 1967) had demonstrated to the world that he was not a senile old man, but a literary genius even during and after the war. *Processen mod Hamsun* succeeds in convincing us that the destiny of Hamsun was fundamentally tragic. In the Sisyphean aspect of the story, Knut Hamsun is reminiscent of Hansen's other tragic heroes, such as Jens Munk and Carsten Niebuhr. Hamsun continued to struggle against impossible odds, namely public opinion and the judicial system, even when his defeat was most certain.

However, there is a troubling aspect to Hansen's "reconstruction" of the case against Hamsun; it concerns his depiction of the role of Marie Hamsun. Hansen speculates that Marie and Knut Hamsun had different reasons to support Nazi Germany. In *Processen mod Hamsun* Hansen advances the theory that Marie's impassioned Nazi convictions were rooted in her feelings of inferiority, her tendency to devote herself to strong authoritarian male figures, and, most importantly, in her belief that her husband had betrayed her. Hansen maintains that in 1936, suspecting Knut of infidelity, she cast her vote for Quisling and National Socialism; he concludes that Adolf Hitler was "den store faderskikkelse, som hun kunne vie sit liv" (the great father figure, to whom she could devote her life). Hansen uses a psychological theory of Fascism to explain Marie's "revenge" on Knut. Hansen maintains that Marie's bitterness over the fact that Knut had forced her to devote herself to him, sacrificing her acting career early in their marriage, led to resentment and hatred later in life; he depicts the Hamsun couple engaged in a Strindbergian dance of death: "Hun hadede så dybt, fordi hun elskede så højt" (She hated so deeply, because she loved so strongly).

The heart of Hansen's defense of Knut is the hypothesis that Marie's "revenge" was to isolate Knut totally during the occupation. Whereas Knut Hamsun is portrayed in Hansen's work as rational (that is, "sane") in terms of his political sympathies, Marie is depicted as emotionally disturbed. It is well documented that Marie was the most politically active of the two; during the war, not only did she open their home at Nørholm to the occupying forces, but she also made several tours in Nazi Germany, reading from her husband's works. Hansen argues that Marie must have been familiar with the political situation in Europe and with the barbarous aspects of Nazism. He questions Marie's silence on these matters during the occupation and asks why she kept her husband uninformed about the atrocities of the war and claims to know the answer: Marie's isolation and manipulation of the older Hamsun was her revenge for the years she had sacrificed for the sake of his literary career.

The specific challenge presented by *Processen mod Hamsun* is that many of the key sources and "documents" are literary texts, which are furthermore tainted by a charged political and emotional environment. In his discussion of Knut and Marie Hamsun's memoirs, Hansen remarks that their lives were a mixture of "sandhed og digtning" (truth and fiction). In attempting to reconstruct the political persuasions and emotional lives of the two Hamsuns, Hansen encountered a mixture of fact and artifice, promulgated by the main actors themselves in the form of memoirs, letters, postcards, responses to questionnaires, many of them undoubtedly artfully constructed with the verdict of posterity in mind. Hansen is aware of the inherent difficulty in his task and draws attention to the problematic relationship between truth and artifice, between history and narrative: "Historien er ikke enfoldig. Den skelner ikke, som moralisterne tror, mellem sandhed og løgn, rigtigt og forkert. . . . Det kan også hænge sammen med, at historien handler om mennesker" (History is not one-sided. It does not distinguish, as the moralists believe, between truth and lies, right and wrong . . . This may also have to do with the fact that history is about people).

Hansen's premonitions regarding the explosive nature of the Hamsun work were amply confirmed. The work appeared on 26 September 1978 in Copenhagen, Oslo, and Stockholm. The simultaneous publication in Danish, Norwegian, and Swedish indicates the importance attached to this tour de force, an event long awaited by Scandinavian critics and readers. A review by Victor Andreasen, entitled "Stjæl den bog" (Steal that book) in *Ekstra Bladet* on the day of publication reads,

> Thorkild Hansen har før bevist, at han som ingen anden dansk forfatter kan gøre et historisk forløb og en historisk personlighed så levende og nærværende. I værket om Hamsun overgår han med indgående dokumen-

tation og lidenskabeligt kunstnerisk engagement alt hvad han tidligere har præsteret.

(Thorkild Hansen has demonstrated before that, like no other Danish writer, he is able to make an historical event and an historical personality alive and immediate. In the work on Hamsun he exceeds all his earlier works by means of exhaustive documentation and passionate artistic engagement.)

However, such critical assessments of Hansen's *Processen mod Hamsun* did not last. The overwhelmingly positive weeklong initial reception was followed by an onslaught of negative criticism. The author describes in his published journal *Mellem Brøndkjær og Nørholm* how the enthusiastic reception of the book quickly soured when critics discovered many historical inaccuracies. The so-called Hamsun debate—which concerned Hamsun's politics as well as Hansen's methods—was particularly vitriolic in Norway. The first errors discovered concerned Hansen's depiction of the execution by firing squad of the Nazi collaborator Quisling on 24 October 1945: Hansen was inaccurate in such details as the position of Quisling's body after being shot. A heated debate in the Scandinavian press ensued and raged for months; the resulting articles were collected by Simen Skjønsberg in *Det uskyldige geni? fra debatten om "Prosessen mod Hamsun"* (The Innocent Genius? From the Debate about "The Case against Hamsun," 1979). Many critics felt that Hansen seemed to exonerate Nazi sympathies, if embraced by a hero and artistic genius such as Hamsun, and argued that the writer, regardless of the nature of his genius, ought to be held accountable for his political activities and views.

This debate was stirred up again nearly two decades later, when Jan Troell's motion picture *Hamsun* was released in April 1996. A new paperback edition of *Processen mod Hamsun* was published for the occasion with the front-cover advertisement: "The book behind the film." Although the Swedish author Per Olov Enquist wrote the screenplay for Troell's production, the credits acknowledge that the motion picture is "based on the novel by Thorkild Hansen." It is difficult to dismiss that the overriding interpretation of the case against Hamsun, as presented in Enquist's sympathetic portrait of Hamsun, is indebted to Hansen's 1978 work.

In the late 1970s and early 1980s, following the "defeat" of his Hamsun book, Hansen was nevertheless the wealthiest Danish writer of his generation and a notable public figure. In 1979 he published an interview with Denmark's constitutional monarch, *Samtale med Dronning Margrethe* (Conversation with Queen Margrethe). After wintering in Southern France in 1980–1981, Hansen bought a stylish house there in the Alps Mari-

times; in 1982 he and Jæger made "Le Mas du Chasseur" their permanent home.

The last work of Hansen's published during his lifetime was an autobiographical picture book, *Søforhør: Nærbillede af Thorkild Hansen* (Maritime Inquest: Close-up of Thorkild Hansen, 1982). The book is staged as a candid dialogue between the author and an anonymous interviewer. Details of the author's private life are (supposedly) frankly explored, and the work takes on a confessional and, at times, apologetic tone. *Søforhør* created a stir among critics who immediately suspected that the work was a self-arranged interview, an autobiography in disguise. The more than one hundred photographs of the author (many of them full-page) that accompany the text seem intended to "document" the authenticity and reliability of the account. Critics immediately panned *Søforhør* as too contrived and self-obsessed.

In the last years of his life, Hansen devoted much time to his lifelong passion: sailing. Like the sea captains depicted in his documentary works, Hansen crossed the Atlantic several times in ships or sailboats. In 1981 he served as a training officer on the sailing ship *Danmark* on a cruise to the Virgin Islands. In 1986–1987, marking the occasion of his sixtieth birthday, he circumnavigated the globe, making stops throughout South America and the South Pacific Islands. The following year he was at sea again, this time on a cruise to Central America, Brazil, and the Caribbean. On 4 February 1989, while cruising between the islands of Antigua and Guadeloupe, Thorkild Hansen died suddenly of a heart attack. He was sixty-two years old. It was fitting in a sense that a writer who lived and wrote according to the motto *Navigare necesse est, vivere non necesse* (Sailing is necessary, living is not necessary) should die at sea. He is buried at Brøndkjær on Samsø.

The authenticity of *Et atelier i Paris: Dagbog 1947–52*, the journals that Hansen edited himself before his death, and the intimate facts of the young author's life in Paris, became the subject of critical debates in the mid 1990s. Apparently, in 1974 Hansen signed a contract with his publisher, the agreement stating that Gyldendal would own the rights to his diaries. He had planned to publish his diaries in ten to twelve volumes, a project cut short by his untimely death in 1989. In 1995 Danish critic and author Poul Behrendt published a controversial book dealing with Hansen's Parisian years, titled *Djævlepagten: En historie om Thorkild Hansen* (Pact with the Devil: A Story about Thorkild Hansen), claiming that Hansen had made a "pact with the devil" when he "sold" his private life for public consumption. Behrendt examines the facts of the young Hansen's life, scrutinizing personal documents, letters, and interviews (a technique practiced by Hansen himself) and juxtaposing these facts with the older author's "reconstructions" of these events in his published journals. In *Djævlepagten* Behrendt attempts to solve the riddles of Hansen's relationship with Jean Seillière and Hansen's hasty marriage in 1951, suggesting–with little real evidence–that Hansen and Seillière had a homosexual relationship and that Seillière arranged Hansen's marriage to Lund as a coverup. Besides exposing personal details about Hansen's life in Paris, Behrendt's pseudobiography demonstrates what critics had already suspected, namely that Hansen's published diaries constitute aesthetically constructed narratives, a contrived autobiography of the author's life. Considering Hansen's status as a master of documentary fiction, it is not surprising to learn that he thoroughly edited and rearranged his own journals. He attempted to ensure that only an idealized autobiography would remain for posterity; once he had thoroughly reworked his journals for publication, he destroyed the original manuscripts.

Hansen's sudden death in 1989 gave added impetus in Denmark and abroad to the publication of scholarly articles and monographs dealing with his authorship. Although the publication of selections from his diaries stirred up considerable debate regarding the relationship between the author's life and works, it will be for his substantial documentary best-sellers that Hansen will be remembered.

Interview:

Claus Clausen, "Thorkild Hansen," in *Digtere i forhør 1966: Samtaler med 12 danske forfattere* (Copenhagen: Gyldendal, 1966), pp. 246–265; reprinted as "Status midtvejs," in *Landkending: En bog om Thorkild Hansen,* edited by Iben Holk and Lars Peter Rømhild (Odense: Odense University Press, 1992), pp. 227–242.

Biography:

Poul Behrendt, *Djævlepagten: En historie om Thorkild Hansen,* 2 volumes (Copenhagen: Gyldendal, 1995).

References:

Iben Holk and Lars Peter Rømhild, eds., *Landkending: En bog om Thorkild Hansen* (Odense: Odense University Press, 1992);

Mikael Jalving, *Mellem linierne: Thorkild Hansen som historiefortæller* (Odense: Odense University Press, 1994);

Johnny Kondrup, "Thorkild Hansen," in his *Erindringens udveje: Studier i moderne dansk selvbiografi* (Valby: Amadeus, 1994), pp. 326–371;

Henk van der Liet, "Just Me, Myself, and I: On Thorkild Hansen as Creator and Creation," *Tijdschrift voor Skandinavistiek,* 18, no. 1 (1997): 71–95;

Lars Peter Rømhild, "Thorkild Hansen," in *Danske digtere i det 20. århundrede,* 3rd edition, 5 volumes, edited by Torben Brostrøm and Mette Winge (Copenhagen: Gad, 1984), IV: 29–42;

Søren Schou, "Eksistentiel historieskrivning: Om Thorkild Hansens forfatterskab," in *Linjer i nordisk prosa: Danmark 1965–75,* edited by Peter Madsen (Lund: Bo Cavefors Bokförlag, 1977), pp. 137–158;

Simen Skjønsberg, ed., *Det uskyldige geni? Fra debatten om "Prosessen mot Hamsun"* (Oslo: Gyldendal Norsk Forlag, 1979);

Marianne Stecher-Hansen, "Double-voiced Discourse in Thorkild Hansen's *Jeus Munk," Scandinavian Studies,* 66, no. 4 (1994): 533–551;

Stecher-Hansen, *History Revisited: Fact and Fiction in Thorkild Hansen's Documentary Works* (Columbia, S.C.: Camden House, 1997);

Stecher-Hausen, "Whose Hamsun? Author and Artifice: Knut Hamsun, Thorkild Hansen and Per Olov Enquist,: *Edda,* no. 3 (Summer 1999): 37–43.

Piet Hein

(16 December 1905 – 17 April 1996)

Charlotte Schiander Gray

BOOKS: *Gruk,* 10 volumes, as Kumbel Kumbell (Copenhagen: Politikens Forlag, 1940–1949);
Vers i verdensrummet (Copenhagen: Gyldendal, 1941);
Den tiende muse (Copenhagen: Gyldendal, 1941);
Kumbels almanak, as Kumbel (Copenhagen: Gyldendal, 1942);
Man skal gaa paa jorden: Aforismer, illustrated by Arne Ungermann (Copenhagen: Gyldendal, 1944);
4 Digte under Sydkorset (Copenhagen: Naver, 1945);
Helicopteren (Copenhagen: Gyldendal, 1947);
Vers af denne verden (Copenhagen: Gyldendal, 1948);
5 juni: Et grundlove kogleri (Copenhagen: Gyldendal, 1949);
Kumbels fødselsdagskalender, as Kumbel (Copenhagen: Gyldendal, 1949);
Ord, as Notorious Jubelco (Copenhagen: Naver, 1949);
Selv om den er gloende: Aforismer, illustrated by Ungermann (Copenhagen: Gyldendal, 1950);
Kumbels lyre: 166 gruk, selected by Svend Clausen and Aage Marcus (Copenhagen: Politiken, 1950);
Gruk, volumes 11–20 (Copenhagen: Gyldendal, 1954–1963);
Gruk, fra alle aarene, 2 volumes, as Kumbel (Copenhagen: Gyldendal, 1960, 1964);
Du skal plante et træ, illustrated by Sikker Hansen (Copenhagen: Gyldendal, 1960);
Husk at elske (Copenhagen: Gyldendal, 1962); republished as *Husk at elske: Udvalgte digte og Gruk* (Copenhagen: Borgen, 1968);
Vis electrica, illustrated by Ungermann (Copenhagen: Elektricitetsselskabet Isefjordværket interessentskab, 1962);
Kilden og krukken: Fabler og essays (Copenhagen: Gyldendal, 1963);
Husk at leve: Udvalgte digte og gruk fra de første 25 år (Copenhagen: Borgen, 1965);
Lad os blive mennesker: Udvalgte digte og gruk (Copenhagen: Borgen, 1967);
I folkemunde, Korte gruk, no. 1 (Copenhagen: Borgen, 1968);

Piet Hein (Collection of Hugo Piet Hein)

Man's Communication to Man, Alexander Graham Bell Lecture, no. 8 (Boston, 1968);
Det kraftens ord, Korte gruk, no. 2 (Copenhagen: Borgen, 1969);
Digte fra alle årene: Et udvalg (Copenhagen: Borgen, 1972);
Menneskesag: En Piet Hein antologi, selected by A. Kaysen-Petersen, Knud Meister, and T. E. Jørgen-Jensen (Copenhagen: Bonde, 1975);
Johannes Buchholtz's Urolige hjerte, illustrated by Thormod Kidde (Struer: Johanes Buchholtz Selskabet, 1977);
Prosa-gruk (Copenhagen: Borgen, 1984);

Gruk fra alle årene, volume 3, as Kumbel (Copenhagen: Gyldendal/Borgen, 1985); as Hein (Copenhagen: Borgen, 1991);

Hjertets lyre: Kærlighedsdigte og -gruk (Copenhagen: Borgen, 1985);

Lars Løvetand-gruk: For voksne der holder af børn (Copenhagen: Borgen, 1987);

Words: Grooks Gruk, edited by Hugo Piet Hein (Copenhagen: Borgen, 1995);

Gruk, fra alle årene, volume 4, edited by Hugo Piet Hein (Copenhagen: Borgen, 1995);

Gruk, fra alle årene, volume 5, edited by Hugo Piet Hein (Copenhagen: Borgen, 1999).

Editions in English: *Grooks,* 7 volumes, by Piet Hein and Jens Arup—comprises volume 1 (Cambridge, Mass.: M.I.T. Press, 1966; Copenhagen: Borgen, 1966); volume 2 (Copenhagen: Borgen, 1968; Garden City, N.Y.: Doubleday, 1969); volume 3 (Copenhagen: Borgen, 1970; Garden City, N.Y.: Doubleday, 1971); republished as *Still More Grooks* (London: Hodder Paperbacks, 1970); volume 4 (Copenhagen: Borgen, 1972; Garden City, N.Y.: Doubleday, 1973); republished as *Motes and Beams* (Oxford: Blackwell, 1973); volume 5 (Garden City, N.Y.: Doubleday, 1973); republished as *Mist and Moonshine* (Oxford: Blackwell, 1973); volumes 6–7 (Copenhagen: Borgen, 1978, 1984).

Runaway Runes, Short Grooks, no. 1, by Hein and Arup (Copenhagen: Borgen, 1968);

Viking Vistas, Short Grooks, no. 2, by Hein and Arup (Copenhagen: Borgen, 1983).

OTHER: *Lille Vise, Op. 35, Nr. 2,* text by Hein, music by Kjell Roikjer (Copenhagen: Skandinavisk & Borups Musikforlag, 1943);

Ludwig Bemelmans, *Madeline,* translated by Hein (Copenhagen: Illustrationsforlaget, 1963);

Ruth Krauss, *Jorden er til at stå på,* translated by Hein and illustrated by Maurice Sendak (Copenhagen: Carlsen / Illustrationsforlaget, 1966);

Christian Winther, *The Flight to America,* translated by Hein (Copenhagen: Gyldendal, 1976).

Polymath scientist, poet, and furniture designer Piet Hein was a true Renaissance man, a versatile figure whose interests embraced both the sciences and the humanities. He was also one of the few contemporary Danes who achieved world renown. Throughout his long, illustrious career, Hein invented games and puzzles, created designs and artifacts, and promoted international peace. He secured his place in Danish literature, however, with his pithy poems and aphorisms, well known in Denmark as *gruk* (translated as grooks). These elliptical poems recall the epigrammatic verses of Old Norse. To this day, Hein's more than seven thousand *gruk*–printed in newspapers and in many other sources–are still being collected for publication. With growing recognition in Denmark and abroad, through his grooks, designs, and games, Hein came to embody the character of his country and to represent it in an official capacity.

Piet Hein was born on 16 December 1905 in Copenhagen to Hjalmar Hein, an engineer, and his wife, Estrid (née Octavius), an ophthalmologist. Hein received a well-rounded education. After passing his university entrance examination in mathematics at the private secondary school Metropolitanskolen in 1924, he attended the Royal Swedish Academy of Fine Arts in Stockholm. He returned to Denmark in 1927 to study philosophy, science, design, and theoretical physics at the Niels Bohr Institute, the University of Copenhagen, and the Technical University of Denmark. A first marriage, to Gunver Holck in 1937, produced no children; Hein's second marriage, to Gerda Ruth Conheim in 1942, produced two sons, Juan Alvaro and Andrés Humberto, both born in 1943. Hein then married Anne Catherina Krøyer Pedersen, and the couple had one son, Lars, born in 1950. The marriage ended a few years later, and Hein married his fourth wife, Gerd Ericson, in 1955. They had two children: Jotun, born in 1956, and Hugo Piet, born in 1963. Gerd Hein died 3 November 1968, and Hein lived in England from 1969 to 1976.

Hein first made a name for himself as an industrial designer. In 1936 he created the three-dimensional SOMA Cube puzzle. In 1942 he invented a board game called Hex (at the time, Hein was contemplating the four-color theory of topology). The game, introduced at the Niels Bohr Institute, first became popular under the name Polygon in Denmark. Albert Einstein kept a copy of the game in his study. Hein's best-known work as a technical designer and inventor was the super-ellipse, a precise geometric shape that is a combination of the circle and the square. Hein designed this particular form for Sergels Torv (Sergel's Square), a point in the center of Stockholm where two motorways intersect at a rectangle only two hundred meters in length. Neither the ellipse nor various circles were adequate solutions to the spatial problem, which Hein solved by employing the opposite shapes of square and circle harmoniously. The super-ellipse design has been employed in Canada, France, the United States, and Mexico for residential constructions and sports centers (for example, the well-known Olympic Stadium in Mexico City). A smaller version of the super-ellipse shape appears in the design of tabletops and other furniture. In a three-dimensional version, the super-ellipse becomes the super-egg, created in metal for board

*Problems worthy
of attack
prove their worth
by hitting back.*

*Manuscript for one of Hein's aphoristic poems, known as "grooks"
(Collection of Hugo Piet Hein)*

games, drink coolers, and an anti-stress ball—an excellent example of the super-egg can be found on the grounds of Egeskov Castle on the Danish island of Funen, which also has a bamboo maze designed by Hein. Hein's work, which contributed to the mid-twentieth-century flourishing of Danish design, places him in the company of other world-class Danish designers such as the furniture designer Arne Jacobsen, the silversmith Georg Jensen, and the designers of Royal Copenhagen Porcelain.

In literature, Hein is best known as the creator of *gruk,* short aphoristic poems expressing a lyrical thought or sage advice. A combination of text and artistic presentation, the poems appear in a distinct graphic form called "technical-handwriting," employing Helvetica print. This style gives the impression of something anonymously carved, something representing both the personal and the collective. As a style it is elegant but not formal. Above the text on the page appears a sketch with the trademark drawing of a flying poet, traditionally dressed in hat and butterfly, with his harp, and a seed representing inspiration sailing in the air above him. A sketched illustration also appears above the poem.

The first *gruk* were printed in the Danish daily *Politiken* (Politics) in the late 1930s; Hein's first collection of *gruk* was published by Politikens Forlag in 1940. During the German occupation of Denmark

(1940–1945), Hein's *gruk* gained importance as a democratic, individualistic, and humane voice against fascism. During the occupation, Hein joined the underground movement and became chair of the anti-Nazi organization Frisindet kulturkamp (Liberal Cultural Action). He spoke out for democracy by stressing the values of the Danish Resistance. Hein's resistance to Nazi ideology and barbarism became a lifelong commitment; he remained suspicious of all political ideologies and advocated democratic mediation in international conflicts. Internationally, his commitment found expression in his work for the Danish section, Én Verden (One World), of the Campaign for World Federal Government. Hein believed that the individual should be aware of belonging to a nationality but should also feel that he or she is a part of the world community. Hein traveled extensively and also lived in England for many years. Through his friendship with Niels Bohr he made many important friends abroad; in particular, Einstein and Charles Chaplin.

The early *grooks* were published in 1940–1949 under the pseudonym of Kumbel Kumbell–later abbreviated to Kumbel–which is actually a pun based on his own name. Piet and Hein are both Dutch names: Piet is derived from Peter, the apostle known as the *rock* upon which Jesus built the Christian Church, while Hein is the same as the old Danish word *hen,* which means whetstone. The Old-Norse *kumbl* means a stone with an inscription, as in a monument with carvings. This pseudonymous play on words became evident when Kumbel was depicted as a carver of runes on the front page of the later collections of *Korte Gruk* (Short Grooks).

The enormous popularity of Hein's grooks owes much to their folkish appeal to common sense. Though they appear lighthearted, their content is serious. *Gruk* are personal–often taken from a daily situation–yet, they are simultaneously universal in their enduring relevance. They function well as applied art–anybody can use them in the context of daily life–but their effect is also immediate. In terms of form they are often constructed around contrasts which nevertheless may be mediated, such as the following: "Den som kun / tar spøg for spøg / og alvor / kun alvorligt / han og hun / har faktisk fattet / begge dele / dårligt." Here is Hein's English translation: "Taking fun / as simply fun / and earnestness / in earnest / shows how thoroughly / thou none / of the two / discernest." This particular *gruk,* translated into many languages, expresses a fundamental attitude (life's essential reliance on contrasts) underlying Hein's *gruk* in general.

A certain wittiness and a relevance to both everyday life and particular circumstances have ensured a lasting role for Hein's inventive *gruk* in both quotations and speeches. In contemporary secular Danish society *gruk* have often replaced traditional quotations from the Bible. In Denmark many everyday implements and knickknacks display *gruk* (Royal Copenhagen Porcelain has an entire line of faience-ware shaped like the super-ellipse and featuring Hein's grooks). They have also provided clever, catchy slogans and brief lyrics for industry, trade, and commerce. The Holbæk Trade Society placed the first commercial order for *gruk* in 1945 in order to encourage Christmas sales. Hein served as chair of Én Verden in 1948–1949 and participated in the international writers' association, PEN, the League of Tolerance, the Frensham Group, and Open Door International. Hein came to play an increasingly official role; in 1967, for example, he composed the slogan Denmark used at the World Exhibition in Montreal. Hein continued to write for the Danish Ministry of Foreign Affairs and Ministry of Industry. He also wrote the script for *Industrilandet Danmark* (Denmark: The Land of Industry, 1970), a motion-picture documentary translated into ten languages. Hein wrote *gruk* for many international organizations and, with characteristic panache, paraphrased the opening line of Hamlet's soliloquy as: "Coexistence/ or no existence." Nonideological and apolitical, Hein's *gruk* are suitable for both industry and international relations; they never refer to specific social classes or economic circumstances. His *gruk* seem to speak to an anonymous moral and sensible individual and to reflect the belief that the individual can make a difference in the world.

Kumbel's *gruk* were eventually published in twenty volumes with the title *Gruk,* half of them from 1940 to 1949 and the second half from 1954 to 1963. These *gruk* later appeared in two volumes: *Gruk, fra alle aarene* (1960, 1964). Two volumes of short *gruk* were published in *I folkemunde* (To Be the Subject of Gossip, 1968) and *Det kraftens ord* (A Word of Power, 1969). Hein published two additional collections of poems under the pseudonym of Kumbel: *Kumbels almanak* (Kumbel's Almanac, 1942) and *Kumbels fødselsdagskalender* (Kumbel's Birthday Calendar, 1949). More than seven thousand *gruk* exist, and they comprise a genre unique to Piet Hein.

After 1950 Hein continued to publish poetry under his own name. The earlier *Vers i verdensrummet* (Poetry in Space, 1941) and *Den tiende muse* (The Tenth Muse, 1941) were followed by *Vers af denne verden* (Poetry from this World, 1948) and *Du skal plante et træ* (You Must Plant a Tree, 1960). In addition,

Hein published a combination of *gruk* and poems in *Husk at elske* (Remember to Love, 1962), *Husk at leve: Udvalgte digte og gruk fra de første 25 år* (Remember to Live: Collected Poems and Grooks from the First 25 Years, 1965) and *Lad os blive mennesker: Udvalgte digte og gruk* (Let Us Become Human: Collected Poems and Grooks, 1967). A selection of his earlier poems was published in *Digte fra alle årene: Et udvalg* (Poems from All the Years: A Collection) in 1972.

According to Danish critic Finn Hauberg Mortensen in *Danske digtere i det 20. århundrede* (Danish Writers of the Twentieth Century, 1981), Hein is a traditional poet whose originality lies in his play on well-known Danish phrases and idioms. In terms of its content and style, Hein's poetry constitutes a coherent, uniform body of literature. Hauberg Mortensen explains that Hein's collections of poems follow a certain system. For example, *Vers i verdensrummet* comprises five groups of poems; the first three groups form a gradual expansion of the "I" from a relationship with nature (I – it) to an attitude toward love (I – you), and, finally, to an affinity with mankind (I – we). The microcosm of the person is then expanded first to the macrocosm of scientific knowledge and finally to poetic perception. This pattern is evident in "Forårs under" (The Miracle of Spring): "Man taler om / naturens spil . . . / men går det mon / naturligt til? / At muldjord / blir til gule krokus, / det er det rene / hokus-pokus" (We glibly talk / of nature's laws / but do things have / a natural cause? / Black earth turned into / yellow crocus / is undiluted / hocus-pocus). The poetic construction of the grooks reflects Hein's attempt to connect the individual to the world while simultaneously mediating between science, the arts, and the humanities. *Vers af denne verden* continues the pattern of *Vers i verdensrummet,* but Hein adds new perspectives on the origin of poetry, on human realization, and on the potential for dealing with war and a postwar society as daily and long-term experiences. According to Hauberg Mortensen, Hein's tendency to seek harmony in his writing and other activities resembles the idealism of early Romanticism; Romantic poets and idealistic scientists such as Adam Oehlenschläger and H. C. Ørsted believed in the neutralization of irreconcilable differences. For example, there is a notably Blakean feel, in both thought and density, to Hein's epigrammatic "I evighedens perspektiv er øjeblikket som et liv" (From the perspective of eternity, a moment is like a lifetime). Hein's paradoxical, harmonious stance in his humanistic poetry corresponds to his scientific resolution of opposite physical forms into the super-ellipse.

Piet Hein died on 17 April 1996. Volumes of his poetry have sold over two and a half million copies—at least one volume of poetry for almost every Danish household in a country of five million people. His work has been translated into many languages, among them Indonesian, Farsi, Chinese, and Japanese. Hein, who wrote some grooks in English and also translated other *gruk* from Danish into English, published five collections in the United States, Canada, and England. As one of the best-known Danes of this century, the cosmopolitan Hein received more international honors and Danish accolades than any of his contemporaries. Some of his more important awards include the Alexander Graham Silver Bell, Boston University (1968); the Danish Årestrup Medal (1969); the Knight of Norwegian Artists' Society (1969); the Golden Wreath of Denmark (1970); the Industrial Design Prize (1971); the Doctor of Human Letters of Yale University (1972); the international Aphis-Pris, Paris (1980); the Danish Design Council's Annual Award (1989); and the Tietgen Medal (1990). When Hein became an honorary member of Denmark's Student Union in 1970, his friend the author Per Stig Møller wrote: "Piet Hein isn't only a crazy mathematician and an original architect who discovered that someone had already invented the ball when he started and therefore brought another perfect form to life among us. He is also a lyricist who brings with him the most beautiful, most romantic and most earthbound in the Danish tradition, in an independent way, *and* who has created a genre or rather recreated the wise, aphoristic verses of the old Icelanders."

Hein is a unique figure not only because of his wide-ranging talents, but also because of his belief in the positive interaction of the various disciplines: science, art, and the humanities. In all his endeavors, he used integration as both a tool and a goal. For example, his mathematical formula leading to the integration of the square and the circle also serves as a design in the arts. At the same time, this formula both reflects and transcends the oppositions appearing in his *gruk* and other poems. Hein believed, ultimately, that harmonious mediation could take place on the cultural and political level. His efforts in this regard reflect his role as an idealist and cosmopolitan Dane. In 1997 the Danes held an exhibition in memory of Piet Hein, the poet, philosopher, mathematician, and inventor, in Farum, Denmark. On this occasion Farum Library and Farum Archives and Museum produced a pamphlet about the man and his work. The following *gruk* was chosen to celebrate the legacy of Piet Hein:

ARS BREVIS
There is
one art
no more,
no less
to do all things
with art-
lessness.

References:

Claus Ahlefeldt, *Sin egen: Piet Hein 90 år* (Valby: Borgen, 1996);

Finn Hauberg Mortensen, "Den permanente: Om digte, gruk og essays af Piet Hein," *Analyser af moderne dansk lyrik I* (1976): 353–386;

Hauberg Mortensen, "Piet Hein," *Danske digtere i det 20 århundrede,* 5 volumes, edited by Torben Brostrøm and Mette Winge (Copenhagen: Gad, 1981), III: 227–240;

Mogens Frohn Nielsen, *Mennesket Piet Hein* (Lyngby: Holkenfedt, 1996).

William Heinesen
(15 January 1900 – 12 March 1991)

W. Glyn Jones
University of East Anglia

BOOKS: *Arktiske Elegier* (Copenhagen: Levin & Munksgaard, 1921);

Høbjergning ved Havet: Digte (Copenhagen: Levin & Munksgaard, 1924);

Sange mod Vaardybet (Copenhagen: Levin & Munksgaard, 1927);

Stjernerne vaagner (Copenhagen: Levin & Munksgaard, 1930);

Blæsende Gry: Nutidsroman fra Færøerne (Copenhagen: Levin & Munksgaard, 1934; revised edition, Copenhagen: Munksgaard, 1961);

Den dunkle Sol: Digte (Copenhagen: Levin & Munksgaard, 1936; revised edition, Copenhagen: Gyldendal, 1965);

Noatun (Copenhagen: Munksgaard, 1938); translated by Jan Noble as *Niels Peter: A Chronicle of the Faroes* (London: Routledge, 1939);

Den sorte gryde (Copenhagen: Gyldendal, 1949); translated by W. Glyn Jones as *The Black Cauldron* (Sawtry, U.K.: Dedalus, 1992; New York: Hippocrene, 1992);

De fortabte spillemænd (Copenhagen: Gyldendal, 1950); translated by Erik J. Friis as *The Lost Musicians,* Library of Scandinavian Literature, no. 12 (New York: Twayne, 1971);

Moder Syvstjerne: En fortælling fra tidernes morgen (Copenhagen: Gyldendal, 1952); translated by Hedin Brønner as *The Kingdom of the Earth,* Library of Scandinavian Literature, no. 22 (Boston: Twayne, 1974);

Digte i udvalg, compiled by Regin Dahl and Ole Wivel (Copenhagen: Gyldendal, 1955);

Det fortryllede lys (Copenhagen: Gyldendal, 1957);

Det dyrebare liv: Jørgen-Frantz Jacobsen i strejflys af hans breve (Copenhagen: Gyldendal, 1958);

Gamaliels besættelse (Copenhagen: Gyldendal, 1960);

Hymne og harmsang (Copenhagen: Gyldendal, 1961);

Det gode håb (Copenhagen: Gyldendal, 1964);

Kur mod onde ånder (Copenhagen: Gyldendal, 1967);

Don Juan fra Tranhuset (Copenhagen: Gyldendal, 1970);

William Heinesen in 1976 (courtesy of Gyldendal Publishers)

Panorama med regnbue (Copenhagen: Gyldendal, 1972);

Fortællinger fra Thorshavn, edited by Erik Vagn Jensen (Copenhagen: Gyldendal, 1973);

Tårnet ved Verdens Ende: En poetisk Mosaik-roman om den yngste Ungdom (Copenhagen: Gyldendal, 1976); translated by Maja Jackson as *The Tower at the Edge of the World: A Poetic Mosaic Novel about My Earliest Youth* (Findhorn, U.K.: Thule Press, 1981);

Her skal danses: Seks fortællinger (Copenhagen: Gyldendal, 1980);

Laterna Magica: Nye Erindringsnoveller (Copenhagen: Vindrose, 1985); translated by Tiina Nunnally as *Laterna Magica* (Seattle: Fjord Press, 1987);

Godaften Måne, Godaften min Ven, selected by Jens E. Donner (Frederiksberg: Fiskers, 1989).

Editions and Collections: *Det fortabte spillemænd,* edited, with an afterword, by Otto Gelsted (Copenhagen, 1965);

Grylen og andre noveller, edited by Inger M. Hansen (Copenhagen: Gyldendal, 1978);

Vinter-drøm: Digte i udvalg, 1920–30, afterword by Erik Sønderholm (Copenhagen: Brøndum, 1983);

Samlede digte (Rødovre: ROLV, 1984);

Digte af William Heinesen, selected by Asger Schnack (Copenhagen: Hans Reitzel, 1990);

Ekskursion i underverdenen fortællinger fra Færøerne, selected, with an afterword, by Jógvan Isaksen, illustrations by Heinesen (Frederiksberg: Fisker Schou, 1998).

Editions in English: *Arctis: Selected Poems 1921–1972,* translated by Anne Born (Findhorn, U.K.: Thule Press, 1980);

The Wingéd Darkness and Other Stories by William Heinesen, translated, with an introduction and notes, by Hedin Brønner (New York: Irvington / Paisley, U.K.: Wilfion, 1983).

MOTION PICTURE: *Tro, Håb og Trolddom,* screenplay by Heinesen, Nordisk Film, 1959.

OTHER: *Nýføroyskur skaldskapur: Úrval,* preface by Heinesen (Tórshavn: Varðin, 1930);

Tann deiliga Havn, text by Heinesen and John Davidsen, illustrations by Ingálvur av Reyni (Tórshavn: H. N. Jacobsens Bókahandil, 1953);

"Færøerne," in *Dette er Island, Færøerne og Grønland,* edited by Niels Th. Mortensen (Copenhagen, 1954);

"Tórshavn," *Færøerne,* volume 2 (Copenhagen: Det Danske Forlag, 1958), pp. 259–277;

Fire Færø-sange for blandet kor. Op. 43, text by Heinesen, music by Walter Zacharias (Copenhagen, Musikhøjskolens Forlag, 1959);

Jørgen-Frantz Jacobsen, *Barbara,* edited, with an afterword, by Heinesen (Copenhagen: Gyldendal, 1964);

Høyr um annan–hygg um teg sjálvan: Glantrileikur, text by Heinesen and H. A. Djurhuus (Tórshavn, 1968);

Færøerne: De magiske øer / Føroyar: Gandaoyggjarnar / The Faroe Islands: The Magic Islands, text by Heinesen, photographs by Gerard Franceschi (Copenhagen: Rhodos, 1971);

Sange mod vårdybet. Sól og kavi. Op. 85, text by Heinesen and T. N. Djurhuus, music by Vagn Holmboe (Copenhagen: Wilhelm Hansen, 1972);

Knut Odegard, trans., *Færoysk lyrikk: Gjendiktningar av færoysk notidslyrikk,* selected by Karsten Hoydal, illustrated by Heinesen (Oslo: Aschehoug, 1974);

Fra billedmagerens værksted: Tegninger, malerier og farveklip, text by Heinesen, photographs by Jørgen Lützen, Ásmundur Poulsen, and Myndamót (Tórshavn: Bókagarður, 1980);

Filsni og Hampafólk. Tekningar, málningar og litklipp. Føroyskað hevur Hans Thomsen. (Tórshavn: Bókagarður, 1980);

Færøsk kunst, text by Heinesen, photographs by Poulsen (Tórshavn: Bókagarður, 1982); translated by W. Glyn Jones as *The Art of the Faroe Islands* (Tórshavn: Bókagarður, 1982);

Ebba Hentze, *Antonia og Morgenstjernen,* illustrated by Heinesen, translated by Per Knutsen (Oslo: Gyldendal, 1984).

SELECTED PERIODICAL PUBLICATIONS–
UNCOLLECTED: *Ranafelli. Sjónleikur í tveimum pørtum.* Umsett havur Rikard Long, *Varðin,* 9 (1929): 65–99;

"Ingálvur av Reyni," *Fra Færøerne: Úr Føroyum,* 1 (1964): 6–13;

"Ljóð av ævinligum vøtnum," *Varðin,* 41 (1973): 5–13;

"Nyere færøsk digtning," *Nordisk tidskrift för vetenskap, konst och industri* (1928): 351–368;

"On being a Faroese," *American-Scandinavian Review,* 60 (1972): 137–143;

"Skaldið Chr. Matras," *Varðin,* 34 (1961): 138–142.

When William Heinesen was told that he was among the handful of candidates under consideration for the Nobel Prize in literature for 1980, he wrote a letter to Artur Lundqvist of the Nobel Committee, asking not to be considered for the award. Heinesen said that if the award were to go to a Faroese writer, it should go to one who actually wrote in Faroese, and not to someone who wrote in Danish, as he did. This anecdote places Heinesen in both an international and a Dano-Faroese context, and at the same time exemplifies the writer's own personal integrity. Although Faroese through and through, Heinesen had been brought up in a bilingual home, and he had chosen to write in Danish because he felt better able to let himself go in that language than was possible with the rather more conservative Faroese. As a result, he was for a long time a controversial figure in the Faroe Islands, where his outstanding talent was overshadowed by his decision to eschew his "native" language, whereas in Denmark he was recognized as one of the outstanding writers of the twentieth century both in his prose works–novels and short stories–and in his poetry. Toward the end of his life, the Faroese forgave him both

Tórshavn, capital of the Faroe Islands, as it looked during Heinesen's childhood

for his use of Danish and for the often humorous, satirical portrayal of the Faroese people, to which many of his fellow countrymen had earlier taken exception.

Born on 15 January 1900, Andreas William Heinesen came of purely Faroese stock on his father's side and could claim descent from the famous seventeenth-century Faroese freebooter Magnus Heinesen, who ended his days on a Danish gallows. William Heinesen's father, Zacharias, was a merchant and shipowner; his mother, Caroline Jacobine Restorff, was half Danish, and it was because of the presence in the home of her mother that Danish became the everyday family language. In one of his autobiographical sketches, Heinesen says that his Danish grandmother, who hailed from Copenhagen and was accustomed to more cosmopolitan and sophisticated surroundings than she encountered in the tiny capital of Tórshavn with its population of between two and three thousand, never really learned to speak Faroese and never felt completely at home in the Faroe Islands, which Heinesen himself once described at that time as having been a "virtually medieval world." All of these family members play a part in one way or another in Heinesen's work, and it is from his mother's side of the family that he inherited his artistic qualities. At the same time, his

father was clearly a colorful character who provided his son with ample inspiration, something on which Heinesen commented in an interview with Birgit Ronild published in the newspaper *Søndags BT* on 23 January 1970: "My father appears in many of my books. I can never tire of thinking back on his many strange excesses." In 1932 William Heinesen married his twenty-five-year-old cousin, Elise Susanne Johansen, who still lives in the family home in Tórshavn. The couple had two sons.

It was Zacharias Heinesen's hope that his son would follow him in the family business, which he had built up from a small shop into a thriving shipowning concern, and to this end William was, in his own words, "shanghaied" to Copenhagen at the age of sixteen to study at the Commercial College. However, business life was not for him, and he turned to journalism for a time, writing in the newspaper *Ringsted Folketidende* (The Ringsted Popular News). That career path, too, was soon abandoned. In 1919 he visited his native Tórshavn, but then returned to Copenhagen, where he met many Danish writers, including the Communists Otto Gelsted and Hans Kirk, both of whom were to be of great significance for his writing and thinking. Finally, after a time spent traveling between the Faroes and other European countries, Heinesen settled in

Tórshavn in 1932 and devoted himself to writing–and to painting, which for many years was his main source of income. He traveled widely, but always insisted on the close link he felt with his native surroundings, which indeed are the setting for almost everything he wrote.

Like Gelsted and Kirk, Heinesen's lifelong Faroese friend, Christian Matras, was at that time a staunch Communist. Heinesen never committed himself to communist doctrines, preferring to call himself a "battling humanist." In a letter to W. Glyn Jones dated 23 February 1973 he commented: " . . . there is no key that opens *all* locks, as dogmatists believe and maintain. The same applies here as everywhere where the human spirit seeks a 'meaning' in life, a common denominator: you never reach the end of the road, only move 'towards' it. . . . Conclusion (without premises): I would be dishonest if I called myself a 'convinced communist,' but faced with censorious reactionaries, it amuses me to conclude a hopeless discussion by saying, 'Well then, I am a hard-boiled Communist.' Then follows a silence replete with loathing and armed peace." He did, however, maintain a radical political attitude, and his sympathies were always with the underdog, never with the powerful and influential. Nevertheless, his works cannot really be considered political. At most it can be said that they betray a clear social awareness and compassion with those who suffer as a result of the social structure, but any social implication is secondary to the cosmic preoccupations that are the essence of all his work. This is true even though it is possible to trace Heinesen's approach back to the Socialist "collective" novels in vogue in Denmark in the 1930s and thereafter, in particular to Kirk's *Fiskerne* (The Fishermen, 1928). Heinesen quickly broke with the rigid, politically related pattern inherent in this genre, replacing it with imaginative content that adds new life to the social picture, placing the later novels into the category of "magic realism."

It was as a poet that Heinesen first made his name, producing four volumes of poetry before any of his published novels. Four years elapsed between the publication of the fourth of these collections, *Stjernerne vaagner* (The Stars Awaken, 1930), and the appearance of the first novel, *Blæsende Gry: Nutidsroman fra Færøerne* (Windswept Dawn: Contemporary Novel from the Faroe Islands, 1934). The only prose work he had published meanwhile was the now-forgotten Ibsenesque drama *Ranafelli,* which appeared in Faroese in the periodical *Varðin* in 1929.

These early volumes of poetry betray little if anything in the way of political or social content. Instead, they are melancholy and reflective, with more than a trace of metaphysical preoccupation. Indeed, such was

the element of melancholy in the first of them, *Arktiske Elegier* (Arctic Elegies, 1921), that Heinesen did not republish any of the poems from it until the appearance of his collected poems, *Samlede digte,* in 1984. In many ways the early poems represent a reversion to the melancholy poetry common in Denmark during the 1890s, with their Symbolist overtones, their synesthesia, and their preoccupation with death, though the reflections on death do already contain traces of the idea of the cycle of life that became a central feature of Heinesen's later work. The poems do, however, constitute a landmark in poetry written in Danish in that they are the first Danish-language poems to be based on an uncompromisingly Faroese set of concepts and imagery, with metaphors derived from Faroese experience such as the mist, the rain, and the light peculiar to the islands together with an expressed longing on the part of the exiled writer to be there. They are highly Faroese in spirit, and the imagery employed is that of everyday Faroese experience.

Taken as a whole, *Arktiske Elegier* lacks the dynamism stemming from the direct confrontation between conflicting principles that is the hallmark of Heinesen's mature work, but it nevertheless contains the germs of what was to come: the urge to discover a meaning in life, a sense of finiteness and a yearning to overcome it. In the construction of the volume as a whole there is a foreshadowing of Heinesen's later work insofar as the early introspection and the somber character of the middle section give way to a more optimistic conclusion. Both in the poetry and the prose works, melancholy and dark presentiment are regularly replaced by light and hope: "Upright my delight / rising with the day, / new lands I greet, / gold-rimmed." The poet Gelsted, who was the publisher's reader for the collection, compared these poems with those of the early hymn writers Thomas Kingo and Hans Adolph Brorson, though there is clearly no similarity in thought, finding in them a de-Christianized religiosity.

The next collection, *Høbjergning ved Havet: Digte* (Hay Harvest by the Sea: Poems, 1924), continues the line of *Arktiske Elegier,* but the mood is different. The elegiac melancholy has been replaced by more disciplined reflection, and the specific Faroese imagery has given way to one of a more generalized, universal nature, though the Faroese experience of autumn and winter is clearly fundamental to the poetry. The mood is established by the first poem, which describes the approach of autumn to the sound of the scythes as the harvesters work to cut the hay. However, the final line of the poem brings out its real, metaphysical significance: "Hurry, harvesters, ere night is upon you." Certainly, the physical harvesters are encouraged to hurry before the arrival of winter, but the real significance goes far beyond that. The harvesters are themselves symbols, and their plight is that of mankind in general. Throughout these poems there is a sense of the inevitability of night and death, of instability and change, but there is at the same time a growing sense of something behind this process, an increasing emphasis on regeneration and re-creation suggesting the first signs of the cosmic vision of Heinesen's mature work: "Now we are drawn . . . to the superabundance of light behind life and death, and if we are no longer drawn, then it is death." This is not a belief in a life after death in a Christian sense, but rather a feeling that the cycle of the seasons is symbolical of the life-death cycle of which mankind is part—and it is only mankind that gives a significance to the universe. The poem marks the start of Heinesen's search for a solution to the problem of existence.

This search remains at the center of the next two poetry collections, *Sange mod Vaardybet* (Songs Toward the Depths of Spring, 1927) and *Stjernerne vaagner,* in which the metaphysical and philosophical reflections are intensified as a result of the death of Heinesen's brother Heine in 1927. The overriding impression of *Sange mod Vaardybet,* however, is one of light and rebirth, as is betokened by the titles of many of the poems: "Sol og Sne" (Sun and Snow), "Vaarligt Læ" (Spring Shelter), "Blomster i Sne" (Flowers in Snow), and "Vaarhilsen" (Spring Greeting). The texts suggest the same: "light in abundance" and "the world as an aerial vision," while the aurora borealis is described as "splitting the eternal darkness with flames / of wildly budding heaven-spring." Along with these works are such great elegiac poems as "Vaarmorgen-Elegi" (Spring Morning Elegy), in which the poet sees the hope of spring overcoming the loss he has sustained: "Soon shall the summer come, ye young dead! / A swell shall arise of shimmering days, a mountain shall rise up of shimmering days from the darkness of the spring morning, ye young dead."

The theme of the hope to be found in the stars and the light they give in the universe is reprised in the poems of Heinesen's fourth collection, *Stjernerne vaagner.* These poems are filled with images of stars shining in the special mix of light and darkness found on a starlit night. All is dark, but there is a promise of light and the coming of morning.

A change in Heinesen's poetry came in 1936 with the publication of *Den dunkle Sol: Digte* (The Dark Sun: Poems), written in the shadow of impending disaster in Europe with the emergence of Nazism and Fascism and showing a clear ethical preoccupation of a kind that had not been present earlier. Writing in the periodical *Oyggjaskeggi* in January 1950, Christian Matras argued that this was the beginning of the ethical period in Heinesen's work, while in an article in the newspaper *Land og Folk* (27 June 1964) Gelsted looked back on this volume

as a breakthrough. In his brief commentary on this volume that he included in the collected edition of his poems in 1984, Heinesen himself wrote:

Efterhånden har du vendt dig bort fra den lyriske grubler–og lønkammertilværelse, frigjort dig for den traditionelle, bundne forms tvang og begivet dig ud i samtiden med dens nye udfordrende og animerende livsaspekter, de medmenneskelige. Som dog–det erfarer du snart–er bedre tjent med den rene prosa.

(With the passing of time, you have turned away from your enclosed, lyrical brooding, freed yourself from the traditional regular verse forms and moved into the present with its new, challenging and inciting aspects of life, the human. Which, however,–as you were soon to discover–are better served by straightforward prose.)

All of this commentary is true, but it is not without significance that the volume opens with a poem elegantly combining the cosmic and the human. "Stenpigen" (The Girl of Stone) depicts the statue of a girl that in the twilight reminds the poet of the stone from which she is made, and hence the cosmos, while at the same time she is representative of humanity:

Saa star hun der–en Gæst
fra et vildt og ukendt Rige,
og dog kun en Pige,
en Gaade i Sten,
og dog simpel og mild
som et Blad paa en Gren.

(Then there she stands–a visitor
from a wild and unknown realm,
yet only a girl,
a riddle in stone
yet simple and mild
like a leaf on a bough.)

Other links with Heinesen's earlier poems are present, especially in the idyllic content of the second part of *Den dunkle Sol,* but Heinesen now embarks on poems striking a completely different note, clearly influenced by the threatening atmosphere present in Europe at the time and showing an awareness of human suffering and neglect. The poems are modern in style, modern in tone, and modern in content, with the predominant attribute being darkness, a great contrast indeed to the starlight of the earlier poems. Daylight is "surrounded by darkness," and a train is depicted traveling through the night–though, with a touch of optimism typical of him, Heinesen finishes by saying that "life's heart will always beat, always beat." For all the glimpses of a threatening world in his poetry, he cannot relinquish hope.

WILLIAM
HEINESEN

BLÆSENDE GRY

NUTIDSROMAN FRA FÆRØERNE

LEVIN & MUNKSGAARDS FORLAG
EJNAR MUNKSGAARD

Cover for Heinesen's first novel, about a small Faroese fishing community wracked by religious conflicts

In a purely stylistic sense, too, this volume also heralds Heinesen's move into the world of modern poetry, clearly influenced by Johannes V. Jensen and at the same time reflecting Heinesen's constant interest in the visual arts. One suite of poems is expressly inspired by the Spanish painter Francisco Goya, while the associations created by a concert in London inspired a poem with a series of images that could be taken from the paintings of Pablo Picasso: the cello is a woman without head or limbs; the clarinet, a goose with no body; the trombone, a homunculus with a wide-open mouth; and the drum, a man of whom only the stomach has been retained—an example not only of the influence of modern painting but also of the regular visual attributes of Heinesen's work itself and a reminder that he was, too, a painter of considerable talent.

As Heinesen points out in his introduction to the volume of poems titled *Hymne og harmsang* (Hymn and Song of Resentment, 1961), it was twenty-five years before he published poetry again, a gap during which he found it more appropriate to voice his ethical preoc-

cupations in prose works. During that period, World War II, the advent of nuclear weapons, and the Korean War had taken place, and Heinesen was deeply concerned with what he saw as the prospect facing humanity and the indifference with which human beings were bringing about their own destruction. The first of the three sections into which the collection is divided begins with "Dedication," a song of praise to Man and his achievements over millennia but ending with the prospect of annihilation. The same tone is maintained throughout the first section, sometimes accompanied by splendid visions, sometimes more modest in scope and couched in terms of melancholy. The form is still experimental, and the cosmic perspectives are mixed with a sense of the continuity of life, as for instance in "Hymnus amoris" (Hymn to Love), subtitled "Anna Magdalena og Johann Sebastian Bach piæ memoriæ"(Anna Magdalen and Johann Sebastian Bach in Pious Memory), written in the form of a fantasia and fugue, in which the fugal section is a series of affirmations of the life force. The final poem in this short introductory section, "Blomstersælgerske i frost" (Flower Seller in Frost), is sharper in tone, portraying a flower seller offering violets and asking the prospective buyer not to despise them, for it will soon be too late to live.

The second section, "Den hvide Mand" (The White Man), is a scathing attack on modern values. "Verdens Undergang" (The End of the World) shows mankind totally oblivious to what is really going on in the world—and unable to distinguish the important from the unimportant, a depiction conveyed by means of a series of statements in the form of newspaper headlines:

> Teknikken har nedbragt tidsfristen for kulturens definitiv undergang
> til alle tiders minimum.
> Automater i uniform planlægger deres egen udslettelse.
> Husvild familie taget gas.
> Ny hungerbølge hærger Indien.
> Premierminister Macmillan lettere forkølet.
>
> (Technology has reduced the time for the definitive end of culture
> to all-time minimum.
> Automata in uniforms planning their own destruction.
> Homeless family gases itself.
> Fresh famine ravaging India.
> Prime Minister Macmillan has a slight cold.)

When the end of the world actually comes, no one really notices. In his familiar pattern, however, Heinesen adopts a more optimistic tone in the final section, "Arken søsat" (The Ark Launched), ending on a note of reconciliation and with the conviction that even in this final hour he has a cosmic vision that suggests continuance. There is hope even in despair.

Hymne og harmsang is stylistically less experimental than was *Den dunkle Sol,* the collection before it, and it should be seen as pointing the way forward to Heinesen's final collection of poetry, *Panorama med regnbue* (Panorama with Rainbow, 1972), the title of which suggests both the cosmic perspective and the optimism Heinesen still possessed, although he was now feeling seriously old and—according to his introduction to his collected poems—intended this work to be an epilogue. The modernist approach Heinesen had taken earlier is maintained in some of the poems in *Panorama med regnbue,* but the collection as a whole is introduced with a vision in the nature of an ode recalling friends from the poet's youth, written with a verve, richness of metaphor, and linguistic invention that had not been seen in his work for some time. "Vinteren tænder sine blus på vore bjerge" (Winter Is Lighting its Beacons on Our Mountains) is followed by the visionary "Fortuna," dedicated to the memory of Heine Heinesen, in which the poet imagines a voyage to the moon, there encountering a ship he had known in his younger days. A further vision follows in "Det er igen en af disse oceaniske dage" (It Is Again One of These Oceanic Days), in which the poet sees himself standing on the border between the beginning and the end of the world, in the midst of things for yet a brief while, and reflecting on the link between himself and all other living things, both good and evil. Subsequent poems are of a critical and sarcastic nature, while others show the modernist approach—all related to what has gone before—but the collection finally ebbs out in a great vision of the end, "Thi natten kommer" (For Night Approaches), in which the poet sees himself together with all the friends he has lost. The cosmic vision and the continuity of life, the unending cycle of life, which are at the center of Heinesen's work, are here put in their most compelling form.

On the whole, the development of Heinesen's prose works follow a similar course to that of the poetry. His first attempt at prose was never published, for it was written under the impression of his brother's death and Heinesen apparently thought that it revealed his thoughts much too clearly, especially the religiosity that preoccupied him at the time; however, parts of this unpublished work were incorporated into the novel *Blæsende Gry* in 1934. Set on an imaginary small island at the north of the Faroes, *Blæsende Gry* is a novel without a hero, a "collective novel," in which the community is the central feature, while the interactions within that community provide the dynamics. This type of structure is found in many Danish novels, but Heinesen already shows here that he is unable to contain himself

within the framework of the social realist novel. Accordingly, his characters are marked less by their sociopolitical interaction than by their personal peculiarities and the resultant relationships between them: Vitus, the meek wandering salesman with his unflinching faith; Morberg, the unpredictable, alcoholic lawyer who befriends him while also flirting with joining the extremist sect that dominates the island's society; Sylverius, the honest and wealthy shipowner who is drawn into the sect because of his bad conscience when one of his ships is lost at sea; Simona, first Sylverius's fiancée and then his wife, who follows him out of loyalty and not out of faith; and Pastor Martens, who is mentally deranged because of personal religious conflicts. *Blæsende Gry* is a tempestuous, confusing novel that nevertheless succeeds thanks to the freshness and vigor of Heinesen's writing and the wealth of ideas he entertains.

While the typical collective novel must be seen as a social novel, *Blæsende Gry* is a socioreligious novel, as Heinesen is not merely providing a broad picture of life in a Faroese island community but is also portraying and analyzing the religious attitudes and movements that were, and are, part of the Faroese culture. Pastor Martens is the main representative of the State Church, but he is not up to the task and has to be retired from his post. One of his problems is that at an early age he was a prey to Jesuits in Copenhagen, and the education they gave him has resulted in his suffering from persecutional delusions and sexual frustration. Opposed to him is the leader of the local sectarian movement, Reinhold Vaag, whose activities in winning converts are aided by the loss of Sylverius's ship with all its crew. Reinhold Vaag is adept at fishing in troubled waters and persuading people to cope with their sufferings by turning their backs on life, and his main catch is Sylverius himself, who is overwhelmed by what he sees as his responsibility for the death of his crew. Sylverius's young and level-headed wife, Simona, opposes her husband's joining the sect. When she fails in her attempts to prevent it, however, she joins him out of a sense of loyalty and without any suggestion that she really believes in the sectarian teachings. The sect is shown throughout to dominate the economic scene, attracting many of the wealthiest trawler-owners and businessmen of the local community, and it appears that they have overcome the difficulty of squaring their wealth with Christian teaching. A further religious perspective is represented by the curious figure of Balduin Hansen, a strangely warped character who has returned to the island from Denmark as a Theosophist and who falls in love with Jane, a girl who is dying of tuberculosis. The link between his fascination for her and the fact that she is dying is clearly underlined, and after her death Balduin undergoes serious personal torment because he feels that he still desires her even though she has now gone. He is a further example of a character warped by religious beliefs.

The true contrast in a religious sense is found in the insignificant and naively believing figure of the salesman, Vitus, and the solicitor, Morberg, who is preoccupied with religious questions but belongs to no church. After Morberg's death, however, when representatives of the State Church have refused to allow his funeral to be held in one of their churches, his body is taken by Vaag, who argues that Morberg was always on the verge of becoming a member of the sect. In fact, in one of his many discussions with Vitus, Morberg expressed what seems to be the metaphysical message of the novel: Vitus puts forth the orthodox argument that God is love, which is countered by Morberg's declaration that love is God.

It is also Morberg who draws attention to another theme at the center of Heinesen's writings: the significance of Woman as the bearer of life—and thereby of hope. Simona joins her husband in the life-denying sect, but before this her role has been a quite different one. While waiting outside the church at her wedding, Morberg comments that she is a kind of luxury in which nature occasionally indulges, and he later emphasizes her gentleness and kindness to such an extent that she takes on a symbolical role, the role of the "good woman" that forms a recurring theme in Heinesen's work. He talks of her as a sun around which everything revolves, and he even refers to her as a Madonna. It is clear from this reference that she is raised above all the other characters in the novel, none of whom attracts this kind of appellation, and she thus becomes a humanist Madonna. Morberg drowns in a brook toward the end of the novel, and various other tragedies ensue. However, hope returns when the honest young sailor Gotfred manages to establish himself and comes home to marry the radiant but uncomplicated Gregoria. Life will go on and triumph.

This is a novel redolent of the freshness of youth, and like many other first novels, it holds more than the inexperienced novelist has been able to control. It is chaotic and lacking in clear structure while at the same time wonderfully dynamic. In its rapid shifts from one group and theme to another it deserves to be called fugal—though Heinesen himself referred to it both to Gelsted and in private letters as "dødbagt" (overbaked). The result of Heinesen's dissatisfaction with the novel was that a second version was published in 1961. The story remains essentially the same, though Heinesen radically abridged the novel and recast certain characters. Morberg, the lawyer in the first version, has been replaced by the character of the ship's pastor, Salomon,

probably because Morberg was too easily recognizable as a caricature of the poet J. H. O. Djurhuus, while the relationship between Sylverius and Simona is brought more within the bounds of realism by allowing Simona to leave her husband rather than assume an almost metaphysical role in standing by him. This new version was, for both Heinesen himself and various critics, including Christian Matras, a great improvement structurally, but it attracted little attention at the time of its publication. It provides a contrast to the first version, for the more substantial construction, the sharper observations of society, and the more acceptable psychology behind the portrayal of Simona—and Balduin Hansen—are achieved at the expense of the freshness of the first version. Even while observing the constraints of the social-collective novel, Heinesen was unable in the first version to refrain from allowing free reign to his imagination. In the second version this imaginative element has been kept under tighter control, which is a loss. The second version is much more in line with the usual collective novel, while the embryonic portrayal of the conflict between life-asserting and life-opposing forces that marks the first version of *Blæsende Gry,* and which was to become a dominant feature of Heinesen's later work, is largely removed from the second version.

Heinesen's second novel, *Noatun* (1938; translated as *Niels Peter: A Chronicle of the Faroes,* 1939), moves further into the collective tradition and indeed is closer to the typical pattern for such novels than is any other of Heinesen's works, being clearly derivative of Hans Kirk's *Fiskerne* from 1928. The setting is again a Faroese village, but this time the action is more closely linked to historical conditions, as the novel reflects both the new land laws of the 1930s that gave the landless population access to land that had hitherto been closed to them and the struggle of the ordinary people to implement these laws in the face of relentless opposition by well-to-do farmers. The villagers of Noatun collectively form the central character of this novel, and it cannot be said that any one is more important than another, though Niels Peter (after whom the English translation is titled) is a figure to whom all look up and whose advice and leadership are sought. He is the one who emerges as the "leader" toward the end when a financial solution to the villagers' problems is found in the building of a lighthouse.

Even while adhering to the collective-novel pattern, however, Heinesen introduces more out-of-the-way characters than is usual in novels of this genre: such as Tilda, the man-sick but childless wife who goes off to the capital, where she both finds a new husband and joins the Salvation Army, and Maria, the girl who is brought to the village to replace her and live with Tilda's first husband, Samson, with whom she has a

Heinesen standing in front of the natural harbor at Tórshavn, where many of his works are set

child. Maria–the "good woman" of this novel–exemplifies Heinesen's name symbolism, suggesting clear parallels to the biblical Mary. Other characters include Bernhard, the young man who seems destined to unhappiness, losing first his fiancée Abria, a hussy who betrays him; the second-sighted Sara, who goes out of her mind after losing first her fiancé, Halvdan, and then her lover, Frederik. Finally Bernhard loses his gentle, blind cousin, Herdis, who dies during an influenza epidemic. Bernhard leaves the village and the islands, becoming one of the symbols of hope in this otherwise somewhat bleak novel. Frederik himself is a character who scarcely belongs in the stern setting of a collective novel in that he first appears as a figure of mystery and finally becomes a wanted murderer. He is tracked down, arrested, and carried off from the village tied to a stretcher to face justice; however, as the party is crossing a high point in the mountains he manages to wriggle free and falls to his death in the sea below. Shortly afterwards the same party that was carrying him to justice is seen carrying his coffin for burial–and the life-death confrontation typical of Heinesen is brought clearly into focus. This confrontation is seen in a more tangible form in the way in which the aging Sinklar saves the boy Ole Jacob from drowning, only to be drowned himself later in another rescue attempt.

There was a gap of ten years before the appearance in 1949 of *Den sorte gryde* (translated as *The Black Cauldron,* 1992). Set during the wartime British occupation of the Faroe Islands, this novel proclaimed Heinesen's maturity as a novelist. A trace of the collective novel is present in *Den sorte gryde,* in that the main "character" is the Berghammer family, with Liva (a name suggestive of the Danish word for life, *liv*) at its center. Heinesen has, however, limited his central "character" here to a single family rather than seeking to make it an entire village community, and the various strands of the action all relate to various members of this family.

The contrast to Liva is the shipowner Opperman, for whom she and her brother Ivar (another life symbol) both work, who seeks to seduce her and who is constantly associated with death. When she realizes his intentions, Liva leaves his employment. She is engaged to a sailor, Johan, who is suffering from tuberculosis after being torpedoed in a ship belonging to Opperman. Johan eventually dies while Liva is visiting him in the sanatorium at Østervaag. As a result of her personal tragedy she joins an extreme sect run by Simon the baker, and in the novel Heinesen examines the relationship between Liva and Simon, which has clear erotic overtones, though once they come to the fore, Simon rejects Liva with the words, "Get thee behind me,

Satan." As a result of this rejection Liva goes out of her mind and finally falls prey to Opperman, who seduces her in one room while his wife lies dying in the next. Liva finally ends her days in a sanatorium that Opperman has established in memory of his late wife. Simon takes the final step of deciding to allow himself to be crucified, though in a scene of glorious black humor the crucifixion is stopped at the last moment.

Liva is the "good woman" of the novel, who is worthy of being worshiped, as Johan's brother, Jens Ferdinand, says of her, but her sister, Magdalena, is another central figure. She has not been better than she should be and, with an echo of her biblical namesake, is a sinner who repents. She falls in love with Ivar's companion, Frederik, and despite her dubious reputation she and he finally come together as life symbols with the express desire to have a child. The life-death confrontation is made obvious at Ivar's funeral, when Frederik is disturbed by his erotic attraction to Magdalena even while the funeral service is taking place, while for her part Magdalena fits into Heinesen's overall project of taking biblical stories and references and putting them into a non-Christian setting with clear humanist overtones.

The action is dramatic, even melodramatic at times, but it is raised above mere melodrama by its poetry and by the clear mythical implications of the events portrayed. The central characters are surrounded by a host of minor characters, some foolish, some ridiculous, some grotesque, with the backdrop of World War II. *Den sorte gryde* is not a war novel properly speaking, though the war does make itself felt in the deaths of two of the main characters and several of its minor ones. The novel also constitutes a bitingly satirical portrayal of the way in which unscrupulous characters seek to exploit the war, not least when Ivar's death is used to work up a mood of false patriotism. His funeral is to be the supreme expression of this emotional wave—but the bubble bursts when the crowd hears the sound of an enemy airplane approaching and disperses with unseemly haste.

The life/death confrontation was by now clearly established as a central feature in Heinesen's work. This confrontation also appears in the following much different novel, *De fortabte spillemænd* (1950; translated as *The Lost Musicians,* 1971). The novel has an historical basis to it, with the musicians at its center being inspired by a group of amateurs who performed in Tórshavn at the beginning of the century. The musicians of the novel, poor but positive in their enjoyment of life, are confronted by the local sectarians led by the bank manager, Ankersen (an easily recognizable historical figure in Tórshavn), in an ultimately successful attempt to introduce the total prohibition of alcohol. Social overtones there certainly are in this confronta-

tion, as there are, too, in the tensions between the lower-class Faroese musicians and the upper-class Danish officials. However, the cosmic conflict between life and anti-life principles is at the center of the novel, as is made clear by Heinesen's sophisticated use of juxtaposition. Music is the ultimate symbol of life, but it is totally without significance to the musicians' opponents, who are bigots and philistines. As the title of the novel suggests, playing on the connotations in Danish of the word *fortabte,* the musicians are "lost" in their music, but they are also "doomed" in this philistine society, and the idea of fate plays an essential role in the novel. One by one, the musicians are removed from the scene as they are overcome by sectarianism or establishment snobbery, the most dramatic episode being the death of Moritz as he leaps into the sea from a burning boat after murdering Matte-Gok, the exploiter whom Ankersen (presumably mistakenly) claims to be his son and who has robbed the bank and framed Moritz's simple-minded brother, Kornelius. This is a novel of great beauty, the poetical passages accompanying the musical element rising to lyrical heights not previously seen in Heinesen's prose, and despite its tragedy it has a great deal of humor, once more ending on an optimistic note when the child prodigy Orfeus leaves the philistine society of the Faroe Islands to be trained as a professional musician in Copenhagen.

The next novel, *Moder Syvstjerne: En fortælling fra tidernes morgen* (1952), literally "Mater Pleiades: A Tale Since the Beginning of Time" but translated into English as *The Kingdom of the Earth* (1974), is a sequel to *De fortabte spillemænd* in the sense that some of the characters are the same, not least Ankersen, who here emerges as an embittered man rather than the slightly amusing, rambunctious, ultimately likable fanatic of the earlier work. It is, however, a much different novel, as the principal figure, Antonia, represents a further stage in the portrayal of the "good woman" and also stands as a further development in Heinesen's creation of secular figures parallel to figures from the Bible. She is portrayed as a secular parallel to the Virgin Mary, a representative of womanhood and life, whose illegitimate child is adopted after her death by the fanatical believer Trine. Deliberately described in terms recalling paintings of Mary as Queen of Heaven, Antonia comes to represent not a metaphysical, but a human dimension. Antonia dies from influenza, and Trine now makes it her aim to rescue Antonia's son, Jacob—whom she sees as the fruit of sin—from an evil world, but the life force is too strong for her, and Trine, a representative of "anti-life," dies. The novel concludes with Jacob awakening suddenly and seeing that it is morning. He is the vehicle of hope, the representative of life triumphing over the representative of death. The life-death confron-

Heinesen and his wife, Lisa (photograph by Finn A. Thomsen)

tation is worked out on a mythic level in a novel that at times has the nature of an intense and passionate prose poem of great beauty.

Although Heinesen wrote both poems and short stories in the intervening years, it was not until 1964 that he again published a novel. *Det gode håb* (Fair Hope), which had been twenty years in the writing, is an historical novel loosely based on events in the Faroe Islands at the end of the seventeenth century. The dates mentioned in the novel do not, however, coincide with historical fact, and neither are the names those of recognizable historical figures. It could be argued that, just as he changed the names and circumstances of easily recognized characters in his novels of contemporary life, so Heinesen is here doing exactly the same thing with figures from the past. There is no difficulty in identifying the central character, Peder Børresen, with the historical Lucas Debes, and other figures are similarly recognizable; however, Heinesen was not interested in historical authenticity and preferred instead the freedom that fiction could give him. He depicts the Faroe Islands under the brutal rule of a regime led by a Holsteiner named Cattorp, with Peder Børresen as the leader of the opposition and representative of the ordinary, oppressed people. On a political and social level, this conflict is between a perverse, not to say perverted, fascistic dictatorship and a popular movement led by a champion of the people–a man who emerges from them, but who does not have any ambitions of his own beyond liberating them. At the same time, Børresen, a pastor who is in conflict with the Lutheran church he supposedly represents but that has surrendered all authority to the dictatorship he opposes, has his own moral battle to fight, being forced to acknowledge the weaknesses of humanity through confronting his own weaknesses. On the one hand he is fighting a dramatic battle with the Cattorp regime, and on the other he has to overcome his own shortcomings, in particular his love of the bottle, which often puts him in compromising situations–that are then exploited by Cattorp.

Written in a language that is as anachronistic a version of seventeenth-century Danish as the action is of historical fact, this novel is one of Heinesen's great achievements, a tour de force of impressive dimensions that incorporates not only the life-death confrontation of the earlier work but also portrays grotesque sectarian activities that have much in common with those depicted in Heinesen's novels of contemporary life. In 1965 Heinesen was awarded the Nordic Råds Litteraturpris (Nordic Council's Literary Award) for *Det gode håb*.

Det gode håb was to be Heinesen's last venture in the grand style, and his later novels are all more modest in scope, often increasingly related to his own life and ultimately closely linked to the short story. He had over the years already shown himself to be a master of the short story, with four collections published between 1957 and 1967. Covering an enormous range of mood and technique, these are no lightweight contributions, and some of them are in fact central to an understanding of Heinesen's work, providing concentrated versions of the conflicts and ideas on which the novels are based. They range from the uproarious to the deeply tragic, from experimental stories in a modernist vein to others projecting Faroese superstitions and obsessions, and from realistic psychological studies to totally unrealistic fantasies.

In the first collection, *Det fortryllede lys* (The Enchanted Light, 1957), the introductory story, "Stormnatten" (translated as "The Night of the Storm," 1983), is closely related to *De fortabte spillemænd* and reuses characters from the novel such as Ankersen. Two of Heinesen's most powerful short stories follow: "Belsmanden" (The Guest from Hell), about a man who grows rich on other people's misfortunes and finally succumbs to the belief that he is damned, and "Grylen" (The Gryla), a story related to Faroese tradition and superstition, about an annual ritual in which one of the villagers is possessed by the obscenely erotic mythological Gryla. In contrast is the delightful "Det vingede Mørke" (translated as "Wingéd Darkness," 1983), a story of two children's experience of darkness falling over the Faroese landscape. "Tartaros" is an absurdist fantasy, one of Heinesen's few ventures in a modernist vein. In addition there are two stories that are at the very center of Heinesen's work. "Himlen smiler" (The Heavens Smile) is on the face of it a childhood reminiscence, depicting the way in which the young Heinesen (here as elsewhere called Marselius) acquires a copy of the French popular astronomer Camille Flammarion's *La fin du monde* (The End of the World, 1894), therein discovering the theory that the world has no beginning and no end. This theory introduces him to the sense of cyclical time and the Nietzschean idea of eternal repetition and provides the philosophical foundation for his own theory of the eternal process of the re-creation of life. It is no accident that this same collection includes the story of "Historien om Digteren Lin Pe og hans

tamme Trane" (The Story of the Poet Li Po and his Tame Crane), depicting the moment when Li Po is called to leave his home and his tame crane and move into eternity. He is told to sacrifice his crane as part of the process, but his feeling of tenderness for the loyal bird is such that he seeks instead to hide it. The deception is discovered, and Li Po is condemned to return to live his life over again—and the story ends with the picture of Li Po as a baby at his mother's breast. His happiness is complete. The idea of repetition is combined with the notion of cyclical time, here in the context of Li Po and Taoism, a philosophy that Heinesen denied knowing well, but one that nevertheless reappears in various guises throughout his work.

The next volume of short stories, *Gamaliels besættelse* (Gamaliel's Bewitchment, 1960), does not continue these themes, but includes a first section exploring various kinds of love, from the tender melancholy of "Sjælen" (The Soul), set in the Canadian forest and thus one of the few stories by Heinesen not taking place in the Faroe Islands, to the studies of obsession in either tragic or comical guise in "Atalanta" and the title story "Gamaliels Besættelse." The fourth story in the first section, "Jomfrufødslen" (The Virgin Birth), is rather different; the scene is Christmas Eve on a ship bound for Copenhagen, and it is discovered that one of the stewardesses is about to give birth. It is a difficult birth, and the conflict between life and death symbols is palpable, as is Heinesen's desire to demythologize the biblical story and provide a humanist parallel to it. There is even a wry pun in the Danish title, as *jomfru* not only means "virgin," but also refers to the Danish term for a stewardess on a ship: *kahytsjomfru*. The remainder of the stories in this volume are more autobiographical, those in the second section being directly so, while those in the third dress up the autobiography in transparent fictional guise.

Autobiographical sketches are also found in the second section of the next collection, *Kur mod onde ånder* (Cure Against Evil Spirits, 1967), while the two stories "Elvesuset" (The Rush of the River) and "Arkadisk eftermiddag" (Arcadian Afternoon) in the first section also have autobiographical overtones. The second story, which recounts how the young Heinesen once had to take a cow to the bull, only to find the bull not interested, shows the author's skill as a humorist, while "Elversuset" is a curious reflection on death. Somewhat as the stretcher-bearers in *Noatun* are seen carrying Frederik first alive and then dead, so, here, the sick boy Daniel is seen alive one moment and dead the next, and the question is raised as to where he is now. Thomas, as Heinesen's alter ego is called here, is sent out with Daniel's sister to make a wreath, and the two find consolation in an embrace. This story is a tender study in fear, loss, and early love. These autobiographical stories are themselves enclosed between two of a completely different kind, the lengthy "Leonard og Leonora: En mini-roman fra de gode gamle petroleums lygters tid" (Leonard and Leonora: A Mini-novel from the Time of the Good Old Paraffin Lamp), a bittersweet story of love and infatuation in Tórshavn at the turn of the century, and "Fluerne" (The Flies), another of Heinesen's ventures into a modernist vein, this time a nightmarish fantasy about a plague of flies in the south of France.

The theme of obsession and possession returns in *Don Juan fra Tranhuset* (Don Juan from the Whale-Oil Factory, 1970) in the story of "Kniven" (The Knife), in which Heinesen explores a child's obsession with a pocketknife and the problems to which it leads. Obsession, though in a much different guise, is also at the heart of "Balladen om Dobbelt-Simon og Kildse-Kalsa" (The Ballad of Double Simon and Kildse-Kalsa), another of Heinesen's bittersweet stories, this time a seemingly objective, almost pedantic, account of a tender, but never fulfilled relationship between the character Simon-Peter Simon-Paul (hence called Double Simon) and Fru Serina, who collects and writes down the ballads for which Simon is famous. For his part, he has previously been obsessed with the demonic figure of Kildse-Kalsa, who has left him with a child of which he is not the father and ruined his life sufficiently for him to join the local sect. Significantly, he has finally given in to Kildse-Kalsa (a symbol of life creation) in a cave associated with suicide and death. In this story, as elsewhere in Heinesen's works, obsession is related to eroticism, and so it is in the title story "Don Juan fra Tranhuset" (translated as "The Man from Malta," 1983), about a Maltese sailor who is washed up on the shore of an island in the Faroes and, after being rescued, proceeds to seduce most of the local women. He is employed at the local whale-oil factory, and it is said that he smears his victims with whale oil before carrying out the seduction. The greatest mystery, however, is why the daughter of a distinguished family, Yrsa Preisler, becomes obsessed with him and embarks on a lengthy affair with him. Once more, this story is told in an objective manner, with quotations from letters and diaries, as though Heinesen is committing to paper a series of actual events. These stories, some humorous, some tinged with melancholy, all dominated with the ideas of obsession and eroticism, are preceded and followed by brief poetical reflections. The first, "Sommerdagen" (Summer's Day), is a brief description of plant and insect life on a summer's day in the Faroe Islands, including a passage putting into specific words a theme that appears elsewhere in Heinesen's poetry: the idea that all this beauty and all this life would be of no significance if people were not there to see it. The final prose

Cover of the first U. S. edition (1987) of Heinesen's last work, Laterna Magica Nye Erindrings novella (1985), with illustrations by Heinesen

poem, "Mørket taler til den blomstrende Busk" (Darkness Speaks to the Flowering Bush), also establishes the idea of the cycle of life. Darkness, the symbol of death, speaks to the flowering bush, the symbol of life, telling it not to be afraid, for it is only through the transformation brought about by death that life can continue. The link with Flammarion and Taoism is obvious.

Heinesen produced one more volume of short stories, *Her skal danses: Seks fortællinger* (Let There Be Dancing: Six Short Stories, 1980), which was awarded the prestigious Kritikerprisen (Critic's Prize) for 1980 by the Litteraturkritikernes Lav (Literary Critics' Guild). Two of the stories are in much the same vein as his earlier fiction—"Teodora," a study in obsession not unlike the story of Atalanta from *Gamaliels besættelse,* and "Dilettanterne" (The Amateurs), a humorous episode from Tórshavn as Heinesen had known it as a boy. Others, however, are different. On the surface, the introductory "Tågehuset" (The House in the Mist) is an autobiographical account of Heinesen's arriving at a Norwegian village with which he was unfamiliar—but it then leaves the realistic sphere. On entering the house he has been seeking, the writer suddenly has the idea that his mother lives there:

> . . . ikke i den skikkelse hvori du har kendt hende. Hun bor her som ung. Hun er ung, ugift, barnløs. Hun sidder her med sine få og fattige erfaringer og med sine drømme. Hun længes grænseløst efter at realisere sit liv. Hun er ensom og fuld af kummer, sådan som den pure ungdom så ofte er det. Men du kan ikke trøste hende, for du er endnu ikke født.

> (. . . not in the shape in which you have known her. She lives here as a young woman. She is young, unmarried, childless. She is sitting here with her few, poor experiences and with her dreams. She is longing endlessly to realize her life. She is lonely and full of sorrow, as people in their early youth often are. But you cannot comfort her, for you are not yet born.)

Heinesen is here not only thinking of his mother, but he is actually playing with time. The borderline between reality in the present and some imagined past is as fluid as the borderline between reality and dream. This same fluid borderline is found in the following story, "Advent," in which the child David has been with his fanatically religious father to visit some sectarians in the larger village on the other side of the island and is on his way back with him across the mountains. A blizzard comes on, and the two are trapped. The father is injured and unable to continue. However, they are missed, and a search party is sent out, sounding a ship's siren to attract attention. By the time they arrive, the father is delirious, but when he hears the siren, he thinks he is hearing the last trump, and he goes out to meet it. For him, it is indeed the last trump, and he is found dead in the snow. The story suggests a curious interplay between reality and unreality which is not unlike the situation in *De fortabte spillemænd,* when Moritz is drifting out at sea and falls asleep. He, too, hears a ship's siren and thinks it is the last trump—but in his case it is the rescue ship approaching.

Another story in this book, the title story, "Her skal danses," has obvious affinities with stories in earlier collections, but it raises the realistic portrayal to a higher, mythical level, in which Heinesen has incorporated the life-death confrontation into a warm portrayal of traditional Faroese culture, prefacing it with a telling refrain from a medieval Faroese ballad traditionally sung as the annual Christmas dancing season draws to a close: "Stígum fast á várt gólv, / sparum ei vár skó! / Gud man ráða, hvar vær drek-

kum / onnur jól." (Let us tread firmly on our floor / let us not spare our shoes! / God will decide where we celebrate / next Christmas.) The setting is the fictional outlying island of Stapa (based on the real island of Mykines, the westernmost of the Faroes), where the narrator has come to take part in a wedding. When the festivities are at their height, however, a ship is wrecked nearby, and a man drowned. The pastor, the representative of the State Church, now forbids any further festivities in the presence of death, but some of the guests go off to a tiny house outside the village, the home of an old man, Niklas i Dunhuset, where they are given a ritual meal of traditional Faroese fare and where they solemnly dance the medieval chain dance in an almost religious, ecstatic mood. On more than one occasion Heinesen pointed out the cultic significance of the Faroese chain dance, and in this story, one of the finest things he ever wrote, it appears as a celebration of the Faroese spirit. Despite being written in Danish, this story is intensely Faroese. All that is left now is for the old narrator to draw the collection to a close, which he does with the comment that the end is near for him and that perhaps he will not awaken the following morning—but nevertheless: good night.

Heinesen preceded and followed *Her skal danses* with what must be seen as two sets of interlinked stories. *Tårnet ved Verdens Ende* (1976; translated as *The Tower at the Edge of the World,* 1981), is subtitled *En poetisk Mosaik-roman om den yngste Ungdom (A Poetic Mosaic Novel about My Earliest Youth)* and portrays Tórshavn as experienced through the eyes of a growing child with his ever-expanding horizons. A nostalgic work, though not without its moments of humor, it shows Heinesen's ability to penetrate the mind of a child and put into words the thoughts and feelings of a child that a child could scarcely formulate. It portrays, too, his early infatuation with a little girl, here called Merrit, and the story is another of the portrayals of the unconscious erotic attraction felt by a boy and a girl in early puberty. Significantly, the whole is preceded by a poem signed Lin Pe (Li Po), reflecting on the happiness of old age; a sign, perhaps, of the cyclical idea of time encountered earlier in Heinesen's work, although Heinesen actually wrote the poem, not Li Po.

The Taoism associated with Li Po is also found in the last of Heinesen's works, *Laterna magica: Nye Erindringsnoveller* (Magic Lantern: New Fictional Recollections, 1985; translated as *Laterna Magica,* 1987), which is in much the same vein as *Tårnet ved Verdens Ende.* Here, the narrator is walking through Tórshavn on his way to the jetty where the ferryman, like Charon, is waiting for him, and on his way there he

Heinesen at work (photograph by Per á Hædd; from the back cover for the U.S. edition of Laterna Magica)

tells stories relating to the various people with whom the surroundings are associated. These stories, too, are provided with an introduction in which there is a metaphysical, unrealistic element, in that the Djurhuus brothers (both of them Faroese poets of a slightly older generation than Heinesen) are depicted as children, receiving a visit from three silent women: the three Norns, the sisters who weave the threads of fate. The remainder of the stories, however, are more realistic, with moods ranging from the melancholy to the humorous–the story of the testing of the new fire pump being one of Heinesen's funniest. However, in the midst of these is the curious tale of "Mester Jakob og Jomfru Urd" ("Master Jakob and Mistress Urd"), in which there is a ritual meal slightly reminiscent of that in "Her skal danses," but in which it is impossible to discover ages and times and in which it is quite obvious that Heinesen is deliberately playing with the concept of time. The sound of Mester Jakob's violin is heard, but the reader is told that he is not there, as he lived around 1800, and as for the ages of Mester Jakob and Jomfru Urd, the reader learns that

together they add up to about 150 years–though on the previous page Jomfru Urd's age is given as less than 50. Time and age seem to have no real significance in this story, and one is again led to the conclusion that the idea of cyclical time, whether stemming from Flammarion or Taoism, is behind it. Perhaps it is merely that time is of no significance for the aging writer on his way to Charon's ferry.

William Heinesen died 12 March 1991. A member of the prestigious Det Danske Akedemi (The Danish Academy) since 1961, he was without question one of the most versatile writers of Danish in the twentieth century, ranging in his work from the most sublime visions to rambunctious accounts of amusing happenings in the tiny capital city of the Faroe Islands. Yet, throughout there is a profound search for compassion and goodness in everyday life and a preoccupation with the great cosmic themes of life and death. Virtually all of his works are set in the Faroe Islands, which, although easily recognizable to those who know them, are sufficiently abstracted to make them accessible to those readers who do not.

The relationship between the Faroes and the cosmos is made plain in the famous introduction to *De fortabte spillemænd:*

> Langt ude i det kviksølvlysende verdenshav ligger et ensomt lille blyfarvet land. Det lillebitte klippeland forholder sig til det store hav omtrent som et sandskorn til gulvet i en balsal. Men set under forstørrelsesglas er dette sandskorn alligevel en hel verden med bjerge og dale, sunde og fjorde og huse med smaa mennesker.
>
> (Far out in the quicksilver-radiant ocean there lies a lonely little lead-colored country. The tiny rocky land relates to the great ocean roughly like a grain of sand to the floor of a dance hall. But seen under a magnifying glass, this grain of sand is nevertheless a whole world with mountains and valleys, sounds and fjords and houses with little people.)

It is through this minute world that Heinesen presents his comic and tragic vision.

Interviews:

Villy Kastborg, "Først når en bog er skrevet kan man skrive den," *Aktuelt,* 26 September 1965;

Ib Dalgaard, "Danskerne tramper på hinanden," *Jyllandsposten,* 29 May 1966;

Hemming Hartmann-Petersen, "Den fortrøstningsfulde spillemand," *Berlingske Tidende,* 15 January 1970;

Birgit Ronild, "God ven mistede fortand og roman blev forkastet," *Søndags BT,* 16 January 1970, pp. 28–29;

Anders Hallengren, "Möte med William Heinesen," *Nordisk tidsskrift för vetenskap, konst och industri,* no. 3 (1978): 149–163;

Jørgen Buch, "Et møde og et interview med William Heinesen," *Nordisk gerontologisk tidsskrift,* no. 4 (1981): 8–12.

Bibliographies:

Mia Thorkenholdt and Lars Øhlenschläger, *William Heinesen: En Bibliografi,* Studier fra Danmarks Biblioteksskole, no. 50 (Copenhagen: Danmarks Biblioteksskole, 1984);

Vitameistarin á heimsins enda og bøkur hansara: William Heinesen ein bókalisti / en bibliografi (Tórshavn: Føroya Landsbókasavn & Býarbókasavnið, 1995).

Biographies:

Hedin Brønner, "William Heinesen" in his *Three Faroese Novelists: An Appreciation of Jørgen-Frantz Jacobsen, William Heinesen and Heðin Brú* (New York: Twayne, 1973), pp. 38–80;

W. Glyn Jones, *Færø og kosmos: En indføring i William Heinesens forfatterskab* (Copenhagen: Gyldendal, 1974);

Bjarne Nielsen Brovst, *Det muntre Nord: William Heinesens liv og digtning: En mosaik* (Copenhagen: Centrum, 1987).

References:

Harry Andersen, "Studier i William Heinesens lyrik," *Fróðskaparrit,* 18 (1970): pp. 102–128;

Andersen, *Tre afhandlinger om William Heinesen* (Rødovre: ROLV, 1983);

Jógvan Isaksen, *Færøsk litteratur: Introduktion og punktnedslag* (Copenhagen: Vindrose, 1993), pp. 36–40, 97–120;

W. Glyn Jones, "Cultural Perspectives in the Late Work of William Heinesen," (Heidelberg: Carl Winter, 1989), pp. 206–214;

Jones, "'Noatun' and the Collective Novel," *Scandinavian Studies,* 41, no. 3 (1969): 217–230;

Jones, "Tid, skæbne og kosmos hos William Heinesen," in *Arbeiten zu Skandinavistik,* edited by Walter Baumgartner and Hans Fix (Vienna: Fassbaender, 1996), pp. 53–64;

Jones, "Trý stig í lyriska skaldskapinum hjá Williami Heinesen," *Varðin,* 47 (1980): 170–182;

Jones, *William Heinesen* (New York: Twayne, 1974);

Jones, "William Heinesen and the Myth of Conflict," *Scandinavica,* 9, no. 2 (1970): 81–94;

Henrik Ljungberg, *Eros og samfund i William Heinesens romaner* (Copenhagen: FS-Forlag, 1976);

Ellen Olsen Madsen, "Sprog og stil i William Heinesens: 'Det gode håb,'" *Danske Studier* (1985): 135–147;

Malan Marnersdóttir, "William Heinesen's *Tårnet ved Verdens Ende,*" *Scandinavian Studies,* 34, no.1 (1995): 71–96;

Vár í Ólavsstovu and Jan Kløvstad, *Tårnet midt i verden—en bog om William Heinesen* (Copenhagen: Nordisk Ministerråd / Stockholm: Nordisk Råd / Tórshavn: Nordens Hus, 1994);

Malan Simonsen, "Vit eiga William. Grein um støðu William Heinesens í danskari bókmentasøgu og um møguliga sess hansara í eina Søgu um føroyskum skaldskap," *Brá,* 20 (1993): 43–50;

Anne-Kari Skarðhamar, "Gåtuføra samanhang lívs og deyða. Greining av stuttsøgum William Heinesens 'Jomfrufødselen' og 'Historien om Lin pe og hans tamme trane,'" *Brá,* 20 (1993): 43–50;

Skarðhamar, "Trúgv og trúarbrøgd í skalsøgum og stuttsøgum efter William Heinesen," *Varðin,* 47 (1980): 3–13;

Hanne Flohr Sørensen, "Det begyndte som leg. William Heinesens og Jørgen-Frantz Jacobsens brevveksling," *Danske Studier* (1992): 59–91.

Agnes Henningsen
(18 November 1868 – 21 April 1962)

Lise Præstgaard Andersen
University of Odense

Translated by Gillian Fellows Jensen

BOOKS: *Glansbilledet: En Historie for Damer* (Copen-
hagen: Det Nordiske Forlag, 1899);
Strømmen (Copenhagen: Det Nordiske Forlag, 1899);
Polens Døtre (Copenhagen: Det Nordiske Forlag, 1901);
De Spedalske (Copenhagen: Det Nordiske Forlag, 1903);
Den uovervindelige: Skuespil i fire Akter (Copenhagen: Gyl-
dendal, 1904);
Lykken: En Elkhovshistorie (Copenhagen: Gyldendal,
1905);
Elskerinden (Copenhagen: Gyldendal, 1906);
Den elskede Eva: Roman (Copenhagen: Gyldendal, 1911);
Den store Kærlighed: Roman (Copenhagen: Gyldendal,
1917);
Den Guderne elsker: Roman (Copenhagen: Gyldendal,
1921);
Barnets Magt: Roman (Copenhagen: Gyldendal, 1923);
Den fuldendte Kvinde: Roman (Copenhagen: Gyldendal,
1925);
Kærlighedens Aarstider: Roman (Copenhagen: Gyldendal,
1927);
Det rige Efteraar: Roman (Copenhagen: Gyldendal,
1928);
Den sidste Aften (Copenhagen: Gyldendal, 1930);
Le kun (Copenhagen: Gyldendal, 1935);
Det rigtige Menneske (Copenhagen: Gyldendal, 1938);
Let Gang paa Jorden: Erindringer (Copenhagen: Gylden-
dal, 1941);
Letsindighedens Gave: Erindringer (Copenhagen: Gylden-
dal, 1943);
Byen erobret: Erindringer (Copenhagen: Gyldendal, 1945);
Kærlighedssynder: Erindringer (Copenhagen: Gyldendal,
1947);
Dødsfjende–hjertenskær (Copenhagen: Gyldendal, 1949);
Jeg er levemand (Copenhagen: Gyldendal, 1951);
Den rige fugl: Erindringer (Copenhagen: Gyldendal,
1953);
Skygger over vejen: Erindringer (Copenhagen: Gyldendal,
1955);

Agnes Henningsen (ca. 1901)

Vi ses i Arizona (Copenhagen: Gyldendal, 1956);
Den lidenskabelige pige (Copenhagen: Gyldendal, 1958);
Bølgeslag (Copenhagen: Gyldendal, 1959).

PLAY PRODUCTIONS: *Moralen,* Copenhagen,
Folketeatret, 24 March 1903;
Elskerinden, Copenhagen, Dagmarteatret, 14 December
1906;
Den uovervindelige, Copenhagen, Dagmarteatret, 22 Janu-
ary 1908;

minde on the island of Fyn, and she is buried not far from there in the family plot in Rynkeby churchyard. Her parents were Peter Andersen and Ophelia Petra Amalia Cathinca Malling, who both belonged to families of landed proprietors, although neither was of aristocratic birth. Peter Andersen was not himself an independent landowner but was a tenant farmer, first of Skovsbo and later of the estate of Lundsgaard, which was in the beautiful neighborhood of Kerteminde. This background, free from some of the narrow constraints of bourgeois life, may have contributed to Agnes Andersen's magnanimous and tolerant attitude toward life and sexuality, although her milieu was in its way ultraconservative as far as political opinions and literary taste were concerned.

Andersen's provocative way of life and her radical opinions might well be thought likely to have brought her at a later period of her life into opposition to the upper classes, but although she had little contact with her childhood friends and neighbors in her adult life, there is no tendency in her memoirs to criticize this milieu. Her two sisters, Tut and Mimi, both of whom married wealthy and steady husbands, are always mentioned with deep respect, while they continued to support their sister both financially and emotionally.

Her early childhood, however, had its sorrows. At the age of nine, Agnes lost her mother, who died in childbirth in 1877. Her father died in 1885 when she was sixteen. He had tried to find solace for the loss of his wife by marrying the children's romantic and soulful governess. Although she bore him four children in six years, Peter Andersen remained unhappy and died a bankrupt alcoholic.

When she was fifteen, Agnes entered into a rash and impulsive engagement with the youngest and most handsome of her father's brothers, Ferdinand Andersen. She was subsequently sent away from home to stay with relatives and later to a boarding school at Antvorskov near Slagelse, where the principal encouraged her to develop intellectually. The rash childhood engagement was broken off, but Agnes, by her own confession, was still far more interested in satisfying her emotional needs than her intellectual ones. She soon became engaged to a private tutor named Mads Henningsen, who was working in the house of a pastor and was studying theology. Agnes married him when she was only nineteen. To her genuine delight, the marriage was soon blessed with children, eventually numbering four. In accordance with their shared belief in free love, the couple had agreed that theirs should be an open marriage, with sexual freedom for both parties. Mads Henningsen did try to live up to his progressive beliefs, unlike most of Agnes Henningsen's subsequent male associates, for he, albeit reluctantly, forgave Agnes

Henningsen, ca. 1899, when she began her career as a writer

Hævnen, Copenhagen, Dagmarteatret, 9 December 1912;
Den rige Fugl, Copenhagen, The Royal Theatre, 24 November 1916;
Troense, Copenhagen, The Royal Theatre, 6 May 1922.

In her old age, Agnes Henningsen wrote eight volumes of memoirs, which were published between 1941 and 1955, when she was between the ages of seventy-three and eighty-seven. In terms of quantity, Henningsen's memoirs constitute the largest autobiographical work in Danish literature; in terms of quality, it is one of the best written and most entertaining works in this genre. The volumes are pervaded by a sense of cheerfulness, zest for life, and inner strength, and they are considered Henningsen's major artistic achievement.

Agnes Kathinka Malling Andersen was born 18 November 1868 at Skovsbo, a landed estate near Kerte-

when he learned that the fourth child, Poul, was the son of the author Carl Ewald, one of their artistic friends. Mads Henningsen supported the family by teaching at a grammar school in Ordrup, a suburb north of Copenhagen, but he turned out to be a completely unreliable husband, squandering away all of the money that he was able to persuade her to extricate from the control of her family, even pawning her jewelry without asking her permission. The young couple was constantly short of money, and Agnes Henningsen soon began to contribute to their income by her earnings as a writer. Her first literary publication was the short story "Storken" (The Stork), published in the newspaper *København* on 21 May 1891 under the pseudonym of Helga Maynert. Her work betrayed her admiration for the literature of *det moderne gennembrud* (the modern breakthrough), the literary movement that introduced naturalism and realism to Scandinavia. She came to know personally most of the leading stars of the literary world and became fascinated with the literary and social life of Copenhagen.

In 1894 Mads Henningsen became involved in a scandal with one of his female students. Although the two were said to have gone no farther than kissing, nevertheless, the affair led to his dismissal from the school, and he fled to the United States. Mads, who had considered himself something of a revolutionary in his youth, ended up as the Danish vice-consul in New York City. A legal separation was arranged because of his sudden flight, and in 1907, when Mads returned to Denmark on a visit, the couple divorced, although they remained good friends for the rest of their lives. After Mads had abandoned Denmark and his family, Agnes sent two of the children, Tage and Ellinor, to be looked after by their paternal grandparents in Fredericia, while she and the other two children, Esther and the youngest boy, Poul, went to live with the Ewalds in what she later referred to as "Carl Ewald's harem." The arrangement, with Agnes living under the same roof as her lover's wife and two other female teachers, was not entirely unproblematic; however, in the beginning, at least, the bohemian life in Copenhagen seems to have been happy and profitable for Agnes Henningsen, despite complicated personal relations and the difficulties involved in making a living.

It was not until almost the turn of the century that Henningsen once again tried writing for a living. She had two somewhat depressing novels published in 1899, namely *Glansbilledet: En Historie for Damer* (The Paper Saint: A Story for Ladies) and *Strømmen* (The Current). Both novels deal with the difficult consequences of female lust. In *Strømmen,* for example, the life of the main character, Karen Sofie, falls apart and she ends up as a prostitute.

Henningsen's 1901 novel, *Polens Døtre* (Daughters of Poland), was her breakthrough novel. Its title is taken from some well-known lines from the Danish writer Carsten Hauch's eulogy to the Polish liberation struggle in his classic novel *En polsk Familie* (A Polish Family, 1839). The setting of Henningsen's novel is based on the pioneering Danish critic Georg Brandes's successful lecture tour of Poland in 1885, when he proclaimed his ideology of freedom, which included political and religious freedom in addition to erotic freedom, and argued for the abolition of all forms of authority, in support of the struggle of the Poles against Russian oppression. Agnes Henningsen claims in her memoirs that she meant to write the book as an argument against patriotism and chastity but no such tendency is evident in the finished work.

The contemporary success of the novel was probably mainly due to an admiring portrait in it of Brandes in the character of Percy Branner. In the novel, the famous and charismatic lecturer Percy Branner attracts the unqualified admiration of women but his message is really of less importance. Two of his admirers are the mature and apparently emancipated author Marja and the young virginal aristocrat Halina. Marja, who is brazenly aggressive in her relationship with Percy, is struggling with some hopeless relationships with various men as well as with a constant shortage of money that leads her to take part in some financial swindles. Halina may be suffering from an emotional blockage as she cannot give herself to Percy sexually. A modern reader, however, may well believe that Halina is the woman who has made the better choice, although such a reading opposes the declared intentions behind the book.

In her day, Henningsen's works—characterized by their descriptions of extramarital relationships—were viewed by many as a challenge to conservative opinions and to the complacency of respectable people. On the other hand, they were critically praised in the daily *Politiken,* the organ of liberalism and Brandesianism, which had been founded in 1884 by Georg Brandes's brother, Edvard, and Viggo Hørup, both prominent left-wing spokesmen, serving as editors. In Henningsen the literary left wing had found an author who was attempting to realize Georg Brandes's program for the erotic liberation of women. Brandes was not blind to the fact that Agnes Henningsen's works did not actually sing the praises of the happy and unconstrained life that ought to have been the result of this same liberation. She therefore received a reprimand from him regarding "det grimme erotiske Jaskeri" (the ugly, erotic slovenliness) depicted in her novels, for when it no longer amused, it became boring. She was, in other words, more radical in her pursuit of truth than was Brandes, the so-called banner bearer of Naturalism.

With *Den elskede Eva: Roman* (The Beloved Eva: Novel, 1911) and *Den store Kærlighed: Roman* (The Great Love: Novel, 1917) Henningsen really did cause scan-

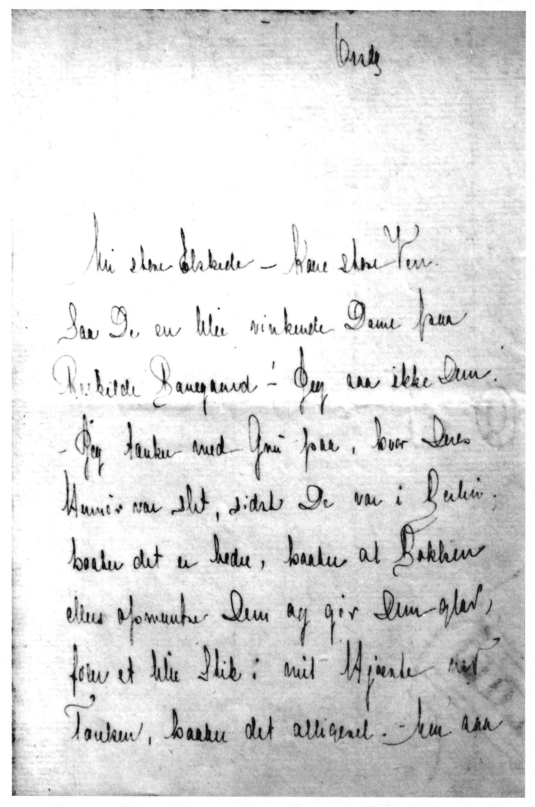

Letter from Henningsen to her lover, literary critic Georg Brandes (Det Kongelige Bibliotek, Copenhagen)

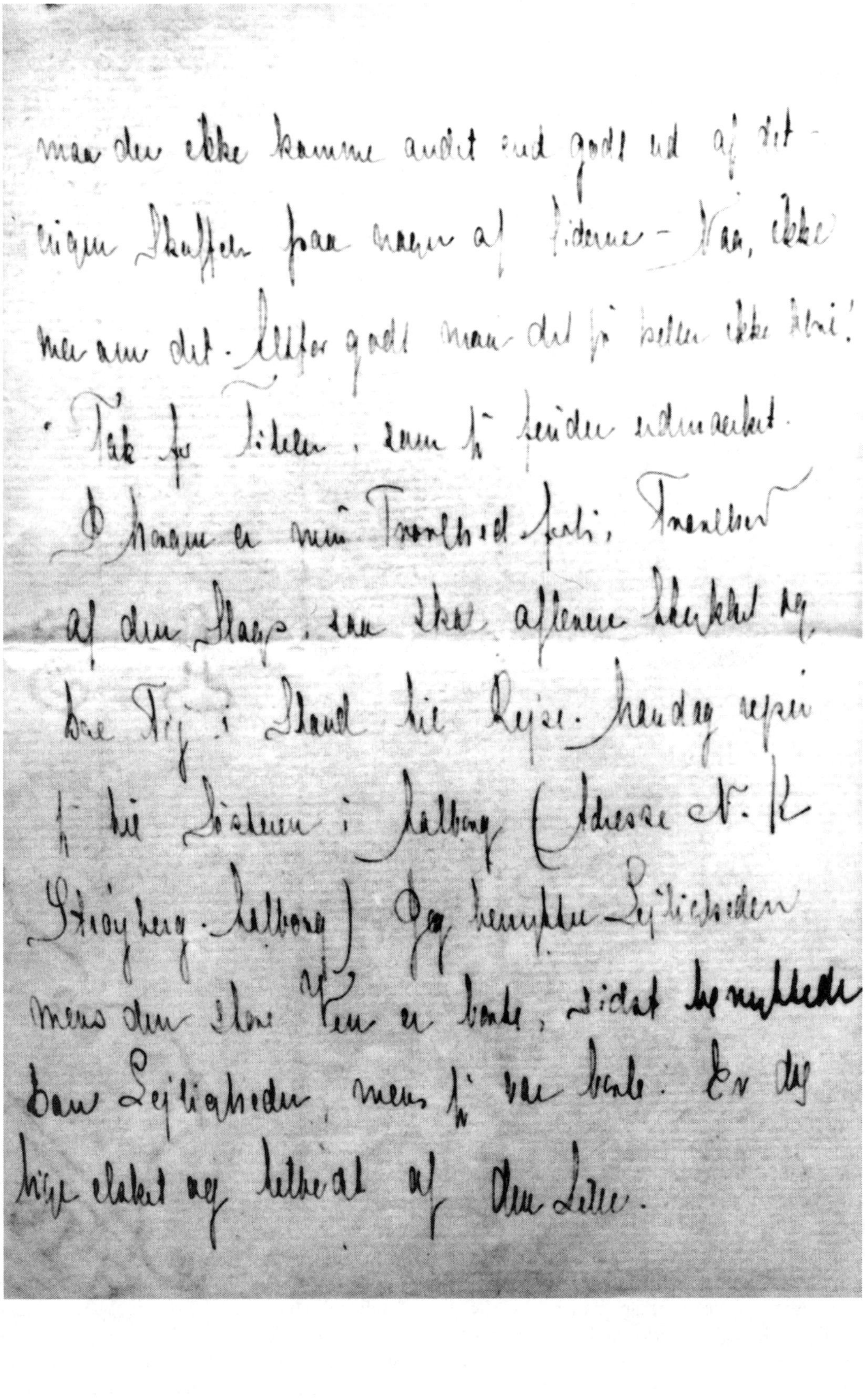

Cover for the novel that Henningsen wrote as a memorial tribute to her second husband, Simon Koch

dal, even though her descriptions of the sexual affairs of so-called liberated people are anything but positive. The reason respectable people were scandalized is simply that these descriptions were in her books. The erotic scenes in these novels would probably not offend most modern readers, and it is clear that the author is much more concerned with depicting subtle emotions than with sexuality. The erotic content of *Den store Kærlighed* was grounds, however, for the denial of the Finansloven, a government grant for which Henningsen had been nominated in 1917.

In the course of her career Henningsen also tried to make money by writing plays, as drama was a genre that was considered by her contemporaries to be a more reliable source of income than fiction. She succeeded in having several plays performed, but their success was only moderate. One that was critically successful was *Den uovervindelige: Skuespil i fire Akter* (The Invincible: Play in Four Acts, 1908), which Georg

Brandes praised unreservedly because the heroine was both good and lovely, that is, absolutely generous to one and all and in addition, exceptionally erotically attractive. As Brandes cynically remarked: "Gode Kvinder plejer ikke at være synderligt erotiske, og de erotiske ikke gode" (Good women are not usually particularly erotic, and the erotic ones are not good). The heroine is a version of the femme fatale character as depicted in many fin de siècle works, and it is possible that the character was conceived as a protest against this stereotype. Henningsen challenged the norms of established society, but she also had an awareness of the tendency of modern "free-thinking" people to construct new norms and roles and hence to impose new limitations on the individual. The drama was by no means conceived as an unequivocal eulogy of the great giver, as the heroine wears herself out because of her generosity, which leads to her shameless exploitation by others.

Between 1927 and 1930 Henningsen published a trilogy of novels, *Kærlighedens Aarstider: Roman* (Seasons of Love: Novel, 1927), *Det rige Efteraar: Roman* (Rich Autumn: Novel, 1928) and *Den sidste Aften* (Last Evening, 1930). When these novels are compared with the later memoirs, they can be seen to be a camouflaged autobiography, although written in a much more somber tone and describing many more tragic events in the life of an author. At the beginning of the trilogy, the heroine, the talented Milli Hahn, lives in a monotonous marriage to a high-school teacher. Milli quickly begins to reveal her talents as a writer and—because of her dissatisfaction with her marriage—falls for a man of the world. Later she becomes an independent woman and writer in an inspiring bohemian milieu, which she soon leaves for a new marriage. In contrast to Henningsen's own life, Milli's personal liberation takes place at the cost of her first husband's suicide and her troubled second marriage. The conclusion of the trilogy seems harsh: as a mature woman, Milli competes with a girlfriend for the attentions of a younger man, a mere gigolo. Nevertheless, she insists on upholding a heroic outlook on life, remarking: "Livet er alligevel overvældende rigt" (Life is nevertheless overwhelmingly rich).

Henningsen's relative silence for five years after the publication of the last volume of the trilogy is probably because in 1935 she lost her sixty-four-year-old husband, Simon Koch, an author and civil servant to whom she had been happily married since 1919. The last novel she published before beginning her memoirs, *Det rigtige Menneske* (The True Person, 1938), is intended as a tribute to Koch, and the title character is a portrait of him.

Henningsen's acclaimed memoirs began to appear during the first years of the German occupation of Denmark, a time when the Danes were undoubtedly hungry for new literature and sources of entertainment.

Their publication extended into the repressive 1950s. Even so, each volume was anticipated with excitement, and the books were the cause of great enjoyment rather than indignation at the author's pervasive desire to "take the carefree path," which is the title of the first volume in the series, *Let Gang paa Jorden: Erindringer* (Take the Carefree Path: Memoirs, 1941). According to Henningsen, "let gang paa Jorden," was an old saying from the island of Langeland, where her father was born, and meant that one should not take life too seriously.

The memoirs begin with the author's birth and come to an end sometime in the 1930s, before the death of Koch. Each slim volume is written in a gripping, impressionistic style and ends in an exciting climactic point. The overall composition is planned in such a way that the climax from the preceding volume is carried over into the immediately succeeding one, almost always with an overlap. The thread is picked up again, not where it broke off but slightly earlier in the story.

The first volume, *Let Gang paa Jorden,* for example, concludes with the seventeen-year-old Agnes seducing her amazed, although actually rather more experienced, fiancé, Mads Henningsen, with the declared intention of becoming pregnant so that she could force a marriage through against the wishes of her wealthy and rationalistic family. The story of the seduction is then repeated in the second volume, *Letsindighedens Gave: Erindringer* (Gift of Lightheartedness: Memoir, 1943), which describes the evolution of the eight-year marriage, entered into with an agreement between the two parties that they should both have sexual freedom.

The couple begins to move in artistic circles, first quite modestly in connection with the newspaper *København* in which Agnes Henningsen's first literary experiments were printed. Her husband cannot keep pace with her either in respect to literature or sexually, even though he has hitherto led the way by engaging in several casual extramarital affairs. These affairs are entered into almost in distraction, and he soon loses all interest in them. In the end, it is Mads who causes a real scandal when he has an affair with one of the female pupils at the grammar school where he is teaching and is dismissed.

The next volume, *Byen erobret: Erindringer* (The Conquered City: Memoir, 1945), opens in the middle of the scandal of Mads Henningsen's dismissal. Mads is sent to America and a legal separation is arranged to give Agnes the right of disposal over her inheritance from her mother, which had been tied up by relatives in order to prevent her husband from gaining access to the money. Now Agnes, a single parent, is about to make a name for herself, and by the end of the book, which covers the period from 1895 to 1901, she has succeeded. After abortive and tragicomical attempts to go into business as a photographer and a

ladies' hairdresser (neither occupation for which she had the slightest talent), she finds success as an author with *Polens Døtre.*

In the penultimate scene of *Byen erobret,* Henningsen invites Georg Brandes to lunch in her newly established home in Roskilde. The luncheon party includes a cluster of young women, since Henningsen knows Brandes's taste in female beauty. He lives up to his reputation as a man of the world and a ladies' man, entertaining the women with chivalrous anecdotes, and he graciously grants his hostess permission to write a book about his Polish lady-friend, to whom he refers as "Dronningen af Saba" (The Queen of Sheba). At this point occurs one of the amusing misunderstandings in which the memoirs are so rich: the young ladies think that the compliment about the queen is a tribute to the hostess and the guest is quite honestly amazed at their mistake, exclaiming that he was talking about someone else entirely. Brandes is depicted, however, as only politely attentive to his hostess as a colleague and more absorbed in the youthful beauties who surround him at the table.

Between *Byen erobret* and the following volume, *Kærlighedssynder: Erindringer* (Sins of Love: Memoir, 1947), there is a gap in time and in the action that would probably pass unnoticed on a first reading. *Byen erobret* ends in 1901 with the success of *Polens Døtre,* while at the beginning of *Kærlighedssynder,* a year or two later, Henningsen is on board one of her wealthy brother-in-law's cargo vessels. She has been offered a free sea voyage in the hope that this will give inspiration to her literary activities. No inspiration is forthcoming, however, and the enterprise would only seem to have been partly successful. The account is also rather uninspiring on the action level. This gap in the action conceals a love affair, which Henningsen apparently was unwilling to write about in a straightforward manner.

From letters in the archives of Det Kongelige Bibliotek (The Royal Library) in Copenhagen, it appears that Brandes and Henningsen actually had a love affair that lasted for a year or two, at about the time of the composition of *Polens Døtre.* It seems that he was the one who put an end to the affair, which he did not take seriously. She, who was otherwise so frank, mentions not a word about this affair in the memoirs; Brandes is, on the contrary, depicted by Henningsen at an admiring distance. He is a model, a teacher, and a father figure, and she has something of a schoolgirl infatuation with him.

Henningsen's memoirs were planned with meticulous care. It can thus hardly have been a matter of chance that the author neglected to reveal the affair that is documented in the letters. When she describes Brandes as an unattainable figure with an artistic and sensual aura, she ensures that the utopia of the grand passion—both sensuous and generous,

Henningsen being interviewed by her youngest son, Poul, for Danmarks Radio in the 1940s

both eros and agape—is preserved. Not only are the teachings of Brandes worthy of imitation, but in her account he personifies a union of the qualities of the exciting and faithless lovers with those of the altruistic Koch.

The next three volumes of the memoirs describe Henningsen's victories and defeats as a woman and as an author; they are characterized by her contagious zest for life and filled with her many romantic adventures. For Danish readers they are particularly valued for their spontaneous portraits of well-known Danish literary figures such as Georg and Edvard Brandes, Herman Bang and—from the younger generation—Johannes V. Jensen and Jeppe Aakjær.

The whole project of the memoirs was designed as an attempt to prove the possibility of realizing Georg Brandes's dream of "free love" in such a way that it brings happiness both to oneself and to one's surroundings. The underlying thesis, however, is discussed and modified in the course of the work, particularly in the final volume of the memoirs, *Skygger over vejen: Erindringer* (Shadows on the Path: Memoir, 1955), in which the author, in spite of her demands for freedom, marries Simon Koch, and in this relationship she becomes acquainted with a different form of love: not the intoxication of infatuation and the heights of passion but mutual affection and loyalty, stability, and durability. The question remains open—not as to whether there is a

trace of resignation mixed in with the development—but to what extent the kind of life she finally chooses is her final and best answer as to how men and women should live together.

At the end of *Skygger over vejen* Koch is incurably ill and, consequently, impotent. After having long nursed him conscientiously, Agnes allows herself to be enticed into one last wild erotic adventure that she believes will not be discovered by her husband. She then says good-bye to her "splendid past" and returns home with a guilty conscience, only to read in her husband's sorrowful eyes that he has seen through the whole intrigue.

The series of memoirs thus concludes in a kind of duality, a duality that can be seen at many other points in the text, even though the dominant mood is one of cheerfulness, joy, and carefree joie de vivre. There are reservations, however, to be read between the lines and many, actually quite complex statements are more or less concealed in the swift-moving and entertaining narrative of Henningsen's varied life. This duality is achieved in part because of the narrative structure, in which the elderly author transposes herself back to the point of view of herself as a young girl and describes everything as seen through her often-naive eyes. The exploitation of the dual time structure, of the relationship between "then" and "now," which is necessarily a feature of an autobiography, is here most subtle, since "the now," the time at which the work was written, is only present implicitly, not explicitly. The impressionistic style does not permit any reflections; but sometimes clues are laid so that, for example, the reader falls a little less under the spell of a new male acquaintance than does the narrator herself. Henningsen wants to show that her life was successful, but between the lines much can be read about the price that she has paid.

After completing her memoirs at the age of eighty-seven, Henningsen once again turned to fiction. One of her daughters, Esther, was married in the United States, and Henningsen visited her there; under the influence of this country, she found the setting for her final series of novels: *Vi ses i Arizona* (See You in Arizona, 1956), *Den lidenskabelige pige* (The Passionate Girl, 1958), and *Bølgeslag* (Breaking Waves, 1959). In this trilogy, she presents a variation of her theme of a woman's right to freedom in love and her duty of absolute honesty toward herself and others.

Agnes Henningsen died 21 April 1962. At the end of her life, she was a highly respected cultural figure and a member of Det Danske Akademi (The Danish Academy). She was awarded the Otto Benzon's Author's Prize in 1938, the Gyldendal Publishing Herman Bang Prize in 1946, the Holger Drachmann Prize in 1953, and the Jeanne and Henri Nathansen Merit Award in 1960. Her youngest son, Poul Henningsen, became famous as a cultural critic, interviewer, and architect. He designed the PH-lamp, which uses shades to diffuse light, and was also a writer of well-known cabaret songs.

Henningsen is best known for her memoirs, in which she clearly finds it wrong to express any wishes of her own or to make any demands on men. The result was indeed a rather hard life. Always suffering financial difficulties, she was simply too generous. The reservations that she might have had about "free love" are expressed in the memoirs, and they are also revealed by the expressions of dissatisfaction by fictional characters in her novels. Sometimes the narrator of the memoirs is also obliged to remind herself about her own theories. This reminding happens typically between two sentences–so to speak, in the middle of a full stop, where she quickly pulls herself together in the next sentence, as, for example, when her lover Carl Ewald tells her that he is expecting a baby with his wife: "Det var en overraskelse. En god Overraskelse sagde jeg til mig selv" (That was a surprise. A nice surprise, I said to myself). In general, however, the atmosphere depicted in the memoirs is bright. Liberation leads to development, both erotically and in her work, and to an exuberant joie de vivre: "Min Verden udvidede sig og blev saa spændende. Nu da jeg igen var fuld af Synd blev jeg nem at omgaas" (My world expanded and became so exciting. Now that I was again full of sin, I was easy to get along with).

Interview:
Christian Rimestad, "Agnes Henningsen," in his *Digtere i Forhør: Interviews og Breve* (Copenhagen: Gyldendal, 1906), pp. 52–56.

Biography:
Bodil Wamberg, *Letsindighedens pris: En bog om Agnes Henningsen* (Copenhagen: Gad, 1983).

References:
Jeppe Aakjær, *Samlede Værker: Artikler og Taler,* volume 4 (Copenhagen: Gyldendal, 1919), pp. 170–171;

Georg Brandes, *Samlede Skrifter,* volume 15 (Copenhagen: Gyldendal, 1905), pp. 278–284;

Stig Dalager and Anne-Marie Mai, *Danske kvindelige forfattere,* volume 2 (Copenhagen: Gyldendal, 1982), pp. 56–63;

Bodil Holm and Lis Thygesen, "Begærets retorik," in *Nordisk kvindelitteraturhistorie,* volume 3, edited by Elisabeth Møller Jensen and others (Copenhagen: Rosinante-Munksgaard, 1996), pp. 328–332;

Beth Juncker, "Bohemen som metafor," in *Nordisk kvindelitteraturhistorie,* volume 3, edited by Møller Jensen and others (Copenhagen: Rosinante-Munksgaard, 1996), pp. 81–89;

Tom Kristensen, *Mellem Krigene* (Copenhagen: Gyldendal, 1946), pp. 59–63, 360–365;

Sven Lange, *Meninger om Litteratur* (Copenhagen: Gyldendal, 1929), pp. 23–27;

Marie-Louise Paludan, "Agnes Henningsen," in *Danske digtere i det 20. århundrede,* volume 1, edited by Ernst Frandsen and Niels Kaas Johansen (Copenhagen: Gad, 1951), pp. 125–128;

Lise Præstgaard Andersen, "Agnes Henningsens Erindringer–og Georg Brandes," *Danske Studier* (1996): 77–100;

Præstgaard Andersen, "Den erotiske utopi–Agnes Henningsens Erindringer og Georg Brandes' evangelium," in *Læsninger i dansk litteratur,* volume 3, edited by Povl Schmidt, Inger-Lise Hjordt-Vetlesen, and Finn Frederik Krarup (Odense: Odense University Press, 1997), pp. 308–325;

Niels Birger Wamberg, "Agnes Henningsen," in *Danske digtere i det 20. århundrede,* second edition, volume 1, edited by Frederik Nielsen and Ole Restrup (Copenhagen: Gad, 1965), pp. 432–442.

Papers:
Agnes Henningsen's papers are at Det Kongelige Bibliotek (The Royal Danish Library), Copenhagen.

Peter Høeg

(17 May 1957 –)

Thomas Satterlee
University of Miami

BOOKS: *Forestilling om det tyvende århundrede* (Copenhagen: Rosinante, 1988); translated by Barbara Haveland as *The History of Danish Dreams* (New York: Farrar, Straus & Giroux, 1995; London: Harvill, 1997);

Fortællinger om natten (Copenhagen: Rosinante, 1990); translated by Barbara Haveland as *Tales of the Night* (London: Harvill, 1997; New York: Farrar, Straus & Giroux, 1998);

Frøken Smillas fornemmelse for sne (Copenhagen: Rosinante, 1992); translated by Tiina Nunnally as *Smilla's Sense of Snow* (New York: Farrar, Straus & Giroux, 1993);

De måske egnede (Copenhagen: Rosinante, 1993); translated by Barbara Haveland as *Borderliners* (New York: Farrar, Straus & Giroux, 1994; London: Harvill, 1995);

Kvinden og aben (Copenhagen: Rosinante, 1996); translated by Barbara Haveland as *The Woman and the Ape* (New York: Farrar, Straus & Giroux, 1996; London: Harvill, 1996).

Editions in English: *Frøken smillas fornemmelse for sne,* translated by Nunnally and others as F. David, as *Miss Smilla's Feeling for Snow* (London: Harvill, 1993);

"Medlidenhed med bornene i Vaden by," translated by Anne Born as "Compassion for the Children of Vaden Town," in *Frontiers,* edited by Christopher MacLehose (London: Harvill, 1994), pp. 185–226.

Peter Høeg (photograph by Jo Selsing; from the dust jacket for Tales of the Night, *1998)*

The most recognized contemporary Danish writer on the international literary scene, Peter Høeg gained widespread acclaim for his second novel, *Frøken Smillas fornemmelse for sne* (1992; translated as *Smilla's Sense of Snow,* 1993; and as *Miss Smilla's Feeling for Snow,* 1993), which was sold to publishers in more than thirty countries. In the United States the novel spent twenty-six weeks on *The New York Times* paperback bestseller list, and both *Time* and *Entertainment Weekly* chose it as their 1993 book of the year. The tremendous popular success of *Smilla's Sense of Snow* led to a 1997 motion picture of the same name, directed by Danish-born Bille August and starring Julia Ormond. All of Høeg's books have been translated into English, and his work has been the subject of lively debate among literary critics, both in Scandinavia and the United States.

In many of his novels Høeg explores Danish society by deliberately including characters from a wide range of social classes. In an interview conducted with Martin Bagger of *Bogens Verden* after the publication of his first novel, Høeg said of his own upbringing,

> Jeg er produkt af den borgerlige kultur, og jeg synes at den på visse områder er unik. Vi har fået en frihed som jeg er dybt taknemmelig for. Men der er både i samfundet og i min bog personer, der går under ved for megen frihed eller for megen pligtopfyldende selvtugt.

> (I am a product of the middle-class culture, which I believe is in certain ways unique. We have been given a freedom, for which I am deeply thankful. But there are people, both in society and in my book, who are ruined by too much freedom or by too much strict self-discipline.)

Peter Høeg was born in Copenhagen on 17 May 1957, the son of Erik Høeg, a lawyer, and Karen Kjellund, a classical philologist. He graduated from Frederiksberg Gymnasium in 1976 and went on to study literary theory at the University of Copenhagen, where he received his master of arts degree in 1984. Before devoting himself to full-time writing, Høeg performed classical ballet, acted and taught acting, competed as a professional fencer, and worked as a crewman on pleasure boats. One interviewer described Høeg as "en ung og meget venligtsindet pirat" (a young and very friendly pirate). An extensive traveler, Høeg often entertains audiences with stories of his mountain-climbing adventures or his travels throughout Africa. Høeg's wife, Akinyi, is a native of Kenya. They live with their two daughters in Copenhagen and make frequent trips to Kenya to visit Akinyi's family.

Høeg was twenty-five years old when he began his first novel, *Forestilling om det tyvende århundrede* (Introduction to the Twentieth Century, 1988; translated as *The History of Danish Dreams,* 1995), which he worked on for six years, rewriting one chapter twenty times and discarding hundreds of pages. In one interview, Høeg referred to this early book as his apprenticeship in writing. Danish critics were quick to praise the work, and some have called it the most significant novel debut of the 1980s. *Forestilling om det tyvende århundrede* includes many of the themes that Høeg develops in greater detail in his later novels—the nature of time, the role of social classes, the mistreatment of children, and the battle between individual and society. *Forestilling om det tyvende århundrede* is told by a first-person narrator, Mads, who recollects stories from the previous four generations of his family's history. In the preface to the novel, Mads explains his intentions: "Det er de danske drømmmes historie, det er et referat af hvad vi har frygtet og drømt og håbet og forventet i dette århundrede" (This is the history of Danish dreams, an account of what we have

dreaded and dreamed of and hoped for and expected during this century). As this preface suggests, the novel recounts many "dreams"—which can be as different as the dreamers themselves—and thus the book reads not so much as a unified narrative as a collection of stories loosely connected by the fact that the main characters are the narrator's ancestors. The tales that Mads relates date from as far back as 1520, but he concentrates on events that occur after New Year's Eve, 1900, when Carl Laurids (the narrator's great-great-grandfather) was born.

Written in the style of magic realism, the novel often recounts stories of the fabulous in a detached, matter-of-fact manner. Grandmother Teandor, for instance, has the power to read the future, and her predictions of deaths, births, and divorces are printed in the family-owned newspaper and read by Danish citizens who believe that her predictions are infallible. Anna Bak, the daughter of an Evangelical priest, has the ability to duplicate herself, and her second self reaches out and heals people. Her father takes her power as a sign that she will bear the Messiah, and he tells everyone of his conviction until Anna's child is born and turns out to be a girl.

A critique of Danish social classes appears fundamental to the book's design. Divided into three sections, it progresses one generation at a time. In the first part, Mads describes four families: the Laurids, Teanders, Baks, and Jensens. Each of the four families has a child—altogether, two boys and two girls—and each child marries a son or daughter from one of the other families. In part 2, each couple has a child, and these two children become the narrator's parents. Part 3 focuses on the narrator's parents and his sister. Built into this genealogy, however, is a broad social critique. Høeg has chosen to represent four distinct social groups in his first generation: an aristocrat, a thief, a nouveau-riche newspaper publisher, and an Evangelical priest. This heritage makes Mads a social hybrid and, more importantly, gives him a reason to narrate stories from different spheres of Danish society.

Mads pays special attention to the lives of children, who, regardless of social class, tend to have a difficult time. The stories that Mads tells cut across social lines to condemn the parents for abandoning or betraying their children. The priest, for instance, locks his daughter in a silver-plated cage and transports her to various revival meetings, where he presents her as the new Virgin. The thief, whose son does not show all the skills of the father, helps the police to catch his own son. The newspaper tycoon becomes so engrossed with planning the most efficient schedules for his workers that he completely ignores his daughter, who suffers from anorexia. A mother has incestuous relations with her son. The cruel and demeaning treatment of children later becomes a major theme in Høeg's work.

Another of Høeg's prominent themes that appears for the first time in *Forestilling om det tyvende århundrede* is the nature of time. The structure of the novel suggests an emphasis on the passing of time and the influence of former generations on succeeding ones. Less subtle, however, are the subtitles of certain chapters: "Om tiden der står stille" (About Time That Stands Still) and "Om tiden der går" (About Time That Passes). Certain characters are obsessed with time. The count of Møkhøj orders all clocks stopped while he searches his property for the exact center of the universe. The count goes to great lengths to keep up the illusion that time has stopped. When the count's estate steward dies, his corpse remains propped on his horse, and from this perch the old steward appears to still watch over the estate's affairs. Grandmother Teander has clocks installed in every room of her house, including the bathroom. Her son becomes so obsessed with schedules that he knows what he and the staff of the family's newspaper will be doing every minute of the day. In *Forestilling om det tyvende århundrede*, as in his other novels, Høeg's discussion of time is dialectical, pitting one character who tries to eradicate linear time against others who attempt to harness time and use it for commercial gain.

The majority of Danish critics praised *Forestilling om det tyvende århundrede* for its skillful blend of social commentary and magic realism. The novel received two awards from Danish newspapers, including the 1988 Literature Prize from *Weekendavisen*. Shortly after its release, plans were in place to have the novel translated into Norwegian and Swedish and distributed through book clubs. In 1997 the Danish version was already in its fifth edition.

In the United States, reviews were mixed. Reviewers agreed that *The History of Danish Dreams* was an ambitious first novel and praised Høeg's prose style as well as his skill in writing humorous social commentary. On the whole, they also agreed that the novel was not as successful as *Smilla's Sense of Snow*, which was Høeg's first book to be translated into English. Beyond these points, reviewers of *The History of Danish Dreams* (as well as Høeg's other novels) disagreed widely, and criticism of the book falls roughly into three categories: reviewers who assume that the book is intended to be a traditional novel and criticize its failure to satisfy one or another convention; reviewers who believe that Høeg's novel is experimental, containing elements of postmodernism, and who praise what may appear to be "errors"; and, finally, reviewers who sense that Høeg is experimenting with style but who do not find his experimentation successful.

Reviewers falling into the first group, for instance, faulted Høeg for creating symbolic characters who seem to exist only to further the novelist's social critique. The multigenerational tale, they contended, was self-defeating since it limited the author's ability to give full characterization. Characters appear briefly, then disappear to make room for the succeeding generation. In the words of Jim Shepard of *The Los Angeles Times Book Review*, "Characters, especially at the beginning, are paraded by at such a pace they're inevitably reduced in the reader's mind (when they stay in the reader's mind at all) to a few key traits, and motivations are accordingly reduced at such times to psychological commonplaces." Another criticism focused on the frequent intrusion of the first-person narrator, who sometimes comments on the meaning of a story he has just related.

Other critics, however, sensed that Høeg was purposeful in his so-called mistakes, his task being to both construct and deconstruct meaning throughout his novel. "There is a constant sense that Høeg has built his beautiful formal structure simply for the pleasure of running molehills and mine shafts beneath the foundations, gleefully undermining his own certainties," noted reviewer Peter Whitlaker for the *New Statesman*, who remarked that glitches in the novel point up the novelist's conviction that history is at best a fiction that people can believe only momentarily. Similarily, a 1995 review in *Time* suggested that the stories in *The History of Danish Dreams* might be seen as purposefully incomplete and loosely related, aspects associating the novel with the postmodern sense of truth as open.

Whether a portrayal of postmodern thought underlies the construction of the novel or not was irrelevant to another group of reviewers who complained that Høeg's novel was at times too clever. The novel might be a sly subversion of the notion that history can never be objectively told, and the self-conscious narrator might represent the postmodern personality, but these projects alone do not necessarily make for good fiction. Although the novel was ambitious, they noted, Høeg had overstretched his abilities, and the result was fiction that was neither as convincing nor as enjoyable as his first work to appear in English, *Smilla's Sense of Snow*.

Between his first and second novels, Høeg published a collection of short stories titled *Fortællinger om natten* (1990; translated as *Tales of the Night*, 1997). As in *Forestilling om det tyvende århundrede*, Høeg provides a preface in which he indicates the subject of his book: "Disse ni fortællinger er fælles om en dato og et motiv. De handler alle om kærligheden. Kærligheden og dens betingelser, om natten den 19. marts 1929" (These nine stories share the same date and the same motive. They are all about love. Love and its conditions on the night of 19 March 1929). Høeg's selection of the year 1929 as the setting for the stories is as purposeful as his inclusion of characters from different social groups in the first generation of *Forestilling om det tyvende århundrede*. In 1929, before Adolf Hitler's rise to power, Europeans had not yet suffered the disillusionment of the Holocaust, and simple romance was still possible. Although essentially love stories, they also illustrate the social and political climate of the time by focusing not only on romantic love but also on the love of science, children, and art.

In "Rejse ind i et mørkt hjerte" ("Travel Into a Heart of Darkness"), as in many of the tales in *Forestilling om det tyvende århundrede,* the ending is left open. The story takes place on a train trip where three characters meet and share stories about what they love most: politics, maps, and algebra. Toward the end of the book the characters discover that the train is headed for a bridge crossing where the train will fall seven hundred feet. At the last moment, the main characters escape. Two of them disappear into the darkness and the third remains behind; the fate of each is left unknown. The train continues on its course to destruction. The story ends in uncertainty, leaving the reader to imagine what will happen to the characters who have told their tales of love. Instilling doubt in his readers, however, may be Høeg's goal. Even the title of the book, which could be translated as "Stories About the Night" or "Stories Told at Night," is ambiguous.

Fortællinger om natten confirmed for Danish critics what they had suspected from Høeg's first book: the author's talent was substantial, and the breadth of his knowledge was impressive. More than *Forestilling om det tyvende århundrede,* critics considered *Fortællinger om natten* a literary work, especially with its similarities to the stories of Karen Blixen (Isak Dinesen) and its many references to distinguished intellectuals. (For instance, Joseph Conrad appears in "Rejse ind i et mørkt hjerte," and the story's main character, the reader is informed, had earlier met with Kurt Gödel.) Høeg's influence on contemporary Danish fiction increased with this second book; critics began to view his ambitious work as a standard by which other Danish writers might be judged.

Although it may not appear so to Anglo-American readers, whose introduction to Høeg came with *Frøken Smillas fornemmelse for sne,* Høeg's second novel signals a departure from his previous work. With *Frøken Smillas fornemmelse for sne,* Høeg entered the world of genre fiction, specifically the thriller. His heroine and first-person narrator, Smilla Qaavigaaq Jaspersen, attempts to solve the mystery behind the death of Isaiah, a young boy, which police consider an accident. A

Dust jacket for the 1993 U.S. edition of Høeg's international best-selling novel, Frøken Smillas fornemmelse for sne, *1992*

trail of clues leads Smilla into various sections of Copenhagen and eventually to Greenland. In her search she uncovers a corrupt Danish corporation, falls in love with a mysterious man, and discovers a scientist's plan to transport a potentially deadly meteorite from its recess in a remote Greenlandic cave to a populated area of Europe.

In its outline, *Frøken Smillas fornemmelse for sne* certainly fits the traditional detective novel, but in many other ways it transcends the genre. Smilla, for instance, struck many readers as a fascinating and unusual sleuth. An expert in glacial morphology, a loner who reads Euclid for fun, her ruminations on mathematics and philosophy would seem dry if it were not for her wit and the way in which Høeg uses her background to delineate character and to move the plot along. Smilla's erudition comes into play at crucial moments, such as when she sees Isaiah's footprints in the snow and determines from subtle clues that he was not playing on the rooftop of a Copenhagen apartment building but was most likely being chased. At other times her background allows her to explain her own character, as when she refers to the German mathematician Georg Cantor's concept of infinity to show why she values her personal space, the English philosopher Bertrand Russell's definition of pure math to indicate why she feels confused about cooking, or an Inuit legend to clarify her relationship with her mother.

Furthermore, Smilla's background figures prominently in the development of certain themes. The daughter of a Greenlandic mother and a Danish father, Smilla has spent the early part of her childhood in Greenland with her mother, a nurturing woman who could hunt as well as any man. While Smilla was still a child, her mother died during a hunting trip, but the adult Smilla has vivid memories of her. These scenes reveal the mother's tenderness toward her daughter and the simple but harsh lives of Inuit people. In an interview with Jes Stein Pedersen for *Smilla's Sense of Snow: The Making of a Film by Bille August, Adapted from the Novel by Peter Høeg* (1997), Høeg said that he tried to portray Greenlanders as realistically as possible: "the book has a subtly shifting view of Greenlanders. I have tried my best to render it unsentimental. There are so many ridiculously romanticized images of the Third and Fourth Worlds which completely forget the harshness that characterizes living conditions in such places."

The novel describes how, after her mother's death, Smilla moves to Denmark to live with her father. Stories of her assimilation (never complete) into Danish culture show her struggles with everything from Danish manners to the language. In boarding school she is mocked for being an outsider—the only one in the class with black hair—and her response is to fight back. She plans a surprise attack on the boy who has treated her the most harshly, and though the boy is much bigger than she, she breaks his nose and leaves him crumpled on the sidewalk in front of his house. The scene reveals the rough Smilla encountered later in the novel, the Smilla who will defend herself against a horde of shady characters and come out alive. More importantly, however, the scene points to the experience of an outsider attempting to live in the highly conformist Danish society.

Smilla is not the only outsider in the novel. Isaiah and his alcoholic mother, Juliane, have moved from Greenland and they also find life in Denmark less than hospitable. Isaiah appears to have no friends his own age and spends most of his free time visiting Smilla, content to listen to her read from Euclid's *Elements*. Juliane, when she is not drunk, frets over the massive paperwork that is required of Greenlanders living in Denmark. Smilla's critique of Denmark's treatment of Greenlanders goes beyond these individual examples, however. She reviews the history of European and Dan-

ish explorations to Greenland, which in her mind amounts to a series of exploitations, and concludes that they will never understand the Inuit. Instead, the Danes believe in a dream,

> En drøm om at inuit skulle blive ved med at være disse hjulbenede, tromme-dansende, sagnfortællende, bredt smilende udstillingsbilleder, som de første opdagelsesrejsende bildte sig ind at møde syd for Qaanaaq ved århundredeskiftet.
>
> (A dream that the Inuit will continue to be the bowlegged, drum-dancing, legend-telling, widely smiling exhibition images that the first explorers thought they were meeting south of Qaanaq at the turn of the century.)

Elsewhere Smilla observes that even after Greenland achieved home rule, Denmark's influence continued in the form of military control and economic incentives—only the Greenlanders who master Danish receive high-paying jobs. Smilla comments freely and critically about these matters, but her insights are so tightly linked both to her character and to the ominous machinations that lie behind the plot, that her criticisms form an integral part of the story.

The exploitation of Greenland has importance throughout the novel, but especially when Smilla discovers that two scientific expeditions have some connection to Isaiah's death. The expeditions were funded by the Cryolite Corporation, which has taken natural resources from Greenland for decades. On one of these expeditions, Isaiah's father died in an accident that Smilla suspects has not been fully explained. The trips required expensive equipment and a team of scientists, but Smilla rules out the possibility of cryolite as their goal. She knows that they must have found something valuable enough to repay their efforts and that this new discovery is another example of Danes using Greenland for their own profit.

Another important theme in *Frøken Smillas fornemmelse for sne* is the treatment of children. Høeg convincingly reveals the inner lives of children, which he renders through flashback scenes to Smilla's childhood and through interactions between Smilla and Isaiah. Smilla has never forgiven her father for leaving her when she was three years old or for taking her away from Greenland four years later, after her mother's death. In one flashback Smilla has run away from home and her father has caught up with her. When he tries to force her to come with him, she slashes his hand with a surgical scalpel. Busy with his career, he puts Smilla in boarding school, an experience she loathes. Isaiah, whose murder at the beginning of the novel represents the ultimate mistreatment of children, lives with his alcoholic mother, who has ignored his ear infections for so long that he suffers permanent hearing loss. Both Smilla and Isaiah's childhoods are characterized by abandonment and neglect, though this treatment does not lead to weakness in either. They survive as loners and pay little attention to the people who have neglected them.

The novel presents at least one other wounded child, Tørk Hvid, whose parents neither feed nor clothe him properly. He goes to school undernourished, and when classmates pick on him, he does not have the strength to fight back. The experience leaves him permanently scarred, and when Tørk grows up, he becomes a scientist with a maniacal need for power and money. Tørk's presence is shadowy for the first three-quarters of the novel, but eventually he is revealed as the mastermind behind a new expedition to Greenland, funded, as were the previous two, by the Cryolite Corporation. This time Smilla goes along and discovers what has prompted the interest: the scientists have found a meteorite that may be radioactive or may be alive, and in their attempts to study it they have risked human lives, including that of Isaiah's father. Although the meteorite has proven deadly, Tørk still wants to put it on display for a general audience because he views the meteorite as the most significant discovery of the century and, more importantly, because he knows that he would profit financially. The scientists who take part in this project, especially Tørk, seem to represent the scientific community at large, which the novel depicts as greedy and dangerous, willing to jeopardize civilization for the sake of money and fame. At various times Smilla, herself a trained scientist, criticizes Western science for its relentless need to measure and calculate and for its desire for money, which outweighs its compassion for human lives. Tørk hardly denies such charges. At one point, asked what his interest in the meteorite is, he blatantly confesses: money.

In his interview with Pedersen, Høeg admitted that he was more preoccupied during the writing of this novel than he had been during his previous work—his wife had just had a baby and returned to work. According to Høeg, "Smilla was very spontaneous and improvised. I just didn't have the energy to research the book thoroughly, I had to fake a lot of things. I was working under much more difficult conditions than anything I have since been faced with."

Far from noticing problems with the research behind the novel, critics praised the author enthusiastically for his wide learning and his brilliant prose. The critical response to *Frøken Smillas fornemmelse for sne* was overwhelmingly positive. The novel won several prizes in Denmark, including De Gyldne Laurbær (The Golden Laurels), a prestigious award given by the Dan-

Poster for the motion-picture adaptation of Høeg's Frøken Smillas fornemmelse for sne

ish booksellers to the author of the year. Critics and reviewers on both sides of the Atlantic praised Høeg for his ability to breathe new life into the thriller novel and to make it a literary as well as a popular medium. In comparing Høeg's work with other writers, critics named Joseph Conrad, John le Carré, and Karen Blixen, the only Danish writer of this century to receive as much attention as Høeg. Current world sales for *Frøken Smillas fornemmelse for sne,* which has been translated into thirteen languages, are estimated at nearly forty million copies.

Critics found little to fault in Høeg's novel, although the conclusion of the work troubled several readers. Writing for the *Partisan Review,* Pearl K. Bell complained about the sudden shift in the novel from the themes of the murder case and corporate corruption (which are consistent with the thriller genre) to the dangers of the meteorite, the existence of strange parasitic worms, and the evil plot of a ruthless scientist (which are more typical of science fiction). Other critics considered the ending ambiguous and unsatisfying. As with *Forestilling om det tyvende århundrede,* however, what one group of critics saw as troubling another group saw as one of the chief merits of the work. This second group of critics viewed the ending of *Frøken Smillas fornemmelse for sne* as further evidence of Høeg's concern with postmodern themes. In a 1994 issue of the Danish journal *Spring,* Bo G. Jansson argued that the purpose behind the transformation from realistic fiction to science fiction at the end of *Frøken Smillas fornemmelse for sne* was to illustrate a condition of postmodern life, namely that the modern sense of reality has disappeared. Smilla has perhaps determined the cause behind Isaiah's death, but she will never comprehend the meteorite, and this inconclusiveness or ambiguity represents a more honest ending to the novel than a traditional dénouement.

Although Høeg has addressed the ending of *Frøken Smillas fornemmelse for sne* in several interviews, his comments suggest various authorial intentions. In an interview with Sarah Lyall of *The New York Times,* Høeg states that the ending was purposefully ambiguous: "There is no clear solution, in my opinion, to the questions raised in the novel. I want to involve the readers in an awareness that there are ambiguities, even as you respect the rules. It is like chemistry: the details shall all have a logical explanation, but it is the overall problems, the principal questions, that are left unanswered." In the 1997 Pedersen interview Høeg gives a slightly different answer:

I wrote a very literary ending, and there are several reasons for this. When I wrote the book I was aware that I was also working with certain stereotypes. In order to make contact with very deep-seated forces in people and capture their attention you have to work with certain emotions that are buried deep inside us. The atrocity committed against the child, man and woman, good and evil, archetypes of that type. Having worked with such profound symbolism throughout the book, I wanted, at the end, to reveal this to the reader by having the realistic plane of the novel crack.

In the same interview, however, he suggested another possible reason behind the ending: "when I wrote *Smilla* I still hadn't learned how to control the entity a novel represents." Høeg then went on to compare himself to a conductor who has assembled a stage full of musicians and "in a sense passed the buck, having not fully resolved the problem of giving the orchestra something to play."

Perhaps the one clear fact about *Frøken Smillas fornemmelse for sne* is that it brought the author unprecedented recognition. When *Smilla's Sense of Snow* first appeared in the United States in 1993, it led sales for all translated novels that year. Both popular and literary magazines printed positive reviews of it, and the National Public Radio program *Talk of the Nation* featured the novel on one of its call-in shows. All of this attention was not entirely welcomed by the author. Since the publication of his first novel, Høeg has maintained that he is not interested in fame. After the worldwide success of *Frøken Smillas fornemmelse for sne,* however, Høeg's popularity in Denmark reached celebrity status. He grew reluctant to give interviews, and in those which he did give he often complained of having to hide his private affairs and to keep his address secret.

The translation of *Frøken Smillas fornemmelse for sne* presents a sort of mystery in itself and warrants attention. Two English-language translations appeared in 1993, one titled *Smilla's Sense of Snow,* published in the United States, and the other titled *Miss Smilla's Feeling for Snow,* published in Great Britain. At first glance one might assume that the translations were done by two separate translators–Tiina Nunnally is credited with translating the American version, and F. David with the British. In reality, however, "F. David" is a pseudonym, and the text for *Miss Smilla's Feeling for Snow* is based largely on Nunnally's translation. Commissioned by Farrar, Straus and Giroux to translate Høeg's novel, Nunnally sent a completed manuscript to the author and his Danish editor, who reviewed it and made suggestions for changes. Nunnally incorporated some of these suggestions, but others she chose not to accept in her final translation. The British edition, *Miss Smilla's Feeling for Snow,* includes all the changes that Høeg and his editor made to Nunnally's manuscript.

Although many of the differences between the two editions appear minor–the British version uses celsius and meters and replaces American idioms with British equivalents–the guiding principle behind the majority of Høeg's changes to the British translation moves it toward a more literal translation. The title itself, *Miss Smilla's Feeling for Snow,* for instance, is closer to the original Danish title than the American, which does not translate the word *Frøken* (Miss) and passes over the cognate "for" in favor of "of." Nevertheless, readers are likely to find the British edition less helpful than the American edition when the novel refers to place names or presents dialogue in German. In *Smilla's Sense of Snow,* the translator has provided clues to assist the reader. For instance, "Christianshavns Torv" becomes "Christianhavn's Square" in the American version, whereas the Danish place names in the British edition are strictly maintained. Nunnally also provides brief translations of German phrases, setting her English translation beside the German. In the British edition, as in the original Danish, the German is left untranslated. Occasionally, too, *Miss Smilla's Feeling for Snow* mishandles the translation of humor and idiom, whereas Nunnally's American translation reads smoothly throughout. The translator of *Smilla's Sense of Snow* gained praise from several reviewers and received an award from the American Translators Association. Significantly, Nunnally's original translation was chosen for the motion picture adaptation of the novel.

After the fanfare surrounding *Frøken Smillas fornemmelse for sne,* Høeg expressed a desire to return to the calmness of his life outside Copenhagen and work on his next project, a novel titled *De måske egnede* (1993; translated as *Borderliners,* 1994). In various interviews, Høeg has described his process of writing a novel as a matter of quiet intensity, usually lasting two years, during which he works every day, striving to remain "totally focused and totally relaxed, to save any buildup of tension." Called "otherworldly calm" by one interviewer, Høeg insists on periods of obscurity for the sake of his work. Out of such a period Høeg emerged with a novel that was quite different from *Frøken Smillas fornemmelse for sne.*

As with his first two novels, *De måske egnede* is told by a first-person narrator, Peter, who is himself the main character of the novel. Peter looks back at his childhood experiences as an orphan shipped from one boarding school to the next. The novel focuses on one school in particular, Biehl's Academy, which Peter describes as an authoritarian nightmare. Biehl, the school's totalitarian headmaster, inspires terror in the children, and each minute of the day is strictly regulated by the clock and a series of bells. Moreover, behind the school there lies a greater evil: the notion of progress, which, although it has created a "civilized" Denmark, is particularly cruel to those who do not fit into its plans. Biehl's Academy, the reader learns, is an educational experiment meant to raise to the Danish standard those children who have social or academic problems. As Peter discovers, the children at Biehl's Academy face their last chance: either they will succeed and go on to study at the university level, eventually to fit comfortably into Danish society, or they will fail—either by flunking out or by breaking the rules—in which case they will be sent to reform school and eventually to the bottom of Danish society.

Although the idea behind the school may seem humanitarian, Peter views the project as forced conformity. Like the Greenlanders in *Frøken Smillas fornemmelse for sne,* no one has asked the children if they want to be civilized and join the ranks of "successful" Danes. At the school Peter bands with two other students, Kata-rina (a sixteen-year-old daughter of wealthy parents, whose mother died of cancer and whose father has since hanged himself) and August (a victim of child abuse who killed both of his parents). Together they try to understand and eventually destroy the system that constrains them with its daily routines. The chief evil, they discover, is linear time, represented by rigorous schedules and a series of school bells coordinated by the clock. Even more than the count of Mørkhøj or Grandmother Teandor of *Forestilling om det tyvende århundrede,* Peter has a fanatical desire to understand time; the novel includes long passages in which the narrator tries to grasp the meaning of time, an obsession that began when he was fourteen years old and has continued into his adult life, where he has a young daughter whose concept of time he carefully charts.

Initially, Danish critics reacted favorably to *De måske egnede,* but with the publication of an article by Erik Skyum-Nielsen in January of 1994 Høeg faced his first serious criticism, and a heated debate over the novel took place in Danish and other Scandinavian publications. Skyum-Nielsen called *De måske egnede* "fejllæst og overvurderet" (misread and overrated), assessing its quality as about average for Danish novels. Defenders of the novel praised it for its treatment of human rationality, an aspect of the novel which Skyum-Nielsen referred to as pompous.

The reaction from American reviewers was similarly mixed, though on the whole more negative than the Scandinavian reaction. Several reviewers found that the emphasis on time distracted from the plot, while others complained that the characters were too sketchily drawn, especially in comparison to Smilla. Unfamiliar with Høeg's earlier work, the American reviewers expected another thriller novel with the literary twists of *Frøken Smillas fornemmelse for sne.* Reviews appearing in *The Los Angeles Times Book Review, The New York Times Book Review, Newsweek, The New York Times,* and *The New Republic* warned Høeg's readers that they might be disappointed by his new novel. On the other hand, reviewers for *The New Statesman* and *The New Republic* praised the novel for its commentary on the Danish educational system and for the intellectual energy with which it was written.

The critical reception of *De måske egnede* in no way dampened enthusiasm for Høeg's next novel, *Kvinden og aben* (1996; translated as *The Woman and the Ape,* 1996). In fact, Danish readers and reviewers alike were eager for new work from their country's only contemporary author with a world-famous name. After the debate that surrounded Skyum-Nielsen's article—with its claim that Danish critics had overrated Høeg's previous book—many observers expected the critics to exercise caution in evaluating *Kvinden og aben.* Some critics already had

The Woman and the Ape

Peter Høeg

Translated by Barbara Haveland

Farrar. Straus and Giroux　　　New York

Title page for the U.S. edition of Høeg's 1996 novel, about a deranged scientist conducting experiments on an unusually intelligent ape

shifted to Skyum-Nielsen's opinion, which they defended in part because the popular success of Høeg's work caused them to doubt its literary quality. Høeg's popularity at home was perhaps most evident in the initial sales figures for *Kvinden og aben,* which had sold more than fifty-two thousand copies only three months after publication.

Kvinden og aben shares many similarities with *Frøken Smillas fornemmelse for sne.* Like his breakthrough novel, the main character in *Kvinden og aben* is a woman who, for the sake of a worthy cause, tracks down clues that lead to the discovery of a sinister plot. Whereas *Frøken Smillas fornemmelse for sne* begins with the death of a child and uncovers the corruption of a Danish corporation and the plot of a deranged scientist, *Kvinden og aben* begins with an ape, Erasmus, who has been caged and made the subject of scientific experiments. As the novel progresses, it reveals the full horror of animal rights violations and the depth of human greed, espe-

cially in the scientific community. Both novels are thrillers with broad philosophical themes. Like *Frøken smillas fornemmelse for sne, Kvinden og aben* starts out as a realistic novel, but by its conclusion the sense of reality in the novel has been greatly altered.

Madeline, the Danish-born heroine of the novel, lives in London with her husband, Adam, who is the head of the Institute of Animal Behavioral Research. Adam, however, is being groomed for a more prestigious position, the directorship of the London Zoo. When an unusual species of ape escapes from a shipping boat and is captured inside the city, Adam begins a series of experiments on the animal, discovering that it possesses extraordinary intelligence. Gathering as much data as possible from his experiments, Adam plans to present his findings to the scientific community with the hope of securing the position at the London Zoo. Madeline watches as her husband daily brings home laboratory equipment and takes it to the conservatory behind their home. One morning while Adam is away, Madeline goes into the conservatory and finds the ape. It looks her in the eyes and a bond forms between them.

Then begins Madeline's plan to free Erasmus. She has to overcome a drinking problem and face a world from which her aristocratic background has sheltered her for a lifetime. Little by little the novel breaks away from this realistic beginning. Erasmus, it turns out, truly is unusual. During their escape, surrounded by a crowd of people, Erasmus utters a perfectly intelligible sentence: "Så går vi" (Let's go). Then he lifts Madeline in his arms and climbs up a wall and away from the crowd. For the remainder of the novel, slightly less than half the book's length, the two remain together, becoming lovers. Madeline teaches Erasmus to speak both Danish and English.

Although the novel enjoyed favorable reviews in a few American publications, the majority of critics panned *The Woman and the Ape.* Perhaps the harshest treatment came from John Skow, who began his review for *Time* by stating, "Cynics may reflect: there is no forgiveness for the marvel who writes a brilliant, successful novel, one of those rare, resonant tales that every literate soul burns to read. On pain of universal outrage and derision, the marvel's next book and all succeeding ones must be even grander than the first, and, while precisely the same, also boldly and completely different." Skow then went on to sum up Høeg's career in the United States as one that began with great promise but led to disappointment, fairly crashing with his latest novel. Others who agreed with Skow faulted the novel for merely retelling such popular science-fiction tales as *King Kong* and *The Planet of the Apes.* Critics also charged the novel with being overly didactic, too concerned with its animal-rights theme. Reviewers who praised *The Woman and the Ape* pointed out that if readers approach the novel as a fable with a subversive ideology and overcome their conventional assumptions, then the book is both original and satisfying. Julia Glass of the *Chicago Tribune* praised Høeg for "persisting on an uncharted course in fiction, using science to elucidate character and add a new dimension to suspense."

Danish critics agreed with their American counterparts in saying that *Kvinden og aben* tended to preach a form of political correctness and that the author's concerns went beyond telling a good story, a charge that might find support in the fact that Høeg has donated the royalties from his book to a charitable foundation benefiting women and children in the developing world. Overall, however, Høeg received a warmer reception among Danish critics, many of whom praised the originality of the novel, command of language, sophistication, and composition. Unlike American critics, the Danes found the author's use of well-known science-fiction tales refreshing and congratulated Høeg for his successful mixture of philosophy, zoology, and the thriller genre.

By the end of the 1990s, Peter Høeg had five books to his credit. Although the assessment of his influence on contemporary Danish literature must be considered incomplete, his existing books have already raised the standards for other Danish writers. In terms of craft, linguistic ability, and scientific knowledge, he has made something new out of the novel. Perhaps most remarkably, however, Høeg has managed to draw a wide audience and his books have thus had success in the elite literary community as well as in the broader commercial market.

Interviews:

Martin Bagger, "Peter Høeg efter debutsforestillingen," *Bogens Verden,* 71 (1989): 197–199;

Sarah Lyall, "Fleeing Literary Limelight for Calm Obscurity," *New York Times,* 6 October 1993, pp. C15, C20;

Synne Rifbjerg, "Hvirvler i en strøm," *Weekendavisen,* 29 March – 2 April 1996, pp. 4–7;

Jes Stein Pedersen, "Film Must Speak to the Heart: A Conversation Between Peter Høeg and Bille August," in *Smilla's Sense of Snow: The Making of a Film by Bille August, Adapted from the Novel by Peter Høeg* (New York: Noonday Press, 1997), pp. 8–32.

References:

Lars Henrik Aagaard, "Peter Høeg and the Critical Apes," translated by W. Glyn Jones, *Danish Literary Magazine,* 10 (1996): 38–39;

Sara Danius, "I tukt och herrans förmaning," *Bonniers Littereara Magasin,* 64 (1995): 13–15;

Jette Eriksen-Benrós, "Hvem drømmer hvem?" *Horisant,* 40 (1993): 46–60;

Marianne Ping Huang, "Hugg och Høeg.Vart tog distansen vägen," *Bonniers Littereara Magasin,* 64 (1995): 23–24;

Bo G. Jansson, "En postmoderne undergangsvision," *Spring,* 7 (1994): 136–47;

Hans Henrik Møller, "Peter Høeg and the Sense of Writing," *Scandinavian Studies,* 69 (Winter 1997): 29–51;

Nader Mousavizadeh, "Strangers in Paradise," *New Republic,* 212 (3 April 1993): 39–41;

Mary Kay Norseng, "A House of Mourning: *Frøken Smillas fornemmelse for sne,*" *Scandinavian Studies,* 69 (Winter 1997): 52–84;

Erik Skyum-Nielsen, "Fripassageraren Høeg: Om-93 Års mest övervärderade bok," *Bonniers Littereara Magasin,* 64 (1995): 5–9;

Skyum-Nielsen, "Grälets Plats. En kommentar till Høeg-debatten," *Bonniers Littereara Magasin,* 64 (1995): 10–11;

Leif Zern, "Giss min gåta: Romanen som redovisar sin egen tolkning," *Bonniers Littereara Magasin,* 64 (1995): 20–22.

Per Højholt

(22 July 1928 –   )

Paul Norlén
University of Washington

BOOKS: *Hesten og solen: Digte* (Copenhagen: Wivel, 1949);

Skrift på vind og vand: Digte (Copenhagen: Schønberg, 1956);

Det ubestemte: Studier i præcision, graphics by Jørgen Brynjolf (Copenhagen: Strube, 1962);

Poetens hoved: Digte (Copenhagen: Schønberg, 1963)– includes "M/S Nelly i modlyd," translated by Nadia Christensen and Alexander Taylor as "M/S Nelly in Countersound"; "November," translated by Christensen, in *Contemporary Danish Poetry,* edited by Line Jensen and others (Copenhagen: Gyldendal / Boston: Twayne, 1977), pp. 194–195;

Provinser: Digte og fotografier (Copenhagen: Schønberg, 1964);

Min hånd 66 (Copenhagen: Schønberg, 1966)–includes "Udenfor," translated by Christensen as "Outside"; "Så og så mange lærker," translated by Christensen and Taylor as "So and so many larks"; "Et 5-finnet blad," translated by Poul Borum as "A 5-pinnate leaf"; "Poeten H," translated by Borum as "The Poet H"; "Frostnat," translated by Borum as "Frosty Night," in *Contemporary Danish Poetry,* edited by Jensen and others (Copenhagen: Gyldendal / Boston: Twayne, 1977), pp. 195–197;

Show (Copenhagen: Schønberg, 1966);

Cézannes metode (Copenhagen: Schønberg, 1967);

Turbo (Copenhagen: Schønberg, 1968)–includes "Turbo 4," translated by T. N., in *Contemporary Danish Poetry,* edited by Jensen and others (Copenhagen: Gyldendal / Boston: Twayne, 1977), pp. 198–199;

6512 (Copenhagen: Schønberg, 1969);

+1 (Copenhagen: Schønberg, 1969);

OG–en tekstantologi, by Højholt and Steffen Hjelskov Larsen (Copenhagen: Schønberg, 1971);

Punkter (Copenhagen: Schønberg, 1971);

Intethedens grimasser: Essays (Copenhagen: Schønberg, 1972);

Volumen (Copenhagen: Schønberg, 1974);

Per Højholt in June 1994 (photograph by Karin Munk; courtesy of Gyldendal Publishers)

Praksis, 1: Revolver (Copenhagen: Schønberg, 1977);

Praksis, 2: Groteskens område (Copenhagen: Schønberg, 1978);

Enhjørningens kvababbelser (Ringkøbing: Edition After Hand, 1979);

Praksis, 3: Den fireogtresindstyvende frokost i det grønne (Copenhagen: Schønberg, 1979);

Smerteskolen og andre digte (Århus: Jorinde & Joringel, 1979);

Gittes monologer og andre kvababbelser (Ringkøbing: Edition After Hand, 1981);

Praksis, 4: Lynmuseet og andre blindgyder (Copenhagen: Schønberg, 1982);

Praksis, 5: Nuet druknet i latter (Copenhagen: Schønberg, 1984);

Kvababbelser (Copenhagen: Schønberg, 1985);

Voldtag stilheden, illustrated by Poul Winther (Viby: Centrum, 1985);

Praksis, 6: Salamanderen og andre blindgyder (Copenhagen: Schønberg, 1986);

Praksis, 7: Hundekunstneren og andre blindgyder (Copenhagen: Schønberg, 1988);

Praksis, 8: Album, tumult (Copenhagen: Schønberg, 1989);

Praksis, 9: Det gentagnes musik (Copenhagen: Schønberg, 1989);

Praksis, 10: Manøvrer (Copenhagen: Schønberg, 1993);

Stenvaskeriet og andre stykker (Copenhagen: Gyldendal, 1994);

Praksis, 11: Lynskud (Copenhagen: Gyldendal, 1995);

Praksis, 12: Anekdoter (Copenhagen: Gyldendal, 1996).

Editions and Collections: *Digte 1963–79* (Copenhagen: Schønberg, 1982);

Gittes monologer: Samlet udgave (Copenhagen: Schønberg, 1984);

Det gentagnes musik, Manøvrer, Lynskud (Copenhagen: Gyldendal, 1998).

RADIO: *Lilys tur,* script by Højholt, Danmarks Radio, 28 & 30 April 1972;

Bestigning af en napoleonskage, script by Højholt, Danmarks Radio, 26 & 28 January 1973, 26 February 1975, 11 April 1981.

RECORDINGS: *Turbo: En space-fiction,* read by Højholt, Peter Christiansen, and Clemens Johansen, 1969;

Gittes monologer, read by Højholt, 1982;

Kvababbelser, read by Højholt, 1982;

Gittes nye og sidste monologer, read by Højholt, 1983.

OTHER: *Spurvens vilje om natur og digtning,* edited by Højholt, Vagn Lundbye, and Jens Smærup Sørensen (Viborg: Arkiv for Ny Litteratur / Copenhagen: Gyldendal, 1980);

Kafka 100 år–essays om Kafka, edited by Per Højholt (Århus: Sjakalen, 1983);

Mig Esbjerg: En antologi, edited by Højholt (Esbjerg: Esbjerg Kommune, 1992);

Kai Führer, *Kun døde fisk flyder med strømmen: Udvalgte billeder,* text by Højholt, Peter Laugesen, and Nicolaj Stochholm (Silkeborg: Silkeborg Kunstmuseum, 1996).

Per Højholt is one of the most influential and radically experimental poets of the post–World War II generation in Denmark. Højholt is difficult to categorize: to some in Denmark, he is known as a popular performer of humorous monologues; to others, as an esoterically modernist poet and essayist; and to still others, as an ironic (even postmodern) writer of short tales of the fantastic. In all his roles as poet, theorist, critic, performer, and prose writer, Højholt has inspired a younger generation of writers, not least in their struggle with the literary modernism that had become dominant by the 1950s and 1960s. Although the subject of several book-length studies as well as many articles in Danish, Højholt remains little known outside of Denmark and is relatively unknown even in the rest of Scandinavia, although some of his poems have been translated into English.

Per Højholt Jørgensen was born 22 July 1928 to Age Højholt Jørgenson and Ragna Thomsen in Esbjerg, a coastal town in southwest Jutland where his father, a talented teacher who was well liked by his students, was *viceinspektør* (assistant headmaster). In 1947 he took the *studentereksamen,* the qualifying examinations for university studies, and in 1951 completed training as a librarian. After a decade of working in various capacities at libraries in Copenhagen, Højholt was able to devote himself full time to writing, supported by a government artists' pension, awarded in 1964, and freelance work. In 1965 Højholt, his wife, Lone, and their daughter, Marie, returned to Jutland, where they have since resided in a renovated stable, situated in a small forest near the town of Silkeborg.

Højholt made his literary debut in 1949 with a poem in *Heretica,* a magazine closely identified with international literary modernism as represented by writers such as Stéphane Mallarmé, Rainer Maria Rilke, and T. S. Eliot. The same year Højholt's debut collection, *Hesten og solen: Digte* (The Horse and the Sun: Poems), appeared, and a second volume of poems, *Skrift på vind og vand: Digte* (Writing on Wind and Water: Poems) was published in 1956. These early works reflect the mood of "den vege yngling gammel før tiden" (the weak youth old before his time), a common stance in Danish poetry of the immediate postwar period, and Højholt pointedly did not include poems from these first two collections in the retrospective volume *Digte 1963–79* (Poems: 1963–79, 1982).

Højholt's next book of poetry, *Poetens hoved: Digte* (The Poet's Head: Poems, 1963), is generally regarded as his real breakthrough. The starkly depersonalized poems in this collection show a clear break with the first-person-centered lyricism of his earlier work. The title refers both to the poet himself (with his initials, PH) and to the Greek myth of Orpheus, the poet and singer whose music won him entry into the Under-world but who was later torn to pieces by a mob of angry women, and his severed head, still singing, then floated out to sea. Højholt alludes to this event in the title poem:

> Langt til havs gynger poetens hoved.
> Fader, din søn.
> Solen græsser i det vestlige led.
> Skyerne grønne som urter.

> (Far out to sea rocks the poet's head.
> Father, your son.
> The sun grazes in the western reach.
> The clouds green as herbs.)

Nils Egebæk has described Højholt's developing method in terms of its "anonymity," as the poet moves away from the first-person-centered lyric characteristic of modernism. Referring specifically to the poem "Spejlet" (The Mirror), in his *Primitivens paradoksale Kostume–Per Højholts for fatterskab: Et essay* (The Paradoxical Costume of Primitivity–on Per Højholt's Authorship: An Essay, 1986), Bo Hakon Jørgensen described the overall theme of this collection as an interplay between the "determined" reality of the words of the poem and an "undetermined" reality outside of language, that is, an attempt to describe what happens "when the world is taken up into language." A poem in *Poetens hoved* in which Højholt explicitly names this concern is "Mala," which begins "Mitt navn for stumhed, Mala, er Tatooga:" (My name for muteness, Mala, is Tatooga). Højholt also displays his strong interest in visual art, especially painting and sculpture, in *Poetens hoved,* as in the suite of poems, "Nødden fra l'estaque," in which the first-person voice is the French impressionist painter Paul Cézanne; *Poetens hoved* also shows Højholt's interest in music, especially jazz, as in the Miles Davis–inspired title, "Blue in Green."

The poems in *Min hånd 66* (My Hand 66, 1966) are even more explicitly concerned with language and with exploring linguistic situations, while the poet's sense of humor and his playfulness are more pronounced as well. The focus on language can be seen in titles such as "Livet til søs genstand for en strid om ord" (Life at sea condition for a war of words) or "Digtet Digtet Digtet" (The Poem The Poem The Poem) and in the form of a poem such as "Udenfor" (Outside), where sixteen lines, typographically justified to be of equal length visually, seem to make little sense until the reader comes to the last line: "vi begynder fra neden og arbejder os op men" (we start from the bottom and work our way up but). The instruction in the first line of the poem, "begynder franeden" (start from the bottom), is to be taken literally. Nature is often seen to be

looking back at the human observer in these poems; as in "Landskab med stor figur" (Landscape with Large Figure), where "sne stirrer ned fra bakkerne" (snow is staring down from the hills) or in the English-titled "Nature's Corner," which has the line "midt i naturens blik et strå ret op i sne" (midway in nature's glance a straw straight up in the snow). The poem as an experience of language-in-time is exemplified by "Så og så mange lærker" (So and so many larks), which begins "383 lærker er kommet 384 / birketræernes kroner syder (385) som balloner faktisk" (383 larks have arrived 384 / the crowns of the birch trees are seething (385) like balloons actually). Finally, the "poet" appears in "Poeten H" (The Poet H) and "Brøndbyøster som åndelig legemsdel" (Brøndbyøster as spiritual body part), not in the form of the Romantic or Symbolist poet but "og til sidst poeten H brugt som waterpas" (and finally the poet H used as a level) or "det / historiske Phoer ANNO 1928" (the / historical PH-er ANNO 1928)–Højholt was born in 1928.

Min hånd 66 is the first book that includes poems Højholt wrote after his move back to Jutland in 1965. The increased concern with nature in his poetry does not mean that nature is the object of the poem but rather that the poet makes use of an experience of nature by pursuing the consequences of that experience in his work, a notion explored more fully in his theoretical essay, *Cézannes metode* (Cézanne's Method, 1967). An anecdote provides a more personal perspective on the poet's intimate connection with the natural world. Prominent in the garden of Højholt's home are several colored, egg-shaped sculptures. When asked about their significance, Højholt's reply was that "I'm always looking at the garden, so I thought it ought to have something to look at too."

Published in 1967, *Cézannes metode* is an essay in ten sections, a reflection on the poetic practice in *Poetens hoved* and *Min hånd 66* in which the poet analyzes several of his own poems. The title refers to the painter Paul Cézanne and the desire expressed in his letters to paint as close as possible to "the color gray, which alone rules in nature." In corresponding terms, "intethed" (nothingness) or "det forskelsløse" (the formless, a term borrowed from the pre-Socratic philosopher Anaximander) cannot be represented in words; the poem is not "about" formlessness, rather it points toward or refers to it. Crucial to Højholt's poetry is the notion of interval: a poem exists in time, the time that it takes to read the poem. The experience of the poem is an opportunity for the reader to experience that he or she exists. Poetry is a medium for experience, not communication: "Digtet er ikke information" (The poem is not information). As Højholt writes at the end of *Cézannes metode,* "Man har ikke anden nytte af kunsten end man

TURBO

PER HØJHOLT

Cover for Højholt's 1968 book-length poem about the events of a single day: 18 March 1968

har fx af lugtesansen: den øger vores bevidsthed om at vi lever og er til som enestående væsener" (Art is of no more use than for example the sense of smell: it increases our awareness of the fact that we are alive and exist as unique beings).

In his *Primitivitetens paradoksale kostume–om Per Højholts forfatterskab,* Jørgensen identified three distinct "phases" in Højholt's work from 1963 to the early 1980s. Excluding Højholt's first two books, which belong to what Jørgensen called "phase zero," the first phase begins with *Poetens hoved,* while the second phase begins with *Show* (1966). A theoretical complement to this second phase can be found in *Intethedens grimasser: Essays* (Grimaces of Nothingness: Essays, 1972). As in *Cézannes metode,* in this book of essays Højholt looks back at, and in a sense sums up, his poetic practice in previous books.

Intethedens grimasser begins with an analysis of "show." While this concept includes the usual sense of the word (as in cabaret or nightclub acts, for example),

there are elements of "show" in diverse aspects of human and social existence. Crucial to "show" is that its nature is the successful fulfillment of audience expectations. What links "show" to writing is its nature of "interval": "Showet eksisterer som tid" (Show exists as time). In terms of writing, the "show" aspects of a text– what Højholt refers to elsewhere in the essay as "inferiøre egenskaber" (secondary qualities)–are those elements that destroy the production of meaning. Højholt does not, however, equate "show" and "art" but instead confronts the differing esthetics of the two. For Højholt, writing is a means to "holde vandet åbent" (keep the water open), that is, to widen the range of the reader's consciousness rather than to reproduce what is familiar and already known. As Jørgensen has observed, another mode of experience is suggested by directing the reader's attention to the qualities of "show" in the poem. Højholt's concept has links to both Søren Kierkegaard's notion of repetition and to the writings of Jacques Derrida in its complex interrelationship of text, writer, reader, and writing. In the final section, Højholt describes a movement in modernist poetry from "desperat baudelauresk fortvivlelse til Mallarmé'sk accept" (desperate Baudelairean doubt to Mallarméan acceptance), and after an analysis of two poems from *Poetens hoved,* he distances himself from that type of modernist poetic practice that "ikke kan destrueres med hvert værk" (cannot be destroyed with each work). Højholt's method is not to establish poetic ideals but rather to explore poetic practice.

Højholt's work in his "second phase" can be characterized as "sprogdigtning" (language poetry; poetry that highlights the visual, graphic, and linguistic elements of the poem as opposed to the communicative or meaningful aspects of the poem) or "systemdigtning" (systematic poetry), though Højholt does not adhere to any particular system. Every book, sometimes each new poem, has its own set of criteria. In the case of *Show,* the "poems" are groups of nonsense texts (or, in Højholt's terms, examples of language), "øjeblikke uden sammenhæng" (moments without context) with titles such as "Fire æg" (Four eggs) and "Seks B-æg" (Six B-eggs). The overall effect is to, in Egebæk's words, "konfrontere læseren med de sproglige mekanismer" (confront the reader with the mechanisms of language).

Turbo (Turbo, 1968) is regarded as a milestone both within Højholt's body of work and in Danish poetry in the 1960s. As the title suggests, this poem is a swirling dynamo of energy and movement, difficult to pin down, quote from, or analyze in the usual sense. It is reported by Jørgensen that during the writing of *Turbo* the author was listening to Jimi Hendrix's *Electric Ladyland* (1968). The poem takes the form of a letter: the cover for the original edition suggests an envelope, while the text refers to a "køkkenskriver" (kitchen writer) and is often suggestive of the sheer (even physical) pleasure of writing. The events recounted in the ten sections of the poem occur within the space of a single day, with the passing of 18 March 1968 seen "fra en døds øjne" (from a dead person's eyes). The reader may be reminded of the structure of James Joyce's novel *Ulysses* (1922), and many allusions to Danish and other literature are made in the text. The energetic movement of *Turbo* comes to a stop—though without "ending"—with a surrealistic image (and an open parenthesis), where "mælken fryser i sin karton" (the milk freezes in its carton).

An offshoot of *Turbo* is the poem *+1,* in which "show" functions in a different way. *+1* was published in 1969 in the form of a reproduction of the author's typescript. The first six pages show various graphic permutations of a single sentence, which happens to be the last line of *Turbo;* on the first page the two clauses of the sentence are typed over one another so as to be illegible.

A section of short poems called "punkter" (points) appeared at the end of the original edition of *Turbo.* These reappeared, augmented to a total of thirty-two pieces, in *Punkter* (Points, 1971). *Punkter* was originally published on transparent plastic pages with a ring binding. Without page numbers on the pieces, their order remains constant while the starting (and ending) point of the work is indeterminate. Four groups of poems can be discerned in this series, each at a distance of eight pages, or "points," from the next. The effect of viewing the book as a whole is that the text disappears into a gray mass, while two lines remain legible, one of which is the characteristically ambiguous "intet er nok" (nothing is enough). The layered effect of *Punkter* is in contrast to the linear motion of *Turbo,* while the poems themselves are more reflective and "transparent."

Another work where "show" predominates is *Volumen* (Volume, 1974), a collage of photographs, many taken from advertising and news media, and texts that mainly function graphically. Steffen Hejlskov Larsen has analyzed *Volumen* in detail in his essay in *Natur/retur: En bog om Per Højholts forfatterskab* (Nature/Return: A Book on Per Højholt's Authorship, 1984), where he points out that "sprog og billede refererer generelt ikke til hinanden i bogen" (language and image generally do not refer to each other in the book). Many of the images in the book can be seen to form a series; for example, photographs of the author with an egg in his mouth appear intermittently throughout. One block of text does appear by itself on a blank page, causing it to leap out at the reader/viewer. Significant for Højholt's method is that "PRAKSIS SKIFTER HELE TIDEN" (PRACTICE CHANGES ALL THE TIME). In *Volumen* Højholt attempts to show how meaning in general is created.

Many writers in the 1950s and 1960s wrote novels that stretched the boundaries of the genre or directly challenged its premises. Højholt's only "novel," *6512* (1969), is an example of this tendency and is, as Danish writer Jens Smærup Sørensen put it, *"sum negation og parodi"* (negation and a parody) of a novel, a parody especially of the novel or short story in diary form. The anonymous first-person narrator of *6512* has found a notebook in which he writes every day, with a self-imposed maximum of one page per day. On the back cover of the novel, Højholt is pictured pointing directly at the reader while the caption explains that this book "består af nogle blade som en eller anden har skrevet, jeg kender ham ikke, hans navn står ikke på bladene . . . Jeg har bare ordnet bladene og lavet en bog af dem" (consists of a few pages which someone or other has written, I don't know him, his name isn't on the pages . . . I have just arranged the pages and made a book of them). The responsibility for this book belongs to the reader: "Hvis De læser bogen er det Deres" (If you read this book it is yours). The narrator's entries are not arranged chronologically; instead, they appear in alphabetical order, based on the first word of the particular entry. Thus the first entry does not represent the "beginning" of the novel, nor is the last entry a conclusion. A more-or-less coherent narrative can be constructed by the reader, applying previously learned conventions of novel reading; but the narrator, on the other hand, seems completely innocent of literary conventions. He lives in an attic room of a house in exchange for a few household tasks and spends most days writing to pass the time or reading at the local library. He prefers to read poetry, because he can "laese langt over 30 sider vers på en halv time" (read way more than 30 pages of verse in a half hour). He also expresses an appreciation for the orderliness represented by alphabetization. Throughout *6512* the narrator's overconcern with details, obsession with bodily functions, and precarious circumstances contrast sharply with the novelist's concern with writing.

From 1969 to 1972, Højholt also was writing pieces for radio performance, including a 1969 radio version of *Turbo,* in collaboration with Peter Christiansen and Clemens Johansen, subtitled *En space-fiction* (A Space Fiction) and also released as a recording; the radio plays have not, however, been published in book form. Of these radio plays it can generally be said that they make use of intervals, silences, and various forms of play with the conventions of radio.

An indication of Højholt's growing reputation is that he was appointed to a position on a three-member commission responsible for the literary activities of the Statens Kunstfond (National Art Fund; roughly equivalent to the National Endowment for the Arts in the United States) from 1974 to 1977, a public service that limited his own creative activities. His next publication, *Praksis, 1: Revolver* (Practice, 1: Revolver, 1977), was the first in a series of volumes published by Højholt under the title *Praksis* (Practice). Each of the books in this series has the same simple format: thin, roughly fifty to seventy-five pages in length, chapbook-sized, with only the author's name and the title on the front cover, although the cover of each volume is a different color.

Some of the poems in *Revolver* are related to the "show" poems in earlier collections (several had previously appeared in *Volumen*), while Jørgensen has noted that other poems in the collection point toward the next two volumes in the *Praksis* series and foreshadow a third phase in Højholt's production. The poems in *Revolver* can be read in groups: a series of poems about a comic-book figure, "Supermules monologer" (Super Mule's

Højholt and translator Steven T. Murray of Fjord Press
(courtesy of Steven T. Murray)

Monologues) as Larsen calls them; poems about nature (but not "nature poetry"), as in "Den tydelige solsort" (The Obvious Blackbird); poems about writing and doubleness, an ongoing theme in Højholt's writing, as in "Broderen i Thailand" (The Brother in Thailand); and a series of first-person poems, such as "Kentaur" (Centaur).

Højholt's next publication, *Praksis, 2: Groteskens område* (Practice, 2: The Region of the Grotesque, 1978), can be seen as a summing up of his poetry from *Poetens hoved* and later. As Højholt points out in a footnote, the word *grotesque* is ultimately derived from the Greek root *kryptos,* meaning *crypt* or *concealed*—in Danish, *skjult,* which is a frequently occurring word in Højholt's writing. *Grotesque* specifically refers to a Roman ornamental style, rediscovered in the sixteenth century, of human and animal figures and stylized plants, wrapped around each other in seemingly random patterns. In the first group of poems, "KHEOPTERYX: Fantasmagorier" (CHEOPSTERYX: Phantasmagorias), Egyptian pyramids are the mask (or "grimace") for first-person musings on the "hard job" of being a pyramid; that is, the pyramids are striving upward, pointing toward the stars, with obvious parallels to the role of an author. The second section, "Stereotypier" (Stereotypes), includes two poems, "var resten" (was the rest), which Jørgensen calls one of the most beautiful "system" poems written in Danish, and "fra En dag med livet som det mindste onde" (from A Day with Life as the Lesser Evil), in which a man returns to his apartment to find everything estranged, in quotation marks, as it were. "Månens gestus: En Sophus Claussen-identification" (The Moon's Gesture: A Sophus Claussen identification) explicitly evokes Højholt's turn-of-the-century modernist predecessor and, as is pointed out in an endnote, refers specifically to Claussen's famous poem, "Mennesket og Digteren" (The Person and the Poet, 1917). The title section, written in the form of a monologue, is the longest in the book and includes an unusually explicit statement of the position of the poet: "Med ryggen til verden spiller jeg det ensomste spil i verden / . . . / Vender jeg mig om ser jeg verden med gåseøjne . . ." (With my back to the world I play the loneliest game in the world / . . . / If I turn around I see the world with goose eyes . . .). To look directly at the world is to see it with "gåseøjne"–that is, "in quotation marks."

After *Groteskens område* Højholt published primarily prose works over the next decade. *Praksis, 3: Den fireogtresindstyvende frokost i det grønne* (Practice, 3: The Sixty-fourth Lunch Outdoors, 1979) is a prose work with an unusual structure. The book begins with a long epigraph from the philosopher Georges Bataille, then sixty-three short sections follow in which four different narrative lines can be traced. The epigraph suggests that there is a fundamental difference between humans and animals: humans prepare food, while animals simply consume. It is the interval between food preparation and consumption that is crucial to human experience. The subtitle of *Praksis, 3* recalls the last poem in *Revolver,* "Frokost i det grønne," where a woman

> fører en lun tomat
> op til munden i samme sekund sekundet
> indstifter det sekund hvor teksten
> slår op og den umulige frokost
> alligevel fortsætter
> og allerede har fundet sted
>
> (conveys a warm tomato
> up to her mouth at the same moment the moment
> constitutes that moment where the text
> opens and the impossible luncheon
> still continues
> and already has taken place.)

This poem refers to Edouard Manet's famous painting *Déjeuner sur l'Herbe* (literally, "Lunch on the Grass"; Picnic Lunch, 1863), and in the thirteenth section of Højholt's book a reproduction of Manet's painting appears and is repeated twelve more times in the book. After section 45 a footnote-like commentary (printed in italics) on Manet's painting begins at the bottom of the page, gradually taking up more and more space on each successive page until page 66 and thereafter, when the commentary is the only text for the final nineteen pages. After this rather dry discussion in art history ends, the rest of the book (a further analysis of the painting and its theoretical implications) turns out to have been written by the Danish critic Per Aage Brandt, as the reader finds in a note at the end of the book.

Praksis, 5: Nuet druknet i latter (Practice, 5: The Present Drowned in Laughter, 1984) consists of five prose texts, including an analysis (thematically related to the third *Praksis* volume) of a painting by Arne Haugen Sørensen, part of an exhibition titled "Dyr og damer" (Animals and Ladies). The image of a creature biting a woman suggests the "animal" both within and without us, and the idea of woman as situated between nature and man. Two of the other texts in this book are also relevant to the themes of *Prakis, 3.* They are, as Højholt describes them, a kind of literary "ready-mades" (as in the French artist Marcel Duchamp, who took found objects, such as urinals, and made art out of them), both rewritten from existing texts dealing with bizarre personalities, namely medical journals and crime studies.

Over the years, Højholt has been active as a reviewer and cultural critic for regional publications such as *Jyllandsposten* as well as for journals and newspapers in Copenhagen. Soon after he relocated to Jutland in 1965, Højholt began giving occasional talks about his apparently difficult poetry. As Højholt has pointed out, these talks became an outlet for his pedagogical instincts, and they also involved a "show" aspect that Højholt began to develop more overtly in the 1970s. Højholt's sense of showmanship made itself apparent during an interview with a newspaper journalist, when Højholt suddenly stood up, walked to the window, and emptied out his teacup in an attempt (he said) to hit a blackbird. Such gestures suggest a performance aspect to Højholt's poetry that should not be overlooked.

In 1979 Højholt began publishing, and performing, occasional poems in a genre he calls "kvababbelser" (a nonsense word). Most of these pieces were commissioned for radio broadcast. A related series is "Gittes monologer" (Gitte's monologues), again written for the radio but also well received in many live performances all over Denmark during this period. The "kvababbelser" are topical, satirical poems, while "Gittes monologer" are the musings of a young married woman from the Århus area of Jutland, addressed to her friend, Susanna, but often referring to her husband, Preben. In her monologues, Gitte discusses such diverse topics as freedom, social democracy, the Alps, and gardening, in her characteristic Jutland dialect and with an oblique relationship between the often abstract subjects of the monologues and her commonsense take on them.

With "Gittes monologer" Højholt demonstrated his command of an oral, popular style and became a nationally known figure. Despite the popularity of this series—or perhaps because of its popularity—Højholt wrote the last of these monologues in 1983. In "Gittes monologer" Højholt plays with conventional, "common sense" uses of language, and their success with the public meant that Gitte, and her monologues, were themselves becoming a new "convention" to be superseded.

A new phase of Højholt's production began in the early 1980s with the short, fantastic tales that Højholt calls "blindgyder" ("dead ends" or "blind alleys") and which comprise three volumes of the *Praksis* series (numbers 4, 6, and 7). Højholt openly acknowledges his debt to literary forebears such as Edgar Allan Poe, Jorge Luis Borges, and Karen Blixen (Isak Dinesen). The title story of Højholt's first collection of "blindgyder," *Praksis, 4: Lynmuseet og andre blindgyder* (Practice, 4: The Lightning Museum and Other Dead Ends, 1982), is an example of what Tzvetan Todorov called the fantastic in literature. In Todorov's analysis, the fantastic depends primarily on a delay or hesitation between rational explanation and an acceptance of the unexplainable. "Lynmuseet" (The Lightning Museum) begins with a discussion of the discovery of electricity in the eighteenth century and of the continued, esoteric attempts to harness the principle of lightning. In 1920 a society of English eccentrics dedicated to such pursuits sent 186 "såkaldte isolatorer" (so-called isolators) to members in various parts of Europe, including a Danish machinist and amateur poet, Willy Lund, who sets up six of the isolators in his workshop. In 1949 he discovers that the isolators are warm (the Society, however, is long-since defunct); by 1956 they are giving off enough heat that he can be in the workshop year-round. In 1963 he observes first the sudden appearance of a stainless steel spoon, then the appearance of a complete clothes iron. (The years mentioned correspond to the publication dates of Højholt's first three books.) Now retired, Lund spends most of his time observing these spontaneous

processes. At this point the narrator (who closely resembles Højholt) describes a meeting with Lund in his home. The workshop is now filled with objects, "lutter trivielle ting" (nothing but trivial things), created in a process that Lund compares to popping corn in a frying pan. The workshop is, however, so hot that the narrator cannot stay to actually observe the process, and a few months later he reads of Lund's death in an explosion in the workshop. The "blindgyder" are written in a matter-of-fact tone that belies Højholt's concern with the inexplicable nature of creativity.

In 1988 a collection of writings in honor of Højholt's birthday was published under the title *Rocky Mountains: Festskrift til Per Højholts 60 års dag 22.7.1988* (Rocky Mountains: Festschrift for Per Højholt's Sixtieth Birthday, 22.7.1988). The photograph on the front cover of the festschrift, a snow-covered peak against a deep blue sky, is that used on packs of Rocky Mountains, a popular brand of cigarettes in Denmark. Contributors included many of Denmark's best-known writers, scholars, and critics. While some of the essays included analyze Højholt's work, many of the contributions show the most sincere form of flattery by writing in styles obviously inspired by Højholt, especially imitating his "blindgyder."

Højholt returned to poetry with *Praksis, 8: Album, tumult* (Practice, 8: Album, Tumult, 1989), a series of fifty-nine prose poems, some of which were written to accompany drawings by the artist Poul Winther and had previously been published in *Voldtag stilheden* (Rape the Silence, 1985). Højholt's next three books, *Praksis, 9: Det gentagnes musik* (Practice, 9: The Music of the Reiterated, 1989), *Praksis, 10: Manøvrer* (Practice, 10: Maneuvers, 1993), and *Praksis, 11: Lynskud* (Practice, 11: Lightning Bolts, 1995), resemble each other in many ways (and in fact were republished by Gyldendal as a single volume in 1998). In these collections Højholt seems to return to earlier concerns but in the sense that exact "repetition" is never possible. The "doubleness" of the lyrical "I" seen in books such as *Revolver* is attenuated, most pointedly perhaps in "Dobbeltgængerens død" (Death of the Doppelgänger). The poem "Bruce Springsteen" is not only an indication of Højholt's love of popular music but also an improvisation on the first verse of the American rock star's hit song "Thunder Road" (1975). Højholt is a writer acutely aware of writing in a tradition that includes not only Danish writers such as Johannes Ewald and Steen Steensen Blicher but also modernists such as Jorge Luis Borges and Federico Garcia Lorca. Several poems in these three collections pay a kind of hom-

age to various predecessors, with titles such as "&
Borges" and "& Lorca," where the ampersand suggests the link with Højholt's own writing. As in
Højholt's "blindgyder," such homage can at times
approach parody.

In *Praksis, 12: Anekdoter* (Practice, 12: Anecdotes, 1996) Højholt puts his characteristic mark on
a seemingly trivial genre, the anecdote. Several of the
pieces, such as "Guds ånde" (The Spirit of God),
recall Højholt's "blindgyder," while others draw on personal experience, though without the narrative context
of conventional autobiography.

Højholt has received many awards, including the
Grand Prize of Det Danske Akademi (The Danish
Academy) in 1982 and the Holberg Medal from the
Danish Writers' Union in 1997. Højholt's essays, arti-
cles, and reviews from a period of almost thirty years
have been collected and published under the title *Sten-
vaskeriet og andre stykker* (The Stone Laundry and Other
Pieces, 1994).

When asked if he ever traveled, Højholt replied
that he had been to Hamburg, once. "The Danish language is my work and my life, so I don't need to go
anywhere." Rooted in the Danish province of Jutland,
but part of an international poetic tradition, Højholt's
writings are, as Carsten Madsen has noted, "utvivlsomt
noget af det væsentligste, der skrives i samtiden"
(undoubtedly some of the most essential being written
in our time).

Interviews:
Iben Holk, "En tur i naturen: Samtale med Per Højholt" in *Natur/retur: En bog om Per Højholts forfatterskab,* edited by Holk (Odense: Centrum, 1984),
 pp. 215–284;
Lars Johansson, *Udsatte egne—det er mig: Samtaler med Per
 Højholt* (Valby: Borgen, 1998).

References:
Niels Egebak, *Højholts metode* (Copenhagen: Schønberg,
 1974);
Iben Holk, ed., *Natur/retur: En bog om Per Højholts forfatter-
 skab* (Odense: Centrum, 1984);
Bo Hakon Jørgensen, "Opspring fra nulhuller: Om Per
 Højholts forfatterskab," in *Danske digtere i det 20
 århundrede,* third edition, 5 volumes, edited by
 Torben Brostrøm and Mette Winge (Copenhagen: Gad, 1982), pp. 169–183;
Jørgensen, *Primitivitetens paradoksale kostume—om Per Højholts forfatterskab: Et essay* (Odense: Odense University Press, 1986);
Jørgensen, Erik Skyum-Nielsen, Harly Sonne, Pia Tafdrup, and Søren Ulrik Thomsen, eds., *Rocky
 Mountains: Festskrift til Per Højholts 60 års dag
 22.7.1988* (Copenhagen: Schønberg, 1988);
Finn Stein Larsen, "Per Højholt: Af *Turbo,*" in *Prosaens
 mønstre* (Copenhagen: Berlingske Forlag, 1971),
 pp. 175–196;
Steffan Hejlskov Larsen, "Forskellene på forskellene,"
 in *Natur/return: En bog om Per Højholts forfatterskab,*
 edited by Holk (Odense: Centrum, 1984), pp.
 120–142;
Anne-Marie Mai, "En hånd til læseren: Per Højholt *Min
 hånd 66,*" in *Læsninger i dansk litteratur,* volume 5,
 edited by Povl Schmidt and others (Odense:
 Odense University Press, 1997), pp. 229–247;
Johan Rosdahl, ed., *Jeg vil ikke stå i vejen for kaos: Per
 Højholts forfatterskab* (Copenhagen: Munksgaard,
 1998);
Jens Smærup Sørensen, "Dogene går ikke uden videre,"
 in *Natur/retur: En bog om Per Højholts forfatterskab,*
 edited by Holk (Odense: Centrum, 1984), pp.
 94–100.

Jørgen-Frantz Jacobsen
(29 November 1900 – 24 March 1938)

W. Glyn Jones
University of East Anglia

BOOKS: *Danmark og Færøerne,* Kultur og Videnskab, no. 25 (Copenhagen: V. Pio, 1927);

Færøerne: Natur og Folk, English chapter summaries by T. King (Tórshavn: H. N. Jacobsens Bókahandils forlag, 1936);

Barbara: Roman (Copenhagen: Gyldendal, 1939); translated by Estrid Bannister as *Barbara* (Harmondsworth, U. K.: Penguin, 1948);

Nordiske Kroniker, edited by Christian Matras (Copenhagen: Gyldendal, 1943).

Edition in English: *Barbara,* translated by George Johnston (Norwich, U.K.: Norvik Press, 1993).

Jørgen-Frantz Jacobsen occupies a distinct place in Scandinavian literature. He is the only Faroese writer to achieve international best-seller status. This status derives from his sole novel, *Barbara: Roman* (1939; translated, 1948), which has the added cachet of being one of the few Scandinavian novels to be translated twice into English within the space of fifty years. It was also adapted as a motion picture directed by Nils Malmros in 1997. These facts, together with Jacobsen's essays, a study of the Faroe Islands published in the guise of a travel guide, and a volume of his letters, are sufficient to suggest that had he lived longer, he would have been one of the outstanding literary figures in Scandinavia in the twentieth century. He must moreover be seen in the context of his being one of five Faroese writers, all born between 1900 and 1903, who represent a remarkable blossoming of literature in a country which had no tradition of literature in a modern sense. Jacobsen, together with William Heinesen, Christian Matras, Heðin Brú, and Martin Joensen, created modern Faroese literature, whether writing in Danish, as did Jacobsen and Heinesen, or Faroese, as did the others.

Jørgen-Frantz Jacobsen was born 29 November 1900 in Tórshavn. His father, the merchant Martin Meinhardt Jacobsen, had Faroese, Swedish, and Danish blood in his veins and, having been born and spent his childhood in Copenhagen, was mainly Danish speaking. His mother, Maren Frederikke Mikkelsen was thor-

Jørgen-Frantz Jacobsen

oughly Faroese. Their home was thus bilingual, and, according to Heinesen, a distant relative, Jørgen-Frantz spoke Danish to his father and Faroese to his mother and siblings. In general, their extended family was interested in music and theater, and Jørgen-Frantz thus grew up in a highly cultured environment.

He first went to school in Tórshavn, where he took his middle-school examination. He began attending Sorø Academy in Denmark in 1916. His father died the following year, but Jacobsen continued his studies, passing his final examination and leaving school in

1919. Armed with this degree, he went to the University of Copenhagen to study history and French, but in 1922 he developed tuberculosis, and ill health prevented him from finishing his studies until 1932. After graduation he worked for two years as a journalist on the newspaper *Politiken*. He gave up journalism in 1934 in order to write a history of the Greenland monopoly—a work that he never finished, in large part because of continued ill health.

In 1927 Jacobsen was asked by representatives of the Faroese Students' Association to write a study of the relationship between the Faroe Islands and Denmark. The result was *Danmark og Færøerne* (Denmark and the Faroe Islands, 1927) a competent and well-written study that first examines the historical relationship between the two countries and then the cultural awakening of the Faroe Islands, with brief summaries of the works of the main figures concerned, finishing with a review of present-day relations between the two countries. Here, as elsewhere in his writings, he stresses the fact that the Faroese are not Danes, that their cultures and temperaments are quite different. Without being openly anti-Danish, he clearly reveals himself as an ardent Faroese nationalist.

His Faroese sympathies are also evident in his 1936 publication *Færøerne: Natur og Folk* (The Faroes: Nature and People), a warm, fond, and poetical presentation of the Faroe Islands, their scenery, their way of life, their history, their constitution, and their links with Denmark. The final section is a tour of the islands with a brief entry on each of the eighteen inhabited islands. The literary qualities of this book are emphasized in the entry in *Dansk Biografisk Leksikon* from 1937, which reads that the volume "er anlagt som en grundig Vejleder for rejsende, men samtid skrevet med en Kærlighed til Stoffet, der hæver Bogen op over Genren og gør den til en Digters Værk" (is in the form of a thorough guide for travelers, but at the same time written with a love of the material that raises the book above the genre and turns it into the work of a poet).

In 1943 Christian Matras collected and published a volume of Jacobsen's newspaper articles under the title of *Nordiske Kroniker* (Nordic Chronicles). Originally published between 1925 and 1937, the articles cover a wide range of topics, some of which are related to those in *Danmark og Færøerne,* while others have a wider cultural interest, as for instance the essay on the Faroese dance. The term "Nordic" is to be understood in a wide sense, including not only mainland Scandinavia and Iceland, but also Scotland. In these articles Jacobsen discusses the extinction of the Norse language of the Shetland Islands and examines the nature of Faroese as an independent language, ridiculing the suggestion that it is really only a dialect; in another essay, "Den yderste

Kyst" (The Farthest Shore), he produces an outstandingly beautiful and poetical description of the outlying island of Mykines.

Det dyrebare Liv: Jørgen-Frantz Jacobsen i Strejflys af hans Breve (Precious Life: Jørgen-Frantz Jacobsen Illuminated by his Letters, 1958), edited by Heinesen, is an example of the way in which Jacobsen's close friends and contemporaries ensured his survival as a writer. It consists of letters that Jacobsen wrote to Heinesen between 1921 and his death in 1938. They are accompanied by a succinct commentary by Heinesen sufficient to string them together, but not such as in any way to turn this into a scholarly, academic edition of the letters. It is ultimately a deeply personal and poetical work, but nevertheless a work of vital importance to an understanding of Jacobsen and his sole novel. In his introduction, Heinesen makes it clear that this is only a small selection of letters, which in total fill some 1,500 pages, and that it is, strictly speaking, not an autobiography. There is no attempt to follow Jacobsen's life day by day, but rather to give a series of momentary impressions of his life and opinions both as a young student and as a mature man marked by the tuberculosis that was to lead to his early death. It is not intended to idealize Jacobsen, but to show his incredible optimism and love of the life that he must surely at an early stage have been aware he was to leave before long. In the words of Heinesen in the introduction:

> Det udvalg af Jørgen-Frantz Jacobsens breve, der bringes her—for det meste i uddrag, nogle dog in extenso—handler hovedsagelig om brevskriveren selv, om betydningsfulde tildragelser i hans liv, og om det sind, hvormed han møder denne sin *skæbne.*

> (The selection of Jørgen-Frantz Jacobsen's letters here presented—mainly in the form of excerpts, though some in extenso—is principally about the letter-writer himself, the significant events in his life, and the mental qualities with which he meets this his *fate*).

In addition, the letters demonstrate Jacobsen's unswerving sense of style, his linguistic inventiveness, and give the reader insight into the background to the novel *Barbara* and the close relationship between Jacobsen and Heinesen, which a comparison of these letters with Heinesen's own writing suggests had a profound literary as well as personal significance. One is, in fact, at times left with a feeling that these letters contain clues to a literary affinity of a special kind between two friends who had many stylistic traits in common.

The selection opens with the "Nytårsouverture"(New Year's Overture), marking the start of 1921 in a grand, dithyrambic prose poem divided into sections with musical markings: Maestoso, Grave,

Andante, and so on, and describing the writer's experience of the Faroe Islands–which are at the center of everything he wrote–at the beginning of 1921. There is then a gap until mid 1922, when there follows, in a completely different vein, a lengthy, humorous account of French student life in Grenoble, in which Jacobsen shows his skill at instant characterization. Yet, even Grenoble is constantly compared with Tórshavn: the sunrise, the grass on the bastion, the mist-covered mountaintops–all of these images give the reader a sense of the author's homesickness. The following section consists of letters written at the end of 1922 and beginning of 1923, by which time Jacobsen had been diagnosed as suffering from tuberculosis. They are as good-humored as the earlier ones and express for the first time Jacobsen's remarkably positive acceptance of what life sent him:

> Jeg mener, at enhver må glæde sig over sin skæbne, over at han overhovedet har levet og fået en skæbne. Skæbnen er det eneste sikre aktiv.
>
> Mennesker fødes og får livets gave. Livet giver de ud og får det ind igen i møntet guld, i skæbne. Giv livet ud og du tager skæbne ind igen. "Evigt ejes kun det tabte"–evigt ejes kun skæbnerne.

> (I believe that everyone must rejoice in his destiny, in the fact that he has lived at all and achieved a destiny. Destiny is the only sure asset.
>
> People are born and receive the gift of life. They distribute life and they receive it again in stamped gold, in destiny. Distribute life and you take in fate in exchange. "Only what is lost is owned eternally"–only fates are owned eternally.)

In the letters, momentary impressions are balanced against long, poetic epistles such as a nearly eight-page atmospheric description of the streams around Tórshavn that is more in the nature of an essay than a letter and which was actually dedicated to Heinesen's eldest son. Jacobsen also reflects on the qualities of writers such as Sigrid Undset, whose work gives her a unique position in Scandinavian literature, as Jacobsen notes, "der ellers, hvor udmærket den end kan være, oftest kun er skrevet for et snævert publikum . . ." (which otherwise, excellent as it might be, is mostly written for a narrow public . . .).

Inevitably, in the letters Jacobsen becomes increasingly concerned with his lengthy stays in the hospital, his operations, and his sickness, but he writes with humor and without a trace of self-pity. His love of life and his acceptance of his own fate dominate all. It was in the midst of his sickness that he wrote his novel, *Barbara,* while suffering from the fickleness of his lover, Estrid Bannister, and the collection provides a letter-by-letter account of the writing of the novel, ending in his

last letter with the statement that three chapters still wait to be written. Of the intended contents of those chapters, he gives no hint, though he does state clearly that the novel is based on "the great human theme of Vanity"–and later develops this theme irrespective of the novel:

> Livet er i sin storladne og paradoksale mangfoldighed så lunefuldt, at man gør vel i at spørge sig selv om man egentlig bør tage det helt alvorligt! . . . Min egen livsfølelse er også af en paradoksal art. Thi samtidig med at jeg elsker livet og næsten daglig–selv nu–nyder dets mangefarvede dråber, så folder jeg dog hænderne og sukker lykkeligt: Hvad er det dog alt.

> (Life in its grandiose and paradoxical manifoldness is so capricious that one does well to ask oneself if one should take it entirely seriously! . . . My own way of realizing myself is also paradoxical in nature. For at the same time as I love life and almost every day–even now–enjoy its many-colored droplets, I nevertheless fold my hands and happily sigh: What is it at best.)

Later Jacobsen writes:

> Det er jo netop den vældige spænding mellem sorrig og glæde, der gør livet *stort*. . . . Mine største øjeblikke har jeg haft når gnisterne er sprunget mellem sorrig og glæde. Og døden er i grunden livets geniale relief. . . . Livet er stort og dæmonisk, værd at elske og lyde. Og det allerstørste i livet er igen resignationen.

> (It is precisely the enormous tension between sorrow and joy that makes life *great*. . . . I have had my greatest moments when the sparks have flown between sorrow and joy. And death is fundamentally the brilliant relief to life. . . . Life is great and demonic, worthy of being loved and obeyed. And the greatest thing in life is again resignation.)

These themes are fundamental to the novel *Barbara*. It is, however, worth noting that Jacobsen at one time considered giving the novel the title "Far, verden, Far Vel!" (Farewell, World, Farewell), the first line of the great Danish Baroque poet Thomas Kingo's poem on vanity that forms the central theme of the episode in the church in the novel.

Vanity in all its senses is the essence of *Barbara:* the vanity that comes with office, power, or beauty; and the vanity of action, the questioning of whether there is a meaning in life, or whether all action is not in vain, with everything the result of fate. There is also the examination of total infatuation on the part of the principal male character, Pastor Poul, alongside the beautiful, fascinating, and mercurial Barbara, whose feelings for Poul are genuine, but who cannot resist the charms

Front cover of Jacobsen's 1939 novel, which is set in the Faroe Islands during the eighteenth century

of other men, insisting all the time that her feelings for Poul are unchanged.

The action is simple, even predictable. The aptly named ship *Fortuna* arrives in Tórshavn, bringing Poul, the new pastor for the parish of Vágar, and the populace has gathered for the event. Among them is Barbara, the widow of two former pastors for whose untimely deaths she is blamed by many. Pastor Poul is warned about her but falls for her charms, despite the fact that when three French ships come to port she follows the example of most of the other women in the town and allows herself to be seduced by a French sailor. As the widow of the parish, she has a house of her own on Vágar, and she and Poul leave for their respective homes there. Inevitably, they marry, but when in Tórshavn on a subsequent visit, Barbara meets and falls for the foppish Andreas Heyde (the instrument of fate in the second half of the novel), on a research trip from Copenhagen. Poul persuades Barbara to leave with him; however, when Christmas approaches he feels duty-bound to visit the outlying island of Mykines,

despite Barbara's entreaties that he not do so. Andreas has now arrived nearby to spend Christmas at the home of the chief magistrate of the island. Despite his misgivings, Poul answers the call of duty, hoping to return almost immediately, but he is delayed by the weather for eleven days, and on his return he discovers that Barbara has left for Tórshavn with Andreas. Andreas is finally persuaded by his uncle, Johan Hendrik, to leave for Copenhagen, without Barbara, and she makes a desperate and futile attempt to reach his ship, once more the *Fortuna,* as it leaves. When she returns, exhausted, she is greeted by the people of Tórshavn in a mock repetition of the first scene in the book, to the words of her jealous cousin, Gabriel, who has meanwhile been forced into an unwelcome but advantageous marriage: "Hi, hi, nu tror jeg faneme . . . at Glansen endelig en Gang er gaaet af Sankte Gertrud. Nu er hun saagu færdig, den Mær!" (He he, now I think, the devil eat me . . . that the shine has at last gone off Saint Gertrude. Now she is finished, by God, the bitch!)

It is not clear whether Gabriel is right. Barbara has weathered storms before. But this is as far as Jacobsen wrote before succumbing to his tuberculosis. When Heinesen and Matras undertook to have the manuscript published, they came to the conclusion that this open ending was in fact a fitting way of finishing the novel, although a few gaps in the writing were filled in by Heinesen. That they were right to leave the ending open is demonstrated by the general dissatisfaction felt by viewers to the sentimentalized ending of the 1997 motion-picture adaptation, in which it appears that Barbara actually makes the ship and sails off to Copenhagen.

Barbara is a bewildering personality who possesses a special charm of her own along with a total lack of moral sense. She is incapable of withstanding her erotic urges, and her only resort is to flee temptation. On repeated occasions, Poul—a pitiful figure at times— has to accept this, and he is in no doubt as to his own position. As soon as Andreas appears and delights the assembled company, Poul knows he is doomed:

[Barbara] var i dette Øjeblik hans Fjende, det følte han. Det vilde være en haabløs Gerning at gaa op til hende og søge at lokke hende bort fra dette Sted. Han var uden Magt over hende, hun gjorde i et og alt, hvad hun selv vilde. Hun var en kat, hun var frygtelig. . . . Han tiltaltes af Glansen i hans [Andreas'] væsen. Og samtidig vidste han, at dette betød hans egen Ruin.

Det uundgaaelige var nu ganske nær.

([Barbara] was at that moment his enemy, he could feel it. It would be a hopeless undertaking to go up to her and try to lure her away from this place. He had no power over her; in everything she did exactly as she pleased. She was a cat, she was frightful. . . . He was attracted by the brightness of his [Andreas'] presence. But at the same time he knew that it betokened the end for him.

The inevitable was about to happen.)

He is doomed, and he always has been doomed, as is suggested when, on the way to Vágar for the first time, Pastor Poul is told the story of an earlier pastor who outwitted an attempt by two elfin women to seduce him in an enchanted mound. The parallel between this story and Pastor Poul's going to Vágar with Barbara is obvious, but he is not wise enough to escape.

Jacobsen was an historian by training; he was extremely well versed in Faroese history and understood Faroese society, and the novel thus has scene after scene in which the reader is presented with a vibrant portrayal of the mid-eighteenth-century Faroe Islands, descriptions of dress, furnishings, and customs. All of the characters are said to be recognizable portraits of actual historical people. Most are not readily identifiable, but the character of Andreas Heyde is clearly based on J. C. Svabo, who did, in fact, as is noted in Jacobsen's first work, *Danmark og Færøerne,* undertake a study of the Faroese economy in the late eighteenth century, only slightly later than the setting for this novel.

The principal character in the novel, Barbara, is based upon Jacobsen's lover, Estrid, who was also the translator of the first English version of the book. Many passages in *Det dyrebare Liv* refer to the title character of the novel, though it is nowhere directly revealed that she and Estrid were the same. However, Estrid was the Barbara of the novel and by the time *Det dyrebare Liv* was published, the identity of the two was common knowledge. It is worth noting that Jacobsen once remarked that he had tried to fashion Pastor Poul after himself.

Jørgen-Frantz Jacobsen died 24 March 1938, after suffering from tuberculosis for nearly sixteen years. His position in Scandinavian literature is unlike that of any other; much of what has been published results from the decision by Christian Matras and William Heinesen to preserve his memory. The one novel on which his reputation rests is unfinished and yet could scarcely have been finished more successfully, and this incomplete work has had enormous sales both in Scandinavia and beyond, standing as a milestone in twentieth-century Scandinavian fiction.

Letters:

Det dyrebare Liv: Jørgen-Frantz Jacobsen i Strejflys af hans Breve, edited by William Heinesen (Copenhagen: Gyldendal, 1958).

References:

Hedin Brønner, *Three Faroese Novelists: An Appreciation of Jørgen-Frantz Jacobsen, William Heinesen and Heðin Brú* (New York: Twayne, 1973), pp. 21–37;

Bo Elbrønd-Bek, "Jørgen-Frantz Jacobsen—mellem tradition og modernitet," *Bogens verden,* 68, no. 2 (1986): 54–56;

William Heinesen, "Jørgen-Frantz Jacobsen," in *Danske digtere i det 20. århundrede,* second edition, 3 volumes, edited by Frederik Nielsen and Ole Restrup (Copenhagen: Gad, 1966), II: 611–624;

Karsten Hoydal, "Jørgen-Frantz Jacobsen," *Varðin,* 47 (1980): 248–260;

Anna Catrina Jacobsen, "Jørgen-Frantz Jacobsen," *Varðin,* 57 (1990): 113–121;

Ole Jacobsen, "Jørgen-Frantz Jacobsen" in *Danske digtere i det 20. århundrede,* revised edition, 2 volumes, edited by Ernst Frandsen and Niels Kaas Johansen (Copenhagen: Gad, 1955), II: 283–289;

W. Glyn Jones, "Duality and Dualism: Jørgen-Frantz Jacobsen Reassessed," *Scandinavica,* 27 (November 1988): 133–151;

Christian Matras, "Jørgen-Frantz Jacobsen," in his *Den yderste Kyst,* Gyldendals Julebog, 1941 (Copenhagen: Gyldendal, 1941), pp. 8–35;

Kristian Mørk, "Om Jørgen-Frantz Jacobsens 'Barbara,'" *Spring,* 11 (1997): 16–30;

Hanne Flohr Sørensen, "Det begyndte som leg: William Heinesens og Jørgen-Frantz Jacobsens brevveksling," *Danske Studier,* 87 (1992): 59–91.

Frank Jæger

(19 June 1926 – 4 July 1977)

Frank Hugus
University of Massachusetts

BOOKS: *Dydige digte* (Copenhagen: Wivel, 1948);

Morgenens trompet (Copenhagen: Wivel, 1949);

Iners (Copenhagen: Wivel, 1950);

De 5 aarstider (Copenhagen, 1950);

Hverdagshistorier (Copenhagen: Wivel, 1951)–includes "Narren," translated by Frank Hugus as "The Fool," *Northwest Review,* 26, no. 1 (1988): 82–85;

Tune–Det første aar, illustrated by Ib Spang Olsen (Copenhagen: H. Branner, 1951);

Den unge Jægers lidelser (Copenhagen: Wivel, 1953)–includes "En sommer," translated by Hugus as "One Summer," *Mundus Artium,* 14, no. 2 (1984): 98–103; "Djævelens instrument," translated by Paula Hostrup-Jessen as "The Devil's Instrument," in *The Devil's Instrument, and Other Danish Stories,* edited by Sven Holm (London: Owen, 1971);

Tyren (Copenhagen: Wivel, 1953);

19 Jægerviser, edited by Tony Vejslev (Copenhagen: Wivel, 1953);

Jomfruen fra Orléans, Jeanne d'Arc (Copenhagen: Aschehoug, 1955);

Havkarlens sange (Copenhagen: Gyldendal, 1956);

Kapellanen og andre fortællinnger (Copenhagen: Gyldendal, 1957)–includes "Foraarsaften med Faust," translated by Hugus as "Spring Evening with Faust," *Prairie Schooner,* 62, no. 3 (1988): 3–18;

Velkommen, vinter (Copenhagen: Gyldendal, 1958);

Cinna og andre digte (Copenhagen: Gyldendal, 1959);

Seks Sidenius-digte (Copenhagen, 1959);

Hvilket postbud–en Due: Hørespil (Copenhagen: Gyldendal, 1959);

Sommer: Novelle (Copenhagen: Dansk Kautionsforsikring, 1959);

Pastorale–Pelsen: To radiospil (Copenhagen: Gyldendal, 1965);

Drømmen om en sommerdag og andre essays (Copenhagen: Gyldendal, 1965);

Danskere: Tre fortællinger af fædrelandets historie (Copenhagen: Gyldendal, 1966);

Idylia: Digte (Copenhagen: Gyldendal, 1967);

Frank Jæger (photograph by Palle Jæger; courtesy of Gyldendal Publishers)

Naive rejser: Essays (Copenhagen: Gyldendal, 1968);

Alvilda: Sengelæsning for unge og gamle (Copenhagen: Gyldendal, 1969)–includes "Værelse i gavlen," translated by Hugus as "A Room in the Gable," *Mid-American Review,* 9, no. 1 (1989): 150–160;

Hjemkomst, by Jæger and others, illustrated by Ib Spang Olsen (Copenhagen: Selskabet Bogvennerne, 1969);

Døden i Skoven; Sidste Sommer; Tulte (Copenhagen: Gyldendal, 1970);

Staa op og tænd ild, illustrated by Oluf Høst (Copenhagen: Arbejdernes Oplysningsforbund, 1971);

Provinser (Copenhagen: Gyldendal, 1972);

S (Copenhagen: Mistral, 1973);

Udsigt til Kronborg: Sengelæsning (Copenhagen: Gyldendal, 1976);

Miraklernes bog: Kasserede digte, edited by Thorkild Bjørnvig (Copenhagen: Gyldendal, 1977).

Editions and Collections: *Digte 1948–50: Dydige digte, Morgenens trompet, De fem aarstider* (Copenhagen: Gyldendal, 1951);

Til en følsom veninde, edited by Tage Skou-Hansen (Copenhagen: Gyldendal, 1957);

Digte 1953–59: Tyren, Havkarlens sange, Cinna (Copenhagen: Gyldendal, 1960);

Frank Jæger, edited by Jørgen and Elsebeth Ougård (Copenhagen: Gjellerup, 1966);

Essays gennem ti aar (Copenhagen: Gyldendal, 1970)—comprises *Velkommen, vinter; Drømmen om en sommerdag; Naive rejser;*

Udvalgte digte (Copenhagen: Gyldendal, 1971);

Den hvide låge: Udvalgte essays, introduction by Bjarne Nielsen Brovst (Copenhagen: Gyldendal, 1987);

Vi, der valgte natten: Digte Frank Jæger, edited by Pia Juul (Copenhagen: Gyldendal, 1995).

TELEVISION: *Kongen skal dø,* script translated by Jæger, television adaptation by Søren Melson of a play by Eugène Ionesco, Danmarks Radio, 1969;

Hvor er Ulla Katrine? TV-spil, script by Jæger, *TV-teaterafdelingen,* Danmarks Radio, 1973.

RADIO: *Hvilket Postbud—en Due,* script by Jæger, Danmarks Radio, 1958;

Kappen, script translated by Jæger from Max Gunderman's adaptation of a story by Nikolai Gogol, Danmarks Radio, 1962;

Pastorale, script by Jæger, Danmarks Radio, 1963;

Oksens kvinder, script translated by Jæger from a French play by Jacques Audiberti, *Radioteatret,* Danmarks Radio, 1963;

Pelsen, script by Jæger, Danmarks Radio, 1964;

Idyl: Hørespil, script translated by Jæger from a Swedish play by Bengt Anderberg, Danmarks Radio, 1966;

Skilderhuset, script translated by Jæger from a French play by Audiberti, Danmarks Radio, 1966;

Der er en verden også i Verona, script by Jæger, Danmarks Radio, 1969.

OTHER: Hans Jæger, *Novelletter,* edited and translated by Frank Jæger (Copenhagen: Steen Hasselbalch, 1954);

Truman Capote, *Holly: En roman og tre noveller,* translated by Jæger (Copenhagen: Gyldendal, 1960);

R. R. Eklund, *Logbog paa landjorden,* translated by Jæger (Copenhagen: Steen Hasselbalch, 1961);

"Dansk foraar," in *Året i norden,* illustrated by Ernst Clausen (Stockholm: A. Bonnier / Copenhagen: Steen Hasselbalch, 1962);

Vesterhav: Danske digte, edited by Jæger (Copenhagen: Erichsen, 1963);

Eugène Ionesco, *Kongen skal dø* (Fredensborg: Arena, 1964);

Albert Camus, *Faldet* (Copenhagen: Gyldendal, 1965);

Pierre Corneille, *Le Cid eller Sejrherren,* translated by Jæger, in *Fransk klassisk drama,* edited, with an afterword, by Jens Kruuse (Copenhagen: Gyldendal, 1967);

Johann Wolfgang von Goethe, *Den unge Werthers lidelser* (Copenhagen: Hernov, 1972);

Alf Henrikson and Edward Lindahl, *Ask Ygdrasil livets træ en gammel guddommelig historie* (Copenhagen: Lademann, 1975);

Hjalmar Söderberg, *Martin Bircks ungdom: Fortælling* (Copenhagen: Hernov, 1976).

Frank Jæger was one of the most influential and widely read Danish writers of the immediate post–World War II era. After establishing his reputation as a poet, Jæger turned to prose and drama as well, in which genres he also showed himself to be a writer of considerable talent, but for which he rarely received the critical praise that was accorded his poetry. Jæger is, in fact, one of the premier prose writers of the mid twentieth century; several of his stories belong to the most memorable and distinctive that appeared in Denmark in the two decades after World War II. Jæger's forte lay in the shorter prose form; only a handful of his works of fiction surpass seventy printed pages. His essays, fewer in number than his poems or stories, are also among the most accessible of the 1950s, 1960s, and 1970s. Unlike many of his contemporaries, Jæger did not engage in political crusades or embrace social causes in his writings. Rather, he attempted to give voice to the universally valid human experience while at the same time emphasizing the intrinsic worth of the quiet, undramatic events of daily life and the wisdom of living in the here and now. Also a skilled translator, Jæger rendered into Danish works by French and German authors, among whom were Pierre Corneille, Eugène Ionesco, and Johann Wolfgang von Goethe.

Frank Jæger was born in Frederiksberg, Denmark, a municipality contiguous to Copenhagen, on 19 June 1926, the son of Holger Jæger, a business manager, and Carla Jæger, née Jyllerup. Jæger spent much of his childhood in Copenhagen and later incorporated many of his experiences into his fiction and essays. He entered secondary school just as World War II began. A talented musician, he played the bass viol in amateur jazz orchestras while still a student. In school Jæger was captivated by literature and always read more than he was assigned, immersing himself in the works of classic Danish authors such as Henrik Pontoppidan, J. P. Jacobsen, and Herman Bang as well as in those of earlier European literary giants, including Miguel de Cervantes, François Rabelais, and Gustave Flaubert. Partially because of this enthusiasm for literature, he sometimes neglected his other subjects and was held back for a year, having to repeat one class.

Upon graduation from secondary school in 1945, Jæger attended library school. He married Kirsten Vodder on 20 May 1948. (The couple divorced in 1970.) After taking his library degree in 1950 he worked briefly as a librarian before becoming co-editor of the influential Danish literary periodical *Heretica* in 1952. From that point on, he was able to live solely from the earnings of his pen.

By the early 1950s Jæger was already an established author, having published three collections of poetry: *Dydige digte* (Virtuous Poems, 1948), *Morgenens trompet* (The Trumpet of Morning, 1949), and *De 5 aarstider* (The Five Seasons, 1950), as well as the novel *Iners* in 1950.

The poems that Thorkild Bjørnvig and Bjørn Poulsen, editors at Wivel Forlag, chose to include in *Dydige digte* display a disarmingly lyrical, sometimes whimsical, and generally optimistic tone. The occasional darker poems, however, already foreshadow much of Jæger's later writing. *Morgenens trompet* continues in the sanguine vein of *Dydige digte* but is tinged with a more persistent feeling of despair and affords frequent glimpses of frustrated eroticism. In *De 5 aarstider* the buoyancy of *Dydige digte* reasserts itself. Here there is a serene depiction of the four seasons of nature coupled with the exuberance of a miraculous "fifth" season, brought about by the birth of the poet's daughter, Ene, in 1950. The poems of *Tyren* (The Bull, 1953) emphasize the power of the erotic and deal with the confusion of illusion with reality.

Jæger, meanwhile, had been active as a prose writer. The novel *Iners,* although it begins as a seemingly idyllic panegyric to the innocence of youth and the benignity of nature, soon turns disquieting and ends in the disintegration of the main character, who is unable to cope with life in the modern world.

The eponymous protoganist, Iners (whose name the author derived from the Latin *iners,* "inactive, inert"), is a nineteen-year-old idler who drifts from one experience to the next, letting himself be manipulated by forces of which he seems only dimly aware. Initially

he thrives, but after encountering the young woman Ene (whose name can be equated with "solitude"), who loves him and with whom Iners initially seems to be infatuated, Iners's experiences become more disjointed and take on a surrealistic quality that verges on the demonic. Iners and Ene impulsively set out on their own and end up living at the estate of a cruel landowner called simply "Manden" (The Man), who, with Iners's tacit consent, seduces Ene.

As Iners withdraws into himself, in part because of his guilt at his complicity in Ene's seduction, in part because of his implied affair with the sensuous and earthy Sulle So (Sulle Sow), he grows sullen and estranges himself from the rest of humanity. Finally even Ene abandons him. The novel ends on New Year's Eve with Iners hoping desperately for someone to visit him and celebrate the new year. On his final trip to the provincial railroad station near midnight, Iners is met by two older people who seem to be his parents, who dry his tears and lead him off toward home.

Iners is a tightly written and carefully composed work of barely 120 pages that progresses rapidly from an almost exuberant optimism to a deep pessimism about the human condition. Its conclusion, like the endings of so many of Jæger's prose works, is ambiguous. Here as elsewhere the author challenges his readers to draw their own conclusions. *Iners,* as is much of Jæger's early prose, is inspired by the lives and works of the poets of the German Romantic period. Jæger, however, unlike his eighteenth- and nineteenth-century German and Danish predecessors, stresses the demonic and the grotesque at the expense of the idyllic innocence that the poets of the Romantic period extolled.

Jæger's fascination with Romantic writing suffuses his next prose work, *Hverdagshistorier* (Everyday Stories, 1951), a collection of eighteen short narratives (none longer than seven pages). *Hverdagshistorier* is prefaced by a passage from Hans Christian Andersen's 1865 tale "Lygtemændene ere i Byen, sagde Mosekonen" (The Will-o-the-Wisps Are in Town, Said the Bog Woman). Jæger clearly strove to write these stories in the manner of Andersen, Denmark's most famous teller of tales. Several of them, in fact, do bear a resemblance to the subject matter, if not to the style, of Andersen's tales. "Enhjørningen" (The Unicorn), for instance, describes how the woodsman and his betrothed capture a unicorn and, by unscrewing its horn, release nature from the icy grip of winter. In "Porcellænskrukken" (The Porcelain Pot) the princess loves a commoner who frees her from the castle by passing her off as a porcelain statue.

In "Narren" (translated as "The Fool," 1988) Jæger comes closest to the spirit of the tales of Andersen. The story is simply told: a poor mother wishes to give her dying son one last pleasure and sets out to bring part of the Shrovetide festival to him. In her humility she feels that she can ask only the procession's ragged fool to accompany her. As they draw nearer to the house, music fills the air, and the fool and his nag are transformed into a golden prince on a magnificent steed. The story ends with the mother able only to ask, "Hvem er dog du?" (But who are you?) of the fool when she sees her son laughing and holding the fool's bells on the doorstep of the house. The beauty of the redemptive power of death evokes the theme of several of Andersen's most moving tales, most notably his "Historien om en Moder" (The Story of a Mother, 1848) and "Den lille Pige med Svovlstikkerne" (The Little Matchgirl, 1845).

Other stories from *Hverdagshistorier,* however, are harsh in their censure of human foibles. In "Elisa med benet" (Elisa and Her Leg) three local good-for-nothings tease the childlike widow Elisa that if the stump of her leg were several inches shorter she would receive a handsome sum of money annually. The credulous Elisa slices the requisite amount of flesh from her stump. In their remorse at having caused her suffering, the three good-for-nothings go to work dredging stones from the bottom of the sea so that they can pay Elisa her annual income. *Hverdagshistorier* is a disquieting mélange of the idyllic and the menacingly grotesque.

Den unge Jægers lidelser (The Sufferings of Young Jæger, 1953)—whose title alludes to *Die Leiden des jungen Werthers* (The Sorrows of Young Werther, 1774), a famous epistolary novel by the German author Johann Wolfgang von Goethe—is a collection of nine short stories that are loosely held together by the theme of the coming of age of the first-person narrator who can be taken as a fictionalized self-portrait of Jæger. In the first story, "Min broder" (My Brother), the narrator limns the significance that his older brother (who is otherwise not mentioned in Jæger's subsequent fiction) had on his early years and on his development as an artist. A nostalgic look back at the security of early childhood, "Min broder" also reveals Jæger's philosophy of art as "løgnens kunst," the art of lying.

"En sommer" (translated as "One Summer," 1984) begins as the perfect summer idyll of the city boy sent to the country for his school vacation, but the reader is soon aware that the youthful narrator's vivid imagination has turned reality into rather sinister fantasy. Together with the slightly older Sille, the first of Jæger's several erotically charged muses of that name, the narrator experiences his sensual awakening. "Flugten" (Flight) presents another stage in the young narrator's passage to adulthood. Fleeing to the rooftops of the school to avoid his dental examination, the narrator is tempted, like Christ, in his urban mountains by his own "Satan," the swarthy chimney sweep, but saved

Cover for Jæger's 1950 novel, about a nineteen-year-old who is drifting through life

by the intervention of the angelic dental assistant who takes him back to face the painful reality of the dentist's chair. "Wiener-Walde" (Vienna Woods) describes the almost surreal wartime voyage of the teenage narrator and his Danish-Austrian school friend, called simply Wiener-Walde, to Austria, where Wiener-Walde attempts to trace his family's roots. Wiener-Walde seems to recognize as his father the young apprentice knife-sharpener whom they meet by chance in rural Austria. Wiener-Walde and the narrator relinquish their illusion and leave Austria only after their money is exhausted and as the reality of the war comes closer.

In "Djævelens instrument" (translated as "The Devil's Instrument," 1971) the narrator's brief romantic encounter with yet another Sille causes him to forsake a promising musical career as a jazz bass player. After spending a night of intimacy with Sille, the narrator discovers that his bass (which up to now has been his alter ego) and Sille have exchanged forms, and the panicked narrator sells the instrument that the Devil (the unbridled forces often inherent in the creative process) has "besjælet" (animated). Frightened by what he cannot control and unwilling to accept the intrusion of the sensual into the aesthetic, he chooses to abandon his art. In "Samvær med Corneille" (A Time Together with Corneille) reality and fantasy again collide. The narrator's banishment from school (elucidated in the volume's preceding story "I Asklepios fodspor" [In Æsculapious's Footsteps]) has led him to a provincial Danish town where he ekes out an existence by translating foreign stories for the local newspaper. After another Sille captures his heart, he is commissioned to find a play suitable for the local stage. At this point the seventeenth-century French dramatist Pierre Corneille arrives and helps the narrator translate "Le Cid." As the narrator immerses himself in his work, Corneille, another of the narrator's alter egos, dallies with Sille. When "Le Cid" is produced, neither the narrator nor Corneille recognizes it. The narrator returns to Copenhagen to re-enter school. Corneille, the epiphany of art made life, leaves him with hope for the future. The artist seems finally to have come of age.

In the final story, "Farlig ungdom" (Dangerous Youth), the narrator's search for his true self continues. Having graduated from school, he journeys to Aarhus to study theology. When he fails his theology examination for the third and last time, he must withdraw from the university. His father arrives to take him home, but the narrator leaves his bewildered father standing on the deck of the Aarhus-to-Copenhagen ferry and returns to Aarhus to retrieve his business cards, upon which are printed "Relegeret fra Aarhus Universitet" (Expelled from Aarhus University). He is determined to make a name for himself and effects a definitive break with his past. *Den unge Jægers lidelser* ends without resolution but with a sense of optimism that is not present at the conclusion of *Iners*. The tone of *Den unge Jægers lidelser* is lighthearted, and the work overflows with gentle irony and quiet humor, most of which is directed at the narrator himself.

In 1954, finding his surroundings too urbanized, Jæger moved from Farum, northwest of Copenhagen, to the island of Langeland, southeast of Funen, where he felt that he could more readily commune with nature. He lived on Langeland until 1970. He described his island lovingly in the essays and poetry of this period. Paradoxically, however, the darker side of Jæger's art began to manifest itself with increasing frequency in this idyllic setting.

This brooding quality is present in Jæger's longest novel (which is, nonetheless, less than two hundred pages), *Jomfruen fra Orléans, Jeanne d'Arc* (The Maid of Orléans, Jeanne d'Arc, 1955). It is also one of his least known works. Not well received by either the critics or the public, *Jomfruen fra Orléans* represents a stylistic departure for the author. The novel retells the story of Joan of Arc in four separate episodes (which Jæger designates as books) narrated by four men who knew the Maid of Orléans. After his death each narrator relates his highly individualized account of the events surrounding Jeanne to either the Virgin Mary, God, or both. Each book is prefaced by an excerpt from what is purported to be a contemporary chronicle.

The first, and longest, book is narrated by François Watriquet, an orphaned and aimless young nobleman who is driven from his hereditary castle and who inadvertently stumbles into the dauphin's war against the English when he meets Jeanne and her family. Against his will, François accompanies Jeanne to the dauphin's court. The first book breaks off early in Jeanne's campaign when François is struck between the eyes by an arrow. François concludes his narrative with a plea to the Virgin Mary that he be allowed to return to life so that he may finish his quest to find his beautiful cousin who had been abducted.

The second book is narrated by Thomas Ladvenu, a minstrel who is also a spy for Georges la Trémoille. Thomas, however, soon becomes convinced that Jeanne is divinely inspired. He seems also to have fallen in love with her. He recounts how Jeanne wins victories over the English, has the dauphin crowned king of France, but is captured and taken to Rouen. Thomas relates that although official reports say that Jeanne was burned as a witch, he has heard that she is still alive and married and has borne two children.

The third book, also the shortest, is told by the mercenary Bartolomeo Baretta, who regrets that he did little to prevent Jeanne's capture. He reveals that Jeanne had broken with the king and laments that her plans to recapture all of France were never realized; perhaps she would have made him her king.

The fourth book is recounted by the unnamed English jurist who had been sent to Rouen to observe Jeanne's trial. Convinced that Jeanne was a witch, he could not comprehend how the French could have had any doubts. At her death, he reports, the common people felt that a saint had been executed.

The disjointed narrative style of *Jomfruen fra Orléans* as well as the multiple narrators and their different perspectives lend this novel a feel of chaotic authenticity, as if the author had unearthed long-lost French and English chronicles from the mid fifteenth century. The first-person narratives give the work a sense of immediacy despite the passage of more than five hundred years since the events recounted. In *Jomfruen fra*

Orléans Jæger emphasizes the realpolitik aspects of the struggle of the French to wrest their country from the English. The religious and mystical aspects of the story of the Maid of Orléans are relegated to the background. Despite its stylistic innovation, *Jomfruen fra Orléans* lacks a coherent core, and although the individual books are self-contained narratives, the work as a whole is anything but unified.

In the late 1950s Jæger published two collections of poetry, *Havkarlens sange* (Songs of the Merman, 1956) and *Cinna og andre digte* (Cinna and Other Poems, 1959). The spirit of many of the poems in these two volumes is quiet melancholy, a mood that is, however, often counterbalanced by the life-affirming nature of still others of the poems. The Cinna of the 1959 collection is the misunderstood and murdered poet in William Shakespeare's play *Julius Caesar* (1623). Central to this cycle, the poem "Cinna, poeten" (Cinna, the Poet), in the "Shakespearesuite" of the volume, encapsulates the dual problems of identity and the agony of the artist that permeate many of Jæger's works.

Each of the five short stories of *Kapellanen og andre fortællinnger* (The Curate and Other Stories, 1957) involves a literal or figurative odyssey and details how the young male protagonist, who is, to some extent, an outsider, copes with a crisis of love. Each odyssey is also a voyage that leads to the discovery of the inner man.

The first story in the collection, "Kidholm" (Kidholm), is set in the Denmark of the late 1830s. Its protagonist, the precocious fifteen-year-old Bernhard Aschegaard, is sent away from home because of his parents' marital difficulties. Instead of landing in Bergen, the ship on which Bernhard is traveling puts into the quarantine establishment of the island of Kidholm (modern Kyholm). Bernhard's odyssey and exile leave him exposed and vulnerable on this island of death and disease, where he regresses and slowly loses his will to live. He recovers some of his former self-assuredness when he falls in love with a much older woman but despairs when he receives the news that he is about to be sent home to Copenhagen—or to be exiled yet again. On the evening of his confirmation into the church, he seeks out and is bitten repeatedly by two poisonous snakes that he has brought to Kidholm as pets. The symbolism is obvious: Bernhard is destroyed by that from which he cannot escape, by that which he has carried with him from the outset.

"Foraarsaften med Faust" (translated as "Spring Evening with Faust," 1988), the most recondite of the stories in this collection, thrusts art intrusively into life. The unnamed protagonist travels from one provincial town to another reading from Goethe's drama *Faust* (1808, 1832), serving art for art's sake but growing poorer and more despondent with each performance. He refuses to admit failure, for to do so would mean a return to his family and a job in his father's window-blind factory. One March evening, after he has read for three hours straight to a single listener, a beautiful young woman, his art abruptly becomes his reality: he becomes Faust and she, Margarethe. (Because he is drunk, he is unsure in retrospect whether he seduced the girl or imagined he did.) The next morning reality is reestablished when the young woman's father appears and requests a performance at his daughter's twenty-first birthday celebration. The Faust-artist agrees but then flees on the bus to go home to his family. Having been defeated by the passion in his art (as was the musician in "Djævelens instrument"), his journey of self-realization has only just begun.

In the final story, "Kapellanen" (The Curate), the newly ordained priest Thorkild Christophersen, who had been only an indifferent theology student, is exiled from his native Copenhagen to a parish in rural Jutland. Thorkild's odyssey begins with a perilous sea voyage (with the author perhaps parodying Homer) during which only his prodigious physical strength saves the boat on which he is journeying from being swamped in a savage storm. Reaching his provincial home, Thorkild is initially charmed by his new surroundings and meets and falls in love with Hanne. The gray weather of autumn, however, depresses him, and, having received an anonymous letter that Hanne's family had been German sympathizers during the Occupation, he begins to doubt her. He flees to Copenhagen but finds everything there shabbier than he remembered it. Realizing that he no longer belongs there, that like his namesake, Thorkild Mortensen, he too is letting himself be haunted by insubstantial ghosts from the past, he precipitately runs back to the main railroad station to return to Hanne. Thorkild's self-realization has come at the last moment. Indeed, the reader is left to entertain some doubt that he will in fact still have Hanne's love.

Kapellanen og andre fortællinnger was one of Jæger's most widely read works and contains some of his most powerful and most lyrical prose. Even though the situations of several of the protagonists are desperate, it is worth noting that only one, the young Bernhard, actually seems to succumb to his adversities. The other protagonists, although the endings of the four remaining stories are ambiguous, persevere. Jæger seems to have wanted to show the progression from utter spiritual exile to a reconciliation with one's lot in life.

In 1958 Jæger's first radio drama, *Hvilket postbud—en Due* (What a Mailman—a Dove), was performed. Perhaps in part inspired by Friedrich Dürrenmatt's 1956 drama, *Der Besuch der alten Dame* (translated as *The Visit,*

Jæger and his daughter, Ene, looking at the dust jacket for his 1958 essay collection, Velkommen, vinter

1958), this slightly absurdist play tells of the return of postman Due's former wife. Due, who feels that he must be alone and remain unsullied by others, rejects her. Three other radio plays, *Pastorale* (Pastorale), *Pelsen* (The Fur), and *Der er en verden også i Verona* (There Is a World in Verona, Too) were performed in 1963, 1964, and 1969, respectively.

The stories of *Danskere: Tre fortællinnger af fædrelandets historie* (Danes: Three Narratives from the History of the Fatherland, 1966) pose unsettling questions of the place of art in life and the destructive power of the erotic. The first two stories, "Didrik" (Didrik) and "Degnen" (The Parish Clerk), are connected thematically. Each takes place during the reign of the fictionalized "divine Emperor." "Didrik" recounts the fate of several of the leaders of the peasants' revolt against the emperor. The titular figure of Didrik, a societal misfit and artist who is forced into the revolt against his will, becomes to his and the reader's surprise a rebel leader. He is just as bemused as a military man, however, as he

was as an artist. The story ends with his defeat, death, and burial. Didrik's tale at times borders on the surreal, especially in the episode of the ritual murder and cannibalism of an eighteen-year-old virgin in a grotesque inversion of the sacrament of the Holy Communion. "Degnen" is the story of the corruption and opportunism of the clergy during the divine emperor's reign. The unnamed first-person narrator drifts through the crises in his life doing little to change his situation. At first a parish clerk, he later becomes, in a Kafkaesque episode, a male prostitute, only to end as a man of the cloth again. The narration is disjointed and opaque, which is entirely in keeping with the flawed moral compass of the narrator, on whom drunken excesses and cold-blooded murder leave no lasting impression.

The third story, "Danserinden" (The Ballerina), has almost nothing in common with "Didrik" and "Degnen" other than off-handed references to several of the characters in the two earlier narratives. Set in Jutland in the early 1800s, "Danserinden" records the decline and psychological destruction of the successful expatriate industrialist Valdemar by the antiquated technology of his Danish homeland (represented by his friend Herman's outdated foundry) and the aggressive eroticism of a young woman (Herman's niece). At the end of the novella, the once self-assured Valdemar has been reduced to a frightened shell of his former self and is ignominiously driven away by the demonic sensuality of Herman's red-haired niece. Valdemar's fate is, however, amply foreshadowed by the narrative's many examples of prefiguration: for instance, his first meeting with the niece, when she cures his badly bruised arm by forcing the blood from the bruise back into his heart, and his predilection for reflective walks in the cemetery.

The poems of *Idylia* (Idylia, 1967) are closely linked thematically to the stories of *Danskere:* they too breathe a disquieting sensuality. Characteristic of this emphasis on the destructive potential of rampant physical desire is the volume's lengthy, final poem, "Idylia" (of which the last section, called "4. aften" [Fourth Evening], is strongly reminiscent of the same motif in "Danserinden"), in which human existence itself is threatened by powerful erotic urges.

Alvilda: Sengelæsning for unge og gamle (Alvilda: Bedtime Reading for Young and Old, 1969) is a collection of short works that Jæger had previously published in a variety of Danish periodicals between 1949 and 1965. The volume is divided into three parts. The first part consists entirely of fiction, including several stories that rank among Jæger's finest: "Værelse i gavlen" (1957; translated as "A Room in the Gable," 1989), "Alvilda" (Alvilda, 1959), and "Susanne efter badet" (Susanne after the Bath, 1962). Two selections, "Fødderne" (The Feet, 1950) and "Præsten i Herløw" (The Pastor of Herløw, 1952), are ghost stories, although neither was written with the cheap thrill in mind. The second section is given largely to autobiographical essays, and the third part is composed of essays on such diverse topics as "Finsk boheme" (Finnish Bohemian, 1952) and "Digtekunst og jazz" (The Poetic Art and Jazz, 1958).

In "Værelse i gavlen" the narrator is an aspiring artist who ultimately realizes that his ambitions as a painter exceed his talents and who, after an encounter with a mysterious old woman and several experiences of déjà vu, resigns himself to his lot in life as a competent, and well-paid, commercial artist. "Alvilda" parallels the situation in the earlier novella "Danserinden"; here also the woman outwits and defeats the suitor. Alvilda, a beautiful young widowed countess, is desired by all the eligible noblemen of the area. Just as it appears that her late husband's cousin, Gottlieb, has won her love, she secretly leaves

to seek refuge with her family in Germany. Unlike Valdemar, however, Gottlieb has not been defeated by overpowering feminine eroticism; he has been overcome by the more subtle feminine cunning, a force that thwarts many of Jæger's male protagonists.

The prose works in Jæger's next collection, *Døden i Skoven; Sidste Sommer; Tulte* (Death in the Forest; Last Summer; Tulte, 1970), are set in the realistic milieu of mid-twentieth-century Denmark. The longest of the three at some 140 pages, "Døden i Skoven" should be considered a short novel. It is one of the most exquisite works of fiction that Jæger ever composed. Written with great care and admirable artistic economy, "Døden i Skoven" details the decline of the middle-aged actor Cornelius. Thrown out of the house by his wife for one-too-many extramarital escapades, Cornelius lets others decide his fate. His lawyer sends him to an isolated forest house on the island of Funen, where Cornelius withdraws into himself. Although this novel, like much of Jæger's prose, ends ambiguously with Cornelius, who suspects that he is incurably ill, about to enter the hospital, the reader is in no doubt as to Cornelius's ultimate fate. "Døden i Skoven" abounds with foreshadowings of his death. In this story the crises in human relationships and the problem of identity are central motifs. Cornelius has never been able to establish more than superficial bonds with another human being; more ominously, he has never fully learned his own identity.

"Sidste Sommer" (originally published in 1959) is the story of yet another of the hapless, basically passive male protagonists who inhabit Jæger's fictional world. Herman Oldén, who has lived surrounded and controlled by women, from his mother to his elderly maiden aunts, makes a desperate but futile attempt to break free during his first summer vacation alone only to end up in the clutches of a young woman who seems to have marriage uppermost in her mind.

Jæger spent the last seven years of his life in Elsinore, north of Copenhagen. He initially felt drawn to the venerable trading center and seaport with its color and bustle, but emotional crises forced themselves on him with ever-increasing urgency. Toward the end of his life Jæger saw himself as isolated and forgotten. His artistry records this somber frame of mind. During his Elsinore period, Jæger wrote little poetry, and his prose works became fewer and more inward-looking.

None of the seven stories in *Provinser* (Provinces, 1972), in fact, measures up to Jæger's previous fiction. Only sporadically do they show the same creative verve and energy or the same sure-handed narrative style that characterize the majority of Jæger's earlier prose writings, and they do not have much of the humor or irony that infuse the rest of Jæger's works. And despite their realistic tone and setting in contemporary provincial Denmark, these stories prove just a shade too contrived to be credible. "Moffer med kikkert" (Grampa's Telescope), for instance, tells the story of a widower in war-time Elsinore who sends money to Sweden to help a woman whom he has seen through his telescope. The woman holds up signs suggesting she is starving and that money can be sent to her post-office box. When the war ends, the widower hurries to Sweden to meet this intriguing woman—only to discover that he is only one of a score of elderly Elsinoreans whom she has tricked before vanishing. This insubstantial episode is the stuff of a swiftly told anecdote and hardly warrants the eighteen pages that the author devotes to it.

The two pieces of fiction in *Udsigt til Kronborg: Sengelæsning* (View of Kronborg: Bedside Readings, 1976), the final book that Jæger published, are similar to those of *Provinser*. They too stress the quotidian, almost banal, aspects of human existence.

Frank Jæger's life ended on 4 July 1977; unsubstantiated rumors attributed his death to either heavy drinking or suicide. Despite the depression of his final years, however, he left an impressive legacy of prose and poetry that ranks among the best that have emerged from mid-twentieth-century Denmark. Rarely the social critic, Jæger nevertheless caused readers to re-evaluate their own worldviews by plumbing the depths of human experience as few writers of his generation were able to do.

Letters:

Den unge Jæger: Breve 1944–56, edited by Frans Lasson (Viborg: Gyldendal, 1994).

Bibliography:

Jørn Knudsen and Leif Hansen Nymark, *Frank Jæger: En bibliografi* (Copenhagen: Danmarks Biblioteksskole, 1982).

References:

Lotte Thyrring Andersen, *Det grønne mørke. Rummelighed og intethed i Frank Jægers digtning* (Odense, Denmark: Odense Universitet, 1996);

Søren Baggesen, "Om Frank Jægers 'Dit Land erobret,'" in *Analyser af moderne dansk lyrik,* 2 volumes, edited by Per Olsen (Copenhagen: Borgen, 1976), I: 294–307;

Thorkild Bjørnvig, *Virkeligheden er til* (Copenhagen: Gyldenal, 1973), pp. 79–88;

Jørgen Gustava Brandt, "Frank Jæger," in his *Præsentation. 40 danske digtere efter krigen* (Copenhagen: Gyldendal, 1963), pp. 81–85;

Bjarne Nielsen Brovst, *Frank Jægers forfatterskab: En monografi* (Copenhagen: Hernov, 1977);

Lars Hamberg, "Några år med Frankie: Ett diktarporträtt," *Nordisk Tidskrift,* 58 (1982): 169–182;

Steen Harvig, *Frank Jæger* (Copenhagen: Gyldendal, 1974);

Harvig, ed., *Om Frank Jæger* (Herning: Systime, 1986);

Sven Holm, "Frank Jæger," in *Danske digtere i det 20. århundrede,* 5 volumes, edited by Torben Brostrøm and Mette Winge (Copenhagen: Gad, 1982), III: 445–457;

Frank Hugus, "The Dilemma of the Artist in Selected Prose Works of Frank Jæger," *Scandinavian Studies,* 47, no. 1 (1975): 52–65;

Hugus, "Frank Jæger's Defeated Protagonists," *Scandinavian Studies,* 54, no. 2 (1982): 148–159;

Dirk van Maelsaeke, *The Strange Essence of Things* (London: Billing, 1977), pp. 142–165, 168–174, 192–201;

Jacob Paludan, *Draabespil: Fjorten stykker, skrevet ved anledning* (Copenhagen: Gyldendal, 1971), pp. 45–54;

Tage Skou-Hansen, "Frank Jæger," in *Danske digtere i det 20. århundrede,* 3 volumes, edited by Frederik Nielsen and Ole Restrup (Copenhagen: Gad, 1966), III: 291–309;

Skou-Hansen, *Det midlertidige fælleskab* (Copenhagen: Gyldendal, 1972), pp. 142–163.

Johannes V. Jensen

(20 January 1873 – 25 November 1950)

Sven Hakon Rossel
University of Vienna

BOOKS: *Danskere* (Copenhagen: Det Nordiske Forlag, 1896);

Einar Elkær: Roman (Copenhagen: Det Nordiske Forlag, 1898);

Himmerlandsfolk: Historier (Copenhagen: Det Nordiske Forlag, 1898);

Intermezzo: Dolores, Forsvundnes, Skove, Louison (Copenhagen: Det Nordiske Forlag, 1899);

Foraarets Død (Copenhagen: Det Nordiske Forlag, 1900);

Den store Sommer (Copenhagen: Det Nordiske Forlag, 1900);

Den gotiske Renaissance (Copenhagen: Det Nordiske Forlag, 1901);

Vinteren (Copenhagen: Det Nordiske Forlag, 1901); enlarged as *Kongens Fald* (Copenhagen: Det Nordiske Forlag, 1901)—comprises *Foraarets Død, Den store Sommer, Vinteren;* translated by P. T. Federspiel and Patrick Kirwan as *The Fall of the King* (London: Grayson & Grayson, 1933; New York: Holt, 1933);

Kirken i Farsø: Skitse (Minneapolis & Chicago: C. Rasmussen, 1903);

Madame D'Ora (Copenhagen: Gyldendal, 1904);

Nye Himmerlandshistorier (Copenhagen: Gyldendal, 1904)—includes "Kirstens sidste Rejse," translated by Lee Marshall as "Kirsten's Last Journey," in *Anthology of Danish Literature: Bilingual Edition,* edited by F. J. Billeskov Jansen and P. M. Mitchell (Carbondale: Southern Illinois University Press, 1971), pp. 300–379;

Skovene (Copenhagen: Gyldendal, 1904);

Hjulet (Copenhagen: Gyldendal, 1905);

Digte (Copenhagen: Gyldendal, 1906); revised and enlarged as *Digte: Anden Udgave,* 1917; revised and enlarged as *Digte: Tredie Udgave,* 1921; revised and enlarged as *Digte: 1901–1941,* 1943; revised and enlarged as *Digte,* 1948—includes "Ved Frokesten" and "Paa Memphis Station," translated by Alexander Taylor as "At Lunch" and "At Memphis Station," in *Contemporary Danish Poetry,* edited by

Line Jensen and others (Copenhagen: Gyldendal, 1958), pp. 91–92;

Myter og Jagter (Copenhagen: Gyldendal, 1907)—includes "Fusijama," translated by Elias Bredsdorff as "Fujiyama," in his *Contemporary Danish Prose: An Anthology* (Copenhagen: Gyldendal, 1958), pp. 91–92;

Den ny Verden: Til international Belysning af nordisk Bondekultur (Copenhagen: Gyldendal, 1907);

Singapore Noveller (Copenhagen: Gyldendal, 1907);

Nye Myter (Copenhagen: Gyldendal, 1908);

Bræen: Myter om Istiden og det første Menneske (Copenhagen: Gyldendal, 1908);

Lille Ahasverus (Copenhagen: Gyldendal, 1909);

Myter: Ny Samling (Copenhagen: Gyldendal, 1910);

Himmerlandshistorier: Tredie Samling (Copenhagen: Gyldendal, 1910);

Nordisk Aand: Kroniker og Karakteristiker (Copenhagen: Gyldendal, 1911);

Skibet (Copenhagen: Gyldendal, 1912);

Myter: Fjerde Samling (Copenhagen: Gyldendal, 1912);

Rudyard Kipling (Copenhagen: Gyldendal, 1912);

Olivia Marianne (Copenhagen: Gyldendal, 1915);

Introduktion til vor Tidsalder (Copenhagen: Gyldendal, 1915);

Aarbog 1916 (Copenhagen: Gyldendal, 1916);

Eksotiske Noveller (Copenhagen: Gyldendal, 1916)–comprises *Singapore Noveller, Lille Ahasverus, Olivia Marianne;*

Aarbog 1917 (Copenhagen: Gyldendal, 1917);

Norne-Gæst (Copenhagen: Gyldendal, 1919);

Det tabte Land: Mennesket før Istiden (Copenhagen: Gyldendal, 1919);

Johannes Larsen og hans Billeder (Copenhagen: Gyldendal, 1920);

Christofer Columbus (Copenhagen: Gyldendal, 1921); enlarged as *Den lange Rejse* (Copenhagen: Gyldendal, 1935)–comprises *Det tabte Land, Bræen, Norne-Gæst, Cimbrernes Tog, Skibet, Christofer Columbus;* translated, with the exception of *Skibet,* by Arthur G. Chater as *The Long Journey,* 3 volumes (London: Gyldendal, 1922–1924; New York: Knopf, 1923–1924)–comprises *Fire and Ice, The Cimbrians, Christopher Columbus;*

Sangerinden (Madame d'Ora): Drama i fem Akter (Copenhagen: Gyldendal, 1921);

Cimbrernes Tog (Copenhagen: Gyldendal, 1922);

Æstetik og Udvikling: Efterskrift til Den lange Rejse (Copenhagen: Gyldendal, 1923);

Aarstiderne, illustrated by Johannes Larsen (Copenhagen: Gyldendal, 1923);

Myter: Tredie Bind, 1914–1924 (Copenhagen: Gyldendal, 1924);

Hamlet: Til Forklaring af Hamletskikkselen (Copenhagen: Gyldendal, 1924);

Evolution og Moral (Copenhagen: Gyldendal, 1925);

Aarets Højtider (Copenhagen: Gyldendal, 1925);

Verdens Lys: Nye Digte (Copenhagen: Gyldendal, 1926);

Jørgine (Copenhagen: Hage & Clausens Forlag, 1926);

Dyrenes Forvandling: Til udviklingens Plastik (Copenhagen: Gyldendal, 1927);

Ved Livets Bred og andre Myter (Copenhagen: Gyldendal, 1928);

Aandens Stadier (Copenhagen: Gyldendal, 1928);

Retninger i Tiden: Artikler 1925–30 (Copenhagen: Gyldendal, 1930);

Den jydske Blæst: Digte 1926–1930 (Copenhagen: Gyldendal, 1931);

Form og Sjæl: Portræter og Personligheder (Copenhagen: Gyldendal, 1931);

Paa danske Veje, illustrated by Larsen (Copenhagen: Gyldendal, 1931);

Pisangen (Copenhagen: Gyldendal, 1932);

Kornmarken (Copenhagen: Gyldendal, 1932);

Sælernes Ø (Copenhagen: Gyldendal, 1934);

Det Blivende: Tankens Revolutionering i det 19de Aarhundrede og Tilbagefaldet i det 20de (Copenhagen: Gyldendal, 1934);

Dr. Renaults Fristelser (Copenhagen: Gyldendal, 1935);

Gudrun (Copenhagen: Gyldendal, 1936);

Darduse, Bryllupet i Peking: Eventyrkomedie i fire Akter (Copenhagen: Gyldendal, 1937);

Paaskebadet: Digte 1931–1937 (Copenhagen: Gyldendal, 1937);

Jydske Folkelivsmalere: Dalsgaard, Michael Ancher, Hans Smidth (Copenhagen: Arthur Jensens Forlag, 1937);

Thorvaldsen: Haandværkeren og Manden (Copenhagen: Arthur Jensens Forlag, 1938);

Nordvejen: Indtryk af norsk Natur (Copenhagen: Gyldendal, 1939);

Fra Fristaterne: Rejsebreve, med et tilbageblik (Copenhagen: Gyldendal, 1939);

Gutenberg: Til bogtrykkerkunstenes Historie, by Jensen and Aage Marcus (Copenhagen: Bianco Lunos Bogtrykkeri, 1939);

Mariehønen (Copenhagen: Gyldendal, 1940);

Mindets Tavle: Portræter og Personligheder (Copenhagen: Gyldendal, 1941);

Vor Oprindelse (Copenhagen: Gyldendal, 1941);

Om Sproget og Undervisningen (Copenhagen: Gyldendal, 1942);

Kvinden i Sagatiden (Copenhagen: Gyldendal, 1942);

Folkeslagene i Østen (Copenhagen: Gyldendal, 1943);

Møllen (Copenhagen: Gyldendal, 1944);

Myter, 2 volumes (Copenhagen: Gyldendal, 1946);

Bogbinderen, illustrations by Madia Stange (Copenhagen: Printed by J. H. Schultz, 1947);

Afrika: Opdagelsesrejserne (Copenhagen: Gyldendal, 1949);

Danske køretøjer (Copenhagen: Thaning & Appel, 1949);

Swift og Oehlenschläger (Copenhagen: Gyldendal, 1950);

Tilblivelsen (Copenhagen: Gyldendal, 1951);

Mytens ring: Efterladte myter og beskrivelser (Copenhagen: Gyldendal, 1957);

Ungt er endnu Ordet: Portræter og Personligheder, edited by Carl Bergstrøm-Nielsen (Copenhagen: Gyldendal, 1958).

Editions and Collections: *Udvalgte Prosastykker,* edited by Morten Borup and Peter Ilsøe (Copenhagen: Gyldendal, 1940);

Bræn, edited by Martin Larsen (Copenhagen: Gyldendal, 1963);

Himmerlandshistorier, edited, with an afterword, by Jørgen Elbek, Gyldendals Bibliotek, no. 24 (Copenhagen: Gyldendal, 1963);

Johannes Larsen og Aarstiderne, edited, with a foreword, by Aage Marcus, Gyldendals Uglebøger, no. 56 (Copenhagen: Gyldendal, 1963);

Den jydske blæst og andre digte, selected by Ole Wivel (Copenhagen: Gyldendal, 1957);

Jordens Kreds, selected by Marcus, introduction by Niels Birger Wamberg (Copenhagen: Gyldendal, 1967);

Myter i Digte i Udvalg, selected by Leif Nedergaard (Copenhagen: Gyldendal, 1969);

Himmerlandshistorier, edited by Povl Marstal (Copenhagen: Gyldendal, 1970);

Mørkets frodighed; Tidlige myter, selected, with an introduction, by Wamberg (Copenhagen: Gyldendal, 1973);

12 Himmerlandshistorier, edited by Sven Moller Kristensen (Copenhagen: Gyldendal, 1979);

Tretten Myter: Johannes V. Jensen, selected and illustrated by Jens Jensen (Copenhagen: Gyldendal, 1982);

Himmerlandshistorier: Et udvalg, selected by Sonja Carlberg (Copenhagen: Gyldendal, 1984);

Kender du Johannes V. Jensen, selected by Margit Mørk (Copenhagen: Grafisk, 1986);

Christofer Columbus, foreword by Ib Michael (Copenhagen: Gyldendal, 1992);

Madame D'Ora; Hjulet, edited by Sven Hakon Rossel (Copenhagen: Det Danske Sproge-og Litteraturselskab/Borgen, 1997);

Digte: Johannes V. Jensen, edited by Frits Johansen (Copenhagen: Gyldendal, 1998).

Editions in English: "Ane og Koen," translated by Victor Folke Nelson as "Ann and the Cow"; "Forsvundne Skove," translated by Henry Commager as "Lost Forests," in *Denmark's Best Stories,* edited by Hanna Astrup Larsen (New York: American-Scandinavian Foundation/Norton, 1928), pp. 327–340;

Garden Colonies in Denmark, translated by F. Aubrey Rush (Copenhagen: Danske selskab, 1949);

Denmark's Johannes V. Jensen, translated by Marion L. Nielsen (Logan: Utah State Agricultural College, 1955);

The Waving Rye, selected by C. A. Bodelsen, translated by Ronald Bathgate and others (Copenhagen: Gyldendal, 1958; New York: American-Scandinavian Foundation, 1959);

The Fall of the King, translated by Alan Bower and edited by Sven H. Rossel (Seattle: Mermaid Press, 1992); revised (Traverse City: Stonehill, 1995).

OTHER: Jack London, *Naar Naturen kalder,* foreword by Jensen (Copenhagen: Peter Hansens Forlag, 1907);

Ditleff von Zeppelin, *Fugletræk,* edited, with an introduction, by Jensen and Otto Gelsted (Copenhagen: Gyldendal, 1916);

Thorvaldsens Portrætbuster, introduction by Jensen, biographical notes by Aage Marcus (Copenhagen: Gyldendal, 1926).

TRANSLATIONS: Frank Norris, *Af Hvedens Saga: Polypen, en Bog om Kalifornien* (Copenhagen: Gyldendal, 1907);

Rudyard Kipling and Wolcott Balestier, *Nauhlaka: Fortælling fra Vesten og Østen,* translated by Jensen and Aslaug Mikkelsen (Copenhagen: V. Pios Forlag, 1911);

Kipling, *Fribytterbreve; De rædselsfulde Nætters By og andre Skizzer,* translated by Jensen and Mikkelsen (Copenhagen: V. Pios Forlag, 1912);

Kipling, *Fra Hav til Hav,* translated by Jensen and Mikkelsen (Copenhagen: V. Pios Forlag, 1913);

Kipling, *Liv og Drøm,* translated by Jensen and Mikkelsen (Copenhagen: V. Pios Forlag, 1913);

Kipling, *Med Natexpressen Aar 2000 og andre Fortællinger,* translated by Jensen and Mikkelsen (Copenhagen: V. Pios Forlag, 1914);

Rudolf Requadt, *Krigsflyveren* (Copenhagen: Fr. Ravns Forlag, 1916);

Adelbert von Chamisso, *Peter Schlemihls vidunderlige Historie,* translated, with an introduction, by Jensen (Copenhagen: Høst & Søn, 1918);

Walt Whitman, *Digte,* translated, with an introduction, by Jensen and Gelsted (Copenhagen: Nyt Nordisk Forlag, 1919);

De islandske Sagaer, 3 volumes, translated by Jensen, Knud Hjortø, and Hans Kyrre (Copenhagen: Gyldendal, 1930–1932);

William Shakespeare, *Hamlet* (Copenhagen: Gyldendal, 1937);

Egil Skallagrimssons Saga (Copenhagen: Gyldendal, 1943);

Snorre Sturlason, *Heimskringla: Norges Kongesagaer,* translated and edited by Jensen and Kyrre (Copenhagen: Gyldendal, 1948).

Jensen in 1886

By revolting against the introspection of Danish turn-of-the-century literature and the psychological and social naturalism of the nineteenth century, Johannes V. Jensen became one of the most prolific innovative spirits in Danish cultural life. His worship of modern science and technology, the bustling life in the international metropolis, and pragmatic materialism and capitalism made him instrumental in the reorientation of Danish literature away from continental, French and German models toward Anglo-American cultural life. His enthusiasm for American literature resulted in the introduction and promotion in Denmark of the works of many American writers.

Charles Darwin's theories were an important source of inspiration for Jensen's depictions of nature scenes and animals but had a disastrous impact on his questionable evolutionary and anthropological theories. Despite his scientific and anti-idealistic orientation, Jensen was never able to let go of his deep-rooted dependence on his childhood's Jutland peasant traditions and an equally deep-rooted fascination with Christian metaphysics. This contradiction or split resulted in an existential insecurity that manifests itself in a fragmentation both with regard to content and form, which gives Jensen's fictional work continuing relevance. It places him in the modernist tradition of the twentieth century, adding to some of his texts a vibrant and eclectic, almost postmodern, quality. However, when Jensen was able to bridge this split as, for instance, in his myths and poetry, he created pieces of timeless art in which observation and vision, present time and eternity, reality and dream are seamlessly merged.

Johannes Vilhelm Jensen was born 20 January 1873 in Farsø in the northern Jutland province of Himmerland. He received decisive impulses from his parents who were both of peasant stock. His mother, Marie Kirstine Jensen, had a prosaic and practical view of life, but she also possessed a vivid imagination and a hot temper; his father, Hans Jensen, was the district veterinarian and was an expert in botany and zoology. He inspired Jensen's later studies of nature and discovery of Darwin's evolutionary theories. Although the family was strongly anti-religious, in the late 1880s Jensen's father became interested in spiritualism, an interest that became lifelong for Jensen's sister, the writer Thit Jensen. Johannes V. Jensen later criticized this occult interest, although it was undoubtedly one of the causative factors for the longing for eternity and spiritual expansion that became an essential feature in his writing.

In the autobiographical sketch *Kirken i Farsø: Skitse* (The Church in Farsø: Sketch, 1903), Jensen described his boyhood with his brothers and friends from the small town and the neighborhood farms, emphasizing his boldness and extroversion. A somewhat different description comes from one of Jensen's friends, Peder Bach, quoted in Oluf Friis's 1974 biography of Jensen: "Han var en besynderlig Dreng, ikke som de andre, men for det meste tavs og indesluttet, og han gik gerne og saa ned i Jorden i sine egne dybe Tanker; men til Tider kunde han vaagne op, og da husker jeg at hans Snebolde blev temmelig haarde" (He was a strange boy, not like the others, but mostly silent and reticent, and he usually walked around looking down deep in his thoughts; but at times he could wake up, and then I remember that his snowballs became rather hard). A characteristic trait was his joy in reading. Jensen himself, in *Mytens ring: Efterladte myter og beskrivelser* (The Ring of the Myth: Posthumous Myths and Descriptions, 1957), has told about his first books: children's readers, accounts by Captain James Cook, Henry Morton Stanley, and David Livingstone of their expeditions, a history of Denmark and Hans Christian Andersen's tales—all works that he found on his father's bookshelves.

After two years at Farsø School, followed by private tutoring, Jensen, in 1890, went to Viborg Katedralskole (cathedral school) for three years, where he became familiar with the humanistic, bourgeois educational tradition that for hundreds of years had formed

Jensen (on extreme left), after a hunting trip in Singapore during his first voyage around the world in 1902–1903

the basis for spiritual life in Denmark. Jensen's years in Viborg, depicted in the first two chapters of his first novel, *Danskere* (Danes, 1896), were not harmonious, and his opposition was nourished in particular by reading the German poet Heinrich Heine, whom Jensen called, in his monograph *Rudyard Kipling* (1912), "denne Dynamitsjæl" (this explosive spirit), and the British author Rudyard Kipling, in whose works Jensen experienced a new world of activity and international settings. Although classes in Viborg did not include modern literature, Jensen read works by contemporary writers in private. Both the Neo-Romantic Danish poet Johannes Jørgensen and the Norwegian Knut Hamsun, whom Jensen regarded as the first to break with the older realism and naturalism, what

Jensen called "den galliske knirkende Fornuftspoesi" (the Gallic, creaking literature of reason), became additional models for the future writer.

Jensen passed his university entrance exams in 1893 and began the study of medicine at the University of Copenhagen in the fall. In January of 1894 he published four poems, basically derivative of Neo-Romantic literature, that contain motifs foreshadowing his later settlement with the introvert and spiritual attitude, that was prevalent in Danish literature at the time of his debut and remained part of Jensens's own personality. Likewise without artistic quality are ten serial novels, written under the pseudonym Ivar Lykke between 1895 and 1898. In his *Mytens ring* Jensen hints at the main ingredients of these serial novels, remarking that: "Hvert Kapitel havde sit horrible Mord" (Each chapter contained a horrible murder). The novels hold no trace of his later mastery of style but are not without importance, as in them Jensen introduces motifs that he would take up again.

Jensen had his true literary debut in 1896 with the novel *Danskere*. After he abandoned his medical studies in 1898, he published *Einar Elkær: Roman* (Einar Elkær: Novel, 1898). Between the publication of the two novels was a brief trip to New York City in 1896, the first of many travels that, altogether, took Jensen to the United States six times. Both the character Buris in the first novel and Einar Elkær, the title character in the second novel, are students from the provinces who are confronted with the modern metropolis, Copenhagen. They are obsessed by paralyzing self-absorption that prevents them from establishing a spontaneous rapport with other people, in particular with women. Whereas Jensen hints at the possibility that the disintegration of Buris's personality may stop, Einar constantly lapses into his ravings and dreams and dies at a mental hospital, where "Sektionen viste blød Hjærne" (the autopsy showed a soft brain). Even though the two novels are strongly dependent on literary models—their melancholy atmosphere, big city sceneries, and self-reflective protagonists can be found in the early works of Jørgensen and Hamsun—their rebellion against both the fin-de-siècle spirit of the 1890s and literary and philosophical authority in general has a genuine ring. Jensen later excluded his first two books from his authorship, perhaps because he recognized too much of his own introverted personality in his two protagonists. They are desperate outsiders, whose longing for happiness finds no fulfillment. This longing, which in so many of Jensen's characters manifests itself as a longing to travel, is in reality a longing for the expansion of the soul.

Introspection remains a major issue in the two travelogues, *Intermezzo: Dolores, Forsvundnes, Skove, Louison* (Intermezzo: Dolores, Lost Forests, Louison, 1899) and *Skovene* (The Woods, 1904), both written under the influence of Heine's capricious, ironic style. The first was based on Jensen's two visits as a reporter for the liberal newspaper *Politiken* to Spain, Germany, and France in 1898 and also includes the first of his many attacks on the works of Friedrich Nietzsche, whose theories of the superman constituted the "bad Darwinism" that Jensen later saw as the indirect cause of the two world wars. The second book was inspired by Jensen's five-week stay in Singapore and on the Malay Peninsula during his first trip around the world in 1902–1903, which also took him to China, Japan, and the United States. In his description of a tiger hunt Jensen incorpo-

rates lyrical and satirical passages, witticisms, and brilliantly executed, precise but poetic descriptions of animals and nature. The strong stylistic contrasts in the volume reflect the self-ironic and didactic approach Jensen takes toward his own glorification of the primitive, against which he sets his homesickness and longing.

The reworked travel letters from his visit to Spain in 1898 and another to the World's Exhibition in Paris in 1900, which Jensen incorporated into his *Den gotiske Renaissance* (The Gothic Renaissance, 1901), on the other hand, include an enthusiastic endorsement of progress and reality: "Det tyvende Aarhundrede suser over Hovedet. Jeg bekender mig til Virkeligheden, jeg bekender" (The twentieth century roars above our heads. I profess to reality, I profess). This work glorifies the expansive spirit of the Gothic, that is, Anglo-Saxon, race, the fullest expression of which Jensen found in the American pragmatic and progressive view of life as it brought liberation from the decadence of the previous century. The volume climaxes in Walt Whitman–inspired prose hymns to progress and technology. Jensen's theory was that the Gothic race had its origin in his home region, Himmerland. Its nature and people are portrayed in the realistic short stories in *Himmerlandsfolk: Historier* (Himmerland People: Stories, 1898), which constitute a counterbalance to Jensen's introspective writings from the same period, and in the two collections *Nye Himmerlandshistorier* (New Himmerland Stories, 1904) and *Himmerlandshistorier: Tredie Samling* (Himmerland Stories: Third Collection, 1910). The early texts are marked by Jensen's preoccupation with the tragic meaninglessness of day-to-day existence and death. Later stories include masterful character studies of grotesque, roaming eccentrics, heroic accounts of man's stubborn fight against either sordid surroundings or the callous forces of nature, and comic or satiric exposures of human folly. Jensen's intimate knowledge of the flaws and meanness of his characters is balanced by a profound veneration for the old peasant traditions they also represent. In such texts Jensen has distanced himself from the uncritical glorification of technology and progress in *Den gotiske Renaissance,* and these stories are far above traditional regional literature.

In 1900–1901 Jensen published an historical novel in three parts, *Foraarets Død* (Spring's Death, 1900), *Den store Sommer* (The Full Summer, 1900), and *Vinteren* (Winter, 1901). Jensen combined the works into a single volume under the title of *Kongens Fald* (1901; translated as *The Fall of the King,* 1933). With *Kongens Fald* Jensen successfully merged the extrovert/naturalistic and introvert/spiritual elements in his writing into a splendid mythic composition. In Jensen's works there are many attempts at defining "the mythic." In his 1932 article on Jensen, Aage Marcus reports Jensen as saying: "Leave out the plot, concentrate on those short flashes of the essence of things that illumine man and time, and you have the myth." As Jensen writes in his *Aarbog 1916* (Yearbook 1916), his point of departure is generally a concrete observation from which an expansion in time and space takes place, a technique that entails a revelation, "ingen lang møjsommelig Opregning men et Spring ind i et Billede" (rather a leap into an image than a long painstaking account). Crucial components of the myth are the tensions between the close and the distant, the tangible and the transcendental, and the concrete and the inexplicable, frequently establishing a perspective of time in which present, past, and future are bound together.

Kongens Fald can be read as a purely historical novel, attacking the passivity and indecisiveness that Jensen perceived as a major component of Danish mentality. These negative qualities are embodied in the Renaissance king Christian II and his companion, the mercenary Mikkel Thøgersen. However, Jensen ignores both historical accuracy and a structured psychological character delineation. Instead, by mingling dreamlike passages of exquisite poetic beauty with harsh, naturalistic scenes of violence and destruction, he creates magnificent, deeply pessimistic visions of man's inability to reach happiness. Like Buris in *Danskere,* the introverted outsider Mikkel completely lacks the ability to devote himself to enjoying the present: He can only act when his anguish turns into hatred and blind destructiveness. Therefore, he must rape the fiancée of his rival Otte Iversen, Ane Mette, and, many years later, kill Otte's son, the carefree and spontaneous Axel, who has success with women, thereby stirring Mikkel's feelings of alienation, envy, and hatred. As a result he assaults the unarmed Axel, who later, without any bitterness, dies of blood poisoning, fever-stricken and dreaming that he is sailing into "den store Sommers Land, Dødens Land" (the land of full summer, the land of death). Axel's "fall," one of the lyrical highlights of the novel, corresponds on the historical level to the king's "fall" during the fateful night in 1523 when Christian II, accompanied by Mikkel, irresolutely sails back and forth between two regions of Denmark wondering whether or not to take up the fight against the rebellious nobility—a dramatic highlight and at the same time a penetrating analysis of the paralysis of action by doubt. However, of crucial importance is not the outward fall as demonstrated in the king's destiny. Jensen's masterpiece must be read as a book about the inner fall, about man's impermanence and about death as his inexorable destiny in the midst of burgeoning life, illustrated in Axel's fate. *Kongens Fald* is a book about the total absurdity of life and love, illustrated in Mikkel's person. All

Illustration by Valdemar Andersen for the 1916 edition of Jensen's Kongens Fald, *an historical novel set in sixteenth-century Denmark*

of humanity is subject to the law of the fall, and only death brings the desired peace.

On his first trip around the world Jensen crossed the Pacific Ocean from Japan, stopping in the Hawaiian Islands and disembarking in San Francisco on 26 October 1902. His stay in the United States, primarily in Chicago and New York during the winter and spring of 1902–1903, provided him with the splendidly depicted sceneries for the two novels *Madame D'Ora* (1904) and *Hjulet* (The Wheel, 1905), with which Jensen—only in part successfully—intended to continue the anti-metaphysical trend in his authorship. Intentionally he disregards the rules of the traditional, naturalistic novel as he sets out to portray not individuals but various stages in man's evolution within the framework of a fierce Darwinian struggle for the "survival of the fittest." In *Madame D'Ora* this struggle takes place between "the missing link"; the cynical lay preacher, charlatan, and murderer Evanston; and the scientist Edmund Hall, a Faustian character fascinated with the transcendental, a neurasthenic dreamer who not only fails to reciprocate passionate and unconditional feelings of the opera singer Leontine D'Ora but also falls an easy prey to Evanston because of his preoccupation with spiritual experiences. In the sequel, *Hjulet,* the young poet Lee, Jensen's alter ego, kills Evanston, who has now changed his name to the symbolic Cancer and has become an even clearer example of the Nietzschean vulgarization of Darwinism that Jensen had earlier attacked in *Intermezzo.* Through his struggle Lee overcomes his earlier passivity and turns into a man of action who condemns all aesthetics as nothing but "en Sygdom i Sansen for Virkeligheden" (a disease in the perception of reality). Passages parodying the detective novels of Sir Arthur Conan Doyle alternate with lengthy monologues, in particular by the constantly talking Cancer, congenial translations of poems by Whitman, and Lee's sweeping visions ranging from prehistoric, evolutionary stages in man's development to his view of Columbus as a man of Nordic descent and a bridge builder between Europe's past and America's present. These visions—indeed prose poems of compelling poetic force—as well as the totally negative portrayal of the representative of pure materialism, Evanston/Cancer, prove that Jensen could not let go of the aesthetics that he lets Lee reject. The enthusiasm for the United States expressed in the two novels foreshadows later works of fiction and nonfiction, as Jensen would return to both theories of Columbus and Faustian motifs.

After Jensen returned to Copenhagen from New York City in the summer of 1903, he published a series of newspaper articles. In these articles his violent criticism of Danish superficiality and provincialism demonstrates how difficult it was for him to resign himself to staying home. He was particularly irritated by Danish literary life, partly because of his own aggressive nature, which isolated him among colleagues, and partly because he rejected both the Neo-Romantics and the radical circle around the influential critic Georg Brandes, whom he had earlier admired. He was also unhappy because his books received mostly negative reviews and sold poorly.

Nevertheless, the period from 1904 to 1906 was characterized by a hectic productivity: two novels, a travelogue, a new volume of stories from Himmerland, and finally an epoch-making collection of poetry. All these publications were projects that Jensen felt he wanted to leave behind. *Digte* (Poems, 1906; revised and enlarged, 1917, 1921, 1943, 1948) includes almost all of his youthful poetry, except for those poems that he had published during his first year at the university, which have never been collected. Two of Jensen's earliest prose poems from 1901, "Interferens" (Interference) and "Ved Bordet" (At the Table), published in a newspaper, were revised and incorporated in *Digte.* Prose poetry came to dominate this volume, especially with

the inclusion of the Whitman translations, first published in the novel *Hjulet.* This preponderance of free verse has contributed to the popular but erroneous view that Jensen's poetry consists mostly of prose poetry, with Whitman as the predominant model. The truth is rather that Jensen's prose poems, modeled after the free verse of Johann Wolfgang von Goethe and Heine, belong to the period 1901–1906, after which he increasingly devoted himself to poems in regular meters with either Old Norse alliterative verse or the classical rhymed stanza as models.

Digte is a milestone in the development of Danish lyric poetry. Here a highly developed, bold imagery can be found, filled with contrasts and tension both in content and in style, a style that veers from cynical statement to ecstatic exclamation to heart-rending simplicity and tenderness—the heritage of the 1890s. This metaphoric language is based on a sharp sensory perception that often takes the shape of a merciless self-analysis at the same time as it incorporates images from modern technology and everyday life.

At the center of the volume are three texts, the two prose poems "Interferens" and "Paa Memphis Station" (At Memphis Station), and the balladlike "Christofer Columbus." In "Interferens" Jensen seeks, as he does in several of the poems, to combine the clash between extroversion and introversion, optimism and pessimism, belief in progress and wish for death—the two poles in his writing. When they intersect or rather become fused in one single state of mind, the myth emerges, as in "Christofer Columbus," originally published in *Madame D'Ora,* where it was a warning to Hall to abandon his insatiable ambitions to transgress the boundaries of empirical science. It can, however, also be read as an anticipation of the novel *Christofer Columbus* (1921; translated as *Christopher Columbus,* 1924), as a portrait of Jensen's tragic alter ego, Columbus, who is invoked in the poem "Afsked" (Departure). Here, another crucial theme from Jensen's novels, the longing to travel, is introduced in an attack on humdrum everyday life in provincial Denmark. The poem was written in 1902 just before Jensen's voyage around the world. Inspired by the voyage itself is "Paa Memphis Station," a commitment to a reality that must encompass even the experience of death. This realization ignites the poet's zest for a life that must be conquered through travel. Thus Columbus must move on, but the outcome of his travel turns out to be tragic as Jensen points out in the succeeding, stirring poem "Hverdagene" (Everyday Life). Its concluding request to "gaa frygtløst ind i Hverdagene" (enter into everyday life fearlessly) is preceded by lines about the merciless passage of time and unavoidable death:

Somren slaar sine Kister i.
Unge er vi saa ikke mere.
Men har Haabet ikke beskæmmet os tilstrækkeligt?
Nu kommer vor rige Dødstid, Broder.

(Summer is closing its chests.
So we are young no longer.
But has hope not shamed us sufficiently?
Now comes a plentiful dying time, brother.)

Lines such as these point ahead to perhaps the most difficult of all lyrical genres, the memorial poem, a genre that Jensen mastered to a degree not reached by any other Danish writer. In the second edition of Jensen's collected poems, *Digte: Anden Udgave* (Poems: Second Edition), in 1917 there are two such poems, "Leonora Christine" and "Bjørnstjerne Bjørnson," written in traditional iambic meter. The first is a portrait of Leonora Christine, a Danish Renaissance princess who spent twenty-two years in prison and whose tragic destiny Jensen perceives in a mythic perspective. The second poem is a glorification of the active and extroverted Norwegian writer written on the occasion of Bjørnson's death in 1910. The poem is pervaded with pantheism; however, Jensen concludes with these lines negating that pantheism: "O Solopgang paa Bjergets Sne –/ham skal du aldrig mere se" (Oh sunrise on the mountain's snow– / you shall never see him again). The last poem in the volume is "Envoi," which Jensen kept revising again, until it received its final form in the third edition of his collected poems. This poem is noteworthy for its haiku-like simplicity, with a perfect form embracing time and space, a myth concentrated around the eternity of love placed in the cycle of nature.

Jensen's productivity after his return from his journey around the world in 1902–1903 was also caused by the need to make a living for his family. On 15 April 1904 he married twenty-six-year-old Else Marie Ulrik, with whom he had three sons, Jens, Villum, and Emmerick. On 2 July 1906 Jensen began his own newspaper, *Pressen* (The Press), with John Martin. Modeled on contemporary American tabloids, *Pressen* was filled with sensational news, cartoons, and many advertisements. As Jensen did not have any political or cultural program for the newspaper, however, he did not find any readers, and *Pressen* lasted only until 31 July. This project was preceded by several trips to Himmerland and Berlin, and at the same time Jensen began translating Frank Norris's novel *The Octopus* (1901), eventually published as *Af Hvedens Saga: Polypen, en Bog om Kalifornien* (From the Wheat's Saga: The Octopus, a Book about California, 1907). By writing the foreword to *Naar Naturen kalder,* a translation in 1907 of Jack London's *The Call of the Wild* (1903), Jensen called attention in Denmark to another American writer; he introduced

JOHANNES V. JENSEN

MYTER

GYLDENDALSKE BOGHANDEL
MCMXXIV

Cover for Jensen's Myter: Tredie Bind, 1914–1924, *illustrated by his friend Johannes Larsen*

a third American writer, Ernest Hemingway, to the Danish public with an essay in *Politiken* (30 May 1930).

As a result of a 1905 trip to New York City, Jensen began writing a series of articles in March 1906 for *Politiken* about journalism, literature, and social issues in the United States. These were republished in the essay collection *Den ny Verden: Til international Belysning af nordisk Bondekultur* (The New World: For an International Illustration of Nordic Peasant Culture, 1907). The heroes of the book are the American reporter Norris, who successfully portrayed the hectic pioneer spirit during the growth of the United States, and Theodore Roosevelt, who is seen as the epitome of American civilization because of his dynamic and extroverted nature. From the fall of 1906 to the summer of 1907 Jensen was preoccupied with polemical exchanges with various Danish writers and critics. For this reason the collection of prose *Myter og Jagter* (Myths and Hunts), from 1907, includes primarily texts that had previously been published. *Singapore Noveller* (Singapore Stories), also from 1907, was likewise based on older material. Together with the texts in *Lille Ahasverus* (Little Ahasuerus, 1909) and *Olivia Marianne* (1915), the stories in *Singapore Noveller* were collected in *Eksotiske Noveller* (Exotic Stories, 1916). They form an exotic counterpart to the stories about Himmerland. The United States provides the setting for some of the stories, but most of them are set in Java and China, inspired by Jensen's Far East trip in the summer and fall of 1902, and owe their quality mainly to the exquisitely drawn scenery and linguistic virtuosity. In their somewhat simplistic view of the life of Europeans among the natives, the stories are an example of the strong influence Kipling had on Jensen's early writings.

In the summer of 1907 Jensen, tired of literary disputes—although he had provoked them himself—made a trip to Norway, and in the following winter he went to Sweden. These visits resulted in several realistic hunting descriptions for *Politiken,* later included in the volume *Nye Myter* (New Myths, 1908), which also includes one of Jensen's finest prose texts, "Darwin og Fuglen" (Darwin and the Bird). It opens with a magnificent spring scene, then is extended into a portrait of Darwin, the man whose theories influenced Jensen's writing for the remaining forty-three years of his life. With this volume and *Myter og Jagter,* Jensen had begun to issue a series of brief, somewhat uneven prose texts, so-called *myter* or myths, which usually were first printed in newspapers; from 1910 to 1944 nine additional volumes were published. In essays and sketches based on reading and traveling, Jensen incorporates

> Øjebliksbilleder fra Gaden, indre dæmrende Erindringer omspændende alle fem Verdensdele, Historien, Urtiden og en fjern Barndom . . . mellem hinanden, men *sandt* til Hobe forsaa vidt som det hænger sammen og har Tone og Farve.

> (snapshots from the street, inner dawning memories encompassing all five continents, history, the earliest times and a distant childhood . . . intermingled, but every bit of it *true* in so far as it has coherence and resonance and color.)

Jensen presents his basic ideas in a symbolic, concentrated form: a full acceptance of present reality as the source and final goal of all longing as in "Fusijama" (1907; translated as "Fujiyama," 1958) and a belief in eternity as it is found in the cyclic reappearance of the seasons as in "Nordisk Foraar" (Nordic Spring, 1912). Jensen's myths are based on his belief in the necessity of placing ourselves in a meaningful context with nature as in "Haren" (The Hare, 1908) and creating links to the most distant memories from history and prehistory as in "Dansk Natur" (Danish Nature, 1910). This myth gives a superb description of Denmark seen in the light

of the country's past incarnated in ancient monuments and in visions of life of Stone Age people. It is actually one of several myths exemplifying the impossibility of seizing and preserving the present moment in isolation and thus—characteristic of the split in Jensen between materialism and spirituality—partially contradicting the "Fusijama" myth. Directly dealing with man's quest for the indefinite and eternal are the myths "Moderen og Barnet" (Mother and Child, 1917) and "Den store Kristoffer" (The Great Christopher, 1917). "Moderen og Barnet," which in his *Æstetik og Udvikling: Efterskrift til Den lange Rejse* (Aesthetics and Evolution: Postscript to The Long Journey, 1923) Jensen called "nok det gyldigste jeg har gjort" (probably the most valid thing I have ever written), is based on the Roman Catholic concept of the Madonna and child, "Livets skønneste Symbol, Slægten i et Afbillede, som var Slægten selv, det højeste Under, og samtidigt den højeste Moral" (life's most beautiful symbol, the family in a single image that is the family itself, the highest miracle and at the same time the highest ethics). In his retelling of the legend of St. Christopher, Jensen makes a Northerner of him. His staff, which changed into a palm, is interpreted mythically as the Northerner's longing for the South, which is finally satisfied when the South comes to him in the person of the infant Jesus, whom Christopher carries across the river and into the North, an achievement that is duplicated when his namesake, Columbus, brings Christianity to the New World.

These two myths, as well as several others, were reworked and incorporated into the six books that became *Den lange Rejse* (1935; translated as *The Long Journey,* 3 volumes, 1922–1924). This multivolume novel comprises an evolutionary history or rather a fantasy of mankind. It was intended as a scientific counterpart to the biblical legends but turned out to be a collection of legends itself. Jensen sees the challenge of nature as the driving force of progress that brings about evolution. *Bræen: Myter om Istiden og det første Menneske* (The Glacier: Myths of the Ice Age and of the First Man, 1908; translated in *Fire and Ice,* 1922) is the first written in the series and also its most popular. Here the Glacial Age has forced the humans to migrate southward; only Dreng (Boy) turns in defiance to the north and founds, together with the woman Moa (Mother), a large family. In a splendid scene Dreng rediscovers fire by striking sparks from flint, while Moa collects seeds and begins to till the soil.

Det tabte Land: Mennesket før Istiden (The Lost Land: Man Before the Ice Age, 1919; translated in *Fire and Ice,* 1922) is a Darwinian myth of creation about the transition from animal to Homo sapiens in the pre-glacial rain forests of Jutland. The major character of the volume is Fyr (Fire), who climbs a volcano and, like

Prometheus, steals the fire. Up on the mountain he sees the ocean in the distance, and the feeling of longing is stirred in him for the first time.

In *Norne-Gæst* (1919; translated in *The Cimbrians*, 1923) Jensen follows the lives of the Northerners from the Glacial Age to the Great Migration. The opening lines describe the newborn title character's first glimpse of the blue sky between the leaves. This vision is to become crucial for his insatiable longing to travel that will drive Norne-Gæst both around the world, encountering, for instance, Greek and Roman civilization, and up through the Bronze and Iron Ages. *Cimbrernes Tog* (The Raids of the Cimbri, 1922; translated in *The Cimbrians*, 1923), the last volume of the series to be published, is also mainly set abroad. It opens with Norne-Gæst wandering up through Jutland in order to attend the spring festivals in Himmerland, home of the Cimbrians. Suddenly climatic deterioration sets in with floods and famine, and the Cimbrians set off under the command of Bojerik, a name modeled after a Boiorix mentioned in one of Jensen's sources, Plutarch's *Parallel Lives*. The narrative then follows the everyday life of the Cimbrians as they raid down through Europe, with intervening mythic scenes as observed and commented upon by the omnipresent Norne-Gæst. Other tribes join the Cimbrians, and together they win their first battles against the Romans. Here the Northerner and the Southerner, separated in *Bræen,* meet again. Eventually, the Cimbrians, having acquired the decadence of the foreign lands, are defeated in a bloody battle, yet the volume concludes on a conciliatory note in which the spirits of antiquity and of the North merge harmoniously.

In *Skibet* (The Ship, 1912) the Nordic longing to travel is embodied in the Vikings and their raids to the Mediterranean. In the North, Christianity is introduced through a monk, Brother Parvus. Jensen's description of his works of charity belongs among his most exquisite passages, forming an essential correlation to his frequently stressed anti-Christian attitude. The first church is erected by turning the Viking ship upside down. In the deepest sense the forest itself becomes a cathedral, while the longing to go abroad takes on a religious dimension.

Longing as the basic trait of the Nordic people becomes personified by the title character of the 1921 novel *Christofer Columbus*—whom Jensen had previously described as a reddish-blond Northerner in *Hjulet*—and his voyages of discovery. Jensen's view of the defiant and struggling individual as the creator of culture, fundamental to *Den lange Rejse,* is paralleled by his concept of the basic trait of the Nordic people—"the Gothic race"—as being the dream about warmth and sun. This dream, which is Jensen's explanation of the religious sentiment, is expressed through a longing for distant places, in the final account a longing for paradise that becomes embodied in the structures of the ship and the upward-reaching Gothic cathedral. The Viking migrations, the "raids of the Cimbri," were a result of this longing, as was the voyage of the Goth, Columbus. His attempt at finding legendary lands resulted, however, in the discovery of America, of reality; and yet, at the conclusion of his life, Columbus realizes that his new discovery has brought him nothing but homelessness and loneliness. Now the initial optimism turns into tragic resignation, as Columbus subsequently chooses not a metaphysical solution but a return to his memories of the past. He does not realize that he must let his journey continue toward the eternal as it is depicted in the myth, "Ave Stella," that concludes the volume.

Den lange Rejse is not a novel with a traditional plot centered around the adventures of a hero, nor should the work be read as a scientifically correct depiction of various cultural stages. The fact that so many of its theories are contrary to modern history, anthropology, and archeology is irrelevant and cannot weaken the work as literature. Rather, *Den lange Rejse* is a vision written by an artist with a formidable ability to identify with other periods and conditions. The outcome proves the impossibility of creating a meaningful coherence based on evolution alone, and Jensen's project defies any organizing structure; however, the six volumes form a grandiose and gripping artistic work that is outstanding as a depiction of the ages of history and of mankind.

Jensen gradually turned away from the writing of fiction in favor of a growing involvement in current cultural and scientific issues; this reorientation was accompanied by a focusing on the feature article and the essay with the purpose of popularizing the theories of evolution. In Jensen's collection of essays *Nordisk Aand: Kroniker og Karakteristiker* (Nordic Spirit: Chronicles and Characteristics, 1911) the American society that he had glorified in *Den ny Verden* was analyzed further and seen as an implementation of the program in *Den gotiske Renaissance,* indeed as the true expression of the Nordic character; the Scandinavian prototype of this character is Bjørnson, who is portrayed with several other Danish and Norwegian writers. The volume concludes with a fierce attack on contemporary Danish literary critics for not appreciating Jensen's work.

In April 1911 Jensen traveled with his wife to Paris and London via Berlin and Cologne. His fascination with the cathedral in Cologne finds powerful expression in his next essay collection, and in a 10 May 1911 travel letter to *Politiken* from Normandy, where he looked for traces of the ancient Nordic population, can be seen the first impulses for the novel *Skibet,* which is set during the Viking Age. In 1912 Jensen also published a monograph, *Rudyard Kipling,* written in connec-

Jensen and his wife, Else

tion with several translations of various Kipling stories that he and Aslaug Mikkelsen had begun in 1911. Although Jensen was strongly influenced by the English writer during the composition of *Singapore Noveller* and the two additional volumes of short stories from 1909 and 1915, he is strongly critical of Kipling's imperialistic attitude and deprecation of women.

In the fall of 1912 Jensen began his second great journey to Asia, from which he returned the following year. His reflections en route were later included in the philosophical travelogue *Introduktion til vor Tidsalder* (Introduction to Our Epoch, 1915). "I det indiske Hav" (In the Indian Ocean) is a magnificent section with pure poetry in some passages, where Jensen describes the voyage until the vessel sails into the Ceylonese port of Colombo in December. Singapore is revisited, and the homesickness that Jensen had experienced a decade earlier overtook him again. In China he found the theme for a lyrical short story, "Darduses Myndlinge" (Darduse's Wards), which was later adapted for the stage as the comedy *Darduse, Bryllupet i Peking: Eventyrkomedie i fire akter* (Darduse, Wedding in Peking: Fairy Tale Comedy in Four Acts, 1937). From Manchuria, Jensen continued on his trip, describing in the chapter "fra Østen til Evropa" (from the East toward Europe) his experiences traveling on the Trans-Siberian Railroad, seeing again with joy the European peasant culture and describing jubilantly his return to Scandinavia. In its analysis of the Northerner's longing, the book forms a striking link between *Den gotiske Renaissance* and *Christofer Columbus*. At the same time, Jensen's attempt to give religious feelings a purely physiological explanation is one more bit of evidence that the question of immortality kept troubling him.

Jensen planned to make still another journey to Asia, by way of the United States, the following summer, but did not complete his trip. In March 1914 he embarked for New York City, but the joy of rediscovery is moderate. Even though Jensen still admired the American press and the hectic and progressive atmosphere in the country, he sharply attacked what he saw as the childishness and bigotry of the Americans. In mid April, Jensen decided to return to Copenhagen, and a few months later World War I broke out. Since Denmark remained neutral, Jensen could leave for Berlin in August in order to negotiate with his German publisher, Samuel Fischer. During his visit he became strongly critical of the bellicosity that was shared by all of the German political parties, and he bitterly regretted the clash between Germany and Britain, since both nations have the same Gothic origin.

During the war Jensen was mainly occupied with writing the last volumes of *Den lange Rejse*. He also prepared a greatly enlarged edition of his collected poems, *Digte: Tredie Udgave* (Poems: Third Edition, 1921). It includes—in addition to several memorial poems and other portraits—nine poems from *Den lange Rejse*. Of these, the alliterative "Drengs Gravsang" (Dreng's Elegy) from *Bræen* binds up the experience of love and boundless longing in a mythic vision. "Vor Frue" (Our Lady), structured on the prosody of the medieval hymn "Dies irae," and the balladlike "Den sørgeligste Vise" (The Saddest Song) from *Christofer Columbus* treat other recurrent themes in Jensen's writing: the first glorifies woman as a saving force and culminates in an apotheosis of the Madonna, while the second is one of the most overwhelming interpretations in Danish poetry of the futility of life. Disillusion and resignation also characterize the majority of remaining poems in the volume, many of which are in alliterative form.

Negative reviews of *Cimbrernes Tog* and the *Den lange Rejse* project as a whole by a critic for *Politiken*

led to another of Jensen's many literary feuds and culminated in a break with the newspaper that lasted until 1926. Shortly after the break, in December 1922, Jensen began the publication of his own periodical, *Forum: Tidsskrift for Litteratur, Biologi og Samfundsspørgsmål* (Forum: Periodical of Literature, Biology, and Social Issues), which survived for only one and a half years. In the first issue of *Forum* he published his most succinct and best-written settlement with the misuse of Darwinism, "Den daarlige Darwinisme" (The Bad Darwinism). In addition, *Forum* included a few insignificant poems about birds that, together with other animal poems illustrated by Jensen's intimate friend the painter Johannes Larsen, were collected in the volume *Aarstiderne* (The Seasons, 1923). Jensen's interest in this painter and in the visual arts in general—he was himself a painter and was also an accomplished sculptor—resulted in several art books, two of which deal with the renowned Danish sculptor Bertel Thorvaldsen. Related to these works is the collection of newspaper articles about art, *Form og Sjæl: Portrætter af Personligheder* (Form and Soul: Portraits of Personalities, 1931), one more expression of Jensen's love for classicism and of sculpture.

Essential for an understanding of Jensen's fiction is his 1923 work *Æstetik og Udvikling*. The book is a sort of afterword to *Den lange Rejse,* in which Jensen also launches his "gradus" theory, a conception designating the gliding steps of evolution that he wanted to stress rather than the static species—further developed in later volumes, such as *Aandens Stadier* (Stages of the Mind, 1928). In *Æstetik og Udvikling* Jensen writes: "*Den lange Rejse* handler ikke eksklusivt om en Race, den handler om Udviklingstrin. Den ene Race er Udviklingstrinet af den anden" (*Den lange Rejse* does not deal exclusively with a race, it deals with stages of evolution. One race is the evolutionary stage of another). At the same time Jensen sharply attacks the novel that focuses exclusively on individuals as being pre-Darwinian and thus hero-worshiping and outdated. The concept of "bad Darwinism" is discussed again in the obscure and insignificant collection of previously published articles about Darwinism, *Evolution og Moral* (Evolution and Ethics, 1925).

At the end of 1925 Jensen once again set out on a long journey; this time the goal was the Egyptian health resort of Helwan. From Egypt and later from Palestine, he sent several travel letters home to the newspaper *Social-Demokraten,* revised versions of which were included in *Aandens Stadier.*

Jensen continued to write memorial poems, and his perfection of this genre can be seen in the under-

Jensen surrounded by representatives of the peoples he wrote about in his ethnographic and historical works, a 1924 caricature by Alfred Schmidt for the magazine Blæksprutten

valued collection *Verdens Lys* (The Light of the World, 1926). *Verdens Lys* includes six alliterative poems from *Cimbrernes Tog* that—in a mythic perspective—juxtapose and celebrate the union between North and South. Unique among Jensen's works in its focus on artistic expression and a true masterpiece is "Graven i Sne" (The Snow-Covered Grave), a memorial poem to the Danish Romantic poet Adam Oehlenschläger. It is both an idealized portrait of Oehlenschläger, Jensen's beloved model as both a harmonious artist and human being—"To Gange gav han Livet Form, / i Livet selv, i ædel Norm" (Twice he gave to life a form, / in life itself, in noble norm)—and a poem about the eternal value of art in spite of the inevitability of death. It becomes a glorification of Jensen's own poetic art, as it is expressed in a structure that combines observation, vision, and reflection into a perfect artistic entity that may turn out to be the only way to overcome the absurdity of life. The poems in memory of Jensen's father offer an affectionate por-

trait of a man who lived in close intimacy with the miracles of life in nature, a closeness to nature inherited by the poet although not without discord. A much more somber tone is heard in the obituary for Jensen's mother, the concluding poem of the volume, "Ved min Moders Død"(At My Mother's Death), as well as in the hymnlike "Kirken i Hardanger" (The Church in Hardanger), in which the reader can perceive, behind the stoic resignation that results from placing oneself in the hands of the cycle of nature, the author's fear of annihilation, which is so strong and powerful that it threatens to break up the poetic form.

In 1927 *Dyrenes Forvandling: Til udviklingens Plastik* (The Transformation of Animals: A Contribution to the Plasticity of Evolution) was published; it was another presentation of evolutionary theories but without the fierce attacks on Christianity that characterize some of his earlier writings. Jensen attempts—and the task appears scientifically absurd—to describe the animal soul and ethics as they change through all stages of evolution. Trips to Madeira and Rome followed in 1928, and impressions from both trips were likewise included in the anthropological study of human origin and development, *Aandens Stadier.*

In May 1929 Jensen received an honorary doctorate from the University of Lund. At the same time Jensen began to focus again on Nordic issues and started his translation of *Egil's Saga* for a planned edition of *De islandske Sagaer* (The Icelandic Sagas), which were published in three volumes from 1930 to 1932. At the same time he returned to his preoccupation with Nordic archeology in a series of articles subsequently published in the volume *Paa danske Veje* (On Danish Roads, 1931) with his own photos and drawings by Larsen. With this work Jensen got involved in a fierce public debate about the preservation of the ancient burial mounds and stirred up so much political attention that stringent conservation laws were put into effect in 1937. His introduction to *De islandske Sagaer,* in which he discusses the sagas as products of a genuine Nordic mentality untouched by the traditions of antiquity and Christianity, points ahead to his book about women in the Viking age, *Kvinden i Sagatiden* (The Woman in the Saga Period, 1942), which also includes retellings of selected saga texts. For a new edition of Snorre Sturlason's *Heimskringla,* published in 1948, Jensen took upon himself the difficult task of translating all 539 stanzas.

The transcendental aspect in his earlier poetry is not found in *Den jydske Blæst: Digte 1926–1930* (The Jutland Wind: Poems 1926–1930, 1931), Jensen's last important poetry collection. Whereas death in, for instance, the memorial poem "Knut Hamsun" is still accepted as a pantheistic amalgamation into nature, most of the texts are structured on the tragic contrast between active life and the corruption of death, as in the memorial poem "Otto Benzon," and now nature brings no consolation: "I Kammerdøren peb Vindens Røst, / en ensom Jammer, ingen Trøst" (The voice of the wind whistled in the chamber door / a lonesome lamentation, no comfort). When the memorial poem over others becomes a poem about Jensen himself, as in the concluding title poem, one finds the same death motif, the portrayal of death as man's tragic but only certain verity. Jensen's writing has this motif in common with Baroque literature, albeit without Heaven as the final destination. With the howling wind that accompanies Cimbrians, Vikings, emigrants, and the author himself and that stretches from the Jutland moor to the Cape of Good Hope and the Andes as the continuous symbolic accompaniment, the poems swell into a grandiose lamentation at the nothingness of life.

On his sixtieth birthday, 20 January 1933, Jensen had reached such an esteemed position that a torchlight procession was held in his honor in Copenhagen and a Festschrift published, *Unge Digteres Hyldest til Johannes V. Jensen* (Young Writers' Homage to Johannes V. Jensen). In response to virulent public criticism of his lack of political commitment, Jensen, in an article published in *Politiken* on his birthday, emphasized—as he had done throughout his career—his independence as a freelance writer outside the political parties. Nevertheless, in a review of Hartvig Frisch's *Pest over Europa* (Plague over Europe, 1933) in the same newspaper on 3 December, he once again attacked Nietzsche's philosophy and its consequences in the Germany of the early 1930s. Here Jensen strongly dissociated himself from contemporary political developments in Europe toward dictatorship, and, in the 1938 article "Hagekorset" ("The Swastika"), he publicly expressed his disgust with anti-Semitism.

In 1930 Jensen published the collection of essays and articles *Retninger i Tiden: Artikler 1925–30* (Trends of the Times: Articles 1925–30); however, during the first part of the 1930s Jensen turned away from the essay form, with the exception of his short history of ideas, *Det Blivende: Tankens Revolutionering i det 19de Aarhundrede og Tilbagefaldet i det 20de* (The Permanent: The Revolution of Thought in the 19th Century and the Backslide in the 20th, 1934), written in a more concise and concentrated style than his other philosophical works. With the underrated novel *Dr. Renaults Fristelser* (The Temptations of Dr. Renault, 1935) he again took up fiction, reworking the Faust motif into a plot that, in contrast to the version presented by Goethe, lets the title character win over Mephistopheles because he is ready to fully accept the present. As in *Hjulet,* aestheticism is regarded as a barrier between man and reality, and in a significant scene Dr. Renault throws a valuable statue of Aphrodite into the sea, so that nothing will stand between him and life.

In October 1936 Jensen went on a short trip to the United States in order to collect material for a sequel to *Dr. Renaults Fristelser,* in spite of the negative reception that the book had received. The continuation never materialized. Instead Jensen published the novel *Gudrun* (1936), a realization of a much older project: a contemporary novel of the Copenhagen woman, and thus also a novel about the city of Copenhagen, but completely different from Jensen's first two novels. The city is no longer seen through the eyes of a student from the provinces. Now a citizen of Copenhagen for many years—and a matured artist—Jensen delivers a splendid and deeply intimate

Jensen's Nobel Prize certificate, awarded to him by the Swedish Academy in 1944

eulogy of this city as a swarming, animated organism. Most of Jensen's poems written in the 1930s were collected in 1937 as *Paaskebadet: Digte 1931–1937* (The Easter Bath: Poems 1931–1937).

That same year Jensen's play adaptation of *Darduse,* a "Fairy Tale Comedy in Four Acts, " had its premiere on 22 January 1937 at the Royal Theater in Copenhagen and was performed sixteen times. It was a weak play, carried by excellent acting and Knudåge Riisager's rousing music. Jensen's relationship with the theater was, on the whole, marked by a lack of success. A dramatization of *Madame D'Ora,* titled *Sangerinden* (The Singer) and published as *Sangerinden (Madame d'Ora): Drama i fem Akter* (The Singer (Madame d'Ora): Drama in Five Acts, 1921), was performed unsuccessfully in 1923, premiering at the Odense Teater on 16 November of that year, and when, on 24 April 1937, Jensen's translation of William Shakespeare's *Hamlet* was performed at the Royal Theater it provoked such fierce criticism that the production had to be canceled.

Shortly before the outbreak of World War II, Jensen managed to visit Norway, described in the travelogue *Nordvejen: Indtryk af norsk Natur* (The Way North: Impressions of Norwegian Nature, 1939), and then the United States; in March 1939 he left Denmark for his sixth journey to the New World. His travel letters were first printed in *Politiken* and subsequently as a book, titled *Fra Fristaterne: Rejsebreve, med et tilbageblik* (From the Free States: Travel Letters with a Retrospect, 1939). This time Jensen's encounter with the United States was marked by ambivalence. In the chapter "Fra Stillehavet til Atlanten" (From the Pacific Ocean to the Atlantic), which is among the most brilliant sections of the book, the impressions from the trip are summed up. Although his overall impressions were still positive, Jensen was disappointed by what he saw as the increasing vulgarity and materialism of American society, where technology had become an end in itself, not an expression of man's inventiveness and ingenuity. After having arrived on the East Coast, Jensen became ill and had to return home earlier than planned. Back in Copenhagen in May 1939 he added a concluding chapter on Thomas Jefferson, meant as a counterweight to the current antidemocratic trends in Europe.

Jensen had planned a tour to France for September 1939 in order to visit the regions where traces of prehistoric man had been discovered, but this plan was thwarted by the outbreak of World War II and had to be postponed until spring 1948. When the Germans occupied Denmark in April 1940, apparently fearing arrest, Jensen took the precaution of burning his diaries from the previous thirty years, together with all personal letters written to him. In this way much data related to the writing of his books and—most important—notes from his many travels were lost for posterity. Nevertheless, he continued to write throughout the occupation from 1940 to 1945. In 1941 came *Mindets Tavle: Portrætter og Personligheder* (Plaque of Commemoration: Portraits and Personalities) with portraits of Nordic and British explorers, scientists, writers—and Darwin once again—and in 1943 the collection of some unimportant ethnographic articles, *Folkeslagene i Østen* (The People of the Orient). Of greater quality is the study *Vor Oprindelse* (Our Origin, 1941), describing humanity's gradual acquisition of civilization. Again Jensen's myth-creating fantasy bloomed in a visionary description of cultural progress. At the same time he offers a subtle analysis of his authorship, clearly drawing up a balance sheet and expressing his feeling that he was at the end of the road, a feeling that is also expressed in the essay "Tak til Sproget" (Thanks to Language), Jensen's farewell to literature; this essay was included, together with some linguistic studies, in a small book, *Om Sproget og Undervisningen* (About Language and Teaching, 1942).

After having been nominated several times for the Nobel Prize in Literature, Jensen finally received it on 9 November 1944. The Nobel Committee announced that the prize was awarded in recognition of "the remarkable force and richness of his poetic imagination, combined with a wide-ranging intellectualism and bold, innovative sense of style," and clearly, *Den lange Rejse* proved to be the decisive factor for the committee.

During the last years of Jensen's life his productivity decreased significantly. After an operation in September 1948 he managed to finish a book about the great explorers, *Afrika: Opdagelsesrejserne* (Africa: Journeys of Discovery, 1949), demonstrating that one of the favorite topics of his childhood reading was still inspiring him. Otherwise, Jensen was primarily occupied with the preparation of a combined, revised edition of the three books, *Dyrenes Forvandling, Aandens Stadier,* and *Vor Oprindelse,* but he managed to complete only the first volume, published posthumously in 1951 in the volume

Tilblivelsen (Genesis). Troubled by an ear disease, he also suffered from shingles during the summer of 1949 and was hospitalized. He still managed to write a few more articles; the most valuable of these, "Adam Oehlenschläger 1779–1850," published in the book *Swift og Oehlenschläger* (Swift and Oehlenschläger, 1950), is a finely drawn portrait of his artistic model as a man of simple nature, without stiltedness, who calmly accepted death as Jensen had described it in the poem "Graven i Sne." On 31 January 1950 Jensen commented on his second great model, Darwin, in a short article, "Træk fra vor Oprindelse" (Traits from Our Origin). These two personalities, the poet Oehlenschläger and the scientist Darwin, perfectly symbolize the two facets of Jensen's authorship. In his later years natural science came to dominate, but the first element stands as the most valuable, the one that will survive.

Johannes V. Jensen died on 25 November 1950. Georg Brandes once claimed that as a thinker and preacher Jensen could not be taken seriously. Brandes had a point: the content of Jensen's many collections of essays and articles dealing with natural science, archeology, and anthropology are often based on dubious scientific theories and deductions. In addition, in these volumes Jensen linguistically turns from lyrical expressiveness to a terse, matter-of-fact diction. But one must not fail to notice that in spite of the scientific topic, his stylistic mastery often breaks forth in evocative passages that can be read as sublime prose poetry. Jensen's critics have also frequently overlooked that he was brilliant as a journalistic writer. He was unusually well informed about current trends, and his knowledge of American society and literature was unique for a Dane of his time. Neither should his contributions as a translator be overlooked. Besides his accomplished translations from Old Norse, his outstanding rendering of Whitman's poetry in Danish must be acknowledged.

It was as a lyrical poet and a creator of myth that Jensen reached perfection, both in his collections of poetry and myths and when he succeeded in combining the two genres, as in *Kongens Fald, Skovene, Den lange Rejse,* and several of his stories of Himmerland. With his debut collection of poems, Jensen introduced modernism in Danish poetry, and he became the writer who, arguably, has had the strongest impact on twentieth-century Danish literature.

Bibliographies:

Frits Johansen and Aage Marcus, *Johannes V. Jensen: En Bibliografi,* 2 volumes (Copenhagen: Gyldendal, 1933–1951);

Aage Jørgensen, *Litteratur om Johannes V. Jensen En bibliografi* (Odense: Odense University Press, 1998).

Biographies:

K. K. Nicolaisen, *Johannes V. Jensen: Bidrag til hans Biografi og Karakteristik* (Aalborg: Viggo Madsens Boghandel, 1914);

Oluf Friis, *Den unge Johannes V. Jensen 1873–1902,* 2 volumes (Copenhagen: Gad, 1974);

Villum Jensen, *Min fars hus: Erindringer om Johannes V. Jensen og hans miljø* (Copenhagen: Gyldendal, 1976);

Leif Nedergaard, *Johannes V. Jensen,* third edition (Copenhagen: C.A. Reitzels Forlag, 1993).

References:

Harry Andersen, *Afhandlinger om Johannes V. Jensen* (Rødovre: Rolvs Forlag, 1982);

Andersen, *Studier i Johannes V. Jensens Lyrik: Verseteknik, Sprog og Stil* (Copenhagen: Levin & Munksgaard, 1936);

Jørgen Elbek, *Johannes V. Jensen* (Copenhagen: Gyldendal, 1966);

Otto Gelsted, *Johannes V. Jensen: Kurven i hans Udvikling* (Copenhagen: Arthur Jensens Forlag, 1938);

Alf Henriques, *Johannes V. Jensen* (Copenhagen: H. Hirschsprungs Forlag, 1938);

Poul Houe, *Johannes V. Jensens lange rejse: En postmoderne myte* (Copenhagen: Museum Tusculanum, 1996);

Niels Ingwersen, "America as Setting and Symbol in Johannes V. Jensen's Early Works," *American Norvegica,* 3 (1971): 272–293;

Bent Haugaard Jeppesen, *Johannes V. Jensen og den hvide mands byrde: Eksotisme og imperialisme* (Copenhagen: Rhodos, 1984);

Aage Jørgensen and Helene Kragh-Jacobsen, eds., *Columbus fra Himmerland* (Farsø: Farsø Bibliotek, 1994);

Aage Marcus, "Johannes V. Jensen," *American-Scandinavian Review,* 20 (1932): 339–347;

Felix Nørgaard and Aage Marcus, eds., *Johannes V. Jensen. 1873–20. Januar–1943* (Copenhagen: Gyldendal, 1943);

Sven H. Rossel, "Andersen og Jensen–Eventyret og myten," in *Hvad Fatter gjør . . . Boghistoriske, litterære og musikalske essays tilegnet Erik Dal,* edited by Henrik Glahn and others (Herning: Poul Kristensen, 1982), pp. 392–402;

Rossel, *Johannes V. Jensen* (Boston: Twayne, 1984);

Aage Schiøttz-Christensen, *Om sammenhængen i Johannes V. Jensens forfatterskab* (Copenhagen: Borgen, 1956);

Henrik Wivel, *Den titaniske eros: Drifts–sog karakterfortolkning i Johannes V. Jensens forfatterskab* (Copenhagen: Gyldendal, 1982).

Papers:

The major collection of correspondence and manuscripts is in the Johannes V. Jensen Archives at Det kongelige Bibliotek (The Royal Library), Copenhagen. Additional material is located at Statsbiblioteket, Århus, and the Farsø Bibliotek. Forty-three letters from Jensen to various Norwegian writers and friends are located at the University Library, Oslo.

Thit Jensen

(19 January 1876 – 13 May 1957)

Paal Bjørby

University of Bergen

BOOKS: *To Søstre: Fortælling* (Copenhagen: Salmonsen, 1903);

Familien Storm (Copenhagen: Salmonsen, 1904; republished, Copenhagen: Gyldendal, 1943);

Martyrium: Samfundsroman (Copenhagen: Gyldendal, 1905);

Ørkenvandring: Samfundsroman (Copenhagen: Gyldendal, 1907);

Prins Nilaus af Danmark: Sagnfortælling (Copenhagen: Gyldendal, 1907);

Sagn og Syner: Mystiske fortællinger fra Island (Copenhagen: Gyldendal, 1909);

I Messias' Spor: Nutids-roman fra Island (Copenhagen: Gyldendal, 1911);

Det banker: Fire Historietter (Copenhagen: Dansk Literært Forlag, 1911);

Elskovs Forbandelse (Copenhagen: Dansk Literært Forlag, 1911);

Hemskoen: Roman (Copenhagen: Gyldendal, 1912; republished, Copenhagen: Hasselbach, 1921);

Højeste Ret: Fortælling fra en dansk Herregaard (Copenhagen: Gyldendal, 1913);

Stærkere end Tro: Roman (Copenhagen: Gyldendal, 1915);

Jorden: Roman fra Nutiden (Copenhagen: Gyldendal, 1915);

Jydske Historier (Copenhagen: Gyldendal, 1916);

Hr. Berger intime (Copenhagen: Gyldendal, 1917);

Gerd, Det tyvende Aarhundredes Kvinde (Copenhagen: Gyldendal, 1918);

Kærlighedens Kaabe: Roman (Copenhagen: Gyldendal, 1918);

Den erotiske Hamster: Nutidsroman (Copenhagen: Gyldendal, 1919);

Kongen af Sande (Copenhagen: Nyt Nordisk Forlag, 1919);

Det evigt Mandige (Copenhagen: Danske Forfatteres Forlag, 1919);

Den evige Længsel: Moderne Studie Over mand og Kvinde (Copenhagen: Hasselbalch, 1921);

Aphrodite fra Fuur, den moderne Kvindes Udviklingshistorie: Roman (Copenhagen: Hasselbach, 1924);

Mit Foredrag: Frivilligt Moderskab (Copenhagen: E. Jespersen, 1924);

Af Blod er du kommet: Roman fra Højrenaissancens Tid i Danmark (Copenhagen: Gyldendal, 1928)–chapter 6, "De Rinds Knaber hylder Blod af deres Blod," translated by Anne Born as "The Knights of Rind Welcome a Kinsman," in *Contemporary*

Danish Prose: An Anthology, edited by Elias Bredsdorff (Copenhagen: Gyldendal, 1958), pp. 93–99;

Jørgen Lykke; Rigens sidste Ridder: Roman i tre Bøger fra Højrenaissancen i Danmark, 2 volumes (Copenhagen: Gyldendal, 1931; republished, 1 volume, 1948);

Nial den Vise: Udstyrsskuespil fra Islands Storhedstid (Copenhagen: Gyldendal, 1934);

Stygge Krumpen, 2 volumes (Copenhagen: Gyldendal, 1936; republished, 1 volume, 1937);

Valdemar Atterdag: En Kærligheds Roman, 2 volumes (Copenhagen: Gyldendal, 1940);

Drotten: Historisk Roman fra det 14. Aarhundrede (Copenhagen: Gyldendal, 1943);

Rigets Arving: Historisk Roman, 2 volumes (Copenhagen: Gyldendal, 1946);

Hvorfra? Hvorhen? (Copenhagen: Gyldendal, 1950);

Atter det skilte: Fjerde og sidste bog om Kong Valdemaar og Dronning Helvig (Copenhagen: Gyldendal, 1953);

Den sidste Valkyrie: Roman om Dronning Thyra Danebod (Copenhagen: Gyldendal, 1954);

Gylden Høst: Et Sommersmil (Copenhagen: Grafisk Forlag, 1956);

Fru Astrid Grib, foreword by Jens Andersen (Copenhagen: Gad, 1990);

Jeg længes . . . Fra Thit Jensens dagbøger 1891–1927, edited by Andersen (Copenhagen: Gad, 1991).

Editions and Collections: *Spøgelseskareten og andre noveller* (Copenhagen: Grafisk Forlag, 1955);

Gerd, Det tyvende Aarhundredes Kvinde, edited, with afterword, by Susanne Fabricius (Copenhagen: Gyldendal, 1975);

Stygge Krumpen, afterword by Kay Nielsen, 2 volumes (Copenhagen: Lademann, 1986).

PLAY PRODUCTION: *Storken,* Copenhagen, Folketeatret, 4 January 1929.

SELECTED PERIODICAL PUBLICATIONS–
UNCOLLECTED: "Ane Marie," *Tilskueren* (September 1903);

"Kammeratægteskab," *Politiken,* 24 March 1929.

During her life Thit Jensen was one of the most widely read and most controversial of Danish writers. Both her tumultuous life and writing career are representative of central issues in Danish literary history between *Det moderne Gennembrud* (The Modern Breakthrough) of the 1870s, the literary movement that introduced naturalism and realism to Danish literature, and World War II, after which modernism became the dominant literary mode. More specifically, Jensen is a leading representative of the Scandinavian female literary tradition of the late nineteenth century and early

twentieth century. In Jensen's case, life and writing are inextricably interwoven. Her fictional experimentation with various notions of the "true" nature of femininity, female sexuality, female-male relations, marriage, and motherhood owes much to the writings of the women of the Modern Breakthrough but equally mirrors private experience and the contemporary social, legal, and economic conditions of women.

Maria Kristine Dorothea Jensen was born 19 January 1876 in Farsø in North Jutland, the oldest daughter of Hans Jensen and Marie Kristine Jensen. The parents were descended from peasants, fishermen, and tradesmen of the Himmerland region. Thit was one of eleven siblings, preceded by three brothers, one of whom was Johannes V. Jensen, who became one of the foremost Danish authors of the twentieth century and a Nobel prize recipient. The parental influence was considerable. Both parents were remarkable personalities, who in dramatically different ways left their imprint on the children. The father, aside from his work as a veterinarian, pursued a wide variety of cultural interests such as botany, dialects, and folklore as well as history and foreign languages. He subscribed to various foreign journals and would make his children read articles in order to learn French, English, and German. His library, which was open to the children, included works by Arthur Conan Doyle, Rudyard Kipling, Friedrich Nietzsche, Heinrich Heine, Charles Darwin, Camille Flammarion, Ralph Waldo Emerson, Thomas Huxley, Annie Besant, Madame Blavatsky, Cesare Lombroso, and others. Between the ages of twelve and fifteen Thit's unorthodox and homespun education included literature, history, nature, science, religion, painting, and languages. Like many others at that time her father was keenly interested in spiritism and mysticism, and by the time she was fifteen Thit had become a convinced spiritist and would remain so throughout her life.

An important source in understanding Jensen's life, and especially her spiritist beliefs, is her diary, edited by Jens Andersen and published in 1991 as *Jeg længes . . . Fra Thit Jensens dagbøger 1891–1927* (I am Longing . . . From Thit Jensen's Diary 1891–1927). The diary, a series of notebooks covering forty of her eighty-one years, was of the greatest importance to her. She used it as a check and balance of herself, as a watchful eye on her conflict-filled dual nature. Throughout her life Jensen felt as if she had two souls, two distinct and opposing temperaments. This sense of a split was repeatedly described by Jensen in terms of gender characteristics, as irreconcilable feminine and masculine elements. She recorded her worst psychic crises in the pages of the diary. Importantly, it is there she would establish contact with the spirit "voices" in whom she confided and whose advice she always sought.

Of similar importance is her published memoir *Hvorfra? Hvorhen?* (Where from? Where to?, 1950), in which Jensen describes her childhood, family life, and the early struggle to become a writer. The book includes extensive references to the nature and pivotal role of the "voices" and the supernatural in her life and fiction. These voices, Jensen claims, protected her. They had chosen her and laid before her their grand plans for her life. She explains how she gradually, with time, would learn to argue with the voices and at times refuse their authority over her, such as their demand that she remain celibate.

Having witnessed her mother's physical and psychological suffering in her marriage, Thit became a fighter for women's rights. In *Hvorfra? Hvorhen?* Thit sketches a searing portrait of her mother, a woman whose presence may be detected in many of the female characters in her fiction. Although Marie Jensen wanted her children to understand her suffering as that of a woman without any rights under patriarchal law, she refused to consider feminism or the emancipation movement as possibilities for change. Her overriding concern for her children appears to have been to raise them to become solid citizens. Their happiness, she claimed, was secondary to their becoming competent, contributing members of society. She especially opposed any inkling of emancipatory notions in her daughters. Upon discovering that Thit was secretly keeping a diary, she forced open the hiding place and read it—she did not want an *original* (freak) for a daughter. The morally upright, strong-willed, but tormented mother figure would remain the focal point of feminist concerns and indignation in Thit Jensen's realist novels. It was because of her, the author often claimed, that she became a writer.

A source as meaningful for her writing, and far more conflict-filled and enduring than her mother's suffering, was Jensen's sense of the gross injustice committed against her, as a girl and later as a woman, both by her family and by society. While her brothers were sent away to receive formal schooling, she was forced to stay at home to help her mother and to teach her younger siblings. Thit understood early in life that the inequality she experienced was based on the assumed natural superiority of men. The anger she felt and the perceived split in her own sense of female identity remain at the core of her writing. Gender, self, sexuality, the yearning to be free and independent, free of the alienation she felt within herself as one of the so-called weaker sex, and the desire for a meaningful life as woman, lover, wife, and mother are all issues ceaselessly explored, continuously defined and redefined

Jensen and her brother, Johannes V. Jensen

both in her early realist-naturalist social-problem novels and later in her series of historical novels. From the beginning Jensen's identity crisis, her sense of being split between competing female and male traits, would be a determining factor in her female portraits and in how she perceived female-male relations and the role of women's sexuality, marriage, and motherhood. It is difficult to divorce her writing from her personal development and experience. In her struggle to come to grips with traditional conceptions of what constituted woman's and man's nature (femininity, masculinity, sexuality), she should be viewed within the context of her time. Her own understanding of human relationships betrays an inability to transcend well-entrenched beliefs and clichés, often biologistic and heavily dependent on late-nineteenth-century and contemporary popularized "truths" from the medical and sexological sciences. In that respect she is hardly alone. Nonetheless, her exploration of the topic of female sexuality as fit for literature was daring and often the cause of alarm. The novella *Fru Astrid Grib* (Mrs. Astrid Grib), written in 1903 but left unpublished until 1990, is an important example of a woman writer attempting to express in literary form the nature and force of female sexuality in the forming of the female self. With its description of a woman's erotic desires and indictment of social mores, it is a remarkable text at the outset of Jensen's long authorship.

In 1895, in an attempt to strike out on her own, the nineteen-year-old Jensen became a photographer's assistant. This career was short-lived, and at the age of twenty-two she went to work as a housemaid and assistant to an older female cousin in Christiania (now Oslo), Norway, where she stayed for two years. While there she suffered terrible bouts of depression and contemplated suicide. By 1900 she was back in Copenhagen working as a housemaid and later as a library assistant. She was finally able to claim her own living space, a small room of her own, where writing could begin in earnest. A pattern developed that was to last a lifetime: her pursuit of solitude, fueled by an overwhelming need to write, and her communication with the voices. While Johannes V. Jensen was celebrated as his generation's great literary hope, enjoying exchanges with such literary figures as Georg Brandes and Knut Hamsun, his sister Thit Jensen, living in poverty and starving, received polite but firm rejections from the major publishing houses. Eventually, she caught the attention of the editor and critic Valdemar Vedel, who in 1903 published one of her short stories "Ane Marie" in the periodical *Tilskueren* (September 1903). More importantly, he advised her where to turn with her unpublished novels, and in 1903 and 1904 she was able to publish *To Søstre: Fortælling* (Two Sisters: A Story) and *Familien Storm* (The Family Storm). Both are strongly autobiographical texts, central to an understanding of Jensen's development as a writer and a human being. Both texts are undisguised self-analyses as well as exposés of her family. In particular, the latter, *Familien Storm,* seeks to explain the deteriorating relations between herself and her beloved brother Johannes. The first novel, *To Søstre,* is not a developmental novel but rather a psychological demonstration of two different kinds of female destinies. Jensen chose to shape the entire narrative around two female figures and the issue of female sexuality. In the characters of the two sisters, Johanne and Agda, the author delineates strikingly different female fates: Johanne, who suffers from a nervous sensibility and lack of self-confidence, struggles in vain to become a whole person. She seeks cover in the traditional female role but feels increasingly split and paralyzed as she confronts the choices she has made. Yearning for a marriage on her terms, that is, to the man she loves, and for a world that would understand her "true" self, she ends by losing all three: man, love, and happiness. She acts against her desire for liberation by accepting a marriage of convenience. There is a messy love affair and an aborted pregnancy as well as a painful break with her sister, Agda. As a wife under the legal authority of her husband, Johanne slowly disintegrates and slips into apathy and madness. Against this familiar literary female plight Jensen positions Agda, a woman determined to be herself fully, free of all constraints in her determined pursuit of the truth. She is energetic and willful, and her ambitions leave no room for the traditional female role. Agda chooses herself first as is shown in her determination to acquire an education: only after completing school is she ready to acquiesce to marriage. Throughout the novel she has, with the none-too-subtle blessing of the intrusive narrative voice, sublimated her sexuality. Marriage means that she has to give up some of her independent characteristics and become more female, less male-like. Agda's strong will has led to happiness. She has remained true to herself and thus gained harmony. She is clearly meant to be an example for women, and a solution to what Jensen saw as a common female predicament. However, the intrusive narrative persona results in a portrait less convincing than the one drawn of Johanne. Combined, the two figures of Johanne and Agda express a deeply felt sense of the split in Jensen herself, a split she could never close. The sense that she was half man, half woman, a sort of third sex, as she herself put it, made her too strong, that is, too lacking in the virtues of femininity for a man to love her. In her diary entry for 3 May 1896 she wrote:

> Jeg vil hævde eksistensen af mænd, kvinder og midt imellem, ikke gamle jom Fruer og snerpede guvernanter skal repræsentere dette 3die køn, men kvinder som kaldes det ved navn, men i virkeligheden ikke er det. Kønløse skabninger, halvt mand, halvt kvinde, uden sanser, men fuld af arbejdsiver, fuld af lyst til at hæve sig, ikke egentlig at hæve sig, men skille sig ud fra det evig ægte kvindelige, som de ikke passer til.

> (I want to raise the existence of men and women and between these, not old maids and repressed governesses shall represent the third sex, but women who are called so by name, but who in reality are not, but rather a sexless being, half man, half woman, without sensual senses, but full of desire to work, full of desire to make a name for herself, perhaps not to announce herself loudly, but to separate herself from the eternally feminine, to which they are not suited.)

Jensen never questioned her dependence upon and reiteration of orthodox and conventional conceptions

Jensen doing needlework with her mother, Marie Kristine, in 1892

about masculinity and femininity, man and woman. These were simply unchanging, given naturals.

In *Familien Storm* Jensen continued the analysis of women's conditions by telling the story of her early years and the valiant struggle to gain independence. Jensen's focus in the book is on gender-specific differences in the lives of a brother and sister who both desire to become writers. The brother enjoys the privileges of education and the luxury of space, time, and money to widen his literary horizon, whereas the sister struggles simply to stay alive, in a constant battle not only with the world but also with her own inner demons. She is subjected to the brother's denigration of her desire to be a writer and his attempt to impose on her the traditional definition of femininity. Simultaneously, he steals material from her diary for his own writing about women. The material he takes consists of the uncensored private experiences she herself feels she must leave out in her own fiction. In her solitary fight the young woman seeks support in spiritism. In the novel Jensen acknowledges female sexuality, its needs and desires, but puts a firm foot down when it comes to the question of free love. Work is valued more highly than

marriage and love; the goal is self-sufficiency. Unlike Agda in *To Søstre,* Birgitte, the young female character in *Familien Storm,* continues on alone without love and family. Career and marriage cannot be combined. Above all, in *Familien Storm* Jensen spells out her ethics as a writer, an ethics arrived at in cooperation with the spiritistic voices. Her realist credo was to be *sund* (healthy), to do good, and to serve humanity with her literary talent.

With this credo as her foundation Jensen began writing a series of novels exploring a range of social issues such as women's rights, the hypocrisy of the church toward women, and the question of sexuality, prostitution, and free love. Her main concern was the need for changes in women's lives within the home and in society. She was convinced that the lack of equality before the law was the first important correction to be made. In novel after novel the reader encounters portraits of women who, in order to survive and in their desire to get ahead, are forced to develop the masculine side of their nature. They are self-aware, strong, intent on becoming whole, and through work they will seek to alter the norms guiding society.

The novel *Martyrium: Samfundsroman* (Martyrdom: Social Novel, 1905) is representative of this period of Jensen's authorship, pinpointing and critiquing the political, legal, sexual, and economic oppression of women. Rarely do any of the protagonists resolve the issues they are up against. Since marriage is the only feasible form of relationship between a man and a woman, Jensen wants it redefined. Unmarried women who become mothers do not fare well in her books; marriage is the end goal and should be seen as a union between *kammerater* (friends), not the realization of grand love, though that too remains an ideal. Furthermore, in some of her books Jensen places positive value on the exploring of free sexual relationships where equality prevails, but she is experienced enough to know that society would not tolerate such unions. Jensen was no less critical of women than she was of men. She realized that women were often the most vociferous objectors to change, willingly embracing the ideology that imprisons them. In Jensen's novels the attack is twofold: against both the men who abuse their power and authority and against the women who support men's continued assumed natural right to women's spiritual and physical lives. Like her Danish contemporaries Karin Michaëlis and Agnes Henningsen, Jensen acknowledged the existence of female sexuality and its centrality to the unfolding of women's lives, but it was never more important than women's need for financial freedom. For Jensen, the times being what they were, the only place for sexuality to be expressed was within a mutual love relationship between a husband and a wife. Increasingly, she castigated sex for sex's sake as vulgar and animalistic. Furthermore, sex must come second to the other much contested female role that, according to Jensen, was the most important role in life, namely that of being a mother. The attack is against society and in particular the role men play. In the novels *Hr. Berger intime* (Mr. Berger Intimate, 1917) and *Det evigt Mandige* (The Eternal Masculine, 1919) Jensen humorously skewers patriarchal ideology. It is not biological man per se that is the problem; it is the role he is given and the power he abuses. Jensen's ideologically orthodox understanding of what constitutes male and female nature remains fundamentally unquestioned and this orthodoxy unintentionally creates a problem in the choice of literary language (symbols, metaphors) that she employs to describe men and women, descriptions that are meant to express Jensen's understanding of the oppression of women. The result is that the objectification of women already built into that literary language is never questioned and is furthermore not paralleled with a similar objectification of the male characters. This failure, however, is one shared by most female writers who at that time sought to alter the status quo.

Between 1905 and 1928 Jensen's authorship can be grouped in three fairly homogenous parts. One group of novels is outright polemical; existing conditions are exposed, and the young women fail in their pursuit of independence because of their lack of will power or other obstacles. Everything ends tragically, as in *Martyrium; Ørkenvandring: Samfundsroman* (Desert Wandering: Social Novel, 1907); *Elskovs Forbandelse* (Love's Curse, 1911); *Hemskoen: Roman* (The Hindrance: Novel, 1912); and *Jydske Historier* (Histories from Jutland, 1916). A second group of novels is shaped around the story of an individual woman's attempt at emancipation and about the costs of such a struggle for the female rebel. These works, which conclude with a sense of optimism, include *To Søstre; Familien Storm; I Messias' Spor: Nutids-roman fra Island* (In the Footsteps of Messias: Contemporary Novel of Iceland, 1911); and *Gerd, Det tyvende Aarhundredes Kvinde* (Gerd, the Twentieth-Century Woman, 1918). Until the publication of *Gerd* in 1918, the author expressed unwavering faith in liberation. The structure of these novels is strikingly reminiscent of that in the typical nineteenth-century male bildungsroman.

Jensen married the painter Gustav Fenger on 4 October 1912. The couple separated in 1918 after Jensen discovered that her husband was having an affair with her best friend, Johanne Svenné, and the divorce was finalized in May 1922. With the failure of her marriage Jensen changed course and sought new values that turned out to be old values intended to replace the liberal spirit in which she had lived and worked. This third group of novels is comprised of narratives describing the dire consequences of women's emancipation. Jensen no longer seemed willing to support the psychological and social costs of women's sexual and financial independence, and the novels end pessimistically. After her marriage to Fenger in 1912 she did not write in her diary. When the marriage failed, however, she resumed her diary writing, and it was through this writing that she found solace and staged her self-justification. She subsequently fictionalized her account of her marriage in what is perhaps the most exhibitionistic novel in Danish literature, *Den erotiske Hamster: Nutidsroman* (The Erotic Guinea Pig: Novel of Today, 1919), which was a huge sales success at home and abroad, going into its tenth edition by the end of 1919. Other novels in the third, pessimistic, group include *Den evige Længsel: Moderne Studie Over mand og Kvinde* (The Eternal Longing: Modern Studies of Man and Woman, 1921), *Aphrodite fra Fuur, den moderne Kvindes Udviklingshistorie: Roman* (Aphrodite from Fuur, the Story of the Modern Woman's Development: Novel, 1924). The conflict, for a woman, between wanting independence and longing for love and family cannot be resolved. By the mid 1920s Thit Jensen no longer believed in the panacea of erotic emancipation or that work came first.

In the 1924 novel *Aphrodite fra Fuur* Jensen introduces the spiritist voices upon which she relied. When the main female figure Gerd is forced to choose between two men, Jensen convenes a meeting with the voices to get their advice. In novels such as *Aphrodite fra Fuur,* however, there is no real alternative for a woman other than being a mother. Disillusioned, Jensen now insists that a woman cannot live without love or without motherhood. The gap that opens between a career woman's need to repress her sexuality with its resultant aggression and depression and the yearning for security and love can only be closed when the woman returns home. In her works Jensen cannot combine love and work for women. She wants oppression removed, but she also wants a woman back in the home in her most important role as wife and mother. At this juncture Jensen stopped writing novels dealing with contemporary issues. At the same time she turned to writing historical novels and she enjoyed great success with a production in 1929 of her play *Storken* (The Stork), which is about theories of voluntary pregnancy and how abortion in some cases should go unpunished.

Some books do not fit into such a grouping of Jensen's novels. These works deal with religion and occultism: *Prins Nilaus af Danmark: Sagnfortælling* (Prince Nilaus of Denmark: Legendary Story, 1907), *Sagn og Syner: Mystiske fortællinger fra Island* (Legends and Visions: Mystical Stories from Iceland, 1909), *Det banker: Fire Historietter* (It Knocks: Four Stories, 1911), and *Kærlighedens Kaabe: Roman* (The Cloak of Love: Novel, 1918). A vehement attack on perverse sexuality and what the author sees as effeminate or weak masculinity is offered in *Højeste Ret: Fortælling fra en dansk Herregaard* (Highest Law: Story from a Danish Manor, 1913) and *Stærkere end Tro: Roman* (Stronger than Faith: Novel, 1915). Jensen's treatment in her novels of homosexuality and of homosexual or effeminate men seems both unfathomably ignorant and intolerant and also indicative of the author's inability to probe her chosen issues beyond conventional and often poorly argued presumptions. In common with many of her contemporaries, she saw the effeminate man as a threat to society and as an insult to "real men." At stake is her own masculine ideal, expressed as the will to ceaselessly strive toward a goal, preferably the common good, but also in the determination to be a faithful husband and tireless provider. From the outset critics repeatedly complained about the obtrusive tendentiousness of her novels. They accused her of using literature as a camouflage for her social agitation. Worse, some critics opined that she was incapable of writing fine literature, that hers was not an artistic talent. Such damning claims never deterred Jensen, but she did heed the advice to keep agitation and fiction as two separate activities.

In 1909 she began what became an illustrious career as a public speaker. For the next twenty years she traveled tirelessly and lectured on women's conditions, marriage, voluntary motherhood, morality, eugenics, and contraception, as well as on feminism and the threat of the feminizing of Danish men—in all, she wrote thirty different lectures, analyzed by Birgitte Borgen in her 1976 study. Not only did Jensen gain national notoriety, she also discovered a considerable source of income. More importantly, the lectures allowed her to try out topics and concerns, as a sort of laboratory for her fiction writing. For many years she would set aside the fall, winter, and spring months for her lecture tours and would also manage to write two novels per year. The lectures, and at times the public outrage against them that was sparked by church officials and politicians, made her the target of anti-female and anti-feminist attacks and neverending caricaturing in the national press. Her outspokenness, her increasingly intractable position on woman's rightful place in the home, and her view of eugenics forced the official Danish feminist organization Dansk Kvindesamfund (Danish Women's Society) to distance itself from what was seen as Jensen's reactionary tendency. Similarly, while on a lecture tour in the United States in 1925, American feminists were surprised at the conservative tone of her views. Inspiration for her more famous talks can be traced to her meetings with the Dutch feminist Alette Jacobs in 1923 and the American Margaret Sanger in 1925 while touring the United States. Inspired by her meeting with Jacobs, Jensen formed Foreningen for sexuel Oplysning (The Organization for Sexual Enlightenment) in 1924, and in that connection wrote her much debated public lecture "Feminismens Program" (Feminism's Program), which was immediately attacked for its perceived threat to patriarchal notions of marriage and family. Prominent members of the establishment vehemently rejected the idea of equal rights for women and that women should have a say in family planning as well as an equal share of authority over the children.

In her lectures there seems to be little development in her views on female-male relations in marriage and her insistence on woman's "meaning" as that of mother, first and foremost; however, in her lecture "Kammeratægteskab" (Marriage of Friends), published in

Jensen reading from her works

els were conceived as a whole and given the collective working title "Himmerlands Nitakkede Krone" (Himmerland's Ninepointed Crown); the project totals nine books, all set in the Himmerland region, encompassing its history, myths, legends, and lore. The supernatural is everywhere at work, as Jensen set aside the pessimism of social realism and sought only to entertain.

Her historical characters are an odd mixture of fact and fiction. Although based on historical figures, such as Valdemar II Atterdag, the king who reunited Denmark in the fourteenth century and who is the title character of *Valdemar Atterdag: En Kærligheds Roman* (Valdemar Atterdag: A Love Story, 2 volumes, 1940), her male characters often seem to be drawn less on historical models, and more to represent idealized depictions of the sort of man Jensen herself longed to meet. She did extensive and systematic research of monasteries, battlegrounds, castles, churches, libraries, architecture, family trees, and clothing styles to gain historical background to write the novels *Drotten: Historisk Roman fra det 14. Aarhundrede* (The King: Historical Novel of the Fourteenth Century, 2 volumes, 1943), *Rigets Arving: Historisk Roman* (The Heir to the Kingdom: Historical Novel, 2 volumes, 1946), and *Atter det skilte: Fjerde og sidste bog om Kong Valdemaar og Dronning Helvig* (Again Divided: Fourth and Last Book on King Valdemaar and Queen Helvig, 2 volumes, 1953). Along with her historical research, however, Jensen also collected cutouts of men from ladies magazines and newspapers and pasted them in a homemade catalogue: beautiful, healthy, classical bodies and faces to be used as inspiration for writing about her male characters. In connection with the novel *Jørgen Lykke; Rigens sidste Ridder: Roman i tre Bøger fra Højrenaissancen i Danmark* (Jørgen Lykke; The Last Knight of the Realm: Novel in Three Books about the High Renaissance in Denmark, 1931) she gave a lecture titled *Hvordan en historisk Roman bliver til* (How a Historical Novel Is Written, 1948). In this lecture she makes it plain that it is the human being that remains her object and goal, and she asserts that the human "heart" of the Renaissance was no different from that of the twentieth-century Danish man and woman. She refused to write about evil individuals from history because she would not attain the right insight or inspiration (and help from the voices) if she were to write about someone of whom she could not approve. It was her intent to uncover the life stories of the wives and daughters of the important men of history. She blamed men's habits of "illegitimate" love for all the misery that had befallen women through the ages. A thread running throughout the historical novels is the invented utopian matriarchy on the island of Virginia Insula (modeled on Fuur, an island in the Limfjord in North Jutland).

Politiken (24 March 1929), she gives a small nod of approval to the right of women who work outside the home to decide the number of children in their marriage. By 1930 Jensen had reached an impasse both in her personal life and in her writing and thinking. She could not resolve the conflicts her fictional female characters encountered. It was especially the reality of women's sexual and erotic drives that stymied the author. Woman, contrary to man, should be concerned with matters far greater than sex, such as motherhood and the rearing of the next generation.

Jensen's earliest venture in the genre of historical novels actually came in 1907 with *Prins Nilaus af Danmark,* but with the publication of her *Af Blod er du kommet: Roman fra Højrenaissancens Tid i Danmark* (Of Blood You Have Come: Novel of the High Renaissance in Denmark, 1928) she embarked fully on a new and successful stage of her career. Between 1928 and her death in 1957 Jensen reached new heights as a popular author of the most extravagant historical narratives set in the Danish late Middle Ages and the Renaissance. The wildly fantastic and dramatic tales of betrayal, greed, luxury, love, battles of the sexes, political maneuverings, and their gallery of idealized male figures found a large and enthusiastic readership both at home and abroad and were translated into Finnish, Swedish, German, and Dutch. The historical nov-

Despite her intention of uncovering the lives of women in history with each new installment of her project, Jensen's concern with the wives, daughters, and mistresses runs into sharp competition with her growing fondness for the idealized male characters. In her last historical novel, aptly titled *Den sidste Valkyrie: Roman om Dronning Thyra Danebod* (The Last of the Valkyries: Novel of Queen Thyra Danebod, 1954), Jensen scrutinizes yet again the vanity of men and the price it extracts, the great deeds it foils, and how, in the end, women are called upon to step forward and manifest the needed traits of selfless service for the common good–again, it is motherhood that is held high as the greatest feat of all.

Jensen's historical novels cumulatively totaled more than four thousand pages, going into several editions, with more than two hundred fifty thousand copies sold by 1990, making Jensen one of the most widely read authors in Denmark. Critics, however, convinced that she was destroying the historical genre, bemoaned the wildly ahistorical concoctions, the many factual mistakes, and the anachronistic and at times wholly invented language as too inauthentic to be taken seriously. Worse yet, critics accused the author of not being up to the task, alleging that the stories were clumsy and the characters often lacking in depth. As with earlier adversity, none of this criticism affected Jensen. The huge success of her novels was proof enough to her of their merit, and her defenders accused scholarly critics of being pedants.

Thit Jensen died in her sleep of a stroke on 13 May 1957 in her house in Bagsværd, a suburb of Copenhagen. The critical reception and evaluation of her work has been quite varied. Women scholars have concentrated on her early authorship between 1900 and 1928, her feminist period. While seeming to repeat a general view that her historical novels constitute the lasting important part of her authorship, feminist scholars seem uninterested in Jensen's monumental historical novels. Little work has been done comparing her historical fiction with that of Sigrid Undset, for example. Serious feminist critical evaluation came and went with the wave of feminist and Marxist criticism in the 1970s with an emphasis on class and the concomitant dismissal of bourgeois-liberal individualism. Jensen was found wanting for not paying attention to the lower classes and for being unable to critique her own liberal assumptions about human nature. Critics had a field day with Jensen's feminist campaign in her early years, and she was often met with ridicule and dismissal. But such criticism seemed not to daunt the author herself. To her, literature was to serve her intent to do good. She did not experiment with literary form but adopted late nineteenth-century realist and naturalist aesthetics from which she never wavered. She wrote because she wanted the lives of women to change and because she wanted society (men and patriarchy) to change its views of women. Above all, she wanted the state to allow for the rights of women: financial, educational, and legal. By exposing the mechanisms of female oppression and by proposing solutions, she simply felt she was doing her duty and what the voices kept insisting that she do. Literature was her handmaiden in her all-consuming quest for change.

Bibliography:

Hanne Corneliussen, *Thit Jensen: En bibliografi,* Studier fra Danmarks Biblioteksskole, no. 20 (Copenhagen: Danmarks Biblioteksskole, 1976).

Biographies:

Cai M. Woel, *Thit Jensen* (Copenhagen: Gyldendal, 1954);

Moltke, *Thit Jensen–og de andre* (Copenhagen: Hernovs Forlag, 1982);

Jens Andersen, *Thit, den sidste Valkyrie* (Copenhagen: Gad, 1990).

References:

Birgitte Borgen, *Thit Jensens samfundsengagement Studier i kvinde- og klasseproblemer* (Copenhagen: Vinten, 1976);

Hans Brix, "Thit Jensen," in *Danske digtere i det 20. Århundrede,* edited by Frederik Nielsen and Ole Restrup (Copenhagen: Gad, 1965), pp. 379–397;

Annegret Heitman, "Search for the Self: Aesthetics and Sexual Identity in the Early Works of Johannes V. Jensen and Thit Jensen," *Scandinavica,* 24, no. 1 (1985): 17–34;

Lisbeth Møller Jensen, *Roser og laurbær: Om grundstrukturen i Thit Jensens kvindepolitiske forfatterskab* (Copenhagen: Gyldendal, 1978);

Else Moltke, ed., *Bogen om Thit Jensen* (Copenhagen: Grafisk Forlag, 1954).

Christian Kampmann

(24 July 1939 – 12 September 1988)

Mark Mussari

Villanova Academy, Pennsylvania

BOOKS: *Blandt venner* (Copenhagen: Gyldendal, 1962);
Al den snak om lykke (Copenhagen: Gyldendal, 1963);
Ly (Copenhagen: Gyldendal, 1965);
Sammen (Copenhagen: Gyldendal, 1967);
Uden navn (Copenhagen: Gyldendal, 1969);
Nærved og næsten (Copenhagen: Gyldendal, 1969);
Vi elsker mere (Copenhagen: Gyldendal, 1970);
Nok til hele ugen (Copenhagen: Gyldendal, 1971);
Pinde til en skønskrivers ligkiste (Copenhagen: Gyldendal, 1971);
En tid alene (Copenhagen: Gyldendal, 1972);
Visse hensyn (Copenhagen: Gyldendal, 1973);
Faste forhold (Copenhagen: Gyldendal, 1974);
Rene linjer (Copenhagen: Gyldendal, 1975);
Andre måder (Copenhagen: Gyldendal, 1975);
Fornemmelser (Copenhagen: Gyldendal, 1977);
Videre trods alt (Copenhagen: Gyldendal, 1979);
I glimt (Copenhagen: Gyldendal, 1980);
Sunshine (Copenhagen: Gyldendal, 1983);
Engle (Copenhagen: Gyldendal, 1984);
Gyldne løfter (Copenhagen: Gyldendal, 1986);
Skilles og mødes (Copenhagen: Gyldendal, 1992).

TELEVISION: *Voksen,* script by Kampmann, Danmarks Radio, 1984.

OTHER: "Sidste dag i det gamle land," in *Christian Kampmann: Om at være sig selv–et udvalg,* edited by John Chr. Jørgensen and Lene Nordin (Varde: Dansklærerforeningen/Skov, 1984), pp. 8–30.

SELECTED PERIODICAL PUBLICATION–UNCOLLECTED: "Hvordan jeg blev forfatter," *Berlingske Aftenavis Weekend* (12–13 July 1969): 9.

Christian Kampmann (from the cover for Christian Kampmann: Om at være sig selv–et udvalg, *edited by John Chr. Jørgensen and Lene Nordin, 1984)*

Christian Kampmann was one of the eminent voices of the *ny-realisme* (new realism) movement that developed in the 1960s in Danish literature. A strong reaction against the subjective and exclusive points of view that defined modernism, *ny-realism* emphasized a shift toward a more objective narrative approach. Kampmann brought to this movement a penetrating insight into the psychology at work behind the life choices of the individual. His careful writing and social sensibility enabled him to peel away the veneers of a character's existence and to disclose the repressed desires in most middle-class lives. In a 28 November 1966 interview in the Danish daily newspaper *Information* Kampmann told a reporter: "En realistisk forfatter

238

skriver på erfaringer. Jeg kan personligt ikke anerkende noget metafysisk" (A realistic author writes from experience. Personally, I cannot acknowledge anything metaphysical).

Christian Peter Georg Kampmann was born in Hellerup, a suburb of Copenhagen, on 24 July 1939, to Niels Ølgaard Kampmann and Leila Ingersoll Jones, an American. In a 1978 interview with Ingmar Björkstén he recalled: "Mit hem var ett så kallat kultiverat hem. Mina föräldrar läste en hel del, de tog oss med på teatrar, konserter, utställningar" (My home was a so-called cultured home. My parents read a great deal; they took us to the theater, concerts, exhibitions). As a child Kampmann immersed himself in reading; by age eight he was reading a book a day. After passing his exam in linguistics from Rungsted State School in 1957, Kampmann apprenticed as a journalist with two local newspapers, *Herning Avis* (1959–1960) and *Aalborg Stiftstidende* (1961–1963). Between these two journalistic stints, he spent a year in Paris, where he wrote the short stories that would launch his literary career. In 1962 he married the music teacher Therese Herman Koppel (they had two children, David and Abelone, and eventually divorced in 1972). His early newspaper experience led to a year of studying in New York at Columbia University's Graduate School of Journalism (1963–1964), after which he returned to Denmark and worked as a television reporter. While honing his writing skills, Kampmann also worked as a freelance reviewer of English, American, and French literature. Much of his literary output reflects the terse quality of his journalistic writing.

Despite his broad background in journalism, Kampmann remarked in an interview in *Aktuelt* (18 December 1971) that he "har været fuldstændig ligeglad med, om noget var en nyhed. Og så er man ikke født journalist" (could not care less whether or not anything was news. And so one is not born a journalist). From 1967 to 1969 he wrote literary reviews for *Aktuelt*. With the release of his seventh book, *Nok til hele ugen* (Enough for the Whole Week) in 1971, Kampmann established his literary reputation and no longer needed journalism to survive. He returned once more to the field in 1975 when he became co-editor of the journal *Seksualpolitik* (Sexual Politics), a publication dedicated to the fight for gay rights in Denmark. A trio of novels dealing with his own bisexual awakening followed in the late 1970s, making Kampmann one of the first and most respected voices in legitimizing gay world literature.

Kampmann was particularly prolific in the 1960s and 1970s and produced three short-story collections, eleven novels, and two memoirs in novel form. His fiction owed much to his own background in an upper-middle-class environment. As he told Björkstén in 1978,

"Bakgrund till alla mina böcker är att man lever genom något vedertaget mönster i stället för att vara öppen och omedelbar. Man lever ut roller i ställat för att leva riktigt, och kräver att andra också skall leva på samma sätt för att sedan uppleva dem genom deras roller" (the background to all my books is that people live through some accepted pattern instead of being open and natural. One lives out roles instead of living correctly and demands that others should also live in the same way, in order then to experience them through their roles).

Both his first work, *Blandt venner* (Among Friends, 1962), a collection of short stories, and the ensuing novel *Al den snak om lykke* (All That Talk about Happiness, 1963), portray loneliness and depression as symptomatic of life among the bourgeoisie. The paralytic effect of societal norms, especially on sex roles and personal development, becomes obvious in Kampmann's early satiric output. His novels and short stories often depict characters trapped by or in personal conflict with their milieu, the main theme of much of his writing. For example, in some of the stories in the ironically titled *Blandt venner,* the provinciality of a small Jutland town presents a narrow existence for its inhabitants.

"Paraply, vinduesniche, snørebånd" (Umbrella, Window Alcove, Laces), a short story from *Blandt venner,* points to the strong psychological bent of Kampmann's authorship. Along with his contemporary Poul Vad, Kampmann was preoccupied in his early work with the development of the narcissistic character. Childhood serves as the source for most of the narcissistic adult's problems. In "Paraply, vinduesniche, snørebånd" a fourteen-year-old boy lacks any identification with a father figure: "Han åndede på ruden og skrev FAR på det kolde glas" (He breathed on the window pane and wrote FATHER on the cold glass). He calls strangers on the telephone and, upon hearing a deep male voice, imagines that it belongs to his dead father. The socializing process plays an equally important role in Kampmann's work; in this story the mother's dissolute lifestyle exacerbates the child's identity crisis.

With the release of the short-story collection *Ly* (Shelter, 1965), Kampmann moved full force into *ny-realisme,* which was creating a stir in Denmark in the mid 1960s. In an interview appearing in the weekly *Berlingske aftenavis weekend* (12 July 1969), Kampmann comments that the predominant Danish literary genre in the early 1960s had been lyric poetry, which had never interested him as much as prose. He adds that he was living in the United States in the early part of the decade. While studying at New York's Columbia University, he began to write the stories that would eventually comprise *Ly:* "De kom til at danne hvad jeg anser for min 'rigtige' debut" (They came to create what I

Kampmann in 1969 with his wife, Therese, and their two children, David and Abelone (from Christian Kampmann:
Om at være sig selv–et udvalg)

consider to be my "real" debut). Like his contemporaries Anders Bodelsen and Benny Andersen, Kampmann depicted modern people in restrictive social environments. His satire resonated with the Danish public, as when one character comments: "Jeg hader teaktræ, det er så småborgerligt" (I hate teakwood. It's so middle class).

Several of the stories in *Ly* deal with marriage, and they mark the beginning of Kampmann's keen insight into the symbiotic relationship between the social and the psychological. In "Støtte" (Support) the power play in a marriage takes center stage and is depicted through shifting points of view. In the title story "Ly" Kampmann applied his knowledge of life in suburban America to a story about a Danish couple's rapid assimilation into a vacuous American middle-class lifestyle. In "Fravær" (Absence) an alienated couple seeks refuge from the emptiness that has taken over their marriage. He tries to escape the situation, and she takes up painting; still, nothing can bring presence to their empty bourgeois world.

In his next novel, *Sammen* (Together, 1967), Kampmann strove for a more realistic narrative style. At this time a debate emerged in Denmark about the value of *ny-realisme,* and some literary figures sided with modernism against the environment-oriented movement. Kampmann, who lamented the absence of environmental factors in most contemporary Danish literature, felt that *ny-realisme* supplied a moral point of view from which to write. In *Sammen* he presents a matter-of-fact depiction of narrow-minded, middle-class consciousness–for example, suburban housewives whose lives have been drained of meaning by consumerism and advertising. The setting of *Sammen* is Hellerup, a suburb of Copenhagen, where eighteen-year-old Peter decides to flee from both the town and his pregnant girlfriend, Inge. Yet, Inge's seemingly bourgeois parents disclose an unexpected tolerance for their daughter's situation. Kampmann again employs shifting points of view to expose the complexities of the situation.

In *Information* (20 October 1967) the literary critic Hans Hertel praised Kampmann's technique in *Sammen.* Hertel notes that Kampmann writes "med en kunstnerisk gehalt enhver nu burde kunne få øje på, og med en analyseform der kan grave stadig dybere ned i forholdet mellem menneske og miljø, ned i skjulte konfliktstof og i de sammensatte mellemtilstande som litteraturen ikke rigtig har gidet behandle før, men som udgør de flestes daglige vilkår" (with an artistic substance everyone ought to take a look at, and with an analytic form that digs deeper still down into the relationship between person and environment, down into the hidden subject matter of conflict and the complex middle conditions that literature has not really chosen to treat before, but which constitutes most people's daily conditions). Kampmann had expanded the genre of *ny-realisme*. He had shown that a relativist point of view did not prevent an author from finding some overriding coherence in the depiction of a character's interaction with his or her environment.

In an interview in *Information* in 1968, Kampmann tried to explain his approach toward the relationship between character and environment: "For mig er det primære menneskene og deres indre, det kan bare umuligt *skilles* fra deres omgivelser, personerne må studeres i dem, fordi deres problemer opstår der og fordi de røber sig i forholdet til dem" (For me it is primarily people and their minds. There is simply no separation from their surroundings. People must be studied within [their surroundings], because their problems arise there and because they reveal themselves in relation to them). Kampmann frequently employed a stream-of-consciousness technique, owing much to his compatriot H. C. Branner and to the French author Nathalie Sarraute, to convey the individual's perception of reality.

After *Sammen* Kampmann entered a new phase in his authorship and began to experiment with different genres. His next work, *Uden navn* (Without name, 1969), was a suspense novel written for a competition held by the Danish weekly magazine *Hjemmet;* it was rejected. He followed *Uden navn* with *Nærved og næsten* (Almost and Nearby, 1969), a novel about writing in which he discusses his own narrative technique. Thematically, Kampmann continued to address consumerism. In *Nærved og næsten* he peels away the facade of comfort and *hygge* (the Danish word for a satisfying sense of coziness) among a small group of characters trying to wrench more out of their existence. For example, one infatuated young man "læser Karen Blixen og længes. Er der virkelig en anden verden end den flade og skuffende han hidtil har måttet nøjes med?" (reads Karen Blixen and feels longing. Is there really another world than the flat and disappointing one he has had to be satisfied with up until now?). It is especially in their relationship to love that Kampmann's characters stumble and fall.

Kampmann's early career received recognition and a financial boost from Denmark's Statens Kunstfond (National Art Fund), which awarded him a three-year grant in 1967. The scholarship enabled him to take a leave of absence from his duties as a reporter. In 1968 he received the prestigious Henri Nathansen award (which he received again in 1978). In 1970 he also took a position as a culture reporter writing on American, French, and British literature for *Information.*

In the short story "Roller" (Roles), from the collection *Vi elsker mere* (We Love More, 1970), Kampmann exposes the ego and longing in a marriage where the husband's acting career has taken precedence. Unfaithful and alcoholic, the actor-husband lacks the strength to end his marriage; he has grown to regret his wife's dependence on him. By the end of the story the wife has become the drinker, and the husband has become reenamored of her mysterious side. He has settled for no solution to their marital problems: "Løsning? Hvem brød sig om den slags begreber længer?" (Solution? Who cared about that kind of concept any more?). Kampmann is at his authorial best here. His writing is sharp and insightful, and his understanding and compassion toward his subjects parallel that of the American writer John Updike, in his refined stories of marital turmoil.

In "Gamle billeder" (Old Pictures), also from *Vi elsker mere,* Kampmann writes about a father who believes he is wise but has a tenuous grasp on reality. His unhappy life is counterpointed by his daughter's self-discovery. She has accepted her lesbianism and has found an older, secure, lover whom she brings home to a birthday party. Only at this moment, when she believes her father has finally accepted her, does she truly feel that she actually has a father (which she tells him in a stunning moment). Later, when he cannot understand why his wife is so accepting of their daughter's newfound lifestyle, she tells him, "Forstår du da slet ikke hvad det drejer sig om? Noget så sjældent som en ægte kærlighed" (Do you not understand what it is all about? Something so rare as a genuine love). Kampmann has observed that the story is "mere ironisk end trist" (more ironic than sad).

In 1975, three years after Kampmann divorced his wife, he announced his bisexuality and took an active role in Denmark's Bøssernes Befrielsesfront (Gays' Freedom Front). It was a brave move for the author, not to mention a media event: Danish newspapers were covered with headlines announcing Kampmann's personal declaration. From 1975 to 1978 Kampmann edited and wrote for the antipatriarchical and anticapitalist periodical *Seksualpolitik.* His private and political life had merged in his coming out. He told the daily *Berlingske tidende* (26 October 1975): "Jeg føler mig meget præget af, at jeg har haft en borgerlig opvækst, men det er ikke mit miljø mere. Jeg har ikke noget miljø. Jeg er klasseløs, for selv om jeg nu går ind for socialismen, får jeg jo ikke en fortid som arbejder af den grund. Og jeg kan heller ikke begynde at skrive arbejder-romaner. Det eneste, jeg kan skrive om, er det, jeg kender til" (I feel marked by my middle-class child-

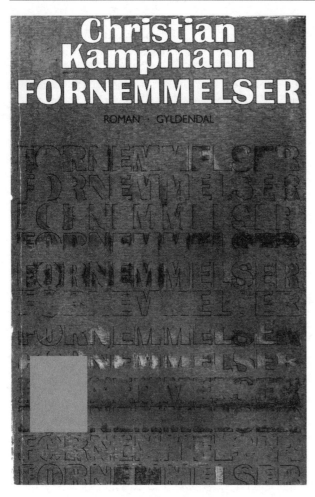

Cover for the first volume (1977) of Kampmann's trilogy of semi-autobiographical novels

hood, but it is no longer my milieu. I have no milieu. I am classless. Even if I advocate socialism, I don't acquire a past as a worker for that reason. Nor can I start to write working-class novels. The only thing I can write about is what I know about).

What Kampmann knew best was his own environment, the upper-middle-class suburb in which he grew up. In 1972 he began working on a trilogy (which would grow into a tetralogy) about the Gregersens, a family living in a well-to-do town north of Copenhagen. With the release of the first volume, *Visse hensyn* (Certain Considerations, 1973), Kampmann struck an immediate chord with the Danish public. The critic Jens Kistrup observed in *Berlingske Tidende* (26 October 1973) that the novel was "en løfterig optakt til en stor dansk familieroman af den type læserne længes efter" (a promising prelude to a great Danish family novel of the type readers are longing for). In no other work had Kampmann so skillfully juxtaposed his characters' private and social lives.

The setting of the novel cycle spans the growth period of the Cold War 1950s through the economic decline of the 1970s. Even in plot, the four books that comprise the Gregersen saga constitute a cycle. In the beginning of *Visse hensyn,* Erik Gregersen's fiancée, Marianne, is pregnant, and at the end of the fourth volume her daughter, Susanne, is also pregnant. The twenty years that pass between the two births are seen through the eyes of the five Gregersen children: Karen, Erik, Bo, Rune, and Maj. In these novels Kampmann mastered the varied perspectives with which he had experimented throughout his previous works. *Visse hensyn* opens with an upper-middle-class idyll, a bubble of domestic security that is about to burst. It is Easter 1954, and the children have gathered with their parents for a family dinner (an important motif throughout the series). By the next gathering, Christmas 1957, the reader learns that their father, Mogens, is having an affair with a family friend; that the second-oldest son, Bo, has faced the truth of his homosexuality; and that Karen is having marital problems.

In the ironically titled second volume, *Faste forhold* (Secure Relations, 1974), the family moves into the turbulent 1960s. It is 1968: Rune and his girlfriend Britta live together in a commune, and Bo is having an affair with a married man. Karen's marriage has fallen apart, due in large part to the chasm between her economic background and that of her husband. The family matriarch, Tilde Gregersen, also learns of her husband's affair when their friend Tjumse, his paramour, confesses. In a revealing television interview, Mogens unknowingly exposes his own shady business deals.

In the next novel, *Rene linjer* (Clean lines, 1975), Mogens and Tilde divorce, as do two of their children, Erik and Karen. Tjumse commits suicide. In Bo, Kampmann creates one of the first openly gay characters in Danish literature (thus paving the way for the author's later autobiographical series).

In the final volume, *Andre måder* (Other Ways, 1975), Kampmann proffers alternative lifestyles as the possibility for the future. It is 1973, and Denmark faces an economic and political crisis. Rune, Marianne, and Karen have found happiness in communal living. The final point of view belongs to Susanne, Marianne's daughter, who will soon give birth to the next generation of Gregersens. Mogens Gregersen's business-driven patriarchy has been replaced by a matriarchical and children-oriented collectivism.

The critic Karen Syberg observed in an essay for the journal *Poetik* that Kampmann's "identifikation med undertrykkelsen går derfor først og fremmest på borgerfamiljens kvinder og børn" (identification with oppression concerns first and foremost the middle-class family's women and children). Through the four novels, Kampmann had stretched the limits of all traditional notions of "family." His messages were well received. By 1980 more than 450,000 copies of the series had been sold in Denmark, more than all of Kampmann's previous combined sales.

After Kampmann finished the final volume in the Gregersen saga, he decided to take a respite from writing. As he told John Chr. Jørgensen and Lene Nordin in 1984: "After Gregersen-bøgerne vidste jeg ikke, om jeg kunne skrive mere. Jeg havde siddet flere år bag et skrivebord. Nu ville jeg hellere leve livet" (After the Gregersen-books I didn't know if I could write anymore. I had sat for years behind a writing desk. Now I would much rather live life). That life would serve as the inspiration for his next literary achievement.

Kampmann's authorship took a significant turn with the publication of *Fornemmelser* (Sensations, 1977). The novel began an autobiographical trilogy completed by *Videre trods alt* (Further Despite Everything, 1979) and *I glimt* (In Glimpses, 1980). A citation by Kampmann appearing at the beginning of *Fornemmelser* best explains his intentions:

Jeg har prøvet at lave en roman om mig selv som helt ung. Vise hvordan jeg tøvende blev klar over hvem jeg var–og så gik i gang med at benægte det ikke bare over for de andre, men over for mig selv. Det er en roman om at stole mere på de andres opfattelse end sin egen, på trods egne fornemmelser. Om at længes efter at være sig selv og blive accepteret som den man ved man er, og at leve i det skjulte indtil videre.

(I have tried to write a novel about myself in the grips of my youth. To show how I hesitantly became clear about who I was–and so began to work at denying it not only to others, but also to myself. It is a novel about relying more on others' perceptions than on your own, despite your own feelings. About longing to become yourself and to be accepted for who you are, and living secretly for the time being.)

Fornemmelser is first and foremost a novel of sexual awakening. The narrator, a young recruit in the Danish Civil Defense force, begins by assuring the reader that he by no means separates himself from others. This statement sets up the main conflict in the book, an inner struggle with accepting his homosexual side in the face of a conventionally hostile bourgeois environment. The honesty of the novel is matched by Kampmann's natural narrative, a masterful blend of experience and reflection, of situation and commentary. The narrator moves in emotional jerks and starts through what are frequently considered "classic" instances of self-discovery: he suffers repressed infatuations with other men; he attempts to connect with women to mask his same-sex

tendencies; he experiences a promiscuous stage of anonymous sex; and he sets up commitments and then runs in fear from them. This last trait becomes a leitmotiv throughout the three books.

At one point the narrator throws himself into Catholicism (much to the chagrin of his atheist grandfather) and tries to commit himself theologically to the "sin" of his behavior. This avenue of escape also fails him and ultimately draws him back to the difficult truth about his socially unacceptable proclivities. In a 1984 interview published in the biographical *Christian Kampmann: Om at være sig selv* (On Being Oneself) Kampmann described his own early awakenings:

I min allertidligste barndom havde jeg fået en fornemmelse af, at min opførsel ikke behagede de andre. Derfor har jeg meget hurtigt udviklet en selvcensur. Jeg forelskede mig f. eks. ikke i nogen skolekammerat.

(In my earliest childhood I had a feeling that my behavior wasn't pleasing the others. Therefore, I quickly developed a self-censorship. For example, I didn't fall in love with any schoolmate.)

The ensuing novel, *Videre trods alt,* takes place ten years later. While pursuing several male relationships, the narrator struggles to maintain his relationship with his former wife and their children, who still live with him. The impossibility of having it all in every possible way rests like a heavy weight on the structure of the novel. At the end of the book, Kampmann is involved in another relationship with a man but is still on the road to self-discovery. *I glimt* pushes the limits even further as the narrator leaves his same-sex relationship and pursues a broader, pan-erotic existence. Commenting on the trilogy in *Danske digtere i det 20. århundrede* (Danish Writers in the Twentieth Century), Jørgensen observed: "Romanrækkens komplicerede centralsymbol er *hinden,* den usynlige væg mellem jeg og omverden, som Christian i sidste bind forstår han har været nødt til at danne for at undgå at blive fordømt for sin kønslige identitet" (The series' complex central symbol is *the membrane,* the invisible wall between the self and the surrounding world, which Christian in the final volume understands he has had to create to avoid being damned for his sexual identity).

In an interview appearing in *Politiken* (19 April 1980), Kampmann encapsulated his feelings about writing the self-revelatory trilogy:

Med *Fornemmelser* syntes jeg for første gang jeg havde en konkret opgave som forfatter: at fortælle om noget, jeg–og andre–havde oplevet, og som mange intet vidste om. Jeg vidste, bøgerne kunne have en bestemt funktion.

(With *Fornemmelser* I felt for the first time that I had a concrete task as an author: to describe something that I–and others–had experienced, and that many knew nothing about. I knew the books could have a distinct function.)

Toward the end of *Fornemmelser,* in a scene in which he visits his eighty-one-year-old grandfather, the narrator comments: "Jeg er treogtyve, og jeg ved at jeg aldrig bliver så gammel som han" (I am twenty-three, and I know that I will never become as old as he).

Kampmann's words proved to be prophetic. On 12 September 1988 a jealous lover with mental problems bludgeoned Christian Kampmann to death. Kampmann was only forty-nine, and both the Danish press and public lamented the loss of his enormous talent.

At the time of his death Kampmann had been working on a new novel. In the early summer of 1988 he told his publisher that he was almost finished and only needed to do a little editing. He then left for Nepal, where he went hiking in the Himalayas. He was murdered shortly after he returned to his summer cottage on the Danish island of Læsø. His family discovered the manuscript for the almost-completed novel among Kampmann's papers. They sent it to the Danish publishing firm Gyldendal, where it received a final edit and was published in 1992 as *Skilles og mødes* (Separate and Meet). In this last novel, set in 1985, Kampmann addresses the burgeoning AIDS crisis. Jakob, married but living a double life, is released from a hospital after a bout of pneumonia and being diagnosed with AIDS. Set at the intersection between the gay urban milieu and traditional married life, *Skilles og mødes* tests the tenuous boundary between the two environments. The novel depicts the existential crisis of living with death as an everyday threat, a reality that somehow draws together disparate characters.

Although he died young, Christian Kampmann left behind two important landmarks in Danish literature, his autobiographical trilogy and the tetralogy comprising the Gregersen saga. Through his work he exposed both himself and his environment in insightful prose filled with passion and honesty. His body of work represents a literary time capsule depicting life, personal and social, in the turbulent 1960s and 1970s, a time when both Denmark and Kampmann came of age.

Interviews:

Hans Hertel, "Tale til Christian Kampmann," *Det danske bogmarked,* 9 (1973);

Ingmar Björkstén, "Christian Kampmann: Denmark," in *Leopardväckning* (Borås: Rabén & Sjögren, 1979), pp. 167–196;

John Chr. Jørgensen and Lene Nordin, "Sandheden er altid subjektiv–samtale med Christian Kampmann," in *Om at være sig selv-et udvalg,* edited by Jørgensen and Lene Nordin (Varde: Dansklærerforeningen/ Skov, 1985), pp. 107–118;

Hans Henrik Lerfeldt, *Blue World: og en samtale med Christian Kampmann* (Copenhagen: Tidende Skrifter, 1985).

References:

Palle Dinesen, "Hedonistisk livsopfattelse–en overvejelse af Christian Kampmanns *Andre måder," Kritik,* 38 (1976): 117–126;

Steen Harvig, *Christian Kampmanns Nok til heleugen–forudsætninger og arbejsopgaver* (Varde: Dansklærerforeningen/Skov, 1979);

John Chr. Jørgensen, "Christian Kampmann," in *Danske digtere i det 20. århundrede,* 5 volumes, edited by Torben Brostrøm and Mette Winge (Copenhagen: Gad, 1982), V: 16–28;

Anne Birgitte Richard, "Historiens urokkelige gang og den villede positivitet," in *Romanen som offentlighedsform: studier i moderne dansk prosa,* edited by Jørgen Bonde Jensen and Karen Nicolajsen (Copenhagen: Gyldendal, 1977), pp. 210–243;

Karen Syberg, "Virkeligheden der voksede over hovedet. Om Christian Kampmann's forfatterskab," *Poetik,* 27 (1976): 1–73.

Hans Kirk

(11 January 1898 – 16 June 1962)

Elias Bredsdorff
University of Cambridge

BOOKS: *Fiskerne* (Copenhagen: Gyldendal, 1928);

Jørgens Hjul (Copenhagen: Monde, 1932);

Daglejerne (Copenhagen: Gyldendal, 1936);

De ny Tider (Copenhagen: Gyldendal, 1939);

Borgmesteren gaar af (Copenhagen: Gyldendal, 1941);

Processen mod Scavenius, by Kirk and Martin Nielsen (Copenhagen: Thaning & Appel, 1946);

Kristendom og Kommunisme, by Kirk and Erik Jensen (Aarhus: Aros, 1948);

Slaven (Copenhagen: Gyldendal, 1948);

Vredens søn (Copenhagen: Gyldendal, 1950);

Djævelens penge (Copenhagen: Tiden, 1952);

Klitgaard & sønner (Copenhagen: Tiden, 1952);

Skyggespil (Copenhagen: Gyldendal, 1953);

Borgerlige noveller (Copenhagen: Gyldendal, 1958);

Prostens søn (Copenhagen: Aschehoug, 1958);

Danmarksrejsen (Copenhagen: Erichsen, 1966);

Breve fra Horserød: Fange nr. 6, edited by Børge Houmann (Århus: Sirius, 1967);

Skipper Klemmen: Tre artikler skrevet til Arbejderbladet 1941 (Copenhagen: Land og Folk, 1967);

Det borgerlige frisinds endeligt, edited by Houmann (Copenhagen: Gyldendal, 1969);

Litteratur og tendens: Essays og artikler, edited by Houmann (Copenhagen: Gyldendal, 1974);

Undertrykkere og undertrykte: Et Hans Kirk-udvalg, edited by Ole Ravn (Copenhagen: Dansklærerforeningens/ Gyldendal, 1977);

Jeppe, Nille og deres hund Tobias, illustrated by Palle Bregn-høi (Copenhagen: Gyldendal, 1977);

Godtfolk: Samtaler og portrætter, edited by Houmann (Copenhagen: Vindrose, 1980);

Hug til højre og venstre: Artikler om nazisme, krig og klassekamp, edited by Houmann (Copenhagen: Vindrose, 1981);

Esbern Fribonde: Historisk hørespil i 5 akter om bonden, der forrådte Skipper Klemmen, by Kirk and Sigurd Thomsen (Risskov: Sirius, 1982);

En kommis' dagbog, illustrated by Herluf Bidstrup (Bagsværd: Forlaget Rosa, 1987).

Editions and Collections: *Fiskerne,* edited, with an introduction, by Jytte Englberg (Copenhagen: Gyldendal, 1964);

Jeg ved en smule om klassekamp: 8 samtaler (Ålborg: KOMM., S. Aalborg, 1984);

En plads i verden og andre fortællinger (Højberg: Hovedland, 1987).

OTHER: B. Traven, *Dødsskibet,* translated by Kirk (Copenhagen, 1932);

Howard Fast, *Clarkton,* translated by Kirk (Copenhagen, 1948);

Manden og jorden: 13 noveller af unge danske forfattere, edited by Kirk (Copenhagen: Gyldendal, 1954);

Hilsen til Otto Gelsted, edited by Kirk and Børge Houmann (Copenhagen, 1957).

Hans Kirk is the main representative of Marxist fiction in Denmark in the 1920s and 1930s. His novels are based on a thorough knowledge of social conditions in Denmark at the time and of the social and psychological contrasts as reflected in the religious views of different social classes. His first novel, *Fiskerne* (The Fishermen, 1928), is a novel without a main character, a truly collective novel that deals with a tightly knit group of poor fishermen, whose fate he himself had shared for a period, and whom he therefore knew intimately. In the period immediately preceding his literary debut he had written several sociological articles in various left-wing periodicals, in which he had drawn attention to the close interrelationship between social conditions and religious views, with special reference to the two most important religious groups in Denmark, the adherents of *Indre Mission* (Home Mission), whose supporters were pietists and religious fundamentalists, believers in the importance of keeping to the straight and narrow path and in putting up with the hardships of daily life in the expectation of going straight to Paradise after death. The other group called themselves *Grundtvigianere,* that is, supporters of the theories of N. F. S. Grundtvig, the Danish nineteenth-century hymnist and educationalist,

choanalytical point of view, man seen as a result of the surroundings in which he lives.)

At an early age Kirk was sent as a boarder to Sorø Academy, the nearest Danish equivalent of an English public school. In 1916 he was admitted to the University of Copenhagen to study law, thus following in the footsteps of an uncle who was a solicitor. After graduating in 1922 he worked for a short while in his uncle's firm and was afterward employed for a year in the Danish legation in Paris, then worked for two years as a civil servant in the town hall of Copenhagen. He then decided to give up his career as a lawyer in order to become a writer. In 1925 he worked as a freelance journalist and literary critic in various serious journals while also earning some extra money by writing short stories for popular weekly newspapers under various pseudonyms.

An important influence at this time was his friendship with Otto Gelsted, a Danish poet who dedicated one of his poems to "H. R. K." (Hans Rudolf Kirk), with an implied portrait of him as a young revolutionary student whose aim is to blow up the entire modern materialistic establishment. In the 1920s Gelsted acted as a pioneer in introducing the ideas of Sigmund Freud to Denmark, and the psychoanalytical philosophy of both Freud and Alfred Adler is clearly discernible in Kirk's early novels, especially in *Fiskerne*.

Kirk felt that he was living an empty life; influenced by his reading of Henri Barbusse's novel of trench warfare in World War I, *Le Feu* (1916), Kirk agreed with Barbusse's view that in order to be a true writer one must have personal contact with real life, and he therefore decided to become a fisherman. His uncle, who was a North Sea fisherman, had recently decided to move, together with his wife and a group of other North Sea fishermen, away from the hardships of the West Coast to an island called Gjøl in the Limfjord. The group, who were now to become Fjord fishermen instead of North Sea fishermen, brought with them not only their fishing skills but also their religious views, which differed drastically from the less strict and more tolerant views of the local population on the island to which they had moved. In 1925 Kirk gave up his career and moved to the island of Gjøl, where he lodged at the local inn and became a boarder at the home of his uncle and aunt, while he helped with the fishing and acted as a jack-of-all-trades for the fishermen.

Having lived with the fishermen for several months, he began to write his first novel, *Fiskerne,* which was immediately accepted for publication by Gyldendal, the leading Danish publisher. In the same way as there is no "hero" in the novel, there is no plot in the ordinary sense of the word. Kirk may have been

Hans Kirk (courtesy of Gyldendal Publishers)

who optimistically saw life as a beautiful gift from God, which it is the duty of humanity to enjoy.

Hans Rudolf Kirk was born in the East Jutland provincial town of Hadsund on 11 January 1898. His father, Christen P. Kirk, came from a family of fishermen and poor peasants on the west coast of Jutland, and his mother, who was born Anna Johanne Andersen, came from a background of well-to-do farmers and landowners. Politically his father was a left-wing radical, whereas his mother was conservative. In an interview in the Danish newspaper *Politiken* (12 March 1939) Kirk said:

> *Fiskerne* var mit allerførste arbejde, men der lå et teoretisk grundlag bagved. Min fars familie var missionske bønder og fiskere, og de blev levende for mig ved en krydsning mellem en marxistisk og en psykoanalytisk opfattelse, mennesket som et resultat af de omgivelser det lever i.

> (*Fiskerne* was my first work, but it had a solid theoretical background. My father's family were fundamentalist peasants and fishermen, and they became alive to me by means of a crossing between a Marxist and a psy-

Cover for Kirk's first book, his 1928 novel about the lives of poor Jutlandic fishermen

influenced by John Dos Passos, whose *Manhattan Transfer* (1925) is also a collective novel, and by the Polish author Władysław Reymont and the Norwegian novelist Knut Hamsun.

In the novel *Fiskerne* Kirk describes how a group of North Sea fishermen survives, having moved from a rough and hard existence to a milder climate without in any way changing their religious fundamentalism, which brings them into conflict with the religious indifference or agnosticism of the local population on the island. The group consists of four married couples, a widower and his stepdaughter, a bachelor, and several children. Unlike the local population, their religious views are all-important to them, they can accept no compromise, and being dissatisfied with the tolerance of the local parson, they decide to build their own nonconformist chapel, where they elect their own lay preachers or invite their own fire-and-brimstone preacher from former days to come and preach to them. The spiritual leader of the group is Thomas Jensen, who once had a vision of the fire of Hell. Another important character is Tea Røn, the wife of Jens Røn,

the poorest of the fishermen. She is a religious fanatic, much concerned with other people's sins. A third member of the group is Anton Knopper, who becomes sexually attracted to a girl who is employed as a maid at the local inn. When he is on the point of embracing her he becomes aware of the gold cross she wears between her breasts. This to him becomes a sign from God, a warning that he is being lured into sinning, and from then on, any cross, even the cross on the chapel, becomes a warning against stimulating his sexual desire.

The fishermen are never held up to ridicule but are described with profound sympathy. They are at the bottom of the social scale, but they are proud men and women who are able to tolerate their situation in life, for they know that they will get their reward in life after death. An important point in the novel is that the new generation, the children of the fundamentalist fishermen and their wives, begin to move away from the religious and moral tradition of their parents. One of the characters in the novel, Mariane, the wife of Poul Vrist, belongs to the group socially but differs from the others by not sharing their religious view. Her tolerance and human understanding of other people stand out in contrast to the others.

An illustration of the close connection between social conditions and religious views comes in an important paragraph in *Fiskerne:*

> Vesterhavsfiskerne vidste, hvad de vidste. Gud havde pisket dem med Vestenvind, Undergang og Fattigdom. Fiskeriet var slaaet Fejl Aar efter Aar, Sandflugt og Havgus havde hærget Sognet, og Brødre og Venner var druknede for deres Øjne. Kun eet var sikkert: Guds ord. Kun eet gav Kraft: Guds Naade. Lagde man ikke sin Byrde paa Jesu Skuldre, var Jordelivet ikke til at leve.

> (The North Sea fishermen knew what they knew. God had whipped them with easterly gales, destruction and poverty, fishing had been a failure year after year, sand drift and sea fog had played havoc with the parish, and brothers and friends had been drowned in front of their eyes. Only one thing was certain: the word of God. Only one thing gave strength: God's mercy. If you did not put your burden on the shoulders of Jesus, earthly life was not worth living.)

The novel was available in the bookshops in November 1928 and was received in a surprisingly positive way by the literary critics, in spite of the fact that they were all aware of Kirk's atheism and of his political views. Several of the critics pointed to Hamsun as a forerunner of Kirk. The novel was regarded as an important literary event, and the author was hailed as a new creative Danish writer of great importance.

Fiskerne was first published in an edition of 1,000 copies; it soon became a best-seller, and was republished many times. In 1960 it was republished in a ninth edition and reached a circulation of more than 33,000 copies. Two years later it was republished in a paperback edition of 30,000 copies. A television adaptation produced by Danmarks Radio, with a scenario by Jens Ravn and a script by Bo Leck Fischer, appeared in six installments in 1977 and revived popular interest in the novel; by the mid 1980s *Fiskerne* had reached a circulation of about 370,000 copies, thus becoming the top best-seller among Danish novels. *Fiskerne* has been translated into eleven languages; Kirk's books have been translated into a total of sixteen languages. None of Kirk's works has been published in English; although Penguin Books announced a forthcoming translation of "The Fishermen" in 1950, apparently the translation was so unsatisfactory that the plan was abandoned. Anticommunist political bias during the Cold War may also have played a part in keeping any work by Kirk from being published in English.

After the publication of the novel in 1928, Kirk earned his living for several years as a journalist and freelance writer of children's books and short stories for popular weekly magazines, often written under a pseudonym. In 1930 he was employed as a literary critic with *Social-Demokraten,* the leading social-democratic paper, but his political sympathies for communism removed him gradually from those of the paper for which he worked. He gave notice to leave the paper, joined the Danish Communist Party, and offered to work as an unpaid literary critic and cultural commentator for *Arbejderbladet,* the Danish Communist Party newspaper.

For some time he had been working on a novel about the transition from agricultural economy to industrialism in Denmark. His idea was to describe what happened locally in a small Danish community in Jutland, where the building of a cement factory changed the entire social pattern. Previously the lowest paid group of workers in the country, the day laborers, who did not own any land of their own, worked as underpaid slaves for the farmers and big landowners whenever they needed them, but with the coming of the factory these workers gradually became wage earners, thus having a regular income. As a child Kirk had witnessed the building of a cement factory near Mariager Fjord in his own home district. He decided that a development that began at the end of the nineteenth century and went until the 1930s could not possibly be told in a single novel, and he therefore planned the work as a trilogy, of which the first volume, titled *Daglejerne* (The Day Laborers) was published in December 1936.

The scene is laid in a fictional village called Alslev near Mariager Fjord in the early part of the twentieth century. The times are hard, and the smallholders must leave their homesteads and work as day laborers. Among the many characters are Marinus and Tora, who have been forced by the crisis to abandon their smallholding in order to become day laborers instead. The most important character in the novel, however, is Cilius, a tough former navvy and drunkard, who has led a wild and crazy life, and who now becomes the leader of a trade union branch. Unlike the other workers he had not previously been a day laborer, but his natural talent as a courageous leader is soon recognized by the others. A counterpart to Cilius is Mr. Høpner, an engineer, who becomes the manager of the cement factory and thus a representative of capitalism. He is looked upon by the workers as the man who was responsible for arranging that the workers, instead of earning their living more or less at the mercy of the local farmers, are now employed with regular weekly wages. Høpner, however, has a double role: in the eyes of the factory workers he is a kind of savior who guarantees them a regular income, but he is also an instrument of capitalism, who is only on their side as long as they follow the rules and refrain from demanding

Hans Kirk: Roman om Fiskere.

Der stod en lille Flok yderst paa Broen og spejdede ud over Fjorden
i den lune Sommeraften. De var klædt i fint, blaat Jakketøj med blanke
Støvler og mørke Hatte. Det var Fiskerne vesterfra, som ventede paa Skibet med Konerne og Børnene.

Nu var det besluttet, at de vilde slaa sig ned her og blive alle
Dage. De havde købt Vand, gammel Herregaardsret til Aalestader og Bund-
garn. Povl Vrist havde allerede boet her nogle Aar og var tilfreds og
tjente gode Penge. De andre havde fisket her en Tid, var kommet rejsende hvert Foraar, naar Sildefiskeriet skulde begynde, og var draget hjem
om Efteraaret, naar Aaleruserne var taget ind. Men først nu skiftede de
Bolig. Saalænge Familien var i Vesterhavssognet, havde Hjemmet jo været
der. Men nu skulde det saa være anderledes.

De var højtidelige allesammen. Det blev man let, naar man havde de
gode Tøj paa, som kun blev brugt ved Kirkegang og Begravelser. Der var

~ / ~

Page from the typescript for Fiskerne *(Det Koninglige Bibliotek, Copenhagen)*

higher wages and—most important of all—do not strike. Also featured in the novel is a local grocer, who is a representative of pietist fundamentalism and hypocrisy, as well as a parson representing official Christianity, and a Grundtvigian schoolteacher, whose humane views are described with profound sympathy.

The novel was hailed as the greatest success of the year. It was printed in an edition of 6,000 copies, and within a year it was republished twice. Kirk was pronounced a worthy heir to two of the greatest Scandinavian writers, Martin Andersen Nexø and Hamsun, and Kirk was called the creator of the modern social novel in Danish literature.

In the years following the publication of *Daglejerne* Kirk devoted much of his time to the fight against Nazism, and in 1939 a sequel to *Daglejerne* was published, a novel titled *De ny Tider* (The New Times, 1939), which continued the story of the land laborers, who have now been transformed into industrial workers. The trade union has now become so strong that the cement workers are able to strike for higher wages, but they have no strike fund, and the situation is so bad that the families are at the point of starving. The farmers are pleased when some of the frightened workers think that the outlook is so bleak that the time has come to consider giving up the strike, but Cilius, who is still their leader and spokesman, is not so easily crushed, and the strike ends in a victory for the workers. They decide to found a cooperative shop, also intended as a punishment for the local grocer, who stopped all credit to the workers and their families during the strike.

The story then moves up to 1914, with World War I causing many changes in Denmark generally and also in the local society. The manager of the cement factory finds it difficult to keep it going, and unemployment becomes a new and frightening reality. The farmers, on the other hand, who have otherwise always complained about the times, are now making big money on the war, and estate agents are doing good business, helped by cynical lawyers. When the war is over conditions for the workers are again improved. As in the first volume in the trilogy, in *De ny Tider* Kirk demonstrates his intimate knowledge of both the local area he describes and of its inhabitants. The novel was as well received as its predecessor and sold equally well and was translated into several languages.

The final part of the trilogy, however, was never published—World War II intervened. Immediately after the German occupation of Denmark began on 9 April 1940 no one was arrested, but when German troops attacked the Soviet Union on 22 June 1941 the Nazi authorities demanded that the Danish government order the police to arrest all leading Communists, and they gave them a list of members of the Danish Communist Party who should be arrested immediately. The Danish government agreed to do what the Nazi invaders demanded and made a list that included not only the members of the Danish Communist Party whom the Germans had requested be arrested but also many names of individuals who were only suspected of being communist sympathizers.

Among the hundreds of people who were arrested by the Danish police in the early hours of Sunday, 22 June 1941 was Hans Kirk. After a short stay in a prison cell in Copenhagen, he was sent with all the other arrested Communists and suspected communist sympathizers to a camp in North Sealand, in clear violation of the Danish constitution. Sometime before his arrest he had submitted the manuscript of a new novel to his publisher, and the book, *Borgmesteren gaar af* (The Mayor Resigns, 1941) was published shortly before he was arrested. It is a humorous story, based on his experience as a civil servant in the town hall of Copenhagen.

After a while the Danish Parliament "legalized" the arrest of all the Danish Communists and communist sympathizers by means of a law that stated that all Communists were criminals. Kirk was a difficult prisoner who did not mince his words when he criticized the camp inspector or when he wrote angry letters to the Danish Minister of Justice, whom he called a traitor to his country, and the Danish authorities decided to remove him from the camp. He was transferred to a prison cell in Copenhagen, where he was held in isolation for over six months to prevent him from "having a bad influence" on the other detainees. In the prison he began a hunger strike and was eventually sent back to the camp.

Although the Minister of Justice never replied to any of his letters, Kirk managed after a prolonged battle to get permission to write literature, and he was eager to write the final part of the trilogy he had begun with *Daglejerne* in 1936. He finished the manuscript of the third volume, but on 29 August 1943, when the Germans took complete power and the Danish government resigned, about half the members of the camp managed to escape before the German army took control of the camp. The escapees who were caught were sent to a German concentration camp in Poland, where many of them died, and the ones that managed to escape, including Kirk, joined the Danish Resistance for the rest of the war. Kirk had to leave his manuscript behind in the camp when he fled, and the German guards burned it. After the war Kirk felt that he could not write the novel again, and so the third volume of the trilogy was never published.

Before he escaped Kirk looked for material for a new book. He remembered having read in an American journal a description of a shipwreck in 1679, when a ship, loaded with gold and silver and precious stones, sank while sailing from the Spanish possessions in America to Spain with a Native American slave on board. The ship had been bought by a certain Dona Inez Escobedo as a present for her brother. Kirk succeeded in getting more material about the period, and after the liberation of Denmark, when Kirk resumed his journalistic work in the resurrected Communist Party newspaper (which had now increased its circulation enormously) he finished the manuscript, and the book, titled *Slaven* (The Slave), was published in November 1948 in an edition of 6,000 copies.

The story takes place in 1679. The pinnace *San Salvatore* sails with a crew of ninety-two from South America to Spain, loaded with riches from the colonies. On board is the viceroy, Don Pedro de Carajaval, the inquisitor Don Jesus, a lawyer whose name is Don Francisco de Elinaz, all of them representatives of power, whereas capital is represented by Dona Inez, a rich widow, the owner of a big financial empire. Another important character is Mr. Rayburn, an English businessman who sells Negro slaves. Representatives of the ordinary people are, in addition to the crew, a soldier called Juan Gomez and the title character, Pancuiaco, the Native American slave, who is owned by Dona Inez. She intends to give him as a present to her brother but is sexually attracted to Pancuiaco. Between the representatives of power and capital on one side and ordinary people on the other side is Pablo Avarano, an intellectual who is a drunkard and who suffers from a venereal disease, but also is a man who has a clear understanding of the conflict on board the ship. His thoughts are described in the following words to the crew:

> På fem minutter kunne I rydde kahytterne deroppe for alle de fine passagerer og kaste dem alle overbord. Men I gør det ikke, for I ved, at de ejer jer. De har banket det ind I jeres dumme hoveder: de ejer os, og de kan gøre ved os, hvad de har lyst til. Og hvis en eller anden finder på at spørge, hvordan det nu I grunden forholder sig med al den ejendomsret, har de lært jer at svare: sådan er Guds vilje, og et menneske skal ikke sætte sig op mod Gud. Men har Gud selv fortalt dig, hvad der er hans vilje? Nej, det har præsten. Han tjener først og fremmest de rige og

The false identification card that Kirk used while hiding from the German army after escaping from an internment camp in 1943 (from Morten Thing, Hans Kirks mange ansigter: En biografi, *1997)*

mægtige, og han får sin føde uden møje ved at forkynde rigdommens bud, som ikke er Guds.

(It would take you five minutes to empty the cabins up there and throw all the fine passengers overboard. But you don't do it, for you know that they own you. They have knocked it into your silly heads: they own us, and they can do to us whatever they like. And if anybody would think of asking how all this ownership has come about, they have taught you the answer: It is God's will, and no one shall question the will of God. But has God himself told you what his will is? No, that is what the priest has done. He serves first and foremost the rich and mighty ones, and he gets his food without difficulty by preaching the commandment of wealth, which is not the commandment of God.)

Pancuiaco refuses to become the lover of Dona Inez. He will do nothing which violates his dignity, and so she has him whipped. He kills the captain, who had violated a Native American girl whom he had won in a card game. When they look for Pancuiaco he has disappeared, and when they find him he has cut a hole in the bottom of the ship and has been drowned, and the entire ship sinks quickly. Only a few people survive, among them Pablo Avarano and Rayburn.

The main theme of *Slaven* is the concept of power. The old order is doomed, but Rayburn survives as a representative of modern British capitalism. He is a man to whom the book of prayer is as important as the ledger. But the book is also inspired by events during the occupation of Denmark. In an interview made shortly before the book was published Kirk said:

Slaven er skrevet i Vestre Fængsel i de sidste måneder af 1941 og foråret 1942. I hvert fald for os, der sad indespærret var det en desperat situation, hvor vi måtte stille os selv det spørgsmål om det blev nødvendigt at kapitulere overfor nazismen, hvad Socialdemokratiet på det tidspunkt var rede til. Bogen er ment som en slags svar på det spørgsmål.

(*Slaven* was written in a prison cell in a Copenhagen jail during the last months of 1941 and the spring of 1942. To us who were jailed, it was at least a desperate situation, in which we had to ask ourselves if it would become necessary to capitulate vis-à-vis Nazism, which the Danish Social Democrats at that time were ready to do. The book was intended as an answer to that question.)

The novel had a mixed reception by the critics. Some of them praised it as a literary masterpiece, while others regarded it as mere communist propaganda.

Kirk's next book was a novel entitled *Vredens søn* (The Son of Wrath, 1950). The scene of the novel is Israel at the time of Jesus Christ. The country is occupied by the Romans, and there is much poverty and social unrest in the country. Various groups have different views about the Romans. The Pharisees, headed by Kaifas, believe in peaceful cooperation with the foreign troops. But the Zealots are eager to take up the fight against the invaders. The Essenes have withdrawn themselves from the community to fight the evil in themselves. And there are the Ebjonim, the poor, who are led by the prophet Jeshua bar Josef, who may be a new *meschica* (messiah). The narrative follows two apostles: Simon, the Zealot, and Matthew, the publican, on their journey in Israel, where they preach the words of the Master. On their way they meet Gaal, a robber, who hates the rich and loves the poor. They all hope that Jeschua will gather together the people to take up the fight against Jerusalem. In Jeschua's camp Simon Peter and a young intellectual from Carioth called Judas are introduced into the plot, and Jeschua is

depicted as speaking to the people with anger rising in him. Jeschua and his disciples go to Jerusalem, where they witness the extreme poverty, and they meet Kaifas and Pilate—and Jeschua is crucified. Judas turns out to be a spy in the service of the Jewish Council.

The novel is not about Jesus of the gospels, but about a well-intentioned rebel who fails to be consistent in his fight against the oppressors. He preaches that divine justice is intended for those who have carried the heavy burdens of life, for the Lord is the God of the poor. In the end, however, he fails to raise the people in a common fight against the Roman occupying power and against the Jewish upper classes and the priests who collaborate with the Romans.

As was *Slaven*, Kirk's novel about Jesus, whom he sees as the first communist, is clearly inspired by the situation during the period when Denmark was occupied by German troops. Jesus is described as a revolutionary, and therefore he was crucified. The Romans who are occupying Israel correspond to the Germans who are occupying Denmark, the Pharisees correspond to the Danish Social Democrats, and so on. The novel was well received and found many readers, and the author had again established himself as one of the important writers of the time.

Kirk's next two novels were both written for the Danish Communist Party newspaper, where they were published in installments between 1951 and 1952. They differ in form and style from all his previous works. *Djævelens penge* (The Devil's Money, 1952) and *Klitgaard & sønner* (Klitgaard & Sons, 1952) were both serialized in the Danish Communist paper before they appeared in book form. They were inspired by a series of articles in *Arbejdbladet* about a Danish firm of alleged war profiteers. The editor of the newspaper was sued for libel and was found guilty and sentenced in 1951 to three-months imprisonment. Kirk, who disagreed with the verdict, decided to tell the story of a firm of Danish war profiteers in a fictionalized (but easily recognizable) form. The story begun in *Djævelens penge* is about a family of three generations, beginning with the description of a decent and God-fearing Jutlandic fisherman, whose children and grandchildren fail to live up to the ethics of their ancestor, becoming ruthless capitalists, eager to get profits from whichever source they can get it. When Denmark is occupied in 1940 by German troops, their Danish engineering firm accepts an offer from the Germans of expanding a provincial airport, which is clearly in the interest, not of their own country, but of Nazi Germany. The grandsons, who have inherited the firm, are not united in their decision, for one of the brothers turns down the profitable offer on patriotic grounds, whereas the two others have no hesitation about working for the enemy. *Klitgaard & sønner* is a sequel to *Djævelens penge.*

While writing the two propaganda novels for the Communist paper, Kirk was also busy writing a new important literary work entitled *Skyggespil* (Play of Light and Shade, 1953), a charming book of personal childhood reminiscences. Here he is at his best as a master of style. In this book Kirk is much concerned with exploring his own identity. *Skyggespil* may be classified as a collection of short stories, but it is much more than that, for the short stories hang together, thus making it into a novel, and at the same time the book is also a key to the understanding of Kirk's development as a writer. *Skyggespil* was extremely well received. Danish literary critics who had complained that a great creative writer had been reduced to a political propagandist, now hailed him as a writer who had once again returned to be an eminent artist.

Apart from a children's book, *Prostens søn,* published in 1958, one more book was published before Kirk died in 1962, a collection of short stories titled *Borgerlige noveller* (Bourgeois Short Stories, 1958), several of them revisions of stories originally written in the 1920s and 1930s. *Danmarksrejsen* (Traveling in Denmark, 1966), published posthumously, was based on a series of articles in which Kirk described various parts of Denmark he had visited over the years.

Hans Kirk had been frail for some years before he died of cancer on 16 June 1962. His name is still known by most Danes as the author of *Fiskerne,* the best-selling Danish novel of all time. He himself, however, considered *Slaven* his most important book.

Morten Thing called his biography of Kirk *Hans Kirks mange ansigter: En biografi* (Hans Kirk's Many Faces: A Biography, 1997), and Kirk was indeed a multifaceted writer. In addition to being one of the greatest Danish novelists of his time he was also a writer of less important short stories for popular weeklies, and he wrote serialized political novels for the Communist newspaper. He was a distinguished literary critic and journalist and, since the early 1930s, a faithful member of the Danish Communist Party, who consistently toed the party line.

Bibliography:
Frank Büchmann-Møller, *Hans Kirk: En bibliografi* (Copenhagen: Gyldendal, 1974).

Biographies:
Werner Thierry, *Hans Kirk* (Copenhagen: Gyldendal, 1977);
Morten Thing, *Hans Kirks mange ansigter: En biografi* (Copenhagen: Gyldendal, 1997).

References:
Jens Kristian Andersen and Leif Emerek, *Hans Kirks forfatterskab* (Copenhagen: Stjernebøger, 1972);
Ib Bondebjerg, "Hans Kirk," in *Danske digtere i det 20. århundrede,* volume 2, edited by Torben Brostrøm and Mette Winge (Copenhagen: Gyldendal, 1981), pp. 198–230;
Elias Bredsdorff, "Marx, Freud og Adler i Hans Kirks roman 'Fiskerne'," in his *Fra Andersen til Scherfig* (Copenhagen: Gyldendal, 1978), pp. 168–190;
Bo Elbrønd-Bek and Ole Ravn, eds., *Omkring Fiskerne* (Copenhagen: Hans Reitzel, 1977);
Carsten Jensen, *Folkelighed og utopi: Brydninger i Hans Kirks forfatterskab* (Copenhagen: Gyldendal, 1981).

Tom Kristensen
(4 August 1893 – 2 June 1974)

W. Glyn Jones
University of East Anglia

BOOKS: *Fribytterdrømme: Digte* (Copenhagen: J. L. Lybeckers Forlag, 1920);

Livets Arabesk: Roman (Copenhagen: Hagerup, 1921);

Mirakler: Digte (Copenhagen: Gyldendal, 1922);

Paafuglefjeren: Digte fra Kina (Copenhagen: Hagerup, 1922);

En Anden: Roman (Copenhagen: Hagerup, 1923);

Bokserdrengen (Copenhagen: Erichsen, 1925; republished as *Kina i Oprør: En Fortælling fra det kinesiske Oprør,* 1938; republished as *Bokserdrengen: Kina i oprør: En fortælling fra det kinesiske oprør,* with afterword by Preben Ramløv, 1968);

En Kavaler i Spanien (Copenhagen: Hagerup, 1926);

Verdslige Sange (Copenhagen: R. Naver, 1927);

Sophus Claussen (Copenhagen: Gyldendal, 1929);

Hærværk (Copenhagen: Gyldendal, 1930); translated by Carl Malmberg as *Havoc* (Madison: University of Wisconsin Press, 1968);

En Fribytters Ord (Copenhagen: Gyldendal, 1932);

Kunst, Økonomi, Politik (Copenhagen: R. Naver, 1932);

Vindrosen: Konfrontationer (Copenhagen: Gyldendal, 1934);

Mod den yderste Rand (Copenhagen: Gyldendal, 1936);

Digte i Døgnet (Copenhagen: Gyldendal, 1940);

Harry Martinson: Den fribaarne Fyrbøder (Copenhagen: Gyldendal, 1941);

Hvad er Heta? (Copenhagen: Boghallen, 1946); enlarged as *Hvad er Heta? Og andre fortællinger* (Copenhagen: Gyldendal, 1959);

Mellem Krigene: Artikler og Kronikker, selected by Regin Højberg-Petersen (Copenhagen: Gyldendal, 1946);

En Omvej til Andorra (Copenhagen: Westermann, 1947);

Rejse i Italien (Copenhagen: Carit Andersen, 1951; republished as *Italien,* 1969);

En bogorms barndom (Copenhagen: Lindberg-Pedersens Boghandel, 1953);

Til dags dato: Artikler og kronikker, selected by Carl Bergstrøm-Nielsen (Copenhagen: Gyldendal, 1953);

Den sidste lygte (Copenhagen: Gyldendal, 1954);

Tom Kristensen in 1930 (courtesy of Gyldendal Publishers)

Det skabende øje: Kroniker (Copenhagen: Gyldendal, 1956);

Oplevelser med lyrik: Artikler og kronikker (Copenhagen: Gyldendal, 1957);

Den evige uro, edited by Bergstrøm-Nielsen (Copenhagen: Gyldendal, 1958);

Svendborg; Thurø-Taasinge, by Kristensen and Svend Eilersgaard (Svendborg: Arnbergs Bogtrykkeri, 1959);

Bøger, bøger, bøger, 2 volumes (Skjern: Selskabet Bogvennerne, 1961);

Mord i Pantomimeteatret; eller, Harlekin Skelet (Copenhagen: Gyldendal, 1962);

I min tid: Fra klunketid til øgledage, edited by Bergstrøm-Nielsen (Copenhagen: Gyldendal, 1963);

AÅbenhjertige fortielser (Copenhagen: Gyldendal, 1966);

Kritiker eller anmelder: Udvalgte essays, edited by Bergstrøm-Nielsen (Copenhagen: Gyldendal, 1966);

Fra Holger Drachmann til Benny Andersen: Udvalgte artikler om dansk lyrik, edited by Bergstrøm-Nielsen (Copenhagen: Gyldendal, 1967);

Hvad var mit ærinde? Rejseglimt, edited by Bergstrøm-Nielsen (Copenhagen: Gyldendal, 1968);

Tom på Thuroø: En samtale mellem Tom Kristensen og Thorkild Bjørnvig (Odense: Andelsbogtykkeriet i Odense, 1971);

Blandt københavnere: Nogle erindringresglimt, edited by Bergstrøm-Nielsen (Copenhagen: Gyldendal, 1973).

Editions and Collections: *Mellem Scylla og Charybdis: Samlede Digte fra Tyverne* (Copenhagen: Gyldendal, 1943);

De forsvundne ansigter: Symfonisk udvalg af Tom Kristensens asiatiske lyrik og prosa, illustrated by Povl Christensen (Copenhagen: Gyldendal, 1953);

Hærværk, 2 volumes, edited, with afterword, by Hanne Marie Svendsen (Copenhagen: Gyldendal, 1964);

Med disse øjne: Digte, selected by Kristensen and Bergstrøm-Nielsen (Copenhagen: R. Naver, 1972);

Den gådefulde Sara og andre historier, edited, with afterword, by Ole Storm (Copenhagen: Vindrose, 1981);

Mellem meninger: En Tom Kristensen antologi, edited by Tom Alsing and Flemming Bolding (Copenhagen: Gyldendal, 1993);

En anden, foreword by Jens Andersen (Copenhagen: Aschehoug, 1994);

Glimtvis åbner sig nuet: Tom Kristensen, selected and edited by Alsing and Andersen (Copenhagen: Gyldendal, 1994);

Samlede digte Tom Kristensen (Copenhagen: Gyldendal, 1997).

OTHER: Rudyard Kipling, *Værker i Udvalg,* Ny Serie 1–6, edited, with introduction, by Kristensen (Copenhagen, 1938);

Gustav Wied, *Værker i udvalg,* 5 volumes, edited by Kristensen (Copenhagen: Gyldendal, 1938);

Soya, *Smaa venlige Smaafisk: Fortællinger og Humoresker,* foreword by Kristensen (Copenhagen, 1941);

Frank Harris, *Mit Liv, Dansk Udgave,* edited by Kristensen (Copenhagen, 1942);

Henri Nathansen, *Memento–Digte i udvalg,* edited by Kristensen (Copenhagen, 1951);

Christian Winther, *Tusind og én nats eventyr,* edited by Kristensen (Copenhagen: Gyldendal, 1958);

Kai Friis-Møller, *Udvalgte essays 1915-1960,* foreword by Kristensen (Copenhagen: Hans Reitzel, 1960);

Amerikanske fortællere: Fra Edgar Allan Poe til Hemingway, edited by Kristensen and Tage La Cour (Copenhagen: Carit Andersen, 1963);

Kirsten Stamer and Rasmus Fischer, trans., *I digterens værksted: Udvalgte interviews fra "The Paris Review,"* foreword by Kristensen (Copenhagen: Rasmus Fischer, 1964);

Mark Twain, *Mark Twain fortæller: Millionpundsedlen og andre muntre historier,* foreword by Kristensen, edited by Orla Lundbo (Copenhagen: Carit Andersen, 1965);

Wied, *Livsens ondskab: Billeder fra gammelkøbing,* edited, with afterword, by Kristensen (Copenhagen: Gyldendal, 1965);

TRANSLATIONS: Norah Hoult, *Saa lukker vi mine herrer* (Copenhagen: Gyldendal, 1931);

Seán O'Faoláin, *Skærsommernats galskab* (Copenhagen: Gyldendal, 1932);

James T. Farrell, *Unge Lonigan* (Copenhagen: Gyldendal, 1942);

Rudyard Kipling, *Digte,* translated by Kristensen, Kai Friis Møller, and Valdemar Rørdam (Copenhagen: Gyldendal, 1942);

Erich Maria Remarque, *Livets gnist,* (Copenhagen: Gyldendal, 1952);

Theodore Dreiser, *En amerikansk tragedie: På dansk* (Copenhagen: Gyldendal, 1960);

D. H. Lawrence, *Sønner og elskere: På dansk* (Copenhagen: Gyldendal, 1960);

Remarque, *Intet nyt fra vestfronten: På dansk* (Copenhagen: Gyldendal, 1961);

Richard Wright, *Sort ungdom: På dansk* (Copenhagen: Gyldendal, 1961);

Dreiser, *Søster Carrie: På dansk* (Copenhagen: Gyldendal, 1962);

Junichiro Tanizaki, *Nøglen: På dansk* (Copenhagen: Grafisk Forlag, 1962);

Wright, *Søn af de sorte: På dansk* (Copenhagen: Gyldendal, 1963);

Walter van Tilburg Clark, *Strikken om halsen* (Copenhagen: Spektrum, 1964);

A. A. Milne, *Peter Plys og hans venner: På dansk,* translated by Kristensen and Else Heise (Copenhagen: Gyldendal, 1964);

T. S. Eliot, *Ødemarken og andre digte,* translated by Kristensen and Møller (Copenhagen: Gyldendal, 1964);

Dreiser, *Jennie Gerhardt: På dansk,* 2 volumes (Copenhagen: Hernov, 1973).

Tom Kristensen occupies a place as a leading avant-garde poet and novelist in the interwar years in Danish literature. His poetry ranges from flamboyant

173 ~~200~~

strax vilde springe ind paa ham, skubbede han ham ~~nakken~~ til Side og gik
ud i Entreen.

"Jeg havde glemt det," raabte Jastrau. Det lød som en Undskyld-
ning, en pludselig, klynkende Overgang.

"Løgn! Infam Journalistløgn!"

Og Entredøren smældede i, saa at ~~det~~ Ruderne
klirrede.

Jastrau satte sig ned paa Divanen, støttede Hovedet mod Hæn-
derne og rokkede det frem og tilbage.

Saadan blev Sejren altsaa! Saadan overvandt han Steffensen. Men havde han villet det? Og var Steffensen ikke stærkere
nu end nogensinde, Steffensen, det stupide Dyr? Blev han nu
ikke nødt til en Gang at opsøge ham og retfærdiggøre sig? Retfærdiggøre sig!! Det var dog for galt. Men hvorfor havde Steffensen saa stor Betydning for ham? Hvorfor havde han om-
gaaedes ham saa intimt i de Par Dage? Det var langtfra nogen Tilfældighed. Det var noget, der stod i sær Kontrast til
Møblerne her, Rococcostolene, Borgerligheden. Tænke sig den
nu lange, grove Laban tilfredsstillede noget i ham. Udløste
hans Skrig mod Uendelighed? Var det saadan at forstaa?
Steffensen var Vejen hinsides Meninger. Meninger, det var
Veje, andre havde traadt. Var det saadan at forstaa? Ungdommen, der uden at vakle gik seende frem imod det usynlige? Var
Steffensen saadan? Men han, Jastrau, var Oldingen, den fire
trediveaarige, den gemene, der tilsyneladende havde antaget ham
Digt, fordi hans Faders Navn var kendt; gemen, gemen. Han,

Page from the manuscript for Kristensen's 1930 novel Hærværk *(permission of Eve Lene Kristensen; Det Kongelige Bibliotek, Copenhagen)*

early poems achieving their effect through sound, color, and fantastic imagery to later works that are more subdued but still inventive; his novels range from clear derivatives of realism to one of the most important Danish novels of the twentieth century, *Hærværk* (1930; translated as *Havoc*, 1968), with its Joycean exploration of the psyche of a single man. In his prose and poetry Kristensen shows a command of language and must be regarded as one of the great renewers of Danish as a literary medium. He was also a highly respected essayist and for years a principal reviewer for the newspaper *Politiken*, using his authority to try to establish the principle that the reviewer's task was to judge the end result in relation to authorial intent, and not pontificate on what the author ought to have done.

The son of twenty-six-year-old Niels Peter Larsen Kristensen and nineteen-year-old Kirstine Marie Petersen, Aage Tom Kristensen was born 4 August 1893 in London, where his father was a metal spinner. According to Erik Halvorsen in *Danske digtere i det 20. århundrede* (Danish Writers in the Twentieth Century, 1966), Kristensen was given his middle name after Uncle Tom, the eponymous character of Harriet Beecher Stowe's novel *Uncle Tom's Cabin; or, Life among the Lowly* (1852). The family returned to Copenhagen when the boy was only three years old. Kristensen once remarked in a conversation with W. Glyn Jones that on arriving in Denmark as an English speaker, he uttered not a word for six months, but thereafter he never ceased trying to make up for lost time. He was brought up in one of the working-class areas of Copenhagen by an outgoing father and an introspective mother who had high ambitions for him. He learned easily and proceeded through various schools until entering the University of Copenhagen, where, after some hesitation, he settled on studying literature. Part of the then compulsory curriculum were courses in philosophy, where Kristensen's teachers inculcated the ideas of the meaninglessness of life—a problem enhanced by World War I, and one to which Kristensen was to return time after time, along with the question of the relationship between art and ethics. On graduating he taught at the Copenhagen School of Commerce from 1919 to 1921, during which time he published his first collection of poems, the expressionistic *Fribytterdrømme: Digte* (Dreams of a Freebooter: Poems, 1920).

The publication of *Fribytterdrømme* caused some stir in the Danish literary world. The ancestry of the poems could certainly be traced back to the work of Johannes V. Jensen and Sophus Claussen, but Kristensen went further than either of these earlier Danish writers both in his use of contemporary life and the vocabulary accompanying it and in his experimenting with sound without meaning. The most striking example of this is "Itokih," in which the refrain (which Kristensen maintains is that of a Maori canoeing song) becomes the vehicle bearing the entire poem: "Tohihah, hiohah, itokih!" It has been suggested that Kristensen at times could approach Dadaism in his use of meaningless sound, but the inspiration for "Itoki" is more likely either Holger Drachmann's poem "Sakuntala" or Claussen's "Ekbátana," both of which make use of an associative sound technique in order to create atmosphere in the poem as a whole and to supplement its general sense. He made similar use of the name "Rio Janeiro" in the poem of the same title.

If one is to relate *Fribytterdrømme* to a literary or artistic movement, however, it would not be Dadaism but rather Expressionism, with its highly subjective visions, unfettered use of color, and unflinching use of modern idiom and pictures of a seamier side of life than had hitherto been seen in Danish poetry. To this influence can be added the obvious signs of Cubism, particularly in a poem such as "Drømmen om Adén" (The Dream of Aden), with its use of color and shape to build up a picture: "Et torv, hvis fliser kaster lys tilbage / og svarer solens gule pisk med pisk, / og hvide huse, som med flade tage / står firkant imod firkant, stejl og bidsk. . . ." (A market square, whose flagstones throw back the light / and reply with a whiplash to the yellow lash of the sun / and white houses with flat roofs / standing square against square, steep and vicious. . . .) These poems are all "dreams," as the exotic locations dominating the first part of the collection–Rio de Janeiro, San Francisco, Aden, Zanzibar, Singapore–are all places that Kristensen had not visited. At the same time Kristensen expresses through the poems his urge to follow Friedrich Nietzsche's idea of revaluing all values and to see the emergence of a new age through chaos. The most famous of these poems, "Landet Atlantis" (The Land of Atlantis), a poem about revolution and chaos, ends with a vision:

Saadan er længselens land, Atlantis,
hvor alle harmoniske fordomme svigter.
Farverne sprænges, og formerne sprænges,
og skønheden skabes af grelle konflikter.
I kaos jeg løfter min bøsse
mod skønhedens stjerne og sigter.

(Thus is the land of longing, Atlantis,
where all harmonious prejudices yield,
colors are shattered and forms are destroyed,
and beauty is made from glaring conflict.
In chaos I raise my gun
toward the star of beauty and take aim.)

These poems of exotic locations and of chaos are supplemented with a series portraying lowlife in Copen-

the same time as apparently partly following the old nineteenth-century technique, first seen in Romantic Realism, of dividing his own personality in two and endowing two leading characters each with part of it. The chaotic, unpredictable Jørgen Baumann and his sober, rationalistic friend Pram are fundamentally two halves of the same character, both far removed from reality, but coping–or not coping–in quite different ways. When, toward the end of the novel, Baumann's home is overrun by revolutionaries who actually throw him out, Pram has already foreseen such developments and, in order to save his own skin, has settled in a flat in a proletarian district–though he has also taken care to furnish it with the opulence to which he is accustomed.

The actual action in this novel is slight, and although it is not specifically set in Copenhagen, it clearly reflects that city and the near-revolutionary situation that arose from the Danish king's intervention in politics in 1920, which led to the so-called Easter Crisis. The situation had been kept under control, but Kristensen indulges in a vision of what might have happened had things gone differently; however, as this is an impressionistic–or Expressionistic–novel, there is little sign of a logically developing plot.

As the novel opens Jørgen Baumann, a respected surgeon, has given up his practice and withdrawn to his luxurious villa to immerse himself in his nihilistic despair. The mood and the style are established in the first lines:

> Doktor Jørgen Bamanns høje, fede Skikkelse tegnede sig mod den hvide Villamur som en stor, sort Masse, som Skyggen af en Trækrone, og midt i denne Skygge glimtede en hvid Flade, et bredt Skortebryst. Han var festklædt.

> Han stod stille, med Haanden støttet mod Muren, og lyttede til Musikken indenfor i Villaen. Der var jo Fest i hans eget Hjem. Det myldrede med Mennesker i de store, øde Sale.

> (Doctor Jørgen Baumann's tall, corpulent figure was outlined against the white wall of the house, formed like a great, black mass, like the shadow of a treetop, and in this midst of this shadow a white expanse could be glimpsed, a broad shirt front. He was dressed for a party.

> He was standing motionless, his hand resting on the wall, listening to the music inside the house. There was a party in his own home. People were milling about in the great, desolate rooms.)

At this party, Baumann's wife leaves him for a Cubist painter.

TOM KRISTENSEN

HÆRVÆRK

GYLDENDAL

Cover for Kristensen's quasi-autobiographical novel, which was attacked by contemporary reviewers for depicting drunkenness and debauchery but hailed by later critics as one of the most important Danish works of the twentieth century

hagen: the pub in "Arbejdets Sol" (Work's Sun), the billiard hall in "Det blomstrende Slagsmaal" (The Flowering Fight), the pimp in "Hans Højhed" (His Highness), and the prostitute in "Paa Tvangen" (By Compulsion). And these poems are again tempered by the sympathetic portrayal of the flower seller in "Violsælgersken" (The Violet Seller) and the warmer and more intimate pictures of Copenhagen in sunlight and a series of half-philosophical, half-humorous poems of which the most famous is "Min Pibe" (My Pipe), in which Kristensen portrays himself as "Jeg er Kun en lille Digter halvt en Tænker, halvt en Når" (only a very small poet, half a thinker, half a clown).

The confusion of themes in *Fribytterdrømme* in 1920 was followed in 1921 by an equally chaotic, impressionistic work, *Livets Arabesk: Roman* (Life's Arabesque: Novel). Here, Kristensen breaks new ground at

The second chapter establishes the contrasting pole of the novel, introducing the bullying pimp Ibald and the prostitute Elise, whom he controls. Elise leaves him and is before long taken over by Baumann, whose home she herself takes over. Ibald is left in the wings, and the scenes now shift between Baumann's house and city lowlife, with prostitutes, pimps, alcoholics, a fanatical monk, revolutionaries, and not least, the Cubist painter with whom Baumann's wife eloped, all competing for the reader's attention. Inevitably, Ibald discovers that Elise is living in Baumann's house and exploits the situation to the advantage of his revolutionary friends who are quickly shown to be as brutal and corrupt as the bourgeois citizens whom they seek to displace. For all his left-leaning sympathies, Kristensen was no real revolutionary, and his stance is aesthetic rather than political or ethical. This novel is no more realistic in its approach to revolution and revolutionary ideas than is the poem "Landet Atlantis." As the revolution approaches, Ibald and his companions take over Baumann's house entirely, and Baumann is turned out. The city seems now to be in the hands of the revolutionaries, but "imperialist" troops are approaching to regain control. Baumann joins the revolutionaries out of a sense of excitement rather than true commitment to their cause and is overcome by fear in a skirmish with the imperialist troops. Struck by a bullet not intended for him, Baumann dies a death that is as meaningless as his life has been.

Just as the action of this novel is entirely unrealistic, so Baumann must be seen as a nihilistic symbol rather than a figure of flesh and blood, and his role is largely to give expression to the author's own search for meaning in a society in disarray. His home is described as "desolate" from the start, and at its center it contains a "cabinet of horrors," a small, eight-sided room without windows and entirely sealed off from the outside world, to which Baumann repairs when he is at his most nihilistic and lonely, in the sole company of his "dysmorphic" paintings and his collection of grotesque dolls. He seeks some kind of spiritual peace, playing around with mainly grotesque forms of religion–and talking of finding a Buddhist nirvana in whisky–while he sits passively and allows prostitutes and exploiters to take possession of his home. The weakness of the novel is its formlessness, but the writing shows enormous energy and linguistic brilliance. As are the poems of *Fribytterdrømme,* this novel is distinguished by the stylistic verve and inventiveness of a young poet who is seeking a new way forward and whose sense of color, sound, and linguistic impact allow him to take liberties that no Danish writer had previously dared.

Kristensen's second volume of poetry, *Mirakler: Digte* (Miracles: Poems, 1922), betokened both a contin-

uation and a modification of *Fribytterdrømme,* in that it took further the poems inspired by city life at the same time that the general tone became more subdued and even at times suggested a hesitation that had been absent in the earlier collection. There are moves toward a more personal expression, in particular in the first of the poems, "Til Ruth" (To Ruth), in which, in a poem suggesting a difficult period in their relationship, Kristensen succinctly and tenderly expresses his feelings toward Ruth Lange, who became his first wife in 1921, and from whom he was divorced in 1927. His personal feelings also emerge in the title poem, "Mirakler," in which the "miracle" is the fact that thirty shining wet stones lose their sheen when the water dries–but can be brought back to life, as by a miracle, when the poet turns the water tap on them. This poem can, of course, be taken at face value, but it is also possible to see in it the idea of the miraculous effect of language on an otherwise uninspiring collection of ideas. The final poem, "Min Sang" (My Song)–in some ways reminiscent of the earlier "Min Pibe"–suggests both the poet's lack of a sense of his own achievement and a mockery of the populace at large when he plays his harp by the side of a dark pool. All he plays are the notes "di di di"–but the carp in the pool think it is food for them and rise to the bait.

In other poems, however, Kristensen shows the same linguistic brilliance as he had in his first collection. "Lirekassen" (The Hurdy-Gurdy) is outstanding in its re-creation of the sounds of the hurdy-gurdy as well as the atmosphere surrounding it, a masterpiece of linguistic creation with internal rhyme, rich rhyme, and assonance, a technique he also employs in "Sancta Katarina fra Alexandria" (Saint Catherine of Alexandria), a poem about the courtesan who converts two hundred soldiers and fifty philosophers. "Nyhavns-Odyssé" (Nyhavn Odyssey) is related in style to the earlier "Hans Højhed" and is a portrait of lowlife in the Nyhavn district that the poet had known in his childhood, here re-created in tones of something approaching nostalgia.

In 1921 Kristensen was awarded a grant to enable him to make a trip to the Far East in 1922. This journey had a profound impact on him, showing him the contrast between the fragmented life he knew in Europe and what he saw as Asiatic calm and fatalistic acceptance of life's trials. The resultant poems, *Paafuglefjeren: Digte fra Kina* (The Peacock Feather: Poems from China, 1922), were of a quite different nature from his earlier poetry.

Many of the poems in *Paafuglefjeren* depict Shanghai or Beijing; in these pictures of Chinese cities the urban confusion is not entirely unlike Kristensen's earlier portrayals of city life in Copenhagen, but the language is more restrained. Already in *Livets Arabesk* Kristensen had talked of Asiatic calm, and this theme runs through much of his work, a sense of stoical acceptance of fate in the East to which he aspires but never achieves.

The East with which Kristensen was confronted by no means entirely represented Asiatic calm, and even in the title poem Kristensen suggests both the confusion and lack of understanding along with the attraction to the East that radiates from the volume as a whole: "Og jeg blev forledt til at ane en Sjæl / i alle de Blikke, jeg mødte og saa, / og jeg blev forledt til at synge om det, / jeg ej kan forstaa." (I was led to sense a soul / in all the glances I met and saw, / and I was led to sing of what / I cannot understand.) One of the reasons for his confusion, perhaps at times repulsion, is the lack of respect for human life in this vast society, as is seen in "En Damper, en Djunke, en Sampan" (A Steamer, A Junk, A Sampan), describing the collision between a steamship and a junk and the resulting loss of life and lack of interest in those who die. This revulsion is balanced by Kristensen's own obvious sympathy in "Den blinde" (The Blind Man), which seeks to present life as experienced by a blind man who looks forward to dying and waking up in a different form. The same sympathy found in the earlier "Violsælgersken" is present in "Tiggersken" (The Beggar Woman), while in "Den blaa Tigger" (The Blue Beggar) it is given a slightly wry, humorous twist. The most heartrending of the poems reflecting the lack of humanity is "Henrettelsen" (The Execution), one of the most famous of all Kristensen's poems. He appears not to have witnessed the public execution by beheading of twenty pirates himself, but he had heard a graphic account of it, and in this poem he puts himself in the place of the sixth miscreant to be executed. As the executioner approaches and heads roll, the sixth figure's experience of reality becomes sharpened to an excruciating degree, and after the fifth victim has fallen he feels that life itself has come to a standstill as preparations are made for his own execution. The poem then ends with a last, seemingly meaningless but meaningful observation: "Jeg ser en Bille vandre tryg / med grønt Metal paa hvælvet Ryg, / den vandrer mod / en Bøddelfod." (I see a beetle walking confidently / with green metal on an arched back, / it is walking towards / an executioner's foot.) Not all the poems are tragic, however, and "De to Oldinge og Det blomstrende Træ" (The Two Old Men and the Blossoming Tree) is a humorous portrayal of two old friends who have each cheated the other in their youth—and probably know it—but who now, as old friends, exchange courteous smiles.

In the midst of all these poems about China, however, Kristensen returns twice to a theme on which he had touched in previous works—the significance and function of the poet. He is writing these poems at a time of European fascination with things Chinese, not least with Chinese poetry, and so it is natural that he should turn in one way or another to the most famous of all Chinese poets, Li Po (in his poems referred to variously as Li Tai Pé, Li-Tai-Pé, and Litaipé). Li Po emerges twice in this volume, first in "Li-Tai-Pés død" (The Death of Li Tai Pé), in which the aging and famous poet has distanced himself from the splendor he has known as the Emperor's favorite to live the life of a minstrel, finding inspiration in wine. Yet, for all his achievements, he regrets that he has perhaps not written the most important of all his potential poems, in which he sees the symbolical value of a "moderlos Rede med plettede" (motherless nest with speckled eggs). He indulges in an excursion by boat to the accompaniment of plentiful wine, and yet he still thinks of the nest. As the drinking continues, he proclaims: "Det ryger med Digte, det ryger med Sange / som Støv, naar jeg slaar til min snavsede Las. / Dog findes et Digt, som jeg aldrig faar sunget, / et moderløst Æg i en Rede af Kvas." (There are poems and songs / as plentiful as dust when I strike my filthy rags. / Yet one poem I never managed to sing, / a motherless egg in a nest of twigs.) Now, the speaker declares, he will sing the songs he has been able to write, but, intoxicated, he falls from his boat and drowns.

The theme of inspiration is taken a step further in the last poem in the book, "Den dobbelte Fjende" (The Double Enemy), in which the beautiful Hua Ling, a symbol of poetry, refuses the advances of the poet because he only drinks "genopkoler Te" (warmed-up tea), as a result of which he writes in the style of Li Tai Pé. Hua Ling rejects his advances and tells him to eschew tea and turn to wine to find inspiration, which he does and writes a poem: "but it *was* Li-Tai-Pé." The poet now embarks on a debauched life and in his intoxication he produces poetry of a different kind: "Jeg Kommer, en Hader of Te, en Elsker ap Vinog of Piger, en Modstander af Li-Tai-Pé" (I come, a hater of tea, a lover of wine and of girls, an opponent of Li-Tai-Pé). He is still rejected, however, as having misunderstood the command of Hua Ling. This is a long, complex, and somewhat obscure poem, but taken together with "Li-Tai-Pés død" must be seen as suggesting Kristensen's own dilemma as to how to be original and avoid following the beaten path—and also bringing in the question of seeking inspiration in alcohol, a theme already found in *Livets Arabesk*.

On his return to Copenhagen from his Far Eastern trip, Kristensen wrote his *En Anden: Roman* (Someone Else: Novel, 1923) and also turned to the literary criticism for which he became famous, first working for

Nörholm, 6 Decbr. 1930.

Hr. Tom Kristensen.

Jeg har i halvandet Døgn levet sammen med Jastrau og de andre, men nu er det slut, og jeg sitter her syk av Savn efter mere av dem. Det er saa tomt at det nu er slut.

Jeg vet ikke at jeg i mit Liv har været saa optat av en Bok, min Kone vet hvorledes jeg har læst — læst og refereret —, hun læser den nu. En Genistrek og et Kjæmpeverk. Jeg beder Dem motta min ærbødige Hyldest. Jeg har selv skrevet Bøker, det mangler ikke, men nu er jeg ydmyg, ingen Bok er som Deres.

Knut Hamsun.

Letter to Kristensen from the Norwegian author Knut Hamsun, praising Hærværk
(permission of Eva Lene Kristensen; Det Kongelige Bibliotek)

the periodical *Tilskueren* (The Observer) and then moving to the newspaper *Politiken* (Copenhagen) as literary critic and cultural editor. He left this post in 1927, but after the publication of his novel *Hærværk* he resumed his work as literary critic in 1931 and continued in that job until 1963. For a period, he showed signs of increasingly left-wing political tendencies, but he became disillusioned with communist ideas and withdrew from politics in general. Nor was it long before he withdrew from the temptations of living in Copenhagen itself to live and work in the seclusion of his house on the tiny island of Thurø outside Svendborg, where he spent the rest of his life.

In the same way as *Paafuglefjeren* suggested a different approach from that in the earlier poems, so Kristensen's second novel, *En Anden,* is couched in tones entirely different from those met in *Livets Arabesk,* and indeed the language and approach are generally speaking those of the realist novel. *En Anden* moreover continues the long line of bildungsromans that had started in Danish literature in the mid-nineteenth century, novels such as Hans Christian Andersen's *At være eller ikke være* (To Be, or Not to Be, 1857) or Jens Peter Jacobsen's *Niels Lyhne* (1880). Like his counterparts in these earlier works, the main character, Valdemar Rasmussen, is a sensitive, physically weak character trying to find himself, and until the end he is convinced that he is really "another."

The structure of this novel is interesting, as each chapter except for the last is divided into two parts, the first short section presenting fragments of Valdemar's life in China where he works as a customs officer, and the second consisting of his own memoirs of his childhood and youth. In each chapter Kristensen depicts the parallel between Valdemar's contemporary experiences and those of his childhood and youth in Copenhagen, the object of this parallel being to demonstrate that nothing changes. Valdemar's youthful infatuation with the fickle Klara is paralleled by his experience in China with the half-caste May, the constant removals in Copenhagen have their counterparts in his changes of place in China, and the reflections of one Chinese on the artistic appearances of a stone are paralleled by Valdemar's reflections on art when he is wrongly seen as a potential artist toward the end of the novel. A scene in the Chinese section of chapter 11 shows the indifference with which people pass by someone who has collapsed and died in the street—the parallel to this emerges later in the chapter when Valdemar's mother dies, and for most people life goes on as before with few tears being shed.

Only in one sense, that of the principal character's search for his own identity, can this be seen as an autobiographical novel, but the portrayals of the child's life in the seedier parts of Copenhagen are clearly reminiscent of Kristensen's own childhood in those same districts—both the experience of being a sensitive, physically weak child in the midst of boys much stronger than himself and not least, of course, in the many moves he experienced that are reflected in the book.

Valdemar grows up in the district around Nyhavn, a district populated by rough bullies, social outcasts, and prostitutes. His unmarried mother is a milliner, originally the owner of a shop, but, when the business fails, she is forced to wear her eyes out doing fine work for others to eke out a living. She has a friend of sorts in the tobacconist Samuelson, and the relationship remains something of a mystery: Valdemar dislikes Samuelson, but on one occasion he is actually pointed out as being Valdemar's father—though the mother says otherwise. On the death of the mother, Samuelson gives Valdemar a home, where the boy discovers Samuelson is having a string of nighttime female visitors. The relationship with Valdemar's mother again emerges as something different when Valdemar goes through Samuelson's photograph album containing pictures of his conquests—and discovers that his mother does not figure among them. As a small boy, Valdemar is drawn to Klara, though she scorns him and as a young man he discovers that she is a semi-prostitute earning her living in part from visiting Samuelson. Valdemar himself strikes up a doomed relationship with her for a time, and this relationship is instrumental in making him leave Samuelson's shop. He lives a life of destitution for a time, pictured in impressionistic scenes reminiscent of those in Norwegian author Knut Hamsun's *Sult* (1890; translated as *Hunger,* 1899), but is put on his feet again on meeting a brutal expressionist painter called Raavad, who cynically exploits the boy's meager artistic gifts in an attempt to fool a rich and arrogant customer. Again, Valdemar rebels, and again he is given a home, this time by a wealthy young man who realizes that Valdemar is not gifted but who also seeks to exploit him. Once more, Valdemar here encounters a young woman he has seen at a distance and fallen in love with; he discovers that she, like Klara, is devoid of feeling and has prepared to spend her nights with Valdemar's patron. The parallel is obvious, and Valdemar again leaves. On this occasion he meets a sailor who befriended him on the night of his mother's death, and he goes to sea as a ship's boy.

As a result of his going to sea he comes to live in Shanghai, which is the scene of most of the "Chinese" episodes with which the various chapters begin—though here, Valdemar moves around as he did in Copenhagen, going to Nanking and Charbin. In Shanghai he is, as he was in Copenhagen, without true friends. His closest contact appears to be with Robert Scott, a man with a reputation for ruthlessness and a love of gin slings—and who introduces him to his friend, the half-caste May Darling. A relationship develops between Valdemar and the enigmatic May, and before long Robert Scott is encouraging him to marry her—but before this happens, Valdemar sees her together with Robert Scott again and realizes that he has been fooled—a clear echo of his earlier relationship with Klara.

In its psychological penetration, this is one of the most important novels of its day, though it suffers from the flaws that the brief glimpses of life in Shanghai do not live up to the vibrant portrayals of Copenhagen, while the encounters toward the end of the novel with Raavad and the young Richard Dam seem implausible and unrealistic. It is as though, at this juncture, the author has been too keen to draw the parallels that emerge elsewhere and has thereby sacrificed the realism that has been the mark of this novel otherwise.

In 1925 Kristensen followed up his trip to China with one to Spain, ostensibly with the intention of writing a novel based on the life of the medieval mystic Ramón Llull. He traveled alone, and he traveled in search of himself. As he puts it in the book resulting from this journey, which was not the intended novel but the travel account *En Kavaler i Spanien* (A Cavalier in Spain, 1926): "You must overcome your weakness if you want to conquer and win." He counted this as one of his best books, and the one that revealed the most about himself. In *En Kavaler i Spanien* he definitively broke with the expressionism that had marked his earlier production.

This break with expressionism does not, however, mean that this mixture of prose and poetry is a colorless book. On the contrary, Kristensen produces a series of vibrant and colorful descriptions of the people he meets, both those he talks to at length or encounters briefly, and he once more demonstrates his linguistic skills, visual awareness, and his ability to create images, whether in the description of a legless beggar on crutches as swinging like a bell or one of the contrasting street scenes in Barcelona:

Men den Dag gik jeg ind i de snævreste Gyder, og jeg geraadede hurtigt ind i en sydlandssk Forvirring. Ærbare Kvinder sad paa Stole ude ved Rendestens-kanten og syede. Deres Rygge og Nakker var uden Nysgerrighed. Mindre ærbare Kvinder fortrak pludselig Ansiget i meningsløse Grimacer og lokkede med et Netværk af Rynker. Ludfattig Borgerlighed og Prostitution Side om Side.

(But that day I went into the narrowest alleyways, and I soon encountered a confusion typical of the South. Respectable women were sitting on chairs by the gutter, sewing. Their backs and the backs of their necks were without curiosity. Less respectable women suddenly contorted their faces in meaningless grimaces and sought to entice me with a network of wrinkles. Desperately poor bourgeois respectability and prostitution side by side.)

Much of this encounter with Spain, which is portrayed as a country filled with gestures and little action, a country in which melancholy is part of the general character, is turned into images, and Kristensen admits to feeling a sense of something unreal between himself and the things he saw. He is on the outside, and he never really comes to feel as if he is on the inside. He visits Barcelona, seeking out the proletarian life in the city and feeling appalled by it. When, inevitably, he is taken to a bullfight, his description is, like so much else in this book, curiously unemotional, though he admits to finding himself both repelled and fascinated. In the cathedral at Barcelona he is overcome by the darkness and the mystery that seem to reflect the mystery of his own soul. He goes to Montserrat to visit the monastery there; although he is terrified of heights, he decides to prove himself by going to the top of the mountain he wants to conquer. He cuts a pitiful figure, however, when at the most dangerous place he has to crawl along on hands and knees in contrast to other, carefree, climbers. The same sense of irony at his own achievements and failings is seen in Majorca, when he finally seeks to find traces of Ramón Llull, clambering with great difficulty up to the top of the mountain only to find that there was a perfectly good road leading up the other side. His visit here, as elsewhere, leads to little beyond the description. Finally, in answer to the question put to him by a French acquaintance as to whether he has achieved anything here in Spain, his answer is an unambiguous "No." He returns to Denmark, apparently unchanged.

After the intensity of his previous works, Kristensen turned on the whole to lighter themes in the volume of poems titled *Verdslige Sange* (Secular Songs, 1927), giving free rein to his skill at rhyming and creating playful rhythms in poems such as "Vaarvise" (Spring Song) and "Narrevise" (Fool's Song). Many of the poems in this collection are of a teasing, erotic nature. There is for instance "Konfirmandinden" (The Confirmandess), in which the poet wishes he were an altar candle, able to look directly at the young lady being confirmed, instead of being a grown man who had to lower his eyes. There are four verses in this vein, elegant and witty. Or there is "O Pinsesol og lysegrønt" (Oh Whitsun Sun and Light Green), in which his and his girl's bicycles are intertwined in "et my forniklet Elskovseventyr" (a newly-nickeled love adventure), while he must be content to kiss her knee though he

TOM KRISTENSEN
VINDROSEN

GYLDENDAL

Cover for Kristensen's 1934 essay collection

longs to kiss her lips. There is something of a contrast in "Prædikeren" (The Preacher), an equally elegant and witty, but much more caustic, attack on a pastor, apparently newly installed, stern, pale, and unbending—but a man who has lived a much less reputable life while young. It is impossible to know whether this was aimed at any one person in particular. The first poem in the volume, however, does have a name attached to it and is a poem in homage to the actress Betty Nansen; the poet expects no thanks, but will be grateful for even the slightest reply.

Weightiest among the erotic poems is "Nat i Berlin 1921" (Night in Berlin 1921), a disturbing poem and one of Kristensen's best known. It is a nightmare vision of a night in a Berlin hotel when the poet is unable to sleep because he hears the sound of horses' hooves on the roads outside and the sound of women's shoes on the hotel corridors. Both sounds have erotic connotations, and they are fused in the poet's mind to produce

visions of sensuous centaurs. "Nat i Berlin 1921" is followed by another poem suggesting insistent erotic associations, "Amsterdam," in which "Elskovens hede Pause tra stóvede Trær aander" (The hot pause of love breathes from dusty trees), while "Hinsides" echoes the theme of love and death. Even among these poems of varied mood, the melancholy that Kristensen felt while in Spain makes itself felt again.

In 1927, the same year that *Verdslige Sange* was published, Kristensen left his post as literary critic and cultural editor for *Politiken.* After spending two and a half years on its composition, Kristensen published his most important novel, *Hærværk,* in 1930. It was unlike anything that had been written in Danish before, and as a consequence became and remained a controversial work for many years. It is now recognized as one of the most important twentieth-century works of fiction in Danish. Although a work of fiction, there is a considerable autobiographical element to the novel, and readers quickly recognized that it was a highly revealing roman à clef. No one with the slightest knowledge of Copenhagen could be in any doubt that the newspaper *Dagbladet* (The Daily) depicted in the novel was in fact *Politiken,* whose famous editor, Henrik Cavling, is clearly portrayed. Nor could anyone with the slightest knowledge of Kristensen be in any doubt that the central character, Ole Jastrau, is at least in part a self-portrait.

In one sense, the action is slender. Jastrau, a literary editor for *Dagbladet,* is disillusioned as a result of his constant reviewing. An election is taking place as the novel begins, and Jastrau is visited by two communist acquaintances, Sanders and Steffen Steffensen, who are wanted by the authorities and who are assuming the election will lead to a Social Democrat government and the removal of the threat to them. They need a place to stay for the night and have sought it from Jastrau, who at one time had communist leanings. They are the start of the havoc that gives the novel its title. The two communists virtually take over both Jastrau and his apartment, as a result of which Jastrau's wife finally leaves him, taking their son with her. There follows a series of episodes illustrating Jastrau's subsequent life and degradation, partly in the company of his visitors, partly in that of heavy-drinking colleagues and friends in a bar near the newspaper offices, and partly by consorting with prostitutes and others of low repute. All this action takes place against the background of a beautiful springtime and the promise it bears with it. Jastrau has rejected the communism of his two visitors, and he subsequently rejects Catholicism, to which he is introduced by a journalist colleague who plays with Catholicism without ever committing himself to it and who in fact betrays Jastrau on one important occasion. Ultimately

Jastrau is saved by a colleague, Kryger, for whom he has little liking and with whose conservative views he disagrees—and with whose wife he has had a brief affair. He is finally sent off to Berlin as secretary to Geberhardt, a highly respected professor of economics. Whether this move is his salvation is, of course, never made clear. Readers are justified in having their doubts. Kristensen himself expresses reservations. Admitting that Jastrau is a self-portrait (from which, however, he says he has removed a steel spring), he states that: "Will is a word I am reluctant to use of Jastrau. It is still to be found in him. But it is of an extremely doubtful quality, and he himself does not know the meaning of the word 'will.'"

Jastrau's actions are related to the idea expressed in the poem "Landet Atlantis" in that he feels, or convinces himself, that destruction is the only way forward. In a world of grotesque meaninglessness, he is on the road to self-destruction and needs violent, dramatic events in order to survive. The general atmosphere in the novel is summed up in the poem "Angst," early in the book, ascribed to one of Jastraus's two communist visitors, Steffen Steffensen:

Men min Angst maa forløses i Længsel
og i Syner af Rædsel og Nød.
Jeg har længtes mod Skibskatastrofer
og mod Hærværk og pludselig Død.
Jeg har længtes mod brændende Byer
og mod Menneskeracer paa Flugt,
mod et Opbrud, som ramte Alverden,
og et Jordskælv, som kaldtes Guds Tugt.

(But my fear must find release in longing
and in visions of terror and suffering.
I have longed for disaster at sea
and for havoc and sudden death.
I have longed for burning cities
and for human races in flight,
for a break up that struck the whole world
and an earthquake called God's punishment.)

The novel was criticized on publication as being a succession of scenes depicting drunken orgies and worse. Jastrau visits prostitutes, contracts venereal disease and undergoes treatment for it, and wastes the money with which he is provided in order to escape from Copenhagen. The same donor, Kryger, then provides him with a further ticket. Is this unexpected action due to his innate respect for Jastrau, or has he suspected the liaison between Jastrau and his own wife? Jastrau is by no means the only alcoholic in the novel, perhaps not even the worst. He at least does not suffer from delirium tremens, as do others. *Hærværk* was, perhaps predictably, castigated for monotony and formlessness. Later critics, however, understood it in a completely dif-

ferent light and recognized the novel as a powerful and highly original psychological study introducing elements of the works of both Sigmund Freud and James Joyce against the background of a society in dissolution, the society of the 1920s. This society and the figures constituting it are seen through the eyes of the sensitive but self-destructive Jastrau; the parallel can clearly be drawn to the expressionism of the early poems in that it is all experienced through the eyes of a supersensitive and not entirely predictable main character, some of whose thoughts are reproduced as stream of consciousness. The parallel to the earlier novels has also been drawn by Erik Halvorsen:

Jastrau er Bauman, Pram, Valdemar Rasmussen i ny forklædninger, og som man husker om disse personer, var det karakteristiske *ikke*, at de sprængtes af voldsomme kræfter, lidenskaber, i deres indre, men netop det modsatte, at de forsumpede og opløstes, fordi de var forsagte væsener, der *længtes* efter at være ild men ingenlunde var det. De havde ikke meget lidenskab—men derimod nerver.

(Jastrau is Bauman, Pram, Valdemar Rasmussen in new disguises, and as will be remembered in these figures, the characteristic feature was *not* that they were blasted by violent forces, passions, within them, but precisely the opposite, that they went downhill and were broken because they were faint-hearted beings who *longed* to be fire, but simply were not. They had not much passion—but on the other hand they had sensitive nerves.)

In 1931, after completing *Hærværk,* Kristensen returned to his former post at *Politiken* as literary reviewer. He continued to write poetry and a few short stories, but his activity as a novelist was now finished with the exception of the lightweight *Mord i Pantomimeteatret; eller, Harlekin Skellet* (Murder in the Pantomime Theater; or, Harlequin Skeleton) in 1962. Nor were his poems the same as they formerly were; the untrammeled experiments of the earlier work are more and more replaced by poems in a classical manner—a development in some ways parallel to what had taken place in the work of Johannes V. Jensen two decades earlier. Nor were the new volumes of poetry as homogenous as the earlier ones, largely consisting of poems already published elsewhere. This latter feature is most noticeable in *En Fribytters Ord* (The Words of a Freebooter, 1932), in which most of the poems are taken either from *En Kavaler i Spanien* or *Hærværk,* whereby they lose their true significance in no longer being seen in context.

The next collection of poems *Mod den yderste Rand* (Towards the Furthest Edge, 1936) also lacks a central theme to hold it together, but it is introduced by one of

Kristensen and his dog, Mot, in 1939

Kristensen's finest poems, "Det er Knud, som er død" (It is Knud Who is Dead), a memorial poem to the Arctic explorer Knud Rasmussen, who had been a close friend of Kristensen. In long, rolling, rhymed lines, Kristensen expresses dignified sorrow at the same time as he suggests the Arctic surroundings in which the message of Rasmussen's death will be heard. The collection is rounded off with another memorial poem, "Emilie Sannom," in homage to a woman flier who had been killed in a parachute jump. In this collection Kristensen fully reveals his skill at writing memorial poems; there is one to the sculptor Kaj Nielsen, while the poem "Hvem var Ludvig Holberg" (Who Was Ludvig Holberg) is of a similar nature, a reflection on the personality of the great eighteenth-century dramatist and historian, about whose actual personality little is known. Other poems in the collection, many with a winter setting, are reminiscent of late Romantic nature poetry, for instance "Isblomster" (Ice Flowers); however, these poems are not mere charming miniatures, and there is often the suggestion of unease or even fear, as when the poet is filled with apprehension while walking in a wintry landscape in "Den syngende Busk" (The Singing Bush). His lack of inner harmony is elsewhere

suggested in "Dobbelt" (Double), in which on the one hand he is reflecting on the execution of Erich Baron by the Nazis and on the other hand preoccupied with the young woman who is with him.

There are mixed opinions about these poems; Jens Andersen has argued that they mark the start of a decline in Kristensen's writing, whereas Halvorsen listed this volume and the later *Den sidste lygte* (The Last Light, 1954) among Kristensen's most important collections of poems. It is true that they show no sign of rigid composition, and the style shows nothing of the experimental zeal displayed by Kristensen in his earlier work—but nevertheless, they are serious poems, and Kristensen's poetic mastery can be in no doubt, even if it is kept within more traditional bounds.

The same applies to the contents of the next volume, *Digte i Døgnet* (Poems Throughout the Day, 1940), though they are of a different kind and in one sense more homogenous. Kristensen had already shown his ability to write memorial poems or poems in homage to people he knew. Such poems form the foundation of this volume, and apart from a small number of patriotic poems toward the end, they are all of the eulogistic or memorial type. They are, however, neither superficial nor trite, and Kristensen again shows an impressive ability to indicate in his poems the achievements or the wider significance of the people of whom he writes: the poets Johannes V. Jensen, Sophus Claussen, and Ludvig Holstein; the composer Carl Nielsen; the ballerina Anna Pavlova; and the literary historian Vilhelm Andersen among many others. A few are names of international significance, while others are mainly of Danish interest. Among the names of mainly Danish significance, however, one does lead to a wider perspective. The poet Gustaf Munch-Petersen had been killed in the Spanish Civil War, and Kristensen was one of several poets to write in memory of him—but he widens the perspective to include the Spanish children who were suffering innocently as a result of the war. The Spanish children lead in turn to a poem dedicated to the children of expatriate Danish parents, reflecting on what these children know of Denmark—and this in turn leads to a few poems in praise of Denmark and what it stands for.

The modest 1954 collection, *Den sidste lygte,* bears further evidence of Kristensen's skill in writing memorial poems, with one dedicated to the poet Nis Petersen and written in the style Petersen employed in some of his own narrative poetry; this is immediately followed by a gentle, lyrical poem in memory of the critic Christian Rimestad. The majority of the poems are of a personal nature, however, and are often melancholy in tone, poems in which Kristensen reflects on his own person. In one, "En høg slog ned" (A Hawk Struck), he identifies himself with the songbird that he has just witnessed being killed by a hawk, though noting, too, that his horror at the sight is soon transformed into a calm memory–a duality of feeling reminiscent of that seen in "Dobbelt" from *Mod den yderste Rand*. Nor, in "Drankeren" (The Drinker), is Kristensen afraid to portray himself as the drinker that he was well known to have been for much of his life. The final reflection in the final poem, "Et manna-korn" (A Grain of Manna), is that

> Begik du Livet,
> bedrev du Livet,
> som det er givet,
> du maa og skal,
> så husk, at Livet
> er blevet Givet
> til dig i kraft af
> et Syndefald.
>
> (If you lived life
> pursued life
> as it is given
> you must and shall,
> remember that life
> was given
> to you by virtue of
> a sin, a fall.)

Tom Kristensen died 2 June 1974. He had led a tumultuous personal life, married at various times to four different women–he actually married and divorced one of them, Gerda Westermann, twice. His only son, Toth, from his first marriage, was born in 1924 and died in 1966. His final volume of poems, *Med disse øjne* (With these Eyes), was published in 1972, two years before his death. They are a selection of previously unpublished poems written between 1923 and 1959, all bearing the dates of composition. As is to be expected in this kind of collection, the poems are not among Kristensen's best, and they introduce nothing new. The elegance of "Ærteblomst" (Sweet Pea), written during travels in the East, is balanced by the sympathy for the captive monkey in "Aben" (The Monkey), written in 1943, but conjuring up memories of Singapore. Kristensen's writings otherwise consist of many newspaper articles and reviews, several of which have been collected, many translations, and a few short stories.

Kristensen's work peaked, however, with the 1930 publication of *Hærværk*, which stands as one of the great and influential novels of the twentieth century in Denmark, a fitting climax to the highly original and experimental work that had preceded it. It is not clear whether after writing *Hærværk* Kristensen was no longer able to

pursue his course of renewal in literature or whether, as seems more likely, he began to doubt the value of the aesthetical in modern culture, turning instead to journalism and essays alongside his later, much more conservative, poetry. There are certainly fine poems in this work from the second half of his life, and they show a man of great inventiveness and sensitivity, but they are no longer the work of an avant-garde innovator. However, it is as just such an innovator that Kristensen will be remembered.

Biographies:

Søren Hallar, *Tom Kristensen. En farvepsykologisk studie* (Copenhagen, 1926);

Niels Egebak, *Tom Kristensen* (Copenhagen: Munksgaard, 1971);

Jørgen Breitenstein, *Tom Kristensens udvikling* (Copenhagen: Gyldendal, 1978);

Bent Haugaard Jeppesen, *Orfeus i underklassen: Tom Kristensens proletardæmoni* (Århus: Århus University Press, 1990);

Jens Andersen, *Dansende stjerne: En bog om Tom Kristensen* (Copenhagen: Gyldendal, 1993).

Bibliographies:

Hanne Jürs and Bente Engelund Knudsen, *Tom Kristensen: En bibliografi* (Copenhagen: Gyldendal, 1979);

Aage Jørgensen, *Litteratur om Tom Kristensen: En bibliografi*, revised edition (Århus: CUK/ Center for Undervisning og Kulturformidling, 1991).

References:

Michael Byram, "The Reality of Tom Kristensen's *Hærværk*," *Scandinavica*, 15, no. 1 (1976): 29–37;

Byram, *Tom Kristensen* (Boston: Twayne, 1982);

Byram, "Tom Kristensen's *Livets Arabesk* Seen as a Political Gesture," *Scandinavica*, 16, no. 2 (1977): 109–118;

Erik Halvorsen, "Tom Kristensen," in *Danske digtere i det 20. århundrede*, 2nd edition, 3 volumes, edited by Frederik Nielsen and Ole Restrup (Copenhagen: Gad, 1966), II: 7–64;

Mogens Bjerring Hansen, *Person og vision: "Hærværk" og dens forudsætninger* (Copenhagen: Forlaget 6MT, 1972);

Aage Jørgensen, ed., *Lyrikeren Tom Kristensen* (Copenhagen: Akademisk Boghandel, 1971);

Jørgensen, ed., *Omkring Hærværk* (Copenhagen: Hans Reitzel, 1969);

Klaus Rifbjerg, "Tom Kristensen," in *Danske digtere i det 20. århundrede*, third edition, 5 volumes, edited by Torben Brostrøm and Mette Winge (Copenhagen: Gad, 1981), II: 11–29.

Svend Åge Madsen

(2 November 1939 –   )

Kim Andersen
Washington State University

BOOKS: *Besøget* (Copenhagen: Gyldendal, 1963);
Lystbilleder (Copenhagen: Gyldendal, 1964);
Otte gange orphan (Copenhagen: Gyldendal, 1965);
Tilføjelser (Copenhagen: Gyldendal, 1967);
Et livstykke og andre stykker (Copenhagen: Borgen, 1967);
Liget og lysten (Copenhagen: Gyldendal, 1968);
Tredje gang så tar vi ham . . . (Copenhagen: Gyldendal, 1969);
Maskeballet (Copenhagen: Gyldendal, 1970);
Sæt verden er til (Copenhagen: Gyldendal, 1971);
Dage med Diam eller Livet om natten (Copenhagen: Gyldendal, 1972); translated by W. Glyn Jones as *Days with Diam, or, Life at Night* (Norwich, U.K.: Norvik Press, 1994);
Blodet på mine hænder, by Madsen and Lise Madsen, as Marianne Kainsdatter (Copenhagen: Lademann, 1973);
Jakkels vandring (Copenhagen: Gyldendal, 1974);
Tugt og utugt i mellemtiden (Copenhagen: Gyldendal, 1976); translated by James M. Ogier as *Virtue and Vice in the Middle Time* (New York: Garland, 1992);
Hadets bånd (Copenhagen: Gyldendal, 1978);
Se dagens lys (Copenhagen: Gyldendal, 1980);
Af sporet er du kommet (Copenhagen: Gyldendal, 1984);
Svejk i tredie verdenskrig (Århus: Arkona, 1984);
Dr. Strangula (Århus: Arkona, 1985);
Det sidste suk (Århus: Arkona, 1986);
Lad tiden gå (Copenhagen: Gyldendal, 1986);
Madsens Kongespil (Århus: Hovedland, 1986);
Nøgne masker (Århus: Arkona, 1987);
Slægten Laveran (Århus: Hovedland, 1988);
At fortælle menneskene (Copenhagen: Gyldendal, 1989);
Mellem himmel og jord (Copenhagen: Gyldendal, 1990);
Et ved jeg som aldrig dør, by Madsen and Lise Madsen, as Kainsdatter (Copenhagen: Gyldendal, 1991);
Edens gave (Copenhagen: Gyldendal, 1993);
Syv aldres galskab (Copenhagen: Gyldendal, 1994);
Den usynlige myre, by (Copenhagen: Gyldendal, 1995);
Kvinden uden krop (Copenhagen: Gyldendal, 1996);
Finder sted (Copenhagen: Gyldendal, 1997);
Genspejlet (Copenhagen: Gyldendal, 1999).

Svend Åge Madsen (photograph by Karin Munk; from the cover for Kvinden uden krop, *1996)*

OTHER: "Henrik Pontoppidan," in *Forfatternes forfatterhistorie,* edited by Per Stig Møller (Copenhagen: Gyldendal, 1980).

SELECTED PERIODICAL PUBLICATIONS–
UNCOLLECTED: "På jagt efter en stil (Hvordan jeg blev forfatter)," *Berlingske Aftenavis,* 19 July 1969;
"Hvorfor jeg ikke vil skrive en kronik," *Århuus Stiftstidende,* 24 July 1969;

"Kend dig selv eller få success," *Information,* 24 September 1969;

"Jeg elsker selvhypnosen," *Jyllands-Posten,* 16 March 1978;

"Det vi allerhelst vil læse," *Information,* 3 December 1991;

"Den eksistentielle fortælling eller Det særligt Danske," *Weekendavisen,* 24 January 1992.

Since his first novel, *Besøget* (The Visit, 1963), Svend Åge Madsen has become one of Denmark's most prolific and productive authors. From his initially experimental style of writing, which dissolved the novel genre's traditional comforting sense of identity, time, and space, to his introduction of actual, recognizable locales and more-psychologically developed protagonists, Madsen's authorship has been characterized by a conscious philosophical mode of experimentation in which his focus is on the writing process itself as the mediator of identity.

This evolution within his authorship–from his early modernistic experiments populated by protagonists almost void of personality toward the embedding of characters into a social context–has been mirrored by the general public's increasing interest in Madsen's writing. Practically every book since *Jakkels vandring* (Jakkel's Journey, 1974) has gone into a third edition; his largest work, *Tugt og utugt i mellemtiden* (1976; translated as *Virtue and Vice in the Middle Time,* 1992), one of only two of Madsen's books to appear in English, was the popular choice for Gyldendals Bogklub, the largest Danish book club, and was eventually printed in four editions, which in the relatively small Danish book market is remarkable. Another fourteen books have appeared in other languages, mostly in German. Madsen's lack of English translations neither reflects his popularity among the general Danish public nor the importance of his position in Danish literature as assessed by the literary establishment. He has been awarded several prestigious prizes, including the Grand Prize of the Danish Academy in 1972, the Søren Gyldendal Prize in 1985, the Adam Oehlenschlager Stipend in 1985, the Danish Dramatists Prize in 1987, and the Holberg Medallion in 1990.

Madsen has also achieved some success as a dramatist. From 1983 to 1986 Madsen was "dramatist-in-residence" at Århus Theater, which together with Odense Theater has staged most of his productions. His published plays include *Et livstykke og andre stykker* (A Piece of Life and Other Pieces, 1967); *Svejk i tredie verdenskrig* (Svejk in World War III, 1984); *Dr. Strangula* (Dr. Strangula, 1985); *Det sidste suk* (The Last Sigh, 1986); *Madsens Kongespil* (Madsen's Royal Plays, 1986); and *Nøgne masker* (Naked Masks, 1987). Madsen's dra-

mas mirror the themes of his more dominant prose works. Madsen has also published some children's books.

Born on 2 November 1939, Svend Åge Madsen's life seems to have progressed uneventfully along an almost predictable Danish middle-class route. His father was an insurance agent providing sufficient means for family life in peaceful Århus. In 1958 Madsen graduated from the Danish Gymnasium (Upper-Secondary High School) and studied mathematics (for which he showed considerable talent during his gymnasium years) at the University of Århus. Soon, however, he quit his studies after failing the first set of comprehensive exams. Having begun writing in the meantime, he instead pursued life as an author. To complement the "failed-exams-theory," Madsen told Kim Andersen in an unpublished interview (July 1993) that it was "consuming love" that made him give up his studies of mathematics to travel to Madison, Wisconsin, where he awaited the return of an American girl he had met while she was travelling in Europe. As he was ready to depart for the United States, he was not sure whether to bring his trumpet or his typewriter–he chose the latter and wrote his first novel, *Besøget,* in a month and a half, his first text to be accepted for publication after the rejection of a collection of short stories.

Others of Madsen's works have in part been produced abroad during longer stays in Algeria and India. Madsen married Ingerlise Larsen Madsen in 1966; he has twice collaborated with her under the pseudonym "Marianne Kainsdatter," and he has two children with her. Madsen readily gives talks on his authorship, and he is a much sought after and busy speaker.

Among literary critics a consensus has emerged that Madsen's authorship falls into three phases, marking a gradual progression toward Madsen's acceptance of the inevitability of a social and historical context in which individuals are participants who form existential patterns as they make choices–thus conditioning each others' lives and possibilities. It is a remarkable development from his first phase, in which "history"–broadly defined–is an absent phenomenon. This phase is constituted by *Besøget; Lystbilleder* (Images of Lust, 1964); *Otte gange orphan* (Eight Times Orphan, 1965); and *Tilføjelser* (Additions, 1967). The common theme for these books is the experience of meaninglessness in a world of identity crises, as anonymous protagonists speaking in the first person gain existential substance only as the text is being written.

In his novel *Besøget,* Madsen explores the accidental nature of human identity as it is shaped by interaction with others. The first-person narrator of the novel, a young man, meets a woman at a bus stop and is, through her, brought into contact with a family staying

Cover for Madsen's 1996 science-fiction novel, about a man who transfers the soul and mind of his dying lover into his own body

successfully depicts a universe devoid of tradition and social roles. Instead, it is inhabited by a searching individual who considers social stimuli an offense to the formation of his identity. Thus, the constructing media for social interaction—as well as reality—is language. However, the absence in the novel of a social environment and a "history" establish the philosophical focus on these entities as determining factors in the production of identity. In a negative sense, environment is a key agent. This environmental presence, initially only implied, becomes more directly pronounced later in Madsen's authorship.

In Madsen's second phase he abandoned the negative angle of the problem of history to proceed in a method much more manageable to his reader. Three novels and a collection of short stories constitute this phase: *Liget og lysten* (The Corpse and the Lust, 1968); *Tredje gang så tar vi ham . . . * (Third Time We'll Grab Him . . . , 1969); *Maskeballet* (The Masquerade, 1970); and *Sæt verden er til* (What If the World Exists, 1971). The revelation in these works is that the complete deconstruction of meaning in fact results in a hopeful condition for mankind: fundamental relativism sets the individual free. The author thus sees himself as free to explore his thoughts in well-proven genres, establishing a more direct, unhindered contact with his readers. In a 1997 lecture Madsen described his first phase as being characterized by "honesty," his attempts to "penetrate existence." By meticulously displaying language as the precondition of all human communication, he disclosed what would happen, for example, when an individual pedantically insists on actual meaning behind individual words while denying their social context.

In his second phase, then, Madsen surrenders to the previously conditioned forms of literary communication and plays with the genres and their characteristics in new attempts to discern the boundaries of existential freedom. In other words, historical or social contemplation, which was absent in the narrations of his first phase, indirectly achieves some presence through the literary forms of his second phase. In this manner *Liget og lysten* utilizes pornography, the love story, the crime story, and science fiction as forms lending their characteristics to the female protagonist, who travels between realms. In *Maskeballet,* Madsen forges a similar technique as three persons caught by an explosion in a castle exchange science-fiction and crime stories (among others), so that the telling of stories becomes the structural element governing their imprisoned reality. *Sæt verden er til* constitutes an almost kaleidoscopic number of intrigues spanning the eighteenth through twenty-first centuries and is told in a variety of styles by five different storytellers, each responsible for their part; a sixth person has edited the tales.

at the hotel where he is lodged. The three-part novel depicts his defense against the threat he feels the family poses to himself and his integrity, as he politely yet suspiciously responds to their attempts at communication. His courtesy, however, only draws him further into their web of politeness as he attempts to ascribe meaning to simplistic communications. The family embodies a floating, asocial state of identity as its members practice incestuous promiscuity—witnessed by the young man.

The second and third parts of the novel suggest different effects of the asocial tendencies in the narrator. In the second part he retracts from his surroundings to draw self-portraits (eventually burned), and in the third part his relationship with the family is resolved in the impersonal rhetoric of polite formal language, his original suspicions seemingly abandoned. In *Besøget* Madsen

With the structure of the novel, Madsen stresses a fundamental cognitive relativism as individuals coexist, each guided by their own mode of interpretation. In his article "Svend Åge Madsen" (1982) noted Danish critic Niels Barfoed concisely summed up Madsen's philosophy:

> Det er en holdning igennem fiktionen og de greb, der tilrettelægger den, at verdens forbedring kun kan ske med udgangspunkt i den enkelte, og at undertrykkelse af andre verdener, andre synsvinkler og dermed andre omverdensforståelser er inhuman og potentielt voldelig.
>
> (It is the view throughout the fiction and in those decisions that arrange it, that the improvement of the world will only occur when the vantage point is in each individual human being, and that suppression of other worlds, other viewpoints and thereby other kinds of understanding is inhumane and potentially violent.)

The transition from Madsen's second to his third phase, less dramatic than the transition between the first and second, occurs with *Dage med Diam eller Livet om natten* (1972; translated as *Days with Diam, or, Life at Night,* 1994). In this novel the notion of "choice" structures the composition. The narrator, Alian Sandme (an anagram for "Alias Madsen"), lives in Dahle, somewhere in Denmark, and has the choice of either meeting his girlfriend, Diam, at the train station or staying home and continuing to write. Every time a situation involving choice arises, the text splits into two new chapters, each pursuing one of the two options. Consecutively, each chapter again splits into two further chapters; this structure is graphically displayed in the initial list of contents, affording the reader much autonomy in following any sequence to happy or sad endings, depending upon individual tastes. The categorical conflict at the outset—write or live?—is dissolved as the complexity of choices in reading the novel asserts the intertwined and complex nature of human expressions and consciousness.

Madsen's masterpiece, *Tugt og utugt i mellemtiden,* refines the structural elements of his early authorship to produce a grand and entertaining composition. The novel involves characters whose existential conditions are set by the psychosocial reality of Århus in the 1970s, and it forms Madsen's most complex attempt at social criticism. At the center of the literary exploration is the vintage Madsen-style phenomenon: the conscious, experimentally "naive" approach, in which someone gazes at life from a (mental) distance—in essence like that of the first-person narrator in Madsen's first novel, *Besøget.* In this case, however, the distance is not merely mental, but also temporal. Ato Vari is an historian living two centuries in the future who is trying to understand life in the Middle Time in Århus, including the nature of a dead literary form that had been known as "novels." To re-create life in those days he writes a novel whose main character, Ludvig Alster, is caught in a situation similar to that of the protagonist in Alexandre Dumas's *Le Comte de Monte-Cristo* (The Count of Monte Cristo, 1844–1845), in which Ludwig—as is the case with the protagonist of Dumas's novel—has been condemned to jail for a murder he did not commit. Obviously, law that (in principle if not in effect) inhibits freedom—that which challenges man's virtue or tempts him with vice—is the structural element around which the novel turns. Its narrative frame consists of Ludvig escaping from prison and seeking revenge on the three people responsible for his conviction: a judge, a journalist, and a police officer.

The frame narrative is but an excuse for the introduction of an intricate web of human motivations and desires, distilled from the force of transcendent love as well as the political and social background of Århus in the 1970s and digested by the frame narrator, someone whose deductions and interpretations often appear charmingly foreign or completely erroneous, as when the Jutland dialect is considered a language different from Danish, or when the priest solemnly ends the marriage ritual: "Hermed erklærer jeg jer for at være ægtefolk, tvunget til at være sammen til døden giver jer fred" (I hereby declare you to be a married couple, forced to be together until death gives you peace).

The novel is full of such quirky ideas, designed to throw the reader off from what he or she considers normality, and this humorous rewriting of reality constitutes Madsen's essential literary accomplishment. He creates a matrix of various actions and interpretations that forces his reader to observe life in a different light: his works suggest that life, happiness, and consciousness are generated in interaction with others; that law and social structure in a similar manner is subject to the temporary, deliberate, or accidental choices made by the many; and that those structures will have disappeared two hundred years from now.

Disillusioned by unrealized love and the essential dissatisfaction inherent in revenge, Ludvig ultimately rejects his environment, choosing to hide behind a wall of bricks beneath the city next to Århus Creek:

> De havde ødelagt hans liv. Men han havde ikke været bedre. Han havde forsøgt at hævne i stedet for at forbedre. Præcis som de. Men det eneste han nu følte var lettelse og trang til uforstyrrethed. Han anbragte de to sidste sten i hullet. Han murede dem godt fast. Da han var helt sikker på at afsondringen fra omverdenen var effektiv og uigenkaldelig, lod han murskeen falde i det lille vandhul. Han trak vejret dybt og satte sig i mørket.

SVEND ÅGE MADSEN
Finder sted

ROMAN GYLDENDAL

Dust jacket for Madsen's 1997 novel

(They had destroyed his life. But he hadn't been any better. He had striven for vengeance instead of improvement. Just like them. But the only thing he felt now was relief and the desire not to be disturbed. He placed the last two stones in the hole. He mortared them tightly into place. When he was very sure his separation from the outside world was complete and irreversible, he dropped the trowel into the little water hole. He took a deep breath and sat down in the dark.)

Ludvig's final recognition of personal improvement as the existential imperative echoes Barfoed's assertion on suppression in relation to *Sæt verden er til*. Thus, in the midst of the comedy, Ludvig delivers his own tragic answer to the question: What if the world exists?

It would not be like Madsen to leave the reader without hope, however, and Ludvig has made sure to stock up on canned food and keeps a tiny stream of water running through his "grave." As he enters it, a woman named Katharina and her resurrected husband come walking out, smiling.

Tugt og utugt i mellemtiden also marks Madsen's construction of his authorship on an even grander scale. From this novel onward, his novels enter into a sort of dialogue with each other, as characters from one

appear in another, as questions raised in one text regarding a certain character may find an answer or development in another novel. This complexity inspired the critic Niels Dalgaard, in *Dage med Madsen eller Livet i Århus* (1996) to produce a complete dictionary of information on individual characters, places, titles, and concepts in Madsen's works. One example of such a recurring character is the author Sten Pekoral. In *Tugt og utugt i mellemtiden* he is one of the many minor characters, described as a man trying "to be bald and grow long hair" at the same time. He is also present in the novels *Slægten Laveran* (The Family Laveran, 1988) and *At fortælle menneskene* (To Invent Humanity, 1989), embodying similar characteristics in all four texts. In this manner Madsen creates a "macro-universe" superimposed over the individual texts, suggesting, according to Dalgaard, "a mosaic" or a "naturalist universe," which on a grander scale than individual texts forms a description of life in Århus in past, present, and future, providing faithful readers with surprising insights.

One might argue that Madsen's attempt at tying his authorship to such a coherency constitutes a strategy resembling that of Søren Kierkegaard, assembling and ascribing meaning to a literary effort that otherwise might seem diversified. While the differences between the two writers are obvious, there are similarities in their communicative approach. There is little doubt that Madsen has been inspired by the compositional methods of Kierkegaard. His preference for letting events be presented by different narrative voices displaying different points of view indicates an affinity for the earlier writer. Furthermore, and more profoundly, liberated from the Kierkegaardian theological foundation, Madsen's existentialism, defined by a sense of physical and social relativism, shows no less concern for individual freedom and the inevitability of choices that determine individual lives.

More than developing a stringent theoretical universe, however, Madsen's essential interest lies in the telling of stories as a reflection of man's existential conditions. Madsen has demonstrated another Kierkegaardian affinity in his preference for the kind of indirect communication inherent in his nonrealistic approach to narrative creativity. In *Forfatternes forfatterhistorie* (The Authors, History of Authors; 1980), a collection of brief interpretive readings by contemporary Danish authors of Danish literary greats, Madsen writes about the Danish grand master of realism, Henrik Pontoppidan (1857–1943). In his essay he points to three factors that he initially felt made realism ineffective as the mode for telling a story: if one maintains the "realistic illusion," the narrative becomes "heavy and circumstantial"; realism creates "unfree" characters, "bound to destiny" as it pursues its goal of "explaining" the characters; and, finally, realism is based upon an author's viewpoint instead of such an insight being sought in the writing process. Upon reading Pontoppidan's *Det forjættede Land* (The Promised Land, 1891–1895) in 1980, however, Madsen admits that his previous assessment of the limitations of realism in Pontoppidan's case is wrong, as Pontoppidan manages to write fascinating, psychologically astute prose, create a main character who transcends the destiny that the reader comes to expect he will suffer, and, as Madsen concedes:

Jeg har sjældent læst en roman der virkede så åben på mig som *Det Forjættede Land*. Den lægger nogle muligheder frem til læserens egen bedømmelse. Den stiller personer op og belyser dem fra så mange sider, at man ikke tvinges til at danne sig en ganske enkel opfattelse af dem.

(Rarely have I read a novel that seemed so open to me as *Det forjættede Land*. It suggests possibilities for the reader to judge for himself. It introduces characters which it illuminates from so many angles that the reader isn't forced to form a simplistic opinion of them.)

Madsen's essay reflects the evolution of his authorship, as he has come to embrace the historical and physical world's entities and make them components of his fictions. Despite this tendency, however, Madsen is hardly a realist. His *Kvinden uden krop* (The Woman without a Body, 1996) exemplifies the characteristics of his style and thematic complexity. In this novel Madsen examines the theme of love conquering physical confinement with a touch of science fiction, crime story, and the dramatic and pathetic atmosphere of soap opera. The setting is an unnamed city with excursions to Iceland and North Africa. Gary and Thelma have been married for eight years, but she is dying from cancer. Both are employed at the forefront of technology; he researches the possibilities for "ånds transformation" (spiritual transformation) or "virtual spiritualitet" (virtual spirituality), and she constructs "infra- polariseret glas til et medicinsk instrument" (infra-polarized glass for a medicinal instrument). The opening paragraph introduces the existential ambiance:

Man siger at inde under huden er ethvert menneske ensomt. Det er ikke længere sandt. For han elskede hende så usigeligt at han bad hende rykke ind hos sig, da hun skulle dø.

(They say that beneath the skin every human being is lonely. This is no longer true. Because he loved her so much, far beyond words, he asked her to move in with him, when she was going to die.)

Although Gary has not completely mastered the technique of spiritual transformation, he convinces Thelma that she—her mind, spirit, consciousness, emotions, and memory—must enter his body, since her body is dying. Although apprehensive, she agrees, and after the transformation they—the two in his body—place her body in the laboratory freezer. Both, in one, leave for Iceland (where Gary had spent some time at a conference), in order to get used to the unusual situation; namely, that neither can hide anything from the other, now that both minds and memories share the same physical vehicle.

Kvinden uden krop examines the ramifications of such closeness, exploring the notion that even the closest of partners have the option of not fully disclosing their emotions and motives. Madsen's humor finds fruitful grounds in this scenario; to Thelma's dismay, Gary cannot hide his sexual excitement on seeing an Icelandic girl:

Du elsker mig ikke længere, sagde Thelma.
    Jeg elsker dig så højt at jeg har tilbudt dig at dele mit legeme med mig.
    Aldrig så snart har du knyttet mig uløseligt til dig før du begynder at løbe efter det første det bedste skørt.

(You don't love me anymore, Thelma said.
    I love you so much that I have offered you to share my body.
    Hardly have you tied me inseparably to you before you start chasing the first skirt.)

Thelma takes revenge in North Africa, where a police officer senses her welcoming sexual vibrations within Gary. Overall, however, Gary and Thelma manage to get along and even return to their jobs. Gary acquires Thelma's old job, using a letter of recommendation that she writes, although his manual skill at developing lenses is not up to her previous standard (her physical qualities could not be transferred).

Their intimate knowledge of each other—"de havde opnået en enestående evne til at aflæse indvirkninger fra barndomstraumer og gennemskue erindringsblokeringer og fortielser" (they had achieved a unique ability to decipher effects of childhood traumas and see through walls of silence caused by memories)—induces them to pursue "et formål" (a purpose), in which her knowledge of lenses leads them to the invention of a set of spectacles, "inkvisitator" (the inquisitionator), which enables them to detect even the most minimal displays of emotion in their fellow human beings. No longer can anyone hide behind words or facial expressions.

At this point their bliss is shattered, as the law catches up with them. The police, who have discovered

Thelma's empty body, suspect a crime has been committed. In addition, Thelma's father, the author, Sten (both Thelma and Sten appear to be characters from prior Madsen texts), fears the "naked society" that will be the result of their invention, or even worse, the possibility that the authorities will keep the invention to themselves. In a climax of escape and regret the *inkvisitator* is destroyed, and Gary/Thelma is shot and killed by Sten, who cries as the novel concludes: "Inde under huden er ethvert menneske ensomt" (Beneath the skin every human being is lonely).

With obvious references to Hans Christian Andersen's tales "Skyggen" (1847; translated as "The Shadow," 1847), in relation to each other Gary and Thelma both constitute a shadow dimension, and in "Snedronningen" (1845; translated as, "The Snow Queen," 1847), the splinter of glass that distorts one's psychic capability, Madsen creates a psychologically thoughtful, puzzling, and entertaining text that questions a fundamental existential dogma: is truth an illusion? He points to the telling and interpretation of stories—preferably with a satirical twist—as the only endeavor through which humans may gain an understanding of reality.

Svend Åge Madsen continues to be a highly productive author, with his keen philosophical eye firmly entrenched in hope. His works examine the limitations of human existence as he imaginatively explores human attempts at transcending mind and flesh. Given Madsen's uncanny imagination and his productive sense of the qualities of well-proven genres and essential stories, it will be interesting to see where his next dissection of man in the modern transitional world will take his readers.

Interviews:

Paul Carlsen, "Jeg er da ganske nem og enkel," *Århuus Stiftstidende,* 29 October 1967;

Ebbe Mørk, "Jeg er glad for min dårlige samvittighed," *Politiken,* 17 September 1972;

Claus Grymer, "Realismen er en trussel for mig," *Kristeligt Dagblad,* 19 May 1984;

Hanne Stouby, "At være i hak med tidsånden," *Århuus Stiftstidende,* 25 January 1987;

Egon Balsby, "Jeg forstår ikke min nye bog," *Weekendavisen,* 10 November 1989;

Lars Henrik Ågård, "Madsen er oppe i tiden," *Berlingske Tidende,* 22 October 1993.

References:

Niels Barfoed, "Svend Åge Madsen," in *Danske digtere i det 20 århundrede,* 5 volumes, edited by Torben Brostrøm and Mette Winge (Copenhagen: Gyldendal, 1982),V: 162–174;

Thomas Bredsdorff, *Sære fortællere* (Copenhagen: Gyldendal, 1967), pp. 172–175;

Niels Dalgaard, *Dage med Madsen eller Livet i Århus* (Copenhagen: Museum Tusculanums Forlag, 1996);

Dalgaard, *Fra tekst til fortælling–Svend Åge Madsen og science fiction* (Copenhagen: Science Fiction Cirklen, 1989);

Renny Edal and Ole Nielsen, *Identitet og virkelighed: En tematisk læsning I Svend Åge Madsens forfatterskab* (Odense: Odense Universitetsforlag, 1980);

Anker Gemzøe, *Metamorphoser i Mellemtiden: Studier i Svend Åge Madsens forfatterskab 1962–1986* (Ålborg: Medusa, 1997);

Hugo Hørlych Karlsen, *Skriften, spejlet og hammeren* (Copenhagen: Borgen, 1973);

Leonie Marx, "Literary Experimentation in a Time of Transition: The Danish Short Story after 1945," *Scandinavian Studies,* 49, no. 2 (1977): 131–154;

Karsten Schmidt, *Mandlighedens positioner* (Copenhagen: Akademisk Forlag, 1982);

Erik Skyum-Nielsen, *Modsprogets process* (Copenhagen: Arena, 1982);

Ole Sylvest, *Det litterære karneval: Den groteske realisme i nyere danske romaner* (Odense: Odense Universitetsforlag, 1987), pp. 44–67.

Ib Michael

(17 January 1945 –)

Else Vinæs
University of Copenhagen

BOOKS: *En hidtil uset drøm om skibe* (Copenhagen: Rhodos, 1970);
Den flyvende kalkundræber (Copenhagen: Rhodos, 1971);
Mayalandet (Copenhagen: Rhodos, 1973);
Hjortefod, illustrated by Per Christensen (Copenhagen: Sommersko, 1974);
Rejsen tilbage (Copenhagen: Gyldendal, 1977);
Rejsen til det grønne firben: En dokumentarisk beretning (Copenhagen: Gyldendal, 1980);
Snedronningen (Copenhagen: Tiderne Skifter, 1981);
Kejserfortællingen: Roman (Copenhagen: Gyldendal, 1981);
Troubadurens lærling: Roman (Copenhagen: Gyldendal, 1984);
Himmelbegravelse: Digte fra Tibet (Copenhagen: Brøndum, 1986);
Kilroy, Kilroy: Roman (Copenhagen: Gyldendal, 1989)— excerpts translated by Frank Hugus as "New Danish Fiction," in *Review of Contemporary Fiction,* 1995: 91–101;
Vinden i metroen: Digte (Copenhagen: Gyldendal, 1990);
Vanillepigen (Copenhagen: Gyldendal, 1991);
Den tolvte rytter (Copenhagen: Gyldendal, 1993);
Det lukkede øje: Rejsedagbog Mexico 1971 (Copenhagen: Brøndum/Aschehoug, 1994);
Brev til månen (Copenhagen: Gyldendal, 1995);
Prins: Roman (Copenhagen: Gyldendal, 1997);
Atkinsons biograf: En vandrehistorie (Copenhagen: Gyldendal, 1998).

PLAY PRODUCTION: *Operation: Orfeo,* libretto by Michael, music by John Cage, Bo Holten, and Christof Willibald Gluck; Copenhagen, Hotel Pro Forma, 1993.

RADIO: *Warum ist die Banane so krumm?,* script by Michael, Danmarks Radio, 1973;
Samerne–en minoritet, script by Michael, Danmarks Radio, 1974;
Den udødelige soldat, script by Michael, Danmarks Radio, 1976.

Ib Michael (photograph by Morten Holtum Nielsen; courtesy of Gyldendal Publishers)

OTHER: *Popol Vuh–Quiché-mayaernes Folkebog,* translated by Michael (Copenhagen: Rhodos, 1975);
Johannes V. Jensen, *Christofer Columbus,* foreword by Michael (Copenhagen: Gyldendal, 1992).

SELECTED PERIODICAL PUBLICATIONS– UNCOLLECTED: "To teser og en formel til frigørelse af eventyret," *Kritik,* 64 (1983): 11–21;
"Synspunkter på mit forfatterskab," *Spring,* 5 (1993): 10–15.

One of the best-known Danish authors of the 1990s, Ib Michael has adapted his life to the idea that reality is a fantasy; his writing consists of journeys, fantasies, recollections, and poetry. His narratives depict different personalities from many parts of the world. They are entertaining, humorous, and full of descriptions of exciting experiences and adventures both on the inward and the outward plane.

Ib Michael Rasmussen was born 17 January 1945. His father, Michael Rasmussen, was raised by a foster uncle in the country. His mother, Inge Rasmussen, née Jørgensen, grew up in indigent circumstances with her mother. Ib's father eventually became a somewhat prosperous merchant in the cathedral town of Roskilde. Ib's younger sister, Ulla, had polio as a child. Still suffering from her handicap, she lives on her own and works as a teacher in Roskilde. Ib has often said that his sister's illness served as the catalyst to his becoming a writer: when they lay in their beds in the evenings, he told her stories simply to survive. He was afraid of the dark and afraid that she would suddenly stop breathing.

Ib graduated from the local secondary school in 1964. A keen, enthusiastic, and skilled horseman, he participated in competitions in his early years, and he and his father passed some of their best moments at the riding school, sharing their passion for horses. The father was, however, an authoritarian and a domineering man, and Ib rebelled against him and moved away from home to a small, ramshackle flat in Copenhagen. As an adult Ib gradually changed his opinion of his father; before his father died, they made up and learned to respect each other's philosophies of life.

Ib Michael, who dropped his family name upon becoming a writer, grew up in the 1960s, which was a time of transformation that changed both the world and his view of it. As did other writers of his generation such as Ebbe Kløvedal Reich, he participated in the youth revolution, devoted himself to meditation, experimented with LSD, and took a passionate interest in Eastern religions. In 1968 he began attending the University of Copenhagen, graduating in 1972 with a degree in the languages and cultures of the Central American Indians. In the course of his studies he had traveled several times to Central America with the noted Danish painter Per Kirkeby, and Michael's first books are based on these travel experiences. Both *En hidtil uset drøm om skibe* (An Unseen Dream of Ships, 1970) and *Den flyvende kalkundræber* (The Flying Turkey Killer, 1971) are written in a style that challenges the reader's attention with constant shifts between prose and poetry with science fiction and cartoonlike images, all spiced with psychedelic hallucinations.

After his graduation from the university, Michael decided to make a living as a writer. Although only twenty-seven years old, he felt that he had to commit himself; as he told Else Vinaes in a September 1997 conversation, he was grappling with the question: "Hvad er jeg? Videnskabsmand, rejsende eller forfatter?" (What am I? A scientist, a traveler or a writer?). The answer, however, never became quite clear, for even as he wrote fiction he translated the sacred book of the Maya, *Popol Vuh–Quiché-mayaernes Folkebog* (Popol Vuh–The Book of the Quiché Maya Indians, 1975). During these years Michael participated actively in the anarchistic left wing in Copenhagen. He married Pi Michael, a radio journalist, and they had a daughter, Sita. Michael's long travels resulted in the couple growing apart, but he has stayed in touch with his daughter.

With his next four books Michael gradually developed a distinctive writing style. His stories still reflected a desire to challenge conventional genres, and there is a fusion between fiction and fact. Michael based these books on his many expeditions to Latin America, incorporating myths from this part of the world into his stories. In 1978 Michael received the Otto Gelsted Memorial Award from Det Danske Akademi (The Danish Academy) for his contribution toward making a distant culture understandable to contemporary Danish readers.

Mayalandet (The Land of the Maya, 1973) is an account of a journey and at the same time a work of scientific documentation. Myths and reality merge, as Michael, the scientist-narrator, an ethnographer and philologist, identifies himself with his material. He demonstrates how imperialism and European scientific methods are two sides of the same coin.

The short novel *Hjortefod* (The Deer's Foot, 1974) is different from the three major myth stories. Historic events, concrete portrayals of modern geography, and the adventurer's experiences and fantasy fuse into a colorful interlacing pattern. Michael interweaves his plot with a recounting of Mexican history, covering the period from Mexico's gaining independence from the Spanish Empire to the installation of Emperor Maximilian to the throne in 1864. With this novel Michael established himself as an epic narrator and a master of composition, able to knit together fact and fiction in gripping language.

In *Rejsen tilbage* (The Journey Back, 1977) Michael tells the story of a journey across time and space, the story of a journey back to the mythical, aboriginal past as well as of the narrator's inner journey. The narrator uses myths and the surrounding world as mirrors in which he finds his own reflection. The work in its entirety can be considered a story, a literary myth, created as the narrator floats between time and space, and the reader cannot determine whether the narrative is related from an actual journey or whether the narrator has invented the story lying in a hammock with his eyes closed for a couple of hours. Michael believes in the strength of myth but not in a naive way. He does not believe that human beings can make the world a tabula rasa but that humans move in the right direction by recalling forgotten values. Myth indicates that everything begins again in every instant and that the past is a mere reflection of the future. According to Michael, the world is changeable, and realistic description must occur in constant transformation.

In *Rejsen tilbage* the figure of the "udødelige soldat" (immortal soldier) is established as part of Michael's central narrative cycle. Neither young nor old, the soldier is untouched by age and is beyond death. He attributes his immortality to a meeting with an Indian soothsayer, who put a curse on him, foretold his entire life, and deprived him of the gift of death. According to the narrator, immortality is neither desirable nor beneficial, and the soldier constantly seeks to remove the curse. Michael's story of the eternal wanderer recalls the legend of Ahasuerus, the Wandering Jew, who taunted Jesus Christ while the Savior was on his way to the Crucifixion and, therefore, was doomed to live until the end of the world. The result of the soldier's immortality is that he cannot progress and that none of his experiences has any influence on the formation of his personality. His life's purpose is to acknowledge this stagnation and to be able to create change and transformation.

Rejsen til det grønne firben: En dokumentarisk beretning (The Journey to the Green Lizard: A Documentary Account, 1980) is, despite the subtitle, only remotely related to the documentary genre and is actually a novel in which the narrator accompanies an Indian, Ernesto Tseremp Juanka, and visits tribal communities in the Peruvian jungle. The main point of the work is that the object of one's life is not determined by others but can be changed if one trusts one's own beliefs and acts accordingly.

The immortal soldier figure from *Rejsen tilbage* reappears in a central role in Michael's next major work, *Kejserfortællingen: Roman* (The Tale of the Emperor: Novel, 1981). In *Kejserfortællingen* Michael has created a long, ingenious, and intriguing narrative in which the myth of the immortal soldier is the leading principle. The novel is an enormous epic covering several thousand years, as it takes the protagonist that long to obtain insight. The novel is set in three different geographical locations: in a jungle in South America, in New York, and in China. Four epic stories are told, each with its own protagonist: Travers, an explorer and a vagabond; Mashiant, a warrior under the first Chinese emperor; Joy,

Cover for the 1995 final novel in Michael's semi-autobiographical trilogy about a writer reliving his past

Travers's daughter; and Mao Zedong, former leader of China. Through his nonlinear narration Michael indicates that he believes in history as a sequence of events that transforms the world. He tries to convince the reader that humanity possesses the power to change the course of history—forward as well as backward. Mashiant and Travers reflect each other's souls; the narrator describes the link between the two souls as something that can take place only because every person contains all people. Both Mashiant and Travers represent aspects of the immortal soldier, the bearer of the most important theme of the work. Michael shows that an oscillation between nothing and something is possible as two equally evident and inseparable thoughts. The possibility of contradictions—that everything entwines like yin and yang—becomes part of his attempt to describe another reality. This book was Michael's breakthrough and brought him critical recognition, as well as an award of 25,000 kroner from the Statens Kunstfond (National Art Fund) of the Danish government.

Michael set his next novel, *Troubadurens lærling: Roman* (The Troubadour's Apprentice: Novel, 1984), in fourteenth-century Europe. The protagonist and first-person narrator is a medieval artist, a traveling troubadour. The troubadour, Trofaldino, and his apprentice, the gypsy girl Tijar, are fleeing from the plague, and in their travels through Italy they witness the plague and its fermenting decay, boils, vomit, death, and despair. The epidemic changes the power structure in society; the world and reality are turned into a circus as religious hysteria escalates. In *Troubadurens lærling* the immortal soldier is called the Man from Cathay. Trofaldino senses that the Man from Cathay is a strange and timeless person, older than a normal human. The Man from Cathay tells a story without beginning and without end; however, Trofaldino does not understand what he is trying to tell him.

Michael's narratives consist of fantastic, metonymic descriptions, constructed so that the reader only sees the tip of the iceberg. Michael tries, as do the Latin American writers Miguel Angel Asturias and Gabriel García Márquez, to write in a manner similar to the oral narrative tradition, taking the storyteller's position. In Michael's works, language functions as the connecting link between the inner and outer self, and a movement occurs from a subconscious perception toward a conscious linguistic manifestation.

An example of how Michael works with linguistic expression is *Troubadurens lærling,* in which language, song, music, and art are the most important elements. In this novel Michael thematizes the problems of artistry in the contradiction created between the carnivalesque folk culture and the religious power structure. The troubadour's narrative is not only a story of travel or the course of contradictions, it also tries to realize the contradictions and the movement in language by becoming the performer's flying leap and the tightrope walker's balancing act. At points in the novel the description is so extensive and detailed that the reader loses sense of the focal point of the narrative. Michael's lyric sense surfaces in his use of rhyme and rhythm and in his many metaphors of nature.

Michael's work *Himmelbegravelse: Digte fra Tibet* (Sky Burial: Poems from Tibet, 1986) is a collection of poems, the background of which is several travels to Tibet. In a series of images, Michael describes the geography and the conditions of the people of Tibet, as well as the suppression of Tibetan culture by the Chinese. In some of the poems the existential understanding and worldview of the Tibetans become closely linked to Michael's own views. In the title poem, "Himmelbegravelse," the first-person narrator is an onlooker at an open-air funeral that takes place according to Tibetan traditions. In the poem Michael describes in a shockingly realistic way the dismem-

bering of a corpse and its transformation into food for hungry vultures. Events are related in such a graphic manner that it is almost as though the narrator were being cut into pieces:

> Han skærper knivene op
> skærer ind bag det ene øre
> vrikker en gang
> og begynder så at rulle
> mens han holder bladet ind til benet
> og hovedhuden kommer af
> i én, lang appelsinskræl
>
> (He sharpens his knives
> penetrates behind the ear
> works the knife once
> and starts to roll
> whilst he holds the blade to the bone
> and the head skin comes off
> in one, long orange peel)

Michael has said that his emotions while at the funeral are the strongest he has ever experienced. The event was burned into his memory, and death became real to him, a reality impossible to repress.

The immortal soldier character reappears in the novel *Kilroy, Kilroy: Roman* (1989). The novel is a narrative about being, about a man trying to find his place in history. The title character is a pilot who lands on an island in the Pacific Ocean. He has amnesia and is trying to find his identity; Kilroy is nobody but wants to be somebody. He is everyone's friend and can assume any identity in all classes of society. Kilroy's problem is not immortality but his missing identity, although he is undoubtedly immortal. Born in the explosion that created Earth, he is older than time, a being without beginning, or end. The soldier's role is extended to include a universal figure: the eternal soldier inside every person, representing certain universal primitive instincts that exist in everyone at all times. The soldier's story is the tale of coming into existence.

Kilroy, Kilroy is purportedly set on Penrhyn Atoll in the Cook Islands, an island in the Pacific that Michael visited in 1988. During his visit there he married for the second time; on a previous journey to Mexico he had met the journalist Hanne Danielsen, and they married in a festive ceremony on Penrhyn. Michael claims that he was "homeless" before he met Hanne and says that their relationship has become more and more beautiful throughout the years. Michael explains that his wife reads everything he writes and that he considers her a ruthless, but indispensable, editor. He has stated in interviews that he needs someone like her to keep him on his toes. Hanne brought into the marriage a daughter,

Dust jacket for Michael's 1998 collection of nine interconnected short stories

Sofie, and the three of them live in a penthouse in the center of Copenhagen. Michael spends only part of his time in Denmark, however, stating that he does not care for the Danish winter and prefers to travel to the South Seas, often accompanied by Sofie and Hanne. An avid sailor, he has made several sea voyages to the Pacific Ocean, as well as to the Caribbean Sea, and Central and South America, often sailing with his friend, Danish travel writer and skipper, Troels Kløvedal, on the sailing vessel *Nordkaperen.*

Near the end of the 1980s Michael sojourned in Rome, and his next publication was a collection of poems, *Vinden i metroen* (The Wind in the Metro, 1990), about his encounter with Rome and a reminiscence of all the other artists who have visited the city in the past. The reader is guided through the city by a first-person narrator who feels imprisoned, and a sinister atmosphere often accompanies overpowering descriptions and somber impressions of Rome. In the poems Michael mentions several intellectual leaders who have

exercised an influence on this city, and he follows the footsteps of artists through Rome.

By the early 1990s Michael had reached a stage in his literary career when he was ready to look within and address the personal recollections from his childhood. In three quasi-autobiographical novels Michael reaches the realization that joy and pain are closely related. Even though he based these works on actual events from his childhood and youth, they are not traditional memoirs; Michael does go back in time, but he embellishes the narrative and creates yet another fantasy. The trilogy is structured around a frame story, in which the narrator writes his own story at a hotel in the town of Roskilde in the 1990s.

In *Vanillepigen* (The Vanilla Girl, 1991), the first volume of Michael's trilogy, the protagonist reflects on his boyhood. At the center of the boy's life are stories of the supernatural, with and without the presence of ghosts, some recounted by his grandmother as she tells family legends, some told by the boy himself. The boy has an intimate relationship with his sister, Lulu, whose life begins in an ethereal, dormant state, for she has polio, although the boy's storytelling seems to give her the strength to survive her illness. In the family backyard stands a big chestnut tree, and the boy digs at its roots, where he slowly uncovers a dead man under the light soil. The boy begins to fantasize about this skeleton and concludes that it is a Spaniard, a soldier with a golden earring. The soldier serves as an initiation to and a warning of the grown-up world where Eros, death, and the cry for liberation play a predominant role. The skeleton, reburied, becomes the best-kept secret of his childhood.

The novel also has stories and legends about the family's black sheep, an uncle Viggo Rasmussen who sailed to a remote island in the South Seas; there on Penrhyn Atoll "Papa Viggo" married a beautiful island princess and became the island's ruling aristocrat. The narrator of *Vanillepigen* recalls that as a boy the image of this South Seas princess evoked the picture of "the Vanilla Girl" displayed on the packages of Vanilla sugar stored in the family's pantry. The figure of "Papa Viggo" bears a striking resemblance to a character of the same name depicted in the short novel *Lost Island* (1944) by James Norman Hall, which also has a South Seas setting, although it is uncertain that Michael was familiar with this minor American novel.

With the release of *Vanillepigen*, which was awarded the Danish literary critics' Kritikerprisen, Michael quickly became one of the most widely read writers in Denmark. His previous works had only been read by a limited audience who liked fantasy literature and magic realism, but by the middle of the 1990s he had become one of the most popular living authors in Denmark, and every time a new work by Michael is published, the press gives it great attention.

The childhood stories in *Vanillepigen* were followed by *Den tolvte rytter,* (The Twelfth Knight, 1993) the story of family origins. Still sitting in a room in the hotel in Roskilde, the narrator is now digging out new items of family history, which include accounts of broken hearts and disastrous sexual affairs, descriptions of the Biedemeier culture in Denmark, and stories of events in Latin America during the Spanish conquest. Michael again resumes his fantasy, telling the fictional story of generations of family members; by immersing himself in the family saga, the narrator develops a sense of an overall destiny. The different life stories in the narrative sum up the whole presence in the various figures, and the narrator unites them with his image of destiny. In a vision, he sees all the soldiers he has written about marching by.

In 1994 Michael was honored with Denmark's most important literary prize, Det Danske Akademis's Grand Prize, and its accompanying 200,000 kroner. At the presentation he was called a world traveler and circumnavigator of the globe, a connoisseur and a lover of Indian cultures, and first and foremost a great storyteller.

The last book of the trilogy, *Brev til månen* (A Letter to the Moon, 1995), is, contrary to the first two books, the first-person narrator's own story. He realizes that life should be lived in the future and based on the past; completing his search in the past, the narrator becomes a man and an author. As the story begins, the narrator has come to the town of Roskilde to participate in his father's funeral. His mother and sister, Lulu, are there too; after the urn is lowered into the ground, they return to the nearly empty childhood home and reminisce, which brings back memories of the narrator's youth, recollections of which form the remainder of the novel. The narrator recalls how he rebelled against his father and moved to Copenhagen with his friend, Olaf. They both had great expectations, with one wanting to become a painter, the other a poet. Eventually, the two go to Venice, Italy, where, living through the free-spirited 1960s, they read beat poetry, study modern art, listen to Bob Dylan and the Rolling Stones, and read aloud poems by Ezra Pound. Olaf has a girlfriend, Kate, and the narrator is fascinated by her and falls in love, but out of loyalty to Olaf he does not reveal his affection for her. They spend all their time in Venice together, living grandly in the Venetian community of artists. The mentally unstable Kate commits suicide; after the funeral the sojourn in Venice is over, as is the narrator's reminiscences. Throughout the trilogy the narrator finds himself caught between past and present. Once all the recollections of the trilogy have passed through the narrator's mind, he is able to exorcize his father's presence and become a whole person.

Brev til nånen lived up to the expectations of the Danish public, and in 1995 a poll of readers taken by the Danish Booksellers' Association named Michael as "Favorite Author of the Year." In February of 1997 Michael made his first lecture tour to the United States, visiting university campuses in Wisconsin, Minnesota, Washington, California, and Texas, where he captivated his audiences with readings from his stories and tales. The trip was sponsored by the Department of Scandinavian Studies at the University of Washington, Seattle, and funded by the Danish Ministry of Education. In October of that same year Michael participated in the Danish-Australian Cultural Exchange program, "Denmark Meets Australia 1997," giving talks at the National Library of Australia in Canberra about the European storytelling tradition and his own work.

Michael continues to produce excellent books. His *Prins: Roman* (Prince: Novel, 1997) has a ghost for a narrator, who is not subject to the limitations that exist for the living–an angle inspired by Rainer Maria Rilke's *Duineser Elegien* (1923; translated as *Duineser Elegien: Elegies from the Castle of Duino,* 1931). Also featured in the novel are a shipwreck, a mutiny, and fairies. Other characters in the novel include Malte, the young son of poor parents who in 1912 spends his holiday in a pension in north Zealand; a maid who marries the Peruvian musician who has made her pregnant; and a Greenlandic witch who dies. The spirit-narrator is frozen in the iceberg that caused the loss of the *Titanic,* and his narrative returns to the beginnings of human existence. The narrator incarnates into any form, and some of the passages in the novel are told from the interior of a stone, while others are told from inside a fox's stomach. The plot leads the boy step-by-step out of his mental isolation at the same time that the narrator is let out of his solitude. The message of the novel is that he who once was prince shall become king of his own life.

Michael says that in *Prins* he has expressed what are, for him, new views of life. He does not seek confrontation as much as he did when he was younger. He no longer seeks ambiguous answers. With reference to the title Michael says that he has an enormous respect for the great writers he follows and continues: "Hvem kan være konge uden først at være prins?!" (Who can become king without first being a prince?!). The authors who inspired Michael are García Márquez, Rilke, Jorge Luis Borges, Edith Södergran, T. S. Eliot, and Franz Kafka and the great Danish authors Johannes V. Jensen, Karen Blixen (Isak Dinesen), and Villy Sørensen.

Atkinsons biograf: En vandrehistorie (Atkinson's Biography: A Wandering Story, 1998) is a collection of nine interconnected short stories. The same characters appear throughout the stories, but in different contexts and in different times and places.

In all his works Ib Michael focuses on the same phenomena and problems, but throughout his career his style has continued to develop. From his early works, when the narrative is presented as an accumulation of surrealistic images, to his complex and fluid later works, Michael has developed his own style, crafting his own version of magic realism, breaking down the boundary between the natural and the supernatural. Breaking down the boundary between fiction and reality, Michael's narratives depict a world in constant motion and transformation, where the unforeseen is everywhere; once one reads Michael's books, normality seems strangely destitute.

References:

Anne Borup, "Læsere og forfattere i foråret 95," *Synsvinkler,* 11 (1995): 5–30;

Lars Bukdahl, "Søn af romanen: Ti punkter om Ib Michaels erindringstrilogi," *Kritik,* 119 (1996): 79–83;

Claus Clausen, "Undervejs er altings mål," *HUG,* 10 (1987): 51–55;

Hans Henrik Møller, "A Touch of Vanilla: On the writings of Ib Michael," *Scandinavica,* 2 (1995): 237–261;

Ebbe Kløvedal Reich, "Ib Michael," in *Danske digtere i det 20. århundrede,* 5 volumes, edited by Torben Brostrøm and Mette Winge (Copenhagen: Gad, 1982), IV: 301–307;

Erik Svendsen, "All My Wishes Turn to Images," *Danish Literary Magazine,* 9 (1996): 22–23;

Else Vinæs, *Forvandlingsfortøllinger: En undersøgelse af Ib Michaels forfatterskab med sørligt henblik på myte, sprog og fantastik* (Odense: Odense University Press, 1997).

Karin Michaëlis

(20 March 1872 – 11 January 1950)

Phyllis Lassner
Northwestern University

BOOKS: *Højt Spil* (Copenhagen: Salmonsen, 1898);

Fattige i Aanden (Copenhagen: Salmonsen, 1901);

Birkedommeren (Copenhagen: Salmonsen, 1901), translated by Amy Skovgaard-Pedersen as *The Governor* (London & New York: John Lane, 1913);

Barnet (Copenhagen: Gyldendal, 1902), translated by J. Nilsen Laurvik as *The Child Andrea* (New York: McClure, Philips, 1904; London: Duckworth, 1904);

Lillemor (Copenhagen: Gyldendal, 1902);

Sønnen: Fortælling (Copenhagen: Gyldendal, 1903);

Hellig Enfold (Copenhagen: Gyldendal, 1903);

Backfische, sommerfortælling af Trold (Copenhagen: Gyldendal, 1904);

Gyda (Copenhagen: Gyldendal, 1904);

Munken gaar i Enge (Copenhagen: Gyldendal, 1905);

De smaa Mennesker (Copenhagen: Gyldendal, 1906);

Tommelise: Fortælling (Copenhagen: Gyldendal, 1906);

Ghettoens Blomst, as Edmond Ralph (Copenhagen: Gyldendal, 1907);

Over al Forstand: Fortælling (Copenhagen: Gyldendal, 1907);

Kyllingesorger: En lille Romàn (Copenhagen: Gyldendal, 1907);

Betty Rosa: En ung Kvindes Roman (Copenhagen: Gyldendal, 1908);

Tro som Guld: Fortælling (Copenhagen: Gyldendal, 1909);

Den farlige Alder: Breve og Dagbogsoptegnelser (Copenhagen: Gyldendal, 1910), translated by Beatrice Marshall, with an introduction by Marcel Prévost, as *The Dangerous Age: Letters and Fragments from a Woman's Diary* (New York: John Lane, 1911; London: John Lane, 1912);

Kvindehjerter, anonymous with Betty Nansen (Copenhagen: Gyldendal, 1910);

Danske Foregangsmænd i Amerika, by Michaëlis and Joost Dahlerup (Copenhagen: Gyldendal, 1911);

Bogen om Kærlighed, as Karin Michaëlis Strangeland (Copenhagen: Gyldendal, 1912);

Karin Michaëlis

Elsie Lindtner (Copenhagen: Gyldendal, 1912); translated by Beatrice Marshall as *Elsie Lindtner* (New York & London: John Lane, 1912);

Grev Sylvains Hævn, as Michaëlis Strangeland (Copenhagen: Gyldendal, 1913);

Glædens Skole, as Michaëlis Strangeland (Copenhagen: Gyldendal, 1914);

Hjertets Drømme: Fortælling, as Michaëlis Strangeland (Copenhagen: Gyldendal, 1915);

En Mo'rs Øjne: Skuespil i fire Akter, as Michaëlis Strange-
land (Copenhagen: Gyldendal, 1915); revised as
Mors Øjne, 3 volumes, illustrated by Ernst Hansen
(Flushing, N.Y.: Fergo, 1940);
Krigens Øfre (Copenhagen: V. Pio, 1916);
Atter det skilte–Novelle (Copenhagen: Gyldendal,
1918);
Don Juan–efter Døden (Copenhagen: Steen Hassel-
balch, 1919);
30 Dages Laan (Copenhagen: Steen Hasselbalch,
1920);
Lille unge Kone (Copenhagen: Gyldendal, 1921);
Mette Trap og hendes Unger (Copenhagen: Gyldendal,
1922); translated by Grace Isabel Colbron as
Venture's End (New York: Harcourt, Brace,
1927);
Syv Søstre sad (Copenhagen: E. Jespersen, 1923);
Træet paa Godt og Ondt, 5 volumes (Copenhagen: E.
Jespersen, 1924–1930)–comprises *Pigen med
Glasskaarene; Lille Løgnerske; Hemmeligheden; Synd
og Sorg og Fare; Følgerne;* selections republished
as *Uddrag til Skolebrug,* by Michaëlis and Hakon
Kirkegaard (Copenhagen: Hirschprung, 1940);
revised and enlarged as *Vidunderlige Verden,* 3
volumes (Copenhagen: Gyldendal, 1948–
1950)–comprises *Pigen med Glasskaarene; Lille
Løgnerske; Farlige Famlen; Lys og Skygge;* selection
"Det første Selskab," translated by Ann and
Peter Thornton as "The First Party," in *Contem-
porary Danish Prose: An Anthology,* edited by Elias
Bredsdorff (Copenhagen: Gyldendal, 1958),
pp. 81–84;
Kvindelil din Tro er stor (Copenhagen: Litterært forlag,
1925);
Bibi, a Little Danish Girl, translated by Lida Siboni
Hanson, illustrated by Hedvig Collin (Garden
City, N.Y.: Doubleday, Page, 1927; London:
Heinemann, 1927); republished in Danish as
Bibi (Copenhagen: Jespersen & Pio, 1929);
Perlerne (Copenhagen: Jespersen & Pio, 1927); anony-
mous abridgement and translation as *The Pearl
Necklace* (New York: E. Pauker, n.d.);
Familie Worm (Potsdam, Germany: Gustav Kiepen-
heur Verlag, 1928); republished in Danish as
Familien Worm (Copenhagen: Jespersen & Pio,
1933);
Pigen der smilede (Copenhagen: Jespersen & Pio,
1929);
Bibis store Rejse, en lille Piges Liv, illustrated by Collin
(Copenhagen: Jespersen & Pio, 1930); trans-
lated by Fyleman as *Bibi Goes Travelling* (London: Allen & Unwin, 1934);
Hjertets Vagabond (Copenhagen: Jespersen & Pio,
1930);

Justine (Copenhagen: Jespersen & Pio, 1931);
Bibi og Ole, en lille Piges Liv illustrated by Collin
(Copenhagen: Jespersen & Pio, 1931);
Bibi og de Sammensvorne, illustrated by Collin (Copen-
hagen: Jespersen & Pio, 1932);
Mor (Copenhagen: Jespersen & Pio, 1935);
The Green Island, translated by Rose Fyleman, illus-
trated by Collin (London: Allen & Unwin,
1935); republished in Danish as *Den grønne Ø*
(Copenhagen: Gyldendal, 1937);
Bibi paa Ferie, illustrated by Collin (Copenhagen: Jes-
persen & Pio, 1935);
Lotte Ligeglad, illustrated by Marie Hjuler (Copen-
hagen: Gyldendal, 1936);
Bibi bliver Landmand, illustrated by Collin (Copen-
hagen: Jespersen & Pio, 1939);
Bibi og Valborg, illustrated by Collin (Copenhagen:
Jespersen & Pio, 1939);
Little Troll, by Michaëlis and Leonore Scorsby (New
York: Creative Age Press, 1946).
Editions in English: *Bibi,* translated by Fyleman
(London: Allen & Unwin, 1933);
*The Dangerous Age: Letters and Fragments from a Woman's
Diary,* translated by Marshall, foreword by
Phyllis Lassner (Evanston, Ill.: Northwestern
University Press, 1991).

PLAY PRODUCTIONS: *Die heilige Lüge,* Vienna,
Deutsches Volkstheater, January 1913; revised
as *En Mo'rs Øjne: Skuespil i fire Akter,* Copenhagen, Dagmar Teater, 15 January 1916;
I rette Øjeblik, script by Michaëlis and Herdis Berg-
strøm; Copenhagen, Det Kongelige Teater,
1921.

Karin Michaëlis was a celebrated novelist,
short-story writer, author of a widely translated
1930s series of children's books with the eponymous
heroine, Bibi, and a journalist and lecturer, who
wrote and spoke especially on feminist and antifascist
subjects. Yet, as did the writing of many gifted
women writers, her work disappeared from view
until rediscovered in the 1980s and 1990s by feminist
scholars. Michaëlis's most famous novel, *Den farlige
Alder: Breve og Dagbogsoptegnelser* (1910; translated as
*The Dangerous Age: Letters and Fragments from a Woman's
Diary,* 1911), dramatizes women's concerns for equality on social and cultural grounds and sold more
than one million copies. It was made into two movie
versions, one in German and one in Danish. Republished in English in 1991, *The Dangerous Age* once
again attracted the acclaim and controversy that
marked its original publication. A hallmark of European modernism in its experimental form, the novel

also dramatizes ongoing feminist debates about the social construction of women's natures and roles. As does Michaëlis's other fiction, it features women characters who express sexual desire and frustrated ambition in an elliptical language that represents the style of Danish symbolists at that time, but also the difficulty discussing subjects that were socially taboo. As were many Danish women writers of her time, Michaëlis was deeply affected by the women's movement.

Karin Michaëlis was only thirty-three when she wrote *Den farlige Alder,* a novel of a woman's midlife crisis, but the various crises of her own youth inspired her creation of a fictional woman who decides that it cannot be too late to discover herself. Karin Michaëlis was born Katharina Marie Bech Brøndum in 1872 in the Danish provincial town of Randers. Her memoir, *Little Troll* (1946; in Danish *Vidunderlige Verden,* 1948–1950), establishes her birthplace as a metaphorical stage–"crooked lanes and twisted streets"–for the alternating privations and triumphs that would define her life. Michaëlis's father, Jacob Anthoniesen Brøndum, a telegraphist, suffered from tuberculosis, which curtailed his career as a civil servant and impoverished the family; her mother, Nielsine Bech Brøndum, made and sold wreaths to pay the bills. Michaëlis later paid tribute to her mother in several works in which the oppression of domestic responsibility is seen from the perspective of a child. Her Bibi character, like so many of Michaëlis's fictional children, dramatizes the child's struggle against domestic oppression by living a vagabond life.

Michaëlis's childhood was marked by an affliction of "crossed eyes" which, though surgically corrected, left her with a squint and the fear that she was ugly. This fear was most likely a motivating factor in her adolescent pursuit of promises of romance. Looking back with pain and ironic humor, Michaëlis portrays herself as a sexually provocative adolescent. At fifteen, she became secretly engaged to two men, one of whom was scarred like herself and had a limp that she found romantic, while she considered the other man as her sex object. Within the context of conservative and pragmatic Danish society, this behavior so shocked Michaëlis's parents, they were convinced that the respectability of their family name was threatened.

Michaëlis translated her assessment of these experiences into the Bibi figure who, like Gunhild in Michaëlis's fictional memoirs, *Træet paa Godt og Ondt* (The Tree of Good and Evil, 5 volumes, 1924–1930), rebels against conventional "good girl" roles. Truants from school and home, both girls tramp the Danish railways and roads in search of self-definition. Michaëlis herself left home in "voluntary exile," to tutor the daughter of a Danish consul, a position that encouraged her romantic imagination and independent spirit. When she returned home a year later, she rejected her parents' assumption that she would either do government work or get married. Yielding to her ambitions, they allowed her to move to Copenhagen to train as a piano teacher.

Both the city and her teacher, Victor Bendix–pianist, composer, and conductor–transformed her creative ambition. Assessing her musical talent as mediocre, he encouraged her to stay in Copenhagen and write. On 29 October 1895 Michaëlis married Sophus Michaëlis, a poet associated with the Danish symbolists of the 1890s, who also supported her literary ambitions. She then published two collections of short stories, *Højt Spil* (High Stakes, 1898) and *Fattige i Aanden* (Weak in Spirit, 1901), which, though praised by such critics as Georg Brandes, were also criticized for her choice of sordid subjects.

Michaëlis then began to write in other genres, including reviews and a novel of medieval life, *Birkedommeren* (1901; translated as *The Governor,* 1913), which was vilified by critics. Her fourth work, the novel *Barnet* (1902; translated as *The Child Andrea,* 1904), was published by the respected Danish firm of Gyldendal and marked her literary breakthrough. Publication of *Barnet* also led to a long and productive relationship with editor Peter Nansen, whose promotion of the novel guaranteed its international success. Translated into sixteen languages, *Barnet* concerns a young girl dying from the effects of an accident. Although this scenario might easily have led to a sentimentalized story, Michaëlis instead shows the girl welcoming death to escape from the oppression of adult life as reflected in her parents' loveless relationship. It struck such a sympathetic chord that Michaëlis was accused by some readers of having stolen the diaries of their dead daughters. By and large, Michaëlis's child characters show the exploitative effects of grim, unhappy adults on the psychological development of the young. Some of her children's fiction was written for a more adult audience, while others targeted younger readers. Her particular contribution to the genre was the development of a language and syntax to show in both dialogue and monologue the child as both distinct and inextricably connected to the world of adults. Using the slang of Danish youth at the time, Michaëlis also introduced a kind of street talk that made her writing distinctly modern. This technique showed the complex interaction between a child's psychology and the social pressures that shaped it and brought it into a conflicted relationship with the world of adults. She deals directly with her own childhood in volumes one and two of *Træet paa Godt og Ondt,* her fictionalized memoirs, *Pigen med Glasskaarene* (The Girl With the Glass Shards, 1924), and *Lille Løgnerske* (Little Liar, 1925).

Michaëlis's emphasis on relational and social factors also attributes women's potential to biology. This biological factor is explored as a compelling and unresolved tension in her fiction about women's nature, especially in debates about marriage and motherhood, as can be seen in such novels as *Lillemor* (Dear Mother, 1902), which was translated into twenty-two languages; whereas *Munken gaar i Enge* (The Monk is Loose upon the Meadows, 1905) reveals her satirical bent. Michaëlis's concerns about women's character were most fully expressed in her most powerful novel, *Den farlige Alder.*

When *Den farlige Alder* was first published in Denmark in 1910 and quickly translated into twelve languages, it shocked readers for reasons that remain powerful today. Its concern with the "true natures" of women made Michaëlis a celebrity, called upon to defend her views in lectures and interviews in Europe and the United States. Reviewers, such as George Middleton writing in *The Bookman* in October 1911, were taken with Michaëlis's "moving picture of a woman's emotions over strange hidden places," and the novel had more than fourteen printings in Denmark. Its appearance coincided with controversies about women's character and destiny. The feminist movement's call for equal rights and choices clashed with the claims of Sigmund Freud and other psychologists that women's destiny was biologically determined. Theories that considered marriage and motherhood the defining moments of women's lives also drove the formulation of fictional female characters. Although "New Women" novels of the period protest woman's sexual oppression, they limit her sexuality to the story of her youth. *Den farlige Alder* is remarkable in exposing such narratives of female development as oppressive.

Den farlige Alder remains striking today because of the bravura voice of the central character, forty-three-year-old Elsie Lindtner. From the first page of her letters and diaries to the last, she challenges herself and her readers unrelentingly, without intervention by any other narrator, about the politics of women's aging. As she veers from one extreme mood to another, from anger at her women friends' destructive strategies to desperate loneliness and remorse and then to empathy with the plights of other women, Elsie creates a new kind of woman's narrative. The unfolding drama of her midlife crisis

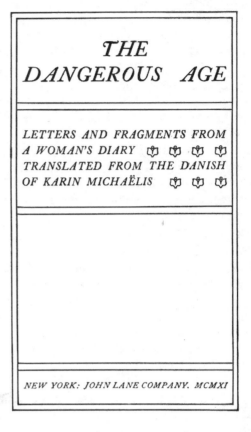

Title page for the first U.S. edition of Michaëlis's Den farlige Alder: Breve og Dagbogsoptegnelser *(1910), translated by Beatrice Marshall*

becomes a woman's own story of the imprisoning scenarios of her development.

Most disturbing to contemporary readers of *Den farlige Alder* was its depiction of menopause, a topic suppressed even when studies of human sexuality were becoming conventional in modernist narratives, and in Scandinavian literature in particular. Although Michaëlis never mentions the word menopause in the novel, she dramatizes symptoms attributed at the time to the biological bases of middle-aged women's psychological changes, which was received with discomfort by readers. Even when favorable, reviews registered embarrassment at the confessional style of the novel and some reviewers even diagnosed and recommended treatment for the women's malaise.

Den farlige Alder dispenses with the conventional narrator who foresees and analyzes characters' development. Through Elsie's responses to her own and other women's experiences, Michaëlis offers a new social-psychological model of women's midlife. Rather than identifying their problems as the onset of decline, she presents women's "hysteria" as a symptom of women's character in flux and struggling to reposition the sexual desire that had been killed by the marriage of convenience. Like those of the other women in the novel, Elsie's character is shaped by the need for social and economic security that drives them to comply with men's expectations and prevent them from knowing their emotional needs. At the core of this unknown self is a woman's sexuality, which only "bursts free" at the boundary between middle age and old age, only to find no acceptable avenues of expression.

During this period of professional success, Karin and her husband, Sophus, worked and traveled together, but the marriage was to end in bitter disappointment and divorce in 1911. Despite personal happiness and professional success as a playwright, Sophus became infatuated with a young woman. Karin responded by encouraging the affair at first, but then realized that her lingering doubts about her own attractiveness and independent spirit made reconciliation impossible.

Her belief that confidence began in a child's need for independence led her to friendship with Eugenia Schwarzwald, who founded an anti-authoritarian school in Vienna, so admired by Michaëlis that she immortalized it in her nonfiction book *Glædens Skole* (The School of Happiness, 1914). This book formulates Michaëlis's belief in sexual equality, arguing that women like Schwarzwald should play prominent roles in science and industry. If a young woman shows more domestic talent, however, she should be encouraged to marry and develop "her naturally given femininity." Some of Michaëlis's personal decisions proved destructive, as in 1912, when she impulsively married Charles Strangeland, an American economist who later blamed his successful wife for his failure to find work in Denmark. Michaëlis's play, *En Mo'rs Øjne: Skuespil i fire Akter* (A Mother's Eyes: A Play in Four Acts, 1915), about a blind woman, allegorizes their mutual self-deception. When the blind woman visits her children in America without telling them of her successful eye surgery, she sees them waiting on the pier dressed in rags. To keep her from worrying about them, they attempt to deceive her and pretend to be prosperous. After she sells her property to help them, she dies without ever letting them know she could see. Michaëlis faced her own illusions when she divorced Strangeland in 1917.

In 1912 Michaëlis published a sequel to *Den farlige Alder,* titled *Elsie Lindtner* (translated, 1912). This work might seem to subvert the feminist analysis of women's social roles and constraints of its predecessor. Instead of discovering outlets of expression for her continuing frustrated desires on her trip of adventure around the world, Elsie adopts a homeless waif in New York and returns to Denmark to devote herself to mothering him. The combination of maternal responsibility and child's needs, however, express concerns that Michaëlis had heretofore separated in her fictional and autobiographical writing. If *Elsie Lindtner* subsumes a woman's sexuality into maternal selflessness, it also establishes a woman's community where Elsie and her friends live in harmony and mutual understanding. If their maternal priorities are viewed as constraining, Michaëlis emphasizes that the women achieve a political and social culture defined by and for themselves.

During World War I Michaëlis visited refugee camps in Austria with her friend Schwarzwald. Following the war, she spoke out against anti-Semitism and personally challenged the policies of the president of Czechoslovakia, Tomas Masaryk, concerning the lack of German instruction in schools in the largely German-populated Sudetenland. In the interwar years Michaëlis lectured on "Love, Marriage, and Divorce," using her experiences and those of her friends. She argued that marital economic equality was fostered by a common expense fund that respected each partner's spending habits. Having seen women degraded by economic dependence and miserly divorce settlements, she campaigned for insurance policies that would assure women's education and economic self-sufficiency. She did not, however, join the women's movement.

Michaëlis demonstrated political courage throughout the interwar years. Branded by Adolf Hitler as "a dangerous woman," she continued to lecture in Nazi-occupied territory, her dais surrounded by Gestapo agents. Michaëlis opened her home at Thurø to those fleeing Nazi imprisonment and death; some were fellow artists, such as Bertolt Brecht and his wife, Helene Weigel; others were strangers except for their shared political sympathies. Michaëlis reported that many had been tortured and then released only as object lessons to other writers. She often heard them screaming in their sleep.

Once it became clear that Denmark would be invaded in early 1940, Michaëlis went to the United States for the remainder of the war. Though she enjoyed the cultural vibrancy of New York City and being with her sister Alma and brother-in-law, she was cut off from her European audience and publishing income. She had no American audience, and American publishers were not interested in publishing translations of her works.

After World War II Michaëlis returned to Denmark. In her last years she lived in Thurø in poverty; although her books had sold in the millions, she had given away much of her earnings. Karin Michaëlis died in Copenhagen on 11 January 1950.

Michaëlis's writings are varied in genre. In addition to her novels, she wrote short stories, essays, and reviews. She produced about seventy titles in book form alone. Although she did not consider herself a feminist, she delivered scathing critiques of contemporary attitudes toward women in many of her interviews and magazine articles. She followed Freud's theories of the psychosexual determination of character, yet found it necessary to trace women's characters through alternative possibilities.

The literary culture in which Karin Michaëlis lived and worked was Scandinavian. For Danish writers, major European trends such as Romanticism enhanced the epic and folkloric forms that expressed their cultural history. Later, Danish critic Georg Brandes's naturalism and the Norwegian playwright Henrik Ibsen's social criticism combined with portrayals of women's sexual roles and working-class perspectives by the Norwegian novelist Amalie Skram and the Danish writer Marie Bregendahl. By the time Michaëlis wrote *Den farlige Alder,* literary experimentation had been formalized by modernism. *Den farlige Alder* combines the symbolic and socially critical aspects of Scandinavian traditions and transforms them by introducing a new narrative approach, authenticating a woman's voice as the medium of social critique.

Karin Michaëlis should be considered a significant voice in the literary history of Denmark as well as in the modern feminist canon. She deserves recognition for her experiments with language and fictional form and for her cogent questioning of women's social roles in the European cultural context and in the modern history of the novel.

References:

Jørgen Claudi, *Contemporary Danish Authors* (Copenhagen: Det Danske Selskab, 1952);

Inga Dahlsgard, *Women in Denmark: Yesterday and Today* (Copenhagen: Det Danske Selskab, 1980);

Susanne Fabricius, "Karin Michaëlis" in *Danske digtere i det 20. århundrede,* 5 volumes, edited by Torben Brostrøm and Mette Winge (Copenhagen: Gad, 1982), I: 343–352;

Phyllis Lassner, "Women's Midlife and the Crisis of Writing: Karin Michaëlis's *Den farlige Alder* and Rose Macaulay's *Dangerous Ages,*" *Atlantis,* 14 (Spring 1989): 21–31;

Karin Sanders, "Blodets uro. Karin Michaëlis *Den farlige Alder,*" in *Læsninger i dansk litteratur, 1900–1940,* volume 3, edited by Inger-Lise Hjordt-Vetlesen and Finn Frederk Krarup (Odense: Odense University Press, 1997), pp. 114–130, 351–352.

Papers:

Karin Michaëlis's manuscripts are held by Det Kongelige Bibliotek (The Royal Library), Copenhagen.

Kaj Munk

(13 January 1898 – 4 January 1944)

Allen E. Hye
Wright State University

BOOKS: *En Idealist, nogle indtrykt fra en konges liv* (Copenhagen: Aschehoug, 1928); translated by R. P. Keigwin as *Herod the King,* in his *Five Plays* (New York: American-Scandinavian Foundation, 1953), pp. 23–86;

I Brændingen (N.p.: Privately printed, 1929);

Cant: Et Skuespil om Henry VIII og Anne Boleyn (Copenhagen: Nyt Nordisk Forlag, 1931); translated by Keigwin as *Cant,* in his *Five Plays* (New York: American-Scandinavian Foundation, 1953), pp. 149–208;

Ordet (Copenhagen: Nyt Nordisk Forlag, 1932); translated by Keigwin as *The Word,* in his *Five Plays* (New York: American-Scandinavian Foundation, 1953), pp. 87–148;

De Udvalgte (Copenhagen: Nyt Nordisk Forlag, 1933);

Vedersø–Jerusalem retur (Copenhagen: Nyt Nordisk Forlag, 1934);

Os bærer den himmelske Glæde: Digte fra den hellige land (Copenhagen: Nyt Nordisk Forlag, 1934);

Sejren (Copenhagen: Nyt Nordisk Forlag, 1936);

10 Oxford-Snapshots klippet af en dramatiker (Copenhagen: Nyt Nordisk Forlag, 1936);

Liv og glade Dage (Copenhagen: Nyt Nordisk Forlag, 1937);

Pilatus (Copenhagen: Nyt Nordisk Forlag, 1937);

Filmen om Christiern den Anden (Copenhagen: Nyt Nordisk Forlag, 1938)

Himmel og Jord: Kronikker m.m. (Copenhagen: Nyt Nordisk Forlag, 1938);

Han sidder ved Smeltediglen (Copenhagen: Nyt Nordisk Forlag, 1938); translated by Keigwin as *He Sits at the Melting Pot,* in his *Five Plays* (New York: American-Scandinavian Foundation, 1953), pp. 209–259;

Fugl Fønix (Copenhagen: Nyt Nordisk Forlag, 1939)*;*

Tempelvers (Copenhagen: Nyt Nordisk Forlag, 1939);

Egelykke (Copenhagen: Nyt Nordisk Forlag, 1940); translated by Llewelleyn Jones as *Egelykke,* in *Modern Scandinavian Plays* (New York: American-Scandinavian Foundation, 1954), pp. 97–171;

Kaj Munk

Navigare necesse–Tolv Digte om Danmark 1940 (Copenhagen: Det Berlingske Bogtrykkeri, 1941);

Sværg det, Drenge, edited by Studenterforeningen (Copenhagen: Nyt Nordisk Forlag, 1941);

Ved Babylons Floder (Copenhagen: Nyt Nordisk Forlag, 1941); translated by John M. Jensen as *By the Rivers of Babylon: Fifteen Sermons by Kaj Munk* (Blair, Nebr.: Lutheran Publishing House, 1945);

Niels Ebbesen: Skuespil (published illegally, 1942); translated by Hanna Astrup Larsen as *Niels Ebbesen* in *Scandinavian Plays of the Twentieth Century,* second series (Princeton: Princeton University Press for the American-Scandinavian Foundation, 1944);

Med Ordets Sværd: Danske prædikener 1941–42 (Copenhagen: Nyt Nordisk Forlag, 1942);

Med Sol og megen Glæde (Copenhagen: Nyt Nordisk Forlag, 1942);

Foraaret saa sagte kommer: Erindringer (Copenhagen: Nyt Nordisk Forlag, 1942);

Før Cannæ (Copenhagen: Samlerens Forlag, 1943); translated by Keigwin as *Before Cannae,* in his *Five Plays* (New York: American-Scandinavian Foundation, 1953), pp. 261–272;

Ewalds død, as [Danish actor] Holger Gabrielsen (Copenhagen: Westermann, 1943);

Jesus' Historier: Genfortalt for de Smaa (Copenhagen: Nyt Nordisk Forlag, 1943);

Danmark (Copenhagen: Nyt Nordisk Forlag, 1943);

Den Skæbne ej til os (Copenhagen: Studenternes Forlag, 1944);

I Guds Bismer: Sidste danske prædikener (Copenhagen: Nyt Nordisk Forlag, 1946);

Alverdens Urostifterne (Copenhagen: Nyt Nordisk Forlag, 1947);

Lanlige Interiører I Lollandsk Bondemaal (Nakskov: Lolland-Falsters Historiske Samfund, 1948);

Mindeudgave, 9 volumes, edited by Niels Nøjgaard and Knud Bruun-Rasmussen, (Copenhagen: Nyt Nordisk Forlag, 1948–1949)—comprises *Kærlighed og andre skuespil; Prædikener; Cant og andre skuespil; En digters vej og andre artikler; Dagen er inde og andre artikler; Egelykke og andre skuespil; Pilatus og andre Skuespil; Digte; Foraaret saa sagte kommer.*

Editions in English: *Four Sermons,* translated by Jensen (Blair, Nebr.: Lutheran Publishing House, 1944);

Kaj Munk: Playwright, Priest and Patriot: Some Examples of His Work, translated and edited by Keigwin (London: Free Danish Publishing, 1944).

PLAY PRODUCTIONS: *En Idealist,* Copenhagen, Det Kongelige Teater, 8 February 1928;

Cant, Copenhagen, Det Kongelige Teater, 10 October 1931;

I Begyndelsen var Ordet, Copenhagen, Betty Nansen-Teatret, 2 September 1932;

De Udvalgte, Copenhagen, Det Kongelige Teater, 9 November 1933;

Kærlighed, Copenhagen, Det Kongelige Teater, 14 September 1935;

Sejren, Oslo, Det Norske Teater, 5 April 1936;

I Brændingen, Copenhagen, Betty Nansen Teatret, 25 February 1937;

Han sidder ved Smeltediglen, Oslo, Det Norske Teater, 27 April 1938;

Diktatorinden, Copenhagen, 3 November 1938;

Fugl Fønix, Copenhagen, Studenterforeningen, 26 November 1938;

Puslespil, Copenhagen, Folketeatret, 5 May 1939;

Egelykke, Copenhagen, Det Kongelige Teater, 17 September 1940;

Pilatus, Sorø, Sorø Akademi, 1941;

Døden, Copenhagen, Det Kongelige Teater, 2 May 1942;

Niels Ebbesen, Stockholm, Svenska Dramatiker Studio, 14 September 1943;

Ewalds død, Copenhagen, Det Kongelige Teater, 18 November 1943;

Kardinalen og Kongen, Copenhagen, Odd-Fellow Palæet, 25 May 1945;

Før Cannæ, Oslo, Det Norske Teater, 16 June 1945;

Atterdag, Copenhagen, Folketeatret, 26 January 1957;

De Herrer Dommere, Copenhagen, Folketeatret, 26 January 1957;

Havet og Menneskene, Odense, Odense Teater, 29 January 1960.

MOTION PICTURES: *Det gyldne smil,* screenplay by Munk, Nordisk Film, 1935;

Filmen om Christiern den Anden, screenplay by Munk, 1938.

TRANSLATION: William Shakespeare, *Hamlet* (Copenhagen: Nyt Nordisk Forlag, 1938).

Kaj Munk was, along with Kjeld Abell, one of the leading Danish playwrights of the twentieth century. Although they were different in almost every respect, the two men are credited with reinvigorating the Danish theater in the 1930s and freeing it from a slavish adherence to naturalism. Munk's influence, however, extends far beyond the plays he created for the stage. He was a fervent writer of lyric poetry from childhood, and although his more than four hundred surviving poems are not as highly regarded as his plays, several collections were published, providing inspiration and encouragement to occupied Denmark during World War II. Munk was also a pastor in the Danish Folkekirke (National Church), publishing three collections of sermons and bringing national prominence to the tiny west Jutland village of Vedersø with his plays. The versatile pastor produced two motion-picture screenplays, a translation of William Shakespeare's *Hamlet,* books on hunting and travel, and, at the age of forty-four, he published his memoirs, *Foraaret saa sagte kommer: Erindringer* (So Gently Comes the Spring: Memoirs, 1942), the best-selling of all his works. Finally, Munk was an active commentator on theological, cultural, and political affairs in Denmark and Europe, frequently writing opinion pieces for the largest newspapers in Denmark.

Rune Lindstrom and Olof Molander in a scene from the 1943 Swedish movie adaptation of Munk's 1932 play Ordet *(Svensk Filmindustri)*

This activity, perhaps even more than his plays, polarized public and critical opinions about him and, together with his outspoken sermons criticizing the German occupation, led to his martyrdom at the hands of Nazi henchmen on 4 January 1944. Few figures in modern Danish life have aroused such contradictory passions as the controversial yet beloved pastor-playwright from Vedersø.

Kaj Munk was born Kaj Harald Leininger Petersen on 13 January 1898 in Maribo on the Danish island of Lolland, the only child of Carl Emanuel Petersen, a tanner, and his wife and former housekeeper, Anna Mathilde Petersen. The elder Petersen died when Kaj was one and one-half years old, and Mathilde succumbed to tuberculosis four years later. The orphaned Kaj was raised by his mother's cousin Marie Munk and her husband, Peter, who resided in nearby Opager; Kaj adopted their surname when he was fourteen. The Munk home was a loving one, fostering the fervent Christian faith that Kaj received from his mother, and supporting the youngster's passion for learning that was so evident to those who knew him.

Outside the home Munk was blessed by mentors and institutions that recognized and developed his spiritual and intellectual talent, introducing him to great literature, such as the Danish Romantic poet Adam Oehlenschläger,

and encouraging him in his writing. Munk also was nurtured by and equally comfortable in the two major currents of Danish Protestantism, the pietistic Indre Mission (Home Mission) tradition in which his family worshiped and the more intellectual heritage of the great Lutheran bishop, hymnist, and educator N. F. S. Grundtvig, to which he was exposed at school.

Beginning in 1917, Munk attended the University of Copenhagen, and the time he spent at Regensen, the celebrated seventeenth-century student residence where he was elected *klokker* (house president), was what he later called the happiest of his life. After passing his theological exams in 1924, Munk became the pastor in Vedersø. As he states in his memoirs, adjustment to country life was difficult and lonely: "Mine to første Præsteaar, det var ikke mine to lykkeligste—langt fra, langt fra. Men det var mine to rigeste, langt, langt de værdifuldeste i mit Liv, værdigfulde for mig selv i indre Væxt, værdifulde i, hvad jeg gav andre" (My first two years as pastor were not my two happiest—far from it, far from it. But they were my two richest, by far, by far the most valuable in my life, valuable for my own inner growth, valuable in what I gave to other people). On his birthday in 1929, Munk married one of his parishioners, Lise Jørgensen, and the couple eventually had five children. For the rest of his life, Munk strove in his daily routine to balance the "calls" he felt on his life, spending mornings with his writing, afternoons attending to his flock, and evenings with his family.

Munk was known for his fascination with great personages—men of power, vitality, and (often blurred) vision—and swashbuckling historical themes that produced theater on a grand scale. In a 1928 article that became something of an artistic manifesto, he articulated his desire to give Denmark such bold drama:

> Maalet har været intet ringere end at give den nye Tid dens Drama og brænde det ind i unge modtagelige Sind: Bagatelleriets og Æsteticisteriets Tid er forbi; vi vil ikke længere være store i det smaa, nu vil vi være store i det store.
>
> (The goal has been nothing less than to give the new age its own dramatic form and impress this upon young, receptive minds: the age of bagatelles and aesthetes is past; we no longer want to be great in the small things, we want to be great in the great things.)

Munk's plays can be divided into four categories: religious plays; plays about powerful political figures, sometimes called "dictator plays"; local color plays about the life and faith of the natives of western Jutland; and patriotic resistance plays. Most of the dramas were completed in astonishingly short time (some in two days or two weeks), in a rush of inspiration and at times of great stress. Although Munk's plays bristle with the energy of powerful, sometimes violent men and often dwell on death, the awareness of which was with Munk from childhood, the primary motif that coursed through his works was faith in God and mankind's need for him: "Uden Tro kann Mennesker ikke leve. Tager man Troen fra dem, vender de sig med deres Trosbegær til Djævlen" (Without faith, people cannot live. If you take faith from them, they will turn to the Devil with their desire for faith).

After writing five youthful dramas that were not published or performed until many years later, Munk finally succeeded with *En Idealist, nogle indtrykt fra en konges liv* (An Idealist, Some Impressions from a King's Life, 1928; translated as *Herod the King,* 1953). He wrote the first eight acts of his play in five feverish days while studying for his theological exams. Shortly after settling in at Vedersø, he added two more acts and sent it to the Royal Theater. A year and a half passed before the play was accepted—on what Munk later called the greatest day of his life—and another two years before it finally premiered, on 8 February 1928. The production was a critical fiasco, due in large measure to an injudicious selection of scenes from the overlong text. It would be three years before another Munk play would reach the stage and ten years before *En Idealist* would be successfully revived.

As Munk uses the term, an idealist is someone passionately committed to a goal and devoted entirely to its attainment, regardless of the cost. The goal for Herod the Great—his ideal—is power, which he twice defines. First, he challenges the priest Zakarja, who contends that God alone, "Jakobs Gud" (Jacob's God), has the power in Judea. As an Edomite, a descendant of Esau, Herod rejoices in his dominion over the Jews, descendants of Jacob. "Edoms Fod paa Jacobs Nakke! Mit Maal, mit Maal: at holde Herskerstaven haardt i en hadet Haand over dette Folk, til jeg dør" (Edom's foot on Jacob's neck! My goal, my goal is to hold the ruler's scepter in a hated hand over this people until I die). Then, in explaining to his wife Mariamne why he murdered their son, Herod reveals that any means are justified to ensure he retains power. "Jeg har et Maal: denne Krone ufravristelig om min Tinding. Jeg maa ofre alt i Verden for dette ene Maal" (I have one goal: to prevent this crown from being wrested from my head. I must sacrifice everything in the world for this one goal).

As ruthless as Herod is at home, he is also cunning and politically savvy abroad, as is evident in the two scenes with Cleopatra and Marcus Antonius, who first established Herod's reign in 37 B.C., and with Octavian, whose camp he visits, risking death to enlist support for his rule. Yet, the king's power and cunning are rendered useless in the final scene of the play. On his deathbed, he encounters the Virgin Mary and her baby Jesus on their flight to Egypt. Enchanted by the woman's grace and the child's beauty, he bestows his royal cloak on Jesus, hands

him his scepter, and kisses his tiny hand, in effect giving his blessing to the future King. "Jødernes Konge—han har afsat mig. . . . Han er større end jeg" (The King of the Jews—he has deposed me. . . . He is greater than I). Sunk in frustration at being too weak to resume his throne, Herod finds himself alone with the God of Jacob he had scorned and despised. Touched by grace, he realizes the folly of his passion for power and begs for mercy.

The epigraph for this play is a quote from Søren Kierkegaard, "Hjertets Renhed er at ville eet" (Purity of heart is to will one thing), which would appear to endorse a single-minded striving for a goal, even if that goal is less than honorable. Yet, as Svend Erichsen has pointed out, "alt tyder på, at han har misforstået det. For Kierkegaard var hjertets eneste mulige renhed at ville det gode, fordi det onde sår splittelse i sindet. Anvendt på Herodes får citatet den stik modsatte betydning" (everything suggests that he misunderstood it. For Kierkegaard the heart's only possible purity was to will the good, because evil sows division in the mind. Applied to Herod the quote has the exact opposite meaning). It is also, according to Erichsen, characteristic of the central dualism in Munk's personality: "den verdslige heltedyrker, der tror på Gud" (the worldly hero-worshiper who believes in God).

Although Munk continued to write after the failure of *En Idealist*—in 1929 he published *I Brændingen* (In the Breakers), about the great Danish critic Georg Brandes—he did not publish another play until *Cant: Et Skuespil om Henry VIII og Anne Boleyn* (Cant: A Play about Henry VIII and Anne Boleyn, 1931; translated as *Cant,* 1953) in 1931. The title, as the author explained to his readers, was the English word for empty, hypocritical rhetoric that seeks to attribute noble motives to egotistical, self-serving actions. In *Cant* Munk criticizes King Henry's maneuvers around church doctrine to attain one wife after another and the willingness of courtiers such as Thomas Cromwell to play along with the king in order to attain power and influence for themselves. *Cant* is a well-crafted play that was popular with audiences and critics alike, and it catapulted Munk into the forefront of Scandinavian theater, where, as Rolf Dorset points out, on the average at least one of his plays was performed every evening from 1932 to 1940, and in one of those years, 1938, five were performed in Denmark alone.

In 1925, impatiently awaiting the disposition of *En Idealist,* Munk dashed to Copenhagen to confront the theater's adviser, Hans Brix, about the delay. Brix could only respond that any play needed to go through several levels of review, but he planted an idea with the young playwright that immediately bore fruit. What was needed, said Brix, was a play about farmers who took themselves and their rural life seriously. Munk returned to Vedersø and in six days wrote the work for which he is probably best known, *Ordet* (1932; translated as *The Word,* 1953), a play

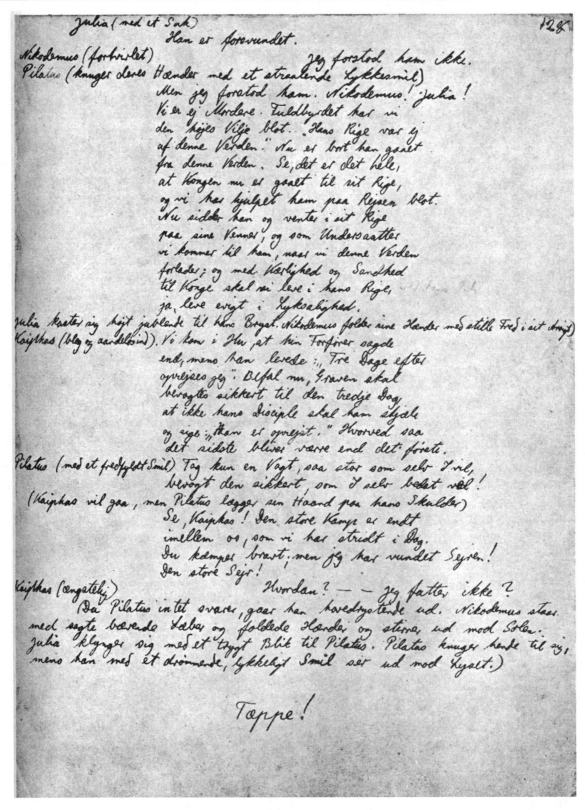

Page from the manuscript for the 1937 play Munk wrote about Pontius Pilate (from Munk's Foraaret saa sagte kommer: *Erindringer, 1942; Det Kongelige Bibliotek, Copenhagen)*

about a faith strong enough to raise a woman from the dead. It premiered in 1932 under the title of *I Begyndelsen var Ordet* (In the Beginning Was the Word) and became Munk's greatest success, playing to full houses for months and eventually reaching fifteen printings. A 1943 Swedish movie adaptation directed by Gustaf Molander was moderately successful, and in 1955 the famous Danish producer Carl Theodor Dreyer produced a motion picture version of *Ordet* that was a box-office hit.

Like *Cant*, *Ordet* is extremely well constructed—Ebbe Neergaard called it "Munks mest perfekte skuespil, teknisk set" (Munk's most technically perfect play). The difference is that the inspiration for *Ordet* is drawn from the playwright's own experiences, including his inability to resurrect a young friend and, in his first year as pastor, the death of a mother and her newborn. These events were the impetus for his great play of faith and resurrection, for which the words of a Vedersø widow furnished the epigraph: "Nej, hans Stadsklæder skal hænge parat, for En ved dog aldrig, om han ikke skulde komme en Paaskemorgen" (No, his Sunday best must hang ready for him, for one never knows, he might just show up one Easter morning).

Three of the four acts of *Ordet* are set at Borgensgaard, the prosperous west Jutland farm of Mikkel Borgen, whose daughter-in-law Inger is expecting her third child. While Inger's fate is the catalyst of the drama, there are many subplots woven around her that make *Ordet* a rich blend of local color and Christian faith. One subplot concerns the future of the farm and the faith of Borgen's three sons. Old Mikkel, a loyal Grundtvigian (follower of Grundtvig), will not leave his estate to Mikkel Jr., for the son, to his father's great distress, is not a believer. The second son, Johannes, is unfit to inherit since he has been suffering from mental illness since the death of his fiancée. Johannes is a believer, but he believes that he is Jesus Christ. The third son, Anders, has proposed marriage to the daughter of Peter Skrædderen, a spiritual rival of Old Mikkel's and leader of the Indremissionsk assembly, who initially opposes the union. Although both the Grundtvigians and the Missioners fall within the Danish National Church, they are so antithetical—in theology as well as culture—that each believes the other to be outside the faith. The second act of the play, set at Peter's modest home, is an emotional portrayal of these differences.

The third and fourth acts are dominated by Inger's crisis and the characters' reaction to it. Her baby dies at birth and, after a brief rally, so does Inger. Her illness and death focus another key theme of the play, namely the question of miracles in the modern age. Old Borgen, for all of his Grundtvigian faith, had stated early on that he does not believe in miracles, and the local clergyman, Pastor Bandbul, agrees: "Gud kunde selvfølgelig gøre Mirakler, men gør det ligesaa selvfølgelig ikke" (God could,

obviously, work miracles, but just as obviously he doesn't). The physician not only does not accept the possibility of miracles, he takes offense when God, rather than the doctor's skill, is credited for someone's good health. His faith rests in science and in himself.

Those who do believe in miracles, although they are lesser figures in the eyes of society, are elevated by Munk to sages and miracle workers. The lay preacher, Peter, had admonished Borgen, "husk, vi lever i Undernes Land. . . . Herren er Undernes Gud" (remember, we live in a land of miracles. . . . The Lord is a God of miracles). Not the least of these miracles occurs in human hearts, as demonstrated by Peter in praying for Borgen's family and in the conciliatory act of offering his daughter to Anders after Inger's death.

Johannes also believes in miracles and, like the youthful Munk, is convinced that he can raise Inger from the dead. His ally is Inger's daughter Maren, who alone believes his pronouncements of great faith. Johannes's sanity is restored at Inger's death, but in the face of unbelievers at Inger's casket, his faith in his power begins to falter. It is Maren's prompting that revives his faith and encourages him to declare, "Kvinde: staa op!" (Woman, arise!), which Inger does, to the consternation of the pastor and doctor and to the rejoicing of the family.

Munk followed the success of *Ordet* one year later with *De Udvalgte* (The Chosen Ones, 1933), a play about King David and his adulterous relationship with Bathsheba. This play, which Munk called "mit kristeligste og lødigste Stykke" (my purest and most Christian play), dramatizes his view of man's sin and God's grace. As Neergaard suggests, David is a positive counterpoint to King Herod of *En Idealist*. Whereas Herod sought and achieved evil but ended in humiliating defeat, David represents the ruler who wants good but succumbs to evil. His redemption comes not from anything he does but from what he is—namely a man after God's own heart—and what God is—the source of love and grace. Grace is extended to David because he is aware of his own sin and, as Munk stresses with italics in the printed text, "Fordi du i Fald som i Sæde *altid greb efter min Kjortel*" (because you whether falling or sitting *always grasped at my coat*).

In January of the same year, Adolf Hitler came to power in Germany, and two months later Munk was in Berlin to record and applaud the excitement surrounding the new regime. In hailing the emergence of the strong man he had longed for since childhood, Munk displayed the same enthusiasm he had earlier expressed for the Italian Fascist leader Benito Mussolini and the utter naiveté that characterized his attitude toward powerful political leaders. In 1934 Munk and his wife took an extended trip to Palestine, which he recorded both in a book of articles, *Vedersø–Jerusalem retur* (Vedersø to Jerusalem and Back, 1934), and in a book of poetry, *Os bærer den himmelske*

Cover for Munk's best-selling 1942 autobiography

Herod is motivated purely by power and evil, the Chancellor is depicted sympathetically as a patriotic man of peace forced into war by domestic intrigue and international politics. Once committed to war, however, he pursues it with a fervor that ruins his family and corrupts his character.

The play throbs with dramatic conflicts and difficult choices. Angelica, the Chancellor's wife, had to decide between two admirers, old friends, one of whom eventually became pope, the other chancellor. As war approaches, she must choose between her husband and her children, who reject their father's decision to attack. The Chancellor must choose between duty to family and duty to the fatherland, and the renewed rivalry with his old friend, who is now the Pope, focuses the play on conflicts between church and state: *Aand* (spirit) and *Muskler* (muscles). The ambitious Chancellor co-opts first the words of Christ—"Men jeg har et Rige af denne Verden" (But I have a kingdom of this world)—and then his role as savior. When, after the victory in Ethiopia, Angelica makes one final effort to rescue him from his megalomania, he retorts, "Ved du, hvem jeg er? Frelseren er jeg, Roms Ægtefælle, Guden Augustus" (Do you know who I am? I am the savior, Rome's bridegroom, the God Augustus). Angelica stabs him, and, unwilling to let him face eternity alone, falls on the dagger herself. The Pope, in conciliatory words reminiscent of Johann Wolfgang von Goethe's *Faust* (1808, 1832) declares that though human striving is corrupted by sin, it is sacred and must be undertaken. God's mercy grants in death the peace and victory that man has vainly sought in life.

The title of *Sejren* is ironic because the military victory in Africa brings a personal defeat for the Chancellor (and his ironically named son, Victor, who is devastated by his experience as a prisoner of war). Thus, despite the affection that Munk still had for the rugged individualist, and for Mussolini in particular, *Sejren* reveals his growing, if belated, awareness of the danger of dictatorship.

This awareness was sharpened by the time Munk wrote his next major play, whose clear condemnation of anti-Semitism forever alienated him from Nazi Germany. *Han sidder ved Smeltediglen* was written in two days, in Paris and Berlin, in January of 1938. It premiered in April in Oslo and in August in Copenhagen, where it was performed more than two hundred times. The title is from a Danish hymn by B. S. Ingemann, which in turn is based on Malachi 3:3: "He will sit as a refiner and purifier of silver." The biblical epigraph of the play, 2 Corinthians 12:3b, encapsulates its theme: "My grace is sufficient for you, for my power is made perfect in weakness." This time it is not the strong man but the weak one that is to be the hero. Both of these passages refer to the transformation of the protagonist, a German archaeology professor, and, to some extent, to the playwright himself.

Glæde: Digte fra den hellige land (Borne by Heavenly Joy: Poetry from the Holy Land, 1934). The importance of this landmark journey, as Marc Auchet discusses in some detail, was a mystical encounter with the spirit of Christ in the Holy Land and an awareness of the grave international situation. Although terribly slow to see the evil represented by Hitler and Mussolini, Munk's support for them began to wane, and he dramatized the evil of their rule in two important plays, *Sejren* (The Victory, 1936) and *Han sidder ved Smeltediglen* (1938; translated as *He Sits at the Melting Pot*, 1953).

Sejren dramatizes the 1935 Italian invasion of Abyssinia, although Munk maintains in an introductory remark that he was seeking to depict the spirit of the age, not the history of a particular country or person. The dynamic play was a box-office success, but critics have faulted it for having uneven, old-fashioned dialogue and an improbable ending. Parallels to King Herod in *En Idealist* abound, for the Chancellor (based on Mussolini) is shown as an energetic leader with "en overmenneskelige Vilje" (a superhuman will) who achieves military and political success only to suffer personal defeat and death at the end. But while

Professor Ernst Mensch is a loyal German and an admirer of the Führer, but he is most dedicated to his research and the pursuit of scientific truth. When he and his assistant piece together ancient pottery shards that depict the countenance of Jesus Christ, painted by a contemporary, they believe that their astonishing discovery is comparable to finding "a fifth gospel." Cultural politics, however, challenge their findings, for the National Socialists insist that Jesus was not a Jew, despite the evidence of history and the pottery that identifies him as such. Professor Mensch is to be awarded a national research prize and must decide whether to stand up for his scientific truth or accede to the political and racial demands of the Nazis. At the same time, he faces a personal dilemma when he falls in love with his assistant, only to learn that she is Sara Levi, a prominent Jewish entertainer who fled the country and returned with a new appearance and identity. After initial anger at having been deceived, Mensch realizes the depth of his devotion to her and proposes marriage.

In the final, climactic scene of the play, at the award ceremony Mensch intends to present the archaeological find to the Führer as a gift to the people, but he has second thoughts. Fearing that the truth of the discovery would be "too dangerous" for German society in a turbulent time, he smashes the pottery image of Christ, then declares his intention to marry Sara Levi. Mensch explains his first action as "mit Offer" (my sacrifice)—he is sacrificing scientific truth for the sake of domestic tranquility. But the second action, announcing his marriage to a Jewess, is a gesture he owes to humanity, to stand up for life, love, and human rights.

The transformation of Professor Mensch, who had preferred pottery to people and people to God, is profound: he comes to accept a woman as partner and Jews as equals; he smashes the physical image of Christ but attests to his spiritual image living in him; he prefers human life and dignity to scientific prestige. Yet, the ending of the play is not totally satisfying, as it begs the question of why Mensch did not defend the truth of his findings and challenge the Nazi rewriting of history and theology. If one takes the professor at his word, as most critics do, then he is indeed sacrificing one good, that is, scientific truth, for another—social stability—while at the same time protesting the Nazi anti-Semitic stance by marrying a Jewish woman, despite the fact that he smashes the pot in order not to challenge that same stance. Auchet suggests that Mensch's act also recalls Moses casting down the tablets in anger at his people's disobedience of God's law after finding the Israelites dancing around a golden calf, a motif found in two other of Munk's works of the same period. Mensch's final words call to mind the patriarch Abraham and, as Auchet explains at some length, stress the emphasis of the play on birth and life: "Du skal føde mig en Søn i min Alderdom, Sara, han skal blive en god Tysker et sandt Menneske" (You shall bear me a son in my old age, Sara, he shall become a good German and a true human being). Thus, Mensch's defiant actions say that human, not scientific, truth is the more precious.

Munk's next major play was a coming-of-age drama about N. F. S. Grundtvig's time as a private tutor in the Leth household and about his love for the lady of the house, Konstance Leth, who became something of a muse to Grundtvig. *Egelykke* (1940; translated, 1954) was a great challenge that took Munk eleven months to write, more time than he spent on any other play. It was completed in June 1939 and premiered 17 September 1940. In his introductory notes Munk explains the poetic license he took in forming the stage persona of Denmark's religious and cultural leader and says: "At være Digter er at tro paa Inspirationen, og hvad den siger En" (To be a poet is to believe in inspiration and what it says to one), which points up the kinship between Munk's works of poetic inspiration and Gruntvig's works of divine inspiration. The play is also dedicated to Konstance for the inspiration she gave to Grundtvig.

Munk's stand against anti-Semitism made him persona non grata with the Nazis, and the final full-length play published during his lifetime, *Niels Ebbesen* (1942; translated, 1944), written immediately after the military occupation of Denmark began on 9 April 1940, moved him closer to martyrdom. The play depicted the fourteenth-century Danish farmer who assassinated Count Gerhard of Holstein and led an uprising against the occupying forces in Jutland, but the parallel to the current situation was clear. Most of the fifteen thousand copies released on 8 April 1942 sold out immediately; the Germans quickly confiscated the remainder. The play circulated underground, however, and, along with the poetry and sermons Munk published in the final years of his life, was an inspiration to the growing Danish Resistance movement. *Niels Ebbesen* was also performed in neutral Sweden, premiering there on 14 September 1943.

As Munk in life had been the spiritual leader of the Danish Resistance, so in death he became one of its greatest martyrs. His many remarks on martyrdom seem almost prophetic, as do these words to his congregation three days before his assassination: "Jeg ved, at jeg nu i Maaneder ikke har lagt mig til Ro nogen Aften uden at tænke: 'Kommer de efter dig i Nat?'" (I know that for months now I have not gone to bed without wondering, "Are they coming for you tonight?"). When his body was found on 5 January 1944, the nation went into mourning, with thousands lining the route of his return to Vedersø. An unplanned tribute was given at the Royal Theater, when the playwright Kjeld Abell interrupted a production of Carl Erik Soya's *To Traader* (Two Threads) to ask for a moment of silence. Danes are fond of observing that in that moment Denmark's three leading dramatists were all represented on the stage at once.

Munk's legacy in Denmark has been a curious one considering his enormous stature in the 1940s. The years immediately following his death produced a flood of literature, including scholarly studies, remembrances, and the nine-volume *Mindeudgave* (Memorial Edition, 1948–1949), which contains several works not published during his lifetime, but before long theaters stopped producing his plays, scholars ignored him, and the public began to forget him. With the occupation over, there was no need for an eloquent resistance spokesman, and an increasingly secular society probably found it difficult to relate to his Christian worldview. Munk's legacy was also affected by Cold War politics, with his patriotism interpreted as nationalism and his conservatism branded as bourgeois reaction or fascism. His reputation rested mainly on his initial naive appraisals of Mussolini and Hitler and his scorn for the indecisive democracies that allowed them to control Europe. The clear change in his thinking that produced *Han sidder ved Smeltediglen, Niels Ebbesen,* and the courageous defiance of Nazism that ultimately cost him his life are generally overlooked. Several new books and plays about Munk appeared around the fiftieth anniversary of his death in 1994 and the centennial of his birth in 1998, but still there was not the public acclaim one once would have expected–he was, observed one pundit, "politically incorrect."

The testimony of his close friends in the memorial volume, *Bogen om Kaj Munk* (The Book About Kaj Munk, 1946), belies the radical political image he attained. More than anything, those who knew him best emphasize his *tro* (faith), *trofasthed* (loyalty), and *kærlighed* (love): his love of God, of truth, and of people. He was "Folkets sande Ven" (a true friend of the people). Well before Munk's death, one of his friends was quizzed about the controversial playwright-pastor: How could such an outspoken public figure also be a pastor? Did he crave the limelight? Was he genuine? When the skeptical questioner was invited to meet him and see for herself, her response after one meeting with Munk was: "Den Mand vilde jeg gerne have skulde holde mig i Haanden, naar jeg skal dø" (That man is the one I would want to hold my hand when I die).

Letters:

Breve fra Kaj Munk til adjunkt P. Garde, edited by H. F. Garde (Ringkøbing: A. Rasmussen, 1958).

Bibliographies:

Finn H. Blædel, *Kaj Munk: En Bibliografi* (Copenhagen: P. Haase, 1945);

Ove Marcussen, *Kaj Munks bøger: En Bibliografi* (Copenhagen: N. C. Rom, 1945).

Biographies:

Alfred Otto Schwede, *Verankert im Unsichtbaren: Das Leben Kaj Munks* (Berlin: Evangelische Verlagsanstalt, 1971);

Bjarne Nielsen Brovst, *Kaj Munk. Liv og død* (Copenhagen: Centrum, 1984);

Nielsen Brovst, *Kaj Munk og den stærke mand* (Copenhagen: Centrum, 1992);

Nielsen Brovst, *Kaj Munk–Krigen og Mordet* (Copenhagen: Centrum, 1993);

Nielsen Brovst, *Kaj Munk: Retsopgør og eftermæle* (Copenhagen: Centrum, 1998).

References:

Marc Auchet, *De lollandske stjerner* (Copenhagen: C. A. Reitzels Forlag, 1997);

Auchet, ed., *Kaj Munk: Dansk rebel og international inspirator* (Copenhagen: Akademisk Forlag, 1995);

Bogen om Kaj Munk (Copenhagen: Westermanns Forlag, 1946);

Rolf Dorset, "Kaj Munk," in *Danske digtere i det 20. århundrede,* 5 volumes, edited by Torben Brostrøm and Mette Winge (Copenhagen: Gad, 1980), II: 97–110;

Christian Eisenberg, *Die politische Predigt Kaj Munks* (Frankfurt am Main: Peter Lang, 1980);

Svend Erichsen, "Kaj Munk," in *Danske digtere i det 20. århundrede,* edited by Frederik Nielsen and Ole Restrup (Copenhagen: Gad, 1966), pp. 537–569;

Melville Harcourt, *Portraits of Destiny* (New York: Sheed & Ward, 1966), pp. 1–47;

Søren Holm, *Kaj Munk: Den religiøse Problematik i hans Dramaer* (Copenhagen: Nyt Nordisk Forlag, 1961);

Harald Mogensen, *Kaj Munk paa Teatret: En teaterbilledbog* (Copenhagen: Nyt Nordisk Forlag, 1953);

Ebbe Neergaard, *Vildt afsted over Himmel og Jord: Kaj Munk, en Digter mellem to Verdenskrige* (Copenhagen: Nyt Nordisk Forlag, 1946).

Papers:

Kaj Munk's manuscripts and other papers are at Det Kongelige Bibliotek (The Royal Library), Copenhagen.

Martin Andersen Nexø

(26 June 1869 – 1 June 1954)

Niels Ingwersen
University of Wisconsin, Madison

BOOKS: *Skygger* (Copenhagen: Julius Gjellerups Forlag, 1898);

Det bødes der for (Copenhagen: Julius Gjellerups Forlag,
1899);

En Moder (Copenhagen: Julius Gjellerups Forlag, 1900);

Muldskud (Copenhagen: Julius Gjellerups Forlag, 1900);

Familien Frank (Copenhagen: Gyldendal, 1901);

Dryss (Copenhagen: Gyldendal, 1902);

Soldage (Copenhagen: Gyldendal, 1903); translated by
Jacob Wittmer Hartman as *Days in the Sun* (New
York: Coward-McCann, 1929);

Muldskud: Anden Samling (Copenhagen: Gyldendal, 1905)–
includes "De tomme pladsers passagerer," translated
by Hallberg Hallmundsson as "The Passengers of
the Empty Seats" in *An Anthology of Scandinavian Literature: From the Viking Age to the Twentieth Century*
(New York: Collier-MacMillan, 1965), pp. 75–80;

Pelle Erobreren, 4 volumes (Copenhagen: Gyldendal,
1906–1910)–comprises *Pelle Erobreren* (1906);
Læreaar (1907); *Den store Kamp* (1909); *Gryet* (1910);
republished, 2 volumes, 1919; republished, 1 volume, 1933; translated by Jessie Muir and Bernard Miall as *Pelle the Conqueror,* 4 volumes (New
York: Holt, 1913–1916)–comprises *Boyhood*
(1913); *Apprenticeship* (1914); *The Great Struggle*
(1915); *Daybreak* (1916);

Af Dybets Lovsang (Copenhagen: Gyldendal, 1908)–
includes "Flyvende Sommer," translated by W.
Glyn Jones as "Adrift," in *Contemporary Danish Prose,*
edited by Elias Bredsdorff (Copenhagen: Gyldendal, 1958), pp. 67–80; "Trækfuglene," translated by
Linda S. Hanson in *Denmark's Best Stories,* edited
by Hanna Astrup Larsen (New York: American-Scandinavian Foundation, 1928), pp. 287–
332;

Barndommens Kyst (Copenhagen: Gyldendal, 1911);

Bornholmer Noveller (Copenhagen: Gyldendal, 1913);

Lykken; en fortælling fra Bornholms nordland (Copenhagen:
Gyldendal, 1913);

Folkene paa Dangaarden: Drama i Tre Akter (Copenhagen:
Gyldendal, 1915);

Martin Andersen Nexø (courtesy of Gyldendal Publishers)

Under Himmelen den Blaa (Copenhagen: Fr. Ravns Forlag,
1915);

Ditte Menneskebarn, 5 volumes (Copenhagen: H. Aschehoug, 1917–1921)–comprises *En barndom; Lille-
more; Syndefaldet; Skaersilden; Mod stjaernerne;*
republished as *Ditte Menneskebarn: Jubilæumsudg,* 2
volumes (Copenhagen, 1923); republished as
Ditte Menneskebarn, 1 volume (Copenhagen: Gyldendal, 1950); translated by A. G. Chater, Richard Thirsk, Asta Kenney, and Rowland Kenney

as *Ditte,* 3 volumes (New York: Holt, 1920–1922)–comprises *Girl Alive!* (1920); *Daughter of Man* (1921); *Towards the Stars* (1922);

Dybhavsfisk (Copenhagen: H. Aschehoug, 1918)–includes "Gulduret," translated by Minna Wreschner as "The Golden Watch," *American Scandinavian Review,* 11, no. 40 (1923): 350–358;

Lotterisvensken (Copenhagen: H. Aschehoug, 1919);

Undervejs (Copenhagen: Danske Forfatteres Forlag, 1919);

De tomme Pladsers Passagerer (Copenhagen: Gyldendal, 1921);

Muldskud: Samlede Fortællinger, 3 volumes (Copenhagen: H. Aschehoug, 1922–1926);

Mod Dagningen: Skildringer fra Rusland (Copenhagen: H. Aschehoug, 1923);

Digte (Copenhagen: H. Aschehoug, 1926; revised edition, Copenhagen: Gyldendal, 1951);

Midt i en Jerntid (Copenhagen: H. Aschehoug, 1929); translated by Thomas Seltzer as *In God's Land* (New York: Peter Smith, 1933);

De sorte Fugle (Copenhagen: H. Aschehoug, 1930);

Et lille Kræ (Copenhagen: Gyldendal, 1932)–excerpts translated by Evelyn Heepe as "Reminiscences," in *Modern Danish Authors,* edited by Heepe and Niels Heltberg (Copenhagen: Allan C. Christensen, 1946);

To Verdener: Tanker og Indtryk fra en Ruslandsrejse (Copenhagen: Frem Forlag A/S, 1934);

Under aaben Himmel (Copenhagen: Gyldendal, 1935);

For Lud og koldt Vand (Copenhagen: Gyldendal, 1937);

Mod Lyset: En Haandfuld Æventyr og Lignelser (Copenhagen: Mondes Forlag A/S, 1938);

Vejs Ende (Copenhagen: Gyldendal, 1939);

Erindringer, 2 volumes (Copenhagen: Gyldendal, 1945)–comprises *Et lille Kræ, Under aaben Himmel, For Lud og koldt Vand,* and *Vejs Ende;*

Morten hin Røde: En Erindringsroman, 3 volumes (Copenhagen: Gyldendal, 1945–1957)–comprises *Morten hin Røde* (1945); *Den fortabte Generation* (1948); *Jeanette,* edited by Houmann and Hans Kirk (1957);

Breve til en Landsmand (Fredericia: Nordiske Landes Bogforlag, 1945);

Et Skriftemaal (Copenhagen: Carit Andersens Forlag, 1946);

De tomme Pladsers Passagerer (Copenhagen: Forlaget Tiden, 1946);

Taler og artikler, 3 volumes, edited by Børge Houmann (Copenhagen: Forlaget Tiden, 1954–1955).

Editions and Collections: *Lotterisvensken og andre noveller,* introduction and notes by Kaj Larsen (Copenhagen: Gyldendal, 1949);

Lykken, og andre fortællinger (Copenhagen: Gyldendal, 1955);

Ægteskab og Fri Kærlighed: Tale holdt i Studentersamfundet 8. September 1906, afterword by Houmann (Risskov: D. B. K., 1966);

Af en ung mands papirer, edited by Houmann (Copenhagen: D. B. K., 1968);

Pelle erobreren, 2 volumes, edited, with an afterword, by Johan Fjord Jensen (Copenhagen: Gyldendal, 1971);

Bornholmernoveller, edited by Sven Møller Kristensen (Copenhagen: Gyldendal, 1977);

Rejse i syden: Et udvalg af rejsebreve, edited by Houmann (Copenhagen: Gyldendal, 1979).

Editions in English: *Pelle the Conqueror,* translated by Muir and Miall (New York: Peter Smith, 1930);

Under the Open Sky: My Early Years, excerpts from *Et lille Kræ* and *Under aaben Himmel,* translated by J. B. C. Watkins (New York: Vanguard, 1938);

Pelle the Conqueror's Boyhood, translated by Muir, revised by Patricia Crampton (London: New English Library, 1963);

"Flyvende Sommer," translated by David Stoner as "Gossamer," in *An Anthology of Danish Literature: Bilingual Edition,* edited by F. J. Billeskov Jansen and P. M. Mitchell (Carbondale: Southern Illinois University Press, 1972), pp. 380–407;

Pelle the Conqueror: Volume 1: Childhood, translated by Steven T. Murray, edited by Tiina Nunnally (Seattle: Fjord Press, 1989);

Pelle the Conqueror: Volume 2: Apprenticeship, translated by Murray and Nunnally, afterword by Niels Ingwersen (Seattle: Fjord Press, 1991).

In 1987 Martin Andersen Nexø, who had first become popular in the early years of the twentieth century, suddenly achieved new prominence. The movie *Pelle the Conqueror,* based on Nexø's novel *Pelle Erobreren* (4 volumes, 1906–1910; translated as *Pelle the Conqueror,* 4 volumes, 1913–1916), was a hit with critics and the public alike, and it received an Academy Award as the best foreign film of the year. Audiences delighted in watching Lasse, an elderly man, played superbly by Max von Sydow, and Pelle, his small son, survive the brutish farm life on the Danish island of Bornholm. The motion picture is filled with scenes that reveal the inhumanity of life on this remnant of the feudal system–one striking scene shows Pelle being abused and humiliated by the farmhands–and it is made clear that Pelle and his father are surrounded by people who are defective as human beings. The farm on which Pelle and his father work can be seen as an allegorical representation of the sickness of the bourgeois laissez-faire world, where the only motivation is monetary gain.

Nexø and his first wife, Margrethe, née Thomsen, in 1904

At the same time, this work is grandly optimistic, for Pelle conquers his world in a spirit of joy and exuberance. Many scenes are jubilantly affirmative of life, filled with humor, warmth, and a belief in the innate goodness of human beings. The novel shows two sides of Nexø: the vehement critic of Western moneymaking society and the compassionate observer of humanity. Nexø was a consistent and often strident critic of anyone on his right politically, but he also had a keen insight into the minds of others no matter what their political orientation (at least until the 1940s).

Although it was not until the release of the movie *Pelle the Conqueror* that the interest of Western audiences in Nexø was revived, he had a steady international following. His works have been translated into twenty-one languages and he is one of the few Scandinavian authors who has been popular outside of his native country. His admirers include such diverse people as Pablo Picasso, Vladimir Lenin, Thomas Mann, Upton Sinclair, and Arturo Barea.

It is noteworthy that people of diverse political opinions have been attracted to Nexø's work: in 1912 Lenin wrote to the editors of *Pravda* and suggested that the newspaper should serialize *Pelle Erobreren*. In an early novel, *The Fires of Spring* (1949), the aspiring author James Michener has his young protagonist, David Harper, encounter *Pelle Erobreren* in a college course, and that encounter upsets the young American, for even though he, too, has come from humble beginnings, he refuses to identify with Nexø's protagonist. Michener writes:

> . . . he [David] never wanted to finish the book. He knew that it was a merciless indictment of David Harper, who had seen most of what Pelle had seen, but who felt no burning sympathy for the writhing masses for the simple reason that he had long since closed his eyes and told himself over and over again: "it isn't like that! People don't sicken and die from lack of food. In America it isn't like that! It isn't! It isn't!" David felt wretched and vastly disturbed.

In this novel, which predates his commercial blockbusters, Michener aptly captures the way in which *Pelle Erobreren* can invade a young man's conscience, and the very fact that David Harper wants to reject Nexø's vision—one that he knows is true—testifies to the power of *Pelle Erobreren*. Nexø had the right to write about poverty; he knew from personal experience what it meant to be poor both in the city and in the countryside.

Martin Andersen was born in Copenhagen on 26 June 1869, at a time when slums housed many of the industrial workers. Although his father, Hans Jørgen Andersen, was a hard worker, the money he earned tended to be spent in taverns on the way home from work. A glimpse of what childhood meant to poor children growing up in industrial Copenhagen is given in "Flyvende Sommer" (1908; translated as "Gossamer," 1972), which, like *Pelle Erobreren,* vests a tremendous hope for the future in the youngsters of proletarian background.

During an economic slump, the city government of Copenhagen offered to pay the way of some of the unemployed back to their native regions. The Andersens returned to the distant, rocky, and culturally backward island of Bornholm, located south of Sweden in the Baltic Sea.

The family settled in Nexø, a small coastal town, and Andersen later adopted the name of the town as his own surname, a not uncommon practice in Denmark. Even though their economic conditions improved somewhat, the tensions in the home remained, and in his memoirs Nexø included scenes that indicate that the children feared the homecoming of their drunken father and relied on their strong-willed mother, Mathilde, for protection. Nexø knew the plight of his father, which the compassionate and tragic story "Lotterisvensken" (The Lottery Swede, 1894) demonstrates, and it is not accidental that he developed a keen sense of the woman as the protector of the home.

Nexø received a limited education, for as soon as he was strong enough to help his father, a stonecutter, he had to work in the quarry or be a herdsboy in the fields (scenes capturing that experience form part of the movie *Pelle the Conqueror*). After his confirmation in the Lutheran Church at the age of fourteen, he found employment outside the home, but since his health was poor, he became an apprentice to a shoemaker in the island's largest town. He found the work boring, though he stayed with it for six years, but during that time he discovered the magic that would change his life—the world of books. At that time, citizens inspired by the thoughts of N. F. S. Grundtvig, the founding father of the *folkehøjskole* (folk high school) movement, formed small study groups to read and debate literature that delved into the issues of the day.

That meeting with the world of letters was a decisive one for Nexø, and he eagerly accepted an opportunity to attend the local *folkehøjskole,* one of the voluntary residential schools for adults with a curriculum influenced by folk culture, founded after 1844 as part of a movement to counteract the elitism that Grundtvig saw as perpetuating social injustice. At the local *folkehøjskole* Nexø met a German socialist, who taught the young Nexø the meaning of a word he had never heard before—*strike*. That man left Nexø with a message: never forget the plight of the poor. He never did, but it took a while before that message really seeped in. At that point, it seemed as if Nexø would rise into the

bourgeois class. He was given some monetary support to attend Askov, a top-notch *folkehøjskole* in Jutland. Finally Nexø had gotten away from the confinement of Bornholm and entered Danish intellectual culture. It might be easy to forget today, but at the time the best of the *folkehøjskolen* served as universities for those who could never dream of attending the only university of the country, located in Copenhagen.

Even though young Nexø had no use for the Christian idealism that tended to permeate the *folkehøjskole* movement, he was forever thankful for the educational impetus he received at Askov. For a while, he served as an assistant to the folklorists Poul Bjerge and H. F. Feilberg, and this experience likely reinforced his sense of the plot structures and motifs found in the tales he undoubtedly heard told as a child. Nexø's first publication, which appeared in a newspaper, depicted Midsummer Night festivities on Bornholm—a sound topic for a folklorist. Feilberg also taught him that he should observe the transition of the rural landless population into the proletariat of the cities. The understanding of that migration informs *Pelle Erobreren,* as does the optimistic rhetoric he heard at Askov. Throughout his life, Nexø saw himself as an educator of the people.

Nexø obtained a teaching position, but bouts of coughing led to a diagnosis of tuberculosis. At that time the disease was almost always fatal, but well-meaning people gathered enough money together so that the young man could travel to southern Europe in the hope that a warmer climate might help him combat the disease. Through writing articles for newspapers, Nexø managed to supplement his income, and he began to grasp that he could become a professional writer.

In December 1894 Nexø left for Italy and then went on to a prolonged stay in Spain. Those two years in the warmer climate apparently restored his health completely. Those years were also significant spiritually, for Nexø's encounter with the proletariat in Spain made him feel that, once again, he was with his own people. He reveled in the optimism of the poor, who were undaunted in the face of suffering and oppression. In a sense, Nexø's stay in Spain was a kind of homecoming for him.

Nexø was at his best when he captured the fates and the mind-sets of his neighbors on Bornholm in his well-wrought, taut stories that never moralize or allegorize. He may let the doctor in "To Brødre" (Two Brothers, 1897) commiserate over the effects that religion has on people by stating that religion creates insanity, but the voice of condemnation is that of the doctor as a character, not that of Nexø as the author. This detachment was to change, but in his early stories Nexø is a consummate psychological realist.

In 1898 Nexø returned to Denmark, married Margrethe Thomsen, and worked as a schoolteacher, but he then decided that he would try to support himself by writing. The fact that he had published a collection of short stories titled *Skygger* (Shadows, 1898) surely encouraged him in that decision. *Skygger* is an uneven book; however, although some of the stories are faddishly decadent, it suggests what was to come, for other stories record the anger of the Spanish proletariat—not least that of its women.

The young author then returned, mentally, to Bornholm and wrote some brilliant stories in which he recalled events from his youth. Several collections appearing between *Skygger* and *Pelle Erobreren* demonstrate Nexø's remarkable psychological ability to depict the workings of the minds of social outcasts, marginalized individuals, and people steeped in crises. Even though these stories have failed to attract much critical attention, they are artistically among Nexø's best works and are in a league with Johannes V. Jensen's acclaimed stories from Himmerland and Henrik Pontoppidan's angry indictments, in short-story form, of socially complacent Denmark. Nexø often singles out the unique and grotesque and depicts people who have no knowledge of bourgeois morality or norms and who act in accordance with their natures and passions. The author Marie Bregendahl once astutely remarked that Nexø's early works described more homicides than Denmark had experienced during his lifetime. He often portrayed violence as the means by which people took charge of their own destinies.

Nexø understood the ways in which the rural population viewed deviations from the age-old norms of its culture. In "Hovsmeden fra Dyndeby" (The Smith from Dyndeby, 1899), a boy who was persecuted by his neurotic father becomes like his father and delights in abusing the norms of his rural society: he neglects the fields; he harasses his neighbors with lawsuits; and he maltreats his two splendid horses. It is from their trouncing hooves that he meets his well-deserved death. In "Skæbne" (Fate, 1905), two young people, Gjarta and Peter, are profoundly attracted to each other, but since she is married to Old Ole and will not commit adultery or elope, they murder Ole. They are found out, spend time in prison, and once out are finally able to marry. They lovingly tend Ole's grave; after all, in spite of their passion for each other, they both had been fond of the old man. Society accepts them, for they have paid the price for their offense, and they spend their days together tending to their farm.

Nexø's early novels are not of the caliber of his best short stories, but they accurately reflect their times. An early attempt that did not find a publisher was an American frontier novel about a sensual young woman

Nexø writing Pelle Erobreren *in Espergærde in 1908, wearing the Russian shirt he purchased in St. Petersburg the previous summer*

who writes to the man whom she desires about her sexual experiences. That Nexø should use the Old West—then not so old—as a setting tells its own tale about what the Danish reading public craved at the time. Although that attempt to earn money failed, the work remains of interest, for it gives an unsentimental depiction of life at a frontier fort and a puzzled, but frank, attempt to deal with female sexuality—that "guddommelig rits" (divine joke) on males. Parts of the text were published in 1946 as *Et Skriftemaal* (A Confession), and Børge Houmann published a synopsis of the original story using Nexø's original title, *Af en ung mands papirer* (From a Young Man's Papers) in 1968.

Female sexuality was dealt with ambivalently by Nexø, who in that respect was hardly a groundbreaking author. The child and the old woman are depicted in his works with loving care, but the young woman who might pose a threat to the male is often rendered with a mixture of fascination, fear, and incomprehension. It is the modern woman—the product of bourgeois culture—who is seen as problematic, not the farm woman of the rural past.

The novels that Nexø did get published during these years demonstrate that he knew how to produce the decadent texts so common in Denmark in the 1890s. *Det bødes der for* (It Must Be Atoned, 1899) investigates sexual relationships and offers the conclusion, on the part of the protagonist, that human beings are motivated only by their sexual desires and their egoism. What absolves a rather dreary book from the triteness of its plot is the narrator's brutal honesty about his own motivations. *En Moder* (A Mother, 1900), a study of shallow people, is critical of bourgeois morality, and its tone is humorous and satirical. Of more substance is *Familien Frank* (The Family Frank, 1901), which depicts a strong-willed, but socially downtrodden woman, Anna, who tries to offer her son, Thorvald, a different fate from that of her weak drunkard of a husband. In Thorvald much hope is vested—by his mother and by his author—and that figure foreshadows Pelle.

With *Dryss* (Waste, 1902) Nexø created a protagonist who displays all the symptoms of fin-de-siècle weariness with life—the protagonist is uncompromisingly egocentric and defeatist. In this work, Nexø competes with such authors as Johannes Jørgensen and Jensen in terms of recording a Danish inability to cope with life, but even though *Dryss* is Nexø's most nihilistic text, the novel is nevertheless infused with a verbal energy that belies the fatigue of the protagonist. Apparently, Nexø himself saw *Dryss* as one last step in the wrong direction; consequently, he had to take the right step to bring him back to the ordinary human being, the proletarian.

That step is recorded in *Soldage* (1903; translated as *Days in the Sun,* 1929), a travel chronicle in which Nexø retraces his earlier trip to Spain. The book exudes sympathy for the proletariat and solidarity with the anarchists. Perhaps this book is more Nexø's own than any other he wrote. It is a lively, joyful account of a stay in Spain, and even when dark moments are brought up, the narrative seems to shine with the joy of experiencing life and writing about it. In this book, Nexø seems to be speaking with his own voice and enjoying himself very much; later, he wrote for the sake of a cause, and eventually such a restraint became damaging to his talent. In *Soldage,* he throws off the shackles of being a decadent author, but he has not yet firmly enrolled himself as a promoter of the momentous cause of the workers.

In fact, Nexø never emerges as a card-carrying Communist; rather, he appears to be an anarchist who followed the credo: you shall not allow yourself to be ruled by others, and you shall not rule over others. That egalitarian attitude was one he knew well from growing up among the poor on Bornholm, and that belief seems to speak from the joyful pages of *Soldage.* Nexø was, however, a man who felt he had to serve causes. Once he began to examine the plight of the poor from the position of an outsider, he was awakened to how severely deprived they were, so he decided to

serve their cause as best he could—and he did so with gusto and success.

Nexø next embarked on the project that was to make him world famous, the writing of *Pelle Erobreren.* It is a rousing, exciting novel that follows its protagonist from his herdsboy days on Bornholm to his success as a founder of a co-operative movement and as a family man.

Pelle Erobreren faithfully reveals that life is not easy for aging Lasse and his young son, but their sense of solidarity enables them to resist the brutishness that surrounds them, and Pelle himself develops an armor against the world. It seems, then, that Pelle, upon leaving his childhood milieu, is well-equipped to conquer the world. That world, however, is a small provincial town with social hierarchies and prejudices. In the second section of the novel Pelle is apprenticed as a shoemaker, and those years are less than joyful, but he finally emerges as a young man ready to transcend his petty world, and he sails off to his future in the Danish capital of Copenhagen.

As the third part of the novel begins, Nexø conjures up a masterful image of a part of Copenhagen that is long gone: an enormous slum dwelling, the Arc, where the inhabitants nevertheless lived with a sense of social solidarity. It is a paean to the lower classes of that time. Pelle lives there, working as a shoemaker, but eventually realizes that something is wrong with the class system and becomes a member of, and eventually an organizer for, a labor union. Pelle has moved into the modern world of class struggle.

He is extremely successful as a labor organizer—and as the suitor of a labor leader's daughter. Pelle experiences his greatest success when the conservative establishment caves in to strikes, but after a triumphant labor march toward the center of town, he is arrested on trumped-up charges and thrown into prison. While in prison, Pelle reads the Bible and seems to hear admonitions from God. Pelle, the judge of others, humbles himself, and he is a changed man when he finally leaves the prison. He reunites with his family and starts a cooperative movement that is dedicated to providing neat homes and harmonious lives for the working class.

The conclusion may well strike the reader as anticlimactic, but it harbored a primary hope of the times—that cooperative ventures would bring the labor class into a position of social safety and financial security. It was a mundane version of a utopian vision, but one that would give the proletariat the dignity it desired. The ending of the novel also suggests that Pelle has grown into a person who knows himself and who, therefore, is the ideal leader of his people. He is the Moses of the labor movement, and in his speeches he lavishly uses Old Testament rhetoric, as when he says he is letting his people look into a promised land. The Old Testament is a forceful frame of reference and so are the age-old stories that Nexø knew well from the rural tradition.

Pelle Erobreren follows the structure of the beloved "once upon a time" magic tale: it takes its hero into situations of dire distress, but since its protagonist makes the right choices, it ends by his "living happily forever after." If that assessment of the novel seems a bit simplistic, it ought to be noted that the same structure is found in the venerable bildungsroman–the most venerable of which, Johann Wolfgang von Goethe's *Wilhelm Meister* (2 volumes; 1795, 1829), is invoked in the ending of *Pelle Erobreren*. The bildungsroman sketches how a young person, as a rule a male, grows up, falls into temptations, and finds himself in danger of spiritual corruption; but, that young man–often guided by older, wiser people–sees the errors of his ways, reforms, and is eventually integrated into society, often as a leader of others. That paradigm had fallen on hard times in the latter part of the nineteenth century, and in many novels the young protagonists faltered, and their quests ended in disillusionment and tragedy. Nexø brilliantly gave the genre new life by creating a socialist bildungsroman. *Pelle Erobreren,* although primarily a realistic novel, also relies heavily on allegorical symbolism and myth–and, perhaps, the populist ideas of the *folkehøjskole*. The novel also demonstrates that Nexø was well-read in the classics and was familiar with traditional storytelling.

Pelle Erobreren became a popular book, one often serialized in social democrat newspapers in many countries, and it made Nexø internationally known. There are, however, signs in the novel that Nexø viewed his protagonist with a jaundiced eye. When Pelle has become a powerful labor organizer, he is a man for whom the cause is above everything else, and that point is brought home painfully when the lovable, but now decrepit and defeated, Lasse appears in Copenhagen. Pelle has hardly any time for him, and Lasse eventually dies feeling bitterly abandoned. Even though Pelle is with him at that moment, Lasse has, for all practical purposes, become a homeless person. Pelle has also allowed himself to be drawn into the lives of two young women, and he has, without wanting to, caused their deaths. In addition, though he loves his wife, he barely has time to tend to her needs.

It almost seems that, as Nexø was creating his magnificent novel about his victorious and healthy proletarian's path toward the light, he was writing a much darker book–one related to his so-called decadent novels–and revealing flaws in his hero that cause the reader to question his idealism. The tension between text and subtext provides a complexity that heightens the text artistically.

The novel quite naturally became a marvelous ideological weapon for the Social Democrats, and Nexø himself joined that party, which was to make Denmark a welfare state. World War I, however, radicalized Nexø, who had envisioned that socialists everywhere would ally themselves to prevent war. In 1914 war was declared, and the German Social Democrats turned nationalistic. Nexø was profoundly disillusioned, and even though he continued to write in favor of social democratic causes, his support seemed halfhearted, and he began to ally himself with those who were politically left of the Social Democrats and to sympathize with the splinter groups that shunned the party. In 1918 Germany was in chaos, and labor unrest was rampant in Denmark, so it did not seem unrealistic to expect that a revolution–one similar to the one that had swept through Russia and transformed it into the Soviet Union–might be the fate of Western European countries. The Danish Social Democrats vehemently opposed communist goals, and Nexø felt that the party to which he belonged was betraying the cause of the proletariat. Consequently, it is hardly surprising that he sent money to support the jailed members of the Workers' Socialist Party. The year 1918 was a watershed year in his life, for it made him a revolutionary.

The Danish Social Democrats renounced him for his monetary support of the revolutionaries, and he resigned from the party. From then on, in spite of temporary rapprochements, he was a relentless critic of the social democrats. He felt that their rhetoric, which was meant to please the workers, was simply a cover-up for the establishment. It is from that perspective that Pelle is viewed in Nexø's next major novel: *Ditte Menneskebarn* (5 volumes, 1917–1921; translated as *Ditte,* 1920–1922).

The Danish title of *Ditte Menneskebarn* is problematic to translate–perhaps "Ditte, Child of Man" or "Child of Humanity"–but it suggests Ditte as being that Everywoman who is born into poverty and who has to struggle against it. While *Pelle Erobreren* charted a young man's rise to success in a world he helped create, *Ditte Menneskebarn* recorded the ways in which women fared in a world cruelly dominated by capitalistic exploitation; *Ditte Menneskebarn* presents the poor that the Social Democrats betrayed and ignored. Nexø's vision had darkened since *Pelle Erobreren*: Pelle achieves his goals, but Ditte experiences only suffering and an early death. It has been suggested that Pelle should be compared to the hero of the folktale who wins the princess and half the kingdom, whereas Ditte is the long-suffering protagonist of the folk legend.

Ditte's early years are spent in the countryside. Her supportive grandparents play the role of Lasse, but

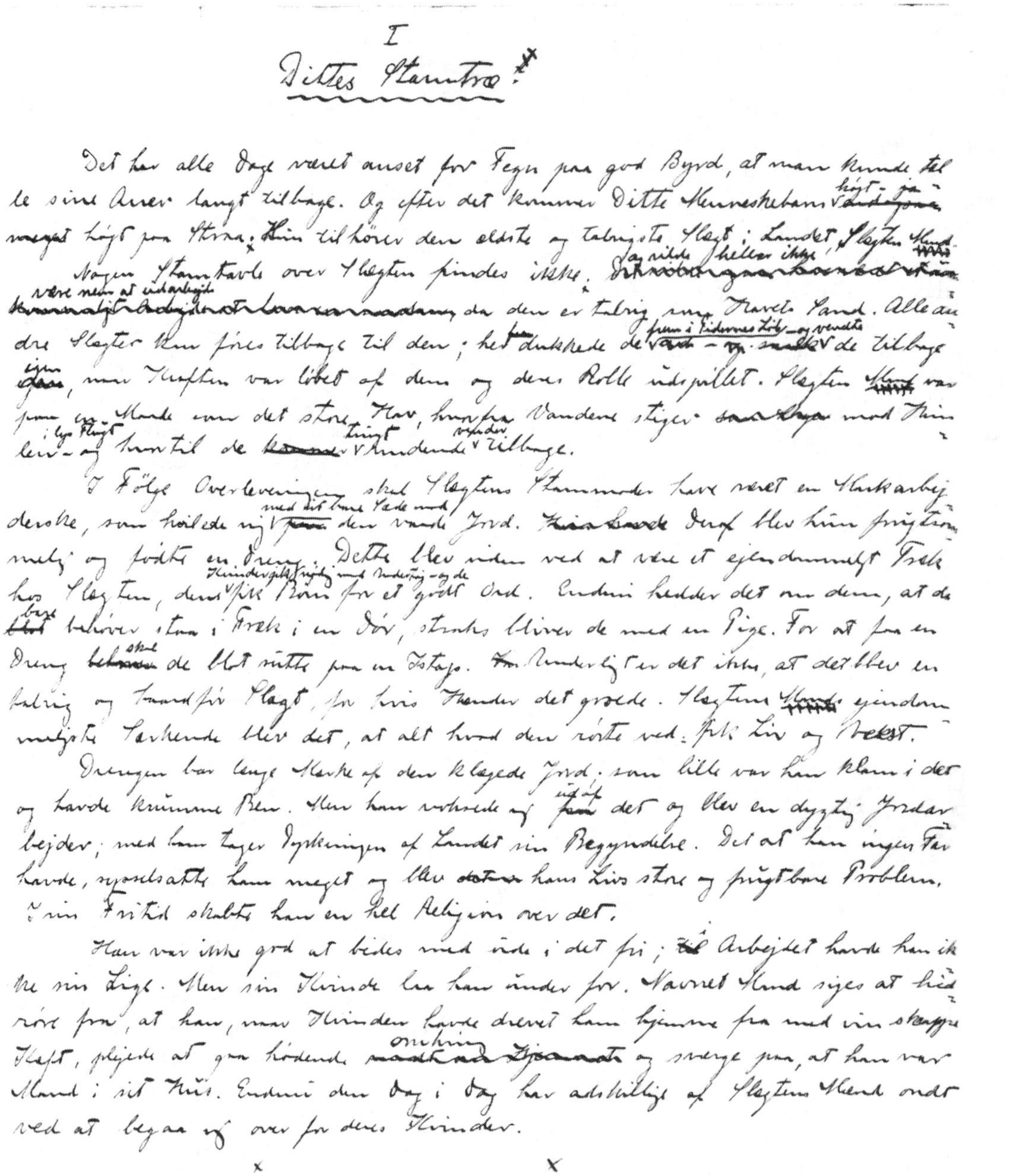
I

Dittes Stamtræ!

Det har alle Dage været anset for Tegn paa god Byrd, at man kunde tælle sine Aner langt tilbage. Og efter det kommer Ditte Menneskebarn højt - ja meget højt paa Strå; hun tilhører den ældste og talrigste Slægt i Landet, Slægten Mand.

Nogen Stamtavle over Slægten findes ikke, og vilde heller ikke være nem at udarbejde, da den er talrig som Havets Sand. Alle andre Slægter kan føres tilbage til den; het dukkede de frem i Tidernes Løb og vendte de tilbage igen, naar Kraften var løbet af dem og deres Rolle udspillet. Slægten Mand var som det store Hav, hvorfra Vandene stiger med Lys Flugt og hvortil de tungt vender tilbage.

I Følge Overleveringen skal Slægtens Stammoder have været en Markarbejderske, som hvilede sig med sit bare Hjerte mod den varme Jord. Deraf blev hun frugtsommelig og fødte en Dreng. Dette blev siden ved at være et ejendommeligt Træk hos Slægten, dens Kvinder fik let og ved det at Børn for et godt Ord. Endnu hedder det om dem, at de bare behøver staa i Træk i en Dør, straks bliver de med en Pige. For at faa en Dreng skal de blot sidde paa en Tøstage. Underligt er det ikke, at det blev en talrig og haardfør Slægt, for hvis Hænder det groede. Slægtens ejendommeligste Særkende blev det, at alt hvad den rørte ved, fik Liv og Vækst.

Drengen bar længe Mærke af den klægede Jord; som lille var han klam i det og havde krumme Ben. Men han voksede af det og blev en dygtig Jordarbejder; med ham tager Dyrkningen af Landet sin Begyndelse. Det at han ingen Far havde, sysselsatte ham meget og blev hans Livs store og frugtbare Problem. I sin Fritid skabte han en hel Religion over det.

Han var ikke god at bides med ude i det fri; i Arbejdet havde han ikke sin Lige. Men sin Kvinde laa han under for. Navnet Mand siges at hidrøre fra, at han, naar Kvinden havde drevet ham hjemme fra med sin skarpe Kæft, plejede at gaa hidende omkring og sværge paa, at han var Mand i sit Hus. Endnu den Dag i Dag har adskillige af Slægtens Mænd ondt ved at begaa sig over for deres Kvinder.

x x

En Gren af Slægten slog sig ned paa den øde Kyst oppe ved Kattegat og grundlagde „Løget". Det var i de Tider, da Skov og Lunge endnu gjorde Landet uvejsomt; og den kom søværts til. Stenrevet, hvor Mændene lagde til med Baade og løftede Kvinder og Børn fra Borde, ligger der endnu; hvide Havfugle skiftes Nat og Dag til at markere Stedet – og har gjort gennem Aarhundreder.

Denne Gren havde i fremtrædende Grad Slægtens typiske Hovedtræk: to

First page of the manuscript for Nexø's Ditte Menneskebarn, *published 1917–1921 (courtesy of Det Kongelige Bibliotek, Copenhagen)*

Ditte's mother–comparable to the evil stepmother in many a folktale–is an agent of destruction and unhappiness. Ditte, however, endures; once she even has the vision of a utopian existence, but she is never able to find her way back to that sacred ground. Eventually she gives in to the enticement of one of her fellow servants and becomes pregnant.

Ditte then moves to the big city–a move from very nearly medieval conditions to the industrial age. Ditte, like so many poor woment of the time, becomes a slave of the sewing machine, that instrument by which clothes were made for the upper classes, with very little payment going to those who produced them. Ditte, however, has a big heart, and she attempts to help those who suffer. She is the embodiment of the nurturing, motherly nature but, worn out by hard work, she dies at the age of twenty-five.

Her child, too, has died; he was stealing coal at the harbor to help his family, and was run over by a train. The workers of Copenhagen recognize that he is a martyr for their social cause, and the night Ditte lies dying, they march through the streets to advance the message of justice. The death of her child has become a symbolic call to arms.

Unlike Pelle, Ditte is hardly aware of the political and ideological implications of her life. Pelle is the idealistic politician, and she is the pure-hearted woman as martyred saint. In this book, Pelle is the recipient of the author's harsh criticism, whereas Ditte is elevated to a sphere of untainted innocence. Morten, who was Pelle's best friend in *Pelle Erobreren,* now emerges as Pelle's severest critic, for Pelle (whom the reader only encounters briefly) has now betrayed his earlier ideals.

One may wonder about the evident changes in Nexø's worldview between *Pelle Erobreren* and *Ditte Menneskebarn.* Much had happened, of course: World War I had ravaged Europe; the revolution in Russia had changed the political map drastically; and Nexø's own marital situation–a divorce from Margrethe Thomsen in 1913 and a new marriage the same year, to Grete Frydenlund Hansen–may have inspired him to reexamine his social philosophy.

Although *Ditte Menneskebarn* may seem less invigorating and inspiring than *Pelle Erobreren,* it offers a gritty realism that is absent in *Pelle Erobreren.* Perhaps childhood in the countryside is more real in *Ditte Menneskebarn* than in *Pelle Erobreren,* but when the protagonists move to the big city, *Pelle Erobreren,* in spite of the description of life in the slum district of the Arc, loses in verisimilitude to *Ditte Menneskebarn.* The Arc is a wonderfully symbolic representation of the plight of the poor, but that plight is captured with much more vivid realism in *Ditte Menneskebarn.*

Nexø had continued to write short stories as he worked on *Pelle Erobreren* and *Ditte Menneskebarn.* Those texts tend to fall into two categories, realistic glimpses of the downtrodden and parables that voiced Nexø's political convictions. The former tend to be more artistically satisfying than the latter, but unquestionably the parables express the aging Nexø's seething anger with capitalism and, what he deemed to be worse, the hypocrisies of the compromising social democrats.

The realistic texts optimistically capture the plight of those who are exploited by individuals or by society and who, in very different ways, are brought to rebel against that exploitation. In "En Strandvasker" (Awash, 1918), a well-to-do farmer's widow is taken advantage of by a ne'er-do-well. She eventually realizes she has been had, and when he returns after a long absence, she ends his life. The key phrase with which Nexø defines her decision to do so is: "hun var ikke Fatalist længer" (she was no longer a fatalist).

That phrase captures the essence of Nexø's worldview, one that the *folkehøjskole* as well as the labor movement had led him to believe in: fatalism is a defense mechanism on the part of the downtrodden, for if anything can happen, one can expect the worst and endure it. Fatalism gives strength–the strength Lasse had and that which made him a protector of Pelle–but the flip side of that coin is that whatever one suffers is accepted as a part of the human condition, as something that is inevitable and unavoidable, and thus no attempt is made to change it. It is that attitude that Nexø combats with the conclusion of "En Strandvasker."

In "Murene" (The Walls, 1907), a cobbler stabs the wealthy fat investor who has transformed the open land into a cityscape; the cobbler does so because he instinctively but justifiably sees that investor as a symbol of capitalism. The story suggests that the poor think allegorically or symbolically and act thereon. Another story, "Idioten" (The Idiot, 1908), which seems to be a personal recollection, tells of a young man, not very bright, who works for a farmer who exploits and abuses him, keeping him in check by letting him have all the cheap liquor he wants. One night the narrator finds the "idiot" passed out, and he empties the boy's bottle of liquor. When the young man revives, the farmer cannot control him, and eventually he burns down the farm. The narrator, typically, does not regret his intervention; the farmer got what he deserved. These rebellions on the part of the proletariat are, of course, not made for the sake of a cause, but are instinctive. Nevertheless, Nexø repeatedly tells stories demonstrating that the downtrodden, though their rebellion may be muted and barely conscious, harbor the right instincts.

Cover for a Russian edition of Nexø's stories, published in 1923

In "Et Møde" (An Encounter, 1910), Nexø makes it painfully clear that he believes that capitalism is sick and vampiric; it is represented by a ghoulish man who has no hands and no need of hands, for he controls machines that carry out his commands. This monster voices his goals with brutal clarity: "Mit Maal er at samle det hele paa én Haand—én eneste forstaar De—og gøre hele den øvrige Verden til Proletarer" (My intentions are to gather everything on one hand—only one, you see—and to reduce the rest of humanity into a proletariat). Other parables, such as "Guds Søn" (God's Son, 1921) or "Stærke Hans og den røde Fane" (Strong Hans and the Red Banner, 1937), suggest that Nexø's fears were alleviated by his firm trust in the exploited masses to awaken and fight the evils of their oppressors. Many stories and parables give evidence of that belief, but these two indicate that Nexø continued to operate within those frames of reference that he knew so well from his childhood. The title character of "Guds Søn" is the proletarian who will fight for humanity so that this world, once again, will become an early paradise. "Stærke Hans og den røde Fane" refers clearly to folklore, to the magic tale, in which the undaunted hero, so often poor, manages to rescue the realm, save all, and then be rewarded with half the kingdom and the princess, so that "they can live happily ever after." In Nexø's scenario, "they" would surely include all the inhabitants of the realm.

In 1922 Nexø traveled to the Soviet Union and found what he wanted—a society in which the leaders were committed to the proletariat. Nexø described the world that he thought he saw, and he was convinced that the Soviet Union was moving toward a utopian state. Nexø, who felt that the labor movement in Western Europe had let the masses down, craved a symbol for the promised land he desired so vehemently. For Nexø the Russian Revolution of 1918 had become a determining event, one that foreshadowed a society that would guarantee peace, joyful work, personal happiness, justice, and equality. In *Mod Dagningen: Skildringer fra Rusland* (Toward the Dawn: Pictures from Russia, 1923), Nexø voiced his exuberant approval of the Soviet Union under its leader, Lenin, as a nation that was striving with courage and joy toward an earthly utopia. The reaction of the bourgeois press in Denmark was chilly.

During these years Nexø was active in leftist politics in Denmark. Various factions were constantly warring, but in 1923 the Danish Communist Party was founded, and Nexø joined it. In spite of his enthusiasm for the Soviet Union, and even though he hailed Karl Marx as a visionary, he had read little more by Marx than *The Communist Manifesto* (1848). Nexø's Marxism was an instinctive, emotional commitment, and one that hardly could be harnessed by dogma. Consequently, it is not difficult for the theoretical Marxist critic to find heresies and inconsistencies in Nexø's writings.

In 1923 Nexø exiled himself to Germany for a seven-year stay. He divorced Grete, his second wife, in 1924, and in 1925 he married Johanna May. During those years he was hard-pressed for money to sustain himself; his attempt to establish a proletarian publishing house met with failure. Nevertheless, he seemed to enjoy living in a country larger than Denmark. He felt respected and treated with a sense of decency, even by the bourgeoisie, in spite of the fact that he espoused the cause of the revolutionaries. Pressed by economic concerns, he managed to get on better terms with the Danish Social Democrats and wrote for their newspapers. Despite their previous animosity toward each other, because Nexø was a powerful figure for social reform, the Danish Social Democrats arranged a celebration in 1929 for his sixtieth birthday.

In 1929, coinciding with the celebration in his honor, Nexø published *Midt i en Jerntid* (translated as *In God's Land,* 1933). It is a novel that looks back to the decadent days during World War I, when hopeful capitalists-to-be tried to exploit the economic situation for their own benefit. The book includes flashes of Nexø's genius where secondary characters are concerned–as in his depictions of an old war veteran and an opportunistic minister–but it remains a pedestrian account of greed and ethical failure on the part of a gifted man, the farmer Jens Vorup, who gradually comes to embody all the flaws of capitalism. In the end, the farmer has to realize that he has run one risk too many and is now bankrupt. That bankruptcy is both a material and a spiritual one, but it seems to foreshadow a redemption and the rebirth of a chastened and better man.

That ending for the novel is, however, barely believable–and even Nexø's comrade-in-political-arms, the novelist Hans Kirk, lambasted its lack of artistic quality. One of its major flaws is that Jens Vorup's wife, Marie, who is an intelligent woman in search of a fulfillment that her husband cannot give her, at the end emerges as a shrew who fails to understand her husband's sincere attempt to start anew. An interesting woman is let down by her creator, a sign of Nexø's ambivalent view of women.

In 1930 Nexø moved back to Denmark, and even though he and his wife found the Danish provinces so inhospitable that they soon moved to Copenhagen, he would undoubtedly have felt less comfortable in Germany, which in the early 1930s was experiencing the rise of Nazism. Nexø's power as an author was reinforced when Adolf Hitler's regime, upon ascending to power in 1933, quickly banned Nexø's works.

Nexø emerged as an adamant opponent of Fascism and Nazism; he became a tireless panelist at international conferences advocating peace and opposition to the forces of repression. As always, during those years he drew his strength from his undaunted belief in the Soviet Union as a bulwark against capitalistic barbarism–and after Lenin's death, Joseph Stalin became Nexø's ideal statesman. In *To Verdener: Tanker og Indtryk fra en Ruslandsrejse* (Two Worlds: Thoughts and Impressions from a Russian Journey, 1934), Nexø triumphantly lets the Western world know about the remarkable social progress in the Soviet Union. Not even the notorious Moscow trials in 1934, engineered by Stalin to remove old comrades from their seats of power, could shake Nexø's trust in his chosen, ideal society. For the believer, the unbeliever's criticism is betrayal. That Nexø was a man of political clout was brought home again after he had attended an antifascist conference in Spain in 1937. Spain was in the midst of a bloody civil war between leftists and fascists. A Danish contingent that went to the aid of the Left called themselves "the Nexø brigade."

Cover for Nexø's 1926 collection of poems

During the 1930s, Nexø proved that he had not lost his skills as a writer. He wrote a four-volume memoir comprised of *Et lille Kræ* (The Little Critter, 1932; extracts translated as "Reminiscences," 1946), *Under aaben Himmel* (1935; extracts, including passages from *Et lille Kræ*, translated as "Under the Open Sky," 1938), *For Lud og koldt Vand* (Dire Straits, 1937), and *Vejs Ende* (The End of the Road, 1939) that are touchingly free of ideological dogma. His life, from his childhood in Copenhagen to his vagabond days on the beaches of Spain, is recounted in a vivid and charming fashion. The memoirs, which only go up to his year in Spain, once again reinforce the impression that those early years were invaluable for the man and the author. When he continued his memoirs, albeit fictionally, in *Morten hin Røde: En Erindringsroman* (Morten the Red: An Autobiographical Novel, 3 volumes, 1945–1957), the joy and exuberance of the previous autobiographical series are entirely absent. Being engaged in a political struggle seemed to have taken its toll.

In the preface to his memoirs, Nexø professes that his writing is an attempt to combat chaos. Nexø, of course, defines chaos ideologically and socially, but chaos may also be a factor to be reckoned with psychologically, for example, in dangerous women who will not stand by their spouses. That combat with chaos was to reemerge on several fronts in *Morten hin Røde.*

Nexø could not keep quiet when he saw what he deemed to be injustice and misrepresentation, and he made himself immensely unpopular when he rose in defense of the Soviet Union during the so-called Winter War of 1939 between Finland and the Soviet Union. Nexø considered the Finnish government to be fascist, but in Denmark, as elsewhere in Scandinavia, Finland was seen as a small, defenseless, but courageous nation being subdued by a superpower.

The Danes were not kind to their famous–now infamous–countryman. A minister arranged a book burning of Nexø's works, and some voices in parliament suggested that his yearly subvention from the state be canceled. On 9 April 1940 Denmark was invaded by Nazi Germany, and according to library records, Nexø's books were suddenly in great demand. In 1941, when Hitler made the Napoleonic mistake of invading the Soviet Union, the Danish police were ordered to round up all members of the Communist Party. It is telling with regard to the ideological bent of the police that they interned many more citizens than were on the official list of communist sympathizers. Nexø was temporarily detained. He was eventually released, but the press was forbidden to refer to him. The occupation forces grew more repressive as the resistance to the German presence gained strength, and a new wave of arrests hit the country. Nexø's name was on the list of those to be arrested again, but he and his family had managed to make a timely exit to neutral Sweden. From there, he went to his beloved Soviet Union.

In 1945 Denmark could once again rejoice in freedom, and at that point the Soviet Union, a partner-in-arms with England and the United States, was probably more popular in Denmark than ever before or since. When Nexø returned to his native country, he was greeted as a hero; in fact, huge masses assembled in Copenhagen to pay tribute to him, and among them were the leaders of the Social Democrats. A reconciliation of antagonists seemed to be in the offing.

Ideas were even floated of a common Social Democrat-Communist front, but apparently Nexø was profoundly suspicious of any such plans. His misgivings about the Social Democrats were brought into the open when he published the first volume of *Morten hin Røde.* A few days later, the first free election was held, one in which the Communist Party gained more seats in parliament than ever before or after.

Nexø had made it clear that he was working on an ambitious project, a trilogy he called the "span of a bridge" (*Brobuen*) from *Pelle Erobreren* and *Ditte Menneske-*

barn to the forthcoming *Morten hin Røde.* That masterful plan, dealing with the dreams and achievements of the Danish proletariat, was about to see its completion.

If readers eager for the excitement of *Pelle Erobreren* or the profound compassion of *Ditte Menneskebarn* hastened to buy *Morten hin Røde,* they were very likely deeply disappointed. The narrative sweep, the ability to capture a milieu–be it the countryside or the big city– and an interest in characters who have no ideological or allegorical bearing were gone. If the reader shared Nexø's interest in the internal history of the Social Democrats from 1917 to the late 1930s or wanted to know the details of Nexø's two failed marriages, the book–and its ensuing two volumes–might evoke some interest, but artistically *Morten hin Røde* was a failure.

Morten hin Røde does, however, capture Nexø's ideological journey. In *Pelle Erobreren,* Nexø may cast some suspicious glances at his protagonist, but Pelle seems to realize that he has failed, and he redeems himself. Pelle and Morten are close friends, and they celebrate together at the end of the book. In *Ditte Menneskebarn* Pelle is merely mentioned by Morten, but he is a leader of the Social Democrats, whom Morten has learned to despise. In *Morten hin Røde,* Morten and Pelle are antagonists, and the scenes in which Pelle appears show him to be a corrupt politician who is willing to sell out to capitalism.

It may seem that Nexø is judging his various authorial selves–and rejecting some of those from the past. He seems to be rejecting that earlier self who knew how to invoke biblical myth and narrative sweep, as well as the delight in storytelling to be found in folklore, for the sake of a painstaking and painful recording of his strong misgivings about the Social Democrats and the women whom he divorced. Nexø apparently felt that both his party and his wives had gravely betrayed him. To the reader's relief, Nexø, while in Germany, finally found the woman who was right for him, but his third marriage seems utterly bourgeois.

One wishes that the conclusion of the envisioned trilogy would have been a crowning, visionary work, but it is exactly the opposite, for the grand mythical vistas of *Pelle Erobreren* and *Ditte Menneskebarn* have given way to a placid realism and a personal perspective that will annoy most readers. Even those readers who may share Nexø's disgust with the corrupt Pelles of this world and with workers' parties that move rightward may find the book lacking, for it can scarcely inspire them to mount the barricades against capitalistic oppression.

The drabness of the novel is saddening. In *Erindringer,* Nexø had admitted that *Bildung* (becoming cultured) is a process that is scarcely ever completed:

Min egen Trang til at vende og krænge Forteelserne har hængt nøje sammen med Manglen paa Ro og Harmoni, med Ufordrageligheden i mit Indre. Man stiller Fænomenerne under Krydsforhør for at finde et Mæglingsgrundlag for alle de fortvivlede Forsøg paa at stifte Fred.

(My own need to turn over and over various phenomena is deeply connected with my lack of harmony and peace of mind. One cross-examines phenomena in order to find a basis for a middle ground, in desperate attempts to find peace.)

Touchingly, Nexø uses the adverb *desperately,* and once again, the truthful author lets his reader know that he is not an omniscient prophet. If only space had been given to a subtext in *Morten hin Røde,* the novel might have been a fascinating study of a leftist who simultaneously believes in and doubts his cause.

In December 1945, Nexø published *Breve til en Landsmand* (Letters to a Countryman), which made it very clear that he felt that the Social Democrats had aided the Germans and betrayed their voters. The working class in Denmark at that point all voted for the Social Democrats; even though the party had lost some popularity, the women and men who belonged to labor remained loyalists; after all, the party had given them the eight-hour workday and decent old-age pensions. In short, Nexø's proletariat existed no longer, but consisted more of well-fed and economically secure people who were hoping to live in nice little homes surrounded by neatly tended gardens—exactly as Pelle had envisioned for his people in the ending of Nexø's first major novel. It is hardly difficult to grasp that the Danish workers had little use for Nexø's denunciation of the party that had allowed them their social move up toward the ranks of the bourgeoisie. This move, however, seemed to Nexø to be an embodiment of treacherous social democratic scheming.

Public opinion once again turned against Nexø. Conservatives raged against his getting a lifelong honorarium from the state. The escalation of the Cold War did not improve matters, especially not since Nexø—nearly eighty years old—defended the Soviet invasion of Czechoslovakia in 1948. The Danish press trumpeted that Nexø was an old man who was losing his mind and had lost his artistic abilities.

In 1951 Nexø managed once again to anger the bourgeois press of Denmark by moving to Radebeul, a suburb of Dresden, in what was then a part of the German Democratic Republic (East Germany). Nexø's friend and biographer, Børge Houmann, has pointed out that the main reason for Nexø's move was that he was old and needed to live in a gentler

FJORD MODERN CLASSICS NO. 4

*Cover for the 1991 translation of the second volume
of Nexø's* Pelle Erobreren

climate. Whether that was the true reason for Nexø's decision to move south is hard to know, but Nexø had earlier found it liberating to leave bourgeois Denmark. Nexø died in Radebeul on 1 June 1954.

After the fall of the Berlin Wall, streets named for Nexø in the former East German Republic were given other names, and the Nexø museum in Radebeul was dismantled. These measures signify ideological acts based on a rejection of the social philosophy Nexø espoused, not a judgment on his skills as a writer.

Authors of Nexø's ilk, those who are passionately involved in the cause of the downtrodden, tend to fare poorly in the literary opinion of bourgeois countries. Commonly, they are complimented for their literary skills, but then they are pitied for their social involvement, which makes them betray their art for the sake of propaganda. That critical judgment may be true of some authors, but in Nexø's case—in spite of his last works—it was his social indignation, or rather wrath, that let him speak so eloquently about the plight of the poor. Indignation was for him inspiration.

Nexø's works have attracted critics of a leftist bent. One such is Houmann, former editor of the Danish Communist daily, *Land og Folk* (Land and People), who for years researched Nexø's life and career, edited his letters and articles, and finally wrote an impressive three-volume biography, which, in spanning Nexø's life, could also serve as a social history of Denmark. Houmann's work is invaluable for any Nexø scholar. Although Houmann's discussion of Nexø's works is not strictly analytical, within the last twenty years several studies of Nexø's two major novels have been published by critics of various orientations. His excellent short stories and his early novels, however, still have not been given the critical attention they deserve. In spite of the unevenness of Nexø's works, his artistic reputation rests securely on his several masterpieces, small and large.

Letters:

Breve fra Martin Andersen Nexø, 3 volumes, edited by Børge Houmann (Copenhagen: Gyldendal, 1969–1972).

Bibliography:

Børge Houmann, *Martin Andersen Nexø bibliography,* 2 volumes (Odense: Forlaget Sirius, 1961, 1967).

Biography:

Børge Houmann, *Martin Andersen Nexø og hans samtid,* 3 volumes (Copenhagen: Gyldendal, 1981–1988).

References:

Anker Gemzøe, *Pelle Erobreren: En historisk analyse* (Copenhagen: Vinten, 1975);

Børge Houmann, ed., *Af en ung mands papirer* (Århus: Sirius, 1968);

Houmann, ed., *Omkring Pelle Erobreren* (Copenhagen: Hans Reitzel, 1975);

Faith and Niels Ingwersen, *Quests for a Promised Land* (Westport, Conn. & London: Greenwood Press, 1984);

Johan Fjord Jensen, "Efterskrift" in *Pelle Erobreren II* (Copenhagen: Gyldendal, 1965), pp. 521–529;

Jacqueline Le Bras-Barret, *Martin Andersen Nexø–écrivain du prolétariat* (Paris: Lettres Modernes Minard, 1969);

Georg Lukács, "Dichtung aus der Solidaritet," in *Omkring Pelle Erobreren,* edited by Houmann (Copenhagen: Hans Reitzel, 1975), pp. 290–299;

"Martin Andersen Nexø: A Symposium," *Scandinavica* 8 (Spring 1969): 121–135;

Lars Peter Rømhild, "Eventyr litteraturhistorisk set," *Meddelelser fra Dansklærerforeningen* (May 1976): 145–155;

Harry Slochower, "On Martin Andersen Nexø's *Pelle the Conqueror,*" in his *Mythopoesis: Myth Patterns in the Literary Classics* (Detroit: Wayne State University Press, 1970), pp. 284–289;

Slochower, "Socialist Humanism: Martin Andersen Nexø's *Pelle the Conqueror,*" in his *Three Ways of Modern Man* (New York: International Publishers, 1937), pp. 105–144;

Henrik Yde, *Det grundtvigske i Martin Andersen Nexøs liv,* 2 volumes (Copenhagen: Vindrose, 1991).

Papers:

Martin Andersen Nexø's manuscripts and other papers are located at Det Kongelige Bibliotek (The Royal Library), Copenhagen; and the Deutsche Akademie der Künste, Berlin.

Henrik Nordbrandt

(21 March 1945 –)

Thomas Bredsdorff
University of Copenhagen

BOOKS: *Digte* (Copenhagen: Gyldendal, 1966)–
includes "Afbrydelse" and "Trappesang," translated by Nadia Christensen and Alexander Taylor
as "Disconnection" and "Stairsong," in *Contemporary Danish Poetry: An Anthology,* edited by Line
Jensen and others (Copenhagen: Gyldendal / Boston: Twayne, 1977), pp. 288–289;

Miniaturer (Copenhagen: Gyldendal, 1967)–includes
"Tyske soldatergrave," translated by Christensen
as "German Soldiers' Graves," in *Contemporary
Danish Poetry: An Anthology,* edited by Jensen and
others (Copenhagen: Gyldendal / Boston:
Twayne, 1977), p. 290;

Sangen om den fortryllede skov, illustrated by Jørgen Boberg
(Copenhagen: Galerie Passepartout, 1967);

Syvsoverne (Copenhagen: Gyldendal, 1969)–includes
"Til en dødsmaske," translated by Christensen as
"To a Death Mask," in *Contemporary Danish Poetry:
An Anthology,* edited by Jensen and others (Copen-
hagen: Gyldendal / Boston: Twayne, 1977), p.
290; "Verden med musen uden hende," trans-
lated by Gay Brewer and Thomas Bredsdorff as
"The World With the Muse Without Her," in
West Wind Review: The Sixteenth Anthology, edited by
Gillian E. Gillette (Ashland: Southern Oregon
State College, 1997), p. 38;

Omgivelser (Copenhagen: Gyldendal, 1972)–includes
"Når et menneske dør," "Narkose," and "I en asi-
atisk landsby," translated by Christensen as
"When a person dies," "Anaesthesia," and "In an
Asian Village," in *Contemporary Danish Poetry: An
Anthology,* edited by Jensen and others (Copen-
hagen: Gyldendal / Boston: Twayne, 1977), pp.
291–293;

Opbrud og ankomster (Copenhagen: Gyldendal, 1974)–
includes "Baklava," "Byzantium," "Et gravpor-
træt," and "Borgerkrig," translated by Christensen and Taylor as "Baklava," "Byzantium," "A
Funeral Portrait," and "Civil War," in *Contemporary
Danish Poetry: An Anthology,* edited by Jensen and

*Henrik Nordbrandt in 1988 (photograph by Rigmor Mydtskov;
courtesy of Gyldendal Publishers)*

others (Copenhagen: Gyldendal / Boston:
Twayne, 1977), pp. 292–295;

Ode til blæksprutten og andre kærlighedsdigte (Copenhagen:
Gyldendal, 1975);

Glas (Copenhagen: Gyldendal, 1976)–includes "Parikia,"
translated by Nordbrant and "Taberne," translated by Taylor as "The Losers," in *Seventeen Danish Poets: A Bilingual Anthology of Contemporary Danish
Poetry,* edited by Niels Ingwersen (Lincoln, Nebr.:
Windflower Press, 1981), pp. 96–99;

Istid: Digte (Copenhagen: Gyldendal, 1977)–includes
"Slægtninge," translated by Brewer and Breds-
dorff as "Relatives," *Cumberland Poetry Review,* 17
(Spring 1998): 37–38;

Guds hus (Copenhagen: Augustinus, 1977); translated by Nordbrandt and Taylor as *God's House* (Copenhagen: Augustinius / Willimantic, Conn.: Curbstone Press, 1979);

Breve fra en ottoman: Indtryk fra Tyrkiet og Grækenland (Copenhagen: Gyldendal, 1978);

Rosen fra Lesbos: Et udvalg, edited, with a foreword, by Nordbrandt and Asger Schnack (Copenhagen: Swing, 1979);

Spøgelseslege: Digte (Copenhagen: Gyldendal, 1979)—includes "Digt mod Bert Brecht" and "Polifobi," translated by Taylor as "Poem against Bert Brecht" and "Poliphobia," in *Seventeen Danish Poets: A Bilingual Anthology of Contemporary Danish Poetry,* edited by Ingwersen (Lincoln, Nebr.: Windflower Press, 1981), pp. 100–103;

Forsvar for vinden under døren (Copenhagen: Gyldendal, 1980);

Udvalgte digte, edited, with a foreword, by Inger Christensen and Erik C. Lindgren (Copenhagen: Gyldendal, 1981);

Armenia: Digte (Copenhagen: Gyldendal, 1982); translated by Nordbrandt and Taylor as *Armenia* (Willimantic, Conn.: Curbstone Press, 1984);

Finckelsteins blodige bazar: En agentroman (Copenhagen: Gyldendal, 1983);

84 digte (Copenhagen: Gyldendal, 1984)—includes "Kvikstøv," translated by Thomas Satterlee as "Mercury," *Literary Review,* 39 (Spring 1996): 335;

Violinbyggernes by (Copenhagen: Gyldendal, 1985)—includes "Carducci," translated by Satterlee as "Carducci," *Prairie Schooner,* 71 (Summer 1997): 101–102;

Håndens skælven i november: Digte (Copenhagen: Brøndum, 1986);

Under mausolæet (Copenhagen: Gyldendal, 1987)—includes "Skruen," translated by Satterlee as "The Screw," *Scandinavian Review,* 86, no. 3 (1998–1999): 78; "Bødlens Klage," translated by Satterlee as "The Hangman's Lament," *Prairie Schooner,* 71 (Summer 1997): 100–101;

Nissen flytter med (Copenhagen: Gyldendal, 1988);

Vandspejlet (Copenhagen: Gyldendal, 1989)—includes "To digte met cikader," translated by Satterlee as "Two Poems with Cicadas," *Osiris,* 43 (Winter 1996): 8;

Tifanfaya: Roman (Copenhagen: Dansklærerforeningen/ Gyldendal, 1990);

Glemmesteder (Copenhagen: Brøndum, 1991)—includes "Guld findes der hvor man graver etter det," translated by Satterlee as "There is gold where you dig for it," *Osiris,* 43 (Winter 1996): 6;

Støvets tyngde (Copenhagen: Brøndum, 1992)—includes "Korsvege," translated by Satterlee as "Cross-

roads," *Osiris,* 43 (Winter 1996): 10; "A," "Ordet," and "Tøbrod," translated by Satterlee as "A," "The Word," and "Thaw," *International Poetry Review,* 21 (1995): 53–55;

Den elektriske mus, illustrated by Flemming Quist Møller (Copenhagen: Gyldendal, 1993);

Ormene ved himlens port (Copenhagen: Gyldendal, 1995)—includes "Biler," "Hjemvendt," "Finks," "Borte/ væk," "Bærestol," and "Tanger," translated by Satterlee as "Cars," "Coming Home," "Fink's," "Gone/Away," "Rickshaw," and "Tangiers," *Seneca Review,* 28 (Fall 1998): 24–29; "Digt," "Ved indgangen," and "Pragmata," translated by Satterlee as "Poem," "At the Gate," and "Pragmatic," *Exchanges,* 8 (Spring 1997): 70–77; "Aftensol" and "Sensommer, 1991," translated by Satterlee as "Evening Sun" and "Late Summer, 1991," *Scandinavian Review,* 86, no. 3 (1998–1999): 78–79;

Ruzname: Dagbog, 4.marts 1995 – 4.marts 1996 (Copenhagen: Brøndum/Aschehoug, 1996);

Drømmebroer (Copenhagen: Gyldendal, 1998).

Editions in English: *Necropolis: 12 Poems [by] Henrik Nordbrandt; Childhood Landscapes: 9 drawings [by] Jørgen Boberg,* translated by Nadia Christensen (N.p.: P. Augustinus, 1977);

Selected Poems, translated by Alexander Taylor (Willimantic, Conn.: Curbstone Press, 1978);

"The Hangman's Complaint," translated by Thomas Satterlee, *Prairie Schooner,* 71, no. 2 (1997): pp. 100–101.

OTHER: "Gammel mand i meditation," in *Eksempler,* edited by Pelle Gudmundsen-Holmgreen (Copenhagen: Wilhelm Hansen, 1972);

Historier om Hodja, edited by Nordbrandt (Copenhagen: Lindhardt & Ringhof, 1973);

Richard Bach, *Jonathan Levingston Havmåge,* translated by Nordbrandt (Copenhagen: Lindhardt & Ringhof, 1973);

Svend Nielsen, *Opstigning mod Akseki,* text by Nordbrandt (Copenhagen: Samfundet Til Udgivelse af Dansk Musik, 1989);

Damelår og andre specialiteter: En Tyrkisk kogebog, edited by Nordbrandt and Hans Jørgen Brøndum (Copenhagen: Brøndum/Aschehoug, 1994).

Henrik Nordbrandt is a major poet, prominent not only within his own generation but among Danish poets of the entire twentieth century. The few prose books he has published are competent works; they include two volumes of essays, a political thriller, two children's books, a cookbook, and a diary, but poetry is by far the most important part of Nordbrandt's output. Taking Danish modernism of the 1960s as his point of departure, dominated as it was by elaborate metaphorical invention, he soon developed his own distinct voice, choosing freely from among the various poetic idioms that have dominated Scandinavian, European, and American poetry since the eighteenth century, combining symbolic, allegorical, and metaphorical techniques into an individualistic blend that he has made the vehicle of the joy and pain of love, the pain and joy of melancholy, and what might be called a certain metaphysics of absence.

Henrik Nordbrandt was born in Frederiksberg on 21 March 1945. The son of Poul Erik Nordbrandt, a captain in the Danish Marine Corps who was bound by clerical duties at headquarters from nine to five, and Greta Marie Werchmeister Nordbrandt, who was a county administrator, Nordbrandt had a sheltered middle-class upbringing in a Copenhagen home. During his childhood he suffered from protracted ear, nose, and throat infections—one reason he has been attracted to dry Mediterranean countries ever since his first short visit to Greece in 1966, about the time his first volume of poetry was published. The following year Nordbrandt dropped out of college and returned to Greece to settle—or rather to stay for some time, since the idea of "settling" seems to go against his grain. In 1967 Nordbrandt married Martha Birgitta Keiding, from whom he was divorced in 1970. In 1977 he married Anneli Fuchs. For several years after 1970 he lived on various Greek islands, and then in Vélez-Málaga in Spain. The past several years he has lived near Bodrum in southwestern Turkey.

Apart from the agreeable climate, another attraction of the southern countries, so Nordbrandt claims, is the light. In an essay (published in the Danish weekly *Information,* 8 September 1995) written in Turkey, he gave an allegorical account of the kind of luminosity he prefers, and why:

Herodot blev født et sted i nærheden. Lidt over 300 km borte gik Sokrates rundt og udformede et livssyn, der i sin essens var en tankes spejlbillede af det samme landskab: Lys her, skygge der, ingen tusmørke, ingen ynglepladser for irrationalitetens dæmoner.

(Herodotus was born not far from here. A little more than three hundred kilometers away Socrates modeled an outlook which basically reflects this very landscape: light here, shadow there, and no twilight in between, no breeding ground for the demons of irrationality.)

In his poetry Nordbrandt has been able to combine this preference for classical clarity with a modern, even postmodern, sense of the center either having fallen apart or never having been there. One of his allegories for the

decentered personality is in a poem set in, and titled, "Troy," from the collection *Glas* (Glass, 1976):

Hver dag er jeg en anden end den foregående
og rykker dag for dag ind i mørket:
Dem jeg var står foran mig i en lang række
de nærmeste endnu hyllet i halvmørke
de lidt fjernere ude i lyset, kastende skygge

(Each day I am someone different than the day before
and day by day I move further into darkness:
Before me is a long line of people I have been—
those nearest still wrapped in twilight,
those farther away, in the light, casting shadows.)

In the poem Nordbrandt pursues the image for a while, elaborating on the notion of the persona moving backward into the dark or, rather, the persons from behind him moving forward through the persona, "Skikkelsen i midten, der spærrer udsynet" (the figure in the middle that blocks the view), who keeps those behind from learning from the mistakes of those ahead. The allegory of the disrupted personality then culminates in a series of paradoxes, visualizing and historicizing the outlook thus created:

Jeg er på en gang Helena og hellenerne
roerne, der ror de udskårne skibsstævne ind i dagningen
og hver enkelt roer, der lænket til sin åre
ror med følelsen af aldrig nogensinde at røre sig af stedet.

(I am Helen and, at the same time, the Hellenes
the rowers who row the carved prows into daybreak
and each separate rower who, chained to his oar,
rows with the feeling of never getting anywhere at all.)

Nordbrandt is not a philosophical poet, despite showing a metapoetic attitude—expressing misgivings about the possibilities of representation—in his poetry. He also provides persuasive images of what being in love is like, particularly love that is doomed, not because it is unrequited but because it remains an essentially one-way affair, as in these lines in "Vores kærlighed er som Byzantium," from the collection of poems *Ode til blæksprutten og andre kærlighedsdigte* (Ode to the Cuttle-fish and Other Love Poems, 1975): "Vores kærlighed er som Byzantium / må have været / den sidste aften" (Our love is like Byzantium / must have been / on the last evening) begins one such poem of doomed love. It ends: "Når jeg vender mig imod dig / i sengen, har jeg en følelse / af at træde ind i en kirke / der er blevet brændt ned / for længe siden" (When I turn toward you / in bed, I have a feeling / of stepping into a church / that was burned down long ago). Characteristic of Nordbrandt's handling of imagery is that he does not stop once the metaphor of the incinerated church is established, but rather elaborates on it:

> der er blevet brændt ned
> for længe siden
> og hvor kun mørket i ikonernes øjne
> er blevet tilbage
> fulde af de flammer, der udslettede dem
>
> (that was burned down long ago
> and where only the darkness in the eyes of the icons
> has remained
> filled with the flames
> which annihilated them.)

Although the love that Nordbrandt depicts in his poems is mostly of this less-than-happy kind, the air with which it is depicted is often one of peculiar satisfaction.

Another poem, also from the collection *Ode til blæksprutten,* titled "Agoraphilia," is only six lines long and depicts another seemingly impossible but real love. In it the speaker deplores the impossibility of the relationship by naming the contradictory aspects of it. Lines five and six run: "Du er disse seks linier / som jeg må begrænse mig til for ikke at skrige" (You are these six lines / to which I must confine myself in order not to scream). Here two of the poet's major concerns—love and metapoetry—combine and possibly explain the absence of despair, so remarkable in view of the desperate plights depicted here and elsewhere in Nordbrandt's love poetry; the ability to turn love's adversities into poetry makes up for the loss of the loved one.

The combination of the two elements—poetic statements about making love and making poetry—occur throughout Nordbrandt's poetry in all conceivable veins and combinations. An attractive and humorous version of the combination occurs in a poem from *Ode til blæksprutten* that begins: "Nu kan jeg ikke bruge dig længere" (Now I can no longer use you). The opening suggests abuse of some kind, while the second line specifies: "som en rose i mine kærlighedsdigte" (as a rose in my love poems). By now the reader may feel that here is a poet speaking who has been taught a lesson by feminists and is promising to change his ways. No longer will he belittle his significant other by turning her into nothing but a metaphor, because "Du er alt for stor, alt for smuk / og alt, alt for meget dig selv" (you are much too large, much too beautiful / and much, much too much yourself). What at this point, at the end of the first stanza, threatens to become a boring example of political, or poetical, correctness of a manner typical of the 1970s is blown to pieces in the second stanza: "Nu kan jeg faktisk kun se på dig / som man ser på en flod / der har fundet sit eget leje . . . "(Now I can really only look at you / as one looks at a river / which

has found its own bed . . .). In other words, I am sorry I have used you as a metaphor, now I shall use you as another metaphor, for such is language. What is left of the poem, another three stanzas, remains within this new metaphor, the river, along which the lovers paradoxically wind up in the end.

The melancholy of Nordbrandt's poetry has a tough masculine character, suggesting that even though joy may be better than grief, there is a certain pleasure involved in transforming grief over lost love into poetry. Elaborate imagery makes objects and themes come alive. Throughout Nordbrandt's poetry, however, there is a strong sense of the illusory nature of language and the beguiling nature of poetic images, as in his poem "vilde rosenbuske" (Wild Roses) from the collection *Syvsoverne* (The Sluggards, 1969): "de vilde rosenbuske i støvregnen / er ikke melankolske, er ikke / triste og ikke engang bedrøvede" (Wild roses in the drizzle / are not melancholy, not grieved / and not even sad). The speaker then asserts that it is impossible for the roses to feel and express the variety of emotions that roses have been forced to convey over the centuries, concluding by stating the philosophy of nonanthropomorphism proverbially—the wild roses in the drizzle, so the speaker insists, "er ikke i stand til at udtrykke noget / andet end det intet de udtrykker / og som er alt, alt hvad der / er at se i det tiltagende mørke" (are capable of expressing nothing / other than the nothing they express / which is all, all there is / to be seen in the growing dark). The traces of Wallace Stevens's poem "The Snow Man" (1923) are obvious; the parallel with Stevens's lines, "For the listener, who listens in the snow, / And, nothing himself, beholds / Nothing that is not there and the nothing that is" is anything but accidental. The poetry of Stevens and T. S. Eliot have been influences on Nordbrandt's poetry, as have the works of the influential twentieth-century Swedish poet Gunnar Ekelöf and the medieval Turkish poet Yunus Emre, most explicitly in Nordbrandt's collection of 1975, *Ode til blæksprutten.*

The theme of representation, prominent in Nordbrandt's poetry, is characterized by a constant shifting of presence and absence. The misgivings about the "metaphysics of presence," which dominate postmodern literary theory, have hardly exerted any influence on Nordbrandt. He attended the University of Copenhagen intermittently between 1967 and 1975, studying Chinese, Arabic, and Turkish, but he never earned a degree, nor has he engaged in academic studies or been under the influence of academe since. He has declared that he takes no interest in literary theory as practiced by academics and "language poets" in the United States and elsewhere.

Time and again, Nordbrandt in his poetry—and particularly in his love poetry—explores the theme of absence and presence. While practitioners of deconstructive theory, especially those who are followers of Jacques Derrida and Paul de Man, seem to deplore, with almost theological despair, the impossibility of bridging the abyss between nature and notion, between the thing and the word, Nordbrandt's poetry seems to thrive in that very abyss. For Nordbrandt, the absence of the thing (or the emotion, or the loved one) is the precondition for it to be put into words.

Thus, although Nordbrandt's poetry at first sight may appear Romantic and even symbolist in its exuberant use of imagery, it is in fact modernist and even postmodernist in its aversion to metaphysics and its embrace of metapoetics. Absence is no tragedy; on the contrary, absence is what makes poetry possible. One of many poems to prove that contention is "verden med musen uden hende" (translated as "The World With the Muse Without Her," 1997) from the collection *Syvsoverne:*

smukkest er du, når du er borte
og violerne i krystalvasen
ser ud som forårsvioler
som du engang har set på

og arrangeret så nænsomt
at aftenlyset som falder
i de visne violers blade

ikke længere spejler sig
i dine pupiller
men farver alting violblåt
undtagen dig, fordi du er borte.

(You are loveliest when absent
and violets in a crystal vase
look like spring violets
that you once admired

arranged so gently
that the evening light
on their leaves

no longer reflects
in your moist eyes,
but shades everything violet
except you, who are absent.)

Although written over the course of three decades, Nordbrandt's poetry has had the same characteristics from the beginning, and these have remained surprisingly constant over the years. There is one exception, however. In 1991 Nordbrandt suffered a loss in his private life that was of a different nature from all previous losses reflected in his poetry. His beloved Ingrid, with whom he had planned to settle down, sud-

HENRIK NORDBRANDT

Drømmebroer

DIGTE · GYLDENDAL

Cover for Nordbrandt's 1998 poetry collection

denly and unexpectedly died from thrombosis at the age of twenty-eight.

In the volume of poetry published that year, *Glemmesteder* (Places of Forgetting), Nordbrandt celebrated her memory and regretted her loss, much in the style and technique of his previous poetry. The loss seems not to have withered away, though. In *Ormene ved himlens port* (The Worms at the Gate of Heaven, 1995) four years later he returned to the experience in poems that seemed, for the first time, to turn "absence" from an aesthetic and philosophical category into an existentialist one.

While previous collections by Nordbrandt are offered as just that—collections of poems on his various recurrent themes—*Ormene ved himlens port* may be read as a mental journey from loss to recovery, a poetic version of *Trauerarbeit* (the work of mourning). The title of the volume refers to the epigraph, taken from some lines by

Stevens, which are spoken by the worms who carry the parts of Badroulbadour from her grave in their bellies: her eyes, her eyelashes, her lips, her feet.

At the beginning of the collection a handful of poems describe the shock of bereavement, the stopping of time, and the intersection of daily routines and irretrievable loss. A major achievement in this section is the poem Katamaranen (The Catamaran), the title of which refers to the topic of an everyday conversation a couple has; seeing a spot on the horizon, they good-naturedly bicker over what it might be, with the woman saying that it is a catamaran. Later, having taken leave of the woman, flying in an airplane over the stretch of water in question, the speaker triumphantly registers that he was right and she was wrong. Later, still concerned with the utterly pointless question, he calls her on the phone to let her know his triumph. The poem ends:

> Du tog ikke telefonen, erfarede jeg senere
> fordi du var død nogle timer før.
> I går overfløj jeg igen den sorte ting på vandet.
> Jeg ønskede at falde, men flyvet ville ikke.
> Du med din katamaran!
>
> (You did not answer the phone, I later learned
> because you had died a few hours earlier.
> Yesterday I flew over the black thing on the water once
>   again.
> I wished I could drop but the aircraft wouldn't.
> You and your catamaran!)

Simple and straightforward in tone, Nordbrandt's poem is like that of the "confessional poets" of the American 1950s and the Danish 1970s, yet different: austere, clean-cut, less garrulous, with the experience of absence and the stopping of time rendered in the temporal medium of language: one word after another.

The first part of *Ormene ved himlens port* is followed by poems of regression, in which an imaginary reversal of time leads back to a time prior to the loss. Then a series of poems follows, set in the present but filled to the brim with the imaginary and illusory presence of the one who has passed away:

> "Hej" råbte jeg, så det genlød
> i hele dalen
> og en krage fløj skrigende op.

> Det var ingen andre end dig
> der ikke svarede
> i hele verden.
>
> ("Hi!" I shouted. The whole
> valley resounded,
> a crow rose, shrieking.
> It was you of
> all people
> who didn't respond.)

The last phase of this extraordinary journey through mourning consists of poems of healing, where the present once again becomes real while the deceased loved one becomes an inner mental partner of the past. The thirty-nine poems of the volume *Ormene ved himlens port,* individually and consecutively, demonstrate a major poet on the point of entering his fourth decade of poetic activity, capable of sharpening and deepening his vision and voice. What might previously have been referred to as a "metaphysics of absence" has been superseded by a poetics of real physical absence.

The next volume, *Drømmebroer* (Dream Bridges, 1998), shows Nordbrandt once again in his full width, with teasing paradoxes, and allegories of life and love, displaying his remarkable ability to transform pain into poetry, here not least the pain of childhood, and always maintaining the distance: "Jeg ville ønske, det aldrig blev sommer / så sommeren altid var på vej" (I wish summer would never come / so summer would always be nearing), from the poem "På Israels Plads" (On Israel Square). The aging persona of the poems is able to visualize scenes from his early life exactly because they are gone forever and cannot be brought back to life. The metaphysics of absence has become a distinct realism.

References:

Thomas Bredsdorff, *Med andre ord: Om Henrik Nordbrandts poetiske sprog* (Copenhagen: Gyldendal, 1996);

Iben Holk, ed., *Ø: En bog om Henrik Nordbrandt* (Odense: Odense University Press, 1989);

Lasse Söderberg, "Henrik Nordbrandt," in *Danske digtere i det 20. århundrede,* third edition, 5 volumes, edited by Torben Brostrøm and Mette Winge (Copenhagen: Gad, 1980–1984), V: 308–315.

Jacob Paludan

(7 February 1896 – 26 September 1975)

Poul Houe
University of Minnesota

BOOKS: *De vestlige Veje* (Copenhagen: Aschehoug, 1922);

Urolige Sange (Copenhagen: Aschehoug, 1923);

Søgelys (Copenhagen: Hasselbalch, 1923);

En Vinter lang (Copenhagen: Hasselbalch, 1924);

Fugle omkring Fyret: Roman (Copenhagen: Hasselbalch, 1925); translated by Grace Isabel Colbron as *Birds around the Light* (New York & London: Putnam, 1928);

Markerne modnes: Roman (Copenhagen: Hasselbalch, 1927);

Feodor Jansens Jeremiader (Copenhagen: Hasselbalch, 1927);

Landet forude: Et Spil om Utopien, by Paludan and Erik Eberlin (Copenhagen: Hasselbalch, 1928);

Aaret rundt: Trykt og utrykt (Copenhagen: Hasselbalch, 1929);

Torden i Syd: Jørgen Stein og hans Kreds (Copenhagen: Hasselbalch, 1932);

Under Regnbuen: Jørgen Stein og hans Kreds (Copenhagen: Hasselbalch, 1933); enlarged as *Jørgen Stein: Torden i Syd–Under Regnbuen* (Copenhagen: Hasselbalch, 1937); translated by Carl Malmberg as *Jørgen Stein* (Madison, Milwaukee & London: University of Wisconsin Press, 1966);

Tanker og Bagtanker (Copenhagen: Hasselbalch, 1937);

Som om Intet var hændt: Kroniker og Essays (Copenhagen: Hasselbalch, 1938);

Fra Amerika til Danmark: Tre Romaner fra Tyverne (Copenhagen: Hasselbalch, 1943)–comprises *De vestlige Veje, Søgelys, En Vinter lang;*

Søgende Aander: Redegørelser og Debatter (Copenhagen: Hasselbalch, 1943; revised, 1944; revised again, 1950);

Smaa Apropos'er, illustrated by Arne Ungermann (Copenhagen: Hasselbalch, 1943);

Landluft, illustrated by Ib Andresen (Copenhagen: Hasselbalch, 1944);

Prosa. Korte Ting fra tyve Aar (Copenhagen: Hasselbalch, 1946);

Facetter (Copenhagen: Hasselbalch, 1947);

Skribenter paa Yderposter. Redegørelser og Debatter (Copenhagen: Hasselbalch, 1949; revised, 1951);

Han gik Ture (Copenhagen: Gyldendal, 1949; revised edition, Copenhagen: Hasselbalch, 1956);

Retur til Barndommen (Copenhagen: Hasselbalch, 1951);

Fremad til Nutiden (Copenhagen: Hasselbalch, 1953);

Sagt i Korthed: 1929-1954 (Copenhagen: Hasselbalch, 1954);

Bøger, Poeter og Stilister (Copenhagen: Selskabet Bogvennerne, 1954; revised, 1968);

Litterært Selskab: 32 Kronikker og Essays (Copenhagen: Hasselbalch, 1956);

Røgringe (Copenhagen: Hasselbalch, 1959);

En Kunstsamlers Meditationer (Copenhagen: Erik Paludans Boghandel, 1960);

Landeveje og Tankeveje: Udvalgte Essays fra tredive Aar, 3 volumes (Copenhagen: Hasselbalch, 1963);

Mørkeblaat og sort (Copenhagen: Hasselbalch, 1965);

Siden De spørger—og andre Omkredsninger (Copenhagen: Hasselbalch, 1968);

Her omkring hjørnet her blæser det mindre (Copenhagen: Hasselbalch, 1969);

Draabespil: Fjorten stykker, skrevet ved anledning (Copenhagen: Gyldendal, 1971);

Skrivebord og stjernehimmel: Essays i udvalg, edited by Niels Birger Wamberg (Copenhagen: Gyldendal, 1972);

I høstens månefase: Lidt af en livsregistrering (Copenhagen: Gyldendal, 1973);

Sløret sandhed: Lidt af en livsregistrering (Copenhagen: Gyldendal, 1974);

Vink fra en fjern virkelighed: Lidt af en livsregistrering (Copenhagen: Gyldendal, 1975);

Låsens klik: Lidt af en livsregistrering (Copenhagen: Gyldendal, 1976).

Editions and Collections: *Jacob Paludan, et udvalg,* edited by Hakon Stangerup (Copenhagen: Dansklærerforeningen/Gyldendal, 1951);

Jørgen Stein, 2 volumes, edited, with an afterword, by Anders Bodelsen (Copenhagen: Gyldendal, 1964);

Jacob Paludan (Collection of Jens Jacob Paludan)

Fugle omkring Fyret: Roman, edited, with an afterword and notes, by Henrik Oldenburg (Copenhagen: Det Danske Sprog-og Litteraturselskab/Borgen, 1997).

OTHER: Sinclair Lewis, *Dodsworth,* translated by Paludan (Copenhagen: Hagerup, 1930);

Kristmann Gudmundsson, *Livets Morgen,* translated by Paludan (Copenhagen: Hasselbalch, 1931);

Alexander Lernet-Holenia, *Baron Bagge,* translated, with a preface, by Paludan (Copenhagen: Schultz, 1937; revised edition, without the preface, Copenhagen: Skrifola, 1963);

Chr. Kongstad Petersens Tegninger, edited by Paludan, (Copenhagen: Hasselbalch, 1937);

Hasselbalchs Kultur-Bibliotek, volumes 1–285, Paludan, general editor (Copenhagen: Hasselbalch, 1941–1969);

Olle Hedberg, *Karsten Kirsewetter,* translated by Paludan (Copenhagen: Hasselbalch, 1941);

Engelske Essays, edited by Paludan (Copenhagen: Hasselbalch, 1941);

Orfeus i Bogverdenen: Udsagn om Musik, edited, with a preface, by Paludan (Copenhagen: Hasselbalch, 1941; enlarged, with a revised preface, 1957);

Paul Valéry, *Omkring Degas,* translated and edited by Paludan (Copenhagen: Hasselbalch, 1942);

*"Mit Kaktusvindu": Mandens blads satiriske kavalkade af * * ** (Copenhagen: Commodore, 1944);

Edwin Fischer, *Johann Sebastian Bach: En Studie,* translated by Paludan (Copenhagen: Wilhelm Hansen, 1948);

Johann Wolfgang von Goethe, *Af Maksimer og Refleksioner,* edited by Paludan (Copenhagen: Hasselbalch, 1949);

Edwin Fischer, *Musikalske Betragtninger,* translated by Paludan (Copenhagen: Wilhelm Hansen, 1950);

Aalborg i min Ungdoms Vaar (Ålborg: Aalborg Amtstidendes Bogtrykkeri, 1955);

Den lille Bog om de gode Glæder, edited by Paludan (Copenhagen: Thaning & Appel, 1956);

Flere gode Glæder, edited by Paludan (Copenhagen: Thaning & Appel, 1957);

Perler i dansk digtning, foreword by Paludan, illustrations by Peter Holm (Copenhagen: Branner & Korch, 1957);

Glæde over Danmark, edited by Paludan (Copenhagen: Thaning & Appel, 1958);

Herman Bang, *Tine,* edited, with an afterword, by Paludan (Copenhagen: Gyldendal, 1964);

Gyldne Snit om Digtning og Bøger i Citater fra Hasselbalchs Kultur-Bibliotek til Forlagets halvtreds-Aars Jubilæum, edited by Paludan (Copenhagen: Hasselbalch, 1966);

Oluf Høst, *Tegninger og notater,* introduction by Paludan (Copenhagen: Hasselbalch, 1966);

Johannes Holbek, *Tegninger,* edited, with a preface, by Paludan (Copenhagen: Hasselbalch, 1968);

Johannes Smith, *Liv og Tanke,* edited, with a preface, by Paludan (Copenhagen: Gyldendal, 1971);

Werner Svendsen, ed., *Danske essays,* afterword by Paludan (Copenhagen: Gyldendal, 1972).

Jacob Paludan was one of Denmark's foremost novelists in the 1920s, and the two parts of his novel, first published as *Torden i Syd: Jørgen Stein og hans Kreds* (1932) and *Under Regnbuen: Jørgen Stein og hans Kreds* (1933), then republished as *Jørgen Stein: Torden i Syd– Under Regnbuen* (1937; translated as *Jørgen Stein,* 1966), constitute one of the classics of twentieth-century Danish literature. Pursuant to his career as a novelist, Paludan became a prolific book editor and writer of literary essays and reviews. Initially published in newspapers, many of his essays reappeared in books over the years. In addition he had hundreds of feature articles and approximately 2,500 book reviews to his credit. While few of Paludan's novels have kept the public's attention, his position as one of Denmark's masters of the literary essay is solid. A conservative humanist with a keen awareness of modernity, he is an often troubled voice of tradition. As evidenced by his last books, a four-volume sequence of memoirs, his stylistic sensibility and compositional complexity occasionally transcend the values he advocates.

Stig Henning Jacob Puggaard Paludan was born in Copenhagen on 7 February 1896 to Julius Paludan and his wife, Gerda Puggaard. His father was appointed to the coveted chair in comparative literature at the University of Copenhagen after a strong conservative opposition had made the post unavailable to the famous radical critic Georg Brandes. The outcome made Julius Paludan an outcast in progressive cultural circles, an isolation that doubtless had an adverse effect on his entire family. While the older son, Hans Aage, who later became a university librarian, seems to have remained on favorable terms with both of his parents, the younger and shyer Jacob tended to turn inward and never overcame his strained relations with his parents and brother. Raised in an academic literary milieu, Jacob's own literary career went in another direction and was no more to his parents' liking than his final choice of Jacob for his personal name, rejecting "Stig," which they preferred. Although not unaffected by the conservative values of his home, Jacob Paludan was inclined from his early years to infuse received truths with an obstinate cultural radicalism akin to that of the heretic Brandes, in whose shadow the Paludans lived, as can be seen in his "Erindringsblade" (Pages of Recollection), reprinted in *Siden De spørger–og andre Omkredsninger* (Since You Ask–and Other Circlings, 1968).

Leaving prestigious Copenhagen schools with only a semi-academic degree, Paludan became an apprentice in pharmacies in the cities of Nykøbing Falster and Aalborg and received his own degree in pharmacy in 1918. After two years as a pharmacist in small provincial towns, he left the country in 1920 for an extended journey to Ecuador, where he worked as a pharmacist in Guayaquil, traveling later to New York, from where he returned to Denmark in 1921. In 1925, after yet another stint as a pharmacist, Paludan finally opted for a career as a professional writer. He wrote on cultural matters for leading Danish newspapers such as *Nationaltidende Dagens Nyheder, Politiken,* and *Aarhuus Stiftstidende* and in 1933 was granted the Finansloven (Finance Law), an annual pension for grant made by the Danish government. With the exception of an ill-advised attempt at poultry farming around 1930, Paludan gradually consolidated his position as a man of letters; in 1943 he married costume designer Vibeke Holck (divorced from Ib Andersen, the principal illustrator of Paludan's books), with whom he had one son, Jens Jacob Paludan.

Paludan's experiences in the United States and in the Danish provinces are the autobiographical extremes that shape his first three novels from the early 1920s, later collected in one volume titled *Fra Amerika til Danmark: Tre Romaner fra Tyverne* (From America to Denmark: Three Novels from the Twenties, 1943). The first novel, *De vestlige Veje* (On Western Roads, 1922), follows Harry Rasmussen, a Danish immigrant, in his failed attempts to carve out a future for himself in the American West. Disillusioned about his life in the new–and modern–world of cynical capitalism and greedy materialism and further dismayed by his final encounter with the metropolitan Babel of New York, Rasmussen is on the verge of returning home to Denmark at the end of the first novel. In the second novel, *Søgelys* (Search Light, 1923), the reader learns of Harry's suicide in America from Hugo Fahlen, a kindred spirit who does make it back to Denmark, albeit only to find his own existential rootlessness aggravated by the degree of Americanization he encounters there. Finally, in *En Vinter lang* (A Winter Long, 1924), where the setting is entirely Danish and largely provincial, the verdict about the changing cultural climate is quite clear. The modern condition of restlessness and shallowness in the midst of European culture has settled in for good.

Such cultural pessimism strikes the balance between tradition and modernity in most of Paludan's works. Only gradually, and never fully, do his early prose fictions reach their novelistic potential. The narrative lines are often strained by lyrical interruptions, and the human characterizations are disrupted by essayistic digressions; meanwhile, omniscient narrators seek to command the behavior of individuals or the outcome of situations. In his uneven struggle with the novelistic form, Paludan was driven by market opportunities as much as by personal and artistic inclinations. Paludan's

Dust jacket for Paludan's first novel, published in 1922, about the unhappy experiences of a Danish immigrant in the United States

spirit. In the end the construction collapses under its own weight. While the outcome of the story is indebted to narrative authority rather than general artistic autonomy, Paludan's next and more pessimistic novel, *Markerne modnes: Roman* (The Fields Ripen: Novel, 1927), proceeds to its conclusion without much undue interference from the narrator. As the fields in its title ripen, they also die, and the rich-boy/poor-boy story at its center turns out to be a story about an Aladdin character who succumbs to a modern Noureddin without much reservation.

After the publication of *Markerne modnes,* Paludan's reputation as a writer was established. His first three attempts at novels were, as the later composite title, *Fra Amerika til Danmark* suggests, essentially different pieces of a usual bildungsroman in geographical reverse. Their general appeal was limited, though not negligible, and public recognition was slow in coming. Børge Benthien, in *Jacob Paludan: En bibliografi* (1980), lists four editions of both *De vestlige Veje* (1922, 1943, 1959, and 1962) and *Søgelys* (1923, 1943, 1960 [reprinted 1962], and 1973) and five of *En Vinter lang* (1924, 1928, 1943, 1956, and 1972). The 1972 edition of the latter title was the largest run, issued in 10,000 copies or about the same number as the total copies for the former two titles, which were both translated into German (in addition to a Russian translation of *De vestlige Veje* in 1923). With the publication of *Fugle omkring Fyret,* Paludan made his public as well as critical breakthrough. This novel received ample and favorable reviews, and by 1977, according to Benthien, it had gone through eight editions and seventeen distinct printings, selling more than 93,100 copies and being translated into five languages, including English. If the success of this novel was not repeated entirely with *Markerne modnes,* which had fewer editions, reprints, and translations, the new book was still considered a major achievement by both readers and critics and helped to solidify Paludan's reputation as a writer.

By 1927 Paludan was finally in a position to take stock of his artistic capital and make his own choices for the future. It is likely that his hard-won battles with the novel genre gave him confidence to pursue the achievement that he reached with the publication of the two parts of *Jørgen Stein* in 1932 and 1933. It is also likely that his recent novelistic successes stimulated his desire to engage in more-agreeable modes of expression. Thus the author explicitly displays his developing idiosyncrasies in *Feodor Jansens Jeremiader* (Feodor Jansen's Jeremiads, 1927), which is a mixture of the novel, philosophical essay, and diatribe, and is thus uninhibited by the constraints of a full-fledged novel. In *Landet forude: Et Spil om Utopien* (The Land Ahead: A Play about Utopia, 1928) Paludan again called upon his friend Eberlin to

biographer, critic Henrik Oldenburg, has revealed the extent of his dependence on one Eric Eberlin, a dubious longtime friend, for narrative material and ideas. His lyrical vein, which yielded merely one forgettable collection of poems, *Urolige Sange* (Unquiet Songs, 1923), needed outlets in prose fiction in order to come to fruition. It was not, however, until Paludan abandoned the novel for shorter stories and literary essays that such a fortunate amalgamation of genres occurred.

In the meantime his apprenticeship as a novelist in the early 1920s had honed his narrative skills; while his recalcitrant treatment of the American version of modern evils—from journalism to feminism—in Danish culture continued to reverberate, his last three novels, written from the mid 1920s to early 1930s, take on a deeper psychology and a broader depiction of their times. The title *Fugle omkring Fyret: Roman* (1925; translated as *Birds around the Light,* 1928) signals how an obsessive attraction to a modern mirage, be it an individual or social attraction, can be a deadly pursuit. A monstrosity of a harbor construction on the west coast of Jutland threatens to corrupt the local culture and

assist him, this time with his first and only play. As in the novels preceding it, the dialogue in the play is poorly written, and it has proven too ethereal for stage production. Though in itself an impossible essay in dramatic form of utopian ideals, it is justified in the context of Paludan's beginning departure from the novel. His next work, *Aaret rundt: Trykt og utrykt* (All The Year Round: Printed and Unprinted, 1929), is the first of his many collections of short prose texts.

In the early 1930s, at the watershed moment of his career, Paludan published *Jørgen Stein,* his last, largest, and most debated novel. In the 1940s publishers and critics considered him to be the most important Danish novelist since the 1920s, and in the 1950s he was the most popular author among Danish high-school students. By 1980, according to Benthien, *Jørgen Stein* had been sold in ten Danish editions, well in excess of 118,000 copies, not to mention translations into German, Swedish, Polish, and English. Both volumes were republished in 1996 to commemorate the centennial of Paludan's birth. A novel about the decline of a family and its times, *Jørgen Stein* has been compared to Thomas Mann's *Buddenbrooks* (1901), and its title character has been said–by Ernst Frandsen–to belong to the antebellum generation that got an impossible start because it was too young to find solace in the past and too old to fit into the future. Jørgen Stein, who has enjoyed a sheltered childhood in the seat of a northern Jutland county (where in reality Eric Eberlin's father had been the mayor), is anxiously preparing to leave his sleepy hometown for boarding school in Aalborg, the modern industrial city (where the young Paludan had worked in a pharmacy). Then World War I breaks out. The immediate impact of this infinitely big event on Jørgen's infinitely small world is that he hopes it will give him an excuse to stay home and not go away to school. He actually goes to Aalborg but begins to dream of reclaiming his childhood. Unable to cope with reality, he turns his attention to memories of nature and values of the past that he considers more primeval and pristine.

While Paludan's indictment in *Jørgen Stein* of the emerging world of modernity, upstart bourgeoisie, and unfettered capitalism was well prepared for in Paludan's earlier work and may well echo the sentiments of Mann in *Buddenbrooks,* the psychological crisis and trauma experienced by the weak protagonist and his corrupted brother find their aesthetic counterpart in Marcel Proust, yet another of Paludan's influences. Jørgen is both a victor and a victim of the individualism he espouses. His distancing himself from contemporary reality gives him the illusion of being in control of the uncontrollable, but he remains ignorant of the price he pays for this control in terms of personal isolation, his

failures in relationships with women, and his social and existential incapacity in general. As his way of life proves increasingly out of time and place, Jørgen entrenches himself in his anachronisms. The dilemmas he reflects within the novel are inextricably linked to his individual shortcomings and are a matter of his personal neurosis rather than the collapse of a way of life.

In understanding the artistic design of the novel, it is critical that credence be given to the protagonist's preference for past and memory over present cultural values. As Lars-Olof Franzén has noted, the 1914 shots in Sarajevo that began World War I seem to resonate louder than the events of 1932, when the first part of the book was published. As the second volume (from 1933) unfolds, including chapters with such Proustian titles as "Paa Sporet af den tabte Tid" (Remembrance of Things Past), the lingering notes of the past appear to coincide with the emotional distance between the protagonist and his surroundings. As a result the text tends to dissolve into an essayistic format that Paludan would soon adopt as a means to describe the reality of his recollections. As reality outside Jørgen's memory is empty, so is nature, and Jørgen, who most needs to find life filled with meaning, chiefly feels the opposite. Both nature and art may offer temporary relief from cultural turmoil, as Lars Peter Rømhild has suggested, but cannot function independent of memory. Thus, rather than resolving Jørgen's predicament, art and nature throw it into relief. Rømhild sums up Jørgen's dilemma: "Jørgen er en Werther uden pistol, en Hamlet uden opgave, undtagen at finde og fastholde sig selv" (Jørgen is a Werther without a pistol, a Hamlet without a cause except to find and remain himself).

Autobiographical elements and references abound in most of Paludan's novels, not the least in *Jørgen Stein,* as Oldenburg has demonstrated. For the most part, however, these autobiographical elements are so intertwined with the artistic schemes of the novels that these works transcend the strictly autobiographical. The external characteristics of the character Jørgen Stein may resemble those of Paludan's friend Eberlin and the internal characteristics of Jørgen Stein may resemble those of Paludan himself, but the character as a whole encompasses attitudes more complex and less familiar than those identifiable with any living model. The good and homely girl with whom Jørgen eventually escapes the upheavals of modern life and (as did Paludan) settles down as a poultry farmer in the seclusion of the country becomes a symbol of a rather dubious resignation from culture. Altogether the interplay between artistic elements and Paludan's private circumstances tends to widen rather than narrow the range of his work.

Jacob Paludan

UNDER REGNBUEN

Jørgen Stein og hans Kreds

II

1933

Title page and opening page of the manuscript for the second part of Paludan's two-volume bildungsroman,
Jørgen Stein og hans Kreds *(Collection of Jens Jacob Paludan)*

Et Overblik.

Det tordnede i Syd paa fjerde Aar. Lang Tid havde man allerede haft til at vænne sig til den Tanke, at den Civilisation, man tilhørte, havde været bygget i Sand. Det kneb for mange at forstaa. Men nye Kuld kom til og fik deres modtageligste Aar præget af Bevidstheden om, at Krig var mulig, at den i høj Grad fandt Sted. Ordet fik for dem en anden, naturligere Klang, den var ingen Lærebogsglose, men jævn, daglig Virkelighed. Uden Forbløffelse saa' de unge inge et Værk udkomme, der hed „Den næste Krig" og skar det op ved Lyset af de stinkende Karbidlamper, der mange Steder maatte erstatte den sugtende Elektricitet og den helt forsvundne Petroleum. Man skulde ikke komme til at kede sig i Fremtiden; denne Krig var, lod det til, allerede nu nærmest at betragte som en stor, lærerig Generalprøve. Og vant som de var til Krig kunde deres Hjerner rumme Tanken, deres Nerver bære den.

De ældre havde det besværligere. De allerfleste havde villet forsværge, at den enkelte, gennemciviliserede, arislockende Borger overhovedet havde Evnen til Barbari i Behold. Man saa vel stadig en Dyd i det Mandsmod, der impulsivt forsvarer sit Lands Grænser, men i det uhyre Verdensopgør glemtes det efterhaanden, hvem der var skyldig og hvem krænket; begejstringsløst, prosaisk vedblev Myrderiet under Faner, hvis Ideal-Inskriptioner forlængst var ulæselige, og syntes blot at ernære sig af de mørke Sindsmagter, man havde tvivlet paa, men som engang vakt truede med at rende alt Kulturens Værk over Ende. Disse Ældre maatte i deres Livs Eftermiddag lære, at de havde gaaet i Søvne hele deres Livs Formiddag. Det var som at have indrettet sig hyggeligt i en sollys Vingaard og opdage, at det var en Slangerede. Begrebet Menneske, Begrebet Kultur maatte erkendes og defineres paany — men de var jo langt ude over den Alder, hvor Hjernesubstansens Smidighed tillader Dannelsen af ny Livsanskuelse. De ældre blev mærkelig meget ældre paa disse Aar; de traadte saa underlig hurtigt ud af Sammenhængen — som falske Læremestre, der efter Afsløringen man vende Hovedet bort. Man spurgte dem ikke længer med Tillid. Og Tiden før Krigen, der dog baade havde rummet Velvære og ideel Stræben, rykkede fjern, som var disse fire Aar en Afgrund, og antog for Erindringen et gistent Udseende. Under dens Overflade havde jo dog den Sygdom luret, der blev alle Tiders sværeste for den beboede Jord.

Mellem de to Slægtled, det detroniserede og det ukklimahsørede, levede et tredje — det, der lige havde naaet at faa en Mundsmag af Tiden før 1914, dens Aand og Stemning, dens Tro paa faste Værdier. —

Amtmand Stein i Havnstrup havde forlængst med en træt Haandbevægelse skudt Europakortet og de smaa Mærkeflag tilside. Han var af Natur tilbøjelig til at se idealistisk paa Begrebet Krig og indrømme den haarde Nødvendighed en bred Margin, men overfor Luftbombardementerne af London og den „tykke Bertha"s Beskydning af Paris med Projektiler, der gik 36 Kilometer op i Atmosfæren [for Nedslaget] stod han dog tavse. Og Hungerblokaden mod Tyskland! Neutrale

Paludan and his son, Jens Jacob, ca. 1961
(Collection of Jens Jacob Paludan)

Niels Barfoed, who has examined the connection between *Jørgen Stein* and the works of Mann, has also pointed out how Paludan ends his most grandiose version of the bildungsroman on a disturbingly modest note: "Jørgens slutpunkt–og nulpunkt–er simpelthen det sted, hvor Paludan omsider under ham ro" (Jørgen's end point–and his point zero–is simply the place where Paludan finally gives him rest). This sort of conclusion has had an increasing attraction for Danish novelists since the late nineteenth century. An often-mentioned Danish literary influence on Paludan is Henrik Pontoppidan, but a more important precursor is Pontoppidan's contemporary, Herman Bang, about whom Paludan wrote in an essay included in *Mørkeblaat og sort* (Dark Blue and Black, 1965). Other influences include the younger and more belligerent Johannes V. Jensen, the Swedish writer August Strindberg, and the Norwegian Knut Hamsun. Individual differences notwithstanding, these sources of inspiration share a touch of nihilism to which Paludan was inherently beholden, as was Tom Kristensen, his own great contemporary, to whose more daring novel *Hærværk* (Havoc, 1930) Paludan devotes a respectful essay in his collection *Draabespil: Fjorten stykker, skrevet ved anledning* (Drops Playing: Fourteen Pieces Written on Occasion, 1971).

The sense of loss and absence that permeates Paludan's novels carries over into many of his essays, in which reflection and depiction interact in various proportions but invariably on the persistent basis of memory. While this shorter genre forms the bulk of Paludan's body of work, it is far from uniform. Many essays border on articles, features, and reviews, and even on the five short stories published by the author at irregular intervals between 1945 and 1971. Unlike the stories, according to Rømhild, the essays are nonfiction, but unlike most of Paludan's articles they are both personal and subjective. Between impartiality and illusion, the essayistic style and tone are suggestive, often charged with metaphors and symbols. With his experiments with different points of view and modes of enunciation, Paludan made the transition between individual short-prose genres one of his trademarks. Part of the transition process is historical, indeed chronological. His essays before 1950 are chiefly descriptive and centered on landscapes, while during the 1950s their locus becomes reflection or abstraction, and after 1960 a more pronounced recollection. Recollection was always, if less significantly in the earlier years, Paludan's prerequisite for both description and reflection; although the two eventually separated, they never divorced.

What happens in the course of time is a gradual liberation from narrative restrictions, first within the novel, later within the alternate modes of shorter writing, then within the genre of the essay–and the attendant swarm of aphorisms and bon mots–and finally within the volumes of memoirs that were Paludan's most independent essayistic forms of memory. In the same way that he reluctantly approached a modernistic point zero by the end of his last novel, he later acknowledged the consequences of this countdown by attempting a personal alternative to the barren artistic conclusion of the novel as genre.

The essay that epitomizes Paludan's nature-descriptive period is "Naturfølelse" (Feeling for Nature), from the collection *Som om Intet var hændt: Kroniker og Essays* (As if Nothing Had Happened: Feuillitons and Essays, 1938). In both this essay and *Jørgen Stein,* as Lars-Olof Franzén has noted, nature here and now is nothing, whereas remembrance is everything. Memories are swept or shrouded in air (as Thorkild Hansen argued in his 1947 study of Paludan), while surroundings, moods, and all the rest are of little consequence, thus heightening the significance of the insignificant and the supremacy of the lyrical over the epic and dramatic. Human recollection alone makes sense of that which is not human. Other essays from the same collection attribute the same perception to localities in Copenhagen and northern Zealand that are particularly close to the author's heart. In "Høne og Hane" (Hen and Rooster), first published in 1930 and republished in 1939 as "Studier fra Hønsegaarden" (Studies from the Chicken Run) but not available in book form until the collection *Landluft* (Country Air, 1944), Paludan draws on his own experience as a poultry farmer but applies his observations about the animals to humans. Wry humor bordering on sarcasm is typical of such connections, but so is the leisurely evocation of other experiences past and present, intimated by the title of yet another collection from this period: *Han gik Ture* (He Took Walks, 1949).

Retur til Barndommen (Back to Childhood, 1951) and *Fremad til Nutiden* (Toward the Future, 1953) are works whose titles reflect the concerns for memory and time in Paludan's essays. Beginning with Copenhagen impressions in "Mørk Jul" (Dark Christmas), the former volume, for instance, includes such pieces as "Rejse-Notater" (Travel Notes), concerning Paludan's encounter with America in 1920–1921, and ends with a piece, "Barndommens Famlen" (The Stumbling of Childhood), comprising recollections of his earliest years.

In *Litterært Selskab: 32 Kronikker og Essays* (Literary Company: 32 Feuillitions and Essays, 1956) the subjects of Paludan's recollection are cultural personalities, most of them modern humanists to his liking. The spiritual and antimaterialistic profiles of these *Wahlverwandtschaften* (elective affinities) allude to different sides of the author's basic credos. Harald Kidde is noted for his metaphysical bent; Johannes Hohlenberg for his revisionist critique of Brandes's influence and that of *Det moderne Gennembrud* (the modern breakthrough) on Danish literature; Martin A. Hansen for his modernity rooted in local mores; Fyodor Dostoyevsky for his irrational view of humans and his Paludanian view of nature as mute; Simone Weil for her sense of suffering, death, and mysticism; Franz Werfel for his poetic defiance of death and vulgarity; and Aldous Huxley for his stylish celebration of culture–to mention but a few.

A piece about the 1920s in the same book, "Tyvernes Stjernbillede" (The Constellation in the Twenties), is a portrait of Paludan's own generation of writers. Another essay, "Kunstneren–Fortidsvrag eller Fremtidsvarsel?" (The Artist–A Wreck from the Past or a Warning about the Future?), quotes the British critic Herbert Read's description of the modern writer as "den eneste aktive Overlevende fra den humanitiske Traditions Vrag–og samtidig Pioner for en ny humanistisk Tradition" (the only active survivor from the wreck of the humanist tradition– and at the same time the pioneer of a humanist renewal). Although Paludan may have believed this dictum, he remained a skeptic. While recognizing the legacy of Johann Wolfgang von Goethe in the works of Mann, he cannot help finding the transition from classical to modern

humanism unsettling. His own assertion of spiritual values occurs in a constant battle with modern materialism.

The last essay in *Litterært Selskab,* titled "Jyllands vejr" (The Weather of Jutland), is less about people and more about nature and how people can use and reflect upon it as they combat their culture's pointless creed of progress. The piece is brimming with the kind of edges and dilemmas that herald Paludan's more reflective future. Bringing lost meaning back to memory in the form of memoirs depends on the joint efforts of intuition and will. Frequently this recovery comes gradually, as in "Ru Mosaik" (Callous Mosaics) and "Sgrafitti" (S-Graffiti), pieces in the 1965 collection *Mørkeblaat og sort* that are composed of edgy and wry aphoristic sentences. One typical sentence reads: "Drømte at jeg saa en Figur, der var en Mellemting mellem et Menneske og et Begreb" (Dreamt I saw a figure that was a cross between a human and a concept). Paludan often regretted that his interest in people was secondary to his interest in the empty frames that they and their actions left behind; for example, in the essay "En af de Sidste naturelsker" (One of the Last Nature Lovers) in *Draabespil* the illustrator Ib Andersen, a true lover of nature, is remembered by Paludan for hearing the raindrops playing on the window panes in the hospital where he is awaiting his death.

Although his last four books–*I høstens månefase* (In the Autumn Phase of the Moon, 1973), *Sløret sandhed* (Veiled Truth, 1974), *Vink fra en fjern virkelighed* (Hints from a Distant Reality, 1975), and *Låsens klik* (The Click of the Lock, 1976)–seemingly come closest to being his true memoirs, he tellingly gave them all the more casual subtitle *Lidt af en livsregistrering* (A Bit of a Life Recording). Johnny Kondrup has described how the discipline of chronological rendition and the central perspective in Paludan's earlier writings have here been replaced by less conventional forms and more parapsychological notions of time. Searching for closer contact with subconscious strata of the human subject, the author allows bold confessions of a sexual nature to intersect with direct reflections of his dreams. The only illusion of a total composition these works leave behind is that of a studied spontaneity. Situated between autobiography and fiction, the four volumes are at the same time reticent and revelatory documents.

Paludan was a founding member of Det Danske Akademi (The Danish Academy) and the recipient of many literary awards over the course of a long career. Among the most noteworthy awards he received were the Holberg Medal in 1939, the Golden Laurels of the Danish Bookseller's Association in 1951, the Adam Oehlenschläger Award in 1956, and the Grand Prize of Det Danske Akademi in 1964. Jacob Paludan died a respected man of Danish letters on 26 September 1975 in Birkerød, north of Copenhagen, where he had resided since 1931.

Interviews:

Kjeld Elfelt, *Skribenter i skriftestolen I* (Copenhagen: Privately printed, 1944), pp. 91–99;

Niels Birger Wamberg, *Samtaler med danske digtere* (Copenhagen: Gyldendal, 1968), pp. 20–33.

Bibliography:

Børge Benthien, *Jacob Paludan: En bibliografi* (Copenhagen: Gyldendal, 1980).

Biographies:

Orla Lundbo, *Jacob Paludan* (Copenhagen: Hasselbalch, 1943);

Henrik Oldenburg, *Jacob Paludan: Historien om et venskab* (Copenhagen: Gyldendal, 1984);

Oldenburg, *Janus fra Thisted: Jacob Paludan som romankunstner: En biografisk analyse* (Copenhagen: Gyldendal, 1988).

References:

Niels Barfoed, "'Jørgen Stein' und Thomas Mann: Eine Vergleichsstudie über einen Roman von Jacob Paludan," *Nerthus,* 3 (1972): 165–171;

Barfoed, "Pietetens helvede. Jacob Paludans *Jørgen Stein,*" in *Tilbageblik på 30'erne: Litteratur, teater, kulturdebat 1930–39,* edited by Hans Hertel (Copenhagen: Stig Vendelkær, 1967), pp. 37–50;

Ernst Frandsen, *Årgangen, der måtte snuble i starten,* second edition (Copenhagen: Gyldendal, 1965), pp. 9–79;

Lars-Olof Franzén, "Skotten i Sarajevo 1932," in his *Danska bilder: Punktnedslag i dansk litteratur 1880–1970* (Stockholm: Wahlström & Widstrand, 1971), pp. 83–91;

Emil Frederiksen, *Jacob Paludan* (Copenhagen: Gyldendal, 1966);

Frederiksen, "Jacob Paludan," in *Danske digtere i det 20. århundrede,* edited by Frederik Nielsen and Ole Restrup, volume 2 (Copenhagen: Gad, 1965), pp. 125–166;

Søren Hallar, *Jacob Paludan* (Copenhagen: Hasselbalch, 1927);

Thorkild Hansen, *Minder svøbt i Vejr: En Studie i Jacob Paludans Digtning* (Copenhagen: Hasselbalch, 1947);

Poul Houe, "Dråbespil og dråbespild," *Bogens Verden,* 78 (February 1996): 9–12;

Houe, *Fra Amerika til Danmark: På rejse gennem Jacob Paludans ungdomsromaner* (Copenhagen: Museum Tusculanum Press, 1993);

Houe, "Jacob Paludan og Eric Eberlins sceniske utopi," *Edda,* 94 (1994): 154–160;

Jørn Jessen, *Die Zeitkritik in den Romanen Jacob Paludans* (Kiel, Germany: Privately printed, 1974);

Johnny Kondrup, "Jacob Paludan," in his *Erindringens udveje: Studier i moderne dansk selvbiografi* (Valby: Amadeus, 1994), pp. 424–484;

Orla Lundbo, *"Fugle omkring Fyret,"* in *Danske Samfundsromaner fra Henrik Pontoppidan til Leck Fischer* (Copenhagen: J. H. Schultz, 1946), pp. 113–127;

Lundbo, ed., *Hilsen til Jacob Paludan paa Halvtredsaarsdagen den 7. februar 1946* (Copenhagen: Hasselbalch, 1946);

Peter Madsen, "Kontinuitetens abstrakte overvindelse," in *Tekstanalyser: Ideologikritiske tekster,* edited by Jørgen Holmgaard (Copenhagen: Munksgaard, 1973), pp. 200–215;

Felix Nørgaard, "Jacob Paludan," in *Danske digtere i det 20. århundrede,* volume 1, edited by Ernst Frandsen, (Copenhagen: Gad, 1951), pp. 331–352;

Marie Normann, "Hvorfor blev Jacob Paludan essayist? En rundtur til kunstnere og skrivende personligheder i Jacob Paludans forfatterskab 1921–33," *Danske Studier* (1990): 130–144;

Jens Overø, ed., *Jacob Paludan–Forfatter, farmaceut og Birkerødborger* (Birkerød: Birkerød Apotek, 1998);

Lars Peter Rømhild, "Jacob Paludan," in *Danske digtere i det 20. århundrede,* edited by Torben Brostrøm and Mette Winge, volume 2 (Copenhagen: Gad, 1981), pp. 61–75;

Rømhild, "Paludans erindring," *Bogens Verden,* 78 (February 1996): 4–8;

Lise Sørensen, "Jørgens Steins damer," in her *Digternes damer,* second edition (Copenhagen: Gyldendal, 1966), pp. 135–143;

Hakon Stangerup, "Jacob Paludan," in his *Den unge Litteratur: Essais* (Copenhagen: Hasselbalch, 1928), pp. 47–60;

Martin Zerlang and Henrik Reinvaldt, "Man kan ikke male ud over rammen. Om klassebevidsthed og karakterstruktur i Jacob Paludans *Jørgen Stein,*" in *Analyser af danske romaner,* edited by Jørgen Holmgaard, volume 3 (Copenhagen: Borgen, 1977), pp. 134–201.

Papers:

The major collections of Jacob Paludan's correspondence and manuscripts are in Det Kongelige Bibliotek (The Royal Library), Copenhagen, and at the Birkerød Bibliotek.

Leif Panduro

(18 April 1923 – 16 January 1977)

Lanae H. Isaacson

BOOKS: *Av, min guldtand* (Copenhagen: Hasselbalch, 1957);

Rend mig i traditionerne (Copenhagen: Hasselbalch, 1958); translated by Carl Malmberg as *Kick me in the Traditions* (New York: Eriksson-Taplinger, 1961);

De uanstændige (Copenhagen: Hasselbalch, 1960);

Øgledage (Copenhagen: Gyldendal, 1961);

Fern fra Danmark (Copenhagen: Gyldendal, 1963);

Fejltagelsen: Den korte og ufuldstændige beretning om tilfældet Marius Berg (Copenhagen: Gyldendal, 1964);

Den gale mand (Copenhagen: Gyldendal, 1965);

Vejen til Jylland (Copenhagen: Gyldendal, 1966); translated by Malmberg as *One of Our Millionaires Is Missing* (New York: Grove, 1967);

Lollypop og andre spil (Copenhagen: Gyldendal, 1966);

Farvel, Thomas, og andre TV-spil (Copenhagen: Gyldendal, 1968)—comprises *En af dagene; I stykker; Farvel, Thomas;*

Daniels anden verden (Copenhagen: Gyldendal, 1970);

Bella og Et godt liv: To TV-spil (Copenhagen: Gyldendal, 1971);

Rundt om Selma (Copenhagen: Gyldendal, 1971);

Vinduerne (Copenhagen: Gyldendal, 1971);

Amatørerne (Copenhagen: Gyldendal, 1972);

Selma, William og Benny: Tre TV-spil (Copenhagen: Gyldendal, 1972);

Den ubetænksomme elsker (Copenhagen: Gyldendal, 1973);

Den store bandit (Copenhagen: Brøndum, 1973);

Den bedste af alle verdener (Copenhagen: Gyldendal, 1974);

I Adams verden og Farvel, Thomas: To TV-spil (Copenhagen: Gyldendal, 1974);

Bertram og Lisa og Anne og Paul: To TV-spil (Copenhagen: Gyldendal, 1974);

Høfeber (Copenhagen: Gyldendal, 1975);

Hvilken virkelighed? Kulturkritiske og selvbiografiske artikler, edited by John Chr. Jørgensen (Copenhagen: Gyldendal, 1977);

Louises hus: TV-spil (Copenhagen: Gyldendal, 1977);

Leif Panduro (courtesy of Gyldendal Publishers)

Den ufuldendte dommer, edited by Jørgensen (Copenhagen: Gyldendal, 1986);

Bare det hele var anderledes: Noveller fra 1950'erne, afterword by Jørgensen (Copenhagen: Gyldendal, 1987);

Leif Panduro, edited by Niels Knudsen (Copenhagen: Gyldendal, 1988).

Editions and Collections: *Rundt om Selma,* edited by Henrik Lundgren (Copenhagen: Gyldendal/Dansklærerforeningen, 1977);

Et ordentligt kaos: Tekster, selected by Lisbeth Aasted and Eigil Christiansen (Herning: Systime, 1994);

Uro i forstderne–og andre noveller, edited by Jørn E. Albert (Copenhagen: Gyldendal, 1995).

PLAY PRODUCTIONS: *Gris på gaflen,* script by Panduro, Jesper Jensen, and Klaus Rifbjerg, Copenhagen, Studenterrevyen, 3 February 1962;

Kufferten, Copenhagen, Allescenen, 11 November 1962;

Kannibaler i kælderen, Copenhagen, Allescenen, 11 November 1962;

Jul i landsbyen–en svinehring, Copenhagen, 1967;

Bøh, sagde Tågehornet, produced by Panduro and Bent Christensen, Copenhagen, Det Ny Teater, 31 January 1970;

Regne med sol, by Panduro, Klaus Rifbjerg, and Benny Andersen, Copenhagen, Rønne Teater, 20 June 1975.

MOTION PICTURES: *Harry og kammertjeneren,* screenplay by Panduro and Bent Christensen, 1961;

Støvsugerbanden, screenplay by Panduro, 1962;

Hvad med os?, screenplay by Panduro, 1962;

Naboerne, screenplay by Panduro and Christensen, ASA Film, 1966;

Oktoberdage, screenplay by Panduro, Christensen, and John Gould, Laterna Films, 1966; re-released as *The Only Way,* 1970;

Spøgelsestoget, screenplay by Panduro and Christensen, 1976.

TELEVISION: *En af dagene,* produced and directed by Panduro and Palle Kjrulff-Schmidt, Danmarks Radio, 1963;

Farfar til Hest, script by Panduro, Danmarks Radio, 1966;

Ka' De li' østers?, series, scripts by Panduro and others, Danmarks Radio, 1967;

I Stykker, script by Panduro, Danmarks Radio, 1968;

Farvel, Thomas, script by Panduro, Danmarks Radio, 1968;

Bella, script by Panduro, Danmarks Radio, 1970;

Et godt liv, script by Panduro, Danmarks Radio, 1970;

Smuglerne, series, produced by Panduro and Bent Christensen, Danmarks Radio, 1970–1971;

Huset på Christianshavn, series, written by Panduro and others, Danmarks Radio, 1970–1977;

Rundt om Selma, script by Panduro, Danmarks Radio, 1971;

Hjemme hos William, script by Panduro, Danmarks Radio, 1971;

Søndagen og Benny, script by Panduro, Danmarks Radio, 1971;

I Adams verden, script by Panduro, Danmarks Radio, 1974;

Bertram og Lisa, script by Panduro, Danmarks Radio, 1975;

Anne og Paul, script by Panduro, Danmarks Radio, 1975;

Louises hus, produced by Panduro and Palle Kjærulff, Danmarks Radio, 1977.

RADIO: *Historien om Ambrosius,* script by Panduro, Danmarks Radio, 1956;

Skygger paa broen, script by Panduro, Danmarks Radio, 1957;

Lollypop eller Mit Navn er Jensen, script by Panduro, Danmarks Radio, 1960;

Hvor er mit hode? script by Panduro, Danmarks Radio, 1962;

Oscar og tyngdeloven, script by Panduro, Danmarks Radio, 1965;

Fortæsttelses-sagoen eller Jul i den blandede landhandel, script by Panduro, Danmarks Radio, 1968.

OTHER: *Om at vre ensom blandt mennesker* (Copenhagen: Byens Antikvariat & Mini-Antikvariat, 1973);

"Det er farligt at bo i Ringsted," in *Da jeg var barn: Kendte danskeres barndomserindringer,* edited by Ole Knudsen (Copenhagen: Aschehoug, 1997), pp. 401–412.

SELECTED PERIODICAL PUBLICATIONS–UNCOLLECTED: "Om at FORNY sig," *Politiken,* 17 October 1965;

"Ka' De li' østers?" *Politiken,* 8 October 1967.

A master of farce, Leif Panduro made his literary mark in novels, motion pictures, television, and radio drama–virtually every genre except critical essay and lyric poetry. Panduro's strengths as a writer lie in dramatic technique and in his portrayal of individuals–usually modern, conflicted souls caught in a tangled web of tradition and convention. Panduro's protagonists wage constant war against custom, propriety, and appearance; they inevitably lose the war–and themselves–because they have also participated in the social game from the start. The fleeting victories of Panduro's characters are couched in terms of a world they reject; they can offer no alternative to that world. Their own pasts doom their efforts to break free, even when freedom seems possible. As the literary critic Jens Kistrup has written,

Næsten hele Leif Panduros forfatterskab kreser omkring én bestemt menneskatype–et menneske, der er splittet, fordi det er bundet, bundet til et på forhånd fastlagt adfærds-mønster, bundet til en bor-

Panduro in 1963 (photograph by Gregers Nielsen)

gerlig livsform, bundet til sin egen fortid. Det er et menneske, der føler sig fanget i en fælde . . . et menneske på flugt fra sig selv—eller på flugt ind i sig selv.

(Nearly all of Leif Panduro's literary oeuvre focuses on a single type of individual—an individual who is split apart because he is bound, conjoined to a predetermined pattern of behavior, to a bourgeois form of life, to his own past. He is a person who feels himself caught in a trap . . . an individual fleeing himself—or into himself.)

Leif Thormod Panduro was born in the Frederiksberg area of Copenhagen on 18 April 1923; his parents, Aage Petersen and Anne Johanne Panduro, divorced soon after his birth, and, because of his mother's mental illness, Panduro spent the first years of "en belastende barndom" (a difficult childhood) in an orphanage (1924–1930). He later went to live with an uncle, Gregers Panduro, in Ringsted, an experience he described in the short narrative "Det er farligt at bo i Ringsted" (It Is Dangerous to Live in Ringsted, 1967); apparently, Panduro's youth in the town consisted of running various gauntlets between rival gangs, ferocious dogs, and dangers or pitfalls on every path. Somehow, Panduro negotiated his difficult childhood and received his middle school examination from Birkerød Kostskole (Birkerød Boarding School) in 1939. He took an apprenticeship in a hardware store and later worked as a pharmacist's assistant. During the war years, Panduro partic-

ipated in the Danish Resistance that executed his own Nazi-sympathizer father; Leif Panduro himself was accidentally shot in the stomach on Liberation Day, 5 May 1945, and suffered severe neuroses that inspired him to pursue both psychoanalysis and cathartic writing.

During World War II, Panduro also began to study dentistry; he entered the Tandlægehøjskolen (College of Dentistry) in Copenhagen in 1942 and received his degree in 1947. He married another dentist, Esther Larsen in 1948. Panduro established his first practice in Copenhagen. From 1952 to 1957 he practiced dentistry in Sweden, and from 1957 to 1962 he served as a school dentist in Esbjerg. In 1962 Panduro returned to Copenhagen, where he intermittently worked as an assistant for the College of Dentistry; he also contributed commentary and critiques to the journals and newspapers of the city.

Panduro's career as a dentist and his humorous first novel, *Av, min guldtand* (Oh, My Gold Tooth, 1957), about a provincial town as seen by its dentist, initially worked at cross-purposes to his own efforts toward a serious literary career. Panduro was branded a gifted amateur, "Den skrivende tandlge" (The writing dentist), and he faced a challenge overcoming the literary typecasting that *Av, min guldtand* inspired.

Panduro's radio plays *Historien om Ambrosius* (The Story of Ambrosius, 1956), *Skygger paa broen* (Shadows on the Bridge, 1957), and *Lollypop eller Mit Navn er Jensen*

(Lollypop or My Name Is Jensen, 1960), preceded his novel, and they suggest the author's more serious side—his concern with the split in the individual psyche and the tendency of the individual to avoid responsibility for his own actions. *Historien om Ambrosius* is an account of a simple man—Everyman—driven to suicide by a vicious slander campaign. *Skygger paa broen* draws on the occupation years in Denmark: a member of the Danish Resistance murders a Nazi and then tries to conceal the murder as a suicide. He becomes what he has tried to eliminate, and, realizing his own culpability, he kills himself. *Lollypop eller Mit Navn er Jensen,* Panduro's breakthrough in the radio-play genre, deals with the theme the Danish critics Torben Brostrøm and Jens Kistrup define as quintessential for Panduro's literary career: "det 'normale' menneskes konstant mislykkede kamp for at tilpasse sig et samfund, der vil dominere og dirigere ham" (the "normal" individual's continually unsuccessful struggle to adjust to a society that tries to dominate and direct him).

With *Rend mig i traditionerne* (1958; translated as *Kick me in the Traditions,* 1961), a work appearing nearly simultaneously with Klaus Rifbjerg's novel about puberty, *Den kroniske uskyld* (Chronic Innocence, 1958), and also strongly reflecting the influence of J. D. Salinger's *The Catcher in the Rye* (1951), Panduro portrays a troubled teen in rebellion against the entire adult world of conventions, traditions, and norms: David Dechel has landed in a Kafkaesque mental institution where adults seek to bury him (or, as they believe, cure him) with words. David had been slated to deliver an address on traditions during Alumni Day at his school; instead, he bolts the scene, abandoning his studies just before his final examinations. As a result, he is committed. At the mental institution David describes his family and school, all the adults who have led him to flee an adult world of words and paramount concerns for propriety: "Nej, hr., om jeg begriber voksne mennesker. At være voksen, det er sådan en sygdom i det indvortes. Den skyldes overdosering med det *rigtige!*" (No, sir, damned if I understand adults. To be an adult, that's such an inner disease. It's caused by overdosing with the *right thing!*). One thing becomes clear: David cannot rebel completely, he cannot destroy the adult world, because he has already accepted all the social trappings of that world; by his own admission David is part and parcel of the proper world, using words ("drivel") himself, even to the extent of addressing his reader formally:

> Det er det samme med mig. Jeg er sådan en pæn fyr at se til. Høflig og velopdragen og alt det der. Men hvis De kommer med alt for mange ord til mig, så kan jeg også gi' mig til at ryge i luften, at De ved det.

> (It's all the same with me. I look like such a nice guy. Polite and well brought up and all that. But if you come at me with way too many words, I'm likely to fly off the handle, so you'll know it.)

Much of David's protest is self-directed; only too clearly does he see the future—he will follow the path of his brother, Hugo, "for jeg er sådan en høflig fyr" (for I'm such a polite guy).

David still manages to poke a great deal of fun at adults: those in his family (his brother, Hugo; his stepfather, Fabby; his mother), those at school, and those in the mental hospital. David's account of waking up at the hospital to the successive, repetitious elation of one and all is telling: all the adults take David's return to "normalcy," his "reawakening" for granted; only David sees the event—and the farce of it all—as "noget værre roderi" (an awful mess). Importantly, the adults around David all rely on clichés that have lost any distinct meaning. David connects such phrases to adulthood and "normalcy," fearing he will be caught in "den fælde der hedder *voksenheden*" (that trap called *adulthood*), in the fate of conforming, of relying on words utterly devoid of idiosyncracy and emotion. Ironically, David has been on the path to conformity all along; his rebellion has nowhere to go.

In Panduro's next book, *De uanstændige* (The Indecent Ones, 1960), the young protagonist, Thomas Simonsen, a conventional, rather shy and proper young man, meets the wildly unconventional, completely abandoned family next door, the Thamms. Thomas's stern, severe father, "klippe-vægsansigtet" (stonewall-face) insists on clockwork precision, regularity, and conformity; his mother worships the god of Health. The Thamms, however, live in a chaotic, frenetic, albeit free, world: Conrad, the father, is an impractical visionary and dreamer who invents "kun idiotiske og ligegyldige ting: en kombineret øloplukker-og-fyldepen og en musikalsk dørlås" (only idiotic and trivial things: a combination beer opener-and-fountain pen and a musical doorlock); Edith, his wife, sunbathes in the nude and provides living space for her lover, Frederik, and Conrad's gay son, Eugene, who has recently lost his lover. The twins, Mikael (Mick) and Gudrun (Topsy), who are Thomas's age, both enchant and repel him, just as a fire or flame enchants and repels a young, inexperienced child. Tragically for Thomas, he will never be part of the Thamms' world; he can never hope to win Topsy from Mick and their amoral, incestuous, devil-may-care world; he realizes his dilemma from the start:

> Det var noget af et dilemma for Thomas. På een gang var han voldsomt tiltrukket og frastødt. . . . Han kunne

ikke placere dem i sin verden, fordi deres forhold til sig selv var helt anderledes, end han var vant til.

(It was something of a dilemma for Thomas. At one and the same time he was powerfully attracted and repulsed. . . . He could not place them in his world because their relationship was completely different from what he was used to.)

The outbreak of World War II lessens Thomas's emotional tension, leading him to a sharper, clearer reality in the chaos of war; for Thomas the war resolves the problems of his relationships with both Mick and Topsy. The conclusion of the war plunges Thomas back into the Thamms' labyrinth, spelling disaster for all three young people and a mystery for the reader: does Thomas actually murder Mick to win Topsy for himself? Or is the final shooting incident, which results in Mick's death, simply an accident? Although neither of these alternatives is made clear, Thomas returns to the home of his parents, "Og da han drejede om hjørnet ved den store snavset-hvide villa, der nu lå hen som en sodet ruin, vidste ham, at fremtiden var kommet" (And when he turned the corner by the large dirty-white villa, that now lay there as a sooty ruin, he knew that the future had arrived). When the character Thomas Simonsen, now an engineer, reappears twenty-six years later in *Amatørerne* (The Amateurs, 1972), he has acquiesced; now the model of propriety and convention, he is amazed by his own long-haired hippie son, David, a virtual stranger.

Panduro devoted much of his attention to the time in life when an individual's future is undetermined, when everything and everyone undergo examination and usually fail. Panduro's three novels *Rend mig i traditionerne, De uanstændige,* and *Øgledage* (Saurian Days, 1961) deal with puberty, what Kistrup terms as "det stadium af menneskets liv, hvor det er trådt ud af barnealderens uskyldigt ansvarsløse tilstand, men hvor det endnu ikke har kapituleret over for de voksnes vedtagne, regelbundne verden" (that stage of a person's life when he has stepped away from the innocent irresponsibility of childhood but still has not capitulated to the accepted rule-bound world of adults.)

The third novel of the series, *Øgledage,* is, according to Michael Bruun Andersen, "Panduros mest modernistiske roman i formsproget og samtidig den, der mest omfattende samler alle de temaer, der både før og siden stykkedes ud i resten af forfatterskabet" (Panduro's most modernistic novel in terms of language and at the same time [the work] that most conclusively contains all the themes that sooner or later appeared individually in the rest of [his] works). With *Øgledage* Panduro broke the bonds of the traditional novel, just as his protagonists generally try to break the bonds of

society to freedom, but, as Kistrup suggests, *Øgledage* finally focuses "om at acceptere–ikke verden, men sig selv, på godt og ondt, som den, man er, og med det, der har gjort én til den, man er" (on acceptance–not of the world but of oneself, for good or ill, as one is, and with [all] that has made one what one is). The work proved to be Panduro's only foray into surrealism.

In *Øgledage* another young man is doomed to fight against the "normalcy" of the adult world, to seek integration, this time by returning to what Panduro describes as "barndommens hav . . . sammen med sin nye kæreste Marie (childhood's sea . . . together with his new love, Marie). The novel begins with this same young man sitting on a toilet, graphically struggling to rid himself of "Fortid" (the past), the waste or blight of his past life, his cultural roots, and a terrible childhood, a conventional one that mars him from getting a girl of his own.

The young man suffers from oedipal and castration complexes, and he addresses a companion, an alter ego named Pluto, who characteristically (for Panduro) languishes in an insane asylum: "Med min ene hjernehalvdel betragter jeg dig, kære Pluto som værende syg, og med den anden betragter jeg verden som værende syg. Hvordan skal jeg kunne holde ud at bestå af to halvdele? (With one-half of my brain I consider you, dear Pluto, as being sick, and with the other I consider the world as being sick. How shall I be able to hold out consisting of two halves?).

In a sense, *Øgledage* revisits the conflict between culture and nature: Panduro recalls the writings of Jean-Jacques Rousseau in seeking a return to nature, a rejection of what Bruun Andersen termed "problemerne [som] stammer fra kulturen, det artificielle, og løses i naturen" (the problems [that] derive from culture, everything artificial, and are solved in nature). However, the return to nature, the entirely expressive efforts of the young man to wrest himself from culture–the adult world–by saying so, by a return to "barndommens by" (the childhood home) with Marie leave "den ødipale problematik" (the Oedipus problematic) intact. The problem is not what to say about the past but, as Jørgen Gustava Brandt has suggested, what to do about it: "som Panduro selv siger: fortidsknuder–vi alle bærer af dem" (as Panduro himself says: the knots of the past–we all bear them). Cutting the psychological ties of the past by verbal means will not work, although the young man of *Øgledage* plans such an act while acknowledging that his alter ego, Pluto, is part and parcel of his past and present identity:

Nu er det tid. Jeg forsvinder med hende i den store kloak og driver med hende på gødningsstrømmen til fortidshavet. Farvel fædre, farvel mødre. Somme tider

One of
Our
Millionaires
Is Missing
a novel by
Leif Panduro

Dust jacket for the 1967 translation by Carl Malmberg of Vejen til
Jylland *(1966)*

skal jeg nok huske jer. For I er jo også Plutos ophav.
Og han er også mig. Dav, mig.

(Now it's time. I disappear with her into the great
sewer and flow out with her on the stream of fertility
to the sea of the past. Farewell fathers, farewell mothers. Sometimes I'll remember you. For you're also
Pluto's source. And he's also me. Hi, to me.)

Panduro followed his surrealistic experiment
with the Identity Trilogy of *Fern fra Danmark* (Fern
from Denmark, 1963), *Fejltagelsen: Den korte og ufuldstændige beretning om tilfældet Marius Berg* (The Mistake:
The Short and Incomplete Account of the Case of
Marius Berg, 1964), and *Den gale mand* (The Crazy
Man, 1965). Each novel in the trilogy focuses on an
individual whose identity has been fractured, either
through loss of memory, hypochondria, or insanity.
Panduro's protagonists, Martin Fern, Marius Berg,
and Edvard Morner, are divided selves (divided by

suppression, sickness and insanity, respectively),
vainly trying to find their identity in a "gigantisk
splittelse . . . en næsten total skizofreni, som tilmed
postuleres som 'det normale'" (gigantic rift . . . a
nearly total schizophrenia which is also postulated to
be "the norm").

Fern has lost his memory–or suppressed it–and
he rejects the identity that "normal" people in a "normal" society posit for him; according to the literary
historian Johannes Møllehave, Fern represents "splittelse som fortrængning" (the rift as suppression).
Marius Berg, "splittelse som sygdom" (the rift as illness), interprets himself through hypochondria.
Edvard Morner, the protagonist of *Den gale mand* and
the embodiment of "splittelse som normalitet" (the
rift as normalcy), asserts his innocence of certain violent crimes (bomb attacks) and his unfair imprisonment. To Morner, society and "normal people" have
detained "den gale mand" (the wrong man)–a play
on the dual meaning in Danish of *gale* as wrong and
crazy. A shadow figure, an insane alter ego of Edvard
Morner, has created all the chaos rocking the "normal" world.

In his trilogy on identity, Panduro focuses on
those on the fringe of "normal" society while also
exploring the individual in search of identity lost.
Individual attempts to come to terms with the division and to integrate the divided self only collide
with the social order and bring the tortured individual to his knees, reinforcing his position of being out
of sync with a schizophrenic world, and ultimately,
"borte fra sig selv" (away from his self).

In his next novel, *Vejen til Jylland* (The Way to
Jutland, 1966; translated as *One of Our Millionaires is
Missing,* 1967), Panduro's protagonist, the wealthy
Danish American Fred S. Jonsson, revisits his childhood home only to discover it changed beyond recognition; what Jonsson remembered as a tranquil
rural and urban idyll has become "et surrealistisk
mareridt" (a surrealistic nightmare). In addition, Jonsson's entire visit becomes a carefully orchestrated
series of official meetings, hardly the intimate family
gatherings he envisioned. Jonsson abandons the official tour, striking out in the company of an old Texas
ranch hand named Classon, who is originally from
Sweden and who despises all Danes, and a young
boy named Rufus, who is on his way to Jutland. The
three manage to elude various frantic search parties
but never quite make it to Jutland. Panduro spins the
whole tale with tongue in cheek, certainly with more
levity than in his earlier novels.

Beginning in the 1960s Panduro made his mark
on the dramatic scene, particularly in movies, television, and radio plays. Panduro's notable talents for

replikken, reply and retort, were "a natural" for his success on the screen. In addition to the early radio plays *Historien om Ambrosius, Skygger paa broen,* and *Lollypop eller Mit Navn er Jensen,* Panduro pursued the theme of individual versus society in such radio dramas as *Hvor er mit hode?* (Where's my Head? 1962), *Oscar og tyngdeloven* (Oscar and the Law of Gravity, 1965), and *Fortsættelses-sagoen eller Jul i den blandede landhandel* (The Continuation Sago or Christmas in the Country General Store, 1968). Panduro also wrote two plays for the live theater, *Kufferten* (The Suitcase, 1962), a play reminiscent of the works of Samuel Beckett, about a man unable to rid himself of a large suitcase, and *Kannibaler i kælderen* (Cannibals in the Cellar, 1962), a Eugène Ionesco–style farce about polite society's tendency to hide—and hide from—negative forces within and without. In the 1960s Panduro wrote scripts for such motion pictures as *Harry og kammertjeneren* (Harry and the Chamber Servants, 1961), *Støvsugerbanden* (The Vacuum Cleaner Band, 1962), *Hvad med os?* (What about Us? 1962), *Nabærne* (The Neighbors, 1966), and *Oktoberdage* (October Days, 1966).

Panduro's debut as a writer for television came with *En af dagene* (One of these Days, 1963), a glance into a war-zone office in which a case file has gone missing and workers ruthlessly compete for advancement. With the television play *Farvel, Thomas* (Goodbye, Thomas, 1968) Panduro offers the viewer a picture of a salesman who has gone missing and lost his hold on life all because he insists that his wife has found someone else (he may have been the one to end the marriage, however). In the last painful scene Thomas seeks out his wife, falling on his knees before her, which is almost too much for the wife to manage.

The television play *Et godt liv* (A Good Life, 1970) examines life in terms of its value and relationships—or denied relationships—with others: Daniel, the owner of a shoe factory, looks forward to retirement in six years. His wife, Elise, urges him to enroll in an insurance program, and, as part of his acceptance, he must undergo a physical to determine whether he has "et godt liv," whether his life is something the insurance company can bank on in crassly financial terms. As it turns out, Daniel suffers from a brain tumor, and his life is of no "value"; he is not a good investment. The question thus turns from monetary value to quality of life: what kind of life has Daniel led?—one of missed opportunities and missing contact with those closest to him.

With *Et godt liv* and its forerunner, *Bella* (1970), Panduro found a special niche as a screenwriter. He wrote individual episodes for such television series as

Ka' De li' østers? (Do You Like Oysters?), *Smuglerne* (The Smugglers), and *Huset på Christianshavn* (The House in Christianshavn) as well as the scripts for such television plays as *Rundt om Selma* (Around Selma, 1971), *Hjemme hos William* (At Home with William, 1971), *Søndagen og Benny* (Sundays and Benny, 1971), *I Adams verden* (In Adam's World, 1974), the connected screenplays *Bertram og Lisa* (Bertram and Lisa, 1975) and *Anne og Paul* (Anne and Paul, 1975), and, finally, *Louises hus* (Louise's House, 1977), the story of a woman trapped in a life of desperation.

Panduro's work for television gave his career a second wind, also enabling him to demonstrate his mastery of modern dialogue. In his television scripts, from his debut, *En af dagene,* to the finale, *Louises hus,* Panduro examines a world where everything and everyone is bought and sold; where "mennesker en slags varer" (people [are] some sort of ware); where everyone must function well. What happens when we break down, when we cling to a lie to cover our "livs-og dødsangst" (fear of life and death) and our failure to function? Panduro repeatedly focuses on such a fate.

Panduro's screenplays represent a change from his exclusive focus on a single protagonist, an emergent individual unwilling to join the normalcy (or lunacy) of society but still preprogrammed by the past for such accommodation, for suppression of every emotion and idiosyncracy. With his screenplays Panduro offers a gallery of ordinary individuals, people whom the viewers would recognize; their stress and tension in a world where everything is not quite what it seems become palpable.

Awards and honors marked Panduro's career as a screenwriter. Such awards as the Critics' Prize (1963), the Danish Booksellers' Association Golden Laurels (1970), the Det Danske Academi (The Danish Academy) Prize for Literature (1971), the Holberg Medallion (1971), the Henri Nathansen Memorial Award (1973), and the Søren Gyldendal Prize (1975) all seem to suggest that Panduro was far more than the amateur dentist-cum-writer of *Av, min guldtand.* Panduro's considerable gifts for dialogue, for developed narrators, and for setting enabled him to capture much of the angst in "normal" society and within the hapless, socially hopeless individual who cannot mesh.

Panduro hardly abandoned the novel in his pursuit of a new dimension and a renewal through scriptwriting; in 1970 he wrote *Daniels anden verden,* depicting a "normal" man living in extreme fear of his father's insanity and his own possible inheritance of it. Daniel's acceptance of insanity and love in the person of Laila frees him from fear and sets him on a course to better health. Similarly, Sanna, the young psychotic girl in *Den ubetænksomme elsker* (The Inconsiderate Lover, 1973), regains her health through a love affair with a young doctor, Jakob Holme. What Panduro seems to suggest is that hard, cold society is sick to death; love heals the rift within the individual—and might even heal the world.

Vinduerne (The Windows, 1971) presents Marcus Lange, a conventional academic whose life seems to revolve around what he terms "Min hemmelighed" (my secret): Marcus is a voyeur, someone who considers his neighbors as actors and actresses carrying out a play for his benefit; his binoculars, the best money can buy, allow him to enjoy the best of all possible dramas, that of everyday people, "mine skuespillere" (my actors). Despite his intentions, Marcus ends up with far more than he bargained for: he becomes involved in the life of one of his "actresses," a young woman hiding from a violent husband, and he witnesses the violent death of her husband through an apparent act of self-defense; more sinisterly, Marcus's lover may have carried out the calculated murder of her own husband, cleverly providing herself with an alibi and first-class witness—not only is Marcus a voyeur, but he is also an actor in his neighbor's (lover's) play.

Alongside Marcus's role as harmless spectator of the human condition, another drama unfolds: one of his young students, Louise Thorsen, falls passionately in love with him—to the point of attempting suicide when he rejects her. Perhaps this drama is a bit too close for comfort. After all, Louise is taking all the initiative, pursuing the bland Marcus at every turn. Or perhaps Marcus's enjoyment of "min hemmelighed," of the actors and actresses he moves as pawns on an imaginary chessboard, allows him to escape to a fantasy world of his own imagination. Marcus crosses the line, however, by involving himself with his neighbor. In short, Marcus becomes a pawn. Panduro offers the reader intrigue in his descriptions of the dramas unfolding in and around Marcus Lange; Marcus's retreat from the frantic attention of Louise pairs with his involvement in the more sinister drama going on just next door.

Panduro's final novel, *Høfeber* (Hayfever, 1975), is like a ride on a carousel circling out of control. Both society and individuals have lost their bearings and guideposts; the results would be tragic if the world of *Høfeber* were not such a farce. The central character, the local judge, Hans Erling Herzberg of Hillerød, encounters what Johannes Møllehave describes as a "farce-galleri af psykotiske elskere og neurotiske embedsmænd, senile oldinge, hypermane forretningsfolk og afsindige funktionærer" (farcical

gallery of psychotic lovers and neurotic officials, senile old people, hypermanic businessmen, and insane functionaries). Herzberg manages to overlook his wife Elise's fling with a hypochondriac internist, Klaus Klausen, because of his own involvement with Lise K, the wife of a good friend, Herman K, who in turn has fallen for a male SAS (Scandinavian Airlines System) flight attendant and followed him to Stockholm. Lise K also pursues an affair on the side, with a millionaire. At this point the judge becomes the victim of various inexplicable attacks: he is sprayed with pepper and contracts an especially virulent form of hayfever. The judge's world is collapsing, disintegrating around him; he has no recourse for the changes as his world fills with a hilarious cast of characters.

Herzberg decides to "drop out," to fake a suicide and leave his roles in society and family life behind. His "death" by drowning, chronicled in the first chapter of *Høfeber*, purposely leads the reader astray, for Herzberg has simply left a chaotic world to "gå ud i byen" (go out on the town). Panduro is perhaps at his funniest, his most absurd, in *Høfeber*: in it, he thumbs his nose at a world run wild.

Panduro also wrote short stories, even before *Historien om Ambrosius* and *Av, min guldtand*. His farcical novellas appeared in the daily press and various journals and in collections such as *Den bedste af alle verdener* (The Best of all Worlds, 1974), which includes his short sketch of his childhood in Ringsted, "Det er farligt at bo i Ringsted." Panduro's prolific literary career concluded with a compilation of his articles on culture and his life, *Hvilken virkelighed? Kulturkritiske og selvbiografi artikler* (Which Reality? Culture-critical and Autobiographical Articles, 1977) and his final television play, *Louises hus*.

Leif Panduro died on 16 January 1977 in Asserbo, Denmark. Despite a late start as a writer and his early death, Panduro managed to secure a firm niche for himself as a novelist and a dramatist with particular talent for motion-picture and television scripts. Panduro's many awards attest to the quality of his work, and his popularity continues after his death, with several adaptations of his works released as motion pictures. In 1979 Edward Flemming wrote the screenplay for and directed *Rend mig i traditionerne,* a motion picture released in the United States as *Up Yours!;* Claus Plug wrote the screenplay for the movie version of *Den ubetænksomme elsker* (1982); *De uanstændige* was adapted by Flemming as a motion picture in 1983; and Annelise Hovmand directed the 1991 adaptation of *Høfeber.*

Panduro generally made use of traditional, classical forms of the novel, with the exception of "den enestående bog" (the exemplary book), *Øgledage.* His strength lies in his insightful portrayal of the modern individual caught in social and psychological webs woven by himself and his culture. Panduro's novels describing adolescence and young people growing up in an insane, oppressive world have become modern classics. *Rend mig i traditionerne, De uanstændige,* and *Øgledage* capture the dilemma of a young person faced with a normalcy verging on insanity and the suppression of feelings–actually unique identity– behind the conventions and clichés of an ominous adult world. The novel *Øgledage* frames the young individual's fate in surrealistic, experimental terms, also suggesting the future form of the novel. Panduro explores the rift in the individual, the inevitable and frightening loss of self, in his three identity novels, *Fern fra Danmark, Fejltagelsen,* and *Den gale mand.* In the 1960s and 1970s Panduro moved on again, using his talents for dialogue and drama to create pictures of the people next door, the ones whose "normal" lives conceal an angst only relieved by love. In *Vinduerne* Panduro depicts a man who retreats to his binoculars and loses control, leaving his imaginary world for the all-too-real one of his neighbor. In Panduro's final novel, *Høfeber,* the protagonist Hans Erling Herzberg leaves chaotic society and apparent propriety for anonymity. In all his works, Panduro succeeds in capturing the insanity of the modern world and depicting the struggles of individuals who risk their identity and, ultimately, their hold on a crazy, chaotic carousel.

Biographies:

John Chr. Jørgensen, *Leif Panduro: Radio, Film, Teater, TV* (Copenhagen: Borgen, 1973);

Orla Lundbo, *Panduro: Tæt på forfatterne* (Copenhagen: Gyldendal, 1973);

Birgitte Hesselaa, *Leif Panduro: Romaner, noveller, journalistik* (Copenhagen: Borgen, 1976);

Paul Hammerich, *Panduros verden* (Copenhagen: Forum, 1977).

References:

Michael Bruun Andersen, "Den indre øgle: Leif Panduro," in *Dansk Litteraturhistorie: Velfrdsstat og kulturkritik 1945–80,* volume 8 (Copenhagen: Gyldendal, 1985), pp. 264–267;

Jørgen Gustava Brandt, "Leif Panduro," in his *Præsentation: 40 danske digtere efter krigen* (Copenhagen: Gyldendals Uglebøger, 1964), pp. 106–109;

Torben Brostrøm and Jens Kistrup, *Dansk litteraturhistorie: Fra Tom Kristensen til Klaus Rifbjerg,* volume 4 (Copenhagen: Politikens Forlag, 1971), pp. 553–559;

Jørgen Holmgaard, "Det indeklemte oprør: om Leif Panduros romaner," in *Linjer i nordisk prosa i Danmark 1965–1975,* edited by Peter Madsen (Lund: Bo Cavefors, 1977), pp. 201–228;

Frank Hugus, "The King's New Clothes: The Irreverent Portrayal of Royalty in the Works of Leif Panduro and Finn Søeberg," *Scandinavian Studies,* 51, no. 2 (1979): 162–176;

Jens Kistrup, "Leif Panduro," in *Danske digtere i det 20. Århundrede,* volume 3, edited by Frederik Nielsen and Ole Restrup (Copenhagen: Gad, 1966), pp. 529–544;

Johannes Møllehave, "Leif Panduro," in *Danske digtere i det 20. århundrede,* volume 4, edited by Brostrøm and Winge (Copenhagen: Gad, 1980), pp. 95–116;

Jørgen E. Tiemroth, *Panduro og tredivernes drøm* (Copenhagen: Vinten, 1977);

Bodil Wamberg, *Den gale kærlighed: Motiver i Leif Panduros forfatterskab* (Copenhagen: Gyldendal, 1978).

Ebbe Kløvedal Reich

(7 March 1940 -   )

Trevor G. Elkington
University of Washington

BOOKS: *Vietnam: Krigen i perspektiv,* by Reich and
Preben Dollerup (Copenhagen: Rhodos, 1965);
Kina–Den ideologiske stormagt (Ålborg: Rhodos, 1967);
Billedalmanak fra en rejse i det europæiske: Digtsuite (Copen-
hagen: Gyldendal, 1967);
Svampens tid (Copenhagen: Rhodos, 1969);
Hvem var Malatesta? (Copenhagen: Gyldendal, 1969);
*Eventyret om Alexander 666: Om en rejse i sjælen, om en civili-
sation i forfald og om hvorledes Alexander blev til et stort
dyr* (Copenhagen: Gyldendal, 1970);
Holger Danske: Tolv fortællinger om en folkehelt (Copen-
hagen: Rhodos, 1970; revised, 1979);
Frederik: En folkebog om N. F. S. Grundtvigs tid og liv
(Copenhagen: Gyldendal, 1972);
Svampen og korset: Fortsatte optegnelser til en Krønike (Copen-
hagen: Rhodos, 1973);
Langelands-manifestet: En skitse til Danmark, by Reich and
Henning Kløvedal Prins (Copenhagen: Rhodos,
1973);
Utopi og virkelighed, by Reich, Søren Krarup, and Per Stig
Møller (Copenhagen: Stig Vendelkær, 1973);
Dialog mellem Karl Marx og Henry George, by Reich, Bern-
hard Hagen, and Knud Vilby (Copenhagen: Infor-
mations Forlag, 1974);
Rejsen til Messias: Tre bøger fra enevældens tid, 3 volumes
(Copenhagen: Gyldendal, 1974)–comprises *Herrens
rakkere og bødler, Brudeturen, Det klare vand;*
Du danske svamp: Afsluttende optegnelser til en ti års krønike
(Copenhagen: Rhodos, 1974);
Henry George (Tranehuse: Forlaget Tranehuse, 1976);
*Til forsvar for masselinien og den rette tro: Tekster om politik,
ideologi, kristendom og erotik* (Copenhagen: Gylden-
dal, 1976);
*Fæ og frænde: Syv en halv nats fortællinger om vejene til Rom og
Danmark* (Copenhagen: Gyldendal, 1977);
*Svaneøglen: Notater fra et eksperiment i tidsrummet 9/4 1976 –
17/2 1978* (Copenhagen: Gyldendal, 1978);
*Nissen fra Nürnberg: Fortællinger om Nissen fra Nürnberg og
hans rejse fra Mille til Laurits til Hanne til Søren og tilbage igen* (Copenhagen: Gyldendal, 1979);

Ebbe Kløvedal Reich (courtesy of Borgen Publishers)

Festen for Cæcilie: Den hemmelige beretning om et kongemord
(Copenhagen: Gyldendal, 1979);
Mediesvampen: Lægprædiken og krønike 1978–80 (Copenhagen: Gyldendal, 1980);
*Viljen til Hanstholm: En beretning om en egns historie, en
havnebys skabelse og om vilkårene for menneskelig planlægning,* illustrations by Poul Skov Sørensen, photographs by Kirsten Klein, Tage Jensen, and others
(Copenhagen: Dansk Byplanslaboratorium, 1981);

De første: 30 fortællinger om Danmarks fødsel, illustrated by Ib Spang Olsen (Copenhagen: Vindrose, 1981);

Danske heltesagn (Copenhagen: Gyldendal, 1981);

David, de fredløses konge (Copenhagen: Danske Bibelselskab, 1982);

Ploven og de to sværd: 30 fortællinger fra Danmarks unge dage, illustrated by Olsen (Copenhagen: Vindrose, 1982);

David, Guds udvalgte konge (Copenhagen: Danske Bibelselskab, 1983);

Den bærende magt: 30 fortællinger om Danmarks syv-otte yngste slægtled, illustrated by Olsen (Copenhagen: Vindrose, 1983);

Hjertets søde morgendrøm; eller, Til kamp mod dødbideriet by Reich and Ejvind Larsen (Charlottenlund: Rosinante, 1983);

Kong Skildpadde: Roman (Copenhagen: Vindrose, 1985);

David, slægtens konge (Copenhagen: Danske Bibelselskab, 1985);

Billeder og fortællinger fra Biblen (Copenhagen: Hernov, 1986);

Danmarks historie, politik og kultur: En introduktion for udlændinge, by Reich and Henning Bro, edited by Mehran Vahman (Copenhagen: Den Iranske Forening/Mellemfolkeligt Samvirke, 1987);

Konfirmationen, by Reich and Per Schultz (Gråsten: Teaterforlaget Drama, 1987);

Bygningen af en bro: En samtidighedsroman (Copenhagen: Vindrose, 1988);

En engels vinger: Roman fra det gotiske Norden (Copenhagen: Vindrose, 1990);

Kontrafej af den danske ånd: Samt krønike og rejsepostil til turen ud i det europæiske (Copenhagen: Vindrose, 1991);

Morgendagens mand: Roman (Copenhagen: Vindrose, 1993);

Rask op ad bakke: En krønike om Århus Kommunehospital, by Reich and Lise Haupt (Århus: Århus Kommunehospital, 1993);

Den fremmede fortryller: Beretning om Knud Rasmussen og hans to folk (Copenhagen: Vindrose, 1995);

Botanisk Have—En oase i storbyen, by Reich, Ghita Nørby, and Jette Dahl Møller (Copenhagen: Lamberth, 1996);

. . .mens legen er god: 25 år med Det Kriminalpræventive Råd, edited by Karsten IVE and Bent Lystrup Andersen (Copenhagen: Det Kriminalpræventive Råd, 1996);

Drag ind ad disse porte: 14 beretninger om kirkerne i den indreby, photographs by Ole Woldbye (Copenhagen: Vindrose, 1996);

Tobaksarbejderens drøm / The tobacconist's Dream, translation by Ingrid von Tangen Page (Holstebro: Holstebro Museum, 1996);

Zenobias liv: Roman (Copenhagen: Vindrose, 1998).

TELEVISION: *Dette er et tv-apparat: Et spil for lukkede kredsløb,* script by Reich, Danmarks Radio, *TV-Teaterafdelingen,* 1979;

Liget i lyskassen, script by Reich and Morten Arnfred, *TV-Teaterafdelingen,* 1983.

OTHER: Viggo Hørup, *Retning til venstre: Artikler og taler,* edited, with an introduction, by Reich (Copenhagen: Gyldendal, 1968);

Danmarks Grundlov, foreword by Reich (Allingåbro: Det Ny Notat, 1977);

Snart dages det– : . . . om arbejderbevægelsens historie, 2 volumes, text by Reich, Bjørn Erichsen, and Poul Vitus Nielsen (Copenhagen: Danmarks Radio, 1986, 1987);

Dante Alighieri, *Billeder og fortællinger fra Dante Den guddommelige komedie,* abridged by Reich, illustrated by Gustave Doré (Copenhagen: Hernov, 1991);

Vilhelm Holst, *Felttogene 1848, 1849 og 1850,* foreword by Reich (Vedbæk: Strandberg, 1998).

One of Denmark's most prolific, and at times controversial, contemporary authors, Ebbe Kløvedal Reich is a challenging figure to describe in precise or encompassing terms. Although his life and literary career have roots in political activity, journalism, and the "flower-child" movements of the 1960s, his topics have included biography, religion, mysticism, the drug culture, classical literature, contemporary events, sociology, and most notably, history. As the Danish critic Uffe Andreasen noted, "det måtte ringe for hans ører: folketingskandidat for Det radikale Venstre, anarkist, blomsterbarn, syrehoved, mystiker, Marxist, nationalist og kristen. Kunne der rummes mere under én hat uden at den lettede?" (It must have rung in his ears: parliamentary candidate for The Radical Liberals, anarchist, flower-child, acidhead, mystic, Marxist, nationalist, and Christian. Could more fit under one hat, without it flying off?). To this list of titles, one could add teacher, historian, politician, journalist, and cultural agitator.

Ebbe Reich was born 7 March 1940, in Odense, a month before the German occupation of Denmark, yet Reich states in his autobiographical work *Svaneøglen: Notater fra et eksperiment i tidsrummet 9/4 1976 – 17/2 1978* (The Swan Lizard: Notes from an Experiment in the Period from 4/9 1976–2/17 1978), that his memory begins not with the five dark years of Denmark's foreign occupation, but with the liberation of Denmark in 1945. In *Svaneøglen,* Reich provides a detailed description of his parents and of his early life. He was born into an educated, middle-class family. His father, Helge Reich Nielsen, was a senior public official who had an interest in art, literature, and music. He was an amateur painter and musician, and attempted to pass his interest

Cover for Reich's 1979 historical novel, about the events leading up to the murder of the Danish king Erik Klipping in 1286

in the arts along to Ebbe. His mother, Karen, was a pragmatic woman whose life centered on the home and raising her family. When Reich was eleven, the family moved to a villa in Gentofte that his father had designed. For the most part, Reich concerned himself with the typical interests of adolescence, and in 1959, he finished his secondary-school examinations at Aurehøj Gymnasium. He then underwent his mandatory two-year period of military service, serving in the Danish air force as a sergeant in an aircraft maintenance crew.

During his military service, Reich began to form an active interest in the world and the political events that were taking place around him. He enrolled at the University of Copenhagen in 1961 as a history student, and was particularly interested in recent history and in the history of Asian countries. That same year he married his first wife, Maria Thorsen, and shortly thereaf-

ter, their son Jacob was born. In 1965 Reich reached a decisive turning point. The cultural revolution of the 1960s was beginning right outside the doors of the university, and he was caught up in the issues that dominated political discussions. Reich left his academic studies before receiving a degree and pursued a career as a journalist and writer, joining the editorial board of the leftist political journal, *Politisk Revy* (Political Review), and publishing his first book, *Vietnam: Krigen i perspektiv* (Vietnam: The War in Perspective, 1965), with co-author Preben Dollerup. *Vietnam* is an attempt to discuss U.S. involvement in the war in Vietnam from a perspective of recent historical events in Asia, as well as an attempt to present the conflict in terms other than of the conservative rhetoric that had dominated discussion of Vietnam up to that time. Reich and Dollerup argued instead that France's original colonialism in Vietnam, followed by the U.S. intervention, was evidence of a "new imperialism" among industrialized nations. That same year Reich began his short-lived career in active politics by joining Det Radikale Venstre Parti (The Radical Liberal Party), which, despite its name, was a more moderate element of the liberal uprising among Danish youth. Reich quickly rose to the top ranks of the party; in 1966 he was chosen as a parliamentary candidate for his party and came close to winning.

However, the moderate-liberal views of the Radical Liberals were destined to conflict with Reich's increasingly extreme radical beliefs, particularly as he became more involved in the outer edges of hippy youth culture. Reich began to experiment with hashish and LSD, as did many writers of his generation. He also began to abandon his image as a serious young political analyst and explore other venues of expression and lifestyle. In 1967 the author published *Kina–Den ideologiske stormagt* (China: The Ideological Superpower) which, though the title would imply an academic political analysis, delivers a laudatory picture of Communist China and Mao Tse-Tung, formulated along Marxist ideological lines. The book was published a few years after the Cultural Revolution in China, and already the process of mythicizing Mao and Communist China had begun in the West. Reich's book stood out as the first Danish attempt to discuss Mao, Maoism, and the new China without conservative prejudice. Reich would continue to pursue his interest in Marxism, Communism, and communal living throughout his life, both as a large-scale political possibility and as a small-scale social experiment. He also published his first experiment in literature in 1967, with a volume of lyric and nature poems that together form a poetic ship's journey, entitled *Billedalmanak fra en rejse i det europæisk: Digtsuite* (Picture-almanac from a Journey in Europe: Poetry

Suite, 1967). Soon after, Reich accepted a teaching position at the prestigious and long-established Askov Folkehøjskole (Folk High School), an educational institution that had been created in the late nineteenth century in accordance with the principles of the Danish theologian, N. F. S. Grundtvig, who believed in the education of Danes beyond the mandatory school years and advocated the formation of *folkehøjskoler* (folk high schools) where farmers and other ordinary Danes could pursue further education. Askov Folkehøjskole was one of the first of these institutions, and Reich taught there from 1967 to 1969. However, the school is located in the countryside of Jutland, far away from the cultural center of Copenhagen, and he found it difficult to resign himself to witnessing the exciting cultural developments of those years from afar. Moreover, in the intervening years at Askov, Reich had eliminated the last remains of the ideologies of his bourgeois upbringing and his beliefs had become more radical. In the end, he resigned his position at Askov. He also split with the Radical Liberal Party, with which his views had increasingly come into conflict, leaving in protest when the Radical Liberals joined moderate and conservative political parties to form a coalition government. Reich returned to Copenhagen and found himself in the midst of cultural upheaval.

During his years at Askov, Reich had continued to publish political essays and cultural commentaries, discussing issues of domestic and foreign policy. These essays eventually led to his conflict with the Radical Liberal Party, as well as to his conflict with the editors of *Politisk Revy,* who saw his views as too radically Marxist. However, his essays and political views had found an audience in the new youth culture in Copenhagen. In 1968 he published *Retning til venstre: Artikler og taler* (Orientation to the Left: Articles and Speeches), an edited collection of orations and articles by the nineteenth-century radical Viggo Hørup, who in his socialist battle against National Liberalism and the conservative Right, served as an ideological forefather. In 1969 Reich published a collection of his own political essays and observations on contemporary events titled *Svampens tid* (Age of the Mushroom), the first of a series that the author refers to as his "Samtidskrønike" (Contemporary Chronicles), as well as the first book in his "Svampe-trilogi" (Mushroom Trilogy). As he was throughout his entire career, Reich was intensely prolific during this time, as attested to by the publication shortly thereafter of the book, *Hvem var Malatesta?* (Who Was Malatesta?, 1969), a biography of the Italian anarchist Errico Malatesta. From this time on, Reich would publish an average of one to two books a year, alternating between fiction, biography, history, essay collections, and a host of other projects.

This early wealth of production, which followed consistent themes of rebellion, communism, and criticism of the course of contemporary politics, found a ready audience among Copenhagen intellectuals and leaders of the youth movement. Reich immediately began to move among the many constellations of collectives and communes. He became a much-sought-after rally leader and orator for the protests and political gatherings that were occurring with increasing regularity. He made his first contact with the Kløvedal commune, a collective named for the elven community of Rivendale in J. R. R. Tolkien's *Lord of the Rings* (1954–1956) trilogy, which had developed a large cult following in Denmark. The commune eventually found a home in Hellerup, north of Copenhagen, and established a collective community which they dubbed "Maos lyst" (Mao's Delight) to mirror their interest in Marxism and solidarity with communism throughout the world. Reich lived in the commune periodically for many years, alternating with living in Copenhagen, as well as in the radical squatter free state "Christiania." He also adopted the middle name, Kløvedal, as a sign of solidarity with the commune, as did most of its members. Reich's membership in the Kløvedal commune mirrors the beginning of a change in the direction of his philosophy, from a hard-hitting and cynical criticism of political developments to a more poetic, Romantic, and mystic interaction with nature.

This more Romantic and mystic interest is mirrored in Reich's increasing publication of fiction. Though he continued to write political and social commentary, which was published in the ongoing "Samtidskrønike" series, as well as biographies of his political and philosophical heroes, Reich's fiction became the truer expression of his new views. Perhaps the clearest bridge between his previous work and his new interest in novels and fiction, as well as his interest in mysticism and new approaches to living, is found in the semibiographical novel, *Eventyret om Alexander 666: Om en rejse is jælen, om en civilisation i forfald og om hvorledes Alexander blev til et stort dyr* (The Adventure of Alexander 666: About a Journey into the Soul, about a Civilization in Decline and about How Alexander Became a Great Beast, 1970). The novel is loosely based upon the life of one of Reich's many heroes, the English adventurer, writer, and mystic Aleister Crowley, but is also a free exploration of mysticism and magic with a considerable influence from Reich's own political views. In *Eventyret om Alexander 666,* Crowley embarks upon a journey to battle a dragon and save a princess. On a metaphorical level, the novel is a journey of the soul toward enlightenment, and along the way, the author delves into magic, astrology, the cabbala, and the tarot. Reich's interest in metaphysics and the occult was also exhibited in his position as editor of the periodical, *MAK*, which published political essays, "anti-poetry," metaphysical discussions, and astrology. However, although Reich became increasingly interested in the drug and occult cultures of the era, he never entirely abandoned his interest in politics and current events.

In 1970 Reich also published his first purely fictional novel, *Holger Danske: Tolv fortællinger om en folkehelt* (Holger the Dane: Twelve Stories about a Folk Hero), the story of the legendary Danish hero, Holger the Dane. In the novel, Holger, son of the Danish king, Gudfred, and heir to the throne, is sent to Charlemagne's court as a political hostage, exchanged by his father as security against tribute owed by the Danish king. Holger eventually proves his worth to the Frankish emperor and becomes one of the greatest heroes of the Holy Roman Empire, only to turn against Charlemagne over a series of injustices at the emperor's hands. He returns to Denmark, where he is blessed by the fairies with eternal life. Holger goes to his father's court and falls into a deep slumber, promising to arise in Denmark's hour of need. This novel is a departure from Reich's previous work in that it is neither biography nor an explicit political commentary. However, Reich does make it clear that the novel is a protest against Denmark's move toward entering the European Common Market (EC). Reich had argued against a unified Europe in the past, and it has come to be one of the major themes of his work. Reich sees the urge to unify as an urge to create an empire, and, as he would argue in his subsequent novels and histories, Denmark's encounters with imperialism always brought about disaster on some level. This novel is also important as it is the first clear example of a technique Reich refers to as "den analogiske metode" (the analogic method), in which historical, biographical, or in this case folkloric, events are retold to provide commentary on current events. This method would be of central importance in his later historical novels.

In 1972 Reich published the documentary novel, *Frederik: En folkebog om N. F. S. Grundtvigs tid og liv* (Frederik: A Popular Novel About N. F. S. Grundtvig's Time and Life), an account of the life of the Danish theologian and hymnist, Grundtvig. Though some critics were initially surprised that Reich, a leader of hippy culture in Denmark, should claim the devoutly religious Grundtvig as a personal hero, their surprise was soon overshadowed by the uproar over the actual work itself. Grundtvig, as a religious philosopher, has been the most influential figure in Denmark since Martin Luther and founded many important cultural institutions such as the *folkehøjskoler*. He also established his own faction within the State Lutheran Church, Grundtvigian humanism. Yet, in his biography, Reich chose to focus upon what he perceived as Grundtvig's sensual and erotic nature. He speculated upon sexual relationships that have not been proven to have existed and blended metaphysical elements with Grundtvig's teachings. None of Reich's speculations were well accepted by the established religious community in Denmark, who saw the work about Grundtvig as a sensationalist mockery of one of the great leaders of Danish culture. Public outcry against Reich was vigorous. Reich responded that he was not attempting to mock Grundtvig, that in fact Grundtvig was a personal hero, a claim lent credence by the time he had spent teaching at Askov Folkehøjskole, one of the institutions established under Grundtvig. Reich argued that the book was subtitled "folkebog"(popular novel) specifically because it aimed at making Grundtvig and his teachings accessible to a popular audience.

In 1973 Reich joined the editorial board for the anti–European Common Market journal, *Notat* (Note), where he served until 1975, writing about the threat of Denmark's submission to a European conglomerate. He also published two collections of political and cultural commentary: *Svampen og korset: Fortsatte optegnelser* (The Mushroom and the Cross: Continued Observations, 1973), the second in his "Svampe-trilogi," and *Langelands-manifestet: En skitse til Danmark* (The Langeland Manifesto: A Sketch of Denmark, 1973) with Henning Kløvedal Prins.

In 1974 Reich published the final work of the "Svampe-trilogi," a collection of essays titled *Du danske svamp: Afsluttende optegnelser til en ti års krønike* (You Danish Mushroom: Concluding Observations on a Chronicle of the Decade). The recurring term "svamp," which can be interpreted as "mushroom" or "fungus," is a reference to a speech given by Reich's hero Viggo Hørup in 1891, in which Hørup declares that now is the time for all differences between humanity to be leveled with the earth, and that equality must reign supreme. Critics have argued that this is exactly what Reich attempted to do with his work: rip down the inequalities of his own culture. Reich published *Henry George,* a biography of the English political essayist and socialist, in 1976. George is best known for his Marxist analysis of the English proletariat system, in which capitalists profit from the poverty of the workers, which blended seamlessly into Reich's own Marxist beliefs. That same year, Reich published *Til forsvar for masselinien og den rette tro: Tekster om politik, ideologi, kristendom og erotik* (In Defense of the Mass Line and the Correct Beliefs: Texts on Politics, Ideology, Christianity, and Eroticism), which further elucidates his theories of revolution and cultural progress.

The body of work Reich had produced by 1976 had clearly established his intellectual, thematic, and

Reich at the writing table that belonged to the Danish explorer Knud Rasmussen (from the dust jacket for
Den fremmede fortryller: Beretning om Knud Rasmussen og hans to folk, *1995)*

philosophical concerns. Chief among them was a belief in communism and the ideals of communal living, as well as a need for actual equality in society among classes, races, and genders, and a call for the questioning—or outright destruction—of the established gender roles and class distinctions. He had established his interest in transcendental or metaphysical experiences, whether through mysticism, religion, or drug experimentation. He had also established his strong opposition to a unified Europe, in its first guise as the EC, and later as the European Union (EU), seeing it as a threat to Danish autonomy and its historical and cultural uniqueness. These issues and themes continue to reappear throughout the rest of Reich's career, as does his ability to publish in a variety of genres, eventually ranging from novels to essay collections, from biographies to political treatises, from children's books to plays and songbooks. However, starting in the late 1970s and continuing through the 1990s, Reich produced works that encompassed all of these issues at once in a way that melded the fictional elements of the novel genre with political commentary and accommodated his interest in history and cultural development by exploring the genre of historical fiction via his "analogic method."

In 1970 Reich had already shown the path that his fiction was going to take with the novel, *Holger Dan-*

ske, which blended history, folklore, and the author's imagination with the purpose of providing an analogy to contemporary issues in order to comment on them. This technique was used in a more detailed historical fashion with the novel *Rejsen til Messias: Tre bøger fra enevældens tid* (Journey to Messiah: Three Books from the Age of the Absolutist Monarchy), published in three volumes in 1974. This work deals with the establishment of the Absolutist Monarchy in Denmark in 1660, the beginning of the spread of Danish imperialism, and the triumph of capitalism over democracy. In Reich's account, King Christian IV drives Denmark to bankruptcy, using the Crown Jewels of Denmark as collateral on a loan to continue his building projects, and a battle of espionage and intrigue erupts between the two great merchant houses in Europe: Teixera in Hamburg and Marselis in Amsterdam. The protagonist, Joseph Lazarus, a Jewish man born in Denmark but raised in Hamburg, is sent by the head of House Teixera to protect and further Teixera interests in Copenhagen. Once there, Lazarus is drawn into political intrigues that eventually send him out of Denmark and across the European continent. He breaks with Teixera and travels to the Middle East, where he crosses paths with Sabbatai Zwi, a Jewish scholar and self-proclaimed Messiah, who is gathering followers and controversy in

Middle Eastern capitals and who eventually forsakes his faith under threat of death. The title of the book, *Rejsen til Messias,* is a reference to Zwi's journey toward his proclaimed fate as the second Messiah, but also a reference to Lazarus's own symbolic journey toward identity and toward a proximity to God. In the concluding volume, *Det klare vand* (The Clear Wind), Lazarus finds his destiny amidst the backdrop of the struggle of great men for power and prestige; he leaves all active service and winds up in an early commune on south Fyn, living in harmony with ten others as his life draws to a close. It has been said of this novel, and of many other of Reich's works, that it is not a novel about people, but rather a novel about the interaction of ideas, the currents of spirituality, politics, and religion and how they interplay with capitalism. Reich is commenting on the re-establishment of imperialism and capitalism in Denmark in his own day.

The same could be said of his next novel, *Fæ og frænde: Syv en halv nats fortællinger om vejene til Rom og Danmark* (Fools and Kinsmen: Seven and a Half Nights' Tales about the Roads to Rome and Denmark, 1977). With this novel, Reich returned to the issue of Denmark's interest in a united Europe, as well as a host of other issues. *Fæ og frænde* is one of Reich's most ambitious works, blending two years worth of research on Ancient Rome, its historians, politicians, philosophers, and slaves, with the tale of the Cimbrian Migration, which began among Celtic tribes living on the Jutland peninsula and spread down into the southernmost reaches of Europe. He uses historical comparisons between these two cultures, the Roman and the Cimbrian, to construct a comparison between the Danish mentality and the predominant European mentality, and to explain in what specific ways Denmark is unlike other European nations. He argues in this novel that Denmark has a long tradition of democracy, equality, and tolerance, a tradition that began even before the birth of Christ.

In *Fæ og frænde,* the tribes living along the Jutland peninsula are spurred into motion by an unscrupulous, deposed Celtic prince who hopes to use them to regain his kingdom to the south. Once moving, however, the migration takes on a life of its own—a chaotic, absolute democracy impossible for one person to control. The Cimbrian Train, as they come to call themselves, meanders throughout Europe, a blend of different Celtic and Nordic tribes, men, women, and children, who along the way create a culture of gender equality and fierce opposition to tyranny and empire. Eventually, the Cimbrians forget their initial impetus and instead decide that their purpose is to strike a blow against the Roman Empire, perched on the brink of becoming the most important power in Europe and beyond. The Cim-

brians march on Rome, only to split into two groups and separate. Both groups eventually confront Roman troops, and, encouraged by their initial encounters against disorganized Roman outposts and distant colonies, decide to attack Rome outright. However, as a backdrop to the Cimbrian migration, the reader is given a picture of developing Roman politics, leading to the rise of General Marius, who reorganizes the Roman armies and leads them against the Cimbrians. The Cimbrians, nowhere near a match for Marius's tactics and the discipline of his troops, are decimated at two battles known as the Battle of Aqua Sextiae and the Battle of Vercellae. The survivors are taken to Rome as slaves. Eventually two of the now-grown children escape and return to Denmark, where they lay the foundations of the Nordic tribes and the Nordic mythology, based upon the hard lessons learned by the Cimbrian Train.

Reich argues in *Fæ og frænde* that democracy and equality have had roots in Denmark since before the country could be called such, and moreover, that Denmark and her people have been opposed to imperialism and tyranny since the earliest roots of Danish culture. According to Reich, any step away from that vision of democratic equality is a step in the wrong direction. Rome in this case provides the symbol of bureaucracy and imperialism run amok, under which the Cimbrians are eventually subjugated. Yet, one of the most impressive elements of this work is the way in which passages by Roman historians, events from the Roman history, and the actual events from the lives of notable Roman figures such as Marius, Julius Caesar, and a host of others, are woven into the fictional configuration of the Cimbrian Migration. Likewise, the origins of historical artifacts such as the Gundestrup Kettle and the Tollund Man are fictively explained, fiction existing seamlessly alongside historical facts and objects. It is Reich's talent for blending history and fiction that makes his works accessible and intriguing.

Reich's production of historical fiction continued in 1979 with the publication of *Festen for Cæcilie: Den hemmelige beretning om et kongemord* (The Celebration for Cecilie: The Secret Account of a Regicide), an historical novel centering on the events leading to the regicide of King Erik Klipping on Saint Cecilie's Night, 22 November 1286. This death is one of the great mysteries of Danish history; Erik Klipping, after agreeing to the creation of a "Danehof" (Danish aristocratic parliament) in 1282, an agreement that would limit his powers as king and give nobles a say in political decisions, was murdered. Reich attempts, by blending historical facts with fictional supposition, to uncover what events or motives could have led to the murder. He elaborates on his theme of the threat of foreign intervention as he implicates Pope Boniface and an order of Cistercian monks, among others, in the murder of the Danish king.

Whether Reich believes the Papacy was actually behind the murder of Erik Klipping is beside the point. He uses history as a starting point for creating a novel in which the point of discussion is more important than a firm commitment to the facts, as the message is rooted in an analogy between past events and contemporary events. Reich did not intend that his reader would believe that he is reading pure history, and in order to insure that skepticism, Reich often included a preface to his historical works, explaining how the story being told is based on "documents" only recently uncovered by the author that make his assertions reasonable, but that cannot be revealed to the public. He does so in *Rejsen til Messias* and *Festen for Cæcilie,* and in more recent fiction as well.

Reich followed these works in 1978 with two books. The first is *Svaneøglen,* a free experimentation with autobiography in which he discusses his life up to that time. Reich explores his childhood and his life in the radical segments of society, as well as his divorce from Maria and his subsequent relationships, and the birth of his children. He also published *Nissen fra Nürnberg* (The Elf from Nürnberg)—a children's book—in the same year. In 1980 Reich continued his "samtidskrønike" with the volume *Mediesvampen: Lægprædiken og krønike 1978–80* (The Media Mushroom: Lay Sermons and Chronicles 1978–1980). In 1981 he published *Viljen til Hanstholm: En beretning om en egns historie, en havnebys skabelse og om vilkårene for menneskelig planlægning* (The Will to Hanstholm: An Account of a Region's History, a Seaport's Creation and the Conditions for Humane Planning), an experiment in provincial literature and local history. In 1981 he also began one of his most important and ambitious projects: a complete discussion of the entire history of Denmark, from the earliest Bronze Age settlers on the Jutland peninsula to the most recent political events. This work, which would eventually span three volumes, began with *De første: 30 fortællinger om Danmarks fødsel* (The First Ones: 30 Tales about Denmark's Birth) in 1981. As the title implies, the volume begins with the earliest archaeological traces of life in Denmark some quarter of a million years ago. Reich then goes on to explore myths and sagas, detailing legendary figures such as King Dan, Hagbert and Signe, and Amled. The trilogy continued in 1982 with *Ploven og de to sværd: 30 fortællinger om Danmarks unge dage* (The Plow and the Two Swords: 30 Tales about Denmark's Days of Youth). *Ploven og de to sværd* centers upon the very early history of Denmark, yet a time in which the nation of Denmark clearly existed both in name and spirit, covering the span from

1042 to 1738. Reich covers well-known historical events. For example, he treats Erik IV's tax upon plows, which earned him the nickname Plowpenny, and the creation and subsequent annulment of the Danehof, Denmark's earliest attempt at a governing parliament, enacted by the murdered King Erik Klipping. Riech ties these historical events together through the experiences of a fictional farmer-couple, Hoter and Estrid. The trilogy concludes with the volume *Den bærende magt: 30 fortællinger om Danmarks syv–otte yngste slægtled* (The Bearing Power: 30 Tales about Denmark's Seven–Eight Youngest Generations, 1983), the title of which alludes again to Reich's political hero, Viggo Hørup. This volume concerns the years between 1750 and 1983, detailing the lives of various important historical figures and families in Denmark. Again, the stories are tied together by fictional characters, in this case Hoter and Estrid's offspring, who represent the Danish people. The volume concludes with Reich being sent by the newspaper, *Søndag-BT,* to cover Queen Margrethe's visit to China, and in doing so, neatly refers back to the beginning of his professional career.

As in his historical novels, in the history trilogy Reich wanted to use history as a means of employing the analogic method, a means to discuss other issues he saw as important to contemporary life, among them the threat of the European Union (EU) to Danish independence and the traditions of democracy and equality that are evident in Danish history, and which must continue to flourish. Unlike in his novels, Reich breaks Denmark's history up into small stories, often centering on just one figure or event from Danish history, and offers an explanation, usually quite different from that found in conventional history texts, as to why this figure or that event is important in Danish history.

After finishing this historical trilogy, Reich turned away from history to a certain degree. His works dealt more with biblical figures and classical literature, as well as with current or recent historical events. In 1982, one year after the publication of the first volume of the trilogy on Danish history, this turn of interest became evident, as the first volume in yet another trilogy was published, *David, de fredløses konge* (David, King of the Outcasts), followed shortly by *David, Guds udvalgte konge* (David, God's Chosen King) in 1983, and *David, slægtens konge* (David, King of the Lineage) in 1985. This trilogy, which would alternate years of publication with Reich's trilogy of Danish history, explores the biblical figure of King David, and in taking up this topic, Reich departed radically from his previous focus. However, his technique remained the same, providing original, often controversial, insights and explanations into the events recorded in the Bible. This biblical theme is con-

I årene omkring 270 e.Kr. skabte den syriske dronning Zenobia et politisk og religiøst magtcentrum i byen Palmyra. Mange år senere sad hun som romerrigets fange og dikterede sit liv til en slave.

Skriftrullen med Zenobias livshistorie – som siges at være fyldt med okkulte spådomme, profetier, ritualer og mysterier – er den røde tråd igennem Ebbe Kløvedal Reichs nye roman, der fører os på en rejse fra oldtiden til nutiden, fra Syrien igennem hele Europa og til Danmark, hvor en række nutidsdanskere hvirvles ind i jagten på Zenobias liv.

VINDROSE

ISBN 87-7456-583-4

9 788774 565833

EBBE
KLØVEDAL
REICH

ZENOBIAS LIV

EBBE

KLØVEDAL

REICH

ZENOBIAS LIV

ROMAN

VINDROSE

Dust jacket for Reich's 1998 novel about the third-century queen of Palmyra

tinued in *Billeder og fortællinger fra Biblen* (Pictures and Tales from the Bible, 1986).

At the same time, Reich began to explore recent events, beginning with his book, *Kong Skildpadde: Roman* (King Tortoise: Novel, 1985), an account of the years leading up to Denmark's decision to join the European Common Market, and also a discussion of the days of the youth rebellion in Denmark, the so-called hippie days, on which Reich is certainly an unparalleled authority. In 1988 he published *Bygningen af en bro: En samtihedsroman* (The Building of a Bridge: A Contemporary Novel), a novel that explores the events leading up to, and the aftermath of, the Danish government's final decision to build a bridge over the *Storebælt* (Great Belt), the second longest suspension bridge in existence. Reich again blends mythology and history, but primarily this novel is an exploration of events that predate the publication of the novel by only one year, a great departure from his earlier historical novels that treat events in the distant past. Reich is always interested in contemporary events, as is seen in his own political activities, as well as the publication of his "samtidskrønike" and the wealth of essays he has published

elsewhere; however, *Bygningen af en bro* represents the first time that Reich chose to explore contemporary events directly through the novel genre. Moreover, he did not abandon his interest in history, as evidenced by *En engels vinger: Roman fra det gotiske Norden* (An Angel's Wings: A Novel from the Gothic North, 1990). In 1993 Reich published *Morgendagens mand* (The Man of Tomorrow), in which he returned to his technique of "discovering" documents that shed new light on historical events, documents that only he has seen, which in this novel are a discussion of the years between 1878 and 1885 and the blossoming of science and rationalism in Denmark. In 1995 Reich published *Den fremmede fortryller: Beretning om Knud Rasmussen og hans to folk* (The Foreign Enchanter: Account of Knud Rasmussen and his Two Men), a biography of the Danish explorer and settler Knud Rasmussen. In 1998 he published another historical novel, *Zenobias liv: Roman* (Zenobia's Life: Novel).

Reich resides in Copenhagen and continues to write prolifically. Though originally springing from the 1960s youth rebellion, his work continues the important tradition of Danish authors who have worked within the genre of historical fiction, beginning with B. S.

Ingemann and continuing through such notable authors as Johannes V. Jensen, Martin A. Hansen, and Thorkild Hansen, and his work has in turn influenced a new generation of novelists such as Mette Winge. Moreover, as Danish critics have noted, "Ebbe Kløvedal Reichs stilling i den samtidige litteratur er temmelig enestående, dels fordi hans person har offentlighedsstatus i samme grad som hans forfatterskab" (Ebbe Kløvedal Reich's position in contemporary literature is particularly unique, in part because his person has public status equal to his authorship). Reich is an author whose work is comprehensively informed by his political beliefs and yet brings an individual contribution to the aesthetic consideration of literature. Indeed, he has been one of the most productive and challenging writers of his generation, with a body of work that covers a wide range of topics and issues, from political events to historical debates, from philosophical quandaries to the classics of literature and art. He comments on the world around him and on the world that has gone before him as a way of discussing the world that is to come. A fresh voice of change in his youth, he has remained true to his beliefs, continuing to discuss socialism and Marxism and to comment upon issues of gender, class, and economic equality. Likewise, he continues to encourage his readers to broaden the boundaries of their perception. Reich provides an engaging voice of criticism and commentary, whether his target is U.S. involvement in Vietnam, Denmark's involvement in the EU, or the building of a bridge, and he consistently proves that his essays and fictional works, though controversial, will continue to be topical and challenging.

References:

Uffe Andreasen, "Ebbe Kløvedal Reich," *Danske digtere i det 20. århundrede,* 3rd edition, 5 volumes, edited by Torben Brostrøm and Mette Winge (Copenhagen: Gad, 1980–1982), IV: 286–300;

Svend Auken, "Historiens tilbud: Om synet på fortid og nutid hos Ebbe Kløvedal Reich," *Kritik,* 69 (1984): 33–42;

Niels Brunse, "Politikeren, der blev en rigtig digter: Om Ebbe Kløvedal Reichs forfatterskab," in *Linjer i dansk prosa,* edited by Peter Madsen (Copenhagen: Pax, 1977), pp. 229–252;

Johannes H. Christensen, "Historiens mure: Erindring, kunst og politik i Ebbe Kløvedal Reichs forfatterskab (I)," *Kritik,* 47 (1978): 5–24;

Christensen, "Historiens mure: Erindring, kunst og politik i Ebbe Kløvedal Reichs forfatterskab (II)," *Kritik,* 48 (1979): 46–89;

"Ebbe Kløvedal Reich," in *Litteraturhåndbogen,* fifth edition, edited by Ib Fischer Hansen and others, volume 2 (Copenhagen: Gyldendal, 1996), pp. 140–143;

Jørgen Bonde Jensen, "Nu står alt i Guds hånd, biskop! Om historieløsheden i Ebbe Kløvedal Reichs dokumentarroman om Grundtvig," *Vindrosen,* 19, no. 2 (1972): 105–112;

Mogens Lange, "Et forsøg på folkelig historieskrivning hos Ebbe Kløvedal Reich," *1066. Tidsskrift for Historisk Forskning,* 5 (April 1976): 3–21;

Allan Olsen, "Historieopfattelsen og den analogiske metode," *Kritik,* 57 (1981): 62–86;

Ole Pedersen, *Den historiske fortælling. Dannelsen i Ebbe Kløvedal Reichs forfatterskab* (Copenhagen: Dansklærerforeningen, 1985);

Niels Petersen, *Ebbe Kløvedal Reich, hans Frederik, og N. F. S. Grundtvig* (Copenhagen: Konrad Jørgensens Bogtrykkeri, 1976);

Henrik Poulsen, "Historien som historier: Om epik og historie i forening hos Ebbe Kløvedal Reich," *Meddelelser fra Dansklærerforeningen* (1978): 413–424;

Søren Schou, "To alternative historiefortællere–Thorkild Hansen og Ebbe Kløvedal Reich," *Danmarks historier,* volume 2 (Frederiksberg: Roskilde University Press, 1997), pp. 313–398;

Mette Winge, "Frederik af Ebbe Kløvedal Reich," *Fortiden som spejl. Om danske historiske romaner* (Copenhagen: Samleren, 1997), pp. 123–132.

Klaus Rifbjerg

(15 December 1931 –   )

Charlotte Schiander Gray

BOOKS: *Under Vejr med mig selv: En utidig selvbiografi* (Copenhagen: Schønberg, 1956);

Efterkrig (Copenhagen: Schønberg, 1957);

Den kroniske uskyld (Copenhagen: Schønberg, 1958);

Konfrontation (Copenhagen: Schønberg, 1960);

Camouflage (Copenhagen: Gyldendal, 1961);

Voliere, et fuglekor på femogtyve stemmer (Copenhagen: Gyldendal, 1962);

Portræt (Copenhagen: Gyldendal, 1963);

Hva' skal vi lave? by Rifbjerg and Jesper Jensen (Copenhagen: Gyldendal, 1963);

Diskret ophold: Et krybbespil i to akter, by Rifbjerg and Jensen (Copenhagen: Gyldendal, 1964);

"Boi-i-ing'64": Den fantastiske virkelighed (Copenhagen: Gyldendal, 1964);

Og andre historier (Copenhagen: Gyldendal, 1964);

Amagerdigte (Copenhagen: Gyldendal, 1965);

Udviklinger: Et skuespil for fire jazzmusikere, fire skuespillere og lille teater (Copenhagen: Gyldendal, 1965); translated by Pat Shaw as *Developments* (Copenhagen: Gyldendal, 1965);

Operaelskeren (Copenhagen: Gyldendal, 1966);

Hvad en mand har brug for: Et skuespil i to akter (Copenhagen: Gyldendal, 1966);

Arkivet (Copenhagen: Gyldendal, 1967);

Drømmen om København og andre Digte fra Byen (Copenhagen: Gyldendal, 1967);

Fædrelandssange (Copenhagen: Gyldendal, 1967);

Rif: Klaus Rifbjerg-journalistik, edited by Hanne Marie Svendsen (Copenhagen: Gyldendal, 1967);

Lonni og Karl (Copenhagen: Glydendal, 1968);

Voks: Et skuespil i tre skter (Copenhagen: Gyldendal, 1968);

Anna (jeg) Anna (Copenhagen: Gyldendal, 1969); translated by Alexander Taylor as *Anna (I) Anna* (Willimantic, Conn.: Curbstone Press, 1982);

Rejsende (Copenhagen: Gyldendal, 1969);

Marts 1970 (Copenhagen: Gyldendal, 1970);

År: Et sentimentalt panorama i ti billeder fra Danmarks besættelse (Copenhagen: Gyldendal, 1970);

Mytologi (Copenhagen: Gyldendal, 1970);

Klaus Rifbjerg in 1994 (courtesy of Gyldendal Publishers)

I skyttens tegn: Digte i udvalg 1956–1967, by Rifbjerg and Carl Bergstrøm-Nielsen (Copenhagen: Gyldendal, 1970);

I medgang og modgang: Blide og barske træk af ægteskabets historie i Norden, by Rifbjerg and Lilli Friis (Copenhagen: Gyldendal, 1970);

Leif den Lykkelige jun (Copenhagen: Gyldendal, 1971);

Til Spanien: En personlig dokumentation af mødet med landet (Copenhagen: Gyldendal, 1971);

Lena Jørgensen, Klintevej 4, 2650 Hvidovre (Copenhagen: Gyldendal, 1971);

Svaret blæser i vinden: Et skuespil i tre akter (Copenhagen: Gyldendal, 1971);

Narrene: Et skuespil i tre akter (Copenhagen: Gyldendal, 1971);

Dengang det var før (Copenhagen: Gyldendal, 1971);

Brevet til Gerda (Copenhagen: Gyldendal, 1972);

R. R. (Copenhagen: Gyldendal, 1972);

Den syende jomfru og andre noveller eller Ude og hjemme (Copenhagen: Gyldendal, 1972);

Rifbjergs lytterroman, by Rifbjerg, Ole Larsen, Hanne Marie Svend, and Jens Schoustrup Thomsen (Copenhagen: Gyldendal, 1972);

Scener fra det daglige liv (Copenhagen: Gyldendal, 1973);

Spinatfuglene (Copenhagen: Gyldendal, 1973);

Dilettanterne (Copenhagen: Gyldendal, 1973);

Privatlivets fred, by Rifbjerg and Franz Ernst (Copenhagen: Gyldendal, 1974);

Du skal ikke være ked af det, Amalia (Copenhagen: Gyldendal, 1974);

En hugorm i solen (Copenhagen: Gyldendal, 1974);

Sommer (Copenhagen: Gyldendal, 1974);

25 desperate digte (Copenhagen: Gyldendal, 1974);

Vejen ad hvilken (Copenhagen: Gyldendal, 1975);

Tak for turen (Copenhagen: Gyldendal, 1975);

Den søndag (Copenhagen: Brøndums forlag, 1975);

De beskedne: En familiekrønike, 4 volumes (Copenhagen: Gyldendal, 1976)–comprises *Ventedid: Fra 4. maj 1952 til 4. juni 1954; Noget er ved at finde sin bane . . . : Fra oktober 1954 til maj 1957; Boom!: Fra juli 1958 til september 1962; Hvorhen, kammerat?: Fra november 1963 til maj 1968;*

Stranden (Copenhagen: Gyldendal, 1976);

Kiks (Copenhagen: Gyldendal, 1976);

Twist (Copenhagen: Gyldendal, 1976);

Det korte af det lange (Copenhagen: Gyldendal, 1976);

Et bortvendt ansigt (Copenhagen: Gyldendal, 1977);

Deres Majestæt! Åbent brev til Dronning Margrethe II af Danmark (Copenhagen: Corsaren, 1977);

Drengene (Copenhagen: Gyldendal, 1977);

Tango eller Syv osmotiske fortællinger (Copenhagen: Gyldendal, 1978);

Dobbeltgænger eller Den korte, inderlige, men fuldstændig sande beretning om Klaus Rifbjergs liv (Copenhagen: Gyldendal, 1978);

Joker (Copenhagen: Gyldendal, 1979);

Voksdugshjertet (Copenhagen: Gyldendal, 1979);

Livsfrisen (Copenhagen: Gyldendal, 1979);

Det sorte hul (Copenhagen: Gyldendal, 1980);

Vores år, 2 volumes (Copenhagen: Gyldendal, 1980);

De hellige aber (Copenhagen: Gyldendal, 1981); translated by Steve Murray as *Witness to the Future* (Seattle: Fjord Press, 1987);

Odysseus fra Amager (Copenhagen: Vindrosen, 1981);

Spansk motiv (Copenhagen: Gyldendal, 1981);

Jus og/eller Den gyldne middelvej (Copenhagen: Gyldendal, 1982);

Mænd og kvinder (Copenhagen: Gyldendal, 1982);

Kesses krig (Copenhagen: Gyldendal, 1982);

Landet Atlantis (Copenhagen: Gyldendal, 1982);

Sangen om sengen (Copenhagen: Gyldendal, 1982);

Hvad sker der i kvarteret? (Copenhagen: Gyldendal, 1983);

En omvej til klostret (Copenhagen: Gyldendal, 1983);

Patience eller Kortene på bordet: En Beckett-idyl (Copenhagen: Gyldendal, 1983);

Det svævende træ (Copenhagen: Gyldendal, 1984);

Falsk forår (Copenhagen: Gyldendal, 1984);

Udenfor har vinden lagt sig (Copenhagen: Brøndum, 1984);

Intet nyt fra køkkenfronten (Copenhagen: Gyldendal, 1984);

Jeg skal nok (Copenhagen: Gyldendal, 1984);

Harlekin skelet: En pantomimeroman (Copenhagen: Gyldendal, 1985);

Borte tit (Copenhagen: Gyldendal, 1986);

Som man behager (Copenhagen: Gyldendal, 1986);

Byens tvelys (Copenhagen: Gyldendal, 1987);

Engel (Copenhagen: Gyldendal, 1987);

Japanske klip, by Rifbjerg and Georg Oddner (Copenhagen: Brøndum, 1987);

Septembersang (Copenhagen: Gyldendal, 1988);

Det svage køn (Copenhagen: Gyldendal, 1989);

Linda og baronen (Copenhagen: Gyldendal, 1989);

Det ville glæde (Copenhagen: Gyldendal, 1989);

En udflugt (Copenhagen: Gyldendal, 1990);

Det ved jeg da godt (Copenhagen: Gyldendal, 1990);

Da Oscar blev tosset (Copenhagen: Gyldendal, 1990);

150 korte og meget korte tekster (Copenhagen: Gyldendal, 1991);

Rapsodi i blåt (Copenhagen: Gyldendal, 1991);

Bjerget i himlen (Copenhagen: Gyldendal, 1991);

Den hemmelige kilde (Copenhagen: Gyldendal, 1991);

Krigen (Copenhagen: Gyldendal, 1992); translated by Steven T. Murray and Tiina Nunnally as *War* (Seattle: Fjord Press, 1995);

Karakterbogen: Et virrehoveds notater (Copenhagen: Gyldendal, 1992);

Hjemvé (Copenhagen: Gyldendal, 1993);

Vi blir jo ældre (Copenhagen: Gyldendal, 1993);

Synderegistret: En angivers betragtninger (Copenhagen: Gyldendal, 1994);

Kandestedersuiten (Copenhagen: Gyldendal, 1994);

Tuschrejse, by Rifbjerg, Teddy Sørensen, and Peter Laugesen (Århus: Århus Kunstmuseum, 1994);

Facitlisten: En gammel snyders papirer (Copenhagen: Gyldendal, 1994);

Berlinerdage: Dagbogsimpressioner marts-maj 1995 (Copenhagen: Gyldendal, 1995);

Divertimento i Mol (Copenhagen: Gyldendal, 1996);

Leksikon (Copenhagen: Gyldendal, 1996);

Andre tider (Copenhagen: Gyldendal, 1997);

Terrains Vagues (Copenhagen: Gyldendal, 1998);

Billedet (Copenhagen: Gyldendal, 1998).

Editions and Collections: *I skyttens tegn: Digte i udvalg 1956–67,* edited by Carl Bergstrøm-Nielsen (Copenhagen: Gyldendal, 1970);

Drenge—et tema i Klaus Rifbjergs forfatterskab, edited by Claus Westh (Copenhagen: Dansklærerforeningen/Gyldendal, 1981);

Rifbjerg rundt: En montage af Niels Birger Wamberg, edited by Niels Birger Wamberg (Copenhagen: Gyldendal, 1981);

På sporet: Udvalgte noveller, edited by Torben Brostrøm (Copenhagen: Dansklærerforeningen/Gyldendal, 1987);

Spinatfugl, edited by John Christian Jørgensen (Copenhagen: Gyldendal, 1995);

Under vejr med mig selv; Efterkrig; Voliere: Tre digtsamling (Copenhagen: Gyldendal, 1997).

Edition in English: *Selected Poems,* translated by Nadja Christensen and Alexander Taylor (Willimantic, Conn.: Curbstone Press, 1976).

PLAY PRODUCTIONS: *Gris på gaflen,* by Rifbjerg, Jesper Jensen, and Leif Panduro, Copenhagen, Studenterforeningen, 3 February 1962;

Hva' skal vi lave? by Rifbjerg and Jensen, Copenhagen, Studenterforeningen, 8 June 1963;

iskret ophold, by Rifbjerg and Jensen, Copenhagen, Folketeatret, 23 November 1964;

Udviklinger, Stockholm, Dramatiska Teatern, 1 April 1965;

Hvad en mand har brug for, Copenhagen, Det Kongelige Teater, 1 October 1966;

Bænken, Århus, Svalegangen, 6 September 1967;

Voks, Copenhagen, Det Kongelige Teater, 9 March 1968;

Tørresnoren, Copenhagen, Folketeatret, 21 February 1969;

Udstilling, by Rifbjerg, Schmidt, and Jensen, Copenhagen, Det Kongelige Teater, 25 March 1970;

Narrene, Copenhagen, Folketeatret, 5 March 1971;

Svaret blæser i vinden, Copenhagen, Det Kongelige Teater, 1 December 1971;

Middelklassekampen, Copenhagen, Teatret på Strøget, 1 June 1972;

Regn med sol, by Rifbjerg, Benny Andersen, and Panduro, Rønne, Rønne Teater, 20 June 1975;

En aften med Lise Ringheim og Henning Moritzen, Ålborg, Ålborghallen, 16 October 1975;

Vi er jo allesammen mennesker, by Rifbjerg, Jensen, and Per Schultz, Copenhagen, A.B.C.-teatret, 8 July 1976;

Sangen om sengen, Copenhagen, Det Kongelige Teater, 18 December 1983;

Mor, Copenhagen, Folketeatret, 17 November 1984;

Intet nyt fra køkkenfronten, Copenhagen, Det Kongelige Teater, 4 May 1984;

Det nye spil, libretto by Rifbjerg, Copenhagen, Nyt Dansk Danseteater, 25 February 1997.

MOTION PICTURES: *De sjove år,* screenplay by Rifbjerg and Palle Kjærulff-Schmidt, ASA, 1959;

Weekend, screenplay by Rifbjerg and Bent Christensen, 1962;

To, screenplay by Rifbjerg, Laterna Film, 1964;

Nordisk kvadrille, screenplay by Rifbjerg, Bengt Forslund, and Jan Troell, Kurkvaara-Filmi, 1965;

Sommerkrig, screenplay by Rifbjerg, Laterna Film, 1965;

Der var engang en krig, screenplay by Rifbjerg, Nordisk Film, 1966;

Historien om Barbara, screenplay by Rifbjerg, Nordisk Film, 1967;

Jeg er s'gu min egen, screenplay by Rifbjerg, Nordisk Film, 1967;

I den grønne skov, screenplay by Rifbjerg, Nordisk Film, 1968;

Det var en lørdag aften, screenplay by Rifbjerg and Erik Balling, Nordisk Film, 1968;

Danske billeder, screenplay by Rifbjerg, Nordisk Film, 1970;

Hærværk, screenplay adapted by Rifbjerg from Tom Kristensen's novel, Nordisk Film, 1977;

Ludvigsbakke, screenplay by Rifbjerg, Nordisk Film, 1978;

Ingenjör Andrées luftfärd, screenplay by Rifbjerg and others, SFI/Bold Productions/SVT Drama/Norsk Film, 1982;

Tukuma, screenplay by Rifbjerg, Kjærulff-Schmidt, and Josef Tuusi Motzfeldt, Nordisk Film, 1984;

Ved vejen, screenplay adapted by Rifbjerg from Herman Bang's novel, Nordisk Film, 1988.

TELEVISION: *Hele den tyrkiske musik,* script by Rifbjerg, Danmarks Radio-TV, 1970;

Premiere, script by Rifbjerg, Danmarks Radio-TV, 1970;

Den frygtelige fiesta, documentary by Rifbjerg, Danmarks Radio-TV, 1971;

Ferien, script by Rifbjerg, Danmarks Radio-TV, 1971;

Vores år, script by Rifbjerg, Danmarks Radio-TV, 1971–1973 and 1977–1979;

Laila Løvehjerte, script by Rifbjerg, Danmarks Radio-TV, 1972;

På vej til Hilda, script by Rifbjerg, Danmarks Radio-TV, 1972;

Gibs, script by Rifbjerg, Danmarks Radio-TV, 1973;

Brudstykker af en landsbydegns dagbog, script adapted by Rifbjerg from Steen Steensen Blicher's novella, Danmarks Radio-TV, 1975;

Ludvigsbakke, script adapted by Rifbjerg from Herman Bang's novel, Danmarks Radio-TV, 1978;

Sangen om Sengen, script by Rifbjerg, Danmarks Radio-TV, 1983.

RADIO: *De beskedne,* series, scripts by Rifbjerg, Danmarks Radio, 1974–1975;

Det drømmende hus, script by Rifbjerg and Carsten Grønning, Danmarks Radio, 1993;

Sarajevo, script by Rifbjerg and Palle Kjærulff-Schmidt, Danmarks Radio, 1994;

Tiden går, script by Rifbjerg and Grønning, Danmarks Radio, 1995;

Komså, Holger, script by Rifbjerg, Danmarks Radio, 1997.

Klaus Rifbjerg occupies a central and prominent position in contemporary Danish literature and cultural life. As the most prolific Danish writer in virtually all literary genres, Rifbjerg is also a literary trendsetter and an important contributor to the cultural life of Denmark. Scandinavian critics agree that his poetry is his crowning achievement and central to Danish and Scandinavian literature; his manifold prose works, screenplays, and radio dramas constitute one of the most significant contributions to Danish literature in the twentieth century. His works have registered the experiences, perceptions, and sensations of predominantly middle-class Danes for more than half a century. The author has referred to his writings as "a continuing novel of development"; his personal life provides a seemingly endless source of themes centered around the contemporary individual and changing sensibilities. Although Rifbjerg's themes remain focused on his own identity and personal experiences, his means of exploring and formulating them artistically are rich and varied. Each work offers new angles of approach, different styles and moods, and varying themes. In his writing, Rifbjerg alternates between realism and modernism; monologues and dramatic dialogues; simple, straightforward presentation and fantastic imagery; subdued pessimism and exhilarating slapstick; sober empathy and biting satire. He has shown a growing predilection for a playful mixture of realistic features, contemporary events, historical characters, and fantastic plots, as he adds to an expansive modern version of the bildungsroman. Although some of his best-known works belong to the earlier part of his authorship, Rifbjerg's creative vitality is unabated.

Klaus Thorvald Rifbjerg was born on 15 December 1931 to a middle-class family in Amager, a suburb of Copenhagen. His father, Thorvald Rifbjerg, and his mother, Lilly (née Nielsen), were both schoolteachers. Because both parents worked, the family had a

Cover for the U.S. edition (1995) of Rifbjerg's poetry collection Krigen *(1992), about the effects of war on everyday life*

nanny-housekeeper, Agnes, to whom Rifbjerg felt very close. His parents were in their forties and already had two daughters when he was born. In spite of growing up during World War II and the German occupation of Denmark, he experienced a stable, secure childhood. Rifbjerg's novels *En hugorm i solen* (A Viper in the Sun, 1974), *Drengene* (The Boys, 1977), *Kesses krig* (Kesse's War, 1982), and *Hvad sker der i kvarteret?* (What is Happening in the Neighborhood?, 1983) portray his life during and soon after the war.

Rifbjerg has described his childhood home as happy and intellectually stimulating. His parents were politically active and subscribed to the Communist Party daily *Land og Folk* (Country and People) and the radical-liberal *Politiken.* As he grew up, Rifbjerg emulated his parents' concerns and also identified with the intellectual movement called *kulturradikalismen* (Cultural Radicalism) and its progressive ideas concerning sexuality, pedagogy, women's rights, and child psychology; his aunt, Sofie Rifbjerg, was a pioneer in the field of child psychology and its practice in institutions and schools. The major tenets of Cultural Radicalism were promoted in the periodical *Kritisk Revy* (Cultural Review, 1926–1928), by the articulate and witty spokesman Poul Henningsen, son of the writer Agnes Henningsen. Originating in the nineteenth century and culminating in the 1930s, Cultural Radicalism underwent a resurgence in the 1960s, as part of a general trend toward growing social awareness and a reaction against the materialism of the welfare society. Rifbjerg has acknowledged his indebtedness to and continued belief in Cultural Radicalism, and his writings bear testimony to his loyalty to the movement. The intellectual atmosphere in Rifbjerg's home also reflected the ideals of Grundtvigianism and its advocacy of democratic education.

Rifbjerg attended Vestre Borgerdydsskole, an excellent secondary school. The outgoing and energetic Rifbjerg was involved with the school union, school magazines, and revues. He befriended Villy Sørensen, who became another leading writer of his generation, as well as Jesper Jensen, with whom Rifbjerg later collaborated on several revues, culminating with the satirical, didactic *Gris på gaflen* (Pork on the Fork, 1962) and *Hva' skal vi lave?* (What Shall We Do?, 1963). Another schoolfellow of Rifbjerg was Niels Barfoed, who took over as editor of the literary journal *Vindrosen* (The Compass), after Rifbjerg's tenure as co-editor (1959–1963) with Sørensen.

Rifbjerg won a one-year scholarship to Princeton University in 1950; his stay in the United States made a deep impression on him and strengthened his predilection for modern American literature, which he found realistic, daring, and invigorating. His novel *Leif den Lykkelige jun* (Leif the Lucky Jr., 1971) is a fictionalized account of his trip home from America.

Back in Denmark in 1951, Rifbjerg began to study English at the University of Copenhagen, but he found his studies too stifling for his creative talents, eventually giving up his studies in 1955. His many-faceted talents and interests induced him to experiment with all of the literary genres. After his student revues, he wrote the play *Hvad en mand har brug for: Etskuespil et to akter* (What a Man Needs: A Play in Two Acts, 1966). He also became involved with motion-picture production as an assistant director and producer at Laterna Film; he wrote the screenplays for *Weekend* (1962) and *Der var engang en krig* (Once There Was a War, 1966), beginning a long career of writing screenplays.

Rifbjerg also wrote reviews of radio, television, motion picture, and theater productions for daily newspapers. From 1957 to 1959 he worked as a critic for the newspaper *Information;* after 1959 he wrote for *Politiken.* In 1955 Rifbjerg married Inge Gerner Andersen, the daughter of C. F. Gerner Andersen and Anna Marie Creutz. She had just finished her education and worked as a schoolteacher and thus could support her freelancing husband. Klaus and Inge Rifbjerg have three children: Lise, Synne, and Frands.

The lyrical work *Under Vejr med mig selv: En utidig selvbiografi* (Getting Wind of Myself: An Ill-timed Autobiography, 1956) introduced the author as a poet. Readers considered the author's self-assured and humorous depiction of himself, from conception and birth to marriage and maturity, to be innovative and unusual. His biological and physical descriptions as well as his focus on the concrete and the present were praised by critics. The subject matter and tone of the poems in *Under Vejr med mig selv* were radically different from the more conventional poetry published in *Heretica* (1948–1953), a literary journal characterized by postwar existential concerns and philosophy. Rifbjerg's departure from traditional poetry was deliberate and at the cutting edge of trends in Denmark in the 1950s. He had initiated a long career dedicated to contemporary trends and new literary impulses.

Rifbjerg's first novel, *Den kroniske uskyld* (Chronic Innocence, 1958), is considered a classic in modern Danish literature. At the time of its publication, critics immediately noticed the similarity between *Den kroniske uskyld* and J. D. Salinger's *The Catcher in the Rye* (1951). Salinger's novel had been translated into Danish in 1953, although Rifbjerg had not read it before he wrote *Den kroniske uskyld*. The resemblance between Rifbjerg's and Salinger's somewhat capricious and neurotic young characters and their respective aversions to things they regard as "phony" reflect similar social phenomena in the United States and Denmark, as does the use of colloquial dialogue. In both novels, privileged middle-class youths rebel against social conventions and insincerity.

Den kroniske uskyld focuses on the first major stage in Rifbjerg's ongoing exploration of human development. The novel concerns puberty, a transition from youth to adulthood, fraught with danger but also with potential. The dominant theme concerns the entrance into the world of sexual maturity without the loss of the innocence, purity, and immediacy of childhood. The double-voiced narrator of *Den kroniske uskyld* is Janus (he is "Janus-faced" like the Roman god of portals); his best friend is Tore (a name that alludes to Thor, the Nordic god of war and thunder, as well as to the Danish *to* [two]); and together they create a self-contained fantasy world that offers an escape from the banal, trite hours at school and the hackneyed conversation of teachers and parents. Janus and Tore meet a girl named Helle (alluding to the German word *hell* [light] as well as to Helena of antiquity), who becomes part of their fantasy world; she becomes Tore's sweetheart and Janus remains a champion and "guardian" of the couple. The problem becomes how to incorporate sexuality into this platonic relationship; while Tore and Helle persevere in their innocence, Janus develops an abusive sexual relationship with another woman, a relationship devoid of the pure feelings he cultivates with Tore and Helle. At their high-school graduation party, Helle's mother, a shameless femme fatale, seduces the innocent Tore. After finding Tore in her mother's bed, Helle commits suicide. At the conclusion of the novel, Rifbjerg's naive protagonist, Tore, has been forced to learn that he is only human and that

> Man kan ikke både være ren og stærk, der må være en brist et eller andet sted, Janus, man kan ikke rage ind i himlen.

> (One cannot be both pure and strong, there must be a flaw in one place or another, Janus, one cannot reach perfection.)

The realistic description of teenage friendship in Denmark in the 1950s is embedded in layers of symbols evoking the Oedipus complex and the Fall. In *Den kroniske uskyld,* initiation into sexuality turns into a Fall; not surprisingly, sexuality remains problematic in Rifbjerg's ensuing works. *Den kroniske uskyld* was filmed in 1985 and directed by Edward Flemming. Rifbjerg has referred to *Den kroniske uskyld* as a "novel of reminiscence"—not strictly autobiographical but a fictive work reflecting past feelings and moods through "lyrical realism" and "emotional realism."

Danish critics agree that poetry constitutes the core of Rifbjerg's works, and he has concurred with this assessment in various interviews. The title of Rifbjerg's first collection of poetry, *Konfrontation* (Confrontation, 1960), became a key work of Danish modernist poetry. With the word "confrontation," Rifbjerg expresses the act of meeting surroundings and other people in an open, immediate manner. He emphasizes registration rather than reflection, favoring concrete details over lengthy descriptions. In *Konfrontation,* Rifbjerg continues the sensuous approach of *Under Vejr med mig selv.* He enumerates disconnected details of the modern technical world, offering no interpretation, but allowing words to gain significance through enumeration. In the poem "Terminologi" (Terminology), the poet confronts the words:

> Ja, ja, ja nu kommer jeg
> ned til jer
> ord.
> Trompet: forblæst.
> Skov: vissen.
> Karyatide: antik.
> Kærlighed: løgn.

> Hallelujah: ræb.
> Poesi: hvor er mit brokbind?

> (Yes, yes, yes now I'm coming
> down to you
> words.
> Trumpet: windblown.
> Woods: withered.
> Caryatid: antique.
> Love: lies.
> Hallelujah: belch.
> Poetry: where is your truss?)

The poet continues connecting words that arbitrarily come to mind. Registration and confrontation lead to an increased awareness of the present moment: "the experience of the second / in the balancing point / between used up past / and useless future."

Rifbjerg's technique of isolating words and items corresponds to a view of the world as disconnected and meaningless. In the process of cutting the superfluous away, the experience of isolated details becomes unbearable. The result—as well as the precondition to Rifbjerg's confrontation technique—is an essentially desolate world devoid of emotions. This bleak experience is occasionally counteracted by a new awareness, which Rifbjerg refers to as *bevidsthedslykken* (happiness derived from becoming aware). The confrontation with meaninglessness and repressed contents may also produce catharsis.

Camouflage (1961) is an extended poem in which Rifbjerg reaches into the subconscious by way of memories triggered by sensations and associations. He assumes a "dancing posture" to create an opening for new perspectives and to overcome taboos and other psychological obstacles in his quest for material from the subconscious. The major theme of *Camouflage* is the search for the self, spatially and historically larger than the individual. The images Rifbjerg creates range from those of family and past generations to those of remote species of animals. His Surrealistic method, in which free associations expand into a successive pattern of ever larger entities (repeating almost musical movements), recalls the poetic techniques employed by T. S. Eliot and Ezra Pound. Rifbjerg has acknowledged the inspiration of these poets for his own experimentation with radical poetic techniques. His exploration of the subconscious brings forth guilt and despair—the problem of innocence from *Den kroniske uskyld*—but also a satisfaction with having brought the problem into consciousness.

Before ending his major experimentation with modernist poetry in *Portræt* (Portrait, 1963), Rifbjerg published an original collection of poems that depict various birds, *Voliere, et fuglekor på femogtyve stemmer* (Avi-

Rifbjerg, with his wife, Inge (left), and Tiina Nunnally (right), one of his translators (photograph by Steven T. Murray)

ary, a Bird Chorus in Twenty-Five Voices, 1962). The author is an avid bird-watcher and the change of style and subject matter testify to his versatility and need for variation. *Portræt* outlines a wide range of human experiences that includes a symbolic and universal meaning. Archetypal events such as birth, the Fall, marriage, death, and rebirth shape human experiences. Rifbjerg's realistic settings and events paint an inner psychological portrait. The blend of "outer" and "inner" depictions distinguishes *Portræt,* in which concrete objects have symbolic meaning, and psychological states take on a concrete dimension; the one mirrors the other.

Simultaneously with his prolific production of poetry, Rifbjerg worked in many other genres during this period. His journalistic output was large, and he wrote motion-picture screenplays and revues as well. Selections of Rifbjerg's journalistic contributions were published in *Rif: Klaus Rifbjerg–journalistik* (Klaus Rifbjerg–Journalistic, 1967). He also wrote short stories before or concurrently with his novels; his short stories often share the thematic content of his novels. Rifbjerg's first collection of short stories, *Og andre historier* (And Other Stories, 1964), is thematically related to *Den kroniske uskyld* and *Operaelskeren* (The Opera Lover, 1966).

The stories in *Og andre historier* describe the development of an individual from childhood to puberty and adulthood to marriage; characteristically Rifbjerg focuses on sexuality within the context of innocence and guilt. For Rifbjerg, marriage generally represents a loss of immediacy and openness. Failure to mature harmoniously consequently becomes the main theme in Rifbjerg's next novel, *Operaelskeren.* The first story of *Og andre historier,* "Consciousness," portrays a borderland between the conscious and the subconscious of a little boy. The boy's use of the word "mother" represents the ambiguous functions of regression and progress. Most of the stories in the collection concern the interplay between a powerful subconscious and conscious, rational behavior. Distortions of perceptions and omission of facts indirectly reveal involuntary repressions and regressions made by adults (including the author). The tendency of a short story to concentrate on a protagonist's sudden insight (epiphany) or his failure of self-recognition suits Rifbjerg's psychological focus.

Operaelskeren represents a new stage in the ongoing bildungsroman of Rifbjerg's prose work: the midlife crisis. At the time of the writing of this novel, the author was approaching middle age; however, his own life as successful writer in a stable marriage with three children does not resemble that of the protagonist of his novel. *Operaelskeren* is written as a diary, a form Rifbjerg frequently uses. The novel deals with Helmer, a scientist who is attracted to an opera singer named Mira; he is also drawn to opera because of its predictable patterns. Not surprisingly, the singer is not predictable, and the relationship between the two deteriorates as Helmer fails to respond to Mira's changing emotions. Helmer's neglect of Mira's emotional needs reflects his own failure to face his anima (the female part of his psyche). The theme of a rational man's search for his irrational self by pursuing a woman recurs in Rifbjerg's works; for example, in the play *Hvad en mand har brug for,* in novels such as *R. R.* (1972), *Twist* (1976), and *Et bortvendt ansigt* (An Averted Face, 1977), and in many short stories.

As Rifbjerg's literary career took shape, certain patterns became apparent. One clear pattern is Rifbjerg's tendency to alternate between modernist and realistic modes of writing. His modernist poetry was followed by the movingly simple and personal *Amagerdigte* (Amager Poems, 1965) and the novel *Arkivet* (The Archives, 1967). In "De glemte år" (The Forgotten Years), an article connected to the publication of *Arkivet,* Rifbjerg explains how he wants to describe invisible, ordinary, inarticulate, and conformist people. One group of people is the so-called *mappefolket* (the briefcase people), white-collar workers. The uneventful lives and ordinary thoughts and perceptions of average people predominate in Rifbjerg's work; in this regard, he is a forerunner of a so-called neorealist movement in Danish literature, which includes such writers as Anders Bodelsen, Christian Kampmann, and Henrik Stangerup. Rifbjerg shares the experience of an affluent welfare society, suburban life, and pop culture with these writers.

Arkivet deals with another transitional stage in life: two young archivists are on the threshold of marriage. They perform the work required of them and follow conventions without deeper reflection. Their uneventful lives are only disturbed by one minor violent incident and the death of an uncle who was "old enough" to die. Their lives are normal, and they strive to keep them that way by means of conventions and rituals, controlling their emotions just as they file and store documents in the archives. Rifbjerg's understated description of the ordinary suggests hidden meaning under an apparently calm surface. A friend's single irrational outburst hints at a potential for violence. The historical setting of *Arkivet* in the 1950s, in the so-called waiting period after World War II and during the Cold War, underscores the psychological component of the novel.

Technically, Rifbjerg's realism in *Arkivet* is masterful. Much of the narrative consists of a methodical registering of concrete surroundings and the actions of the characters; such an account slows down the speed of the novel, and the reduced tempo imitates the languor of everyday life. Features such as repetition serve the same function of underscoring triviality and lack of change—for example, Rifbjerg shares the thoughts and plans of action of a central character; the narrator then echoes verbatim these thoughts and plans as the character carries out his intentions. In this way, the ordinary attains new interest, and commonplace objects and events gain symbolic significance.

The novel *Lonni og Karl* (Lonni and Karl, 1968) presents a striking contrast to *Arkivet. Lonni og Karl* is as full of fantasy and exaggeration as *Arkivet* is mundane and understated. Karl is a dreamer and, true to the spirit of the late 1960s—a period of romantic dreams and antiestablishment demonstrations—Karl dreams of revolution. To the daydreamer Karl, the revolution will not only change the world for the better; it will help him escape the boredom and constraints of everyday life. Karl is employed in the motion-picture industry, enabling the author to create a palimpsest of reality, composed of both movies and Karl's daydreaming. As Karl's fantasies expand, the irrational takes over in weird surrealistic scenes, many centered on dogs. In one such scene Karl sees a man stuffing stray dogs into his furnace; he tries to repress his urges, but the result is similar to fueling a fire. The scenes are replete with "fear, furor, and lubricity," to use Rifbjerg's words, and his explicit descriptions of sexual perversity and his exploration of sexual taboos alienated many Danish readers.

As the revolution turns ugly and spins out of control, Karl regrets his dreams and comes to the realization that no revolution can be fair because: "den delte folk op i to grupper: dem der henrettede, og dem der blev henrettet" (it divided people into two groups: those who execute and those who are executed). As a novel of development, *Lonni og Karl* maintains a focus on the psychological rather than the political—the revolution in the novel is in the psyche of the protagonist.

The next novel, *Anna (jeg) Anna* (1969; translated as *Anna (I) Anna,* 1982), holds a prominent place in Rifbjerg's writings, alongside *Den kroniske uskyld.* A travel, psychological, and detective novel, the book deals with a woman named Anna, the wife of the Danish ambassador in Karachi; she suffers from a strange urge to kill her young daughter. This female protagonist points towards many future works by Rifbjerg, who has become known for his many female portrayals, such as in *Lena Jørgensen, Klintevej 4, 2650 Hvidovre* (Lena Jørgensen, Klinte Road 4, 2650 Hvidovre, 1971), *Du skal*

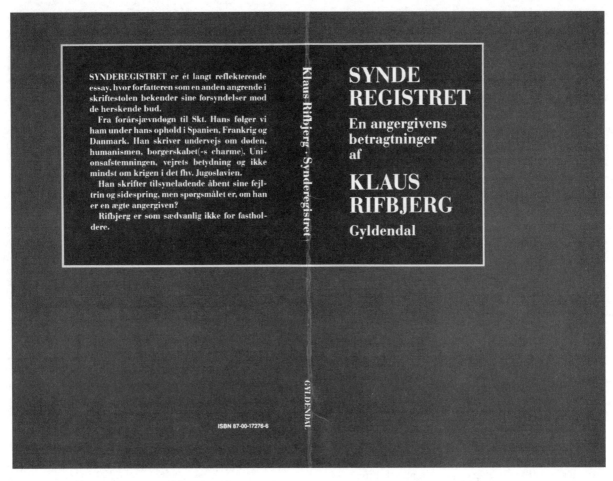

SYNDEREGISTRET er ét langt reflekterende essay, hvor forfatteren som en anden angrende i skriftestolen bekender sine forsyndelser mod de herskende bud.

Fra forårsjævndøgn til Skt. Hans følger vi ham under hans ophold i Spanien, Frankrig og Danmark. Han skriver undervejs om døden, humanismen, borgerskabet(-s charme), Unionsafstemningen, vejrets betydning og ikke mindst om krigen i det fhv. Jugoslavien.

Han skrifter tilsyneladende åbent sine fejltrin og sidespring, men spørgsmålet er, om han er en ægte angergiven?

Rifbjerg er som sædvanlig ikke for fastholdere.

ISBN 87-00-17276-6

Klaus Rifbjerg · Synderegistret

SYNDE REGISTRET

En angergivens betragtninger af

KLAUS RIFBJERG

Gyldendal

GYLDENDAL

Cover for Rifbjerg's 1994 memoir, in which he reflects on his life and recent Danish history

ikke være ked af det, Amalia (Do Not Feel Sorry, Amalia, 1974), *Vejen ad hvilken* (The Road Along Which, 1975), and *Voksdugshjertet* (The Oilcloth Heart, 1979). The travel motif of *Anna (jeg) Anna* is frequent in Rifbjerg's works, not only because the author himself travels frequently, but also because it is suited to the psychological development of the protagonist as well as to the cyclical structure of narrative. *Rejsende* (The Travelers, 1969), one of Rifbjerg's most outstanding collections of travel stories, anticipates *Anna (jeg) Anna* and includes a story called "Omstigning" (Transfer) about a woman's frantic flight from place to place. "Omstigning" illustrates how a short story may expand into a full-length novel. Originally written for the radio, *Anna (jeg) Anna* includes résumés at the beginning of each chapter, as well as a climax at the end of each chapter. The first-person narrative continues through direct action, flashbacks, conversation, or stream of consciousness. The reader is close to the narrator and has to question her reliability, for she is mentally ill.

Anna's husband, Tom, is a rational man and finds it difficult to understand his wife's mental problems, but he agrees to allow her to leave Pakistan, where they are living, in order to seek psychiatric help back home in Denmark. On the plane home, Anna feels strangely attracted to Jørgen, a hippie traveling in the custody of a policeman; on an impulse, and with the help of her diplomatic pass, Anna helps him escape. Jørgen will have little to do with such a crazy woman, but he returns to her hotel to get some money. Pursued by the policeman and Anna's brother-in-law, Jørgen and Anna embark on a criminal escapade, stealing and shooting while working their way north. They stay temporarily with a circus called "Colpa & Pena," and Anna, a criminal, now becomes a victim. Jørgen saves her but shoots the Danish policeman as they try to escape. They make a hazardous climb over the St. Bernard pass, where a Swiss peasant couple finds them. As Jørgen and Anna spend the winter in the Alps, their relationship develops into a love affair, but with the melting of the snow, they are forced to continue north. They encounter some American servicemen who try to rape Anna, forcing Jørgen to kill again; they finally reach the northern coast of Europe during a military exercise. Jørgen is killed by machine-gun fire, but Anna escapes on a fishing boat, finally reaching Denmark. She walks to Copenhagen, where she tries to shoot herself, but there are no bullets left in her gun. She then starts walking toward her brother's house.

The clues to Anna's mental illness and possible cure are gradually revealed through the symbols and events of this metaphorical journey. Anna's desire to kill her daughter, Minna (which means "little Anna"), is the result of her own self-loathing, which she projects onto her daughter.

Male protagonists seek psychological balance through a quest for their animas in several of Rifbjerg's novels; in *Anna (jeg) Anna,* Anna seeks her animus (her male side) through her male counterpart, Jørgen. Anna feels guilty because she has severed her own working-class ties in her role of diplomat and colonizer. Through Jørgen, Anna can reconnect with her repressed emotions; Jørgen's petty crimes and inferiority "fit" her guilty feelings. Anna and Jørgen's sojourn on the mountain summit provides the climax to their love story and a kind of therapy for Anna; the trip home recalls feelings and passions of which Anna is no longer aware. The theme of guilt and innocence continues in the novel but is especially effective in the symbolic interlude concerning the circus. "Colpa & Pena"–which may be translated as "guilt & punishment"–allows Anna to relive her feelings and regain some of her innocence and capacity for experiencing life unconditionally. Jørgen's death symbolizes the loss of her guilt; Anna no longer needs him. Anna's suicide attempt simultaneously suggests death and rebirth. Finally, the question of guilt and innocence also emerges on Anna's and Jørgen's trip north through Germany and in the encounter with the American GIs; Anna's personal problem is played out in the national and historical context.

Whether or not Anna's cure is psychologically convincing, it works well as a fictional fantasy. *Anna (jeg) Anna* is written with gusto and beautiful lyrical passages. One of Rifbjerg's most popular books, it has sold more than 70,000 copies. With *Anna (jeg) Anna,* Rifbjerg ended his impressively productive period of the 1960s. During this decade, Rifbjerg had formulated nearly all of his basic themes and mastered prose, poetry, and drama. He seemed to settle into a routine of producing about three works a year. During this decade, Rifbjerg also received many literary awards, among the most well-known prizes were the Aarestrup Medal, 1964; the Kritikerprisen, awarded by the Danish Literary Critics Association, 1965; The Grand Prize of Det Danske Akademi (The Danish Academy), 1966; The Golden Laurels awarded by the Danish Booksellers' Association, 1967; and the prestigious Nordisk Råds Litteraturpris (Nordic Council's Literary Award, 1970. He became a member of Det Danske Akademi in 1967.

Rifbjerg's published works of the 1970s, 1980s, and 1990s elaborate on, diverge from, and refine techniques and structures that the author had employed earlier in his career. The central source of his production remains his personal life. One narrative among many is his travelogue *Til Spanien: En personlig dokumentation af mødet med landet* (To Spain: A Personal Documentation of Encounters with the Land, 1971). Rifbjerg knows Spain intimately from extensive travels in the country and from his annual stays and vacations there. He belongs to a tradition of Danish writers who have written about Spain that includes Hans Christian Andersen, Martin Andersen Nexø, and Tom Kristensen; these writers all share an attraction to the unknown, the exotic. To Rifbjerg, Spain represents "the Other," a different style, mood, and history that can be transformed into art. Spain also presents a paradox; Rifbjerg recognizes the ambiguity in his attraction to a country with a record of brutal military dictatorship. The conflict between private and political is reflected in Rifbjerg's writings, especially in the novel *Dilettanterne* (The Dilettantes, 1973).

Rifbjerg tends to satirize his relationship to his critics; he regards his readers seriously, however, in such works as *Lena Jørgensen,* in which Lena represents the ordinary reader who may sometimes find the author too bohemian. Not surprisingly, Rifbjerg's experimental approach has also led him to try co-writing a novel with his readers and listeners. *Rifbjergs lytterroman* (Rifbjerg's Listeners' Novel, 1972) is a pragmatic attempt at democracy in the creative act. Readers and listeners were asked to call up with suggestions for the novel. The result testifies to the author's openness to experimentation.

An outspoken critic of cultural affairs and a frequent contributor to newspapers, Rifbjerg has often found himself in lively, antagonistic, or controversial disputes. He has written a series of romans à clef, satires based on real-life figures, as a means of responding to his opponents and critics. Such novels as *Marts 1970* (March 1970), *Spinatfuglene* (The Spinach Birds, 1973), *Du skal ikke være ked af det, Amalia,* and *Det ville glæde* (I Would be Pleased, 1989) fall into this category. Rifbjerg has a tremendous sense of humor; his use of easily recognizable characters in hilarious and fantastic scenes provide some of the funniest narratives in contemporary Danish literature (as well as outlets for the author's own frustration and occasional anger).

Dobbeltgænger eller Den Korte, inderlige, men fuldstæn-dig sande beretning om Klaus Rifbjergs liv (The Double or The Short Heartfelt but Completely True Account of Klaus Rifbjerg's Life, 1978) is a satire of the candid autobiography, popular with contemporary feminist writers. Rifbjerg himself is the most easily recognizable character in a grotesque plot. The collection of poems *Scener fra det daglige liv* (Scenes from Daily Life, 1973) connects the simple realism of *Amagerdigte* and *Arkivet* to novels such as *En hugorm i solen*. As is usual in Rifbjerg's realism, *Scener fra det daglige liv* verges on the symbolic, on a meaning beyond everyday realism. In this case, a strange sound emerges from the underground and anticipates a similar effect in Rifbjerg's *De hellige aber* (1981; translated as *Witness to the Future,* 1987).

Dilettanterne stands out as one of Rifbjerg's most socially involved works. In this novel, the author deals with the general and personal question of social respon-sibility and potential guilt. The protagonist in *Dilettan-terne* is a scientist whose research is wanted by terrorists working for the dictatorial Spanish government. The naive scientist, John, believes in the integrity of science and his personal autonomy in spite of adverse social and political conditions. Amid increasingly ill omens and suspense, John's wife and friend are kidnapped by a terrorist group. After such horrifying events, John thinks that

> han ville gerne vokse ovenud af sit dilettanteri som af et sæt gammelt konfirmationstøj og blive voksen. Men så måtte han også *ind* i verden og ikke længere betragte den fra sin post mellem de yderste sætstykker.

> (he would like to grow out of his dilettantism as out of an old confirmation suit and become a grown-up. But then he would have to *enter* the world and no longer watch from his post between the most remote set pieces.)

The political awareness of *Dilettanterne* is a question of maturity and engagement, and John's problem is only part and parcel of Rifbjerg's ongoing bildungsroman. *En omvej til klostret* (A Detour to the Convent, 1983) con-tinues the story of a scientist who does not want to become involved in politics.

Realistic descriptions of ordinary people and their everyday lives in contemporary Denmark also form the backdrop for the radio series *De beskedne* (Humble Lives, 1974–1975). *De beskedne* traces the lives of three genera-tions of a family in dialogue that captures the vernacular perfectly. The historical panorama of a bookstore owner's family through the 1950s and 1960s demon-strates how an individual life is connected to social cir-cumstances. The television play *Vores år* (1971–1973 and 1977–1979; translated as *Our Years,* 1980) further explores

how an ordinary man depends on economic fluctuations: in an economic recession, a fisherman who owns a boat, loses it, and becomes a victim of social pressures.

In addition to his prose and poetry, Rifbjerg has produced plays for stage, screen, and the radio on a yearly basis. The plays present yet another approach to Rifbjergian themes. The author has also been involved in motion-picture production; he is attracted to the use of visual images and perspectives in cinematography. Like-wise, he uses movie techniques and approaches in his poetry and prose. With his ear for the vernacular, he is a master of dialogue and monologue. As a modernist, he tends to structure his plays as a succession of scenes rather than as a tightly knit unity. He enjoys working with other artists and has produced television adapta-tions of nineteenth-century Danish literary classics such as *Brudstykker af en landsbydegns dagbog* (1975), based on a novella of Steen Steensen Blicher, and *Ludvigsbakke* (1978), based on a novel by Herman Bang. Rifbjerg also wrote the screenplay for Max von Sydow's motion-pic-ture adaptation of Bang's novel *Ved vejen* (1988) and the screenplay for Ole Roos's movie version of Tom Kris-tensen's novel *Hærværk* in 1977.

In the modernist detective novel *Kiks* (Biscuits, 1976), a crime committed does not have social but rather physical and psychosomatic causes. The biologi-cal-behaviorist approach builds on Rifbjerg's early "con-frontation" poetry, in which larger entities are split into smaller, isolated items. People are not motivated by social circumstances, but rather by somatic and psychosomatic processes such as irritations, aversions, and aggressions. The focus of this novel is on preconscious sensations (sexuality, digestion, and physical discomforts). Rifbjerg is interested in the idiosyncrasies of the characters, not in ideology or ideas, and his emphasis on irrationality and absurdity leads to exaggerated metaphors and a dissolu-tion of conventional language. In this novel, language secures an autonomy all its own; the result is a metalan-guage which both obscures and reveals meaning.

The grotesque works *Twist* (1976) and *Tango eller Syv osmotiske fortællinger* (1978) build on Rifbjerg's work in the comic-absurd vein. *Twist* is based on Rifbjerg's experi-ences during the filming of *Weekend* in 1962; the Baccha-nalian scenes read like a variation of *Lonni og Karl.* While *Twist* takes place in the 1950s; *Tango,* a collection of short stories, takes place in the 1930s and 1940s. In these short stories, Rifbjerg recounts some of his own experiences and portrays such well-known public fig-ures as Prime Minister Thorvald Stauning and writer Karen Blixen (Isak Dinesen). More importantly, Rifb-jerg re-creates the temperament of those times. His often playful humor is part of his self-conscious stance on the prevailing ideological and literary criticism of the time. His challenge to the powers that be is an "Aufforderung zum Tanz" (invitation to dance):

> Det var ikke en vild zapateado, en sørgmodig jota eller en burlesk rumba, men disse katteelastiske, kunstfærdige, minderige og fjernt melankolske tangotoner, som ikke siger nogen ret meget, men pludselig fik en hel by til at lytte.

> (It was not a wild zapateado, a sad jota, or a burlesque rumba, but these catlike elastic, artful, memorable and distantly melancholy tango tones that do not tell anyone anything in particular but suddenly make a whole city listen.)

Tango is humorous and entertaining, and the composition and narration are sophisticated; it is perhaps not surprising that this collection of short stories became a best-seller in an edition of 82,000 copies.

In his writings, Rifbjerg retains the "dancing stance" of *Konfrontation.* With *Joker* (1979) and *Det sorte hul* (The Black Hole, 1980), he switches from the humorous playful mood of *Tango* to gloom and pessimism. The plot of *Joker* concerns a male midlife crisis similar to that of the protagonists of *Operaelskeren, R. R., Et bortvendt ansigt,* and *Det sorte hul.* The journalist Jeremias Lister has trouble following all the latest trends; he has resigned himself to being an "old-fashioned male chauvinist." Lister is getting divorced reluctantly–but in step with the prevailing trend of the times. *Joker* represents Rifbjerg's coming to terms with Marxism, feminism, and the other "isms" of the previous decade and his final realization that people do not change as fast as ideas. *Joker* is full of wisdom and is one of Rifbjerg's best novels.

Det sorte hul is especially effective in depicting triviality: the ordinary from an uninspired or depressing point of view. The work enumerates consumer goods in a materialistic society, using techniques from poetry:

> Den langsomme nedglidning i skidt mod nulpunktet, det store, fælles sammenbrud i hver sin isolerede blikæske, det kollektive selvmord i sololie og samlebåndsproducerede beboelsesmaskiner.

> (The slowly sliding descent in dirt toward the zero point, the big, common collapse in each one's isolated metal box, the collective suicide in sun oil and mass-produced living-machines.)

Rifbjerg continued to receive literary awards in the 1970s and 1980s; in 1979 he was awarded the PH-pris (Poul Henningsen Award) and the Holberg Medal. His lyrical frieze of life continued in this period with a significant collection of poems, *Livsfrisen* (The Frieze of Life, 1979). These poems represent an attempt

Cover for Rifbjerg's 1998 novel

to stabilize something fleeting, to solidify something fluid; the resulting reliefs, created out of experiences and sensations, resemble a continuous row of sculptures. As in Rifbjerg's earlier poetry, the poems of *Livsfrisen* offer no sense of coherent identity; at most, they suggest there is a succession of separate pieces. The lack of cohesiveness and, consequently, of logical predictability, is illustrated by the presence of a satyr, who recalls the protagonist of *Joker.*

In a subsequent collection of poems, *Landet Atlantis* (The Land of Atlantis, 1982) Rifbjerg touches on death and the theme of renunciation. He had already anticipated this theme in the novel *Et bortvendt ansigt,* in which the protagonist considers the possibility of renouncing material goods and sexual temptations. Similarly, the protagonist from *Hvad en mand har brug for* has reached a new stage in his development in *Et bortvendt ansigt,* he has matured and is less greedy. In the 1980s Rifbjerg gradually entered a new phase of his continued bildungsroman: maturity and old age.

Throughout his life, Rifbjerg has been an enthusiastic traveler. He has journeyed extensively in Europe; he has visited America many times, the Far East, and much of the rest of the world. Whether he has traveled on literary tours, as an observer for a newspaper (often *Politiken*), or on private trips, he has gained inspiration and new insights. Rifbjerg provides travel chronicles for the newspapers, and he frequently uses foreign settings in his novels. The confrontation with the unknown constitutes an important theme in Rifbjerg's novels, short stories, and poetry. *Odysseus fra Amager* (Odysseus from Amager, 1981), is a collection of travelogues and stories from many parts of the world; more such collections are sure to follow. Rifbjerg's great appetite for new experiences and his keen perceptions lead to vivid, often humorous descriptions of places, people, and their customs. The portrayal of a foreign setting frequently functions as a palimpsest to the familiar surroundings at home.

The pessimistic aspect of Rifbjerg's outlook is also evident in the decade of the 1980s with a work of science fiction describing contemporary society in the shadow of the atomic bomb. *De hellige aber* (The Holy Apes, 1981; translated as *Witness to the Future*, 1987) was the second of Rifbjerg's novels to be translated into English. *De hellige aber* provides a futuristic vision of contemporary 1980s society: in 1942, two boys climb through a hole into a sort of time tunnel; they reach the "future" world of 1988. The boys witness present-day society from the perspective of the 1940s, a perspective with which the author identifies. The two periods share a background of war: World War II and the threat of World War III. Rifbjerg takes his inspiration from the present fear of an atomic war. From this point of view, the past naturally assumes nostalgic, idyllic qualities. The reader sees the present through a nightmarish vision of an alienated society, technically advanced and socially deprived. In this hostile world, the boys make only one friend, whose symbolic name is "the shadow," a patient at a narcotics rehabilitation center. Because the boys do not have enough money (only bills from the 1940s) they end up commiting crimes; the inhumane society does not leave them any other alternative. The irony of this situation is that a technical and so-called rational society leads to irrational behavior, and the two boys and their friend are reduced to a struggle for survival.

De hellige aber also employs the theme of innocence and its loss; Rifbjerg juxtaposes past "innocent" times with a destructive inhumane present. Innocence refers to complete openness and lack of reserve, qualities the two boys possess. With their untainted senses, the boys see, smell, and hear everything intensely, just as Rifbjerg does. His novel abounds in descriptions of sounds, smells, and tactile sensations; the boys recall the "good old days" of

sommersmørrets gule farve, skabiosa-svaermerens sorte bagkrop og de røde pletter på vingerne, skovjordbaerrenes aromatiske ruhed mod tungen, den søde klump af fløde i jersey-flaskens top, hjertegraessets ringlen, grøftekanternes overflod af blomster, lugten af sengetøjet, når det havde ligget til luftning i solen.

(the yellow color of summer butter, the black abdomen of the scabiosa moth and the red spots on its wings, the aromatic roughness of wild strawberries on his tongue, the sweet clump of cream at the top of the Jersey milk bottle, the rustling of quaking-grass, the profusion of flowers along the edge of ditches, the smell of a down comforter after it had been aired out in the sunshine.)

This richness of pleasant perceptions has been displaced by acrid smells and the shrill discord of the futuristic society. The title, *De hellige aber,* refers to the three wise monkeys who "see no evil, hear no evil, speak no evil"; it might also refer to adults who have lost the keenness of their senses.

The collection of short stories *Maend og kvinder* (Men and Women, 1982) continues Rifbjerg's exploration of the problematic relationship between the sexes. These pieces describe everyday life of couples in interaction or lonely isolation. The focus is psychological, but the omniscient narrator often omits something decisive and important; in this regard *Maend og kvinder* resembles *Og andre historier*. In *Jus og/eller Den gyldne middelvej* (Jus and/or The Golden Mean, 1982), Rifbjerg portrays a contemporary middle-aged man, Jus, who wants to kill his wife; it happens that the wife has similar intentions toward her husband. This farce deals with a "normal life" that verges on madness. Jus's speculations concern the philosophy of *Oprør fra Midten* (Rebellion from the Middle, 1978), by Niels I. Meyer, K. Helveg Petersen, and Villy Sørensen. The middle-of-the-road rational philosophy of caution and compromise gets the better of poor Jus; his lack of commitment and passion ultimately leads to his death.

Hvad sker der i kvarteret? (What is Happening in the Neighborhood?, 1983) is a realistic novel based on Rifbjerg's memories of Amager. As fantasy takes over everyday normality, however, the plot turns into grotesque drama; Rifbjerg suggests the presence of the irrational under the surface, the madness beneath normality. The self-conscious staging of scenes and settings and the use of frequent metacommentary illustrate Rifbjerg's increasingly modernist approach to his descriptions of ordinary middle-class people in their everyday lives.

The progression of the stages of life in Rifbjerg's bildungsroman is underscored by his next novel, *Patience eller Kortene på bordet: En Beckitt-idyl* (Patience or The Cards on the Table, 1983). It approaches the topic of old age and death with both disillusionment and humor; in typical Rifbjergian fashion the word "krybe" (shrink) symbolizes the final stage or state of being. The character is not slimming but shrinking in preparation for the coffin: an old reduced person lives in a spatially reductive world, where activities have been limited to essential needs such as grocery shopping. The overall reduction leads to minimalist descriptions.

Rifbjerg is not only a prolific writer; he has also served as an important intermediary between Danish and foreign literatures, between the critics and the reading public. He continues to write for Danish newspapers and he works as literary reviewer for Gyldendal Publishers, where he served as Literary Director from 1984 to 1991. *Jeg skal nok* (I Shall, 1984), is a selection of Rifbjerg's reviews of English and American works. His reviews are subjective, sensitive, and entertaining; they reveal that Rifbjerg is well-versed in Anglo-American literature.

The novel *Falsk forår* (False Spring, 1984) adds another female protagonist to Rifbjerg's gallery. In this work the protagonist, Elizabeth, returns home to Denmark; as a young woman she had become pregnant by an English soldier just as the war was ending. Elizabeth's daughter was given up for adoption, and she has had no further contact with her. She has repressed her vulnerability, and her return to Denmark becomes an act of revenge for her past humiliation. Elizabeth, one of the characters in Rifbjerg's continued novel of development, has not matured in a harmonious way; she has suppressed her feelings and plays the role of "iron lady." Elizabeth's psychological development runs parallel with the historical turn toward neoconservatism. As in many other works, Rifbjerg uses the political mood of an era to serve his artistic agenda.

At the end of the 1980s and well into the 1990s, Rifbjerg continued to write in various genres: poetry, novels, short stories, and plays. The collection of poems *Det svævende træ* (The Hovering Tree, 1984) describes gracefully the magic of everyday life. The prose poems in *Udenfor har vinden lagt sig* (Outside the Wind Has Subsided, 1984) continue the dialogue between the conscious and subconscious. These metaliterary poems explore perceptions of the surrounding world in a slightly different manner from Rifbjerg's contemporary novels. The novel *Harlekin skelet: En pantomimeroman* (Harlequin Skeleton, 1985) presents mime characters in a realistic setting. They pantomime as a reflection of their deathlike existence. The lack of real life is a major theme throughout Rifbjerg's work and relates to the question of immediacy, which also represents missing vitality. The short-story collection *Borte tit* (Peekaboo, 1986) balances the ordinary with the irrational, the familiar with the unseen. Everyday life is

seen as a peekaboo game. The stories are written with inspiration and spirit and reconfirm Rifbjerg's mastery of the short prose narrative.

In 1987 Rifbjerg served as Assistant Professor of Aesthetics at Danmarks Lærerhøjskole (The Teachers' Institute of Denmark). After finishing *Byens tvelys* (Twilight in the City, 1987), a collection coinciding with Rifbjerg's return from the countryside to work as literary director for Gyldendal, he published *Septembersang* (September Song, 1988); the work marks the change in seasons and in the life of the author. Among Rifbjerg's works at the end of the 1980s is the novel *Engel* (Angel, 1987), another visit to the past through travel, and *Det svage køn* (The Second Sex, 1989), short stories testifying to Rifbjerg's continual fascination with his feminine side.

Rifbjerg was productive in the 1990s, adding a new genre to his repertoire: children's books such as *Linda og baronen* (Linda and the Baron, 1989), *Da Oscar blev tosset* (When Oscar Went Mad, 1990), *Det ved jeg da godt* (I Do Know That, 1990), and *Den hemmelige kilde* (The Secret Spring, 1991). A novel for adults, *Rapsodi i blåt* (Rhapsody in Blue, 1991) is an emotional and imaginative work, a rhapsody continuing in the same vein as *Twist* and *Tango*. It takes place in the Copenhagen of the 1930s and borrows its title and mood from the music of the time. The milieu of the novel resembles that of *Harlekin skelet,* but *Rapsodi i blåt* focuses on language. The mixture of serious themes (related to the Fall) and farce is a characteristic of the rhapsody and illustrates the creativity and sophistication of the author. Rifbjerg's experience and knowledge seem to increase his playfulness.

The status of the author's bildungsroman in the 1990s may be ascertained through *Synderegistret: En angivers betragtninger* (List of Sins: An Informer's Reflections, 1994), a long reflective essay taking stock of the past. Moved by civil war in the former Yugoslavia and the contemporary efforts to establish a European Union, Rifbjerg rejects the extremes and various "isms" in favor of common sense and "good old-fashioned" social democratic ideals. *Synderegistret* can also be read as Rifbjerg's literary and personal manifesto, an apotheosis to "almindelighedens egen poesi" (the poetry of ordinary life), an uneventful poetry that finally becomes meaningful because of its roots in bourgeois life. This unassuming stance presupposes an innocence that Rifbjerg has retained throughout his literary career.

Readers and critics generally view Rifbjerg foremost as a lyrical writer, because of his manner of writing and to the subjective sources of his inspiration. In a 1981 interview with Jørgen Dines Johansen, Rifbjerg points to the writing method of another lyrical writer, Henry Miller. The creative process for Miller means that "he opens a tap and then it flows. And that's a wonderful feeling, and I think I experience it [the creative process] in a similar way." Both writers do not plan exactly what to write, but give themselves over to the creative act. Rifbjerg writes his novels like he writes his poetry: they are conceived as an entity. That is why the beginning of a work is so important; it contains the entire work within its initial tone and premises. Rifbjerg's manner of composing also means that he does not rework his works: once they have been created, he rarely makes changes.

The most important sources for Rifbjerg's creativity are his recollections; but, as he explains in the same interview, "the past makes me feel part of the present." Rifbjerg "connects" the two through his memories. In the collection of short stories *Andre tider* (Other Times, 1997), in which the focus is the familiar everyday (physical) experience, the narrative typically seems derived from the interaction between past and present. Rifbjerg's writing is personal but not private. He notes, "the more personal the expression, the more common it is."

Rifbjerg clearly stages and composes his material; this trend has become more evident in his novel *Divertimento i Mol* (Divertimento in the Minor Mode, 1996). In this work, Rifbjerg focuses on the narrator–how he approaches his material and how he deals with critic and reader (who also become characters). Dead people speak, and figures from Danish literature appear with a resulting overlap of reality and fantasy. Rifbjerg explores the human experience of reality–often humorously and playfully, but also seriously. If reality is what the subject experiences, are fantasy and imagination not as real as anything else?

Rifbjerg continues to pursue his artistic and epistemological quest with unabated energy and unsurpassed verbal skills. He resides with his wife at a permanent residence in Malaga, Spain, and maintains a summerhouse in Kandestederne, Denmark.

Interviews:

Per Øhrgaard, "Interview med Klaus Rifbjerg," in his *Klaus Rifbjerg* (Copenhagen: Gyldendal, 1977), pp. 104–127;

Niels Birger Wamberg, *Sandheden er fuld af løgn: Et Portræt af Klaus Rifbjerg* (Copenhagen: Samleren, 1980);

Jørgen Dines Johansen, "Hvalerne venter: To samtaler med Klaus Rifbjerg," in his *Hvalerne venter: Studier i Klaus Rifbjergs forfatterskab* (Odense: Odense University Press, 1981), pp. 179–243.

References:

Poul Borum, *Danish Literature* (Copenhagen: Det danske selskab, 1979), pp. 93–98;

Torben Brostrøm, *Klaus Rifbjerg: En digter i tiden* (Copenhagen: Gyldendal, 1970);

Brostrøm, *Klaus Rifbjerg: En digter i tiden II* (Copenhagen: Gyldendal, 1991);

Bernhard Glienke, "Anna, Balthazar und die Deutschen: Ein Aspekt zweier neuer dänischer Romane," *Skandinavistik,* 10 (1970): 19–35;

Glienke, "Noras Heimflug: Die Frauenperspektive in der Prosa Klaus Rifbjergs," *Aspekte der skandinavischen Gegenwartsliteratur* (Heidelberg, 1978): 119–143;

Charlotte Schiander Gray, *Klaus Rifbjerg* (Westport, Conn.: Greenwood Press, 1986);

Gray, "Klaus Rifbjerg: A Contemporary Writer," *Books Abroad* (Winter 1977): 25–28;

Jørgen Bonde Jensen, *Klaus Rifbjergs poesi* (Copenhagen: Babette, 1986);

Jensen, *Klaus Rifbjergs prosa* (Copenhagen: Babette, 1989);

Jørgen Dines Johansen, *Hvalerne venter: Studier i Klaus Rifbjergs forfatterskab* (Odense: Odense University Press, 1981);

John Chr. Jørgensen and Erik Olesen, eds., *Omkring Den kroniske uskyld* (Copenhagen: Hans Reitzel, 1974);

Lone Klem, "Klaus Rifbjerg," in *Danske digtere i det 20. århundrede,* volume 4, edited by Brostrøm and Mette Winge (Copenhagen: Gad, 1980), pp. 65–94;

Per Øhrgaard, *Klaus Rifbjerg* (Copenhagen: Gyldendal, 1977);

Sven Hakon Rossel, ed., *A History of Danish Literature* (Lincoln: University of Nebraska Press, 1992), pp. 451–457.

Hans Scherfig

(8 April 1905 – 28 January 1979)

Frank Hugus
University of Massachusetts

BOOKS: *Hvad lærer vi i Skolen?* (Copenhagen: Monde, 1933);

Den døde Mand: Kriminalfortælling (Copenhagen: Arthur Jensen, 1937);

Den forsvundne fuldmægtig (Copenhagen: Gyldendal, 1938); translated by Frank Hugus as *The Missing Bureaucrat* (Seattle: Fjord Press, 1988);

Det forsømte foraar (Copenhagen: Gyldendal, 1940); translated by Hugus as *Stolen Spring* (Seattle: Fjord Press, 1986);

Idealister (Stockholm: Bonnier, 1944; Copenhagen: Gyldendal, 1945); translated by Naomi Walford as *The Idealists* (London: Elek, 1949);

Danmark i lys og skygge (Copenhagen: Vor Tid, 1948);

Hellas (Copenhagen: Terpo Tryk, 1949);

På vej ind i vandmanden (Copenhagen: H. J. Krohn, 1951);

Rejse i Sovjetunionen (Copenhagen: Tiden, 1951);

Bothus Occitanus, eller, Den otteøjede Skorpion, illustrated by Elisabeth Karlinsky (Copenhagen: Tiden, 1953);

Det befriede Rumænien (Copenhagen: Tiden, 1953);

Dammen, illustrated by Karlinsky (Risskov: Sirius, 1958);

Den gloende drage over Roskilde (Risskov: Sirius, 1959);

Krigs–ABC (Copenhagen: Tiden, 1961);

Frydenholm (Copenhagen: Gyldendal, 1962);

Tre digtere (Risskov: Sirius, 1963);

Den fortabte abe (Copenhagen: Gyldendal, 1964);

Naturens uorden og andre essays (Copenhagen: Gyldendal, 1965;

Hos kirgiserne (Copenhagen: Gyldendal, 1965);

Rumænsk Billedbog, illustrated by Scherfig (Copenhagen: Gyldendal, 1967);

Morgenrødens land: Litterær rejse i Grusien (Copenhagen: Gyldendal, 1971);

Den fattige mands bil: udvalgte essays (Copenhagen: Vinten, 1971);

Månen og Trediveårskrigen: Udvalgte essays (Copenhagen: Vinten, 1972);

Butleren og andre historier (Copenhagen: Vinten, 1973);

Holberg og andre forfattere: udvalgte essays, edited by Jens Kr. Andersen and Leif Emerek (Copenhagen: Vinten, 1973);

Hans Scherfig in 1924

Det borgerlige samfund og dets institutioner: Udvalgte essays, edited by Anderson and Emerek (Copenhagen: Vinten, 1974);

Marxisme, rationalisme, humanisme: Udvalgte essays, edited by Andersen and Emerek (Copenhagen: Vinten, 1975);

Journalistik fra 30'erne (Copenhagen: Tiden, 1975);

Terminen på Ajlegården og andre indlæg, edited by Nils Frederiksen (Copenhagen: Vinten, 1975);

361

En rænkefuld prælat: artikler og tegninger fra Land og Folk, by
Scherfig and Herluf Bidstrup (Valby: Danmarks
Kommunistiske Ungdom Valby / Copenhagen: I
kommission hos Tiden, 1977);

Unden for kunstcaféen (Amagerbro: Danmarks Kommunistiske Ungdom, 1979);

Den lange dag, illustrated by Karlinsky (Copenhagen:
Gyldendal, 1979);

Presse-og ytringsfrihed (Copenhagen: Tiden, 1983);

*Lyttere og lurere: 22 artikler om politi, militær og efterretnings-
væsener* (Ålborg: KOMM. S., Aalborg, 1983);

*Den kolde krig i Danmarks Radio: Udvalgt radiokritik 1947–
1964,* edited by Nils Frederiksen (Copenhagen:
Tiden, 1986).

Edition in English: *Idealister,* translated by Frank
Hugus as *Idealists* (Seattle: Fjord Press, 1991).

OTHER: Norman Douglas, *I begyndelsen,* translated
and illustrated by Scherfig (Copenhagen:
Rosendahl & Jørgensen, 1945);

Ludvig Holberg, *Niels Klims underjordiske rejse,* illustrated,
with preface by Scherfig (Risskov: Sirius, 1961).

In his native Denmark, Hans Scherfig is remembered as one of his generation's polymaths. In addition
to being an influential novelist, he was also a preeminent painter of naivistic oils and watercolors, an amateur naturalist of note, and a widely read journalist.

Scherfig began his artistic career as a largely self-
taught painter of unspoiled nature scenes, and turned
his hand to writing in part by accident, in part by necessity. From his childhood, Scherfig harbored a great love
for literature. He was as well read in the classics as he
was in the prose and poetry of his Danish contemporaries. As a young man in the 1920s and 1930s, he composed several poems which, for the most part, have
remained unpublished. He also wrote movie reviews
and opinion pieces for various periodicals during that
time. To help meet expenses in the early 1930s while he
continued to paint, he wrote, under several pseudonyms, several short stories for several popular weekly
magazines; some of these rapidly produced stories foreshadowed the novels he later published.

Throughout his life, he combined writing with
painting. He became well known for his oil paintings
and lithographs, as well as for his occasional murals,
decorations for public buildings, and commercial art.
Equally well known are the many essays and columns
he wrote in support of the Danish Communist Party.
Scherfig frequently illustrated his own novels and essay
collections and occasionally supplied drawings for
works by other authors, among them George Bernard
Shaw and Norman Douglas, whose novel *In the Beginning* (1927) Scherfig translated and illustrated in 1945.

Scherfig was born in Copenhagen on 8 April
1905 to Christian Didrik Scherfig, director of a publishing house, and Claudine Scherfig, née Nielsen, his
father's second wife. Scherfig had four older half sisters.
He spent his childhood and youth in the solidly middle-
class setting of the Østerbro section of the city. As an
adolescent, he was sent to Metropolitanskole, one of the
most elite secondary schools in Copenhagen, which he
castigates in two of his novels for its rigidity and cruelty of its faculty. Upon graduation, he attended the
University of Copenhagen for several years, where he
studied zoology as well as Danish and German literature, but did not take a degree. During his university
years Scherfig was first exposed to Marxist ideology.

In 1928 he held the first exhibition of his paintings, which attracted little critical notice. From November 1929 through June 1930, in order to be near the
woman he was eventually to marry, the Austrian-born
painter Elisabeth Karlinsky, Scherfig made a fateful trip
to New York City. There he witnessed firsthand the gulf
between rich and poor, as well as the social inequities
that ever after infused his perception of the United
States. With little money Scherfig occasionally worked
as a dishwasher and sometimes slept on park benches;
at other times he was able to live at the John Reed Club
where he discussed Marxism and read John Reed's *Ten
Days that Shook the World* (1919). He produced two hundred drawings and woodcuts and thirty paintings during his months in New York and was occasionally hired
to give art lessons to the children of wealthy families. In
the spring of 1930, he had a two-week exhibit of his art
in New York City, realizing only $20 in sales.

Scherfig and Karlinsky returned to Copenhagen
and were married in 1931. Scherfig had sought entry
into the Danish Communist Party as early as 1927, but
the party rejected him because of his suspect middle-
class background. Eventually admitted into the Communist Party in 1932, he remained an active and loyal
member for the rest of his life.

Scherfig's literary debut came in 1933 with the
first of the many short stories of the fantastic and mysterious that he wrote for the weekly women's magazine
Ude og Hjemme, and with the appearance of his unpreten-
tious children's book *Hvad lærer vi i Skolen?* (What Do
We Learn in School?, 1933). The sparse text–with
barely two printed lines to each page–is accompanied
by politically explicit drawings by the author. Despite its
brevity, the author includes in these sixteen pages a
severe reproof of the educational system–that the
school teaches the inferiority of other nations and peoples, and the school's instruction is biased.

In the late 1930s, with an eye disease threatening
his eyesight, he was forced to curtail his painting and so
began the first of his seven novels, *Den døde Mand: Krim-*

inalfortælling (The Dead Man: Crime Story, 1937), for which he was awarded the Jules Verne Prize. When Scherfig wrote Den døde Mand in 1937, he did so with little expectation that this modest novel would capture the imagination of its readers. This novel is his only one to be written in the first person and the only one in which a character named Scherfig appears, here as an alternately sardonic and bemused narrator. The story is set in the bohemian, artistic milieus of both Copenhagen and Paris, the latter of which he had visited in 1931. It chronicles the rise and fall of the "demonic" and intellectually shallow painter, Hakon Brand, who abruptly rejects his dissolute life and converts to an American-inspired revivalist Protestantism known as the Oxford Movement.

Concurrently, Brand changes his painting style and is immediately accepted by the middle and upper classes who eagerly purchase his paintings. As a fashionable society painter, Brand gains entry into the leading families and marries into money. Although his outward success increases, Brand becomes obsessed with thoughts of death. His behavior begins to revert to that of his early days. Convinced he is pursued by the corpse of Poul Vollbeck (a one-time acquaintance and rival for the motherly affections of Sylvia Drusse), whom he thinks he has murdered, the distraught Brand dies of fright in a dingy Paris hotel while on his honeymoon. On the last page of the novel, the supposedly deceased Vollbeck reappears alive, much to the consternation of the narrator, for, as it would seem, Hakon Brand has been the real "dead man" of the novel all along.

Scherfig tells this story of artistic humbug and intellectual hypocrisy with the amusement and apparent objectivity that were to become the hallmarks of his entire literary body of work. His description of the incongruously named "Grand Hotel" in Paris, for example, fairly overflows with humorous observations, from missing stair treads to hazardous electric fixtures to the foibles of the guests themselves. Likewise, his portrait of the eccentric recipe writer and self-styled psychic, Sylvia Drusse, is a study in understated comedy. Drusse claims to be a reincarnated Inca princess and prophesies she will die on 27 December. When she apparently remains alive, she declares to a skeptical narrator that he is talking to a dead woman.

Less apparent in this first novel is the criticism of middle-class society that came to characterize Scherfig's subsequent writings. Nor is Den døde Mand, despite the appearance of several characters drawn from real life, the roman à clef that his latter novels are. One notable exception is Drusse, who Scherfig seems to have modeled on the editor of Ude og Hjemme. She is also one of the first of the characters to make a reappearance in one

Design by Scherfig for the dust jacket of his first book (Hans Scherfig Collection, Det Kongelige Bibliotek)

or more of Scherfig's later novels, as is the figure of Brand himself, who may also be a caricature of the Danish painter Eugene de Sala.

Encouraged by the success of Den døde Mand, Scherfig, who was living in straitened circumstances with his wife and children in the Tisvilde area of north Zealand, wrote his second novel, Den forsvundne fuldmægtig (1938; translated as The Missing Bureaucrat, 1988). Because of his diminished eyesight, Scherfig composed the novel in his head and dictated it to his wife, who also illustrated many of her husband's works. Den forsvundne fuldmægtig went through at least three revisions before Scherfig was satisfied.

The novel opens with the simultaneous disappearance in Copenhagen of two middle-aged men, Teodor Amsted, a head clerk in the War Ministry, and Mikael Mogensen, an impoverished eccentric. One of these men has blown himself to bits with dynamite. The police are initially stymied, and only when they discover that Mogensen was a classmate of Amsted's in the Metropolitanskole, does their patient detective work begin to pay off. As Amsted later tells the police, he had received a letter from Mogensen that his old friend had determined to kill himself in a deserted area near the waterfront. Amsted raced to the scene only to find a large hole in the ground and fragments of clothing. On the spur of the moment, Amsted decides to pass off Mogensen's scattered remains as his own and set out to build a new life far from his work and family. In the meantime, Amsted's "widow" has made the best of the scandalous situation by burying the bits and pieces of her "husband" in one of Copenhagen's most prominent cemeteries, Assistenskirkegård (where, among others, Hans Christian Andersen, Søren Kierkegaard, and Scherfig himself are buried).

The bulk of the novel alternates between Mrs. Amsted's attempts to reestablish the hollow respectability of her old life and her husband's futile efforts at adapting to a life on his own in Tisvilde. Mrs. Amsted soon comes under the spell of Sylvia Drusse, who has brought her a message from the deceased. Through the effeminate young medium, Einer Olsen, and several helping spirits (one of whom is Hakon Brand), Mrs. Amsted succeeds in communicating with her late husband. She seems on the point of marrying Olsen when the police telephone her with the shocking news that her husband is alive.

Amsted, meanwhile, has found himself even more isolated in his new life. When the police finally track him down, he is relieved to be convicted of insurance fraud and he is jailed for several months. His career destroyed, his family estranged, and his future uncertain, Amsted cannot cope with life when he is released from jail and craves the security and predictability of prison life. To return to this womblike existence, he resolves to murder his former supervisor at the War Ministry but at the last minute loses his nerve. In a final desperate act, however, Amsted uses what remains of the imagination of his boyhood and concocts the story of having murdered Mogensen. He is sentenced to life imprisonment. The novel ends on Christmas Eve with the inmates singing "Silent Night." The final line is a fitting epitaph for Amsted and all such stunted souls: "Salig fred, himmelsk fred" (Holy peace, heavenly peace).

Den forsvundne fuldmægtig documents the protagonist's desperate but fruitless search for the self. Stylistically, it is a briskly paced narrative written in a straightforward, almost conversational tone. Solidly fixed in the easily recognizable milieus of middle-class Copenhagen and rural north Zealand of the late 1930s, this novel is a realistic work with convincingly drawn, highly individualized, character portraits. In his book, Scherfig has embedded a subtle but harsh criticism of a society that condemns its best and brightest to conformity and intellectual and spiritual dullness. Prison becomes a telling metaphor for the stultifying effects of a ruthlessly competitive capitalistic system on the guileless individual.

Scherfig also takes to task the shameless exploitation that members of the broad middle class practice on one another, from the pettiness and cruelty of the north Zealand farming community in which Amsted (and the author) lived, to the merchants and bureaucrats of the capital city. As chairman of the county board of Tisvilde, Jens Jensen makes certain that the poor do not abuse the system by, for example, collecting welfare instead of working. The able-bodied unemployed are required to sit on the seashore all day long, winter and summer, splitting stones, which are never used for anything, before they can claim their benefits. Another pillar of this society, Martin Hageholm, all but admits responsibility for the death of his wife—and may have murdered his daughter—in order to get her inheritance. Several characters in the novel, Hageholm and Mogensen, for instance, are taken from real life. The book was, in fact, so clearly modeled on the people, events, and places of Tisvilde, that, after its publication, Scherfig felt it prudent to move to the village of Tikøb near Elsinore. His reputation as a novelist was firmly established.

Scherfig's only extant attempt at drama dates from these years, as well. In 1939 he wrote a brief parody of the radio-play genre that he titled "Terminen paa Ajlegaarden" (Due Date at Liquid Manure Manor), which appeared in the Communist newspaper, *Arbejderbladet* (The Worker's Paper), on 31 January 1940. In this breezy satire, the faithful foreman, Morten, saves the family estate of Mads Bøvelse from bankruptcy and earns the right to marry Mads's daughter by donating his entire earnings (plus interest) over fifteen years to the worthy landowner. In his radio-play, Scherfig shows himself to be a skillful writer of dialogue and capable of creating a credible sense of dramatic tension.

After German troops entered Denmark on 9 April 1940, Scherfig, along with his fellow Communists, was in constant danger of being arrested. Despite this risk, Scherfig continued to write and six months later published his third novel, *Det forsømte foraar* (1940; translated as *Stolen Spring*, 1986), which he also had to dictate to his wife because of his virtual blindness. *Det forsømte foraar*, although it follows his second novel chronologically, is really its precursor. *Det forsømte foraar*, like *Den forsvundne fuldmægtig*, opens with a murder: Mr. Blomme, an elderly Latin teacher in an elite boys' secondary school, dies after eating a poisoned malt drop. Although foul play is suspected, the police are unable to find any clues to the perpetrator, and the crime remains unsolved. The scene of the story then leaps a quarter century into the future to the twenty-five year reunion of a class that graduated from the same secondary school. One of those in attendance is the murderer. Using a skillful flashback technique, Scherfig brings the

Scherfig; his wife, Elisabeth Karlinsky; and their son, Peter, in 1936

reader back to the years leading up to Blomme's murder. Characters already familiar from *Den forsvundne fuldmægtig,* notably Teodor Amsted and Mikael Mogensen, appear as awkward teenagers who are subjected to both physical brutality and mental cruelty from their teachers.

The teachers are portrayed as embittered older men who cannot relate to their pupils, and who prepare their charges for careers as professional men by breaking down the boys' self-esteem and stifling their imagination and creativity. As an act more of desperation than rebellion, one of the pupils, Edvard Ellerstrøm (who, oddly enough, later becomes a judge), poisons Blomme's malt drop to avoid failing his year-end Latin examination. Once the identity of the murderer has been revealed, the scene of the novel reverts to the class reunion. *Det forsømte foraar* ends with the participants returning to their empty personal lives. Amsted is trapped in a loveless marriage and a meaningless job. Ellerstrøm still lives with his domineering mother. Mogensen now has the privacy and independence he could never enjoy in the crowded home of his economically stressed youth; but to attain his independence he

has had to drop out of society altogether and lives as a strange creature on the fringes of the system. What Mogensen's choice leads to has already been described in Scherfig's previous novel. There are also many instances of deviant moral values and warped emotional relationships. Blomme, for example, finds the young Ellerstrøm "appetitlig" (appetizing). Some of the older boys treat the younger ones in curiously intimate ways. Many of the teachers give the boys "playful" slaps on the behind. The hapless pupil Jørgen Hurrycane, who is subject to the deleterious influence both of the school and of his unprincipled family (representing what Scherfig sees as the morality of the conniving petit-bourgeois), ends up behind bars even before the class reunion has taken place.

The "gray school," though unnamed in the novel, is the same Metropolitanskole that Scherfig and his father before him attended. In *Det forsømte foraar,* he described many of the teachers he had and some of the events he had witnessed or participated in. The school and its goal of producing "useful" (that is, unthinking and conformist) citizens is seen as the instrument of an oppressive, unfeeling bureaucratic society. The victims of this oppression are treated sympathetically by the author, particularly as young boys. This book also repeats aspects of Scherfig's earlier children's work *Hvad lærer vi i Skolen?* as well as themes from a polemic essay he wrote in 1935, "Om at gå i Skole" (On Going to School).

When German troops attacked the Soviet Union in 1941, Scherfig was imprisoned from June through August after a police roundup of Danish Communists. In August, however, he was transferred to a hospital for the operation that was to restore most of his eyesight. After being quietly released, Scherfig successfully avoided jail for the remainder of the German occupation of Denmark. Danish police, however, continued to keep him under surveillance. During the rest of the German occupation, Scherfig was officially prohibited from writing. He continued to do so under pseudonyms (among them, that of his wife). He began his fourth novel, *Idealister,* while in prison in 1941. He completed it in 1942 but could not get the manuscript published in Denmark until 1945 (The Danish Foreign Ministry barred its publication fearing that *Idealister,* with its clear allusions to the Occupation, might offend the German government). A manuscript of the novel was smuggled to Sweden where it was published in 1944.

Set in 1938, *Idealister* begins with the murder of the wealthy landowner and businessman, C. C. Skjern-Svendsen, in the bedroom of the mansion on his huge estate. The police are unable to establish the identity of the murderer, and not until the confession of the estate's gardener, a religious fundamentalist obsessed with notions of sin and the apocalypse—who has had a brief affair with Skjern-Svendsen's much younger wife—does the mystery unravel. What holds the reader's interest is not the thin, straightforward main plot but the various subplots, few of which are resolved in *Idealister.*

Scherfig uses most of the 240 pages of the novel to describe the odd assortment of "idealists" who populated Copenhagen and its environs in the immediate prewar years: the altruistic print-shop owner, Damaskus, (who conducted the seances Mrs. Amsted attended in *Den frosvundne fuldmægtig*); the harmless astrologer and cabalistic wizard, Kados; the quack sexual psychologist, Dr. Robert Riege; the unctuous representative of the Danish State Church, Pastor Nørregård-Olsen, and the right-wing literary critic, Harald Horn (all three of whom attended the reunion in *Det forsømte foraar*). Although the narrator does not subscribe to any of the alternative social systems put forth by these idealists, he nonetheless accords most of them an indulgent, if tongue-in-cheek, respect. For Riege and Nørregård-Olsen, however, the narrator reserves a special censure. The fraudulent purveyor of quirky sexual behavior, who Scherfig may have modeled at least in part on the

psychologist, Wilhelm Reich (or on one of Reich's Danish disciples), represents a danger to society; it is he who has been "treating" Skjern-Svendsen's wife and who is indirectly the cause of Skjern-Svendsen's murder. The self-serving pastor is a study in the hypocrisy that Scherfig sees in the religious—and by extension the societal—establishment of Denmark.

Counterbalancing the "idealists" are the inhabitants of the Præstø region of Zealand, which is not to say that the country folk are portrayed as paragons of virtue. Like the residents of the Tisvilde area, few of them, in fact, are depicted sympathetically. The wealthy farmer, Niels Madsen, said by everyone to be a good, hardworking Christian, displays great cruelty. This pillar of society mistreats the poor, young public wards who are sent by the government to work on his "model" farm. More ominously, Madsen senses the winds of change coming from the south and buys himself a pair of black jackboots, a black belt, and a cap to be ready for the new system to come. Madsen's neighbor, Marius Petersen, nicknamed "Bukse Marius" (Marius Panties), because of his proclivity of stealing women's undergarments and cutting holes in them, is a dull-witted, middle-aged farmer with a perpetually runny nose, who is easily led by others. One exception to this array of contemptible characters is Old Emma, who, though querulous and close to eighty, is a decent, caring human being. Another is Martin Olsen, a young worker who, though he and his family live a hand-to-mouth existence, displays high principles that time and again put the self-serving actions of the more established pillars of society to shame. It is gardener Holm, however, Skjern-Svendsen's murderer, for whom the narrator has the greatest sympathy. Tormented by the contradiction between the world's injustices, as opposed to what he has read in the Bible and heard in church, Holm gradually loses his mind by asking himself theological questions that cannot be answered: why should only a chosen few attain salvation? Is the Christian God really a just and loving god?

Idealister exposes and explores the seamy underside of Danish society as none of Scherfig's previous novels had done. More significantly, it lays the groundwork for Scherfig's later and much longer novel, *Frydenholm* (1962), for which it functions as an effective prelude. That Scherfig knew he would write a sequel to *Idealister* is clear from many allusions in the novel itself, as well as from *Idealister*'s concluding sentence: "Senere vil der måske ske andre begivenheder, som der engang kan skrives om" (Later on there may be other events that can be written about someday).

Between 1945 and 1953 Scherfig divided his creative energies between painting and journalism. Writing for the now-defunct Communist daily newspaper, *Land*

Scherfig in December 1940 (photograph by Helmer Lund Hansen)

og Folk (Country and People), Scherfig produced a series of columns that hurled barbs at many of Danish society's shortcomings. His targets could be radio and television commentators, politicians, the monarchy, various cultural institutions, leaders of conservative movements, and many others. From 1966 through the year of his death, these weekly columns were published annually in book form.

In 1949 Denmark joined the North Atlantic Treaty Organization and, much to Scherfig's vocal displeasure, officially backed policies and alliances that put the Danish Communists on the defensive. During the 1950s and 1960s, Danish police kept a close watch on Scherfig. His writings, while they were not, technically speaking, banned, were not readily available to the reading public. Denmark's largest publisher, Gyldendal, with whom he had worked since 1938, did not publish or republish anything by him between the publications of *Idealister* in 1945 and *Frydenholm* in 1962.

Scherfig's fifth novel, *Bothus Occitanus, eller, Den otteøjede Skorpion* (Bothus Occitanus; or The Eight-eyed Scorpion, usually referred to simply as *Skorpionen,* 1953) was serialized in *Land og Folk* and published in book form by Forlaget Tiden, the literary press of the newspaper. *Skorpionen* is Scherfig's most incisive attack on

what he saw as the collusion of Denmark during the Cold War.

Skorpionen is a novel of political intrigue and economic corruption. It is a thinly disguised fictionalized account of one of Denmark's largest scandals of the Cold War era, "Edderkoppesagen" (The Spider Affair), which involved the black market and wrongdoing by the police, which was exposed by the Danish press in 1949. To the sordid details of "Edderkoppesagen," Scherfig added a mysterious and still unsolved double-murder in Copenhagen from the same period; this murder allowed *Skorpionen* to begin along the same sanguinary lines as his three immediately preceding novels.

Skorpionen opens in an "unnamed country on a beautiful Sunday morning in May with the completely unjustified arrest and jailing of the innocent school teacher, Axel Karelius, for the murder of a mysterious Mr. Schulze, the owner of a photography supply store, and Mrs. Schulze. Cast by the narrator as a latter-day Candide, Karelius clings to his conviction that he is living in the best of all possible democratic societies. Despite experiencing police brutality and the miscarriage of justice, Karelius emerges from his jail cell at the end of the novel only slightly the wiser. From the point of Karelius's imprisonment, however, *Skorpionen* deals less with Karelius and his plight than with the machinations of the elements of society who are involved in the scandal.

The unnamed European country, which has not yet fully recovered from its occupation by hostile German troops, is now overrun by American commercial and political interests. The country's leaders eagerly do the bidding of the Central Intelligence Agency (CIA), the United States military colossus, and American businessmen. A venal press encourages the Americanization of the country while turning a blind eye to the social injustices and corruption in its midst.

Skorpionen sets itself apart from Scherfig's earlier and later novels in several ways. Most obvious is its location in the "unnamed country" (which the author implies in a two-page preface is not Denmark), where almost all of the characters have un-Danish names: Justice Minister Bothus, Police President Occitanus, School Principal Timian, even Axel Karelius. In addition, none of the personas in the novel had appeared in any of the four previous novels (and only a few of the characters in *Skorpionen* appear in later works). Several character types are recognizable from previous novels: School Principal Timian's behavior and his pompous and highly stylized speech call the principal of *Det forsømte foraar* to mind; police psychologist Dr. Moritz is at least as egregious a medical fraud as is Dr. Robert Riege. The most important departure from his earlier novels, however, is Scherfig's explicit political message: his unremitting, at times bitter, condemnation of the sins of Western capitalism and his insistence that the liberal democracy of the non-Communist world is rotten to the core. None of his prior novels so openly displays the social indignation of *Skorpionen;* only *Frydenholm* comes close.

As the "Scorpion" affair unravels, an ever-increasing number of powerful members of the bureaucracy are imprisoned or put to death. The opportunistic black marketeers who had collaborated with the Gestapo, and who presently work hand in hand with the CIA, can operate with impunity. Two of the underworld's most prominent participants in the "Scorpion" affair, the "carpet merchant" Ulmus and the "green grocer" Løvkvist, are indeed arrested and imprisoned toward the conclusion of the novel, and many corrupt police officers and military leaders are convicted and jailed for complicity, but their neutralization does little to impede the effectiveness of the organization. As spring comes to the country, Karelius is suddenly released from prison, and almost offhandedly, as if it were no longer of any significance whatsoever, the narrator discloses that detective Jonas, now serving jail time himself, has discovered that the Schulzes were murdered by foreign competitors.

Rather than ending *Skorpionen* with a bang, Scherfig seems to have chosen to end this novel with an anticlimactic whimper. But a closer reading of the concluding pages of *Skorpionen* reveals a subtle, if fragile, sense of optimism. Karelius's faith in the justice of the liberal democratic system has been shaken. He has begun to think independently, and he now concedes that, "Det var vel alligevel ikke det bedste ag alle mulige demokratier her, der kunne nok laves bedre. Der var andre muligheder" (This was probably not the best of all possible democracies here; things probably could be done better. There were other possibilities). Karelius is not the man to bring about these changes, but the very fact that he realizes changes are necessary is a positive first step.

Nine years elapsed between the appearance of *Skorpionen* and the publication of the novel that many consider to be Scherfig's masterpiece, *Frydenholm*. Nearly five hundred pages in length, it is the most ambitious of his literary efforts. To the characters already known from earlier novels (primarily from *Idealister*), Scherfig adds many new ones. *Frydenholm*'s portrait gallery is so densely crowded that the author once observed, and with some satisfaction, that this novel has more characters than Leo Tolstoy's epic *War and Peace* (1868).

Frydenholm begins in the spring of 1939 in a mythical village of the same name, in the region of Præstø in southern Zealand. The first few pages of the novel put into perspective certain events from *Idealister,* with a focus on the murder of Skjern-Svendsen that occurred less than a year before. The castle of Frydenholm has, in the meantime, been sold to the younger brother of Skjern-Svendsen's widow, the vacuous, self-indulgent Preben Flemming Fido, Count Rosenkop-Frydenskjold, whose family had formerly owned the estate. The count arrives in the village, not in an elegant horse-drawn carriage, but astride a farm tractor, which he drunkenly drives into the window of the village bakery. This incident, together with the narrator's prior discussion of Skjern-Svendsen's murder, provides a prefigurative allegory: unpleasant changes are in store for this rural community (which symbolizes Denmark itself). By immediately reminding the reader that the castle of Frydenholm played hospitable host to the Swedish enemy during the Dano-Swedish war of 1658, the narrator reveals the coming role of Frydenholm.

As the count settles in as lord of Castle Frydenholm, Egon Charles Olsen, the watery-eyed print-shop worker from *Idealister* (who was arrested in connection with the murder of Skjern-Svendsen), is being groomed by the Danish police as a spy. From the radio, the rantings of Adolf Hitler come into the living rooms of the village, filling most people with disgust, but filling others, notably Niels Madsen and Marius Petersen (both of

Covers for the first Swedish (1944) and U.S. (1991) editions of Scherfig's novel

whom figured prominently in *Idealister*), with an eager anticipation for great events.

During the winter of 1939–1940, as the war draws nearer to Denmark, the sea surrounding the country freezes fast, creating chaos and holding the kingdom in its icy grip–foreshadowing the debilitating confinement of the coming five-year German Occupation. The German troops easily overtake Denmark early in the morning of 9 April 1940. At first, most Danes submit to what seems to be the inevitable; the German armies have proven all but invincible elsewhere in Europe, and a new order appears about to begin. King Christian X of Denmark; Thorwald Stauning, the fatherly prime minister; and the non-Communist press publicly advocate accommodation with the occupying forces. The Danish police secretly compile an extensive file of known Communists.

The Danish Nazis prepare to seize power. In the Præsto district, Nazi activity centers on the castle of Fry-

denholm, where Count Rosenkop-Frydenskjold has assembled a small band of farmworkers, who train for battle with spades instead of rifles. Prominent German military officers and Danish Nazis receive a warm welcome at the castle. Madsen and Marius openly declare their Nazi sympathies; other residents do so less overtly. Pastor Nørregård-Olsen gives a fascist twist to his sermons, and baker Andersen makes a handsome profit by baking German specialties and selling them to the occupiers.

Other inhabitants are, however, solidly against the German forces and their Danish sympathizers. The region's Communists, led by Martin Olsen and Oscar Poulsen (both of whom appeared in *Idealister,* the latter now married to Johanne, the daughter of Gardener Holm), maintain their vigilance. Not until the Germans break the mutual nonaggression pact with the Soviet Union, however, do they embark on a more overt path of resistance. The area's freethinking physician, Dr.

Damsø, proclaims his disdain for Nazism. Old Emma, still feisty, although well into her eighties, makes no effort to hide her contempt for the occupiers. Yet, other Danes, like the rotund farmer Jens Olsen and his obese daughters, think first and foremost of their own well-being and do not want to get themselves mixed up in anything. This group represents the majority of the population.

When the Danish Nazis stage a mass rally in Copenhagen in November 1940, Madsen and Marius join in, expecting that this gathering will sweep them into power. The citizens of Copenhagen, however, break up the rally and force the Nazis to flee in disarray. Marius, sporting his Nazi uniform, becomes separated from Madsen (who has taken the precaution of attending dressed in his civilian clothes), and is nearly beaten by an angry crowd. He is saved by the police who arrest him and charge him with unlawful assembly, urinating in public, and threatening to use a pistol. He is sentenced to several months in jail and is later decorated as an Aryan hero and martyr to the fascist cause. Marius is given his medal by Count Rosenkop-Frydenskjold who, had he not been drunk at the time, would have been in the vanguard of the Nazi rally in Copenhagen.

In June 1941 the Danish police stage a massive nighttime operation to pick up and imprison as many leading Danish Communists as possible. Martin Olsen is among those dragged out of bed, but Poulsen escapes. The captive Communists are eventually interned in Horserød Lejren, (Horserød Prison Camp) north of Copenhagen.

The Danish authorities repeatedly violate the constitutional rights of the internees who are charged with no crime other than membership in the Danish Communist Party. Prison Warden Henningsen, described by the prisoners as an insecure dwarf, stands as the symbolic representative of the cowardly and repressive Danish collaborative government. Under Henningsen, conditions in Horserød Camp become so unbearable that the justice minister is finally forced to replace the diminutive warden. Life for the families of the interned Communists is hard. Their wives are denied social benefits, and they have difficulty finding enough work to eke out a living. Martin Olsen's wife, Margarete, for example, earns barely enough money cleaning the small local school to feed her growing family. Visiting privileges are restricted and the camp is so remote that few wives manage to see their husbands more than once a month.

After the German defeat at Stalingrad, the public mood in Denmark changes. Acts of sabotage increase (many of them attributed to Poulsen, who becomes an almost mythical figure in the minds of his fellow Danes), and conditions for the interned Communists

improve. Despite assurances that no Danish citizens will be handed over to the Germans, the Danish authorities begin to deport the Communists. Martin Olsen is sent to Stutthof Concentration Camp.

Egon Charles Olsen, now a powerful figure among the Danish collaborators, helps the Germans arrest the print-shop owner, Damaskus. Olsen is later gunned down by the Danish Resistance. As the war moves toward its conclusion, Oscar Poulsen is captured and sent to a German concentration camp. Margarete Olsen receives a terse communication from the Danish Foreign Ministry that Martin has died in Stutthof. Numbly, Margarete thinks of their last evening together. Martin was just one of many innocent Danes who would never again hear the larks sing, who would never smell the fragrances of elderberry blossoms, and for whom the cuckoo would never sing. Martin's obituary, brief as it is, is the most moving tribute to the senseless death of an innocent human being that Scherfig ever wrote.

Damaskus and many other captured Danes return to their homes and families. Soon thereafter the German forces in Denmark capitulate, and the settling of accounts begins. The author does not dwell on the chaos that marked the first few days of freedom in Denmark. Rather, he moves quickly to the message of the novel: despite their complicity, those who were in positions of authority both before and during the Occupation have retained their hold on power.

The final chapter of *Frydenholm* should be viewed both as an allegory for the novel and as a grim warning from the author. The village decides to erect a monument for Poulsen across from Skjern-Svendsen's mausoleum. In attendance are both the true resistors to the German Occupation (Old Emma; Johanne Poulsen, Oscar's widow; and the old Communist, Jakob Enevoldsen) and the tacit collaborators (Pastor Nørregård-Olsen, Harald Horn, Rasmus Larsen). The pastor and Larsen give speeches, insincerely praising Poulsen's bravery and rationalizing their own less honorable conduct during the sccupation. As the plaque with Poulsen's name is unveiled, the supposedly dead freedom fighter appears on the podium and declares that the war against Nazism has only been partially won; the struggle must continue against those who make fascism possible. If the fight is not waged to the finish, Nazism will come again. At this point Poulsen loses his voice and the crowd disperses, unwilling to heed his admonition. Denmark seems to have learned little from the brutal lessons of the occupation and may be condemned to endure similar trials in the future.

Despite the deep emotions Scherfig felt about the German Occupation and his conviction about the continued dangers of fascism, *Frydenholm* must not be

2

Den myrdede var anset for et fredeligt menneske. Han blev
61 år gammel. Ifølge den retsmedicinske rapport døde han did
efter at være tilføjet et antal kraftige slag i hovedet med
et stumpt redskab. Der skete det uhyggelige og i kriminal-
historien enestående, at hans enke bagefter uafvidende spis-
te mordvåbnet. Der blev sagt, at denne omstændighed vanske-
liggjorte politiets arbejde. Men der blev også hvisket, at
man måske i virkeligheden ikke var interesseret i affærens
opklaring.

        Forfatteren havde ikke noget stort navn i literatu-
ren og kunne i sin levetid gå på gaden og køre med nordbane-
toget uden at vække opsigt. Før mordet var navnet Christian
Grønholt-Hansen kun kendt af en beskeden kreds af læsere
med interesse for egnshistorie og hjemstavnsfortællinger.
I mange år leverede han venlige bidrag til heftet "Jul i Hillerød". Han forulempede ikke nogen med sit forfatterskab og
skaffede sig ikke fjender.
        Christian Grønholt-Hansens literære form var ikke
særpræget og kunne ikke af kritikerne fremhæves som forure-
ligende og engageret og kontroversel. Fire romaner om for-
dums landboliv i Nordsjælland og nogle noveller og et bind
"Kulsvier-beretninger" og nogle særdeles grundige topografiske
beskrivelser er blevet betegnet som hyggelige og hæderlige.
At denne literære virksomhed var forbundet med livsfare,
kunne selv den mest skarpsindige kritiker ikke forudse.
        Livet går videre i Fredensborg uden forfatteren
Grønholt-Hansen. Solen står op, og togene kører hver time
uden hans bevidsthed. Husmødrene foretager deres indkøb i
Jernbanegades butikker og giver sig tid til at vælge og
udpege de rette stykker. Der er ingen hektisk travlhed.
Folk hilser høfligt på hinanden og standser og fører samtaler på fortovet. Gamle mænd sidder med deres ølbajere på

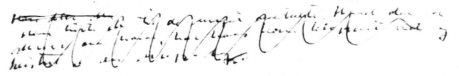

*Corrected typescript page for "Døden i Fredensborg," the novel Scherfig began to write just before his death in 1979
(permission of Christine Scherfig; Hans Scherfig Collection, Det Kongelige Bibliotek)*

viewed as a tendentious Marxist tract. The author's sympathies obviously lie with the Communists in the novel, yet, other characters are accorded an equally positive treatment: Old Emma, Dr. Damsø (who is murdered by Danish Nazis), the retired schoolteacher Tofte, who befriends a young German soldier who later joins the Danish Resistance. All are virtuous human beings who maintain their moral bearings in the face of the turbulence of the war. *Frydenholm* is first and foremost a work of art. As carefully constructed and as tightly written as the author's earlier novels, Frydenholm differs from Scherfig's previous efforts by the relatively sparse use of humor, the depth of emotion, the sometimes ruthlessly realistic depiction of events, and the directness of the author's political message (surpassed in this regard only by *Skorpionen*).

The style of *Frydenholm* is more soberly "documentary" than Scherfig's other novels, for the author was, in a sense, writing the slightly fictionalized history of Denmark's treatment of its Communist citizens during the occupation. In composing this novel, he drew upon his own personal experiences as well as the experiences of fellow Communists. He researched this novel by delving into newspaper accounts and public archives for the many official citations found throughout the novel. Many of the 150 characters in *Frydenholm* were taken directly from real life; some with their identities clearly revealed despite the author's use of pseudonyms.

Two years after he completed *Frydenholm,* Scherfig published *Den fortabte abe* (The Lost Monkey, 1964), a modest narrative of barely 120 pages that tells a lighter, less complicated story than either *Idealister* or *Frydenholm*. In *Den fortabte abe,* he returns to the theme he explored in *Den døde Mand* nearly thirty years earlier: commercial chicanery in the painting world.

After the publication of *Den fortabte abe,* Scherfig wrote no more novels. At this stage in his career, he concentrated on essays, travel narratives, and newspaper columns. A volume of short stories, *Butleren og andre historier* (The Butler and Other Stories), appeared in 1973. All the stories in this collection had, however, been written earlier, and most had been published in magazines or newspapers in the 1930s.

The title story, "Butleren" ("The Butler," which appeared for the first time in 1934), recounts an incident in Daverill Hall near London where the first-person narrator has been hired to paint pictures of elephants on the walls of the children's nursery (as a painter, Scherfig was famous for his colorful jungle animals, especially his elephants, and was often asked to carry out such projects). James, the aloof butler and the model of British correctness, runs amok one day. He gets drunk on Lord Daverill's whiskey and locks himself in the china closet, where he fires a revolver and then smashes the china. The Daverill family takes this all in stride and patiently waits for James to run his course. After a little more than a day, James sobers up and reverts to his officious ways; life in Daverill Hall can again return to normal. The narrator uses this incident to ridicule both the British upper classes (who think, for example, that "Henry Ibsen" is Danish), and to express his solidarity with James, who showed that he was human after all.

Between the appearance of *Butleron og andre historier* in 1973 and his death on 28 January 1979, Scherfig published no other works of fiction. He did, however, have plans for an eighth novel, which he had tentatively titled "Døden i Fredensborg" (Death in Fredensborg), the small north Zealand village in which he and his wife had lived since the 1960s. At his death, he left behind only four typewritten pages of this novel. "Døden i Fredensborg" might have been a novel of the "perfect crime," since the killer used a blunt instrument (a frozen supermarket chicken) to bludgeon his victim to death, and the victim's wife unknowingly ate the murder weapon. Little beyond this intriguing beginning exists, however; but it is enough to show that Scherfig still possessed the ability to write an unforgettable first chapter.

Scherfig had a profound influence on his contemporaries and on the generation of Danish authors who followed him. Many of these authors paid their tribute to him in essays, such as: Anders Bodelsen, "Den falske loyalitet: Hans Scherfig" ("False Loyalty: Hans Scherfig," 1967), and Finn Søeborg in his autobiography, *Sådan var det bare* (That's Just the Way It Was, 1986). Others incorporated references to or scenes from his novels into their own works. Leif Panduro, for example, modeled his novel *Høfeber* (Hay Fever, 1975), in which a respected judge disappears and takes on a new existence, in *Den forsvundne fuldmægtig*. Anders Bodelsen was also inspired by *Den forsvundne fuldmægtig* when composing his novel *Straus* (1971), which describes the disappearance of a writer of mystery novels. The narrator of *Straus* laments at one point that he cannot employ a certain plotline because it would inevitably remind his readers of one of Scherfig's novels.

Two of Scherfig's novels have been filmed: *Den forsvundne fuldmægtig* in 1971 and *Det forsømte foraar* in 1993. *Frydenholm* was dramatized as *Rejsen til Frydenholm* (Journey to Frydenholm) and produced at Copenhagen's Fiolteatret in 1975. In 1979 Danmarks Radio broadcast a four-part opera based on *Skorpionen*. Dramatizations of both *Det forsømte foraar* and *Idealister* were produced in the 1980s.

Scherfig has remained a favorite with the reading public of Denmark. His ability to tell a good story in a straightforward and uncomplicated style makes his novels accessible to a large and varied audience. All Scherfig's novels, with the exception of *Skorpionen,* have frequently been reprinted since the 1960s and have been translated into several languages: among them English, German, Dutch, Swedish, Norwegian, Polish, Czech, Hungarian, Bulgarian, Romanian, and Russian. Middle-class readers seem not to be deterred by his often barbed critiques of the capitalist system, and, instead, consider him to be one of the "grand old men" of Danish letters.

Bibliography:

Nils Frederiksen, *Hans Scherfig: En bibliografi* (Copenhagen: Gyldendal, 1977).

References:

Jens Kr. Andersen and Leif Emerek, *Hans Scherfigs forfatterskab: En analyse* (Copenhagen: Vinten, 1973);

Carl Erik Bay, Nils Frederiksen, and Ejgil Søholm, *Hans Scherfig 1905–1979* (Copenhagen: Tiden, 1989);

Arngeir Berg and Espen Haavardsholm, *Partiskhed* (Oslo: Gyldendal, 1975);

Anders Bodelsen, "Den falske loyalitet: Hans Scherfig," *Tilbageblik på 30'erne,* volume 2, edited by Hans Hertel (Copenhagen: Stig Vendelkær, 1967), pp. 134–148;

Elias Bredsdorff, "Hans Scherfig's roman *Frydenholm,*" in his *Fra Andersen til Scherfig* (Copenhagen: Gyldendal, 1978), pp. 191–221;

Carsten Clante, *Normale mennesker: Hans Scherfig og hans romaner* (Copenhagen: Gyldendal, 1975);

Clante and Frederiksen, eds., *Omkring Det forsømte forår* (Copenhagen: Hans Reitzel, 1974);

Frederiksen and John Poulsen, eds., *Hans Scherfig: Forfatteren, maleren og kommunisten* (Copenhagen: Tiden, 1985);

Otto Gelsted, "Et talent med tre hoveder," in his *Goddag liv!* (Copenhagen: Sirius, 1958), pp. 84–93;

Daniel Hjorth, "Trivselskommunism: Hans Scherfig," in his *Bifigurer och några andra* (Stockholm: Atlantis, 1980), pp. 223–230;

Frank Hugus, "Hans Scherfig's *Det forsømte forår:* Investigating the Genesis of the Novel," *Scandinavica,* 33 (1994): 57–88;

Hugus, "Literary Sources of Hans Scherfig's *Den forsvundne fuldmægtig,*" *Scandinavian Studies,* 1 (Winter 1996): 19–50;

Vilhelm Joost, *Scherfig* (Copenhagen: Stig Vendelkær, 1974);

Claus Ingemann Jørgensen, *Scherfig og fru Drusse af Ude og Hjemmes historie* (Ålborg: Aalborg Universitetsbibliotek, 1993);

Aven Møller Kristensen, "How to Castigate Your Public—and Write Best Sellers," *Danish Journal,* 76 (1973): 26–29;

Birthe Wind Lindegaard, "Nøglen eller romanen—en genre til revision," *Kritik,* no. 40 (1976): 45–70;

Antje Mayfarth, "Antifascistischer Widerstandskampf als geschichtliche Aufgabe: Zum Hans Scherfigs weltanschaulish-künstlerischer Konzeption," *Nordeuropa,* 12 (1979): 65–74;

Jørgen Moestrup, *Hans Scherfig* (Copenhagen: Gyldendal, 1977);

Hans-Jørgen Nielsen, "Hans Scherfig," *Danske digtere i det 20: århundrede,* volume 3, edited by Torben Brostrøm and Mette Winge (Copenhagen: Gad, 1981), pp. 180–211;

Dieter K. H. Riegel, "Society and Crime in the Novels of Hans Scherfig," *Scandinavian-Canadian Studies* (1983): 109–114;

Birger Wamberg, *Samtaler med danske digtere* (Copenhagen: Gyldendal, 1968).

Papers:

Hans Scherfig's papers are held by Det Kongelige Bibliotek (The Royal Library), Copenhagen.

Peter Seeberg

(22 June 1925 – 8 January 1999)

James Massengale

University of California, Los Angeles

BOOKS: *Bipersonerne* (Viborg: Arena, 1956);

Fugls føde (Viborg: Arena, 1957); translated by Anni Whissen as *The Impostor,* with an afterword by Niels Ingwersen (Lincoln: University of Nebraska Press, 1990);

Eftersøgningen og andre noveller (Viborg: Arena, 1962);

Jens Munks minde-ekspedition, by Seeberg and Thorkild Hansen (Copenhagen: Gyldendal, 1965);

Ferai: Et dramatisk forløb (Viborg: Arena, 1970);

Hyrder: Roman (Viborg: Arena, 1970);

Dinosaurusens sene eftermiddag (Viborg: Arena, 1974);

Erobringen af Fyn: en øjenvidnerapport fra maj 1974 (Viborg: Nørhaven Bogtrykkeri, 1974);

TV-version af St. St. Blicher: En landsbydegns dagbog (Viborg: Arkiv for Ny Litteratur/Arena, 1975);

Argumenter for benådning: Noveller (Viborg: Arena, 1976);

12. – 17. November 1917: Forslag til en film, photographs by Jørgen Bang (Viborg: Arena, 1977);

På selve dagen: Et skuespil for amatører i tre akter (Gråsten: Drama, 1978);

Ved havet: Roman (Viborg: Arena, 1978);

Hovedrengøring: Stumper af erindring (Viborg: Nørhaven Bogtrykkeri, 1979);

Om fjorten dage (Viborg: Arena, 1981);

Roland kommer til verden: En ny historie om Roland, illustrated by Ursula Hanne Seeberg (Copenhagen: Gyldendal, 1986);

Værkfører Thomsens endelige hengivelse (Brøndum: Brøndum forlag, 1986);

Den sovende dreng (Copenhagen: Gyldendal, 1988);

Frosten hjælper: En fortsættelse til Den sovende dreng (Copenhagen: Gyldendal, 1989);

Rejsen til Ribe: Noveller (Viborg: Samleren, 1990);

En dag med Svava, illustrated by Tryggvi Olafsson (Copenhagen: Brøndum, 1991);

Vingeslag—og andre noveller, illustrated by Seeberg (Copenhagen: Gyldendal, 1995);

Oh, at være en kænguru, illustrated by Seeberg (Copenhagen: Gyldendal, 1996);

Halvdelen af natten (Copenhagen: Gyldendal, 1997);

Peter Seeberg (courtesy of Gyldendal Publishers)

En efterårsdag i jernalderen, illustrated by Seeberg (Copenhagen: Gyldendal, 1998).

Collection: *Udvalgte noveller,* edited by Johannes Riis (Copenhagen: Samleren, 1994).

PLAY PRODUCTION: *Ferai,* Odin Theatre, Holstebro, 1969.

MOTION PICTURE: *Sult,* screenplay by Seeberg, based on Knut Hamsun's novel, Svenska Filminstitut/Sandrews, 1966.

TELEVISION: *En Landsbydegns Dagbog,* script by Seeberg, based on a short story by Steen Steensen Blicher, 1975.

OTHER: *Gruppe 66: Introduktion: En antologi,* edited by Seeberg, Anders Bodelsen, and Ivan Malinovski (Copenhagen, 1966);

En lille musebog, edited by Seeberg (Viborg: Arena, 1977);

Her på lag: noder og unoder i Viborg Amt, edited by Seeberg (Viborg: Komplot, 1977);

Højtlæsning for en flue og andre jobs, edited by Seeberg and Per Højholt (Viborg: Arena, 1985);

Husk Klaus: En hilsen til Klaus Rifbjerg på hans tresårsdag, 15. December 1991, edited by Seeberg and Niels Barfoed (Copenhagen: Samleren, 1991).

SELECTED PERIODICAL PUBLICATIONS–UNCOLLECTED: "Den tavse generation," *Informationens kronik,* 19 April 1955; "Wittgenstein," *Information,* 31 March and 2 April 1959.

Within the realm of modern Danish literature, no author has for a longer time or more tenaciously held onto the position of short fiction specialist, in the widest definition of the term, than did Peter Seeberg. Within his novels, Seeberg employed a variety of pseudorealistic documents, which distance his works from the structure of ordinary novels, at the same time linking them to the nonfiction documents most people deal with in the real world. On the appearance of a new book in 1997, literary critic Lars Bukdahl exulted that "Peter Seeberg både er vores mest radikale avantgardist og vores fremmeste realist, side om side" (Peter Seeberg is our most radical avant-gardist and our most outstanding realist, at the same time). The latest in a venerable line of short-story masters from the Jutland peninsula that includes Steen Steensen Blicher, Johannes V. Jensen, and Henrik Pontoppidan, Seeberg shares their sense of peasant sturdiness and earthy pleasure; their psychologically realistic, often pessimistic view of humankind; and their ironic whimsy. Seeberg's "myte-syn" (mythical perspective) reaches beyond Jensen's, however, and is a term so well established in the critical assessment of his authorship that it was used as a book title for a set of major essays about him. "Mytesyn" is not a reference to any consistent linkage to older mythical systems, nor is it an indication of his wish to create a modern mythology. It is rather an acknowledgment of his talent in representing those ontological oddities that arise out of everyday contexts and assume–often in absurd twists of adventure–a timeless dimension. Although Seeberg was always diffident about discovering deeper meaning or higher truth, he is considered a modern master at probing the nature of reality and in depicting humans in their search for existential guideposts. The Scandinavians placed him in the front rank of their modern writers and rewarded him with their most prestigious literary prizes. However, his work is not well known in the English-speaking world and does not garner as much critical attention as it deserves.

Peter Ejnar Lauritzen Seeberg was born on 22 June 1925 in Skrydstrup, in the district of Haderslev, near the southern border of present-day Denmark. His parents were Christian Seeberg and Karen Kristine Seeberg, née Kjær. His father was a teacher and writer. The area in which Seeberg was born and grew up had long been torn by the territorial dispute between Germany and Denmark. The northern portion of the duchy of Schleswig-Holstein between Kongeå (The King's River) and the present border near the city of Åbenrå had been taken by force from Denmark in 1864 and subjected to a program of cultural and linguistic Germanization by the Prussian authorities. This program was met with resistance by the Danish-speaking populace, and after the end of World War I a referendum officially returned the 4,000-square-kilometer area to the Danish monarchy on 9 July 1920. By the time Seeberg had completed his secondary-school education, the Germans were back, this time occupying all of Denmark on 9 April 1940. Seeberg's youthful inclination was toward writing and literary study, but following an adventurous and also dangerous whim, he spent the summer and fall of 1943 as a volunteer worker at the UFA motion-picture *ateljés* (studios) outside the blacked-out city of Berlin. After the war, he attended the University of Copenhagen, where he studied comparative literature, taking his advanced degree in 1950. A dearth of academic jobs led him to find work at the National Museum in Copenhagen, and he became an archaeologist. His second career was more than merely successful. He could boast of participation in major excavations in the Middle East, Scandinavia, and the Arctic, and his settled position as the head of the regional Viborg Museum afforded him an outlet for research in cultural history, local excavations, exhibits, and scientific articles.

While his archaeological career was developing, however, Seeberg had no intention of abandoning his literary interest. "Spionen" (The Spy), an existential short story published in *Perspektiv* in 1953, was his debut piece, although he had experimented with writing as a teenager. In a particularly openhearted interview with the writer Hanne Marie Svendsen in the mid 1960s, he sketched his early development:

> Jeg offentliggjorde blandt andet nogle bondehistorier i 'Landet,' men samtidig skete der det, at jeg fik skrevet en novelle, 'Spionen,' og det var første gang jeg overhovedet havde på fornemmelsen at have truffet en tone, man kunne arbejde videre på. Jeg prøvede mig så frem i forskellige retninger, og her var det rimeligt, at jeg gav mig i lag med et stof, som var helt selvfølgeligt for mig, nemlig mit halvårs lange ophold i Berlin i sommeren og efteråret 1943, hvor jeg jo havde oplevet både det ene

og det andet, men også–at man ikke kunne opleve noget på den måde.

(I published among other things some "farmer's tales" in [the provincial magazine] *Landet,* but at the same time it happened that I wrote one short story, "Spionen," and that was the first time I had the feeling that I had caught a tone that I could keep on working on. So I experimented in several directions, and, reasonably enough, I set to work on material that was inevitable for me, namely my six-month stay in Berlin during the summer and fall of 1943, when I had experienced one thing or another–but also had found that nothing could be experienced in that way.)

In literary theory, Seeberg was already mature, as may be seen in a critical article he published in *Information* (19 April 1955), "Den tavse generation" (The Silent Generation): "Den nye epoke, som man taler om, begynder vel først der, hvor man indser, at man ikke kan give sit besyv med . . . fordi man har gjort sine erfaringer på andre felter. Hvor man er blevet fremmed, uden at føle trang til modsigelse, som blot ville bringe en på bølgelængde med det man modsagde" (The new epoch that is being spoken of begins first at the point where we come to the understanding that we can't offer any opinion . . . because our experiences lie elsewhere. Where one has become estranged, without feeling the need for formulating a counterargument, that sort of statement that would simply place us on the same wavelength as the argument with which we were in disagreement). Seeberg coined the term "Silent Generation" to refer to the Danish writers of the 1950s. It stuck and is usually used to refer to those writers who played no active role in the ideology of World War II, but who were young enough to be affected by the horrors it brought. Their paralysis expressed itself in a reaction of antipathy to all ideologies or even to the possibility of getting in touch with any sort of workable reality. This paralysis characterized Seeberg's first two novels and put him, together with Villy Sørensen, at the forefront of new Danish prose writers of the 1950s. The "material that was inevitable" for him to rework into fiction was published as a novel in 1956 under the title *Bipersonerne* (Secondary Figures). Although loosely conceived as a collective novel, it has only an oblique or negative relationship to the proletarian, heroless novels of the 1930s, of which Hans Kirk's *Fiskerne* (The Fishermen, 1928) is often considered the Danish prototype. There is indeed no hero in Seeberg's book. A group of men is recruited by the Germans to serve as backstage crew for their Berlin propaganda movie studios. But the motion picture being worked on in the detailed, realistic account of six consecutive days at the studio has no propaganda value. It is a fluffy, escapist musical fantasy about Hawaii–and very little filming is actually done. The stagehands are engaged in busywork: "Schnell, Schnell!" shouts the foreman, more to justify his own existence than to indicate any particular hurry. The reality of a dying Berlin that lies outside the building where they work to create the fantasy world of a movie is ignored in their desperation to perpetuate the fantasy that the country in which they live is not war ravaged. The only concession to that reality is the sense of captivity felt by the secondary figures. And even this sense is partially illusory, since the setting of the novel is in no way a concentration camp. The workers have been taken from occupied countries, since all healthy German men are on active duty. But the living conditions at the studio are neither totally restrictive nor completely unhealthy. There is only one escape incident in the novel, and there is basically nowhere to escape to. Out of the anonymous cast, the Dane, Sim, gradually crystallizes as a sort of authorial alter ego. Seeberg has explained that the un-Danish name Sim may be considered the subjunctive of the Latin verb "to be," hence something like: "if I were," and a playful naming of characters is a characteristic trait of Seeberg's early work. Sim sees himself as a kind of protagonist, but his coworkers and the novel itself undermine this view. They want to know why he had come from occupied Denmark to war-torn Berlin. To spy? To show sympathy for the Germans? To experience excitement? There is a shadow of guilt in the exchange between Sim and Marcel:

–Det kan være du bliver skudt for landsforræderi. Det er mig ubegribeligt, at du er kommet herned . . .
–Tal du med Andres om det, han mener, jeg burde skydes.
–Så vigtig en personage er du nu alligevel ikke, min højt elskede ven. Efter min mening er du ikke en kugle værd, basta! Så rejs du bare hjem, inden Berlin går helt i smadder, for det gør den.

("Maybe they'll shoot you for treason. I can't understand why you would come down here . . ."
"Talk to Andres about it; he thinks I ought to be shot."
"You're not really an important enough person for that, my dearest friend. That's my opinion: you aren't worth the price of a bullet, basta! Just trot along home, before Berlin gets bombed to smithereens, because that's what's going to happen.")

The problem is that Sim is so thoroughly a simulator that even the reality of guilt cannot manifest itself. *Bipersonerne* has been called "historieløs, fordi den nægter at se sine personer som betingede af og indvirkende på den historiske situation" (outside history, because it refuses to observe its characters as being conditioned by or as interacting with the historical situation). One could say with equal right, however, that the sense of the historic condition lies everywhere in the book—in the very fact that the war and Germany's now inevitable defeat are actively ignored, both by the characters and by the author. The "secondary figures" are, in a real sense, the proper Everymen for a cataclysmic, apocalyptic world. Beyond a certain point in an historical sequence of events, the events themselves are the "main characters," and even the humans that set them in motion or carry them out have lost their significance. They can do nothing significantly different from what these petty workers can do: take nails out of scenery, put nails into scenery, and wait for the end. *Bipsersonerne* is both the foundation stone of Seeberg's literary production and the exception to the rest. As he himself noted in the early interview with Svendsen:

> med hensyn til "Bipersonerne" der vil jeg sige, at det var en bog, som ingen forløbere har og ingen efterfølgere vil få. Den situation, der skildredes, og de forutsætninger, som jeg havde for at skildre den, danner tilsammen en kombination, der ikke kommer igen.

> (with regard to *Bipersonerne,* I must say that it was a book that has had no antecedents, and will not have any successors. The situation I described, and the particular conditions under which I described it are, in combination, a set of circumstances that will never arise again.)

This is not a boasting remark; it reflects a simple truth. Sim, for all his lack of presence and reality, is the closest to an autobiographical portrait that Seeberg came in over forty years of authorship, and the combination of the unrelenting realism and existential blockage that he refined and made into a cogent form was conditioned by the specific experience it reflects.

Seeberg's second novel, *Fugls føde* (1957; translated as *The Impostor,* 1990), brought his Danish readership back to a more recognizable landscape and a familiar authorial problem: writer's block. The book caught on with academics and intellectuals, and, as Niels Ingwersen points out in his afterword to the English translation: "Many cult books soon lose their admirers, but Danes—like many others—continue to be fascinated with *The Impostor,* just as Americans still find pleasure in, or get riled by, reading J. D. Salinger or Joseph Heller." The novel is not a simple depiction of a frustrated, penniless, written-out novelist; the plot of the book centers on a sort of cat-and-mouse game played with the luckless Tom by an old acquaintance, Hiffs. Hiffs is like Tom in his nihilism, his capability to deal on the fringes of the ethical (or beyond them), and his lack of inherent creativity. But he has money, and he has Tom eating out of his hand, ready in his desperation to prostitute his talent (if he has talent—the reader

Cover for Seeberg's first novel, about workers at a Berlin motion-picture studio during World War II

never learns this) for the prospect of cash payment. Hiffs offers Tom 10,000 kroner, to write something:

> —Du skal skrive noget, der er vigtigt, sagde Hiffs.
> —Hvad mener du med det, sagde Tom,—har du tænkt dig at udgive det?
> —Det er ikke det, det drejer sig om, sagde Hiffs,—har du hørt, hvad jeg har sagt?
> —Ja, sagde Tom, —noget virkeligt; skal det være langt?
> —Passende, sagde Hiffs,—hverken længere eller kortere, det kommer ikke an på det.

> ("I want you to write something important," said Hiffs.
> "What do you mean by that?" said Tom. "Were you thinking of publishing it?"
> "That's not the point," said Hiffs. "Were you listening to what I said?"
> "Yes," said Tom, "Something real. Should it be long?"
> "Long enough," said Hiffs. "Neither longer nor shorter, that isn't the important thing.")

The reader's first reaction—like Tom's—is that this is child's play. The second reaction is that it appears to be somewhat problematic, perhaps a trap, or a misunderstanding on Tom's part (is "important" the same as "real"?). And the third—as the reader follows Tom's despairing, hopeless failure in the job as the book unfolds—is that it is like one of those Buddhist philosophical puzzles that are designed to have no solution. Writing is an act of distancing oneself from reality. There is no set of words to bring one closer. After agonizing over his task, Tom finally produces this tiny prose poem:

> Mine øjne er blinde,
> mine hænder er visne,
> mit sind er hjemsøgt af tilintetgørelse.

> (My eyes are blind,
> my hands are withered,
> my soul is afflicted with annihilation.)

After thinking a bit more, he adds another line:

> Jeg skriver dette for at tjene titusind.
> (I am writing this in order to earn ten thousand.)

Naturally, the project fails to bring Tom the desired result. He loses Etna, his "volcanic" girlfriend, and he is brought to a point where his despair is so complete that it might even be posited that at least this angst is some sort of reality for Tom. Seeberg still holds an ironic hand over Tom, however. The story ends with Tom at the seashore, throwing stones out into the water. When they make their plunking sound he cries out: "Jeg er her!" (I am here!). It is not a reassuring affirmation, but a desperate and doubting cry of pain. But it is just this fear, this incapability of establishing one's position in an ideology by a particular activity, that rang true enough for the young Danes of the 1950s to make Seeberg famous for his empty character, Tom (*tom* means "empty" in Danish). The title of the book, literally "Bird Feed," does not lend itself well to direct translation, but obliquely reflects the famous lines from W. S. Gilbert: "Food for fishes / Only fitted, / Jester wishes / He was dead."

Seeberg's production slowed—and shortened—after *Fugls føde*. His debut story, "Spionen," had been published for over a decade when he added sixteen remarkable stories to it and published the resulting collection as *Eftersøgningen og andre noveller* (The Investigation and Other Stories, 1962). While "Spionen" is well written, its absurd but angst-ridden style is rather like that of *Fugls føde*. By contrast, "Patienten" (The Patient), Seeberg's most frequently anthologized tale, is a harbinger of a radical new trend in his writing. The story of a patient who keeps getting body parts removed and replaced with mechanical devices shows

a new control of absurd humor. The cast of fanatic, often endearing characters in *Eftersøgningen* is long and varied: the workmen who are supposed to dig a hole all the way through to China, the man who gets an automobile tire as a present and builds his life around it, the couple who hear a big noise; the confidence trickster who devises a plan to build new apartments out of air and assurances. The most endearing characters are two searchers in "Investigation," the title story. The search the two men are conducting to find someone emerges as a meaningful activity, not because they believe the person is ever going to be found, but because the search itself gives purpose and definition to their lives.

Seeberg explained that one key that unlocked his new approach was his reading of the works of Ludwig Wittgenstein in the late 1950s. In a pair of articles on Wittgenstein published in *Information* in 1959, Seeberg turns toward the idea of language as play, as communicative gamesmanship, not in order to solve problems of existence in a dialectical way, but to call attention to existence through language. *Eftersøgningen og andre noveller* is a tour de force that comes from this new direction, a distillation of absurd humor, poignant moments (in which absurdity lurks as well), and a tendency for human situations to "mythologize" themselves.

In response to Svendsen, who asked him how he began to write extremely short tales after his first two novels, Seeberg said:

> Ja det gik sådan til: Jeg havde arbejdet længe med en storroman, "Eftersøgningen," som altså bevægede sig på alle mulige planer og var et projekt a la "Der Mann ohne Eigenschaften." Men så kom min dovenskab ind i billedet. Det her skulle jo overstås, og så sagde jeg til mig selv: Men i himlens navn, det kan skrives på 14 sider. Sa skriver vi det på 14 sider. Det var en lykke at gøre det. Og så var lysten vakt til at skrive noveller.

> (This is how it happened: I had worked for a long time with a large novel, "The Investigation," that played itself out on every possible level, a project like "Der Mann ohne Eigenschaften." But then my laziness got in the way. I had to get it done, and so I said to myself: but in Heaven's name, the whole thing can be said in 14 pages. So let's put it down in 14 pages. It was sheer bliss to do that. And with that, my desire was awakened to write short fiction.)

Seeberg's self-deprecating irony should not be taken too literally. But the type of compressed expression he refers to is employed from that point on, both in his longer and his shorter pieces. The novel *Hyrder: Roman* (Shepherds: Novel, 1970) could be viewed as a continuation of the problem posed in the story from *Eftersøgningen* called "Nød" (Need), about a patient who never regains consciousness after a traffic accident, and his nurse. The macabre situation is projected into the novel in such a way that the main character, Leo Gray, becomes a quadriplegic, semiconscious package less than a quarter of the way into the work, and only regains center stage for a few seconds at the end. In an essay included in Ibn Holk's book on Seeberg's authorship, Bo Hakon Jørgensen has stated that *Hyrder* is a kind of new configuration of the concept of "secondary character," where the "gray" central figure is removed from the center of his own life story and attains a kind of "everyday mythological" status. The actions of those who find him, attend to him, think of him, and care for him—the "Shepherds" of his ruined existence—in themselves are reconfigured in a new way such that one might say that Gray, in his absolute inability to connect with reality either by thinking or doing, provides them with a purpose in life—to ensure that Gray's spiritual self exists by thinking about him as a person and that his physical self exists by taking care of his bodily needs. Seeberg also skillfully reformatted his tale for reading on the radio, a type of performance that has been popular for several decades on Danmarks Radio, the state-supported broadcast system.

Seeberg's growing audience in Denmark was used to his trademark style of "mythologizing modern life" by the 1970s, despite his rather sparse production. His book of short stories published in 1974, *Dinosaurusens sene eftermiddag* (The Late Afternoon of the Dinosaur), was still "farther out" in the modernistic sense, and could represent, for the reader who enjoys finding watersheds in authors' productions, a clear line of demarcation in his writing. Seeberg had transformed into a full-fledged avant-gardist, and a kind of fusion occurs between his two careers. Jørgen Christian Hansen correctly noted, in his essay in Holk's book, that "Seebergs dinosaurus-bog røber museumsmanden og digteren, arkivaren og skaberen. Da bogen udkom, mente de forvirrede anmeldere, at kun en del af bogens tekster kunne kaldes noveller. Mange af dem er da også en slags optegnelser, noter, glimt, eller kataloger" (Seeberg's dinosaur-book reveals the museum director and the poet, the archivist and the creator. When the book was published, the confused reviewers wrote that only a portion of the texts in the volume deserved to be called short stories. Many of them are also a sort of memoranda, notes, glimpses or catalogues). More particularly, there are necrologies, a last will and testament, and a genealogy. However, not only are these documents fictional (they only appear to be real), they also tell stories in a way that forces the reader to use the archaeologist's and anthropologist's mental tools to discover through them what really happened, as when such fragmentary records are assembled in a museum.

The "dinosaur-book" represents Seeberg in perfect balance between his technical skill as a researcher and his creativity as a modernist writer. In one sense, one could call Seeberg a humorous radical of no particular political inclination, who might imagine his readers struggling in vain to fit his stories into the category of "short story" that the book cover tells them they are going to read. In another sense, he is an archaeologist who knows what poetry lies hidden in dusty archives. But the crucial matter is that the "documents" Seeberg publishes are consciously not real, and their ostensibly archival tone always vibrates with emotion and authorial wit.

The technique used in Seeberg's later fiction follows a three-part pattern: sets of realistic, traditionally formatted short stories in the middle of each book are flanked on the one side by quasi-documentary, fragmentary or aphoristic material and on the other by whimsical fables and poetic pieces. While the boundaries for this "flanking" procedure are somewhat fluid, the general principle holds true. Set against this formal plan, there can be a thematic idea that colors our understanding of all of the pieces in each book. For example, the main story line about a superannuated species of dinosaur opens a perspective that appears as latent content in much of the other material: the concept of fading personalities, dying races, and leave-taking. The consistency of Seeberg's newer, varied perspective was noticed by the critic Hansen, who pronounced *Dinosaurusens sene eftermiddag* the first of a triptych that includes *Argumenter for benådning: Noveller* (Arguments for Clemency: Stories, 1976) and *Om fjorten dage* (In Fourteen Days, 1981). This pronouncement was true in 1985, but in light of Seeberg's later production, the correct term is now polyptych; Seeberg did not decide to limit himself to three such books, and there is no clear line of demarcation between those from the 1970s and later products.

New trends and aspects, however, arise as central themes in each succeeding volume. Karen Horsens responded to *Argumenter for benådning* by remarking, in an essay in Holk's collection, that "i Seebergs senere bøger har man fundet 'noget,' som anmeldere og andre litteraturkritikere har vurderet og defineret vidt forskelligt" (in Seeberg's later books "something" has been seen that reviewers and other literary critics have assessed and defined in widely different ways). Some critics, Horsens went on to note, saw these new aspects as a manifestation of a humanist tolerance on Seeberg's part, while others "dømmer Seeberg for med sine seneste bøger at have kastet sig ud i et religiøst fantasteri og dermed have svigtet menneskene i bearbejdelsen af deres virkelige problemer" (criticize Seeberg for having jumped into some sort of religious fantasy, whereby

PETER SEEBERG

Halvdelen af natten

GYLDENDAL

PETER SEEBERG

Halvdelen af natten

GYLDENDAL

© Katrine Ussing

ISBN 87-00-31082-4

Dust jacket for Seeberg's 1997 short-story collection

he has failed humanity by not working with realistic problems). As Horsen perceptively concluded, "Ingen af definitionerne forekommer umiddelbart træffende" (But none of the definitions appears to hit the mark exactly).

Part of the difficulty many Danish critics of the 1970s had in understanding the new elements in Seeberg's work was that contemporary consensus held that old Lutheran concepts such as *nåde* (grace) were suspect as a kind of invocation of a nonexistent God that had been created by a feudal system to solidify its own power. Here Seeberg was out in front of the pack, with a position that neither denied his early avowed nihilism nor succumbed to an outmoded existential angst. Always skeptical of political ideologies, his "invocations" were directed neither at God nor at Karl Marx. In *Argumenter for benådning* Seeberg neither says that there is nor is not "clemency"; the work is rather a sort of elegant and humorous verbal ballet in which the justifications the characters present to the courts and their peer groups and wives constitute their formulation of

an existential meaning. Naturally, the abstract quality of a court of law makes it easy to extrapolate a final step and understand a direct appeal is being made to God. The reply will not be found, however, in Seeberg's work.

In 1978 Seeberg experimented with the collective novel once again. *Ved havet* is the most radically composed of his novels, but it could be said to refer structurally to each of his previous longer pieces. One long (eighteen-hour) summer day at the beach—around the sandy islands Rømø and Sild on the southwest coast of Jutland and northern Germany—is noted down almost minute by minute (the time of day is recorded in the text margins), as a whimsically chosen cast of about forty vacationers disport themselves on the sand. The parallel to *Bipersonerne* is more striking than might at first be imagined. The people are by no means prisoners in any ordinary sense, unless one were to make a philosophical extrapolation based upon the prison house of societal norms. But they are all "secondary characters," once more, and part of the irony in the novel is inherent in the narrator's scientific enthusiasm for getting all the details and the time of day down correctly, as if that kind of accuracy would give the reader more insight into the meaning of what is going on. In direct opposition to the accepted truism that a Sunday at the beach is a time when people can be themselves (or at least something other than they ordinarily must be), Seeberg shows that the only character that truly possesses a clear and immutable identity is the sea itself, the only completely mute and passive participant in the day:

> Stranden har altid været der. Den er før end alt andet og bliver længere end alt andet. Den er det første og det sidste. Men før den og efter den er havet. Menneskene fylder så lidt i strandens tid. Og ingenting i havets. Hvis havet har tid? . . . 18.01 Det er blot en tanke her tidligt på aftenen.

> (The beach has always been here. It was here before everything else and it was stay after everything else is gone. It is the first and the last. But before it and after it is the sea. People make so little difference in the time frame of the beach. And nothing in that of the sea. That is, if the sea even has a time frame? . . . 6.01 P.M. It is only a thought, here early in the evening.)

The philosophical Friedrich, a character who could be fused at times with the narrator in his frenetic note-taking and philosophizing, does not give the reader a meaningful interpretation of the day, any more than does the skydiver who almost forgets to pull his rip cord. Everyone, even the most secondary of secondary characters, becomes a bit more mythological with the sea as background.

By 1983 when Seeberg won the Nordic Council's prestigious Literary Award, the committee reflected a general academic consensus in saying that his work that "på en nyskabende måde, med præcisionens mesterskab og gennem et spil med mange tidsperspektiver, giver stille menneskelige eksistenser en mytisk dimension" (in a creative way, with the mastery of precision and through a play of many time perspectives, gives quiet human existences a mythic dimension). The work specifically cited was *Om fjorten dage,* which was published in 1981. The realistic core of the book, in this instance, is a group of ten stories from a southern Jutland town set during November of 1927. The one hundred pages that comprise these tales constitutes, yet again, a kind of "collective novel," in which several of the characters recur in central and peripheral positions. The setting is the landscape of Seeberg's childhood. The month is November; as Seeberg remarked to Marianne Juhl in an interview for *Weekendavisen* (9 September 1990):

> November er hovedtidspuktet for alt, hvad jeg har skrevet. De grå sfærers måned, som svarer til at jeg altid har befundet mig et sted, hvor der er meget lidt betydningsfuldt. Alligevel har jeg ønsket at give dette sted karakter og farve–at give det betydningsløse betydning.

> (November is the principal point in time for everything I have written. The month of the gray spheres, that reflect the fact that I have always found myself someplace where there is little that is meaningful. Even so, I have wanted to give that place character and color–to give meaning to the meaninglessness.)

The year 1927 is also central to Seeberg's mythos. In his address to the Danish Language Association in 1982, when he was presented with its prize for literature, Seeberg outlined his plan for the composition of his realistic stories: "Jeg havde den drøm, at jeg ville skrive en bog om hvert 17. år inden for 7 gange 17 år, 119 år, og det tidspunkt, jeg beregnede det efter, det var 1893, den 18. maj, hvor min far var født og min bedstefar var i Metz som ulan . . ." (I had a dream, that I would write a book about each seventeenth year for a period of 7 times 17 years, or 119 years, and the point in time I counted from was 1893, on the 18th of May, when my father was born and my grandfather was in Metz as an uhlan . . . .). Other realistic stories from *Om fjorten dage* are "I Middagsstilheden" (In the Quiet of Noon), set in 1853, the erotically charged tale of three girls and a photographer; and "Drømmen om folket" (The Dream of the People), set in 1875–1876, which concerns the collecting of folk material. These stories show that Seeberg was following his plan. The stories from 1927, however, take the central position in this novel.

Rejsen til Ribe: Noveller (The Trip to Ribe: Stories, 1990) continues Seeberg's schematic in the stories "Smerten som gæst" (Pain as a Guest), which is dated 1910, and "Drengen på forsædet" (The Boy in the Front Seat), dated 1944–1945. The title story, concerning a thirteen-year-old boy whose family throws him out, breaks the seventeen-year cycle (it is dated August 1957), but otherwise is part of the "repertoire," as Seeberg calls it, as is "I passende afstand" (At a Proper Distance), dated 1988, about a Danish journalist who gets himself in trouble with a guerrilla army in El Salvador. The "flanking" technique is retained, but has taken on an increasingly lyrical character. Seeberg's prose-lyrical style became increasingly clarified, and what remained was an intimation that the material displayed before the reader consists of pieces of a great puzzle. Like a collection of different shells from the seashore, the nature of the sea itself is revealed in the markings of its creatures. The second "flanking" group, placed after the realistic texts, is a new set of mythical or legendary pieces, arranged in a gentle transition from the amusing but believable to the wildly franciful: from a story about a man who lives without electricity, to a story about a dog genius who turns green from eating cucumbers.

Peter Seeberg died on 8 January 1999. *Halvdelen af natten* (Half of the Night, 1997) is the last, and in certain respects, the most radical of his experimental story-books. In his own laconic manner, Seeberg had noted, upon completion of *Rejsen til Ribe:* "Jeg laver ikke flere bøger af den art. Jeg har sagt at jeg vil skrive større noveller, med det ved man ikke en pind om. Før man har sat pen til papiret konsekvent i nogen tid, så svindler man sig selv" (I'm not going to write any more books of that type. I have said that I want to write longer stories, but of course one never knows what happens. Before one has put pen to paper for a while consistently, one deceives oneself). The 1997 collection holds to the gradual organic development of the experimental *novelle* (short story) that Seeberg began with *Dinosaurusens sene eftermiddag.* His "flanking" stories moved from documentary notation toward aphorism on the one side, and from fable and myth to poetry on the other: three of the texts in the last collection were even typeset as poems. Seeberg's self-professed nihilism had not disappeared, but had instead become a richly nuanced concept. Not only was the concept of God welcome in the mix (for the disbeliever, who has to have something to fix his disbelief on, or for the humorist, for whom Fate takes on personal attributes), but an inner point of absolute contentment was allowed–like that which can be expressed by a dog that is oblivious to a human being's suicidal thoughts or can be felt by a man who enjoys watching a bevy of nude ladies bathing, even if he only has one eye with which to do it. The imbalances of Seeberg's early work–the wide pendulum swings driven by guilt or fanaticism–were gradually metamorphosed into a road map for existence, for those "secondary persons" every supposedly primary person finds himself to be.

Interview:

Marianne Juhl, "Interview with Peter Seeberg," *Weekendavisen,* 9 September 1990.

Biographies:

Vagn Thule, *Peter Seeberg* (Copenhagen: Munksgaard, 1972);

Ole Sarvig, *Den forunderlige Peter Seeberg* (Viborg: Arena, 1977).

References:

Søren Baggesen, "Dansk prosamodernisme" in *Modernisme i dansk litteratur,* edited by Jørgen Vosmar (Copenhagen: Fremad, 1967);

Baggesen, "Peter Seeberg," in *Danske digtere i det 20. århundrede,* volume 3, edited by Frederik Nielsen and Ole Restrup (Copenhagen: Gad, 1965);

Ib Bondebjerg, *Peter Seeberg: En ideologikritisk analyse* (Grenaa: GMT, 1972);

Thomas Bredsdorff, "Peter Seeberg," in *Sære Fortællere: Hovedtræk af ny dansk prosakunst* (Copenhagen: Gyldendal, 1967);

Lars Bukdahl, "Peter Sørensen var helt godt ved det i dag," in *Weekendavisen,* 21–27 November 1997;

Sigurd Enggaard and Kr. Friis-Jensen, *Dagen letter i sindet* (Herning: Poul Kristensen, 1979);

Iben Holk, ed., *Mytesyn: En bog om Peter Seebergs forfatterskab* (Viborg: Centrum, 1985);

Søren Hove, *Min personlige tigerhun, Maja* (Copenhagen: Munksgaard, 1997);

Hanne Marie Svendsen, *Romanens veje: Værkstedssamtaler med danske forfattere* (Copenhagen: Fischer, 1966).

Tage Skou-Hansen

(12 February 1925 –   )

Jørgen Gleerup
University of Odense

Translated by Tiina Nunnally

BOOKS: *De nøgne træer* (Copenhagen: Gyldendal, 1957); translated by Katherine John as *The Naked Trees* (London: Cape, 1959);
Dagstjernen (Copenhagen: Gyldendal, 1962);
På den anden side (Copenhagen: Gyldendal, 1965);
Hjemkomst (Copenhagen: Gyldendal, 1969);
Tredje halvleg (Copenhagen: Gyldendal, 1971);
Tolvtemanden, illustrated by Anders Kirkegaard (Copenhagen: Brøndum, 1972);
Det midlertidige fællesskab: Kritisk prosa fra 40'erne til 70'erne, edited, with an introduction, by Hans Hertel (Copenhagen: Gyldendal, 1972);
Medløberen (Copenhagen: Gyldendal, 1973);
Den hårde frugt (Copenhagen: Gyldendal, 1977);
Nedtælling (Copenhagen: Gyldendal, 1978);
Over stregen (Copenhagen: Gyldendal, 1980);
Nedenom og hjem (Copenhagen: Gyldendal, 1982);
Springet: En historie fra det runde bord (Copenhagen: Gyldendal, 1986);
Krukken og stenen: En historie fra det runde bord (Copenhagen: Gyldendal, 1987);
Det andet slag: En historie fra det runde bord (Copenhagen: Gyldendal, 1989);
Sidste sommer: En historie fra det runde bord (Copenhagen: Gyldendal, 1991);
Den forbandede utopi: Kritisk prosa fra 70'erne til 90'erne, edited, with an introduction, by Hertel (Copenhagen: Gyldendal, 1995);
På sidelinjen (Copenhagen: Gyldendal, 1996).
Edition: *Det runde bord,* 2 volumes (Copenhagen: Gyldendal, 1992).

PLAY PRODUCTIONS: *Nedtælling,* Århus, Svalegangen Theatre, 1 April 1978;
Nedenom og hjem, Århus, Svalegangen Theatre, 15 May 1982.

Tage Skou-Hansen in 1996 (photograph by Jakob Skou-Hansen; courtesy of Tage Skou-Hansen)

TELEVISION: *Højskolejournal 69,* script by Skou-Hansen and Franz Ernst, Danmarks Radio, 1969;
På hospitalet, script by Skou-Hansen and Dan Tschernia, Danmarks Radio, 1974;
Konflikten der blev væk, script by Skou-Hansen and John Carlsen, Danmarks Radio, 1982;
Hvem var Krag?, script by Skou-Hansen and Carlsen, Danmarks Radio, 1985.

RADIO: *Hvor kragerne vender,* script by Skou-Hansen and John Carlsen, Danmarks Radio, 1974.

OTHER: Frank Jæger, *Til en følsom veninde,* edited by Skou-Hansen (Copenhagen: Gyldendal, 1957).

SELECTED PERIODICAL PUBLICATION–
UNCOLLECTED: "Kjeld," *Heretica,* 6, no. 3 (May 1953): 235–265.

Tage Skou-Hansen won international acclaim with the publication of his first novel, *De nøgne træer* (1957; translated as *The Naked Trees,* 1959), which deals with the German occupation of Denmark from 1940 to 1945. The book was published in many countries in both the East and the West. At the same time, this debut novel laid the groundwork for a career that has made Skou-Hansen one of the most prominent literary commentators of the latter half of the twentieth century and also won him a place among the most important contemporary novelists in Denmark.

Skou-Hansen's work is primarily concerned with the crisis-filled transition from the modern to the postmodernist or late-modernist period, although these general labels of specific epochs do not do full justice to his concerns. Skou-Hansen's work digs deep and questions the attempt to distinguish between the universal and that which is typical of a specific era, while at the same time it seeks to pinpoint the basic features of historical development. This complexity of intent has made Skou-Hansen a modern chronicler whose work has broad appeal among general readers as well as literary scholars and leading politicians. The idea that history is revealed only reluctantly is trenchant in all of his books, which nevertheless spring from the author's strong urge to defy this reluctance toward history. Most of Skou-Hansen's novels have been reprinted multiple times, and he has received many literary prizes, including the Kritikerprisen (Critics' Award) in 1977 and the Danske Akademis Pris (Danish Academy's Prize) in 1978. He has also held important honorary positions associated with art, culture, education, and politics in Denmark. He has been a member of Det Danske Akademi (The Danish Academy) since 1982.

Tage Skou-Hansen was born on 12 February 1925 in the provincial town of Fredericia in Jutland. He was the son of a bank manager and later finance officer, Johannes Hansen, and Martha Skou and spent his early years in Holsted. When he was seven years old, his father was convicted of fraud and sentenced to a prison term; the crime made front-page news, and young Tage, his sister, and mother were forced to live with relatives in Kolding while the father served his sentence. Undoubtedly this early traumatic experience prompted the author later in life to explore ethical questions concerning guilt and innocence, action and consequence. The family later settled in the university town of Århus (then Aarhus), where Skou-Hansen completed his secondary education at Marselisborg Gymnasium in 1942. In 1950 he was awarded a master of arts degree in Danish and comparative literature from Århus University. That same year he married Ellen Porsgaard, a librarian, and they moved to Copenhagen. There Skou-Hansen suddenly became a member of the Danish literary elite when he was appointed co-editor of the journal *Heretica* (Heresy).

Memories from Århus are interwoven throughout his works. The paradoxical nature of youth, with its combination of strong will and impressionable searching, found particular resonance in the dark universe of the German occupation of Denmark. Skou-Hansen writes in his essay "Den poetiske besættelse" (The Poetic Occupation) from 1964: "Vi overvandt netop anonymiteten, gentertheden, jargonen fordi mørket lå så tæt om os. Mørket var en beskyttelse. Det gav os mod til at sige ting vi ellers ikke turde have sagt, og det lærte os at lytte" (We vanquished anonymity, self-consciousness, and superfluous chitchat because the darkness was drawn so tightly around us. The darkness was protection. It gave us courage to say things that we otherwise wouldn't have dared to say, and it taught us to listen). The complex universe of the occupation opened up several other dimensions of existence with the promise of "a meaningful life"–a promise that proved hard to fulfill after the liberation in 1945, when social development quickly reverted to its usual course.

There is a pervasive perception in Skou-Hansen's work that life is double-sided, whether literature, love, the resistance movement, or various types of national groups are challenging the surface of normalcy. The tension between idea and reality, hope and utopia, is ever present in his novels, in their search for an authentic life and genuine language. This tension is also the theme behind the catastrophes and losses that, with their inner mystery, drive the characters and narrators of his works.

The author's two great novel series–the novels about Holger Mikkelsen, published between 1957 and 1996, and the "Historier fra det runde bord" (Stories from the Round Table) series, published between 1986 and 1991, both start with idealistic groups that are in search of something, and their dreams and ultimate destinies are pursued in the novels. From a broader perspective, the books deal with the belief in progress, reason, and civilization, which has carried Western democracies through several centuries but which went up in flames with the world wars of the twentieth century, leaving only unanswered questions about what might emerge from the ashes.

Skou-Hansen's memoirs provide concrete material for these general concerns, and he has never been reticent about commenting on his own works in articles and interviews. According to him, fiction and reality are not diametrically opposed; they are different layers of the same endeavor to understand life, which is both self-interpretive and existentialist. Selections of Skou-Hansen's autobiographical articles, his ongoing commentaries on society, and his literary criticism have been collected by Hans Hertel in *Det midlertidige fællesskab: Kritisk prosa fra 40'erne til 70'erne* (Temporary Solidarity: Critical Essays from the 1940s to the 1970s, 1972) and *Den forbandede utopi: Kritisk prosa fra 70'erne til 90'erne* (The Cursed Utopia: Critical Essays from the 1970s to the 1990s, 1995). These articles provide the best background for understanding Skou-Hansen's work and development, together with an early study of the author's writings by the literary critic Ejgil Søholm, *Fra frihedskamp til lighedsdrøm: En læsning af Tage Skou-Hansens forfatterskab* (From the Dream of Freedom to the Dream of Equality: A Study of the Works of Tage Skou-Hansen, 1979).

In Skou-Hansen's memoirs he describes how an adolescent friend put him in contact with the illegal activities of the occupation. As a communist with an interest in economics and a great lover of poetry, he and several of his literary colleagues from the *Heretica* group supplied material for the central conflict between poetry and social involvement in *De nøgne træer,* which is the first novel narrated by Holger Mikkelsen. The reader is told of Aksel, an intelligent student who joined the German Wehrmacht to serve on the Eastern Front. This story becomes the source for the Stories from the Round Table series, which all circle around an inscrutable question: Why did Aksel choose to commit high treason?

The combination of existential and historical concerns creates a fundamental tension in Skou-Hansen's novels, and this dichotomy makes it difficult to place him in the literary landscape of the postwar era. In 1952 he was introduced to the powerful literary circles associated with *Heretica,* which included such authors as Martin A. Hansen, Paul la Cour, Ole Sarvig, Ole Wivel, and Thorkild Bjørnvig. Another member of this group was the writer Frank Jæger, with whom Skou-Hansen edited the journal during its last two years, until 1953. The war had clearly revealed the depths of the crisis in Western culture. Although *Heretica* sought redemption in a metaphysical turning away from society and its ideologies and a turning toward the individual, Skou-Hansen could not abandon his commitment to the outside world. For him this commitment meant turning away from poetry toward prose. In his first published article, "Forsvar for prosaen" (In Defense of Prose), published in *Heretica* in 1950, he bluntly expressed this view, which opened doors to the literary milieu for him but at the same time positioned him on the sidelines.

Skou-Hansen could not abandon the idea-oriented social involvement of the 1930s, no matter how disastrous these ideologies had proved to be during the war. For this reason he naturally joined forces with the journal that succeeded *Heretica, Vindrosen* (The Com

pass), published by Gyldendal. This new literary journal was supposed to create a bridge between the metaphysical and the radical cultural ideas of the time. Together with Peter P. Rohde, Skou-Hansen edited the journal during its early years, from 1954 to 1958, to great acclaim, but he was personally dissatisfied with this fabricated compromise. Life's duplicity was to be redeemed in fiction, which he had attempted with some trepidation during the *Heretica* period with the short story "Kjeld" (1953). He later used this story as the basis for his first novel, *De nøgne træer.*

The events depicted in the novel take place over the course of ten months, from December in the crucial war year of 1943, when the official Danish policy of cooperation was broken by the resistance movement, until October 1944. The novel describes the formation of a resistance group and follows several of its sabotage actions. Through Holger and his relationship to the members of the group, Skou-Hansen's concerns about sabotage and the war are expressed in terms of love and in the central tension between writing and social involvement.

Holger tries to persuade his friend Kjeld to join the group, but Kjeld is more interested in his poetic dreams than in the resistance struggle. This attitude provokes Holger's bullying instincts, vented in a merciless critique of his friend's moral constitution. There is a schism between an ideal vision of what life should be and the necessity for someone to handle its nastier aspects. Neither one is right—not Kjeld, who allows himself to be led by his own idealistic illusions, nor Holger, who follows the impulses of the day. Like all of Skou-Hansen's works, *De nøgne træer* can be viewed as a quest for those in-between spheres of existence in the tension between the ideal and reality.

Kjeld has a difficult time realizing what he wants from life. His confusion leads him to confront the perilousness of life by joining the group after all, in the summer of 1944. He comes under the rough tutelage of the mechanic Leo, who has little patience for the sensitive, upper-class boy. Kjeld is not seeking real membership in the group; instead, he wants a personal confrontation with his foundering perception of life. Disaster strikes when an unarmed Kjeld, on his first sabotage action, assaults a German soldier and is shot. During the failed mission the group's leader, Christian, is also seriously wounded, an event that has ramifications for the illicit relationship between Holger and Christian's wife, Gerda.

Gerda does not feel comfortable or free to develop in the refined world that her unselfish husband has tried to open for her lovingly and with the best of intentions. When Holger meets her, she is a loud and vociferous subverter of the social norms and conven

Covers for translated editions of Skou-Hansen's first book, De nøgne træer

tions that constrain her sensuous self. Gerda's violent attempts to liberate herself appeal to Holger so strongly that their love affair becomes inevitable. Their relationship is revealed only to Leo, who, as a saboteur, understands what lies behind the respectable facade of life. He feels as if he is in another world whenever he finishes his sabotage work and seeks cover among the unsuspecting ordinary people on the street. When Christian attempts to explain the real meaning of the resistance movement, Leo interrupts or tries to sabotage him with inappropriate questions. In the same way, Gerda drops dishes or throws plates whenever her husband tries to introduce her to the perfectly tuned customs of the upper-class social circles. Life during the occupation is divided into two universes that cannot be conjoined.

Sabotage lures the characters with its sense of danger and liberation as well as catastrophe. Gerda and Holger stand at an awkward crossroads at the end of the novel. Christian has survived his injuries, and the couple must decide whether to seize hold of their right to love each other or, in a more respectable move, to deny it. They choose the latter, but for Holger the decision is made with the awareness that from now on he will go through life merely surviving and not actually living:

Livet gik videre, godmodigt og sangvinsk, med sine gentagelser og små kompromiser. Det overkommelige liv, hvor man slog sig igennem som man kunne, hyggede sig med andre og græmmede sig for sig selv. Det vanskelige liv, hvor man langsomt og tålmodigt skulle lade sig slide op, affinde sig og lære at nøjes. Sådan var det altså jeg selv skulle leve videre engang. Måske. For halv kraft. Uden for den alvor og spænding, krigen og Gerda havde ført mig ind i. Uden at tages helt i brug.

(Life went on, good-natured and sanguine, with its repetitions and little compromises. The modest life, in which people made it through as best they could, enjoyed the company of others, and mourned alone. The difficult life, in which people were slowly and patiently supposed to wear themselves out, put up with things, and be content. That was the way I was going to have to live. Maybe. At half-strength. Without the danger and excitement that the war and Gerda had introduced me to. Without fully making use of myself.)

This tone of impotence and underlying defiance permeates the subsequent novels about Holger. Skou-Hansen returned to the character in *Tredje Halvleg* (The Third Half, 1971), which was originally conceived as a collection of shorter texts or stories meant to be read on the radio. Skou-Hansen used Holger's background and story to turn the work into a continuous narrative.

Before this book was written, however, an interlude occurred in Skou-Hansen's life as an author. After completing his editorship at *Vindrosen,* he moved back to Jutland with his family. From 1958 until 1967 Skou-Hansen taught literature at the stronghold of Danish adult education: Askov Folkehøjskole (folk high school). Afterward he returned to writing full time and moved to Århus, but while he was at Askov Folkehøjskole he wrote *Dagstjernen* (Day Star, 1962). In this book the concerns of *De nøgne træer* are further intensified as the author addresses the subject of the liquidation of informers during the war—a complex ethical issue also explored by his fellow writer Martin A. Hansen. Can acts of violence be legitimized by society? This question echoes from *De nøgne træer,* but it is based on a moral examination that Danish society had chosen to suppress.

In *På den anden side* (On the Other Side, 1965) the author makes use of his own family background to transform the ethical and psychological issues associated with people living together and trying to have genuine communication into an examination of marriage—in which honesty and equality are crushed by a misunderstood self-sacrifice. The novel has been linked to the central ideas of the twentieth-century Danish philosopher K. E. Løgstrup, whose book *Den etiske fordring* (The Ethical Demand, 1956) was much used in Danish *folkehøjskolen* during the 1960s. The two authors also have written about each other's work.

After a trip to India in 1966, Skou-Hansen wrote the novel *Hjemkomst* (Homecoming, 1969), which brings a new, broadened perspective to bear on the provincialism and blind self-righteousness of the Western industrial and welfare system, for which Denmark and the other Nordic countries have become so famous in modern times. The depths of the conflict with which the author struggles can be glimpsed in the murder that, without concrete reasons, triggers the themes in the novel. The distance between the two worlds is so great that it can only be expressed through unavoidable violence. After his return to Jutland from India, Ernst Fenger, the protagonist, can solve his problems only by killing the woman who is most precious to him.

With *Hjemkomst* the central issues of Skou-Hansen's work assume a political dimension, and the author was on the verge of discovering his own literary expression for the heretical program that he had drafted in 1950 in "Forsvar for prosaen." He had not found any easy way to realize his agenda, but when it finally did emerge, it was multilayered—existential concerns were combined with topics of an international political nature as well as portrayals of the more concrete aspects of industrial development in Danish society. These social developments included, for example, the transformation of the

Danish landscape with the tremendous surge in construction of single-family homes in the 1960s and 1970s. Skou-Hansen has been widely recognized as the author who has portrayed these changes best.

In 1969 Skou-Hansen and Franz Ernst filmed the documentary *Højskolejournal 69* (High School Journal '69). Even in the *Heretica* period, Skou-Hansen had shown an openness toward and interest in modern mass media such as cinema and television. From 1970 until 1972 he was on the board of directors of the Danish Film Foundation, Filmfonden. He has written many scripts for radio and television, including *Hvem var Krag?* (Who Was Krag?), a portrait of the Danish prime minister Jens Otto Krag, which he wrote with John Carlsen in 1985. For the Svalegangen Theatre in Århus, Skou-Hansen wrote the plays *Nedtælling* (Countdown, 1978), about a group of political activists, and *Nedenom og hjem* (Going to the Dogs, 1982), about the power games in an advertising agency. The plays and the essayistic story *Tolvtemanden* (The Twelfth Man, 1972), with illustrations by Anders Kirkegaard, are all thematically linked to the author's novels.

While working on the novel *Medløberen* (The Opportunist, 1973), the author found that Holger Mikkelsen had forced his way in again as the narrator of the stories about soccer player Alan and his difficulties fitting in with the Århus team, AGF. On the soccer field Alan is a loner and a bully, just as Holger was in *De nøgne træer*. Off the field, however, Alan is plagued and hampered by a need to be normal. Holger recognizes in this quality his own sense of resignation that, after his break with Gerda, has put him on the sidelines of life. He tells Alan's story to his law partner's daughter, the homeless Bente, who has been radicalized by the events of the Student Movement in Denmark in 1968. She has moved in with Holger, bringing along her fatherless son. The telling of the story gradually transforms the practical nature of their living arrangement into an intimate relationship—"a meaningful life." For both of them the soccer stories serve as a well-camouflaged courtship, and the novel then comes to an end with Bente's sly statement to Holger that he is a "difficult seducer."

Medløberen draws an analogy between relationships and a soccer game, in which the good players (in contrast to Alan) do not force their way but rather let themselves be carried along by the game. When it is successful, soccer is a genuine form of communication, which on the societal level is only glimpsed occasionally in temporary partnerships. Skou-Hansen's later works deal with the increasingly restrictive conditions of the popular political movements and their possible transformation close to the millennium. In the series narrated by Holger this theme is stretched to the limit, while

there are hints of redemption in the Stories from the Round Table.

In *Medløberen* Skou-Hansen finds a social space for the issues that concern him by making use of the rebellious attitudes of the 1968 generation. In *Den hårde frugt* (The Hard Fruit, 1977) and *Over stregen* (Over the Line, 1980) he enters the increasingly individualized world of the late-modernist period. In these two novels Holger and Bente grow apart, not because Holger gets too old for the somewhat younger Bente but because she moves to the west coast of Jutland to take a temporary job and settles into a life in which her original rebellion loses all power. Her social involvement and sensual presence vanish into a goal-oriented job, a sense of political superiority, and a planned love life. In her place Skou-Hansen introduces a new figure or temptation in Holger's life: Eva, Gerda's daughter, whom he defends in his role as lawyer after she and a friend try to blow up a bourgeois newspaper office.

Eva is the last "hard fruit" of the twentieth-century dream of an active, grassroots solidarity. In prison she is moved by a woman's nightly scream for help until she finally realizes that she is listening to her own voice. *Over stregen* marks a temporary end to Holger's efforts to find traces of a meaningful life in a social environment that seems to be closing in on itself as the millennium approaches. A reunion with Gerda, the love of his youth, holds no real temptation for him. In Skou-Hansen's next novels the freedom fighter Holger is replaced with a different protagonist, Aksel, who during the occupation sought his destiny on the front lines of the enemy and in defeat.

With the Stories from the Round Table a reversal begins to take shape in the dominant themes of Skou-Hansen's work, which also has consequences for his style of writing. His novels become more loosely structured, more free and direct; and this freedom of form is accompanied by a certain thematic conciliation. The tension between the ideal and reality is displaced with intimations of new possibilities for escape, in spite of the often straitened situation of the characters.

The series begins with the novel *Springet: En historie fra det runde bord* (The Leap: A Story from the Round Table, 1986), which was also broadcast on Danish radio. The protagonist, Sivert, tries to understand why Aksel, whom he had known in his youth, decided to join the German Wehrmacht. After spending some time on the Eastern Front, Aksel lost his life during the Allied invasion of France. Sivert's name (derived from the Danish word *siv*, which means *reed*) connotes an existence that has never managed to seize hold of life but merely bends with the wind. In Sivert's opinion, history itself has grown senile. For this reason he is content to observe from a distance the media's constantly

Efter flere års tavshed har Holger Mikkelsen
igen noget at fortælle.

Den oprørske Eva, datter af Mikkelsens ung-
domskærlighed Gerda, bliver kæreste med Mads,
en sympatisk, lidt kantet og meget lidt intellek-
tuel fyr. De to synes ikke ligefrem skabt for hinanden, alligevel bliver de gift og får børn. Senere
begynder forholdet at knage, men inden det
kommer til opbrud, sker katastrofen. Og den
gamle advokat får en sag, som fører ham et andet
sted hen, end han har været før.

Det er tabet, sorgen og følelsen af magtesløs-
hed, der er udgangspunkt for Mikkelsens beretning. I tilgift får man hans tanker om den udvikling, der er sket med ham selv og hans verden,
siden han sidst lod høre fra sig.

Tage Skou-Hansen

På sidelinjen

Tage Skou-Hansen
På sidelinjen
GYLDENDAL

ROMAN · GYLDENDAL

ISBN 87-00-27546-8

Dust jacket for Skou-Hansen's 1996 novel, featuring his recurring protagonist Holger Mikkelsen

shifting versions of the same events repeated over and
over. Sivert is a *husejer* (home-owner) but nothing else, a
fact that he admits at his fortieth high-school reunion,
which shakes up his isolated existence like an invitation
from his past. Through memory Sivert relives his
youthful preoccupation with the unapproachable group
of fellow students who sit at a round table; he remembers the fruitless but important conversations with
Aksel and the overwhelming moment when he declared
his unrequited love to Tove.

Unlike the others he had known from his youth—
those who sat at the round table and wondered why
Aksel joined the German Wehrmacht—Sivert is preoccupied with the decision itself, the leap. He has never
dared to take this leap into life, but in the course of the
story he comes to share in Aksel's. There is a slight shift
of focus from the tension between two irreconcilable
universes to the actual leap between them. This shift
summons up an undercurrent present in all of Skou-
Hansen's previous works and brings it to a culmination: the sporadically glimpsed merging of the author

and his narrator in the descriptions of nature. In several
crucial passages in *Springet,* nature—or rather sensory
perception—emerges as redemptive, since the revelations also have to do with daily life and its more banal
aspects:

> Men samtidig begyndte solskinnet bagved at brede sig
> og det fik alle skyerne til at lyse med et diffust gennem-
> sigtigt lys, som på en gang var hvidt og blåt.
>
> Elmetræet i hjørnet af legepladsen løftede de lange
> skrå stivere og det lådne mørke løv brusede længe.
> Sivert så ind i skyggerne. At gå derind nu, tænkte han.
> Tage sig tid til at være åben og opmærksom på alt det
> sanserne uden ophør blev bombarderet med og som
> var så let at overse eller glemme.

> (But at the same moment the sunshine in the distance
> began to spread, making all the clouds light up with a
> diffuse, transparent light, which was both white and
> blue.
>
> The elm tree in the corner of the playground lifted its
> long, slanting struts, and its shaggy dark leaves rustled
> for a long time. Sivert stared into the shadows. What if

he went inside there right now, he thought. What if he took his time to be open and alert to everything that his senses were constantly being bombarded with; things that were so easy to overlook or forget.)

The dream of a meaningful life no longer has to be realized with violence and force. On the other hand, it can actively live as a hope, an insight, or a calling. For Skou-Hansen, sensory perception has a dialogic quality, and life will not "speak freely" unless the individual prepares for it and insists that it do so. Thus, his work can preserve its characteristic dichotomy of involvement versus existential or metaphysical responsiveness, but in a new form that points toward a new and more complex millennium.

Another of the central figures in the Stories of the Round Table is Sigurd, the protagonist of *Det andet slag* (The Second Beat, 1989). He is not successful in adapting to the millennial changes. Tove's story, as told in *Krukken og stenen* (The Pitcher and the Stone, 1987), is more complex. As a child Tove lost her father, but as she grows up, her memories of him provide her with a strong guarantee for a happy life. This conviction carries her through the loss of Aksel, to whom she had secretly devoted all the love of her youth; it also carries her through her divorce from the architect Ejnar, whom she married after Aksel's death. Tove is wooed by all the male members of the circle, perhaps because she expresses a vigorous balance between the necessity of continuing and a sensitivity toward whatever else life has to offer, as indicated by hopes and longings. Tove's story has a peculiar duplicity that reflects the raw power of her being–something that her husband, Ejnar, can counter physically and sexually but cannot grasp emotionally. Their marriage dissolves without drama, and Tove settles into a life that she can steer herself. In *Springet* she hints at the secret of her life when she tells Sivert this line from a poem by Sophus Claussen: "Alt er unyttigt undtagen vor skælven" (Everything is useless except our trembling).

Skou-Hansen's change of thematic interest is represented by his depiction of Ejnar's architecture business. Ejnar is a cultural radical; through his buildings he wants to manifest his dream of the politically correct society. Gradually, however, he realizes that people do not want ready-made solutions but rather the opportunity to create their own lives. The utopian vision of the "true life" cannot be realized without ending up in something demonic. In the course of the novel Ejnar develops a growing preference for those concerns that fall outside his building plans–which goes back to Sivert's rejuvenated understanding of life in *Springet* and presages the culmination of this transformation in the final novels of the series.

Skou-Hansen has said that the order of the last two novels in the series was determined by readers wanting to know about Aksel's story. *Det andet slag* follows Aksel's closest friend, Sigurd. In the novel he comes to understand that with Aksel's death he lost the rhythm, or "second beat," of his own heart, although this awareness has no real consequence for his life. Tove has found Aksel's letters and sent them to Sigurd. By reading them he develops a greater insight into his relationships with Aksel and with his own son, Anders, in whom he recognizes traits of his dead friend. Anders has a love-hate relationship with his father and those of his parents' generation, who feel that the welfare society of the twentieth century has given them so much, when in reality they have squandered everything. Their solicitous zeal thus seems to have the character of an ineffectual guardianship. During a confrontation between father and son, Anders hits Sigurd in the face; his merciless condemnation of his father's life is a more serious blow to Sigurd's otherwise unshakable self-confidence.

Aksel's letters from the front reveal that he voluntarily chose defeat and went to his death in order to realize his ideals in a tragically heroic way. Sigurd is moved by this but does not buy Aksel's final, legitimizing belief in a God who is greater than the cruelty he has experienced. Aksel's letters open Sigurd's eyes to the fact that his son, who is apparently a social misfit, has a greater feel for the pulse of the times than he does; yet Sigurd cannot abandon his entrenched position as a left-wing cultural radical. He chooses instead to continue living without being influenced by the "second beat" of his life.

Det andet slag looks closely at the cultural transformations that mark the end of the twentieth century. Of particular concern is the relationship between the generations, as well as the changing view of work, family life, and politics. The novel does not solve these problems, but it treats them in new ways that are both rooted in the previous century and point forward to the future.

The Stories from the Round Table series reached its conclusion in *Sidste sommer* (Last Summer, 1991). The following year all of the novels were collected and republished in a two-volume set as *Det runde borde. Sidste sommer* is the story of Herman, an expatriate Dane who, as a pastor and *estancia* owner in Argentina, feels no longing for his native country. When the Berlin Wall falls in 1989, however, he perceives the new era as a kind of Whitsuntide miracle, when anything can happen, even in a "province" of Denmark. He hopes that the new era will vanquish his memories of the suicides following the liquidation of informers and the faithless flirtatiousness of Kirsten–memories that drove him into exile.

The concrete reason for his return home is his brother's sale of their ancestral farm to a former communist economist who has become a European Union bureaucrat. Herman and the bureaucrat reunite, both homeless now, but without any kind of mutual sympathy for their respective attempts at exile. They meet the adopted Aksel's biological parents and finally get to the bottom of this inscrutable person and his life, but this does not prompt any kind of redemption. Yet, the return home becomes a decisive event for Herman. He takes a walk in a meadow and suddenly realizes that it is not Denmark as a nation that he loves, much less its supranational extension—what he loves is the Danish countryside.

In *På sidelinjen* (On the Sidelines, 1996), another Holger Mikkelsen novel, Holger suffers a defeat as a lawyer. He cannot clearly establish culpability in a hospital lawsuit, which is filed when young Mads—whom Eva has met and married—dies while hospitalized. True to her rebellious nature, Eva refuses to give up the lawsuit, but Holger does give up, although there are indications of a new awareness on his part.

Mads is the youthful rebel of the late-modernist period who does not aggressively attack society but instead turns his back on it in a search for the intimate and spontaneous qualities of life. With his usual awareness of any new social trends, Holger is preoccupied with Mads, whose alternative projects begin to assume an increasingly absurd character. At one point he sets up a small rabbit farm without any purpose other than to keep it running, an act that isolates him not only from society but also from Eva. Holger senses that Mads is beginning to recognize that his quest for a pure life is pointless and that his illness is a conscious attempt at suicide. In spite of the seductiveness of all social utopias, life cannot be lived without structure, goals, or a sense of purpose. Perhaps the surrender to such ideal conditions, no matter how seductive or restrictive they may be, is not the only way to a greater sympathy toward Nature or one's fellow human beings. Perhaps, instead, the introspective relationship to oneself and to those blind spots can occasionally open life to the forces that reach beyond the individual. With these types of questions the works of Skou-Hansen have brought the great ideas of the twentieth century and their innate dilemmas to the verge of the new millennium.

Skou-Hansen has often referred to William Faulkner as his literary model, pointing to his work methods, historical consciousness, and stream-of-consciousness realism. In the Danish literary tradition, Skou-Hansen is considered a successor to the great realist Henrik Pontoppidan and his dualistic worldview. He has said of his own work that writing a novel is like entering into a dialogue in which the time must be ripe to tell the story. The dialogic relationship between idea and reality, introspection and empathy, marks Skou-Hansen's artistic process in the same way as it carries the themes of his work.

Interviews:

K. E. Løgstrup, "Kunst og etik," *Dansk Udsyn,* new series 1 (1969): 18–33;

Ejgil Søholm, "Interview med Tage Skou-Hansen," in his *Fra frihedskamp til lighedsdrøm: En læsning af Tage Skou-Hansens forfatterskab* (Copenhagen: Gyldendal, 1979), pp. 142–165;

Søholm, *Ordkvartet Århus: Peter Laugesen, Svend Åge Madsen, Henning Morensen, Tage Skou-Hansen: Fire forfatterinterviews* (Århus: Statsbibliotek, 1990), pp. 81–109;

Erik Skyum Nielsen, "Som skyernes flugt. Samtale med Tage Skou-Hansen," *Bogens verden* (March 1993): 92–102.

References:

Johs. H. Christensen, "Tage Skou-Hansen," in *Danske digtere i det 20. arhundrede,* 5 volumes, edited by Torben Brostrom and Mette Winge (Copenhagen: Gad, 1981), III: 375–396;

Jørgen Gleerup, "Det levende sprog–om Tage Skou-Hansens fembindsværk om Holger Mikkelsen," *Almanak for teologi og litteratur* (1987): 9–24;

Niels Gunder Hansen, "Gennem tidens mur: Om sammenhængen mellem Tage Skou-Hansens to romanserier 'Holger Mikkelsen' og 'Historier fra det runde bord,'" *Kritik,* new series 117 (1995): 7–19;

Bo Hakon Jørgensen, "Det, der er mere end lysten–eller er Holger en bølle?," in *Læsninger i dansk litteratur,* 5 volumes, edited by Povl Schmidt and others (Odense: Odense University Press, 1997), IV: 122–140;

Klaus Otto Kapel, "Oktoberluft," *Dansk Udsyn,* 40, no. 1 (1960): 22–38;

K. E. Løgstrup, "Kærlighed og karakter," *Dansk Udsyn,* 46, no. 1 (1966): 21–36;

Løgstrup, "Sansning or symbol," *Dansk Udsyn,* 59, no. 1 (1979): 25–35;

Løgstrup, "System og symbol," *Dansk Udsyn,* 59, no. 2 (1979): 83–99;

Lars J. Onslev, "Af en overlevendes papirer: Om Tage Skou-Hansens 'Det andet slag,'" in *Prosa fra 80'erne til 90'erne,* edited by Anne-Marie Mai (Copenhagen: Borgen, 1994), pp. 11–24;

Ejgil Søholm, *Fra frihedskamp til lighedsdrøm: En læsning af Tage Skou-Hansens forfatterskab* (Copenhagen: Gyldendal, 1979);

Ole Wivel, "De nøgne træer," in his *Tranedans: Erindringsmotiver* (Copenhagen: Gyldendal, 1975), pp. 124–131.

Knud Sønderby

(10 July 1909 – 8 August 1966)

Poul Bager
State Grammar School, Randers

BOOKS: *Midt i en Jazztid* (Copenhagen: Jespersen & Pio, 1931); revised edition (Copenhagen: Teknico, 1944); revised again (Copenhagen: Gyldendal, 1948; revised, 1961);

To Mennesker mødes (Copenhagen: Jespersen & Pio, 1932); revised edition (Copenhagen: Thaning & Appel, 1946); revised again (Copenhagen: Fremads Folkesbibliotek, 1953); revised again (Copenhagen: Gyldendal, 1962);

En Kvinde er overflødig (Copenhagen: Jespersen & Pio, 1936);

De kolde Flammer: Roman fra Grønland (Copenhagen: Jespersen & Pio, 1940);

Grønlandsk Sommer (Copenhagen: Jespersen & Pio, 1941);

En Kvinde er overflødig: Skuespil i tre Akter (Copenhagen: Gyldendal, 1942); translated by A. I. Roughton as *A Woman Too Many* (London: Thames & Hudson, 1955);

Den usynlige Hær (Copenhagen: Thaning & Appel, 1945);

Forsvundne Somre (Copenhagen: Gyldendal, 1946);

Hvidtjørnen (Copenhagen: Gyldendal, 1950);

Kvindernes oprør: Skuespil i tre akter (Copenhagen: Gyldendal, 1955; revised as *Kvindernes oprør: Skuespil i 2 akter (10 billeder),* 1963);

Gensyn med havet (Copenhagen: Gyldendal, 1957);

Tanker on tiden, illustrations by Marlie Brande (Copenhagen: E. H. Petersen, 1959);

De blå glimt: Essays (Copenhagen: Gyldendal, 1964)— comprises *Barndommens by; Vinduet på klem; Fartens narkomanl; Christianshavn; Kylling på rejse; Møde med mørket; Tredive år efter; De blå glimt; Italienske noter; Den sorte svane; Forår på Christiansø; Misantropen;*

Barndommens by (Esbjerg: Hartvig Nielsens Boghandel, 1965);

Vinduet på klem (Gentofte: Lise og Niels Munk Plum, 1965);

Tingene: Knud Sønderby in memoriam (Copenhagen: Gyldendal, 1966);

Gardin for åbent vindue: Tre enaktere (Copenhagen: Gyldendal, 1969)—comprises *Krista; Hjertets renhed; Gardin for åbent vindue;*

Knud Sønderby, circa 1925

De danske havne, edited, with a foreword, by Inge Sønderby and Mogens Knudsen (Copenhagen: Gyldendal, 1969);

Editions and Collection: *Samlede essays* (Copenhagen: Gyldendal, 1961)—comprises *Forsvundne somre; Hvidtjørnen; Gensyn med havet;*

Stumper af et spejl: Et Knud Sønderby-udvalg, edited by Gunnar Jakobsen (Copenhagen: Dansklærerforeningen/ Gyldendal, 1964);

Den usynlige hær, edited by Birthe Valbo (Copenhagen: Dansklærerforingen/Gyldendal, 1967);

Danmarkskortet: Udvalgte essays om landskaber og mennesker, edited by Inge Sønderby and Knudsen (Copenhagen: Gyldendal, 1970);

Den usynlige hær, afterword by Claus Pico Stæhr (Varde: Dansklærerforeningen, 1985);

Den sorte svane: Essays, edited, with a foreword, by Inge Sønderby and Ole Knudsen (Copenhagen: Gyldendal, 1987).

Edition in English: *The Blue Flashes; The Hawthorn; Danish Harbours,* translated by Reginald Spink (Copenhagen: Udenrigsministeriets Pressebureau, 1966).

PLAY PRODUCTIONS: *En kvinde er overflødig,* Copenhagen, Det Kongelige Teater, 10 November 1942;

Krista: Hende vi glemmer, by Sønderby, Leck Fischer, and C. E. Soya; Copenhagen, Det Ny Teater, 14 October 1947;

Hjertets renhed: Han, hun og hende, by Sønderby, Fischer, and Soya; Copenhagen, Det Ny Teater, 1 February 1949;

Trold kan tæmmes, translation by Sønderby of William Shakespeare's *The Taming of the Shrew,* Copenhagen, Det Ny Teater, 30 December 1959;

Macbeth, translation by Sønderby of Shakespeare's *The Tragedy of Macbeth,* Copenhagen, Det Ny Teater, 1 February 1961;

Kvindernes oprør, Copenhagen, Det Kongelige Teater, 3 April 1963;

Glasmenageriet, translation by Sønderby of Tennessee Williams's *The Glass Menagerie,* Copenhagen, Det kongelige Teater, 10 February 1966.

MOTION PICTURES: *Den usynlige Hær,* screenplay by Sønderby, A/S Filmcentralen-Palladium, 1945;

Næste gang er det dig, screenplay by Sønderby, Ministeriets Filmudvalg, 1948;

En kvinde er overflødig, screenplay by Sønderby, A/S Nordisk Film Kompagni, 1957.

TELEVISION: *En kvinde er overflødig,* script by Sønderby, Statsradiofonien Television, 16 October 1955;

Krista: Skuespil i een akt, script by Sønderby, Danmarks Radio Television, 1 September 1965.

RADIO: *En Kvinde er overflødig,* script by Sønderby, Statsradiofonien, 2 May 1941;

Kirsebærhaven, script translated by Sønderby from the play *The Cherry Orchard* by Anton Chekhov, Danmarks Radio, 1960;

Gardin for åbent vindue, script by Sønderby, Danmarks Radio, 14 April 1963.

OTHER: "Eventyret og Virkeligheden" in *Der brænder en Ild* (Copenhagen, 1944), pp. 65–69;

Arthur Miller, *En Sælgers Død,* translated, with an introduction, by Sønderby (Copenhagen: Wangel, 1949); revised edition (Copenhagen: Gyldendal, 1965);

"Mennesket," in *Frederik Schyberg* (Copenhagen: Gyldendals Julebog, 1950), pp. 43–50;

Miller, *Heksejagt: Skuespil i 4 akter,* translated by Sønderby (Copenhagen: Wangel, 1954);

William Shakespeare, *Trold kan tæmmes,* translated by Sønderby (Copenhagen: Gyldendal, 1959);

Shakespeare, *Macbeth,* translated by Sønderby (Copenhagen: Gyldendal, 1961);

Shakespeare, *Stor ståhej for ingenting,* translated by Sønderby (Copenhagen: Gyldendal, 1963);

Tennessee Williams, *Glasmenageriet,* translated by Sønderby (Copenhagen: Gyldendal, 1966).

Knud Sønderby was one of the founding members of Det Danske Akademi (The Danish Academy) in 1960. At that time he had long been a respected man and a recipient of many literary awards, including the seldom-awarded Humoristlegatet (Prize for Humor) in 1934 and the Colleagues Award of Honor in 1958. His production was small, but it was both exclusive and popular; in particular, his essays were highly esteemed. Therefore, it was a shock for almost the whole nation when he died of a heart attack at the age of fifty-seven.

Knud Sønderby was born on 10 July 1909 in Esbjerg, the main port for Danish agricultural export on the western coast of Jutland, and at that time the main harbor for the North Sea fishery. His father, Niels Christian Sønderby, was a successful wholesale merchant in this enterprising town, but he died in 1917 of the Spanish influenza. In the same year Sønderby's mother, Inge Nielsen Barfod, moved with her children to Hellerup, a wealthy suburb just north of Copenhagen.

Sønderby became a law student in 1927, but after his early debut he also worked as a journalist on the newspaper *Dagens Nyheder,* where he wrote short humor columns and motion picture reviews. In 1935 Sønderby received his master's degree in law, but he soon decided to continue working as a journalist, and in 1937 he was employed by *Berlingske Tidende.* On 20 April 1940 Sønderby married Ingeborg (Inge) Marie

Title page for the revised edition of Sønderby's 1932 novel, about the love affair of a medical student from a wealthy family and a poor shopkeeper's assistant

writings is that he still visualizes the situations of his youth. The time in his books was always the present tense, and Sønderby learned to use in his accounts the techniques of cutting motion pictures. In a 1932 review of his novel *To Mennesker mødes* (Two People Meet, 1932) the reviewer writes of Sønderby's literary techniques that his descriptions are "Nærbilleder, der er skrapt knipset af, og som ligner det, de skal ligne" (close-ups which are sharply snapped off and imitate what they should imitate).

In "Stumper af et Spejl" Sønderby writes that his father died when he was six years old (he was in fact seven) and continues,

> Havde han levet længere kunne han have lært mig andre ting som ville have indprentet sig lige saa dybt [som eksemplet med cyklen], jeg kunne have faaet mere af den samme tilfredse tryghed, den samme stolthed. Og jeg kunne maaske have lært vigtige ting om mig selv blot ved at have kendt ham, medens jeg voksede til. Ved at kende ham kunne jeg maaske have pejlet mig til klarhed over konstellationer i mig, som nu svæver i luften.

> (Had he lived for a longer time, he could have taught me other things which would have impressed me so profoundly [as the situation with the bicycle], and I could have received more of the same contented confidence, the same pride. And maybe I could have learned important things about myself simply if I had known him when I grew up. Had I known him, I might have taken a bearing of lucidity over constellations in me which now are floating in the air).

The absence of a father figure in Sønderby's family was a great problem, and he is an invisible but important character in the novel *En Kvinde er overflødig* (A Woman is Superfluous, 1936).

In this novel—adapted by Sønderby as a radio play in 1941, as a play at Det Kongelige Teater (The Royal Theater) in Copenhagen in 1942 (translated as *A Woman Too Many,* 1955), as a production for television in 1955, and as a motion picture in 1957—Sønderby dramatizes his and his sister's difficult youth with a tyrannic but self-sacrificing mother. More dramatic than the dramatized versions of the same privately oppressive subject matter, the novel presents a complex and harrowing portrait of a proud woman with aristocratic and romantic ideals who in reality is a tyrannic and worn-out petit bourgeois. She fights to give her children the best upbringing in the same environment that would have prevailed had their father lived, but at the price of losing wholehearted attention and devotion. They must validate her false idea that she has sacrificed her own life to maintain the home, although they all

Johansen. During World War II the Sønderby family was indirectly involved in the Danish Resistance, and in December 1944 Sønderby had to flee to neutral Sweden. He was also a contributor to the illegal and anonymous resistance anthology *Der brænder en Ild* (A Fire is Burning, 1944). After the war Sønderby worked as a writer and a translator. Most of his essays in their first version were published in the newspaper *Politiken.*

In Esbjerg, Sønderby's father had his warehouses along the harbor, and there he taught his young son to cross the rusted railway tracks with a new bicycle. In the essay "Stumper af et Spejl" (Bits of a Mirror, 1940; revised, 1944) Sønderby recalls this situation, remarking on the light over a wilderness of cobblestones looking out on the North Sea. This glimpse of Sønderby's childhood is typical of the author's practice: a central characteristic of his

help each other on equal terms. Therefore, the children have an ambivalent attitude toward her, admiring her for her straightforward ideals and proud self-awareness, but hating her for her selfish expectations.

When Sønderby was a twenty-year-old law student, he wrote his first novel, *Midt i en Jazztid* (In the Middle of the Jazz Age, 1931). The book caused a scandal because the reviewers saw it as a proof of the immorality of youth. The publisher, Jespersen og Pio, ordered the destruction of the printing plates for the book, but later had them reset. Within three months the book went into four printings, and Sønderby suddenly became a young representative of the rich youths who wasted their time riding, skiing, playing tennis, listening to jazz, dancing, and, not least, having sexual adventures. Although Sønderby was employed by *Dagens Nyheder* as a movie reviewer, in the years following the publication of *Midt i en Jazztid* he also wrote about jazz, skiing, fashionable events, and everything American (for example, Louis Armstrong concerts and movie adaptations of Ernest Hemingway novels). The editor understood how to profit from Sønderby's new public image. The young author had become a symbol.

Sønderby, however, was shocked by and resented the scandal. He had not had any negative or scandalous intentions, he had only—as he explained to an interviewer for the student periodical *Studium-Ugeblad for Studerende* (30 September 1931)—written about youth as it was, and youth was more healthy than the older generation with its false brilliance and hypocritical moral principles. In the same interview Sønderby dismisses reviewer Tom Kristensen's allegations that he had plagiarized from Hemingway. Sønderby asserted that he had not read Hemingway at all. Others would later conjecture that Sønderby must have read about F. Scott Fitzgerald and his *Tales of the Jazz Age* (1922) in *Moderne amerikansk Litteratur* (Modern American Literature, 1930), a book by his mentor, Frederik Schyberg. It may have been Schyberg, however, who, having read Sønderby's manuscript, proposed the title of the work, having seen the parallel between the young Fitzgerald and the young, but more modest, Danish author.

The central character in *Midt i en Jazztid* is a twenty-one-year-old law student, Peter Hasvig, who serves as Sønderby's alter ego. Peter comes from the middle class of an unnamed town in Jutland, but he now resides in Copenhagen, where he is a member of a circle of young people from the upper middle class: daughters and sons of rich lawyers, wholesale merchants, and managers. To use an expression from the Norwegian-American sociologist Thorstein Veblen,

Peter has joined the "leisure class." These young people have a lot of free time; they do not work. When they stay in Copenhagen, they loiter and go shopping, but most of the time they live in country houses in north Zealand (north of Copenhagen). With a characteristic statement, which Sønderby reiterates, there they "spillede tennis, red og gik i vandet" (played tennis, went riding, and went bathing). Lurking behind this life of luxury, however, is boredom and vacuity.

On the one hand, Peter, like Sønderby, is fascinated not by money as such, but by the aesthetic comforts that the young people have as a matter of course. They live in houses with spacious rooms, grand pianos, fine art, tennis courts, and saddle horses. The girls are cheerful in a lazy, self-confident way, and their dresses are expensive without being gaudy. On the other hand, Peter is a stranger in these houses. He registers everything in visual descriptions, which are typical of Sønderby, but he also feels the emptiness in the moments when nothing happens. In spite of these feelings, he cannot afford to be critical, for fear of jeopardizing his role as a beautiful, sportive partner for the girls. He again experiences the isolation and emptiness of his own life, from which he tries to escape, at the end of the novel, where he is totally alone with the impression that even time is fleeing. The narrative is written by the disillusioned Peter, perhaps to fill his empty time, and the reader cannot avoid noting the tone of melancholy that is characteristic of Sønderby's work.

Midt i en Jazztid has been read as a novel about the oppositions between social classes. This theme is also evident, but first of all it is a novel of disillusionment, and the disillusion of a generation which has not experienced the values that existed before World War I. Thus, at the end of the novel, the reader discovers that the author generalizes the destiny of Peter Hasvig, so that his lack of values is valid for everybody—both rich and poor—in the period that followed the great crash of values as a consequence of the war. A symptom of this cultural situation is that parents do not exist as characters. They only form the background of the young people who live in their own right and follow their own ethics. But, of course, Sønderby cannot generalize; Peter Hasvig's and Sønderby's aesthetic and erotic way of experiencing life is too personal. The style is the man, and therefore the author is much different from the social realists of the 1930s with whom he has been compared.

Sønderby's next novel, *To Mennesker mødes*, has likewise been seen as a novel about the opposition between social classes. It is the love story of the medical student Kaj Ruben, who is from a circle of

Sønderby in 1965 (photograph by Henrik Folker; courtesy of Gyldendal Publishers)

wealthy young people, and the shop assistant Kirsten Bruun, who already has an illegitimate child. Their relationship apparently comes to an end at a party where Kirsten feels ostracized because she pronounces the word *musiker* (musician) with the wrong accent. The chapter-long descriptions of the manners of different classes underline the fact that the social gap and different expectations may threaten the relationship that Kaj, typical of Sønderby, has based on an irresistible aesthetic and erotic attraction.

To Mennesker mødes is not an example of social realism—as its structure and symbolic metaphors (parallel lines, circles) demonstrate. Rather, it is a modern, experimental novel in which "Kaj Ruben" and "Kirsten Bruun" are two accidental names (passport codes), selected among thousands of combinations. The social opposition reinforces this experiment, but in reality Sønderby wants to confront two human beings, each with their personal and inscrutable, but also binding, past. As the author writes,

> To mennesker kan gaa ved siden af hinanden som parallelle linjer, og ude i mørket til begge sider, hvor de har færdedes og levet deres liv og sat deres spor,

sker der ting: Der sidder en mand eller der sidder en kvinde, eller der er et barn, der græder, og de to mennesker, der gaar side om side, kan være som parallelle linjer blot, men sommetider kan det være, de standser og rører ved hinanden, og holder fast paa hinanden, og i de øjeblikke er der ingen, der kan gøre dem noget.

> (Two human beings may walk side by side as parallel lines, and out there in the darkness on both sides where they have lived and left their traces, things happen: a man is sitting, a woman is sitting or a child is weeping, and the two people walking side by side may be like parallel lines only, but sometimes it happens that they stop and touch each other and embrace each other, and in those moments nobody can harm them.)

Whether Kirsten and Kaj reunite after the disastrous party is not made clear, but this point is not essential. The expression "sub specie æterni" (*aeternitatis*) forms a leitmotiv of the novel—only one couple out of a thousand is suited to each other, and perhaps they will never meet. Such is the condition in a world where the relativity of time and space has complicated knowledge endlessly. The skeptical and disillusioned Sønderby has experienced this perplexity and seen that he lives in the age of relativity and probability. Thus, his novel is an experiment, in which Kirsten and Kaj are two of a thousand people whose circles for a moment accidentally converge.

In 1935 Sønderby received his master's degree in law, and during the following months he lived in Greenland, at that time an island unknown to most Danes. It would provide the setting for his third novel, *De kolde Flammer: Roman fra Grønland* (The Cold Flames: Novel of Greenland, 1940), and the subject matter for his first volume of essays, *Grønlandsk Sommer* (Greenlandic Summer, 1941).

In *De kolde Flammer* Sønderby rejects the romantic idea that two people are destined for each other—the probability is now one in a million. Kristian Vase, an adventurer and photographer who knows Greenland, and his wife, Vera, have come to understand that love is a labor, not a naturally given truth. Vera and Kristian, too, are driven from Paradise, the myth that creates the connection in this book between the love story and the social themes. This resigned perspective is underlined in Sønderby's descriptions of nature. Seen with a bird's-eye view from the gigantic mountains, human beings are tiny, and their culture, by the same token, frail.

De kolde Flammer is a work planned along generous lines, but there is more philosophy than art in this novel, in which the reasoning expands at the expense of the sharp sensations and vivid descriptions characteristic of Sønderby's earlier works. This lack of structure could be the reason why *De kolde Flammer* was Sønderby's last novel. From 1941 to his death in 1966 he preferred the essay, in which genre he finally experienced a continuous success, discovering the form that suited his temperament and his concept of time.

In *Tingene: Knud Sønderby in memoriam* (The Things: In Memory of Knud Sønderby, 1966), a book published in honor of Sønderby, the medical professor Mogens Fog, one of the leaders of the Danish Resistance who had had his papers hidden in Sønderby's apartment during World War II, recalls Sønderby the year before his death. At a fair in Provence the rest of the group had been looking for objects to buy, while Sønderby, apparently without plan and purpose, had wandered about. Months later a feature article Sønderby published in the newspaper *Politiken* revealed that he had seen and sensed everything at the fair, in particular the small and droll things that created the atmosphere. He had realized his experience in such a way that the most worthless things became the most valuable because from Sønderby's point of view these things were the

core of the experience. The book introduces this article as Sønderby's last essay.

The situation, Fog explains, is typical of both the older and the younger Sønderby. In Sønderby's own words, he was lazy, and he liked to be a loafer and a spectator, but when he stopped he was an extraordinarily sensitive observer. This quality is already apparent in "Vinterens Fugle" (The Winter's Birds, 1933), Sønderby's first essay, published in the newspaper *Dagens Nyheder*, in which Sønderby with the greatest precision registers all the characteristic details of the different birds but also creates comical episodes because he had a keen eye and an unerring ear for details that break down illusions.

Also typical is the fact that Sønderby did not write down his impressions at once. He kept his vision and his experiences in his mind and wrote about them months or years later. They were, he has written, like filmstrips that he could replay when he felt an inspirational constraint. The title essay in *Gensyn med havet* (The Sea Revisited, 1957) is an example of this practice. It was written while he was in Italy, Sønderby said, because he suddenly felt a deep need to recall walking tours along the western coast of Jutland. As he wrote, the unfamiliar surroundings of Italy were out of sight; he was simply at the beach in Lønstrup in Jutland. At first, his descriptions of the sea are intense, bringing the past vividly to life; yet later in the essay the reader understands that Sønderby cannot adhere to the original situation: the light fades and emptiness lurks. In a lucky moment Sønderby has experienced the fullness of time, but then he has to release his hold on the past. In other words, the filmstrip had run out, and Sønderby was in Italy again.

Sønderby died on 8 August 1966 in Visbyå, located on the island of Mors in the northwestern part of Jutland. He traveled all his life, particularly in Denmark, to experience and see what others had failed to experience and see; ultimately, however, he traveled to recall, and he recalled to stop fleeting time. In this way his minute examinations of the past became an attempt to stabilize identity through spontaneous presence. Such existential topics are frequently explored in his essays, in which experiences and reflections intersect and enrich each other. As an essayist, Sønderby can be favorably compared to other great Danish practitioners of the form: Johannes Smith, Jacob Paludan, and, most of all, his teacher in regard to the form, the Nobel Prize winner Johannes V. Jensen. Sønderby has his own tone, however—the combination of deep melancholy, honest hedonism, and wise humor is the mark of Sønderby's essays.

Interviews:

"Sønderby, Knud: Midt i en Jazztid," *Studium-ugeblad for Studerende,* 30 September 1931, p. 6;

Niels Birger Wamberg, "Knud Sønderby," in his *Samtale med danske digtere* (Copenhagen: Gyldendal, 1968), pp. 101–109.

Bibliography:

Dan Hellum, *Knud Sønderby: Bibliografi og produktionsregistrant 1925–74,* Studier fra Danmarks biblioteksskole, no. 23 (Copenhagen: Danmarks Biblioteksskole, 1976).

References:

Poul Bager, *Fylde og tomhed: Om Knud Sønderbys forfatterskab* (Copenhagen: Gyldendal, 1984);

Bager, "Midt i en Jazztid," in his *Læsninger* (Århus: Centrum, 1991), pp. 82–99;

Flemming Bergsøe, *Det underlige Aar* (Copenhagen: Thaning & Appel, 1945), pp. 126–127, 145–154;

Thorkild Bjørnvig, "Knud Sønderby," in his *Digtere* (Copenhagen: Gyldendal, 1991), pp. 145–157;

Peter Gadman, *Knud Sønderbys forfatterskab* (Copenhagen: Vinten, 1976);

Birgitte Rasmussen Hornbek, "Ting og erindring," *Spring,* no. 4 (1993): 79–85;

Hornbek, "Melankolsk poetik," in *Tidsskrift för litteraturvetenskap* (Lund, Sweden, 1991): 61–81;

Susanne Bodholdt Jakobsen, "Møde midt i byen," in *Københavnerromaner,* edited by Marianne Barlyng and Søren Schou (Copenhagen: Borgen, 1996), pp. 226–245;

Niels Kaas Johansen, "Knud Sønderby," in *Danske Digtere i det 20. århundrede,* volume 2, edited by Ernst Frandsen and others (Copenhagen: Gad, 1951), pp. 451–464;

Finn Nordentoft, "Midt i en Jazztid," *Meddelelser fra Dansklærerforeningen,* 10 (1972): 307–318;

Ralf Pittelkow, "Narcissus og kapitalen," in *Analyser af danske romaner,* volume 3, edited by Jørgen Holmgaard (Copenhagen: Borgen, 1977), pp. 7–133;

Ole Risak, *Knud Sønderby* (Kongerslev: GMT, 1973);

Lars Peter Rømhild, "En kvinde er overflødig," *Meddelelser fra dansklærerforeningen,* 4 (1966): 125–133;

Frederik Schyberg, "En kvinde er overflødig," in his *Teatret i Krig (1939–1946)* (Copenhagen: Gyldendal, 1949), pp. 75–80;

Hakon Stangerup, *Portrætter og Protester* (Copenhagen: Haase, 1940), pp. 168–175;

Hanne Marie Svendsen, "Livsstil og klasseforskel," in *Tilbageblik på 30'erne,* volume 1, edited by Hans Hertel (Copenhagen: Stig Vendelkærs, 1967), pp. 80–93;

Bodil Wamberg, "Knud Sønderby," in *Danske digtere i det 20. århundrede,* third edition, volume 2, edited by Torben Brostrøm and others (Copenhagen: Gad, 1981), pp. 322–338;

Niels Birger Wamberg, "Knud Sønderbys gratie," *Vinduet,* no. 17 (1963): 86–89;

Wamberg, "Knud Sønderby," in *Danske digtere i det 20. århundrede,* second edition, edited by Frederik Nielsen and others, volume 2 (Copenhagen: Gad, 1966), pp. 269–300;

Papers:

Letters, manuscripts, and other materials are in the Knud Sønderby collection at Det Kongelige Bibliotek (The Royal Library), Copenhagen.

Villy Sørensen
(13 January 1929 –   )

Finn Hauberg Mortensen
University of Southern Denmark, Odense

Translated by Trevor Elkington

BOOKS: *Sære historier* (Copenhagen: Gyldendal, 1953; revised and enlarged edition, 1963); translated by Maureen Neiiendam as *Strange Stories* (London: Secker & Warburg, 1956); republished as *Tiger in the Kitchen and Other Strange Stories* (New York: Abelard-Schuman, 1957);

Ufarlige historier (Copenhagen: Gyldendal, 1955); translated by Paula Hostrup-Jessen as *Harmless Tales* (Norwich: Norvik, 1991);

Digtere og Dæmoner: Fortolkninger og vurderinger (Copenhagen: Gyldendal, 1959);

Hverken–eller: Kritiske betragtninger (Copenhagen: Gyldendal, 1961);

Friedrich Nietzsche (Copenhagen: Gad, 1963); revised edition (Copenhagen: Gyldendal, 1982);

Formynderfortællinger (Copenhagen: Gyldendal, 1964); translated by Hostrup-Jessen as *Tutelary Tales* (Lincoln: University of Nebraska Press, 1988);

Kafkas digtning (Copenhagen: Gyldendal, 1968);

Mellem fortid og fremtid: Kronikker og kommentarer (Copenhagen: Gyldendal, 1969);

Schopenhauer (Copenhagen: Gyldendal, 1969);

Uden mål–og med: Moralske tanker (Copenhagen: Gyldendal, 1973);

Seneca: Humanisten ved Neros hof (Copenhagen: Gyldendal, 1976); translated by W. Glyn Jones as *Seneca, the Humanist at the Court of Nero* (Chicago: University of Chicago Press, 1984; Edinburgh: Cannongate, 1984);

Oprør fra midten, by Sørensen, K. Helveg Petersen, and Niels I. Meyer (Copenhagen: Gyldendal, 1978); translated by Christine Hauch as *Revolt from the Center* (London: Boyars, 1981);

Den gyldne middelvej og andre debatindlæg fra 70erne (Copenhagen: Gyldendal, 1979);

Vejrdage (Copenhagen: Gyldendal, 1980);

Villy Sørensen in 1985 (photograph by Gunvor Jorgsholm)

Aladdin–og den vidunderlige lampe (Århus: Centrum, 1981; London: Faber & Faber, 1981);

Ragnarok: En gudefortælling (Århus: Centrum 1982); translated by Hostrup-Jessen as *The Downfall of the Gods* (Lincoln: University of Nebraska Press, 1989);

Røret om oprøret, by Sørensen, Petersen, and Meyer (Copenhagen: Gyldendal, 1982);

De mange og De enkelte–og andre småhistorier (Copenhagen: Brøndum, 1986); translated by Tiina Nunnally and Steven T. Murray as *Another Metamorphosis and Other Fictions* (Seattle: Fjord, 1990); selections translated by Hostrup-Jessen as *Four Biblical Tales* (Seattle: Mermaid, 1991);

Demokratiet og kunsten (Copenhagen: Gyldendal, 1988);

Tilløb: Dagbog 1949–53 (Copenhagen: Gyldendal, 1988);

Den berømte Odysseus (Copenhagen: Gyldendal, 1988);

Apollons oprør: De udødeliges historie (Copenhagen: Vindrose, 1989);

Forløb: Dagbog 1953–61 (Copenhagen: Gyldendal, 1990);

Den frie vilje (Copenhagen: Reitzel, 1992);

Jesus og KRISTUS (Copenhagen: Gyldendal, 1992);

Perioder: Dagbog 1961–74 (Copenhagen: Gyldendal, 1993);

Historien om Ødipus (Copenhagen: Gyldendal, 1995).

Edition in English: *The Soldier's Christmas Eve,* translated by Nadia Christensen and Alexander Taylor (Willimantic, Conn.: Trekroner, 1973).

TELEVISION: "At gå op ad væggen," script by Sørensen, produced by Peter Bech Film in conjunction with Danmarks Radio, TV-Facts, and Statens Filmscentral, 24 October 1997.

OTHER: *Vindrosen,* co-edited by Sørensen (1959–1963);

Søren Kierkegaard, *Begrebet Angest,* introductory essay by Sørensen (Copenhagen: Gyldendal, 1960);

Karl Marx, *Økonomi og filosofi: Ungdomsskrifter,* introductory essay by Sørensen (Copenhagen: Gyldendal, 1962);

Hans Christian Andersen, *Eventyr og Historier,* introductory essay by Sørensen (Copenhagen: Gyldendal, 1965);

Herman Bang, *Haabløse Slægter,* introductory essay by Sørensen (Copenhagen: Gyldendal, 1965);

Midler uden mål: Kommentarer til perspektivplanlægningen, edited by Sørensen (Copenhagen: Spektrum, 1971; Copenhagen: Gyldendals Kulturbibliotek, 1987–1991);

Seneca, *Om vrede–Om mildhed–Om sindsro,* translated, with an introductory essay, by Sørensen (Copenhagen: Gyldendal, 1976);

På vej, co-edited by Sørensen (1979–1981);

"Villy Sørensen, f. 13. 1. 1929," in *Festskrift* (Copenhagen: University of Copenhagen, 1979);

Desiderius Erasmus, *Tåbelighedens lovprisning,* translated, with an introductory essay, by Sørensen (Copenhagen: Gyldendal, 1979);

Richard Wagner, *Kunsten og revolutionen,* translated, with an introductory essay, by Sørensen (Copenhagen: Gyldendal, 1983);

Erasmus, *Skøn er krigen for den uerfarne,* translated, with an introductory essay, by Sørensen (Copenhagen: Gyldendal, 1984);

Herman Bang, *Tine,* introductory essay by Sørensen (Copenhagen: Det danske Sprog-og Litteraturselskab/Borgen, 1986).

Villy Sørensen's linguistic subtlety and sharp intellect have earned him a prominent place among the top Danish authors of the twentieth century. His absurd, modernistic parables and fantastic tales—translated into many languages—invoke the works of Hans Christian Andersen and Karen Blixen. The stories are "strange"—they break with realism in order to follow a specific, unusual logic. As with the works of Andersen, clichés gain new meaning through the slightest twists, and as with the writings of Søren Kierkegaard, irony makes the text ambiguous and yet revealing, coaxing the reader to take a position.

In a 1969 interview with Ninka og Bendix, Sørensen said, "Jeg kommer altid i forlegenhed, når jeg skal angive min stilling. Filosofferne vil jo i hvert fald ikke kalde mig filosof, men måske nok digter. Mens nogle litterater måske nærmere vil kalde mig for filosof" (I always find it difficult when I must state my position. The philosophers would, in any case, certainly not call me a philosopher, but an author. Meanwhile, some literary scholars might consider me closer to a philosopher). One might call Sørensen, like Kierkegaard, a writer-philosopher, as he finds himself in the field of tension somewhere between literature and philosophy.

Sørensen writes of delusions, repressions, and other irrationalities that serve as obstacles in the path of individual freedom. The individual's recognition of his surroundings and his self are often united, and Sørensen views the European cultural crisis and the crisis of humanity as crises within the individual. His works present these crises as a fall, on the levels of both the species and the individual, a loss of innocence experienced as discord due to the breakdown of an understanding of unity up to the current age. Yet, they can also remove the individual's alienation and neurotic repression of the unconscious. This fall is therefore a prerequisite of liberation, while freedom before this fall is understood as merely "dyrets og den primitives amoralske frihed" (the amoral freedom of the animal and the primitive).

Villy Sørensen was born on 13 January 1929 in Frederiksberg, a municipality within Copenhagen, and grew up in Valby, in the western corner of Copenhagen. His father was Johannes Peder Sørensen, a porter and later conductor for DSB, the state railway, and his mother was Anna Mathilde Thomsen. Sørensen's older brother, Henning Sørensen, became a professor of geol-

First page of the manuscript for Sørensen's retelling of the myth of Theodora and Theodorus in his first book,
Sære historier, *published in 1953 (Collection of Villy Sørensen)*

ogy with special emphasis in petrography at the University of Copenhagen in 1962, and in 1976 he was appointed state geologist for the Danish Geological Survey. Sørensen's childhood experiences as the son of a blue-collar family in the 1930s are linked to his close-knit family; brother, mother, and father are mirrored in many of his stories about twins, sexuality, and father-son relationships.

Kierkegaard's father is said to have forsaken God as a poor shepherd boy on the Jutland heath, thereby calling down a curse on himself and his family. With a sidelong glance at Kierkegaard, Sørensen recalls how he as a boy he had regarded his father as a heathen. Just as Kierkegaard undertook a pilgrimage to his father's home district, so did Villy accompany his father in 1954 to his childhood home on Reersø, an isolated peninsula in west Sjælland. The young author was closely connected to his father and there met

> Villy i bageriet som jeg siges at være opkaldt efter–jeg havde jo hørt det før, men ligesom ikke følt noget ved det før nu. Og det var vel fars følelser jeg prøvede at føle efter da vi gik gennem byen og mødte gamle bekendte som jeg ikke kendte og som sagde: "ja tiden den guer, Johannes."

> (Villy at the bakery, whom I am said to have been named after–I had heard it before, but had not felt anything about it before now. And it was father's feelings I tried to sense after that, when we walked through the town and met old acquaintances that I didn't know, and who said: "yes, time surely passes, Johannes.")

Sørensen's published diary depicts Reersø as a paradise, despite the war: "Besættelsestid. De rød-hvide bomme står i paradisets have hvor far kører med tog–smedens nøddetræ allerede er en første barnlig udgave af kundskabens træ, dens frugter er den engelsk-tyske lærdom." (The Occupation. The red-white barriers across the railroad tracks appear as in a garden of paradise where father rides the train–the smithy's walnut tree is a first, childish edition of the tree of knowledge, its fruits are English-German erudition). The description is used again as the prelude to the story "Hjemvejen" (The Road Home) from *Ufarlige historier* (1955; translated as *Harmless Tales,* 1991) as the experience of two boys on their way home from school.

Sørensen went to Ålhom School. While the other two thousand students sang "Dejlig er jorden" (Wonderful is the Earth) in the assembly hall, the nine-year-old boy asked himself, "Er den nu det?" (Is that a fact?). In the following year, he became an eager athlete as a way to break his melancholy and sense of isolation from his peers. His parents owned world literature in the form of Gyldendal's fifty-two-volume series of world classics and encouraged their two sons to read, fruitlessly attempting to wean them from playing indoor fantasy games with "paper dolls"–pictures from *Illustreret Tidende* (Illustrated Times) of Danish and German soldiers from the battles in Sønderjylland in 1864. Villy pursued an education with an emphasis in modern languages at Vester Borgerdydskole, where he met two boys who would later become critics and novelists: Niels Barfoed and Klaus Rifbjerg. The paper dolls were exchanged for dramas on paper: the sixteen-year-old Sørensen wrote a drama about freedom fighters in 1945 and began his first novel, "Mørkets barn" (Child of Darkness), which he destroyed because he was dissatisfied with it. After his graduation from secondary school in 1947, the author pursued studies in liberal arts at the University of Copenhagen, which were broken off in 1954 without his having taken a degree. His interest in German philosophy and psychology was nurtured during a study visit at the University of Freiburg in 1952–1953.

Sørensen's authorship from 1952 on can be divided into five cyclical stages. Each of the five cycles has a specific generic and thematic profile. In an interview on the occasion of his fortieth birthday, Sørensen pointed out the cyclical stages of his authorship: "En cyklus begynder nemlig med symbolske fortællinger. Så kommer der en bog med analyse af digteriske symboler, altså litteraturkritik. Så kommer der en med social kritik, og endelig kommer der så en rent filosofisk" (A cycle begins with symbolic tales. Then there comes a book with analysis of poetic symbols, that is, literary criticism. Then there comes one with social criticism, and finally comes one that is purely philosophical). He asserted that writers normally break through at age twenty-three or twenty-four–as he himself had done–and that at age forty they revise, but do not necessarily reject, that which they started with. The author continued: "Hvis De nu er stiv i mine papirer, så kan De se, hvordan det passer" (If you are now well into my papers, you can see for yourself how it goes). This overview held true up to 1969, in that he had two such cycles behind him, the time periods from 1953 to 1963 and from 1964 to 1969. In 1969 he was perhaps on his way into a new cycle, but the cycle was disrupted. Sørensen lost his father; he was too old to belong to the 1968 revolt of students and intellectuals, although he took sides in the rebellion. The politicization of the 1960s and the 1970s inspired a craving in the philosophizing author and initiated a pause in his authorship. The result was another revolution–*Oprør fra midten* (1978; translated as *Revolt from the Center,* 1981), the middle-aged entering the political spectrum. After 1980, fiction and the cyclical movement in Sørensen's authorship returned in a more liberated form.

In October 1949 the author wrote in his journal that Kierkegaard plays "en så overvældende rolle for vor tid, fordi han havde dette skizoide væsen, der i vore dage er karakteristisk for os alle" (such an overwhelming role for our time, because he had that schizoid nature, which in our time is characteristic for us all). Sørensen's reading of Kierkegaard during that summer exerted a strong and lasting influence on him and provided subsequent entrance to the Bible and the writings of Friedrich Nietzsche, Marcel Proust, Franz Kafka, Carl Jung, and Georg Friedrich Wilhelm Hegel.

The first of the five shorter cycles of Sørensen's work, from 1953 to 1963, begins with two collections of prose fiction, *Sære historier* (1953; first translated as *Strange Stories,* 1956) and *Ufarlige historier* (1955; translated as *Harmless Tales,* 1991); it continues with two collections of essays, *Digtere og Dæmoner: Fortolkninger og vurderinger* (Poets and Demons, 1959), and *Hverken–eller: Kritiske betragtninger* (Neither–Nor, 1961), together with editions of Kierkegaard and Karl Marx; it concludes with the monograph on *Friedrich Nietzsche* (1963).

When the Danish Authors' Guild donated a typewriter to Sørensen in December 1954, the chairperson called upon his young colleague to continue with short stories and "evt. gøre dem mindre sære og mere favnende" (possibly make them less strange and more embracing). After his debut in 1953 with *Sære historier,* Sørensen became known for the "strange": fictional elements that point out the "normal," which the stories in turn make noteworthy and remarkable. Beginning with Sørensen, however, this "strangeness" became so common among young, modernistic writers in Denmark that Thomas Bredsdorff chose *Sære fortæller* (Strange Storytellers, 1967) as the title of the first critical overview of their work.

Sørensen, like Andersen, uses the designation *historier,* or "stories," for many types of texts. Some of them are fairy-tales that have undergone a long process of development. A sketch of "Det ukendte træ" (The Unknown Tree) exists from 3 August 1949, while the story itself was "skrevet i en fart" (written in a hurry) on 17 March 1952. Often Sørensen observes only that the writing process is quick.

The content of his journals focuses on dreams, which the author carefully trains himself to remember and uses as the raw material for his work. Many other elements then enter into the work, whether they be experienced, thought, remembered, or dreamed: Sørensen writes affirmatively, negatively, or ironically about an enormous range of subjects, spanning from antiquity to the twentieth century.

Sære historier is comprised of two "myths/legends," two novellas, and five short, fantastic stories that frame and separate the longer compositions. Altogether, the

Painting by Arne Ungermann for the cover of Sørensen's first book (Collection of Villy Sørensen)

texts tell of a mythical age and the distinction of each. First, a primordial, or golden, age, depicted in the myths "Silvanus af Nazareth" (Silvanus of Nazareth) and "Theodora og Theodorus" (Theodora and Theodorus), together with the Paradise myth "Det ukendte træ" (The Unknown Tree); next, a modern age, depicted in the positivist-critical "Blot en drengestreg" (Just a Boyish Prank) in the Kafkaesque novella "Mordsagen" (The Case of Murder), and in the media parody "Vidunderbarnet" (The Wonder Child); and a future or utopian age, depicted in the novella "Koncerten" (The Concert), and in the short stories "De to tvillinger" (The Two Twins) and "Tigrene" (The Tigers). An historical passage is connected to each of these three ages, telling of both successful and unsuccessful developments.

Ufarlige historier was written quickly in the early summer of 1955. Among the longest of the stories is "Købmanden" (The Merchant). The merchant sells only what he thinks his customers have use for, instead

of what they think they want. He is against advertisements, does not sell beer to bricklayers who work on
scaffolds, and throws a customer out of his shop when
he tries to buy cigarettes. He raises an only son, the
mute Filip, who wants to be like his father but is unable
to refuse anything. The merchant's shop soon receives
competition from a self-service shop, where the customers can buy anything and everything they want. The
merchant responds by portioning out all of his wares to
the poor, free of charge, but he keeps the liquor. He
turns his house into a pub, and his old customers are
free to drink all they want. The son journeys out into
the world with his trumpet. He is to be an entertainer
on a luxury liner, but is soon set ashore because he will
not play the melodies requested by the guests. Learning
of his son's refusal, the merchant is filled with fatherly
pride.

Sørensen's studies of philosophy, psychology, and
literature are interrelated through Jung's analytical psychology. The literary gestalt of symbols played a large
role in Sørensen's development, and in his younger
years, Kafka was his greatest inspiration. Sørensen
writes in his journal for September 1953 of his rebellion
against the naturalists—"Kafka har myrdet det gamle
rum og ladet liget stå" (Kafka has murdered the old
space and left the corpse standing)—but when he
"trænger gennem ordenes overflade og lader det
uforståelige selv træde frem, bebrejder man ham at han
er uforståelig og at han ikke forstår sig på rigtige mennesker" (pushes through the superficiality of words and
lets the incomprehensible self step forth, he is admonished that he is incomprehensible and that he does not
understand real people).

In December 1953, when Sørensen looked back
upon the work that made up *Sære historier,* he immediately went "hinsides Kafka-universet" (beyond the
"Kafka universe") to Hermann Broch, whose novel *Die
Schuldlosen* (1950, written 1917–1949) is praised for its
fragmentary nature. Sørensen translated the German
writer in 1959, calling himself "Broch's imitator," but
adds that there is "noget tilfredsstillende i at jeg i så fald
var Broch-epigon før jeg lærte ham at kende" (something satisfying in knowing that I was in this case an
imitator of Broch before I really got to know him).

Sørensen's next work, *Digtere og Dæmoner: Fortolkninger og vurderinger,* changed in preparation from "a
collection" of essays to "a context" for essays. In his
analysis of folk ballads, among other things, Sørensen
develops an understanding of the individual as an historical process in relation to what is ontologically called
"the Fall" and psychologically, "the trauma." Sørensen
discovered that Kierkegaard's abstract theories could be
developed through folk ballads, and that the Fall in
both instances is tied to a particular age—and to sexual-

ity—which he takes as an argument for a connection
between ontology and biology: "Hvordan skulle de
evige kategorier kunne bestemme menneskelivet om de
ikke trådte frem i tiden—og hvordan skulle noget kunne
bestemme mennesket som ikke kan iagttages i det biolo-
giske?" (How should the eternal stages [of Kierkegaard]
be able to determine the life of the individual if they did
not appear in our times—and how should some force be
able to "determine" the individual that cannot be
observed in the biological?). All of the stories in *Sære
historier* revolve around the Fall and how to overcome it.

The influence of Thomas Mann was decisive for
the young Sørensen. Sørensen's analyses of Kierkegaard and Andersen distinctly position the notions of
recollection, division, and repetition. In the section dealing with aesthetic criticism, Sørensen has Mann meet
with two other authors who are characterized by these
notions (Harald Kidde and Broch), after which they are
confronted with "Folkeviser og forlovelser" (Folk Ballads and Betrothal), a long essay on the Fall in connection with betrothal, which belongs among the most
influential research on folk ballads. Sørensen's psycho-
logical-philosophical method has had enormous meaning for subsequent literary scholarship.

Finally, in *Digtere og Dæmoner* the individual is
socially located in the welfare state and in Europe,
which in its loss of superpower status has experienced
its own Fall. Sørensen asserts that postwar European
reconstruction demands the abolition of "den
europæiske selvbevidsthed, som i store nationer kan få
karakter af storhedsvanvid, og den selvtiltrækkelighed
som i små nationer kan få karakter af provinsialisme"
(the European self-awareness, which in great nations
can achieve the character of megalomania, and the
self-sufficiency that in small nations can take on the
character of provincialism).

In the summer of 1960 Sørensen began to feel he
had lost his inspiration as an author. Although he was
at the time sought out as a trendsetter, he only felt himself drifting "længere og længere bort fra det litterære,
der egentlig også interesserer mig mindre og mindre"
(farther and farther away from literature, which actually
interests me less and less). Even though Sørensen has
been closely tied throughout his career to the personal
circle surrounding the Gyldendal publishing house, the
Louisiana Museum, and the newspaper *Politiken,* these
collaborations were not always free of tension. On 4
June 1961 he was sharply criticized by the author Knud
Poulsen, and he reacted with an unexpected and violent
anger. Sørensen's public status was so high by this time
that the left-wing newspaper *Information* and the conservative *Berlingske Tidende* both immediately lined up
behind him.

The author's anger prompted the reprinting of a collection of previously published journal essays and newspaper articles from 1958 to 1961, together with new, longer essays, titled *Hverken–eller: Kritiske betragtninger* (Neither–Nor: Critical Observations, 1961). The process of publication went quickly: on 13 June the decision to publish the book was made; the next day Gyldendal accepted the manuscript, and it was received on 25 July. By 22 October, however, the mood was low. Sørensen wrote in his journal: "Forsinket 2. korrektur på HvE. Hverken fugl eller fisk. Læser lidt Bliktromme på dansk–og føler mig så mager (53 kg)" (Second set of proofs delayed on *HvE*. Neither fish nor fowl. Reading a bit of *The Tin Drum* in Danish–and feel so thin [53 kg]). By 5 December *Hverken–eller* was receiving favorable reviews.

"Et hus splidagtigt med sig selv? Om 'Politiken'" (A House Divided Against Itself? On *Politiken*) was included in *Hverken–eller*. It was clearly a response to Poulsen, but it was also an attempt to resurrect the original free-minded ideals of political openness of *Politiken*, which had long since been devalued in the modern omnibus-newspaper, with its tendency toward entertainment and petty journalism.

Nietzsche, Kierkegaard, and Marx are "die Heilige Familie" (the Holy Family), wrote Sørensen, in a journal entry from 15 February 1962. A well-known figure in Danish cultural life, Hal Koch, had just requested Sørensen to write a book on Nietzsche, who had been introduced internationally by the Danish critic Georg Brandes. In the journal *Tilskueren* (1889) Brandes and the philosopher Harald Høffding had engaged in a momentous debate on "Aristocratic Radicalism" and "Democratic Radicalism." The problem was whether the "Übermensch" (Superman) should be understood as the means or the end of cultural development.

Sørensen's monograph on Nietzsche was published in the autumn of 1963. The idea was to reconstruct his philosophy so as to examine its consequent misinterpretation by the Nazis. The book was revised and expanded in 1982; in the new material Sørensen explores Nietzsche's relation to Richard Wagner and adds a chapter in which he relates Nietzsche to his own revolutionary project. Nietzsche, according to Sørensen, jumped from a revolt against contemporary Biedermeier culture to the criticism of the foundation of European culture, which is "uden midte, uden 'apolinsk' formidling mellem de 'dionysiske' drivkræfter og det styrende–'sokratiske'–intellekt" (without middle, without an "Apollonian" mediation between the "Dionysian" driving forces and the steering–"Socratic"–intellect).

In 1960 Sørensen introduced and annotated a new edition of the chief work in the philosophy of personality, *Begrebet Angest* (1844; translated as *The Concept of Dread*, 1947), by Kierkegaard, who is among the most frequently discussed and criticized figures in Sørensen's journals from the 1950s to the 1960s. Though the Kierkegaard text was simply reprinted from an earlier edition and was encumbered with many typographical errors, the book was a success in a first print run of 4,500 copies–a bittersweet success, remarked Sørensen, that this was "den første af 'mine' bøger der har fundet vej til et større publikum" (the first of "my" books that has found its way to a broad audience). Gyldendal wanted to follow this success by offering Sørensen responsibility for the largest Danish paperback publication in history: Kierkegaard's *Samlede Værker* (Collected Works) in twenty volumes. In December 1961 Sørensen wrote in his journal that the project would stand or fall on his talents, but in the end he declined the offer in order to free himself from commissioned work.

Sørensen's selection of texts by Marx, published as *Økonomi og filosofi: Ungdomsskrifter* (Economy and Philosophy, 1962), addressed a significant need for original sources among the then new, anti-authoritarian left-wing, as the emphasis of the selection on the young Marx provided a humanistic angle to Marxism. Sørensen was not fond of "isms," however. In his journal entry for 21 November 1958, he criticizes both Kierkegaard, Marx, and positivism for bowing down to "filosofiske overvurdering" (philosophical overestimation): "Eksistentialismen vil være ontologi, marxismen vil være videnskab, positivismen vil, i strid med sig selv, levere grundlag for en livsanskuelse" (Existentialism wants to be ontology, Marxism wants to be science, positivism wants, contrary to itself, to furnish the basis for a philosophy of life). The alternative is "at være uintresseret, hvilket vil sige at være fortrinlig interesseret i det menneskelige og ikke fortrinsvis i sig selv" (to be uninterested, which is to say, to be supremely interested in the human and not supremely in oneself). Sørensen's assertion of abstract humanity rejects egoism and materialism and transfers Immanuel Kant's notion of disinterested pleasure from the aesthetic realm to those of the ethical and political.

Sørensen had become politically engaged during a youth festival in East Berlin in 1951. Berlin, before the wall was built, was a crucial meeting place of the large, modern foreign powers. Despite extensive study and reading, Sørensen had his first political experiences in the form of concrete events, for example, the conditions of children and youth in communist East Germany, an experience that jolted him. Only later came theory. Even in March 1954 he had not yet read much Marx, though he knew a great deal about the man. As a schoolboy he had, however, read the *The Communist Manifesto* (1848) that Marx had written with Friedrich Engels. Sørensen's study sabbaticals in the 1950s had contrib-

Dust jacket for the U.S. edition (1989) of Sørensen's Ragnarok:
En gudefortælling *(1982)*

als led a debate on the overarching goals of union membership. This hesitant position is grounded in relation to Germany–the large neighbor to the south that has served as source for a large portion of the European culture that has been integrated into Denmark, but which has also conquered Denmark on several occasions, partially in the war of 1864 and entirely during the occupation, from 1940 to 1945. The author evoked this history in 1953 with the question: "Hvordan ville danskerne være hvis vi tilfældigvis ikke var fire, men fyrre eller endda firs millioner?" (What would the Danes be if we happened not to be four, but instead forty or eighty million?)

Both in the global East/West conflict and in the national Danish/German opposition, Sørensen concentrates on the "Neither–Nor." He seeks, in a Hegelian manner, to elevate these divisions to a higher plane rather than choosing between polar oppositions. In a note from his journal in 1961 about the migrations from East to West Berlin, he expresses the wish that "der skulle findes et ingenmandsland, et stort Hverken–eller som man kunne flygte til fra begge lejre. Ingenmandslandet er das Nichts, der ikke-eksisterende Nirvana" (a no-man's-land could be found, a great Neither–Nor to which one could flee from both camps. The no-man's-land is *das Nichts* [the Nothing], the non-existing Nirvana).

This Neither–Nor appears as a motif in portions of Sørensen's dreams, due to the German presence in Denmark during his boyhood. In his journal entry for 12 March 1958, he depicts a dream in which he is arrested by the Germans and pointed out for sacrifice by a beautiful young woman in a white overcoat. A few nights earlier he had dreamed of being accused of leading freedom fighters to their deaths–and he adds, "Også den 27. jan. blev jeg skudt af SS" (Also on 27 January, I was shot by the SS).

On the global level, Sørensen was affected by the atomic bomb and Vietnam, as was typical of his generation. On 2 August 1955 he wrote a journal notation on the ten-year anniversary of Hiroshima; the Cuban Missile Crisis in 1962 had made a deep impression on him; when the local gasworks in Valby exploded on 26 September 1964, he associated it with the mushroom cloud. The war in Vietnam is often commented on in his journals. As early as 1965 Sørensen, in connection with President Lyndon B. Johnson's escalation of the U.S. war effort, pointed to "den indre opløsning" (the inner dissolution) as "langt farligere for USA end Nordvietnam" (far more dangerous for USA than North Vietnam), and he understood immediately in December 1969 the importance of the My Lai Massacre in relation to that dissolution.

The second cycle in Sørensen's authorship, the period between 1964 and 1969, begins with a collection

uted to his internationalism. In the postwar years the European unification was "en stor tanke, som dog ikke kan siges at have fremkaldt begejstring" (a grand thought, which could not yet be said to have called forth great excitement), Sørensen wrote in his journal in 1958, in a critique of contemporary intellectuals: "En radikal omvurdering af nationalitetstanken har de ikke foretaget, skønt de vel skulle være de nærmeste til det" (They have not undertaken a radical reevaluation of the idea of nationality, even though they should be closest to it).

The critique is still relevant. The Danes, since they joined in 1972 by narrow majority, have been among the most union-skeptical members in the European Union. In 1997–1998, Sørensen and other artists and intellectu-

of prose fiction, *Formynderfortællinger* (1964; translated as *Tutelary Tales,* 1988). Like Andersen, who experimented with expansions of his original, confining fairytale genre, Sørensen included in *Formynderfortællinger* several long texts, among them "Et formynderskabs historie" (A Tutelary Tale). This account is historically costumed and relies upon a detailed study of German culture–in particular a study of the history of the Hapsburgs that Sørensen had begun in the summer of 1955, immediately after delivering *Ufarlige historier.* The new book was in the works for a long time. On 30 August 1963 the basic plan of the book was laid out, and on 18 May 1964 a second draft of "Et formynderskabs historie" was completed, but with the note that it might be written again entirely anew. The author considered dropping the three myths up until 2 August 1964, even though they, together with the long account of the Hapsburgian tutelage, finally received a prominent place in the book. On the day the work was finally finished, 11 August 1964, Sørensen's journal records a list of authorial provisoes, reducing the literary significance of the work to its psychotherapeutic function for the author.

Formynderfortællinger concerns guardianship when it is replaced by authority and liberation on the personal and political level. It begins with "En glashistorie" (A Tale of Glass), a tale that inverts the themes and symbols used in Andersen's tale "Snedronningen" (The Snow Queen, 1845). "En glashistorie" tells of the dissemination of a type of glass that makes each owner believe everything is good and beautiful, but the glass actually replaces reality with a delusion. New eyeglasses become fashionable. People willingly allow themselves to be blinded and long for windows made of the wonder glass. Those few who remain in opposition to the authorities must go to an institute for the blind, together with the truly blind. The catastrophe spreads to the "mindre fremskredne, optisk uudviklede lande, hvori glasset endnu er en luxusvare som alle kæmper om" (less advanced, optically undeveloped countries, where the glass is still a luxury item that everyone fights over). It is easy for these outsiders to conquer the country where only the blind are left, but when the invaders see the glass, they lose sight of everything else.

In opposition to this doomsday scenario stands the concluding story of the book, "En fremtidshistorie" (A Tale of the Future), where guardianship and the guardian state are dissolved and freedom conquers all. The hero is Filius, who holds a pistol to his chest, yet survives as a free man because he has the choice of whether or not to fire. He chooses therefore not to shoot the president, even though this has been foreordained. As a free man he becomes master over the

prophesy and thus over his future, and so he deposes the president and takes his place.

In 1970 Sørensen often wrote the words "revolt" or "youth rebellion" in his journal. He did not only confine himself to the word; he also concurred with the student advisory board's complaints over the new university guidance regulations, which claimed to be the most democratic in the world. Despite criticism, Sørensen read and imparted the ideas of the international figures of the student revolution such as Ernest Bloch, Herbert Marcuse, and Theodor W. Adorno. He does not speak on behalf of the working class, despite his origins and his edition of Marx. Through the youth revolution he felt the pull of an international, socially engaged humanism, corresponding to his beliefs during the polarized postwar period. Whereas the youth revolution brought him closer to the political scene and contributed to the blossoming of his critical essays, it also removed him from the rebels by one generation.

In 1957 Sørensen called his generation "den tavse" (the silent one); in 1968 he wrote of "den oprørte ungdom" (the rebelling youth), who had reduced the silent ones to middle age. These two generational accounts were used as the prelude to a large retrospective collection of essays and columns from the period 1954–1968, published under the title *Mellem fortid og fremtid: Kronikker og kommentarer* (1969). Moving freely between the political and philosophical spheres of existence, Sørensen, in his journal entry for 2 July 1969, curses the split between "hoved og hjerte" (head and heart) and Arthur Schopenhauer's delineation of the opposition between them. Schopenhauer's pessimism is described through an inversion of Romans 7:18–"det gode som jeg ikke gør vil jeg ikke, det onde som jeg gør vil jeg" (the good that I do not do, I do not want; the evil that I do, I do). The concept of the will is central to Sørensen's monograph, *Schopenhauer* (1969), which introduces the philosopher as an anti-Hegelian and positions him in contemporary and later German philosophy. Sørensen describes Schopenhauer's chief work, *Das Welt als Willie und Vorstellung* (The World as Will and Idea, 1819; expanded, 1844), as a symphony in four movements. The first book presents the theory of cognition: the world is understood as identical with the subject's conception of it. The second book treats the philosophy of nature: the world is seen as split between a superior will and concrete objects–animals and people–which the will has split off from itself and, in the case of people, given individual will. The third book, "Aesthetics," describes how the cognizant subject, free of interest–and therefore free from will–can observe ideas and artificial objects. In the fourth book, "Ethics," the subject has set itself above the individual in order to become one with pure will, the cosmos.

Andersen also belongs among Sørensen's most important chosen kinships, yet his admiration is neither limitless nor unconditional. Sørensen is particularly critical of the early stories, and he is aware of the older poet's flight "fra noget væsentligt i sig selv" (from something essential in himself): "Hvor den sandte midte mangler, flygter A. til sine to poler: det spidst bedske ('Sneglen og Rosenhækken') og det patetisk sentimentale ('Psyche')" (Where the true midpoint is missing, Andersen flees to his two poles: the tartly bathetic ["The Snail and the Rosebush"] and the pathetically sentimental ["Psyche"]). Andersen's language, imagination, and insight into the child's consciousness and unconsciousness inspired Sørensen's strange and harmless stories, both as congenial play and as Kafkaesque retort. In 1965 Andersen's *Eventyr og Historier* (Tales and Stories) was published in Gyldendal's fifty-volume series of Danish literature–thirty-eight texts chosen by Sørensen, who in his introduction offers an overview of this fairy-tale landscape into which *Digtere og Dæmoner* had entered. Sørensen's selection and introductory essay belong among the best works that research on Andersen has produced.

When Brandes in 1883 published *Det moderne Gjennembruds Mænd* (The Men of the Modern Breakthrough), he did not take Herman Bang into consideration, despite the fact that Bang had distinguished himself as a journalist and critic, and as the author of *Haabløse Slægter* (Hopeless Generations). When printed in 1880, Bang's novel was viewed as immoral and was impounded, after which an edited version was published in 1884. The original edition was made available to the public for the first time in 1965, with an introduction by Sørensen. The novel is naturalistic in Emile Zola's meaning of the term. It deals with a family's decline due to inner weakness and degeneration. In the introductory essay Sørensen shows why this novel about puberty, written by a twenty-two-year-old man, had to be seen as unsettling, particularly in its inclusion of the angst-ridden attraction men can inspire in other men, just as he accentuates the novel as "vor litteraturs mest indtrængende analyse af Oedipus-komplekset, dets forudsætninger og virkninger" (our literature's most penetrating analysis of the Oedipus complex, its presumptions and consequences).

The third cycle of Sørensen's authorship, the period between 1969 and 1979, does not involve prose fiction in book form, but furthers Sørensen's essay production in the collections *Midler uden mål: Kommentarer til perspektivplanlægningen* (Means Without Ends, 1971); *Uden mål–og med: Moralske tanker* (Without Ends–and With: Moral Thoughts, 1973); and *Den gyldne middelvej og andre debatindlæg fra 70erne* (The Golden Mean and Other Contributions to Debates from the 1970s, 1979) together with the utopian debate collection *Oprør fra midten*. A monograph on Lucius Annaeus Seneca the Younger, *Seneca: Humanisten ved Neros hof* (1976; translated as *Seneca, the Humanist at the Court of Nero,* 1984), includes Sørensen's translation of that author's writings. The cycle also includes a translation of works by Desiderius Erasmus.

In *Midler uden mål,* edited by Sørensen, politicians, public officials, experts, and students offered their commentary on the *Perspektivplanlægning 1970–1985* (Perspective Planning 1970–1985), which had been implemented by the Danish state as the first collected evaluation of the welfare state. The book covers issues relating to economics, technology, public health, research, education, and information communication. Its awareness of the fact that in a welfare society there are limited boundaries for growth was confirmed a few years later by the international oil crisis. A portion of its proposed solution lies in an increased ecological consciousness, which was not widespread in Denmark in the beginning of the 1970s. The editor's own contribution to the book criticizes the notion of wealth as an end in itself and the loss of defined and accepted goals of social development.

Work on "the perspective-plan book" was finished in June 1971, the time *Midler uden mål* was delivered for publication. At the same time, a new collection of articles was in the works, which by 1971 had been given the title *Uden mål–og med*–inspired by "the perspective-plan book," from which it inherited Sørensen's essay. *Uden mål–og med* dives deeply into culture, science, aesthetics, politics, and ethics. Criticism of the ends/means rationality is manifested as a renunciation of positivism and behavioralism, and technocracy and institutions are criticized.

Sørensen's alliance with a broad spectrum of the Danish population began in this period with "revolt from the center," both in life and in the political spectrum. The "strange" author was now set aside to make room for a political reformer. The troika behind *Oprør fra midten* consisted of Sørensen, who delivered the important intellectual framework of the book, the former radical minister of culture and education Kresten Helveg Petersen, and Professor Niels I. Meyer of Denmark's Technical University, who both before and since have played a role in the grassroots debate in Denmark regarding ecology and the European community.

Oprør fra midten, first published in a Danish edition of 120,000 copies, was translated into several languages. The work is positioned outside of the traditional party system as a voice of human reason in the transition from an industrial to an information-based society. The wish of centrist revolution to cover social debate in its entire breadth conflicted with the new folk movements of the 1970s, which employed narrowly defined views of society–for example, in the atomic energy or gender-role debates. Just as fundamentally, the revolt positioned itself outside the four-party system that has characterized Denmark throughout the twentieth century, in that it was not rooted in the class interests of an industrial society. *Oprør fra midten* is the most thoroughly developed and pronounced attempt by Danish citizens outside the ranks of active politicians to allow reason to renew democracy and the welfare state. The goal is the "humane ligevægtssamfund" (humane society of equilibrium). The authors insist that moral, psychological, and social problems are all tightly interconnected.

The ambitious intentions of *Oprør fra midten* have roots in the accelerated growth of the postwar economy, bringing with it overconsumption and a lack in social engagement as well as a loss of ideological opinion, which political wings have been unable to reinstate. The leaders of the revolt wanted to stand on the side of humanity against political "isms." Instead of ideologies, they desired a social order that is unified with nature and fulfills the emotional, social, and material needs of humanity, as well as a world order in which small, self-governing communities participate in a realistic, international collaboration. The tools of government are reason and morality; the means are economic and social equality, greater social responsibility for the individual via an expansion of democracy, improved education, and a viable interaction between production and nature, together with a new economic world order based on equilibrium and the decreasing of tension.

The three authors collaborated again in 1982 on *Røret om oprøret* (The Commotion over the Revolt), in which they took positions with regard to the debates that had risen, for example, in relation to problems of leadership, educational policy, human understanding, morality, economy, production, and internationalization. The bibliography of the book encompasses the four years of debate following the publication of *Oprør fra midten,* totaling approximately 1,300 books, as well as journal and newspaper articles. The movement even had its own journal, *På vej,* co-edited by Sørensen from 1979 to 1981.

Den gyldne middelvej collects excerpts and previously published essays and draws a picture of Sørensen's multifaceted activities in the public spectrum in the last half of the 1970s. The columns from Danish newspapers are combined with contributions to relevant anthologies and lectures from radio, high-school, and parish work. The themes include power/state, means/ends, science/humanity, quantity/quality, and Stoicism/Christianity. The title essay draws connections with Stoicism and Erasmus. Sørensen takes issue with polarization, which he finds typical of young and restless people, adding that "Det er ikke radikalt at neutralisere modsætninger,

Sørensen with the German author Günter Grass in 1997 (photograph by Erling Groth; Collection of Villy Sørensen)

så at facit bliver det dårligste fra begge sider, men at forebygge dem ved radikale initiativer" (It is not radical to neutralize oppositions, such that the answer is the worst option for both sides, but rather radicality is to prevent them through radical initiatives).

Sørensen had begun an acquaintance with Seneca's tragedies in 1964, but the material first caught hold of him in 1969, and in his journal entries from 1970, the Roman emperor Nero and his teacher, Seneca, become recurrent figures of fascination. In the summer of 1971 Sørensen considered using the material as the basis of a novel, but instead he wrote a long monograph on the tyrant and the sage, placing them in relation to Greek and Roman myths and to court history, in which Nero's atrocities, particularly toward his closest family members, are understood as a myth created by historians and by Nero himself as a real-life tragedy that points toward the theatrical tradition. Nero's displays toward men and women seem to have been connected with his peculiar, sexually sadistic enjoyment, in which he, identifying with the victims, became aroused by their impending death.

Sørensen makes an effort to understand by way of psychology the mechanisms that lay behind Nero's brutality and his artistic and sexual excesses. Nero is a figure of contrast to Seneca, with whom Sørensen has a greater affinity than with any other of the the many individuals he has analyzed and published. Sørensen's kinship with Seneca springs not only from the ancient author's roles as statesman, poet, and philosopher but also to the bonds between Stoicism and European intellectual development that had prevailed since the Age of Enlightenment. Sørensen's monograph encompasses the Danish reception of Seneca, of which the most remarkable work is *Moralske Tanker* (Moral Thoughts, 1744) by the Danish comic playwright and philosopher Ludvig Holberg. Sørensen, of course, did not need to name himself in this context. He had used Holberg's title as a subtitle to *Uden mål—og med*. Common to Seneca, Holberg, and Sørensen is the notion that reason and morality are preeminent in humanity. For the Stoics, the individual is sovereign. When good is replaced by evil, the Stoic finds the opportunity to display his moral qualities. The decisive element is not what happens, but how one reacts to it.

In 1976 Sørensen published, in his own Danish translations, selections from three Seneca texts, which are interpreted in his monograph as the three dialogues *Om vrede—Om mildhed—Om sindsro* (1976): translations of *De ira* (Concerning Anger), *De clementia* (Concerning Compassion), and *De tranquillitate animi* (Concerning Peace of Mind). *De clementia* is a royal mirror, held up to the face of the eighteen-year-old Nero, while *De ira* and *De tranquillitate animi* discuss personal authority.

Sørensen's studies of the Renaissance and Reformation periods focus on the humanist Erasmus of Rotterdam as the main figure. Martin Luther and Niccolò Machiavelli are introduced for the sake of contrast. Erasmus's *Tåbelighedens lovprisning*—a translation of *Encomium Moriae* (In Praise of Folly)—for which Sørensen provided an introduction, was written during Erasmus's residence with Sir Thomas More in England, from 1509 to 1514. The Latin title refers both to the fool (Greek: *moros*) who praised himself and to More, who completed his book *On the Best Form of the State and the New Island Utopia* in 1516.

The fourth cycle in Sørensen's authorship is between 1980 and 1988. It begins with a collection of notes from his journals, *Vejrdage* (Weather days, 1980), encompasses a collection of prose fiction, *De mange og De enkelte—og andre småhistorier* (1986; translated as *Another Metamorphosis and Other Fictions*, 1990), and includes Sørensen's retellings of Aladdin, Ragnarok, and the story of Odysseus. The idea of the utopia continues with *Røret om oprøret,* and the cycle includes editions of Wagner and Erasmus.

In the summer of 1979 a new breakthrough occurred in Sørensen's authorship. He had first pub-

lished verse and short prose on everyday life and weather in *Vejrdage,* but with the publication of his journals in 1988, it was revealed for the first time that these texts had existed in his workshop for quite some time. They are neither guided epically like the stories, nor conceptually like the long essays. Instead of the storyteller, politician, and debater, a private individual seeks associative and reflective "ro til den personlige virkelighedsoplevelse som er betingelsen for et virkeligt personligt engagement—uden at afsondre sig fra den verdensuro som er vilkåret" (peace in the personal experience of reality, which is the basic stipulation for real personal engagement—without isolating oneself from the world's unrest which are its circumstances). *Vejrdage* is a lyrical book in verse and prose, in which observation, sentiment, and reflection unfold. Both everyday experience and the weather are used as mirrors of the mind. In the final text, "Istid" (Ice Age), dated 29 October 1979, the narrative voice knows that the Ice Age "begyndte det år / der sprang sommeren over" (began the year / that sprang over summer).

De mange og De enkelte was originally published in a deluxe edition with woodcuts by Seppo Mattinen; in 1987 it was republished as an anthology, providing an abbreviated cross section of Sørensen's older and relevant prose. Roughly half of the texts had not been published previously; the rest are taken from journals, newspapers, and anthologies, dating from the years 1957 to 1984. The biblical tales, written to be read over Danmarks Radio in 1978, recall the myths in Sørensen's earlier works.

The retelling of tales for children is a new voice in this cycle of Sørensen's authorship. In *Aladdin—og den vidunderlige lampe* (Aladdin and the Wonderful Lamp, 1981) Sørensen created a new Danish text for an English edition, beautifully bound and with illustrations by Erroll le Cain. The storyteller's enthusiasm builds a bridge between the reader and the listening child, as had Andersen's fairy tales in his day. Adam Oehlenschläger, in the Danish Romantic author's *Aladdin* (1805), allows the hero to slay Noureddin because the sorcerer uses his life force to spread terror and death, subjugating his natural impulses in order to satsify his own desire. In Sørensen's retelling of *A Thousand and One Nights,* the sorcerer stands by the claim that his efforts in the forbidden arts were the reason that the treasure was found. Here, the sorcerer is not slain but is imprisoned and allowed to continue his research in the final hope that he will discover internal insight. Aladdin likewise learns to use science maturely—the spirit of the lamp and the ring—"at udføre opgaver, som næppe var menneskeligt mulige, men som dog var til gavn for menneskene" (to carry out duties that were hardly humanly possible, but were nevertheless to the benefit of humanity).

Ragnarok: En gudefortælling (1982; translated as *The Downfall of the Gods,* 1989) also refers to Oehlenschläger, the national skald of the Danish Golden Age, who often used material from Nordic mythology and who wrote a poetic account of Ragnarok in *Nordens Guder* (Gods of the North, 1819). Sørensen's retelling combines various dramatic elements into one enthralling story that is addressed to both children and adults and plays itself out between the two Nordic races of gods: the Aesir and the giants. The Aesir perceive themselves as eternally young and as the original deities of the world. The giants are immortal, although they can become old, and they claim to have ruled the world long before the Aesir arrived. Odin, the leader of the Aesir, and his son, Balder, have foreseen Ragnarok in a dream. When Balder is killed, Ragnarok breaks out, because he had been the embodiment of good and the only Aesir with whom the giants will negotiate. The Aesir avenge themselves by punishing Loki for his involvement in Balder's death, in a scene that distinguishes itself from the otherwise epic prose through its dramatized exchange of dialogue. In the end, however, the giants gain their revenge upon the Aesir, who can do nothing against the Fenris Wolf and the Midgaard Serpent. Their arguments delay the final defeat for a time, and so the drama is concluded in lyrical prose. It is not difficult to see the connection between the two races of gods and the polarities between East and West, which in the 1980s could easily have led to a Ragnarok for the human race.

Den berømte Odysseus (The Famous Odysseus, 1988) is a tale in which the events of Homer's epic poem are seen from the point of view of Odysseus's son, Telemachus, who was raised while Odysseus was away on his long and difficult journey—surrounded by men who courted the kingdom by proposing to the queen. In Sørensen's story Odysseus finally returns home to unite with his son, and their reciprocal relationship is the central point of the story. Together they take gruesome revenge on the suitors. Woven into this plot are (as in *The Odyssey*) tales of the returned king's adventures, as told by Odysseus to his son. The language and pace of the book make it well suited for older children as an introduction to the Greek epic.

Sørensen's translation of a selection of Wagner's writings on art theory written ca. 1850, *Kunsten og revolutionen* (Art and the Revolution, 1983), shows how the Revolution of 1848 was the great event in the life of the composer, who is usually associated with the conservatism and Christianity of his day. In the introduction Sørensen relates these writings to Wagner's chief work, *Der Ring der Niebelungen* (1853). Despite changing political opinions, Wagner maintained the opinion that the purpose of art was to rescue religion by finding a deeper truth in its mythical symbolism.

In 1984 Sørensen translated and introduced another important work by Erasmus, the long essay *Dulce bellum inexpertis,* as *Skøn er krigen for den uerfarne* (War is Beautiful to the Inexperienced) in which the Renaissance humanist argues for peace in a Europe that, at the time, was divided by a power struggle between France and the Hapsburgs, between Christians and Turks. Erasmus combined his hope for peace with the belief in cultural rebirth: salvation was for all, Christian or not, and it would prevail when the warring parties accepted Jesus as the highest example of humanity.

The fifth cycle of Sørensen's career, the years after 1988, encompass three collections of his journal entries, *Tilløb: Dagbog 1949–53* (Approach, 1988), *Forløb: Dagbog 1953–61* (Progress, 1990), and *Perioder: Dagbog 1961–74* (Periods, 1993), as well as his versions of the stories of Apollo and Oedipus. Sørensen's essay collections continued with *Demokratiet og kunsten* (Democracy and Art, 1988), the monograph *Jesus og KRISTUS* (Jesus and CHRIST, 1992), and *Den frie vilje* (The Free Will, 1992), together with his editorial work and an introductory essay for Bang's novel *Tine* (1889).

The three volumes of journals—*Tilløb, Forløb,* and *Perioder*—were written in the years between 1949 and 1974, but also belong to the time in which they were published—they have changed status from their existence as private texts to having become a part of public authorship, moving associatively and reflexively in the space between life and work. As such, the three volumes should be read as one coherent text that does not necessarily require a further context, neither with Sørensen's volumes on the period after 1974 nor with further insight from his private life, which some critics have desired.

The three published volumes represent a fifth of Sørensen's original diaries. Such vigorous editing provided the mature author with the opportunity to contextualize his earlier work, but he does not do so. The journal genre can appear unproblematic to the writer, yet Sørensen's feelings of being locked outside himself led to a showdown on 26 November 1956: "Intet sted er man så alene som i sin dagbog, derfor bryder jeg mig ikke om at være i den. Erindringernes mangfoldighed kan dog ikke finde plads i den, den kan kun være til gavn for den enfoldige hukommelse" (In no place is one so alone as in his journal, so I do not care to be in it. The diversity of recollection can find no place in it, it can only embrace the simple memory). Only a year later is the journal taken up again, if one is to believe the published version. The publication of the three volumes brings Sørensen's work on personal development

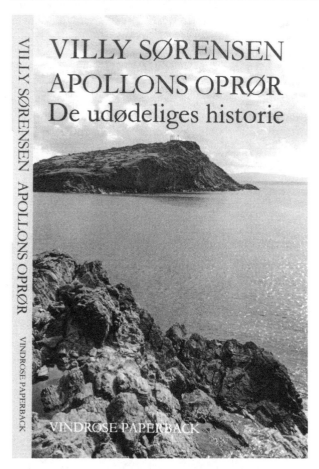

Cover for Sørensen's 1989 work that combines his retellings of Greek myths with essays analyzing those myths

to the forefront—a new literary voice characterizes this cycle of his career.

According to his journals, in December 1949 Sørensen read Jung's *Psychologische Typen* (Psychological Types, 1921) and was euphoric over the confirmation of his view of the connections between intuition and symbol. A portion of the accounts of dreams in the journal deal with sex, even though Sørensen also writes that the significance of sexuality as defined by Sigmund Freud has been exaggerated. Instead, sexuality should be seen as either harmless or as an expression of our need for control. A passionate relation to women is found only rarely in the dreams the author shares with his readers. Where such passion appears, it is often associated with interruption, anxiety, and punishment. Often, hostile mother figures enter into Sørensen's dreams, as in the entry of 15 April 1963, in which the father assists and the mother prevents his access to a beautiful woman, and in which he is also bitten by a vicious dog, somehow cutting him off from the therapy found in recording the dream. He finds an explanation for the bite in Jung's psychology, which prescribes that

one should expose oneself to animal impulses from the unconscious without submitting or fleeing. The author as dreamer notes in another context: "Hundene er jo også tolkninger af noget i kroppen" (The dogs are certainly interpretations of something in the body). Within that context, it is not surprising that these dogs can transform themselves into mischievous boys who are handsome but whose sexuality is yet latent or unstable.

In the journals Sørensen often comments on the author's calling. Despite his early success as a writer, melancholy and a fear of writer's block continue to plague him. The accounts in the journal of his victories are set in relief against the costs, especially the chronic back pain that has since 1960 periodically halted Sørensen's production. When Sørensen became a member of Det Danske Akademi (The Danish Academy) on 13 October 1965, irony joins pride and modesty: "Medlem af Akademiet–i resten af mit liv. Men de udødelige er vistnok den menneskegruppe der har højest dødelighedsprocent her i landet" (Member of the Academy–for the rest of my life. But the immortals are most certainly the group of humanity that has the highest mortality rate in this country).

While publishing his journals, Sørensen returned to the study of ancient myth. *Apollons oprør: De udødeliges historie* (The Revolt of Apollo: The Story of the Immortals, 1989) is addressed to adults and is positioned between fiction and essay, in that it is constructed of two lines of text–twenty-four textual pairs in all–that tell and simultaneously analyze the story of the Greek gods' immortality. Each pair consists of an epic "account" and an essayistic "reflection." The reflections establish at the same time a chronologically organized fictional history, with the point that the gods only later became immortal. The essay texts are synchronistically organized as point-by-point commentaries to the progress of the epic. The myth analysis in the book is subtle and opinionated, while it expresses great joy in re-creating one of the great stories of Western civilization.

In *Historien om Ødipus* (The Story of Oedipus, 1995) Sørensen's interest in ancient myth is united with the pedagogical project and an affection for children. The book is quite substantial, considering that it is directed at the weakest readers of the public school's graduating class. The sentences are short and sharp, and the story is so enticing that it should lure many students away from their comic books and televisions to partake of their first literary experience.

Demokratiet og kunsten is a collection of seven previously published articles and speeches from the period between 1979 and 1988. In his argument for democracy–and in order to expand it to embrace economic, activity-based, and localized structures–Sørensen points out that parliamentary rule has difficulty in becoming a cause of the people. When democracy is introduced, the democrats are soon found to be in short supply, because they segregate themselves according to political belief and only see democracy as an ideology in opposition to dictatorship. In the collection's concluding essay, democracy is seen as a challenge and an inspiration to art. Art should be a critical presence in society and an advocate for democracy, yet Sørensen acknowledges that it is also elitist in its essence.

In the line of radical atheists who have devoted vast energies to religious subjects belong the German David Friedrich Strauss, the Frenchman Joseph Ernest Renan, and their Danish disciple Brandes, whose book *Sagnet om Jesus* (The Legend of Jesus, 1925), was read by Sørensen in July 1964; he criticized it for depicting Jesus as a myth without historical foundation. His own monograph on the subject, *Jesus og KRISTUS,* has roots in his Kierkegaardian summer of 1949, when he read the book *Jesus Menneskesønnen* (Jesus, Son of Man, 1935) by the Danish historian of religion and culture Vilhelm Grønbech. Inspired by Jung, Sørensen removes the opposition between Jesus as myth and Jesus as historical reality: precisely because Jesus is a myth, he is also historically authentic–a person who embodied an archetype. Supplemented with the study of Israeli history, Sørensen's reading of the Bible explores the duality between, on the one side, Jesus, who–bound in time and place– proclaimed God's kingdom in the sense of a new Israel, and, on the other side, the Christians, who proclaimed Jesus as Christ (Messiah) and God's son, and who believed in him as the savior of the world. The crucifixion of Jesus appears to be an historical fact, yet Paul asserts that he died "som et sonoffer for dem der tror (og ikke blot for jøder) og han var opstanden: ved at overvinde døden, der var straf for synden, havde han ophævet synden" (as a sacrifice of appeasement for those who believe [and not just for Jews], and he was risen from the dead: by conquering death, which was punishment for sin, he had abolished sin). Sørensen's book deals with the Kierkegaardian theories of the ethical and the specifically religious. In the second edition Sørensen adds that in Jesus the religious stage is the specifically ethical.

The publication of a new edition of Bang's *Haabløse Slægter* in 1965 was followed in 1986 by Sørensen's afterword to a new critical edition of Bang's impressionistic novel *Tine.* Sørensen sees the novel in the light of the collapse of national values, which was associated with the defeat of the Danish by the Germans in 1864–the open wound from the defeat at Dybbøl.

In a 1998 interview Sørensen the writer-philosopher stressed the power of collective effort:

At arbejde sammen med andre giver noget. Det oplevede jeg, da jeg løb stafetløb som dreng: Man kunne løb hurtigere, når man havde den pind i hånden, fordi en anden skulle have den, end hvis man løb alene.

(Working with others provides something. I experienced this when I ran relay races as a boy: One could run faster when one had the baton in his hand, because someone else had to take it next, than if one ran alone.)

Sørensen became a member of Det Danske Akademi in 1965 and received an honorary doctorate from the University of Copenhagen in 1979. He has been awarded The Critics' Award in 1959, Det Dansk Academi's Award in 1962, the Søren Gyldendal Award in 1965, Jeanne and Henri Nathansen's Memorial Scholarship in 1969, the Holberg Medal and the Georg Brandes Award in 1973, the Nordic Council Literary Prize and the West German Heinrich Steffen's Award in 1974, the Amalienborg Award from the Queen Margrethe and Prince Frederik Fund in 1977, the *Weekendavisen* Literary Award in 1982, the H. C. Andersen Medal in 1983, the Swedish Academy's Nordic Literary Award in 1986, the Poul Henningsen Award in 1987, the Christian Wilster Award in 1988, the H. C. Andersen Award in 1993, and the Paul Hammerich Award in 1994.

Interviews:

Claus Clausen, *Digtere i forhør 1966* (Copenhagen: Gyldendal, 1966), pp. 11–34;

Ninka og Bendix, *33 portrætter* (Copenhagen: Rhodos, 1969), pp. 262–270;

Villy Sørensen, "Synspunkt på mit forfatterskab," Spring, 4 (1993): 7–19.

Ejvind Larsen, "Villy Sørensen," *Information,* 21 February 1998;

Bibliographies:

Danske digtere i det 20. århundrede, third edition, volume 4, edited by Torben Brostrøm and Mette Winge (Copenhagen: Gad, 1982), pp. 394–395.

References:

Niels Barfoed, "Villy Sørensen," *Danske digtere i det 20. århundrede,* second edition, volume 3, edited by Frederik Nielsen and Ole Restrup (Copenhagen: Gad, 1966), pp. 445–466;

Poul Behrendt, "Den fængslede tiger," *Kritik,* 13 (1970): 16–38;

Behrendt, "Det ukendte træ," *Kritik,* 3 (1967): 3–23;

Thorkild Bjørnvig, "Tale for Villy Sørensen," in *Det danske akademi 1960–67* (Copenhagen: Gyldendal, 1967), pp. 37–49;

Thomas Bredsdorff, *Sære fortællere* (Copenhagen: Gyldendal 1967), pp. 21–51;

Torben Brostrøm, *Men dansen den går–Litterære memoirer* (Copenhagen: Gyldendal, 1994);

Iselin Maria Gabrieli, "La tigra in cucina–il 'modernismo' danese di Villy Sørensen," *La Cultura,* 10 (1972): 448–462;

Jørgen Bonde Jensen, "Fortilfælde og forskel: Om forholdet mellem fortid and nutid i Villy Sørensens bog om Seneca, humanisten ved Neros hof," *Mellemting: Æstetiske and politiske forsøg* (Copenhagen: Gyldendal, 1980), pp. 189–209;

Jensen, "Glem ikke at det aldrig kan være en fordel at være blind," *Analyser af dansk kortprosa,* 2 (1972): 165–184;

Jensen, *Litterær arkæologi: Studier i Villy Sørensens "Formynderfortællinger,"* (Copenhagen: Gyldendal, 1978);

Johan Fjord Jensen, *Efter guldalderkonstruktionens sammenbrud,* volume 3 (Århus: Modtryk 1981), pp. 82–161, 180–186;

Jensen, *Homo manipulatus: Essays omkring radikalismen* (Copenhagen: Gyldendal, 1966);

Svend Johansen, "Adskilligt om Villy Sørensen," in his *Millionbevidsthed* (Copenhagen: Arena, 1969), pp. 135–146;

Flemming Lundgreen-Nielsen, "Villy Sørensen: Ragnarok," *Danske Studier* (1984): 167–170;

Peter Madsen, "Humanisten mellem Kierkegaard and Marx: Villy Sørensens filosofi," *Kultur og klasse,* 34 (1979): 28–43;

Finn Hauberg Mortensen, "Dele hele: Villy Sørensen 'Sære historier'," in *Læsninger i dansk litteratur,* volume 4, edited by Povl Schmidt, Anne-Marie Mai, Finn Hauberg Mortensen, and Inger-Lise Hjordt-Vetlesen (Odense: Odense University Press, 1997), pp. 91–109;

Per Øhrgaard, "Villy Sørensen," *Danske digtere i det 20. århundrede,* third edition, volume 4, edited by Torben Brostrøm and Mette Winge (Copenhagen: Gad, 1982), pp. 43–64;

Ulrich Horst Petersen, "Om (nogle af) Villy Sørensens historier," in his *Frihed og tabu* (Copenhagen: Gyldendal, 1971), pp. 108–166;

Ebbe Sønderiis, *Villy Sørensen: En ideologikritisk analyse* (Grenå: GMT, 1972);

Åsfrid Svensen, "Villy Sørensens 'Duo,'" *Norsk litterær årbok 1968* (1968): 167–175;

Catarina Testa, "The Comic Conception of Reality," *Scandinavian Studies,* 82 (1992): 228–242;

Testa, "Den smertelige indre proces: Om fire historier af Villy Sørensen," *Nordica,* 13 (1996): 146–164;

Testa, "Villy Sørensen: 'I det fremmede,'" *Scandinavica,* 35 (1996): 53–70;

H. B. Vergote, "Un lecteur danois de Kierkegaard: Villy Sørensen," *Les études Philosophiques* (Paris: Presses Universitaires de France, 1971), pp. 461–464;

Jørn Vosmar, ed., *Modernismen i dansk litteratur* (Copenhagen: Fremads, 1967), pp. 128–136.

Henrik Stangerup

(1 September 1937 – 4 July 1998)

Søren Schou
Roskilde University Center, Denmark

Translated by Tiina Nunnally

BOOKS: *Lille håbs rejse: Tre fabler* (Copenhagen: C. A. Reitzel, 1958);

Grønt og sort (Fredensborg: Arena, 1961);

Veritabel Pariser (Fredensborg: Arena, 1966);

Slangen i brystet (Copenhagen: Gyldendal, 1969); translated by Anne Born as *Snake in the Heart* (London & New York: M. Boyars, 1996);

Løgn over løgn (Copenhagen: Gyldendal, 1971);

Manden der ville være skyldig (Copenhagen: Gyldendal, 1973); translated by David Gress-Wright as *The Man Who Wanted to Be Guilty* (London & Boston: M. Boyars, 1982);

Kunsten at være ulykkelig (Copenhagen: Gyldendal, 1974);

Mens tid var: Kronik og journalistik 1961–77 (Copenhagen: Gyldendal, 1974);

Jorden er flad, eller, Erasmus Montanus: En film (Copenhagen: Gyldendal, 1976);

Fjenden i forkøbet: En roman om angst og skyld of sjælens misere (Copenhagen: Gyldendal, 1978);

Retten til ikke at høre til (Copenhagen: Berlingske forlag, 1979);

Fangelejrens frie halvdel (Copenhagen: Berlingske forlag, 1979);

Vejen til Lagoa Santa (Copenhagen: Gyldendal, 1981); translated by Barbara Bluestone as *The Road to Lagoa Santa* (New York: M. Boyars, 1984);

Det er svært at dø i Dieppe (Copenhagen: Gyldendal, 1985); translated by Sean Martin as *The Seducer: It Is Hard to Die in Dieppe* (New York: M. Boyars, 1990);

Tag din seng og gå: En personlig beretning (Copenhagen: Gyldendal, 1985);

Den kvarte sandhed: Fra et tiår (Copenhagen: Lindhardt & Ringhof, 1989);

Broder Jacob (Copenhagen: Lindhardt & Ringhof, 1991); translated by Born as *Brother Jacob* (London & New York: M. Boyars, 1993);

Henrik Stangerup in 1958 (photograph by Knud Meister)

I flugtens tegn: Udvalgte beretninger og essays 1965–1993 (Copenhagen: Lindhardt & Ringhof, 1993);

Datter af–Scener om en mor (Copenhagen: Lindhardt & Ringhof, 1995).

MOTION PICTURES: *Manden der tænkte ting,* dialogue by Stangerup, ASA, 1969;

Giv Gud en chance om søndagen, screenplay and direction by Stangerup, ASA, 1970;

Græsset må ikke betrædes/Pelouse interdite, screenplay and direction by Stangerup, ORTF, 1970;

Farlige kys, screenplay and direction by Stangerup, ASA, 1972;

Jorden er flad, screenplay by Stangerup and Fausto Wolff, direction by Stangerup, Alter Filmes, 1976.

OTHER: Poul Henningsen, *Vi er selv historie,* edited by Stangerup (Copenhagen: Thaning & Appel, 1963);

Kulturkampen: En antologi af tidsskriftet Kulturkampen, edited by Stangerup and Ole Grünbaum (Copenhagen: Fremad, 1968);

Søren Kierkegaard, *Dansemesteren: Sider af Søren Kierkegaard,* edited by Stangerup and Roger Poole (Copenhagen: Gyldendal, 1985);

Naturens historie-fortællere, 2 volumes, edited by Stangerup, Niels Bonde, and Jesper Hoffmeyer (Copenhagen: Gad, 1985, 1987);

Ludvig Holberg, *Holbergs helte-og heltindehistorier,* preface by Stangerup (Copenhagen: Lindhardt & Ringhof, 1990).

Henrik Stangerup is one of the most widely read and most versatile Danish authors of his generation. His body of work ranges from satirical contemporary realism and autobiographical essays to biographical novels about controversial or forgotten figures in Danish history. With his novels, films, and essays, Stangerup passionately championed attitudes and points of view that are often contrary to those prevailing in Danish cultural life. He asserted the right of the artist "ikke at høre til" (not to belong)—as in the title of one of his essay collections—and to write without being influenced by whatever opinions are fashionable at the moment. His work has also drawn attention outside of Denmark, and several of his novels have been translated into many languages.

Henrik Stangerup was born in Copenhagen on 1 September 1937 and grew up in a milieu that was artistically and intellectually stimulating. He was the son of Hakon Stangerup, a professor of Danish literature, and actress Betty Söderberg. His younger sister, Helle Stangerup, is also a prominent author, especially known for her historical novels.

In 1967 Stangerup married the actress Lotte Tarp, and their son, Jacob, was born in 1971. The marriage ended in 1976. He was married for a second time in 1982 to the painter Susanne Krage. Over the years he received many honors for his literary work, including the Danske Akademis Store Pris (Danish Academy Grand Prize) in 1986.

After finishing his secondary education, Stangerup entered the University of Copenhagen to study theology, but he never completed his degree. Studying at the university turned out to be incompatible with the extensive journalistic activity into which he threw himself, first as a writer for the tabloid *Ekstrabladet,* from 1961 to 1964, and later for other newspapers. His primary interest was modern literature and motion pictures. He wrote about the critics involved with the journal *Cahiers du Cinéma* and about La Nouvelle Vague in French movies. What fascinated him about the French New Wave directors was their improvisational way of making motion pictures, their love for classic Hollywood movies, and their concept of the filmmaker using the camera like a pen.

Stangerup's interest in movies led him to try his hand as a scriptwriter and director. His movies occupy a special niche in his artistic production, although in a thematic sense there are many lines of association between them and his novels. His first independent film, *Giv Gud en chance om søndagen* (Give God a Chance on Sundays, 1970), is a humorous and unsentimental account of a Danish pastor's problems and scruples in contemporary, virtually de-Christianized Denmark. *Farlige kys* (Dangerous Kisses, 1972), which was influenced by the debate over psychiatrist R. D. Laing's ideas on insanity and normality, deals with the love relationship between a psychiatrist and a patient at an insane asylum. Both movies—like many of Stangerup's novels—are stories about intellectuals who suffer defeat in their work.

The last and most controversial of his motion pictures is a personal interpretation of the comedy *Erasmus Montanus,* a play written in 1722 by the Norwegian-Danish author Ludvig Holberg. *Jorden er flad* (The Earth Is Flat, 1976) is about a peasant student who, after finishing his education, returns to the impoverished roots of his childhood. He is arrogant and overbearing, and his lofty theories prove to be impractical when confronted with the reality of ordinary people. Stangerup views the play as a tale about the student's betrayal of his native people. To emphasize the universal aspect of the story, he relocates the setting from Holberg's Denmark to the brilliantly colorful and exotic Brazil of the sixteenth century. This personal interpretation of one of the indisputably major works in Danish literature seemed too provocative to Stangerup's contemporaries. At its premiere, the film was a failure in the eyes of critics and audiences alike, but it was later received positively in France.

For a period in the 1960s Stangerup lived in Paris and worked as a reporter for the Danish newspaper *Politiken.* He was not interested in the prevailing stereotypes of Paris as the capital of the fashion houses and of carefree frivolity. He redefined the traditional role of the Paris corre-spondent with his social commentaries on the lives of the poor on the outskirts of the city, which also became the topic of his short documentary, *Pelouse interdite,* financed by French television. In articles and interviews he also intro-duced Danish readers to a long list of major figures in modern French art and philosophy.

Stangerup's years as a journalist provide the back-ground for his first novel, *Slangen i brystet* (1969; translated as *Snake in the Heart,* 1996). The story follows a Danish reporter in Paris who is in a state of mental disintegration. Max Møllerup, the protagonist, has become middle-aged and is no longer as promising as he once was. He keeps trying to get his life together but makes a fool of himself and attracts embarrassing attention, most dramatically during a press conference with Charles de Gaulle. After Mollerup has made himself a laughingstock in Paris, the newspaper brings him back to Denmark to a less demand-ing position, but this too he is unable to handle. Finally his descent is complete, and his paranoia erupts full-blown. Mollerup returns to Paris and installs himself in an isolated room, where he plots his enemies' positions and maneu-vers on a "general staff" map.

Slangen i brystet is part of a wave of novels labeled New Realism in Denmark during the 1960s. It describes in great detail the everyday life of the foreign correspon-dent. The reader gains a vivid impression of the way in which Mollerup is pressured from all sides and the way in which the newspaper's editors, readers, and the colony of resident Danes in Paris make conflicting demands on him. The novel is a realistic depiction of Paris and the newspa-per milieu, but it is first and foremost a psychological study of the guilt—the snake in the heart—that eventually overwhelms Mollerup completely. Although large sections of the plot take place in Paris, much of the novel is devoted to discussion of the local Danish colony and Danes in gen-eral. The novel presents unkind portraits of Stangerup's countrymen as scandalmongers and life-fearing conform-ists. It points ahead to his subsequent novels of contempo-rary life by using as its basis personally experienced material taken from the media world with which Stangerup was intimately familiar. Even here, however, the autobiographical aspect is already reproduced in an artisti-cally reworked form and with an awareness of literary tra-dition; hence, Tom Kristensen's novel *Hærværk* (1930; translated as *Havoc,* 1968) can be glimpsed as an inspira-tion behind the description of Mollerup's personal col-lapse.

In the novel *Løgn over løgn* (Lie upon Lie, 1971), Stangerup sharpens the polemics against his Danish con-temporaries. The novel depicts a cultural life that is domi-nated by a politically leftist faction that has no room for people with different opinions. The book is composed as a work of metafiction, a novel about a novel. The narrator is

Dust jacket for the English-language edition (1996) of Stangerup's first novel, Slangen i brystet *(1969), about a Danish novelist undergoing a mental breakdown in Paris*

trying to write a story about an aging movie director, Joachim Jerlang, who is vainly attempting to make a come-back with a movie that will deal with the generation of the youth revolution and communal movement. What is sup-posed to be a ruthless portrait of a has-been artist gradu-ally becomes for the narrator a source of grave self-recriminations. The narrator begins to question whether his portrait of the movie director as a parasite preying on other people's lives is merely an attempt to jus-tify his own existence. Does he stop living a lie simply because he exposes the spurious existence of another per-son? In this way the conflict in this novel inspired by the thinking of Søren Kierkegaard is aimed both externally against the "medieimperialisterne" (media imperialists) who have monopolized the public debate by pretending to represent the people and internally against the writer him-self.

Criticism of the Social Democratic administration of the welfare state is the main theme in the gloomy futuristic work *Manden der ville være skyldig* (1973; translated as *The Man Who Wanted to Be Guilty,* 1982). Those in power keep ordinary people down by means of a conformist prosper-ity. Personal responsibility is stripped from the individual, and any feeling of guilt is suppressed with tranquilizers.

Conscious life has become a public concern, and it is society's task to see to it that all citizens find themselves in a permanent state of bliss. Yet, the novel's protagonist, Torben, insists on feeling guilty after he, in a moment of insanity, murders his wife and is admitted to a psychiatric hospital. *Manden der ville være skyldig* is a dystopian novel in the tradition of Aldous Huxley's *Brave New World* (1932) and George Orwell's *Nineteen Eighty-Four* (1949). Thematically, however, the story is more directly inspired by existentialist philosophy; it emphasizes that only the person who takes on his own guilt can be called independent and free. The novel castigates a bureaucratic welfare society based on the Scandinavian model, which, in the eyes of the author, stifles individual freedom with a tyranny of opinion and social therapy. One of the novel's arguments is that this coercion is not exercised by cynical powermongers but by well-meaning bureaucrats who genuinely wish to create a harmonious society for everyone. The novel provoked discussion and was particularly criticized by people from the cultural left, who regarded its attack on the welfare state as reactionary. Stangerup himself always refused to define his political involvement based on a left-right axis. In an interview with Iben Holk published in her 1986 book about him, he said, "Det bedste af konservatismen blandet med det bedste af anarkismen passer mig godt: At mennesket har en fri vilje, at vi selv er ansvarlige for vores liv" (The best of conservatism mixed with the best of anarchism suits me fine: that a human being has free will, that we are responsible for our own lives). *Manden der ville være skyldig* was filmed in 1990 by the director Ole Roos.

Fjenden i forkøbet (The Preemptive Enemy, 1978) is the most self-revealing and the most desperate of the author's works. It was written as a direct extension of—and speaks openly about—a crisis in Stangerup's life, prompted by three distressing events that happened in rapid succession: the death of his father, the breakup of his marriage to Lotte Tarp, and the critics' almost unanimous negative appraisal of *Jorden er flad*. In long memoir sections the author discusses his experience growing up as the son of a famous literature professor who, during the German occupation of Denmark, acted in a manner that was regarded by many as opportunistic. After the liberation, the Stangerup name was widely compromised, and the son candidly describes how the animosity toward his father was felt by the entire family, including his children, who had no possibility of defending themselves against the vicious gossip. Particularly harrowing is the depiction of an infamous schoolteacher who vents his hatred for the father on the defenseless Henrik.

In this book Stangerup reveals the personal background that explains why, in his work, he so often characterizes public opinion as a faceless, slanderous, and resentment-tinged entity. The fact that *Jorden er flad* was butchered by the critics and ignored by the public is, according to the novel, a sign that his family curse was still active many years after the occupation. *Fjenden i forkøbet* is not only a book of self-scrutiny; it is also an extroverted and polemical novel. At the same time that Stangerup conjures up his own inner demons, he expands the accusations of his previous novels against Danish society, which is marked by a hostility toward the nonconformist deeply rooted in a puritanical fear of life. He praises Brazil as a people-friendly and colorful alternative to the renunciation of life, which he dubbed "den danske syge" (the Danish malady) in an essay. In general, it is a pervasive feature of his work that people in the Catholic countries are regarded as substantially more generous and tolerant than Northern Europeans, who drag around the heavy burden of a puritanical fear of life.

Despite its harsh polemics, the novel was positively received in Denmark, and it solidified Stangerup's reputation as an author who was capable of writing on a grand scale. The novel was among a wave of so-called confessional works that arose in connection with the women's movement and came to characterize Denmark in the 1970s. The confessional literary authors wrote about their own experiences with great candor and a minimum of fictional adaptation. Many consider *Fjenden i forkøbet* to be one of the most important works in this genre, especially because of the gripping and starkly told sections on the author's childhood.

The maverick who acts in opposition to prevailing opinion is the principal figure and focus of identification throughout Stangerup's novels. In a trilogy of novels comprising *Vejen til Lagoa Santa* (1981; translated as *The Road to Lagoa Santa*, 1984), *Det er svært at dø i Dieppe* (1985; translated as *The Seducer: It Is Hard to Die in Dieppe*, 1990), and *Broder Jacob* (1991; translated as *Brother Jacob*, 1993), he describes the conflict between the loner and the masses in an historical framework and using a style that is marked by a greater linguistic richness and artistic nuance than his previous novels. Thematically the trilogy is constructed as an artistic illustration of the three stages of human development that Kierkegaard formulated in *Enten-Eller* (1843; translated as *Either/Or*, 1944). Stangerup first presents the ethical, then the aesthetic, and finally the religious person.

Vejen til Lagoa Santa depicts the nineteenth-century Danish naturalist P. W. Lund, who was Kierkegaard's brother-in-law. Lund turns his back on Danish society and takes up residence in Brazil, where he becomes the founder of the country's paleontology research. In a limestone cave in the province of Minas Gerais he finds the fossilized remains of the extinct giant sloth. A conflict then arises between belief and knowledge, for the discovery of these fossils cannot be easily assimilated with the belief in the Christian story of Creation.

In Stangerup's interpretation, Lund is the personification of the European, the world conqueror who channels his sexual desires into a passion for systematizing and classifying. When he encounters the tropical world, however, he is faced with a reality that is greater and more secretive than the one that European science wishes to know. The conflict between old and new views of the world results in a violent crisis of personality and a mysterious illness that silences Lund for the latter part of his life. The novel is a stylistic tour de force, a magical and rapturous depiction of the Brazil that had already enthralled Stangerup when he filmed *Jorden er flad*. In its view of nature as magical and sublime, *Vejen til Lagoa Santa* is inspired more by the Romantics' perception of nature than by Charles Darwin's. Stangerup was also preoccupied with this topic in the two-volume anthology he co-edited with Niels Bonde and Jesper Hoffmeyer, *Naturens historie-fortællere* (Chroniclers of Natural History, 1985, 1987), the first volume of which deals with the history of ideas from Plato to Darwin.

Whereas Stangerup portrays Lund as an ethical person in the Kierkegaardian sense, the second volume of the trilogy is about the aesthete—understood as an eroticist and hedonist. Stangerup again chose a controversial figure from nineteenth-century Danish cultural life as the protagonist for *Det er svært at dø i Dieppe*: the literary critic P. L. Møller. Møller was a Janus figure, conflicted over the struggle between tradition and modernity. In his writings Møller showed that he understood and loved Danish Romantic literature as few among his contemporaries did. He was in conflict with the cultural Parnassus in his homeland and felt repelled by the predominant staid moralism. Møller is a restless hedonist and erotic seducer who sates all of his senses in the Parisian life of the Second Empire. He is also an attentive observer of life around him, until jealousy clouds his mind, and he is confined to a madhouse. The novel follows Møller on a journey through the turbulent Europe of the mid nineteenth century, marked by the conflict between revolutionary zeal and conservatism and between idealism and the egotistical pursuit of wealth.

In Stangerup's novels both Møller and Lund recognize that they are living at the end of an epoch but lack the will or desire to identify wholeheartedly with the new era. What they surmise is later fully realized by others. It was Darwin, with his work on the origin of species, who created the new natural history paradigm, and Lund was only his timid precursor. Similarly, it was the younger critic Georg Brandes, and not Møller, who heralded "det moderne Gennembrud" (the Modern Breakthrough) in Danish literature and intellectual life.

The trilogy was completed with *Broder Jacob*, which deals with the religious individual. Originally Stangerup had intended to make Kierkegaard his protagonist, but he abandoned him and his era and looked to the Reformation in Denmark three hundred years earlier to depict the pious, unselfish person in an artistically convincing manner. The plot of the novel is constructed around a legendary figure, the Franciscan monk Brother Jacob, who, it was claimed, was the brother of the Danish king, Christian II. Along with the other "gray friars," Brother Jacob is driven from his monastery in Denmark by Lutheran temple-scourgers who take a hostile, puritanical view of the image-worship and *festivitas* of Catholicism. The novel's main symbol of this enmity toward imagination is the destruction of the church's magnificent ancient chalk frescos as the puritans of the new era cover them over with plaster. As in the previous volumes of the trilogy, the references to contemporary conditions are clear and unmistakable. For Stangerup, there is a direct line from sixteenth-century religious reformers to today's puritanical perpetrators of political and artistic correctness.

The novel follows Brother Jacob on his long, eventful wandering through Europe. Both the merry Rabelais, whom he knew from his study years in Paris, and the rational Erasmus of Rotterdam are introduced along the way as positive alternatives to the prevailing intolerance. Jacob rediscovers the fanaticism and lack of humanity that he encountered in Denmark in southern Europe, where anti-Semitic attitudes are allowed free rein. Jacob reaches Spain and then embarks by ship for Mexico. There he works as a missionary among the Indians; his many years of work are marked by an empathy and respect for the Native American culture and way of life that was quite unusual for the time. Jacob is a nontraditional proselytizer who interprets the message of Christianity through the brilliantly colored symbols of the native population. Missionaries with a more orthodox orientation become embittered by Jacob's behavior and accuse him of being too "indianervenlig" (Indian-friendly). After an exhaustive court proceeding against him, he is driven from the monastery—not a new experience for him.

Broder Jacob can be regarded as a kind of legend and as an act of rectification toward a great, forgotten countryman. Yet, Stangerup still manages to avoid letting the novel devolve into monumental edification, because even though Jacob is pious, he is nagged by constant doubt until his final years. On his deathbed he asks one of his fellow monks the most desperate of all questions: "Kom vi fra Helvede, Broder?" (Did we come from Hell, Brother?). Stangerup enticingly leaves the answer to the question unclear.

Despite the difference among the three protagonists in the trilogy—the ethical naturalist, the aestheticizing man of letters, and the saintly Franciscan monk—crucial traits unite them. They are all outsiders in Danish intellectual life, semiforgotten figures who at most appear in footnotes in history books. Although they

*Stangerup and Fausto Wolff, with whom he collaborated on the
screenplay for the 1976 motion picture* Jorden er flad
(photograph by Ebbe Andersen)

thought of themselves as Danes, they were in conflict
with the dominant cultural trends of their homeland.
Whether from inclination or necessity they were forced
to break out of the narrow domestic confines and find
their bearings in a large, international world. Also common to all three protagonists is their preoccupation with
those who are scorned and neglected, a rare empathy
with marginalized people and ways of thinking.

As an historical novelist Stangerup exhibits a lush
imagination. His books contain surreal elements and
are marked by a strongly expressive stream-of-consciousness technique. These modern stylistic features
do not mean that the depiction of the time period is
experienced as anachronistic; the reader senses that the
books are based on extensive historical research, which
makes the people and milieus of the past brilliantly
come alive. Still, the historical material is presented with
subjective biases, which demonstrate that Stangerup in
many ways perceives his protagonists as his own intellectual kinsmen and contemporaries. They are as fasci-

nated as he is by Southern Europe and Latin America,
and the books present the puritanism and self-sufficiency during the Reformation and the Romantic
period in Denmark with many allusions to present-day
conditions worthy of criticism. The historical distance
makes Stangerup a more multifaceted stylist, but it does
not lead to a weakening of the polemical perspective in
his works.

Stangerup's artistic development through his trilogy shows that he had become increasingly subtle.
Whereas his contemporary novels of the 1970s are
characterized by a vigorous and direct revolt against
Social Democrats and scholastic Marxists, in the trilogy
Stangerup utilizes more muted tones. The quiet narrative voice of *Broder Jacob* reflects Stangerup's faith that
the events of the novel are dramatic enough to sustain
the narrative. The climactic court proceeding against
the unduly "Indian-friendly" Jacob, for example, is
especially powerful because it is presented in a terse,
reportorial style.

The same subdued tone and artistic economy
characterize Stangerup's last book, *Datter af–Scener om en
mor* (Daughter of–Scenes about a Mother, 1995), a
short, densely written portrait of his mother, Betty
Söderberg. The peculiar title refers to the fact that
Betty's father was the Swedish author Hjalmar Söderberg, who in every sense–both as an artist and a private
individual–was a demanding father to live up to.

Alongside his work as a novelist, Stangerup was a
diligent essayist, and at regular intervals he published
the best of his newspaper articles and editorials in a
series of essay collections. Articles from his years as a
correspondent in Paris were compiled in *Veritabel Pariser*
(A Veritable Parisian, 1966), followed by later collections: *Kunsten at være ulykkelig* (The Art of Being
Unhappy, 1974), *Tag din seng og gå: En personlig beretning*
(Take Your Bed and Go: A Personal Narrative, 1985),
and *I flugtens tegn: Udvalgte beretninger og essays 1965–1993*
(Exile by Choice: Selected Narratives and Essays,
1993). This part of Stangerup's literary output is sustained by the same joy in writing and sense of commitment that his novels are, and for the most part the
essays are rewarding independent of their specific topics. They span a wide range of subjects and demonstrate Stangerup's view of the intellectual as a person
who openly and directly speaks his mind about the vital
and often conflict-ridden questions of the day without
being restricted by loyalties to a particular group.

As an essayist Stangerup continuously followed
the international debate over the reassessment of the
so-called master thinkers of European philosophy. The
French philosopher André Glucksmann, in particular,
provoked this reevaluation starting in the mid 1970s,
but it was also an extension of important themes in

Stangerup's own novels, which early on were concerned with the relationship between fanaticism and the destructive use of power. In Stangerup's eyes, those people who wanted to improve the world—from Johann Gottlieb Fichte through Georg Wilhelm Friedrich Hegel, Karl Marx, and Martin Heidegger—are morally responsible for the totalitarian regimes of the twentieth century and thus also for the mass slaughters of Communism and Nazism. Alongside the philosophical and political debate, Stangerup provides a detailed account of the international trends in motion pictures and literature. In his early essays the discussion of French conditions dominates; later, he increasingly turns his attention to authors from developing countries. Stangerup was one of the first Danes to write extensively about author Salman Rushdie with a clear recognition of his stature.

Finally, the essays contain sensitive portraits of distinguished countrymen such as Holberg, Kierkegaard, and Georg Brandes. Among the Danish figures from the twentieth century to whom Stangerup continually returns and whom he portrays with great sympathy are the movie director Carl Dreyer, the cultural critic Poul Henningsen, the actress Asta Nielsen, and, in particular, the author Elsa Gress, who was Stangerup's intellectual mentor and who offered crucial personal support during the crisis period when he was writing *Fjenden i forkøbet*—a wide-ranging group, with no obvious political or artistic traits in common. Stangerup's admiration is directed toward the great iconoclasts, those people who were too different and too difficult to fit in with the cultural patterns of their time.

On the whole, a mixture of generosity and criticism marks Stangerup's work as an essayist. He was the great nay-sayer in modern Danish literature, but his polemics are often presented from unexpected and witty points of view and may target both the right wing and the left. As a staunch supporter of Denmark's integration into the European Union, he fought on two fronts politically: against the socialists and the conservative nationalists, who, for entirely different reasons, had joined forces to defeat European integration.

Stangerup died on 4 July 1998 at age sixty after a long battle with cancer. By that time he had won a large audience abroad, especially in France, but he also found prominent supporters and admirers in the English- speaking world—for example, Anthony Burgess. The themes and problems of his works have international relevance, but Stangerup was greatly aware of his national heritage. Artistically he was constantly involved in a dialogue with classic Danish writers. In addition to Holberg and Kierkegaard, another major source of inspiration was the realistic novelist Henrik Pontoppidan—for whom, incidentally, Stangerup was named.

The contemporary Danish author to whom Stangerup is most closely related is Thorkild Hansen, who also wrote books about repressed episodes of the Danish past, viewed from the perspective of the nonconformist and the heroic loser. In the work of both authors the minor characters of real life are elevated to the stature of main characters. Another intellectually related writer from the present is the Frenchman Jean-Marie-Gustave le Clézio, whom Stangerup greatly admired. There are clear parallels between the works of the two authors, who were almost the same age. Both developed from writers of claustrophobic big-city life into cosmopolitan authors who write on a grand, epic scale about the magical interconnectedness between human beings and nature. Stangerup's later novels are broader in scope and have more sophisticated hues than his earlier novels, but throughout his career the author remained an attentive observer of Danish life, both past and present.

Interviews:

Barbara Bluestone, "In the Shadow of Northern Lights: A Conversation with the Danish Novelist, Henrik Stangerup," *Encounter,* 63 (1984): 73–77;

Bo Elbrønd-Bek, "Det er svært at dø i Dieppe," *Bogens Verden,* 6 (1985): 400–407;

Peter Nielsen, "Jeg vil hellere være reaktionær," *Opus,* 2 (1991): 14–16.

References:

Mogens Davidsen, "Vejen til frelse eller fri os fra modernismen—Om Henrik Stangerups *Broder Jacob*," in *Prosa fra 80'erne til 90'erne,* edited by Anne-Marie Mai (Copenhagen: Borgen, 1994), pp. 128–139;

Bo Elbrønd-Bek, "Knoglesamlerens skygge: Om Henrik Stangerups roman *Vejen til Lagoa Santa*," *Karneval 82* (1982): 97–123;

Birgitte Hesselaa, "Fortælleteknik, manipulation og personpsykologi—Henrik Stangerups *Slangen i brystet*," *Kritik,* (1974): 52–73;

Iben Holk, ed., *Henrik Stangerup* (Odense: Odense Universitetsforlag, 1986);

Johnny Kondrup, *Erindringens udveje: Studier i moderne dansk selvbiografi* (Ballerup: Amadeus, 1994), pp. 372–423;

Martin Schwarz Lausten, "Stangerup, Jacob og Luther," *Kristeligt Dagblad,* 23 November 1991;

Johan de Mylius, "Henrik Stangerup," in *Danske digtere i det 20. århundrede,* 5 volumes, edited by Torben Brostrøm and Mette Winge (Copenhagen: Gad, 1982), V: 44–51;

Hans Hagedorn Thomsen, "Naturens skyld," *Kritik,* 58 (1981): 110–118.

Hanne Marie Svendsen

(27 August 1933 –)

Helle Mathiasen
University of Arizona

BOOKS: *På rejse ind i romanen* (Copenhagen: Munksgaard, 1962);

Geschichte der danischen Literatur, by Svendsen and Werner Svendsen (Neumünster, Ger.: Karl Wachhöltz, 1964);

Romanens veje: Værkstedssamtaler med danske forfattere, photographs by Gregers Nielsen (Copenhagen: Fischer, 1966);

Mathildes drømmebog (Copenhagen: Gyldendal, 1977);

Dans under frostmånen: Roman (Copenhagen: Gyldendal, 1979);

Klovnefisk (Copenhagen: Gyldendal, 1980);

Samtale med Gud og med fandens oldemor: Noveller (Copenhagen: Lindhardt & Ringhof, 1982);

Guldkuglen: Fortælling om en ø (Copenhagen: Lindhardt & Ringhof, 1985); translated by Jørgen Schiøtt as *The Gold Ball* (New York: Knopf, 1989); Danish edition revised (Copenhagen: Gyldendal, 1998);

Kaila på fyret (Copenhagen: Lindhardt & Ringhof, 1987);

Rosmarin og heksevin (Copenhagen: Lindhardt & Ringhof, 1987);

Den røde sten: Roman, illustrated by Nina Sten-Knudsen (Copenhagen: Dansklærerforeningen, 1990);

Under solen: En roman (Copenhagen: Gyldendal, 1991);

Kirstines ting og andre historier om genfærd: Noveller (Copenhagen: Gyldendal, 1992);

Lisa Månestråle og hendes søstre, illustrated by Svend Otto S. (Copenhagen: Gyldendal, 1992);

Spejlsøster: Naja ser på billeder i Skagen, illustrated by Dina Geller (Copenhagen: Forum, 1995);

Karantæne: Roman (Copenhagen: Gyldendal, 1995);

Rejsen med Emma: Roman (Copenhagen: Gyldendal, 1996);

Ingen genvej til Paradis (Copehagen: Gyldendal, 1999).

PLAY PRODUCTION: *Rosmarin og heksevin,* Copenhagen, Bådteatret, 20 March 1987.

Hanne Marie Svendsen *(photograph by Rigmor Mydtskov; courtesy of Gyldendal Publishers)*

TELEVISION: *Kirstines ting,* script by Svendsen, TV 2, Denmark, 18 November 1991.

RADIO: *Stjernebilleder,* script by Svendsen, Danmarks Radio, 11 May 1998.

OTHER: *Mosaik,* edited by Svendsen and Uffe Harder (Copenhagen: Kunst & Kultur, 1963);

Tom Kristensen, *Hærværk,* afterword by Svendsen (Copenhagen: Gyldendal, 1964);

Åke Runnquist, *Moderne udenlandske forfattere i Europa og Amerika,* translated by Svendsen (Copenhagen: Gyldendal, 1964);

Hans Hertel, ed., *Tilbageblik på 30'erne,* chapter by Svendsen (Copenhagen: Vendelkjær, 1967);

Klaus Rifberg, *Rif: Klaus Rifbjerg-journalistik,* edited by Svendsen (Copenhagen: Gyldendal, 1967);

K. Helveg Petersen, ed., *Vor tid. Det tyvende århundredes litteratur,* volume 4, chapter by Svendsen (Copenhagen: Steen Hasselbalch, 1971);

Rifberg, *Rifbjergs lytterroman,* edited by Svendsen, Ole Larsen, and Jens Schoustrup Thomsen (Copenhagen: Gyldendal, 1972);

Kærlighedens stjernetræ: En antologi af moderne danske kærlighedsdigte, edited by Svendsen (Copenhagen: Forum, 1978);

Iben Holck, ed., *Tidstegn,* chapter by Svendsen (Copenhagen: Centrum, 1978);

Det som heddder Israel, chapter by Svendsen (Copenhagen: Samleren, 1980);

Ritt Bjerregaard, ed., *Heltindehistorier,* chapter by Svendsen (Copenhagen: Gyldendal, 1983);

Sven Holm, ed., *Lysten. En erotisk antologi,* chapter by Svendsen (Copenhagen: Informations Forlag, 1985);

"Lykkens tinder," in *Double Danish,* edited by Per K. Brask (Ontario: Cormorant Press, 1991), pp. 79–84;

Edith Wharton, *Munterhedens Hus,* afterword by Svendsen (Copenhagen: Gyldendal, 1994);

Johannes Møllehave, ed., *Barndommens labyrint,* chapter by Svendsen (Copenhagen: Sesam, 1994);

Birthe Melgaard Mortensen, ed., *Brev til min datter,* chapter by Svendsen (Copenhagen: Gyldendal, 1995);

Anne Mørch-Hansen, ed., *Forfattere fortæller,* chapter by Svendsen (Copenhagen: Høst & Søn, 1995).

SELECTED PERIODICAL PUBLICATION–
UNCOLLECTED: "At overvinde døden," *Samtiden,* 1 (1987): 18–24.

Hanne Marie Svendsen is one of the leading Danish women authors of the 1980s and 1990s. She has published seven novels, two collections of short stories, two plays for television, poetry, and three books for children. In addition to fiction, Svendsen has excelled in several other genres, publishing literary history and criticism, interviews with modern Danish novelists, and autobiographical works and editing poetry anthologies and other collections. She is recognized as a modern Danish master of the literary movement known as magic realism; her work might be compared to that of her contemporaries Peter Høeg and Ib Michael. Above all, Svendsen's strength as a writer is her ability to cre-

ate enthralling stories. Her books feature eccentric characters and even ghosts, who love, suffer, and die on islands, at sea, or during voyages. Writing about boats and water is natural to her, as she grew up near the sea.

Svendsen's ability to convey the ambiguity of modern existence through her writing is a remarkable talent. In expressing the uncertainty of life and its accompanying feelings, some of Svendsen's work resonates with Kierkegaardian angst. In an interview with Birgit Rasmussen from the Danish press on 8 March 1992, the author remarked: "Tænk på vores situation. Vi lever her på en skrøbelig klode i et fuldstændig ukendt univers, og aner ikke hvor vi flyder hen eller hvorfor!" (Think about our situation. We live here on a vulnerable planet in a totally unknown universe, and do not know where we are floating or why!). In such chaos, the storyteller can provide an order that, however temporary, provides comfort and enlightenment.

Hanne Marie Jensen was born 27 August 1933 in Skagen, the northernmost point of Denmark, a narrow peninsula that pokes its crooked finger into the two seas of Kattegat and Skagerrak. This charming seaside town became a favorite with Danish writers and painters in the late nineteenth and early twentieth centuries. It has since become a major tourist attraction, though it still retains its artists' colony status. Hans Christian Andersen visited Skagen, and Karen Blixen (Isak Dinesen) wrote most of *Out of Africa* (1937; translated into Danish as *Den afrikanske Farm,* 1937) while living at a hotel there. The famous paintings of Anna Ancher and her husband Michael are exhibited in their former home, now a museum. As a child Svendsen wanted to be a painter like her role model, Ancher, and her penchant toward pictorial art comes across clearly in her metaphorical fiction.

Jensen grew up an only child, and her father, Ditlef Magnus Jensen, played a major role in her childhood. He was born on Fanø, a small island off the west coast of Jutland. As a young man he had planned a career as a first mate, but on one of his voyages he was shipwrecked off the coast of Cuba. While being rescued, he lost three fingers on one hand. He settled in Skagen village and became a teacher. Despite his handicap, Svendsen's father excelled as a violinist, introducing his daughter to jazz and classical music. He also taught her to love tales of adventure, especially the stories of Alexandre Dumas. Jensen was just eight years old when her father died suddenly in 1941. Seeking to overcome her sorrow, she took refuge in daydreams, games, and books. She wrote poetry and drew and painted pictures. She found support for her love of stories in her mother and her mother's older female relatives, who lived in an old house next door on Skagen Harbor. From these remarkably independent women

Svendsen's home near Skagen, where many of her writings are set (Collection of Hanne Marie Svendsen)

Jensen learned that women were the ones who worked, earned money, and made decisions. Men were delicate, requiring great care, or they were simply absent. Her admiration for strong, creative women later found expression in her fiction.

Early on, Jensen was fascinated by images, light and shade, colors, and atmosphere. She loved the rhythms of songs, poetry, and spoken language. She wanted to be a painter or a writer but did not succeed in realizing her dream until after age forty. The urge to communicate was always there, however. She remembers an anecdote told about her grandfather: during World War II a submarine had run aground off the coast of Skagen. For several days, signals from the crew of the submerged submarine could be heard, but the fishermen lacked the proper diving equipment to rescue the boat in the depths of the sea. Jensen's grandfather locked himself in his office and attempted to design a diving bell for the rescue. He felt compelled to respond to the signals from the submarine, even though nothing could be done. Slowly the signals ceased. The two stories of her father's injury while being rescued at sea and her grandfather's attempt to save the submarine crew strongly influenced the young child's imagination, inspiring in her awe at the power of nature and love for the lifeline of language. She expressed her feeling to Rasmussen in the 1992 interview with her: "Vi lever jo allesammen i lukkede miljøer med bestemte sprogvaner og adfærdsmønstre. Og kan ikke finde udgangen, løsningen. Hvordan kommer man igennem "muren"–ud til *noget andet,* det, der ligger udenfor?" (We live, all of us, in closed environments with certain languages and behaviors. And we cannot find the exit, the solution. How do you get through "the wall"–to *something else* which is outside?). In her daring experiments with words and images, Svendsen has managed to break through the walls that often isolate her characters in time and space.

As a teenager Jensen prepared for a career in teaching by attending Frederikshavn Gymnasium, a secondary school. At age seventeen she left Skagen for the capital; her goal was to study at the University of Copenhagen, but she also dreamed of becoming an actress. As a university student during the 1950s, she became involved in leftist groups advocating the independence of Algiers from France and nuclear disarmament and protesting environmental pollution. At twenty-one she married Werner Svendsen, a publisher, and became the mother of three children: Catherine, born in 1956; Morten, born in 1960; and Christian, born in 1963. While raising her family, Svendsen held important posts, serving as literary and dramatic program director at the state broadcasting network, Danmarks Radio, and as an assistant professor at the University of Copenhagen.

She graduated from the University of Copenhagen in 1958 with a master of arts degree in Danish and German. Svendsen began writing seriously after graduation; although her career and family obligations consumed most of her time, at the age of forty-three she found her artistic voice. Svendsen has written and spoken about women's lives and about the "brutality" it requires for a woman to dedicate herself to her art. She has publicly debated about the common female conflict between career and family. With the publication of her first novel, *Mathildes drømmebog* (Mathilde's Dream Book, 1977), Svendsen made the choice to become an artist, and her life as a storyteller had begun.

This work of only fifty-six pages is a masterpiece that breaks with the linear structure of the traditional novel. It is comprised of two related stories: the real events of Mathilde's ordinary life and the surreal images of her dreams. Mathilde's reality is printed in brown; her dreams are printed in blue. Mathilde is a young woman ambitious for career and personal happiness; she falls in love, gets married, and has children. Finally, she reaches a stage of disillusionment with her life as a wife and mother; she realizes that she is not special but that she, too, is subject to disappointment. Being an oppressed wife and mother might have destroyed Mathilde, but she is a dreamer, and her dreams sustain her. Svendsen's technique of presenting two dimensions–Mathilde's outer life, subject to the linearity of time, and her inner life, free from limitations of time and space–create an extraordinarily rich mimesis of human experience. Dreams are a part of life; in Mathilde's case, they keep her alive. Svendsen writes in the epigraph to the novel: "Mennesker, der gennem længere tid forhindres i at drømme, bliver vanvittige" (People who are prevented from dreaming for a significant length of time become insane). This novel introduces several themes recurring in Svendsen's subsequent fiction: the element of myth or allegory; the coexistence of fantasy and reality; and a compassionate insight into the lives of women.

During the 1980s she participated in the public debate concerning the new role of women in the second half of the twentieth century, though she has never claimed to be a feminist. Her ironic outlook prohibits any kind of programmatic declaration. In her published discussions about modern attitudes toward feminine and masculine issues, she has described two distinct concepts of time, the linear and the circular, relating the linear to the male point of view and the circular to the female point of view. Svendsen herself prefers to think of time as a spiral that encompasses death and rebirth, the way of nature. She believes that in order to survive we must see ourselves as part of cyclical nature, not separate from it. She believes modern science shows dawning awareness of this circularity. The perception of time as a circular event, or even as a spiral, gives her hope for the continuation of human life even after the earth has become uninhabitable.

Svendsen's first full-length novel *Guldkuglen: Fortælling om en ø* (The Gold Ball: A Story about an Island, 1985; translated as *The Gold Ball,* 1989) gushes forth with abundant life both inside and outside linear time. Its narrator and leading characters are female visionaries, illustrating Svendsen's philosophy that we would be able to glimpse the great pattern of eternity were we not limited by our human senses. As things are, the artist can reveal such other visions through her disciplined forging of word and image.

Guldkuglen won the Danish Literary Critics' Award in 1985. An immediate success, it has been translated into ten languages. On the literal level, this work is a series of improbable stories about violent, passionate individuals living on an unnamed northern island over a period of three hundred years. Structurally, the story is a circle or sphere. On the level of allegory, familiar to Svendsen from her lifelong reading of Dante's *Divine Comedy* (1310–1314), in *Guldkuglen* Svendsen tells a story about all humanity, its past, its present, and its uncertain future. This ambitious novel takes its title from a gold ball, a piece of jewelry worn by its ageless heroine, Maja Stina. The novel opens with the female narrator's image of Maja Stina wearing her gold ball and surrounded by the island children, all of them whirling through space seated in treetops. This is the ending of the story, which now follows in flashback, returning to that same startling image of women and children carried into space in an uprooted ash tree. The gold ball, it is later revealed, came from Asia, where a man stole it from a fertility goddess. When one looks into the gold ball, time falls away; the shiny ball reflects images that shift and transpose time. It shows the multiplicity of the world. The narrator sets herself the task of forging words to express these timeless images; however, she is well aware of the limits of words and of the novel as genre. She experiments with time and language, using techniques of magic realism.

The narrator tells the story of a group of sturdy individuals headed by Niels Gløe, grandfather of Maja Stina, who arrived to settle a sandy island a long time ago. The island population expands and the island develops, until, ravaged by its ruthless human invaders, it becomes unfit for human habitation. The pioneering fisherman Gløe becomes the unacknowledged feudal lord of the island. He marries several wives and fathers numerous descendants. It is he who formulates the leitmotiv of *Guldkuglen,* by saying: "Og det er, som det er, og det bliver ikke andet" (And that is the way it is, and it won't be otherwise). One of the earliest events in the story of Gløe's life involves his second wife, Hedevig Regitze. Hating her husband's sexual violence, yet longing for affection, Hedevig falls in love with her stepson, Hirtus, but he rejects her effort at seduction. She lies to

Svendsen in 1998 (photograph by Jo Selsing;
Collection of Hanne Marie Svendsen)

the gold ball from the captain and passes it on to Maja Stina.

The island, finally prosperous and modern, a place of tourism and trade, lawyers and accountants, slowly perishes, as do its people. The consequence of industrialization, water pollution, arrives from the sea as a red slime, covering island beaches; poisoning the flounder and cod, fertilizer and cattle feed, and canned food; and destroying the island economy. As the adults leave the polluted island, the children stay and go hungry. Maja Stina takes in the children, feeds them, and washes their clothes. Paradise has been lost. No one knows whether there will be another. From their perch in the tree whirling through the cosmos, the narrator, Maja Stina, and the island children view the earth, now abandoned. Perhaps there is hope yet, for the ash may be Yggdrasil, sanctuary of the Nordic gods, a tree that reaches up into the heavens. The women and children travel beyond all known dimensions. They may land somewhere else and take root.

Mythical and magical, *Guldkuglen* ranges over a vast field of human experience. The novel took Svendsen three years to write. She wrote part of the novel in Italy and part in Skagen, where she owns a thatched cottage among the dunes. She incorporated the history and legends of her hometown, along with contemporary research on concepts of time, into her novel. The beauty of the language was obtained through constant revision—Svendsen rewrote portions of the book ten times. Though she feared the novel might be considered alien to Danish tradition, Danish and international audiences were ready for her work. After interviewing Svendsen in 1985, Danish critic Malin Lindgren wrote in *Politiken* that she was "en ny litterær vulkan" (a new literary volcano); other enthusiastic reviewers in Denmark and in the United States compared her talent to that of Hans Christian Andersen, Johannes V. Jensen, and Karen Blixen.

Guldkuglen launched Svendsen's writing career. After that, she wrote novels, stories, and plays and published continually. *Kaila på fyret* (Kaila from the Lighthouse, 1987), which depicts a young girl's transition to adulthood, earned her the 1988 Danish Literary Prize for Childrens' Literature. *Rosmarin og heksevin* (Rosemary and Witches' Brew, 1987), a play about Ulysses and Circe, was published in the same year. In *Den røde sten: Roman* (The Red Stone: Novel, 1990) Svendsen tells the tale of a ten-year-old girl, Marie, who witnesses a mythic battle between good and evil. This popular children's story displays Svendsen's rare insight into the thoughts and needs of children. In presenting the world of so-called real-

her husband, telling him that Hirtus has tried to assault her. Gløe then confronts his son, beating him severely. As Hirtus runs to the beach, a sea monster emerges to take him from the island. Subsequently, Gløe's other son, Niels Martinus, a crude adventurer who fathers three children with three island women, goes to sea. During a voyage the son encounters the *Blakstar*, a slave ship whose deck is strewn with the dead bodies of mutinied black slaves and their oppressors. Niels Martinus brings back the only two survivors, a brilliantly colored bird and a chained black slave who turns out to be a chief. Other strangers reach the island, among them a captain bringing the gold ball and a master of mosaics, who sees visions. Bewitching island women fall in love with the new inhabitants. One of them, Elle, has been said to dance around the lighthouse with a horned devil. She gets

ity and the more real world of Marie's imagination, *Den røde sten* yet again displays Svendsen's talent for magic realism. *Under solen: En roman* (Under the Sun: A Novel, 1991) is a novel featuring a woman who returns to her small hometown by the sea, where she confronts old enemies and prejudice. Svendsen's play *Kirstines ting* (Kirstine's Things) was performed on Danish television in 1991, and the following year *Kirstines ting og andre historier om genfærd: Noveller* (Kirstine's Things and Other Stories about Ghosts: Short Stories, 1992) her second collection of short stories, was published. Svendsen has published children's books, including *Lisa Månestråle og hendes søstre* (Lisa Moonbeam and Her Sisters, 1992) and *Spejlsøster: Naja ser på billeder i Skagen* (Sister in the Mirror: Naja Looks at Pictures in Skagen, 1995). The latter is a richly illustrated book, with drawings by Dina Geller, about a young girl who goes to Skagen to visit her grandmother during summer vacation. Svendsen depicts the child-adult relationship with tenderness and humor, as the grandmother introduces her granddaughter to the writers and painters of Skagen.

Her next book, *Karantæne: Roman* (Quarantine: Novel, 1995), marks a new departure for Svendsen. It is a psychological thriller about a twentieth-century alienated man. A middle-aged, lost individual without a name takes a boat to a dark, rainy island, where he will meet others who are damned and perhaps find out who he is. In the novel, "Karantæne" refers to the abandoned quarantine hospital on this island, a building used in previous times to house humans and goods thought to be infectious. The story line follows the flashback technique used in *Guldkuglen*. The tale is narrated by the unnamed central character, but he intersperses events about his daily life with evocative passages of memories. An art historian, he has been dispatched to this foreign island to establish a local maritime museum. The residents are unfriendly, and the man finds himself alone most of the time. In his solitude he begins to remember what brought him to his current state of emotional paralysis, gradually unraveling an unsettling story of rejection, loss, and death. Thus, the story operates on a literal level of fact. The second layer reveals his memories; yet a third layer relates the dreams and ghostly sightings of the increasingly distraught narrator. He begins to put his life story into writing and discovers that he has lived on fantasy: his relationships with his parents, wife, and son are not loving but are hate-filled; his career is not successful but is a failure. His anxiety finds expression in nightmares, visions, and suicidal thoughts.

To a certain extent, the protagonist in *Karantæne* is a counterpart to Mathilde in *Mathildes drømmebog*, but where he has refused to take responsibility for his failures, she has accepted hers; where he has denied his feelings, she has been sustained by hers. Most importantly, Mathilde has endured and survived the social pressures placed on her as a woman, whereas the man in quarantine remains infected with narcissism.

Svendsen's seventh novel, *Rejsen med Emma: Roman* (Travels with Emma: Novel, 1996), recalls a game the author used to play with a friend in Skagen Harbor. They would row out in a rowboat and then cross the wakes of the freighters and large boats, making their boat rock violently. *Rejsen med Emma* tells the story of a writer who leaves her bourgeois Danish existence to have an adventure on a freighter named *Emma,* bound for New York, the Panama Canal, and South America. The writer is trying to decide whether to stay with her current lover or pursue her fantasy of taking a foreign lover. The story includes subplots involving the Danish crew and the characters they encounter. The narrator relates tales of a garrulous ghost living in the engine room, her visions of animals and humans merging, and her dead father visiting her onboard as well as the prosaic details of daily life at sea. A dignified elderly lady, Sofie Tobel, is the only other passenger. She is a busybody and a political activist who smuggles a young South American guerrilla, Aurelio Cervallos, on board and takes him back to Denmark to seek political asylum. His questions conclude this novel of adventure, as he wonders about the complacency of his Danish friends: "I er så fremmede. I fremsætter jeres teorier og løsningsmodeller på sikker afstand af problemerne. Hvad ved I om vores tilværelse? Hvad ved I om de mennesker, hvis håb er knyttet til et liv med normale sorger, normale dødsfald, normale tab?" (You are so alien. You present your theories and solutions at a safe distance from the problems. What do you know about our lives? What do you know about people whose hopes hang on a life with normal sorrows, normal deaths, normal losses?) The writer, back in Denmark, returns to her physician-lover and to her work. She begins a book about a young, freedom-loving sailor, based on her experiences aboard *Emma,* in a sense sublimating her attraction to Aurelio.

In *Rejsen med Emma,* Svendsen asks whether literature can break through habitual dimensions and ingrained prejudices. In her novel she portrays life as a risky undertaking but shows that perhaps through political action and the creative imagination, attentive readers can travel beyond their familiar milieu, both literally and figuratively. Finally, what stands out in *Rejsen med Emma* is the author's gift of imagination that enables her to evoke kaleidoscopic images of color and movement, whether she is describing New York City in the snow or the luxuriant foliage of the tropical rain forest.

In her autobiographical essay included in *Forfattere fortæller* (Author Stories, 1995), written about the time *Karantæne* was published, Hanne Marie Svendsen remembers the female storytellers of her childhood. Her older relatives entertained her with many stories; sometimes fables, sometimes family legends. Often these tales had a moral: pride comes before a fall; cowardice is despicable; share with others what you have. Her early experiences with oral history and storytelling and her own extensive reading inspired in her the idea that stories can show the attentive reader the way to truth. But truth is not singular. She quotes the French realist Gustave Flaubert, "There is no truth, only different ways of seeing." Truth appears in so-called realistic writing, but also in dreams and fantasy. Svendsen's work blends realism with dreams and magic, and, at times, these ways of seeing merge to become inseparable. Svendsen has received many literary awards. Her art has done much to advance the possibilities of modern Danish fiction.

Interviews:

Birgit Rasmussen, "Hun vil gerne blive en fandens oldemor," *Berlingske tidende,* 10 October 1982;

Linnea Friis, "Eventyret åbner en ny livstolkning," *Kristeligt dagblad,* 20 April 1985;

Malin Lindgren, "En ny litterær vulkan. Hanne Marie Svendsen forlod toppost for at skrive en bog," *Politiken,* 21 April 1985;

Annagrethe Skov, "Hendes hovede fuld af eventyr," *Frederiksborgs amts avis,* 21 April 1985;

Else Cornelius, "Jeg lærte aldrig at slå fra mig," *Berlingske tidende,* 11 April 1990;

Rasmussen, "Vi har masser af genfærd inden i os," *Berlingske tidende,* 8 March 1992;

Marianne Juhl, "Mødre-og døtre," *Jyllands-posten,* 15 August 1995.

References:

Susi Frastein, "Når Kuinder Skriver," *Tiderne Skifter* (1985): 100–111;

Sara Lidman, "Guldkulan–ett mirakel," in her *Och tradet svarade* (Stockholm: Bonniers, 1988), pp. 157–159;

Artur Lundkvist, "En o mellan fantasi och verklighet," in his *Segling mot nya stjärnor: Artiklar om utländsk litteratur* (Stockholm: Bonniers, 1987), pp. 192–198;

Helle Mathiasen, "Hanne Marie Svendsen in Tucson, Ariz.," *Hoffman Estates (Ill.) Den danske pioneer* (25 May 1998), pp. 11–12;

Marie-Louise Paludan, "Alle Orte liegen mitten in der Welt," in *Blixen, Christensen und andere danischene Dichterinnen,* edited by Bodil Wamberg (Munich: Kleinheinrich, 1988), pp. 155–165;

Jean Renaud, "A World of Dream and Magic," *Danish Literary Magazine,* 5 (1993): 6–7;

Klaus Rothstein, "Det kærlighedsløse. Efter en samtale med Hanne Marie Svendsen," *Alef: Tidsskrift for jødisk kultur,* 6 (1991): 13–16;

May Schack, "On Taking Our Time," *Danish Children's Literature,* 10 (1996): 28–29.

Pia Tafdrup

(29 May 1952 –   )

Anne-Marie Mai
University of Southern Denmark, Odense

BOOKS: *Når der går hul på en engel: Digte* (Copenhagen: Borgen, 1981);

Intetfang: Digte (Copenhagen: Borgen, 1982);

Den inderste zone: Digte (Copenhagen: Borgen, 1983);

Springflod: Digte (Copenhagen: Borgen, 1985); translated by Anne Born as *Spring Tide* (London & Boston: Forest, 1989);

Hvid feber: Digte (Copenhagen: Borgen, 1986);

Sekundernes bro: Digte (Copenhagen: Borgen, 1988);

Døden i bjergene (Gråsten: Teaterforlaget Drama, 1988);

Over vandet går jeg: Skitse til en poetik (Copenhagen: Borgen, 1991);

Jorden er blå (Gråsten: Teaterforlaget Drama, 1991);

Krystalskoven: Digte (Copenhagen: Borgen, 1992);

Territorialsang: En Jerusalemkomposition: Digte (Copenhagen: Borgen, 1994);

Dronningeporten: Digte (Copenhagen: Gyldendal, 1998);

Tusindfødt: Digte (Copenhagen: Gyldendal, 1999).

Collection: *Mindst ét sar har kroppen altid: Pia Tafdrups forfatterskab,* edited by Carsten Dilling (Copenhagen: Borgen, 1995).

Edition in English: *Ten Poems,* translated by Poul Borum and Roger Greenwald (Toronto: Cloudberry Foundation, 1989).

PLAY PRODUCTIONS: *Døden i bjergene,* Odense, Odense Teater, 14 April 1988;

Jorden er blå, Odense, Odense Teater, 2 November 1991.

RADIO: *Døden i bjergene,* script by Tafdrup, *Radioteatret,* Danmarks Radio, 1990;

Min tid, mit vilddyr, script translated by Tafdrup from Eva Ström's *Tiden Min, Mitt Vilddjur, Radioteatret,* Danmarks Radio, 1990.

OTHER: *Konstellationer—en antologi of dansk lyrik 1976–1981,* edited by Tafdrup (Herning: Systime, 1982);

Transformationer: Poesi 1980–1985, edited by Tafdrup (Herning: Systime, 1985);

Pia Tafdrup (Collection of Pia Tafdrup)

Rocky Mountains: Festskrift til Per Højholts 60 års dag 22.7.1988, edited by Tafdrup and others (Copenhagen: Schønberg, 1988);

K. E. Løgstrup, *Den etiske fordring,* foreword by Tafdrup (Copenhagen: Gyldendal, 1991);

"Søvnen i en rosenbusk," in *Museum midt på dagen. 80'er-digtere skriver erindringer i utide,* edited by Johan Rosdahl and Peter Thielst (Copenhagen: Hans Reitzel, 1991), pp. 47–59;

"The Invisible Intervention. Discussion of Joseph Brodsky's Paper 'A Cat's Meow,'" *Of Thought and Words: The Relation Between Language and Mind,* edited by Sture Allén, Proceedings of Nobel Symposium 92 (N.p.: Imperial College Press / River Edge, N.J.: World Scientific, 1995), pp. 27–33;

"Himlens blinde spejl," in *Hvordan jeg blev forfatter,* edited by Agnete Stjernfelt (Copenhagen: Borgen, 1997), pp. 139–155.

SELECTED PERIODICAL PUBLICATION–UNCOLLECTED: "Aarestrup læst af Tafdrup," *Passage,* 8 (1990): 120–125.

Pia Tafdrup is one of the finest Danish poets of the 1980s and 1990s. Her poetry collections have inspired readers and critics in Denmark and Scandinavia as well as at poetry festivals and readings all over the world. From London, Toronto, Moscow, Lahti, and Bergen to Sidney and Auckland, her poetry has been critically acclaimed. Beautifully shaped verses with intense musicality characterize Tafdrup's poetic language; her profound reflections on human existence alternate with her impressions of nature, the body, sexuality, and modern living.

The vitality of young womanhood and a consciousness of the inevitability of death form the center of Tafdrup's poetic universe. Many of her readers and critics have viewed her poetry as a liberating reaction to the feminist poetry of the 1970s, in which the subjection of women was the major theme. In Tafdrup's poems the beauty of the verse itself as well as the sensuality of the body and of art form the main focus.

Pia Tafdrup was born 29 May 1952 in Copenhagen. She grew up in the countryside as the eldest daughter of Finn Tafdrup and Elin Hannover, both born in Copenhagen. Of Jewish descent, both of her parents had to flee from Nazi-occupied Denmark to neutral Sweden during World War II. Finn Tafdrup and Elin Hannover were married in 1950 and became owners of the large farm "Endrupgård" and later of the farm "Rosendal," both situated in the north of Sjælland, one of the most idyllic regions of Denmark. Pia's mother and father were interested in literature and poetry of the classical genres as well as in contemporary prose and poetry. As did many young parents of their generation, they considered it vital to tell their children fairy tales, to sing with them, and to read them bedtime stories. In an essay on how she became a writer, Tafdrup remembers the experience of learning to read at school:

> De første linier, jeg fik for i skolen, blev en sær blanding af svimlende lykke og lidt af et mareridt. Jeg stavede ord som so – ko – lo – mus – hus, men blev aldrig færdig med de lektier, fordi der for bare to-tre bogstaver udspillede sig et univers, jeg blev helt svimmel af at gå ind i. Hvordan læse to eller tre bogstaver, når jeg først skulle se de billeder, der rul-

lede sig op for øjnene af mig? To bogstaver på papiret korresponderede med en uendelighed i mit sind.

> (The first lessons I had to prepare as a pupil gave me the strange experience of both giddy happiness and a nightmare. I spelled words like sow – cow– mouse – house, but I never finished my lessons, because I became so fascinated with the universe which two or three letters created for me. How could I read two or three letters when I first had to concentrate on the pictures that they evoked? Two letters on a piece of paper corresponded to an infinity in my imagination.)

Tafdrup retained a young girl's fascination with letters and spelling and a love for the sound and possibilities of words. When she finished high school, she chose to study Danish language and literature at the University of Copenhagen, graduating with a bachelor of arts degree in 1977. In 1978 she married the literary critic and Karen Blixen scholar, Bo Hakon Jørgensen, an assistant professor at the University of Odense. The couple has two sons, Phillip Tafdrup Jørgensen, born in 1979, and Daniel Tafdrup Jørgensen, born in 1983.

Tafdrup's first collection, *Når der går hul på en engel: Digte* (When an Angel Breaks Her Silence: Poems, 1981), consists of poems dealing with the experiences and reflections of a young woman: impressions from her childhood, her first love, and the birth of her child. It is obvious, however, that these poems do not simply reproduce an experience; the poetry itself becomes an exploration and an interpretation. The boundless imagery of the soul emerges in the poems; the metaphoric language of the poems is fresh and surprising, and the rhythm of the verse is both self-confident and searching. The title of the collection plays with the idea that the angel is often used as a metaphor for the female sex, but in these poems the metaphor has been transformed and new meanings and a new understanding of the body and soul emerge.

Intetfang: Digte (No Hold: Poems, 1982) is Tafdrup's second collection, and it brings a new dimension to her poetry. The title refers to the concept of the Danish philosopher Ludvig Feilberg (1849–1912), who sought to describe the human soul and who stressed the difference between the soul that has "a hold on life" and the soul that has "no hold." The notion of "no hold" indicates a condition by which existence is no longer rooted in the concrete; this idea inspired Tafdrup to write a selection of poems in which the poetic language no longer refers to the concrete nor to the experiential. Instead the poems follow their own logic determined by rhythm and metaphor. The collection consists of four sections, and the second section offers a new way of using poetic language. In the first stanzas of this section the theme is a love affair between a man and a woman, but coitus is transformed into an allegory. The poem unveils an unknown beauty of sound and cosmic vision.

This new dimension in Tafdrup's poetry is related to the tradition of symbolism in Danish literature that dates back to Sophus Claussen (1865–1931), the most important Danish symbolist poet, whose poetry still serves as a major inspiration to many postmodern Danish poets, such as Per Højholt and Inger Christensen. Claussen defined poetry as "sublime mathematics," and by that expression he suggested that poetry should consist of a finished shape and yet reach beyond itself into the unknown realm of the soul and nature. This idea is an important key to Tafdrup's poetry. In addition to Claussen, she often mentions the German symbolists Rainer Maria Rilke and Paul Celan as sources of inspiration.

The title of her third collection, *Den inderste zone: Digte* (The Innermost Zone: Poems, 1983), should be seen as a continuation of her new poetics. Here, poetry becomes a process of approaching an innermost zone for which the body serves as an allegory. The composition of the collection follows the changing seasons from winter to spring and summer, and the poems lead the poet and the reader to the beauty, intensity, and fulfillment of midsummer, where the lovers are absorbed in the innermost zone of their love.

The first collections of poems by Tafdrup were well received by critics and often seen in relation to a new generation of Danish poets of the 1980s led by Michael Strunge. In different ways the young poets of the 1980s protested against the realism that dominated Danish literature in the 1970s. Tafdrup's fourth collection, *Springflod: Digte* (1985; translated as *Spring Tide,* 1989), marked the turning point of her career. The influential Danish critic Poul Borum (1934–1996) lauded this collection, and Tafdrup began to be seen as one of the leading contemporary Danish poets, along with such significant figures as Henrik Nordbrandt, Inger Christensen, and Per Højholt. The composition of *Springflod* is a variation over the metaphor of the tide that expresses the essence of nature, body, and life cycle. The collection consists of seven sections, and the poems in each section relate to the female cycle and the spring tide. A powerful desire for life and for being part of a cosmic life cycle dominate the poems, and the poetic language is full of energy and passion; many of the poems refer

to poets and philosophers such as Friedrich Nietzsche. The rhythm of the verses is strong and almost chanting, and the poems lure the reader into the font of love and longing where life begins and ends. *Springflod* concludes with motifs from the modern world; a new awareness of the threats of increasing militarism and conformity in the modern age is expressed in the poem "De fire vugger" (The Four Cradles), which is dedicated to the artist Ola Enstad's 1983 sculpture of the same title.

The strong experience of life and poetry in *Springflod* was followed by poems depicting the shivering and trembling of the body, the poem, and the soul. In *Hvid feber* (White Fever, 1986) the poetic voice is almost whispering, a fever penetrates the language and often a rupture or a breach of metaphors occurs. The poet picks up the broken fragments of language and creates new patterns that reflect an awareness of death and the limits of art. *Hvid feber* expresses both silence, longing, and despair; it seems to be a poetic and mental reaction to the energy and power of *Springflod.*

The success of *Springflod* brought Tafdrup fame as well as opportunities for travel. She received the Holger Drachmann Grant in 1986, and the Henri Nathansen Grant and the Otto Rung Grant in 1987, and she visited several countries, including the United States. Themes from her journeys and her first visit to the United States are present in her sixth collection of poems, *Sekundernes bro: Digte* (The Bridge of Moments: Poems, 1988). The poet meditates over the places that she has seen in her life, in her dreams, and in her poems. In one of the first poems of the collection she gives the reader an impression of her creative work with language. She literally shows how the poem is shaped by crossing out words and rewriting. The process of writing is the subject in several poems, including a poem that illustrates the use of a computer for writing poetry.

In 1991 Tafdrup published *Over vandet går jeg: Skitse til en poetik* (Walking Over the Water: An Outline of a Poetics). In this book-length essay she draws on her experience and her understanding of poetry, and her reflections are emphatic and yet subtle. The exposition is shaped by symbolist notions that regard the poem as timeless, a sacred moment of insight, and an innermost zone. She discusses the relation between poetry and religion, poetic language, religious language and everyday language, and sex and poetry, and the relationship between the arts. She also reveals that the Jewish family roots of her parents have become more and more important to her. Tafdrup's essay on poetics represents the first attempt in that genre by a Scandinavian woman

Dust jacket for Tafdrup's 1999 poetry collection

writer, and although some critics denigrated *Over vandet går jeg* as pathetic and perhaps pompous, the work remains an important part of the discussion on poetics that engages many young Danish writers and poets. *Over vandet går jeg* was published in a Swedish translation in 1995 and was received enthusiastically by Swedish critics. Its serious and heartfelt tone was perhaps more acceptable to the Swedish than to the Danish critics.

In a lecture, "A Theory of Poetry," given in New Zealand at Auckland University in October 1997, Tafdrup explained how she understands the process of writing poetry:

> When I am left with a feeling that here I have a successful poem, it is precisely because I have written something I had not imagined to be possible. By this I do not intend to say that I as a writer have said everything. I have made my way to a new high point in the landscape, from which I feel there is still a long way to go: a new country awaits me out there on the horizon. We surely always write in the illusion of the absolute poem, or the absolute book in which everything that is crucial to our lives is written, well-aware that this is an impossibility.

A characteristic of Tafdrup's poetry is her attempt to attain this "absolute poem"; she shows a mastery of every detail of the poem. This characteristic is obvious in her seventh collection of poems, *Krystalskoven:*

Digte (The Crystal Forest: Poems, 1992). The poems are carefully executed with a faultless poetic language of harmony and beauty. The poems are like crystals, cold and hard, but unforgettable. A growing consciousness of death accompanies the formal mastery. The poem protects the reader and the poet from death; but, in its perfection, it also reminds the poet and reader about the inevitability of death.

The next collection of poems, *Territorialsang: En Jerusalemkomposition: Digte* (Territorial Song: A Jerusalem Composition: Poems, 1994), marks a high point in Tafdrup's career. It is a poetic excursion that describes the poet's journey to Israel and the ancient town of Jerusalem, where Christian, Islamic, and Jewish cultures and religions meet both in conflict and in mutual inspiration. Tafdrup reminisces and reflects on her Jewish family roots and the poet's journey becomes a discovery of the past: the flight of her parents to Sweden during World War II, the fears and hopes of the Jewish people, and the immense strength of the Jewish culture. The colors, the heat, the lights, and the scents of the city overwhelm the poet, and the poems are both expressive and sensitive. The perfection of Tafdrup's symbolist poetics is transformed into a new, more open poetry attentive to this strange and fascinating old town, its people, its past and its present, its threats and fears, for example in the poem titled "Livet som indsats" (Commitment):

I det mindste torterer truslerne dagligt bevidstheden
forudsiger som et hastigt greb om struben
din dødsstund
Hver religion beder under sit tag
kuplet, spidst eller teltformet
men bønnerne stiger mod den samme himmel
hvor fugle sværmer i zenit.

(If nothing else the threats torture your mind daily,
like a quick stranglehold they predict
your moment of death
Each religion prays under its own roof
domed, pointed, or tent-shaped
but the prayers rise toward the same heavens
where birds swarm at the zenith.)

Territorialsang was nominated for the most prestigious literary prize in Scandinavia, the award of the Nordic Literary Council, and its vivid and emotional poetry makes the reader read it at one sitting, breathless and inspired. During her second stay in Jerusalem in 1993 Tafdrup was again inspired; the result was a major collection of poetry, *Dronningeporten: Digte* (Queen's Gate: Poems, 1998), which deals with love and the dreams of a woman. The collection won Tafdrup the Nordic Council's Literary Award in 1999.

In addition to nine collections of poetry, Tafdrup has written two plays, *Døden i bjergene* (Death in the Mountains, 1988)—later revised for the Danish Radio Theater—and *Jorden er blå* (The Earth is Blue, 1991), both for the Odense Teater. For Tafdrup, drama and poetry are related genres. The plays deal with relationships between children and their parents and focus on the verbal communication of the characters; the dialogue of the characters is carefully crafted and the strength of the metaphors in these plays bears the distinctive mark of the poet.

Pia Tafdrup has received several honors and awards for her poems: in 1989 she became a member of Det Danske Akademi (The Danish Academy), and from 1993 to 1995 she served as chair of the Department of Literature for Denmark's Foundation for the Fine Arts. In her 1997 lecture at Auckland University, Tafdrup emphasized that a poet is identified by his or her aesthetic signature, that is to say, by a special personal characteristic or spiritual fingerprint. Tafdrup's own aesthetic signature is that of a formal mastery and a suggestive beauty.

References:
Marianne Barlyng, "Lysets engel, en Pia Tafdrup komposition," in *Perspektiver i nyere dansk litteratur,* edited by Neal Ashley Conrad and others (Silkeborg: Spring, 1997), pp. 131–152;

Poul Borum, "POe-(RO)-tik, om Pia Tafdrup og tre andre kvindelige lyrikere," *Kritik,* 66 (1984): 125–141;

Carsten Dilling, *Mindst et sår har kroppen altid. Pia Tafdrups forfatterskab* (Copenhagen: Borgen, 1995);

Mads Julius Elf, "Poetik for Gud og hvermand," in *Perspektiver i nyere dansk litteratur,* edited by Neal Ashley Conrad and others (Silkeborg: Spring, 1997), pp. 112–129;

Ole Karlsen, "En gigantisk uro og følelse af nødvendighed," *Norskloraren: Tidsskrift for språk og litteratur* 4 (1995): 5–14;

Erik A. Nielsen, "En stige ind i himlen–om Pia Tafdrups poetik *Over vandet går jeg,*" *Spring,* 1 (1991–1992): 87–90;

Anne-Marie Mai, "... finder hjem til kroppen. Om firserlitteraturen," in *Nordisk kvindelitteraturhistorie,* 4 volumes, edited by Elisabeth Møller Jensen and others (Copenhagen: Rosinante, 1997), IV: 463–478;

Lars Onslev, "Den anden stemme–om Pia Tafdrups *Sekundernes Bro* 1988," in *Digtning fra 80'erne til 90'erne,* edited by Mai (Copenhagen: Borgen, 1993), pp. 214–228;

Erik Skyum Nielsen, "Lyset der gør alting mere synligt," *Litteratur/86. En almanak* (1986): 4–6.

Kirsten Thorup
(9 February 1942 –   )

Charlotte Schiander Gray

BOOKS: *Indeni-udenfor: Digte* (Copenhagen: Gyldendal, 1967);

I dagens anledning (Copenhagen: Gyldendal, 1968);

Love from Trieste: Digte (Copenhagen: Gyldendal, 1969); translated by Nadia Christensen and Alexander Taylor as *Love from Trieste* (Willimantic, Conn.: Curbstone, 1980);

Idag er det Daisy: Digte (Copenhagen: Gyldendal, 1971);

Baby: Roman (Copenhagen: Gyldendal, 1973); translated by Christensen as *Baby: A Novel* (Baton Rouge: Louisiana State University Press, 1980);

Lille Jonna (Copenhagen: Gyldendal, 1977);

Den lange sommer (Copenhagen: Gyldendal, 1979);

Himmel og helvede, 2 volumes (Copenhagen: Gyldendal, 1982);

Marie, translated by Taylor (New York: Top Stories, 1982);

Romantica: Skuespil (Copenhagen: Gyldendal, 1983);

Den yderste grænse, 2 volumes (Copenhagen: Gyldendal, 1987);

Sidste nat før kærligheden (Copenhagen: Gyldendal, 1989);

Elskede ukendte (Copenhagen: Gad, 1994);

Projekt paradis: En trilogi (Copenhagen: Gad, 1997).

PLAY PRODUCTIONS: *Romantica,* Herning, Denmark, Team Teater, October 1983;

Sidste nat før kærligheden, Copenhagen, Aveny Teater, 2 March 1989;

Projekt paradis, Copenhagen, Betty Nansen Teater, Edison Stage, November 1996.

MOTION PICTURE: *Den dobbelte mand,* screenplay by Thorup and Franz Ernst, Steen Herdel Filmproduktion, 1976;

Ballerup Boulevard, screenplay by Thorup, Synne Ryfbjerg, and Linda Wendel, Magnusson, 1986.

TELEVISION: *Sæsonen slutter,* Danmarks Radio, TV-teatret, 1971;

Frisørinden, Danmarks Radio, 1971;

Hvornår dør Maria? Danmarks Radio, 1972;

Helte dør aldrig, Danmarks Radio, 1976;

Kirsten Thorup (photograph by Stine Heger; courtesy of Gyldendal Publishers)

Else Kant, Danmarks Radio, 1978;

Du er smuk, jeg elsker dig, Danmarks Radio, TV-Teaterat delingen, 1980;

Krigsdøtre, script by Thorup and Li Vilstrup, Danmarks Radio, 1981.

RADIO: *Historien om Mally,* 1973;

Længslen efter tatovørens nål, 1990.

Kirsten Thorup, like her contemporaries Suzanne Brøgger and Dorrit Willumsen, has significantly influenced Danish literature since the 1960s through her female perspective. Thorup has developed from an experimental, modernist poet to a prose writer specializing in psychological realism. As an experimental writer she became a favorite of the critics; with her social and psychological novels she became popular with a wide circle of readers. Although Thorup uses realistic descriptions, her characters display imagination and often express a hope for change.

The author was born Kirsten Christensen in Gelsted, a small town on the island of Funen, on 2 February 1942 to Svend Christensen, a bookstore owner, and his wife, Jenny (née Jørgensen), a homemaker. She and her three brothers grew up in modest, petit-bourgeois circumstances in a provincial milieu, which she later described in the Jonna books. As a child Thorup was keenly aware of the vulnerability of the working class and the poorer people of the Danish provinces. She played with the boys who lived in local welfare institutions and quickly realized how they were trapped by their circumstances; later, she grew interested in their experiences, and in the psychological impact of difficult social conditions. She used this knowledge in her novel *Baby: Roman* (1973; translated as *Baby: A Novel,* 1980) to portray the irresponsible and often reckless attitudes of social outsiders.

When Kirsten entered secondary school, life changed fundamentally for her. She was the first member of her family to obtain an advanced education and enter the academy. She did not enjoy her time in school because she felt as if she were an outsider and socially inferior. She felt increasingly alienated and tried to express these feelings in her early poetry. In her first writings she dissected and analyzed her experiences from multiple points of view. Only later, when she turned to realism in the Jonna books, was she ready to place her perceptions in a larger social context. Throughout her life and writings, Thorup has maintained her loyalty to the milieu and people of her childhood.

She graduated from Fredericia Gymnasium in 1961 and spent the next year in England. In 1963 she returned to Denmark and married stage director Ib Thorup. They had a daughter, Aja, and lived in Vesterbro, a working-class district of Copenhagen. For a time Thorup worked for the Word Register, an occupation that increased her awareness of the meaning and absurdity of words and her skill as a poet. Thorup studied English for a while but then turned

to literary history. She also tried her hand at weaving, while continuing to write poetry. Her marriage to Ib lasted until 1974.

Thorup made her literary debut with a modernist collection of poems, *Indeni-udenfor: Digte* (Inside-Outside: Poems, 1967). Her poems seem driven by a need to find some kind of identity in vague, mysterious surroundings. Her fragmented images represent attempts to overcome the feeling of being trapped "inside" or "outside," as, for example, in one of Thorup's poems: "Vanskeligheden ved at beskrive / et bart umøbleret værelse / ligger i at man ikke kan / fastholde billedet af det / når man lukker øjnene" (The difficulty of describing / a bare unfurnished room / is because one can't / maintain the image of it / when one closes one's eyes); the poem continues: "Den der kan gøre / dette værelse betegnende / undslipper" (the one who can / describe this room / escapes). The poems in *Indeni-udenfor* are distinguished by Thorup's use of isolated objects or closely observed actions such as hand movements. Thorup transforms the familiar and the ordinary, bestowing new, even mysterious meanings upon them. Written with stylistic sophistication and self-assured originality, *Indeni-udenfor* focuses on feelings of alienation, the lack of identity, the need for and fear of contact, ambiguity, and nihilism.

Thorup's period of modernist experimentation includes a collection of short stories, *I dagens anledning* (In Honor of the Occasion, 1968), which consists of three short stories told in plain, unemotional style in which everyday details and events are separated from their normal context. The first story, "Festen" (The Feast), depicts unknown guests who are waiting for the "real" invitation to a wedding. As the story progresses, the wedding comes to symbolize something foreboding and absurd. In the next story a bride is spending her honeymoon alone while surrounded by the servants of a big house. Strange images—of the nail she keeps in her jewelry box, for example—convey her sense of alienation. Disconnected from any meaningful context, the images gain independent, symbolic value. The stories in *I dagens anledning* do not portray any specific society, but rather they comment on the human condition, reflecting the influence of the French modernists Michel Butor, Alain Robbe-Grillet, and Nathalie Sarraute. The last story of the collection, "Breve til en sagfører" (Letters to a Lawyer), consists of letters written from an institution by a sixteen-year-old boy to his lawyer; why the boy is confined and whether the lawyer really exists are unclear. The lack of a coherent picture and the vague information provided by the narrator underscore the helplessness of the boy. His captivity is also an inner one because he does not know or understand his situation. As a Danish literary critic described them, the images of Thorup's first period are "inexplicable, mysterious movements with a tropistic tendency."

Thorup's next literary phase consists of two collections of poetry, *Love from Trieste* (1969; translated, 1980), and *Idag er det Daisy* (It's Daisy Today, 1971). *Love from Trieste* is a montage of poetic texts centered around the Italian town of Trieste. Critics have pointed out that the two collections of poems are deeply influenced by psychiatrist R. D. Laing's ideas about the defense mechanisms of the schizophrenic. To protect themselves, the characters of the poems create "ufarlige idyller på snævre, kunstigt afgrænsede områder midt i en i øvrigt flydende, årsagssammenhængsløs og skræmmende verden" (harmless idylls within narrow, artificially limited areas in the midst of an otherwise fluid, causally disconnected and frightening world). The characters are often split into several figures, sometimes with just a letter for a name, in order to exemplify the divided mind of the schizophrenic. Other characters may only exist in the imagination of a protagonist, with the overall effect resembling a hall of mirrors.

The critic Torben Brostrøm described the narrative in *Idag er det Daisy* as "short prose pieces which are rather like laconic poems or fragments of a story which refuses to be put together properly." The characters are types, and reality is composed of momentary experiences. Thorup narrates in monotone the characters' disconnected, isolated, apparently meaningless actions and feelings. The matter-of-fact tone creates a semblance of normality that causes the reader to question his or her own sense of reality. Thorup's deliberately cool detachment from her subject matter is one of her hallmarks as a writer.

Thorup is interested in television and has also written screenplays. The visual medium attracts Thorup and serves her search for objectivity. However, Thorup's sense of the dramatic does not always translate well into visual images, and her plays tend to emphasize interaction between characters rather than a dramatic plot. Thorup's first television script was *Sæsonen slutter* (The Season Ends, 1970); she followed this television debut with several television plays about asocial, drifting, delinquent girls. In 1978 she wrote the television play *Else Kant,* the title character based on the protagonist of Norwegian author Amalie Skram's 1895 semi-autobiographical novels, *Professor Hieronimus* and *På Sct. Jørgen.* Skram's novels deal with oppressive social conditions leading women to madness and the highly vulnerable position of the female mental patient, which the author herself had

experienced. The story of Else Kant therefore clearly appealed to Thorup. Another play for Danish television, *Du er smuk, jeg elsker dig* (You Are Beautiful, I Love You, 1980), is about foreign workers who have not yet mastered Danish. With her awareness of language and her concern for social outsiders, Thorup is naturally interested in immigrants and their struggles to communicate and belong.

Thorup's novel *Baby* is considered her first major work. Critics selected it as the best Danish novel of the 1970s, earning Thorup the Pegasus Prize for Literature for 1979. *Baby* deals with marginalized people in an urban setting. The characters are jobless, are in debt, or prostitute themselves; they survive day to day, lingering in the moment, since they have no future. The first chapter takes place in a discotheque and introduces most of the main characters. At the center of the action is a car salesman, Marc, and his wife, Cadett; Marc "elskede Cadett lidenskabeligt som alt andet han ikke kunne undvære, lækkert tøj og øl og karbad" (loved Cadett passionately, like everything else he couldn't do without—good-looking clothes and beer and hot baths). He is watching a drag singer, Jolly Daisy, and talking with Suzie and Leni. He is attracted to Leni because she is tall and looks like a boy. Suzie, who is pregnant and wants an abortion, is hopelessly in love with David, who was "brought up to be happy" by his well-to-do father. A loan shark, Eddy, enters the disco and offers to loan Marc 1,000 kroner at a high rate of interest; Marc then buys a sandwich for a starving sixteen-year-old delinquent, Nova. Eddy still pursues his former wife, Leni. The novel follows these people through a series of loosely connected episodes. Marc and Cadett's marriage is ruined by financial problems; Cadett becomes a prostitute and falls under Eddy's power. Eddy also owns tenements, and one of his tenants, Karla—who is also David's mistress—loses one of her children because of the unsanitary conditions in the apartments. Nova travels with a girl named Sonja, who stabs a traveling salesman for his money; both girls are apprehended and sent to a women's detention center. There Nova attempts suicide when she discovers that Sonja has tried to seduce one of the supervisors. The characters disperse in all directions; all they hold in common seems to be their strong and continued ability to make bad choices.

While the characters in Thorup's poetry confront absurdity, the characters in *Baby* live in a clearly defined social hierarchy, in which their physical and mental suffering is directly related to their social condition. Their fixation on money is due to their poverty, and their obsession with nice things suggests a need for compensation. Thorup describes social dep-

KIRSTEN THORUP
Elskede ukendte

»Man bliver jublende rædselsslagen.
Elskede ukendte er en hjerteskærende
uhyggelig roman«
– *John Christian Jørgensen i Politiken*

gad

Cover for the 1995 paperback edition of Thorup's 1994 book, a
tragicomic novel about two madmen

rivation in a matter-of-fact, even monotonous tone. She presents her characters in terms of their social interaction, characterizing them through their actions (or, more often, their lack of action), their authentic dialogue, and their individual mannerisms. The narrator avoids interpreting her subjects by linking sentences with the conjunction *and,* creating a succession of disordered, disconnected observations and statements: "og det var meget varmt og der var en elektrisk vifte i loftet og Susi havde lyst til at danse og hun havde engang villet være korrespondent" (and it was very warm and there was an electric fan in the ceiling and Suzie felt like dancing and at one time she had wanted to be a foreign-language secretary). The run-on sentence structure and dispassionate tone avoid sentimentality but also suggest the characters' lack of any coherent vision or meaningful order. Socially powerless, Marc and the other characters live like babies in the pleasure-seeking immediacy of the present.

The translation of *Baby* was well received in America in 1980. In *TLS: The Times Literary Supplement* (30 January 1981) Mary Furness emphasized the focus on money in a book which she described as "totally humorless," adding that the "atmosphere of darkness" is "powerfully evoked by minute description of every detail." In the *Village Voice* Carl Bailey described *Baby* as a punk novel conforming to punk aesthetics. Although Bailey found the novel a little boring in its predictability and "bare bones language," he found the style persuasive: "The cadences here are hypnotic—surely 'and' has never been used more sinisterly—not only of sound but of meaning. The rhythm of information—the order in which the detail is supplied—is startling and original." He compared the rhythm of the narrative to punk music: "The beat of the prose . . . pounds like a pile driver, grating and monotonous at its worst, though more often with a strange underground energy."

Thorup's next two novels, *Lille Jonna* (Little Jonna, 1977) and *Den lange sommer* (The Long Summer, 1979), increased her popularity with the public. In these works Thorup shifts the setting from the city to the petit bourgeois milieu of a small provincial Danish town. The characters in these novels also differ from the city dwellers of *Baby* in that they are part of a family with cultural roots. Although this particular family lives in constant fear of degradation and experiences social decline, the parents remain devoted to one another and the family unit. The style in these novels is closer to traditional realism, although Thorup injects the narrative with her personal sense of humor and poetic passages. *Lille Jonna* deals with the title character's adolescence, and the events of the novel are seen through her perspective. The story begins when Jonna is ten years old. Her father is the manager of a farm, but he loses his job because of some mistakes. He becomes a traveling salesman, but the family loses its home and is forced by the local welfare department to move to the gym of the local public school. The plot of *Lille Jonna* climaxes with the description of Jonna's brother's confirmation dinner in the gym. Her mother, Betty, manages to prepare and serve a family feast on a limited budget; however, the ceremonious occasion is ruined when Jonna's father and brother end up in a fistfight. In the middle of this chaotic scene, the school teacher reveals his secret love for Betty. Jonna's two older brothers had left home prior to the confirmation. The charming Eyvind married a delicate woman of a higher social class. When his younger brother visits later on, Eyvind feels ashamed to introduce him to his in-laws. All of the family members suffer from social insecurity, and their failure to communicate with one another aggravates their problems.

When Betty learns that Eyvind has abandoned his first wife to marry a manager's daughter, she suffers a breakdown. Thorup's spokesperson for humanistic and moral values, Betty ends up in the same mental hospital where her daughter worked. At the end of the novel Jonna's simple, taciturn father leaves his daughter some notes he wrote when he worked as a traveling salesman. Jonna's parents exemplify a statement made by one of the patients at the mental hospital: "Ethvert menneske er større end det liv det lever" (Every individual is bigger than the life he lives). As did several other Scandinavian women writers before her, Thorup focuses on the so-called invisible people in society, those who do not count, and who often happen to be women.

In *Den lange sommer* Jonna's father has opened a bicycle shop, and with Betty's added income as a cleaning lady the family has been able to rent an apartment. Jonna is now sixteen and has finished middle school. During the summer she takes a job at a factory peeling asparagus, where she learns about the life and harsh realities of ordinary workers. She also works as an assistant at the local mental hospital, and she feels drawn toward the hospital. Jonna is confused about her identity and sinks into a lethargy, both a symptom of her insecurity and a means of self-protection: "Til tider tvivlede jeg på om jeg overhovedet eksisterede. Jeg var ligesom uden for alting, som om jeg befandt mig i en glasklokke. Det at blive voksen, var som at falde i en dyb søvn" (Sometimes I doubted if I even existed. It was like I was outside of everything, as if I were trapped inside of a glass jar. Growing up felt like falling into a deep slumber). The experience is similar to emotions depicted in the poems of *Indeni-udenfor.* Jonna's story is strongly autobiographical, if not in exact details then in terms of the experiences and emotions described. *Den lange sommer* portrays an important event in the author's own life, when Jonna continues her schooling beyond the level of any of her family members. Academically capable and interested in literature, Jonna abandons the nonliterary world of her family. Jonna does not feel at home or accepted in her new life; she feels as if she is "cut in two by a big axe."

The Jonna books are more traditional and less experimental than *Baby,* but the character portrayal is deeper and demonstrates a fine balance between slightly understated, realistic narrative and poetic language and dialogue. The speech of Jonna's parents suggests a sparse reality, interspersed with sudden aesthetic images. Jonna's parents are essentially nonverbal, but they become eloquent when they repeat traditional poems and proverbs. Thorup's implicit goal, in her poetry as well as in her novels, is to find truth in life through linguistic formulations.

Himmel og helvede (Heaven and Hell, 1982) and *Den yderste grænse* (The Extreme Limit, 1987) are large novels with female protagonists. *Himmel og helvede,* which served as the basis for a 1988 movie of the same title, is divided into two parts: the first deals with a middle-aged Miss Andersen, who works as a medical secretary until her supervisor, the doctor, closes his clinic. This unexpected event makes her realize that she has never been her own person but has always lived to serve others. She decides to begin a new life and catch up on what she missed. The first part of *Himmel og helvede* also deals with a young girl, Maria, a precocious violinist; with her parents' encouragement, Maria sacrifices her youth for a brilliant musical career. She finally rebels and moves in with her boyfriend, a charming waiter named Jonni. When Jonni reveals he has a secret life as a homosexual, Maria experiences a serious identity crisis. Like Jonna, she asks herself whether she is real. The second part of *Himmel og helvede* describes Maria's trip to England and her stay in a commune. Here, Maria has a terrifying experience on an LSD trip–another threat to her identity. Miss Andersen, on the other hand, becomes the madam of a brothel and learns to enjoy life. Maria returns to Copenhagen in the midst of the demonstrations of the 1960s and ends up marrying John, a cabdriver who happens to be one of Jonna's brothers.

Jonna, the narrator of the two novels, becomes the protagonist of the first half of *Den yderste grænse.* As a single mother and teacher, Jonna perseveres in spite of serious ups and downs and a constant sense of insecurity. She overcomes an identity crisis after the father of her child disappears. In spite of many small defeats and much confusion, Jonna maintains a vision of herself as a whole person, and the novel ends with her optimism about the future. Maria and John's marriage ends when Maria decides to return to her career as a violinist. She does not succeed in integrating her creative life with her work and family. Thorup ties her gallery of characters together at the end of *Den yderste grænse* when all of Jonna's family members gather to celebrate Betty's eighty-fifth birthday. The final chapter, "Ved begyndelsen" (At the Beginning), does not suggest that the family has found harmony; on the contrary, old conflicts remain. John gets into the usual fight with his father, and various family members maintain a cool distance. Eyvind's socially advantageous marriage creates the most tension: his stylish upper-class wife stands in glaring contrast to the old, limited, but authentic atmosphere of the family home. Yet, he remains his mother's favorite, because he is successful. Thorup's portrayal of ambition and hypocrisy is penetrating.

Thorup's interlinked slice-of-life stories depict working- and middle-class life in Denmark in the 1950s, 1960s, and 1970s. The author's description of society convincingly captures the problems faced by individuals. Thorup often uses a fairy-tale motif in her realistic descriptions and psychological portrayals. The vitality and indomitable nature of her characters suggest the spirit of the hero or heroine of the traditional fairy tale. Like those resourceful protagonists, Thorup's characters demonstrate a talent for survival that grows out of humble social origins. They are so vulnerable and have so little to lose that they become daring and adventuresome. Characters who lose their traditional moorings—for example, Miss Andersen and Maria's mother, Jasmine—sometimes behave eccentrically, almost recklessly. After his beloved Maria leaves him, John pulls himself together and envisions a life of limitless potential.

One literary critic concluded that "the message of Kirsten Thorup is that the oppressed, exploited and inarticulate masses will realize their power and change the world by removing capitalism." However, Thorup does not address the question of social change directly; her focus remains on individuals and their potential for personal change. The lack of a secure future teaches the characters to remake themselves. Miss Andersen "discards her old self" to start all over at the age of fifty-seven, and Eyvind "buries his old self" when he leaves his first wife. The characters' quest for identity is not that of the traditional bildungsroman, for they do not develop and mature gradually over a period of time. Instead, Thorup's characters suddenly transform into new people or find another persona in a complex of personalities. The author modifies the atomistic description of character in *Baby* but still retains it in her larger epics. In 1982 she received both the Kritikerprisen (Critics' Prize) and De Gyldne Laurbær (The Golden Laurels) for *Himmel og helvede*.

The core of Thorup's writing concerns the individual's perception of herself vis-à-vis her fellow human beings. In her early poetry Thorup examines the feelings of people trapped "inside" or "outside"; in the Jonna books the novelist explores a young girl's growing feeling of unreality; and in *Himmel og helvede* she uses Miss Andersen to warn against isolation from social interaction. In *Elskede ukendte* (Beloved Stranger, 1994) Thorup examines two extreme cases of social alienation. The two protagonists distance themselves from reality and finally

clash. Thorup partakes in the Danish literary legacy of dreamers and fantasists who end in madness, a motif that may be traced to such novels as Hans Egede Schack's *Fantasterne* (The Dreamers, 1857) and Henrik Pontoppidan's *Det forjættede land* (The Promised Land, 1895). In Pontoppidan's novel the protagonist suffers from messianic delusions similar to Rene's in *Elskede ukendte*.

In the first part of *Elskede ukendte* Rene falsifies his grades so that he can enter the University of Copenhagen to study law. Although he previously did well as a student, he will not run the risk of living a reality different from his wishes. He has thereby set himself outside of the social norm, a circumstance aggravated when he is discovered and expelled from the university. He declines socially and morally and is finally picked up by Karl, who wants to save him.

Part two of *Elskede ukendte* focuses on Karl, who was adopted by a well-to-do wine importer, Otto Valentin. Otto's wife is a painter who lives for her art and leaves the family for extended work periods. Karl, whose previous name was Ronnie, has an ambiguous relationship to his adopted wealthy milieu. He feels he does not belong with the upper class. He rebels and leads a dissolute life as a playboy in Copenhagen until he meets Connie, whose family belongs to the Pentecostal movement. Karl is attracted to the purity and sincerity of the religion, although it conflicts with his own sensuous nature. Not surprisingly, his marriage to Connie turns into a disaster, based more on Karl's wishful thinking than on reality. Connie does not respond to Karl's sexuality, and her conventionality and materialism are antinomic to Karl's desired spirituality. When Karl's father retires and Karl is supposed to take over the wine import business, he effectively destroys it. Karl is then forced into a mental hospital but escapes by pretending to be its authoritarian manager.

At this point Karl's story merges with Rene's. Karl takes Rene to his old playboy apartment, which he now uses to "save souls" as a means of alleviating his inferiority complex. Rene has a similar need after his defeat by society. Karl's treatment and Bible reading awaken within Rene a belief that he is Jesus. Karl's manipulations have led to the creation of an arrogance and megalomania even greater than his own. In the third part of the novel the two men's desire to save each other turns into a comical power struggle. Karl takes Rene out to sea in his yacht in order to finalize Rene's transformation in the midst of "God's elements." Here, apocalyptic, tragicomic encounters take place. In the end the two abandon their delusions and Rene gets a job as Santa Claus at Christmastime. Throughout the novel Thorup sustains this fantastic plot with fine psychological descriptions and humor.

To some critics *Elskede ukendte* is the comprehensive, contemporary social novel Danish literature needed. Although *Elskede ukendte* embraces descriptions of diverse classes, Thorup's focus on Karl's and Rene's distorted perceptions shifts the emphasis away from society toward the delusions of two madmen. While the novel manages to explain how the two men became disconnected from their social context, the goal of the narrative seems to be to portray madness in the extended climactic scenes of life and death. Thorup's work remains focused on the characters' perception of their surroundings rather than on the surroundings themselves. In this regard, Thorup's body of work is remarkably consistent in its orientation.

Thorup remains true to her interest in identity problems and in the experience of social outsiders in *Projekt paradis,* first performed in 1996. The play was developed out of interviews with thirty-five Danish immigrants and refugees who live between cultures. Thorup dramatizes that the immigrant and the native have more in common than the cultural features that separate them, but she also asserts that "there is much energy in being foreign."

Indeed, it seems that much of Thorup's creative energy originates from her own experience as an outsider. Her interest in the psychological effects of social marginalization has remained a constant of her literary career. Despite the often-noted cool detachment her fiction exhibits, her novels, especially the Jonna books and *Himmel og helvede,* suggest an equally distinctive commitment to social justice.

References:

Torben Brostrøm, "Kirsten Thorup: It's Thorup Today," in *Out of Denmark: Isak Dinesen/Karen Blixen (1885–1985) and Danish Women Writers Today,* edited by Bodil Wamberg (Copenhagen: Danish Cultural Institute, 1985), pp. 63–76;

Charlotte S. Gray, "Identity and Narrative Structure in Kirsten Thorup's Novels," *Scandinavian Studies,* 63, no. 2 (1991): 214–220;

Marie-Louise Paludan, "Kirsten Thorup," in *Danske digtere i det 20 århundrede,* 5 volumes, edited by Brostrøm and Mette Winge (Copenhagen: Gad, 1982), V: 259–267.

Dorrit Willumsen

(31 August 1940 –   )

Anne-Marie Mai
University of Odense

Translated by Tiina Nunnally

BOOKS: *Knagen: Noveller* (Copenhagen: Gyldendal, 1965)–includes "Komplication," translated by Paula Hostrup-Jessen as "Complication," in *The Devil's Instrument and Other Danish Stories,* edited by Sven Holm (London: Peter Owen / Copenhagen: Hans Reitzel, 1971), pp. 187–191;

Stranden (Copenhagen: Gyldendal, 1967);

Da (Copenhagen: Gyldendal, 1968);

The, krydderi, acryl, salær, græshopper (Copenhagen: Gyldendal, 1970);

Modellen Coppelia (Copenhagen: Gyldendal, 1973);

En værtindes smil (Copenhagen: Gyldendal, 1974);

Kontakter: Digte (Copenhagen: Gyldendal, 1976);

Neonhaven: Roman (Copenhagen: Gyldendal, 1976);

Hvis det virkelig var en film: Noveller (Copenhagen: Gyldendal, 1978); translated by Anne Marie Rasmussen as *If It Really Were a Film* (Willimantic, Conn.: Curbstone Press, 1982);

Manden som påskud (Copenhagen: Vindrose, 1980);

Programmeret til kærlighed (Copenhagen: Vindrose, 1981)– includes "Skæbelsen af Bianca," translated by Paula Hostrup-Jessen as "The Creation of Bianca," in *No Man's Land: An Anthology of Modern Danish Women's Literature,* edited and with an introduction by Annegret Heitmann (Norwich: Norvik Press, 1987), pp. 165–177;

Ni liv: Udvalgte noveller, edited by Line Schmidt-Madsen (Copenhagen: Vindrose, 1982);

Umage par: Digte (Copenhagen: Vindrose, 1983);

Marie: En roman om Madame Tussauds liv (Copenhagen: Vindrose, 1983); translated by Patricia Crampton as *Marie: A Novel About the Life of Madame Tussaud* (London: Bodley Head, 1986);

Suk hjerte (Copenhagen: Vindrose, 1986);

Caroline: Skuespil i to akter (Århus: Arkona, 1987);

Glemslens forår: Noveller (Copenhagen: Vindrose, 1988);

Klædt i purpur (Copenhagen: Gyldendal, 1990);

Dorrit Willumsen (photograph by Elisabeth Ronde Kristensen; courtesy of Gyldendal Publishers)

Bang: En roman om Herman Bang (Copenhagen: Gyldendal, 1996);

De kattens feriedage: En fortælling, illustrated by Lars Pugholm (Copenhagen: Gyldendal, 1997).

PLAY PRODUCTIONS: *Caroline,* Århus Theatre, September 1985;

Margrethe I, Copenhagen, Grønnegaard Theatre, 7 September 1991.

TELEVISION: *Børn,* series, scripts for three episodes by Willumsen and Sten Kaalø, *TV-Theatre,* Danmarks Radio 1; 21, 23, and 26 February 1982.

RADIO: *Jomfru åben for kontakt,* script by Willumsen, *Radioteatret,* Danmarks Radio, 21 September 1970;

På en grøn bænk, script by Willumsen, *Radioteatret,* Danmarks Radio, 3 April 1972;

For slet ikke at tale om Marcia, script by Willumsen, *Radioteatret,* Danmarks Radio, 21 January 1974;

På grund af Karina, script by Willumsen, *Radioteatret,* Danmarks Radio, 4 August 1975;

Ud af billedet, script by Willumsen, *Radioteatret,* Danmarks Radio, 24 August 1992;

Sålænge smerten er usynlig, script by Willumsen, *Radioteatret,* Danmarks Radio, 27 September 1993.

OTHER: "Jomfru åben for kontakt," in *Dansk Radio-dramatik,* volume 4, edited by Jørgen Claudi (Copenhagen: Forlaget Fremad, 1971), pp. 203–238;

"Alt på betingelse" and "Martas genopvækkelse," in *Bibelhistorier fortalt af danske forfattere,* edited by Mogens Hansen (Copenhagen: Haase, 1979), pp. 113–120;

"Puds ham elskede" in *Den sorte rose. Seksten beretninger om ulykkelig kærlighed,* edited by Bodil Wamberg (Århus: Centrum, 1984), pp. 76–84;

Karin Michaëlis, *Den farlige Alder,* third edition, with an afterword by Willumsen (Copenhagen: Gyldendal, 1987), pp. 207–216.

Modernism was a well-established and much-discussed trend in Danish postwar literature by the time Dorrit Willumsen made her debut in 1965 with *Knagen: Noveller* (The Peg: Stories). These short stories, with their themes of alienation and their criticism of modern life, were well in keeping with the concerns of experimental literature. At the same time, it was evident that the young author had something new to contribute, in terms of both style and theme. The stories in *Knagen* exposed specific aspects of alienation and reification in the welfare society, especially because Willumsen used the point of view of both women and children in a surprisingly new way. The attempt of modernist literature to articulate gender, the body, and the unconscious became an important catalyst for those few, but artistically significant, female modernists in Danish literature during the 1960s. As an author, Willumsen won a place at the forefront among both her male and female contemporaries. Since the publication of her first book, she

has added poems, short stories, plays, memoirs, and novels to her long list of published works. While her early books found an audience and won renown among well-educated readers and scholars of modernist literature, her later works have reached a much wider audience. This increased popularity is particularly true of Willumsen's historical novels, in which plot plays a more prominent role than in her earlier works. Although female forms of experience are of central concern to Willumsen, her work cannot be pigeonholed as specifically feminist. Her complex stories about modern life, with their expressive metaphors and fragmented images, defy any attempt at synthesis; instead, her texts reveal the many repressed and painful aspects of modern life, the unbearable longing for love, and the modern sense of loss.

Dorrit Willumsen was born in Copenhagen on 31 August 1940, the daughter of opera singer Kaj Willumsen and Lillian F. Johansen. Willumsen was five years old when World War II ended, and she finished her secondary education in 1960. In 1963 Willumsen married thirty-one-year-old Jess Ørnsbo, who was studying Slavic literature and languages and already had made his literary debut in 1960 with his modernist collection *Digte* (Poems). After living in Copenhagen for several years, the couple moved to the small provincial town of Viby on Sjælland, where a modern suburban neighborhood became the backdrop for the family's life. Their large house had ample room for plants, fish, and two hardworking authors, although they both continued to maintain offices in Copenhagen. Their son, Tore Ørnsbo, was born in 1970, and he in turn made his literary debut in 1997 with the poetry collection *Inkubationer* (Incubations), which has won him much praise.

Willumsen's childhood and adolescence came during a time in which great changes occurred in Danish society. There was a dramatic contrast between the economic and material deprivations of the 1950s and the rapid buildup of an urbanized welfare society in the 1960s. The loss of tradition and of a sense of historical continuity was felt across a wide spectrum of society as Danish agriculture was reorganized and mechanized and a growing percentage of the workforce instead found jobs in the industrial and service sectors.

Knagen opens with a novella titled "Lukket land" (Closed Territory), which starts with a list of everyday inanimate objects that activate the childlike imagination and the ability to experience life. The collection concludes with a tale titled "Svangerskab" (Pregnanacy). This story was extremely unusual for the time because it contained sensual and metaphorical descriptions of the female body, rather than the customary images of

Willumsen in 1965 (photograph by Gregers Nielsen)

the "sweet maternity period" and "the expectant mother in a charming maternity dress."

The break with tradition that results from modern development is one of the themes in Willumsen's autobiographical novel *Da* (Back Then, 1968). It is partially based on her own childhood memories and her close relationship with her grandfather, H. F. Johansen, who died in 1965. The novel presents a strong portrait of a little girl's childhood spent with her maternal grandparents, in whose care she has been placed by her mother. The focus of the novel, however, is not only on the child-narrator's description of her pain over her mother's absence or her story of the good life she shares with her grandparents, whose lives and memories have their roots in a premodern era. It is typical of Willumsen's work that the story of the child-narrator becomes a medium for her grandfather's reminiscences about his own childhood and the family's past, for bits and pieces from "back then." The narrative technique itself links memory to art and to the child's capacity for experiencing life. The modern world can only offer a loss of certainty and a constant sense of pain and discord, but the child's linguistic imagination and desire to formulate her reality contain an indomitable vitality. Even though the story cannot establish any type of coherence in modern life, art and the child's imagination can shape "back then" into vibrant material, accessible here and now, even for the discordant adult consciousness. Art confronts the adult with the tremen-

dous linguistic and experiential energy possessed by the child.

The reminiscences and narrative of *Da* provide an important foundation for Willumsen's thematic interest in modern conditions, in the mechanisms of repression in adult life, and in the sources and power of art. The depiction of a child and the use of a child as the narrator or as the bearer of the narrative point of view occurs repeatedly in her work, and she often focuses on the specific moment when the child is forced to give up her illusions.

A recurrent image in Willumsen's description of women and children is the doll metaphor, which appears in various forms throughout her work. The doll represents a deadly narcissism, which is associated with a modern female psyche. Incapable of drawing boundaries between themselves and the world, girls and women are psychologically locked into a complex of anxiety, guilt, and aggression—the origin and object of which cannot be pinpointed—and thus these elements attack the fragile psyche from all sides. The ego becomes both all-powerful and impotent in its self-reflections—its attempts to protect itself from an overwhelming environment and to confirm its own existence. The experience of gender in general and female sexuality in particular threatens the unstable order and balance of the narcissistic universe; the doll becomes a metaphor for the psychological paralysis to which the female narcissist is relegated.

A counterpart to the lifeless doll-woman is the all-consuming monster mother, a figure that is also related to psychological narcissism and its origin in the symbiosis between mother and child. The novel *Stranden* (The Shore, 1967), which was Willumsen's second work to be published, focuses on a man's nervous breakdown brought about by the unrelenting grip of his domineering mother. The male protagonist tries to flee from this psychological dilemma, seeking the bare white beaches and glaring, revealing sunlight of the south. But he is only able to evade the enforced maternal symbiosis through the destructive disintegration of schizophrenia. Another male form of self-destruction is thematically portrayed in the novels *The, krydderi, acryl, salær, græshopper* (Tea, Spices, Acrylic, Fee, Grasshopper, 1970) and *Neonhaven: Roman* (The Neon Garden: Novel, 1976). In these works, the male protagonists are devoured by their hideous fantasies and they end up as suicides, while the women become monsters and zombies in the modern narcissistic nightmare. Characters from earlier books reappear in various situations and at different ages. For instance, the young doll-girl Ivy Yvonne, who as a child ate a doll and swallowed its eyes, makes another appearance in both the novel *The, krydderi, acryl, salær, græshopper* and in the story collection *Modellen Coppelia* (The Model Coppelia, 1973).

There is a truly terrifying gap between the underplayed, restrained style that Willumsen uses in her early prose and the shocking dimensions of psychological breakdown, painful repression, and self-annihilation the works reveal. There are elements of both orality and lyrical rhythm in Willumsen's prose. Her metaphors evoke the concrete and the sensual for the reader; her use of metaphors often stems from a child's concrete and literal understanding of the routine, everyday language of adults. This creates a kind of double metaphor, which exposes the psychologically conflicted material of the imagery. Typical of Willumsen's work is the way she demonstrates how the use of metaphors creates existential structures and locks her characters into the patterns of destruction and narcissism. In the short story "Voksdukken" (translated as "The Wax Puppet") from the collection *Hvis det virkelig var en film: Noveller* (1978; translated as *If It Really Were a Film,* 1982), the experience of coldness between the parents and the soft, swaddled baby become existential metaphors that structure a young woman's lust for the dead and cold wax-puppet man (who is the only character in the story with a name). The young, newly married woman murders her husband, who reminds her of both her sex and her mortality. She indirectly

attributes the murder to the wax puppet because his cool lemon scent fills the bridal room. Together with the wax puppet, the narrative "I" has constant access to her baby life and oral satisfaction, a time when her mouth was filled with milk, ice cream, and candy; at the same time, the bed, which is covered with furry animals and soft comforters, resembles a womb.

The novel *Manden som påskud* (The Man as Pretense, 1980) marked a breakthrough in Willumsen's literary career. By the time the book was published, the debate about gender roles and the concerns of the women's movement had already reached a wide audience, but the novel gave the discussion a new perspective. *Manden som påskud* was exceptional because it provided a complex portrait of the modern relationship between the sexes and attempted to encompass the male, female, and child's point of view.

The women in the novel all have a relationship to an unnamed man who dies in a traffic accident. The reader meets his present wife, his former wife, his two daughters, and his lover. All of these women attribute both their happiness and their unhappiness to the man, and they use him as a pretext for their passivity and their dreams—but also for their attempts to escape the restrictions of modern life. By the time his wife, Lisa, finally decides to leave her stifling suburban life and abandon the material security her marriage has provided, the man is already dead. Her fantasy that things would be much easier if he were dead becomes reality, even though she is unaware of it. In the novel Willumsen does not idealize the female need for liberation nor male self-righteousness; instead, she provides a nuanced picture of the restraints, repression, and self-annihilation that are part of the relationship between the sexes.

The fragile Lisa, who feels as if she were dead in her relationship with her husband, has clearly shut him out of her emotional relationship with their daughter. His restlessness and search for security have, in turn, made him spineless in his relations with his lover, Marianne. Marianne wants to get out of the relationship but continues to cling to him with her romantic secret meetings, clean sheets, and expensive perfumes. When Marianne finally sends the man a farewell letter, which his wife reads, it is highly ambiguous. Lisa feels insulted on her husband's behalf because of the discreetly cool tone of the letter and Marianne's poorly disguised demand to "forføre hende uden hendes viden" (seduce her without her knowledge). The shifting points of view in the novel create an interplay of mirrored images that reveal much about the characters, which is apparent in the sardonic confrontation between Marianne's grandiloquent idealization of intercourse and the man's blunt interpretation of her always perfectly washed body and genitals: "som var hendes egentlige partner et bidet" (as if her real partner were a bidet). The long, sensual descriptions occasionally form lyrical passages, and everyday scenes become charged with significance and bodily metaphors. For instance, in the opening scene, when Lisa is preparing escargots for the couple's twelfth wedding anniversary, she feels both repulsed and fascinated as she neatly and carefully stuffs the small, soft, dead animals into their shells. *Manden som påskud* is an example of the artistic power and new prose style present in the works of many women writers in the early 1980s.

Following her success with this novel, Willumsen published more poems, novels, short stories, and plays. The novel *Programmeret til kærlighed* (Programmed for Love, 1981) is a mythical, futuristic vision about the scientist Liv, who creates a female robot she thinks will be able to satisfy all the demands a man might have for a perfect woman. She sends her wonderful monster out to seduce the man whom she herself cannot have. But when the chosen man's dreams are fulfilled, it quickly becomes evident that he has ended up at the mercy of his own overwhelming sense of anxiety, emptiness, and self-loathing. Both the story of Frankenstein and the myth of Orpheus and Eurydice are intertwined with the depiction in the novel of the dishonest and desperate relationships men and women have with each other, with themselves, and with their ideals, expectations, and reality itself. The final scene is a symbolic encounter between the characters in "the house of the dead," which is a metaphor for the human body. In the house of the dead the robot falls apart. Willumsen intends this encounter between the mortal body and the experience of the conditions of death to give the sexes a chance to reach each other and strip away emotional coldness.

In the 1980s Willumsen began to work with the historical novel, as did many other Danish authors during the 1970s and 1980s. Henrik Stangerup and Thorkild Hansen, for example, used the genre to depict the world and modern life in epic prose narratives that were based on historical subjects, authentic documents, and colorful personalities. Some women authors such as Mette Winge, Helle Stangerup, and Jytte Borberg attempted to use the historical novel to bring to life the suppressed and forgotten stories of women's lives and work.

The fascinating protagonist of Willumsen's *Marie: En roman om Madame Tussauds liv* (1983; translated as *Marie: A Novel About the Life of Madame Tus-*

Cover for Willumsen's 1981 science-fiction novel, about a woman scientist who creates a female robot programmed to seduce the man she cannot have

saud, 1986) is the famous Madame Tussaud, creator of the wax museum that bears her name. The novel follows her entire life, from childhood until death. This electrifying story, which begins during the French Revolution and ends in Victorian England, marks a high point in Willumsen's literary production. Willumsen emphasizes the refined detail, delicacy, and courtly discipline of the Rococo era in depictions of the outmoded and doomed aristocratic life—and contrasts these ideals with the violence and unrestrained sensual pursuits of the Revolutionary era. As a young girl, Marie Tussaud learns the art of making wax models, and she founds her famous wax cabinet by making death masks of the aristocrats and royalty who die on the guillotine. She is a modern career woman who frees herself from her husband and fights for her right to make decisions about her

Dust jacket for Willumsen's 1996 novel, based on the life of the nineteenth-century Danish author Herman Bang

own life and business endeavors. She is also depicted as a sensitive and developing artist who never ceases in her attempt to express all aspects of human life. Inherent in her art are the element of horror and the necessity for crossing social boundaries, both of which become themes in the depiction of Marie's work with the severed heads and death masks. The artist's fascination with sensual details, as well as her terror-filled respect for the dead, force any feeling of revulsion or guilt into the background. Marie feels she is succeeding as an artist and that the death mask is the most honest and authentic expression of the personalities of the deceased. This is especially true of Jean-Paul Marat's mask, which Marie makes after he is found murdered in his bath. The hideousness of the man is striking, but he is as open and defenseless as a flower, Marie thinks. His death mask looks light and simple, with a waxen and open gaze.

Willumsen depicts Marie's success as coming at great costs. It affects her relationship to her children, especially her youngest son, whom she leaves behind in France when she moves to London. Marie is also forced to make artistic compromises so that the wax cabinet will satisfy the wishes of the public, hungry for sensationalism. The fine art of sculpting in wax becomes framed with frills and glitter, and the Lon-

don gallery becomes a "virtual reality" setting, where both lowly seamstresses and citizens at the highest level of society can ogle precious jewels, royal finery, and grand drama. The gallery is a dreamworld of mirrors and lacework, which for a moment erases all social differences among the spectators. To a great extent, the themes of the novel explicate Willumsen's own experiences with the creative process, the power of illusion, and the seductive dream of beauty, as well as her fascination with various materials and sounds, sights, and smells of the physical world. The first chapters, in particular, which are set in the court at Versailles, offer beautiful tableaux in which the physical body, desire, and death suddenly appear behind the rich silks, the floral arrangements, the makeup, and the elegant manner of speaking. The doll metaphor from earlier works now takes on a new and different significance. The dolls are not associated with female emotional infantilism or narcissism; instead they are tied to the young woman's zealous attempts to master her world. The dolls become a manifestation of the beauty, extreme sensitivity, and icy callousness that are all part of Marie's artistic work.

In the novel *Suk hjerte* (Sigh Heart, 1986), Willumsen turns her attention to recent history and the Danish milieu. The novel is the story of several generations, played out in a Copenhagen working-class neighborhood, which runs from the 1930s until the mid 1980s. The lives of three women reveal the negative aspects inherent in the development of the welfare society: a loss of culture and community, and a growing sense of coldness and alienation among the people. Again, the female point of view is used to expose the alienating mechanisms of modern life.

In her next novel, *Klædt i purpur* (Dressed in Purple, 1990), Willumsen turns to ancient history and uses the life story of the exotic Empress Theodora as her motif. Theodora has led a shady existence as a proletarian, prostitute, and dancer before she became the wife of Emperor Justinian. She succeeds in making herself the ruler in her own official story, and she invests everything in her career and reign. As a ruler, she recognizes the value of being mysterious, notorious, and the subject of constant discussion in wide circles. This short historical novel can be read as an allegory for a modern, powerful woman—someone who is an effective self-promoter and fearless image creator, who uses her body and sex to benefit her career, and who knows how to hold onto power. Yet, at the same time, the empress paradoxically preserves a certain innocence and sincerity. Intertwined with the portrait of the powerful empress, Willumsen uses elegant metaphors drawn from mosaics, fabrics, gemstones, and colors to represent various forms of self-control.

Following a series of plays and radio dramas, Willumsen's next novel, *Bang,* published in 1996, depicts the life of the renowned Danish author Herman Bang (1857-1912). The book was originally planned as a biography, to be based on Bang's letters, notes, and his own descriptions of his childhood. Willumsen found, however, that she had to fictionalize the account in order to get closer to Bang's private life as an artist. Bang's groundbreaking novels and short stories marked a clear transition between nineteenth- and twentieth-century literary trends in Denmark; he was one of the first writers to introduce realism and impressionism into Scandinavian fiction. He was a journalist as well as an author, and he created an entirely new and quite lively style of reporting. Because he was a homosexual, he was sometimes treated harshly, so he often fled abroad. Bang's wandering existence, his bohemian life in the capital cities of Europe, his loneliness, his disappointments in love, and his artistic genius all provide material for Willumsen's novel, in which fictional scenes are juxtaposed with authentic letters and documents. When *Bang* was awarded the prestigious Nordic Council Literary Prize in 1997, a fierce controversy about this decision arose in Norway. A well-known publisher and a Bang scholar, himself homosexual, both strongly criticized the blending of fictional and authentic materials in the novel, and they objected to Willumsen's portrait of Bang in general. The novel was called a "bastard" and "illicit." These types of derogatory labels clearly demonstrated that Willumsen, as a female author, had transgressed certain norms and boundaries. In interviews published in Norway, the critics emphasized that Willumsen had asserted her own interpretations of Bang's biography. In a heated debate, reminiscent of the *Processen Mod Hamsun* (The Case Against Hamsun) of 1978 that was fueled by Thorkild Hansen's controversial work, it was demonstrated that the modern documentary genre—with its merging of facts and fiction—was still capable of offending the Norwegians. However, in the other Nordic countries, the novel was well received by the critics, and it found a wide audience.

A close study of her style in the novel shows how Willumsen created a distinctive form of prose. She confronts the familiar universe and the portrait of the amenable individual, which were known from nineteenth-century Danish Biedermeier literature, with her own revealing, modernist metaphors. Elements of Bang's subtle, intense impressionism and his almost cinematic narrative style also inspire Willumsen's style, creating a restless and nervous sort of prose, which captures the complexity of Bang's artistic temperament. Willumsen's portrait of Bang shows him to be a modern European artist, dependent on publishers, sales figures, and readers. He is a man who is good at promoting himself in the media, but who is also true to his own ideas and artistic instincts. He is surrounded by admirers and enemies, and yet he is always alone—even in death, which occurs on a lecture tour in the United States. Willumsen's incisive and sensual prose depicts Bang's torturous experience of the American urban jungle:

> Biler tudende som ulve strøg gennem gaderne. Der var huse som klipper i et mærkeligt rosa lys, pudret og strålende af gadelygter og reklamers vulgære simili. Den by var lige til besvimelse og krampe. Da han endelig kom op på værelset og ville tænde lyset, begyndte en propel i loftet at snurre rundt. En iskold blæst rev notaterne til rejsebrevet fra ham, og mens han kravlede rundt på gulvet for at fange dem, ringede telefonen. Og han, der så godt som aldrig talte i telefon, måtte løfte røret for at få den til at holde op med at ringe og lytte til en stemme han ikke forstod.

(Cars howling like wolves raced through the streets. There were buildings resembling cliffs in a peculiar pink light, powdered and luminous from streetlamps and the vulgar, artificial glare of advertisements. The city was enough to make a man dizzy and nauseated. When he finally reached his room and tried to turn on the light, a propeller in the ceiling began spinning around. An icy-cold blast tore the notes for his travel article out of his hand. While he crawled around on the floor, gathering up the pages, the telephone rang. And he, who almost never used a telephone, had to lift the receiver in order to make it stop ringing and listen to a voice that he didn't understand.)

Willumsen has been honored with many awards and prizes for her extensive literary work. In 1981 she was the first woman to receive the prestigious Grand Prize of Det Danske Akademi (The Danish Academy). She was also the first Danish female author to receive the Nordic Council's Literary Prize. In the context of contemporary Nordic literature, she is considered one of the most exciting and innovative authors. Her narratives describe the losses and alienation of modern life and the artificial world to which humankind has been consigned.

In Willumsen's fiction, the world's beauty is cruel and ice-cold; but at the same time, like a mosaic, the image is constantly changing, and a subtle and liberating sense of humor casts a wondrous and humane light on her narratives.

References:

Stig Dalager and Anne-Marie Mai, "Kvindelige modernister," in *Danske kvindelige forfattere: Fra Adda Ravnkilde til Kirsten Thorup,* volume 2 (Copenhagen: Gyldendal, 1982), pp. 123–136;

Maria Davidsen, "Frihed uden ansigt–om Dorrit Willumsens *Marie,* 1983," in *Prosa fra 80'erne til 90'erne,* edited by Mai (Copenhagen: Borgens Forlag, 1994), pp. 116–128;

Anne Birgitte Richard, *På sporet af den tabte hverdag: Om Dorrit Willumsens forfatterskab og den moderne virkelighed* (Copenhagen: Gyldendal, 1979);

Richard, "Livet som ting," in *Nordisk kvindelitteraturhistorie,* volume 4, edited by Elisabeth Møller Jensen and others (Copenhagen: Rosinante, 1997), pp. 123–129;

Sven H. Rossel, *A History of Danish Literature* (Lincoln: University of Nebraska Press, 1992), pp. 478–480;

Maria Schottenius, "A Foggy Dream Landscape. Dorrit Willumsen: *Bang.* A Novel About Herman Bang," *Nordic Literature* (1997): 16–17;

Bodil Wamberg, "Dorrit Willumsen," in *Danske digtere i det 20. århundrede,* volume 5, edited by Torben Brostrøm and Mette Winge (Copenhagen: Gads Forlag, 1982), pp. 244–259;

Carl Otte Werkelid, "Dorrit Willumsen's Prize-Winning Novel about Herman Bang," *Danish Literary Magazine,* 11 (Spring 1997): 4–5.

Books for Further Reading

Barlyng, Marianne, and Søren Schou. *Københavner romaner*. Copenhagen: Borgen, 1996.

Bay, Carl Erik, and John Christian Jørgensen, eds. *Litteratur og samfund i mellemkrigstiden: Litteratursociologiske studier*. Copenhagen: Gyldendal, 1979.

Billeskov Jansen, F. J., and P. M. Mitchell, eds. *Anthology of Danish Literature*. Carbondale: Southern Illinois University Press, 1972.

Bjørnvig, Thorkild. *Digtere*. Copenhagen: Gyldendal, 1991.

Borum, Poul. *Danish Literature: A Short Critical Survey*. Copenhagen: Det danske Selskab, 1979.

Brandt, Jørgen Gustava. *Præsentation: 40 danske digtere efter krigen*. Copenhagen: Gyldendal, 1964.

Brandt and Asger Schnack. *80 moderne danske digtere: Præsentation og portræt*. Copenhagen: Gyldendal, 1988.

Bredsdorff, Elias. *Danish Literature in English Translation, with a Special Hans Christian Andersen Supplement: A Bibliography*. Copenhagen: Munksgaard, 1950.

Bredsdorff, ed. *Contemporary Danish Plays: An Anthology*. Copenhagen: Gyldendal / London: Thames & Hudson, 1955.

Bredsdorff, ed. *Contemporary Danish Prose*. Copenhagen: Gyldendal, 1958.

Bredsdorff, Thomas. *Sære fortællere: Hovedtræk af den ny danske prosakunst i tiåret omkirng 1960,* enlarged edition. Copenhagen: Gyldendal, 1968.

Bredsdorff and others, eds. *Bogens virkelighed*. Copenhagen: Gyldendal, 1999.

Brønsted, Mogens, and Sven Møller Kristensen. *Danmarks litteratur,* second edition, 2 volumes. Copenhagen: Gyldendal, 1975–1976.

Brostrøm, Torben. *Fantasi og dokument: Litteraturen og firserne*. Copenhagen: Gyldendal, 1984.

Brostrøm. *Den ny åbenhed: 1970ernes brugslitteratur*. Copenhagen: Berlingske Forlag, 1981.

Brostrøm and Mette Winge, eds. *Danske digtere i det 20. århundrede,* third edition, 5 volumes. Copenhagen: Gad, 1980–1984.

Cedergreen Bech, Sven, ed. *Dansk biografisk leksikon,* third edition, 16 volumes. Copenhagen: Gyldendal, 1979–1984.

Christensen, Robert Zola, and Gorm Larsen. *Moderne dansk prosa: Teksthistorisk beskrivelse og antologi*. Lund: Studentlitteratur, 1997.

Clareus, Ingrid, ed. *Scandinavian Women Writers: An Anthology from the 1880s to the 1980s*. Westport, Conn.: Greenwood Press, 1989.

Claudi, Jørgen. *Contemporary Danish Authors*. Copenhagen: Det Danske Selskab, 1952.

Dahl, Svend, and Povl Engelstoft, eds. *Dansk skønlitterært forfatterleksikon 1900–1950,* 3 volumes. Copenhagen: Grønholt Pedersens Forlag, 1959–1964.

Dalager, Stig, and Anne-Marie Mai. *Danske kvindelige forfattere: Udvikling og perspektiv,* 2 volumes. Copenhagen: Gyldendal, 1982.

Dansk litteraturhistorie, 9 volumes. Copenhagen: Gyldendal, 1983–1985.

Engelstoft, Povl, and Sven Dahl, eds. *Dansk biografisk Leksikon,* second edition, 27 volumes. Copenhagen: J. H. Schultz, 1933–1944.

Frandsen, Ernst, and Niels Kaas Johansen, eds. *Danske digtere i det 20. århundrede,* 2 volumes. Copenhagen: Gad, 1951.

Franzén, Lars-Olof. *Punktnedslag i Dansk litteratur 1880–1970*. Copenhagen: Lindhardt & Ringhof, 1971.

Hansen, Ib Fischer, Jens Anker Jørgensen, Knud Michelsen, Jørgen Sørensen, and Lars Tonnesen, eds. *Litteratur Håndbogen,* fifth edition, 2 volumes. Copenhagen: Gyldendal, 1996.

Harmer, Henning, and Thomas Jørgensen, eds. *Gyldendals litteraturleksikon,* 4 volumes. Copenhagen: Gyldendal, 1974.

Heepe, Evelyn, and Niels Heltberg, eds. *Modern Danish Authors*. Copenhagen & Chicago: Scandinavian Publishing, 1946.

Heitmann, Annegret, ed. *No Man's Land: An Anthology of Modern Danish Women's Literature*. Norwich, U.K.: Norvik, 1987.

Hertel, Hans, ed. *Tilbageblik på 30erne: Litteratur, teater, kulturdebat 1930–39: En antologie,* second edition, 2 volumes. Copenhagen: Stig Vendelkær, 1967.

Hjordt-Vetlesen, Inger-Lise, and Finn Frederik Krarup, eds. *Laesninger i dansk litteratur 1900–1940,* volume 3. Odense: Odense University Press, 1997.

Holm, Sven, ed. *The Devil's Instrument, and Other Danish Stories*. Copenhagen: Hans Reitzel / London: Owen, 1971.

Holmberg, Hans. *Fra Klaus Høeck til Karen Blixen: Interviews, Portrætter, Biografier*. Copenhagen: Hernov, 1981.

Holmgaard, Jørgen. *Analyser af danske romaner,* 3 volumes. Copenhagen: Borgen, 1977.

Ingwersen, Niels, ed. *Seventeen Danish Poets: A Bilingual Anthology of Contemporary Danish Poetry*. Lincoln, Neb.: Windflower Press, 1981.

Jensen, Bernard Eric, and others. *Danmarkshistorier: En erindringspolitisk slagmark,* 2 volumes. Frederiksberg: Roskilde University Press, 1997.

Jensen, Elisabeth Møller, Eva Hættner Aurelius, and Mai, eds. *Nordisk kvindelitteraturhistorie,* 5 volumes. Copenhagen: Rosinante, 1993–1999.

Jensen, Line, and others, eds. *Contemporary Danish Poetry*. Copenhagen: Gyldendal / Boston: Twayne, 1977.

Johansen, Jørgen Dines, ed. *Analyser af dansk Kort prosa,* 2 volumes. Copenhagen: Borgen, 1971, 1972.

Jørgensen, Aage. *Dansk litteraturhistorisk bibliografi 1967–86*. Copenhagen: Dansklærerforeningen, 1989.

Klysner, Finn. *Den danske kollektivroman 1928–1944*. Copenhagen: Vinten, 1976.

Koefoed, H. A., ed. *Modern Danish Prose: A Selection of Danish Texts for Foreign Students*. Copenhagen: Høst, 1955.

Kondrup, Johnny. *Erindringens udveje: Studier i moderne dansk selvbiografi*. Valby: Amadeus, 1994.

Kristensen, Sven Møller. *Den store generation*. Copenhagen: Gyldendal, 1974.

Madsen, Peter. *Linjer i Nordisk Prosa: Danmark 1965–75*. Lund: Bo Cavefors, 1977.

Mai, ed. *Digtning fra 80'erne til 90'erne: Læsninger af ny dansk lyrik*. Copenhagen: Borgen, 1993.

Mai and Knud Bjarne Gjesing, eds. *Laesninger i dansk litteratur 1940–1970*, volume 4. Odense: Odense University Press, 1997.

Mawby, Janet. *Writers and Politics in Modern Scandinavia*. London: Hodder & Stoughton, 1978.

Mitchell, P. M. *A History of Danish Literature*. Copenhagen: Gyldendal, 1957.

Mogensen, Knud K., ed. *Modern Danish Poems*. New York: Bonniers, 1949.

Møller, Per Stig, ed. *Forfatternes forfatterhistorie*. Copenhagen: Gyldendal, 1980.

Nielsen, Erling, ed. *Dansk litterær debat 1950–75: Holdninger/miljøer/temaer*. Copenhagen: Gyldendal, 1981.

Nielsen, Frederik, and Ole Restrup, eds. *Danske digtere i det 20. århundrede*, second edition, 3 volumes. Copenhagen: Gad, 1965–1966.

Palmvig, Lis, ed. *Lysthuse: Kvindelitteraturhistorier*. Charlottenlund: Rosinante, 1985.

Ravn, Ole. *Dansk litteratur 1920–75: Brydninger og tendenser*, 2 volumes. Copenhagen: Gjellerup, 1976.

Richard, Anne Birgitte. *Kvindelitteratur og kvindesituation: Socialisering, offentlighed og æstetik*. Copenhagen: Gyldendal, 1976.

Rossel, Sven H., ed. *A History of Danish Literature*. Lincoln: University of Nebraska Press, 1992.

Schou, Søren. *Dansk realisme 1960–75*. Copenhagen: Medusa, 1976.

Sylvest, Olve. *Det litterære karneval: Den groteske realisme i nyere danske romaner*. Odense: Odense University Press, 1987.

Tafdrup, Pia, ed. *Transformationer: Poesi 1980–85*. Herning: Forlaget Systime, 1985.

Thomsen, Ejnar. *Dansk litteratur efter 1870 med sideblik til det øvrige Norden*, revised edition, Copenhagen: Rosenkilde & Bagger, 1965.

Traustedt, P. H., ed. *Dansk litteratur historie*, revised edition, 6 volumes. Copenhagen: Politiken, 1976–1977.

Vosmar, Jørn, ed. *Modernismen in dansk litteratur*. Copenhagen: Fremad, 1967.

Wamberg, Bodil, ed. *Blixen, Brøgger og andre danske damer*. Copenhagen: Centrum, 1985.

Wamberg, Niels Birger. *Samtaler med danske digtere*. Copenhagen: Gyldendal, 1968.

Winge, Mette. *Fortiden som spejl: Om danske historiske romaner*. Copenhagen: Samleren, 1997.

Winge, ed. *Fra Brandes til Rifbjerg: En tekstantologi*. Copenhagen: Statens Filmcentral, 1993.

Zerlang, Poul. *Dansk litterær opslagsbog*. Copenhagen: Gad, 1985.

Zuck, Virpi, ed. *Dictionary of Scandinavian Literature*. Westport, Conn.: Greenwood Press, 1990.

Contributors

Kim Andersen . . . . *Washington State University*

Lise Præstgaard Andersen . . . . *University of Southern Denmark, Odense*

Poul Bager . . . . *State Grammar School, Randers*

Paal Bjørby . . . . *University of Bergen*

Elias Bredsdorff . . . . *University of Cambridge*

Thomas Bredsdorff . . . . *University of Copenhagen*

Per Dahl . . . . *University of Århus*

Linda G. Donelson . . . .

Trevor G. Elkington . . . . *University of Washington*

Jørgen Gleerup . . . . *University of Southern Denmark, Odense*

Charlotte Schiander Gray . . . .

Poul Houe . . . . *University of Minnesota*

Frank Hugus . . . . *University of Massachusetts*

Allen E. Hye . . . . *Wright State University*

Faith Ingwersen . . . . *University of Wisconsin at Madison*

Niels Ingwersen . . . . *University of Wisconsin at Madison*

Lanae H. Isaacson . . . .

W. Glyn Jones . . . . *University of East Anglia*

Phyllis Lassner . . . . *Northwestern University*

John Lingard . . . . *University College of Cape Breton*

Anne-Marie Mai . . . . *University of Southern Denmark, Odense*

Leonie Marx . . . . *University of Kansas*

James Massengale . . . . *University of California, Los Angeles*

Helle Mathiasen. . . . . *University of Arizona*

Finn Hauberg Mortensen . . . . *University of Southern Denmark, Odense*

Mark Mussari . . . . *Villanova Academy, Pennsylvania*

Paul Norlén . . . . *University of Washington*

Sven Hakon Rossel . . . . *University of Vienna*

Thomas Satterlee. . . . . *University of Miami*

Søren Schou. . . . . *Roskilde University Center, Denmark*

Marianne Stecher-Hansen . . . . *University of Washington*

Timothy R. Tangherlini . . . . *University of California, Los Angeles*

Tanya Thresher . . . . *University of Wisconsin at Madison*

Else Vinæs . . . . *Rosenlund School, Copenhagen*

Mette Winge . . . .

Cumulative Index

Dictionary of Literary Biography, Volumes 1-214
Dictionary of Literary Biography Yearbook, 1980-1998
Dictionary of Literary Biography Documentary Series, Volumes 1-19

Cumulative Index

DLB before number: *Dictionary of Literary Biography,* Volumes 1-214
Y before number: *Dictionary of Literary Biography Yearbook,* 1980-1998
DS before number: *Dictionary of Literary Biography Documentary Series,* Volumes 1-19

B

Cumulative Index

ISBN 0-7876-3108-6

90000

9 780787 631086